The Sunday Telegraph

GOLF COURSE GUIDE
——— TO ———
BRITAIN & IRELAND

PETER ALLISS

13th E

CollinsWillow
An Imprint of HarperCollins*Publishers*

*The publishers would like to acknowledge the help of the following
in the compilation of the 13th edition of this book:*

Text updating and revision
*Jack Carroll
Cristina Caruso
Val Coxon*

Research co-ordination
Tricia Gibson

Technical and text organisation
*Howard Scott
Richard Weekes*

Map compilation and artwork
*Stefan Bayley
Graeme Murdoch
Katie Murray*

Cover photograph
*The Roxburghe
by Chris Smith*

This edition published 1998 by
CollinsWillow
an imprint of HarperCollins*Publishers*
London

First published 1968
Thirteenth revised edition 1998

A CIP catalogue record for this book
is available from the British Library

ISBN 0 00 218832 5

This edition produced by
Richard Weekes Publishing, London N8

Printed and bound in Spain

CONTENTS

KEY TO THE MAPS

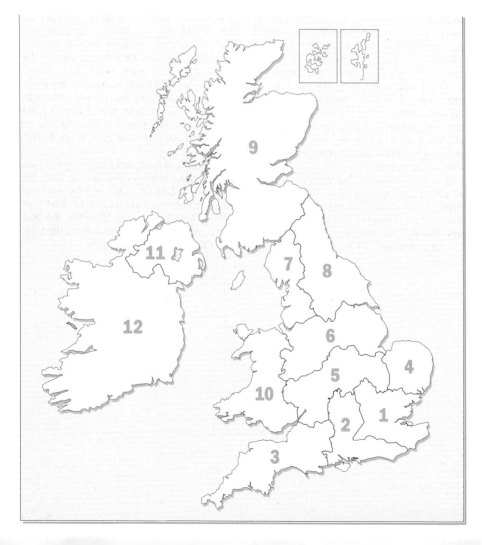

PREFACE

In the thirty years since the *Sunday Telegraph Golf Course Guide* was first published, golf has changed enormously. The 1960s were the years when wooden clubs were made of wood: you could choose the size of golf ball you used and every other professional tournament seemed to be sponsored by a tobacco company. Lengths of courses, too, were more modest. The birth of Big Bertha was still a considerable way off.

There are now more courses and more golfers – significantly more. Golf has become a major industry, its stars multi-millionaires. Television allows us to watch golf almost every week of the year but one thing which hasn't changed is the urge for individual golfers to explore new courses, to get out and sample the unique variety that exists in our islands.

In 1968, the idea behind the *Sunday Telegraph Golf Course Guide* was making people aware of that variety and providing information valuable in planning days out or weeks away. That remains the driving force. It is accepted that, when a major event is seen on television, there is a rush to the host course by those anxious to try their own hand. As a result, courses that are household names are always in demand. However, the search is not confined to the famous. Greater reward lies in locating quiet backwaters.

Motives vary. A few golfers seek competitive glory although even those who say they play only for fun, like to win. Many see golf as an escape, the occasion once or twice a week when worries are forgotten, when the Walter Mitty in them takes over. Alternatively, there are those who regard the game as their means of exercise, a therapy staunchly opposed to the view that golf is a good walk spoiled. But everyone likes to play in nice places and marvel at the scenery. That is a common bond.

The Guide lists something for every taste, the joy lying more in the arrival than the travelling hopefully. Golf Clubs are like hotels in that some are more welcoming, or better value, than others. However, the best way is to judge for yourself. That is the most appealing of golf's special offers.

INTRODUCTION

The 13th edition of the *Sunday Telegraph Golf Course Guide* has been revamped to give easier access to a record number of courses and also added value to the readers. For the first time we include coupons at the back of the book for four magnificent hotels which host outstanding golf courses.

The coupons will offer special and unrivalled discounts on golf packages at Carden Park near the beautiful city of Chester and St David's Park at the gateway to the classic courses of North Wales. Carden Park was the host course for the Hippo Tour Championship in August 1997 while Northop Country Park, a few miles from St David's Park Hotel, has hosted many of the Welsh PGA events.

Both these hotels also offer the exciting opportunity of exploring some of the best golfing venues that the North West of England and North Wales has to offer – and now at a discounted price.

Also included in this new value-for-money scheme for the travelling golfer is the newly refurbished Tweed Valley Hotel in the Scottish borders. It lies in the heart of real golfing country – the closest course is Peebles – but there are no fewer than 20 new venues within a short drive of this wonderfully relaxing venue. There are those who argue that Scotland is the home of golf and with so many outstanding courses, including some household names, to choose from Tweed Valley enjoys a perfect location.

Ashdown Forest Hotel is another outstanding venue for golf. The course is set in the beautiful rolling countryside and woodlands of East Sussex in the village of Forest Row. Again the hotel would form a fine base for the exploring golfer who wishes to return to luxury and comfort.

This year not only does Peter Alliss, the BBC's Voice of Golf, offer a series of classic golfing itineraries but he also combines with the proven knowledge, experience and insight of Donald Steel, who again edits the book with style and contributes some excellent golfing essays.

Derek Lawrenson, the *Sunday Telegraph's* brilliant golf correspondent, also wanders through Ireland and the Midlands highlighting some of the hidden gems and picks out the magnificent K Club as well as describing the 1998 Open Championship venue of Royal Birkdale and the 1999 host course Carnoustie.

With James Mossop returning to the North West to tour the rich golfing area of the Lake District and Clare Middleton finding out the favourite courses of the top women players, this latest version of the *Sunday Telegraph Golf Course Guide* has a new and exciting feel.

And then, of course, there are the Golf Clubs. When this Guide first appeared in 1968 there were less than 1650 clubs. This year we have reached the amazing total of 2685 with many, many more under construction. This boom time for British and Irish golf is reflected in these pages.

To gather the information is a painstaking task. Without the help of the secretaries of so many of the Golf Clubs in Britain and Ireland and the assistance in many cases of the club professionals this book would never have been possible. There is no doubt that this is the most comprehensive guide to British golf clubs ever published. So to all those who took the time to fill in the questionnaire or answer the telephone queries – a big thank you.

Organisation. A new book, a new look. This year the book has been divided into new regions. We retain many of the geographical and county groupings that were introduced in the 11th edition – based on affinities and familiarity rather than carto-graphic convenience or local government divisions, which again altered in 1997. We said goodbye to many of the Welsh coun-ties like Powys and Clwyd, some Scottish boundaries moved and Humberside and Cleveland slipped into the history books.

This time we are starting with London and the Home Counties, followed by the South and then the South West and so on. Many regions, like London for example, are still divided into two distinct areas. We still retain Surrey, Kent and South London as well as a separate section for North London, Essex and Hertfordshire. Each area has a map indicating the location of courses within it (see page 4 for a key to the area groupings and pages on which individual area maps are to be found).

Wales has been given a new identity rather than being slotted in between the border counties of Shropshire, Stafford-shire and Cheshire and the chapter for Lancashire and the North West.

Ireland has reached a record 340 clubs in this edition while the growing populari-ty of golf in the North East is reflected with 270 clubs in Yorkshire, Northumberland and Durham.

As before, each course is numbered and given a letter code for easy reference from the expanded index. Courses are listed alphabetically and numbered in sequence.

Course information. This is a guide that reflects the golf course as well as the golf club. For each club the following informa-tion has normally been provided: the address and post code, relevant telephone and fax numbers, travel directions to the course, a brief description of the type of course and its architect as well as any inter-esting trivia. For the first time we also include the name of the club's professional.

There is also a guide for golfers as to whether they will be welcome at a golf course on a particular day, either as indi-viduals or as a member of the growing number of golfing societies. Just as impor-tant, there is information on the likely cost, both for individuals and societies. However, it is always a common courtesy to telephone any club you plan to visit in advance to check the availability of the course and also any restrictions that may be placed on visitors.

While the prices quoted are correct at the time of going to press there are likely to be variations in them during a season and again it is worth checking the green fees before climbing into the car.

Most of all, this book is aimed at encouraging golfers to explore new courses and to maximise their enjoyment of the sport. Great care has been taken to try and ensure the accuracy of the information in this book and thanks is due, again, to the secretaries, professionals and course managers.

Comments. Feedback on the book is always welcome as are comments on cours-es that have been visited. We would be happy to hear of any errors, alterations or extensions to courses. Comments should be addressed to: Colin Gibson, Sports Editor, *The Sunday Telegraph*, 1 Canada Square, London E14 5DT or sent by email to stsport@telegraph.co.uk

The rise of new courses, such as Loch Lomond, the London and the Roxburghe (which have featured on the covers of the last three editions of the Guide) has clearly brought new stature and new quality to British golf.

Loch Lomond is now a tour venue for the European PGA's pre-Open Champion-ship event and the London enjoyed hosting recent Senior Tour events.

Sometimes, however, the older courses can be forgotten amid the praise lavished on such impressive new clubs. *The Sunday Telegraph* is therefore planning a Golf Course of the Year award in the next edi-tion and we would like the readers to nom-inate their favourite club.

It can be a brand new establishment, an old established favourite, a scenic setting or a club which has improved markedly in the last few years.

All nominations should be sent again to Colin Gibson, the Sports Editor, *The Sunday Telegraph*, 1 Canada Sq, London E14 5DT.

MY CLASSIC GOLF COURSES
by Peter Alliss

One of the eternally rewarding pastimes of golfers everywhere is to chin-wag about their favourite courses. When I was asked to nominate mine, instead of going for those obvious ones that seem to be permanent fixtures in everybody's top ten lists, I decided to look a little outside. To go through the 'accepted' ones is like saying that Bobby Charlton, Stanley Matthews and John Charles were outstanding footballers.

The courses I am nominating from the British Isles are, believe me, capable of passing any test and all have the compelling quality of drawing me back to them. They are magnificent golf courses in wonderful settings. No one could ever tire of such places. As part of the old debate I have decided to nominate three courses in each of England, Scotland, Wales and Ireland plus the added topic of my favourite 19th hole. Every golfer has one of those, too.

You may argue all day about course design, clubhouse comforts, scenery. All these things help to make good golf courses and I feel my nominations qualify. Let's look at three for England first and, as with the others, in no particular order. I have chosen Notts Golf Club, probably better known as Hollinwell, Ganton in Yorkshire and Broadstone, a Dorset classic in its own right and its own style.

Hollinwell is a course for serious golfers, especially those who appreciate the traditions of the game. I have played very well there in professional competitions years ago. Indeed, I remember coming third in the Dunlop Masters behind Eric Brown and John Jacobs in the 1957 Dunlop Masters.

The drive to the solid clubhouse is the beginning of the grandness of Hollinwell. Deep leather armchairs, dark wood-panelling and a proper snooker room all add to the splendour but the real majesty is out on the course where there are 18 superb holes. The rough is thick and heathery as the course snakes cleverly through a natural valley of trees, mainly pine. Shot selection and accuracy are at a premium. Take the 13th, for instance, a stunning par-three of 236 yards. The player hits from a high-sided tee through a valley of heather and gorse to a green that has bunkers short left and right of the green. Sometimes the wind can be so demanding that the hole may require anything from a driver to a five-iron.

When I lived in Yorkshire throughout the Seventies, I was constantly in admiration of Ganton, as indeed I retain that affection to this day. To go to Ganton when the gorse is in full bloom is one of life's real pleasures. The course, eleven miles south-west of Scarborough, hosted the 1949 Ryder Cup and at the time there was a call to get some young blood into the team especially after the 11-1 defeat in Portland, Oregon, two years earlier. I was 19 at the time and mine was one of the names being mentioned. I had to wait until 1953 for the call-up.

My memories of Ganton are all wonderful, not least because of the intriguing nature of the holes created by the joint efforts of a quartet of four marvellous architects, Dunn, Vardon, Braid and Colt. They certainly made sure you had to hit the ball in the right place. Some of the par-four holes looked short on the card but they were never easy.

I enjoyed the kind of 'feudal system' that existed at Ganton. Families, who were housed within the grounds, seemed to have worked at the club for generations. Then there was the classic Ganton cake – a wonderful confection of fruit and spices and more calories than I dare to contemplate. I also recall Max Faulkner being asked to remove his two-seater Allard which he had parked with two wheels on the grass. He accelerated away with such force that clods of earth flew perilously close to the official barking the orders. Ganton, the golf course, has not changed, and those who have played it recently tell me it remains as splendidly aloof as ever.

Two of the above architects, by the way, were involved in the creation of a course that was very much a part of my formative years as a competitor, Broadstone. Dunn was the original planner in 1898, Colt tweaked it in 1925. I loved playing there before and after my National Service and it was at Broadstone that I met Jimmy Cousins, who was my caddie for ten years. The course itself is probably one of the hardest par 68s in the world, with the opening par-four, close on 470 yards, setting the standard of what is to follow. If your game is off, don't worry. There is ample compensation in the long views across to the Purbeck Hills and Poole Harbour. I remember them as vividly as the pleasures of the boiled eggs and toast in the clubhouse.

Much further North in Scotland I have a special affection for Blairgowrie, especially after Dave Thomas and myself were invited to design the newer of the two courses, Lansdowne, which sits very comfortably with the original course, Rosemount. They complement each other perfectly and the visitor cannot fail to be impressed with the scenery which has a special whiteness from the sand in the huge bunkers and the silver birch trees that are everywhere.

It may seem invidious to make any special selections North of the Border since the country is gloriously blessed with famous courses, both links and inland, but there remains something wonderfully traditional about Blairgowrie. It has a lovely rolling lay-out through the birches and pines and a delightful clubhouse. I cannot leave Scotland without including two of the great, historical Open Championship courses, Muirfield and St Andrews. Muirfield, close to the East Lothian village of Gullane, is the home of The Honourable Company of Edinburgh Golfers. This not only boasts far more tradition than most courses but also comprises some of the greatest holes in the ancient game. It was created, by hand and horse, by Old Tom Morris and opened in 1891, but it was not until Harry Colt was brought in to make changes in 1925 that it became the great course of 14 Open Championships we know today (nine of them since Colt's alterations).

I was fed on stories of Muirfield by my father, of secretaries who were eccentric enough to be almost certifiable, of the long table with its cold cuts and port drunk from half-pint glasses. But most of all I remember Gary Player almost in tears after taking six at the last in the 1959 Open when he thought he had lost (he hadn't) and Jack Nicklaus praising its qualities so highly than he called his home course in Ohio, Muirfield Village. Of the Scottish Muirfield, he said that it was marvellous to experience a links course where it was possible to see everything with no blind holes.

It would be impossible to leave Scotland without mentioning St Andrews. The whole atmosphere of the Old Course and the town is magical. There are calm days when the course looks easy and, indeed, Curtis Strange went round in 62 in the 1987 Dunhill Cup, although that was from the forward tees. It has been criticised by some American professionals but I consider such folk as heathens without souls. The pot-bunkers, the Road Hole (17th), the gorse, the whins, the lurking traps, the sheer geography of the place make it absolutely special in the history of the game. I once held the record with a 66 – a dozen fours and six threes.

Golf in Wales begins and ends with Royal Porthcawl, some people might say. It is not a monster course. It does not need to be, it has so much going for it. It was here that my father started his professional career around 1920, so there are other reasons for it being special to me. The sea is visible from every hole and, while you might need a bit of wind to make it a great test, there is so much history in the course and the clubhouse that it is worth its place in golfing lore.

For scenery to accompany the quality of the golf course, you would travel North to Royal St Davids. It may be a fairly flat course but with Harlech Castle sitting on the hill it really is a majestic spot with some very testing holes and distant views of Snowdonia.

There is another Harry Colt masterpiece, Pyle and Kenfig, which manages to combine seaside links with downland, and with a standard scratch score of 73 it is a test of anyone's golf, especially when the wind drives in from Swansea Bay. It was opened in 1922 and as far as I am concerned it is a 'must' for anyone with a love of outstanding but unpretentious golf courses.

Ireland, like Scotland, teems with courses of every kind, from nine-holers where sheep may graze to the truly great tests such as Royal County Down, south of Belfast and in the shadows, almost, of the Mountains of Mourne. No one could fail to be impressed by the demands of a course that taxes the imagination and presents massive dunes, gorse and heather as a warning to the wayward.

Lahinch, too, out on the West coast of the Republic of Ireland, is another gem. It is one of those courses that has so many wonderful holes that you will have absolute pleasure and joy whatever your standard.

There are so many good courses around Dublin, frequently overshadowed by Portmarnock, that to make an arbitrary choice is not easy. However, I am going for Royal Dublin, where my old friend and Ryder Cup partner for many years, Christie O'Connor, was based. Tales of his deeds with golf clubs on that wondrous acreage of golfing terrain are legend. And wondrous terrain it is, as you arrive at it along a causeway that takes you from the 'mainland' to the clubhouse. A visit to Royal Dublin will be rewarding at any time.

MY FAVOURITE 19TH HOLES
by Peter Alliss

Within the relatively modest clubhouse at Trevose, there is a rare cosiness, a welcoming warmth. Whether it is on a fine summer's day or the winter wind is hurling rain at the big bow windows, there is something deeply rewarding about sitting there, looking out. It is a place 'made' by the people and the staff, on Constantine Bay just south of Padstow in Cornwall. There is only a modest mark-up on a bottle of champagne so everybody can afford a glass and the variety of food and snacks at 'competitive' prices makes Trevose a joy to behold. When you come in from a round of golf there are few more embracing places.

There will be many a 19th hole habitué with his own ideas as ambience, food, even the range of malt whiskies are weighed and considered along with the views and comfort. For my own part, I have to say that Swinley Forest is a jewel of a special hue. After 18 holes on this attractive course near Ascot, on the beautiful heathland of Berkshire, there is nothing more rewarding than a Swinley Special, a non-alcoholic refresher that can only do you good, followed by a lunch upstairs accompanied by the wines of an outstanding cellar. Coffee and liqueur downstairs and then to be chauffeur-driven home. What bliss!

LEADING LADIES' FAVOURITE COURSES

LAURA DAVIES MBE: *Muirfield*
You might expect Laura Davies to choose a course which rewards long, powerful driving, and with Muirfield she does not disappoint. Never mind that it is littered with bunkers and that reaching safety from the depths of fairway sand is nigh impossible; she loves the different challenges imposed by every single hole. "You can't improve on this one," she says.

The hardest hole is also the best, she believes. She is not one who thrives on tight courses where making fewer errors than her fellow competitors is the name of the game: she prefers to be set a task that sorts wheat from chaff, the more difficult the better. "The 18th is a par-four, it is tough and the sort of hole every course should have – long and testing. I play it with a driver and my five-iron – but beware the big bunker with the island of turf on the right of the green."

It is the dog-leg 17th which has probably decided more men's Open Championships than most – don't be tempted to cut the corner – and that with the 18th is a memorable way to finish any round. Surprisingly, Davies has never played a strokeplay competition there but loves the place, just 20 or so miles from Edinburgh, because it stirs up happy memories of the Curtis Cup.

"Enjoy it," she advises the amateur. "But don't expect too much, especially if the wind blows. I have had nightmares there myself."

JOANNE MORLEY: *Royal Liverpool*
The second-oldest seaside course in England is the favourite of Joanne Morley, the Cheshire-born Solheim Cup player who divides her time between the women's European and American tours.

The venue for the 1992 Curtis Cup, in which Morley played, she had fallen in love with it well before then, having competed there in numerous county championships.

"I love all the history attached to it and the feel of the place," she says, "but I also love a challenge and Royal Liverpool provides it. You can play the first nine holes with barely a breeze and then the weather can change and you finish in a gale. That is why I enjoy links golf."

Morley's best over the par-74 links is five under, secured in the 1989 Cheshire county championship. She is not about to reveal her worst – except to say it was pretty bad.

"My favourite holes are the four after the turn – which comes at the eighth. The ninth, 10th, 11th and 12th run along the River Dee and are a stiff test, especially when the wind gets up. It is no use just plonking your tee-shot on the fairway, you have to do more than stand up and hit it."

The 11th gets her vote as the best – a 150-yard par-three known as the Alps. Take plenty of club – a long iron, or even a wood – and swing easy, she says. "The wind usually blows left to right there, there's a bunker to the right of the green so you have to send the ball out left and hope the wind brings it in."

TRISH JOHNSON: *Royal North Devon*
A quirky seaside course in Westward Ho!! is the favourite of four-time Solheim Cup player Trish Johnson. It is her home course, and apart from erosion by the sea – the eighth is in danger of flooding and a new hole will be created during 1998 – it has changed little since it was founded in 1864.

Johnson warns it is not for everybody: "There are burrows everywhere and sheep and horses running wild," she says. "It is unique." Her favourite hole is the fifth, a 130-yard par-three – the Table – which is slightly uphill, its raised green protected by an enormous bunker. "Once you get to the green, there are bunkers all around. There and up on the sixth tee you get the feeling of being almost on top of the sea. A fabulous hole."

18-hole courses over 5,800 yards beginning with a par 3

Aboyne
Accrington
Addington
Anglesey
Ashburnham
Ballards Gore
Berkshire (Blue)
Churston
City of Derry
Cochrane Castle
Colville Park
Crow Wood
Dartford
Davenport
Davyhulme Park
Deer Park
Easingwold
Eastham Lodge
Falkirk Tryst
Hayling
Hollingbury Park
Horam Park
Houldsworth
Huntercombe
Kettering
Kingsknowe
Knole Park
Largs
La Moye
Liphook
Llandudno (Maesdu)
Llanymynech
Longcliffe
Macroom
Manor of Groves
Meyrick Park
Monkstown
Pebbles
Pontypridd
Preston
Purley Downs
Royal Lytham and
    St Annes
Royal Mid-Surrey
Royal Norwich
Southport and
    Ainsdale
South Moor
Thetford
Upton by Chester
Wearside
Wellow
West Bowling
West Cornwall
Whitchurch
    (Cardiff)
Withington
Yelverton

18-hole courses over 5,800 yards ending with a par 3

Aberystwyth
Airdrie
Alloa
Arkley
Ashford (Kent)
Bandon
Barnard Castle
Beadlow Manor
Berkshire (Red)
Boyce Hill
Breightmet
Bremhill Park
Bright Castle
Brinkworth
Brora
Carlyon Bay
Cawder (Cawder)
Chapel-en-le-Frith
Chelmsford
Cold Ashby
Courtown
Darenth Valley
Deeside
Dewsbury
Dorset Heights
Douglaston
Downes Crediton
Dunstable Downs
Dunwood Manor
East Herts
Ellesmere
Erewash Valley
Fairlop Waters
Forest of Arden
    (Arden)
Fortrose and
    Rosemarkie
Glamorganshire
    (Penarth)
Goodwood
Great Barr
Hayston
Hoebridge
Howley Hall
Ilfracombe
Kennilworth
Killarney
    (Mahony's Point)
Kilsyth Lennox
Kirkcaldy
Lancaster
Langley Park
Leasowe
Leeds
Lindrick
Lochwinnoch
Louth
Milford Haven
Moor Park (High)
Mount Oswald
Northcliffe
Nottingham City
Old Padeswood
Old Ranfurly
Padeswood and
    Buckley
Parkstone
Penwortham
Piltdown
Prestwick St
    Nicholas
Rhos on Sea
Rolls of Monmouth
Royal Eastbourne
Royal Guernsey
Royal St David's
Ryton
Saffron Walden
St Pierre
Saltburn-by-the-Sea
Sandy Lodge
Shanklin and
Sandown
Sickleholme
Stocksfield
Stoke by Nayland
    (both)
Stone
Tredegar Park
Vale of Llangollen
Wallsend
Welwyn Garden City
West Linton
Wetherby
Whitburn
Woodbury (Oaks)
Woodhall Hills
    (both)
Worksop

18-hole courses beginning and ending with a par 3

Aboyne
Aldwark Manor
Bala
Bearsted
Bingley St Ives
Didsbury
Eltham Warren
Harpenden Common
Hawick
Peacehaven
Southwold
Upminster

18-hole courses over 5,800 yards with two consecutive par 3s

Ashford Manor
Ballybunion (Old)
Balmoral
Bandon
Barnard Castle
Bawburgh
Birr
Bishop Auckland
Brancepeth Castle
Bristol & Clifton
Brough
Burntisland
Chester-le-Street
Clonmel
Consett and District
Cruden Bay
Elgin
Erewash Valley
Harburn
Hartsbourne
Hayston
Holywood
Ganstead Park
Glamorganshire
    (Penarth)
Haywards Heath
Ilkley
Kidderminster

Killymoon
Knott End
Lee-on-the-Solent
Leyland
Linlithgow
Loudoun (twice)
Lurgan
Machrihanish
Market Rasen
Millport
North Oxford
Potters Bar
Roehampton
Royal Eastbourne
Royal Jersey
Rushmere
Sandy Lodge
Stoneham
Tain
Thurlestone
The Manor, Laceby
Tredegar Park
Waterlooville
West Linton
West Monmouthshire
West Sussex
Willesley Park

18-hole courses over 6,000 yards with fewer than 3 par 3s
St Andrews (Old) – 2
Golf House Club, Elie – 2

18-hole courses over 5,900 yards with more than five par 3s
Barnard Castle – 6
Berkshire (Red) – 6
Bigbury – 6
Darlington – 6
Downes Crediton – 6
Killymore – 6
Richmond – 6
Sandy Lodge – 6
Tredegar Park – 6
NB: The Red Course at The Berkshire has six par 3s, six par 4s and six par 5s.

Courses with holes over 600 yards
Aldenham G & CC
 (13th, 636 yards)
Belton Woods (Wellington)
 (18th, 613 yards)
Bright Castle
 (16th, 735 yards)
East Dorset
 (6th, 604 yards)
Gedney Hill
 (2nd, 671 yards)
Manor of Groves
 (18th, 614 yards)
Overstone Park
 (11th, 601 yards)
Portal
 (6th, 603 yards)
Welwyn Garden City
 (17th, 601 yards)

Courses over 7,000 yards
Austin Lodge
 (7,118 yards)
Ballards Gore
 (7,062 yards)
Barkway Park
 (7,000 yards)
Bidford Grange
 (7,233 yards)
The Belfry (Brabazon)
 (7,177 yards)
Belton Woods (Lancaster)
 (7,021 yards)
Bowood
 (7,317 yards)
Bright Castle
 (7,143 yards)
Carnoustie
 (7,272 yards)
Chart Hills
 (7,086 yards)
Dartmouth
 (7,012 yards)
East Dorset
 (7,027 yards)
East Sussex (West)
 (7,154 yards)

Forest of Arden (Arden)
 (7,102 yards)
Gleneagles (The Monarch's Course)
 (7,081 yards)
Hanbury Manor
 (7,011 yards)
Killarney (Killeen)
 (7,079 yards)
Loch Lomond
 (7,053 yards)
The London Club (Heritage 7,208 yards) (International 7,005 yards)
Millbrook
 (7,100 yards)
Moatlands
 (7,060 yards)
Mount Juliet
 (7,100 yards)
The Oxfordshire
 (7,143 yards)
Notts (Hollinwell)
 (7,020 yards)
Perton Park
 (7,007 yards)
Portal (7,145 yards)
Royal Liverpool
 (7,100 yards)
Slaley Hall
 (7,038 yards)
Stocks Hotel
 (7,016 yards)
Thorpe Wood
 (7,086 yards)
Waterville
 (7,184 yards)
West Berkshire
 (7,059 yards)
Loch Lomond
 (7,053 yards)

18-hole courses with holes under 100 yards
Bridport and West Dorset
 (2nd, 81 yards)
Dun Laoghaire
 (7th, 95 yards)

Erewash Valley
 (4th, 89 yards)
Ilfracombe
 (4th, 81 yards)
Tilsworth
 (13th, 97 yards)

Courses with par 3s numbered all odds or all evens
Addington
Auchterarder
Cape Cornwall
Cirencester
County Armagh
County Louth
Hoebridge
Liphook
Lyme Regis
Oake Manor
Scunthorpe
Stockwood Park
Sundridge Park (West)
West Cornwall
Uttoxeter

18-hole courses with notable differences between the lengths of their two nines
Chapel-en-le-Frith
 (821 yards
Davids Heath
 (786 yards)
Flackwell Heath
 (786 yards)
Goodwood Park
 (712 yards)
Kings Lynn
 (584 yards)
Kirkhill
 (648 yards)
Old Ranfurly
 (507 yards)
Reddish Vale
 (534 yards)
Thurlestone
 (821 yards)
Woodhall Hills
 (754 yards)
Worcestershire
 (655 yards)

1

LONDON AND THE HOME COUNTIES

It is not often that a golfer can say he changed his shoes in the 15th-century home of Cardinal Wolsey or the headquarters of the American 2nd Airborne Division (World War II) but that is one of the many pleasures awaiting the visitor to Moor Park, a golfing joy along the Metropolitan line heading from the city to North London.

With gardens laid out by Capability Brown, three courses designed by the celebrated Harry Colt and the clubhouse mansion, a Grade 1 Listed Building, you can see why Moor Park, Rickmansworth, is an extraordinary place.

Whether on the Tube, or taking the hour's drive from Central London, the visitor will find a delightful parkland with rolling terrain and the High Course, the one used for championship golf, a supreme test that has hosted several professional events. Indeed, in 1963, the South African golfer, Harold Henning, holed out in one at the par-three 18th and collected £10,000 which, at the time, was more than the entire prize-money for the Open Championship.

To hit the ball close to the hole on the 12th would satisfy most golfers. It is a classic short hole of 210 yards across a valley to a green set slightly higher than the teeing position. The ball must carry all the way as there is a severe upslope just short and bunkers either side. The green is two-tiered with a steep incline between the two. Many a card has been ruined here.

Ross Whitehead, who was professional at Moor Park for more than 25 years, once said: "Positional play is the key to a good round on the High Course. It is no longer as wide open as it used to be and you have to think about every shot."

Closer to London, just a taxi ride from the West End hotels, is a comparatively undiscovered Colt gem, Hendon Golf Club, a parkland course of two loops of nine with mature trees and copses – two par-fives, four par-threes. It has been the venue of county matches but generally the members have it to themselves and are fortunate indeed to have such an excellent facility which Colt created in 1903. He was a young man then and was soon making his mark on grander estates such as Sunningdale, Wentworth, Muirfield, Pine Valley (USA) and so on.

It looks fairly short on the card – 6,266 – but the professional record of 66 by the current pro Stuart Murray has stood for several years. The course is well bunkered, some of the fairways are tight and it is cleverly shielded from any buildings with tree-lined borders.

Anyone wanting to play the North London courses should visit Porters Park, another high-quality oasis just off the regular rail and road tracks in the small town of Radlett, where the countryside meets London. It is a wonderfully mature parkland course with a stream that frequently comes in to play. The landscape is undulating and there is an air of tranquillity about the course which remains a serious test of golf and has been used as an Open Championship pre-qualifying venue as well as the scene of county golf competitions. It would be difficult to play at Porters Park and not leave without some outstanding memories. The opening hole appears to be an easy, uphill par-four, requiring a driver or three-wood and then a short iron. After that the course begins to ask questions and full concentration is required to keep a round together.

1A 1 Abbey Moor

Green Lane, Addlestone, Surrey KT15 2XU
☎(01932) 570741, Pro 570765, Bar/Rest 570293.
Leave M25 at junction 11 and proceed on St Peters Way towards Weybridge; take right turn at large roundabout towards Addlestone on A318, then over railway bridge; take 2nd turning right at small roundabout into Green Lane; course 0.5 mile on right.
Public parkland course.
Pro Steve Carter; Founded 1991.
Designed by David Taylor.
9 holes, 5104 yards, S.S.S. 66
Visitors: welcome WD and WE; advisable to book early.
Green Fee: WD £7.50; WE £8.50.
Societies: WD only; terms on application.
Catering: full bar and restaurant facilities.
Hotels: White Lodge.

1A 2 The Addington

205 Shirley Church Rd, Croydon, Surrey CRO 5AB
☎(0181) 777 1055, Sec 777 6057
Through Addington village, 2.5 miles from East Croydon station.
Heather, bracken, silver birch and pine parkland.
Founded 1913
Designed by J.F. Abercromby
18 holes, 6242 yards, S.S.S. 71
Visitors: WD only.
Green Fee: WD £35; WE £35.
Societies: WD only; terms on application.
Catering: restaurant and bar.

1A 3 Addington Court

Featherbed Lane, Croydon, Surrey CRO 9AA
☎(0181) 627 0281, Fax 651 0282, Pro 657 9000, Sec 651 0282
2 miles E of Croydon off the B281 in Addington village.
Undulating parkland.
Pro Adam Aram/John Scappatura; Founded 1931
Designed by F. Hawtree Snr
18 holes, 5577 yards, S.S.S. 67
Falconwood academy course: 9 holes, 5360 yards.
Visitors: welcome.
Green Fee: WD £12; WE £13.60.
Societies: welcome by prior arrangement; catering packages available; terms on application.
Catering: full catering facilities.
Hotels: Selsdon Park.

1A 4 Addington Palace

Gravel Hill, Addington Park, Croydon, Surrey CRO 5BB
☎(0181) 654 3061, Fax 655 3632, Pro 654 1786, Bar/Rest 655 1290
2 miles E of Croydon on the A212.
Undulating parkland.
Pro Roger Williams; Founded 1927
Designed by J H Taylor
18 holes, 6304 yards, S.S.S. 71
Visitors: welcome with members.
Green Fee: WD £15; WE £15.
Societies: welcome Tues, Wed, Fri; details on application; £55.
Catering: bar and catering facilities.

1A 5 Aquarius

Marmora Rd, Honor Oak, London SE22 0RY
☎(0181) 693 1626
SE of London, just off A2.
Set around a reservoir.
Pro Fred Private; Founded 1912
9 holes, 5422 yards, S.S.S. 65
Visitors: welcome with members only.
Green Fee: WD £10; WE £10.
Societies: on request
Catering: on request.
Hotels: Selsden Park.

1A 6 Ashford (Kent)

Sandyhurst Lane, Ashford, Kent TN25 4NT
☎(01233) 620180, Fax 622655, Pro 629644, Sec 622655
1.5 miles from junction 9 on M20
Parkland course.
Pro Hugh Sherman; Founded 1903.
Designed by C.K. Cotton.
18 holes, 6263 yards, S.S.S. 70
Visitors: welcome with h'cap certs.
Green Fee: WD £20; WE £20.
Societies: Tues,Thurs; packages available; £25-£45.
Catering: bar and restaurant.

1A 7 Austin Lodge

Upper Austin Lodge Road, Eynsford, Kent DA4 0HU
☎(01322) 863000, Fax 862406
A225 to Eynsford station; course is in road behind station
Rolling parkland course.
Pro Paul Edwards; Founded 1991.
Designed by Peter Bevan & Mike Walsh.
18 holes, 7118 yards, S.S.S. 73
Visitors: welcome.
Green Fee: WD £16; WE £25.
Societies: Mon-Friday; after 2pm at WE; coffee, lunch, dinner and golf; £25-£39.

Catering: meals and bar.
Hotels: Castle, Eynsford.

1A 8 Banstead Downs

Burdon Lane, Belmont, Sutton, Surrey SM2 7DD
☎(0181) 642 2284, Fax 642 5252, Pro 642 6884, Bar/Rest 643 9286
On A217 from M25 junction 8.
Downland course.
Pro Robert Dickman; Founded 1890
Designed by J H Taylor/ J Braid
18 holes, 6194 yards, S.S.S. 69
Visitors: welcome WD; WE with member only.
Green Fee: WD £30; WE £30.
Societies: welcome, Thurs preferred; full day's golf and catering; £51.
Catering: full clubhouse facilities.
Practice range.

1A 9 Barnehurst

Mayplace Rd East, Bexleyheath, Kent DA7 6JU
☎(01322) 551205, Fax 528483, Sec 523746, Bar/Rest 552952
N of Crayford town centre.
Mature inland course.
Founded 1904
Designed by James Braid
9 holes, 5474 yards, S.S.S. 68
Visitors: welcome.
Green Fee: WD £7.50; WE £7.50.
Societies: welcome; terms on application.
Catering: full facilities and function room.
Hotels: Swallow, Bexleyheath.

1A 10 Bearsted

Ware St, Bearsted, Kent ME14 4PQ
☎(01622) 738389, Fax 738198, Pro 738024, Sec 738198
M20 to junction 7 and follow Bearsted Green signs.
Parkland course.
Pro Tim Simpson; Founded 1895
Designed by Golf Landscapes
18 holes, 6486 yards, S.S.S. 71
Visitors: welcome with h'cap certs.
Green Fee: WD £27; WE £27.
Societies: Tues-Fri; 36 holes of golf, coffee, lunch and dinner; £54.50.
Catering: full facilities.
Hotels: Stakis Country Court, Tudor Park, Great Danes.

1A 11 Beckenham Place Park

Beckenham Hill Rd, Beckenham, Kent BR3 2BP
☎(0181) 650 2292

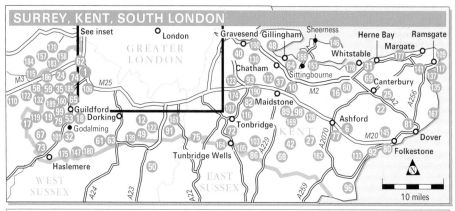

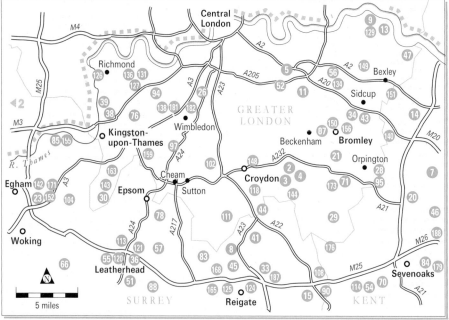

1 mile from Catford towards Bromley, right at Homebase.
Parkland course.
Pro Hugh Davies-Thomas; Founded 1932
18 holes, 5722 yards, S.S.S. 68
Visitors: welcome.
Societies: terms on application.
Catering: meals and snacks.
Hotels: Bromley Court.

1A 12 **Betchworth Park**
Reigate Rd, Dorking, Surrey RH4 1NZ
☎(01306) 882052

1 mile E of Dorking on A25, entrance opposite horticultural gardens.
Parkland course.
Pro A Tocher; Founded 1913
Designed by H. Colt
18 holes, 6266 yards, S.S.S. 70
Visitors: welcome except Tues am, Sat and Sun am.
Green Fee: WD £33; WE £45.
Societies: Mon and Thurs; pacakages including meals available; terms on application.
Catering: lunch and tea facilities available.
Hotels: White Horse.

1A 13 **Bexleyheath**
Mount Rd, Bexleyheath, Kent DA6 8JS
☎(0181) 303 6951
1 mile from Bexleyheath station off Upton road.
Undulating course.
Founded 1907
9 holes, 5239 yards, S.S.S. 66
Visitors: welcome WD.
Green Fee: WD £20.
Societies: welcome WD by appt.
Catering: full bar and catering facilities, except Monday.
Hotels: Swallow.

KEY					
		39 Coombe Wood	78 Horton Park CC	117 Prince's	155 Sunbury
1	Abbey Moor	40 Corinthian	79 Hurtmore	118 Purley Downs	156 Sundridge Park
2	The Addington	41 Coulsdon Manor	80 Hythe Imperial	119 Puttenham	157 Sunningdale
3	Addington Court	42 Cranbrook	81 Jack Nicklaus GC	120 Pyrford	158 Sunningdale Ladies
4	Addington Palace	43 Cray Valley	82 Kings Hill	121 RAC Country Club	159 Surbiton
5	Aquarius	44 Croham Hurst	83 Kingswood Golf & CC	122 Redhill & Reigate	160 Sutton Green
6	Ashford (Kent)	45 Cuddington	84 Knole Park	123 Redlibbets	161 Tandridge
7	Austin Lodge	46 Darenth Valley	85 Laleham	124 Reigate Heath	162 Tenterden
8	Banstead Downs	47 Dartford	86 Lamberhurst	125 Reigate Hill	163 Thames Ditton & Esher
9	Barnehurst	48 Deangate Ridge	87 Langley Park	126 Richmond	164 Tunbridge Wells
10	Bearsted	49 Dorking	88 Leatherhead	127 Richmond Park	165 Tyrrells Wood
11	Beckenham Place Park	50 The Drift	89 Leeds Castle	128 The Ridge	166 Upchurch River Valley
12	Betchworth Park	51 Duke's Dene	90 Limpsfield Chart	129 Riverside	167 Walmer & Kingsdown
13	Bexleyheath	52 Dulwich & Sydenham Hill	91 Lingfield Park	130 Rochester & Cobham Pk	168 Walton Heath
14	Birchwood Park	53 Dunsfold Aerodrome	92 Littlestone	131 Roehampton	169 Weald of Kent
15	Bletchingley	54 Edenbridge G&CC	93 The London	132 Roker Park	170 Wentworth
16	Boughton	55 Effingham	94 London Scottish	133 Romney Warren	171 West Byfleet
17	Bowenhurst	56 Eltham Warren	95 Lullingstone Park	134 Royal Blackheath	172 West Hill
18	Bramley	57 Epsom	96 Lydd	135 Royal Cinque Ports	173 West Kent
19	Broadwater Park	58 Farnham	97 Malden	136 Royal Mid-Surrey	174 West Malling
20	Broke Hill	59 Farnham Park	98 Marriott Tudor Pk CC	137 Royal St George's	175 West Surrey
21	Bromley	60 Faversham	99 Merrist Wood	138 Royal Wimbledon	176 Westerham
22	Broome Park CC	61 Fernfell G & CC	100 Mid-Kent	139 Rusper	177 Westgate & Birchington
23	Burhill	62 Foxhills	101 Milford	140 Ruxley	178 Whitstable & Seasalter
24	Camberley Heath	63 Gatton Manor	102 Mitcham	141 St Augustine's	179 Wildernesse
25	Canterbury	64 Gillingham	103 Moatlands	142 St George's Hill	180 Wildwood
26	Central London GC	65 Goal Farm Par 3	104 Moore Place	143 Sandown Golf Centre	181 Wimbledon Common
27	Chart Hills	66 Guildford	105 Nevill	144 Selsdon Pk Hotel & GC	182 Wimbledon Park
28	Chelsfield Lakes	67 Hankley Common	106 New Zealand Golf Club	145 Sene Valley	183 Windlemere
29	Cherry Lodge	68 Hawkhurst	107 Nizels	146 Sheerness	184 Windlesham
30	Chessington	69 Herne Bay	108 North Downs	147 Shillinglee Park	185 The Wisley
31	Chestfield	70 Hever	109 North Foreland	148 Shirley Park	186 Woking
32	Chiddingfold	71 High Elms	110 Oak Park	149 Shooters Hill	187 Woodcote Park
33	Chipstead	72 Hilden	111 Oaks Sports Centre	150 Shortlands	188 Woodlands Manor
34	Chislehurst	73 Hindhead	112 Oastpark	151 Sidcup	189 Worplesdon
35	Chobham	74 Hoebridge Golf Centre	113 Pachesham Golf Centre	152 Silvermere	190 Wrotham Heath
36	Clandon Regis	75 Holtye	114 Park Wood	153 Sittingbourne & Milton	
37	Cobtree Manor Park	76 Home Park	115 Pine Ridge Golf Centre	Regis	
38	Coombe Hill	77 Homelands B'golf Centre	116 Poult Wood	154 Staplehurst Park	

1A 14 Birchwood Park

Birchwood Rd, Wilmington, Dartford, Kent DA2 7HJ
☎(01322) 660554
Off A20 or M25 at Swanley turn-off.
Meadowland course.
Pro Gary Orr; Founded 1990
Designed by Howard Swan
18 holes, 6364 yards, S.S.S. 71
Visitors: welcome.
Green Fee: WD £14; WE £18.
Societies: welcome WD; WE limited, contact Sec; terms on application.
Catering: full facilities.
Practice range, 38 bays; floodlit.
Hotels: Stakis.

1A 15 Bletchingley

Church Lane, Bletchingley, Surrey RH1 4LP
☎(01833) 744666, Fax 744284, Pro 744848
From M25 junction 6 take A25; course 3 miles.
Parkland course.
Pro Alisdair Dryer; Founded 1993
18 holes, 6531 yards, S.S.S. 71
Visitors: welcome by appt.
Green Fee: WD £18; WE £25.

Societies: welcome by appt; terms on application.
Catering: bar and restaurant.
Hotels: Priory, Redhill.

1A 16 Boughton

Brickfield Lane, Boughton, Nr Faversham, Kent ME13 9AJ
☎(01227) 752277
At intersection of the A2/M2 follow signs for Boughton and Dunkirk.
Upland course.
Pro Tim Poole; Founded 1993
Designed by P Sparks
18 holes, 6452 yards, S.S.S. 71
Visitors: welcome.
Green Fee: WD £15; WE £20.
Societies: welcome; terms on application.
Catering: bar and restaurant.

1A 17 Bowenhurst

Mill Lane, Crondall, Nr Farnham, Surrey GU10 5RP
☎(01252) 851695, Fax 851695, Pro 851344
M3 junction 5.4 miles on A287 to Farnham.

Parkland course.
Pro Cameron Cowie; Founded 1994
Designed by N Finn/G Baker
9 holes, 4014 yards, S.S.S. 60
Visitors: welcome by prior arrangement.
Green Fee: WD £10; WE £13.
Societies: welcome by arrangement with Sec.
Catering: full facilities.
Practice range, 38 bays; floodlit.

1A 18 Bramley

Bramley, Nr Guildford, Surrey GU5 0AL
☎(01483) 893042, Fax 894673, Pro 893685, Sec 892696, Bar/Rest 898313
3 miles S of Guildford on A281.
Parkland course.
Pro Gary Peddie; Founded 1914
Designed by Charles Mayo,
Redesigned by James Braid
18 holes, 5990 yards, S.S.S. 69
Visitors: welcome with member.
Green Fee: WD £27; WE £27.
Societies: contact Sec; full bar and catering with driving range and practice area; £43-£54.

Catering: full catering with grill menu.
Hotels: Harrow, Compton; Parrot, Shalford.

1A 19 Broadwater Park

Guildford Rd, Farncombe, Nr Godalming, Surrey GU7 3BU
☎(01483) 429955, Fax 429955
On A3100 between Godalming and Guildford.
Par 3 parkland course.
Pro K Milton; Founded 1989
Designed by K.D. Milton
9 holes, 1301 yards
Visitors: welcome.
Societies: by prior arrangement.
Catering: bar and snacks.
Practice range, 16 bays; floodlit.

1A 20 Broke Hill

Sevenoaks Road, Halstead, Kent TN14 7HR
☎(01959) 533225, Fax 532880, Pro 533810
Close to M25 junction 4 opposite Knockholt station.
Parkland course/downland.
Pro Chris West; Founded 1993
Designed by D Williams
18 holes, 6454 yards, S.S.S. 71
Visitors: welcome WD.
Green Fee: WD £30; WE £30.
Societies: welcome Tues, Thurs (pm), Fri; packages available; from £34.
Catering: full clubhouse facilities.
Hotels: Post House, Borough Green; Bromley Court Hotel; Brands Hatch Thistle.

1A 21 Bromley

Magpie Hall Lane, Bromley, Kent BR2 8JF
☎(0181) 462 7014
A21 2 miles S of Bromley.
Public parkland course.
Pro Danny Williams
9 holes, 5490 yards, S.S.S. 67
Visitors: all welcome; no restrictions.
Green Fee: WD £4.85; WE £6.35.
Societies: welcome by appointment; terms on application.
Catering: snacks available.

1A 22 Broome Park CC

Broome Park Estate, Barham, Canterbury, Kent CT4 6QX
☎(01227) 831701, Fax 821973
Just off A2 E of Canterbury.
Parkland course.
Founded 1982
Designed by Donald Steel

18 holes, 6610 yards, S.S.S. 72
Visitors: welcome.
Green Fee: WD £26; WE £32.
Societies: welcome by prior arrangement; terms on application.
Catering: clubhouse facilities.
Practice range, 13 bays.

1A 23 Burhill

Walton-on-Thames, Surrey KT12 4BL
☎(01932) 227345, Fax 267159, Pro 221729
On A245 off A3 towards Byfleet.
Parkland course.
Pro Lee Johnson; Founded 1907
Designed by Willie Park
18 holes, 6224 yards, S.S.S. 70
Visitors: welcome by appointment Mon-Thurs with h'cap certs.
Green Fee: WD £45.
Societies: by prior arrangement only; details on application; £78.
Catering: bar and catering.
Hotels: Oatlands Park Hotel, Weybridge.

1A 24 Camberley Heath

Golf Drive, Camberley, Surrey GU15 1JG
☎(01276) 23258, Fax 692505
Off A325 Portsmouth road between Bagshot and Frimley.
Pine and heather.
Pro Glenn Ralph; Founded 1913
Designed by H. S. Colt
18 holes, 6637 yards, S.S.S. 70
Visitors: welcome WD only.
Green Fee: WD £36.
Societies: welcome weekdays by appt; terms on application.
Catering: full facilities.
Hotels: Frimley Hall Hotel.

1A 25 Canterbury

Scotland Hills, Canterbury, Kent CT1 1TW
☎(01227) 453532, Fax 784277, Pro 462865, Bar/Rest 781871
1 mile from Town Centre on A257 road to Sandwich.
Parkland course.
Pro Paul Everard; Founded 1927
Designed by H.S. Colt
18 holes, 6249 yards, S.S.S. 70
Visitors: welcome with h'cap certs.
Green Fee: WD £27; WE £27.
Societies: welcome Tues and Thurs; minimum 15; package of coffee, 36 holes, light lunch, 3-course evening meal; £46.50.
Catering: full facilities and bar.
Hotels: many in Canterbury.

1A 26 Central London GC

Burntwood Lane, Wandsworth, London SW17 0AT
☎(0181) 8712468, Fax 874 7447
Take Garratt Lane from A3 in Wandsworth. Burntwood Lane is off Garratt Lane after Earlsfield.
Parkland course.
Pro Jeremy Robson; Founded 1992
Designed by Patrick Tallack
9 holes, 4468 yards, S.S.S. 62
Visitors: welcome anytime.
Green Fee: WD £9; WE £9.
Societies: by arrangement.
Hotels: in Wimbledon.

1A 27 Chart Hills

Weeks Lane, Biddenden, Kent TN27 8JX
☎(01580) 292222, Fax 292233
M20 to junction 8; follow signs to Leeds Castle before turning on to A274 through Sutton Valence. 3 miles turn into Weeks Lane.
Parkland course; European HQ of D Leadbetter Academy.
Pro Danny French; Founded 1993
Designed by Nick Faldo
18 holes, 7086 yards, S.S.S. 72
Visitors: restricted Sun, Tues-Fri.
Green Fee: WD £60; WE £70.
Societies: restricted; full facilities including lunch and coffee; £75-£105.
Catering: full facilities.
Hotels: Great Danes; Forstal B&B.

1A 28 Chelsfield Lakes

Court Rd, Orpington, Kent BR6 9BX
☎(01689) 896266, Fax 824577
From M25 junction 4 follow signs to Orpington; course 300 yds from 2nd roundabout.
Parkland course.
Pro Nigel Lee; Founded 1993
Designed by MRM Leisure
18 holes, 6077 yards, S.S.S. 69
Warren course: 9 holes, par 3
Visitors: welcome.
Green Fee: WD £14; WE £17.
Societies: welcome by prior application; minimum 8; golf and catering packages available; terms on application.
Catering: full clubhouse facilities.

1A 29 Cherry Lodge

Jail Lane, Biggin Hill, Kent TN16 3AX
☎(01959) 572250, Fax 540672, Pro 572989
3 miles N of Westerham off A233.
Parkland course.
Pro Nigel Child; Founded 1970

Designed by John Day
18 holes, 6652 yards, S.S.S. 73
Visitors: WD by prior arrangement;
with a member only at WE.
Green Fee: WD £18; WE £18.
Societies: welcome by arrangement;
£30.
Catering: full bar and restaurant facilities.
Hotels: Kings Arms, Westerham.

1A 30 **Chessington**
Garrison Lane, Chessington, Surrey
KT9 2LW
☎(0181) 391 0948
Opposite Chessington South station,
very near Chessington Zoo.
Parkland course.
Pro Simon Defoy; Founded 1983
Designed by Patrick Tallack
9 holes, 1353 yards, S.S.S. 25
Visitors: welcome.
Green Fee: WD £4.50; WE £5.40.
Societies: welcome; terms on application.
Catering: full facilities.
Practice range, 18 bays; floodlit.
Hotels: Seven Hills; Oatlands Park.

1A 31 **Chestfield**
103 Chestfield Rd, Whitstable, Kent
CT5 3LU
☎(01227) 794411, Fax 794454, Pro
793563, Bar/Rest 792243
0.5 miles S of A299 at Chestfield station.
Parkland course, with sea views.
Pro John Brotherton; Founded 1924
18 holes, 5834 yards, S.S.S. 68
Visitors: WDs only.
Green Fee: WD £15.
Societies: welcome weekdays except
Thurs; packages available; terms on
application.
Catering: facilities available.
Hotels: Marine, Tankerton.

1A 32 **Chiddingfold**
Petworth Rd, Chiddingfold, Surrey
GU8 4SL
☎(01428) 685888
Take A283 off A3 and course is 10
minutes away, 50 yards S of
Chiddingfold.
Downland course.
Pro Paul Creamer; Founded 1994
Designed by J Gaunt & P Alliss
18 holes, 5482 yards, S.S.S. 67
Visitors: welcome WD.
Green Fee: WD £15; WE £22.
Societies: welcome; packages available; terms on application.

Catering: full facilities; conference
suite.
Practice range, 4 bays.
Hotels: Lythe Hill.

1A 33 **Chipstead**
How Lane, Coulsden, Surrey CR33PR
☎(01737) 555781
Follow signs to Chipstead from A217
Undulating parkland course.
Pro Gary Torbett; Founded 1906
18 holes, 5491 yards, S.S.S. 67
Visitors: welcome WD.
Green Fee: WD £20; WE £20.
Societies: welcome WD by appt;
terms on application.
Catering: lunch served; booking reqd.
Hotels: Reigate Manor.

1A 34 **Chislehurst**
Camden Place, Camden Park Rd,
Chislehurst, Kent BR7 5HJ
☎(0181) 467 3055, Fax 295 0874,
Pro 467 6798, Sec 467 2782,
Bar/Rest 467 2888
Off A20/A222 from Junction 3 of M25.
0.5 miles from Chislehurst station.
Parkland course.
Pro Mark Lawrence; Founded1894
18 holes, 5106 yards, S.S.S. 65
Visitors: welcome WD; with a member at WE.
Green Fee: WD £25; WE £25.
Societies: welcome Mon-Fri; 36 holes
available Thurs; £33.
Catering: full facilities.

1A 35 **Chobham**
Chobham Rd, Knaphill, Woking,
Surrey GU21 2TZ
☎(01276) 855584, Fax 855663, Pro
855748
Take A322 from M3 junction 3 towards
Guildford; at first roundabout take
A319 to Chobham, course 2 miles on
right towards Knaphill.
Wooded parkland with lakes.
Pro Tim Commes; Founded 1994
Designed by Clive Clark & Peter Alliss
18 holes, 6021 yards, S.S.S. 69
Visitors: members' guests only in
midweek.
Green Fee: WD £17.
Societies: welcome by appointment;
terms on application.
Catering: restaurant, bar and function
rooms.

1A 36 **Clandon Regis**
Epsom Road, West Clandon, Nr
Guildford, Surrey GU4 7TT

☎(01483) 224888, Fax 211781, Pro
223922
4 miles E of Guildford on A246.
Parkland course.
Pro Steve Lloyd; Founded 1994
Designed by D Williams
18 holes, 6412 yards, S.S.S. 71
Visitors: welcome by prior arrangement.
Green Fee: WD £25; WE £30.
Societies: welcome by prior arrangement; terms on application.
Catering: full bar and restaurant.

1A 37 **Cobtree Manor Park**
Chatham Rd, Maidstone, Kent ME14
3AZ
☎(01622) 753276
Take A229 from M20.
Municipal parkland course.
Pro Paul Foston; Founded 1984
Designed by F. Hawtree
18 holes, 5586 yards, S.S.S. 67
Visitors: welcome.
Green Fee: WD £13.50; WE £18.
Societies: terms on application.
Catering: available.

1A 38 **Coombe Hill**
Golf Club Drive, Kingston, Surrey KT2
7DF
☎(0181) 942 2284, Fax 949 5815,
Pro 949 3713, Bar/Rest 9422284
1 mile W of New Malden on A238.
Undulating, tree-lined.
Pro Craig Defoy; Founded 1911
Designed by J.F. Abercromby
18 holes, 6293 yards, S.S.S. 71
Visitors: WD by prior arrangement.
Green Fee: WD £65.
Societies: welcome by prior arrangement with Sec; terms on application.
Catering: restaurant and bar.
Hotels: Kingston Lodge.

1A 39 **Coombe Wood**
George Rd, Kingston Hill, Kingston-on-
Thames, Surrey KT2 7NS
☎(0181) 942 0388, Fax 942 0388,
Pro 942 6764, Bar/Rest 942 3828
From A3 take A308 (E) or A238 (W).
Mature parkland.
Pro David Butler; Founded 1904
Designed by T. Williamson
18 holes, 5299 yards, S.S.S. 66
Visitors: welcome WD; with a member only at WE.
Green Fee: WD £21.50; WE £21.50.
Societies: welcome Wed, Thurs, Fri;
packages available; £25.
Catering: full bar and restaurant.
Hotels: Kingston Lodge.

1A 40 Corinthian

Gay Dawn Farm, Fawkham, Longfield, Kent DA3 8LY
☎(01474) 707559, Fax 708431
Take A20 off junction 3 of M25 towards Brands Hatch and turn left towards Fawkham/Longfield.
Wooded parkland.
Pro Cameron McKillop; Founded 1986
Designed by Greg Turner
18 holes, 6323 yards, S.S.S. 70
Visitors: welcome WD, after 1pm at WE.
Green Fee: WD £12; WE £18.
Societies: welcome midweek; packages available; terms on application.
Catering: bar facilities.
Hotels: Brands Hatch Hotel; Brands Hatch Thistle.

1A 41 Coulsdon Manor

Coulsdon Rd, Coulsdon, Surrey CR5 2LL
☎(0181) 6680414, Pro 6606083
Just off A23, 2 miles S of Croydon, 2 miles N of M25 and M23.
Parkland course.
Pro David Copsey; Founded 1926
Designed by H.S. Buck
18 holes, 6037 yards, S.S.S. 68
Visitors: welcome.
Green Fee: WD £13; WE £16.
Societies: welcome by prior arrangement; terms on application.
Catering: full facilities.
Hotels: Coulsdon Manor.

1A 42 Cranbrook

Golford Rd, Cranbrook, Kent TN17 4AL
☎(01580) 712833, Fax 714274, Bar/Rest 715771
Off A262 at Sissinghurst; turn right at Bull towards Benenden; 1 mile on left.
Tree-lined parkland.
Pro Alan Gillard; Founded 1969
Designed by John D. Harris
18 holes, 6295 yards, S.S.S. 70
Visitors: welcome except Mon.
Green Fee: WD £23; WE £30.
Societies: welcome Tues-Fri; packages available; from £19.50.
Catering: full clubhouse facilities.
Hotels: Kennel Holt; The George.

1A 43 Cray Valley

Sandy Lane, St Paul's Cray, Orpington, Kent BR5 3HY
☎(01689) 839677, Fax 891428, Pro 837909
A20 off Ruxley roundabout; course is on Sandy Lane, 0.5 miles on left.

Parkland course.
Pro Gary Sherriff; Founded 1972
Designed by Golf Centres Ltd
18 holes, 5669 yards, S.S.S. 67
Visitors: pay and play.
Green Fee: WD £13; WE £19.
Societies: bookings 7 days in advance.

1A 44 Croham Hurst

Croham Rd, South Croydon, Surrey CR2 7HJ
☎(0181) 6575581, Pro 6577705, Sec 657558
1 mile from S Croydon; from M25 exit 6 N onto A22, take B270 to Warlingham at roundabout, then B269 to Selsdon; at traffic lights turn left into Farley Road, clubhouse 1.75 miles on left.
Parkland course.
Pro Eric Stillwell; Founded 1911
Designed by Hawtree & Sons
18 holes, 6290 yards, S.S.S. 70
Visitors: welcome, h'cap certs required; with member only at WE.
Green Fee: WD £33; WE £33.
Societies: welcome Wed, Thurs, Fri by arrangement; terms on application.
Catering: full facilities every day 10am-6pm; banqueting.
Hotels: Selsdon Park.

1A 45 Cuddington

Banstead Rd, Banstead, Surrey SM7 1RD
☎(0181) 393 7097, Fax 786 7025, Pro 393 5850, Sec 393 0952, Bar/Rest 393 0951
200 yards from Banstead station.
Parkland course.
Pro Mark Warner; Founded 1929
Designed by H.S. Colt
18 holes, 6394 yards, S.S.S. 70
Visitors: welcome with h'cap certs.
Green Fee: WD £35; WE £35.
Societies: welcome Thurs; full day's golf and meals, including dinner; £60.
Catering: full catering service.
Hotels: Heathside; Driftbridge.

1A 46 Darenth Valley

Station Rd, Shoreham, Kent TN14 7SA
☎(01959) 522944, Fax 525089, Pro 522922
Along A225 Sevenoaks-Dartford road, 4 miles N of Sevenoaks.
Parkland course.
Pro Scott Fotheringham; Founded 1973
18 holes, 6394 yards, S.S.S. 71

Visitors: welcome; bookings daily.
Green Fee: WD £13; WE £18.
Societies: welcome by arrangement with manager; terms on application.
Catering: bar meals, society catering, functions (up to 100 persons).

1A 47 Dartford

Dartford Heath, Dartford, Kent DA1 2TN
☎(01322) 223616, Pro 226409, Sec 226455
0.5 miles from A2 Dartford-Crayford turn-off.
Park/heathland course.
Pro Gary Cooke; Founded 1897
Designed by James Braid
18 holes, 5914 yards, S.S.S. 69
Visitors: WDs with h'cap certs; with member only at WE.
Green Fee: WD £28; WE £12.50.
Societies: Mon and Fri by prior arrangement; full day's package of golf and catering, including evening meal; £47.
Catering: full clubhouse facilities.
Hotels: Swallow, Bexleyheath; The Stakis Dartford Bridge.

1A 48 Deangate Ridge

Hoo, Rochester, Kent ME3 8RZ
☎(01634) 251180, Fax 255370
A228 from Rochester to Isle of Grain, then road signposted to Deangate.
Municipal parkland course.
Pro Richard Fox; Founded 1972
Designed by Hawtree & Sons
18 holes, 6300 yards, S.S.S. 70
Visitors: welcome anytime; bookings essential at WE.
Green Fee: WD £10.20; WE £13.50.
Societies: welcome; terms on application.
Catering: lunch and dinner served, bookings essential at weekends.
Practice range, 12 bays; floodlit.

1A 49 Dorking

Chart Park, Dorking, Surrey RH5 4BX
☎(01306) 886917, Pro 885914
1 mile S of Dorking on A24.
Parkland course.
Pro Paul Napier; Founded 1887
Designed by James Braid
9 holes, 5163 yards, S.S.S. 65
Visitors: welcome WD only.
Green Fee: WD £12; WE n/a.
Societies: welcome by prior arrangement; full restaurant and bar facilities; from £17.
Catering: restaurant and bar.
Hotels: Burford Bridge, Boxhill.

1A 50 **The Drift**

The Drift, East Horsley KT24 5HD
☎(01483) 284641, Fax 284642, Pro
284772, Bar/Rest 282432
On B2039 East Horsley road off A3.
Woodland course.
Founded 1975
Designed by H. Cotton/R Sandow
18 holes, 6425 yards, S.S.S. 72
Visitors: WD only unless member's
guest.
Green Fee: on application.
Societies: Mon-Fri by appt; club
cleaning service, coffee, lunch, dinner;
£37-£58
Catering: full restaurant and bar.
Hotels: Jarvis Thatcher Hotel, E
Horsley; Hautboy, Ockham.

1A 51 **Duke's Dene**

Slines New Rd, Woldingham, Surrey
CR3 7HA
☎(01883) 653501, Pro 653541
From M25 junction 6 towards
Caterham roundabout take
Woldingham exit.
Valley course.
Pro Paul Thornley; Founded 1996
18 holes, 6393 yards, S.S.S. 70
Visitors: welcome except after 12 at
WE.
Green Fee: WD £25; WE £25.
Societies: welcome WD but only after
2pm at WE in summer.
Catering: bar and brasserie.
Practice range.

1A 52 **Dulwich & Sydenham Hill**

Grange Lane, College Rd, London
SE21 7LH
☎(0181) 6933961, Fax 6932481, Pro
6938491
Off S Circular road at Dulwich College
and College Rd.
Parkland course.
Pro David Baillie; Founded 1894
18 holes, 6008 yards, S.S.S. 69
Visitors: welcome WD only by appt.
Green Fee: WD £25; WE £25.
Societies: welcome WD by prior
arrangement; terms on application.
Catering: lunch daily, dinner by appt.

1A 53 **Dunsfold Aerodrome**

British Aerospace, Dunsfold
Aerodrome, Nr Godalming, Surrey
GU8 4BS
☎(01483) 265451, Sec 276118
12 miles S of Guildford on A281.
Parkland course.
Founded 1965

Designed by John Sharkey
9 holes, 6099 yards, S.S.S. 69
Visitors: with member only.
Green Fee: member's responsibility.
Societies: welcome from British
Aerospace.
Catering: bar and snacks.

1A 54 **Edenbridge G & CC**

Crouch House Rd, Edenbridge, Kent
TN8 5LQ
☎(01732) 865097, Fax 867029
Travelling N through Edenbridge High
St, turn left into Stangrove Rd (30 yds
before railway station), at end of road
turn right, course is on left.
Undulating meadowland.
Pro Keith Burkin; Founded 1975
Old: 18 holes, 6577 yards, S.S.S. 72
New: 18 holes, 5695 yards, S.S.S. 68
9 hole beginners course, 1546 yards
Visitors: welcome, except WE morn-
ings on Old course.
Green Fee: WD £17.50; WE £23.50.
Societies: welcome WD by appoint-
ment; packages available; terms on
application.
Catering: clubhouse bar and catering.
Practice range, 14 bays; floodlit.
Hotels: Langley Arms, Tonbridge.

1A 55 **Effingham**

Guildford Rd, Effingham, Surrey KT24
5PZ
☎(01372) 452203, Fax 459959, Pro
452606
On A246 8 miles E of Guildford.
Downland course.
Pro Stephen Hoatson; Founded 1927
Designed by H.S. Colt
18 holes, 6524 yards, S.S.S. 71
Visitors: WD only by arrangement;
h'cap certs required.
Green Fee: WD £35; WE £35.
Societies: welcome Wed, Thurs and
Fri; terms on application.
Catering: lunch, tea, evening meal,
snacks, etc.
Hotels: Thatchers (East Horsley);
Preston Cross (Great Bookham).

1A 56 **Eltham Warren**

Bexley Rd, Eltham, London SE9 2PE
☎(0181) 850 1166, Pro 859 7909,
Sec 850 4477
0.5 miles from Eltham Station on
A210.
Parkland course.
Pro Gary Brett; Founded 1890
9 holes, 5840 yards, S.S.S. 68
Visitors: welcome on WD.
Green Fee: WD £25; WE £25.

Societies: Thurs only; green fees,
morning coffee, ploughman's lunch,
evening meal; £42.
Catering: full bar and catering.
Hotels: Swallow, Bexleyheath.

1A 57 **Epsom**

Longdown Lane South, Epsom, Surrey
KT17 4JR
☎(01372) 721666, Fax 817183, Pro
741867, Bar/Rest 723363
0.5 miles S of Epsom Downs Station
on road to Epsom College.
Downland course.
Pro Ron Goudie; Founded 1889
18 holes, 5658 yards, S.S.S. 68
Visitors: welcome except before noon
on Thurs, Sat and Sun.
Green Fee: WD £20; WE £20.
Societies: welcome WD except Tues,
and WE pm; min 12, max 40; packages available; terms on application.
Catering: full clubhouse facilities.
Hotels: Heathside hotel.

1A 58 **Farnham**

The Sands, Farnham, Surrey GU10
1PX
☎(01252) 783163, Fax 781185, Pro
782198, Sec 782109
On A31 from Runfold.
Heathland, pines, parkland.
Pro Grahame Cowlishaw; Founded
1896
18 holes, 6325 yards, S.S.S. 70
Visitors: welcome WDs.
Green Fee: WD £28.
Societies: Wed, Thurs, Fri only; 2
rounds of golf, coffee and roll on
arrival, snack lunch and evening meal;
golf clinics available; £57.
Catering: bar and restaurant facilities.
Hotels: Hogs Back Hotel.

1A 59 **Farnham Park**

Folly Hill, Farnham, Surrey GU9 0AV
☎(01252) 715216, Fax 718246
On A287 next to Farnham Castle.
Parkland course.
Pro P Chapman; Founded 1966
Designed by Henry Cotton
9 holes, 2326 yards, S.S.S. 54
Visitors: public pay and play.
Green Fee: WD £3.90; WE £4.40.
Societies: none.

1A 60 **Faversham**

Belmont Park, Faversham, Kent ME13
0HB
☎(01795) 890561, Fax 890760, Pro
890275

Leave M2 at junction 6, A251 to Faversham, then A2 to Sittingbourne for 0.5 mile, turn left at Brogdale Rd, and then follow signs.
Parkland course.
Pro Stuart Rokes; Founded 1902
18 holes, 6030 yards, S.S.S. 69
Visitors: only with member WE and Bank Holidays.
Green Fee: WD £28; WE £35.
Societies: by arrangement; terms on application.
Catering: by arrangement with Steward.
Hotels: Granary; Porch House.

1A 61 Fernfell G & CC
Barhatch Lane, Cranleigh, Surrey GU6 7NG
☎(01483) 268855, Pro 277188
Take A281 out of Guildford, 1 mile through Cranleigh take Ewhurst road, then turn into Barhatch Road/Barhatch Lane.
Parkland course.
Pro Trevor Longmuir; Founded 1985
18 holes, 5648 yards, S.S.S. 68
Visitors: welcome WD; restrictions WE.
Green Fee: WD £20; WE £25.
Societies: welcome WD; terms on application.
Catering: bar, restaurant, snacks, banquets.

1A 62 Foxhills
Stonehill Rd, Ottershaw, Surrey KT16 0EL
☎(01932) 872050, Fax 874762, Pro 873961
M25 junction 11 follow signs for Woking; at 2nd roundabout take 3rd exit into Foxhills Road.
Treelined course.
Pro A Good; Founded 1972
Designed by F Hawtree
Chertsey: 18 holes, 6883 yds, S.S.S. 73
Longcross: 18 holes, 6743 yds, S.S.S. 72
Visitors: welcome WD with h'cap certs.
Green Fee: WD £55; WE £55.
Societies: WD only; packages available; driving range facilities; £52-£115.
Catering: full clubhouse facilities.
Hotels: accommodation on site.

1A 63 Gatton Manor
Ockley, Dorking, Surrey RH5 5PQ
☎(01306) 627555, Fax 627713, Pro 627557

1.5 miles SW of Ockley on A29.
Parkland course.
Pro Rae Sergeant; Founded 1969
Designed by D.B. & D.G. Heath
18 holes, 6653 yards, S.S.S. 72
Visitors: welcome except Sunday am.
Green Fee: WD £21; WE £28.
Societies: welcome WD; coffee, lunch, dinner, 36 holes of golf; conference facilities, tennis and fishing with gym and health suite; £29-£55.
Catering: bar and restaurant.
Hotels: Gatton Manor.

1A 64 Gillingham
Woodlands Rd, Gillingham, Kent ME7 2AP
☎(01634) 853017, Fax 574749, Pro 855862, Bar/Rest 850999
On A2 at Gillingham, about 2 miles from M2 turn off to Gillingham.
Parkland/meadowland course.
Pro Brian Impett; Founded 1908
Designed by James Braid
18 holes, 5514 yards, S.S.S. 67
Visitors: welcome WD with h'cap certs; with member only at WE.
Green Fee: WD £18; WE £18.
Societies: welcome WD except Thurs; terms on application.
Catering: Wed-Sun lunch, evening meals.
Hotels: The Crest.

1A 65 Goal Farm Par 3
Gole Rd, Pirbright, Surrey GU24 OPZ
☎(01483) 473183
1 mile from Brookwood station off A322 towards Pirbright.
Parkland course.
Founded 1977
9 holes, 1146 yards, S.S.S. 48
Visitors: welcome except Thurs am or Sat am.
Green Fee: WD £3.50; WE £3.75.
Societies: welcome; terms on application.
Catering: bar and bar snacks.
Hotels: Lakeside.

1A 66 Guildford
High Path Rd,, Merrow, Guildford, Surrey GU1 2HL
☎(01483) 563941, Fax 453228, Pro 566765, Bar/Rest 531842
2 miles E of Guildford on A246.
Downland course.
Pro P G Hollington; Founded 1886
Designed by James Braid
18 holes, 6090 yards, S.S.S. 70
Visitors: welcome WD; members' guests only at WE.

Green Fee: WD £25; WE £25.
Societies: welcome by prior arrangemen; packages including practice areas and indoor practice rooms and snooker; terms on application.
Catering: full bar and catering facilities.
Hotels: White Horse; Angel.

1A 67 Hankley Common
Tilford Rd, Tilford, Farnham, Surrey GU10 2DD
☎(01252) 792493, Fax 795699, Pro 793761, Bar/Rest 793145
Off M3 or A3 to Farnham, along A31 Farnham by-pass to lights; left to Tilford.
Heathland course.
Pro P Stow; Founded 1897
Designed by James Braid
18 holes, 6438 yards, S.S.S. 71
Visitors: welcome only with telephone booking and h'cap cert.
Green Fee: WD £40; WE £40.
Societies: Tues, Wed; packages available; £65-£70.
Catering: full catering and bar.
Hotels: Bush, Farnham; Frensham Ponds; Pride of Valley, Churt.

1A 68 Hawkhurst
High St, Hawkhurst, Cranbrook, Kent TN18 4JS
☎(01580) 752396, Fax 754074, Pro 753600
On A268 3 miles from A21 at Flimwell, 0.5 mile from junction with A229.
Undulating parkland course.
Pro Tony Collins; Founded 1968
Designed by Rex Baldock
9 holes, 5751 yards, S.S.S. 68
Visitors: welcome weekdays; only with member at weekends.
Green Fee: WD £10; WE £10.
Societies: welcome by prior arrangement; mostly Fri; £18.
Catering: by arrangement.
Hotels: Royal Oak; Tudor Court; Queens.

1A 69 Herne Bay
Eddington, Herne Bay, Kent CT6 7PG
☎(01227) 373964, Pro 374727, Bar/Rest 374097
Off A299 Thanet road at Herne Bay-Canterbury junction.
Parkland course/links.
Pro S Dordoy; Founded 1895
18 holes, 5567 yards, S.S.S. 66
Visitors: welcome WD, and pm at WE.
Green Fee: WD £15; WE £20.

Societies: by prior arrangement; terms on application.
Catering: full facilities.

1A 70 **Hever**

Hever, Edenbridge, Kent TN8 7NP
☎(01732) 700771, Fax 700775, Bar/Rest 700016
Off A21 between Sevenoaks and Edenbridge adjacent to Hever Castle.
Parkland course, with water hazards.
Pro Richard Tinworth; Founded 1992
Designed by Dr Peter Nicholson
18 holes, 7002 yards, S.S.S. 75
Visitors: societies only.
Societies: by prior appt; coffee, golf, dinner; use of gymnasium included.
Also on site: sauna, spa, snooker, tennis; £38-£68.
Catering: restaurant and bar.
Hotels: hotel on site.

1A 71 **High Elms**

High Elms Rd, Downe, Kent BR6 7SL
☎(01689) 858175, Pro 853232
5 miles out of Bromley off the A21 to Sevenoaks.
Public parkland course.
Pro Peter Remy; Founded 1969
Designed by Fred Hawtree
18 holes, 6209 yards, S.S.S. 70
Visitors: welcome.
Green Fee: WD £9.75; WE £12.75.
Societies: welcome WD only; terms on application.
Catering: full meals and snacks.
Hotels: Bromley Court.

1A 72 **Hilden**

Rings Hill, Hildenborough, Kent TN11 8LX
☎(01732) 833607
Off A21 towards Tunbridge Wells adjacent to Hildenborough station.
Parkland course.
Pro Brendan Wynne; Founded 1994
9 holes, 1558 yards, S.S.S. 54
Visitors: welcome.
Green Fee: WD £5.75; WE £7.25.
Societies: welcome; terms on application.
Catering: full facilities.
Practice range, 40 bays; floodlit.

1A 73 **Hindhead**

Churt Rd, Hindhead, Surrey GU26 6HX
☎(01428) 604614, Fax 608508, Pro 604458
1.5 miles N of Hindhead on the A287.
Heathland course.

Pro Neil Ogilvy; Founded 1904
18 holes, 6373 yards, S.S.S. 70
Visitors: welcome WD; by appt WE.
Green Fee: WD £36; WE £44.
Societies: Wed, Thurs only; 36 holes of golf, coffee, snack lunch, evening meal; £50-£52.
Catering: full catering and bar.
Hotels: Mariners, Farnham; Devils Punch Bowl, Hindhead; Frensham Pond.

1A 74 **Hoebridge Golf Centre**

Old Woking Rd, Old Woking, Surrey GU22 8JH
☎(01483) 722611, Fax 740369
On B382 between Old Woking and West Byfleet.
Public parkland, two par 3 courses.
Pro Tim Powell; Founded 1982
Designed by John Jacobs
18 holes, 6536 yards, S.S.S. 71
Visitors: welcome but booking advised.
Green Fee: WD £15; WE £17.
Societies: WD by prior arrangement; snooker room also available; terms on application.
Catering: restaurant and bar facilities.
Practice range, 25 bays.

1A 75 **Holtye**

Holtye Common, Cowden, Kent TN8 7ED
☎(01342) 850635, Fax 850576, Pro 850957, Sec 850576
On the A264 1 mile S of Cowden.
Forest/heathland with 10-acre practice ground.
Pro K Hinton; Founded 1893
9 holes, 5325 yards, S.S.S. 66
Visitors: welcome Mon, Tues, Fri; Restrictions other days.
Green Fee: WD £15; WE £18.
Societies: by prior arrangement; terms on application.
Catering: catering and bar facilities.
Hotels: White Horse Inn (next door).

1A 76 **Home Park**

Hampton Wick, Kingston-upon-Thames KT1 4AD
☎(0181) 977 2423, Fax 977 4414, Pro 977 2658, Bar/Rest 977 6645
Entrance to Home Park is through Kingston Gate at Hampton Wick roundabout.
Parkland course/links.
Pro Len Roberts; Founded 1895
18 holes, 6611 yards, S.S.S. 71
Visitors: welcome.
Green Fee: WD £20; WE £25.

Societies: welcome with prior appt; packages available; terms on application.

1A 77 **Homelands Bettergolf Centre**

Ashford Rd, Kingsnorth, Kent TN26 1NJ
☎(01233) 661620, Fax 66162
M20 junction10 following signs for International station until 2nd roundabout where course is signposted.
Parkland course.
Pro Mark Belsham; Founded 1995
Designed by D Steel
9 holes, 4410 yards, S.S.S. 64
Visitors: Public pay as you play.
Green Fee: WD £7; WE £14.
Societies: welcome; bar snacks, driving range, academy pitch and putt; terms on application.
Catering: bar with drinks and snacks; BBQs can be arranged.
Practice range, 14 bays; floodlit.
Hotels: Eastwell Manor.

1A 78 **Horton Park Country Club**

Hook Road, Epsom, Surrey KT19 8QG
☎(0181) 3938400, Fax 394 1369
M25 junction 9; follow signs to Chessington, turning right at Malden Rushett lights. 2 miles, then left into Horton Lane.
Parkland course.
Pro G Clements/H Omidiran/J September; Founded 1987
Designed by P Tallack
9 holes, 5100 yards, S.S.S. 68
Visitors: Pay and play WD; bookings WE.
Green Fee: WD £11; WE £13.
Societies: welcome; packages include golf and lunch/dinner; £17.50-£32.
Catering: restaurant, bar, private suites.
Practice range, 26 bays; floodlit.
Hotels: Chalk Lane Hotel, Epsom.

1A 79 **Hurtmore**

Hurtmore Rd, Hurtmore, Godalming, Surrey GU7 2RN
☎(01483) 426492, Fax 426121, Sec 424440
4 miles S of Guildford on A3 at Hurtmore exit.
Parkland course.
Pro Maxine Burton; Founded 1990
Designed by Peter Alliss & Clive Clark
18 holes, 5514 yards, S.S.S. 67
Visitors: Public pay and play.

Green Fee: WD £10; WE £15.
Societies: welcome by appt; from £12.75.
Catering: full facilities
Hotels: Squirrel.

1A 80 Hythe Imperial

Princes Parade, Hythe, Kent CT21 6AE
☎(01303) 267554, Pro 267441
Turn off M20 to Hythe, to E end of seafront.
Seaside course.
Pro Gordon Ritchie; Founded 1950
9 holes, 5560 yards, S.S.S. 68
Visitors: welcome; must be member of a club, h'cap certs required.
Green Fee: WD £10; WE £15.
Societies: welcome by prior appt; terms on application.
Catering: hotel/club bar.
Hotels: Hythe Imperial.

1A 81 Jack Nicklaus Golf Centre

Sidcup By-pass, Chislehurst, Kent BR7 6RP
☎(0181) 3090181, Fax 3081691
On the main A20, London road.
Parkland course.
Pro David Bailey; Founded 1995
Designed by M Gillett
9 holes, 1055 yards
Visitors: welcome; pay as you play.
Green Fee: WD £5; WE £6.
Societies: welcome; terms on application.
Catering: full facilities.
Practice range, 54 bays; floodlit.

1A 82 Kings Hill

Kings Hill, West Malling, Kent ME19 4AF
☎(01732) 875040, Fax 875019, Pro 842121
From M20 junction 4 take A228 towards Tonbridge.
Parkland course.
Pro Chris Lightfoot; Founded 1996
Designed by David Williams
18 holes, 6622 yards, S.S.S. 72
Visitors: welcome WD; WE with member.
Green Fee: WD £25.
Societies: welcome by appt; £35-49.
Catering: full bar and catering.
Practice range.

1A 83 Kingswood Golf & CC

Sandy Lane, Tadworth, Surrey KT20 6DP
☎(01737) 832188, Fax 833920, Pro 832334, Bar/Rest 832316
From A217 take Bonsor Drive (A2032) to Kingswood Arms. Club 0.25 miles down Sandy Lane.
Parkland course.
Pro James Dodds; Founded 1928
Designed by James Braid
18 holes, 6904 yards, S.S.S. 73
Visitors: welcome but WE restrictions.
Green Fee: WD £32; WE £45.
Societies: welcome; terms on application.
Catering: bar and restaurant.
Hotels: club will provide list.

1A 84 Knole Park

Seal Hollow Rd, Sevenoaks, Kent TN15 0HJ
☎(01732) 452709, Fax 463159, Pro 452150, Sec 452150, Bar/Rest 740221
0.5 miles from Sevenoaks town centre.
Parkland course.
Pro P Gill; Founded 1924
Designed by J.A. Abercromby
18 holes, 6259 yards, S.S.S. 70
Visitors: welcome after 9am WD.
Green Fee: WD £32; WE £32.
Societies: Tues, Thurs, Fri by appt (min 20, max 40); £63.
Catering: full facilities.
Hotels: Royal Oak, Sevenoaks.

1A 85 Laleham

Laleham Reach, Chertsey, Surrey KT16 8RP
☎(01932) 564211, Fax 564448, Pro 562877, Bar/Rest 502188
From M25 junction 11 take A320 to Thorpe Park roundabout then to Penton Marina and signposted.
Parkland course.
Pro Hogan Scott; Founded 1908
18 holes, 6211 yards, S.S.S. 70
Visitors: welcome with h'cap certs.
Green Fee: WD £18; WE £18.
Societies: Mon, Tues, Wed; catering facilities; £21-£37.
Catering: full facilities.

1A 86 Lamberhurst

Church Rd, Lamberhurst, Kent TN3 8DT
☎(01892) 890241, Fax 891140, Pro 890552, Sec 890591
6 miles S of Tunbridge Wells on A21; turning on to B2162 at Lamberhurst.
Parkland course.
Pro Mike Travers; Founded 1890/1920
Designed by Frank Pennink

18 holes, 6345 yards, S.S.S. 70
Visitors: welcome WD, and pm at WE.
Green Fee: WD £22; WE £36.
Societies: welcome Tues, Wed and Thurs, April to October; 36 holes, coffee, lunch and 3-course dinner; min 16, max 36; £47.
Catering: full clubhouse facilities.
Hotels: Pembury Resort, Pembury; George & Dragon, Lamberhurst.

1A 87 Langley Park

Barnfield Wood Rd, Beckenham, Kent BR3 6SZ
☎(0181) Pro 650 1663, Sec 658 6849, Bar/Rest 650 2090
1 mile from Bromley South station.
Parkland course.
Pro Colin Staff; Founded 1910
Designed by J.H. Taylor
18 holes, 6488 yards, S.S.S. 71
Visitors: welcome WD by arrangement with Pro shop.
Green Fee: WD £35; WE £35.
Societies: Wed and Thurs only; maximum 24 Thurs; 36 holes of golf, lunch and dinner; £52.
Catering: full bar and restaurant.
Hotels: Bromley Court Hotel.

1A 88 Leatherhead

Kingston Rd, Leatherhead, Surrey KT22 0EE
☎(01372) 843966, Fax 842241, Pro 843956
From M25 junction 9 take A243 towards London, course entrance 500 yards.
Parkland course.
Pro Simon Norman; Founded 1903
18 holes, 6203 yards, S.S.S. 70
Visitors: welcome by appointment; WE not before 12 am.
Green Fee: WD £30; WE £45.
Societies: welcome; terms on application.
Catering: restaurant, brasserie, bar.
Hotels: Woodlands Park (Oxshott).

1A 89 Leeds Castle

Leeds Castle, Maidstone, Kent ME17 1PL
☎(01622) 880467, Fax 735616
M20 junction 8 and follow signs to Leeds Castle on A20.
Parkland course.
Founded 1933
Designed by Neil Coles
9 holes, 5362 yards
Visitors: book 6 days ahead; no jeans.

Societies: WD only; coffee, golf, nets; £16-£22.50.
Hotels: Tudor Park, Maidstone.

1A 90 **Limpsfield Chart**

Limpsfield, Oxted, Surrey RH8 0SL
☎(01883) Sec 723405, Bar/Rest 722106
On A25 between Oxted and Westerham, over traffic lights 300 yards on right, E of Oxted.
Heathland course.
Founded 1889
9 holes, 5718 yards, S.S.S. 69
Visitors: WE by prior arrangement or with member.
Green Fee: WD £18; WE £20.
Societies: can be arranged; terms on application.
Catering: meals served.
Hotels: Kings Arms (Westerham).

1A 91 **Lingfield Park**

Racecourse Road, Lingfield, Surrey RH7 6PQ
☎(01342) 834602, Fax 836077, Pro 832659
From A22 at E Grinstead take the B 2028 to Lingfield.
Parkland course.
Founded 1987
18 holes, 6487 yards, S.S.S. 72
Visitors: welcome.
Green Fee: WD £27; WE £27.
Societies: welcome by prior arrangement; packages include golf and catering; from £35.
Catering: facilities available.
Hotels: Felbridge; Copthorne.

1A 92 **Littlestone**

St Andrews Rd, Littlestone, New Romney, Kent TN28 8RB
☎(01797) 363355, Fax 362740, Pro 362231, Bar/Rest 362310
In New Romney on A259 between Brenzett and Hythe; 15 miles S of Ashford
Links course.
Pro Stephen Watkins; Founded 1888
Designed by Laidlaw Purves
18 holes, 6470 yards, S.S.S. 72
Visitors: welcome by prior arrangement at WE.
Green Fee: WD £30; WE £45.
Societies: welcome WD; golf and catering packages; from £34.
Catering: full facilities.
Practice ground; chipping bunker.
Hotels: Romney Bay House; Broadacre; Rose and Crown; White House B&B.

1A 93 **The London**

South Ash Manor Estate, Ash, Nr Sevenoaks, Kent TN15 7EN
☎(01474) 879899, Fax 879912
Off A20 near Brands Hatch at W Kingsdown.
Parkland course.
Pro K Morgan/Paul Way is touring pro; Founded 1993
Designed by Jack Nicklaus
Heritage: 18 holes, 7208 yards, S.S.S. 72
International: 18 holes, 7005 yards, S.S.S. 74
Visitors: welcome only with member.
Green Fee: Heritage: WD £50; WE £60; International: WD £40; WE £45.
Societies: corporate days arranged.
Catering: restaurant, bar, function rooms and coffee shop.
Hotels: Brands Hatch Thistle; Brands Hatch Place.

1A 94 **London Scottish**

Windmill Enclosure, Wimbledon Common, London SW19 5NQ
☎(0181) 7880135, Fax 7897517, Pro 7891207
1 mile from Putney station.
Parkland course.
Pro Steve Barr; Founded 1865
18 holes, 5458 yards, S.S.S. 66
Visitors: welcome WD, except BH; must wear red upper garment.
Green Fee: WD £15; WE £15.
Societies: welcome except WE, Mon; terms on application.
Catering: lunch served, dinner if ordered.
Hotels: Wayfarer.

1A 95 **Lullingstone Park**

Park Gate, Chelsfield, Orpington, Kent BR6 7PX
☎(01959) 533793, Bar/Rest 532928
Signposted from M25 junction 4.
Municipal parkland course.
Pro Mark Watt; Founded 1923
Designed by Fred Hawtree
18 holes, 6779 yards, S.S.S. 72
Visitors: welcome.
Green Fee: WD £9; WE £11.
Societies: welcome by prior arrangement; terms on application.
Catering: bar, snacks; meals ordered.
Practice range, 32 bays.
Hotels: Thistle (Brands Hatch).

1A 96 **Lydd**

Romney Road, Lydd, Romney Marsh, Kent TN29 9LS
☎(01797) 320808, Pro 321921

Take Ashford exit off M20 and follow A2070 signs to Lydd Airport. At Brenzett turn left and take B2075, club is on left.
Links type course.
Pro Andrew Jones; Founded 1993
Designed by M Smith
18 holes, 6517 yards, S.S.S. 71
Visitors: welcome.
Green Fee: WD £14; WE £18.
Societies: welcome by prior appt; terms on application.
Catering: bar and restaurant.
Practice range, 25 bays; floodlit.

1A 97 **Malden**

Traps Lane, New Malden, Surrey KT3 4RS
☎(0181) 942 0654, Fax 336 2219, Pro 942 6009, Bar/Rest 942 3266
0.5 miles from New Malden station, close to the A3 between Wimbledon and Kingston.
Parkland course.
Pro Robert Hunter; Founded 1926
18 holes, 6295 yards, S.S.S. 70
Visitors: welcome WD; WE restrictions.
Green Fee: WD £25; WE £45.
Societies: Wed, Thurs, Fri only; terms on application.
Catering: full clubhouse facilities.
Hotels: Kingston Lodge.

1A 98 **Marriott Tudor Park Hotel & CC**

Ashford Rd, Bearstead, Maidstone, Kent ME14 4NQ
☎(01622) 734334
Follow A20 Ashford road; 3 miles from Maidstone centre.
Parkland course.
Founded 1988
Designed by Donald Steel
18 holes, 6041 yards, S.S.S. 69
Visitors: welcome with h'cap certs.
Green Fee: WD £25; WE £35.
Societies: welcome WD by appt; terms on application.
Catering: hotel bar and restaurant.
Hotels: Marriott Tudor Park.

1A 99 **Merrist Wood**

Coombe Lane, Worplesdon, Guildford, Surrey GU3 3PE
☎(01483) 884045, Pro 884050, Bar/Rest 884048
Off A323 at Worplesdon.
Parkland/woodland course.
Pro Andrew Kirk; Founded 1997
Designed by David Williams
18 holes, 6909 yards, S.S.S. 73

Visitors: welcome weekdays.
Green Fee: WD £35.
Societies: welcome from 1999.
Catering: bar and restaurant.
Hotels: Worplesdon Place.

1A 100 **Mid-Kent**
Singlewell Rd, Gravesend, Kent DA11 7RB
☎(01474) 568035, Fax 564218, Pro 332810, Bar/Rest 352387
On A227 after leaving A2 signposted Gravesend.
Parkland course.
Pro Mark Foreman; Founded 1909
Designed by Frank Pennink
18 holes, 6218 yards, S.S.S. 70
Visitors: welcome midweek.
Green Fee: WD £20; WE £20.
Societies: Tues only; minimum 24; £30.
Catering: full facilities.
Hotels: Manor; Tolgate.

1A 101 **Milford**
Milford, Nr Guildford, Surrey GU8 5HS
☎(01483) 419200, Fax 419199, Pro 416291
From A3 take Milford exit and head for station.
Parkland course.
Pro Nick English; Founded 1993
Designed by Peter Alliss & Clive Clark
18 holes, 5960 yards, S.S.S. 69
Visitors: welcome.
Green Fee: WD £20; WE £35.
Societies: welcome; from £35.
Catering: full clubhouse facilities.
Hotels: Inn on the Lake.

1A 102 **Mitcham**
Carshalton Rd, Mitcham Junction, Surrey CR4 4HN
☎(0181) 6481508, Pro 6404280, Sec 6484197
A237 off A23, by Mitcham Junction station.
Meadowland course.
Pro Jeff Godfrey; Founded 1886
18 holes, 5935 yards, S.S.S. 68
Visitors: welcome WD by appt.
Green Fee: WD £13; WE £13.
Societies: terms on application.
Catering: full facilities.
Hotels: Hilton.

1A 103 **Moatlands**
Watermans Lane, Brenchley, Kent TN12 6ND
☎(01892) 724400, Fax 723300, Pro 724252

From A21 take B2160 to Paddock Wood travelling through Matfield.
Parkland course.
Pro Simon Wood; Founded 1993
Designed by K. Saito/Taiyo International
18 holes, 7060 yards, S.S.S. 74
Visitors: welcome WD; pm at WE.
Green Fee: WD £29; WE £39.
Societies: welcome Mon, Tues,Thurs; terms on application.
Catering: clubhouse bar and restaurant.
Hotels: Jarvis Pembury Resort.

1A 104 **Moore Place**
Portsmouth Rd, Esher, Surrey KT10 9LN
☎(01372) 463533, Fax 460274
On A3 Portsmouth road, 0.5 mile from centre of Easher towards Cobham.
Public undulating parkland course.
Pro David Allen; Founded 1926
Designed by David Allen
9 holes, 2148 yards, S.S.S. 30
Visitors: welcome.
Green Fee: WD £5.80; WE £7.70.
Societies: welcome WD; terms on application.
Catering: full facilities.
Hotels: Haven.

1A 105 **Nevill**
Benhall Mill Rd, Tunbridge Wells, Kent TN2 5JW
☎(01892) 525818, Fax 517861, Pro 532941, Bar/Rest 517860
S of Tunbridge Wells on A21.
Parkland course.
Pro Paul Huggett; Founded 1914
Designed by C.K. Cotton
18 holes, 6349 yards, S.S.S. 70
Visitors: welcome with h'cap certs.
Green Fee: WD £25; WE £46.
Societies: welcome Wed, Thurs; £53.
Catering: full facilities.
Hotels: Spa Hotel, Tunbridge Wells.

1A 106 **New Zealand Golf Club**
Woodham Lane, Addlestone, Surrey KT15 3QD
☎(01932) 345049, Fax 342891, Pro 349619
On A245 from W Byfleet to Woking.
Wooded heathland course.
Founded 1895
Designed by Muir-Ferguson/Simpson
18 holes, 6012 yards, S.S.S. 69
Visitors: welcome by appt.
Societies: welcome by appt; terms on application.
Catering: full facilities.

1A 107 **Nizels**
Nizels Lane, Hildenborough, Nr Tonbridge, Kent TN11 8NU
☎(01732) 833138, Fax 833764, Pro 838926
A21 southbound from M24 junction 5.
Take B 245 towards Tonbridge. At roundabout head for Hildenborough and first right is Nizels Lane.
Parkland course.
Pro Richard and Sue Hodge; Founded 1992
Designed by Lennan/Purnell
18 holes, 6362 yards, S.S.S. 71
Visitors: welcome except am and WE.
Green Fee: WD £25; WE £35.
Societies: welcome by prior arrangement; minimum 12; from £36.
Catering: full facilities and bar
Hotels: Rose & Crown, Tonbridge; Philpots Manor, Hildenborough.

1A 108 **North Downs**
Northdown Rd, Woldingham, Surrey CR3 7AA
☎(01883) 652057, Fax 652832, Pro 652004, Sec 652298, Bar/Rest 652027
2 miles N of M25 junction 6 to roundabout, 5th exit to Woldingham (2miles); clubhouse 0.5 mile through village on left.
Downland course.
Pro Mike Homewood; Founded 1899
Designed by J.J. Pennink
18 holes, 5843 yards, S.S.S. 68
Visitors: welcome WD with h'cap certs or prior enquiry to Manager.
Green Fee: WD £20; WE £20.
Societies: WD, half or full day (half day only Thurs); terms on application.
Catering: restaurant, snacks.
Hotels: Lodge Road Chef (M25).

1A 109 **North Foreland**
Convent Rd, Broadstairs, Kent CT10 3PU
☎(01843) 862140, Fax 862663, Pro 604471
A28 from Canterbury, or A2/M2/A299 from London to Kingsgate via Broadstairs; course 1.5 miles from Broadstairs station.
Seaside/clifftop course.
Pro Neil Hansen; Founded 1903
Designed by Fowler and Simpson
18 holes, 6430 yards, S.S.S. 71
Short course: 18 holes, 1752 yards, par 54
Visitors: prior booking, not Sun, Mon, Tues am; h'cap certs required; short course unrestricted.

Nizels Golf Course and Georgian Manor House - a Grade II listed House offering a wide choice of elegantly appointed meeting rooms - is sited in 127 acres of tranquil Kentish Parklands, yet easily accessible from the M25 and train network from London.

Our excellent facilities, high standards and personal service combine to provide a memorable experience for corporate, society and individual golfers.

For further details please contact:
The Membership & Events Office,
Nizels Lane, Hildenborough, Kent TN11 8NU
Tel: 01732 833138
• Member of the Clubhaus Group •

Green Fee: WD £25; WE £35; short course £5.50.
Societies: welcome by appt; terms on application.
Catering: full clubhouse facilities.
Hotels: Castle Keep.

1A 110 **Oak Park**
Heath Lane, Crondall, Nr Farnham, Surrey GU10 5PB
☎(01252) 850880, Fax 850851, Pro 850066, Bar/Rest 850850
1.25 miles off A287 Farnham-Odiham road; 5 miles from M3 junction 5.
Woodland course; also 9 hole Village parkland course.
Pro Simon Coaker; Founded 1984
Designed by Patrick Dawson
18 holes, 6318 yards, S.S.S. 70
Visitors: h'cap certs required for Woodland course.
Green Fee: WD £20; WE £30.
Societies: welcome by appt; from £23.50.
Catering: conservatory bar, restaurant with cocktail bar.
Hotels: Bishops Table, Bush; both Farnham.

1A 111 **Oaks Sports Centre**
Woodmansterne Rd, Carshalton, Surrey SM5 4AN
☎(0181) 6438363, Fax 770 7303, Sec 642 7103
On B2032 past Carshalton Beeches station, Oaks Sports Centre signposted N of A2022, halfway between A217 and A237.
Public meadowland course.
Pro Geoff Horley; Founded 1972
Designed by Alphagreen
18 holes, 6033 yards, S.S.S. 69
Visitors: welcome.
Green Fee: WD £12; WE £14.
Societies: welcome by appt; terms on application.
Catering: restaurant and bar.

1A 112 **Oastpark**
Malling Rd, Snodland, Kent ME6 5LG
☎(01634) 242818, Fax 240744, Pro 242661, Bar/Rest 242659
On A228 close to M20 junction 4 and M2 junction 2.
Parkland course.
Pro John Gregory; Founded 1992
Designed by Terry Cullen
18 holes, 6173 yards, S.S.S. 69
Visitors: welcome.
Green Fee: WD £8.50; WE £12.
Societies: welcome WD and after 11 at WE; minimum 8; from £13.
Catering: full clubhouse facilities.
Hotels: Swan; Larkfield Priory; Forte Crest.

1A 113 **Pachesham Golf Centre**
Oaklawn Road, Leatherhead, Surrey KT22 0BT
☎(01372) 843453, Fax 844076
M25 junction 9; A244 towards Esher.
Parkland course.
Pro Phil Taylor; Founded 1992
Designed by Phil Taylor
9 holes, 5608 yards, S.S.S. 67
Visitors: welcome; book 48 hours ahead.
Green Fee: WD £7.50; WE £9.
Societies: welcome by appt; terms on application.
Catering: full facilities.
Hotels: Woodlands Park.

1A 114 **Park Wood**
Chestnut Avenue, Westerham, Kent TN16 2EG
☎(01959) 577744, Fax 572702
From the centre of Westerham take Oxted Road then turn right into Croydon Road, go under M25 to small crossroads. Course is right and immediate right.
Parkland and lakes course.
Pro Nick Terry; Founded 1993
Designed by L Smith & R Goldsmith
18 holes, 6835 yards, S.S.S. 72
Visitors: welcome.
Green Fee: WD £20; WE £30.
Societies: welcome Mon-Sat.
Catering: 120-seat restaurant, full bar.
Hotels: Kings Arms (Westerham).

1A 115 **Pine Ridge Golf Centre**
Old Bisley Rd, Frimley, Camberley, Surrey GU16 5NX
☎(01276) 675444
5 mins from M3 junction 3; location map available on request.
Public pine-forested course.
Pro Andrew Fannon; Founded 1992
Designed by Clive D. Smith
18 holes, 6012 yards, S.S.S. 71
Visitors: welcome.
Green Fee: WD £17.50; WE £22.
Societies: welcome WD, min 12; terms on application.
Catering: bar and restaurant, all day.
Hotels: Lakeside; Frimley Hall.

1A 116 **Poult Wood**
Higham Lane, Tonbridge, Kent TN11 9QR
☎(01732) 364039, Bar/Rest 366180
1 mile N of Tonbridge off the A227.
Municipal wooded course.
Pro Chris Miller; Founded 1972
Designed by Fred Hawtree
18 holes, 5569 yards, S.S.S. 67
Visitors: welcome by appt.
Green Fee: WD £10; WE £15.
Societies: welcome WD by appt; terms on application.
Catering: restaurant and bar.
Hotels: Langley; Rose & Crown.

1A 117 **Prince's**
Sandwich Bay, Sandwich, Kent CT13 9QB
☎(01304) 611118, Fax 612000, Pro 613797

M2, A2 to A256 then follow signs for Sandwich; course signposted.
3 loops of 9 holes; links course.
Pro Chris Evans; Founded 1904
Designed by Sir Guy Campbell & John Morrison
18 holes, 6690 yards, S.S.S. 72
Visitors: welcome.
Green Fee: WD £25; WE £36.
Societies: welcome by appt; from £25.
Catering: spike and lounge bar; restaurant.
Hotels: The Bell; The Blazing Donkey, Ham; Royal, Deal.

1A 118 **Purley Downs**
106 Purley Downs Road, South Croydon, Surrey CR2 0RB
☎(0181) 657 1231, Fax 651 5044, Pro 651 0819, Sec 657 8347
3 miles S of Croydon on A235.
Downland course.
Pro Graham Wilson; Founded 1894
18 holes, 6212 yards, S.S.S. 70
Visitors: welcome WD.
Green Fee: WD £30; WE £30.
Societies: welcome Mon, Thurs; terms on application.
Catering: 19th hole bar, lounge bar and restaurant.
Hotels: Selsdon Park; Trust House Forte; Croydon Hilton.

1A 119 **Puttenham**
Heath Rd, Puttenham, Guildford, Surrey GU31A L
☎(01483) 810609, Fax 810988, Pro 810277, Sec 810498, Bar/Rest 811087
Off A31 Hogs Back at Puttenham sign (B3000).
Tight heathland course.
Pro Gary Simmons; Founded 1894
18 holes, 6214 yards, S.S.S. 69
Visitors: welcome WD by prior arrangement; with a member only at WE.
Green Fee: WD £23; WE £23.
Societies: welcome Wed, Thurs; terms on application.
Catering: full catering and bar.
Hotels: Hogs Back Hotel.

1A 120 **Pyrford**
Warren Lane, Pyrford, Woking, Surrey GU22 8XR
☎(01483) 723555, Fax 729777, Pro 750170
From A3 take Ripley/Wisley exit (B2215) through Ripley, follow signs for Pyrford.
Parkland course.

Pro Jeremy Bennett; Founded 1993
Designed by Peter Alliss & Clive Clark
18 holes, 6230 yards, S.S.S. 70
Visitors: welcome.
Green Fee: WD £36; WE £52.
Societies: welcome; £45.
Catering: full bar and catering.
Hotels: Cobham Hilton.

1A 121 **RAC Country Club**
Woodcote Park, Epsom, Surrey KT18 7EW
☎(01372) 276311
On the A24 1.75 miles from Epsom
Parkland courses.
Founded 1913
Coronation course:18 holes, 5474 yds, S.S.S. 67
Old course: 18 holes, 6709 yds, S.S.S. 72
Visitors: with a member only.
Societies: none.
Catering: full facilities.

1A 122 **Redhill & Reigate**
Clarence Lodge, Pendleton Rd, Redhill, Surrey RH1 6LB
☎(01737) 240777, Fax 240777, Pro 244433, Bar/Rest 244626
1 mile S of Redhill between A23 and A25.
Wooded parkland course.
Pro Warren Pike; Founded 1887
Designed by James Braid
18 holes, 5272 yards, S.S.S. 66
Visitors: welcome WD and after 11am at WE.
Green Fee: WD £12; WE £18.
Societies: welcome by prior arrangement; packages available; from £37.50.
Catering: full facilities.
Hotels: Reigate Manor.

1A 123 **Redlibbets**
Manor Lane, West Yoke, Ash, Sevenoaks, Kent TN15 7HT
☎(01474) 872278, Fax 879290, Sec 879190
Take A20 off M25 towards Brands Hatch, course is on Paddock side next to Fawkham Manor Hospital, 8 miles from Sevenoaks.
Parkland course.
Pro Ross Taylor; Founded 1996
Designed by J Gaunt
18 holes, 6619 yards, S.S.S. 72
Visitors: welcome with a member.
Societies: Tues, Thurs; terms on application.
Catering: full facilities.
Hotels: Brands Hatch Place.

1A 124 **Reigate Heath**
Reigate Heath, Reigate, Surrey RH2 8QR
☎(01737) 242610, Fax 226793, Pro 243077, Sec 226793, Bar/Rest 226793
1.5 miles W of Reigate on Flanchford Road off A25.
Heathland course.
Pro Barry Davies; Founded 1895
9 holes, 5658 yards, S.S.S. 67
Visitors: welcome in midweek.
Green Fee: WD £20; WE n/a.
Societies: Wed, Thurs; max 30; terms on application.
Catering: full facilities.
Hotels: Cranleigh Hotel, Reigate.

1A 125 **Reigate Hill**
Gatton Bottom, Reigate, Surrey RH2 0TU
☎(01883) Fax 642650, Sec 645577
1 mile off junction 8 of the M25.
Parkland course.
Pro Martin Platts; Founded 1995
Designed by D Williams
18 holes, 6175 yards, S.S.S. 70
Visitors: WE with restrictions.
Green Fee: WD £25; WE £35.
Societies: welcome by appt; terms on application.
Catering: full facilities.
Hotels: Bridge House (Reigate Hill): The Priory (Nutfield).

1A 126 **Richmond**
Sudbrook Park, Richmond, Surrey TW10 7AS
☎(0181) 9401463, Pro 9407792, Sec 9404351
On A307 1 mile S of Richmond, look for Sudbrook Lane on left.
Parkland course.
Pro Nick Job; Founded 1891
Designed by Tom Dunn
18 holes, 5785 yards, S.S.S. 69
Visitors: WD by appt.
Green Fee: WD £25; WE £25.
Societies: Tues, Thurs, Fri by appt; terms on application.
Catering: bar snacks, lunches every day.
Hotels: Petersham; Richmond Gate.

1A 127 **Richmond Park**
Roehampton Gate, Richmond Park, London SW15 5JR
☎(0181) 8763205, Fax 878 1354, Pro 876 1795
Inside Richmond Park. Enter through Roehampton Gate off Priory Road.
Parkland courses.

Royal Cinque Ports

When the founders of Royal St George's finally spied out the incomparable stretch of linksland that became their home, it signalled the end of a search that had started in the Bournemouth area although, more than a century later, it is impossible to tell how diligent their reconnaissance had been. If it was really thorough, it means they overlooked the claims of Rye and Littlestone – even perhaps the charms of Deal whose plans to build a course there may have been hatched about the same time.

However, one assertion about which there has never been any argument is that Rye, Littlestone, Deal, Sandwich and Prince's, the latter founded in 1904, offer a variety and quality of golf which is second to none. They typify the very best the game has to offer, a mixture of inviting challenge and rich enjoyment. In easy reach of London, they are reminders of the era when shotmaking was much more of an art than it is today.

A comfortable journey by car across Romney Marsh is all that separates Rye from Sandwich, a note to remember when planning a few days off. Rye is a world of its own, a unique golfing fairy tale land. Its subtleties are many, its conquerors few. Essentially a members' Club, it has never sought to attract major events, unlike Royal St George's which, within seven years of opening in 1887, had staged the Open championship, the first to be held outside Scotland.

This heralded an immediate recognition for a quiet corner of England whose bleak beauty, if something of an acquired taste, becomes compelling. Deal staged the Opens of 1909 and 1920, Prince's receiving the call in 1932 – an honour that was bound to have been repeated had not it been so badly scarred by enemy bombing in World War II, an act of disfigurement

that Lord Brabazon likened to "throwing darts at a Rembrandt".

Nevertheless, nowhere in the world are three championship courses quite so cheek by jowl. Prince's and Royal St George's common boundary is all too apparent every time you drive on the 14th at Royal St George's while, if Tiger Woods stood on the fifth tee at Sandwich and launched one of his exocets over the houses, it would be precious near to landing on the 11th fairway at Deal. This is part of an inward nine that is full of intrigue and mighty hitting.

Sandwich is a place for giant dunes, larks where a high degree of golfing ingenuity is essential. Conventional shots, measured to the metre, can be singularly ill advised and unsuccessful in stout winds although Greg Norman caught it off guard in somewhat calmer conditions in his final round of 64 in the 1993 Open, Sandwich's third in twelve years after a period in the wilderness.

Some of the greens at Sandwich are eccentrically shaped and contoured, a classic way of nullifying the power of the modern player. It is often said that today, you couldn't build them like that today, but why not? Littlestone may not have anything to match the fourth or ninth at Royal St George's but their greens were beautifully shaped in the first instance by Alister Mackenzie, confirmation of their pedigree. Littlestone puts me in mind of the small Scottish towns or hamlets built around a golf course. Somewhat unusually for a links, the holes change direction attractively and cleverly, a sure sign of the need to adapt and not simply be blown out or blown home.

It is an undoubted gem in the South East's locker, withstanding and remaining fresh in the face of changing equipment but, if it is courses built in the modern idiom that you prefer, Chart Hills and East Sussex National offer notable contrast.

Pro David Bown; Founded 1923
Designed by Hawtree & Sons
Dukes's: 18 holes, 6036 yards, S.S.S.
68
Prince's: 18 holes, 5868 yards, S.S.S.
67
Visitors: pay and play course.
Green Fee: WD £13; WE £16.
Societies: welcome; £15-£45.95.
Catering: some catering available.
Hotels: Richmond Gate Hotel.

1A 128 **The Ridge**
Chartway St, East Sutton, Maidstone,
Kent ME17 3DL
☎(01622) 844382, Fax 844168, Pro
844243
From M20 junction 8 take B2163 to
Sutton Valence.
Old apple orchards.
Pro Matthew Rackham; Founded 1993
Designed by Tryton Design Ltd
18 holes, 6254 yards, S.S.S. 70
Visitors: h'cap certs required; mid-
week only.
Green Fee: WD £25; WE n/a.
Societies: welcome by appt; £19-£44.
Catering: full catering facilities.

1A 129 **Riverside**
Summerton Way, Thamesmead SE28
8PP
☎(0181) 3107975
Off A2, 10 mins from Blackheath, 15
mins Bexleyheath; near Woolwich.
Pay-as-you-play course on reclaimed
marshland.
Founded 1991
Designed by Heffernan & Heffernan
9 holes, 5482 yards
Visitors: welcome subject to reason-
able standard of golf.
Green Fee: WD £6.50; WE £8.50.
Societies: welcome by appt WD, only
small societies WE; terms on applica-
tion.
Catering: 2 bars, à la carte.
Hotels: Black Prince (Bexleyheath);
Swallow.

1A 130 **Rochester & Cobham
Park**
Park Pale by Rochester, Kent ME2
3UL
☎(01474) 823411, Fax 824446, Pro
823658, Bar/Rest 823412
3 miles E of Gravesend east exit off
A2.
Parkland course.
Pro Joe Blair; Founded 1891/1997
Designed by Donald Steel
18 holes, 6596 yards, S.S.S. 71

Visitors: WD with h'cap certs; WE
with member only.
Green Fee: WD £26; WE £26.
Societies: Tues and Thurs; £39-£45.
Catering: full catering facilities.
Hotels: Inn on the Lake, A2; Tolgate
Motel, Gravesend.

1A 131 **Roehampton**
Roehampton Lane, London, SW15
5LR
☎(0181) 876 1621, Fax 392 2386,
Pro 876 3858, Sec 876 5505, Bar/Rest
876 2057
Just off the South Circular road
between Sheen and Putney.
Private members parkland course.
Pro Alan Scott; Founded 1901
18 holes, 6011 yards, S.S.S. 69
Visitors: members' guests only.
Green Fee: WD £19; WE n/a.
Societies: by members' introduction
only; £29.

1A 132 **Roker Park**
Holly Lane, Aldershot Rd, Guildford,
Surrey GU3 3PB
☎(01483) 236677, Fax 232324, Sec
232324, Bar/Rest 237700
2 miles W of Guildford on A323.
Parkland course.
Pro Kevin Warn; Founded 1992
Designed by W.V. Roker
9 holes, 6074 yards, S.S.S. 72
Visitors: public pay and play course.
Green Fee: WD £6.50; WE £8.
Societies: WD only; minimum 12;
£17.50.
Catering: facilities available.

1A 133 **Romney Warren**
St Andrews Rd, Littlestone, New
Romney, Kent TN28 8RB
☎(01797) Pro 362231, Bar/Rest
366613
Take A259 to New Romney, turn right
into Littlestone Road and after 0.5
miles into St Andrews Road.
Links course.
Pro Stephen Watkins; Founded 1993
Designed by J.D. Lewis, B.M. Evans
18 holes, 5126 yards, S.S.S. 65
Visitors: welcome with booking.
Green Fee: WD £12; WE £17.
Societies: apply at pro shop; from
£13.

1A 134 **Royal Blackheath**
Court Rd, Eltham, London SE9 0LR
☎(0181) 850 1795, Fax 859 0150,
Pro 850 1763, Bar/Rest 850 1042

Junction 3 M25-A20 to London; 2nd
lights turn rt; club is 600 yards on
right.
Parkland course; oldest known golf
club in world.
Pro Ian McGregor; Founded
1608/1892
Designed by James Braid
18 holes, 6219 yards, S.S.S. 70
Visitors: welcome midweek by
arrangement/ h'cap cert; WE only with
member.
Green Fee: WD £30; WE £30.
Societies: welcome Wed-Fri by appt;
from £65.
Catering: full catering and bar facilities.
Hotels: Bromley Court, Bromley;
Clarendon, Blackheath.

1A 135 **Royal Cinque Ports**
Golf Rd, Deal, Kent CT14 6RF
☎(01304) 379530, Pro 374170, Sec
367856, Bar/Rest 374007
Follow coast road through Deal to end
and turn left on to Goldwyn Rd, at the
end turn right on to Golf Rd.
Seaside links.
Pro Andrew Reynolds; Founded 1892
Designed by Tom Dunn, Guy
Campbell
18 holes, 6754 yards, S.S.S. 72
Visitors: welcome WD; WE by appt;
h'cap certs required.
Green Fee: WD £50; WE £60.
Societies: welcome WD by appt;
terms on application.
Catering: full facilities; dress code.
Hotels: Royal; Kings Head, both Deal;
Bell, Sandwich.

1A 136 **Royal Mid-Surrey**
Old Deer Park, Richmond, Surrey
TW9 2SB
☎(0181) 9401894, Fax 332 2957, Pro
940 0459
On A316 300 yards before the
Richmond roundabout heading to
London.
Parkland courses.
Pro David Talbot; Founded 1892
Designed by J.H. Taylor
Inner: 18 holes, 5544 yards, S.S.S. 68
Outer: 18 holes, 6385 yards, S.S.S. 68
Visitors: WDs with h'cap cert; WE
only with a member.
Green Fee: WD £60.
Societies: contact Sec; terms on
application.
Catering: lunches served every day
except Mon; bar and snacks available.
Hotels: Richmond Hill; Richmond
Gate.

1A 137 **Royal St George's**
Sandwich, Kent CT13 9PB
☎(01304) 617308, Fax 611245, Pro
615236, Sec 613090
2 miles E of Sandwich on road to
Sandwich Bay.
Open Championship course 1993;
Links course.
Pro Andrew Brooks; Founded 1887
Designed by Dr Laidlaw Purves
18 holes, 6560 yards, S.S.S. 74
Visitors: welcome midweek but with
maximum 18 handicap; certificate
required.
Green Fee: WD £60-£85 per day.
Societies: Mon, Tues, Wed, but not
mid-July to end of August; £110.
Catering: full facilities.

1A 138 **Royal Wimbledon**
29 Camp Rd, Wimbledon SW19 4UW
☎(0181) 946 2125
0.75 mile of War Memorial in
Wimbledon village.
Parkland course.
Pro Hugh Boyle; Founded 1865
18 holes, 6362 yards, S.S.S. 70
Visitors: Members only.
Societies: Wed, Thurs only; terms on
application.
Catering: full facilities.
Hotels: Wayfarer Hotel.

1A 139 **Rusper**
Rusper Rd, Newdigate, Surrey RH5
5BX
☎(01293) 871871
M25 exit 9 and A24 towards Dorking,
follow signs to Newdigate and Rusper.
Parkland course.
Pro Janice Arnold; Founded 1992
Designed by S. Hood
18 holes, 6218 yards, S.S.S. 69
Visitors: welcome.
Hotels: Ghyll Manor, Rusper.

1A 140 **Ruxley**
Sandy Lane, St Paul's Cray,
Orpington, Kent BR5 3HY
☎(01689) 839677, Fax 891428, Pro
871490, Bar/Rest 871490
M20 exit 1, follow signs to St Pauls
Cray and then signs to course.
Parkland course.
Pro Andy Langdon; Founded 1973
Designed by Gilbert Lloyd
18 holes, 5712 yards, S.S.S. 68
Visitors: public pay and play.
Green Fee: WD £11; WE £18.
Societies: welcome; terms on applica-
tion.
Catering: facilities available.

1A 141 **St Augustine's**
Cottington Rd,, Cliffsend, Ramsgate,
Kent CT12 5JN
☎(01843) 590333, Fax 590444, Pro
590222
On B2048 off Ramsgate to Sandwich
road.
Parkland course.
Pro Derek Scott; Founded 1907
Designed by Tom Vardon
18 holes, 5197 yards, S.S.S. 65
Visitors: welcome with h'cap certs.
Green Fee: WD £21.50; WE £23.50.
Societies: welcome by appt; from
£25-£40.
Catering: clubhouse facilities.
Hotels: Jarvis Marine, Ramsgate;
Blazing Donkey, Ham.

1A 142 **St George's Hill**
St George's Hill, Weybridge, Surrey
KT13 0NL
☎(01932) 847758, Fax 821564, Pro
843523
B374 towards Cobham, 0.5 miles from
station.
Wooded heathland courses.
Pro A C Rattue; Founded 1913
Designed by H.S. Colt
18 holes, 6569 yards, S.S.S. 71
Visitors: Wed, Thurs, Fri by appt.
Green Fee: WD £65.
Societies: Wed, Thurs, Fri only; £100-
£110.
Catering: full facilities available.
Hotels: Oatlands Park Hotel; Hilton,
Cobham.

1A 143 **Sandown Golf Centre**
More Lane, Esher, Surrey KT10 8AN
☎(01372) 461234
In centre of Sandown Park racecourse.
Parkland course.
Pro R Catley-Smith/D Kent; Founded
1967
Designed by John Jacobs
9 holes, 5656 yards, S.S.S. 67
Visitors: welcome.
Green Fee: WD £6; WE £7.75.
Catering: available.
Hotels: Haven Hotel, Sandown.

1A 144 **Selsdon Park Hotel & GC**
Addington Road, Sanderstead, South
Croydon, Surrey CR2 8YA
☎(0181) 657 8811 x 659, Fax 657
3401, Pro 657 8811 x 694, Sec 657
8811, Bar/Rest 657 8811
Take A2022 towards Selsdon. Hotel
entrance is 0.5 miles opposite junction
with Upper Selsdon Road.

Parkland/downland course.
Pro Malcolm Churchill; Founded 1929
Designed by J.H. Taylor
18 holes, 6473 yards, S.S.S. 71
Visitors: welcome by prior arrange-
ment.
Green Fee: WD £25; WE £30.
Societies: welcome by prior arrange-
ment; terms on application.
Catering: catering in hotel.
Hotels: Selsdon Park.

1A 145 **Sene Valley**
Sene, Folkestone, Kent CT18 8BL
☎(01303) 268513, Fax 237513, Pro
268514
M20 junction 12, take A 20 towards
Ashford and left at 1st roundabout.
Downland course.
Pro Nick Watson; Founded 1888
Designed by Henry Cotton
18 holes, 6196 yards, S.S.S. 69
Visitors: welcome with h'cap certs.
Green Fee: WD £20; WE £25.
Societies: Wed,Thurs, Fri only; £45.
Catering: catering and bar facilities.
Hotels: Sunny Bank House.

1A 146 **Sheerness**
Power Station Rd, Sheerness, Kent
ME12 3AE
☎(01795) 662585, Fax 666840, Pro
666840
M2/M20 to A249 to Sheerness
Seaside course.
Pro Roger Tattershall; Founded 1906
18 holes, 6460 yards, S.S.S. 71
Visitors: welcome; WE with a mem-
ber.
Green Fee: WD £15; WE £15.
Societies: welcome Tues, Wed, Thurs
by prior arrangement; from £34.
Catering: clubhouse bar and catering.
Hotels: Kingsferry GH, Isle of
Sheppey.

1A 147 **Shillinglee Park**
Chiddingfold, Godalming, Surrey GU8
4TA
☎(01428) 653237, Fax 644391
Leave A3 at Milford, S on A283 to
Chiddingfold; at top end of Green turn
left along local road, then after 2 miles
turn right signposted Shillinglee;
entrance to course on left after 0.5
mile.
Public undulating parkland course.
Pro David Parkinson; Founded 1980
Designed by Roger Mace
9 holes, 2516 yards, S.S.S. 64
Visitors: welcome, book in advance.
Green Fee: WD £8; WE £9.

Societies: welcome; terms on application.
Catering: bar and restaurant 8.30am-6pm (3pm Sun); evening meals and parties by arrangement.
Hotels: Lythe Hill.

1A 148 Shirley Park
194 Addiscombe Rd, Croydon, Surrey CR0 7LB
☎(0181) 654 1143, Fax 654 6733, Pro 654 8767
On A232 1 mile E of E Croydon station.
Parkland course.
Pro Paul Webb; Founded 1914
18 holes, 6210 yards, S.S.S. 70
Visitors: welcome WD; with a member only at WE.
Green Fee: WD £30; WE £15.
Societies: WD except Wed; £53.
Catering: full catering and bar.

1A 149 Shooters Hill
Lowood, Eaglesfield Rd, London SE18 3DA
☎(0181) 854 6368, Fax 854 0469, Pro 854 0073
Just past water tower on A207 Shooters Hill.
Hilly parkland/woodland course.
Pro Michael Ridge; Founded 1903
18 holes, 5721 yards, S.S.S. 68
Visitors: welcome WD with h'cap cert.
Green Fee: WD £22.
Societies: Tues, Thurs only; terms on application.
Catering: full clubhouse facilities.
Hotels: Clarendon, Blackheath.

1A 150 Shortlands
Meadow Road, Shortlands, Kent BR2 0PB
☎(0181) 4602471, Pro 4646182
2 miles S of Bromley.
Parkland course.
Pro John Murray; Founded 1894
9 holes, 5261 yards, S.S.S. 66
Visitors: with member only.
Societies: by arrangement; terms on application.
Catering: bar and catering.

1A 151 Sidcup
7 Hurst Rd, Sidcup, Kent DA15 9AE
☎(0181) Pro 3090679, Sec 3002150
A222 off A2, 400 yards N of station.
Parkland course.
Pro Nigel Willis; Founded 1891
Designed by James Braid And H. Myrtle
9 holes, 5722 yards, S.S.S. 68

Visitors: welcome; WE with member only; h'cap certs required, smart casual dress except after 7pm.
Green Fee: WD £18; WE £18.
Societies: welcome; terms on application.
Catering: bar, restaurant, except Mon.
Hotels: Bickley Arms; Swallow.

1A 152 Silvermere
Redhill Rd, Cobham, Surrey KT11 1EF
☎(01932) 867275, Fax 868259, Pro 866894
At junction 10 of M25 and A3 take A245 to Byfleet; Silvermere is 0.5 mile.
Parkland course.
Pro Doug McClelland; Founded 1976
18 holes, 6377 yards, S.S.S. 71
Visitors: welcome WD; WE by appt from Apr-Oct.
Green Fee: WD £20; WE £30.
Societies: welcome WD only; terms on application.
Catering: bar, restaurant except Mon.
Hotels: Bickley Arms; Swallow.

1A 153 Sittingbourne & Milton Regis
Wormdale, Newington, Sittingbourne, Kent ME9 7PX
☎(01795) 842261
1 mile N of exit 5 off M2 on A249.
Undulating course.
Pro John Hearn; Founded 1929
Designed by Harry Hunter
18 holes, 6279 yards, S.S.S. 70
Visitors: welcome WD with h'cap cert.
Green Fee: WD £20; WE £20.
Societies: welcome Tues and Thurs; terms on application.
Catering: facilities available Tues-Sat.
Hotels: Coniston (Sittingbourne); Newington Manor.

1A 154 Staplehurst Park
Craddock Lane, Staplehurst, Kent TN12 0DR
☎(01580) 893362
9 miles S of Maidstone on A229 Hastings Rd, turning on to Headcorn Rd, at Staplehurst and then right into Craddock Lane.
Parkland course.
Founded 1993
Designed by John Sayner
12 holes, 5780 yards, S.S.S. 66
Visitors: welcome.
Green Fee: WD £10; WE £12.
Societies: welcome except Sun; terms on application.
Catering: bar and snacks.
Hotels: Bell Inn.

1A 155 Sunbury
Charlton Lane, Shepperton, Middlesex TW17 8QA
☎(01932) 770298, Pro 772898
2 miles from M3 junction 1.
Public parkland course.
Pro Alistair Hardaway
18 holes, 4996 yards, S.S.S. 64
Visitors: welcome; no restrictions.
Green Fee: WD £10; WE £12.
Societies: welcome by appt; terms on application.
Catering: in 16th century clubhouse.
Hotels: Warren Lodge Hotel, Moat House.

1A 156 Sundridge Park
Garden Rd, Bromley, Kent BR1 3NE
☎(0181) 460 0278, Fax 289 3050, Pro 460 5540, Bar/Rest 460 3060
N of Bromley on A2212.
Parkland courses.
Pro Bob Cameron; Founded 1901
Designed by Willie Park
East: 18 holes, 6538 yards, S.S.S. 71
West: 18 holes, 6016 yards, S.S.S. 68
Visitors: welcome WD; WE only with a member.
Green Fee: WD £40; WE £40.
Societies: welcome WD by appt; terms on application.
Catering: full catering and bar.

1A 157 Sunningdale
Ridgemount Rd, Sunningdale, Ascot, Surrey SL5 9RR
☎(01344) 621681, Fax 624154, Pro 620128
From M3 junction 3 or M 25 junction 13. Take A30.
Heathland courses.
Pro Keith Maxwell; Founded 1923
Designed by H S Colt
New: 18 holes, 6617 yards, S.S.S. 70
Old: 18 holes, 6609 yards, S.S.S. 72
Visitors: Mon-Thurs only; with max18 handicap and letter of introduction.
Green Fee: WD £75.
Societies: Tues, Wed, Thurs only; min 20 players, max 20 handicap; £175.
Catering: full catering and bar.

1A 158 Sunningdale Ladies
Cross Rd, Sunningdale, Surrey SL5 9RX
☎(01344) 620507
S of A30 600 yards W of Sunningdale level crossing.
Heathland course.
Founded 1902
Designed by Edward Villiers/H S Colt
18 holes, 3616 yards, S.S.S. 60

Visitors: welcome with h'cap certs but not before 11am at WE.
Green Fee: WD £18/men £22; WE £20/men £27.
Societies: ladies societies only; terms on application.
Catering: full facilities.

1A 159 Surbiton
Woodstock Lane, Chessington, Surrey KT9 1UG
☎(0181) 3983101, Fax 3390992
From A3 westbound, take Esher/Chessington turn-off, turn left to Claygate, club 400 yards on right.
Parkland course.
Pro Paul Milton; Founded 1896
18 holes, 6055 yards, S.S.S. 70
Visitors: welcome WD only; h'cap certs required; members' guests only at WE.
Green Fee: WD £35; WE £35.
Societies: welcome by prior arrangement; terms on application.
Catering: full facilities.
Hotels: Haven (Esher); Travelodge.

1A 160 Sutton Green
New Lane, Sutton Green, Nr Guildford, Surrey GU4 7QF
☎(01483) 747898, Fax 750289, Pro 766849
Midway between Guildford and Woking on A320.
Parkland course with water features.
Pro Tim Dawson; Founded 1994
Designed by Laura Davies /D Walker
18 holes, 6400 yards, S.S.S. 70
Visitors: unrestricted midweek; after 1pm at WE.
Green Fee: WD £25; WE £30.
Societies: welcome WD; packages available; from £49.50.
Catering: full catering and bar.
Hotels: Forte Post House, Guildford; Cobham Hilton; Worplesdon Place.

1A 161 Tandridge
Oxted, Surrey RH8 9NQ
☎(01883) 712274, Fax 730537, Pro 713701, Bar/Rest 712273
From M25 junction 6, take A22 and then A25.
Parkland course.
Pro Allan Farquhar; Founded 1924
Designed by H.S. Colt
18 holes, 6250 yards, S.S.S. 70
Visitors: welcome Mon, Wed, Thurs.
Green Fee: WD £45.
Societies: welcome Mon, Wed, Thurs; £69.
Catering: full clubhouse facilities.

1A 162 Tenterden
Woodchurch Rd, Tenterden, Kent TN30 7DR
☎(01580) 763987, Fax 763987
Take A28 to Tenterden and at St Michaels take B2067.
Woodland course.
Pro Andrew Scullion; Founded 1905
18 holes, 6152 yards, S.S.S. 69
Visitors: welcome by appt.
Green Fee: WD £20; WE £20.
Societies: contact Sec J M Wilson; terms on application.
Catering: catering facilities and bar.
Hotels: White Lion; Little Silver.

1A 163 Thames Ditton & Esher
Scilly Isles, Portsmouth Rd, Esher, Surrey KT10 9AL
☎(0181) Pro 3981551
Off A3 by Scilly Isles roundabout (0.25 mile from Sandown Park Race Course).
Parkland course.
Pro Mark Rodbard; Founded 1892
9 holes, 2537 yards, S.S.S. 33
Visitors: welcome Mon-Sat and Sun pm.
Green Fee: WD £10; WE £12.
Societies: max 28 booked in advance with Sec; terms on application.
Catering: snacks available.

1A 164 Tunbridge Wells
Langton Rd, Tunbridge Wells, Kent TN4 8XH
☎(01892) Pro 541386, Sec 536918, Bar/Rest 523034
Behind Marchants Garage next to Spa Hotel.
Undulating parkland course.
Pro Mike Barton; Founded 1889
9 holes, 4728 yards, S.S.S. 62
Visitors: welcome.
Green Fee: WD £15; WE £25.
Societies: contact Sec; terms on application.
Catering: by arrangement.
Hotels: Spa; Periquito; Royal Wells.

1A 165 Tyrrells Wood
The Drive, Tyrrells Wood, Leatherhead, Surrey KT22 8QP
☎(01372) 376025, Fax 360836, Pro 375200, Bar/Rest 360702
2 miles SE of Leatherhead off the A24; M25 junction 9 1 mile.
Undulating parkland.
Pro Max Tayler; Founded 1924
Designed by James Braid
18 holes, 6063 yards, S.S.S. 70

Visitors: welcome WD.
Green Fee: WD £34; WE £34.
Societies: welcome by appt; from £37.
Catering: full clubhouse facilities.

1A 166 Upchurch River Valley
Oak Lane, Upchurch, Sittingbourne, Kent ME9 7AY
☎(01634) 360626, Fax 387784, Pro 379592
From M2 junction 4 take A278 Gillingham road; then A2 for 2.5 miles towards Rainham.
Moorland/seaside courses.
Pro Roger Cornwell; Founded 1991
Designed by David Smart
18 holes, 6237 yards, S.S.S. 70
9 holes, 3192 yards, par 60
Visitors: welcome; book 2 days in advance.
Green Fee: WD £10.95; WE £13.95.
Societies: welcome WD; min 12; terms on application.
Catering: restaurant and bar.
Hotels: Newington Manor; Rank Motor Lodge.

1A 167 Walmer & Kingsdown
The Leas, Kingsdown, Deal, Kent CT14 8EP
☎(01304) 373256, Fax 363017, Pro 363017, Bar/Rest 374832
Off A258 Dover to Deal road; follow signs to Kingsdown from Ringwould, signposted thereon.
Downland course with panoramic views of English Channel.
Pro M Paget; Founded 1909
Designed by James Braid
18 holes, 6444 yards, S.S.S. 71
Visitors: welcome by appt with Pro.
Green Fee: WD £22; WE £24.
Societies: welcome by appt; terms on application.
Catering: full catering and bar.

1A 168 Walton Heath
Off Deans Lane, Walton-on-the-Hill, Tadworth, Surrey KT20 7TP
☎(01737) 812380, Fax 814225, Pro 812152, Bar/Rest 813777
M25 exit Junction 8 and take A217, London bound. After 2nd roundabout turn left into Mill Road and at next junction left into Dorking Road. Deans Lane is 1.5 miles on right.
Heathland course.
Pro Ken MacPherson; Founded 1903
Designed by Herbert Fowler/James Braid
18 holes, 6801 yards, S.S.S. 73

Visitors: by appt only.
Green Fee: WD £65; WE £65.
Societies: by prior arrangement only; terms on application.
Catering: full facilities in clubhouse.
Hotels: club can provide list.

1A 169 **Weald of Kent**

Maidstone Rd, Headcorn, Kent TN27 9PT
☎(01622) 890866, Fax 891793
7 miles from Maidstone on A274.
Parkland course.
Founded 1991
Designed by John Millen
18 holes, 6169 yards, S.S.S. 70
Visitors: public pay and play course.
Green Fee: WD £14.50; WE £18.50.
Societies: welcome; from £15.
Catering: catering and bar facilities.
Hotels: Chilston Park; Great Danes; Shant.

1A 170 **Wentworth**

Wentworth Drive, Virginia Water, Surrey GU25 4LS
☎(01344) 842201, Fax 842804, Pro 846306, Bar/Rest 846300
21 miles SW of London on A30/A329 junction.
Heathland courses.
Pro D Rennie; Founded 1924
Designed by H.S. Colt (East and West); J.R.M. Jacobs (Edinburgh)
East: 18 holes, 6169 yards, S.S.S. 70
West: 18 holes, 6957 yards, S.S.S. 74
Edinburgh: 18 holes, 6979 yards, S.S.S. 73
Visitors: welcome WD by appt.
Green Fee: WD £145.
Societies: welcome by appt Mon-Thurs; min 20; from £115.
Driving range, caddies, buggies and golf clinics.
Catering: top-class catering facilities.
Hotels: 8 rooms available at course.

1A 171 **West Byfleet**

Sheerwater Rd, West Byfleet, Surrey KT14 6AA
☎(01932) 345230, Fax 340667, Pro 346584, Sec 343433
On A245 in West Byfleet.
Woodland course.
Pro David Regan; Founded 1906
Designed by Cuthbert Butchart
18 holes, 6211 yards, S.S.S. 70
Visitors: welcome by appt.
Green Fee: WD £30; WE £30.
Societies: welcome Mon, Tues, Wed; £58.
Catering: full clubhouse facilities.

1A 172 **West Hill**

Bagshot Rd, Brookwood, Surrey GU24 0BH
☎(01483) 474365, Fax 474252, Pro 473172, Bar/Rest 472110
5 miles W of Woking on A322.
Heathland course.
Pro John Clements; Founded 1909
Designed by Willie Park/ Jack White
18 holes, 6368 yards, S.S.S. 70
Visitors: welcome WD with h'cap certs; WE only with member.
Green Fee: WD £35; WE £35.
Societies: WD except Wed by prior arrangement; packages available; £67-£71.
Catering: full facilities and bar.
Hotels: Worplesdon Place, Perry Hill.

1A 173 **West Kent**

West Hill, Downe, Orpington, Kent BR6 7JJ
☎(01689) 851323, Pro 856863
A21 to Orpington, head for Downe village; leave on Luxted Lane for 300 yards then right into West Hill.
Parkland/downland course.
Pro Roger Fidler; Founded 1916
18 holes, 6399 yards, S.S.S. 70
Visitors: welcome WD with letter from Sec or h'cap cert; must phone in advance.
Green Fee: WD £26; WE £26.
Societies: welcome by appt; terms on application.
Catering: full facilities.
Hotels: Bromley Continental.

1A 174 **West Malling**

London Rd, Addington, Maidstone, Kent ME19 5AR
☎(01732) 844785, Fax 844795, Pro 844022
Off A20 8 miles NW of Maidstone.
Parkland courses.
Pro Duncan Lambert; Founded 1974
Hurricane: 18 holes, 6256 yards, S.S.S. 70
Spitfire: 18 holes, 6142 yards, S.S.S. 70
Visitors: welcome WD; WE afternoon.
Green Fee: WD £20; WE £30.
Societies: welcome by appt; terms on application.
Catering: full facilities.
Hotels: Larkfield.

1A 175 **West Surrey**

Enton Green, Godalming, Surrey GU8 5AF
☎(01483) 421275, Fax 415419, Pro 421278

0.5 miles SE of Milford Station.
Wooded parkland course.
Pro A Tawse; Founded 1910
Designed by Herbert Fowler
18 holes, 6259 yards, S.S.S. 70
Visitors: by appt with Sec.
Green Fee: WD £27; WE £47.50.
Societies: welcome Wed, Thurs, Fri by appt; £56.
Catering: full catering facilities.
Hotels: Inn on the Lake.

1A 176 **Westerham**

Valence Park, Brasted Rd, Westerham, Kent TN16 1LJ
☎(01959) 563700, Fax 563787
On A25 between Brasted and Westerham.
Woodland course.
Pro Ewan Campbell; Founded 1997
Designed by David Williams
18 holes, 6272 yards, S.S.S. 70
Visitors: welcome WD.
Green Fee: WD £27.
Societies: welcome WD by appt with Sec; from £27.
Catering: restaurant, bar in temporary clubhouse; new clubhouse open Sept 98.
Hotels: Jarvis Fellbridge.

1A 177 **Westgate & Birchington**

176 Canterbury Rd, Westgate-on-Sea, Kent CT8 8LT
☎(01843) 831115
0.25 miles from Westgate station off A27.
Seaside links.
Pro Roger Game; Founded 1892
18 holes, 4926 yards, S.S.S. 64
Visitors: welcome after 10am Mon-Sat; after 11am Sun.
Green Fee: WD £13; WE £15.
Societies: welcome by appt; Tues preferred; terms on application.
Catering: clubhouse facilities.
Hotels: Ivyside.

1A 178 **Whitstable & Seasalter**

Collingwood Rd, Whitstable, Kent CT5 1EB
☎(01227) 272020, Fax 272020
On A290 to Whitstable.
Seaside links.
Founded 1910
18 holes, 5314 yards, S.S.S. 63
Visitors: by arrangement.
Green Fee: WD £15; WE £15.
Societies: not welcome.
Catering: full catering facilities.
Hotels: Marine Hotel, Tankerton.

1A 179 Wildernesse
Seal, Sevenoaks, Kent TN15 0JE
☎(01732) 761526, Pro 761527, Sec
761199
Off A25 in Seal village.
Rolling parkland course.
Pro Craig Walker; Founded 1890
Designed by W Park
18 holes, 6448 yards, S.S.S. 72
Visitors: letter of intro required.
Societies: apply to Sec; terms on
application.
Catering: bar and restaurant.

1A 180 Wildwood
Horsham Rd, Alfold, Cranleigh, Surrey
GU6 8JE
☎(01403) 753255, Fax 752005
On A281 Guildford to Horsham road
10 miles from Guildford.
Parkland course.
Pro Nick Parfrement; Founded 1992
Designed by Martin Hawtree
18 holes, 6655 yards, S.S.S. 72
Visitors: welcome.
Green Fee: WD £19; WE £29.
Societies: welcome WD; packages
available; Japanese societies very
welcome; from £26.
Catering: full catering and bar.
Large practice area.
Hotels: Random Hall, Slinfold.

1A 181 Wimbledon Common
Camp Rd, Wimbledon Common,
London SW19 4UW
☎(0181) 946 0294, Fax 947 8697,
Sec 946 7571
1 mile NW of War Memorial past Fox
and Grapes.
Links type wooded course.
Pro J S Jukes; Founded 1865
Designed by Tom and Willie Dunn
18 holes, 5438 yards, S.S.S. 66
Visitors: welcome WD.
Green Fee: WD £15; WE £15.
Societies: welcome Tues-Fri by appt;
terms on application.
Catering: full facilities.

1A 182 Wimbledon Park
Home Park Rd, Wimbledon, London
SW19 7HR
☎(0181) 946 1002, Fax 944 8688,
Pro 946 4053, Sec 946 1250
Near Wimbledon Park District Line
tube.
Parkland course.
Pro Dean Wingrove; Founded 1898
Designed by Willie Park Jnr
18 holes, 5492 yards, S.S.S. 66
Visitors: welcome with h'cap certs.

Green Fee: WD £40; WE £40.
Societies: welcome Tues, Thurs by
appt; terms on application.
Catering: full facilities except Mon.
Hotels: Canizaro House.

1A 183 Windlemere
Windlesham Rd, West End, Woking,
Surrey GU24 9QL
☎(01276) 858727
Take A322 from Bagshot towards
Guildford; turn left on A319 towards
Chobham, course is on left opposite
Gordon Boys School.
Gently undulating public parkland
course.
Pro David Thomas; Founded 1978.
Designed by Clive D. Smith
9 holes, 2673 yards, S.S.S. 34
Visitors: open to public on payment of
green fees.
Green Fee: WD £8.50; WE £10.
Societies: by appt with Pro; terms on
application.
Catering: bar snacks always avail-
able.

1A 184 Windlesham
Grove End, Bagshot, Surrey GU19
5HY
☎(01276) 452220, Fax 452290
At junction of A30 and A322.
Parkland course.
Pro Lee Mucklow; Founded 1994
Designed by Tommy Horton
18 holes, 6564 yards, S.S.S. 71
Visitors: welcome except before
11am at WE; h'cap certs required.
Green Fee: WD £40; WE £50.
Societies: welcome Mon-Thurs by
appt; terms on application.
Catering: bar and restaurant.
Practice range, 3 covered bays, 10
outdoor.
Hotels: Berrystead.

1A 185 The Wisley
Mill Lane, Ripley, Nr Woking, Surrey
GU23 6QU
☎(0483) 211022, Fax 211622
Exit A3 at Ockham, Send and Ripley,
3rd exit from the roundabout and first
left into Mill Lane.
Parkland course; 3 x 9 holes.
Founded 1991
Designed by Robert Trent Jones, Jr.
27 holes, 6858 yards, S.S.S. 73
Visitors: private members' club.
Societies: none.
Catering: full clubhouse catering and
bar facilities.
Large practice ground.

1A 186 Woking
Pond Rd, Hook Heath, Woking, Surrey
GU22 0JZ
☎(01483) 760053, Fax 772441, Pro
769582
Off A322 after West Hill GC.
Oldest heathland course in Surrey.
Pro John Thorne; Founded 1893
Designed by Tom Dunn
18 holes, 6340 yards, S.S.S. 70
Visitors: welcome only with member.
Green Fee: WD £50; WE £50.
Societies: by appt with 12 months'
notice; £74.
Catering: full facilities.
Hotels: Glen Court, Woking;
Worplesdon Place, Worplesdon.

1A 187 Woodcote Park
Meadow Hill, Bridleway, Coulsden,
Surrey CR5 2QQ
☎(0181) 668 2788, Fax 668 2788,
Pro 6681843, Bar/Rest 660 0176
2 miles N of Purley on Coulsdon-
Wallington road.
Parkland course.
Pro David Hudspith; Founded 1912
18 holes, 6699 yards, S.S.S. 72
Visitors: welcome by appt and with
h'cap certs.
Green Fee: WD £30; WE £30.
Societies: welcome by appt; £57.50.
Catering: catering and bar facilities.

1A 188 Woodlands Manor
Tinkerpot Lane, Sevenoaks, Kent
TN15 6AB
☎(01959) 523805, Pro 524161, Sec
523806
Off A225, 4 miles NE of Sevenoaks, 5
miles S of M25 junction 3.
Undulating parkland course in AONB.
Pro Phil Womack; Founded 1928
Designed by N. Coles, J. Lyons
18 holes, 6037 yards, S.S.S. 68
Visitors: welcome WD; not WE.
Societies: welcome Mon-Fri by appt;
terms on application.
Catering: meals served.
Hotels: Thistle (Brands Hatch).

1A 189 Worplesdon
Heath House Rd, Woking, Surrey
GU22 0RA
☎(01483) Fax 473303, Pro 473287,
Sec 472277
Leave Guildford on A322 to Bagshot,
6 miles turn rt into Heath House Rd.
Heathland course.
Pro Jim Christine; Founded 1908
Designed by J.F. Abercromby
18 holes, 6440 yards, S.S.S. 71

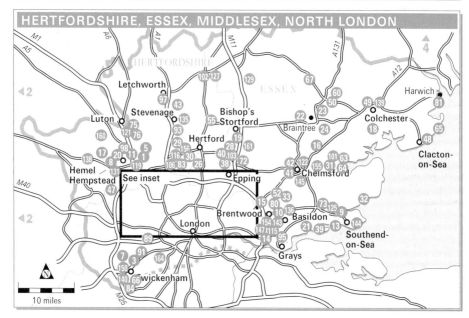

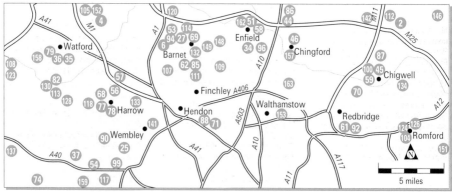

Visitors: welcome WD only with intro from Club Sec.
Green Fee: WD £44; WE £44.
Societies: welcome WD by appt (except Tues); terms on application.
Catering: bar every day, lunch every day except Tues.
Hotels: Worplesdon Place.

1A 190 Wrotham Heath
Seven Mile Lane, Borough Green, Sevenoaks, Kent TN15 8QZ
☎ (01732) 884800, Fax 887370
Off A20 near junction with A25.
Woodland/heathland course.
Pro Harry Dearden; Founded 1906

Designed by Donald Steel
18 holes, 5954 yards, S.S.S. 69
Visitors: welcome WD with h'cap certs, not WE or BH without member.
Green Fee: WD £25; WE £25.
Societies: welcome Fri only; terms on application.
Catering: full catering by arrangement with Steward, except Mon.
Hotels: Post House.

1B 1 Abbey View
Holywell Hill, Westminster Lodge, St Albans, Herts AL1 2DL
☎ (01727) 868227
In centre of St Albans.

Public parkland course.
Pro Mark Sibley; Founded 1990
Designed by Jimmy Thomson
9 holes, 1383 yards
Visitors: open to public at all times.
Green Fee: WD £4.50; WE £4.50.
Societies: welcome; terms on application.
Catering: tea/coffee on site; café in main centre.

1B 2 Abridge G & CC
Epping Lane, Stapleford Tawney, Essex RM4 1ST
☎ (01708) 688396, Fax 688550, Pro 688333

KEY							
1	Abbey View	33	The Burstead	66	Fulwell	100	Loughton	134	Stapleford Abbotts
2	Abridge G & CC	34	Bush Hill Park	67	Gosfield Lake	101	Maldon	135	Stevenage
3	Airlinks	35	Bushey G & CC	68	Grim's Dyke	102	Malton	136	Stock Brook Manor
4	Aldenham G & CC	36	Bushey Hall	69	Hadley Wood	103	Manor of Groves G & CC		Golf & Country Club
5	Aldwickbury Park	37	C & L Golf & CC	70	Hainault Forest	104	Maylands Golf & CC	137	Stockley Park
6	Arkley	38	Canons Brook	71	Hampstead	105	Mid-Herts	138	Stocks Hotel & CC
7	Ashford Manor	39	Castle Point	72	Hanbury Manor G& CC	106	Mill Green	139	Stoke-by-Nayland
8	Ashridge	40	Chadwell Springs	73	Hanover	107	Mill Hill	140	Strawberry Hill
9	Ballards Gore	41	Channels	74	Harefield Place	108	Moor Park	141	Sudbury
10	Basildon	42	Chelmsford	75	Harpenden	109	Muswell Hill	142	Theydon Bois
11	Batchwood Hall	43	Chesfield Downs	76	Harpenden Common	110	The Nazeing	143	Thorndon Park
12	Batchworth Park	44	Cheshunt	77	Harrow Hill	111	North Middlesex	144	Thorpe Hall
13	Belfairs Park	45	Chigwell	78	Harrow School	112	North Weald Golf Club	145	Three Rivers Gulf & CC
	(Southend-on-Sea)	46	Chingford	79	Hartsbourne G & CC	113	Northwood	146	Toothill
14	Belhus Park (Thurrock)	47	Chorleywood	80	Hartswood	114	Old Fold Manor	147	Top Meadow
15	Bentley	48	Clacton-on-Sea	81	Harwich & Dovercourt	115	Orsett	148	Trent Park
16	Benton Hall	49	Colchester	82	Haste Hill	116	Panshanger	149	Tudor Park Sports
17	Berkhamsted	50	Colne Valley (Essex)	83	Hatfield London CC	117	Perivale Park		Ground
18	Birch Grove	51	Crews Hill	84	Hazelwood	118	Pinner Hill	150	Twickenham Park
19	Bishop's Stortford	52	Crondon Park	85	Hendon	119	Porters Park	151	Upminster
20	Boxmoor	53	Dyrham Park	86	The Hertfordshire	120	Potters Bar	152	Verulam
21	Boyce Hill	54	Ealing	87	High Beech	121	Redbourn	153	Wanstead
22	Braintree	55	East Herts	88	Highgate	122	Regiment Way	154	Warley Park
23	Braintree Towerlands	56	Edgewarebury	89	Hillingdon	123	Rickmansworth	155	Warren
24	Braxted Park	57	Elstree	90	Horsenden Hill	124	Risebridge (Havering)	156	Welwyn Garden City
25	Brent Valley	58	Enfield	91	Hounslow Heath	125	Rochford Hundred	157	West Essex
26	Brickendon Grange	59	Epping Forest Golf & CC	92	Ilford	126	Romford	158	West Herts
27	Bridgedown	60	Essex Golf & CC	93	Knebworth	127	Royston	159	West Middlesex
28	Briggens House Hotel	61	Fairlop Waters	94	Laing Sports Club	128	Ruislip	160	Whipsnade Park
29	Brocket Hall	62	Finchley	95	Langdon Hills	129	Saffron Walden	161	Whitehill
30	Brookmans Park	63	Five Lakes Hotel Golf	96	Lee Valley	130	Sandy Lodge	162	Whitewebbs
31	Bunsay Downs		& CC	97	Letchworth	131	Shendish Manor	163	Woodford
32	Burnham-on-Crouch	64	Forrester Park	98	Little Hay Golf Complex	132	South Herts	164	Wyke Green
		65	Frinton	99	London Golf Centre	133	Stanmore		

M11 from London exit 5 via Abridge; from the N, M11 exit 7 via Epping. Parkland course.
Pro Stuart Layton; Founded 1964
Designed by Henry Cotton
18 holes, 6686 yards, S.S.S. 72
Visitors: welcome WD only; h'cap certs required.
Green Fee: WD £30; WE £30.
Societies: Mon, Wed and Fri; terms on application.
Catering: available every day.
Hotels: Post House (Epping).

1B 3 Airlinks

Southall Lane, Hounslow, Essex TW5 9PE
☎(0181) 5611418
M4 junction 3 on to A312 and A4020; part of David Lloyd Tennis Centre.
Public meadowland/parkland course.
Pro Chris Woodcock; Founded 1984
Designed by P. Alliss
18 holes, 6001 yards, S.S.S. 68
Visitors: welcome; some restrictions at weekends.
Green Fee: WD £10; WE £15.
Societies: welcome Mon-Fri; fees negotiable.
Catering: bar, snacks, hot and cold meals available.
Practice range 24 bays; floodlit.
Hotels: London Airport hotels nearby.

1B 4 Aldenham G & CC

Church Lane, Aldenham, Nr Watford, Herts WD2 8AL
☎(01923) 853929, Fax 858472
M1 junction 5 on to A41, left at roundabout to A462 and then into Church Rd.
Parkland course.
Pro Pat Winston; Founded 1975
18 holes, 6480 yards, S.S.S. 71
Visitors: welcome WD but afternoon only at WE.
Green Fee: WD £22; WE £30.
Societies: welcome WD and WE afternoons; full catering packages and 36 holes of golf; from £50.
Catering: full facilities.
Hotels: Watford Hilton National; Jarvis International.

1B 5 Aldwickbury Park

Piggottshill Lane, Harpenden, Herts AL5 1A B
☎(01582) 760112, Fax 760113, Sec 765112, Bar/Rest 766463
10 mins off M1 junction 9 on road between Harpenden and Wheathampstead.
Parkland course.
Pro Sean Clark; Founded 1995
Designed by K Brown / M Gillett
18 holes, 6352 yards, S.S.S. 70
Visitors: welcome WD; after 1pm WE.
Green Fee: WD £20; WE £26.

Societies: welcome WD: 36 holes, coffee and biscuits, lunch, 3-course dinner; other packages available; £49.
Catering: full catering and bar.
Hotels: Harpenden House.

1B 6 Arkley

Rowley Green Rd, Barnet, Herts EN5 3HL
☎(0181) 449 0555, Fax 440 5214, Pro 440 8473, Sec 449 0394, Bar/Rest 449 0394
Off A1 at Arkley.
Parkland course.
Pro Martin Porter; Founded 1909
Designed by James Braid
18 holes, 6117 yards
Visitors: welcome WD but with members only at WE.
Green Fee: WD £20; WE £20.
Societies: welcome Wed and Fri; terms on application.
Catering: full catering facilities.

1B 7 Ashford Manor

Fordbridge Rd, Ashford, Middx TW15 3RT
☎(01784) 257687, Fax 420355, Pro 255940, Bar/Rest 252049/ 258410
Off A308 between Staines and Sunbury. 0.5 miles from Fordbridge roundabout.

Wooded parkland course.
Pro Mike Finney; Founded 1898
18 holes, 6352 yards, S.S.S. 70
Visitors: welcome WD with h'cap certs.
Green Fee: WD £25; WE £25.
Societies: welcome WD except Thurs by prior arrangement; golf, morning coffee, lunch, afternoon tea, dinner; £40-60.
Catering: full catering facilities.
Hotels: Shepperton Moathouse; The Ship, Shepperton.

1B 8 Ashridge
Little Gaddesden, Berkhamsted, Herts HP4 1LY
☎(01442) 842244, Fax 843770, Pro 842307, Bar/Rest 842379
4 miles N of Berkhamstead on B4506.
Parkland course.
Pro Andrew Ainsworth; Founded 1932
Designed by Sir Guy Campbell, Colonel Hotchkin and Cecil Hutch
18 holes, 6547 yards, S.S.S. 71
Visitors: welcome WD only.
Green Fee: WD £30; WE £30.
Societies: WD only; terms on application.
Catering: full facilities.

1B 9 Ballards Gore
Gore Rd, Canewdon, Essex SS4 2DA
☎(01702) 258917, Pro 258924
From London via A127 to Southend Airport, then through Rochford on to Great Stambridge road; course 1.5 miles from Rochford centre.
Parkland course.
Pro Andrew Curry; Founded 1980
Designed by D. and J.J. Caton
18 holes, 6845 yards, S.S.S. 73
Visitors: welcome WD; guest of member only at WE, Sun after 2 pm.
Green Fee: WD £22; WE £22.
Societies: WD by arrangement with Sec, subject to availability; terms on application.
Catering: bar and restaurant; private functions.
Hotels: Renouf.

1B 10 Basildon
Clay Hill Lane, Basildon, Essex SS16 5JP
☎(01268) 533297, Fax 533849, Pro 533352
On A176 S of Basildon via either A127 or A13.
Undulating wooded parkland.
Pro W Paterson; Founded 1967
Designed by A H Cotton

18 holes, 6236 yards, S.S.S. 70
Visitors: welcome.
Green Fee: WD £9; WE £15.
Societies: welcome, packages available; terms on application.
Catering: restaurant and bar.
Hotels: Haywain; Campanile, Basildon.

1B 11 Batchwood Hall
Batchwood Tennis and Golf Centre, St Albans, Herts AL3 5XA
☎(01727) 833349, Fax 850586, Pro 844250
NW corner of St Albans; 5 miles S of M1 junction 9.
Parkland course.
Pro Mark Flitton; Founded 1935
Designed by J.H. Taylor
18 holes, 6487 yards, S.S.S. 71
Visitors: welcome.
Green Fee: WD £9.50; WE £12.50.
Societies: welcome by prior arrangement; packages available; tennis courts; 2 squash courts; fitness gym; dance studio.
Catering: bar and restaurant.
Practice range.
Hotels: Aubrey Park.

1B 12 Batchworth Park
London Rd, Rickmansworth, Herts WD3 1JS
☎(01923) 711400
From M25 junction 17 towards Rickmansworth to the Batchworth roundabout; course 400 yards.
Parkland course.
Founded 1996
Designed by Dave Thomas
18 holes, 6723 yards, S.S.S. 72
Visitors: private; members and guests only.
Green Fee: n/a.
Catering: bar and restaurant.
Practice range for members and guests.

1B 13 Belfairs Park (Southend-on-Sea)
Starter's Hut, Eastwood Rd North, Leigh-on-Sea, Essex SS9 4LR
☎(01702) 525345, Pro 520202
4.5 miles from Southend centre; Eastwood Rd links A127 and A13
Set in Belfairs Park; parkland/woodland course.
Pro Martin Foreman; Founded 1926
Designed by H.S. Colt
18 holes, 5840 yards, S.S.S. 68
Visitors: unrestricted; bookings every day, week in advance or on day.

Green Fee: WD £9; WE £13.80.
Societies: welcome; terms on application.
Catering: public restaurant.
Hotels: Westcliff Hotel.

1B 14 Belhus Park (Thurrock)
Belhus Park, South Ockendon, Essex RM15 4QR
☎(01708) 854260
A13 to Avely.
Public parkland course.
Pro Gary Lunn; Founded 1972
Designed by Frank Pennink
18 holes, 5589 yards, S.S.S. 69
Visitors: bookings can be made at course WD; in advance by phone WE (booking card required).
Green Fee: WD £8; WE £12.
Societies: welcome; terms on application.
Catering: bar and restaurant
Practice range 12 bays; floodlit.
Hotels: Thurrock Hotel.

1B 15 Bentley
Ongar Rd, Brentwood, Essex CM15 9SS
☎(01277) 373179, Fax 375097, Pro 372933
On A128 between Brentwood and Ongar.
Parkland course with water hazards.
Pro Nick Garrett; Founded 1972
Designed by Alec Swan
18 holes, 6709 yards, S.S.S. 72
Visitors: welcome WD and afternoons at WE.
Green Fee: WD £21; WE £21.
Societies: welcome WD; terms on application.
Catering: full catering facilities.

1B 16 Benton Hall
Wickham Hill, Witham, Essex CM8 3LH
☎(01376) 502454, Fax 521050
Off A12 at Witham; course is well signposted.
Woodland course.
Pro J Hudson/P McBride; Founded 1993
Designed by Alan Walker and Charlie Cox
18 holes, 6570 yards, S.S.S. 72
Visitors: welcome by prior arrangement.
Green Fee: WD £20; WE £20.
Societies: welcome WD by prior arrangement; packages available; from £40.
Catering: clubhouse facilities.

1B 17 Berkhamstead
The Common, Berkhamstead, Herts
HP4 2QB
☎(01442) 865832, Fax 863730, Pro
865851, Bar/Rest 862648
1 mile N of Berkhamstead.
Heathland course.
Pro Basil Proudfoot; Founded 1890
Designed by G.H. Gowring (1890-92
Founder), 1912 C.J. Gilbert with
advice from Harry Colt)
18 holes, 6605 yards, S.S.S. 72
Visitors: welcome with handicap of 24
or better.
Green Fee: WD £22.50; WE £35.
Societies: welcome Wed and Fri;
maximum 50; £60.
Catering: meals and bar facilities.
Hotels: Hemel Hempstead Post
House.

1B 18 Birch Grove
Layer Rd, Colchester, Essex CO2 0HS
☎(01206) 734276
On B1026 3 miles S of Colchester.
Parkland course.
Founded 1970
Designed by course owners
9 holes, 4038 yards, S.S.S. 60
Visitors: welcome.
Green Fee: WD £10; WE £10.
Societies: welcome by arrangement;
golf and 4-course dinner, bar, dining
area; £15-21.
Catering: facilities.

1B 19 Bishop's Stortford
Dunmow Rd, Bishop's Stortford, Herts
CM23 5HP
☎(01279) 654715, Fax 655215, Pro
651324, Bar/Rest 461779
From M11 junction 8 follow signs to
Bishop's Stortford. Course 1.5 miles
on left.
Flat parkland course.
Pro Vince Duncan; Founded 1910
Designed by James Braid
18 holes, 6404 yards, S.S.S. 71
Visitors: welcome with h'cap certs.
Green Fee: WD £20; WE £20.
Societies: welcome by prior arrange-
ment; varied packages available; from
£35-65.
Catering: full restaurant and bar
bistro.
Hotels: Stansted Airport; Downhall,
Hayfield Heath.

1B 20 Boxmoor
18 Box Lane, Hemel Hempstead,
Herts HP3 0DJ
☎(01442) 242434

On A41 0.75 miles from Hemel
Hempstead station.
Undulating parkland.
Founded 1890
9 holes, 4812 yards, S.S.S. 64
Visitors: welcome except Sun.
Green Fee: WD £10; WE £15.
Societies: welcome with month's
notice.
Catering: limited service; meals avail-
able by prior arrangement.
Hotels: Boxmoor Lodge.

1B 21 Boyce Hill
Vicarage Hill, South Benfleet, Essex
SS7 1PD
☎(01268) 793625, Fax 750497, Pro
752565
7 miles W of Southend-on-Sea; A127
to Rayleigh Weir (3 miles from
course); A13 to Victoria House Corner
(1 mile from course).
Undulating parkland course.
Pro Graham Burroughs; Founded
1922
Designed by James Braid
18 holes, 5983 yards, S.S.S. 68
Visitors: welcome WD; WE with member; h'cap certs required and 24 hours
notice.
Green Fee: WD £25; WE £25.
Societies: Thurs only; terms on application.
Catering: service 7.30am-8pm.
Hotels: Crest Maisonwyck.

1B 22 Braintree
Kings Lane, Stisted, Braintree, Essex
CM7 8DA
☎(01376) 324117
A120 eastbound after Braintree by-
pass, 1st left, 1 mile to course sign-
posted.
Parkland course.
Pro Tony Parcell; Founded 1891
Designed by Hawtree and Son
18 holes, 6191 yards, S.S.S. 69
Visitors: welcome; h'cap certs
required Sat and Sun pm.
Green Fee: WD £18; WE £40.
Societies: by arrangement Mon, Wed
and Thurs (Tues Ladies Day); terms
on application.
Catering: meals served.
Hotels: White Hart.

1B 23 Braintree Towerlands
Panfield Rd, Braintree, Essex CM7
5BJ
☎(01376) 326802, Fax 552487, Pro
347951, Sec 552794
1 mile NW of Braintree on B1053.

Picturesque parkland course.
Pro Tom Mansford-Stewart; Founded
1985
Designed by G.R. Shiels/Golf
Landscapes
9 holes, 5559 yards, S.S.S. 66
Visitors: welcome.
Green Fee: WD £10; WE £12.
Societies: welcome by appointment;
contact C W Hunnable or J C Sillett;
terms on application.
Catering: clubhouse facilities.
Practice range.
Hotels: Old House; Old Court; Hare
and Hounds.

1B 24 Braxted Park
Braxted Park, Witham, Essex CM8
3EN
☎(01376) 572372, Fax (01621)
892840
1.5 miles off A12 near Kelvedon.
Parkland course.
Pro Michael Woollett; Founded 1953
Designed by Sir Allen Clark
9 holes, 5704 yards, S.S.S. 68
Visitors: public pay as you play WD;
members only WE.
Green Fee: WD £12; WE £9.
Societies: welcome WD; pool, tennis,
sauna, snooker; terms on application..
Catering: restaurant, bar.
Hotels: Braxted Park; Rivenhall.

1B 25 Brent Valley
Church Rd, Hanwell, London W7 3BE
☎(0181) 5674230, Pro 5671287
A4020 Uxbridge Rd, Hanwell, on to
Greenford Ave then on to Church Rd.
Public meadowland course.
Pro Peter Bryant; Founded 1938
Designed by P. Alliss and D. Thomas
18 holes, 5446 yards, S.S.S. 66
Visitors: welcome 7 days.
Green Fee: WD £9.25; WE £14.
Societies: organised via the Pro;
terms on application.
Catering: restaurant from 8am.

1B 26 Brickendon Grange
Brickendon, Nr Hertford, Herts SG13
8PD
☎(01992) 511258, Fax 511411, Pro
511218, Bar/Rest 511228
3 miles S of Hertford near Bayford BR
station.
Undulating parkland course.
Pro John Hamilton; Founded 1968
Designed by C.K. Cotton
18 holes, 6394 yards, S.S.S. 70
Visitors: welcome WD; h'cap certs
required.

Green Fee: WD £24; WE £24.
Societies: WDs except Wed; terms on application.
Catering: bar lunches.
Hotels: White Horse.

1B 27 Bridgedown
St Albans Rd, Barnet, Herts EN5 4RE
☎(0181) 441 7649, Pro 440 4009
1.5 miles from M25 junction 23 at South Mimms exit.
Parkland course.
Pro David Beal; Founded 1994
18 holes, 6626 yards, S.S.S. 72
Visitors: welcome.
Green Fee: WD £15; WE £17.
Societies: welcome by prior arrangement.
Catering: bar and catering facilities.
Practice range, 12 bays.

1B 28 Briggens House Hotel
Stanstead Road, Stanstead Abbots
Ware, Herts SG12 8LD
☎(01279) 829955, Fax 793685, Pro 793742, Sec 793742, Bar/Rest 793742
Situated on A414.
Parkland course.
Pro Alan Battle; Founded 1988
18 holes, 5586 yards, S.S.S. 69
Visitors: welcome at all times.
Green Fee: WD £10.50; WE £15.
Societies: terms on application.
Catering: facilities available.

1B 29 Brocket Hall
Brocket Hall, Welwyn Garden City,
Herts AL8 7XG
☎(01707) 390055, Fax 390052, Pro 390063
On B653 to Wheathampstead off A1 (M) junction 4.
Parkland course.
Pro Keith Wood; Founded 1992
Designed by Peter Alliss / Clive Clark
18 holes, 6584 yards, S.S.S. 72
Visitors: members' guests only.
Societies: corporate days can be arranged; terms on application.
Catering: clubhouse restaurant and bar.
Practice range available.

1B 30 Brookmans Park
Golf Club Rd, Hatfield, Herts AL9 7AT
☎(01707) 652459, Fax 661851, Pro 652468, Sec 652487.
10 min from M25 through Potters Bar.
Parkland course.
Pro Ian Jelley; Founded 1930

Designed by Hawtree & Taylor
18 holes, 6460 yards, S.S.S. 71
Visitors: welcome by prior arrangement.
Green Fee: WD £27; WE £27.
Societies: terms on application.
Catering: full facilities, bar and catering.
Hotels: Brookmans Park Hotel.

1B 31 Bunsay Downs
Little Baddow Rd, Woodham Walter,
Nr Maldon, Essex CM9 6RW
☎(01245) 222648, Sec 223258
Leave A414 at Danbury towards
Woodham Water; course 0.5 W of village.
Gently undulating meadowland.
Pro Mickey Walker; Founded 1982
9 holes, 5864 yards, S.S.S. 68
Also Badgers course: 1319 yards, par 27.
Visitors: welcome.
Green Fee: WD £10; WE £11.
Societies: welcome WD except BH; packages available.
Catering: full facilities all week.
Practice range, 3 indoor bays.

1B 32 Burnham-on-Crouch
Ferry Rd, Creeksea, Burnham-on-Crouch, Essex CM0 8PQ
☎(01621) 782282, Fax 782282, Pro 786280, Bar/Rest 785508
1 mile before entering Burnham on B1010.
Undulating parkland.
Pro K Smith/S Cardy; Founded 1923
Designed by Howard Swan (2nd 9)
18 holes, 6056 yards, S.S.S. 69
Visitors: welcome WD.
Green Fee: WD £22; WE £22.
Societies: welcome WD except Thurs; full catering facilities; from £30.
Catering: full bar and restaurant facilities.

1B 33 The Burstead
The Common Rd, Little Burstead,
Billericay, Essex CM12 9SS
☎(01277) 631171, Fax 632766
Leave A127 at Research
Centre/Laindon exit; 1st exit at roundabout and then immediate right into
DuntonRoad; left into Rectory Road.
Parkland course.
Pro Keith Bridges; assisted by D Bullock; Founded 1993
Designed by Patrick Tallack
18 holes, 6275 yards, S.S.S. 70
Visitors: welcome WD with h'cap certs.

Green Fee: WD £18; WE £18.
Societies: welcome WD by prior arrangement; packages available; from £18.
Catering: clubhouse bar and restaurant.
Practice range; practice area.
Hotels: Trust House Forte and Camponile, both A127; Hill House, Horndon on the Hill.

1B 34 Bush Hill Park
Bush Hill, Winchmore Hill, London
N21 2BU
☎(0181) 3605738
0.5 mile S of Enfield town.
Parkland course.
Pro Adrian Andrews; Founded 1895
18 holes, 5828 yards, S.S.S. 68
Visitors: welcome WD except Wed am.
Green Fee: WD £24; WE £24.
Societies: on application. except Wed; terms on application.
Catering: bar snacks, full restaurant.
Hotels: West Lodge.

1B 35 Bushey G & CC
High St, Bushey, Herts WD2 1BJ
☎(0181) 9502283, Pro 9502215
On A411, 1.5 miles from M1/A411 junction.
Parkland course.
Pro Mike Lovegrove; Founded 1980
Designed by Donald Steel
9 holes, 6400 yards, S.S.S. 69
Visitors: welcome WD except Wed;
WE and Bank Holidays after 3.30pm.
Green Fee: WD £7; WE £9.
Societies: maximum 50 by arrangement; not available Wed; terms on application.
Catering: meals served.
Practice range 30 bays; floodlit.
Hotels: The Hilton.

1B 36 Bushey Hall
Bushey Hall Drive, Bushey, Herts WD2
2EP
☎(01923) Fax 229759, Pro 225802,
Sec 222253
1 mile SE of Watford.
Undulating parkland course.
Pro Christian Mower; Founded 1886
Designed by Robert Stewart Clouston
18 holes, 6099 yards, S.S.S. 69
Visitors: welcome; must book with Pro shop.
Green Fee: WD £12; WE £18.50.
Societies: welcome WD; terms on application.
Catering: full facilities.

1B 37 C & L Golf & Country Club
Junction of West End Road & A40, Northolt, Middlesex UB5 6RD
☎(0181) 8455662, Fax 8415515
A40 from London; opposite Northolt Airport.
Parkland course.
Pro Richard Kelly; Founded 1991
Designed by Patrick Tallack
9 holes, 2251 yards
Visitors: welcome Mon, Wed and Fri; no jeans or T-shirts; golf shoes only.
Green Fee: WD £6.50; WE £7.50.
Societies: welcome WD; terms on application.
Catering: bar, restaurant, banqueting hall.
Hotels: Master Brewer.

1B 38 Canons Brook
Elizabeth Way, Harlow, Essex CM19 5BE
☎(01279) 421482, Fax 626393, Pro 418357, Bar/Rest 421542
1 mile W of Harlow Town station.
Parkland course.
Pro A McGinn; Founded 1963
Designed by Sir Henry Cotton
18 holes, 6763 yards, S.S.S. 73
Visitors: welcome WD.
Green Fee: WD £27; WE £27.
Societies: welcome Mon, Wed, Fri; golf and catering; £45.
Catering: full catering facilities.
Hotels: Churchgate Hotel; Moat House.

1B 39 Castle Point
Somnes Avenue, Canvey Island, Essex SS8 9FG
☎(01268) Pro 510830
A13 to Southend, right on A130 to Canvey Island at Saddler's Farm roundabout, over Waterside Farm roundabout to Somnes Ave, course on left.
Public seaside links course.
Pro Michael Otteridge; Founded 1988
Designed by Golf Landscapes
18 holes, 6096 yards, S.S.S. 69
Visitors: no restrictions; booking required at WE.
Green Fee: WD £8.50; WE £12.80.
Societies: on request; telephone in advance; terms on application.
Catering: bar and restaurant facilities.
Hotels: Crest (Basildon); Oyster Fleet.

1B 40 Chadwell Springs
Hertford Rd, Ware, Herts SG12 9LE
☎(01920) 461447, Pro 462075
On A119 halfway between Hertford and Ware.
Parkland course.
Pro Mark Wall; Founded 1975
Designed by J.H. Taylor
9 holes, 3209 yards, S.S.S. 71
Visitors: welcome WD; WE by arrangement.
Green Fee: WD £10.
Societies: welcome Mon and Wed; terms on application.
Catering: full facilities.
Hotels: Salisbury (Hertford); Moat House (Ware).

1B 41 Channels
Belsteads Farm Lane, Little Waltham, Chelmsford, Essex CM3 3PT
☎(01245) 440005, Fax 442032, Pro 441056
2 miles NE of Chelmsford off A130.
Undulating parkland course.
Pro Ian Sinclair; Founded 1974
Designed by Henry Cotton
Belsteads: 18 holes, 4779 yards, S.S.S. 70; Channels: 18 holes, 6272 yards, S.S.S. 70
Visitors: welcome anytime.
Green Fee: Belsteads course WD £16, WE £16; Channels course WD £24, WE £24.
Societies: welcome WD; packages involve playing both Channels and Belsteads courses; £26-55.
Catering: full catering facilities.
Hotels: County Hotel, Chelmsford.

1B 42 Chelmsford
Widford Rd, Chelmsford, Essex CM2 9AP
☎(01245) 256483, Fax 256483, Pro 257079, Bar/Rest 268581
Off A1016 Chelmsford road.
Parkland course.
Pro Dennis Bailey; Founded 1893
Designed by Harry Colt (1924)
18 holes, 5981 yards, S.S.S. 68
Visitors: welcome WD only.
Green Fee: WD £27; WE £27.
Societies: welcome Wed and Thurs only; terms on application..
Catering: full facilities.
Hotels: South Lodge, Chelmsford.

1B 43 Chesfield Downs
Jack's Hill, Graveley, Herts SG4 7EQ
☎(01462) 482929, Fax 482390
From A1M follow signs on B197 to Graveley.
Parkland course.
Pro Jane Fernley/H Arnott; Founded 1991
Designed by Jonathan Gaunt
18 holes, 6646 yards, S.S.S. 72
Visitors: welcome.
Green Fee: WD £14.75; WE £21.
Societies: welcome; various packages; terms on application.
Catering: full facilities.
Hotels: Blackmore Hotel, Little Wymondley.

1B 44 Cheshunt
Park Lane, Cheshunt, Herts EN7 6QD
☎(01992) 629777, Sec 624009
From M25 junction 25 towards Hertford, at 2nd lights turn left to mini-roundabout, turn right then signposted.
Municipal parkland course.
Pro Andy Trainer; Founded 1976
18 holes, 6613 yards, S.S.S. 71
Visitors: welcome WD and by arrangement at WE.
Green Fee: WD £10.50; WE £13.50.
Societies: by arrangement; terms on application.
Catering: café service all day.
Hotels: Marriott.

1B 45 Chigwell
High Rd, Chigwell, Essex IG7 5BH
☎(0181) 5002059, Fax 5013410, Pro 5002384
On A113, 13.5 miles NE of London
Undulating parkland course.
Pro Ray Beard; Founded 1925
18 holes, 6279 yards, S.S.S. 70
Visitors: welcome WD with h'cap certs; only with member at WE.
Green Fee: WD £30.
Societies: welcome Mon, Wed and Fri by prior arrangement; terms on application.
Catering: bar and catering facilities.
Hotels: Prince Regent; Roebuck.

1B 46 Chingford
Bury Rd, Chingford London E4 7QJ
☎(0181) Pro 5295708, Sec 5292107
Off Station Road, 300 yards S of Chingford station.
Public parkland course.
Pro John Francis/Robin Gowers; Founded 1888
Designed by James Braid
18 holes, 6342 yards, S.S.S. 69
Visitors: welcome; red outer garment must be worn.
Green Fee: WD £9.80; WE £13.40.
Societies: welcome by appointment; terms on application.
Catering: snacks, no bar; café next to club.
Hotels: Ridgeway (Chingford).

1B 47 **Chorleywood**

Common Rd, Chorleywood, Herts
WD3 5LN
☎(01923) 282009
0.5 mile from Chorleywood station
near Sportsman Hotel.
Wooded heathland course on common
land.
Founded 1890
9 holes, 5712 yards, S.S.S. 67
Visitors: welcome WD except Tues.
Green Fee: WD £16; WE £20.
Societies: small societies; terms on
application.
Catering: bar and catering.

1B 48 **Clacton-on-Sea**

West Rd, Clacton-on-Sea, Essex
CO15 1A J
☎(01255) 424331, Fax 424602, Pro
426804, Sec 421919 Bar/Rest 424793
On the seafront at Clacton.
Parkland course.
Pro Stuart Levermore; Founded 1892
Designed by Jack White
18 holes, 6532 yards, S.S.S. 71
Visitors: welcome WD.
Green Fee: WD £20; WE £30.
Societies: welcome WD; full day of
golf plus lunch and dinner; £45.
Catering: full facilities and bar.
Hotels: Kingcliff; Plaza; Chudleigh.

1B 49 **Colchester**

Braiswick, Colchester, Essex CO4 5AV
☎(01206) 852946, Fax 852698, Pro
853920, Sec 853396
0.75 miles NW of Colchester North
station on the B1508.
Parkland course.
Pro Mark Angel; Founded 1907
Designed by James Braid
18 holes, 6307 yards, S.S.S. 70
Visitors: welcome with h'cap certs.
Green Fee: WD £18; WE £18.
Societies: welcome by arrangement;
terms on application.
Catering: full facilities.
Hotels: George Hotel; Rose & Crown;
both Colchester.

1B 50 **Colne Valley (Essex)**

Station Road, Earls Colne, Essex CO6
2LT
☎(01787) 224343, Fax 224126, Pro
224233, Bar/Rest 224233
10 miles W from A12/A604 junction.
Parkland course.
Pro Scott Clark; Founded 1991
Designed by Howard Swan
18 holes, 6301 yards, S.S.S. 70
Visitors: welcome midweek and after

10.30 at WE with prior arrangement.
Green Fee: WD £16; WE £21.
Societies: welcome; in-house cater-
ing, corporate days for up to 200; pool
and snooker; terms on application.
Catering: restaurant and bar.
Hotels: Bull Hotel; Forte Posthouse;
Marks Tey Hotel.

1B 51 **Crews Hill**

Cattlegate Rd, Crews Hill, Enfield,
Middx EN2 8AZ
☎(0181) 3636674, Sec 9973959
Off A1005 Enfield to Potters Bar road
into East Lodge Lane, turn right into
Cattlegate Rd.
Parkland course.
Pro Neil Wichelow; Founded 1921
Designed by H. Colt
18 holes, 6244 yards, S.S.S. 70
Visitors: must be members of recog-
nised club; WE and BH only with
member.
Green Fee: WD £22; WE £33.75.
Societies: welcome with advance
booking; terms on application.
Catering: full facilities, except Mon.
Hotels: Royal Chase.

1B 52 **Crondon Park**

Stock Road, Stock, Essex CM4 9DP
☎(01277) 841115, Fax 841356, Pro
841087
Off B1007 outside village of Stock.
Parkland course.
Pro Mike Herbert; Founded 1984
Designed by M Gillett
18 holes, 6585 yards, S.S.S. 71
Visitors: WDs and after 11 am at WE.
Green Fee: WD £19; WE £25.
Societies: WDs only, full clubhouse
facilities; from £23.50.
Catering: full bar and restaurant.
Hotels: South Lodge; County Hotel;
Miami Hotel.

1B 53 **Dyrham Park**

Galley Lane, Barnet, Herts EN5 4RA
☎(0181) Pro 4403904, Sec 4403361
2 miles outside Barnet near Arkley, off
A1 and M25.
Parkland course.
Pro Bill Large; Founded 1963
Designed by C.K. Cotton
18 holes, 6428 yards, S.S.S. 71
Visitors: only as guest of member or
member of Golf Society.
Societies: Wed only; two rounds golf,
light lunch and dinner or lunch and
afternoon tea; terms on application.
Catering: full restaurant facilities.
Hotels: Post House.

1B 54 **Ealing**

Perivale Lane, Greenford, Middx UB6
8SS
☎(0181) 9970937, Fax 9980756, Pro
9973959
Off A40 W opposite Hoover building.
Parkland course.
Pro Ian Parsons; Founded 1898
Designed by H. Colt
18 holes, 6216 yards, S.S.S. 70
Visitors: welcome WD only, phone for
advance booking.
Green Fee: WD £30; WE £30.
Societies: Mon, Wed and Thurs only;
terms on application.
Catering: full facilities.
Hotels: The Bridge (Greenford).

1B 55 **East Herts**

Hamels Park, Buntingford, Herts SG9
9NA
☎(01920) 821923, Fax 823700, Pro
821922, Sec 821978, Bar/Rest
821922
On A10 N of Puckeridge.
Parkland course.
Pro Stephen Bryan; Founded 1899
18 holes, 6456 yards, S.S.S. 71
Visitors: WDs with h'cap certs; WE
with member only.
Green Fee: WD £26; WE £26.
Societies: on application; 18 holes of
golf, bar, catering; £54.50.
Catering: full facilities.

1B 56 **Edgewarebury**

Edgeware Way, Edgeware, Middlesex
AL4 0BR
☎(0181) 9583571, Sec 9053393
On A41 between Edgeware and
Elstree.
Pitch and putt course.
Pro Peter Andrews; Founded 1946
9 holes, 2090 yards, S.S.S. 27
Visitors: welcome 9am until dusk; no
booking necessary.
Green Fee: WD £4; WE £4.
Societies: welcome; terms on applica-
tion.
Catering: no facilities.
Hotels: Edgewarebury Hotel.

1B 57 **Elstree**

Watling St, Elstree, Herts WD6 3AA
☎(0181) 953 6115, Fax 207 6390
On A5183 between Elstree and
Radlett.
Parkland course.
Pro Marc Warwick; Founded 1984
18 holes, 6556 yards, S.S.S. 72
Visitors: welcome WD and after mid-
day at WE.

ENFIELD GOLF CLUB
Old Park Road South, Enfield, Middlesex EN2 7DA Tel: 0181-363 3970
A warm welcome awaits you at Enfield. Course designed by James Braid. Casual green fees (with Handicap Certificate) and Society Days welcome. Call secretary for details.

1893

Green Fee: WD £20; WE £25.
Societies: welcome WD except Wed by prior arrangement; minimum 8 players in party; golf and catering packages available; Ingolf Simulator room; from £15.
Catering: full catering and bar. Practice range, 60 bays.
Hotels: Edgwarebury Hotel, Elstree; Oaklands, Boreham Wood; North Medburn Farm B&B.

1B 58 Enfield
Old Park Rd South, Enfield, Middx EN2 7DA
☎(0181) Fax 342 0381, Pro 366 4492, Sec 363 3970, Bar/Rest 3633970
Leave M25 at junction 24; take A1005 to Enfield, turn right at roundabout in Slades Hill, then 1st left into Old Park View, at end of road turn right into Old Park Road South.
Parkland course.
Pro Lee Fickling; Founded 1893
Designed by James Braid
18 holes, 6154 yards, S.S.S. 70
Visitors: WD, except Tuesday.
Green Fee: WD £25.
Societies: WD only with references; full clubhouse facilities; from £50.
Catering: full catering facilities.
Hotels: West Lodge Park, Cockfosters; Royal Chase, Enfield.

1B 59 Epping Forest G & CC
Woolston Manor, Abridge Rd, Chigwell, Essex IG7 6BX
☎(0181) 500 2549, Fax 501 5452, Pro 559 8272
From M11 junction 5 take the A113; course is 1 mile on between Abridge and Chigwell.
Parkland course.
Pro Craig Stephenson; Founded 1994
Designed by Neil Coles
18 holes, 6408 yards, S.S.S. 71
Visitors: with member only.
Societies: welcome by prior arrangement; terms on application.
Catering: full catering and bar facilities.
Hotels: Swallow Hotel, Waltham Abbey.

1B 60 Essex G & CC
Earls Colne, Nr Colchester, Essex CO6 2NS
☎(01787) 224466, Fax 224410
On B1024 2 miles N of A120 at Coggeshall.
Parkland course.
Pro Danny Peck; Founded 1990
Designed by Reg Plumbridge
18 holes, 6879 yards, S.S.S. 73
Also 9-hole academy course, par 34
Visitors: welcome by prior arrangement.
Green Fee: WD £16; WE £20.
Societies: welcome WD by prior arrangement; packages available; health and beauty facilities; terms on application.
Catering: restaurant and bar. Practice range, floodlit.
Hotels: The Lodge.

1B 61 Fairlop Waters
Forest Rd, Barkingside, Ilford, Essex IG6 3HN
☎(0181) 5009911, Pro 5011881
Signposted from M11 and along A12; near Fairlop station (Central Line).
Public heathland course.
Pro Bradley Preston; Founded 1988
Designed by John Jacobs
18 holes, 6281 yards, S.S.S. 69
Visitors: welcome; tidy dress required.
Green Fee: WD £8.95; WE £12.95.
Societies: welcome WD by arrangement; sailing, children's play area, country park; terms on application.
Catering: bar, Daltons American Diner, 2 banqueting suites. Practice range 36 bays; floodlit.
Hotels: Granada Travel Inn (Redbridge).

1B 62 Finchley
Nether Court, Frith Lane, Mill Hill, London NW7 1PU
☎(0181) 346 2436, Fax 343 4205, Pro 346 5086, Bar/Rest 349 2314
2 miles from M1 junction 2.
Parkland course.
Pro David Brown; Founded 1929
Designed by James Braid
18 holes, 6411 yards, S.S.S. 71
Visitors: by prior arrangement only.
Green Fee: WD £24; WE £30.
Societies: terms on application.
Catering: full facilities.

1B 63 Five Lakes Hotel G & CC
Colchester Rd, Tolleshunt Knight, Maldon, Essex CM9 8HX
☎(01621) 862326, Fax 862320, Bar/Rest 868888
Off A12 at Kelvedon, take B1023 to Tiptree following tourist signs.
Links style course.
Pro Gary Carter; Founded 1991
Designed by N Coles
Lakes course: 18 holes, 6767 yards, S.S.S. 70; Links course: 18 holes, 6188 yards, S.S.S. 70
Visitors: welcome by prior arrangement.
Societies: welcome by prior arrangement; corporate days organised; minimum of 8; terms on application.
Catering: clubhouse and hotel facilities.
Hotels: Five Lakes.

1B 64 Forrester Park
Beckingham Rd, Great Totham, Nr Maldon, Essex CM9 8EA
☎(01621) 891406, Fax 891406, Pro 893456
Off A12 at Rivenhall End, follow signs to Great Braxted until B1022. Turn right to Malden, course is 1.8 miles on left.
Parkland course.
Pro Gary Pike; Founded 1968
Designed by D.A.H. Everett & T.R. Forrester-Muir
18 holes, 6073 yards, S.S.S. 69
Visitors: welcome by arrangement.
Catering: facilities available.
Hotels: Rivenhall Motor Inn, Rivenhall; Bull Boer, Malden.

1B 65 Frinton
1 The Esplanade, Frinton-on-Sea, Essex CO13 9EP
☎(01255) 674618, Fax 674618, Pro 671618, Bar/Rest 650405
On B1033 in Frinton.

Seaside course, not traditional links.
Pro Peter Taggart; Founded 1895
Designed by Tom Dunn (1895)/ Willie
Park Jnr (1904)
18 holes, 6265 yards, S.S.S. 70
Visitors: welcome by prior arrange-
ment with Sec.
Green Fee: WD £25; WE £25.
Societies: welcome Wed, Thurs and
some Fri by arrangement with Sec;
catering by arrangement; £25-45.
Catering: available.
Hotels: Maplin Hotel; Rock Hotel;
Glenco Hotel.

1B 66 Fulwell
Wellington Rd, Hampton Hill, Middx
TW12 1JY
☎(0181) Pro 9773844, Sec 9772733
2 miles S of Twickenham on A311,
opposite Fulwell bus station.
Meadowland course.
Pro Nigel Turner; Founded 1904
Designed by D. Morrison
18 holes, 6544 yards, S.S.S. 71
Visitors: welcome WD; book through
Pro shop.
Green Fee: WD £30; WE £35.
Societies: welcome by prior arrange-
ment; terms on application.
Catering: by arrangement.
Hotels: The Winning Post.

1B 67 Gosfield Lake
The Manor House, Hall Drive, Gosfield
Halstead, Essex CO9 1SE
☎(01787) 474747, Fax 476044, Pro
474488, Bar/Rest 474400
7 miles N of Braintree on A1017; 1
mile W of Gosfield village.
Parkland course.
Pro Richard Wheeler; Founded 1988
Designed by Sir Henry Cotton,
Howard Swan
18 holes, 6756 yards, S.S.S. 72
Also Meadows course: 4180 yards
Visitors: welcome.
Green Fee: WD £25; WE £25.
Societies: welcome; 36 holes, lunch,
carvery; from £42.
Catering: full catering facilities.
Hotels: Bull, Halstead.

1B 68 Grim's Dyke
Oxhey Lane, Hatch End, Pinner,
Middx HA5 4AL
☎(0181) 428 4539, Fax 421 5494,
Pro 428 7484, Bar/Rest 428 4093
On the A4008 between Hatch End and
Watford.
Gently undulating parkland.
Pro J Rule; Founded 1910

Designed by James Braid
18 holes, 5590 yards, S.S.S. 67
Visitors: welcome WD.
Green Fee: WD £20; WE £20.
Societies: welcome Tues-Fri; 36
holes, 2 meals; £47.
Catering: full catering facilities.

1B 69 Hadley Wood
Beech Hill, Barnet, Herts EN4 0JJ
☎(0181) 449 4328, Fax 364 8633,
Pro 449 3285, Bar/Rest 441 8023
Off A111 Cockfosters road, a mile from
M25 junction 24.
Parkland course.
Pro Peter Jones; Founded 1922
Designed by A MacKenzie
18 holes, 6457 yards, S.S.S. 71
Visitors: welcome WD.
Green Fee: WD £36.
Societies: welcome Mon, Thurs and
Fri; terms on application.
Catering: full catering and bar facili-
ties.
Hotels: West Lodge Park,
Cockfosters.

1B 70 Hainault Forest
Chigwell Row, Hainault, Essex IG7
4QW
☎(0181) 500 2097, Pro 500 2131,
Sec 500 0385
On A12 12 miles central London.
Parkland course.
Pro Chris Hope; Founded 1912
Lower: 18 holes, 6618 yards, S.S.S.
72
Upper: 18 holes, 5893 yards, S.S.S.
68
Visitors: welcome.
Green Fee: WD £11.50; WE £14.
Societies: welcome by prior arrange-
ment; packages available.
Catering: meals and bar service.

1B 71 Hampstead
Winnington Rd, Hampstead, London
N2 0TU
☎(0181) 455 0203, Fax 731 6194,
Pro 455 7089
400 yards down Winnington Road
near Kenwood House.
Undulating parkland course with
mature trees.
Pro Peter Brown; Founded 1893
Designed by Tom Dunn
9 holes, 5822 yards, S.S.S. 68
Visitors: welcome with h'cap certs or
letter of introduction; restrictions Tues
and WE.
Green Fee: WD £30; WE £35.
Societies: not available.

1B 72 Hanbury Manor
G & CC
Ware, Herts SG12 0SD
☎(01920) 487722, Fax 487692
Junction 25 off M25 and take A10 N
for 12 miles.
Parkland course.
Pro Peter Blaze; Founded 1990
Designed by Jack Nicklaus II
18 holes, 7016 yards, S.S.S. 74
Visitors: hotel resident or member's
guest.
Green Fee: WD £50; WE £50.
Societies: on application to the golf
co-ordinator; terms on application.
Catering: hotel and clubhouse facili-
ties.
Hotels: Marriot Hanbury Manor.

1B 73 Hanover
Hullbridge Rd, Rayleigh, Essex SS6
9QS
☎(01702) 232377
Undulating course.
Pro Tony Blackburn; Founded 1991
Designed by Reg Plumbridge
Georgian course: 18 holes, 6696
yards, S.S.S. 72
Regency course: 3700 yards, par 61
Visitors: members' guests only.
Societies: affiliated society enquiries
only; terms on application.
Catering: full clubhouse service.
Hotels: The Watermill.

1B 74 Harefield Place
The Drive, Harefield Place, Uxbridge,
Middx UB10 8AQ
☎(01895) 272457, Fax 810262, Pro
237287
B467 towards Ruislip off A40. 1st left
down The Drive.
Undulating parkland.
Pro Phil Howard
18 holes, 5753 yards, S.S.S. 68
Visitors: welcome.
Green Fee: WD £11.85; WE £16.85.
Societies: welcome midweek; after-
noons at WE; terms on application.
Catering: full catering facilities, includ-
ing carvery, and bar.
Hotels: Master Brewer, Hillingdon.

1B 75 Harpenden
Hammonds End, Redbourn Lane,
Harpenden, Herts AL5 2AX
☎(01582) 712580, Fax 712725, Pro
767124, Bar/Rest 462014
On A487 Redbourn road.
Parkland course.
Pro Peter Cherry; Founded 1894/1931
Designed by Hawtree & Taylor

18 holes, 6381 yards, S.S.S. 70
Visitors: welcome WD except Thurs; with a member at WE.
Green Fee: WD £24; WE £24.
Societies: welcome WD except Thurs; £52-£58.
Catering: full facilities.
Hotels: Gleneagles, Harpenden; Harpenden House Hotel

1B 76 Harpenden Common
Cravells Rd, East Common, Harpenden, Herts AL5 1BL
☎(01582) 712856, Fax 715959, Pro 460655, Sec 715959
4 miles N of St Albans on A1081.
Parkland course.
Pro D Fitzsimmons; Founded 1894/1931/ 1995
Designed by Ken Brown (1995)
18 holes, 6214 yards, S.S.S. 67
Visitors: welcome WD with h'cap certs.
Green Fee: WD £23; WE £23.
Societies: welcome on Thurs and Fri; £45.
Catering: full facilities.
Hotels: Gleneagles, Harpenden.

1B 77 Harrow Hill
Kenton Road, Harrow Middlesex HA1 2BW
☎(0181) 864 3754
Off main Harrow by-pass near Northwick Park roundabout.
Park beginners course.
Pro Simon Bishop; Founded 1982
Designed by S. Teahan
9 holes, 850 yards
Visitors: public beginners par 3.
Green Fee: WD £3.50; WE £3.50.
Catering: cold soft drinks and sweets.

1B 78 Harrow School
Harrow School, 5 High St, Harrow-on-the-Hill, Middlesex HA1 3JE
☎(0181) 4222196
Parkland course.
Founded 1979
Designed by Donald Steel
9 holes, 3690 yards, S.S.S. 57
Visitors: no visitors.

1B 79 Hartsbourne G & CC
Hartsbourne Ave, Bushey Heath, Herts WD2 1JW
☎(0181) 950 1133, Pro 950 2836
Turn off A411 at entrance to Bushey Heath village; 5 miles SE of Watford.
Parkland course.

Pro Alistair Campbell; Founded 1946
Designed by Hawtree and Taylor
18 holes, 6325 yards, S.S.S. 70
Also 9 holes, 5773 yards, par 70
Visitors: members guests' only.
Green Fee: WD £20; WE £30.
Societies: welcome Mon and Fri only; catering packages available.
Catering: full catering and bar facilities.
Hotels: Hilton National.

1B 80 Hartswood
King George's Playing Fields, Ingrave Road, Brentwood, Essex CM14 5AE
☎(01277) 214830, Pro 218714, Sec 2188501 mile from Brentwood town centre on A128 Ingrave road.
Parkland course.
Pro Steve Cole; Founded 1965
18 holes, 6192 yards, S.S.S. 69
Visitors: municipal course.
Green Fee: WD £7.50; WE £11.50.
Societies: welcome WD, minimum 20; meals and 18 or 36 holes, no coffee on arrival; £25-£35.
Catering: facilities available.

1B 81 Harwich & Dovercourt
Station Rd, Parkeston, Harwich, Essex CO12 4NZ
☎(01255) 503616, Fax 503616
Left off A120 roundabout for Harwich International port; course 100 yards.
Parkland course.
Founded 1907
9 holes, 5900 yards, S.S.S. 69
Visitors: welcome with h'cap certs.
Green Fee: WD £17; WE £17.
Societies: welcome by prior arrangement; catering by prior arrangement; from £14.
Catering: clubhouse facilities.
Hotels: Tower; Cliff both at Dovercourt.

1B 82 Haste Hill
The Drive
Northwood, Middx HA6 1HN
☎(01923) 829808, Pro 822877, Sec 825224, Bar/Rest 739484
On A404 at Northwood
Tree-lined parkland.
Pro Adam Hart; Founded 1933
18 holes, 5797 yards, S.S.S. 68
Visitors: welcome; book in advance.
Green Fee: WD £10.95; WE £15.95.
Societies: welcome; terms on application.
Catering: available.
Hotels: Tudor Lodge, Eastcote.

1B 83 Hatfield London CC
Bedwell Park, Essendon, Hatfield, Herts AL9 6JA
☎(01707) 642624
A1000 from Potters Bar, B158 towards Essendon.
Undulating parkland course.
Pro Norman Greer; Founded 1976
Designed by Fred Hawtree
18 holes, 6385 yards, S.S.S. 70
Visitors: welcome by advance booking only.
Green Fee: WD £17; WE £28.
Societies: welcome; terms on application.
Catering: full facilities.

1B 84 Hazelwood
Croysdale Ave, Sunbury-on-Thames, Middlesex TW16 6QU
☎(01932) 770981, Fax 770933, Pro 770932, Bar/Rest 783496
1 mile from M3 junction 1.
Parkland course.
Founded 1993
Designed by Jonathan Gaunt
18 holes, 5700 yards
Visitors: welcome.
Societies: welcome; terms on application.
Catering: full facilities
Practice range 36 bays.
Hotels: Thames Lodge, Staines; Runnymede Hotel, Egham; Moat House, Shepperton.

1B 85 Hendon
Ashley Walk, Devonshire Road, Mill Hill, London NW7 1DG
☎(0181) 3466023, Fax 3431974, Pro 3468990
From Hendon Central take Queens Rd through Brent St, continue to roundabout, take 1st exit on left, club 0.5 mile on left in Devonshire Rd.
Parkland course.
Pro Stuart Murray; Founded 1903
Designed by H.S. Colt
18 holes, 6266 yards, S.S.S. 70
Visitors: welcome Tues-Fri, limited Mon, not Sat/Sun morning.
Green Fee: WD £28; WE £35.
Societies: welcome Tues-Fri by arrangement; terms on application.
Catering: snacks only Mon; other days lunch, snacks, high tea to 6pm.
Hotels: Holiday Inn (Brent Cross); Hendon Hall.

1B 86 The Hertfordshire
Broxbournebury Mansion, White St, Broxbourne, Herts EN10 7PY

☎(01992) 466666, Fax 470326
M25 junction 25, take a A10 towards
Cambridge. Take A10 exit for
Turnford and then A1170 to Bell Lane.
Turn left, Bell Lane becomes White
Stubbs Lane. Course on right.
Parkland course.
Pro Adrian Shearn; Founded 1995
Designed by Jack Nicklaus (his first
pay and play course In Europe)
18 holes, 6388 yards, S.S.S. 70
Visitors: welcome.
Green Fee: WD £21; WE £25.
Societies: welcome; corporate days
available; health club, tennis club, golf
academy with chipping green; terms
on application.
Catering: restaurant and bar.
Practice range 30 bays.
Hotels: The Cheshunt Marriott.

1B 87 **High Beech**

Wellington Hill, Loughton, Essex IG10
4AH
☎(0181) 508 7323
5 mins from M25 junction 26 at
Waltham Abbey.
Parkland course.
Founded 1963
9 holes, 1477 yards
Visitors: public pay and play.

1B 88 **Highgate**

Denewood Rd, London N6 4AH
☎(0181) 3401906, Pro 3405467, Sec
3403745
Off Hampstead Lane near Kenwood
House, turn into Sheldon Ave then 1st
left into Denewood Rd.
Parkland course.
Pro Robin Turner / Mark Tompkins /
Darren Turner; Founded 1904
18 holes, 5985 yards, S.S.S. 69
Visitors: welcome WD (after noon on
Wed); no visitors at WE.
Green Fee: WD £27; WE £27.
Societies: welcome Tues, Thurs, Fri;
terms on application.
Catering: full facilities 12am-8pm.

1B 89 **Hillingdon**

18 Dorset Way
Hillingdon, Middx UB10 0JR
☎(01895) 239810, Pro 460035, Sec
233956
Turn off A40 to Uxbridge past RAF
station, up Hillingdon Hill to turn left at
Vine Public House into Vine Lane.
Undulating parkland.
Pro Phil Smith; Founded 1892
Designed by Harry Woods & Chas E.
Stevens.

9 holes, 5490 yards, S.S.S. 68
Visitors: welcome WD except Thurs
pm; WE with a member only after
12.30pm.
Green Fee: WD £15.
Societies: welcome Mon by prior
arrangement; special golf and catering
packages available; from £22.
Catering: bar and catering facilities.
Hotels: Master Brewer; Old Cottage.

1B 90 **Horsenden Hill**

Woodland Rise, Greenford, Middx
UB6 0RD
☎(0181) Pro 9024555
Signposted off Whitton Ave East, rear
of Sudbury Golf club.
Public undulating parkland course.
Pro Simon Hoffman; Founded 1935
9 holes, 1632 yards
Visitors: welcome, no restrictions.
Green Fee: WD £3.70; WE £6.40.
Societies: welcome any time by prior
arrangement.
Catering: bar and restaurant.

1B 91 **Hounslow Heath**

Staines Rd, Hounslow, Middx TW4
5DS
☎(0181) 5705271
A315 main road between Hounslow
and Bedfont, on left hand side.
Heathland course.
Founded 1979
Designed by Fraser Middleton
18 holes, 5901 yards, S.S.S. 68
Visitors: welcome.
Green Fee: WD £7.70; WE £11.20.
Societies: welcome by arrangement;
terms on application.
Catering: no bar; snacks and soft
drinks available.
Hotels: several in Hounslow or
Heathrow.

1B 92 **Ilford**

291 Wanstead Park Rd, Ilford, Essex
IG1 3TR
☎(0181) Pro 5540094, Sec 5542930
0.5 mile from Ilford railway station.
Parkland course.
Pro Stuart Dowsett; Founded 1906
18 holes, 5297 yards, S.S.S. 66
Visitors: welcome with advance book-
ing; restricted Tues and Thurs; Sat
10.30am-12.30pm, Sun 12.30pm-
1.30pm.
Green Fee: WD £13.50; WE £16.
Societies: welcome WD by arrange-
ment with Sec; terms on application.
Catering: restaurant most days.
Hotels: Woodford Moat House.

1B 93 **Knebworth**

Deards End Lane, Knebworth, Herts
SG3 6NL
☎(01438) 812752, Fax 815216, Pro
812757
1 mile S of Stevenage on B197, leave
A1M at junction 7.
Undulating parkland.
Pro Garry Parker; Founded 1908
Designed by Willie Park
18 holes, 6492 yards, S.S.S. 71
Visitors: welcome WD.
Green Fee: WD £30; WE £30.
Societies: welcome Mon, Tues and
Thurs only; terms on application.
Catering: full catering and bar .

1B 94 **Laing Sports Club**

Rowley Lane, Arkley, Barnet, Herts
EN5 3HW
☎(0181) 4416051
Off A1 S at Borehamwood.
Parkland course.
Designed by employees of John Laing
and members.
9 holes, 4178 yards, S.S.S. 60
Visitors: Only with member.
Green Fee: WD £6; WE £6.
Societies: limited.
Catering: limited.

1B 95 **Langdon Hills**

Lower Dunton Road, Bulphan, Essex
RM14 3TY
☎(01268) 548444, Fax 490084, Pro
544300
8 miles from M25 junction 30, A13 E
towards Tilbury, after approx 7 miles
turn off on B1007 towards Horndon on
the Hill; after approx 1 mile turn left
into Lower Dunton Rd.
Parkland course.
Pro Terry Moncur; Founded 1991
Designed by MRM Sandow
27 holes, 6504 yards, S.S.S. 71
Bulphan course: 6426 yards, par 73
Horndon course: 6186 yards, par 71
Visitors: welcome WD; not before
10.30 WE.
Green Fee: WD £11; WE £14.
Societies: welcome WD by prior
arrangement; European School of golf;
special packages; function suite; terms
on application.
Catering: bar and restaurant.
Practice range 22 bays; floodlit.
Hotels: Langdon Hills.

1B 96 **Lee Valley**

Lee Valley Leisure Golf Course,
Edmonton London N9 0AS
☎(0181) 8033611

1 mile N of North Circular road, junction with Montagu Rd.
Public parkland course with large lake and river.
Pro Richard Gerken; Founded 1974
18 holes, 4902 yards, S.S.S. 64
Visitors: open to public every day, no restrictions except dress code in operation.
Green Fee: WD £10.50; WE £13.20.
Societies: welcome WD only; max 30 persons; sporting facilities at leisure centre; terms on application.
Catering: breakfast until midday, bar and bar snacks daily.
Practice range 20 bays; floodlit.
Hotels: Holt Whites Hotel (Enfield).

1B 97 Letchworth

Letchworth Lane, Letchworth, Herts SG6 3NQ
☎(01462) 683203, Fax 484567, Pro 682713
1 mile S of Letchworth off A505.
Parkland course.
Pro John Mutimer; Founded 1905
Designed by Harry Vardon
18 holes, 6181 yards, S.S.S. 69
Visitors: welcome WD with restrictions Thurs.
Green Fee: WD £24; WE £24.
Societies: welcome Wed, Thurs and Fri; 36 holes of golf, snack lunch and dinner; £50.
Catering: full clubhouse catering facilities.
Hotels: Ambassador, Letchworth; Letchworth Hall.

1B 98 Little Hay Golf Complex

Box Lane, Bovingdon, Hemel Hempstead, Herts HP3 0DQ
☎(01442) 833798
Just off A41, turn left at 1st traffic lights, past Hemel Hempstead station, turn right up hill at lights; 1.5 miles up hill, complex on right.
Public parkland pay and play course.
Pro David S Johnson / Stephen Proudfoot; Founded 1977
Designed by Hawtree & Son
18 holes, 6311 yards, S.S.S. 70
Visitors: welcome.
Green Fee: WD £10; WE £14.25.
Societies: welcome by prior arrangement; bookings accepted on the day after 9 am by phone; golf and catering packages available on request; terms on application.
Catering: full meals.
Practice range 22 bays; floodlit.
Hotels: Bobsleigh.

1B 99 London Golf Centre

Ruislip Rd, Northolt, Middx UB5 6QZ
☎(0181) 845 3180, Fax 845 0542, Sec 842 0442
0.5 miles S of Polish War Memorial on A4180.
Parkland course.
Pro Neil MacDonald; Founded 1982
18 holes, 5836 yards, S.S.S. 69
Visitors: welcome.
Green Fee: WD £10; WE £14.
Societies: welcome WD; unlimited golf, 2-course lunch; from £20.
Catering: bar and catering facilities.

1B 100 Loughton

Clay's Lane, Debden Green, Loughton, Essex IG10 2RZ
☎(0181) 502 2923
From M25 junction 26 take A121 towards Loughton; 3rd exit at roundabout; 1st turning on left.
Hilly parkland course.
Pro Richard Layton; Founded 1982
9 holes, 4652 yards, S.S.S. 63
Visitors: welcome; book after Thurs for WE.
Societies: terms on application.
Catering: available but limited.

1B 101 Maldon

Beeleigh, Langford, Maldon, Essex CM9 6LL
☎(01621) 853212
2 miles NW of Maldon on B1019. Turn off at Essex Waterworks.
Parkland course.
Founded 1891
9 holes, 6253 yards, S.S.S. 70
Visitors: welcome WD; with a member only at WE.
Green Fee: WD £15; WE £12.
Societies: welcome; maximum of 32; packages; terms on application.
Catering: clubhouse catering and bar.
Hotels: Blue Boar, Maldon.

1B 102 Malton

Malton Lane, Meldreth, Royston, Herts
☎(01763) 262200, Fax 262209
A10 towards Cambridge, turn at Melbourne towards Meldreth, 4 miles.
Parkland course.
Founded 1994
18 holes, 6708 yards, S.S.S. 72
Visitors: welcome.
Green Fee: WD £10; WE £12.
Societies: welcome WD; packages available; from £12.
Catering: bar and bar snacks.
Driving range, 10 bays.
Hotels: Cambridge Motel.

1B 103 Manor of Groves G & CC

High Wych, Sawbridgeworth, Herts CM21 0LA
☎(01279) 722333, Fax 726972, Pro 721486
On A1184 to High Wych; leave M11 at junction 7 on A414.
Parkland course.
Pro Craig Laurence; Founded 1991
Designed by S. Sharer
18 holes, 6280 yards, S.S.S. 70
Visitors: welcome WD; pm at WE.
Green Fee: WD £18; WE £25.
Societies: welcome WD; packages arranged for parties; from £26.
Catering: full hotel facilities.
Hotels: Manor of Groves Hotel.

1B 104 Maylands Golf & CC

Colchester Rd, Harold Park, Romford, Essex RM3 0AZ
☎(01708) 342055, Fax 373080, Pro 346466, Sec 373080, Bar/Rest 346273
1 mile W of M25 junction 28.
Parkland course.
Pro J S Hopkin/R Cole Touring Pro; Founded 1936
Designed by Colt, Alison and Morrison
18 holes, 6361 yards, S.S.S. 70
Visitors: welcome with prior arrangement and h'cap certs.
Green Fee: WD £20; WE £30.
Societies: welcome; packages available; terms on application.
Catering: full catering facilities.
Hotels: Brentwood Post House; Mary Green Manor.

1B 105 Mid-Herts

Gustard Wood, Wheathampstead, St Albans, Herts AL4 8RS
☎(01582) 832242, Fax 832260, Pro 832788
6 miles N of St Albans on B651.
Parkland course.
Pro Nick Brown; Founded 1892
18 holes, 6060 yards, S.S.S. 69
Visitors: welcome except Tues morning and Wed afternoon.
Green Fee: WD £24; WE £24.
Societies: welcome Thurs and Fri; terms on application.
Catering: catering and bar facilities.
Hotels: Hatfield Lodge Hotel.

1B 106 Mill Green

Gypsy Lane, Welwyn Garden City, Herts AL7 4TY
☎(01707) 276900, Fax 276898, Pro 270542

Moor Park and Sandy Lodge

In one of the popular television programmes which John Betjeman narrated towards the end of his life, he highlighted the Metropolitan line and the station of Moor Park and Sandy Lodge, shared in its earliest days largely for the convenience of golfers. While the walk to Moor Park involves quite a lengthy climb, Sandy Lodge is no more than a long pitch shot from the station which, until it was elaborately modernised, was a somewhat odd looking basic wooden structure. Sandy Lodge is a most pleasant course remembered by most golfers for the carry over large, deep bunkers to the 1st green, a prominent sleeper-faced bunker at the second, consecutive short holes at the seventh and eighth and a short hole to finish across a quarry that is much less stark than it used to be.

It also has its 16th green beside the railway and a par-five 17th alongside a wood. Laddie Lucas and Alec Hill were its best known members and John Jacobs its best known professional. It was at Sandy Lodge that he built up his considerable reputation as a teacher but, in the days when he was a regular figure on the tournament circuit, the opening tournament of what was then a more truncated season, was invariably at Moor Park.

The architectural splendour of the clubhouse makes it one of the most photographed in the world. In addition to the professional tournaments which were always attractions for schoolboys in the Easter holidays, the Carris Trophy was one of the blue riband events of junior golf.

It involved a round on each of the High and West courses, the High regarded as the sterner of the tests, like Sandy Lodge ending with a short hole at which Harold Henning once earned £1,000, a small fortune in the 1960s, during the Esso Round Robin event.

The High and West epitomise the char-acteristics of parkland golf although the High is unusually undulating, a factor that adds to the problems it presents. The West dominates the front of the clubhouse, the first tee and 18th green on the High being quite a step from its noble pillars. The first, crossing the road, has a narrow-looking fairway, lined on the right by stately trees, while the second has another demanding drive. If it is not held up sufficiently on the left, it will fall to the right, adding problems to the second shot. But the problem of guardian bunkers at the green is nothing compared to the short third, whose green is virtually encircled.

From the fourth green, one of the lowest points, the next couple of fairways border elegant houses into which it is easy to slice. The eighth green lies beside a pond which, before water features became so fashionable, caused quite a stir. The ninth is one of the best holes, with an awkward green to hit and an expensive one to miss, the inward nine beginning near one of the main entrances to the park with a short hole where I once saw Arthur Havers, the Club's professional, hole in one during a tournament.

The 11th, 12th and 13th confront some of the severer slopes and hollows while the 14th green is remembered for being very much wider than it is deep. There is an inviting downhill second to the 15th, an up and back element about the 16th and 17th and finally a downhill short hole where out of bounds lurks on the right.

It is a hole which, mercifully, cannot be lengthened by more than a few yards. The modern giants may rarely need more than a lofted iron from the tee but it is not always easy to judge, the fear of being short often leading to being just that. It is plain to see what must be done but last holes impose a pressure all of their own and many a bold ambition has been ambushed in the quest for glory.

Off A100 Welwyn Garden City past Bush Hall, at lights turn left, 2nd rt and then into Gypsy Lane.
Parkland course.
Pro Alan Hall; Founded 1994
Designed by Peter Alliss & Clive Clark
18 holes, 6615 yards, S.S.S. 72
Also Romany par 3 course.
Visitors: welcome.
Green Fee: WD £27.50; WE £32.50.
Societies: welcome by prior arrangement; packages available; par 3 course; terms on application.
Catering: full catering and bar.
Practice range, grass.
Hotels: Jarvis Comet, Hatfield.

1B 107 Mill Hill
100 Barnet Way, Mill Hill, London NW7 3AL
☎(0181) 9592282, Fax 9060731, Pro 9597261, Sec 9592339
From junction of A1/A41, going N, immediately filter right and cross into Marsh Lane, after 0.5 mile turn left into Hankins Lane, leading to clubhouse; going S, 1 mile from Stirling Corner.
Parkland course.
Pro Gary Harvey; Founded 1925
Designed by J.F. Abercromby (1931 remodelled by H.S. Colt)
18 holes, 6247 yards, S.S.S. 70
Visitors: welcome WD; WE reservations only.
Green Fee: WD £21; WE £30.
Societies: welcome Mon, Wed, Fri (except BH); terms on application.
Catering: facilities daily.
Hotels: Jarvis; Hilton National.

1B 108 Moor Park
Rickmansworth, Herts WD3 1QN
☎(01923) 773146, Fax 777109, Pro 774113
1 mile SE of Rickmansworth off Batchworth roundabout on A4145.
Parkland course.
Pro L Farmer; Founded 1923
Designed by H.S. Colt
High: 18 holes, 6713 yards, S.S.S. 72
West: 18 holes, 5815 yards, S.S.S. 68
Visitors: WDs only with h'cap certs.
Green Fee: WD £30; WE £30.
Societies: welcome WD only; packages available; terms on application.
Catering: full restaurant facilities.

1B 109 Muswell Hill
Rhodes Ave, Wood Green London N22 4UT
☎(0181) 888 1764, Fax 889 9380, Pro 888 8046

1 mile from Bounds Green tube station, 1.5 miles from N Circular Rd.
Undulating course.
Pro David Wilton; Founded 1893
18 holes, 6432 yards, S.S.S. 70
Visitors: WDs restricted; WE and BH limited bookings through Pro.
Societies: welcome WD by arrangement; packages available; terms on application.
Catering: meals and snacks, bar.
Hotels: Raglan Hall.

1B 110 The Nazeing
Middle St, Nazeing, Essex EN9 2LW
☎(01992) 893915, Fax 893882, Pro 893798, Sec 893798
On B194 in Nazeing.
Parkland course.
Founded 1992
Designed by Martin Gillett
18 holes, 6598 yards, S.S.S. 71
Visitors: welcome after 8.30am WD and 12 at WE.
Green Fee: WD £20; WE £28.
Societies: welcome WD with a minimum of 12 players; packages involving breakfast, lunch and dinner and 18, 27 or 36 holes can be arranged; terms on application.
Catering: full catering and bar.
Hotels: Swallow Hotel, Waltham Abbey.

1B 111 North Middlesex
The Manor House, Friern Barnet Lane, Whetstone, London N20 0NL
☎(0181) 445 1732, Fax 445 5023, Pro 445 3060, Sec 445 1604, Bar/Rest 343 7275
5 miles S of M25 junction 23 between Barnet and Finchley.
Parkland course.
Pro Steve Roberts; Founded 1905
Designed by Willie Park Jnr
18 holes, 5625 yards, S.S.S. 67
Visitors: welcome by prior arrangement.
Green Fee: WD £22; WE £30.
Societies: welcome WD by prior arrangement with Sec; discounts available for groups of 15+; from £27.50.
Catering: full clubhouse facilities.

1B 112 North Weald GC
Rayley Lane, North Weald, Essex CM16 6AR
☎(01992) 522118, Fax 522881, Pro 524725
On A414 Chelmsford road from M11 junction 7.
Parkland course.

Pro M Janes; Founded 1996
Designed by D Williams
18 holes, 6311 yards, S.S.S. 70
Visitors: welcome; book with Pro.
Green Fee: WD £17.50; WE £25.
Societies: welcome with prior arrangement with Sec; bar and restaurant facilities; driving range; from £20.
Catering: bar and restaurant.

1B 113 Northwood
Rickmansworth Rd, Northwood, Middx HA6 2QW
☎(01923) 821384, Fax 840150, Pro 820112, Bar/Rest 825329
0.25 miles S of Northwood on A404.
Parkland course.
Pro C Holdsworth; Founded 1891
Designed by James Braid
18 holes, 6553 yards, S.S.S. 71
Visitors: welcome WD.
Green Fee: WD £26; WE £26.
Societies: welcome Mon and Thurs; packages available; terms on application.
Catering: full catering facilities.
Hotels: Tudor Lodge, Eastcote.

1B 114 Old Fold Manor
Old Ford Lane, Hadley Green, Barnet, Herts EN5 4QN
☎(0181) 449 1650, Fax 441 4863, Pro 440 7488, Sec 440 9185, Bar/Rest 440 2266
On A1000 1 mile N of Barnet close to M25 junction 23
Heathland course.
Pro Gary Potter; Founded 1910
18 holes, 6481 yards, S.S.S. 71
Visitors: welcome with h'cap certs.
Green Fee: WD £20; WE £20.
Societies: welcome Thurs and Fri; packages for golf and catering available; £51.50.
Catering: full clubhouse facilities.
Hotels: Hadley Hotel; West Lodge Park.

1B 115 Orsett
Brentwood Rd, Orsett, Essex RM16 3DS
☎(01375) 891226, Fax 892471, Pro 891797, Sec 891352, Bar/Rest 891352
4 miles NE of Grays on A128
Heathland/parkland course.
Pro Paul Joiner; Founded 1899
Designed by James Braid
18 holes, 6614 yards, S.S.S. 72
Visitors: welcome if accompanied by a member.
Green Fee: WD £12.50; WE £12.50.

Societies: welcome Mon, Tues and in afternoon on Wed; packages include all meals; £40-50.
Catering: full catering and bar facilities.
Hotels: Orsett Hall; Stifford Moat House, nr Grays.

1B 116 Panshanger
Old Herns Lane, Welwyn Garden City, Herts AL7 2ED
☎(01707) Pro 333350, Sec 332837
Off B1000 close to A1, 1 mile NE of town.
Municipal undulating parkland course.
Pro Mick Corlass/Bryan Lewis; Founded 1976
18 holes, 6347 yards, S.S.S. 70
Visitors: welcome; no restrictions.
Green Fee: WD £11; WE £15.
Societies: welcome by prior arrangement; terms on application.
Catering: Lunch every day.
Hotels: Homestead Court.

1B 117 Perivale Park
Stockdove Way, Argyle Road, Greenford, Middx UB6 8EN
☎(0181) Pro 575 7116
On Ruislip Rd East between Greenford and Perivale, entrance from Argyle Rd.
Public parkland course.
Pro Peter Bryant; Founded 1932
9 holes, 2733 yards, S.S.S. 67
Visitors: welcome, no restrictions.
Green Fee: WD £4.75; WE £7.
Societies: no societies.
Catering: café serving meals, tea, coffee etc; no bar.
Hotels: Kenton (Hanger Hill).

1B 118 Pinner Hill
South View Rd.
Pinner Hill, Middx HA5 3YA
☎(0181) 866 0963, Fax 868 4817,

Pro 866 2109, Sec 866 0963
1 mile W of Pinner Green.
Parkland course.
Pro Mark Grieve; Founded 1928/47
Designed by J.H. Taylor/ Hawtree
18 holes, 6266 yards, S.S.S. 70
Visitors: welcome WD, particularly Wed and Thurs.
Green Fee: WD £25; WE £32.
Societies: welcome WD for groups of 12-40 players; package of full meals and full day's golf; £40-£42.
Catering: full facilities.
Hotels: Barn House, Eastcote; Harrow Hotel: Frithwood GH, Northwood.

1B 119 Porters Park
Shenley Hill, Radlett, Herts WD7 7AZ
☎(01923) 854127, Fax 855475, Pro 854366
From M25 junction 22 to Radlett via A5183, turn at railway station, 0.5 mile to top of Shenley Hill.
Undulating parkland course.
Pro David Gleeson; Founded 1899
18 holes, 6313 yards, S.S.S. 70
Visitors: welcome WD; h'cap certs required, phone 24 hours in advance; guest of member only at WE.
Green Fee: WD £29; WE £29.
Societies: Wed, Thurs only; min 20, max 50; £68 inc.
Catering: full catering for societies, breakfast (pre-ordered), bar menu.
Hotels: Red Lion.

1B 120 Potters Bar
Darkes Lane, Potters Bar, Herts EN6 1DE
☎(01707) 652020, Fax 655051, Pro 652987
1 mile N of M25 junction 24 close to Potters Bar station.
Parkland course.
Pro G Airis; Founded 1924
Designed by James Braid
18 holes, 6291 yards, S.S.S. 70

Visitors: welcome WD with h'cap certs.
Green Fee: WD £20; WE £20.
Societies: welcome WD except Wed; full lunch and dinner with 36 holes of golf; £55.
Catering: full clubhouse facilities.

1B 121 Redbourn
Kinsbourne Green Lane, Redbourn, Herts AL3 7QA
☎(01582) 793493, Fax 794362, Sec 794888, Bar/Rest 793363
Off A5183, turn into Luton Lane and club is 0.5 miles.
Parkland course.
Pro Mike Varney; Founded 1971
Designed by H. Stovin
18 holes, 6506 yards, S.S.S. 71
Visitors: welcome with prior bookings, accepted 3 days in advance.
Green Fee: WD £18; WE £23.
Societies: welcome WD; full golfing day either on 18-hole course and 9-hole par 3 Kinsbourne or at Aldwickbury Park; golf clinics, golf ranger, buggies; £21-49.
Catering: full restaurant and bar.
Practice range, 20 bay target range.

1B 122 Regiment Way
Pratts Farm Lane, Little Waltham, Chelmsford, Essex CM3 3PR
☎(01245) 361100
On A130 off the A12 at Boreham.
Parkland course.
Pro I Warn/D March; Founded 1995
9 holes, 4887 yards, S.S.S. 64
Visitors: welcome; pay and play.
Green Fee: WD £10; WE £11.
Societies: welcome by arrangement.
Catering: snack facilities.
Practice range, 16 bays floodlit.

1B 123 Rickmansworth
Moor Lane, Rickmansworth, Herts WD3 1QL

☎(01923) 775278, Pro 773163
0.5 miles S of Rickmansworth on
A4145
Undulating parkland.
Pro Alan Dobbins; Founded 1944
Designed by H S Colt
18 holes, 4493 yards, S.S.S. 62
Visitors: welcome.
Green Fee: WD £9; WE £13.
Catering: available in the Fairway Inn.
Hotels: Long Island Hotel.

1B 124 Risebridge (Havering)
Risebridge Chase, off Lower Bedfords
Road, Romford, Essex RM1 4DG
☎(01708) 727376, Pro 741429
From A12 Gallows Corner, left and
then left again.
Parkland course.
Pro Paul Jennings; Founded 1972
Designed by F W Hawtree
18 holes, 6271 yards, S.S.S. 70
Visitors: welcome except between 8
and 10am at WE.
Green Fee: WD £11; WE £13.
Societies: welcome by prior arrange-
ment with Pro; packages available;
terms on application.
Catering: full clubhouse catering.
Hotels: Forte Lodge, Brentwood.

1B 125 Rochford Hundred
Rochford Hall, Hall Rd, Rochford,
Essex SS4 1NW
☎(01702) 544302, Fax 541343, Pro
548968
On B1013 off the A127.
Parkland course.
Pro Graham Hill; Founded 1893
Designed by James Braid
18 holes, 6302 yards, S.S.S. 70
Visitors: welcome with h'cap certs
except Sun.
Green Fee: WD £30; WE £30.
Societies: welcome; packages avail-
able include 36 holes of golf and
meals; £48.
Catering: full clubhouse facilities.

1B 126 Romford
Heath Drive, Gidea Park, Romford,
Essex RM2 5QB
☎(01708) 740986, Pro 749393
1.5 miles Romford centre, off A12.
Parkland course.
Pro Harry Flatman; Founded 1894
Designed by MacKintosh (redesigned
By H.S.Colt 1921)
18 holes, 6185 yards, S.S.S. 69
Visitors: WDs with h'cap certs and by
arrangement with Pro; with member
only at WE.

Green Fee: WD £25; WE £25.
Societies: welcome by prior arrange-
ment; packages available; terms on
application.
Catering: facilities available.
Hotels: Coach House.

1B 127 Royston
Baldock Rd, Royston, Herts SG8 5BG
☎(01763) 242696, Fax 242696, Pro
243476
On A505 on outskirts of town to W,
course on Therfield Heath.
Undulating heathland course.
Pro Mark Hatcher; Founded 1892
18 holes, 6066 yards, S.S.S. 69
Visitors: welcome WD; WE with mem-
ber only.
Green Fee: WD £20; WE £20.
Societies: by prior arrangement with
Sec; packages available; terms on
application.
Catering: full clubhouse facilities
available.
Hotels: Old Bull Inn; The Banyers.

1B 128 Ruislip
Ickenham Rd, Ruislip, Middx HA4
7DQ
☎(01895) 638835, Fax 635780, Pro
638081
Opposite West Ruislip Tube station.
Parkland course.
Pro Paul Glozier; Founded 1936
Designed by Sandy Herd
18 holes, 5571 yards, S.S.S. 67
Visitors: public pay and play.
Green Fee: WD £12; WE £12.
Societies: terms on application. Ring
(01923) 822877.
Catering: available.
Hotels: Barn, Ruislip.

1B 129 Saffron Walden
Windmill Hill, Saffron Walden, Essex
CB10 1BX
☎(01799) Pro 527728, Sec 522786
Take B184 from Stumps Cross round-
about on M11 (junction 9), entrance
just before entering town.
Parkland course.
Pro Philip Davis; Founded 1919
18 holes, 6606 yards, S.S.S. 72
Visitors: welcome WD with h'cap
certs; with member WE and BH.
Green Fee: WD £30; WE £30.
Societies: welcome Mon, Wed, Thurs;
terms on application.
Catering: lunch available WD;
evening meals for societies.
Practice range 6 bays; no floodlights.
Hotels: Saffron.

1B 130 Sandy Lodge
Sandy Lodge Lane, Northwood, Middx
HA6 2JD
☎(01923) 825429, Fax 824319, Pro
825321
Off A404 adjacent to Moor Park under-
ground station.
Inland links.
Pro J Pinsent; Founded 1910
Designed by Harry Vardon
18 holes, 6347 yards, S.S.S. 71
Visitors: welcome WD by prior
arrangement.
Green Fee: WD £28; WE £28.
Societies: welcome Mon and Thurs;
full catering and bar available; £28-40.
Catering: full clubhouse facilities
Practice range opening 1998.
Hotels: Hilton National, Watford;
Bedford Arms, Rickmansworth.

1B 131 Shendish Manor
Shendish House, Apsley
Hemel Hempstead, Herts HP3 0AA
☎(01442) 251806, Fax 217446,
Bar/Rest 232220
3 miles from M25 junction 20 on
A4251. M1 junction 8 is 5 miles away.
Parkland course.
Pro Murray White; Founded 1984/96
Designed by Henry Cotton, Extension
by Donald Steel
18 holes, 5660 yards, S.S.S. 67
Visitors: welcome by prior arrangement.
Green Fee: WD £15; WE £20.
Societies: welcome WD and by special arrangement at WE; packages
available include 18-hole course,
health club, 9-hole pitch and putt, conference
and banqueting rooms. Lessons also
available; from £21.
Catering: full clubhouse facilities with
private function rooms.

1B 132 South Herts
Links Drive, Totteridge London N20
8QU
☎(0181) 445 0117, Fax 445 7569,
Pro 445 4633, Sec 445 2035, Bar/Rest
446 3951
On Totteridge Lane 2.5 miles E of
A1M at Mill Hill.
Parkland course.
Pro R Mitchell; Founded 1899
Designed by Harry Vardon
9 holes, 6432 yards, S.S.S. 71
Visitors: welcome with h'cap of 24 or
less.
Green Fee: WD £25; WE £25.
Societies: welcome Wed, Thurs and
Fri; terms on application.

Catering: full clubhouse catering and bar.
Hotels: Queens Moat House, Boreham Wood; South Mimms Post House.

1B 133 Stanmore
Gordon Ave, Stanmore, Middx HA7 2RL
☎(0181) 954 2599, Pro 954 2646, Bar/Rest 954 4661
Between Stanmore and Belmont off Old Church Lane.
Parkland course.
Pro V R Law; Founded 1893
18 holes, 5860 yards, S.S.S. 68
Visitors: welcome WD but reduced rates on Mon and Fri.
Green Fee: WD £25; WE £25.
Societies: welcome Wed and Thurs; packages include breakfast, lunch, dinner; 3-balls favoured; £29-45.
Catering: full catering service and bar.

1B 134 Stapleford Abbotts
Horseman's Side, Tysea Hill, Stapleford Abbotts, Essex RM4 1JU
☎(01708) 381108 (Abbots), Pro 373344 (Priors)
3 miles from M25 junction 28 off the B175 Romford to Ongar road; left at Stapleford Abbots up Tysea Hill.
Parkland course.
Pro Ian Anderson; Founded 1972
Designed by Howard Swan
18 holes, 6501 yards, S.S.S. 71
Visitors: welcome.
Green Fee: WD on application.
Societies: welcome by prior arrangement; packages available; sauna; function room; also Friars course: 2280 yards, par 3; Priors course: 5720 yards; WD: £11; WE: £13.
Catering: full bar and restaurant facilities.
Hotels: Post House, Harlow.

1B 135 Stevenage
Aston Lane, Aston, Stevenage, Herts SG2 7EL
☎(01438) 880424, Fax 880040Sec. 880322, Bar/Rest 880223
Leave A1(M) Stevenage South, then on A602 to Hertford, course signposted about 1.5 miles.
Public parkland/meadowland course.
Founded 1980
Designed by John Jacobs
18 holes, 6341 yards, S.S.S. 71
Visitors: welcome every day; book in advance.
Green Fee: WD £10.40; WE £13.40.

Societies: welcome WD; packages available; terms on application.
Catering: full meals and bar snacks.
Practice range 24 bays; floodlit.
Hotels: Roebuck.

1B 136 Stock Brook Manor G & CC
Queens Park Avenue, Stock, Billericay, Essex CM12 0SP
☎(01277) 653616, Fax 633063
M25 junction 28 then A12 to Gallywood/Stock exit following the B1007 to Stock.
Parkland course.
Pro Kevin Merry; Founded 1992
Designed by Martin Gillett
27 holes, 6728 yards, S.S.S. 72
Visitors: welcome.
Green Fee: WD £25; WE £30.
Societies: welcome by prior arrangement; country club facilities; bowls; tennis; croquet; also 2 more 18-hole courses: Stock/Manor: 6481 yards, par 71; Brook/Manor: 6241 yards, par 71.
Catering: full clubhouse facilities.
Hotels: Trust House, Basildon.

1B 137 Stockley Park
Uxbridge, Middx UB11 1A Q
☎(0181) 813 5700, Fax 813 5655, Sec 561 6339, Bar/Rest 813 570
5 mins from Heathrow, 2 mins M4 junction 4 towards Uxbridge.
Hilly parkland championship course.
Pro Alex Knox; Founded 1993
Designed by Robert Trent Jones Snr
18 holes, 6539 yards, S.S.S. 71
Visitors: welcome, pay as you play, correct dress, no denims, golf shoes required.
Green Fee: WD £23; WE £33.
Societies: welcome WD, booked in advance; packages available; terms on application.
Catering: bar and restaurant.
Hotels: Novotel.

1B 138 Stocks Hotel & Country Club
Stocks Rd, Aldbury, Nr Tring, Herts HP23 5RX
☎(01442) 851341, Fax 851253, Pro 851491
From either junction 20 of M25 or junction 11 of M1. Follow signs to Tring.
Parkland course.
Pro Peter Lane; Founded 1993
Designed by Mike Billcliff
18 holes, 7016 yards, S.S.S. 73
Visitors: welcome WD.

Green Fee: WD POA; WE n/a.
Societies: WD by prior arrangement; terms on application.
Catering: full club and hotel facilities.
Hotels: Stocks Hotel.

1B 139 Stoke-by-Nayland
Keepers Lane, Leavenheath, Colchester, Essex CO6 4PZ
☎(01206) 262836, Fax 263356, Pro 262769
Off A134 on B1068 between Colchester and Sudbury.
Parkland with lake features.
Pro Kevin Lovelock; Founded 1972
Designed by W Peake
Constable course: 18 holes, 6544 yards, S.S.S. 71
Gainsborough course: 18 holes, 6498 yards, S.S.S. 71
Visitors: welcome at all times with h'cap certs.
Green Fee: WD £22; WE £27.50.
Societies: welcome WD; 36 holes of golf on 2 courses, also driving range and full facilities; from £30.
Catering: full clubhouse facilities available.
Practice range 20 bays.

1B 140 Strawberry Hill
Wellesley Rd, Strawberry Hill, Twickenham, Middx TW2 5SD
☎(0181) 894 0165, Pro 898 2082, Bar/Rest 894 1264
Near Strawberry Hill BR station.
Parkland course.
Pro Peter Buchan; Founded 1900
Designed by J.H. Taylor
9 holes, 4762 yards, S.S.S. 62
Visitors: welcome WD only.
Green Fee: WD £20; WE £20.
Societies: Fri only; maximum 25; terms on application.
Catering: bar and catering facilities available.

1B 141 Sudbury
Bridgewater Rd, Wembley, Middx HA0 1A L
☎(0181) Fax 903 2966, Pro 902 7910, Sec 902 3713
At junction of Bridgewater Rd (A4005) and Whitton Ave East (A4090).
Undulating parkland course.
Pro Neil Jordan; Founded 1920
Designed by H. Colt
18 holes, 6282 yards, S.S.S. 70
Visitors: welcome WD with h'cap certs; Mon open day (no h'cap cert required); WE with member only.
Green Fee: WD £23.

An 18th Century Georgian Mansion set amidst 182 acres of beautiful parkland just outside the lovely village of Aldbury.

Our championship Golf Course has spectacular views of Ashridge Forest & due to its high build specification has not closed due to rain in the last 4 years.

Societies, Companies Days and Residential Golfing Breaks are our speciality any time of year.

STOCKS

Hotel Golf & Country Club

Stocks Road, Aldbury, Nr. Tring
Herts HP23 5RX
Tel: 01442 851341 Fax: 01442 851253
Professionals Shop: 01442 851491

- 18 hole Golf Course
- Resident PGA Golf Professionals
- Golf Academy with Golf Range, Chipping & Putting Greens
- Conference Facilities
- Gymnasium
- Heated Outdoor Swimming Pool (May-September)
- Jacuzzi, Steam Room & Sauna
- Tennis Courts • Riding Stables
- Full size Snooker Table
- Two Restaurant

Societies: welcome Tues pm, Wed, Thurs, Fri by appointment; terms on application.
Catering: full catering service, bar.
Hotels: The Cumberland (Harrow).

1B 142 Theydon Bois

Theydon Rd, Epping, Essex CM16 4EH
☎(01992) 812279, Pro 812460, Sec 813054, Bar/Rest 812260
1 mile S of Epping on B1721.
Woodland course; no par 5s.
Pro Richard Hall; Founded 1897
Designed by James Braid
18 holes, 5487 yards, S.S.S. 68
Visitors: welcome with h'cap certs.
Green Fee: WD £23; WE £23.
Societies: welcome Mon, Tues, Fri; £32.
Catering: full clubhouse facilities available.
Hotels: The Bell, Theydon Bois.

1B 143 Thorndon Park

Ingrave, Brentwood, Essex CM13 3RH
☎(01277) 811666, Pro 810736, Sec 810345
2 miles SE of Brentwood on A128.
Parkland course.
Pro Brian White; Founded 1920
Designed by H. Colt
18 holes, 6492 yards, S.S.S. 71
Visitors: welcome WD and with member WE; h'cap certs required.
Green Fee: WD £35; WE £50.
Societies: welcome Tues and Fri; terms on application.
Catering: meals served WD.
Hotels: Post House.

1B 144 Thorpe Hall

Thorpe Hall Ave, Thorpe Bay, Essex SS1 3AT
☎(01702) 585331, Fax 582205, Pro 588195, Sec 582205

4 miles E of Southend on Sea on seafront at Thorpe Bay.
Parkland/meadowland course.
Pro Bill McColl; Founded 1907
18 holes, 6286 yards, S.S.S. 71
Visitors: welcome on WD by prior arrangement.
Green Fee: WD £30; WE £30.
Societies: Fri only; maximum 40; catering by arrangement; terms on application.
Catering: full catering facilities available.
Hotels: Rosylin Hotel.

1B 145 Three Rivers Golf & Country Club

Stow Rd, Cold Norton, Purleigh, Nr Chelmsford, Essex CM3 6RR
☎(01621) 828631, Fax 828060, Pro 829781
From M25 junction 29 take A127 and then A132 to South Woodham Ferrers. Take signs for Cold Norton. Course 4 miles.
Parkland; new heathland course.
Founded 1973
Designed by Fred Hawtree
18 holes, 6500 yards
Jubilee course: 4600 yards, par 65
Visitors: welcome.
Green Fee: WD £22; WE £22.
Societies: welcome; combination of 18, 27, 36 holes, driving range, video analysis, clubhouse and private rooms; squash and tennis; from £28.
Catering: full facilities.
Hotels: Three Rivers.

1B 146 Toothill

School Road, Toot Hill, Ongar, Essex CM5 9PU
☎(01277) 365523, Fax 364509, Pro 365747
2 miles off A414 between N Weald and Ongar.
Parkland course.

Pro Mark Bishop; Founded 1991
Designed by Martin Gillett
18 holes, 6053 yards, S.S.S. 69
Visitors: welcome.
Green Fee: WD £15; WE £20.
Societies: welcome Tues and Thurs; lunch/dinner included; from £34.
Catering: full catering facilities.
Hotels: Post House, Epping.

1B 147 Top Meadow

Fen Lane, North Ockendon, Essex RM14 3PR
☎(01708) Pro 859545, Sec 852239
Off B186 in North Ockendon.
Parkland course.
Pro Paul King/Kevin Smith; Founded 1986
18 holes, 6498 yards
Visitors: welcome WD; only with member at WE.
Green Fee: WD £12 inc breakfast.
Societies: welcome WD by advance booking; terms on application.
Catering: bar and restaurant.
Practice range under construction.
Hotels: Top Meadow Guest House.

1B 148 Trent Park

Bramley Rd, Oakwood London N14 4UT
☎(0181) 367 4653, Fax 366 3823
200 yards from Oakwood underground station between Barnet and Enfield on A110.
Parkland course.
Pro Ray Stocker; Founded 1973
18 holes, 6176 yards, S.S.S. 69
Visitors: public course (booking available).
Green Fee: WD £11; WE £14.50.
Societies: welcome; restaurant and bar facilities; driving range, buggies, video analysis; terms on application.
Catering: facilities available.
Practice range; video teaching bay and range heaters.

1B 149 Tudor Park Sports Ground

Clifford Rd, New Barnet, Herts EN5
☎(0181) 4490282
Off Potters Rd.
Public parkland course.
9 holes, 3772 yards, S.S.S. 58
Visitors: welcome.
Green Fee: WD £5.30; WE £6.80.
Societies: apply for details.
Catering: clubhouse for members only.

1B 150 Twickenham Park

Staines Rd, Twickenham, Middx TW2 5JD
☎(0181) Fax 941 9134, Pro 783 1698
On A305 near Hope and Anchor roundabout
Municipal parkland course.
Pro Suzy Watt; Founded 1977
Designed by Charles Lawrie
9 holes, 6076 yards, S.S.S. 69
Visitors: welcome.
Green Fee: WD £6; WE £7.
Societies: welcome by arrangement; catering packages available; terms on application.
Catering: full licensed bar, snacks, function room.
Practice range 24 bays; floodlit.
Hotels: Richmond Gate.

1B 151 Upminster

114 Hall Lane, Upminster, Essex RM14 1A U
☎(01708) 222788, Pro 220000, Bar/Rest 220249
On A127 towards Southend from M25 junction 29.
Parkland course.
Pro Neil Carr; Founded 1927
Designed by H.A. Colt
18 holes, 6013 yards, S.S.S. 69
Visitors: welcome WD by arrangement, with h'cap certs.
Green Fee: WD £25.
Societies: welcome Wed- Fri by arrangement; some small societies possible Mon and Tues.
Catering: full clubhouse facilities.
Hotels: Post House, Brentwood.

1B 152 Verulam

228 London Rd, St Albans, Herts AL1 1JG
☎(01727) 853327, Fax 812201, Pro 861401, Bar/Rest 839016
Turn off London Road A1081 at railway bridge.
Parkland course.
Pro Nick Burch; Founded 1905

Designed by James Braid/upgrade by D Steel
18 holes, 6448 yards, S.S.S. 71
Visitors: welcome WD; with member at WE.
Green Fee: WD £25 (Mon £13); WE £25.
Societies: By arrangement with Sec; full day golf and catering packages available; from £55.
Catering: full facilities.
Hotels: Apple Hotel; Sopwell House.

1B 153 Wanstead

Overton Drive, Wanstead, London E11 2LW
☎(0181) 989 3938, Fax 532 9138, Pro 989 9876, Bar/Rest 989 0604
Close to Wanstead Tube station.
Parkland/heathland course.
Pro David Hawkins; Founded 1893
Designed by James Braid
18 holes, 6262 yards, S.S.S. 69
Visitors: welcome Mon, Tues and Fri.
Green Fee: WD £25; WE £25.
Societies: welcome Mon, Tues and Fri; facilities include 36 holes of golf, lunch and dinner; £45.
Catering: full clubhouse facilities.

1B 154 Warley Park

Magpie Lane, Little Warley, Brentwood, Essex CM13 3DX
☎(01277) 224891, Fax 200679, Pro 200441, Bar/Rest 231352
Off B186.
Parkland with 3 x 9 holes.
Pro Jason Groat; Founded 1975
Designed by R. Plumbridge
27 holes, 6232 yards, S.S.S. 69
Visitors: welcome WD only.
Green Fee: WD £25; WE £25.
Societies: welcome WD; packages available; terms on application.
Catering: restaurant, bar and spike bar.
Hotels: Forte Post House; New World Inn; Marygreen Manor.

1B 155 Warren

Woodham Walter, Maldon, Essex CM9 6RW
☎(01245) 223258, Fax 223989, Pro 224662
A414 6 miles E of Chelmsford towards Maldon.
Undulating parkland course.
Pro Mickey Walker OBE; Founded 1934
18 holes, 6263 yards, S.S.S. 70
Visitors: welcome WD and WE after 2pm; booking essential.

Green Fee: WD £25; WE £30.
Societies: Mon, Tues, Thurs, Fri; packages available; terms on application.
Catering: full facilities 7 days.
Hotels: Pontlands Park; Blue Boar.

1B 156 Welwyn Garden City

Mannicotts, High Oaks Rd, Welwyn Garden City, Herts AL8 7BP
☎(01707) 322722, Fax 393213, Pro 325525, Sec 325243
1 mile north of Hatfield from A1M junction 4.
Parkland course.
Pro Richard May; Founded 1922
Designed by Hawtree & Son
18 holes, 6074 yards, S.S.S. 69
Visitors: welcome by arrangement.
Green Fee: WD £25; WE £35.
Societies: welcome Wed and Thurs; 36 holes, coffee, lunch and dinner; £52.
Catering: full clubhouse bar and catering.
Hotels: Homestead Court, Welwyn; Bush Hall Hotel, Hatfield.

1B 157 West Essex

Bury Rd, Sewardstonebury, Chingford, Essex E4 7QL
☎(0181) 529 7558, Fax 524 7870, Pro 529 4367, Bar/Rest 529 1029
1.5 miles N of Chingford station.
Parkland course.
Pro Robert Joyce; Founded 1900
Designed by James Braid
18 holes, 6289 yards, S.S.S. 70
Visitors: welcome WD except Tues am and Thurs pm.
Green Fee: WD £25; WE £25.
Societies: welcome Mon, Wed and Fri; package includes coffee, lunch, dinner and 36 holes of golf, plus driving range; £50.
Catering: bar and catering facilities.
Hotels: Swallow Hotel, Waltham Abbey.

1B 158 West Herts

Cassiobury Park, Watford, Herts WD1 7SL
☎(01923) 236484, Fax 222300, Pro 220352, Bar/Rest 224264
Off A412 between Watford and Rickmansworth.
Parkland course.
Founded 1890
Designed by Tom Morris & Harry Vardon
18 holes, 6528 yards, S.S.S. 71
Visitors: welcome.

Green Fee: WD £20; WE £30.
Societies: welcome Wed, Thurs, Fri; full facilities; £50.
Catering: full facilities.

1B 159 West Middlesex

Greenford Rd, Southall, Middx UB1 3EE
☎(0181) 574 3450, Pro 574 1800, Bar/Rest 574 0166
At junction of Greenford and Uxbridge road.
Parkland course.
Pro I P Harris; Founded 1891
Designed by James Braid
18 holes, 6119 yards, S.S.S. 69
Visitors: welcome.
Green Fee: WD £15.50; WE £15.50.
Societies: welcome; minimum 20; coffee, lunch, evening meal, 2 rounds of golf; £44.
Catering: full catering and bar.

1B 160 Whipsnade Park

Studham Lane, Dagnall, Herts HP4 1RH
☎(01442) 842330, Fax 842090, Pro 842310, Bar/Rest 842331
Between villages of Studham and Dagnall.
Parkland course.
Pro Mark Lewendon; Founded 1974
18 holes, 6704 yards, S.S.S. 72
Visitors: welcome WD; WE with member.
Green Fee: WD £23; WE £23.
Societies: welcome Tues, Wed, Thurs, Fri; coffee, 2 rounds of golf with lunch and 4-course dinner; £50.

Catering: full catering facilities.
Hotels: Post House, Hemel Hempstead.

1B 161 Whitehill

Dane End, Ware, Herts SG12 0JS
☎(01920) 438702, Fax 438891, Pro 438326, Sec 438495, Bar/Rest 438495
4 miles N of Ware just off A10.
Parkland course.
Pro D Ling/M Belsham; Founded 1990
Designed by Golf Landscapes
18 holes, 6681 yards, S.S.S. 72
Visitors: welcome with h'cap certs.
Green Fee: WD £18; WE £20.
Societies: welcome WD; maximum 16 at WE; golf and catering packages available; £20-40.
Catering: full facilities.
Hotels: County, Ware; Vintage Corner, Puckeridge.

1B 162 Whitewebbs

Beggars Hollow, Clay Hill, Enfield, Middx EN2 9JN
☎(0181) 3532951, Sec 3534454
1 mile N of Enfield town.
Public parkland course.
Pro Peter Garlick; Founded 1932
18 holes, 5863 yards, S.S.S. 68
Visitors: welcome; book 6 days in advance.
Green Fee: WD £10.60; WE £12.60.
Societies: welcome by arrangement; café on site; nature trails and horseriding; various packages.
Catering: public café on site.
Hotels: Royal Chase.

1B 163 Woodford

2 Sunset Ave, Woodford Green, Essex IG8 0ST
☎(0181) 504 0553, Fax 504 3330, Pro 504 4254, Sec 504 3330
11 miles northeast of London; 2 miles N of North Circular Road on A11.
Forest course.
Founded 1890
Designed by Tom Dunn
9 holes, 5867 yards, S.S.S. 68
Visitors: welcome except Tues am; Sat or Sun pm; red clothing must be worn.
Green Fee: WD £15; WE £15.
Societies: welcome by prior arrangement with Sec; packages including meals can be arranged; terms on application.
Catering: dining facilities, bar.
Hotels: Packfords, Woodford Green.

1B 164 Wyke Green

Syon Lane, Isleworth, Middx TW7 5PT
☎(0181) 561 8777, Fax 569 8392, Pro 847 0685, Bar/Rest 847 1956
0.5 miles north of A4 near Gillettes corner.
Flat parkland.
Pro Neil Smith; Founded 1928
Designed by W.H. Tate
18 holes, 6211 yards, S.S.S. 70
Visitors: members' guests only.
Green Fee: WD £13; WE £18.
Societies: welcome Tues and Thurs; 3 different packages available; minimum 20 players; £32-42.
Catering: full catering and bar.
Hotels: Master Robert; Osterley Four Pillars.

2
THE SOUTH

The connoisseur, making his way east from Brokenhurst Manor in the New Forest to Rye on the East Sussex border with Kent, passes through as good and varied a golfing tapestry as could be imagined – a veritable Aladdin's Cave. Compared with other parts of the country, the volume of courses is none too dense but any shortcomings in quantity are more than absorbed by quality.

For the purposes of playing qualification at county level, Hampshire embraces the Channel Islands, the Isle of Wight and Hayling Island, the latter a links, or part links, which Tom Simpson rated enormously highly. I also remember Henry Longhurst singing its praises and I can join in the chorus but Hampshire's inland gems are North Hants at Fleet, Blackmoor and Liphook – all extensions of the rich seam of heather, gorse and silver birch country which starts with Wentworth and Sunningdale in the east and continues down through Swinley Forest and Camberley Heath.

Liphook, straddling the busy A3 and involving one or two mad dashes to cross it, has had strong naval connections in view of its proximity to Portsmouth but it has remained essentially a refuge for the Club golfer in spite of being able to test the best.

Hockley and Royal Winchester typify downland golf at its best, while Stoneham at Southampton is more in the mould of Liphook. Sussex, too, is full of variety with something for everyone. West Sussex at Pulborough is a particular favourite, ideal for any occasion and giving the chance of a good score with its five short holes although, like Rye, the par of 68 can be tantalisingly elusive.

Straight hitting has more merit than unharnessed power, for the heather is punishing but the unique charms of Rye centre more on a battle with the winds that sweep off the sea or across the exposed and chilly reaches of Romney Marsh.

There is a charm about Rye that never varies or fades. Expectation begins with departure from the ancient town and its cobbled streets and heightens as the road to Camber twists and turns through fields of grazing sheep. The character of the golf is distinctive in the range of shots it demands, the ability to flight the ball and gauge how it will run on landing being infinitely more valuable than memorising yardage charts and clubbing by numbers.

Rye is a monument to the links style of British golf but the new East Sussex National is the opposite, an expensive machine-shaped exercise in creating a new landscape over which the European Open was played in 1993. There are those who prefer courses which preserve nature rather than fighting it but nowhere is that aspect better illustrated than Royal Ashdown Forest or Crowborough which crisscross the Sussex Downs, Ashdown Forest notably without bunkers.

Goodwood is another from whose highest points scenic splendour unfurls, a contrast to its neighbour, the Goodwood Park Hotel Golf and Country Club which occupies a large part of the grounds of Goodwood House. Bognor Regis, Selsey and Littlehampton lie a few miles to the south while Chichester Golf Centre is a recently opened venture at Hunston – ideal for those wishing to learn the ropes.

Worthing, Brighton and Eastbourne are well served while Cooden Beach has its host of admirers, along with a particular favourite in Seaford, another downland course overlooking the Channel.

An Edwardian house set in historic Ashdown Forest, in the heart of East Sussex.

The Hotel manages the Royal Ashdown Forest GC West Course.

Venue for the 1932 British Ladies Open Championship.

With 14 courses located nearby, the Hotl is the ideal centre for golf tours of East Sussex.

Societies welcome 7 days.

Residential packages all year.

ASHDOWN FOREST
GOLF HOTEL

Chapel Lane, Forest Row,
East Sussex, RH18 5BB

Tel: 01342 824866 • Fax: 01342 824869
Internet: http://www.ashgolf.co.uk

Save £10 - see voucher section

- Resident PGA Golf Professional
- Practice Ground
- Conference Facilities
- Tennis Courts
- Superb A La Carte Restaurant
- Large Sportsman's Bar and Dining Area
- 19 en-suite bedrooms with tea & coffee making facilities, satelite TV, direct-dial phone
- Quiet snug bar for non-golfers

2A 1 Alresford
Cheriton Rd, Tichborne Down, Alresford, Hants, SO24 0PN
☎(01962) 733746, Fax 736040, Pro 733998, Bar/Rest 733067
One mile S of Alresford on B3046.
Downland course.
Pro Malcolm Scott; Founded 1890
Designed by Scott Webb Young
18 holes, 5622 yards, S.S.S. 68
Visitors: welcome WD; not before 12 noon at WE unless with member.
Green Fee: WD £18; WE £34.
Societies: welcome by prior arrangement with Sec; terms on application.
Catering: full facilities.
Hotels: The Swan, Alresford.

2A 2 Alton
Old Odiham Rd, Alton, Hants, GU34 4BU
☎(01420) 82042, Pro 86518
On B3349 Alton to Odiham road; turn off at Golden Pot.
Parkland course.
Pro Paul Brown; Founded 1908
Designed by James Braid
9 holes, 5744 yards, S.S.S. 68
Visitors: welcome; restrictions on Sun.
Green Fee: WD £12; WE £12.
Societies: welcome by prior arrangement; bar, catering, PGA professional, practice area; terms on application.
Catering: full facilities.
Hotels: Wheatsheaf Inn; Alton House; Grange Hotel.

2A 3 Ampfield Par 3 G & C C
Winchester Rd, Ampfield, Romsey, Hants, SO51 9BQ
☎(01794) 368480, Pro 368750
A31 Winchester/Romsey road, opposite Keats restaurant, next to White Horse public house.
Parkland course.
Pro Richard Benfield; Founded 1965
Designed by Henry Cotton

18 holes, 2478 yards, S.S.S. 53
Visitors: welcome but advisable to telephone first.
Green Fee: WD £9; WE £9.
Societies: welcome by arrangement; terms on application.
Catering: bar and catering by arrangement.
Hotels: Potters Heron, Ampfield.

2A 4 Andover
51 Winchester Rd, Andover, Hants, SP10 2EF
☎(01264) 358040, Pro 324151, Bar/Rest 323890
Turn off A303 at Wherwell/Stockbridge turning; take Andover direction, golf course 0.5 mile.
Parkland course.
Pro Derrick Lawrence; Founded 1907
Designed by J.H. Taylor
9 holes, 5873 yards, S.S.S. 68
Visitors: welcome.
Green Fee: WD £10; WE £22.
Societies: welcome.
Catering: full facilities.
Hotels: White Hart Hotel, Andover.

2A 5 Army Golf Club
Laffans Rd, Aldershot, Hants, GU11 2HF
☎(01252) 336776, Fax 337562, Pro 336722, Sec 337272, Bar/Rest 336744
Access from Eelmoor Bridge off A323 Aldershot-Fleet road.
Heathland course.
Pro Graham Cowley; Founded 1883
18 holes, 6550 yards, S.S.S. 71
Visitors: welcome by prior arrangement.
Green Fee: WD £22; WE £22.
Societies: welcome by prior arrangement.
Catering: facilities available.
Hotels: Trust House Forte, Farnborough; Potters International Hotel, Farnborough.

2A 6 Ashdown Forest Hotel
Chapel Lane, Forest Row, E Sussex, RH18 5BB
☎(01342) 824866, Fax 824869
3 miles S of East Grinstead on A22 in village of Forest Row, E on B2110; Chapel Lane 4th on right.
Heathland/woodland course.
Pro Martyn Landsborough; Founded 1985
Designed by Horace Hutchinson (1930s); Henry Luff (1965)
18 holes, 5606 yards, S.S.S. 67
Visitors: welcome but advisable to phone first, particularly at WE.
Green Fee: WD £16; WE £21.
Societies: welcome by prior arrangement; full facilities; terms on application.
Catering: full restaurant service and bar snacks 7 days; banqueting facilities for up to 100.
Hotels: Ashdown Forest.

2A 7 Avisford Park
Avisford Park, Yapton Lane, Walberton, Arundel, BN18 0LS
☎(01243) 554611, Fax 555580, Pro 55461
On A27 4 miles W of Arundel, 6 miles E of Chichester.
Parkland course.
Pro Richard Beach
18 holes, 5669 yards, S.S.S. 68
Visitors: welcome; pay as you play.
Green Fee: WD £14; WE £15.
Societies: welcome by arrangement; terms on application.
Catering: bar.
Hotels: Stakis Arundel.

2A 8 Barton-on-Sea
Milford Road, New Milton, Hants, BH25 5PP
☎(01425) 615308, Fax 621457, Pro 611210
From New Milton take B3058 towards

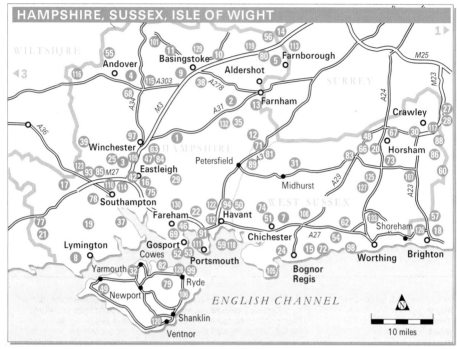

HAMPSHIRE, SUSSEX, ISLE OF WIGHT

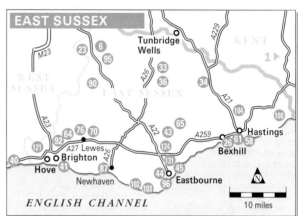

EAST SUSSEX

Milford-on-Sea; club is signposted about 0.75 mile on right.
Clifftop links course.
Pro Pat Coombs; Founded 1897
Designed by J Hamilton Stutt
27 holes 6296 yards, S.S.S. 70
Visitors: welcome with h/cap certs by prior arrangement.
Green Fee: WD £25; WE £30.
Societies: welcome by arrangement.
Catering: snacks and teas available, other catering by arrangement.
Hotels: Chewton Glen; Westover Hall.

2A 9 **Basingstoke**

Kempshott Park, Basingstoke, Hants, RG23 7LL
☎ (01256) 465990, Fax 331793, Pro 351332
3 miles W of Basingstoke on A30; M3 junction 7.
Parkland course.
Pro Ian Hayes; Founded 1928
Designed by James Braid
18 holes, 6334 yards, S.S.S. 70
Visitors: welcome WD; WE with a member.
Green Fee: WD £20.
Societies: welcome Wed and Thurs; 36 holes of golf, light lunch, evening meal; £52.50.

Catering: full clubhouse bar and restaurant facilities.
Hotels: Wheatsheaf, N Waltham.

2A 10 **Basingstoke Golf Centre**

Worting Rd, West Ham, Basingstoke, Hants, RG23 0TY
☎ (01256) 50054
M3 junction 7; 0.5 mile from Basingstoke town centre.
Public parkland course.

9 holes, 908 yards
Visitors: welcome.
Green Fee: WD £2.50; WE £2.90
Practice range 24 bays; floodlit.

2A 11 **Bishopswood**

Bishopswood Lane, Tadley, Basingstoke, Hants, RG26 4AT
☎ (0118) 9815213, Pro 9820312
6 miles N of Basingstoke, off A340.
Public parkland course.

Pro Stephen Ward; Founded 1976
Designed by Blake And Phillips
9 holes, 6474 yards, S.S.S. 71
Visitors: welcome WD.
Green Fee: WD £9; WE £14.
Societies: welcome WD by arrangement; full facilities.
Catering: bar snacks and restaurant
Practice range, 12 bays floodlit.
Hotels: Romans.

2A 12 Blackmoor

Firgrove Road, Whitehill, Bordon, Hants, GU35 9EH
☎(01420) 472775, Fax 487666, Pro 472345
Located on A325 between Petersfield and Farnham - at Whitehill crossroads turn left into Firgrove Road; Blackmoor situated 1000 yards on right.
Parkland/heathland course.
Pro Steve Clay; Founded 1913
Designed by H.S. Colt
18 holes, 6232 yards, S.S.S. 70
Visitors: welcome WD; guest of member only at WE.
Green Fee: WD £40; WE £40.
Societies: welcome Mon/Wed/Thurs by arrangement; full facilities; £50-£58 package.
Catering: full facilities.

2A 13 Blacknest

Binstead Rd, Binstead, Alton, Hants, GU34 4QL
☎(01420) 22888, Sec 520160

Take A31 to Bentley, then the Bordon road, course is immediately on right.
Parkland/heathland course.
Pro Ian Benson; Founded 1994
Designed by P Nicholson
18 holes, 5858 yards, S.S.S. 69
Visitors: welcome; no jeans.
Green Fee: WD £14; WE £18.
Societies: welcome by arrangement; full facilities.
Catering: bar and restaurant.
Practice range, 13 bays, not floodlit.
Hotels: Alton House; The Bush; The Farnham Park.

2A 14 Blackwater Valley

Chandlers Lane, Basingstoke, Hants, GU46 7SZ
☎(01252) 874725
5 miles from Camberley on the Reading road.
Parkland course with lakes.
Pro James Rodger; Founded 1994
9 holes, 2372 yards, S.S.S. 66
Visitors: welcome.
Green Fee: WD £6; WE £8.
Societies: welcome by arrangement; full facilities.
Catering: full facilities.
Practice range, 36 bays floodlit.

2A 15 Bognor Regis

Downview Rd, Felpham, Bognor Regis, PO22 8JD
☎(01243) 865867, Fax 860719, Pro 865209, Sec 821929

A259 Bognor-Littlehampton road; at Felpham traffic lights turn left into Downview Road.
Parkland course.
Pro Stephen Bassil; Founded 1892
Designed by James Braid
18 holes, 6238 yards, S.S.S. 70
Visitors: welcome with h/cap certs WD; with member at WE during summer.
Green Fee: WD £25; WE £30.
Societies: welcome by arrangement, tee-off times allocated; full facilities available; £46 package.
Catering: available by arrangement.
Hotels: The Beachcroft, Felpham.

2A 16 Botley Park Hotel & CC

Winchester Road, Boorley Green, Botley, Hants, SO32 2UA
☎(01489) 780888, Fax 789242, Pro 789771
NW of Botley on B3354 Winchester road, within easy reach of M27 junction 7, or M3/A33.
Parkland course.
Pro Tim Barter; Founded 1990
Designed by Charles Potterton
18 holes, 6341 yards, S.S.S. 70
Visitors: welcome by arrangement; h'cap certs or letter of intro required.
Green Fee: WD £30; WE £30.
Societies: welcome Weds and Thurs by arrangement; full facilities.
Catering: full facilities; banqueting service
Practice range, 10 bays; not floodlit.
Hotels: hotel in complex.

2A 17 **Bramshaw**

Brook, Lyndhurst, Hants, SO43 7HE
☎(01703) 813433, Fax 813958, Pro
813434, Bar/Rest 814628
10 miles SW of Southampton, 1 mile
from junction 1 M27.
Open New Forest course.
Pro Clive Bonner; Founded 1880
Forest: 18 holes, 5774 yards, S.S.S.
69; Manor: 18 holes, 6517 yards,
S.S.S. 71
Visitors: welcome WD; members'
guests only WE.
Green Fee: Forest WD £20, WE £20;
Manor WD £25, WE £25.
Societies: welcome Mon to Fri;
Packages available; £26-£54.50.
Catering: catering and bar facilities.
Hotels: Bell Inn, Brook.

2A 18 **Brighton & Hove**

Devil's Dyke Rd, Brighton, BN1 8YJ
☎(01273) 556482, Fax 556482, Pro
540560, Bar/Rest 507861
A23 / A27 NW Brighton.
Downland course – oldest golf club in
Sussex.
Pro P Bonsall; Founded 1887
Designed by James Braid
9 holes, 5710 yards, S.S.S. 68
Visitors: welcome with some restrictions.
Societies: welcome by arrangement;
restaurant facilities; from £20 per
head.
Catering: full facilities available.

2A 19 **Brockenhurst Manor**

Sway Rd, Brockenhurst, Hants, SO42
7SG
☎(01590) 623332, Fax 624140, Pro
623092
A337 to Brockenhurst then B3055 S
from village centre, club 1 mile on right.
Undulating forest/parkland course.
Pro John Lovell; Founded 1919
Designed by H.S. Colt, Alterations by
J. Hamilton
18 holes, 6222 yards, S.S.S. 70
Visitors: welcome by arrangement;
must have h'cap certs.
Green Fee: WD £30; WE £45.
Societies: welcome on Thurs by
arrangement; also small parties welcome Mon, Wed and Fri by
arrangement; full facilities.
Catering: full facilities.

2A 20 **Brookfield**

Winterpit Lane, Lower Reading,
Horsham, W Sussex, RH13 6LY
☎(01403) 891191, Fax 891499

From M23 take A279 to Handcross,
through village, then 2nd right and 1st
left; from Horsham take A281
towards Brighton, at Mannings Heath
Dun Horse pub turn left, over crossroads into Winterpit Lane.
Public parkland course.
Founded 1991
Designed by P. Webster
9 holes, 4000 yards
Visitors: welcome at all times.
Green Fee: WD £10; WE £10.
Societies: welcome; also corporate
days available; full facilities.
Catering: 2 bars, lounge, restaurants.
Practice range.
Hotels: Brookfield Farm.

2A 21 **Burley**

Cott Lane, Burley, Ringwood, Hants,
BH24 4BB
☎(01425) 402431, Fax 402431,
Bar/Rest 403737
From A31 through Burley towards
New Milton/Brockenhurst; turn immediately after cricket pitch.
Open heathland course.
Founded 1905
9 holes, 6149 yards, S.S.S. 69
Visitors: welcome with h'cap certs.
Green Fee: WD £14; WE £16.
Societies: welcome; maximum 14;
terms on application.
Catering: bar.
Hotels: Burley Manor; Moorhill; White
Buck.

2A 22 **Cams Hall Estates Golf**

Cams Hall, Fareham, Hants, PO16
8UP
☎(01329) 827222, Fax 827111, Pro
827732
Close to M27, junction 11.
18-hole links course, 9-hole parkland
course.
Pro Jason Neue; Founded 1993
Designed by Peter Alliss & Clive Clark
18 holes, 6244 yards, S.S.S. 70
Visitors: welcome.
Green Fee: WD £19-£28; WE £25-£35.
Societies: welcome, subject to availability; full facilities; £21-£47 package.
Catering: full facilities available.
Practice range; £2 bucket of balls.
Hotels: Marriott Hotel, Cosham; Trust
House Forte, Fareham; Solent Hotel,
Whiteley.

2A 23 **Chartham Park**

Felcourt Rd, Felcourt, E Grinstead,
RH19 2JT
☎(01342) 870340, Fax 870719

1 mile out of E Grinstead town centre
on the Lingfield road.
Mature parkland course.
Pro Ian Dryden; Founded 1992
Designed by N Coles
18 holes, 6680 yards, S.S.S. 72
Visitors: welcome but not before 12
noon at WE.
Green Fee: WD £27; WE £40.
Societies: welcome Mon, Tues,
Thurs; full facilities.
Catering: full facilities.
Hotels: Felbridge.

2A 24 **Chichester Golf Centre**

Hoe Farm, Hunston, Chichester, PO20
6AX
☎(01243) 533833, Fax 539922,
Sec 536666
3 miles S of Chichester (A27) on
B2145 to Selsey, on left after Hunston.
Public Floriday-style course with membership.
Pro Stephen James; Founded 1990
Designed by Philip Sanders
Cathedral: 18 holes, 6461 yards,
S.S.S. 71; Tower: 18 holes, 6175
yards, S.S.S. 69
Visitors: welcome; tee reservations
required; h'cap certs required for
Cathedral.
Green Fee: Cathedral WD £20, WE
£28; Tower WD £15; WE £19.50; .
Societies: welcome by prior arrangement; society clubroom available;
terms on application.
Catering: full catering/refreshments.
Practice range, 27 bays; floodlit; academy course.
Hotels: Millstream (Bosham); Hunston
Mill B&B (Hunston); Post House
(Hayling Island).

2A 25 **Chilworth Golf Centre**

Main Rd, Chilworth, Southampton,
Hants, SO16 7JP
☎(01703) 740544, Fax 733166
On A27 between Romsey and
Southampton.
Parkland course.
Pro M Butcher/J Barnes; Founded
1989
18 holes, 5740 yards, S.S.S. 69
Visitors: welcome.
Green Fee: WD £12; WE £15.
Societies: welcome by prior arrangement; terms on application.
Catering: available.

2A 26 **Cooden Beach**

Cooden Sea Rd, Nr Bexhill-on-Sea,
TN39 4TR
☎(01424) 842040, Fax 842040, Pro

843938, Bar/Rest 843936
A259 Eastbourne-Hastings road; follow Cooden Beach sign at Little Common roundabout; 1 mile on. Seaside course.
Pro Jeffrey Sim; Founded 1912
Designed by Herbert Fowler
18 holes, 6450 yards, S.S.S. 71
Visitors: welcome with h/cap certs, telephone first.
Green Fee: WD £29; WE £35.
Societies: welcome by arrangement; full facilities; £50 package.
Catering: full facilities available.
Hotels: Jarvis Cooden Resort; Brickwall Hotel, Lansdowne Hotel; Netherfield Place.

2A 27 Copthorne

Borers Arms Rd, Copthorne, Crawley, RH10 3LL
☎(01342) 712033, Fax 717682, Pro 712405, Bar/Rest 712508
M23 junction 10; follow A264 to East Grinstead; course 3 miles on left. Heathland course.
Pro Joe Burrell; Founded 1892
Designed by James Braid
18 holes, 6221 yards, S.S.S. 71
Visitors: welcome with h/cap certs.
Green Fee: WD £30-40.
Societies: Mon-Fri by arrangement with Sec; full facilities available; £45-£60 packages.
Catering: facilities available.
Hotels: Copthorne; Effingham Park.

2A 28 Copthorne Effingham Park

West Park Rd, Copthorne, W Sussex, RH10 3EU
☎(01342) 716528, Fax 716039
From M23 junction 10 on to A264. Parkland course.
Pro Mark Root; Founded 1980
Designed by Francisco Escario
9 holes, 3630 yards, S.S.S. 57
Visitors: welcome with prior booking.
Green Fee: WD £8; WE £9.
Societies: welcome by prior arrangement; terms on application.
Catering: 2 restaurants and bar.
Hotels: Copthorne Effingham Park; Copthorne Gatwick.

2A 29 Corhampton

Sheeps Pond Lane, Droxford, Southampton, Hants, SO32 1LP
☎(01489) 877279, Pro 877638
Right off A32 at Corhampton on B3135 for 1 mile.
Downland course.

Pro Ian Roper; Founded 1891
18 holes, 6444 yards, S.S.S. 71
Visitors: welcome WD; with member at WE.
Green Fee: WD £21; WE £21.
Societies: welcome by arrangement Mon and Thurs; full facilities; terms on application.
Catering: lunch, tea and dinners available.
Hotels: The Uplands Hotel; Little Uplands Country Guest House.

2A 30 Cottesmore

Buchan Hill, Pease Pottage, Crawley, Sussex, RH11 9AT
☎(01293) 528256, Fax 522819, Pro 535399
Take M23 junction 11 and follow signs for Pease Pottage Services; go past services and take 3rd exit; course 1.5 miles on right.
Undulating meadowland course; start and finish par 5.
Pro Andrew Prior; Founded 1975
Designed by M.D. Rogerson
Griffin: 18 holes, 6248 yards, S.S.S. 70; Phoenix: 18 holes, 5514 yards, S.S.S. 67
Visitors: welcome WD and after 11am WE and Bank Holidays.
Green Fee: Griffin WD £25, WE £31; Phoenix WD £16, WE £21.
Societies: welcome Mon to Fri; four different packages available; health club and tennis facilities; conference suites and private function rooms; £31.75-£53.75.
Catering: full restaurant, coffee shop and bar, including spike bar, facilities.
Hotels: country club has 12 bedrooms on site.

2A 31 Cowdray Park

Midhurst, W Sussex, GU29 0BB
☎(01730) 813599, Fax 815900, Pro 812091
About 1 mile E of Midhurst on A272. Parkland course.
Pro Richard Gough; Founded 1920
18 holes, 6212 yards, S.S.S. 70
Visitors: welcome.
Green Fee: WD £20; WE £25.
Societies: welcome by arrangement; full facilities; terms on application.
Catering: bar snacks daily, evening meals by arrangement; restaurant.
Hotels: Angel, Spread Eagle.

2A 32 Cowes

Crossfield Ave, Cowes, Isle of Wight, PO31 8HN

☎(01983) 280135, Pro 292303, Sec 292303, Bar/Rest 292303
Next to Cowes High School. Parkland course.
Founded 1908
9 holes, 5923 yards, S.S.S. 68
Visitors: welcome.
Green Fee: WD £15; WE £18.
Societies: welcome; packages available; from £12.
Catering: full clubhouse facilities.
Hotels: New Holmwood; Fountain.

2A 33 Crowborough Beacon

Beacon Rd, Crowborough, E Sussex, TN6 1UJ
☎(01892) 661511, Fax 667339, Pro 653877
8 miles S of Tunbridge Wells on A26. Heathland course.
Pro Dennis Newnham; Founded 1895
18 holes, 6256 yards, S.S.S. 70
Visitors: welcome WD; h'cap certs or letter of introduction required.
Green Fee: WD £25; WE £25.
Societies: welcome WD by arrangement; not Thurs; terms on application.
Catering: for up to 60; breakfast available by prior arrangement.
Hotels: Winston Manor.

2A 34 Dale Hill Hotel

Ticehurst, Wadhurst, TN5 7DQ
☎(01580) 200112, Fax 201249, Pro 201090
On A21 from Tunbridge Wells. Parkland course with lake features.
Founded 1974
Old: 18 holes, 5856 yards, S.S.S. 69; Woosnam: 18 holes, 6512 yards, S.S.S. 69
Visitors: welcome by arrangement.
Green Fee: Old WD £20, WE £30; Woosnam WD £45, WE £55.
Societies: welcome by prior arrangement; restaurant, golf clinics, pool and leisure facilities; terms on application.
Catering: restaurant and full facilities.
Hotels: Dale Hill.

2A 35 Dean Farm (Kingsley)

Main Rd, Kingsley, Bordon, Hants, GU35 9NG
☎(01420) 489478, Sec 472313
On B3004 between Alton and Bordon on W side of Kingsley.
Parkland course.
Founded 1984
9 holes, 1600 yards
Visitors: public pay and play.
Green Fee: WD £4; WE £4.
Societies: n/a.

2A 36 **Dewlands Manor Golf Course**
Cottage Hill, Rotherfield, E Sussex, TN6 3JN
☎(01892) 852266, Fax 853015
Sec, 853308
0.5 mile S of village of Rotherfield just off B2101 to Five Ashes, 10 miles from Tunbridge Wells.
Parkland/woodland course with water hazards.
Pro Nick Goding; Founded 1991
Designed by R.M. And Nick Goding
9 holes, 3186 yards, S.S.S. 70
Visitors: welcome all year; 15 minute tee intervals.
Green Fee: WD £13; WE £15.
Societies: small business groups welcome, maximum 20 persons; full facilities; terms on application.
Catering: bar, light snacks at all times, special orders by arrangement.
Hotels: Spa; Royal Wells (Tunbridge Wells); Winston Manor (Crowborough).

2A 37 **Dibden**
Main Rd, Dibden, Southampton, Hants, SO45 5TB
☎(01703) 207508, Pro 845596, Bar/Rest 845060
Turn off A326 at Dibden roundabout, course situated 0.5 mile on right.
Public parkland course.
Pro Alan Bridge; Founded 1974
Designed by J. Hamilton Stutt
18 holes, 5965 yards, S.S.S. 69
Visitors: welcome; no restrictions.
Green Fee: WD £7.75; WE £11.30.
Societies: welcome by arrangement with Pro; full facilities; terms on application.
Catering: full facilities
Practice range, 20 bays; floodlit.
Hotels: Four Seasons; Pilgrim.

2A 38 **Dummer**
Dummer, Nr Basingstoke, Hants, RG25 2AR
☎(01256) 397888, Fax 397889, Pro 397950
M3 exit 7.
Parkland course.
Pro Gary Stubbington; Founded 1992
Designed by Peter Alliss and Clive Clark
18 holes, 6427 yards, S.S.S. 71
Visitors: welcome WD only.
Green Fee: WD £21; WE £21.
Societies: welcome by arrangement; full facilities; terms on application.
Catering: full facilities.
Hotels: Audley's Wood; Hilton National (Basingstoke).

2A 39 **Dunwood Manor Golf Club**
Danes Road, Awbridge, Romsey, Hants, SO51 0GF
☎(01794) 340112, Fax 341215, Pro 340663
Sec 340549, Bar/Rest 340549
Off A27 Romsey to Salisbury road; after 2 miles turn right at Shootash crossroads into Danes Road; club is 800 yards on left.
Undulating parkland course.
Founded 1972
18 holes, 5474 yards, S.S.S. 68
Visitors: welcome WD by prior arrangement.
Green Fee: WD £20-£28.
Societies: welcome Mon/Tues/Thurs/ Fri all day and Wed pm; packages available.
Catering: facilities available.
Hotels: luxury farmhouse accommodation available – details on request. Abbey Hotel; Bell Inn.

2A 40 **The Dyke Golf Club**
Devil's Dyke, Devil's Dyke Rd, Brighton, BN1 8YJ
☎(01273) 857296, Fax 857078, Pro 857260, Bar/Rest 857230
A27 Brighton by-pass; follow directions for Devil's Dyke; course 2.5 miles west of by-pass.
Downland course.
Founded 1906
Designed by Fred Hawtree
18 holes, 6611 yards, S.S.S. 72
Visitors: welcome by prior arrangement; not Sundays before 12 noon.
Green Fee: WD £25-£35.
Societies: welcome by arrangement; full facilities available; £48 package.
Catering: full facilities.
Hotels: Tottington Manor, nr Henfield.

2A 41 **East Brighton**
Roedean Rd, Brighton, BN2 5RA
☎(01273) 604838, Fax 680277, Pro 603989, Bar/Rest 621461
1.5 miles east of Palace Pier, just off A259 behind Brighton Marina.
Undulating downland course.
Pro Robin Goodway; Founded 1894
Designed by James Braid
18 holes, 6020 yards, S.S.S. 69
Visitors: welcome WD except Tues am; WE and Bank Holidays after 11am.
Green Fee: n/a.
Societies: welcome Mon-Fri, except for Tues am, by arrangement.
Catering: facilities available.
Hotels: Old Ship; Grand; Metropole.

2A 42 **East Horton Golfing Centre**
Mortimers Lane, Fair Oak, Hants, SO50 7EA
☎(01703) 602111
From M27 junction 7 follow signs for Fair Oak.
Parkland course.
Pro Trevor Pearce; Founded 1993
18 holes, 5920 yards, S.S.S. 70
Visitors: welcome; 7 day advance booking system.
Green Fee: WD £11; WE £14.
Societies: welcome everyday by prior arrangement.
Catering: bar and restaurant facilities. Practice range, 15 bays; floodlit.
Hotels: Marwell Lodge; Botley Grange.

2A 43 **East Sussex National**
Little Horsted, Uckfield, E Sussex, TN22 5ES
☎(01825) 880088, Fax 880066, Pro 880256
Sec, 880233 Bar/Rest 880224
Situated on the A22 between East Grinstead and Eastbourne just outside Uckfield
American style layout in English countryside
Pro Iain Naylor; Founded 1989
Designed by Bob Cupp
East: 18 holes, 7138 yards, S.S.S. 74;
West: 18 holes, 7154 yards, S.S.S. 74
Visitors: WD only.
Green Fee: WD £45; WE £45.
Societies: welcome with h'cap certs; minimum 20 players; societies can select their own corporate package; £85.
Catering: full catering and entertaining as well as bar facilities, sauna and steam rooms.
Hotels: club will provide comprehensive list of hotels and B&B.

2A 44 **Eastbourne Downs**
East Dean Rd, Eastbourne, E Sussex, BN20 8ES
☎(01323) 720827, Fax 412506, Pro 732264, Bar/Rest 730809
0.5 miles W of Eastbourne on the A259
Downland course.
Pro Terry Marshall; Founded 1908
Designed by J.H. Taylor
18 holes, 6601 yards, S.S.S. 72
Visitors: welcome.
Green Fee: WD £16; WE £20.
Societies: welcome WD; some WE by arrangement; packages available; from £30.

Catering: full clubhouse facilities.
Practice range.
Hotels: Landsdown.

2A 45 **Eastbourne Golfing Park**

Lottbridge Drove, Eastbourne, BN23 6QJ
☎(01323) 520400, Fax 520400, Bar/Rest 504134
East side of Eastbourne.
Parkland course.
Pro Barrie Finch; Founded 1993
Designed by David Ashton
9 holes, 5046 yards
Visitors: welcome.
Green Fee: WD £8-£15; WE £8-£15.
Societies: welcome by arrangement; full facilities; terms on application.
Catering: full facilities.
Practice range, 24 bays, floodlit all-weather driving range; £2 for 50 balls, £5 for 250 balls.
Hotels: Wish Tower Hotel.

2A 46 **Fleetlands**

N.A.R.O. Fleetlands Division, Gosport, Hants, PO13 0AA
☎(01705) 544384
Off A32 2 miles S of Fareham..
Parkland course.
Founded 1963
9 holes, 4852 yards, S.S.S. 64
Visitors: welcome with a member.
Green Fee: WD £5; WE £7.
Societies: welcome if accompanied by member.
Catering: bar.

2A 47 **Fleming Park**

Magpie Lane, Eastleigh, Hants, SO50 9LM
☎(01703) 643671
A27/M27, turn off at Eastleigh sign, 1 mile to course..
Parkland course.
Pro Chris Strickett; Founded 1973
Designed by Charles Lawrie
18 holes, 4378 yards, S.S.S. 61
Visitors: welcome.
Green Fee: WD £6.60; WE £9.90.
Societies: on application to Sec; full facilities; packages available; terms on application.
Catering: bar snacks and meals.
Hotels: Crest Hotel; Gateway.

2A 48 **Foxbridge**

Foxbridge Lane, Plaistow, W Sussex, RH14 0LB
☎(01403) 753303, Fax 753433

Take B2133 from Billingshurst to Lockswood; then take Plaistow road and course is signposted.
Parkland course.
Pro Max Newman/Janice Arnold;
Founded 1991
Designed by P Clark
9 holes, 6236 yards, S.S.S. 70
Visitors: welcome WD only.
Green Fee: WD £12; WE £12.
Societies: welcome WD by arrangement; full facilities; terms on application.
Catering: full facilities and bar service available.

2A 49 **Freshwater Bay**

Afton Down, Freshwater Bay, Isle of Wight, PO40 9TZ
☎(01983) 752955
3 miles from Yarmouth on A3055 overlooking Freshwater Bay.
Seaside downland course.
Founded 1893
18 holes, 5725 yards, S.S.S. 68
Visitors: welcome after 9.30am on WD and 10am on Sun.
Green Fee: WD £20; WE £24.
Societies: welcome by arrangement; after 9.30am on WD and 10am on Sun; full facilities; terms on application.
Catering: full catering facilities; licensed bar.
Hotels: Albion, Country Garden, Farringford.

2A 50 **Furzeley**

Furzeley Road, Denmead, Hants, PO7 6TX
☎(01705) 231180, Fax 231180
2 miles NW of Waterlooville.
Parkland course.
Pro Derek Brown; Founded 1993
Designed by M Sale
18 holes, 4363 yards, S.S.S. 61
Visitors: welcome, bookings taken 2 days in advance.
Green Fee: WD £9.80; WE £11.50.
Societies: welcome; packages available; terms on application.
Catering: available.

2A 51 **Goodwood**

Kennell Hill, Goodwood, Chichester, West Sussex, PO18 0PN
☎(01243) 785012, Fax 781741, Pro 774994, Sec 774968, Bar/Rest 774105
3 miles NE of Chichester on road to racecourse.
Downland course.

Pro Keith Macdonald; Founded 1892
Designed by James Braid
18 holes, 6000 yards, S.S.S. 69
Visitors: welcome with h/cap certs.
Green Fee: WD £32; WE £42 (£21 with member).
Societies: welcome Wed/Thurs only; minimum 16; full facilities; £50 package.
Catering: full facilities by arrangement.

2A 52 **Gosport & Stokes Bay**

Fort Rd, Gosport, Hants, PO12 2AT
☎(01705) 581625, Fax 527941, Pro 582220, Sec 527941, Bar/Rest 580226
M27 to Fareham; A32 Gosport; Haslar Bridge to Haslar Road to Fort Road.
Links course.
Founded 1885
9 holes, 5999 yards, S.S.S. 69
Visitors: welcome.
Green Fee: WD £15 (£10 with member); WE £18.
Societies: welcome by arrangement; full facilities.
Catering: full facilities.
Hotels: The Old Lodge; The Alverbank; The Anglesey (all in Alverstoke).

2A 53 **Great Salterns**

Burrfields Road, Portsmouth, Hampshire, PO3 5HH
☎(01705) 812435, Fax 650525, Pro 664549
From M27 junction A2030 towards Southsea; turn rt at 3rd set of lights.
Parkland course.
Pro Terry Healy; Founded 1914
18 holes, 5737 yards, S.S.S. 68
Visitors: municipal course.
Green Fee: WD £11.50; WE £11.50.
Societies: bookings welcome; £14.
Catering: at public house adjacent to course.
Practice range; £2.30 for 50 balls.
Hotels: Inn Lodge; Hilton Hotel.

2A 54 **Ham Manor Golf Club**

Angmering, BN16 4JE
☎(01903) 783288, Fax 850886, Pro 783732, Bar/Rest 775653
Off A259 between Littlehampton and Worthing.
Parkland course.
Pro Simon Buckley; Founded 1936
Designed by H.S. Colt
18 holes, 6092 yards, S.S.S. 70
Visitors: welcome with h/cap certs.
Green Fee: WD £30; WE £40.

Societies: welcome Wed/Thurs/Fri by arrangement; full facilities; £50-£55 package.
Catering: full facilities.
Hotels: Arundel Hotel; Lamb Inn, Angmering.

2A 55 **Hampshire**
Winchester Road, Goodworth Clatford, Nr Andover, Hants, SP11 7TB
☎(01264) 357555, Fax 356606
From Andover take the Stockbridge road A3057, 0.5 mile S of Andover.
Downland course.
Pro John Slade/Paul Smith; Founded 1993
Designed by T Fiducia & A Mitchell
18 holes, 6376 yards, S.S.S. 70
Visitors: welcome.
Green Fee: WD £14; WE £25.
Societies: welcome by arrangement; full facilities; packages available; terms on application.
Catering: full facilities.
Practice range, covered bays.
Hotels: White Hart (Andover).

2A 56 **Hartley Wintney**
London Rd, Hartley Wintney, Hants, RG27 8PT
☎(01252) 842214, Pro 843779, Sec 844211
A30 between Camberley (5 miles) and Basingstoke (12 miles).
Parkland course.
Pro Martin Smith; Founded 1891
9 holes, 6096 yards, S.S.S. 69
Visitors: welcome, Sat/Sun/Bank Holiday only with member.
Green Fee: n/a.
Societies: Tues/Thurs only by arrangement with Sec; full facilities.
Catering: full facilities.
Hotels: Lismoyne Hotel, Fleet.

2A 57 **Hassocks**
London Road, Hassocks, Sussex, BN6 9NA
☎(01273) 846630, Fax 846070, Pro 846990, Bar/Rest 846949
Take A273 towards Hassocks from Brighton; club is between Hassocks and Burgess Hill.
Parkland course.
Pro Charles Ledger; Founded 1995
Designed by P Wright
18 holes, 5439 yards, S.S.S. 68
Visitors: welcome anytime; tee time booking recommended.
Green Fee: WD £12.50; WE £16.25.
Societies: welcome by arrangement with Sec; full facilities.

Catering: full facilities.
Hotels: The Birch Hotel, Haywards Heath; Hickstead Hotel, Bolney.

2A 58 **Hastings**
Battle Rd, St Leonards-on-Sea, E Sussex, TH38 0TA
☎(01424) 852981, Fax 852981, Sec 852977
A2100 from Battle to Hastings, 3 miles NW of Hastings.
Municipal undulating parkland course.
Pro Charles Giddings; Founded 1973
Designed by Frank Pennink
18 holes, 6248 yards, S.S.S. 70
Visitors: welcome; no restrictions WD; booking system in usse at WE 7am-10.30am.
Green Fee: WD £10.30; WE £13.
Societies: welcome Mon-Fri; full facilities; terms on application.
Catering: full facilities.
Practice range, 14 bays; floodlit.
Hotels: Beauport Park.

2A 59 **Hayling Golf Club**
Links Lane, Hayling Island, Hants, PO11 0BX
☎(01705) 464446, Fax 464446, Pro 464491, Bar/Rest 463712
From Havant junction on A27 take A3023 to SW corner of Hayling Island.
Links course.
Founded 1883
Designed by J H Taylor/Tom Simpson
18 holes, 6521 yards, S.S.S. 71
Visitors: welcome with h'cap certs.
Green Fee: WD £26; WE £35.
Societies: welcome Tues/Wed by prior arrangement; full facilities.
Catering: full facilities.
Practice range; putting green; 2 covered driving nets.
Hotels: Newton House Hotel; Broad Oak Country Hotel.

2A 60 **Haywards Heath**
High Beech Lane, Haywards Heath, Sussex, RH16 1SL
☎(01444) 414310, Fax 458319, Pro 414866, Sec 414457
1.5 miles north of Haywards Heath on the Ardingly road.
Parkland course.
Pro Michael Henning; Founded 1922
18 holes, 6204 yards, S.S.S. 70
Visitors: welcome with h'cap certs.
Green Fee: WD £26; WE £36.
Societies: welcome by prior arrangement with the Secretary; packages from £27.
Catering: full facilities.

2A 61 **Highwoods**
Ellerslie Lane, Bexhill-on-Sea, E Sussex, TN39 4LJ
☎(01424) 212625, Pro 212770, Bar/Rest 21262
Off A259 from Eastbourne or Hastings; 2 miles from Bexhill; from Battle, A269 via Ninfield, turn right in Sidley.
Parkland course.
Pro Mike Andrews; Founded 1925
Designed by J.H. Taylor
18 holes, 6218 yards, S.S.S. 70
Visitors: welcome with h'cap certs; no visitors Sun before 12 noon unless with member.
Green Fee: WD £25; WE £30.
Societies: welcome by prior arrangement; full facilities; terms on application.
Catering: full facilities.
Hotels: Cooden Resort; Granville.

2A 62 **Hill Barn**
Hill Barn Lane, Worthing, Sussex, BN14 9QE
☎(01903) 237301
N of Worthing off London & Edinburgh Building Society roundabout on A27, take last exit before the Brighton exit; course is signposted.
Municipal downland course.
Founded 1935
Designed by Hawtree & Son
18 holes, 6224 yards, S.S.S. 70
Visitors: welcome.
Green Fee: WD £12.90; WE £13.90.
Societies: welcome WD only; minimum 20; terms on application.
Catering: breakfasts, snacks, hot meals available all day.
Hotels: Beach; Ardington & Chatsworth.

2A 63 **Hockley**
Twyford, Winchester, Hants, SO21 1PL
☎(01962) 713165, Fax 713612, Pro 713678, Bar/Rest 714572
Leave M3 at junction 11 and follow signs for Twyford.
Downland course.
Pro Mr T Lane; Founded 1914
Designed by James Braid
18 holes, 6296 yards, S.S.S. 70
Visitors: welcome.
Green Fee: WD £30; WE £30.
Societies: welcome Wed/Fri by prior arrangement; full facilities; £30.
Catering: full facilities.
Practice range.
Hotels: Winchester Royal Hotel; Harestock Lodge; Potters Heron.

2A 64 Hollingbury Park

Ditchling Rd, Brighton, Sussex, BN1 7HS
☎(01273) 552010, Pro 500086
1 mile from Brighton, astride the Downs between A23 London Rd and A27 Lewes Rd.
Public undulating downland course.
Pro Graeme Crompton; Founded 1908
Designed by J. Braid and J.H. Taylor
18 holes, 6400 yards, S.S.S. 71
Visitors: welcome anytime.
Green Fee: WD £11.50; WE £15.50.
Societies: welcome WD; full facilities; terms on application.
Catering: full restaurant facilities.
Hotels: Old Ship; Preston Resort.

2A 65 Horam Park

Chiddingly Rd, Horam, East Sussex, TN21 0JJ
☎(01435) 813477, Fax 813677
Off M25 at junction 6; A22 to Eastbourne; A267 to Heathfield; before reaching Horam, take Chiddingly road – 200 yards on right.
Parkland course with lakes.
Pro Liam Greasley; Founded 1985
Designed by Glen Johnson
9 holes, 5968 yards, S.S.S. 68
Visitors: welcome.
Green Fee: WD £9-£15; WE £9-£15.
Societies: welcome by arrangement.
Catering: full facilities.
Practice range, bucket of balls £2, members £1.
Hotels: The Boship Hotel, Hailsham.

2A 66 Horsham Golf Park

Worthing Rd, Horsham, , RH13 7AX
☎(01403) 271525, Fax 274528
A24 between Horsham and Southwater; off Hop-Oast roundabout.
Parkland course.
Pro Neil Burke; Founded 1993
we holes 4122 yards, S.S.S. 60
Visitors: welcome at all times except before 11 am Sat.
Green Fee: WD £6/7; WE £8/10.
Societies: welcome by arrangement except before 11am Sat; full facilities; from £11.75.
Catering: full facilities.
Practice range – £2.50 bucket of balls.

2A 67 Ifield Golf & Country Club

Rusper Rd, Ifield, Crawley, RH11 0LN
☎(01293) 520222, Fax 612973, Pro 523088
M23 junction on the outskirts of Crawley near Gossops Green.

Parkland course.
Pro Jon Earl; Founded 1927
Designed by Bernard Darwin.
18 holes, 6330 yards, S.S.S. 70
Visitors: welcome but should phone in advance.
Green Fee: WD £20/30 per day; WE £20.
Societies: Society bookings taken for 16 people or more; Coffee, buffet lunch, 3 course dinner in carvery and 36 holes of golf; £52.
Catering: full facilities.
Hotels: Ifeld Court Hotel.

2A 68 Leckford and Longstock

Leckford, Stockbridge, Hants, SO20 6JF
☎(01264) 810320
2.5 miles N of Stockbridge on Andover road.
Parkland course.
Pro Tony Ashton
9 holes, 6394 yards, S.S.S. 72; also New course: 4562 yards, par 66
Visitors: employees of John Lewis Partnership and guests only.
Green Fee: WD £9; WE £13.
Societies: none.
Catering: none.

2A 69 Lee-on-the-Solent

Brune Lane, Lee-on-the-Solent, Hants, PO13 9PB
☎(01705) 550207, Pro 551181, Sec 551170
3 miles S of M27 junction 11.
Heathland course.
Pro John Richardson; Founded 1905
18 holes, 5933 yards, S.S.S. 69
Visitors: welcome WD.
Green Fee: WD £25; WE £30.
Societies: welcome Thurs by prior arrangement.
Catering: full clubhouse facilities.
Practice range.
Hotels: Belle Vue.

2A 70 Lewes

Chapel Hill, Lewes, E Sussex, BN7 2BB
☎(01273) 483474, Fax 483474, Pro 473245, Bar/Rest 473245
E of town centre on the A27.
Downland course.
Founded 1896
18 holes, 6213 yards, S.S.S. 70
Visitors: welcome WD and after 2pm at WE.
Green Fee: WD £16.50; WE £27.
Societies: welcome; terms on application.

Catering: full bar and restaurant facilities.
Hotels: White Hart Hotel, Lewes.

2A 71 Liphook

Wheatsheaf Enclosure, Liphook, Hants, GU30 7EH
☎(01428) 723785, Fax 724853, Pro 723271, Sec 723271, Bar/Rest 723271
1 mile S of Liphook on B2070 (old A3).
Heath and heather course.
Pro Ian Large; Founded 1922
Designed by Arthur Croome
18 holes, 6167 yards, S.S.S. 69
Visitors: welcome with h'cap certs but not on Tues and only pm at WE.
Green Fee: WD £29; WE £37.
Societies: welcome Wed, Thurs, Fri; min 16, max 36; terms on application.
Catering: bar, bar snacks and restaurant facilities.

2A 72 Littlehampton

170 Rope Walk, Riverside West, Littlehampton, W Sussex, BN17 5DL
☎(01903) 717170, Fax 726629, Pro 716369
From Littlehampton take A259 Bognor Regis road; take 1st left after new river bridge, signs to golf club.
Seaside links course.
Pro Guy McQuitty; Founded 1898
18 holes, 6258 yards, S.S.S. 70
Visitors: welcome any time; after 12 noon on Sun.
Green Fee: WD £24; WE £30.
Societies: welcome WD; full facilities; terms on application.
Catering: full facilities 7 days.
Hotels: Bailiff's Court; Norfolk Arms.

2A 73 Mannings Heath

Fullers, Hammerpond Rd, Mannings, Horsham, W Sussex, RH13 6PG
☎(01403) 210228, Fax 270974
2 miles S of Horsham on A281 from junction 11 on the M23; 4 miles along Grouse Road; turn right at T junction.
Undulating wooded course.
Pro Clive Tucker; Founded 1995
Designed by D Williams
Kingfisher: 18 holes, 6305 yards, S.S.S. 70; Waterfall: 18 holes, 6378 yards, S.S.S. 70.
Visitors: welcome.
Green Fee: WD £32; WE £40.
Societies: welcome; full catering available, tennis, steam rooms and practice facilities; £51-£65.
Catering: full facilities.
Hotels: South Lodge.

Liphook

For most golfers charm is a more important quality in a course than challenge. Liphook is the type which combines the two in equal measure. 6207 yards is not long these days but matching the par of 70 is another matter when the heather and trees, the hallmark of the best Surrey and Hampshire courses, place such a premium on controlled shot-making.

You certainly appreciate the lovely setting more if you keep straight, the countryside possessing more normal contouring than the valleys, plateaux and gulleys that characterise the land surrounding the Devil's Punchbowl at Hindhead just up the Portsmouth Road, and in terms of golf course architecture, Liphook has rightly been hailed as an example for the connoisseur. My late senior partner, Ken Cotton, was always singing its praises but the remarkable part of the story is that its designer, A.C. Croome, was first and foremost a schoolmaster. Liphook was the only new course for which he was entirely responsible. Jack Neville keeps him notable company in this regard, Neville's lone masterpiece being Pebble Beach. It was ill health rather than lack of demand that prevented Croome pursuing the final chapter of his working life.

In addition to being a housemaster at Radley College, he wrote about cricket and golf for several newspapers, both games at which he excelled himself. He was founder member of the Oxford and Cambridge Golfing Society, donating the Croome Shield for annual competition among College pairs at the President's Putter, and was a regular competitor in the Amateur and other championships.

It was J.F. Abercromby, the designer of Addington, among others, who persuaded him to join forces in the firm of Fowler, Abercromby, Simpson and Croome – as elite a quartet as anyone could muster. At first, Croome's role was mainly administrative, but inside every golfer is a golf course architect clamouring to get out, and Liphook was to be the ultimate expression of Croome's talents.

No clubhouse gets a better view of its first and 18th holes, the work of John Morrison, who wanted to provide a fine long short hole to get players moving, but, apart from the difficulty of the opening tee shot, Liphook is quick to let golfers know what is expected of them. There are three par-fours of well over 400 yards in the first six holes, the fourth, High View, being particularly demanding. It leads to the first crossing of the busy road and on to the first of three par-fives where thorn trees feature in the drive.

The sixth, with its little grassy hollow behind the green, doubles back on the fifth, the attractive short seventh starting the section of 10 holes on the other side of the railway. The ninth, 438 yards, another demanding four, prompts a long uphill second over a road and a heathery dell but the 10th offers a more inviting drive even if a ditch lurks on the approach to the green.

A large central bunker dominates the short 11th, in a visual sense, and the 12th, Forest Mere, completes the long par-fours and always with a victim or two. A nice downhill drive and a slightly uphill second give the long hitters a chance of a birdie at the 13th, and, for those negotiating the dogleg successfully, a good pitch can do the same at the 14th.

Then it is a deep breath and a mad dash to the 15th where the drive takes us up over a steep ridge with the temptation to cut off more than is good for us. The 16th is the reverse of the 15th, a quarry and the corner of a wood awaiting any poorly struck second. The walk to the 17th is a last reminder of the Portsmouth Road which explains in part the club's traditionally strong links with the Navy; the 17th's tee shot across a diagonal, corrugated bank of gorse and heather makes the fifth and last short hole difficult to judge, enhancing Liphook's reputation that it's not just nautical men who are all at sea.

2A 74 **Marriott Goodwood Park G & CC**

Goodwood, Nr Chichester, W Sussex, PO18 0QB
☎(01243) 520114, Fax 520125
3 miles N of Chichester.
Parkland course.
Pro Adrian Wratting; Founded 1989
Designed by Donald Steel
18 holes, 6530 yards, S.S.S. 71
Visitors: welcome with h'cap certs.
Green Fee: WD £28; WE £35.
Societies: welcome; packages available for golf, catering and hotel; aerobic studio, driving range; from £55.
Catering: hotel and clubhouse facilities.
Hotels: Marriott Goodwood Park.

2A 75 **Meon Valley Hotel Golf & Country Club**

Sandy Lane, Shedfield, Hampshire, SO32 2HQ
☎(01329) 833455, Fax 834411, Pro 832184
Off M27 at junction 7, take Botley exit A334 towards Wickham; course is on Sandy Lane.
Wooded parkland course.
Pro John Stirling; Founded 1978
Designed by J. Hamilton Stutt
18 holes, 6519 yards, S.S.S. 71; also Valley course: 9 holes.
Visitors: book in advance.
Green Fee: WD £25; WE £35.
Societies: welcome; parties catered for; terms on application.
Catering: full facilities.
Practice range, but no ball collection.
Hotels: Meon Valley Country Club.

2A 76 **Mid-Sussex**

Spatham Lane, Ditchling, East Sussex, BN6 8XJ
☎(01273) 846567, Fax 845767
1 mile E of Ditchling on Lewes road.
Parkland course.
Pro Chris Connell; Founded 1995
Designed by D Williams Partnership
18 holes, 6446 yards, S.S.S. 71
Visitors: welcome midweek and afternoons at WE.
Green Fee: WD £22; WE £22.
Societies: welcome on WD; restaurant and practice facilities; from £28.
Catering: full facilities.
Practice range, grass tees available.
Hotels: many in Brighton area.

2A 77 **Moors Valley Golf Centre**

Horton Road, Ashley Heath, Nr Ringwood, Hants, BH24 2ET

☎(01425) 480448, Fax 472057, Pro 479776
A 31 through Ringwood, right at roundabout to Ashley Heath, course 2 miles on right.
Parkland/heathland course; par 3 course planned.
Pro Michael Torrens; Founded 1988
Designed by Martin Hawtree
18 holes, 6270 yards
Visitors: municipal.
Green Fee: WD £9; WE £11.50.
Societies: bookings welcome in advance; £9-£11.50.
Catering: full bar and catering facilities.
Hotels: Struan, St Leonards.

2A 78 **New Forest**

Southampton Rd, Lyndhurst, Hants, SO43 7BU
☎(01703) 282752
On the A35 between Ashurst and Lyndhurst.
Forest heathland course.
Founded 1888
Designed by Peter Swann
18 holes, 5772 yards, S.S.S. 68
Visitors: welcome.
Green Fee: WD £10; WE £12.
Societies: welcome but must book in advance; bar and lounge facilities; from £12.
Catering: full facilities.

2A 79 **Newport**

Near Shide, Newport, Isle of Wight, PO30 3BA
☎(01983) 525076
On A3056 Newport-Sandown road 0.5 miles from Newport.
Downland course.
Founded 1896
Designed by Guy Hunt
9 holes, 5660 yards, S.S.S. 68
Visitors: welcome with h'cap certs.
Green Fee: WD £15; WE £17.50.
Societies: welcome by arrangement; catering packages available by arrangement with caterer; from £12.
Catering: bar and catering facilities.

2A 80 **North Hants**

Minley Rd, Fleet, Hants, GU13 8RE
☎(01252) 616443, Fax 811627, Pro 616655
0.5 mile N of Fleet Station on B3013, junction 4A, M3.
Heathland course.
Pro Steve Porter; Founded 1904
Designed by James Braid
18 holes, 6257 yards, S.S.S. 70

Visitors: welcome by prior arrangement with Sec; letter of introduction and h'cap certs required.
Green Fee: WD £30; WE £30.
Societies: welcome Mon-Fri by arrangement with Sec; full facilities; packages available; terms on application.
Catering: lunch, tea, dinner; pre-booking required.
Hotels: various in Fleet, Camberley and Farnborough.

2A 81 **Old Thorns**

Old Thorns, Longmoor Rd, Griggs, Liphook, Hants, GU30 7PE
☎(01428) 724555, Fax 725063
Signposted from A3 at Griggs Green.
Parkland course.
Founded 1982
Designed by Commander John Harris; adapted by Peter Alliss and Dave Thomas
18 holes, 6533 yards, S.S.S. 71
Visitors: welcome.
Green Fee: WD £35; WE £45.
Societies: welcome any day; corporate and society days can be arranged; packages available; function rooms; half-way house; conference centre; £75-£140.
Catering: European and Japanese restaurants.
Hotels: Old Thorns.

2A 82 **Osborne**

Osborne House Estates, East Cowes, Isle of Wight, PO32 6JX
☎(01983) 295421
1 miles from Red Funnel Terminal in grounds of Osborne House.
Parkland course.
Founded 1903
2 holes opened for Royal household in 1892 : extended to 9 by Osborne House Governor in 1904
9 holes, 6418 yards, S.S.S. 70
Visitors: welcome by prior arrangement except Tues, Sat and Sunday mornings.
Green Fee: WD £16; WE £19.
Societies: welcome by arrangement but a maximum of 24; bar and restaurant facilities; terms on application.
Catering: facilities available.
Hotels: Memories, East Cowes; Wheatsheaf, Newport.

2A 83 **Osiers Farm**

London Road, Petworth, W Sussex, GU28 9LX
☎(01798) 344097

1.5 miles N of Petworth on A283.
Parkland course over farmland.
Pro Roger Mace; Founded 1991
Designed by Chris Duncton
9 holes, 6191 yards, S.S.S. 64
Visitors: welcome.
Green Fee: WD £9; WE £9.
Societies: welcome; new clubhouse
opening 1998 with full facilities; terms
on application.
Hotels: B & B on course;
Stonemasons Arms, Petworth.

2A 84 **Otterbourne GC**
Poles Lane, Otterbourne, Nr
Winchester, SO21 1DZ
☎(01962) 775225
On A31 between Hursley and
Otterbourne villages.
Parkland course.
Founded 1995
9 holes, 1939 yards
Visitors: public pay and play.
Green Fee: WD £4; WE £5.
Societies: none.

2A 85 **Paultons Golf Centre**
Old Salisbury Rd, Ower, Nr Romsey,
Hants, SO51 6AN
☎(01703) 813345, Fax 813993, Pro
814623, Sec 813992
Exit 2 off M27 in direction of Ower, left
at 1st roundabout, then right at
Heathlands Hotel, then signposted.
Parkland course.
Pro Rod Park; Founded 1993
18 holes, 6238 yards, S.S.S. 70
Visitors: All welcome at all times.
Green Fee: WD £15; WE £18.
Societies: welcome by arrangement;
full facilities; terms on application.
Catering: bars and restaurant
Practice range 24 bays; floodlit.
Hotels: Heathlands (500 yards).

2A 86 **Paxhill Park**
East Mascalls Lane, Lindfield, W
Sussex, RH16 2QN
☎(01444) 484467, Fax 482709, Pro
484000
2 miles outside Haywards Heath on
Lindfield road.
Parkland course.
Pro S Dunkley; Founded 1990
Designed by Patrick Tallack
18 holes, 6117 yards, S.S.S. 69
Visitors: welcome WD and after 12 at
WE.
Green Fee: WD £15; WE £20.
Societies: welcome Mon-Fri; full facili-
ties but no food on Mon evenings;
£45.

Catering: full facilities except Mon
evenings.
Hotels: Birch Hotel, Haywards Heath.

2A 87 **Peacehaven**
Brighton Rd, Newhaven, E Sussex,
BN9 9UH
☎(01273) 514049, Pro 512602
On A259 1 mile W of Newhaven.
Undulating downland course
Pro Ian Pearson; Founded 1895
Designed by James Braid
9 holes, 5488 yards, S.S.S. 67
Visitors: welcome WD; after 11.30am
WE and Bank Holidays.
Green Fee: WD £10; WE £15.
Societies: welcome WD; full facilities;
terms on application.
Catering: available WE; by prior
arrangement WD.

2A 88 **Pease Pottage GC & Driving Range**
Horsham Rd, Pease Pottage, Crawley,
RH11 9AP
☎(01293) 521706
Leave M23 at junction 11, then course
is signposted from large roundabout.
Public parkland course.
Pro David Blair; Founded 1986
Designed by Adam Lazar
9 holes, 3511 yards, S.S.S. 60
Visitors: welcome.
Green Fee: WD £8.50; WE £11.
Societies: welcome by arrangement;
full facilities; terms on application.
Catering: full bar and restaurant facili-
ties.
Practice range, 26 bays; floodlit.
Hotels: Cottismore Hotel.

2A 89 **Petersfield**
Tankerdale Lane, Liss, Petersfield,
Hants, GU33 7QY
☎(01730) 895324, Fax 894713, Pro
895216, Sec 895165
Off A3 between Petersfield/Midhurst &
Liss exit.
Parkland course.
Pro Greg Hughes; Founded 1892;
New course founded 1997
New course designed by Martin
Hawtree
18 holes, 6387 yards, S.S.S. 71
Visitors: welcome with handicap cer-
tificates.
Green Fee: WD £25; WE £30.
Societies: welcome Mon, Wed and
Fri; modern new clubhouse facilities;
terms on application.
Catering: full facilities.
Hotels: Concord Hotel.

2A 90 **Piltdown**
Piltdown, Uckfield, E Sussex, TN22
3XB
☎(01825) 722033, Fax 724192, Pro
722389
1 mile W of Maresfield on the A272.
Heathland course.
Pro J Amos; Founded 1904
Designed by J. Rowe, G.M. Dodd,
Frank Pennink
18 holes, 6070 yards, S.S.S. 69
Visitors: welcome by arrangement.
Green Fee: WD £27.50; WE £27.50.
Societies: welcome Mon, Wed and
Fri; packages available; terms on
application.
Catering: full facilities.

2A 91 **Portsmouth**
Crookhorn Lane, Purbrook,
Portsmouth, Hants, PO7 5QL
☎(01705) 201827, Fax 200766, Pro
372210, Sec 372210, Bar/Rest
375999
1.5 miles from A3(M), junction of
Purbrook/Leigh Park.
Parkland course.
Pro Jason Banting; Founded 1972
Designed by Hawtree
18 holes, 5760 yards, S.S.S. 70
Visitors: welcome with prior booking.
Green Fee: WD £11; WE £11.
Societies: welcome at any time by
prior arrangement; packages avail-
able; from £16.
Catering: bar and restaurant facilities
available.
Hotels: Innlodge Hotel.

2A 92 **Pyecombe**
Clayton Hill, Pyecombe, Sussex, BN45
7FF
☎(01273) 844176, Fax 843338, Pro
845398, Sec 845372
Off A23 at Hassocks and Pyecombe.
Turn left on to A273 and course is 300
yds on right
Downland course.
Founded 1894
18 holes, 6278 yards, S.S.S. 70
Visitors: welcome.
Green Fee: WD £15; WE £20.
Societies: welcome by prior arrange-
ment; terms on application.
Catering: full facilities.

2A 93 **Romsey**
Romsey Rd, Nursling, Southampton,
Hants, SO16 0XW
☎(01703) 734637, Fax 741036, Pro
736673, Bar/Rest 732218
2 miles SE of Romsey on A3057

Southampton road, near M27/M271 junction 3.
Wooded parkland course.
Pro Mark Desmond; Founded 1900
Designed by Charles Lawrie
18 holes, 5856 yards, S.S.S. 68
Visitors: welcome WD.
Green Fee: WD £22; WE £22.
Societies: welcome by arrangement Mon, Tues and Thurs; full facilities; terms on application.
Catering: full facilities.
Hotels: White Horse (Romsey); Travel Inn (Nursling); Novotel (Southampton).

2A 94 Rowlands Castle
31 Links Lane, Rowlands Castle, Hants, PO9 6AE
☎(01705) 412216, Fax 413649, Pro 412785, Bar/Rest 412784
3 miles on the B2149 off junction 2 of the A3M.
Parkland course.
Pro P Klepacz; Founded 1902
18 holes, 6612 yards, S.S.S. 72
Visitors: welcome except for Sat.
Green Fee: WD £25; WE £30.
Societies: welcome Tues and Thurs by prior arrangement; packages include 36 holes plus lunch and dinner; £41-£45.
Catering: full facilities.

2A 95 Royal Ashdown Forest
Chapel Lane, Forest Row, E Sussex, RH18 5LR
☎(01342) 822018, Fax 825211, Pro 822247
A22 East Grinstead-Eastbourne road, 4.5 miles S of East Grinstead turn left in Forest Row opposite church on to B2110, after 0.5 mile turn right into Chapel Lane, top of hill turn left, over heath to clubhouse.
Undulating moorland course with views over forest.
Pro Martyn Landsborough; Founded 1888
18 holes, 6477 yards, S.S.S. 70
Visitors: welcome by arrangement only; restrictions at WE and Bank Holidays.
Green Fee: WD £30; WE £36.
Societies: welcome by arrangement;

Wed-Fri normal catering, Mon limited catering; full facilities, except Mon; terms on application.
Catering: lunch, tea; casual visitors requested to book in advance or before teeing off.
Hotels: Ashdown Forest; Brambletye (E Grinstead); Chequers.

2A 96 Royal Eastbourne
Paradise Drive, Eastbourne, Sussex, BN20 8BP
☎(01323) 729738, Fax 729738, Pro 736986, Bar/Rest 730412
0.5 miles from Town Hall.
Downland course.
Pro Richard Wooller; Founded 1887
18 holes, 6118 yards, S.S.S. 69
Visitors: welcome but h'cap certs needed on the Devonshire course.
Green Fee: WD £20; WE £25.
Societies: welcome on WD only; golf, lunch and 3-course dinner; £30-£40.
Catering: full facilities.
Hotels: Grand; Lansdowne; Chatsworth, all in Eastbourne.

2A 97 Royal Winchester
Sarum Rd, Off Romsey Rd, Winchester, Hants, SO22 5QE
☎(01962) 851694, Fax 865048, Pro 862473, Sec 852462, Bar/Rest 852462
Take M3 to junction 11 and at Pitt roundabout follow sign to Winchester; left into Kilham Lane and then right into Sarum Road.
Downland course.
Founded 1888
Designed by H.S. Colt And A.P. Taylor
18 holes, 6212 yards, S.S.S. 70
Visitors: welcome WD; with a member only at WE.
Green Fee: WD £28.
Societies: Mon, Tues and Wed only by prior arrangement; £48.
Catering: full facilities.

2A 98 Rustington Golf Centre
Golfers Lane, Rustington, W Sussex, BN16 4NB
☎(01903) 850790, Fax 850982

A259 at Rushington, between Worthing and Chichester.
Public parkland course.
Pro David Phillips/Gerry Newham; Founded 1995
Designed by David Williams P'ship
9 holes, 5735 yards, S.S.S. 68
Visitors: welcome 9am to 9pm 7 days a week; bookings taken.
Green Fee: WD £8.50; WE £10.50.
Societies: welcome by arrangement; full facilities; terms on application.
Catering: coffee shop serving hot and cold lunches; licensed bar.
Practice range, 30 covered bays, 6 outdoor bays.

2A 99 Ryde
Binstead Rd, Ryde, Isle of Wight, PO33 3NF
☎(01983) 614809, Pro 562088
Main Ryde-Newport road.
Parkland course.
Pro Peter Hammond; Founded 1895
9 holes, 5287 yards, S.S.S. 66
Visitors: welcome; not Wed pm or Sun am.
Green Fee: WD £15; WE £20.
Societies: welcome WD except Wed; contact Sec; facilities and packages by arrangement; terms on application.
Catering: by arrangement.
Hotels: Newlands.

2A 100 Rye
New Lydd Road, Camber, Rye, E Sussex, TN31 7QS
☎(01797) 225241, Fax 225460, Pro 225218
From Rye take the A259 to New Romney; 2 miles out of town turn right towards Camber; course is 1.5 miles on right.
Links course.
Founded 1894
Designed by H.S. Colt
18 holes, 6308 yards, S.S.S. 71
Visitors: welcome, but only with a member.
Green Fee: n/a.
Societies: none.
Catering: full facilities.
Hotels: Hope; Anchor; Mermaid, all in Rye.

2A 101 **Sandford Springs**
Wolverton, Tadley, Hants, RG26 5RT
☎(01635) 297881, Fax 298065, Pro
297883
Off the A339 at Kingsclere between
Basingstoke and Newbury.
Picturesque varied course overlooking
5 counties.
Pro Gary Edmunds; Founded 1988
Designed by Hawtree & Son
27 holes, 6222 yards, S.S.S. 70
Visitors: welcome WD; booking system in operation.
Green Fee: WD £23.
Societies: welcome by prior arrangement; company days arranged; private
suites; 27 holes form 3 courses; others
Park/Wood: 6143 yards, par 70;
Wood/Lakes: 6005 yards, par 69;
packages; terms on application.
Catering: bar and restaurant facilities.
Hotels: Hilton National, Basingstoke.

2A 102 **Seaford**
Firle Road, East Blatchington,
Seaford, E Sussex, BN25 2JD
☎(01323) 892442, Fax 894113, Pro
894160
1 miles N of Seaford on A259
Downland course.
Pro D Mills; Founded 1887
Designed by J.H. Taylor
18 holes, 6551 yards, S.S.S. 71
Visitors: welcome by arrangement.
Green Fee: WD £25; WE £25.
Societies: by arrangement; terms on
application.
Catering: full facilities available.
Hotels: Dormy House available.

2A 103 **Seaford Head**
Southdown Rd, Seaford, E Sussex,
BN25 4JS
☎(01323) 894843, Pro 890139
S of A259, 12 miles from Brighton.
Public seaside course.
Pro Tony Lowles; Founded 1887
18 holes, 5848 yards, S.S.S. 68
Visitors: welcome at all times.
Green Fee: WD £13; WE £15.50.
Societies: welcome; full facilities;
terms on application.
Catering: light snacks.
Hotels: Traslyn.

2A 104 **Sedlescombe**
(Aldershaw)
Sedlescombe, E Sussex, TN33 0SD
☎(01424) 870898
On main A21 near Sedlescombe.
Parkland course.
Pro James Andrews; Founded 1991

18 holes, 6321 yards, S.S.S. 70
Visitors: welcome.
Green Fee: WD £14; WE £15.
Societies: full facilities; terms on
application.
Catering: bar and snacks.
Practice range, 25 bays; floodlit.
Hotels: Brickwall.

2A 105 **Selsey**
Golf Links Lane, Selsey, Chichester,
W Sussex, PO20 9DR
☎(01243) 606442, Pro 602203
On B2145 7 miles S of Chichester.
Seaside course.
Pro Peter Grindley; Founded 1909
9 holes, yards, S.S.S. 68
Visitors: welcome if member of recognised club.
Green Fee: WD £15; WE £15.
Societies: small societies welcome;
full facilities; terms on application.
Catering: lunch and snacks.
Hotels: Chichester Ship (Bedford).

2A 106 **Shanklin & Sandown**
The Fairway, Lake, Sandown, Isle of
Wight, PO36 9PR
☎(01983) 403217, Fax 403217, Pro
404424, Bar/Rest 403170
Off main Sandown & Shanklin road at
Lake (A3055).
Sandy parkland course with some
steep slopes.
Pro Peter Hammond; Founded 1900
Designed by Dr. J. Cowper, James
Braid
18 holes, 6083 yards, S.S.S. 69
Visitors: welcome with h'cap certs;
restrictions at WE before lunch.
Green Fee: WD £22; WE £25.
Societies: welcome on WD except
Tues by prior arrangement; packages
available; terms on application.
Catering: full facilities available.

2A 107 **Singing Hills Golf**
Centre
Albourne, E Sussex, W Sussex, BN6
9EB
☎(01273) 835353, Fax 835444
On the B2117 off the A23.
Parkland course with 3 x 9 holes
(River, Valley & Lake).
Pro Wallace Street; Founded 1992
Designed by Richard Hurd (Sandow)
18 holes, 6601 yards, S.S.S. 71
Visitors: welcome.
Green Fee: WD £10; WE £12.50.
Societies: welcome for groups of
more than 12; prices and packages
vary each day; £23.50-£60.

Catering: restaurant and bar facilities.
Practice range, 15 bays.
Hotels: Hickstead Hotel, Bolney; Birch
Hotel, Haywards Heath.

2A 108 **Slinfold Park Golf &**
Country Club
Stane Street, Slinfold, Horsham, W
Sussex, RH13 7RE
☎(01403) 791154, Fax 791465, Pro
791555
On A29 S of junction with A281.
Parkland course.
Pro George McKay; Founded 1992
Designed by John Fortune
18 holes, 6418 yards, S.S.S. 71
Visitors: welcome.
Green Fee: WD £25; WE £25.
Societies: welcome Mon-Fri although
some restrictions on Tues; full facilities; from £25.
Catering: full facilities.
Practice range, 19 bays floodlit.
Hotels: Ramson Hall, Slinford.

2A 109 **South Winchester**
Pitt, Winchester, Hants, SO22 5QW
☎(01962) 877800, Fax 877900, Pro
840469
S of Winchester on Romsey road.
Championship style links course.
Pro Richard Adams; Founded 1993
Designed by Dave Thomas, Peter
Alliss, Clive Clark
18 holes, 6729 yards, S.S.S. 73
Visitors: guests of members only.
Green Fee: n/a.
Societies: welcome; terms on application.
Catering: full bar and dining facilities.
Practice range for teaching and members only.
Hotels: Lainstone Hotel; Royal Hotel;
Hotel du Vin.

2A 110 **Southampton**
Golf Course Rd, Bassett,
Southampton, Hants, SO16 7AY
☎(01703) 760546, Pro 768407,
Bar/Rest 767996
N end of city, off Bassett Ave, halfway
between Chilworth roundabout and
Winchester Rd roundabout.
Municipal parkland course.
Pro Jon Waring; Founded 1935
18 holes, 6213 yards, S.S.S. 70
Visitors: welcome.
Green Fee: WD £8.20; WE £11.30.
Societies: welcome by arrangement;
full facilities; terms on application.
Catering: breakfast, lunch, bar snacks.
Hotels: Hilton (Chilworth).

2A 111 Southsea

Portsmouth Golf Centre, Great Salterns GC, Burfields Rd, Portsmouth, PO3 5HH
☎(01705) 664549, Fax 650525
2 miles off M27/A27/A3 on E road into Portsmouth.
Municipal meadowland course
Pro Terry Healy; Founded 1935
18 holes, 5575 yards, S.S.S. 67
Visitors: welcome.
Green Fee: WD £11.50; WE £11.50.
Societies: welcome by arrangement; catering available in adjacent farmhouse pub; terms on application.
Catering: available in adjacent farmhouse pub.
Practice range, 24 bays; floodlit.

2A 112 Southwick Park

Pinsley Drive, Southwick, Fareham, Hants, PO17 6EL
☎(01705) 370683, Fax 210289, Pro 380442, Sec 380131
B2177 to Southwick village.
Parkland course.
Pro J Green; Founded 1977
Designed by Charles Lawrie
18 holes, 5992 yards, S.S.S. 69
Visitors: strictly by prior arrangement.
Green Fee: n/a.
Societies: welcome by prior arrangement; 36 holes with coffee, lunch and dinner; £20-£35.
Catering: full bar and dining facilities.

2A 113 Southwood

Ively Rd, Cove, Farnborough, Hants, GU14 0LJ
☎(01252) 548700, Fax 515855, Bar/Rest 515139
0.25 miles W of Farnborough.
Parkland course.
Pro Bob Hammond; Founded 1977
Designed by Hawtree & Son
18 holes, 5738 yards, S.S.S. 68
Visitors: public course.
Green Fee: WD £11.50; WE £14.50.
Societies: welcome on WD; full facilities available; terms on application.
Catering: full facilities.
Hotels: Potters International.

2A 114 Stoneham

Monks Wood Close, Off Bassett Green Rd, Southampton, Hants, SO16 3TT
☎(01703) 768151, Fax 766320, Pro 768397, Sec 769272
Close to M3 and M27.
Undulating parkland course with heather.
Founded 1908

Designed by Willie Park
18 holes, 6310 yards, S.S.S. 70
Visitors: welcome by prior arrangement.
Green Fee: WD £27; WE £30.
Societies: welcome Mon, Thurs and Fri; 36 holes, coffee, lunch and dinner; golf clinic, video analysis; from £49.
Catering: full facilities.
Hotels: Hilton, Southampton.

2A 115 Test Valley

Micheldever Rd, Overton, Nr Basingstoke, Hants, RG25 3DS
☎(01256) 771737, Bar/Rest 770916
2 miles S of Overton village junction with B3400 or1.5 miles N of A303 from Overton turn-off.
Inland links course.
Pro Alastair Briggs; Founded 1992
Designed by D. Wright (E. Darcy)
18 holes, 6883 yards, S.S.S. 72
Visitors: welcome WD and WE; advisable to phone first.
Green Fee: WD £14; WE £20.
Societies: welcome 7 days; full facilities; packages from £18.
Catering: full bar and dining facilities; dining room for up to 100.

2A 116 Tidworth Garrison

Bulford Rd, Tidworth, Wiltshire SP9 7AF
☎(01980) 842301, Fax 842301, Pro 842393, Bar/Rest 842321
A338 Salisbury to Marlborough into Bulford road.
Treelined downland course.
Pro Terry Gosden; Founded 1908
Recent upgrade by Donald Steel
18 holes, 6101 yards, S.S.S. 69
Visitors: welcome.
Green Fee: WD £20; WE £20.
Societies: welcome Tues and Thurs; full facilities and packages on application; £38.
Catering: full catering facilities.

2A 117 Tilgate Forest Golf Centre

Titmus Drive, Tilgate, Crawley, W Sussex, RH10 5EU
☎(01293) 530103, Fax 523478
M23 junction 11 for Pease Pottage, follow main road to Crawley, at 1st roundabout turn right, follow signs.
Public parkland course.
Pro Shaun Trussll; Founded 1983
Designed by Huggett And Coles
18 holes, 6359 yards, S.S.S. 70
Visitors: welcome.
Green Fee: WD £12; WE £16.75.

Societies: welcome Mon-Thurs; full facilities; terms on application.
Catering: restaurant and bar all day.
Practice range, 36 bays; floodlit.
Hotels: Holiday Inn (Crawley).

2A 118 Tournerbury

Tournerbury Lane, Hayling Island, Hants, PO11 9DL
☎(01705) 462266
Off A27 on Hayling Island.
Seaside course.
Pro Robert Brown; Founded 1994
9 holes, 5912 yards, S.S.S. 66
Visitors: welcome; pay and play.
Green Fee: WD £8.80; WE £11.80.
Societies: welcome by arrangement.
Catering: none; local pub.
Practice range, 16 bays; floodlit.
Hotels: Forte Post House.

2A 119 Tylney Park

Rotherwick, Basingstoke, Hants, RG27 9AY
☎(01256) 762079, Fax 763079, Sec 763827
Take M3 to junction 5 and then 2 miles to Rotherwick via Hook.
Parkland course.
Pro Chris de Bruin; Founded 1974
Designed by W. Wiltshire
18 holes, 6200 yards, S.S.S. 69
Visitors: welcome by prior arrangement on WD; h'cap certs needed WE.
Green Fee: WD £20; WE £28.
Societies: welcome Mon to Thurs; 36 holes of golf plus coffee, lunch and dinner; £46.
Catering: full facilities.
Hotels: Tylney Hall.

2A 120 Ventnor

Steephill Down Rd, Ventnor, Isle of Wight, PO38 1BP
☎(01983) 853326
On A3055 to Ventnor.
Undulating downland course.
Founded 1892
12 holes 5767 yards, S.S.S. 68
Visitors: welcome except between 12-3.30pm Wed; not before 1pm Sunday.
Green Fee: WD £12; WE £14.
Societies: welcome by arrangement.
Catering: bar and bar snacks.
Hotels: Eversly; Bonchurch Manor; Mayfair, Shanklin.

2A 121 Waterhall

Waterhall Road, Brighton, E Sussex, BN1 8YR
☎(01273) 508658

3 miles N of Brighton off A27.
Hilly downland course.
Pro Paul Charman; Founded 1923
18 holes, 5713 yards, S.S.S. 68
Visitors: welcome.
Green Fee: WD £14; WE £18.
Societies: welcome; full catering facilities and packages on request; terms on application.
Catering: full facilities.

2A 122 **Waterlooville**
Cherry-Tree Ave, Cowplain,
Waterlooville, Hants, PO8 8AP
☎(01705) 263388, Fax 347513, Pro 256911
A3 (M) junction 3 take B2150 to
Waterlooville; at 1st roundabout take
exit for Hurstwood.
Parkland course.
Pro John Hay; Founded 1907
Designed by Henry Cotton
18 holes, 6602 yards, S.S.S. 72
Visitors: welcome WD.
Green Fee: WD £25.
Societies: welcome Thurs with prior arrangement with secretary; 36 holes of golf; coffee on arrival, light lunch and evening meal; other packages also available; £46.
Catering: full catering and bar facilities.
Hotels: Hilton National.

2A 123 **Wellow**
Ryedown Lane, East Wellow, Romsey,
Hants, SO51 6BD
☎(01794) 322872, Pro 323833
Take M27 to junction 2 then A36 for 2
miles to Whinwhistle road then 1.5
miles to Ryedown Road.
Parkland course; 27 holes, three 9s:
Ryedown, Embley, Blackwater.
Pro Neil Bratley; Founded 1991
Designed by W. Wiltshire
27 holes, 5966 yards
Visitors: welcome 7 days.
Green Fee: WD £16; WE £19.
Societies: welcome on WD; 27 holes,
full catering; terms on application.
Catering: full catering available.
Hotels: Vine Hotel, Ower Romsey;
Bramble Hill, Bramshaw.

2A 124 **Wellshurst Golf & Country Club**
North St, Hellingly, E Sussex, BN27 4EE
☎(01435) 813636, Fax 812444, Pro 813456
Take A267 Heathfield and Wellshurst road.

Parkland course.
Pro Matt Round; Founded 1992
Designed by Golf Corporation
18 holes, 5771 yards, S.S.S. 68
Visitors: public pay and play.
Green Fee: WD £14; WE £17.50.
Societies: welcome; packages available; from £39.
Catering: available.
Practice range, 16 bays and 2 bunker bays.
Hotels: Boship Farm Hotel, Hailsham.

2A 125 **West Chiltington**
Broadford Bridge Road, West
Chiltington, RH20 2YA
☎(01798) 813574, Fax 812631, Pro 812115
On A29 proceed south and turn left at
Advesane.
Undulating parkland course.
Pro Clay Morris; Founded 1988
Designed by Brian Barnes and Max
Faulkner
18 holes, 5877 yards, S.S.S. 69
Visitors: welcome.
Green Fee: WD £15; WE £20.
Societies: welcome; terms on application.
Catering: full facilities.
Hotels: Roundabout Hotel, W
Chiltington; Chequers Hotel,
Pulborough.

2A 126 **West Hove**
Church Farm, Hangleton, Hove, E
Sussex, BN3 8AN
☎(01273) 419738, Fax 439988, Pro
413494, Bar/Rest 413411
On A27 Brighton by-pass at the
Hangleton Interchange.
Downland course relocated in 1990.
Pro Darren Cook; Founded 1910/1991
Designed by Hawtree
18 holes, 6255 yards, S.S.S. 70
Visitors: welcome.
Green Fee: WD £20; WE £25.
Societies: welcome; packages available for groups; terms on application.
Catering: full bar and catering.
Practice range, 15 bays.

2A 127 **West Sussex**
Pulborough, W Sussex, RH20 2EN
☎(01798) 872563, Fax 872033, Pro
872426
1.5 miles E of Pulborough on A283.
Heathland course.
Pro Tim Packham; Founded 1931
Designed by Sir Guy Campbell, Major
C.K. Hutchison
18 holes, 6221 yards, S.S.S. 70

Visitors: welcome WD only.
Green Fee: WD £35; WE £35.
Societies: welcome Wed and Thurs;
full facilities; terms on application.
Catering: lunch and tea.
Practice range, 10 bays.
Hotels: Amberley Castle; Roundabout.

2A 128 **Westridge**
Brading Rd, Ryde, Isle of Wight, PO33 1QS
☎(01983) 613131, Fax 567017
A3054 Ryde to Sandown road 2 miles
S of Ryde.
Flat parkland course.
Pro Mark Wright; Founded 1992
9 holes, 3228 yards, S.S.S. 55
Visitors: welcome.
Green Fee: WD £7-£10; WE £8-£11.
Societies: welcome by arrangement;
terms on application.
Catering: bar and food available,
Practice range, 19 bays floodlit.

2A 129 **Weybrook Park**
Aldermarston Rd, Basingstoke, Hants,
RG24 9NT
☎(01256) 320347, Fax 812973, Pro
333232, Bar/Rest 331159
2 miles NW of town centre between
A339 and A340.
Parkland course.
Pro Anthony Dillon; Founded 1971
18 holes, 6468 yards, S.S.S. 70
Visitors: welcome by arrangement.
Green Fee: WD £16; WE £22.
Societies: welcome by prior arrangement; catering for breakfast, lunch and
dinner, plus 36 holes of golf; £24-£40.
Catering: available.
Practice range, grass.

2A 130 **Wickham Park**
Titchfield Lane, Wickham, Nr
Fareham, Hants, PO17 5PJ
☎(01329) 833342, Fax 834798
2 miles N of Fareham off M27 junc 10.
Parkland course.
Pro Trevor Hill; Founded 1995
Designed by J Payne
18 holes, 6022 yards, S.S.S. 69
Visitors: public pay and play.
Green Fee: WD £9.50; WE £12.50.
Societies: welcome by prior arrangement WD; packages available; society
room; from £14.50.
Catering: clubhouse facilities.

2A 131 **Willingdon**
Southdown Rd, Eastbourne, E
Sussex, BN20 9AA

☎(01323) 410981, Fax 411510, Pro 410984, Bar/Rest 41098
2 miles N of Eastbourne off A22
Downland course.
Pro Jim Debenham; Founded 1898
Designed by J.H. Taylor; modernised by Dr MacKenzie 1925
18 holes, 6044 yards, S.S.S. 69
Visitors: welcome WD.
Green Fee: WD £24; WE £27.
Societies: by prior arrangement WD except Tues; packages available; terms on application.
Catering: by arrangement.
Hotels: Grand; Queens; Lansdown.

2A 132 Worldham Park
Caker Lane, E Worldham, Nr Alton, Hants, GU34 3AG
☎(01420) 543151, Bar/Rest 544606
Take A31, then A3004 to Bordon; course 100 yards on right.
Parkland course.
Pro Jon Le Roux; Founded 1994
Designed by F Whidborne
18 holes, 5864 yards, S.S.S. 68
Visitors: pay and play.
Green Fee: WD £11; WE £13.
Societies: welcome Mon to Fri; minimum 12, maximum 36; meals and 27 holes of golf; £15-£20.
Catering: full bar and catering.
Hotels: Alton Hotel; Swan Hotel.

2A 133 Worthing
Links Rd, Worthing, W Sussex, BN14 9QZ
☎(01903) 260801, Fax 694664, Pro 260718
On A27 near junction with A24.
Downland course.
Pro Stephen Rolley; Founded 1905
Designed by H Vardon
Lower: 18 holes, 6530 yards, S.S.S. 72; Upper: 18 holes, 5243 yards, S.S.S. 66
Visitors: welcome except at WE April-Oct.
Green Fee: WD £30; WE £40.
Societies: welcome by arrangement; full day's golf and catering arrangements; from £50.
Catering: full facilities.
Hotels: Windsor House; Rosedale GH; Ardington Hotel.

2B 1 Abbey Hill
Monks Way, Two Mile Ash, Stony Stratford, MK8 8AA
☎(01908) 562566, Fax 569538, Pro 563845
2 miles S of Stony Stratford.
Parkland course.
Pro K Bond/M Booth; Founded 1982
18 holes, 6122 yards, S.S.S. 69
Visitors: public pay and play.
Green Fee: WD £9.95; WE £13.95.
Societies: welcome WD; golf and catering packages; £19-£25.
Catering: available.
Practice range, 21 bays floodlit.
Hotels: Friendly Hotel, Milton Keynes.

2B 2 Aspect Park
Remenham Hill, Henley-on-Thames, Oxon, RG9 3EH
☎(01491) 578306, Fax 578306, Pro 577562, Bar/Rest 410308
On A4130 Henley-Maidenhead road 0.75 miles from Henley.
Historic parkland course.
Pro Terry Notley; Founded 1988
Designed by Tim Winsland
18 holes, 6559 yards, S.S.S. 71
Visitors: welcome WD; limited WE.
Green Fee: WD £20; WE £25.
Societies: welcome WD; terms on application.
Catering: facilities available.
Practice range, grass.
Hotels: Red Lion.

2B 3 Aylesbury
Hulcott Lane, Bierton, Aylesbury, Bucks, HP22 5GA
☎(01296) 393644, Bar/Rest 399988
1 mile N of Aylesbury on the A418 Leighton Buzzard road.
Parkland course.
Pro Mitch Kierstenson; Founded 1992
Designed by T S Benwell
9 holes, 5488 yards, S.S.S. 67
Visitors: welcome.
Green Fee: WD £9; WE £10.
Societies: welcome at all times; terms on application.
Catering: facilities available.
Practice range, 30 floodlit bays.
Hotels: Forte Crest; Holiday Inn.

2B 4 Aylesbury Park
Oxford Road, Aylesbury, Bucks, HP17 8QQ
☎(01296) 399196, Fax 399196
Parkland course.
Founded 1996
Designed by Hawtree & Son
18 holes, 6150 yards, S.S.S. 69
Visitors: welcome at all times.
Green Fee: WD £12; WE £16.
Societies: welcome at all times; terms on application.
Hotels: Forte Post House; Hartwell House.

2B 5 Aylesbury Vale
Stewkley Rd, Wing, Leighton Buzzard, Beds, LU7 0UJ
☎(01525) 240196, Fax 240848, Pro 240197
3 miles W of Leighton Buzzard between Wing and Stewkley.
Parkland course.
Pro L Bryant/D Marsden; Founded 1990
Designed by D Wright/ Mick Robinson
18 holes, 6612 yards, S.S.S. 72
Visitors: welcome with prior booking.
Green Fee: WD £10; WE £21.
Societies: welcome midweek; coffee, 36 holes of golf, lunch and roast dinner; £30-£40.
Catering: meals and bar facilities.

2B 6 Badgemore Park
Badgemore Park, Henley-on-Thames, Oxon, RG9 4NR
☎(01491) 573667, Fax 576899, Pro 574175, Sec 572206
1 mile from centre of Henley.
Parkland course.
Pro J Dunn; Founded 1972
Designed by Bob Sandow
18 holes, 6112 yards, S.S.S. 69
Visitors: welcome WD and afternoons at WE.
Green Fee: WD £18; WE £28.
Societies: welcome WD; full catering facilities for lunch and dinner; £30-£47.
Catering: full facilities.
Hotels: Red Lion.

2B 7 Banbury
Aynho Road, Adderbury, Banbury, Oxon, OX17 3NT
☎(01295) 810419, Fax 810056 5 miles S of Banbury on the B4100; 10 mins from M40 junction 10.
Parkland course.
Pro Sarah Jarrett; Founded 1994
18 holes, 6365 yards, S.S.S. 70
Visitors: welcome.
Green Fee: WD £8; WE £10.
Societies: welcome by prior arrangement; terms on application.
Catering: clubhouse facilities.
Practice range.

2B 8 Beaconsfield
Seer Green, Beaconsfield, Bucks, HP9 2UR
☎(01494) 676545, Fax 681148, Pro 676616
Off M40 on to A355 Amersham road adjacent to Seer Green/Jordans railway station.
Parkland course.

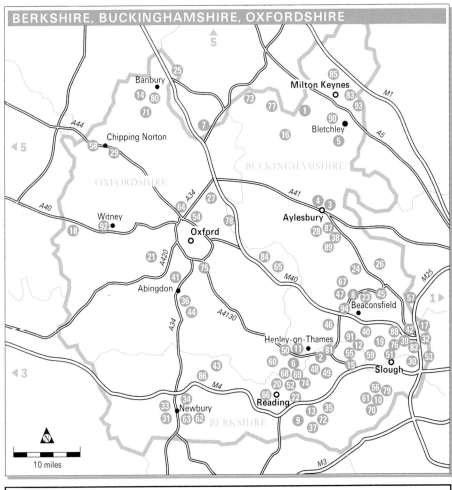

BERKSHIRE, BUCKINGHAMSHIRE, OXFORDSHIRE

KEY				
1 Abbey Hill	19 Burnham Beeches	38 Ellesborough	57 Little Chalfont	78 Studley Wood
2 Aylesbury	20 Calcot Park	39 Farnham Park (Bucks)	58 Lyneham	79 Swinley Forest
3 Aylesbury	21 Carswell Golf &	40 Flackwell Heath	59 Maidenhead Golf Club	80 Tadmarton Heath
4 Aylesbury Park	Country Club	41 Frilford Heath	60 Mapledurham	81 Temple
5 Aylesbury Vale	22 Castle Royle	42 Gerrards Cross	61 Mill Ride	82 Thorney Park
6 Badgemore Park	23 Chalfont Park	43 Goring & Streatley	62 Newbury & Crookham	83 Three Locks
7 Banbury	24 Chartridge Park	44 Hadden Hill	63 Newbury Golf Centre	84 Waterstock
8 Beaconsfield	25 Cherwell Edge	45 Harewood Downs	64 North Oxford	85 Wavendon Golf Centre
9 Bearwood	26 Chesham & Ley Hill	46 Harleyford Golf	65 The Oxfordshire	86 West Berks
10 The Berkshire	27 Chesterton	47 Hazlemere Golf &	66 Pincents Manor	87 Weston Turville
11 Billingbear Park	28 Chiltern Forest	Country Club	67 Princes Risborough	88 Wexham Park
12 Bird Hills	29 Chipping Norton	48 Henley Golf Club	68 Reading	89 Whiteleaf
(Hawthorn Hill)	30 Datchet	49 Hennerton	69 Richings Park	90 Windmill Hill
13 Blue Mountain Golf	31 Deanwood Park	50 Huntercombe	70 Royal Ascot	91 Winter Hill
Centre	32 Denham	51 Huntswood	71 Rye Hill	92 Witney Lakes
14 Brailes	33 Donnington Grove	52 Hurst	72 Sandmartins	93 Woburn
15 Braywick	Country Club	53 Iver	73 Silverstone	94 Wycombe Heights
16 Buckingham	34 Donnington Valley Hotel	54 Kirtlington	74 Sonning	Golf Centre
17 The Buckinghamshire	35 Downshire	55 Lambourne	75 Southfield	
18 Burford	36 Drayton Park	56 Lavender Park Golf	76 Stoke Poges Golf Club	
	37 East Berkshire	Centre	77 Stowe	

BADGEMORE PARK GOLF CLUB
Badgemore, Henley-on-Thames, Oxon RG9 4NR.
Telephone: Henley (STD Code 01491) Professional: 574175, Clubhouse: 573667, Fax: 01491 576899.
Badgemore Park is renowned in the area and prides itself on the friendly welcome all visitors receive. The beautiful but challenging parkland course, founded in 1972, was formerly the McAlpine country estate. A Wide variety of Society days are available. Golfers may also make up specific days to suite their requirements, this can include overnight accommodation.

Pro Michael Brothers; Founded 1914
Designed by H.S. Colt
18 holes, 6030 yards, S.S.S. 71
Visitors: welcome WD with h'cap certs.
Green Fee: WD £30.
Societies: welcome Tues and Wed.
Catering: full facilities.
Practice range, 6 bays; floodlit.
Hotels: Bellhouse.

2B 9 Bearwood
Mole Rd, Sindlesham, Berks, RG11 5DB
☎(0118) 9761330, Pro 9760156, Sec 9760060
On B3030 1.5 miles N of Arborfield Cross.
Parkland course.
Founded 1986
Designed by B Tustin
9 holes, 5600 yards, S.S.S. 72
Visitors: welcome WD; with member at WE.
Green Fee: terms on application.
Catering: facilities and packages available.
Hotels: Reading Moat House.

2B 10 The Berkshire
Swinley Rd, Ascot, Berks, SL5 8AY
☎(01344) 621495
On A332 between Ascot and Bagshot.
Heathland course.
Pro Paul Anderson; Founded 1928
Designed by Herbert Fowler
Red course: 18 holes, 6379 yards, S.S.S. 71; Blue course: 18 holes, 6260 yards, S.S.S. 71
Visitors: welcome by prior arrangement with the secretary.
Green Fee: WD £50.
Societies: welcome by prior arrangement; packages available.
Catering: full clubhouse facilities.
Hotels: Berystede; Cricketers; Royal Foresters.

2B 11 Billingbear Park
The Straight Mile, Wokingham, Berkshire, RG40 5SJ
☎(01344) 869259
From M4 junction 10 take A329M to

Binfield; after Coppid Beech round-about, left at Traveldoge lights; then into Foxley Lane; left at T junction to mini roundabout then right for 1 mile.
Parkland course; second 9-hole course planned.
Pro Martin Blainey; Founded 1994
9 holes, 5750 yards, S.S.S. 68
Visitors: pay and play; advance booking available.
Green Fee: WD £10; WE £12.
Societies: welcome by arrangement.
Catering: none; clubhouse planned.
Hotels: Coppid Beech.

2B 12 Bird Hills (Hawthorn Hill)
Drift Rd, Hawthorn Hill, Nr Maidenhead, Berks, SL6 3ST
☎(01628) 771030, Fax 631023
M4 junction 8/9; take A330 towards Bracknell for 2.5 miles; course on right at crossroads.
Parkland course.
Pro Nick Slimming; Founded 1984
Designed by Clive D. Smith
18 holes, 6176 yards, S.S.S. 69
Visitors: welcome subject to club competitions; pay as you play.
Green Fee: welcome WD; packages available; terms on application.
Catering: extensive facilities including baronial function room.
Practice range, 36 floodlit bays.
Hotels: Holiday Inn, Maidenhead; Frederick's, Maidenhead; Thames Riviera, Maidenhead.

2B 13 Blue Mountain Golf Centre
Wood Lane, Binfield, Berks, RG42 4EX
☎(01344) 300200, Fax 360960
At Binfield on the A322 off the A329.
Parkland course with lake features.
Founded 1992
18 holes, 6097 yards, S.S.S. 70
Visitors: welcome any day.
Green Fee: WD £14; WE £18.
Societies: welcome; £18.50-£50.
Catering: full restaurant and hospitality facilities.
Practice range, 33 bays; floodlit with video and tuition.

2B 14 Brailes
Sutton Lane, Lower Brailes, Banbury, Oxon, OX15 5BB
☎(01608) 685336, Pro 685633, Bar/Rest 685722
On B4035 4 miles from Shipston on Stour towards Banbury.
Parkland/meadowland course.
Founded 1992
Designed by Brian A. Hull
18 holes, 6270 yards, S.S.S. 70
Visitors: welcome.
Green Fee: WD £16; WE £22.
Societies: welcome Mon, Tues, Fri and afternoons on Wed and Thurs; lunch and dinner available; from £30.
Catering: full facilities and bar.

2B 15 Braywick
Braywick Road, Maidenhead, Berks, SL6 1DH
☎(01628) 676910
On A308 Maidenhead to Windsor road.
Parkland course.
Pro Mike Upcott; Founded 1992
Designed by Mike Upcott
9 holes, 2514 yards, S.S.S. 55
Visitors: with member only.
Green Fee: WD £7.50; WE £7.50
Catering: by arrangement.
Practice and driving range.
Hotels: Oakley Court.

2B 16 Buckingham
Tingewick Rd, Buckingham, Bucks, MK18 4AE
☎(01280) 815566, Fax 821812, Pro 815210, Bar/Rest 813282
2 miles SW of Buckingham on A421.
Parkland course.
Pro Tom Gates; Founded 1914
18 holes, 6068 yards, S.S.S. 69
Visitors: welcome WD.
Green Fee: WD £28.
Societies: welcome Tues and Thurs; bar, restaurant, conference facilities, full day's golf; £47.
Catering: full facilities.
Hotels: Four Pillars; Villiers.

2B 17 The Buckinghamshire
Denham Court, Denham Court Drive, Denham, Bucks, UB9 5BG

☎(01895) 835777, Fax 835210
Follow signs to Denham Country Park
from M40 junction 1.
Gently undulating parkland course.
Pro John O'Leary; Founded 1992
Designed by John Jacobs
18 holes, 6880 yards, S.S.S. 73
Visitors: members' guests only.
Green Fee: WD £45; WE £55.
Societies: by prior arrangement only;
full catering and bar facilities; lunch
and dinner; £90-£130.
Catering: catering and clubhouse bar.
Hotels: Bull Hotel; Bellhouse both
Gerrards Cross.

2B 18 **Burford**
Burford, Oxon, OX18 4JG
☎(01993) 822583, Fax 822801, Pro
822344
19 miles W of Oxford at junction of
A40 and A361 at Burford roundabout.
Parkland course.
Pro Norman Allen; Founded 1936
18 holes, 6414 yards, S.S.S. 71
Visitors: by arrangement, Mon-Fri
only.
Green Fee: apply for details.
Societies: limited.
Catering: full facilities.

2B 19 **Burnham Beeches**
Green Lane, Burnham, Bucks SL1
8EG
☎(01628) 661448, Fax 668968, Pro
661661
M40 exit Beaconsfield, follow signs to
Slough, turn right and follow Burnham
signs (not Burnham Beeches) to
Green Lane.
Parkland course.
Pro Ronnie Bolton; Founded 1891
18 holes, 6449 yards, S.S.S. 71
Visitors: welcome WD; at WE only
with member.
Green Fee: WD £30.
Societies: welcome Wed, Thurs, Fri;
full catering facilities; from £62.
Catering: full facilities except Mon.

2B 20 **Calcot Park**
Bath Rd, Calcot, Reading, RG31 7RN
☎(0118) 9427124, Fax 9453373, Pro
9427797, Bar/Rest 9414952
1.5 miles from M4 junction 12 on A4.
Parkland course.
Pro I J Campbell; Founded 1930
Designed by H.S. Colt
18 holes, 6283 yards, S.S.S. 70
Visitors: welcome WD.
Green Fee: WD £36.
Societies: welcome WD; minimum of

15 with £100 deposit; coffee, lunch,
dinner, 36 holes, trolley hire, course
planners and refreshment hut; £55.
Catering: full facilities.

2B 21 **Carswell Golf & Country Club**
Carswell, Nr. Faringdon, Oxon SN7
8PU
☎(01367) 870422
Off A420 near Faringdon.
Parkland course.
Pro Geoff Robbins; Founded 1993
Designed by Ely Brothers
18 holes, 6133 yards, S.S.S. 70
Visitors: welcome at all times.
Green Fee: WD £13; WE £18.
Societies: welcome WD only; full
facilities; terms on application.
Catering: facilities available.
Practice range, 19 bays covered flood-
lit.
Hotels: Sudbury House.

2B 22 **Castle Royle**
Knowl Hill, Reading, Berks, RG10 9XA
☎(01628) 829252, Fax 829299
From M4 junction 8/9 follow A4 signs
to Reading and course is 2.5 miles.
Inland links course; Founded 1992
Designed by Neil Coles
18 holes, 6828 yards, S.S.S. 73
Visitors: welcome WD with booking
and afternoons at WE.
Green Fee: WD £30; WE £30.
Societies: welcome WD; £60-£110.
Catering: facilities available.
Hotels: Bird in Hand; Holiday Inn,
Maidenhead.

2B 23 **Chalfont Park**
Bowles Farm, Three House Holds,
Chalfont St Giles, Bucks, HP8 4LW
☎(01494) 876293, Fax 874692
Beaconsfield junction off M40; course
is off A413 Amersham road.
Parkland course.
Pro Graeme Stevens; Founded 1994
Designed by J Gaunt
18 holes, 5208 yards, S.S.S. 66
Visitors: welcome WD.
Green Fee: WD £18.
Societies: welcome WD; terms on
application.
Catering: facilities available.
Driving range.

2B 24 **Chartridge Park**
Chartridge, Chesham, Bucks, HP5
2TF
☎(01494) 791772, Fax 786462

From M25 junction 19 take A41 W to
Aylesbury until Chesham sign.
Parkland course.
Pro Peter Gibbins; Founded 1990
Designed by John Jacobs
18 holes, 5516 yards, S.S.S. 67
Visitors: welcome with booking.
Green Fee: WD £20; WE £25.
Societies: welcome by arrangement;
unlimited golf and catering; from £10.
Catering: full catering facilities.
Hotels: club can recommend.

2B 25 **Cherwell Edge**
Chacombe, Banbury, Oxon, OX17
2FN
☎(01295) 711591, Fax 712404
3 miles E of Banbury, A442 to
Northampton; 1.5 miles E of M40 junc-
tion 11.
Parkland course.
Pro Joe Kingston; Founded 1983
Designed by Richard Davies
18 holes, 5947 yards, S.S.S. 68
Visitors: welcome any time.
Green Fee: WD £12; WE £15.
Societies: welcome by arrangement;
full facilities; £33 full day.
Catering: lunches, bar snacks,
evening meals.
Practice range, 18 bays; floodlit.
Hotels: Whatley Arms.

2B 26 **Chesham & Ley Hill**
Ley Hill, Chesham, Bucks, HP5 1UZ
☎(01494) 784541, Fax 785506 Off
A41 on B4504 to Ley Hill.
Parkland course.
Founded 1900
9 holes, 5296 yards, S.S.S. 66
Visitors: welcome Mon and Thurs all
day; afternoon Wed and after 4pm Fri.
Green Fee: WD £12.
Societies: welcome on Thurs by prior
arrangement; full catering facilities and
36 holes of golf; various menus; £39.
Catering: facilities.
Hotels: Crown, Old Amersham.

2B 27 **Chesterton**
Chesterton, Nr Bicester, Oxon, OX6
8TE
☎(01869) 241204, Pro 242023
1 mile from M40 exit 9 by A41 towards
Bicester, 2nd left, left again at Red
Cow, 150 yards on right.
Meadowland course.
Pro Jack Wilkshire; Founded 1973
Designed by R.R. Stagg
18 holes, 6229 yards, S.S.S. 70
Visitors: no restrictions.
Green Fee: WD £12; WE £15.

Societies: welcome WD (except Tues) by arrangement; min 12 persons; full facilities; £35. Practice range, complete summer 1998. **Hotels:** Littlebury (Bicester).

2B 28 Chiltern Forest

Aston Hill, Halton, Aylesbury, Bucks, HP22 5NQ
☎(01296) 631267, Fax 631267, Pro 631817, Bar/Rest 630899
Between Aylesbury, Tring and Wendover.
Wooded hilly course.
Pro Chris Skeet; Founded 1920
18 holes, 5760 yards, S.S.S. 70
Visitors: welcome WD; with member at WE.
Green Fee: WD £23; WE £23.
Societies: welcome Mon, Wed and Thurs; full day of golf, lunch and dinner; £40.
Catering: full facilities.
Hotels: Red Lion, Wendover; Forte, Aylesbury.

2B 29 Chipping Norton

Southcombe, Chipping Norton, Oxon, OX7 5QH
☎(01608) 641150, Fax 645422, Pro 643356, Sec 642383, Bar/Rest 644321
Follow A44 to Evesham from Oxford and turn left at Chipping Norton sign; club 50 yards.
Downland course.
Pro Derek Craik Jnr; Founded 1890
18 holes, 6241 yards, S.S.S. 70
Visitors: welcome WD; with members at WE.
Green Fee: WD £20; WE £12.
Societies: welcome WD by prior arrangement; morning coffee, buffet lunch and evening meal with full day of golf (27 or 36 holes); £38.
Catering: full facilities.
Hotels: Crown & Cushion; White Hart; Fox – all Chipping Norton.

2B 30 Datchet

Buccleuch Rd, Datchet, Slough, Berks, SL3 9BP
☎(01753) 5438872 miles from Slough and Windsor, easy access from M4.
Parkland course.
Pro Julian Goodman; Founded 1890
9 holes, 5978 yards, S.S.S. 70
Visitors: welcome WD, 9am-3pm.
Green Fee: WD £16; WE £16.
Societies: small societies welcome on Tues only; full facilities; terms on application.

Catering: bar snacks and lunches available.
Hotels: The Manor.

2B 31 Deanwood Park

Stockcross, Newbury, Berks, RG20 8JS
☎(01635) 48772, Fax 48772 From A4 take B4000 towards Stockcross; 500 yards on rt.
Parkland course.
Pro Nat Summers; Founded 1995
Designed by Dion Beard
9 holes, 4228 yards, S.S.S. 61
Visitors: welcome with prior booking.
Green Fee: WD £13; WE £15.
Societies: welcome by prior arrangement; full practice, clubhouse facilities; packages available; terms on application.
Catering: bar and restaurant.
Hotels: Elcot Park; Folley Lodge.

2B 31 Denham

Tilehouse Lane, Denham, Bucks, UB9 5DE
☎(01895) 832022, Fax 835340, Pro 832801
From M40 take Uxbridge/Gerrards Cross turn off on to A40 towards Gerrards Cross; right on to A412 towards Watford; 2nd turning left.
Parkland course.
Pro Stuart Campbell; Founded 1910
Designed by H.S. Colt
18 holes, yards, S.S.S. 71
Visitors: welcome Mon-Thurs by prior arrangement.
Green Fee: WD £36.
Societies: welcome Tues, Wed, Thurs by prior arrangement; from £53 for full day's package.
Catering: full facilities; lunches served daily.
Hotels: Bull, Gerrards Cross.

2B 33 Donnington Grove Country Club

Grove Road, Donnington, Newbury, Berks, RG14 2LA
☎(01635) 581000, Fax 552259, Pro 551975
Follow signs to Donnington Castle off A34, 2.5 miles, Grove Rd on right.
Moorland/parkland course.
Pro Gareth Williams; Founded 1993
Designed by Dave Thomas
18 holes, 7045 yards, S.S.S. 74
Visitors: must become day member.
Green Fee: WD £30; WE £35.
Societies: welcome; full facilities, tennis courts, lake fishing; from £36.

Catering: Japanese and English restaurant.
Hotels: on site.

2B 34 Donnington Valley Hotel

Oxford Road, Donnington, Newbury, Berks, RG16 9AG
☎(01635) 550464
Off the old Oxford road N of Newbury.
Parkland course.
Pro Edward Lainchbury; Founded 1985
18 holes, 4029 yards, S.S.S. 60
Visitors: welcome.
Green Fee: WD £13; WE £17.
Societies: welcome by prior arrangement; packages on request.
Catering: full facilities.
Hotels: Donnington Valley.

2B 35 Downshire

Easthampstead Park, Wokingham, Berks, RG11 3DH
☎(01344) 302030, Fax 301020
Between Bracknell and Wokingham off Nine Mile Ride.
Municipal parkland course.
Pro Wayne Owers/Chris Gurney; Founded 1973
Designed by F. Hawtree
9 holes, 6416 yards, S.S.S. 70
Visitors: welcome.
Green Fee: WD £10.50; WE £13.50.
Societies: welcome by arrangement.
Catering: full bar and restaurant.
Practice range, 40 bays covered.
Hotels: Ladbroke Mercury; St Annes Manor.

2B 36 Drayton Park

Steventon Rd, Drayton, Oxon, OX14 2RR
☎(01235) 528989, Fax 525731, Pro 550607
2 miles S of Abingdon off A34.
Parkland course.
Pro Dinah Masey; Founded 1992
Designed by Hawtree & Co
18 holes, 5503 yards, S.S.S. 67
Also: 9 holes, 776 yards, par 3
Visitors: welcome.
Green Fee: WD £12; WE £15.
Societies: welcome; packages available.
Catering: full bar and dining facilities.
Practice range, 21 bays; floodlit.

2B 37 East Berkshire

Ravenswood Ave, Crowthorne, Berks, RG45 6BD
☎(01344) 772041, Fax 777378, Pro 774112

M3 junction 3 towards Bracknell and follow Crowthorne signs.
Heathland course.
Pro Arthur Roe; Founded 1903
Designed by P. Paxton
18 holes, 6344 yards, S.S.S. 70
Visitors: welcome WD.
Green Fee: WD £35; WE £35.
Societies: welcome Thurs and Fri only; golf, lunch and dinner; £60.
Catering: clubhouse facilities.
Hotels: Waterloo.

2B 38 Ellesborough
Butlers Cross, Aylesbury, Bucks, HP17 0TZ
☎(01296) 622114, Pro 623126
On B4010 1 mile W of Wendover.
Undulating downland course.
Pro Mark Squire; Founded 1906
Designed by James Braid
18 holes, 6283 yards, S.S.S. 71
Visitors: welcome WD except Tues.
Green Fee: WD £25.
Societies: welcome by prior arrangement; packages available for full day's golf and catering; from £55.
Catering: full clubhouse facilities available.
Hotels: Red Lion, Wendover.

2B 39 Farnham Park (Bucks)
Park Rd, Stoke Poges, Bucks, SL2 4PJ
☎(01753) 647065, Pro 643332, Bar/Rest 643335
M4 junction 5 take A355 to Farnham Pump; at 2nd roundabout turn rightt into Park Road.
Parkland course.
Pro Paul Warner; Founded 1977
Designed by Hawtree & Sons
18 holes, 6172 yards, S.S.S. 69
Visitors: public pay and play.
Green Fee: WD £9; WE £12.
Societies: welcome Tues and Thurs; terms on application.
Catering: full clubhouse facilities available.
Hotels: Burnham Beeches.

2B 40 Flackwell Heath
Treadaway Rd, Flackwell Heath, Bucks, HP10 9PE
☎(01628) 520027, Fax 530040, Sec 520929
Off A40 High Wycombe-Beaconsfield road at Loudwater roundabout; 1.5 miles from M40 junction 3 or 4.
Undulating heathland course.
Pro Paul Watson; Founded 1905
18 holes, 6211 yards, S.S.S. 70

Visitors: welcome WD with h'cap certs.
Green Fee: WD £20.
Societies: welcome Wed & Thurs only.
Catering: full facilities Tues-Sun; limited Mon.
Hotels: Bellhouse; Crest.

2B 41 Frilford Heath
Frilford Heath, Abingdon, Oxon, OX13 5NW
☎(01865) 390864, Fax 390883, Pro 390887, Sec 390866, Bar/Rest 390865
3 miles W of Abingdon on A338 adjacent to Frilford village
Parkland/heathland course.
Pro Derek Craik; Founded 1908
Designed by J.H. Taylor, C.K. Cotton And S. Gidman
18 holes, 6884 yards, S.S.S. 73
Visitors: welcome with h'cap certs.
Green Fee: WD £45; WE £60.
Societies: welcome WD; packages using 3 golf courses available; £70-£80.
Catering: full clubhouse facilities available.
Hotels: Four Pillars, Abingdon.

2B 42 Gerrards Cross
Chalfont Park, Gerrards Cross, Bucks, SL9 0QA
☎(01753) 883263, Fax 883593, Pro 885300, Bar/Rest 884740
Off A413 at Gerrards Cross.
Wooded parkland course.
Pro Matthew Barr; Founded 1922
Designed by Bill Pedlar
18 holes, 6212 yards, S.S.S. 70
Visitors: h'cap certs required.
Green Fee: WD £32; WE £32.
Societies: welcome on Thurs and Fri with h'cap certs; terms on application.
Catering: full facilities.
Hotels: Bull; Bellhouse Gerrards Cross.

2B 43 Goring & Streatley
Rectory Rd, Streatley-on-Thames, Berks, RG8 9QA
☎(01491) 873229, Fax 875224, Pro 873715
On A417 Wantage road 0.25 miles from the Streatley crossroads.
Parkland course.
Pro Roy Mason; Founded 1895
18 holes, 6320 yards, S.S.S. 70
Visitors: welcome WD; WE with member.
Green Fee: WD £30.
Societies: welcome by prior arrangement; packages available; from £52.

Catering: full restaurant facilities.
Hotels: Swan Diplomat, Streatley; Miller at Mansfield, Goring.

2B 44 Hadden Hill
Wallingford Rd, Didcot, Oxon, OX11 9BJ
☎(01235) 510656, Fax 510656, Sec 510410
On A4130 E of Didcot.
Parkland course.
Pro Adrian Waters; Founded 1990
Designed by Michael V. Morley
18 holes, 6563 yards, S.S.S. 71
Visitors: welcome; start times are bookable.
Green Fee: WD £12.50; WE £16.50.
Societies: welcome WD by arrangement; packages available.
Catering: full bar and restaurant.
Practice range, 20 bays; floodlit.
Hotels: George; Springs, both Wallingford; George; White Hart, both Dorchester.

2B 45 Harewood Downs
Cokes Lane, Chalfont St Giles, Bucks, HP8 4TA
☎(01494) 762308, Fax 766869, Pro 764102, Sec 762184
2 miles E of Amersham on A413.
Rolling tree-lined parkland course.
Pro GC Morris; Founded 1903
18 holes, 5958 yards, S.S.S. 69
Visitors: welcome with advance booking.
Green Fee: WD £27; WE £33.
Societies: welcome; 2 rounds of golf and full day's catering with refreshment hut; from £56.
Catering: full clubhouse facilities available.

2B 46 Harleyford Golf
Henley Road, Marlow, Bucks, SL7 2SP
☎(01628), Fax 487434, Pro 402300
On A4155 Marlow-Henley road 2 miles from Marlow town centre.
Downland course.
Pro Alistair Barr; Founded 1996
Designed by Donald Steel
18 holes, 6604 yards, S.S.S. 72
Visitors: welcome by arrangement.
Green Fee: WD £40; WE £60.
Societies: welcome by prior arrangement; minimum 12 maximum 60; winter and summer packages available; terms on application.
Catering: full clubhouse facilities.
Practice range.
Hotels: Danesfield House.

FRILFORD HEATH GOLF CLUB

Visitors and Societies are warmly welcomed to Frilford Heath Golf Club one of a select group of complexes able to boast 54 holes of championship golf. Founded in 1908 on traditional heathland it offers a true test of golf on three distinctive course layouts. The recently enlarged and refurbished clubhouse also provides a warm and attractive atmosphere for refreshment and dining. For further details please contact – **Frilford Heath Golf Club, Abingdon, Oxon OX13 5NW. Tel: 01865**

2B 47 Hazlemere Golf & Country Club

Penn Rd, Hazlemere, Bucks, HP15 7LR
☎(01494) 714722, Fax 713914, Pro 718298
4 miles N of M40 junction 4 on A404.
Parkland course.
Pro A McKay/P Harrison; Founded 1982
Designed by Terry Murray
18 holes, 5873 yards, S.S.S. 68
Visitors: welcome.
Green Fee: WD £15; WE £15.
Societies: welcome; packages available; from £45.
Catering: full restaurant and bar facilities.
Hotels: White Harte, Beaconsfield; Bellhouse; Bull, Gerrards Cross; Crown, Amersham.

2B 48 Henley Golf Club

Harpsden, Henley-on-Thames, Oxon, RG9 4HG
☎(01491) 575742, Fax 412179, Pro 575710, Bar/Rest 575781
1 mile SW of Henley; off A4155 Henley-Reading road.
Parkland course.
Pro Mark Howell; Founded 1907
Designed by James Braid
18 holes, 6329 yards, S.S.S. 70
Visitors: welcome WD with h'cap certs and prior arrangement; WE with member.
Green Fee: WD £30; WE £30.
Societies: Wed and Thurs only; packages available; £57.50.
Catering: full clubhouse facilities.

2B 49 Hennerton

Crazies Hill Rd, Wargrave, Reading, Berks, RG10 8LT
☎(0118) 9401000, Fax 9401042, Pro 9404778
Off A321 into Wargrave village; club signposted.
Parkland course.
Pro William Farron; Founded 1992
Designed by Col. Dion Beard
9 holes, 5460 yards, S.S.S. 67
Visitors: welcome with prior booking.
Green Fee: WD £15; WE £18.

Societies: welcome; terms on application.
Catering: full bar and restaurant facilities.
Practice range, 7 bays.

2B 50 Huntercombe

Nuffield, Henley-on-Thames, Oxon, RG9 5SL
☎(01491) 641207, Fax 642060, Pro 641241
On A4130 6 miles from Henley towards Oxford.
Woodland/heathland course.
Pro J Draycott; Founded 1902
Designed by Willie Park Jnr
18 holes, 6311 yards, S.S.S. 70
Visitors: welcome WD; no 3 or 4 balls.
Green Fee: WD £27.
Societies: welcome Tues and Thurs only.
Catering: restaurant and bar facilities.
Hotels: White Hart, Nettlebed.

2B 51 Huntswood

Taplow Common Rd, Burnham, Bucks, SL1 8LS
☎(01628) 667144
Off M4 junction7; turn left at roundabout and then right at next miniroundabout; straight on for 1.5 miles and course is just past Grovefield Hotel.
Wooded valley course.
Pro Alan Lithins; Founded 1996
9 holes, 5138 yards, S.S.S. 64
Visitors: welcome.
Green Fee: WD £11; WE £14.
Societies: welcome by prior arrangement with club manager Mark Collard; packages available; terms on application.
Catering: full bar and catering; Sun lunches.
Hotels: Grovefield.

2B 52 Hurst

Sandford Lane, Hurst, Berks, RG10 0SQ
☎(0118) 9345143 Sec, 9344355
Between Reading and Twyford signposted from Hurst village.

Parkland course.
Founded 1977
9 holes, 6308 yards, S.S.S. 70
Visitors: welcome.
Green Fee: WD terms on application.
Societies: welcome by prior arrangement.
Catering: bar facilities.

2B 53 Iver

Hollow Hill Lane, Langley Park Rd, Iver, Bucks, SL0 0JJ
☎(01753) 655615, Fax 654225
Near Langley station.
Parkland course.
Pro Karl Teschner; Founded 1984
Designed by David Morgan
9 holes, 6288 yards, S.S.S. 70
Visitors: welcome.
Green Fee: WD £10; WE £13.50.
Societies: welcome; packages available; terms on application.
Catering: full facilities.
Practice range, 18 bays, 9 covered.
Hotels: Marriott.

2B 54 Kirtlington

Kirtlington, Oxon, OX5 3JY
☎(01869) 351133, Fax 351143
On A34 to Kirtlington off M40 junction 9.
Parkland course.
Pro Peter Hughes; Founded 1995
Designed by Graham Webster
18 holes, 6084 yards, S.S.S. 69
Visitors: welcome.
Green Fee: WD £15; WE £20.
Societies: welcome; packages available; terms on application.
Catering: full facilities.
Practice range, 12 bays.

2B 55 Lambourne

Dropmore Rd, Burnham, Bucks SL1 8NF
☎(01628) 666755, Fax 663301, Pro 662936, Bar/Rest 669984
From M4 junction 7 to Slough and Burnham; M40 junction 2 to Burnham.
Parkland course.
Pro David Hart; Founded 1991
Designed by Donald Steel
18 holes, 6771 yards, S.S.S. 72
Visitors: welcome WD with h'cap certs.

Berkshire, Buckinghamshire, Oxfordshire

In the early days of county golf, Berkshire, Buckinghamshire and Oxfordshire were so thin on the ground in terms of courses that an amalgamation was approved. Nowadays, they can boast as many Clubs as Surrey and more than any other county except Lancashire and Yorkshire but, as you would expect from an area which stretches from the verge of London to Gloucestershire, there is plenty of variety.

Castle Royle, Harleyford, Mill Ride, Mentmore, Waterstock, Lambourne, Rye-hill and the Oxfordshire represent the newer front, although the Oxfordshire does not admit casual green fee payers. It is part of the Nitto Kogyo Company which owns Turnberry and lies in the heart of the countryside near Thame, a stone's throw from the M40. Opened in 1993, it has already housed a major event on the Women's professional tour and early in 1995 was preparing for the Benson and Hedges Tournament on the men's European tour.

Another established venue for both men's and women's tours is Woburn with its Duke's and Duchess courses now 20 years old but, not far away, Abbey Hill and Windmill Hill extol the virtues of the more public type of operation, a department in which these counties are better served than most.

There is Downshire near Bracknell, Farnham Park and Wexham Park near Slough, Hawthorn Hill near Maidenhead and Cherwell Edge near Banbury. More and more such courses are necessary if the demands of the army of new golfers can come close to being met but many of these counties' gems remain the longer established Clubs.

There is nothing better than a day's golf over the Red and Blue courses at the Berkshire, with a marvellous lunch to rebuild the spirits if the heather has taken its toll. The same goes for Swinley Forest across the road where the Walter Mitty in you imagines it to be your own private course while the character of heather and birch is echoed by East Berks at Crowthorne, another delightful place to play.

Stoke Poges, Denham and Beaconsfield form a convenient triangle for those staying in the area and seeking a change of scene, the clubhouses at Denham and Beaconsfield lending a cosy, rural air unusual so close to London.

Out beyond Harewood Downs and Amersham, the Vale of Aylesbury beckons, where Ellesborough, near Chequers, offers an ideal stopping place for 18 holes with an unmistakable feeling of having got away from it all.

Over in Berkshire again, Maidenhead, Sonning, Temple and Calcot are always worth a visit while Newbury and Crookham is one of the oldest courses in England. Travellers through Pangbourne along the Thames Valley should look out for Goring & Streatley. Oxfordshire's best known names are Huntercombe and Frilford Heath, the latter with three courses of charm and challenge. Frilford has housed a number of important events, including the 1987 English championship for men.

Since its earliest days, Huntercombe has assumed a more enclosed look, the appearance of the common now liberally laced with trees and bushes. Its distinctive greens bear the hallmark of Willie Park, designer of the Old course at Sunningdale who used to declare that "a man who can putt is a match for anyone".

Mill Ride at North Ascot, a mile or so from the Berkshire, is now well established but one of the most attractive new courses is Harleyford, on the road out of Marlow towards Henley. It is part of the Harleyford Estate which runs down to the Thames, the higher part looking out across the river to Temple, which is situated on the Henley road out of Maidenhead.

Green Fee: WD £36; WE £36.
Societies: not welcome.
Catering: full clubhouse facilities available.
Practice range, grass.
Hotels: Burnham Beeches.

2B 56 Lavender Park

Swinley Rd, Ascot, Berks, SL5 8BD
☎(01344) 884074, Pro 886096
On A329 opposite the Royal Foresters Hotel.
Parkland course.
Pro David Johnson; Founded 1974
9 holes, 2248 yards, S.S.S. 56
Visitors: welcome any time.
Green Fee: WD £5; WE £8.
Societies: welcome by prior arrangement.
Catering: full bar and catering facilities available.
Practice range, 30 bays; floodlit.
Hotels: Royal Foresters.

2B 57 Little Chalfont

Lodge Lane, Little Chalfont, Bucks, HP8 4 AJ
☎(01494) 764877, Fax 762860, Pro 762942
From M25 junction 18 take A404 towards Amersham; course first left after garden centre.
Parkland course.
Pro J Redpath; Founded 1982
Designed by James Dunne
9 holes, 5852 yards, S.S.S. 68
Visitors: welcome by prior arrangement.
Green Fee: WD £10; WE £12.
Societies: welcome by arrangement; package includes day's golf and full catering; £30.
Catering: bar and clubhouse.
Hotels: White Hart.

2B 58 Lyneham

Lyneham, Chipping Norton, Oxon, OX7 6QQ
☎(01993) 831841, Fax 831775
1 mile off A361 Chipping Norton to Burford road.
Parkland course with water hazards.
Pro R Jefferies; Founded 1992
Designed by D. Carpenter, A. Smith
18 holes, 6669 yards, S.S.S. 72
Visitors: welcome.
Green Fee: WD £15; WE £18.
Societies: welcome; full day's golf and catering available; scorecard and scoreboard administration available; £28-£38.
Catering: full facilities.

Hotels: Mill, Kingham; Crown & Cushion, Chipping Norton; Kings Arms; Chipping Norton.

2B 59 Maidenhead Golf Club

Shoppenhangers Road, Maidenhead, Berkshire, SL6 2PZ
☎(01628) 624693, Fax 624693, Pro 624067, Bar/Rest 635321
Off A404 signposted Henley.
Parkland course.
Pro S Geary; Founded 1896
18 holes, 6364 yards, S.S.S. 70
Visitors: welcome WD; not afternoons on Fri.
Green Fee: WD £28; WE £28.
Societies: welcome Wed and Thurs; terms on application.
Catering: full catering and bar facilities.
Hotels: Fredericks; Holiday Inn.

2B 60 Mapledurham

Chazey Heath, Mapledurham, Reading, Berks, RG4 7UD
☎(0118) 9463353, Fax 9463363
Off A4074 NW of Reading 1.5 miles from Mapledurham village.
Undulating parkland course.
Pro Simon O'Keefe; Founded 1992
Designed by MRM Sandow
18 holes, 5621 yards, S.S.S. 67
Visitors: welcome.
Green Fee: WD £14; WE £17.
Societies: welcome by prior arrangement; packages available; terms on application.
Catering: bar and restaurant facilities available.
Practice range.
Hotels: Holiday Inn, Caversham.

2B 61 Mill Ride

Mill Ride Estate, Mill Ride, North Ascot, Berkshire, SL5 8LT
☎(01344) 891494, Fax 886820, Pro 886777, Bar/Rest 886777
From Ascot take A329 until lights, then right into Fernbank Road, which leads to Mill Ride.
Blend of parkland and links course.
Pro Mark Palmer; Founded 1991
Designed by Donald Steel
18 holes, 6762 yards, S.S.S. 72
Visitors: welcome by prior arrangement only.
Green Fee: WD £35; WE £50.
Societies: terms on application.
Catering: full catering and club facilities.
Hotels: Royal Berkshire, Ascot; Berystede, Sunningdale.

2B 62 Newbury & Crookham

Bury's Bank Rd, Greenham, Newbury, Berks, RG19 8BZ
☎(01635) 40035, Fax 40035, Pro 31201
2 miles SE of Newbury.
Wooded parkland course of natural beauty.
Pro David Harris; Founded 1873
Designed by J.H. Turner
18 holes, 5940 yards, S.S.S. 68
Visitors: welcome WD.
Green Fee: WD £25; WE £25.
Societies: welcome by prior arrangement; terms on application.
Catering: full clubhouse facilities.
Hotels: Hilton, Newbury.

2B 63 Newbury Golf Centre

The Racecourse, Newbury, Berks, RG14 7NZ
☎(01635) 551464
Signposted off the A34 for racecourse/conference centre.
Parkland course.
Pro Nick Mitchell; Founded 1994
18 holes, 6500 yards, S.S.S. 70
Visitors: welcome.
Green Fee: WD £12; WE £15.
Societies: welcome by prior arrangement.
Catering: full catering facilities available.
Practice range, 20 floodlit bays.
Hotels: Hilton National.

2B 64 North Oxford

Banbury Rd, Oxford, Oxfordshire, OX2 8EZ
☎(01865) 554924, Fax 515921, Pro 553977
Between Kidlington and N Oxford 2.5 miles N of the city centre.
Parkland course.
Pro Robert Harris; Founded 1907
18 holes, 5456 yards, S.S.S. 67
Visitors: welcome WD.
Green Fee: terms on application.
Societies: welcome by prior arrangement; packages available; terms on application.
Catering: full facilities.
Hotels: Moat House; Linton Lodge; Randolph.

2B 65 The Oxfordshire

Rycote Lane, Milton Common, Thame, Oxon, OX9 2PU
☎(01844) 278300, Fax 278003, Pro 278505
M40 junction 7 turn on to A329; club is 1.5 miles on right.

Championship parkland course; hosts B&H Masters.
Pro Ian Mosey; Founded 1993
Designed by Rees Jones
18 holes, 7187 yards, S.S.S. 76
Visitors: members guests' only.
Green Fee: WD £35; WE £55.
Societies: none.
Catering: outstanding clubhouse bar and catering facilities.
Hotels: Manoir aux Quat Saisons, Great Milton; Oxford Belfry, Milton Common.

2B 66 **Pincents Manor**
Pincents Lane, Calcot, Reading, Berks, RF3 5UQ
☎(0118) 9323511
From M4 junction 12, course is 0.5 miles.
Parkland course.
Founded 1995
18 holes, 4882 yards, S.S.S. 68
Visitors: welcome.
Green Fee: WD £6; WE £7.
Societies: welcome by prior arrangement.
Catering: full bar and restaurant facilities.
Hotels: Pincents Manor on site.

2B 67 **Princes Risborough**
Lee Rd, Saunderton Lee, Princes Risborough, Bucks, HP27 9NX
☎(01844) 346989, Fax 274938, Pro 274567
7 miles NW of High Wycombe on A4010.
Parkland course.
Founded 1990
Designed by Guy Hunt
9 holes, 5440 yards, S.S.S. 66
Visitors: welcome.
Green Fee: WD £14; WE £18.
Societies: welcome by prior arrangement; packages available; terms on application.
Catering: full clubhouse facilities available.
Hotels: Rose and Crown, Saunderton.

2B 68 **Reading**
Kidmore End Rd, Emmer Green, Reading, Berks, RG4 8SG
☎(0118) 9472169, Pro 9476115, Sec 9472909, Bar/Rest 9472909
2 miles N of Reading off Peppard Road.
Parkland course.
Pro A R Wild; Founded 1910
18 holes, 6212 yards, S.S.S. 70
Visitors: welcome Mon-Thurs.

Green Fee: WD £30.
Societies: welcome Mon-Thurs; catering packages available; terms on application.
Catering: full catering and bar facilities.
Hotels: Holiday Inn.

2B 69 **Richings Park**
North Park, Iver, Bucks, SL0 9DL
☎(01753), Pro 655352, Sec 655370
From M4 junction 5 head towards Colnbrook; turn left at the lights to Iver.
Parkland course.
Pro Martin Heys; Founded 1995
Designed by Alan Higgins
18 holes, 6094 yards, S.S.S. 69
Visitors: welcome WD.
Green Fee: WD £20.
Societies: welcome WD by arrangement; packages available; terms on application.
Catering: restaurant and function room.
Practice range, 12 bays; academy course.
Hotels: Marriott.

2B 70 **Royal Ascot**
Winkfield Rd, Ascot, Berks, SL5 7LJ
☎(01344) 25175, Fax 872330, Pro 24656
Inside Ascot racecourse.
Heathland course.
Pro Alastair White; Founded 1887
Designed by J.H. Taylor
18 holes, 5716 yards, S.S.S. 68
Visitors: members' guests only.
Societies: welcome Wed and Thurs by prior arrangement; 36 holes, lunch and dinner; £40.
Catering: available by prior arrangement.
Hotels: Royal Berkshire; Berystede.

2B 71 **Rye Hill**
Milcombe, Banbury, Oxon, OX15 4RU
☎(01295) 721818, Fax 720911
Off A361 between Banbury and Chipping Norton, take road signposted Bloxham.
Links style course; 2 holes redesigned in late 1998.
Pro Les Bond; Founded 1993
18 holes, 6692 yards, S.S.S. 72
Visitors: welcome.
Green Fee: WD £10; WE £14.
Societies: welcome by prior arrangement; packages available; terms on application.
Catering: full facilities.
Hotels: White Horse.

2B 72 **Sandmartins**
Finchhampstead Rd, Wokingham, Berks, RG40 3RQ
☎(0118) 9792711, Fax 9770282, Pro 9770265
1 mile S of Wokingham & 4 miles from Reading on B3016.
Parkland first 9; links style back 9.
Pro Andrew Hall; Founded 1993
Designed by E.T. Fox
18 holes, 6204 yards, S.S.S. 70
Visitors: welcome WD.
Green Fee: WD £22; WE £22.
Societies: welcome; minimum 15; various packages available with dining facilities in the Georgian style clubhouse; terrace; video analysis; terms on application.
Catering: full clubhouse catering and bar facilities.
Hotels: Stakis St Annes Manor.

2B 73 **Silverstone**
Silverstone Rd, Stowe, Buckingham, MK18 5LH
☎(01280) 850005, Fax 850150
1.5 miles beyond race track on Silverstone road from Buckingham and Stowe.
Farmland course.
Pro Rodney Holt; Founded 1992
Designed by David Snell
18 holes, 6213 yards, S.S.S. 71
Visitors: welcome.
Green Fee: WD £9.95; WE £13.45.
Societies: welcome WD by prior arrangement; private dining room; 9-hole pitching course; swing analysis; terms on application.
Catering: full bar and restaurant facilities.
Practice range, 11 bays; floodlit.
Hotels: White Hart, Buckingham; Green Man, Syresham; Travelodge, Towcester.

2B 74 **Sonning**
Duffield Rd, Sonning-on-Thames, Berks, RG4 6GJ
☎(0118) 9693332, Fax 9448409, Pro 9692910, Bar/Rest 9272055
S of A4 between Reading and Maidenhead.
Parkland course.
Pro Richard MacDougall; Founded 1914
18 holes, 6366 yards, S.S.S. 70
Visitors: welcome WD with h'cap certs.
Green Fee: on application.
Societies: welcome Wed; terms on application.
Catering: full clubhouse catering.

2B 75 Southfield

Hill Top Rd, Oxford, Oxon, OX4 1PF
☎(01865) 242656, Fax 242158, Pro
244258, Sec 242158, Bar/Rest
248944
1.5 miles SE of Oxford city centre off
B480
Undulating parkland course.
Pro Tony Rees; Founded 1875
Designed by James Braid (1875),
Redesigned H. Colt (1923)
18 holes, 6328 yards, S.S.S. 70
Visitors: welcome WD; with a member only WE.
Green Fee: WD £24.
Societies: welcome but must apply in
writing; home of Oxford Univ GC,
Oxford City and Oxford Ladies; terms
on application.
Catering: full catering facilities in
Southfield restaurant and 19th bar.
Hotels: Randolph Hotel, Oxford;
Travel Inn, Cowley; Eastgate Hotel,
Oxford.

2B 76 Stoke Poges

Stoke Park, Park Rd, Stoke Poges,
Bucks, SL2 4PG
☎(01753) 717171, Fax 717181, Pro
717172, Sec 717162
Off M4 or A4 into Slough to Stoke
Poges Lane, then into Park Road.
Parkland course.
Pro Tim Morrison; Founded 1909
Designed by H.S. Colt
18 holes, 6770 yards, S.S.S. 71
Visitors: welcome except Tues am.
Green Fee: WD £60; WE £125.
Societies: society and corporate days
welcomed; various packages and
prices available on application to the
events organiser; terms on application.
Catering: full facilities.
Practice range, grass.
Hotels: Bellhouse; Bull Gerrards
Cross; Copthorne, Slough; Chequers
Inn, Wooburn Common.

2B 77 Stowe

Stowe, Buckingham, Bucks, MK18
5EH
☎(01280) 816254 Sec, 813650
At Stowe school.
Parkland course.
Founded 1974
9 holes, 4573 yards, S.S.S. 63
Visitors: private; members only.
Green Fee: WD £10; WE £10

2B 78 Studley Wood

The Straight Mile, Horton-cum-Studley,
Oxon, OX33 1BF

☎(01865) 351144, Fax 351166, Pro
351122
From M40 junction 6 take A40 to
Headington roundabout; follow signs
to Headly-cum-Studley.
Woodland course.
Pro Tony Williams; Founded 1996
Designed by Simon Gidman
18 holes, 6315 yards, S.S.S. 71
Visitors: welcome.
Green Fee: WD £20; WE £27.50.
Societies: welcome by prior arrangement.
Catering: restaurant and function
room.
Practice range, 14 bays; floodlit range.
Hotels: Studley Priory.

2B 79 Swinley Forest

Bodens Ride, Coronation Rd, South
Ascot, Berks, SL5 9LE
☎(01344) 20197, Fax 874733, Pro
874811, Sec 874979
2 miles S of Ascot.
Heathland course.
Pro R C Parker; Founded 1909
Designed by H.S. Colt
18 holes, 5952 yards, S.S.S. 69
Visitors: members' guests only.
Green Fee: WD £65; WE £65.
Societies: by introduction of a member only; packages £120.
Catering: clubhouse bar and catering.
Hotels: Royal Berkshire; Highclere;
Berystede.

2B 80 Tadmarton Heath

Wigginton, Banbury, Oxon, OX15 5HL
☎(01608) 737278, Fax 730548, Pro
730047
Off A361 at Banbury Castle on B4035
for 5 miles to Tadmarton.
Heathland course.
Pro Tom Jones; Founded 1922
Designed by Major C.K. Hutchison
18 holes, 5917 yards, S.S.S. 69
Visitors: welcome by arrangement.
Green Fee: terms on application.
Societies: welcome WD except Thurs
by arrangement; 36 max; full day's
golf, coffee, lunch and dinner; £45.
Catering: full facilities.
Hotels: Banbury Manor; Wheatley
Hall; Cromwell Lodge.

2B 81 Temple

Henley Rd, Hurley, Maidenhead,
Berks, SL6 5LH
☎(01628) 824795, Fax 828119, Pro
824254, Bar/Rest 824248
Off A4130 Maidenhead to Henley
Road or A404.

Parkland course.
Pro James Whiteley; Founded 1908
Designed by Willie Park Jnr
18 holes, 6207 yards, S.S.S. 70
Visitors: by appointment only.
Green Fee: WD £25; WE £30.
Societies: by prior appointment; packages available on request; coffee,
lunch and dinner all available; from
£65.
Catering: full clubhouse catering facilities.
Hotels: Compleat Angler, Marlow; Bell
Inn, Hurley.

2B 82 Thorney Park

Thorney Mill Lane, Iver, Bucks, SL0
9AL
☎(01895) 422095
Off A4 at Langley into Parlaunt Road.
Parkland course.
Pro Andrew Killing; Founded 1993
Designed by Grundon Leisure Ltd
9 holes, 5668 yards, S.S.S. 67
Visitors: welcome.
Green Fee: WD £10; WE £13.
Societies: welcome anytime; terms on
application.
Catering: n/a.
Hotels: any Heathrow hotel.

2B 83 Three Locks

Great Brickhill, Milton Keynes, Bucks,
MK17 9BH
☎(01525) 270470, Fax 270470, Pro
270050
3 miles from Leighton Buzzard on
A4146.
Parkland course with several water
hazards.
Founded 1992
Designed by MRM Sandow/ P.
Critchley
18 holes, 6025 yards, S.S.S. 68
Visitors: welcome; booking strongly
recommended.
Green Fee: WD £12.50; WE £14.50.
Societies: welcome with prior booking; various packages available to
cover day's golf and catering; terms on
application.
Catering: full catering facilities available.
Hotels: limited accommodation on
site.

2B 84 Waterstock

Thame Rd, Waterstock, Oxford, OX33
1HT
☎(01844) 338093, Fax 338036
Direct access from M40 junction 8 on
to A418 Thame road.

Parkland course; further 9 holes due 1999.
Pro Andy Wyatt; Founded 1994
18 holes, 6535 yards, S.S.S. 71
Visitors: welcome.
Green Fee: WD £13; WE £16.50.
Societies: welcome by prior arrangement; packages available for groups of 70; terms on application.
Catering: bar and grill facilities.
Practice range, 24 bays; floodlit.
Hotels: Belfry, Milton; County Inn; Travelodge, both Wheatley.

2B 85 **Wavendon Golf Centre**
Lower End Road, Wavendon, Bucks, MK17 8DA
☎(01908) 281811, Fax 281257, Sec 281297, Bar/Rest 281296
M1 junction 13 to A421, 1st left at roundabout; take first left into Lower End Road.
Parkland course.
Founded 1989
Designed by John Drake/Nick Elmer
18 holes, yards, S.S.S. 67
Visitors: public pay and play.
Green Fee: WD £10; WE £14.
Societies: welcome WD and afternoons at WE; packages available; from £24.99.
Catering: facilities; carvery, bar and bar snacks.
Hotels: The Bell, Woburn.

2B 86 **West Berks**
Chaddleworth, Newbury, Berks, RG20 7DU
☎(01488) 638574, Fax 638781, Pro 638851
M4 junction 14 follow signs to RAF Welford.
Downland course.
Pro Paul Simpson; Founded 1975
Designed by R Stagg
18 holes, 7059 yards, S.S.S. 74
Visitors: welcome; afternoons only at WE.
Green Fee: WD £18; WE £22.
Societies: welcome by prior arrangement; packages available; terms on application.
Catering: full facilities.
Hotels: Queens, E Gaston; Blue Boar, Chiveley; Littlecote House, Hungerford.

2B 87 **Weston Turville**
New Rd, Weston Turville, Aylesbury, Bucks, HP22 5QT
☎(01296) 424084, Pro 425949
2 miles from Aylesbury between Aston Clinton and Wendover.

Parkland course.
Pro Gary George; Founded 1975
18 holes, 6008 yards, S.S.S. 69
Visitors: welcome except Sun am.
Green Fee: terms on application.
Societies: welcome WD, some WE, by prior appt; terms on application.
Catering: lunches and evening snacks.
Hotels: Post House.

2B 88 **Wexham Park**
Wexham St, Wexham, Slough, Berks, SL3 6ND
☎(01753) 663271, Fax 663318
2 miles from Slough towards Gerrards Cross; follow signs to Wexham Park Hospital; course 0.5 mile further on.
Parkland course.
Founded 1976
Designed by Emil Lawrence and David Morgan
9 holes, 5323 yards, S.S.S. 66
Visitors: welcome.
Green Fee: WD £10; WE £13.50.
Societies: welcome; full catering facilities; terms on application.
Catering: bar and catering facilities.
Hotels: Wexham Park Hall.

2B 89 **Whiteleaf**
Upper Icknield Way, Whiteleaf, Bucks, HP27 0LY
☎(01844) 343097, Pro 345472, Sec 274058, Bar/Rest 274058
From Monks Risborough turn right into Cadsden road and 100 yards on turn right into Whiteleaf village; course 0.25 miles on left.
Hilly Chilterns course.
Pro Ken Ward; Founded 1904
9 holes, 5391 yards, S.S.S. 66
Visitors: welcome WD and with member at WE.
Green Fee: WD £18; WE £18.
Societies: welcome on Thurs by prior arrangement; packages available; morning coffee, golf, lunch and dinner; £40.
Catering: full facilities.
Hotels: Red Lion, Whiteleaf; Rose & Crown, Saunderton.

2B 90 **Windmill Hill**
Tattenhoe Lane, Bletchley, Milton Keynes, Bucks, MK3 7RB
☎(01908) 631113, Fax 630034
Off A421 through Milton Keynes towards Buckingham.
Parkland course.
Pro Colin Clinghan; Founded 1972
Designed by Henry Cotton

18 holes, 6720 yards, S.S.S. 72
Visitors: welcome.
Green Fee: WD £10.50; WE £13.60.
Societies: welcome WD and after 11 at WE; packages available for catering and golf; from £19.50.
Catering: full clubhouse facilities available.
Practice range, 23 indoor 6 outdoor bays.
Hotels: Forte Crest, Milton Keynes; Shenley, Bletchley.

2B 91 **Winter Hill**
Grange Lane, Cookham, Maidenhead, Berks, SL6 9RP
☎(01628) 527810, Fax 527811, Pro 527610, Sec 527613, Bar/Rest 527811
M4 junction 8/9 through Maidenhead to Cookham; club signposted.
Parkland course.
Pro Roger Frost; Founded 1976
Designed by Charles Lawrie
18 holes, 6408 yards, S.S.S. 71
Visitors: welcome WD; with member at WE.
Green Fee: WD £24; WE £24.
Societies: welcome Wed and Fri; packages can be arranged; terms on application.
Catering: full facilities.
Hotels: Spencers, Cookham.

2B 92 **Witney Lakes**
Downs Road, Witney, Oxon, OX8 5SY
☎(01993) 779000, Fax 778866, Bar/Rest 702020
W of Witney on B4047 Burford road, 1.5 miles from town centre.
Lakeland style course.
Pro Paul Hunt; Founded 1994
Designed by Simon Gidman
18 holes, 6675 yards, S.S.S. 71
Visitors: welcome.
Green Fee: WD £13; WE £18.
Societies: welcome; various packages available; £17-£44.
Catering: full clubhouse facilities.
Practice range, 24 bays; floodlit.
Hotels: Four Pillars, Witney.

2B 93 **Woburn**
Bow Brickhill, Milton Keynes, MK17 9LJ
☎(01908) 370756, Fax 378436, Pro 647987
4 miles W of M1 junction 13; 1 mile E of Little Brickhill junction.
Woodland course
Pro Luther Blacklock; Founded 1976
Designed by Charles Lawrie
Duchess course: 18 holes, 6651

yards, S.S.S. 72; Dukes course: 18 holes, 6961 yards, S.S.S. 74
Visitors: welcome WD by prior arrangement.
Green Fee: on application.
Societies: welcome WD by prior arrangement; terms on application.
Catering: full clubhouse catering, restaurant and bar facilities.
Practice range.

2B 94 **Wycombe Heights Golf Centre**
Rayners Ave, Loudwater, High Wycombe, Bucks, HP10 9SW
☎(01494) 816686, Sec 813185, Fax 816728
Off A40 from M40 junction 3.
Parkland course.
Pro Joseph Awuku; Founded 1991
Designed by John Jacobs

18 holes, 6253 yards, S.S.S. 72
Visitors: pay and play.
Green Fee: WD £11; WE £14.95.
Societies: welcome WD by prior arrangement; packages available; terms on application.
Catering: bar, restaurant, family room. Practice range, 24 floodlit bays.
Hotels: Post House Forte; Cressex; Alexandria.

3
THE SOUTH WEST

Golf in the South West always suggests to me Saunton and Westward Ho! in Devon, St Enodoc and Trevose further down the same coastline in Cornwall. Many new courses have joined the throng in recent years but, historically and sentimentally, this noble quartet head my list. Westward Ho! is pre-eminent on grounds of seniority, older, in fact, than any seaside Club in England, and famous for its golfing sons. Most notable among these are Horace Hutchinson, captain at the age of 16 on account of winning the Club medal in 1875, and JH Taylor, who rose from the caddie ranks to win the Open championship five times.

One of the course's many charms is that so little about it changes. What is more, it has overridden the need for change in spite of the constant manufacture of new equipment. True, the winds invariably spring to its protection but, as an example of the way courses looked and played a hundred years ago, Westward Ho! provides the most authentic reminder. Saunton, or its present version, was, on the other hand, designed more for modern equipment, the West course being right up to date on that score.

Re-established in the 1970s, its greens were redesigned and reconstructed 10 years ago, making it a match for its distinguished neighbour, the East. As a pair, they are as good as any, worthy of the Amateur championship which now needs a qualifying course. New roads also make the South West more accessible, the journey between Saunton and Westward Ho!, in full view of each other across the estuary, much less fraught. The new bridge also assists the journey to Cornwall and the rival attractions of St Enodoc and Trevose which, like their Devon counterparts, are closer as the crow flies than by quaint Cornish lanes.

A description of holiday golf may sound a little disparaging but, in St Enodoc's case, it is apt, although anyone matching the par of 69 will know that challenge and enjoyment go together, the worthiest combination of all. If variety is added to the equation, St Enodoc is better qualified than most, a distinct downland character wedged between the sand dunes and a sight of the sea. Trevose, too, has its devoted patrons, many drawn by its friendly welcome and value for money.

There is a nice contrast between Trevose and St Enodoc, an obvious appeal to golfers. Golfers are great explorers and even the most active will never exhaust the subject any more than will lovers of wine. In the days after World War II, before Majorca was "invented" and British seaside holidays were all there was to offer, I have fond memories of a round at Newquay and a glance at Perranporth in which James Braid had a hand. Since then, West Cornwall at Lelant and Mullion on the south coast of Cornwall have become warm favourites.

The South West covers such a wide area that it should be tackled in stages. Its north eastern extreme is marked by Burnham and Berrow which is magnificent, a championship links in the classic mould, but there are pastures new as well, not least St Mellion which, in its relatively short life, has fully tested the professionals and now prepares for the English Amateur championship in 1999.

Although St Enodoc might just as easily have done the honours, it is nice that Cornwall has been so recognised at last.

A beautiful 18 hole course overlooking the sea in South Devon

BIGBURY GOLF CLUB LIMITED
Bigbury, Kingsbridge, South Devon TQ7 4BB (01548) 810207

No golfer visiting the South Hams should miss the opportunity of playing at Bigbury. It's an ideal holiday course –
challenging enough for low handicappers but not too daunting for the average golfer. There are outstanding views
from almost everywhere on the course – with Dartmoor to the North, the river Avon running near a number of
holes and breathtaking scenes of Bantham Beach and Burgh Island.

3A 1 Alderney
Routes des Carriers, Longis Rd,
Alderney, Channel Islands, GY9 3YD
☎(01481) 822835
1 mile E of St Annes.
Undulating seaside course.
Designed by Frank Pennink
9 holes, 4952 yards, S.S.S. 65
Visitors: welcome at all times; except
competition days.
Green Fee: WD £12.50; WE £17.50.
Societies: welcome by arrangement
WD and WE for special events; cater-
ing available.
Catering: by arrangement.
Hotels: Bellvue; Seaview.

3A 2 Ashbury
Higher Maddaford, Southcott,
Okehampton, Devon, EX20 4NL
☎(01837) 55453, Fax 55468
Leaving Okehampton, take Holsworthy
Road and turn right to Ashbury; course
half mile on right.
Hilly parkland course.
Pro Reg Cade; Founded 1991
Designed by D.J. Fensom
Ashbury course: 18 holes, 5766 yards,
S.S.S. 68; Oakwood course: 18 holes,
5207 yards, S.S.S. 68
Visitors: welcome; normal dress codes
apply; half price if playing with a mem-
ber; booking essential.
Green Fee: WD £12; WE £15.
Societies: essential to book at least 2
weeks in advance; no societies March,
April, May, June, September and
October; packages available; terms on
application.
Hotels: Manor House Hotel,
Okehampton; golf free to guests.

3A 3 Axe Cliff
Squires Lane, Axmouth, Seaton,
Devon, EX12 4AB
☎(01297) 24371, Pro 21754, Bar/Rest
20499
Off A3052 Axmouth-Seaton road.
Coastal/parkland course.
Pro Mark Dack; Founded 1984
18 holes, 6040 yards, S.S.S. 70
Visitors: welcome by prior arrange-
ment.
Green Fee: WD £19; WE £21.

ment; packages available; terms on
application.
Catering: bar and restaurant facilities
available.

3A 4 Bigbury
Bigbury-on-Sea, Kingsbridge, Devon,
TQ7 4BB
☎(01548) 810207, Pro 810412, Sec
810557
Turn off the A379 Kingsbridge/
Plymouth road near Modbury, on to
the B3392; follow signs to Bigbury-on-
Sea which lead to the course.
Clifftop course.
Pro Simon Lloyd; Founded 1926
Designed by J.H. Taylor
18 holes, 6048 yards, S.S.S. 69
Visitors: welcome, but essential to
belong to a Golf Club and have cur-
rent h'cap certs.
Green Fee: WD £20; WE £24.
Societies: bookings taken in advance
for Tues and Thurs; all players must
have h'cap certs; £20 including 2-
course meal.
Catering: full facilities.
Hotels: Cottage Hotel, Hope Cove;
Thurlestone Hotel, Thurlestone;
Pickwick Inn, St Ann's Chapel.

3A 5 Bowood
Lanteglos, Camelford, Cornwall, PL32
9RF
☎(01840) 213017, Fax 212622
3A39 through Camelford to Valley
Truckle, then right on to B3266
Boscastle-Tintagel road, 1st left after
garage towards Lanteglos; entrance
0.5 mile on left.
Parkland course with woodland and
lakes.
Pro Tony Moore; Founded 1992
18 holes, 6692 yards, S.S.S. 72
Visitors: welcome with h'cap certs.
Green Fee: WD £25; WE £25.
Societies: welcome anytime by
arrangement; full facilities available;
day ticket £35; terms on application.
Catering: full facilities.
Practice range available.
Hotels: Lanteglos; Cornish Arms;
Pendoggett; Countryman.

3A 6 Bude and N Cornwall
Burn View, Bude, Cornwall, EX23 8DA
☎(01288) 352006, Fax 356855, Pro
353635, Bar/Rest 352176
Through the Bude one-way system on
A39 and turn right and right again to
the Golf Club; 1 minute from town cen-
tre.
Seaside links course.
Pro John Yeo; Founded 1892
Designed by Tom Dunn
18 holes, 6057 yards, S.S.S. 70
Visitors: welcome.
Green Fee: WD £20; WE £25.
Societies: some societies are wel-
come but not at WE; available
depending on numbers; terms on
application.
Catering: wide selection of meals
available throughout the day.
Hotels: many in local area.

3A 7 Budock Vean Hotel
Nr Mawnan Smith, Falmouth,
Cornwall, TR11 5LG
☎(01326) 250288
On main road between Falmouth and
Helston; head for Mabe then go
through Mawnan Smith; golf course
approx 1.5 miles on right.
Undulating parkland course.
Founded 1932
Designed by James Braid, D. Cook
and P.H. Whiteside
9 holes, 5222 yards, S.S.S. 65
Visitors: welcome with h'cap certs;
phone for start time am only.
Green Fee: terms on application.
Societies: welcome; full facilities
available.
Catering: full facilities available.
Hotels: Budock Vean.

3A 8 Cape Cornwall Golf & Country Club
Cape Cornwall, St Just, Penzance,
Cornwall, TR19 7NL
☎(01736) 788611, Fax 788611
3A3071 to St Just-in-Penwith, turn left
at memorial clock, 1 mile down road
on left.
Coastal parkland course.
Pro Scott Richards; Founded 1990
18 holes, 5650 yards, S.S.S. 68

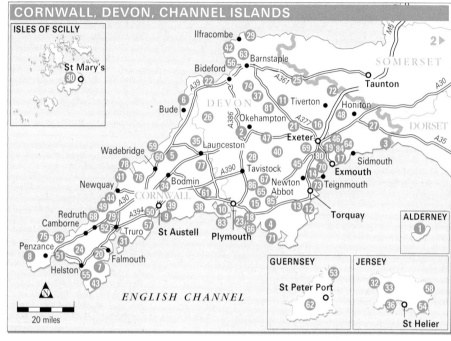

CORNWALL, DEVON, CHANNEL ISLANDS

ISLES OF SCILLY

ENGLISH CHANNEL

20 miles

GUERNSEY
St Peter Port

JERSEY
St Helier

ALDERNEY

KEY

1	Alderney
2	Ashbury
3	Axe Cliff
4	Bigbury
5	Bowood
6	Bude and N Cornwall
7	Budock Vean Hotel
8	Cape Cornwall Golf & Country Club
9	Carlyon Bay Hotel
10	China Fleet Country Club
11	Chulmleigh
12	Churston
13	Dainton Park
14	Dartmouth Golf & Country Club
15	Dinnaton
16	Downes Crediton
17	East Devon
18	Elfordleigh Hotel Golf & Country Club
19	Exeter Golf & Country Club
20	Falmouth
21	Fingle Glen
22	Hartland Forest Golf & Leisure Park
23	Hele Park
24	Helston Golf and Leisure
25	Highbullen Hotel
26	Holsworthy
27	Honiton
28	Hurdwick
29	Ilfracombe
30	Isles of Scilly
31	Killiow Park
32	La Grande Mare
33	La Moye
34	Lanhydrock
35	Launceston
36	Les Ormes Golf and Leisure
37	Libbaton
38	Looe
39	Lostwithiel Hotel Golf & Country Club
40	Manor House Hotel & Golf Course
41	Merlin
42	Mortehoe & Woolacombe
43	Mullion
44	Newquay
45	Newton Abbot (Stover)
46	Okehampton
47	Okehampton
48	Padbrook Park (Cullompton)
49	Perranporth
50	Porthpean
51	Praa Sands
52	Radnor Golf Centre
53	Royal Guernsey
54	Royal Jersey
55	Royal Naval Air Station Culdrose
56	Royal North Devon
57	St Austell
58	St Clements
59	St Enodoc
60	St Kew
61	St Mellion International
62	St Pierre Park Hotel
63	Saunton
64	Sidmouth
65	Sparkwell
66	Staddon Heights
67	Tavistock
68	Tehidy Park
69	Teign Valley
70	Teignmouth
71	Thurlestone
72	Tiverton
73	Torquay
74	Torrington
75	Tregenna Castle Hotel
76	Treloy
77	Trethorne
78	Trevose Country Club
79	Truro
80	Warren
81	Waterbridge
82	West Cornwall
83	Whitsand Bay Hotel Golf and Country Club
84	Woodbury Park Golf & Country Club
85	Wrangaton
86	Yelverton

Visitors: welcome except Sat and Sun between 8am and 11.30am.
Green Fee: WD £20; WE £20.
Societies: welcome by arrangement; full bar all weekend, lunch 12am- 2pm, dinner 7-10pm.
Catering: full facilities.

3A 9 Carlyon Bay Hotel

Carlyon Bay, St Austell, Cornwall, PL25 3RD
☎(01726) 812304, Fax 814938, Sec 814228
Main Plymouth-Truro road 1 mile W of St Blazey.
Clifftop/parkland course.
Pro Mark Rowe; Founded 1926
Designed by J. Hamilton Stutt
18 holes, 6560 yards, S.S.S. 71
Visitors: h'cap certs required; phone for start times.
Green Fee: WD £27; WE £27.
Societies: welcome by arrangement.
Catering: full facilities available.
Hotels: Carlyon Bay.

3A 10 China Fleet Country Club

Saltash, Cornwall, PL12 6LJ
☎(01752) 848668, Fax 848456

1 mile from Tamar Bridge, leave A38 before tunnel and follow signs.
Parkland course.
Founded 1991
Designed by Martin Hawtree
18 holes, 6551 yards, S.S.S. 72
Visitors: welcome by prior arrangement only.
Green Fee: WD £20; WE £25.
Societies: by arrangement with Sec; full facilities available.
Catering: full facilities.
Hotels: accommodation available, telephone for details.

3A 11 **Chulmleigh**

Leigh Rd, Chulmleigh, Devon, EX18 7BL
☎(01769) 580519
From Barnstaple follow Tourist Route Exeter signs; from Exeter follow A377 Crediton road, continue through Crediton, after approx 12 miles turn right into Chulmleigh.
Meadowland course.
Founded 1976
Designed by J.W.D. Goodban OBE
9 holes, 2310 yards, S.S.S. 54
Visitors: welcome.
Green Fee: WD £6.50; WE £6.50.
Societies: welcome by arrangement; bar and light snacks available.
Catering: bar and light snacks.
Hotels: cottage for rent, phone for details; Thelbridge Cross Inn.

3A 12 **Churston**

The Club House, Churston, Nr Brixham, Devon, TQ5 0LA
☎(01803) 842218, Fax 845738, Pro 843442, Sec 842751
5 miles south of Torquay along the main road towards Brixham.
Parkland course.
Pro Neil Holman; Founded 1890
Designed by H.S. Colt
18 holes, 6208 yards, S.S.S. 70
Visitors: welcome with h'cap certs.
Green Fee: WD £22; WE £27.
Societies: Mon, Thurs and Fri only; minimum 12; reductions for 50+; bar, restaurant, pro shop, function and conference room; terms on application.
Hotels: Grand Hotel, Torquay; Imperial Hotel, Torquay; Redcliffe Hotel, Paignton; Berry Head Hotel, Brixham.

3A 13 **Dainton Park**

Ipplepen, Newton Abbot, Devon, TQ12 5TN
☎(01803) 813812

2 miles south of Newton Abbot on the A381.
Parkland course.
Pro Martin Tyson; Founded 1993
Designed by Adrian Stiff
18 holes, 6207 yards, S.S.S. 70
Visitors: unrestricted access.
Green Fee: WD £14.50; WE £17.
Societies: groups of 15 or more welcome; bar and catering available as well as practice ground; £12.50.
Catering: full bar and catering service. Practice range, 12 bays; floodlit.
Hotels: Passagehouse, Kingsteignton; Coppa Dolla, Broadhempston; Sea Trout Inn, Totnes.

3A 14 **Dartmouth Golf & Country Club**

Blackawton, Totnes, Devon, TQ9 7DE
☎(01803) 712686, Fax 712628, Pro 712650
Off A3122 between Totnes and Dartmouth, 5 miles W of Dartmouth.
Moorland/parkland course.
Pro Jason Fullard; Founded 1992
Designed by Jeremy Pern
18 holes, 6663 yards, S.S.S. 74
Visitors: welcome with h'cap certs; phone for starting times.
Green Fee: WD £25; WE £35.
Societies: welcome WD by arrangement; full facilities available.
Catering: bar meals, restaurant, function room.
Hotels: Fingals (Dittisham).

3A 15 **Dinnaton**

Dinnaton Sporting and Country Club, Blachford Road, Ivybridge, Devon, PL21 9HU
☎(01752) 892512, Fax 698334, Pro 691228, Sec 892542
Leave A38 at Ivybridge and head to town centre; follow signs to club from roundabout.
Parkland course.
Pro David Ridyard; Founded 1987
Designed by Cotton & Pink
9 holes, 4089 yards, S.S.S. 59
Visitors: welcome.
Green Fee: WD £7.50; WE £7.50.
Societies: welcome; full day of golf including snack at lunchtime; £12.50.
Catering: snacks available.
Hotels: accommodation on site.

3A 16 **Downes Crediton**

The Clubhouse, Hookway, Crediton, Devon, EX17 3PT
☎(01363) 773991, Pro 774464, Sec 773025

Leave A377 Exeter to Crediton road, 8 miles NW of Exeter at Crediton station; turn left at crossroads to Hookway.
Parkland course with water.
Pro Howard Finch; Founded 1976
18 holes, 5884 yards, S.S.S. 68
Visitors: by arrangement.
Green Fee: WD £18; WE £22.
Societies: welcome by arrangement; catering facilities available; terms on application.
Catering: meals and snacks with coffee available.

3A 17 **East Devon**

North View Rd, Budleigh Salterton, Devon, EX9 6DQ
☎(01395) 443370, Pro 445195, Bar/Rest 442018
M5 junction 30; follow signs to Exmouth and the course is on the right as you enter Budleigh Salterton.
Clifftop, heathland course.
Pro Trevor Underwood; Founded 1902
18 holes, 6239 yards, S.S.S. 70
Visitors: welcome by prior arrangement and with h'cap certs.
Green Fee: WD £27; WE £35.
Societies: welcome on Thurs only; bar and restaurant as well as practice facilities; £27 per round, £35 per day.
Hotels: recommendations available from secretary.

3A 18 **Elfordleigh Hotel Golf & Country Club**

Colebrook, Plympton, Plymouth, Devon, PL7 5EB
☎(01752) 336428, Fax 344581, Sec 348425
Off A38 5 miles NE of Plymouth 2 miles from Marsh Mills roundabout.
Parkland course.
Pro C Rendell; Founded 1932
Designed by J.H. Taylor
9 holes, 5664 yards, S.S.S. 67
Visitors: welcome with h'cap certs.
Green Fee: WD £15; WE £20.
Societies: terms on application.
Catering: full facilities available.
Hotels: Elfordleigh Hotel.

3A 19 **Exeter Golf & Country Club**

Countess Wear, Exeter, Devon, EX2 7AE
☎(01392) 874139, Pro 875028, Sec 874023
Exit 30 off M5; follow road marked Topsham; course is 4 miles south east of Exeter.
Parkland course.

Pro Mike Rowett; Founded 1895
Designed by James Braid
18 holes, 6000 yards, S.S.S. 69
Visitors: welcome with h'cap certs;
not on Tues mornings, Thurs or Sats.
Green Fee: WD £22; WE £22.
Societies: welcome on Thurs only;
function room, four bars and spike
bars; players' guests welcome; terms
on application.
Hotels: Buckerell Lodge; Countess
Wear Lodge; Devon Motel.

3A 20 **Falmouth**
Swanpool Road, Falmouth, Cornwall,
TR11 5BQ
☎(01326) 314296, Fax 317783, Pro
311262
Half a mile west of Swanpool beach
on the road to Maenporth.
Seaside parkland course.
Pro Bryan Patterson; Founded 1894
18 holes, 6061 yards, S.S.S. 70
Visitors: welcome.
Green Fee: WD £20; WE £20.
Societies: welcome by prior arrange-
ment; bar, lunch and tea facilities;
terms on application.
Catering: available.
Practice range.
Hotels: Royal Duchy; Meudon Vean;
Park Grove.

3A 21 **Fingle Glen**
Fingle Glen Family Golf Centre, Nr
Exeter, Devon, EX6 6AF
☎(01647) 61817, Fax 61135
4 miles from Exeter on the A30 to
Okehampton, 400 yards from Fingle
Glen Junction.
Parkland course.
Founded 1989
Designed by W. Pile
9 holes, 2483 yards, S.S.S. 63
Visitors: welcome.
Green Fee: WD £8.50 (9 holes), £9.50
(18 holes); WE £12.50 (9 holes), £15
(18 holes).
Societies: welcome; fishing also avail-
able; golfing packages can be
arranged; terms on application.
Catering: bar, lounge and restaurant.
Practice range.
Hotels: own accommodation on site.

3A 22 **Hartland Forest Golf &
Leisure Park**
Woolsery, Bideford, Devon, EX39 5RA
☎(01237) 431442, Fax 431734
6 miles S of Clovelly off A39.
Parkland course.
Pro Steve Barker; Founded 1987

Designed by John Hepplewhite
18 holes, 6015 yards, S.S.S. 69
Visitors: no restrictions except
acceptable standard of golf.
Green Fee: WD £12; WE £12.
Societies: welcome by arrangement;
full facilities available.
Catering: full facilities.
Hotels: 34 units of accommodation
available on site sleeping 130.

3A 23 **Hele Park**
Ashburton Road, Newton Abbot,
Devon, TQ12 6JN
☎(01626) 336060, Fax 332661
On edge of Newton Abbot on the
A383 Newton Abbot-Ashburton road.
Parkland course.
Pro J Langmead; Founded 1992
Designed by M Craig/N Stanbury
9 holes, 5168 yards, S.S.S. 65
Visitors: welcome - no h'cap certs
required.
Green Fee: on application.
Societies: welcome on application to
the secretary; terms on application.
Catering: full facilities.
Practice range, floodlit driving range
and outdoor grass tees.
Hotels: Passage House, Kingsteign-
ton, Newton Abbot.

3A 24 **Helston Golf and
Leisure**
Wendron, Helston, Cornwall, TR13
0LX
☎(01326) 565103
1 mile N of Helston on B3297 Redruth
road.
Short park and downland course.
Founded 1988
18 holes, 2100 yards, S.S.S. 54
Visitors: welcome anytime.
Green Fee: WD £6; WE £6.
Societies: Mon-Sat before 11am or
after 5pm, by prior arrangement; full
facilities available at Whealdream Bar.
Catering: full facilities available at
Whealdream Bar.

3A 25 **Highbullen Hotel**
Chittlehamholt, Umberleigh, Devon,
EX37 9HD
☎(01769) 540561, Fax 540492
10 mins west on A361 from South
Molton.
Parkland course; fishing also avail-
able.
Pro Paul Weston; Founded 1960
Designed by Hugh Neil. New
Extension by M Neil & H. Stutt Desi
18 holes, 5455 yards, S.S.S. 66

Visitors: welcome; free for hotel
guests.
Green Fee: WD £14; WE £16
Hotels: Highbullen Hotel.

3A 26 **Holsworthy**
Killatree, Holsworthy, N Devon, EX22
6LP
☎(01409) 253177
1.5 miles out of Holsworthy on the
A3072 Bude road.
Parkland course.
Pro Simon Chapman; Founded 1937
18 holes, 6062 yards, S.S.S. 69
Visitors: welcome.
Green Fee: WD £15; WE £20.
Societies: by arrangement; packages
available; terms on application.
Catering: clubhouse facilities.
Hotels: Court Barn, Clawton.

3A 27 **Honiton**
Middlehills, Honiton, Devon, EX14
8TR
☎(01404) 44422, Fax 46383, Pro
42943, Bar/Rest 47167
1 mile S of Honiton.
Parkland course.
Pro A Cave; Founded 1896
18 holes, 5902 yards, S.S.S. 68
Visitors: welcome by arrangement.
Green Fee: WD £22; WE £27.
Societies: welcome on Thurs; terms
on application.
Catering: bar facilities available.
Hotels: club can recommend hotels.

3A 28 **Hurdwick**
Tavistock Hamlets, Tavistock, Devon,
PL19 8PZ
☎(01822) 612746
Signposted from centre of Tavistock; 1
mile N of Tavistock on Brentor road.
Parkland course.
Founded 1988
Designed by Hawtree
18 holes, 5217 yards, S.S.S. 67
Visitors: welcome at any time; dress
code applies.
Green Fee: WD £14; WE £14.
Societies: welcome; packages avail-
able; 36 holes of golf and lunch; £18.
Catering: lunch and snacks.
Hotels: Bedford Hotel, Tavistock;
Castle Inn, Lydford.

3A 29 **Ilfracombe**
Hele Bay, Ilfracombe, N Devon, EX34
9RT
☎(01271) 862050, Fax 867731, Pro
863328, Sec 862176, Bar/Rest 862675

1 mile from Ilfracombe towards Combe Martin on A399 coast road. Undulating heathland course with spectacular views of sea.
Pro David Hoare; Founded 1892
Designed by T.K. Weir
18 holes, 5893 yards, S.S.S. 69
Visitors: welcome by prior arrangement, particularly in the summer.
Green Fee: WD £19; WE £22.
Societies: welcome by prior arrangement with the secretary; terms on application.
Catering: full clubhouse facilities.
Hotels: club can recommend in local area.

3A 30 **Isles of Scilly**
St Mary's, Isles of Scilly, TR21 0NF
☎(01720) 422692
1.5 miles from Hugh Town in St Mary's.
Heathland/seaside course.
Founded 1904
Designed by Horace Hutchinson
9 holes, 6001 yards, S.S.S. 69
Visitors: welcome Mon-Sat; phone one hour before.
Green Fee: WD £16; WE £16.
Catering: available.
Hotels: Star Castle Hotel.

3A 31 **Killiow Park**
Killiow, Kea, Nr Truro, Cornwall, TR3 6AG
☎(01872) 270246, Sec 240915
Leave Truro on A39 Truro/Falmouth road, turn right at 1st roundabout 3 miles from Truro, clearly signposted thereafter.
Picturesque parkland course.
Founded 1987
18 holes, 4029 yards, S.S.S. 59
Visitors: welcome at all times; after 10.30am WE and BH; advisable to book in high season.
Green Fee: WD £10; WE £10.
Catering: lounge bar.
Hotels: Hospitality Hotel (St Agnes).

3A 32 **La Grande Mare**
Vazon Bay, Castel, Guernsey, CI, GY5 7LL
☎(01481) 53544, Fax 55194, Pro 53432, Bar/Rest 56576
On the west coast of Guernsey at Vazon Bay.
Parkland course.
Pro Matt Groves; Founded 1994
Designed by Hawtree
18 holes, 5112 yards, S.S.S. 66.
Visitors: welcome.

Green Fee: WD £25; WE £28.
Societies: book in advance; restaurant and bar; hotel has 5 crowns; terms on application.
Catering: bar, restaurant and hotel.
Hotels: La Grande Mare Hotel.

3A 33 **La Moye**
La Moye, St Brelade, Jersey, Channel Islands, JE3 8GQ, JE3 8GQ
☎(01534) 43401, Pro 43130, Bar/Rest 42701
2 miles W of airport off Route des Orange.
Links course.
Pro Mike Deeley; Founded 1902
Designed by James Braid
18 holes, 6664 yards, S.S.S. 72
Visitors: welcome by prior arrangement.
Green Fee: WD £40; WE £45.
Societies: welcome by prior arrangement WD between 9.30-11; 2.30-4; £5 booking fee; meals can be organised through the head steward; £40.
Catering: full clubhouse restaurant and bar facilities.
Hotels: Atlantic; L'Horizon both St Brelade.

3A 34 **Lanhydrock**
Lostwithiel Rd, Bodmin, Cornwall, PL30 5AQ
☎(01208) 73600, Fax 77325
1 mile south of Bodmin.
Parkland course.
Pro Jason Broadway; Founded 1992
Designed by J. Hamilton Stutt
18 holes, 6169 yards, S.S.S. 69
Visitors: welcome.
Green Fee: WD £25; WE £25.
Societies: welcome; packages available for groups between 8-160 players; private suite available with own bar facility; £24.95-£39.95.
Catering: full facilities.
Hotels: Lanhydrock Golfing Lodge adjacent to first tee.

3A 35 **Launceston**
St Stephens, Launceston, Cornwall, PL15 8HF
☎(01566) 773442, Pro 775359
1 mile N of Launceston on Bude road (B3254).
Parkland course.
Pro John Tozer; Founded 1927
Designed by J. Hamilton Stutt
18 holes, 6407 yards, S.S.S. 71
Visitors: welcome WD by arrangement.
Green Fee: WD £24; WE £24.

Societies: welcome WD by arrangement; full facilities available; terms on applicationt.
Catering: available by prior arrangement.
Hotels: White Hart.

3A 36 **Les Ormes Golf and Leisure**
Mont a la Brune, St Brelade, Jersey, Channel Islands, JE3 8FL
☎(01534) 499077, Fax 499122
5 mins from Jersey Airport following the signs for St Brelade.
Parkland course.
Pro Andrew Chamberlain; Founded 1996
9 holes, 5018 yards, S.S.S. 65
Visitors: welcome.
Green Fee: WD £16; WE £18.
Societies: welcome by prior arrangement.
Catering: full catering facilities.
Practice range, 17 bays.
Hotels: many in Jersey; contact local tourist board.

3A 37 **Libbaton**
High Bickington, Umberleigh, N Devon, EX37 9BS
☎(01769) 560269, Pro 560167
A377 to Atherington and then B3217 to High Bickington.
Parkland course.
Pro J N Phillips; Founded 1988
Designed by Col P Badham
18 holes, 6494 yards, S.S.S. 72
Visitors: welcome.
Green Fee: WD £15; WE £16.
Societies: welcome Mon, Wed, Fri; golf, coffee, snack lunch, evening meal; £25.
Catering: facilities available.
Practice range.
Hotels: Northcote Manor, Umberleigh; Exeter Inn, Chittlehamholt.

3A 38 **Looe**
Bin Down, Looe, Cornwall, PL13 1PX
☎(01503) 240239, Fax 240864
3 miles W of Looe just off B3253.
Parkland/downland course.
Pro A MacDonald; Founded 1933
Designed by Harry Vardon
18 holes, 5940 yards, S.S.S. 68
Visitors: welcome.
Green Fee: WD £20; WE £20.
Societies: welcome but minimum of 8 players; catering and packages available; from £14.
Catering: facilities available.
Hotels: St Mellion.

3A 39 Lostwithiel Hotel Golf & Country Club

Lower Polscoe, Lostwithiel, Cornwall, PL22 0HQ
☎(01208) 873550, Fax 873479, Pro 873822
On the A390 from Plymouth to Lostwithiel.
Parkland course.
Pro Tony Nash; Founded 1991
Designed by Stewart Wood R.I.B.a
18 holes, 5984 yards, S.S.S. 71
Visitors: welcome.
Green Fee: WD £20; WE £23.
Societies: welcome; golf only £15; coffee and lunch, evening meal and day's golf £28; terms on application.
Catering: full facilities.
Practice range, 6 undercover bays; floodlit.
Hotels: 18 bedroom country style bedrooms on site with tennis courts, swimming pool.

3A 40 Manor House Hotel & Golf Course

Moretonhampstead, Newton Abbot, Devon, TQ13 8RE
☎(01647) 440998, Fax 440961, Bar/Rest 440355
On B3212 towards Mortonhampstead.
Parkland built around 2 rivers
Pro Richard Lewis; Founded 1921
Designed by J.F. Abercrombie
18 holes, 6016 yards, S.S.S. 69
Visitors: welcome but must book start time.
Green Fee: WD £24; WE £30.
Societies: welcome by prior arrangement; packages can be arranged; terms on application.
Catering: hotel facilities.
Hotels: Manor House Hotel.

3A 41 Merlin

Mawgan Porth, Newquay, Cornwall, TR8 4AD
☎(01841) 540222, Fax 01637, 541031
On coast road between Newquay and Padstow. After Mawgan Porth take St Eval Road.
Heathland course.
Founded 1991
Designed by Ross Oliver
18 holes, 5305 yards, S.S.S. 67
Visitors: no restrictions.
Green Fee: WD £12; WE £12.
Societies: welcome by prior arrangement; includes unlimited golf only; lunch and dinner are available at special rates; £10.
Catering: bar and restaurant.

Practice range, 6 covered bays.
Hotels: Bedruthan Steps; Merrymoor Inn; Whitelodge; Sea Vista, all Mawgan Porth; Falcon, St Mawgan.

3A 42 Mortehoe & Woolacombe

Easewell, Mortehoe, N Devon, EX34 7EH
☎(01271) 870225, Fax 870745
1 mile before Mortehoe on the Ilfracombe road.
Parkland with superb sea views.
Founded 1992
Designed by Hans Ellis/David Hoare
9 holes, 4638 yards, S.S.S. 63
Visitors: welcome.
Green Fee: WD £10; WE £10.
Societies: welcome with pre-booking; terms on application.
Hotels: Woolacombe Bay; Watersmeet; Lundy House; Rockham Bay.

3A 43 Mullion

Cury, Helston, Cornwall, TR12 7BP
☎(01326) 240276, Fax 240685, Pro 241176, Sec 240685, Bar/Rest 241231
S of Helston on A3083 towards The Lizard past Culdrose Naval Air station.
Parkland/links course.
Pro P Blundell; Founded 1895
Designed by W Sich
18 holes, 6037 yards, S.S.S. 70
Visitors: welcome with h'cap certs.
Green Fee: WD £20; WE £20.
Societies: welcome with prior arrangement; packages available; terms on application.
Catering: full catering and bar available.
Hotels: Polurrian; Mullion Cove; Angel.

3A 44 Newquay

Tower Rd, Newquay, Cornwall, TR7 1LT
☎(01637) 872091, Fax 874066, Pro 874830, Sec 874354
Adjacent to Fistral Beach.
Seaside links course.
Pro Andrew Cullen; Founded 1890
Designed by H.S. Colt
18 holes, 6136 yards, S.S.S. 69
Visitors: welcome; handicap certificates required.
Green Fee: WD £21; WE £21.
Societies: by arrangement only; full facilities; terms on application.
Catering: bar and restaurant.
Hotels: Bristol; Esplanade, Narrowcliff.

3A 45 Newton Abbot (Stover)

Bovey Rd, Newton Abbot, Devon, TQ12 6QQ
☎(01626) 65472, Pro 62078, Sec 52460, Bar/Rest 56798
Off A 38 at Drumbridges and turn towards Newton Abbot on the A382; course is 500 yards on right.
Wooded parkland course.
Pro Malcolm Craig; Founded 1931
Designed by James Braid
18 holes, 5862 yards, S.S.S. 68
Visitors: welcome with h'cap certs unless with a member.
Green Fee: WD £22; WE £22.
Societies: Thurs only; minimum 24; full catering facilities to order; £432 for first 24 players plus £16 thereafter.
Catering: bar and restaurant.
Hotels: Dolphin; Edgemoor, both Bovey Tracey.

3A 46 Northbrook

Topsham Rd, Exeter, Devon, EX2 6EU
☎(01392) 257436
From M5 junction 30 take A379 then on to B3182 Topsham road.
Wooded parkland.
Founded 1968
18 holes, 1078 yards, S.S.S. 54
Visitors: welcome; pay as you play.
Green Fee: WD £2; WE £2.
Catering: vending machines and confectionery.

3A 47 Okehampton

Okehampton, Devon, EX20 1EF
☎(01837) 52113, Fax 52734, Pro 53541, Sec 52734
Enter town centre from A30 and follow signs from the main lights.
Parkland course.
Pro Simon Jefferies; Founded 1913
Designed by J H Taylor
18 holes, 5252 yards, S.S.S. 67
Visitors: welcome but only by prior arrangement; booking essential.
Green Fee: WD £17; WE £19-23.
Societies: welcome by prior arrangement; terms on application.
Catering: available.
Hotels: Fox and Hounds, Bridestowe; White Hart, Okehampton.

3A 48 Padbrook Park (Cullompton)

Padbrook Park, Cullompton, Devon, EX15 1RU
☎(01884) 38286, Fax 34359
Exit 28 of the M5; follow signs through Okehampton; across roundabout and then first on right.

MULLION GOLF CLUB

CURY, HELSTON, CORNWALL TR12 7BP. TEL: SECRETARY 01326 240685
THE MOST SOUTHERLY GOLF COURSE IN ENGLAND • 18 HOLES • 6037 YDS • PAR 70
SOCIETIES & VISITORS WELCOME • FULL BAR AND CATERING FACILITIES.
"The most unorthodox and sporting club where golf is played in the most beautiful scenery"
TURLY SMITH - writer and critic 1905. *His wish was granted - so come to Mullion*

Parkland course.
Pro Stewart Adwick; Founded 1991
Designed by Bob Sandow
18 holes, 6108 yards, S.S.S. 69
Visitors: welcome but must pre-book tee time.
Green Fee: WD £12; WE £16.
Societies: welcome with prior arrangements; full catering for society and corporate packages; terms on application.
Catering: bar and restaurant.
Hotels: Exeter Inn, Brampton.

3A 49 **Perranporth**
Budnic Hill, Perranporth, Cornwall, TR6 0AB
☎(01872) 572454, Fax 573701, Pro 572317, Sec 573701
Take Perranporth road off the A30; course is on the right when entering town.
Links course with panoramic sea views.
Pro Derek Michell; Founded 1929
Designed by James Braid
18 holes, 6286 yards, S.S.S. 72
Visitors: welcome with booking.
Green Fee: WD £20; WE £25.
Societies: welcome with booking; packages can be arranged; terms on application.
Catering: bar and restaurant.
Hotels: Ponsmere, Perranporth; White Lodge, Mawgan Porth.

3A 50 **Porthpean**
Porthpean, St Austell, Cornwall, PL26 6AY
☎(01726) 64613
Off A390 2 miles from St Austell.
Parkland course.
Founded 1992
Designed by R Oliver/ A Leather
18 holes, 5184 yards, S.S.S. 67
Visitors: welcome.
Green Fee: WD £12; WE £12.
Societies: welcome by prior arrangement; packages available; terms on application.
Catering: clubhouse facilities.
Practice range, 9 bays; floodlit range.
Hotels: Cliff Head; Pier House; Porth Avallen.

3A 51 **Praa Sands**
Germoe Crossroads, Praa Sands, Penzance, Cornwall, TR20 9TQ
☎(01736) 763445, Fax 763399
7 miles east of Penzance on A394 to Helston
Seaside parkland course.
Founded 1971
9 holes, 4122 yards, S.S.S. 60
Visitors: welcome except Sun mornings.
Green Fee: WD £10; WE £10.
Societies: by arrangement; course will accept Telegraph Golf Network 2 for One cards; packages available; terms on application.
Catering: meals and snacks.
Hotels: Praa Sands Hotel; Queens, Penzance.

3A 52 **Radnor Golf Centre**
Radnor Road, Redruth, TR16 5EL
☎(01209) 211059
Take A30 from Redruth to Porthtowan; after 200 yards turn right; golf centre on left after 1 mile.
Heathland course with gorse.
Pro Gordon Wallbank; Founded 1988
Designed by Gordon Wallbank
9 holes, 1312 yards
Visitors: pay and play.
Green Fee: WD £7.50; WE £7.50.
Societies: none.
Catering: none.

3A 53 **Royal Guernsey**
L'Ancresse Vale, Guernsey, Channel Islands, GY3 5BY
☎(01481) 47022, Fax 43960, Pro 45070, Sec 46523
3 miles north of St Peter Port.
Seaside links course.
Pro Norman Wood; Founded 1890
Designed by MacKenzie Ross
18 holes, 6206 yards, S.S.S. 70
Visitors: welcome; must be accompanied by a member on Thurs and Sat morning; no visitors on Sun.
Green Fee: WD £34; WE £34.
Societies: not welcome.
Catering: coffee, afternoon teas and meals available.
Hotels: Pembroke Bay; L' Ancresse Hotel.

3A 54 **Royal Jersey**
Grouville, Jersey, Channel Islands, JE3 9BD
☎(01534) 854416, Fax 854684, Pro 852234, Bar/Rest 851042.
4 miles east of St Helier on road to Gorey.
Links course.
Pro Tommy Horton; Founded 1878
18 holes, 6089 yards, S.S.S. 70
Visitors: welcome between 10-12 and 2-4pm on WD and after 2.30pm at WE.
Green Fee: WD £35; WE £40.
Societies: apply in writing to Sec; full catering by prior arrangement with Steward; 40+ £5 for tee reservation.
Catering: bar and catering facilities.

3A 55 **Royal Naval Air Station Culdrose**
RNAS Culdrose, Helston, Cornwall, TR12 8QY
☎(01326) 552413, Sec 573929
3A3083 1 mile from Helston towards Lizard
Flat parkland course built around part of airfield.
Founded 1962
14 holes 6132 yards, S.S.S. 70
Visitors: must be accompanied by club member.
Green Fee: terms on application.
Societies: welcome by arrangement.
Catering: clubhouse bar and hot/cold snacks available.

3A 56 **Royal North Devon**
Golf Links Rd, Westward Ho!, Bideford, Devon, EX39 1HD
☎(01237) 473824, Fax 423456, Pro 477598, Sec 473817
Take M5 to A361 and go through Northam Village to Sandymere road and then into Golf Links Road.
Links course.
Pro Iain Higgins; Founded 1864
Designed by Tom Morris
18 holes, 6653 yards, S.S.S. 72
Visitors: welcome with h'cap certs.
Green Fee: WD £28; WE £34.
Societies: welcome; bar, restaurant, snooker room; terms on application.
Catering: full facilities.

Saunton

Name the courses worthy of the Open championship if they were more strategically located, and Saunton would be top of many lists. A strange fact because in many ways Saunton's setting is its prime asset. It is hard to avoid sounding like a travel brochure when describing the vast, wide stretch of golden sand, the estuaries of the Taw and the Torridge, the botanic delights of the Burrows and the mountainous dunes that divide the golf from the sea. A keen eye quickly spots the Pebble Ridge and the links of Westward Ho! across the estuary, which are the oldest seaside links in England.

Bernard Darwin, in his wonderful book *The Golf Courses of the British Isles* published in 1910, describes a visit to Westward Ho! as a "reverent pilgrimage", blossoming forth into pages of ecstatic detail, but he glosses over Saunton in as few lines. "Saunton," he wrote, "looks at first glance like a fine golf course." None the less, he quoted Herbert Fowler as rating Saunton "almost, if not quite, as highly as Westward Ho!" and Harry Vardon as saying that he "would like to retire to Saunton and do nothing but play golf for pleasure".

In fairness to Darwin, Saunton had barely come of age when he wrote those words and I am sure that, had he had occasion to reassess his judgments, he would have written a purple passage or two on the subject of Saunton. It was, after all, one of the very few seaside links laid out for the modern ball, which is why it has withstood the recent advancements in the manufacture of clubs and balls better than any.

As John Goodban's excellent history of the Club – *The First 90 Years* – relates, the changes that have been necessary were mostly caused by the upheaval of the Second World War. The clubhouse became the headquarters of the Coast Defence Unit and the courses a battle training school with the sandhills mined against invasion.

Three years earlier, Saunton reached a deserved peak of eminence by staging the English championship in which Frank Pennink beat Leonard Crawley in the final.

After the war, Saunton rose phoenix like from the ashes, although there was a period of uncertainty when its survival might have been said to be a 'close run thing'. Until 1960 the management of the Club was in the hands of its owners, the Christie Estate – also the owners of Glyndebourne – but the saviour of the Old course was Ken Cotton.

He was able to restore most of it in 1950 with the only radical change being to the first two and last two holes. From a tee on a high ridge near the clubhouse, he made a new first hole which, with the addition of the new second, stretched the first four holes (all par fours) to nigh on a mile. However, one of the charms of Saunton is that two of its three short holes really are short. The fifth and the 13th are classic examples of how short holes need not be a long iron or a wood but still demand plenty of stout hitting.

Cotton's other amendment was to cut a gap in the hills at the eighth and to turn the 17th into a downhill short hole and the 18th into a fine par four which curves right-handed to a green outside the clubhouse windows.

A significant development came in 1974 with the opening of the new West course. Instead of the pre-war Old and New courses came the East and West and, following the decision in 1987 to remodel the greens on the West, there is no doubt that the two courses are as fine as any in Britain.

Lovers of Saunton hope it will one day house the Amateur championship. Its glories are infinite.

Hotels: Anchorage Hotel; Durrant House, Northam; Riversford Hotel, Northam.

3A 57 St Austell
Tregongeeves Lane, St Austell, Cornwall, PL26 7DS
☎(01726) 72649, Fax 74756, Pro 68621, Sec 74756
1 mile out of St Austell on the A390 Truro road; signposted.
Heathland/parkland course.
Pro Tony Pitts; Founded 1911
18 holes, 6089 yards, S.S.S. 69
Visitors: must be a member of a golf club and hold h'cap cert.
Green Fee: WD £18; WE £18.
Societies: welcome by appointment except on Fri and WE; restaurant and lounge bar; meals to be arranged with the caterer; £15.
Catering: available.
Practice range, opening 1998.

3A 58 St Clements
Jersey Recreation Grounds Co Ltd, Graeve d'azette, St Clements, Jersey, JE2 6PN
☎(01534) 21938
Close to St Helier
Public meadowland course.
Founded 1913
9 holes, 2244 yards
Visitors: welcome every day except before 11.30 Tues and 1pm Sun.
Green Fee: WD £10; WE £10.
Societies: welcome by arrangement; buffet bar and restaurant.
Catering: buffet bar and restaurant.
Hotels: Hotel de Normandy, Merton.

3A 59 St Enodoc
Rock, Wadebridge, Cornwall, PL276LD
☎(01208) 863216, Fax 862976, Pro 862402, Sec 862200
6 miles NW of Wadebridge.
Links course.
Pro Nick Williams; Founded 1890
Designed by James Braid
18 holes, 6243 yards, S.S.S. 70
Visitors: welcome; max h'cap 24 on Church course.
Green Fee: WD £35; WE £40.
Societies: welcome by prior arrangement; meals can be arranged through restaurant; £35-£40.
Catering: full restaurant and bar.

3A 60 St Kew
St Kew Highway, Nr Wadebridge, Bodmin, Cornwall, PL30 3EF
☎(01208) 841500, Fax 841500
Main A30 Wadebridge to Camelford road; course 2 and a half miles north of Wadebridge.
Parkland course.
Pro Nick Rogers; Founded 1993
Designed by D Derry
18 holes, 4543 yards, S.S.S. 62
Visitors: welcome at all times.
Green Fee: WD £13; WE £13.
Societies: welcome by arrangement; discounts on application; catering available; terms on application.
Catering: full facilities.
Practice range, covered.
Hotels: Bodare Hotel, Daymer Bay; Molesworth Arms, Wadebridge; St Moritz, Trebetherick.

3A 61 St Mellion International
St Mellion, Nr Saltash, Cornwall, PL12 6SD
☎(01579) 351351, Fax 350537, Pro 352006, Sec 352018, Bar/Rest 352005
3 miles south of Callington on A388.
Parkland course; former home of Benson and Hedges Masters
Pro D Moon/A Milton; Founded 1986
Designed by Jack Nicklaus; Old course designed by J Hamilton Stutt
Nicklaus course: 18 holes, 6651 yards, S.S.S. 72; Old course: 18 holes, 5782 yards, S.S.S. 68
Visitors: welcome by prior arrangement; WE after 1.30pm only.
Green Fee: Nicklaus WD £35, WE £35; Old WD £25; WE £25.
Societies: welcome subject to availability; coffee, 18 holes of golf, 3-course club meal; Nicklaus £43; Old £33.
Catering: full catering; coffee shop, grill room.
Hotels: own hotel and lodges.

3A 62 St Pierre Park Hotel
Rohais, St Peter Port, Guernsey, Channel Islands, GY1 1FD
☎(01481) 727039, Fax 712041, Bar/Rest 728282
1 mile west of St Peter Port on Rohais Road.
Hilly course with water hazards.
Pro Roy Corbet; Founded 1982
Designed by Tony Jacklin
9 holes, 2610 yards, S.S.S. 50
Visitors: welcome.
Green Fee: terms on application.
Societies: welcome; packages available; terms on application.
Catering: full facilities at the hotel.
Hotels: St Pierre Park Hotel.

3A 63 Saunton
Saunton, Nr Braunton, N Devon, EX33 1LG
☎(01271) 812436, Fax 814241, Pro 812013
On B3231 from Braunton to Croyde, 7 miles from Barnstaple
Traditional links course.
Pro Albert MacKenzie; Founded 1897
Designed by Herbert Fowler
East: 18 holes, 6373 yards, S.S.S. 73; West: 18 holes, 6138 yards, S.S.S. 73
Visitors: welcome with h'cap certs.
Green Fee: terms on application.
Societies: welcome by arrangement; full facilities available.
Catering: full restaurant.
Hotels: Saunton Sands; Kittiwell House; Preston House; Croyde Bay House, Woolacombe Bay.

3A 64 Sidmouth
Cotmaton Road, Peak Hill, Sidmouth, Devon, EX10 8SX
☎(01395) 513451
Take Station Road to Woodlands Hotel and then turn right into Cotmaton Road.
Undulating parkland course.
Pro Gaele Tapper; Founded 1889
18 holes, 5068 yards, S.S.S. 65
Visitors: welcome by arrangement with the secretary.
Green Fee: WD £20; WE £20.
Societies: welcome; terms on application.
Catering: full facilities.

3A 65 Sparkwell
Welbeck Manor Hotel, Sparkwell, Plymouth, Devon, PL7 5DF
☎(01752) 837219, Fax 837219
From Plymouth take A38, turn left at Plympton and then signposted to Sparkwell.
Parkland course.
Founded 1993
9 holes, 5772 yards, S.S.S. 68
Visitors: welcome; pay as you play course.
Green Fee: WD £6; WE £7.
Societies: welcome; full facilities available.
Catering: full bar and restaurant facilities.
Hotels: Welbeck Manor.

3A 66 Staddon Heights
Staddon Heights, Plymstock, Plymouth, Devon, PL9 9SP
☎(01752) 402475, Fax 401998, Pro 492630, Bar/Rest 484264

Club is five miles south of the city near the Royal Navy aerials.
Parkland cliff top; no par 5s
Pro Ian Marshall; Founded 1904
18 holes, 5845 yards, S.S.S. 68
Visitors: welcome with h'cap certs.
Green Fee: WD £18; WE £23.
Societies: welcome with prior arrangement and h'cap certs; catering available; £25.
Catering: bar available.

3A 67 **Tavistock**
Down Rd, Tavistock, Devon, PL19 9AQ
☎(01822) 612049, Fax 612344, Pro 612316, Sec 612344
From town centre take Whitchurch road; turn left at Down Road.
Moorland course.
Pro Dominic Rehaag; Founded 1890
18 holes, 6250 yards, S.S.S. 70
Visitors: welcome WD by prior arrangement; must be accompanied by member at WE.
Green Fee: WD £20.
Societies: welcome WD by prior arrangement; minimum 20; terms on application.
Catering: clubhouse facilities.
Hotels: Bedford.

3A 68 **Tehidy Park**
Tehidy, Nr Camborne, Cornwall, TR14 0HH
☎(01209) 842208, Fax 843680, Pro 842914, Bar/Rest 842557
Off A30 at Camborne exit; follow Portrreath signs to club, 2 miles NE of Camborne.
Parkland course.
Pro James Dumbreck; Founded 1922
18 holes, 6241 yards, S.S.S. 71
Visitors: welcome with h'cap certs.
Green Fee: WD £21; WE £26.
Societies: welcome with h'cap certs; packages available.
Catering: full bar snacks and meals available.

3A 69 **Teign Valley**
Christow, Nr Exeter, Devon, EX6 7PA
☎(01647) 253026, Pro 253127
From M5 to A38 Plymouth road taking exit marked Teign Valley.
Parkland course.
Pro Richard Stephenson; Founded 1995
Designed by David Nicholson
18 holes, 5913 yards, S.S.S. 68
Visitors: welcome.
Green Fee: WD £15; WE £18.

Societies: welcome; packages available; discounts for larger groups; catering packages arranged.
Catering: full bar and catering facilities.
Practice range.
Hotels: Ilsington; Passage House; club manager can arrange local B&Bs.

3A 70 **Teignmouth**
Exeter Rd, Teignmouth, Devon, TQ14 9NY
☎(01626) 774194, Pro 772894, Sec 777070
2 miles from Teignmouth on Exeter road B3192.
Heathland course.
Pro Peter Ward; Founded 1924
Designed by Dr Alister MacKenzie
18 holes, 6183 yards, S.S.S. 70
Visitors: must be members of a club and have h'cap certs.
Green Fee: WD £22.50; WE £25.50.
Societies: welcome Tues/Thurs by arrangement; full facilities available.
Catering: full facilities available.
Hotels: London; The Bay Hotel.

3A 71 **Thurlestone**
Thurlestone, Nr Kingsbridge, Devon, TQ7 3NZ
☎(01548) 560405, Fax 560405, Pro 560715
Seaward side of A379 Kingsbridge-Salcombe road.
Downland course; all par fives on back nine.
Pro Peter Laugher; Founded 1897
18 holes, 6340 yards, S.S.S. 70
Visitors: welcome with booking and h'cap certs.
Green Fee: WD £26; WE £26.
Societies: none.
Catering: available.
Hotels: Thurlestone Hotel; Cottage Hotel, Hope Cove.

3A 72 **Tiverton**
Post Hill, Tiverton, Devon, EX14 4NE
☎(01884) 252187, Fax 252187, Pro 254836, Bar/Rest 252114
5 miles from junction 27 on M5 towards Tiverton on A373; take 1st exit left on dual carriageway through Samford Peverell to Halberton.
Parkland/meadowland course.
Pro David Sheppard; Founded 1931
Designed by James Braid
18 holes, 6236 yards, S.S.S. 71
Visitors: welcome with letter of introduction or h'cap certs; not Wed, WE, Bank Holidays or competition days.

Green Fee: WD £23; WE £30.
Societies: no societies unless a standard fixture.
Catering: lunch and teas available.
Hotels: Parkway Hotel; Tiverton; Hartnol.

3A 73 **Torquay**
Petitor Rd, St Marychurch, Torquay, Devon, TQ1 4QF
☎(01803) 314591, Pro 329113
N of Torquay on A379 Teignmouth road, on outskirts of town.
Parkland course.
Pro Martin Ruth; Founded 1910
18 holes, 6165 yards, S.S.S. 70
Visitors: welcome with h'cap certs.
Green Fee: WD £20; WE £25.
Societies: welcome by arrangement; full facilities available.
Catering: full facilities.

3A 74 **Torrington**
Weare Trees, Torrington, Devon, EX38 7EZ
☎(01805) 622229, Fax 622514
Between Bideford and Torrington.
Heathland course.
Founded 1895/1932
9 holes, 4429 yards, S.S.S. 62
Visitors: welcome.
Green Fee: WD £14; WE £16.
Societies: welcome by prior application to secretary Mr B Martin; terms on application.
Catering: facilities available.

3A 75 **Tregenna Castle Hotel**
St Ives, Cornwall, TR26 2DE
☎(01736) 795254, Fax 796066, Sec 797381
In grounds of Tregenna Castle Hotel, signposted to left just before St Ives on A3074 from Hayle.
Parkland course.
Founded 1982
18 holes, 3478 yards, S.S.S. 58
Visitors: welcome; phone for tee times.
Green Fee: WD £12.50; WE £12.50.
Societies: welcome by arrangement; full facilities available; terms on application.
Catering: full bar and restaurant.
Hotels: Tregenna Castle.

3A 76 **Treloy**
Newquay, Cornwall, TR7 4JN
☎(01637) 878554, Fax 871710
On A3059 St Columb Major-Newquay road 3 miles from Newquay.

TREVOSE GOLF & COUNTRY CLUB

Constantine Bay, Padstow, Cornwall. Tel: (01841) 520208 Fax: (01841) 521057
E-mail Info@trevose-gc.co.uk http://www.trevose-gc.co.uk.

- Championship Golf Course of 18 holes. S.S.S.71. Fully automatic watering on all greens.
- 2 x 9 hole courses. One 3100 yds, par 35, the other 1369 yds par 29.
- Excellent appointed Club House with Bar and Restaurant providing full catering facilities. A/C throughout.

- Superior Accom. in 7 Chalets, 6 Bungalows, 11 Luxury Flats & 12 Dormy Suites. Daily Rates available. Mid-week bookings encouraged. **Open all Year.**
- 3 Hard Tennis Courts.
- Heated Swimming Pool open from mid May to mid September.

- In addition to Membership for Golf and Tennis, Social Membership of the Clubis also available with full use of the Club House facilities.
- 6 glorious sandy bays within about a mile of the Club House, with pools, open sea and surf bathing.
- 8 miles from Civil Airport.
- Daily flights to and from London Gatwick.

Public heathland/parkland course.
Founded 1991
Designed by M.R.M. Sandow
9 holes, 4286 yards, S.S.S. 62
Visitors: welcome.
Green Fee: WD £11.50; WE £11.50.
Societies: welcome.
Catering: bar, full facilities.
Hotels: Barrowfield; California Hotel (Newquay).

3A 77 Trethorne

Kennards House, Launceston, Cornwall, PL15 8QE
☎ (01566) 86324, Fax 86903
2 miles west of Launceston, 200 yards off the A30 on the A395.
Parkland course.
Founded 1993
Designed by F Frayne
18 holes, 6432 yards, S.S.S. 71
Visitors: welcome.
Green Fee: WD £16; WE £16.
Societies: welcome
£10-£12 for 18 holes.
Catering: available.
Practice range, 11 bays.
Hotels: guest house on site.

3A 78 Trevose Country Club

Constantine Bay, Padstow, Cornwall, PL28 8JB
☎ (01841) 520208, Fax 521057, Pro 520261.
4 miles W of Padstow off B3276
Seaside links course.
Pro Gary Alliss; Founded 1925
Designed by H.S. Colt
18 holes, 6435 yards, S.S.S. 71
Visitors: welcome; 3 and 4 ball matches restricted; phone first.
Green Fee: WD £22; WE £22.
Societies: welcome anytime except July-Sept; full facilities available.
Catering: full facilities.
Hotels: own self-contained accommodation available; phone for details.

3A 79 Truro

Treliske, Truro, Cornwall, TR1 3LG
☎ (01872) 272640, Fax 278684, Pro 276595, Sec 278684
On edge of Truro adjacent to Treliske Hospital on the A390 Truro to Redruth road
Undulating parkland overlooking Truro; no par fives.
Pro Nigel Bicknell; Founded 1937
Designed by Colt, Alison & Morrison
18 holes, 5347 yards, S.S.S. 66
Visitors: welcome with h'cap certs.
Green Fee: WD £18; WE £22.
Societies: welcome; inclusive price on application; £12-£18.
Catering: two bars and bar snacks available.

3A 80 Warren

Dawlish Warren, Dawlish, Devon, EX7 0NF
☎ (01626) 862738, Fax 888005, Pro 864002, Sec 862255, Bar/Rest 862493
12 miles south of Exeter off the A379.
Links course.
Pro A Naldrett; Founded 1892
Designed by J Braid & Sir Guy Campbell
18 holes, 5965 yards, S.S.S. 69
Visitors: welcome.
Green Fee: WD £21; WE £24.
Societies: welcome; terms on application.
Catering: bar and meals available.
Hotels: Langstone Cliff; Sea Lawn Lodge.

3A 81 Waterbridge

Down St Mary, Nr Crediton, Devon, EX17 5LG
☎ (01363) 85111
Off A377 Barnstaple road 1 mile after Copplestone.
Parkland course.
Founded 1992

Designed by David Taylor
9 holes, 3910 yards
Visitors: welcome.
Green Fee: WD £9; WE £12.
Societies: welcome by arrangement; packages available; terms on application.
Hotels: New Inn, Crediton.

3A 82 West Cornwall

Lelant, St Ives, Cornwall, TR26 3DZ
☎ (01736) 753401, Pro 753177, Bar/Rest 753319
Take A30 to Lelant, turn right at Badger Inn.
Links course.
Pro Paul Atherton; Founded 1889
Designed by Rev Tyack
18 holes, 5884 yards, S.S.S. 69
Visitors: welcome with handicap certificates.
Green Fee: WD £20; WE £25.
Societies: welcome; catering to be negotiated; snooker; from £15.
Catering: restaurant, snack bar and bar.
Hotels: Badger Inn, Lelant; Pedn Olna, St Ives.

3A 83 Whitsand Bay Hotel Golf and Country Club

Portwrinkle, Torpoint, Cornwall, PL11 3BU
☎ (01503) 230276, Fax 230329, Pro 230788
On B3247 6 miles off A38 from Plymouth.
Clifftop course.
Pro S Poole; Founded 1905
Designed by William Fernie of Troon
18 holes, 5885 yards, S.S.S. 69
Visitors: h'cap certs required except for residents.
Green Fee: WD £20; WE £20.
Societies: welcome; bar and leisure facilities; terms on application.
Hotels: Whitsand Bay.

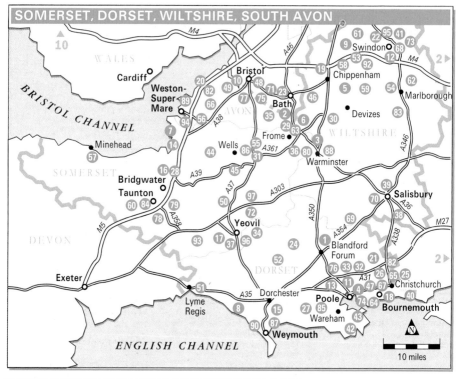

SOMERSET, DORSET, WILTSHIRE, SOUTH AVON

KEY

1	The Ashley Wood Golf Club	32	Ferndown	65	Parley Golf Centre
2	Bath Golf Club	33	Ferndown Forest	66	Puxton Park
3	Blue Circle	34	Folke	67	Queen's Park
4	Bournemouth & Meyrick	35	Fosseway Country Club		(Bournemouth)
	Park	36	Frome	68	RMCS Shrivenham
5	Bowood Golf & Country	37	Halstock	69	Rushmore Park
	Club	38	Hamptworth Golf & Country	70	Salisbury & South Wiltshire
6	Bradford-on-Avon		Club	71	Saltford
7	Brean	39	High Post	72	Sherborne
8	Bridport & West Dorset	40	Highcliffe Castle	73	Shrivenham Park
9	Brinkworth	41	Highworth Golf Centre	74	Solent Meads Par 3
10	Bristol & Clifton	42	Hyde House Country Club	75	Stockwood Vale
11	Broadstone	43	Isle of Purbeck	76	Sturminster Marshall
12	Broome Manor	44	Isle of Wedmore	77	Tall Pines
13	Bulbury	45	King Weston	78	Taunton & Pickeridge
14	Burnham & Berrow	46	Kingsdown	79	Taunton Vale
15	Came Down	47	Knighton Heath	80	Thoulstone Park
16	Cannington	48	Knowle	81	Tickenham
17	Chedington Court	49	Long Ashton	82	Two Riversmeet
18	Chichester	50	Long Sutton	83	Upavon (RAF)
19	Chippenham	51	Lyme Regis	84	Vivary
20	Clevedon	52	Lyons Gate	85	Wareham
21	Crane Valley	53	Manor House Golf Club	86	Wells (Somerset)
22	Cricklade Hotel & Country		(at Castle Combe)	87	Wessex Golf Centre
	Club	54	Marlborough	88	West Wilts
23	Cumberwell Park	55	Mendip	89	Weston-super-Mare
24	Dorset Heights	56	Mendip Spring	90	Weymouth
25	Dudmoor Farm	57	Minehead & West Somerset	91	Wheathill
26	Dudsbury	58	Monkton Park Par 3	92	The Wiltshire Golf Club
27	East Dorset	59	North Wilts	93	Windwhistle
28	Enmore Park	60	Oake Manor	94	Worlebury
29	Entry Hill	61	Oaksey Park	95	Wrag Barn Golf & Country
30	Erlestoke Sands	62	Ogbourne Downs		Club
31	Farrington	63	Orchardleigh	96	Yeovil
		64	Parkstone		

3A 84 Woodbury Park Golf & Country Club

Woodbury Castle, Woodbury, Exeter, Devon, EX5 1JJ
☎ (01395) 233382, Fax 233384
From M5 junction 30, take A3052 Sidmouth road, turn right on to B3180, after approx 1 mile turn right to Woodbury, then immediately turn right to course.
Parkland/moorland/heathland course.
Founded 1992
Designed by J. Hamilton Stutt
18 holes, 6626 yards, S.S.S. 72
Visitors: welcome with h'cap certs.
Green Fee: WD £35; WE £45.
Societies: welcome by prior arrangement; catering packages by arrangement; 9 hole Acorn course 4582 yds par 65 SSS 62; terms on application.
Catering: full facilities.
Practice range, available.
Hotels: Swiss style lodges on site with leisure complex.

3A 85 Wrangaton

Golf Links Road, Wrangaton, South Brent, , TQ10 9HJ

Bowood Golf & Country Club

Set in the heart of Bowood Park, this 18 hole golf course was voted in the Top Ten New Courses in Britain and Top Fifty Golf Destinations in Europe by Golf World Magazine. With a £2m Clubhouse extension opening June 1998, the quality of the facilities will match the quality of the course. Superb practice grounds include 2 putting greens, a floodlit driving range and a three hole academy course.
Also, Queenwood Golf Lodge, your own rural retreat.

Derry Hill, Calne, Wilts. Tel: 01249 822228

☎(01364) 73229, Pro 72161
Turn off A38 between South Brent and Bittaford at Wrangaton P.O,.
Moorland/parkland course.
Pro Adrian Whitehead; Founded 1895
Designed by Donald Steel
18 holes, 6083 yards, S.S.S. 69
Visitors: welcome with h'cap certs or member of recognised club; no beginners.
Green Fee: WD £17; WE £23.
Societies: welcome by arrangement; full facilities.
Catering: bar and catering (except Mon in winter).
Hotels: The Coach House Inn; Glazebrook.

3A 86 **Yelverton**
Golf Links Rd, Yelverton, Devon, PL20 6BN
☎(01822) 852824, Fax 852824, Pro 853593, Bar/Rest 855658
Off A386 8 miles north of Plymouth.
Moorland course.
Pro Tim McSherry; Founded 1904
Designed by Herbert Fowler
18 holes, 6351 yards, S.S.S. 72
Visitors: welcome with h'cap certs.
Green Fee: WD £30; WE £40.
Societies: welcome with h'cap certss; full bar and restaurant facilities; £15-24.
Catering: restaurant and bar.
Hotels: Moorland Links course; Burrator Inn; Rosemount Guest House.

3B 1 **The Ashley Wood Golf Club**
Wimborne Rd, Blandford, Dorset, DT11 9HN
☎(01258) 452253, Fax 450590, Pro 450379
Half a mile from Blandford.
Parkland course; two par 5s in first three holes.

Pro Spencer Taylor; Founded 1896
Designed by Patrick Tallack
18 holes, 6276 yards, S.S.S. 70
Visitors: welcome WD, h/cap certs required at WE.
Green Fee: WD £24; WE £35.
Societies: welcome WD; apply to Sec.
Hotels: Anvil (Pimperne).

3B 2 **Bath Golf Club**
Sham Castle, North Rd, Bath, Somerset, BA2 6JG
☎(01225) 425182, Fax 331027, Pro 466953, Sec 463834 ♦
1.5 miles SE of Bath off A36 Warminster road.
Downland course.
Pro Peter Hancox; Founded 1880
Designed by H S Colt
18 holes, 6438 yards, S.S.S. 71
Visitors: welcome; h'cap certs required.
Green Fee: WD £25; WE £30.
Societies: welcome Wed and Fri only; coffee, 18 holes, soup & sandwiches - £25; 18 holes, 3-course dinner - £40.
Hotels: Bath; Beaufort, Dukes; Spa.

3B 3 **Blue Circle**
Trowbridge Rd, Westbury, Wilts
☎(01373) 822481
Part of Blue Circle Works Sports Complex.
Parkland course.
9 holes, 5600 yards, S.S.S. 66
Visitors: with member only or on county card system.
Green Fee: on application.
Societies: welcome by prior arrangement; terms on application.
Catering: by arrangement.

3B 4 **Bournemouth & Meyrick Park**
Central Drive, Meyrick Park, Bournemouth, BH2 6LH

☎(01202) 292425, Fax 290233
In centre of Bournemouth
Picturesque parkland course (Meyrick Park).
Founded 1890
18 holes, 5757 yards, S.S.S. 68
Visitors: welcome any time; advisable to book previous day.
Green Fee: WD £12.50; WE £13.80.
Societies: welcome by prior arrangement; packages available; full facilities.
Catering: bars and restaurant.

3B 5 **Bowood Golf & Country Club**
Derby Hill, Calne, Wilts, SN11 9PQ
☎(01249) 822228, Fax 822218
Off the A4 between Chippenham and Calne.
Parkland course.
Pro Nigel Blenkarne; Founded 1992
Designed by Dave Thomas
18 holes, 7317 yards
Visitors: welcome on WD and after 12 noon WE.
Green Fee: WD £32; WE £32.
Societies: welcome by prior arrangement; special rates on Mon; coffee & bacon roll, 9 holes, Ploughman's lunch, 18 holes, 3-course dinner; £51.
Catering: full facilities.
Practice range, 10 bays; floodlit range.
Hotels: Queenwood Golf Lodge, Bowood Golf & CC; Lucknam Park Hotel, Colerne.

3B 6 **Bradford-on-Avon**
Avon Close, Trowbridge Rd, Bradford-on-Avon
☎(01225) 868268
From Bradford towards Trowbridge on left near Police station.
Picturesque parkland course next to River Avon.
Founded 1991
9 holes, 2109 yards, S.S.S. 61

Visitors: welcome anytime; pay and play course.
Green Fee: WD £6; WE £6.
Societies: welcome by prior arrangement.
Catering: none.

3B 7 **Brean**
Coast Rd, Brean, Burnham-on-Sea, Somerset, TA8 2QY
☎(01278) 751595, Fax 751595, Pro 752111, Sec 751570
Follow tourist signs for Brean Lesiure Park from junction 22 of M5.
Meadowland course.
Pro Sue Spencer; Founded 1973
Designed by Brean Leisure Park
18 holes, 5715 yards, S.S.S. 68
Visitors: welcome at all times except competition days.
Green Fee: WD £15; WE £18.
Societies: welcome WD and after 1pm at WE; packages available; from £14-£16.
Catering: facilities available.
Hotels: accommodation available on the Brean Leisure Park.

3B 8 **Bridport & West Dorset**
East Cliff, West Bay, Bridport, Dorset, DT6 4EP
☎(01308) 421095, Fax 421095, Pro 421491, Bar/Rest 422597
1.5 miles south of Bridport at West Bay.
Clifftop links course.
Pro David Parsons; Founded 1891
Designed by G.S.P. Salmon / 1996 modified by F Hawtree
18 holes, 6028 yards, S.S.S. 69
Visitors: welcome; dress codes apply.
Green Fee: WD £22; WE £22.
Societies: welcome; bookings must be made in advance; packages can be arranged to meet individual requirements; terms on application.
Catering: full facilities.
Hotels: Haddon House, West Bay.

3B 9 **Brinkworth**
Longmans Farm, Brinkworth, Chippenham, Wilts, SN15 5DG
☎(01666) 510277
Between Swindon and Malmesbury on B4042.
Meadowland course.
Founded 1984
18 holes, 70 yards, S.S.S. 69
Visitors: welcome anytime.
Green Fee: WD £7.50; WE £9.50.
Societies: welcome by arrangement.
Catering: full facilities.

3B 10 **Bristol & Clifton**
Beggar Bush Lane, Failand, Nr Clifton, Bristol, BS8 3TH
☎(01275) 393474, Fax 394611, Pro 393031
Junction 19 off M5, 4 miles along A369 to Bristol turn right at traffic lights, then further 1.5 miles.
Parkland course.
Founded 1891
18 holes, 6316 yards, S.S.S. 70
Visitors: welcome WD with h'cap certs; restrictions at WE.
Green Fee: WD £30; WE £35.
Societies: welcome by arrangement on Thurs only; full facilities available.
Catering: full facilities.
Hotels: Redwood Lodge.

3B 11 **Broadstone**
Wentworth Drive, Broadstone, BH 18 8DQ
☎(01202) 692595, Fax 692595, Pro 692835, Bar/Rest 693363
Take A349 from Poole to village; club signposted off main roundabout.
Heathland course.
Pro Nigel Tokley; Founded 1898
Designed by George Dunn (1898) & H.S. Colt (1925)
18 holes, 6315 yards, S.S.S. 70
Visitors: members may introduce one guest per round.
Green Fee: WD £15; WE £15.
Societies: welcome but only Mon, Tues, Wed, Fri 9.30-11am; Mon-Fri 2.30-4pm; £28-£36.
Catering: full bar and restaurant facilities.

3B 12 **Broome Manor**
Piper's Way, Swindon, Wilts, SN3 1RG
☎(01793) 495761, Fax 433255, Pro 532403, Bar/Rest 490939
Take Junction 15 off M4 and follow signs; course 2 miles off motorway.
Parkland course.
Pro Barry Sandry; Founded 1976
Designed by Hawtree & Son
18 holes, 6283 yards, S.S.S. 70
Visitors: pay and play course.
Green Fee: WD £10.50; WE £10.50.
Societies: welcome Mon-Fri; 27 holes, driving range and most packages include 1st tee video analysis; £15-£40.
Catering: full facilities.
Practice range, 34 bays.

3B 13 **Bulbury**
Halls Rd, Lytchett Matravers, Nr Poole, Dorset, BH16 6EP

☎(01929) 459574, Fax 459000
On main A35 3 miles from Poole.
Parkland course set in ancient woodlands
Pro Nigel Gravelle; Founded 1989
Designed by J. Sharkey
18 holes, 6313 yards, S.S.S. 70
Visitors: welcome.
Green Fee: WD £20; WE £20.
Societies: welcome; full catering packages available on application; terms on application.
Catering: full à la carte and bistro menu.
Hotels: on site accommodation.

3B 14 **Burnham & Berrow**
St Christopher's Way, Burnham-on-Sea, Somerset, TA8 2PE
☎(01278) 783137, Fax 795440, Pro 784545, Sec 785760
M5 junction 32; 1 mile N of Burnham
Seaside links; also has a 9-hole course.
Pro Mark Crowther-Smith; Founded 1890
18 holes, 6393 yards, S.S.S. 71
Visitors: must be members of golf clubs with handicaps of 22 and under.
Green Fee: WD £34; WE £48.
Societies: terms on application.
Catering: full facilities.
Hotels: Batch Farm, Lympsham; Lulworth GH; Warren GH, both Burnham-on-Sea.

3B 15 **Came Down**
Came Down, Dorchester, Dorset, DT2 8NR
☎(01305) 812531, Fax 813494, Pro 812670
2 miles S of Dorchester off A354.
Undulating downland course.
Pro David Holmes; Founded 1896
Designed by J.H. Taylor
18 holes, 6244 yards, S.S.S. 71
Visitors: welcome by arrangement with h'cap certs; midweek after 9am; Sun after 11am.
Green Fee: WD £22; WE £27.50.
Societies: welcome by arrangement on Wed; packages available, approx £32; full facilities.
Catering: bar and restaurant.
Hotels: Rembrandt (Weymouth); Junction Hotel (Dorchester).

3B 16 **Cannington**
Cannington College, Nr Bridgewater, Somerset, TA5 2LS
☎(01278) 655050
M5 junction 23. Take A38 to

Cumberwell Park Golf Club

Bradford-on-Avon, Wiltshire BA15 2PQ. Tel: (01225) 863322 • Fax: (01225) 868160

Superb Parkland Course • A363 Bath Road to Bradford-on-Avon • 18 Holes / 27 Holes Sept '99 •
Par 72 SSS 72 • Catering All Day / Bar Snacks • Functions Rooms Green Fees £20 W/Day £25 Wk/End •
Societies Welcome W/day - Prior Arrangement several packages available • Start times required for
playing • Wedding & Conference Facilities • Corporate and Society packages available.

Bridgwater; course is 4 miles from Bridgwater on A39 road to Minehead.
Links/parkland course.
Pro Ron Macrew; Founded 1993
Designed by Martin Hawtree
9 holes, 5858 yards, S.S.S. 68
Visitors: welcome.
Green Fee: on application.
Societies: apply to Pro; 25% off for groups of 12+; terms on application.
Catering: bar and restaurant.

3B 17 Chedington Court
South Perrott, Beaminster, Dorset, DT8 3HU
☎(01935) 891413
0.5 mile E of South Perrott on A356 Crewkerne-Dorchester road.
Parkland course.
Pro Simon Tucker; Founded 1991
Designed by D. Hemstock, P. & H. Chapman
18 holes, 5924 yards, S.S.S. 70
Visitors: welcome; properly dressed.
Green Fee: WD £12; WE £16.
Societies: welcome by arrangement; terms on application.
Catering: refreshments available. Practice range, basic pitch and putt course; driving and practice area.
Hotels: Chedington Court.

3B 18 Chichester
Iford Bridge Sports Centre, Barrack Rd, Christchurch, Dorset, BH23 2BA
☎(01202) 473817
Off the A35 between Bournemouth and Christchurch.
Parkland course.
Pro Peter Troth/Laurence Moxon; Founded 1977
9 holes, 4360 yards, S.S.S. 61
Visitors: welcome.
Green Fee: WD £6.05; WE £6.80.
Societies: welcome by prior arrangement; also tennis, bowling.
Catering: full bar facilities. Practice range.
Hotels: contact local tourist board.

3B 19 Chippenham
Malmesbury Rd, Chippenham, Wilts, SN15 5LT

☎(01249) 652040, Fax 446681, Pro 655519, Bar/Rest 443481
From M4 junction 17 take A350 towards Chippenham; course on right before town.
Parkland course.
Pro Bill Creamer; Founded 1896
18 holes, 5600 yards, S.S.S. 67
Visitors: welcome.
Green Fee: WD £20; WE £25.
Societies: welcome Tues, Thurs, Fri by prior arrangement; full day golf and catering packages available; from £35.
Catering: clubhouse facilities.

3B 20 Clevedon
Castle Rd, Clevedon, North Somerset, BS21 7AA
☎(01275) 874057, Fax 341228, Pro 874704, Bar/Rest 873140
M5 Junction 20 and follow signs to Portishead. Turn right into Walton Road then Holly Lane.
Hilltop course overlooking Bristol Channel.
Pro Martin Heggie; Founded 1908
Designed by J H Taylor
18 holes, 6117 yards, S.S.S. 69
Visitors: welcome with h'cap certs.
Green Fee: WD £22; WE £30.
Societies: welcome except Fri, must book in advance and minimum of 12; terms on application.
Catering: facilities and bar.
Hotels: Walton Park; Highcliffe House.

3B 21 Crane Valley
West Farm, Romford, Verwood, Dorset, BH31 7LE
☎(01202) 814088, Fax 813407
On B3081 0.5 miles after Verwood.
Parkland course.
Pro Paul Cannings; Founded 1992
Designed by Donald Steel
18 holes, 6424 yards, S.S.S. 71
Visitors: welcome with h'cap certs.
Green Fee: on application.
Societies: welcome WD; packages available; academy course 4120 yards, par 66; terms on application.
Catering: clubhouse facilities. Practice range, 12 bays; floodlit.
Hotels: West Farm SC; St Leonards Hotel.

3B 22 Cricklade Hotel & Country Club
Common Hill, Cricklade, Wilts, SN6 6HA
☎(01793) 750751, Fax 751767
B4040 Cricklade-Malmesbury road, 15 mins from M4 junctions 15/16.
Parkland course.
Pro Ian Bolt; Founded 1990
Designed by Ian Bolt/C Smith
9 holes, 3660 yards, S.S.S. 57
Visitors: welcome Mon-Fri; WE must be accompanied by a member.
Green Fee: WD £10; WE £10.
Societies: welcome; terms on application.
Catering: full bar and restaurant facilities.
Hotels: Cricklade.

3B 23 Cumberwell Park
Bradford on Avon, Wiltshire, BA15 2PQ
☎(01225) 863322, Fax 868160
M4 junction 18. Take A46 to Bath and then A363 to Bradford-on-Avon.
Parkland course.
Pro John Jacobs; Founded 1994
Designed by A Stiff
18 holes, 6810 yards, S.S.S. 71
Visitors: welcome.
Green Fee: WD £12; WE £16.
Societies: welcome Mon-Fri; 18 holes of golf plus 3-course private dinner and coffee on arrival; £33.
Catering: bar and restaurant.
Hotels: Bath Spa Hotel; Swan Hotel, Bradford-on-Avon.

3B 24 Dorset Heights
Belchalwell, Blandford Forum, Dorset, DT11 0EG
☎(01258) 861386, Fax 860900, Pro 861916
On A357 Sturminster Newton-Blandford road.
Woodland course.
Founded 1991
Designed by Project Golf (D.W. Asthill)
18 holes, 6138 yards, S.S.S. 70
Visitors: welcome with prior arrangement.
Green Fee: WD £12; WE £17.
Societies: welcome by prior arrange-

ment; packages available; restaurant; terms on application.
Catering: restaurant, bar.
Hotels: Crown Hotel, Blandford.

3B 25 **Dudmoor Farm**
Dudmoor Farm Rd, Christchurch, Dorset, BH23 6AQ
☎(01202) 483980
Off A35 W of Christchurch.
Woodland course.
Founded 1974
9 holes, 1428 yards
Visitors: welcome anytime.
Green Fee: WD £4.50; WE £4.50.
Societies: welcome by arrangement.
Catering: snacks and soft drinks.
Hotels: Avon Causeway; B&B available on site.

3B 26 **Dudsbury**
64 Christchurch Rd, Ferndown, Dorset, BH22 8ST
☎(01202) 593499, Fax 594555, Pro 594488
On B3073 off A348 from Ferndown.
Parkland course.
Pro Roger Tuddenham; Founded 1992
Designed by Donald Steel
18 holes, 6765 yards, S.S.S. 72
Visitors: welcome with prior booking.
Green Fee: WD £30; WE £35.
Societies: welcome; packages available from secretary; restaurant, lounge bar, 6-hole par 3 course; terms on application.
Catering: spikes and lounge bar, function room and restaurant.
Hotels: Dormy Hotel; Bridge House.

3B 27 **East Dorset**
Bere Regis, Wareham, Dorset, BH20 7NT
☎(01929) 472244, Fax 471294, Pro 471294
A35 or A31 50 Bere Regis, take Wool road and signs to the club.
Parkland course.
Pro Derwyn Honan; Founded 1978
Designed by Martin Hawtree
18 holes, 6580 yards, S.S.S. 73
Visitors: welcome with prior reservation.
Green Fee: WD £27; WE £32.
Societies: welcome any day with reservation; combination of courses and catering on application; £30.
Catering: full facilities.
Practice range; floodlit and covered.
Hotels: own accommodation, the Dorsetshire Golf Lodge, includes free golf.

3B 28 **Enmore Park**
Enmore, Bridgewater, Somerset, TA5 2AN
☎(01278) 671481, Fax 671481, Pro 671519, Bar/Rest 671244
M5 to junction 23 or 24; follow A38/39 to Bridgwater; A39 to Minehead, then left to Spaxton/Durleigh, left at reservoir and course is 2 miles on right.
Parkland course.
Pro Nigel Wixon; Founded 1906
Designed by Hawtree and Son
18 holes, 6406 yards, S.S.S. 71
Visitors: welcome but handicap required at WE.
Green Fee: WD £18; WE £25.
Societies: Mon, Thurs or Fri with advance booking; 27-hole packages available; £22.
Catering: full facilities.
Practice range.

3B 29 **Entry Hill**
Entry Hill, Bath, Somerset, BA2 5NA
☎(01225) 834248
Take A367 Wells road from city centre, fork left into Entry Hill Road after 1 mile; course is 0.5 mile on right.
Compact, hilly parkland course.
Pro Tim Tapley; Founded 1984
9 holes, 2103 yards, S.S.S. 61
Visitors: welcome; book up to 7 days in advance for WE, Bank Holidays and peak periods.
Green Fee: WD £6; WE £6.
Societies: welcome.

3B 30 **Erlestoke Sands**
Erlestoke, Devizes, Wiltshire, SN10 5UB
☎(01380) 831069, Fax 831069, Pro 831027, Bar/Rest 830507
On B3098 off A350 at Westbury signposted Bratton, course 6 miles on left before village of Erlestoke (3 miles) on right after Erlestoke village.
Parkland course.
Pro Adrian Marsh; Founded 1992
Designed by Adrian Stiff
18 holes, 6406 yards, S.S.S. 71
Visitors: welcome.
Green Fee: WD £16; WE £25.
Societies: preferably WD by prior arrangement; full facilities.
Catering: full facilities.

3B 31 **Farrington**
Marsh Lane, Farrington Gurney, Bristol, BS18 5TS
☎(01761) 453440, Fax 241274, Pro 241787, Sec 241274
12 miles south of Bristol on A37.

Parkland course with lakes.
Pro Peter Thompson; Founded 1993
Designed by Peter Thompson
18 holes, 6693 yards, S.S.S. 72
Visitors: welcome but must telephone first.
Green Fee: WD £20; WE £30.
Societies: welcome WD only; 2 courses, driving range, spikes bar, restaurant and private suite seating 150; BBQ area; terms on application.
Catering: bar and restaurant.
Practice range, 16 bays covered; floodlit.
Hotels: Hunstrete House, Hunstrete; Hamham House, Paulton; Stow Easton Park, Stow Easton.

3B 32 **Ferndown**
119 Golf Links Rd, Ferndown, Dorset, BH22 8BU
☎(01202) 874602, Fax 873926, Pro 873825
A31 to Trickett's Cross and A348 to Ferndown.
Heathland course.
Pro Ian Parker; Founded 1913
Designed by Harold Hilton (Old course)
18 holes, 6452 yards, S.S.S. 71
Visitors: with prior permission, h'cap certs required; limited WE.
Green Fee: WD £40; WE £45.
Societies: Tues and Fri only; full facilities; 9-hole course 5604 yards; terms on application.
Catering: full facilities all week.
Hotels: Coach House Motel; Dormy; Bridge House.

3B 33 **Ferndown Forest**
Forest Links Road, Ferndown, Dorset, BH22 9QE
☎(01202) 876096, Fax 894095, Sec 894095, Bar/Rest 874990
Midway between Ringwood and Wimborne directly off the Ferndown by-pass A31.
Parkland course; extension planned for 1998.
Pro Kevin Spurgeon; Founded 1993
Designed by G Hunt & R Grafham
18 holes, 4920 yards, S.S.S. 63
Visitors: welcome.
Green Fee: WD £10; WE £12.
Societies: welcome; catering facilities; £8-£10.
Catering: full bar and restaurant facilities.
Practice range, 19; floodlit bays with targets.
Hotels: Dormy House on course; Coach House Motel, Ferndown.

3B 34 Folke
Folke Golf Centre, Alweston,
Sherborne, Dorset, DT9 5HR
☎(01963) 23330
From Sherborne head towards
Sturminster Newton, 2 miles from
Sherborne turn off towards Alweston;
course is 200 yards away.
Parkland course.
Founded 1993
9 holes, 2847 yards, S.S.S. 66
Visitors: welcome.
Green Fee: WD £7; WE £9.
Societies: welcome by prior arrangement; terms on application.
Catering: sandwiches, snacks, bar.
Practice range, 10 covered bays;
floodlit.

3B 35 Fosseway Country Club
Charlton Lane, Midsomer Norton,
Bath, Somerset, BA3 4BD
☎(01761) 412214, Fax 418357
10 miles south of Bath on the A367.
Parkland course.
Founded 1971
Designed by C K Cotton/F Pennink
9 holes, 4278 yards, S.S.S. 65
Visitors: by prior arrangement.
Green Fee: WD £8; WE £11.
Societies: terms on application.
Catering: facilities.
Hotels: Centurion Hotel (on site).

3B 36 Frome
Critchill Manor, Frome, Somerset, BA
11 4LJ
☎(01373) 453410, Fax 453410
Take A361 from Frome towards
Shepton Mallett; at Nunney Catch
roundabout follow signs to course.
Parkland course.
Founded 1994
18 holes, 4890 yards, S.S.S. 64
Visitors: welcome.
Green Fee: WD £10; WE £12.
Societies: welcome; contact club for
details; terms on application.
Catering: available.

3B 37 Halstock
Halstock Golf Enterprises, Common
Lane, Nr Yeovil, Somerset, BA22 9SF
☎(01935) 891689, Fax 891839
300 yards from centre of Halstock village, turn right at green, from Quiet
Woman Pub, 50 yards on left past
village shop/P.O. signposted.
Parkland course.
Founded 1988
18 holes, 4351 yards, S.S.S. 63
Visitors: welcome.

Green Fee: WD £10; WE £12.
Societies: welcome by arrangement;
terms on application.
Catering: light refreshments available.

3B 38 Hamptworth Golf & Country Club
Hamptworth Rd, Hamptworth, Wilts,
SP5 2DU
☎(01794) 390155, Fax 390022
6 miles from M27 junctions 1 and 2,
off A36 to Salisbury, follow Landford
and then Downton road signs.
Parkland course among ancient woodlands, lakes and river.
Pro Mark Smith; Founded 1994
Designed by Brian Pierson and D.
Saunders
18 holes, 6512 yards, S.S.S. 71
Visitors: welcome by arrangement;
h'cap certs required.
Green Fee: WD £25; WE £25.
Societies: welcome by arrangement,
h'cap certs required for entire group;
full facilities.
Catering: full facilities.
Hotels: Devore Grand Harbour.

3B 39 High Post
Great Durnford, Salisbury, Wilts, SP4
6AT
☎(01722) 782356, Fax 782356, Pro
782219
Halfway between Salisbury and
Amesbury on the A345, opposite the
Inn at High Post.
Downland course.
Pro Ian Welding; Founded 1922
18 holes, 6305 yards, S.S.S. 70
Visitors: welcome WD without restriction; h'cap certs required at WE.
Green Fee: WD £23; WE £28.
Societies: welcome WD by arrangement; full facilities available.
Catering: full facilities.
Hotels: The Inn; High Post; Milford
Hall (Salisbury).

3B 40 Highcliffe Castle
107 Lymington Rd, Highcliffe on Sea,
Dorset, BH23 4LA
☎(01425) 272953, Fax 272210
1 mile W of Highcliffe on A337.
Parkland course.
Founded 1913
18 holes, 4776 yards, S.S.S. 63
Visitors: welcome if member of recognised golf club.
Green Fee: WD £19.50; WE £27.50.
Societies: by prior arrangement with
the secretary; terms on application.
Catering: clubhouse facilities.

3B 41 Highworth Golf Centre
Highworth Community Golf Centre,
Swindon Road, Highworth, Wilts, SN6
7SJ
☎(01793) 766014
Take A361 from Swindon.
Parkland course.
Pro Mark Toombs; Founded 1990
Designed by Swindon Council
9 holes, 3120 yards
Visitors: pay as you play.
Green Fee: WD £6.50; WE £6.50.
Societies: pay as you play.

3B 42 Hyde House Country Club
Hyde, Nr Wareham, Dorset, Club
(01929) 471847, Fax 471849
SE of Wareham.
Woodland/parkland course with river
and lakes.
Designed by J. Hamilton Stutt
18 holes, 6469 yards, S.S.S. 72
Visitors: welcome by arrangement.
Green Fee: WD £15; WE £15.
Societies: welcome any day by
arrangement; full facilities, packages
available; also outdoor activities centre.
Catering: full facilities.
Hotels: accommodation available.

3B 43 Isle Of Purbeck
Studland, Swanage, Dorset, BH19
3AB
☎(01929) 450361, Fax 450501, Pro
450354
3 miles north of Swanage on the
B3351 Corfe Castle road.
Heathland, set in a nature reserve.
Pro Ian Brake; Founded 1892
Designed by H.S. Colt
18 holes, 6295 yards, S.S.S. 71
Visitors: welcome.
Green Fee: WD £26; WE £32.
Societies: welcome; morning coffee,
Ploughman's lunch, 2 rounds of golf,
two course dinner; £45-£48.
Catering: bar, snacks and restaurant.

3B 44 Isle of Wedmore
Lineage, Lascots Hill, Wedmore,
Somerset, BS28 4QT
☎(01934) 713649, Fax 713696, Pro
712452
Junction 22 off M5; take A38 north to
Bristol, after 5 miles turn right in Lower
Weare; follow signposts to Wedmore.
Parkland course.
Founded 1992
Designed by Terry Murray
18 holes, 6009 yards, S.S.S. 68

Visitors: welcome but after 9.30 at WE.
Green Fee: WD £18; WE £22.
Societies: welcome; packages available; private function room and professional lessons also available; £24-£32.

3B 45 **King Weston**
Millfield Enterprises Sports & Recreation, Nr Glastonbury, BA16 0YD
☎(01458) 448300
1 mile SE of Butleigh.
Parkland course.
Founded 1970
9 holes, 4434 yards, S.S.S. 62
Visitors: welcome with member when not required by school.
Green Fee: WD £5; WE £5.
Societies: limited.

3B 46 **Kingsdown**
Kingsdown, Corsham, Wilts, SN13 8BS
☎(01225) 742530, Fax 743472, Pro 742634, Sec 743472
5 miles E of Bath on A365.
Downland course.
Pro Andrew Butler; Founded 1880
18 holes, 6445 yards, S.S.S. 71
Visitors: welcome Mon-Fri; h'cap certs required.
Green Fee: WD £22; WE £22.
Societies: welcome Mon-Fri; full bar and catering facilities; £22.
Catering: bar and catering facilities.

3B 47 **Knighton Heath**
Francis Ave, Bournemouth, Dorset, B11 8NX
☎(01202) 572633, Fax 590774, Pro 578275
From junction of A348/A3049 (Mountbatten Arms) signposted.
Heathland course.
Pro Jane Mills; Founded 1976
18 holes, 6084 yards, S.S.S. 69
Visitors: welcome after 9.30 WD; members guests at WE.
Green Fee: WD £20; WE £20.
Societies: welcome by arrangement; minimum 12 players; packages available; from £35.
Catering: full catering facilities.

3B 48 **Knowle**
Fairway, West Town Lane, Brislington, Bristol, BS4 5DF
☎(0117) 9776341, Fax 9720615, Pro 9779193, Sec 9770660
3 miles S of City Centre on A4 to Bath

or A37 to Shepton Mallett.
Parkland course.
Pro Gordon Brand; Founded 1905
Designed by Hawtree & J.H. Taylor
18 holes, 6016 yards, S.S.S. 69
Visitors: welcome with h'cap certs.
Green Fee: WD £22; WE £27.
Societies: welcome on Thurs; coffee, lunch, evening meal available; from £22.
Catering: full facilities.

3B 49 **Long Ashton**
Clarken Combe, Long Ashton, Bristol, BS18 9DW
☎(01275) 392316, Fax 394395, Pro 392265
Leave M5 at junction 19, take A369 to Bristol, turn right into B3129 at traffic lights and then left on to B3128; club is 0.5 mile on right
Undulating moorland/downland course.
Pro Denis Scanlan; Founded 1893
Designed by Hawtree & Taylor
18 holes, 6177 yards, S.S.S. 70
Visitors: welcome with official club h'cap certs.
Green Fee: WD £26; WE £35.
Societies: welcome by arrangement; full facilities available.
Catering: full facilities daily until 6pm; evening meals by arrangement.
Hotels: Redwood Lodge.

3B 50 **Long Sutton**
Long Load, Nr Langport, Somerset, TA10 9JU
☎(01458) 241017, Fax 241022
Course after Long Sutton village.
Parkland course.
Pro Michaell Blackwell; Founded 1990
Designed by Patrick Dawson
18 holes, 6368 yards, S.S.S. 70
Visitors: welcome with advance tee reservation.
Green Fee: WD £14; WE £17.
Societies: welcome by prior arrangement; full facilities; terms on application.
Catering: bar, restaurant and function rooms.
Hotels: list can be provided.

3B 51 **Lyme Regis**
Timber Hill, Lyme Regis, Dorset, DT7 3HQ
☎(01297) 442963, Pro 443822, Bar/Rest 442043
Off A3052 Charmouth road 1 mile E of town.
Clifftop course.

Pro Andrew Black; Founded 1893
18 holes, 6283 yards, S.S.S. 70
Visitors: welcome with h'cap certs or proof of membership of recognised club; restrictions Thurs and Sun am.
Green Fee: WD £20; WE £20.
Societies: welcome by arrangement, not Thurs or Sun am; full facilities available; £24.
Catering: hot and cold snacks all day; full restaurant.
Hotels: Alexander; Bay; Buena Vista; Devon; Fairwater Head; Tudor House.

3B 52 **Lyons Gate**
Lyons Gate Farm, Lyons Gate, Dorchester, DT2 7AZ
☎(01300) 345239
3 miles N of Cerne Abbas on A352 Sherborne-Dorchester road.
Wooded farmland/parkland course.
Founded 1991
Designed by Ken Abel
9 holes, 2000 yards, S.S.S. 30
Visitors: welcome; no restrictions.
Green Fee: on application.
Societies: welcome by arrangement.
Catering: light refreshments available.
Hotels: Kings Arms.

3B 53 **Manor House Golf Club (at Castle Combe)**
Castle Combe, Wilts, SN14 7PL
☎(01249) 782982, Fax 782992, Pro 783101
On B4039 to N of Castle Combe village.
Ancient woodland/parkland course.
Pro Chris Smith; Founded 1992
Designed by Peter Alliss and Clive Clark
18 holes, 6340 yards, S.S.S. 71
Visitors: welcome anytime with h'cap certs and prior tee reservation.
Green Fee: WD £35; WE £45.
Societies: welcome by arrangement; full facilities.
Catering: 2 bars, restaurant, private dining facilities, bar snacks available all day.
Hotels: Manor House.

3B 54 **Marlborough**
The Common, Marlborough, Wilts, SN8 1DU
☎(01672) 512147, Fax 513164, Pro 512493
On the A346 1 miles north of Marlborough; 7 miles south of M4 exit 15.
Downland course.
Pro Simon Amor; Founded 1888

Designed by T Simpson / upgraded 1920 by H Fowler
18 holes, 6491 yards, S.S.S. 71
Visitors: welcome with prior arrangement.
Green Fee: WD £21; WE £40.
Societies: welcomed midweek, particularly Tues and Thurs; day's golf, coffee, light lunch and dinner; from £25.
Catering: full facilities.
Hotels: Castle and Ball Hotel; Ivy House Hotel, both Marlborough.

3B 55 Mendip

Gurney Slade, Bath, Somerset, BA3 4UT
☎(01749) 840570, Fax 841439, Pro 840793
3 miles N of Shepton Mallet off A37.
Undulating downland course.
Pro Ron Lee; Founded 1908
Designed by H. Vardon with extension by F. Pennink
18 holes, 6381 yards, S.S.S. 70
Visitors: welcome by arrangement; starting times may be reserved.
Green Fee: WD £20; WE £30.
Societies: welcome by arrangement Mon & Thurs; full facilities.
Catering: full facilities.
Hotels: Stone Easton Park Hotel.

3B 56 Mendip Spring

Honeyhall Lane, Congresbury, North Somerset, BS19 5JT
☎(01934) 853337, Fax 853021, Bar/Rest 852322
Take A370 from M5 junction 21 to Congresbury.
Parkland/water features; also 9-hole Orchard course.
Pro John Blackburn; Founded 1991
Designed by Terry Murray
18 holes, 6334 yards, S.S.S. 70
Visitors: welcome by prior arrangement.
Green Fee: WD £21; WE £24.
Societies: welcome; full catering facilities; halfway house facilities for refreshments, buggies; terms on application.
Catering: full facilities.
Practice range, 10 bays.

3B 57 Minehead & West Somerset

The Warren, Minehead, Somerset, TA24 5SJ
☎(01643) 702057, Fax 705095, Pro 704378
Course at end of seafront.
Links course.

Pro Ian Read; Founded 1882
Designed by Johnny Alan
18 holes, 6228 yards, S.S.S. 71
Visitors: welcome.
Green Fee: WD £22; WE £25.
Societies: welcome on written application; full facilities.
Catering: by prior arrangement with caterer; snacks always available.
Hotels: York; Northfield; Marshfield.

3B 58 Monkton Park Par 3

Monkton Park, Chippenham, Wilts, SN15 3PE
☎(01249) 653928, Fax 653928
Into Chippenham, past railway station, turn right.
Parkland course.
Founded 1960
Designed by M. Dawson
9 holes, 990 yards, S.S.S. 27
Visitors: welcome.
Green Fee: WD £3.50; WE £3.75.
Catering: refreshments available.

3B 59 North Wilts

Bishops Cannings, Devizes, Wilts, SN10 2LP
☎(01380) 860257, Fax 860877, Pro 860330, Sec 860627
Take A361 Devizes to Swindon road and after 3 miles turn to Calne.
Downland course.
Pro Graham Laing; Founded 1890/1972
Designed by K Cotton
18 holes, 6333 yards, S.S.S. 70
Visitors: welcome by prior arrangement.
Green Fee: WD £19; WE £25.
Societies: welcome WD by prior arrangement; brochure and price list available; terms on application.
Catering: clubhouse facilities.
Hotels: Bear, Devizes; Landsdown, Calne.

3B 60 Oake Manor

Oake, Taunton, Somerset, TA4 1BA
☎(01823) 461993, Fax 461995, Bar/Rest 461992
5 minutes from Junction 26 off M5.
Gently undulating parkland course with water.
Pro Russell Gardner; Founded 1993
Designed by Adrian Stiff
18 holes, 6109 yards, S.S.S. 69
Visitors: welcome but must phone to reserve tee time.
Green Fee: WD £16.50; WE £20.
Societies: welcome; contact Golf manager Russell Gardner; from £20.

Catering: function rooms, bar and restaurant.
Practice range, 11 bays.
Hotels: Rumwell Manor.

3B 61 Oaksey Park

Oaksey, Nr Malmesbury, Wilts, SN16 9SB
☎(01666) 577995, Fax 577174
Off A419 between Swindon and Cirencester, W of Cotswold Water Park.
Public parkland course.
Founded 1991
Designed by Chapman & Warren
9 holes, 2904 yards, S.S.S. 68
Visitors: welcome.
Green Fee: WD £9; WE £14.
Societies: welcome; full facilities; terms on application.
Catering: full facilities.
Hotels: Oaksey Park Country Cottages Hotel (10 farm cottages).

3B 62 Ogbourne Downs

Ogbourne St George, Marlborough, Wilts, SN8 1TB
☎(01672) 841217, Fax 841327, Pro 841287, Sec 841327, Bar/Rest 841362
Junction 15 off M4; course on A345.
Downland course.
Pro Colin Harraway; Founded 1907
Designed by Taylor, Hawtree and Cotton
18 holes, 6353 yards, S.S.S. 70
Visitors: welcome with h'cap certs.
Green Fee: WD £20; WE £30.
Societies: on application from secretary; bar, dining room, ball hire, buggy hire; from £20.
Catering: full bar and restaurant facilities.
Hotels: Parklands Hotel, Ogbourne St George.

3B 63 Orchardleigh

Frome, Somerset, BA11 2PH
☎(01373) 454200, Fax 454202, Pro 708092
On A363 between Frome and Radstock.
Parkland course.
Pro Peter Green; Founded 1995
Designed by Brian Huggett
18 holes, 6810 yards, S.S.S. 73
Visitors: welcome.
Green Fee: WD £25; WE £25.
Societies: welcome; terms on application.
Hotels: Stone Easton House; Bishopstrow House; Homewood Park.

3B 64 Parkstone
49a Links Rd, Parkstone, Poole,
Dorset, BH14 9JU
☎(01202) 708025, Fax 706027, Pro
708092, Sec 707138, Bar/Rest
700856
On A35 between Bournemouth and
Poole; signposted left off Bournemouth
road.
Links course.
Pro Mark Thomas; Founded 1910
Designed by Willie Park and James
Braid
18 holes, 6250 yards, S.S.S. 70
Visitors: welcome with h'cap certs.
Green Fee: WD £30; WE £40.
Societies: terms on application.
Catering: full catering.

3B 65 Parley Golf Centre
Parley Green Lane, Hurn,
Christchurch, Dorset, BH23 6BB
☎(01202) 591600
Opposite Bournemouth International
Airport.
Parkland course.
Founded 1992
Designed by Paul Goodfellow
9 holes, 4584 yards
Visitors: welcome.
Green Fee: WD £7; WE £8.50.
Societies: welcome by arrangement;
full facilities.
Catering: full catering facilities.
Practice range, 23 bays floodlit, 2
teaching bays.

3B 66 Puxton Park
Woodspring Golf & Leisure Park, Nr
Weston-super-Mare, Avon, BS24 6TA
☎(01934) 876942
2 miles E of M5 junction 21 on A370
Bristol-Weston Rd.
Moorland course.
Founded 1992
Designed by R. Hemmingway &
Partner
18 holes, 6559 yards, S.S.S. 70
Visitors: welcome; pay and play.
Green Fee: WD £8; WE £10.
Societies: welcome.
Catering: bar facilities.

3B 67 Queen's Park
(Bournemouth)
Queen's Park West Drive,
Bournemouth, Dorset, BH8 9BY
☎(01202) 396198, Fax 302611, Pro
396817, Sec 302611, Bar/Rest 394466
Off Wessex Way in Bournemouth.
Parkland course.
Pro R Hill; Founded 1906

18 holes, 6319 yards, S.S.S. 70
Visitors: welcome.
Green Fee: on application.
Societies: terms on application.
Catering: full catering.
Hotels: Embassy; Wessex; Marsham
Court.

3B 68 RMCS Shrivenham
RMCS Shrivenham, Swindon, Wilts,
SN6 8LA
☎(01793) 785725
In the grounds of Royal Military
College of Science on A420, 1 mile
NE of Shrivenham.
Parkland course.
Founded 1953
18 holes, 5684 yards, S.S.S. 69
Visitors: restricted access; welcome
with member.
Green Fee: WD £8; WE £10.
Societies: limited access WD;
from £9.
Catering: coffee and soft drinks.

3B 69 Rushmore Park
Tollard Royal, Salisbury, Wiltshire, SP5
5QB
☎(01725) 516326, Fax 516466
12 miles from Salisbury off the A354
Blandford road through Sixpenny
Handley; course is just before Tollard
Royal.
Parkland course; 9-hole extension
opening summer 1998.
Pro Sean McDonagh; Founded 1994
9 holes, 4976 yards, S.S.S. 68
Visitors: welcome.
Green Fee: WD £12; WE £15.
Societies: welcome by prior arrange-
ment.
Catering: no catering facilities; food
can be brought from Larmer Tree.
Practice range, 6 bays.

3B 70 Salisbury & South
Wiltshire
Netherhampton, Salisbury, Wilts, SP2
8PR
☎(01722) 742645, Pro 742929
On A3094 2 miles from Salisbury and
from Wilton.
Downland course.
Founded 1888
Designed by J.H. Taylor; extra 9 holes
by S Gidman 1991
18 holes, 6430 yards, S.S.S. 71
Visitors: welcome.
Green Fee: WD £25; WE £40.
Societies: welcome by arrangement;
full facilities.
Catering: full facilities.

Hotels: Rose & Crown, Kings Arms
(both Salisbury); Pembroke Arms
(Wilton).

3B 71 Saltford
Golf Club Lane, Saltford, Bristol, BS31
3AA
☎(01225) 873513, Fax 873525, Pro
872043
Off A4 between Bath and Bristol.
Meadowland course.
Pro Dudley Millensted; Founded 1904
18 holes, 6046 yards, S.S.S. 69
Visitors: welcome with h'cap certs.
Green Fee: WD £22; WE £30.
Societies: welcome Mon and Thurs
by arrangement; full facilities.
Catering: full facilities.
Hotels: Grange (Keynsham); Crown;
Tunnel House.

3B 72 Sherborne
Higher Clatcombe, Sherborne, Dorset,
DT9 4RN
☎(01935) 812475, Fax 814218, Sec
814431, Bar/Rest 812274
1 miles north of Sherborne off B3145.
Parkland course.
Pro Stewart Wright; Founded 1894
Designed by James Braid
18 holes, 5882 yards, S.S.S. 68
Visitors: welcome with h'cap certs.
Green Fee: WD £25; WE £30.
Societies: welcome Tues and Wed
only; full playing, practice and dining
facilities; terms on application.
Catering: full facilities.
Hotels: Sherborne Hotel; Eastbury;
Antelope.

3B 73 Shrivenham Park
Pennyhooks, Shrivenham, Swindon,
Wilts, SN6 8EX
☎(01793) 783853, Fax 782999
Off A420 between Swindon and
Oxford.
Parkland course.
Pro Barry Randall; Founded 1969
Designed by Glen Johnson
18 holes, 5769 yards, S.S.S. 69
Visitors: welcome.
Green Fee: WD £12.50; WE £14.
Societies: welcome anytime; pack-
ages available; from £15.
Catering: facilities available.
Hotels: Blunsdown House.

3B 74 Solent Meads Par 3
Rolls Drive, Nr Hengistbury Head,
Bournemouth, Dorset
☎(01202) 420795

Off Broadway at Hengistbury Head.
Seaside course.
18 holes, 2182 yards
Visitors: welcome; pay and play.
Green Fee: WD £4; WE £4.
Societies: limited.
Catering: light refreshments and snacks.
Practice range, 10 bays floodlit.

3B 75 **Stockwood Vale**
Stockwood Lane, Keynsham, Bristol,
BS18 2ER
☎(0117) 9866505, Fax 9860509, Sec
9860509
In Stockwood Lane off A4.
Undulating parkland course.
Pro John Richards; Founded 1991
Designed by J. Wade & M. Ramsay
9 holes, 5520 yards, S.S.S. 67
Visitors: welcome with prior reservation.
Green Fee: WD £12; WE £14.
Societies: welcome by prior arrangement; packages available; terms on application.
Catering: available.

3B 76 **Sturminster Marshall**
Moor Lane, Sturminster Marshall,
Dorset, BH21 4AH
☎(01258) 858444, Fax 858262
In village centre on the A350 midway between Blandford and Poole.
Parkland course.
Pro Graham Howell; Founded 1992
Designed by John Sharkey
18 holes, 4882 yards, S.S.S. 64
Visitors: welcome.
Green Fee: WD £10; WE £10.
Societies: welcome with prior bookings accepted 7 days in advance; terms on application.
Catering: full facilities.

3B 77 **Tall Pines**
Cooks Bridle Path, Downside,
Backwell, Bristol, BS48 3DS
☎(01275) 474869, Fax 474869, Pro
472076, Bar/Rest 474889
Take A38 or A370 from Bristol and course is next to Bristol International Airport.
Public parkland course.
Pro Alex Murray; Founded 1990
Designed by Terry Murray
18 holes, 6049 yards, S.S.S. 68
Visitors: welcome; no restrictions.
Green Fee: WD £14; WE £16.
Societies: welcome; full facilities; terms on application.
Catering: bar and restaurant.

3B 78 **Taunton & Pickeridge**
Corfe, Taunton, Somerset, TA3 7BY
☎(01823) 421537, Fax 421742, Pro
421790
B3170, 4 miles S of Taunton, through Corfe village, then 1st left.
Undulating course.
Pro Gary Milne; Founded 1892
Designed by Hawtree
18 holes, 5926 yards, S.S.S. 68
Visitors: welcome WD by arrangement; h'cap certs required.
Green Fee: WD £20; WE £28.
Societies: welcome by arrangement; full facilities.
Catering: full facilities.
Hotels: Castle.

3B 79 **Taunton Vale**
Creech Heathfield, Taunton, Somerset,
TA3 5EY
☎(01823) 412220, Fax 413583, Pro
412880
Just off A361 junction with A38, exits 24 or 25 from M5.
Parkland course.
Pro Martin Keitch; Founded 1991
Designed by John Pyne
18 holes, 6142 yards, S.S.S. 69
Visitors: welcome; dress code applies.
Green Fee: on application.
Societies: welcome WD; terms on application.
Catering: full facilities.
Hotels: Walnut Tree (North Petherton); Castle (Taunton); Falcon (Henlade); Tudor (Bridgwater).

3B 80 **Thoulstone Park**
Chapmanslade, Nr Westbury, Wilts,
BA13 4AQ
☎(01373) 832825, Fax 832821, Pro
832808
3 miles NW of Warminster on the A36.
Parkland course.
Pro Tony Isaacs; Founded 1991
Designed by M.R.M. Sandow
18 holes, 6312 yards, S.S.S. 70
Visitors: welcome.
Green Fee: WD £16; WE £22.50.
Societies: welcome Mon-Fri; terms on application.
Catering: full facilities.

3B 81 **Tickenham**
Clevedon Rd, Tickenham, N
Somerset, BS21 6SB
☎(01275) 856626
Take M5 junction 20 and follow signs for Nailsea; course on left after Tickenham.

Parkland course.
Pro Andrew Sutcliffe; Founded 1994
Designed by A Sutcliffe
9 holes, 3776 yards, S.S.S. 58
Visitors: welcome.
Green Fee: WD £10; WE £10.
Societies: welcome by arrangement; catering and bar facilities; driving range; teaching academy; terms on application.
Catering: bar, club room and breakfast catering.
Practice range, 24 bays floodlit.
Hotels: Redwood Lodge.

3B 82 **Two Riversmeet**
Two Riversmeet Leisure Centre, Stony
Lane South, Christchurch, Dorset,
BH23 1HW
☎(01202) 477987, Fax 470853
Signposted from the centre of Christchurch.
Public seaside course.
Founded 1986
Designed by local authority
9 holes, 1591 yards
Visitors: pay and play.
Green Fee: WD £4.20; WE £4.20.
Societies: welcome; terms on application.
Catering: bar and restaurant.

3B 83 **Upavon (RAF)**
Andover Rd, Upavon, Nr Pewsey,
Wilts, SN9 6BQ
☎(01980) 630787, Fax 630787, Pro
630281
On the A342 1.5 miles SE of Upavon village.
Undulating chalk downland
Pro Richard Blake; Founded
1918/1997
18 holes, 6407 yards, S.S.S. 67
Visitors: welcome on WD and after noon at WE.
Green Fee: WD £15; WE £15.
Societies: welcome WD; from £18ph.
Catering: by arrangement.
Practice range.

3B 84 **Vivary**
Vivary Park, Taunton, Somerset, TA1
3JW
☎(01823) 289274, Pro 333875, Sec
01984 623552
Centre of Taunton in Vivary Park.
Parkland course.
Pro Mike Steadman; Founded 1928
Designed by Herbert Fowler
18 holes, 4620 yards, S.S.S. 63
Visitors: welcome.
Green Fee: WD £8; WE £8.

Societies: welcome on WD only; contact Professional for golf and club for catering; terms on application.
Catering: full restaurant and bar facilities.
Hotels: Corner House; Castle.

3B 85 Wareham

Sandford Rd, Wareham, Dorset, BH20 4DH
☎(01929) 554147, Fax 554147, Sec 554156
N of Wareham off A351 between Sandford and Wareham.
Mixture of parkland and heathland course; fine views.
Pro Richard Emery; Founded 1908
Designed by C. Whitcombe
18 holes, 5603 yards, S.S.S. 67
Visitors: welcome Mon-Fri 9.30am-5pm.
Green Fee: WD £15.
Societies: welcome WD; packages available; 20 per cent reduction for groups of 20 or more; full facilities for dining; £15-£20.
Catering: full bar and catering.
Hotels: Worgret Manor; Springfield; Priory; Kemps.

3B 86 Wells (Somerset)

East Horrington Rd, Wells, Somerset, BA5 3DS
☎(01749) 672868, Fax 675005, Pro 679059, Sec 675005
E of Wells off B3139.
Parkland course.
Pro Adrian Bishop; Founded 1893
Redesigned by Adrian Stiff
18 holes, 6015 yards, S.S.S. 69
Visitors: welcome.
Green Fee: WD £18; WE £20.
Societies: welcome on Tues and Thurs by prior arrangement; packages available; from £33.
Catering: full facilities.
Practice range, 12 bays floodlit.
Hotels: Swan; White Hart both Wells; Charlton House, Shepton Mallett.

3B 87 Wessex Golf Centre

Radipole Lane, Weymouth, Dorset, DT4 9HX
☎(01305) 784737
Off Weymouth by-pass behind the football club.
Parkland course.
Pro N Statham;
9 holes, 1432 yards
Visitors: public pay and play.
Green Fee: WD £3.85; WE £3.85 .
Practice range, available.

3B 88 West Wilts

Elm Hill, Warminster, Wilts, BA12 0AU
☎(01985) 213133, Fax 219809, Pro 212110, Bar/Rest 212702
In Warminster off Westbury road.
Downland course.
Pro A Lamb; Founded 1891
Designed by J.H. Taylor
18 holes, 5709 yards, S.S.S. 68
Visitors: welcome with h'cap certs or as members' guest.
Green Fee: WD £24; WE £35.
Societies: Wed and Thurs only; 36 holes of golf plus lunch and dinner; £35.
Catering: full facilities.
Hotels: Bishopstrow; Old Bell.

3B 89 Weston-super-Mare

Uphill Rd North, Weston-super-Mare, N Somerset, BS23 4NQ
☎(01934) 621360, Fax 626968, Pro 633360, Sec 626968, Bar/Rest 641826
M5 to junction 21 and then follow road to seafront.
Links course.
Pro M Laband; Founded 1892
Designed by T. Dunn
18 holes, 6208 yards, S.S.S. 70
Visitors: welcome; h'cap certs required at WE.
Green Fee: WD £24; WE £35.
Societies: welcome; terms on application.
Catering: full bar and restaurant facilities.
Hotels: Beachlands; Commodore; Rozel; Timbertops.

3B 90 Weymouth.

Links Rd, Weymouth, Dorset, DT4 0PF
☎(01305) 784994, Fax 788029, Pro 773997, Sec 773981, Bar/Rest 773558
1 mile from Weymouth town centre.
Parkland course.
Pro Des Lochrie; Founded 1909
Designed originally by James Braid; Redesigned by J. Hamilt
18 holes, 5976 yards, S.S.S. 69
Visitors: welcome with h'cap certs.
Green Fee: WD £25; WE £30.
Societies: welcome Mon-Fri; catering by arrangement; £30-£35.
Catering: full facilities.

3B 91 Wheathill

Wheathill, Somerton, Somerset, TA11 7HG
☎(01963) 240667, Fax 240230

Take A37 towards Yeovil; at village of Lydford Cross turn left; course 1 mile on right.
Parkland course.
Founded 1993
Designed by J Payne
18 holes, 5351 yards, S.S.S. 66
Visitors: welcome.
Green Fee: WD £10; WE £15.
Societies: welcome by arrangement; full facilities.
Catering: full facilities.
Hotels: George (Castle Cary).

3B 92 The Wiltshire Golf Club

Vastern, Wootton Basset, Swindon, Wilts, SN4 7PB
☎(01793) 849999, Fax 849988, Pro 851360
On A3102 1 mile S of Wootton Bassett, close to M4 junction 16.
Parkland with water on 8 holes; rolling downs.
Pro Andy Gray; Founded 1992
Designed by Peter Alliss/ Clive Clark
18 holes, 6522 yards, S.S.S. 71
Visitors: welcome by prior arrangement.
Green Fee: WD £30; WE £30.
Societies: welcome by arrangement; golf and catering packages can be arranged; terms on application.
Catering: full clubhouse facilities.
Practice range, practice ground.
Hotels: Hilton; De Vere, both Swindon.

3B 93 Windwhistle

Windwhistle, Cricket St Thomas, Nr Chard, Somerset, TA20 4DG
☎(01460) 30231, Fax 30055
On N side of A30 5 miles from Crewkerne, 3 miles from Chard, opposite wildlife park; follow signs from M5 junction 25.
Downland/parkland course.
Founded 1932
Designed by J.H. Taylor (1932), Leonard Fisher (1992)
18 holes, 6470 yards, S.S.S. 71
Visitors: welcome but advisable to phone first.
Green Fee: WD £14; WE £18.
Societies: welcome by arrangement; full facilities.
Catering: full facilities.

3B 94 Worlebury

Monks Hill, Worlebury, Weston-super-Mare, Avon, BS22 9SX
☎(01934) 623214, Fax 625789, Pro 418473, Sec 625789

From M5 junction 21 follow old road to Weston-super-Mare; turn right at Milton Church.
Hilltop parkland course.
Pro Gary Marks; Founded 1908
Designed by W. Hawtree & Son
18 holes, 5936 yards, S.S.S. 69
Visitors: welcome.
Green Fee: WD £20; WE £20.
Societies: welcome by prior arrangement; terms on application.
Catering: bar and restaurant facilities.
Hotels: Commodore; Beachlands.

3B 95 **Wrag Barn Golf & Country Club**

Shrivenham Rd, Highworth, Wilts, SN6 7QQ
☎(01793) 861327, Fax 861325, Pro 766027

10 miles from M4 junction 15; take A419 towards Cirencester, left turn to Highworth, follow A316 to Highworth, then 3rd exit at roundabout on to B4000 to Shrivenham; course is 0.5 mile on right.
Undulating scenic parkland course.
Pro Barry Loughrey; Founded 1990
Designed by Hawtree & Sons
18 holes, 6548 yards, S.S.S. 71
Visitors: welcome; some restrictions at WE; advisable to phone first.
Green Fee: WD £20; WE £25.
Societies: welcome WD by arrangement; packages available min 20 players; full facilities; £45.
Catering: full bar and restaurant, catering for companies, parties, receptions.
Hotels: Blunsden House Hotel; Jesmond House (Highworth).

3B 96 **Yeovil**

Sherborne Rd, Yeovil, Somerset, BA21 5BW
☎(01935) 475949, Fax 411283, Pro 473763, Sec 422965, Bar/Rest 431130
1 mile from town centre towards Sherborne on A30.
Parkland course; also 9-hole course available.
Pro Geoff Kite; Founded 1919
Designed by Fowler & Alison (18 holes); Sports Turf Rese (9 holes)
18 holes, 6144 yards, S.S.S. 70
Visitors: welcome but must ring for tee time.
Green Fee: WD £25; WE £30.
Societies: welcome on Mon, Wed, Thurs; packages can be arranged; £25-£30.
Catering: full facilities.
Hotels: Ludgate House, Ilchester.

4

EAST ANGLIA

Suffolk and Norfolk provide all the ingredients for a perfect golfing holiday, any number of excellent courses – seaside and inland – in settings that give golfers a special sense of escape. Journeys from London have been considerably assisted by new roads plus a bridge over the River Orwell at Ipswich which is spectacular but East Anglia remains something of a quiet backwater which contributes greatly to its popularity.

Felixstowe Ferry, the place where Bernard Darwin learned to play, is the oldest, retaining a measure of its quaintness in spite of many changes since the clubhouse was based around its famous Martello Tower. The best holes are those nearest the sea, those on the other side of the road filling the flatter land although perhaps the most unusual hole, the short 12th, straddles the road with the tee shot having to clear a safety net to protect passers-by – motorised and pedestrian.

Further up the coast lie Aldeburgh and Thorpeness, contrasting Clubs and courses that, nevertheless, can conveniently be taken together. For all of the nearness of the sea, neither can be classed as seaside, Thorpeness, with a profusion of heather, and Aldeburgh, weaving its crafty way between the gorse across the common.

Crossing the county boundary into Norfolk, the coastal path heads for Great Yarmouth and Caister, founded in 1882, Sheringham, Brancaster and Hunstanton. Lovers of racing will have identified Great Yarmouth and Caister from the stands, the first and last holes hurdling the rails and several others enclosed by the track.

The best is very good after a slightly mundane start but the focus for the connoisseur is fixed on Hunstanton and the Royal West Norfolk links at Brancaster which occupy as remote a tract as any on which the game is played. Hunstanton, one hundred years old in 1991, is a full-blown championship test divided by a central ridge of dunes that gives it a bit of a Jekyll and Hyde character.

Brancaster, on the other hand, derives its character more from deep sleepered bunkers, sandy turf, a unique stretch of marshland and a rich variety in the size, angling, shaping and defence of its greens. A year junior to Hunstanton, it rubs shoulders with nature in all its aspects, adverse weather adding a wild, bleak dimension that, for all its ferocity, can add appeal.

On more modern lines are the two courses and varied leisure facilities at Barnham Broom on the outskirts of Norwich which gain in popularity.

Cambridge University golfers have an understandably soft spot for East Anglia, fixtures, in addition to Hunstanton, including Royal Norwich and, in the old days, a final trial at Thetford which has a fine new clubhouse and changed course since then. The changes, dictated by the Thetford bypass, necessitated intrusion into the forest or, at least, what was forest until the terrible storm of October 1987. Only a few scraggy pines survived the blast but Thetford, ancient and modern, is full of charm that deserves to be sampled.

From Thetford, it is relatively plain sailing to Cambridge either through or round Newmarket but, on the way, there is a port of call at Royal Worlington and Newmarket which you overlook at your peril.

Given the accolade by Bernard Darwin of "the sacred nine", it is a masterpiece of simple design, a triumph in fitting a quart into a pint pot. In winter, it is a veritable haven that offers the ideal of a day of foursomes with the lure of characteristic refreshment to re-fuel the system. Throughout the world, I have enjoyed nothing better.

4 1 Aldeburgh

Saxmundham Rd, Aldeburgh, Suffolk, IP15 5PE
☎(01728) 452408, Fax 452937, Pro 453309, Sec 452890
On A12 N of Ipswich take A1094 to Aldeburgh; 6 miles E of A12.
Open heathland course; no par 5s.
Pro Keith Preston; Founded 1884
Designed by John Thompson/ Willie Fernie
18 holes, 6330 yards, S.S.S. 71
Visitors: welcome by prior arrangement.
Green Fee: WD £35; WE £42.
Societies: welcome by arrangement; terms on application.
Catering: clubhouse facilities.
Hotels: Wentworth; White Lion; Brudewell; Uplands.

4 2 Alnesbourne Priory

Priory Park, Nacton Road, Ipswich, Suffolk, IP10 0JT
☎(01473) 727393, Fax 278372
From A14 take Ransomes Europark exit and follow signs to Priory Park.
Parkland course.
Founded 1987
9 holes, 1760 yards, S.S.S. 58
Visitors: public pay and play (course closed Tues).
Green Fee: WD £10; WE £9.
Societies: course available for hire every Tues; packages available; swimming pool, adventure playground; terms on application.
Catering: bar, restaurant.
Hotels: lodge cabins on site.

4 3 Barnham Broom

Honingham Rd, Barnham Broom, Norwich, Norfolk, NR9 4DD
☎(01603) 759393, Fax 758224
9 miles SW of Norwich.
River valley setting.
Pro P Ballingall/S Beckham; Founded 1977
Designed by Frank Pennink (Valley), Donald Steel (Hill)
Hill course: 18 holes, 6628 yards, S.S.S. 72; Valley course: 18 holes, 6470 yards, S.S.S. 71
Visitors: welcome by prior arrangement.
Green Fee: WD £30; WE £30.
Societies: many golfing breaks and corporate packages available; complete hotel, conference and golfing leisure breaks available at the hotel; from £89.
Catering: full club and hotel facilities.
Hotels: Barnham Broom Hotel.

4 4 Bawburgh

Glen Lodge, Marlingford Road, Bawburgh, Norfolk, NR9 3LU
☎(01603) 740404, Fax 740403, Pro 742323
Off the Norwich southern by-pass (A47) at the Royal Norfolk Showground junction; follow road to Bawburgh.
Parkland/heathland course.
Pro Chris Potter; Founded 1978
Designed by S. Manser
18 holes, 6224 yards, S.S.S. 70
Visitors: welcome by arrangement.
Green Fee: WD £18; WE £22.
Societies: welcome by arrangement; normal packages involve 36 holes; lunch and evening meal; from £34.
Catering: full clubhouse facilities.
Practice range, 14 bays; floodlit.
Hotels: Park Farm, Hethersett.

4 5 Beccles

The Common, Beccles, Suffolk, NR34 9BX
☎(01502) 712244, Sec 712479
Leave A146 Norwich-Lowstoft road at Sainsbury's roundabout.
Parkland course; was Wood Valley (Beccles).
Founded 1899
9 holes, 5562 yards, S.S.S. 67
Visitors: welcome; with a member on Sun am.
Green Fee: WD £11; WE £13.
Societies: welcome with prior notice; terms on application.
Catering: clubhouse facilities.
Hotels: King's Head; Waveney House, both Beccles.

4 6 Bungay & Waveney Valley

Outney Common, Bungay, Suffolk, NR35 1DS
☎(01986) 892337, Fax 892222
Signposted from Bungay by-pass.
Heathland course.
Pro N Whyte; Founded 1889
Designed by James Braid
18 holes, 6044 yards, S.S.S. 69
Visitors: welcome by arrangement.
Green Fee: WD £18; WE £18.
Societies: welcome by prior arrangement; discounted day rates and green fees for groups of more than 20.
Catering: clubhouse facilities.
Practice range.

4 7 Bury St Edmunds

Tuthill, Bury St Edmunds, Suffolk, IP28 6LG
☎(01284) 755979

1st exit off A14 for Bury St Edmunds; 0.25 miles down B1106 to Brandon.
Parkland course.
Pro Mark Jillings; Founded 1924
Designed by Hawtree (9 holes), Ray (18 holes)
18 holes, 6678 yards, S.S.S. 72
Visitors: welcome WD; WE with a member.
Green Fee: WD £24.
Societies: welcome WD by arrangement; also 9-hole course: WD £12; WE £13; terms on application.
Catering: full clubhouse facilities.
Hotels: Butterfly.

4 8 Caldecott Hall

Caldecott Hall, Beccles Road, Fritton, Norfolk, NR31 9EY
☎(01493) 488488, Fax 488561
5 miles SW of Great Yarmouth on A143 Beccles Road.
Parkland course.
Pro M Snazell; Founded 1994
9 holes, 6186 yards, S.S.S. 69
Visitors: welcome by prior arrangement.
Green Fee: on application.
Societies: welcome by prior arrangement; groups of 10 or more; terms on application.
Catering: full clubhouse facilities.
Practice range, 20 bays; floodlit.
Hotels: The Cliff, Gorleston-on-Sea; The Star, Great Yarmouth.

4 9 Costessey Park

Old Costessy, Norwich, Norfolk, NR8 5AL
☎(01603) 746333, Pro 747085
Off A1074 at Round Well public house 3 miles W of Norwich.
Parkland/river valley course.
Pro Simon Cook; Founded 1983
Designed by Frank MacDonald
18 holes, 6104 yards, S.S.S. 69
Visitors: welcome; not before 11.30am at WE.
Green Fee: terms on application.
Societies: welcome by prior arrangement.
Catering: full catering and bar facilities.
Practice range.

4 10 Cretingham

Cretingham, Woodbridge, Suffolk, IP13 7BA
☎(01728) 685275, Fax 685037
2 miles from the A1120 at Earl Soham; 10 miles N of Ipswich.
Parkland course.

Pro Colin Jenkins; Founded 1984
9 holes, 4380 yards, S.S.S. 64
Visitors: welcome.
Green Fee: WD £9; WE £11.
Societies: welcome by arrangement;
catering packages available; snooker;
pitch & putt; swimming pool; tennis;
caravan park.
Catering: full restaurant and licensed
bar.
Practice range.

4 11 Dereham

Quebec Rd, Dereham, Norfolk, NR19
2DS
☎(01362) 695900, Fax 695904, Pro
695631, Sec 695900/4
0.5 miles out of Dereham on B1110.
Parkland course.
Pro R Curtis; Founded 1934
9 holes, 6225 yards, S.S.S. 70
Visitors: welcome by prior arrangement.
Green Fee: WD £20; WE £20.
Societies: welcome by arrangement;
packages available; terms on application.
Catering: clubhouse facilities.
Hotels: Phoenix; Kings Head; George.

4 12 Diss

Stuston Common, Diss, Norfolk, IP22
3JB
☎(01379) 642847, Pro 644399, Sec
641025
2 miles W of the A140 at Scole, halfway between Norwich and Ipswich.
Commonland course.
Pro Nigel Taylor; Founded 1903
18 holes, 6262 yards, S.S.S. 69
Visitors: welcome; WE only with a
member.
Green Fee: WD £20.
Societies: welcome WD by prior
arrangement.
Catering: full facilities.

4 13 Dunham Golf Club (Granary)

Little Dunham, Nr Swaffham, King's
Lynn, Norfolk, PE32 2DF
☎(01328) 701718
On A47 at Necton/Dunham cross-
roads.
Parkland with lakes.
Founded 1987
9 holes, 4812 yards, S.S.S. 67
Visitors: welcome.
Green Fee: WD £9; WE £12.
Societies: welcome by prior arrange-
ment.
Catering: full bar and snack facilities.

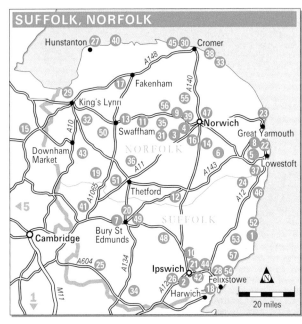

SUFFOLK, NORFOLK

KEY

1	Aldeburgh	20	Flempton	41	Royal Worlington & Newmarket
2	Alnesbourne Priory	21	Fynn Valley	42	Rushmere
3	Barnham Broom	22	Gorleston	43	Ryston Park
4	Bawburgh	23	Great Yarmouth & Caister	44	Seckford
5	Beccles	24	Halesworth	45	Sheringham
6	Bungay & Waveney Valley	25	Haverhill	46	Southwold
7	Bury St Edmunds	26	Hintlesham Hall	47	Sprowston Park
8	Caldecott Hall	27	Hunstanton	48	Stowmarket
9	Costessey Park	28	Ipswich	49	Suffolk Golf & Country Club
10	Cretingham	29	King's Lynn	50	Swaffham
11	Dereham	30	Links Country Park	51	Thetford
12	Diss	31	Mattishall	52	Thorpeness
13	Dunham Golf Club (Granary)	32	Middleton Hall	53	Ufford Park Hotel
14	Dunham Hall	33	Mundesley	54	Waldringfield Heath
15	Eagles	34	Newton Green	55	Wensum Valley
16	Eaton	35	Norfolk Golf & Country Club	56	Weston Park
17	Fakenham	36	Richmond Park	57	Woodbridge
18	Felixstowe Ferry	37	Rookery Park		
19	Feltwell	38	Royal Cromer		
		39	Royal Norwich		
		40	Royal West Norfolk		

4 14 Dunston Hall

Dunston Hall, Ipswich Road, Norwich,
Norfolk, NR14 8PQ
☎(01508) 470178
On the main A140 Ipswich road; 10
minutes drive from Norwich city centre.
Meadowland course.
Pro Peter Briggs; Founded 1994
Designed by M Shaw (1998 extension)
18 holes, 6302 yards, S.S.S. 69
Visitors: welcome; priority to mem-
bers and hotel guests.
Green Fee: WD £20; WE £25.
Societies: welcome by prior arrange-
ment; catering packages; conference

facilities; leisure and health centre.
Catering: full clubhouse facilities.
Practice range, 22 covered; floodlit
bays.
Hotels: Dunston Hall on site.

4 15 Eagles

28 School Road, Tilney All-Saints,
King's Lynn, Norfolk, PE34 4RS
☎(01553) 827147, Fax 829777, Sec
829777
Off A47 between King's Lynn and
Wisbech.
Parkland course.

Pro Nigel Pickerell; Founded 1992
Designed by David Horn
9 holes, 4284 yards, S.S.S. 61
Visitors: welcome.
Green Fee: WD £12; WE £14.
Societies: welcome by arrangement;
catering facilities available by negotia-
tion; terms on application.
Catering: facilities.
Practice range.
Hotels: Bufferfly; Park View, both
King's Lynn.

4 16 Eaton

Newmarket Rd, Norwich, Norfolk, NR4
6SF
☎(01603) 451686, Fax 451686, Pro
452478, Bar/Rest 452881
Off A11 1 mile S of Norwich.
Predominantly parkland course.
Pro Mark Allen; Founded 1910
18 holes, 6114 yards, S.S.S. 69
Visitors: welcome with members.
Green Fee: WD £28; WE £35.
Societies: welcome by arrangement;
terms on application.
Catering: bar and catering facilities.
Hotels: Norwich; Nelson and Post
House.

4 17 Fakenham

Sports Centre, The Race Course,
Fakenham, Norfolk, NR21 7NY
☎(01328) 862867, Pro 863534
On B1146 from Dereham or A1067
from Norwich.
Parkland course.
Pro Colin Williams; Founded 1981
Designed by Charles Lawrie
9 holes, 6174 yards, S.S.S. 69
Visitors: welcome; restrictions Sat
and Sun morning.
Green Fee: WD £18; WE £24.
Societies: welcome by arrangement.
Catering: bar and restaurant in Sports
Centre.
Hotels: Wensum Lodge; Crown;
Limes.

4 18 Felixstowe Ferry

Ferry Rd, Felixstowe, Suffolk, IP11
9RY
☎(01394) 286834, Fax 283975
3A14 to Felixstowe following signs for
the yacht centre.
Links course.
Pro Ian MacPherson; Founded 1880
Designed by Henry Cotton & Sir Guy
Campbell
18 holes, 6272 yards, S.S.S. 70
Visitors: welcome WD.
Green Fee: WD £22.

Societies: welcome Tues, Wed and
Fri by arrangement; catering packages;
also 9-hole Kingsfleet course opened
in April 1997: 5980 yards, par 70.
Catering: full catering facilities.
Practice range.
Hotels: Orwell House; s/c flats above
clubhouse for rent.

4 19 Feltwell

Thor Ave, Feltwell, Thetford, Norfolk,
IP26 4AY
☎(01842) 827644, Pro 827666
Off B1112 Lakenheath-Feltwell road
just before Feltwell village.
Inland links course.
Pro Peter Field; Founded 1972
9 holes, 6256 yards, S.S.S. 70
Visitors: welcome.
Green Fee: WD £14; WE £22.
Societies: welcome WD; by arrange-
ment; terms on application.
Catering: bar and catering.
Hotels: Brandon House, Brandon.

4 20 Flempton

Flempton, Bury St Edmunds, Suffolk,
IP28 6EQ
☎(01284) 728291.
4 miles NE of Bury St Edmunds on
A1101 to Mildenhall.
Breckland course.
Pro Mark Gillings; Founded 1895
Designed by J. H. Taylor
9 holes, 6240 yards, S.S.S. 70
Visitors: welcome WD with h'cap
certss; with member at weekend.
Green Fee: WD £22.
Societies: limited availability.
Catering: by arrangement.
Hotels: Priory & Angel; The Riverside.

4 21 Fynn Valley

Witnesham, Ipswich, Suffolk, IP6 9JA
☎(01473) 785267, Fax 785632, Pro
785463, Bar/Rest 785202
From A14 or A12 take A1214 and then
B1077 to N of Ipswich.
Parkland course.
Pro G Crane/P Wilby; Founded 1991
Designed by Tony Tyrrell
18 holes, 5873 yards
Visitors: welcome except before
10.30am Sun; Ladies day Wed.
Green Fee: WD £17; WE £20.
Societies: welcome WD; catering and
golf packages available; also 9-hole
par 3 course; from £17.
Catering: excellent restaurant.
Hotels: Novotel, Ipswich; Travel
Lodge, Claydon; Marlborough Hotel,
Ipswich.

4 22 Gorleston

Warren Rd, Gorleston, Great
Yarmouth, Norfolk, NR32 6JT
☎(01493) 661911, Fax 611911, Pro
662103, Bar/Rest 441922
Off A12 between Great Yarmouth and
Lowestoft.
Clifftop course.
Pro N Brown; Founded 1906
Designed by J R Taylor
18 holes, 6391 yards, S.S.S. 71
Visitors: welcome with h'cap certs.
Green Fee: WD £21; WE £25.
Societies: welcome by prior arrange-
ment; full golf and catering package;
terms on application.
Catering: full clubhouse catering facili-
ties.
Hotels: Cliffs, Gorleston; Potters HH,
Hopton.

4 23 Great Yarmouth & Caister

Beach House, Caister-on-Sea, Great
Yarmouth, Norfolk, NR30 5TD
☎(01493) 728699, Fax 728699, Pro
720421, Bar/Rest 720214
From Yarmouth N to Caister-on-Sea.
Links course.
Founded 1882
Designed by T Dunn/ H S Colt
18 holes, 6330 yards, S.S.S. 70
Visitors: welcome; h'cap certs pre-
ferred.
Green Fee: WD £27; WE £30.
Societies: welcome by prior arrange-
ment; packages available; dining
room, TV lounge, snooker; terms on
application.
Catering: full catering and bar facili-
ties.
Hotels: Imperial; Burlington; Caister
Old Hall.

4 24 Halesworth

Bramfield Rd, Halesworth, Suffolk,
IP19 9XA
☎(01986) 875567, Fax 874565, Pro
875697
On A144 off the A12 1 mile N of
Darsham.
Parkland course; was St Helena GC
Pro Philip Heil; Founded 1990
Designed by J.W. Johnson
27 holes 6580 yards
Visitors: welcome.
Green Fee: on application.
Societies: welcome by prior arrange-
ment; full day packages available;
company days organised; also 9-hole
par 36 course available; terms on
application.
Catering: full clubhouse facilities.

4 25 Haverhill

Coupals Rd, Haverhill, Suffolk, CB9 7UW
☎(01440) 761951, Fax 714883, Pro 712628
Leave Haverhill on A604 towards Colchester and turn 2nd left after railway viaduct; 1st right into Coupals Road.
Parkland course; new 18 opened April 1998.
Pro Simon Mayfield; Founded 1973
Designed by Charles Lawrie
18 holes, yards, S.S.S. 68
Visitors: welcome.
Green Fee: WD £16; WE £20.
Societies: welcome by prior arrangement.
Catering: bar facilities and catering available.
Hotels: Woodlands.

4 26 Hintlesham Hall

Hintlesham, Ipswich, Suffolk, IP8 3NS
☎(01473) 652761, Fax 652750
4 miles W of Ipswich; 10 mins from A12 or A14.
Parkland course.
Pro Alistair Spink; Founded 1991
Designed by Hawtree & Sons
18 holes, 6638 yards, S.S.S. 72
Visitors: welcome.
Green Fee: WD £27; WE £45.
Societies: welcome WD by prior arrangement with the secretary; packages available; spa; sauna; steam room; swimming pool.
Catering: full bar and restaurant service.
Practice range, 10 bays.
Hotels: Hintlesham Hall.

4 27 Hunstanton

Golf Course Rd, Old Hunstanton, Norfolk, PE36 6JQ
☎(01485) 532811, Fax 532319, Pro 532751, Bar/Rest 533932
On the North Norfolk coast; take the A149 Cromer Road through Old Hunstanton and follow signs to Club Links course; 2 ball play only.
Pro John Carter; Founded 1891
Designed by George Fernie; updated by J Braid

18 holes, 6735 yards, S.S.S. 72
Visitors: welcome from 9.30am to 11.30am and after 2pm on WD in summer; 10-30am-11am and after 2pm at WE.
Green Fee: WD £45; WE £55.
Societies: welcome by prior arrangement but 2 ball play only; packages available; full facilities; terms on application.
Catering: full catering facilities.
Hotels: Le Strange Arms, Hunstanton; Lifeboat Inn, Thornham.

4 28 Ipswich

Bucklesham Rd, Purdis Heath, Ipswich, Suffolk, IP3 8UQ
☎(01473) 728941, Fax 715236, Pro 724017, Bar/Rest 713030
3 miles E of Ipswich off A14.
Heathland course with pine trees; present site since 1927.
Pro S Whymark; Founded 1895/ 1927
Designed by James Braid, Hawtree & Taylor
18 holes, 6435 yards, S.S.S. 71
Visitors: welcome WD by arrangement; WE as member's guest only.
Green Fee: WD £35; WE £35.
Societies: welcome by prior arrangement; packages including breakfast, lunch and dinner available; from £40.
Catering: full catering facilities.
Hotels: Marriott Courtyard.

4 29 King's Lynn

Castle Rising, King's Lynn, Norfolk, PE31 6BD
☎(01553) 631654, Fax 631036, Pro 631655, Bar/Rest 631656
On A149 King's Lynn to Hunstanton, turn at Castle Rising.
Parkland course.
Pro John Reynolds; Founded 1923/1975
Designed by Alliss & Thomas
18 holes, 6609 yards, S.S.S. 72
Visitors: welcome by prior arrangement.
Green Fee: WD £35; WE £45.
Societies: welcome Thurs and Fri only; catering available from society menu; minimum 16; from £35.
Catering: full facilities.

4 30 Links Country Park

Sandy Lane, West Runton, Cromer, Norfolk, NR27 9QH
☎(01263) 838383, Fax 838264, Pro 838215, Bar/Rest 837691
Off A149 road.
Coastal course with heath; 300 yards from sea.
Pro L Patterson; Founded 1899/1903
Designed by J H Taylor (1903 when 18 holes)
9 holes, 4842 yards, S.S.S. 64
Visitors: welcome.
Green Fee: WD £20; WE £25.
Societies: welcome with prior arrangement; full catering and golf packages; hotel on site with pool, sauna, sun bed and tennis court; terms on application.
Catering: full catering facilities.
Hotels: ETB 4 crown Links Country Park Hotel.

4 31 Mattishall

South Green, Mattishall, Dereham, Norfolk
☎(01362) 850111
B1063 to Mattishall; right at church; course 1 mile on left.
Parkland course.
Founded 1990
9 holes, 6218 yards, S.S.S. 68
Visitors: welcome.
Green Fee: WD £10; WE £10.
Societies: limited availability.
Catering: limited.
Hotels: Phoenix, E Dereham.

4 32 Middleton Hall

Hall Orchards, Middleton, Nr King's Lynn, Norfolk, PE32 1RH
☎(01553) 841800, Pro 841801
On A47 between King's Lynn and Swaffham.
Parkland course.
Pro Peter Whittle; Founded 1989
Designed by D Scott
18 holes, 6007 yards, S.S.S. 69
Visitors: welcome.
Green Fee: WD £20; WE £25.
Societies: welcome by prior arrangement; golfing and catering packages available; carvery available for 30 or more players; from £27.50.

Catering: full catering and bar facilities.
Hotels: Butterfly; Knight's Hill, both King's Lynn.

4 33 Mundesley

Links Rd, Mundesley, Norwich, Norfolk, NR11 8ES
☎(01263) 720279, Fax 720279, Sec 720095
Turn off Mundersley-Cromer road at Mundersley church.
Undulating parkland with fine views.
Pro Terry Symmons; Founded 1903
Designed by Harry Vardon (in Part)
9 holes, 5377 yards, S.S.S. 66
Visitors: welcome WD except Weds; after 11.30 at WE.
Green Fee: on application.
Societies: welcome as with guests; catering by arrangement; terms on application.
Catering: clubhouse bar and catering facilities.
Hotels: Manor House, Mundesley.

4 34 Newton Green

Newton Green, Sudbury, Suffolk, CO10 0QN
☎(01787) 377217, Pro 313215
On A134 3 miles E of Sudbury.
Moorland course.
Pro Tim Cooper; Founded 1907
18 holes, 5893 yards, S.S.S. 68
Visitors: welcome WD; WE by prior arrangement.
Green Fee: WD £15; WE £15.
Societies: welcome by prior arrangement; packages available; from £15.
Catering: bar and restaurant facilities.
Hotels: Mill, Sudbury.

4 35 Norfolk G &Cc

Hingham Rd, Reymerston, Norwich, Norfolk, NR9 4QQ
☎(01362) 850297, Fax 850614
Signposted from B1135.
Parkland course; was Reymerston GC.
Pro Alison Sheard; Founded 1993
Designed by Adas
18 holes, 6609 yards, S.S.S. 72
Visitors: welcome with prior arrangement.
Green Fee: WD £16; WE £20.
Societies: welcome WD; full golf, catering and leisure packages; terms on application.
Catering: full facilities; function room. Practice range, golf academy.
Hotels: White Hare, Hingham; Mill, Yaxham.

4 36 Richmond Park

Saham Road, Watton, Thetford, Norfolk, IP25 6EA
☎(01953) 886100, Fax 881817, Pro 881803, Bar/Rest 881803
At bottom of Watton High Street.
Parkland course.
Founded 1990
Designed by R. Jessup, R. Scott
18 holes, 6289 yards, S.S.S. 70
Visitors: welcome.
Green Fee: WD £15; WE £20.
Societies: welcome WD by prior arrangement; coffee on arrival, light lunch and 3-course dinner; other packages available; £35.
Catering: full facilities.
Hotels: accommodation on site.

4 37 Rookery Park

Carlton Colville, Lowestoft, Suffolk, NR33 8HJ
☎(01502) 560380, Pro 515103
2 miles W of Lowestoft on A146.
Parkland course.
Pro Martin Elsworthy; Founded 1975
Designed by Charles Lawrie
18 holes, 6729 yards, S.S.S. 72
Visitors: welcome.
Green Fee: WD £25; WE £30.
Societies: welcome by prior arrangement except Tues; packages by arrangement; also 9-hole par 3 course; snooker.
Catering: full facilities.
Hotels: Hedley House; Broadlands.

4 38 Royal Cromer

145 Overstrand Rd, Cromer, Norfolk, NR27 0JH
☎(01263) 512884, Fax 512884, Pro 512267
1 mile E of Cromer on the B1159 coast road close to the Cromer lighthouse.
Undulating seaside course.
Founded 1888
Designed by James Braid
18 holes, 6508 yards, S.S.S. 71
Visitors: welcome WD and after 11am most WE.
Green Fee: WD £30; WE £36.
Societies: welcome WD by prior arrangement.
Catering: daily facilities.
Hotels: Cliftonville; Cliff House; Roman Camp Inn; Anglia Court; Red Lion.

4 39 Royal Norwich

Drayton High Rd, Hellesdon, Norwich, NR6 5AH
☎(01603) 425712, Fax 429928, Pro 408459, Sec 429928
On A1067 3 miles from Norwich on Fakenham road.
Mature undulating parkland course.
Pro Dean Futter; Founded 1893
Designed by J J W Deuchar 1893; J Braid 1924
18 holes, 6603 yards, S.S.S. 72
Visitors: welcome; bookings needed at WE.
Green Fee: WD £30; WE £36.
Societies: welcome; book through General Manager; packages available; catering and golf facilities; from £40.
Catering: bar and restaurant facilities.
Hotels: Norwich Sports Village; Hotel Norwich; Stakis Hotel.

4 40 Royal West Norfolk

Brancaster, King's Lynn, Norfolk, PE31 8AX
☎(01485) 210223, Fax 210087, Pro 210616, Sec 210087
7 miles E of Hunstanton; in Brancaster village turn at the Beach/Broad Lane junction with the A149; course 1 mile.
Historic links course.
Pro R E Kimber; Founded 1892
Designed by Holcombe Ingleby
18 holes, 6428 yards, S.S.S. 71
Visitors: welcome at secretary's discretion; deposit needed to confirm booking; not last week of July or August or first week of September.
Green Fee: WD £43; WE £53.
Societies: n/a.
Catering: full facilities.
Practice range.
Hotels: Hoste Arms, Burnham Market; Titchwell Manor, Titchwell.

4 41 Royal Worlington & Newmarket

Golf Links Rd, Worlington, Bury St Edmunds, Suffolk, IP28 8SD
☎(01638) 712216, Pro 712224, Sec 717787
6 miles NE of Newmarket on A14 then A11 towards Thetford; follow signs to Worlington
Inland links course.
Pro Malcolm Hawkins; Founded 1893
Designed by H.S. Colt
9 holes, 6210 yards, S.S.S. 70
Visitors: WD only.
Green Fee: WD £35; WE £35.
Societies: welcome Tues and Thurs by arrangement; catering packages; limit 24 players; from £50.
Catering: full clubhouse facilities.
Hotels: Worlington Hall; Riverside, Mildenhall.

4 42 Rushmere

Rushmere Heath, Ipswich, Suffolk, IP4 5QQ
☎(01473) 727109, Fax 725648, Pro 728076, Sec 725648 Bar/Rest 719034
3 miles E of Ipswich off A1214 Woodbridge road.
Heath and commonland course.
Pro N T J McNeill; Founded 1927
18 holes, 6262 yards, S.S.S. 70
Visitors: welcome WD and after 2.30pm WE; h'cap certs required.
Green Fee: WD £20; WE £20.
Societies: welcome by arrangement; pacakages available; terms on application.
Hotels: full clubhouse facilities.

4 43 Ryston Park

Ely Rd, Denver, Downham Market, Norfolk, PE38 0HH
☎(01366) 382133, Sec 383834
On A10 1 mile S of Downham Market.
Parkland course.
Founded 1933
Designed by J Braid
9 holes, 6310 yards, S.S.S. 70
Visitors: welcome WD; with members at WE.
Green Fee: WD £20; WE £20.
Societies: welcome; maximum 45; caterirg packages available from the steward; terms on application.
Catering: full facilities.
Hotels: Castle Hotel, Downham Market.

4 44 Seckford

Seckford Hall Rd, Great Bealings, Woodbridge, Suffolk, IP13 6NT
☎(01394) 388000, Fax 382818, Bar/Rest 384588
Off A12 at Woodbridge Junction.
Parkland course; Mizuno golf academy.
Pro T Pennock/J Skinner; Founded 1991
Designed by Johnny Johnson
18 holes, 5303 yards, S.S.S. 66
Visitors: welcome with prior arrangement.
Green Fee: WD £13; WE £12.
Societies: welcome by prior arrangement; special leisure and golf breaks can be arranged in old Manor House hotel with 34 rooms; spa pool, swimming pool; packages available; terms on application.
Catering: bar, bistro, terrace and hotel restaurant.
Practice range.
Hotels: Seckford Hall.

4 45 Sheringham

Weybourne Rd, Sheringham, Norfolk, NR26 8HG
☎(01263) 823488, Fax 825189, Pro 822980, Bar/Rest 822038
From the A148 follow the signs into Sheringham; left at roundabout; club 0.5 miles.
Clifftop course.
Pro M W Jubb; Founded 1891
Designed by Tom Dunn
18 holes, 6464 yards, S.S.S. 71
Visitors: welcome with prior booking.
Green Fee: WD £37; WE £42.
Societies: welcome with prior arrangement; terms on application.
Catering: clubhouse facilities.
Practice range.

4 46 Southwold

The Common, Southwold, Suffolk, IP18 6TB
☎(01502) 723234, Pro 723790, Sec 723248
From A12 Henham to Blythborough; take A1095 to Southwold.
Links course.
Pro Brian Allen; Founded 1884
Designed by J Braid
9 holes, 6052 yards, S.S.S. 69
Visitors: welcome.
Green Fee: WD £18; WE £22.
Societies: welcome by arrangement; packages available; terms on application.
Catering: clubhouse facilities.
Practice range.
Hotels: Swan; Crown; Cricketers; Pier Avenue Hotel.

4 47 Sprowston Park

Wroxham Rd, Sprowston, Norwich, Norfolk, NR7 8RP
☎(01603) 410657, Fax 788884, Pro 417264
On A1551 Norwich to Wroxham road; 10 minutes from city centre.
Parkland course.
Pro P Grice; G Ireson; M Barnard; Founded 1980
18 holes, 5763 yards, S.S.S. 68
Visitors: welcome.
Green Fee: WD £18; WE £21.
Societies: welcome by prior arrangement; full package of golf and catering, including morning coffee, lunch and dinner; from £37.
Catering: full catering facilities.
Practice range, 27 bays; floodlit covered range.
Hotels: Sprowston Manor (adjoining course); Maid Head; Norwich; Catton Old Hall.

4 48 Stowmarket

Lower Rd, Onehouse, Stowmarket, Suffolk, IP14 3DA
☎(01449) 736733, Pro 736392, Sec 736473, Bar/Rest 736473
2.5 miles SW of Stowmarket off B1115 Stowmarket-Bidlestone road.
Parkland course.
Pro Duncan Burl; Founded 1962
18 holes, 6107 yards, S.S.S. 69
Visitors: welcome after 9.15 am with h'cap certs, except Wed.
Green Fee: WD £23; WE £29.
Societies: welcome Thurs and Fri.
Catering: full facilities.
Practice range, 12 bays; 4 outdoor, 8 indoor; 2 practice grounds.
Hotels: Cedars.

4 49 Suffolk Golf & CC

St John's Hill Plantation, Fornham All Saints, Bury St Edmunds, Suffolk, IP28 6JQ
☎(01284) 706777, Fax 706721
From A14 take B1106 to Fornham.
Parkland course; was Fornham Park; rebuilt course in 1998.
Pro J Bevan; Founded 1969
18 holes, 6077 yards, S.S.S. 70
Visitors: welcome by prior arrangement.
Green Fee: WD £12; WE £15.
Societies: welcome WD; packages with golf, catering and leisure on request; terms on application.
Catering: full clubhouse facilities.
Practice range.

4 50 Swaffham

Cley Rd, Swaffham, Norfolk, PE37 8AE
☎(01760) 721611
1 mile out of town on Cockley Cley road; signposted in market place.
Heathland course.
Pro Peter Field; Founded 1922
9 holes, 6252 yards, S.S.S. 70
Visitors: welcome WD; with member at WE.
Green Fee: WD £20.
Societies: welcome WD by arrangement.
Catering: full catering except Mon and Tues; snacks.
Practice range.
Hotels: George.

4 51 Thetford

Brandon Rd, Thetford, Norfolk, IP24 3NE
☎(01842) 752258, Pro 752662, Sec 752169

A spectacular parkland course with specimen oak, beech and ash trees over 200 years old. Abundant wildlife with roe, red and fallow deer.

WESTON PARK
Golf Club

- **6621 YARDS**
- **PAR 72**
- **Societies & conferences welcomed**
  tel: **01603 872363**
  Tee reservations on **01603 872998**

Wooded heathland course.
Pro Gary Kitley; Founded 1912
Designed by C.H. Mayo, Donald Steel
18 holes, 6879 yards, S.S.S. 73
Visitors: welcome WD with h'cap certs; weekend with member only.
Green Fee: WD £32.
Societies: welcome Wed, Thurs, Fri only; packages available.
Catering: full facilities.
Hotels: Bell; Thomas Paine; Wereham House.

4 52 **Thorpeness**
Thorpeness, Nr Aldeburgh, Suffolk, IP16 4NH
☎(01728) 452176, Fax 453868, Pro 454926
25 miles N of Ipswich on A12; then B1094 to Aldeburgh and then B1069 to Thorpeness.
Heathland course.
Founded 1923
Designed by James Braid
18 holes, 6271 yards, S.S.S. 71
Visitors: welcome with h'cap certs.
Green Fee: on application.
Societies: welcome; packages available; catering facilities, snooker; lounge, function room; tennis courts; terms on application.
Catering: restaurant, patio bar, lounge.
Practice range.
Hotels: 30-room hotel on site; guests have priority tee-times.

4 53 **Ufford Park Hotel**
Yarmouth Road, Ufford, Woodbridge, Suffolk, IP12 1QW
☎(01394) 382836, Fax 383582, Pro 383555, Bar/Rest 383555
2 miles N of Woodbridge on B1438.
Parkland with ponds
Pro S Robertson; Founded 1991
Designed by Phil Pilgrim
18 holes, 6300 yards, S.S.S. 70
Visitors: welcome by arrangement.

Green Fee: WD £16; WE £20.
Societies: welcome on WD; Packages available; leisure facilities inc pool, spa, sauna, gym; terms on application.
Catering: full facilities.
Practice range, driving nets.
Hotels: Ufford Park Hotel on site.

4 54 **Waldringfield Heath**
Newbourne Road, Waldringfield, Woodbridge, Suffolk, IP12 4PT
☎(01473) 736426, Pro 736417, Sec 736768
3 miles NE of Ipswich.
Heathland course.
Pro Robin Mann/Alex Lucas; Founded 1983
Designed by P. Pilgrem
18 holes, 6141 yards, S.S.S. 69
Visitors: welcome WD; after 12 noon WE.
Green Fee: WD £13.50; WE £16.50.
Societies: welcome WD by prior arrangement.
Catering: full facilities.
Hotels: Marlborough, Ipswich.

4 55 **Wensum Valley**
Beech Avenue, Taverham, Norwich, Norfolk, NR8 6HP
☎(01603) 261012, Fax 261664
Take A1067 Fakenham to Taverham road.
Parkland course; golf school.
Founded 1989
Designed by B.C. Todd
Valley course: 18 holes, 6172 yards, S.S.S. 69; 18 holes, 6470 yards, S.S.S. 71
Visitors: welcome.
Green Fee: WD £18; WE £18.
Societies: welcome; packages on request; TV lounge, pool table; bowling green. Other leisure facilities can be organised; conference facilities; golfing breaks available; terms on application.

Catering: clubhouse facilities; Morton restaurant; Wensum suite; bars.
Practice range, 8 bays; floodlit.
Hotels: hotel on site.

4 56 **Weston Park**
Weston Longville, Norwich, Norfolk, NR9 5JW
☎(01603) 872363, Fax 873040, Pro 872998, Bar/Rest 871842
9 miles NW of Norwich off A1067 Norwich-Fakenham road.
Parkland course.
Pro Michael Few; Founded 1993
Designed by Golf Technology
18 holes, 6603 yards, S.S.S. 72
Visitors: welcome.
Green Fee: WD £24; WE £29.
Societies: welcome with a minimum of 12 players; packages available; group lessons; snooker room; conference room; £25-£45.
Catering: full restaurant facilities, Brasted's on the Park; 2 bars, sitting and reading room.
Hotels: Lenwade House.

4 57 **Woodbridge**
Bromeswell Heath, Woodbridge, Suffolk, IP12 2PF
☎(01394) 382038, Fax 382392, Pro 383213, Bar/Rest 383212
2 miles E of Woodbridge on A1152.
Heathland course.
Pro A Hubert; Founded 1893
Designed by F. Hawtree
18 holes, 6299 yards, S.S.S. 70
Visitors: welcome WD with h'cap certs.
Green Fee: WD £30.
Societies: welcome WD by prior arrangement; maximum 36; packages available; from £32.
Catering: restaurant and bar facilities 11am-10pm.
Hotels: Crown & Castle, Orford; Melton Grange, Woodbridge

5

SOUTH MIDLANDS

In the last four or five years, Northampton has gained two new courses on opposite sides of the city. Collingtree is an example of the American style of design and construction while the relocation of the Northampton Golf Club on Lord Spencer's Estate at Althorp epitomises the technique of blending the courses harmoniously into a lovely, natural landscape.

Cold Ashby and Staverton Park are among Northamptonshire's other new courses in the last twenty years but the mantle of seniority belongs to Kettering GC, which in 1991 celebrated its Centenary in spite of the new by-pass running beside one corner of the course.

Gog Magog, east of Cambridge, is the pick of Cambridgeshire's Clubs with its 27 holes but Ramsey, St Ives and St Neots boast a countryside whose largely agricultural character has not been little eroded by the spread of the game. Large, open fen-like fields are not ideal for golf but mention should be made of Ely City and Cambridgeshire Moat House Hotel which meet local needs adequately enough.

Bedfordshire was the birthplace of Henry Longhurst, who played most of his early golf at the Bedfordshire GC, then known a little less grandly as the Bedford GC. Bedford and County followed in 1912 and nowadays Bedford has a public course called Mowsbury.

Memories of Dunstable Downs, South Bedfordshire at Luton and the excellent John O'Gaunt (36 holes) at Biggleswade involve county matches with B B and O in the south-eastern group but Northamptonshire is included in the Midlands Group along with Leicestershire, where golf revolves around the county town of Leicester itself.

The stock of Leicestershire golf was enhanced considerably by the crowning in 1991 as Amateur champion of Gary Wolstenholme, who learned and played all his early golf in the county.

The Three Choirs Festival, the province of the cathedrals of Hereford, Worcester and Gloucester, would have been close to the heart of Sir Edward Elgar, the most English of all composers. Less well known was his love of golf and, in particular, his connections with the Worcestershire Golf Club at Malvern Wells, although how much inspiration his musical scores owed to the latter is not clear.

Judging by the excellent centenary history of the Club, it can be assumed that his game was based more on hope than glory – perhaps even enigmatic and variable but the beauty of the Malvern Hills has been solace to many.

Far more modern is Abbey Park at Redditch which is a valuable addition to the county's facilities but, as an example of true dedication and private enterprise, there is nothing in the entire country to match the tale of Ross-on-Wye. Having existed for almost sixty years as a nine-hole course, they built themselves a new 18-hole home in pleasant woodland in the 1960s. What is more, the cost of course and clubhouse did not exceed £50,000 although the sacrifices and contributions of the original course committee, a gallant, cheerful band, never featured in the calculations.

Two Ryder Cup matches at the Belfry have done a lot to publicise golf in the Birmingham area in recent years but Warwickshire, particularly in the area around Birmingham, is full of variety. Some of the older clubs include Handsworth, Edgbaston, Harborne, Moseley, Kidderminster, Robin Hood and Sandwell Park, a stone's throw from the home of West Bromwich Albion F.C.

ABBOTSLEY GOLF HOTEL

A delightful country house hotel, set amidst two 18 hole courses.

"The Abbotsley course – the design is a revelation, the presentation superb."
GOLF MONTHLY

2 of East Anglia's GOLFING GEMS

Home of VIVIEN SAUNDERS GOLF SCHOOLS.
ST. NEOTS, CAMBS. PE19 4XN.
Tel: 01480-474000 Fax: 01480-471018

CAMBRIDGE MERIDIAN GOLF CLUB

"A stunning championship venue for the 21st century."

"Probably East Anglia's best new course."

"Peter Alliss & Clive Clark have excelled themselves in the design."

"A truly memorable 18 holes in 207 acres."

TOFT, CAMBRIDGE CB3 7RY.
Tel: 01223-264700 Fax: 01223-264701

5A 1 Abbotsley

Eynesbury Hardwicke, St Neots, Cambs, PE19 4XN
☎(01480) 474000, Pro 406463, Sec 210033
2 miles SE of St Neots leaving A428 at Tesco roundabout.
Parkland course.
Pro Vivien Saunders/Geoff Dixon; Founded 1976 (Abbotsley), Founded 1989 (Cromwell)
Designed by Derek Young, Vivien Saunders, Jenny Wisson
Abbotsley: 18 holes, 6311 yards, S.S.S. 72; Cromwell: 18 holes, 6087 yards, S.S.S. 69
Visitors: welcome WD with h'cap certs; restrictions at WE (Abbotsley); pay and play; WE bookings required (Cromwell).
Green Fees: Abbotsley WD £25, WE £30; Cromwell WD £12, WE £15.
Societies: welcome by prior arrangement; packages available; WE residential packages; minimum 12; Vivien Saunders golf school; from £27.50 (Abbotsley); from £16.50 (Cromwell).
Catering: clubhouse restaurant and bar.
Practice range, 23-bay floodlit range; 24-bay grass range.
Hotels: Abbotsley Golf Hotel on site; 17 bedrooms.

5A 2 Aspley Guise & Woburn Sands

West Hill, Aspley Guise, MK17 8DX
☎(01908) 582264, Fax 528974, Pro 582974, Sec 583596
2 miles W of M1 junction 13 between Aspley Guise and Woburn Sands
Undulating parkland course.
Pro David Marsden; Founded 1914
Designed by Sandy Herd
18 holes, 6135 yards, S.S.S. 70
Visitors: welcome WD; WE as member's guest.
Green Fees: WD £23; WE £23.

Societies: welcome Wed and Fri: April to October; catering and golf packages available; from £44.
Catering: full catering facilities.

5A 3 Barkway Park

Nuthampstead Rd, Barkway, Nr Royston, Herts, SG8 8EN
☎(01763) 848215
On B1368 5 miles S of Royston.
Gently undulating course.
Founded 1991
Designed by Vivien Saunders
18 holes, 6997 yards, S.S.S. 74
Visitors: welcome; WE tee times cannot be booked until Fri pm.
Green Fees: WD £15; WE £20.
Societies: welcome by prior arrangement; packages available; terms on application.
Catering: full facilities.
Practice range, opening 1998.
Hotels: Vintage Puckeridge; Flintcroft Motel.

5A 4 Beadlow Manor Hotel

Beadlow, Nr Shefford, Beds, SG17 5PH
☎(01525) 860800, Fax 861345, Pro 861292
On the A507 between Ampthill and Shefford; 1.5 miles W of Shefford.
Parkland course.
Pro Phil Bradley; Founded 1973
Baron Manhattan: 18 holes, 6619 yards, S.S.S. 72; Baroness Manhattan: 18 holes, 6072 yards, S.S.S. 69
Visitors: welcome.
Green Fees: terms on application.
Societies: welcome by prior arrangement; several golf and catering packages available; health club; conference rooms; terms on application.
Catering: bar, restaurants.
Practice range, 25 bays floodlit.
Hotels: 30-room hotel on site.

5A 5 Bedford & County

Green Lane, Clapham, Beds, MK41 6ET
☎(01234) 354010, Fax 357195, Pro 359189, Sec 352617
Off the A6 N of Bedford before Clapham village.
Parkland course.
Pro Eddie Bullock; Founded 1912
18 holes, 6399 yards, S.S.S. 70
Visitors: welcome WD; with a member at WE.
Green Fees: WD £23.
Societies: welcome WD except Wed; all day golf packages available; from £45.
Catering: full facilities.
Hotels: Woodlands Manor.

5A 6 Bedfordshire

Bromham Rd, Biddenham, Bedford, MK40 4AF
☎(01234) 261669, Fax 261669, Pro 353653, Bar/Rest 353241
1.5 miles W of Bedford on A428 Northampton road.
Flattish parkland course.
Pro Peter Sanders; Founded 1891
Designed by Tom Dunn
18 holes, 6305 yards, S.S.S. 70
Visitors: welcome WD; as members' guests at WE.
Green Fees: WD £23; WE £23.
Societies: welcome WD; full clubhouse facilities; green fee plus catering.
Catering: full clubhouse facilities.
Hotels: Shakespeare; Swan; Moat House.

5A 7 Beedles Lake

Broome Lane, East Goscote, Leics, LE7 3NQ
☎(0116) 2606759, Bar/Rest 2607086
Between A46 Leicester-Newark road and A607 Leicester-Melton Mowbray.
Parkland course.

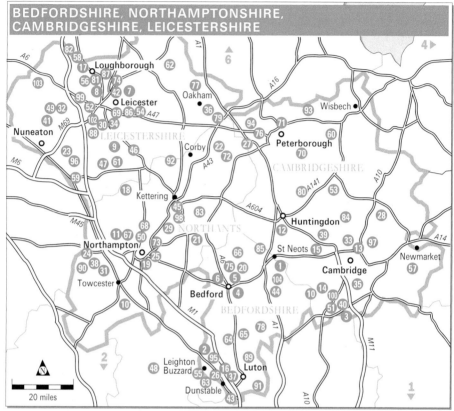

BEDFORDSHIRE, NORTHAMPTONSHIRE, CAMBRIDGESHIRE, LEICESTERSHIRE

20 miles

KEY			
1	Abbotsley	25	Delapre Park
2	Aspley Guise & Woburn Sands	26	Dunstable Downs
3	Barkway Park	27	Elton Furze
4	Beadlow Manor Hotel	28	Ely City
5	Bedford & County	29	Embankment
6	Bedfordshire	30	Enderby
7	Beedles Lake	31	Farthingstone Hotel G & LC
8	Birstall	32	Forest Hill
9	Blaby	33	Girton
10	Bourn	34	Glen Gorse
11	Brampton Heath	35	Greetham Valley
12	Brampton Park	36	Greetham Valley
13	Cambridge	37	Griffin
14	Cambridge Meridian	38	Hellidon Lakes Hotel and Country Club
15	Cambridgeshire Moat House Hotel	39	Hemingford Abbots
16	Chalgrave Manor Golf Club	40	Heydon Grange G & CC
17	Charnwood Forest	41	Hinckley
18	Cold Ashby	42	Humberstone Heights
19	Collingtree Park	43	Ivinghoe
20	Colmworth & N Beds	44	John O'Gaunt
21	Colworth	45	Kettering
22	Corby	46	Kibworth
23	Cosby	47	Kilworth Springs
24	Daventry & District	48	Kingfisher CC
		49	Kingstand
		50	Kingsthorpe

51	Kingsway	77	RAF Cottesmore
52	Kirby Muxloe	78	RAF Henlow
53	Lakeside Lodge	79	RAF North Luffenham
54	Leicestershire	80	Ramsey
55	Leighton Buzzard	81	Rothley Park
56	Lingdale	82	Rushcliffe
57	Links	83	Rushden
58	Longcliffe	84	St Ives
59	Lutterworth	85	St Neots
60	March	86	Scraptoft
61	Market Harborough	87	Shelthorpe
62	Melton Mowbray	88	Six Hills
63	Mentmore	89	South Bedfordshire
64	Millbrook	90	Staverton Park
65	Mount Pleasant	91	Stockwood Park
66	Mowsbury	92	Stoke Albany
67	Northampton	93	Thorney Golf Centre
68	Northamptonshire County	94	Thorpe Wood
69	Oadby	95	Tilsworth
70	Old Nene Golf & Country Club	96	Ullesthorpe
71	Orton Meadows	97	Waterbeach Barracks
72	Oundle	98	Wellingborough
73	Overstone Park	99	Western Park
74	Park Hill	100	Whaddon Golf Centre
75	Pavenham Park	101	Whetstone
76	Peterborough Milton	102	Whittlebury Park G&CC
		103	Willesley Park
		104	Wyboston Lakes

Pro Sean Bryne; Founded 1993
Designed by D Tucker
18 holes, 6625 yards, S.S.S. 71
Visitors: welcome at all times.
Green Fees: WD £9; WE £12.
Societies: welcome any time; terms
on application.
Catering: clubhouse facilities.
Practice range, 17 bays.

5A 8 Birstall

Station Rd, Birstall, Leicester, LE4
3BB
☎(0116) 2674322, Pro 2675245
Off A6 3 miles N of town.
Parkland course.
Pro David Clarke; Founded 1901
18 holes, 6222 yards, S.S.S. 70
Visitors: welcome except WE.
Green Fees: WD £20; WE n/a.
Societies: welcome Wed and Fri by
prior arrangement; reductions for
groups of more than 20; day rate £25;
snooker; billiards; from £20.
Catering: full facilities except Mon.

5A 9 Blaby

Lutterworth Rd, Blaby, Leics, LE8 3DP
☎(0116) 2784804
From Leicester through Blaby village;
course on the left-hand side.
Parkland course.
Founded 1991
9 holes, 5312 yards
Visitors: welcome; pay and play.
Green Fees: WD £4; WE £6.
Societies: welcome; special company
days available; terms on application.
Catering: bar and bar meals.
Practice range, 27 floodlit bays.

5A 10 Bourn

Toft Rd, Bourn, Cambridge, CB3 7TT
☎(01954) 718057, Fax 718908, Pro
718958, Sec 718088
6 miles W of Cambridge off A14
through Bourn village.
Parkland course.
Pro Craig Watson; Founded 1991
Designed by J. Hull and S. Bonham
18 holes, 6417 yards, S.S.S. 71
Visitors: welcome.
Green Fees: WD £15; WE £18.
Societies: welcome; full clubhouse
facilities; terms on application.
Catering: clubhouse facilities.
Hotels: many in Cambridge.

5A 11 Brampton Heath

Sandy Lane, Church Brampton,
Northants, NN6 8AX

☎(01604) 843939, Fax 843885
3 miles N of Northampton just off
A5119.
Undulating heathland course.
Pro R Hudson; Founded 1995
Designed by D Snell
18 holes, 6233 yards, S.S.S. 70
Visitors: welcome at all times.
Green Fees: WD £10; WE £14.
Societies: welcome WD and after mid
day at WE; packages can be
arranged; also par 3 practice course;
terms on application.
Catering: full facilities.

5A 12 Brampton Park

Buckden Rd, Brampton, Huntingdon,
Cambs, PE18 8NF
☎(01480) 434700, Fax 411145, Pro
434705
Take A1 or A14 to RAF Brampton;
club is opposite airbase.
Meadowland course.
Pro A Currie; Founded 1991
Designed by Simon Gidman (Hawtree
& Sons)
18 holes, 6403 yards, S.S.S. 73
Visitors: welcome.
Green Fees: WD £20; WE £30.
Societies: welcome WD; full facilities;
from £27.50.
Catering: clubhouse facilities.
Hotels: limited accommodation on
site.

5A 13 Cambridge

Station Road, Longstanton, Cambs,
CB4 5DR
☎(01954) 789388
10 mins N of Cambridge on B1050 off
A14.
Parkland course.
Pro G Huggett; Founded 1992
Designed by G Huggett
18 holes, 6736 yards, S.S.S. 74
Visitors: welcome.
Green Fees: WD £9; WE £11.
Societies: welcome at all times; vari-
ous packages and reductions avail-
able; terms on application.
Catering: full clubhouse facilities.

5A 14 Cambridge Meridian

Comberton Road, Toft, Cambs, CB3
7RY
☎(01223) 264700, Fax 264701, Pro
264702
On B1046 at Toft 3 miles W of M11
junction 12.
Parkland course.
Pro Michael Clemons; Founded 1994
Designed by P Alliss/C Clark

18 holes, 6651 yards, S.S.S. 72
Visitors: welcome with telephone
booking.
Green Fees: WD £20 ; WE £25.
Societies: welcome WD and, max 24,
after 12.30pm WE; range of packages
available; £21-£49.
Catering: full clubhouse catering facili-
ties.
Practice range, large practice facilities.
Hotels: University Arms Hotel;
Abbotsley Golf Hotel.

5A 15 Cambridgeshire Moat House Hotel

Bar Hill, Cambridge, Cambs, CB3 8EU
☎(01954) 780098, Fax 780010, Sec
249980, Bar/Rest 249988
On A14 5 miles N of Cambridge.
Parkland course.
Pro David Vernon; Founded 1974
Designed by F Middleton
18 holes, 6734 yards, S.S.S. 72
Visitors: welcome.
Green Fees: WD £20 ; WE £30.
Societies: welcome; day packages
can be organised; terms on applica-
tion.
Catering: full hotel and clubhouse
facilities.
Hotels: Cambridgeshire Moat House.

5A 16 Chalgrave Manor

Dunstable Road, Chalgrave,
Toddington, Bedfordshire, LU5 6JN
☎(01525) 876556, Fax 876556, Pro
876554
2 miles W of M1 junction 12 on A5120
between Toddington and Houghton.
Undulating parkland course.
Pro Martin Brewer; Founded 1994
18 holes, 6382 yards, S.S.S. 70
Visitors: welcome.
Green Fees: WD £15; WE £ 30.
Societies: welcome midweek; full golf
and catering packages can be
arranged; £21-£37.
Catering: full catering facilities.

5A 17 Charnwood Forest

Breakback Rd, Woodhouse Eaves,
Loughborough, Leics, LE12 8TA
☎(01509) 890259, Fax 890925
Close to M1 junctions 22/23.
Heathland course with heather, gorse
and bracken.
Founded 1890
Designed by James Braid
9 holes, 5960 yards, S.S.S. 69
Visitors: welcome.
Green Fees: WD £15; WE £15.
Societies: welcome Wed, Thurs and

Fri; full catering package plus 27 holes of golf; £32.50.
Catering: full catering facilities.
Hotels: Friendly Hotel.

5A 18 **Cold Ashby**

Stanford Road, Cold Ashby, Northampton, NN6 6EP
☎(01604) 740548, Fax 740548, Pro 740099
11 miles N of Northampton near A5199/A14 junction 1.
Undulating parkland course with spectacular views.
Pro Shane Rose; Founded 1974
Designed by John Day; Extension by D Croxton 1995
27 holes, 6308 yards, S.S.S. 70
Visitors: welcome; some WE restrictions.
Green Fees: WD £16; WE £18.
Societies: welcome any day by prior arrangement; full day's golf and catering packages available; 27-hole course; 3 loops of 9; Winwick/Ashby par 70; Ashby/ Elkington par 72; Elkington/Winwick par 70; dining room facilities; £37.
Catering: full clubhouse facilities.
Hotels: Pytchley, W Haddon; Post House, Crick; Broomhill, Spratton.

5A 19 **Collingtree Park**

Windingbrook Lane, Northampton, Northamptonshire, NN4 0XN
☎(01604) 700000, Fax 702600, Pro 701202
M1 junction 15 just past Stakis Hotel.
Championship course; owned by European PGA.
Founded 1990
Designed by Johnny Miller
18 holes, 6908 yards, S.S.S. 73
Visitors: welcome with 7 day advance booking.
Green Fees: WD £30; WE £40.
Societies: welcome with prior arrangement; full clubhouse facilities and driving range and practice ground; terms on application.
Catering: full facilities in clubhouse.
Hotels: Stakis Hotel; Swallow Hotel; Midway Hotel.

5A 20 **Colmworth & N Beds**

Mill Cottage, New Rd, Colmworth, Beds, MK44 2NU
☎(01234) 378822, Fax 376235, Pro 378181, Sec 378181, Bar/Rest 378181
From Bedford just off B660.
Links style course.

Founded 1991
Designed by John Glasgow
18 holes, 6435 yards, S.S.S. 69
Visitors: welcome after 9.30 WD and with booking at WE.
Green Fees: WD £10; WE £15.
Societies: welcome every day; packages can be arranged; restaurant facilities all day; terms on application.
Catering: full restaurant and bar.
Practice range, opening 1998.

5A 21 **Colworth**

Unilever Research, Colworth House, Sharnbrook, Bedford, MK44 1LQ
☎(01234) 781781
10 miles N of Bedford off A6 through village of Shambrook.
Parkland course.
Founded 1985
9 holes, 5000 yards, S.S.S. 64
Visitors: private with member only.
Green Fees: terms on application.

5A 22 **Corby**

Stamford Rd, Weldon
☎(01536) 260756
A43 Corby to Stamford road 2 miles E ot Weldon.
Parkland course.
Pro Jeff Bradbrook; Founded 1965
18 holes, 6677 yards, S.S.S. 72
Visitors: welcome.
Green Fees: WD £7.70; WE £9.90.
Societies: welcome anytime; packages for golf and catering available; from £7.70.
Catering: snacks and meals available.
Hotels: Stakis.

5A 23 **Cosby**

Chapel Lane, off Broughton Rd, Cosby, Leics, LE9 1RG
☎(0116) 2864759, Fax 2864484, Pro 2848275
From M1 junction 21 take B4114 for 3 miles until Cosby turning.
Parkland course.
Pro Martin Wing; Founded 1895
Designed by C Sinclair
18 holes, 6410 yards, S.S.S. 71
Visitors: welcome midweek; members guest only at WE.
Green Fees: WD £16; WE £16.
Societies: welcome, maximum 80 with prior arrangement; various packages available; £32-£35.
Catering: full clubhouse bar and catering facilities.
Practice range, practice ground.
Hotels: Stakis, Leicester; Mill on the Soar, Broughton Astley.

5A 24 **Daventry & District**

Norton Rd, Daventry, Northants, NN11 5LS
☎(01327) 702829, Sec 706245
1 mile N of the town next to the BBC station.
Undulating meadowland course.
Founded 1922
9 holes, 5812 yards, S.S.S. 68
Visitors: welcome; except before 11am Sun.
Green Fees: WD £10; WE £12.
Societies: welcome by prior arrangement with the professional; packages by arrangement; discounts for more than 16 players; terms on application.
Catering: bar.
Hotels: Britannia; Hanover.

5A 25 **Delapre Park**

Eagle Drive, Nene Valley Way, Northampton, NN4 7DU
☎(01604) 764036, Fax 706378 , Sec 763957
M1 junction 15 then 4 miles on A45.
Parkland course course; also has 9-hole Hardingstone course.
Pro J Corby/J Cuddihy; Founded 1976
Designed by J. Jacobs/ J. Corby
10 holes, 6299 yards, S.S.S. 70
Visitors: welcome at all times.
Green Fees: WD £7.30; WE £9.50.
Societies: welcome one per day but also welcome WE; packages can be arranged; terms on application.
Catering: full clubhouse catering and bar facilities.
Practice range, 40-bays floodlit range; also grass tees.
Hotels: Swallow; Stakis; Northampton Moat House; Courtyard by Marriott.

5A 26 **Dunstable Downs**

Whipsnade Rd, Dunstable, Beds, LU6 2NB
☎(01582) 604472, Fax 478700, Pro 662806
2 miles from Dunstable on Whipsnade road B4541.
Downland course.
Pro M Weldon; Founded 1907
Designed by James Braid
18 holes, 6251 yards, S.S.S. 70
Visitors: welcome WD; members guests at WE.
Green Fees: WD £18; WE £18.
Societies: welcome WD except Wed; full golf and catering package including lunch and dinner; half-day packages also available; £35-£48.
Catering: full clubhouse facilities.
Hotels: Old Palace Lodge; Hertfordshire Moat House.

5A 27 Elton Furze
Bullock Rd, Haddon, Peterborough,
Cambs, PE7 3TT
☎(01832) 280189, Pro 280614
4 miles W of Peterborough on old
A606; leaving A1 at the
Alwalton/Showground exit.
Parkland course.
Pro Frank Kiddie; Founded 1993
Designed by Roger Fitton
18 holes, 6259 yards, S.S.S. 70
Visitors: welcome by prior arrange-
ment; h'cap certs required.
Green Fees: WD £20.
Societies: welcome by prior arrange-
ment with the secretary on Tues and
Thurs; golf and catering packages
available; terms on application.
Catering: full facilities.
Practice range, practice ground; 4
bays.
Hotels: Swallow, Peterborough.

5A 28 Ely City
Cambridge Rd, Ely, Cambs, CB7 4HX
☎(01353) 662751, Fax 668636, Pro
663317, Bar/Rest 661966
1 mile S of City Centre on old A10.
Parkland course.
Pro Andrew George; Founded 1961
Designed by Henry Cotton
18 holes, 6627 yards, S.S.S. 72
Visitors: welcome with h'cap certs.
Green Fees: WD £24; WE £30.
Societies: welcome Tues-Fri in official
organised groups; full packages avail-
able; also practice area; Sky TV;
snooker; terms on application.
Catering: full bar and restaurant facili-
ties.
Hotels: Nyton Hotel; Lamb Hotel.

5A 29 Embankment
The Embankment, Wellingborough,
Northants, NN8 1LD
☎(01933) 228465
In the Embankment area of the city
alongside the river.
Parkland course.
Founded 1977
9 holes, 3562 yards, S.S.S. 57
Visitors: welcome with members only.
Green Fees: WD £4.
Societies: none.
Catering: bar and limited food.

5A 30 Enderby
Mill Lane, Enderby, Leics, LE9 5LH
☎(0116) 2849388
From M1 junction 21 to Enderby and
then follow the signs to Leisure
Centre.

Municipal heathland course.
Pro Richard Allen; Founded 1986
9 holes, 4212 yards, S.S.S. 61
Visitors: welcome.
Green Fees: WD £4.50 (9); 5.50 (18);
WE £5.50 (9); 7.50 (18).
Societies: welcome by arrangement.
Catering: bar and bar snacks.

**5A 31 Farthingstone Hotel G
& LC**
Farthingstone, Towcester, Northants,
NN12 8HA
☎(01327) 361291, Fax 361645, Pro
361533, Bar/Rest 361560
M1 junction 16; take signs to Weedon,
then Everdon and Farthingstone.
Parkland course.
Pro Gary Buckle; Founded 1972
Designed by M. Gallagher
18 holes, 6299 yards, S.S.S. 70
Visitors: welcome at all times.
Green Fees: WD £10; WE £15.
Societies: welcome any time by prior
arrangement; packages available; also
pool, snooker and hotel facilities;
terms on application.
Catering: full bar, restaurant and hotel
facilities.
Practice range and nets.
Hotels: Farthingstone.

5A 32 Forest Hill
Markfield Lane, Botcheston, Leics,
LE9 9FJ
☎(01455) 824800, Fax 828522
2 miles from Botcheston; 3 miles SW
of the A50
Well-wooded parkland course.
Pro Philip Harness; Founded
1991/1995
18 holes, 6039 yards, S.S.S. 69
Visitors: welcome.
Green Fees: WD £15; WE £20.
Societies: welcome WD by arrange-
ment; packages for golf and catering
available; terms on application.
Catering: bar; restaurant and function
room.
Practice range, 20 bays floodlit.
Hotels: Forest Lodge.

5A 33 Girton
Dodford Lane, Girton, Cambs, CB3
0QE
☎(01223) 276169, Fax 277150, Pro
276991
3 miles N of Cambridge on the A604.
Flat open course.
Pro Scott Thomson; Founded 1936
18 holes, 6080 yards, S.S.S. 69
Visitors: welcome WD.

Green Fees: WD £16.
Societies: welcome WD by prior
arrangement; packages available;
terms on application.
Catering: lunches and dinners served
except Mon.
Hotels: Post House, Impington.

5A 34 Glen Gorse
Glen Rd, Oadby, Leicester, LE2 4RF
☎(0116) 2712226, Fax 2714159, Pro
2713748, Sec 2714159, Bar/Rest
2718875
On A6 Leicester- Market Harborough
road between Oadby and Great Glen,
5 miles S of Leicester.
Parkland course.
Pro Dominic Fitzpatrick; Founded
1933
18 holes, 6648 yards, S.S.S. 72
Visitors: welcome WD by arrangement; WE with member.
Green Fees: WD £24; WE £8.50 with
member.
Societies: Tues-Fri by arrangement
with secretary; full golf and catering
facilities; terms on application.
Catering: full catering facilities.
Hotels: Hermitage, Oadby.

5A 35 Gog Magog
Shelford Bottom, Cambridge, Cambs,
CB2 4AB
☎(01223) 247626, Fax 414990, Pro
246058
On A1307 5 miles from Cambridge.
Chalkdownland course.
Pro Ian Bamborough; Founded 1901
Designed by Hawtree
Old course: 18 holes, 6398 yards,
S.S.S. 70; Wandlebury course:18
holes, 6754 yards, S.S.S. 73
Visitors: welcome WD; booking
required Wed.
Green Fees: WD £30; WE £30.
Societies: welcome WD except Wed;
full day's golf and catering package;
£58.
Catering: full clubhouse facilities
available.
Hotels: Duxford Lodge, Duxford;
many in Cambridge.

5A 36 Greetham Valley
Wood Lane, Greetham, Nr Oakham,
Leics, LE15 7RG
☎(01780) 460444, Fax 460623, Pro
460666, Bar/Rest 460004
1 miles from A1 off the B668 signposted Greetham.
Combinations of 3 x 9 holes; parkland
course with water.

Pro John Pengelly; Founded 1991
Designed by S T R I
27 holes, 6351 yards, S.S.S. 71
Visitors: welcome with phone booking.
Green Fees: WD £15; WE £20.
Societies: welcome WD in groups of
10 or more; various packages and
menus involving 18, 27, 36 holes of
golf (two other courses: 5879 yards,
par 68; 5890 yards, par 69) plus buggies; from £31.
Catering: full restaurant and bar facilities.
Practice range, 27 bays floodlit.
Hotels: Barnsdale Lodge; Barnsdale
CC; Hambleton Hall; Stapleford Hall.

5A 37 **Griffin**

Chaul End Rd, Caddington, Luton,
Beds, LU1 4AX
☎(01582) 415573, Fax 415314
10 mins from M1 junction 9 or 11 via
A5 or A5056.
Parkland course.
Founded 1982
18 holes, 6242 yards, S.S.S. 70
Visitors: welcome WD after 9; by
arrangement at WE.
Green Fees: WD £10/Fri £12; WE
£15.
Societies: welcome WD; packages
can be arranged for full day's catering
and golf; from £27.
Catering: full catering facilities.

5A 38 **Hellidon Lakes Hotel and Country Club**

Hellidon, Nr Daventry, Northants,
NN11 6LN
☎(01327) 262550, Fax 262559, Pro
262551
15 miles from M1 junction 16 by A45
and A361 Banbury road; turn right
before village of Charwelton.
Undulating parkland course.
Pro Gary Wills; Founded 1991
Designed by David Snell
18 holes, 6587 yards, S.S.S. 72
Visitors: welcome; h'cap certs needed
WE.
Green Fees: WD £15; WE £25.
Societies: welcome by arrangement;
packages available through the hotel;
conference facilities can be arranged;
fly fishing; tennis; snooker; health studio; swimming pool; also 9-hole
Holywell course, 2791 yds; terms on
application.
Catering: full bar and restaurant facilities.
Practice range, 14 bays.
Hotels: 4-star hotel on site.

5A 39 **Hemingford Abbots**

Cambridge Rd, Hemingford Abbots,
Cambs, PE18 9HQ
☎(01480) 495000, Fax 496000
Alongside A604 between Huntingdon
and St Ives.
Public parkland.
Founded 1991
Designed by Advanced Golf Services
18 holes, 5414 yards, S.S.S. 68
Visitors: welcome.
Green Fees: WD £11.50; WE £17.
Societies: small groups welcome by
prior arrangement.
Catering: bar and snacks.
Practice range.
Hotels: St Ives; The Bridge.

5A 40 **Heydon Grange G & CC**

Heydon, Royston, Herts, SG8 7NS
☎(01763) 208988, Fax 208926
M11 junction 10 on to A505 towards
Royston; take 3rd left to Hayden.
Downland/parkland courses with
lakes.
Pro Stuart Smith; Founded 1994
Designed by Alan Walker
Cambs/Essex:18 holes, 6512 yards,
S.S.S. 71; Cambs/Herts.18 holes,
6623 yards, S.S.S. 72; Herts/Essex:18
holes, 6387 yards, S.S.S. 71
Visitors: welcome; book in advance.
Green Fees: WD £15; WE £20.
Societies: welcome by prior arrangement; company days arranged; packages available; conferences and functions available; terms on application.
Catering: lounge, cocktail and wine
bar; restaurants; carvery on Sun.
Practice range and practice ground.

5A 41 **Hinckley**

Leicester Rd, Hinckley, Leics, LE10
3DR
☎(01455) 615124, Fax 890841, Pro
615014
From Hinkley Town Centre follow
signs for Earl Shilton.
Lakeside parkland course; (Burbage
Green until 1983).
Pro Richard Jones; Founded
1894/1983
Designed by Southeren Golf
18 holes, 6517 yards, S.S.S. 71
Visitors: welcome WD; members
guest WE.
Green Fees: WD £25; WE £25.
Societies: welcome WD with handicaps; packages available; terms on
application.
Catering: full catering facilities.
Hotels: Sketchley Grange.

5A 42 **Humberstone Heights**

Gipsy Lane, Leicester, Leics, LE5 0TB
☎(0116) 2763680, Pro 2764674, Sec
2897472, Bar/Rest 2761905
Off Uppingham Road opposite Towers
Hospital.
Parkland course.
Pro Philip Highfield; Founded 1978
Designed by Hawtree & Son
18 holes, 6343 yards, S.S.S. 70
Visitors: pay and play.
Green Fees: WD £7; WE £8.
Societies: terms on application.
Catering: clubhouse facilities.
Practice range, 30 bays.
Hotels: city centre hotels in Leicester.

5A 43 **Ivinghoe**

Wellcroft, Ivinghoe, Leighton Buzzard,
Beds, LU7 9EF
☎(01296) 668696, Fax 662755
4 miles from Tring and 6 miles from
Dunstable behind the Kings Head in
Ivinghoe village.
Meadowland course.
Pro Bill Garrad; Founded 1967
Designed by R. Garrad & Sons
9 holes, 4508 yards, S.S.S. 62
Visitors: welcome after 9am WD; after
8am WE.
Green Fees: WD £8; WE £8.
Societies: welcome WD by prior
arrangement; includes 36 holes of
golf; coffee; light lunch and evening
meal; from £22.
Catering: full facilities except Mon.
Hotels: Rose & Crown, Tring; Stocks,
Aldbury.

5A 44 **John O'Gaunt**

Sutton Park, Sandy, Beds, SG19 2LY
☎(01767) 260252, Fax 261381, Pro
260094, Sec 260360, Bar/Rest
261469
Between Biggleswade and Potten on
B1040.
Parkland course.
Pro Peter Round; Founded 1948
Designed by Hawtree
Carthagena: 18 holes, 5869 yards,
S.S.S. 69; Course 1: 18 holes, 6513
yards, S.S.S. 71
Visitors: welcome with h'cap certs
and by prior arrangement.
Green Fees: WD £45; WE £50.
Societies: welcome WD by prior
arrangement through administrators
office; packages for catering and
green fees on application; terms on
application.
Catering: full clubhouse catering.
Hotels: Holiday Inn; Stratton House,
Biggleswade; Rose & Crown, Potten.

5A 45 Kettering

Headlands, Kettering, Northants,
NN15 6XA
☎(01536) 511104, Pro 481014,
Bar/Rest 512074
S of Kettering, adjacent to A14.
Parkland course.
Pro K Theobald; Founded 1891
Designed by Tom Morris
18 holes, 6081 yards, S.S.S. 69
Visitors: welcome WD; with member
at WE.
Green Fees: WD £15; WE £22.
Societies: welcome Wed and Fri; full
catering and golf packages; from £35.
Catering: full clubhouse facilities.
Hotels: Kettering Park; George; Royal.

5A 46 Kibworth

Weir Rd, Kibworth, Beauchamp, Leics,
LE8 0LP
☎(0116) 2796172, Fax 2792301, Pro
2792283, Sec 2792301, Bar/Rest
2792301
10 miles S of Leicester off A6.
Flat woodland/parkland course.
Pro Bob Larratt; Founded 1904/62
18 holes, 6333 yards, S.S.S. 70
Visitors: welcome WD; WE with a
member.
Green Fees: WD £22; WE £22.
Societies: welcome by arrangement;
golf and catering available; from £20.
Catering: full catering facilities.
Hotels: Angel, Market Harborough.

5A 47 Kilworth Springs

North Kilworth, Lutterworth, Leics,
LE17 6HJ
☎(01858) 575094, Fax 575078 , Sec
575082
5 miles from M1 junction 20.
Front 9: Inland links; back 9: Parkland.
Pro Nick Melvin; Founded 1993
Designed by Ray Baldwin
18 holes, 6718 yards, S.S.S. 72
Visitors: welcome.
Green Fees: WD £17; WE £21.
Societies: welcome WD and after 12
at WE; catering and golf packages;
bar, spike bar, private 36-seat board-
room, restaurant, driving
range; from £24.
Catering: full clubhouse bar, spikes
bar and restaurant facilities.
Practice range, sunken range with
specialised short game areas.
Hotels: club can supply list.

5A 48 Kingfisher CC

Buckingham Rd, Deanshanger,
Northants, MK19 6DG

☎(01908) 562332, Sec 560354
On A422 Buckingham road 7 miles
from Milton Keynes opposite the vil-
lage of Deanshanger
Parkland course with lake features.
Founded 1994
9 holes, 5066 yards, S.S.S. 65
Visitors: welcome; pay and play.
Green Fees: WD £7.50; WE £10.50.
Societies: welcome by prior arrange-
ment; corporate days organised; fish-
ing; model steam railway; function
room; terms on application.
Catering: full facilities; 2 restaurants
and 2 bars.
Practice range, 10 bays.
Hotels: Shires.

5A 49 Kingstand

Beggars Lane, Leicester Forest East,
Leicester, LE3 3NQ
☎(0116) 2387908, Fax 2388087
Off main A47 Hinckley road; 5 mins
from M1 junction 21.
Parkland course.
Pro Simon Sherrit; Founded 1991
Designed by S. Chenia
9 holes, 5380 yards, S.S.S. 66
Visitors: welcome.
Green Fees: WD £9; WE £10.
Societies: welcome by prior arrange-
ment with the professional; packages
and discounts available; gymnasium.
Catering: restaurant; Indian restaurant
on site.
Practice range, 16 bays floodlit.
Hotels: Red Cow.

5A 50 Kingsthorpe

Kingsley Rd, Kingsley, Northampton,
NN2 7BU
☎(01604) 719602, Fax 710610 , Sec
710610, Bar/Rest 711173
Off A508 2 miles N of Northampton
town centre.
Parkland course.
Pro Paul Armstrong; Founded 1908
Designed by Charles Alison
18 holes, 5918 yards, S.S.S. 69
Visitors: welcome with h'cap certs.
Green Fees: WD £25; WE £25.
Societies: welcome Thurs and Fri;
catering facilities and golf packages
available; from £20.
Catering: clubhouse catering facilities.
Hotels: Westone Hotel; Broom Hill.

5A 51 Kingsway

Cambridge Rd, Melbourne, Royston,
Herts, SG8 6EY
☎(01763) 262727, Fax 263298, Pro
262943

On A10 N of Royston.
Landscaped farmland course.
Pro Richard Jessop; Founded 1991
9 holes, 4910 yards, S.S.S. 64
Visitors: welcome.
Green Fees: WD £9 (18 holes); WE
£11(18).
Societies: welcome by prior arrange-
ment; corporate days arranged; 9-hole
pitch and putt; terms on application.
Catering: bar and restaurant facilities.
Practice range, 36 bays floodlit.
Hotels: Sheene Mill Hotel.

5A 52 Kirby Muxloe

Station Rd, Kirby Muxloe, Leicester,
LE9 9EN
☎(0116) 2393457, Fax 2393457, Pro
2392813, Bar/Rest 2396577
From M1 junction 21a follow signs to
Kirby Muxloe.
Parkland course.
Pro Bruce Whipham; Founded 1893
18 holes, 6279 yards, S.S.S. 70
Visitors: welcome Mon, Wed and Fri.
Green Fees: WD £22.
Societies: welcome with h'cap certs
only; all day and individual round
packages available; from £37.
Catering: full clubhouse catering facili-
ties.
Hotels: Travel Inn; Red Cow.

5A 53 Lakeside Lodge

Fen Road, Pidley, Huntingdon,
Cambs, PE17 3DD
☎(01487) 740540, Fax 740852, Pro
741541, Bar/Rest 740968
From A14 Cambridge-St Ives road
take B1040 to Pidley
Open parkland with 8 lakes and
15,000 trees.
Pro Scott Waterman; Founded 1991
Designed by Alister Headley
18 holes, 6865 yards
Visitors: welcome any time.
Green Fees: WD £10; WE £16.
Societies: welcome any time; golf,
catering and other corporate activities
can be arranged (ten pin bowling, rally
karting,
hot air ballooning), also 9 holes, 2601
yards, par 34 course; terms on application.
Catering: full catering facilities.
Hotels: Olivers Lodge; Dolphin Hotel.

5A 54 Leicestershire

Evington Lane, Leicester, Leicester,
LE5 6DJ
☎(0116) 2738825, Fax 2738825, Pro
2736730, Bar/Rest 2731307

2 miles E of Leicester.
Parkland course course; no par 5s.
Pro John Turnbull; Founded 1890
Designed by James Braid
18 holes, 6326 yards, S.S.S. 70
Visitors: welcome with h'cap certs
and prior arrangement.
Green Fees: WD £24; WE £30.
Societies: welcome with h'cap certs;
packages can be arranged; terms on
application.
Catering: full clubhouse facilities.
Hotels: Gables Hotel.

5A 55 Leighton Buzzard

Plantation Rd, Leighton Buzzard,
Beds, LU7 7JF
☎(01525) 373811, Fax 373843
1 miles N of Leighton Buzzard.
Parkland/woodland course.
Pro Len Scarbrow; Founded 1925
18 holes, 6101 yards, S.S.S. 70
Visitors: welcome WD with h'cap
certs; WE with member.
Green Fees: WD £20; WE £20.
Societies: welcome WD except Tues;
full day's golf and catering from morn-
ing coffee to evening meals; from £45.
Catering: full clubhouse catering facili-
ties.
Hotels: Cock Horse Hotel.

5A 56 Lingdale

Joe Moore's Lane, Woodhouse Eave,
Loughborough, Leics, LE12 8TF
☎(01509) 890035, Pro 890684, Sec
890703
2 miles off M1 junction 22 towards
Woodhouse Eaves.
Parkland course.
Pro P Sellears; Founded 1967
Designed by D.W. Tucker & G. Austin
18 holes, 6545 yards, S.S.S. 71
Visitors: welcome.
Green Fees: WD £20; WE £20.
Societies: welcome with prior
arrangement with secretary; minimum
12; full day's golf and catering facili-
ties; from £16.
Catering: full clubhouse facilities.
Practice range, practice ground.

5A 57 Links Course

Cambridge Rd, Newmarket, Suffolk,
CB8 0TG
☎(01638) 663000, Fax 661476, Pro
662395, Bar/Rest 662708
On A1304 1 mile S of Newmarket mid-
way between racecourse entrances.
Parkland course.
Pro John Sharkey; Founded 1902
Designed by Col Hotchkin

18 holes, 6574 yards, S.S.S. 71
Visitors: welcome with h'cap certs;
not before 11.30 Sun.
Green Fees: WD £28; WE £32.
Societies: welcome by prior arrange-
ment; booking fee of £35; catering
packages; maximum 60; from £28.
Catering: full restaurant and bar.
Hotels: Bedford Lodge.

5A 58 Longcliffe

Snell's Nook Lane, Nanpantan,
Loughborough, Leics, LE11 3YA
☎(01509) 239129, Pro 231450
1 mile from M1 junction 23 off A512
towards Loughborough.
Heathland course.
Pro Ian Bailey; Founded 1904
18 holes, 6611 yards, S.S.S. 72
Visitors: welcome WD 9-4.30 except
Tues; WE with a member.
Green Fees: WD £25.
Societies: welcome WD except Tues
(ladies day); packages available for
groups of 20 or more; from £25.
Catering: bar, restaurant and snacks.
Hotels: Friendly Hotel.

5A 59 Lutterworth

Rugby Rd, Lutterworth, Leics, LE17
4HN
☎(01455) 557141, Fax 553586, Pro
557199, Sec 552532
On A426 0.5 mile from M1 junction 20.
Parkland course.
Pro Roland Tisdall; Founded 1904
Designed by D. Snell
18 holes, 6226 yards, S.S.S. 70
Visitors: welcome WD; members
guests at WE.
Green Fees: WD £18; WE £18.
Societies: welcome Mon, Wed and
Thurs and Tues pm; indoor academy;
terms on application.
Catering: clubhouse facilities.
Practice range.

5A 60 March

Frogs Abbey, Grange Rd, March,
Cambs, PE15 0YH
☎(01354) 652364
On A141 W of March by-pass.
Parkland course.
Pro Jason Hadland; Founded 1920
9 holes, 6204 yards, S.S.S. 70
Visitors: welcome WD.
Green Fees: WD £15.
Societies: welcome WD by prior
booking.
Catering: bar facilities; meals by prior
booking.
Hotels: Griffin.

5A 61 Market Harborough

Great Oxendon Rd, Market
Harborough, Leics, LE16 8NB
☎(01858) 463684
1 mile S of Market Harborough on
A508 towards Northampton.
Parkland course.
Pro F Baxter; Founded 1898
Updated by H Swan
18 holes, 6022 yards, S.S.S. 69
Visitors: welcome WD; WE as mem-
ber's guest only.
Green Fees: WD £20; WE £20.
Societies: welcome WD by arrange-
ment; Inclusive packages available;
from £35.
Catering: clubhouse facilities.
Hotels: Three Swans, Market
Harborough; George, Oxendon.

5A 62 Melton Mowbray

Waltham Rd, Thorpe Arnold, Melton
Mowbray, Leics, LE14 4SD
☎(01664) 562118, Fax 562118, Pro
569629
2 miles NE of Melton Mowbray on
A607
Undulating parkland course.
Pro James Hetherington; Founded
1925
18 holes, 6222 yards, S.S.S. 70
Visitors: welcome before 3pm.
Green Fees: WD £17; WE £20.
Societies: welcome WD by prior
arrangement; golf and lunch, dinner
packages can be organised; from £21.
Catering: full catering, bar and dining
facilities.
Hotels: Syonsby Knoll; George;
Harborough;Stapleford Park.

5A 63 Mentmore

Mentmore, Leighton Buzzard, Beds,
LU7 0QN
☎(01296) 662020, Fax 662592
1 mile from Cheddington, E of A41 to
Aylesbury.
Parkland course.
Pro Pip Elson; Founded 1992
Designed by Bob Sandow
Rosebury: 18 holes, 6855 yards,
S.S.S. 73; Rothschild 18 holes, 6791
yards, S.S.S. 72
Visitors: welcome WD; after 11am
WE.
Green Fees: WD £30; WE £30.
Societies: welcome WD; full facilities;
also pool, sauna, 2 tennis courts,
sports bar, fitness room, jacuzzi; 55-
75.
Catering: full bar, restaurant facilities.
Hotels: Pendley Manor; Rose and
Crown, both Tring.

5A 64 Millbrook
Millbrook, Bedford, Beds, MK45 2JB
☎(01525) 840252, Fax 406249, Pro
402269, Bar/Rest 841850
In Millbrook Village off A507 road just
before Ampthill.
Inland links course.
Pro David Armor; Founded 1980
Designed by W. Sutherland
18 holes, 6134 yards, S.S.S. 73
Visitors: restricted; phone profession-
al for details.
Green Fees: WD £17.50; WE £25.
Societies: welcome by prior arrange-
ment WD except Thurs; golf and cater-
ing packages can be arranged; from
£15.
Catering: clubhouse facilities.
Hotels: White Hart, Ampthill.

5A 65 Mount Pleasant
Station Rd, Lower Stondon, Henlow,
Beds, SG16 6JL
☎(01462) 850999
0.75 miles W of Stondon-Henlow
Camp roundabout off A600 Hitchin to
Bedford road; 4 miles N of Hitchin
Undulating meadowland course.
Pro Mike Roberts; Founded 1992
Designed by Derek Young
9/18 holes, 6003 yards, S.S.S. 69
Visitors: welcome at all times; book-
ing advisable.
Green Fees: WD £10.50; WE £14.50.
Societies: welcome WD; packages
available; 24 maximum for full cater-
ing, 36 for buffet; terms on application.
Catering: clubhouse bar facilities.
Hotels: Sun, Hitchin.

5A 66 Mowsbury
Cleat Hill, Kimbolton Rd, Ravensden,
Bedford, MK41 8DQ
☎(01234) 771493, Pro 216374, Sec
771041, Bar/Rest 771041
On B660 at northern limit of city
boundary.
Parkland course.
Pro M Summers; Founded 1975
Designed by Hawtree
18 holes, 6514 yards, S.S.S. 71
Visitors: welcome.
Green Fees: WD £7.15; WE £9.35.
Societies: welcome anytime; golf and

catering packages; driving range,
squash court; terms on application.
Catering: full facilities.

5A 67 Northampton
Harlestone, Northampton, Northants,
NN7 4EF
☎(01604) 845155, Fax 820262, Pro
845167, Bar/Rest 845102
On A428 Rugby road 4 miles from
Northampton.
Parkland course.
Pro Kevin Dickins; Founded 1893
Designed by Donald Steel
18 holes, 6615 yards, S.S.S. 72
Visitors: welcome WD.
Green Fees: WD £30.
Societies: welcome by prior arrange-
ment WD except Wed; packages for
golf and catering available; snooker;
banqueting; terms on application.
Catering: full facilities.
Hotels: Northampton Moat House;
Heyford Manor.

5A 68 Northamptonshire County
Golf Lane, Church Brampton,
Northampton, NN6 8AZ
☎(01604) 842951, Fax 843025, Pro
842226, Sec 843025, Bar/Rest
842170
5 miles NW of Northampton in village
of Church Brampton.
Heathland course with woods, gorse
and streams.
Pro Tim Rouse; Founded 1909
Designed by H.S. Colt
18 holes, 6503 yards, S.S.S. 71
Visitors: welcome by arrangement
with h'cap certs.
Green Fees: WD £37.50; WE £37.50.
Societies: large groups on Wed;
smaller groups Thurs; terms on application.
Catering: full catering facilities.
Hotels: Broomshill; Limetrees.

5A 69 Oadby
Leicester Rd, Oadby, Leicester, LE2
4AB
☎(0116) 2709052, Sec 2703828,
Bar/Rest 2700215

On A6 from Leicester inside Leicester
racecourse.
Meadowland course.
Pro Allan Kershaw; Founded 1975
18 holes, 6311 yards, S.S.S. 70
Visitors: welcome.
Green Fees: WD £6; WE £9.
Societies: welcome by prior applica-
tion to the professional; terms on
application.
Catering: bar meals and snacks;
meals on request.

5A 70 Old Nene Golf & Country Club
Muchwood Lane, Bodsey, Ramsey,
Cambs, PE17 1XQ
☎(01487) 813519, Pro 710122,
Bar/Rest 815622
1 mile N of Ramsey.
Parkland course course with water
hazards.
Pro Stuart Mills; Founded 1992
Designed by Richard Edrich
9 holes, 5675 yards, S.S.S. 68
Visitors: pay and play.
Green Fees: WD £10; WE £14.
Societies: welcome; reductions for 10
or more players; packages available;
terms on application.
Catering: bar and bar snacks avail-
able.
Practice range, floodlit; 2 piece balls.
Hotels: several in area.

5A 71 Orton Meadows
Ham Lane, Orton Waterville,
Peterborough, Cambs, PE2 0UU
☎(01733) 237478
On the A605 Peterborough-Oundle
road 2 miles W of Peterborough.
Parkland course.
Pro Neil Grant; Founded 1987
Designed by Dennis & Roger Fitton
18 holes, 5664 yards, S.S.S. 68
Visitors: welcome; advance bookings
available.
Green Fees: WD £9.80; WE £12.50.
Societies: welcome WD except Tues
and before 11am Sun; terms on appli-
cation.
Catering: In adjoining steakhouse The
Granary.
Hotels: Travelodge.

5A 72 **Oundle**

Benefield Rd, Oundle, Northants, PE8 4EZ
☎(01832) 273267, Fax 272267, Pro 272271, Bar/Rest 274882
On A427 Oundle-Corby road, 1.5 miles from Oundle.
Parkland course.
Pro Richard Keys; Founded 1893
18 holes, 6235 yards, S.S.S. 70
Visitors: welcome WD and after 10.30 WE.
Green Fees: WD £22; WE £30.
Societies: welcome WD except Tues; golf and catering packages available; from £35.
Catering: full clubhouse facilities.
Practice range, 2 practice areas.
Hotels: Talbot, Oundle; Travel Lodge, Thrapston.

5A 73 **Overstone Park**

Billing Lane, Northampton, Northants, NN6 0AP
☎(01604) 647666, Pro 643555
Take A45 Northampton road to Billing Lane.
Parkland course in walled Victorian estate.
Pro Brian Mudge; Founded 1993
Designed by Donald Steel
18 holes, 6602 yards, S.S.S. 72
Visitors: welcome WD and from 11am WE.
Green Fees: WD £25; WE £25.
Societies: welcome by prior arrangement; packages; health and leisure club.
Catering: bar and brasserie.
Practice range, practice area.

5A 74 **Park Hill**

Park Hill, Seagrave, Leics, LE12 7NG
☎(01509) 815454, Fax 816062, Pro 815775, Bar/Rest 815885
Off A46 from Leicester; turn left at Seagrave.
Parkland course; five par 5s more than 500 yards.
Pro David Mee; Founded 1895
18 holes, 7219 yards, S.S.S. 74
Visitors: welcome.
Green Fees: WD £20; WE £20.
Societies: welcome; terms on application; from £20.
Catering: clubhouse catering facilities.
Hotels: Rothley Court; Willoughby.

5A 75 **Pavenham Park**

Pavenham Park, Pavenham, Beds, MK43 7PE
☎(01234) 822202, Fax 826602

On A6 6 miles N of Bedford.
Parkland course.
Pro Zac Thompson; Founded 1994
Designed by Derek Young/Z Thompson
18 holes, 6353 yards, S.S.S. 70
Visitors: welcome WD.
Green Fees: WD £15.
Societies: welcome WD; full catering and golf packages; from £14.
Catering: clubhouse facilities.
Practice range, practice area.

5A 76 **Peterborough Milton**

Golf Club, Milton Ferry, PE6 7AG
☎(01733) 380224, Fax 380489, Pro 380793, Sec 380489
2 miles W of Peterborough on A47.
Parkland course.
Pro Mike Gallagher; Founded 1938
Designed by James Braid
18 holes, 6463 yards, S.S.S. 72
Visitors: welcome with h'cap certs.
Green Fees: WD £20; WE £20.
Societies: welcome Tues-Fri; full catering facilities and golf packages; from £30.
Catering: full facilities.
Practice range, large practice area.
Hotels: Haycock, Wansford; Swallow; Butterfly, both Peterborough.

5A 77 **RAF Cottesmore**

Oakham, Leicester, Leics, LE15 7BL
☎(01572) 812241
7 miles N of Oakham off B668.
Parkland course.
Founded 1980
9 holes, 5622 yards, S.S.S. 67
Visitors: with member only.
Green Fees: terms on application.

5A 78 **RAF Henlow**

Henlow Camp, Beds, SG16 6DN
☎(01462) 851515
3 miles SE of Shefford on A505, follow signs to RAF Henlow.
Meadowland course.
Founded 1985
9 holes, 5618 yards, S.S.S. 67
Visitors: only with member.
Green Fees: terms on application.
Societies: can be arranged through Sec.
Catering: light refreshments available.
Hotels: Bird in Hand.

5A 79 **RAF North Luffenham**

North Luffenham, Oakham, Leics, LE15 8RL
☎(01780) 720041

Follow signposts for RAF North Luffenham from A606, station is close to Rutland Water.
Meadowland course.
Founded 1975
9 holes, 6010 yards, S.S.S. 70
Visitors: with member or by appointment through Sec.
Green Fees: terms on application.
Societies: can be arranged through Sec.
Catering: bar and restaurant facilities.
Hotels: George; Crown.

5A 80 **Ramsey**

4 Abbey Terrace, Ramsey, Huntingdon, Cambs, PE17 1DD
☎(01487) 812600, Fax 815746, Pro 813022
Off B660 Ramsey road from the A1 between Huntingdon and Peterborough.
Parkland course.
Pro Stuart Scott; Founded 1964
Designed by J. Hamilton Stutt
18 holes, 6163 yards, S.S.S. 70
Visitors: welcome WD; WE as member's guest.
Green Fees: WD £25; WE £12.
Societies: WD only; minimum 8; golf package, catering, professional can offer coaching, practice area; from £25.
Catering: clubhouse facilities.
Practice range, 4 large practice areas.
Hotels: George, Huntingdon; Bell, Stilton; Dolphin, St Ives.

5A 81 **Rothley Park**

Westfield Lane, Rothley, Leicester, LE7 7LH
☎(0116) 2375086, Fax 2302809, Pro 2303023, Sec 2302809, Bar/Rest 2302019
Off A6 N of Leicester.
Parkland course.
Pro Andrew Collins; Founded 1912
18 holes, 6476 yards, S.S.S. 71
Visitors: welcome WD except Tues; h'cap certs required.
Green Fees: WD £25.
Societies: welcome Wed, Thurs, Fri; 10 per cent discount for more than 40 players; full catering available; terms on application.
Catering: full clubhouse facilities.
Hotels: Rothley Court; Quorn Country Hotel; Quorn Grange.

5A 82 **Rushcliffe**

Stocking Lane, East Leake, Loughborough, Leics, LE12 5RL

☎(01509) 852959, Pro 852701,
Bar/Rest 852209
From M1 junction 24 take A453
towards West Bridgford; turn at
Gotham, East Leake signs.
Parkland course.
Pro Chris Hall; Founded 1910
18 holes, 6013 yards, S.S.S. 69
Visitors: welcome.
Green Fees: WD £22; WE £22.
Societies: welcome WD; packages
available; from £22.
Catering: clubhouse facilities.

5A 83 Rushden
Kimbolton Rd, Chelveston,
Wellingborough, Northants, NN9 6AN
☎(01933) 312581, Sec 418511
On A45 2 miles E of Higham Ferrers.
Undulating meadowland course.
Founded 1919
10 holes 6350 yards, S.S.S. 70
Visitors: welcome WD except Wed
pm; WE with member.
Green Fees: WD £18.
Societies: welcome WD except Wed
pm by prior arrangement.
Catering: full facilities except Mon.

5A 84 St Ives
Westwood Rd, St Ives, Cambs, PE17
4RS
☎(01480) 468392, Pro 466067
On B1040 off A45 in St Ives.
Parkland course.
Pro Darren Glasby; Founded 1923
9 holes, 6100 yards, S.S.S. 69
Visitors: welcome WD; with member
WE.
Green Fees: WD £20; WE £20.
Societies: welcome Wed and Fri by
prior arrangement; packages avail-
able; from £20.
Catering: full clubhouse facilities.
Hotels: Slepe Hall.

5A 85 St Neots
Crosshall Rd, St Neots, Huntingdon,
Cambs, PE19 4AE
☎(01480) 474311, Fax 472363, Pro
476513, Sec 472363
On B1048 off the A1.
Parkland course with water hazards.
Pro Graham Bithrey; Founded 1890
Designed by Harry Vardon (original 9)
18 holes, 6026 yards, S.S.S. 69
Visitors: welcome WD; WE with mem-
ber.
Green Fees: WD £20; WE £20.
Societies: welcome Tues, Wed, Thurs
by prior arrangement; packages avail-
able; snooker; terms on application.

Catering: full clubhouse facilities.
Hotels: Eaton Oak; Kings Head.

5A 86 Scraptoft
Beeby Rd, Scraptoft, Leicester, LE7
9SJ
☎(0116) 2418863, Pro 2419138
Turn off A47 main Peterborough-
Leicester road at Scraptoft at Thurnby.
Meadowland course.
Pro Simon Wood; Founded 1928
18 holes, 6235 yards, S.S.S. 70
Visitors: welcome; dress code after
7pm.
Green Fees: WD £20; WE £25.
Societies: welcome WD by prior
arrangement; packages available;
terms on application.
Catering: full facilities.
Hotels: White House.

5A 87 Shelthorpe
Poplar Road, Loughborough, Club
☎(01509) 267766
From Leicester on A6 turn left at first
traffic lights, over island and then 2nd
left.
Municipal parkland course.
18 holes, 4160 yards,
Visitors: welcome.
Green Fees: WD £3; WE £3.

5A 88 Six Hills
Six Hills, Melton Mowbray, Leics, LE14
3PR
☎(01509) 881225
From M1 take A46 N; course 0.5 mile
from A46.
Parkland course.
Pro Matt Alls; Founded 1986
18 holes, 5808 yards, S.S.S. 68
Visitors: welcome; pay and play.
Green Fees: WD £8; WE £10.
Societies: welcome but no advance
booking system.
Catering: limited to coffee, tea and
light refreshments.
Hotels: Ragdale Hall.

5A 89 South Bedfordshire
Warden Hill Rd, Luton, Beds, LU2 7AA
☎(01582) 591500, Pro 591209
3 miles N of Luton on A6 signposted
into Warden Hill Rd.
Undulating course with trees and
hawthorn hedges.
Pro Eddie Cogle; Founded 1892
18 holes, 6389 yards, S.S.S. 71
Visitors: welcome WD; WE by prior
arrangement.
Green Fees: WD £19; WE £26.

Societies: welcome mainly Wed and
Thurs by prior arrangement; packages
available; snooker; also Warden
course: 9 hole, 4914 yards, par 64
WD:£7; WE:£10; terms on application.
Catering: snacks, catering and bar
facilities.
Hotels: Chiltern; Strathmore.

5A 90 Staverton Park
Staverton, Daventry, Northants, NN11
6JT
☎(01327) 302000, Pro 705506
On A425 Daventry to Leamington
road; 1 mile S of Daventry.
Undulating meadowland course.
Pro Richard Mudge; Founded 1978
Designed by Comm. John Harris
18 holes, 6100 yards, S.S.S. 72
Visitors: welcome.
Green Fees: WD £25; WE £27.50.
Societies: welcome WD by prior
arrangement; snooker; solarium;
sauna; banqueting suites; terms on
application.
Catering: full facilities at all times.
Practice range, 11 bays floodlit.
Hotels: Staverton Park offers golfing
weekends.

5A 91 Stockwood Park
Stockwood Park, London Rd, Luton,
Beds, LU1 4LX
☎(01582) 413704, Fax 481001
M1 junction 10; towards town centre
and then left at 1st traffic lights.
Meadowland course.
Pro Glyn McCarthy; Founded 1973
Designed by Charles Lawrie
18 holes, 6049 yards, S.S.S. 69
Visitors: welcome.
Green Fees: WD £7.50; WE £9.90.
Societies: welcome Mon, Tues and
Thurs by prior arrangement with pro;
packages for catering and golf by
arrangement; 9-hole pitch & putt;
terms on application.
Catering: full facilities.
Practice range, 24 bays floodlit.
Hotels: Strathmore.

5A 92 Stoke Albany
Ashley Rd, Stoke Albany, Market
Harborough, Leics, LE16 8PL
☎(01858) 535208, Fax 535505
Off A427 Market Harborough-Corby
road just through Stoke Albany.
Parkland course.
Founded 1995
18 holes, 6132 yards, S.S.S. 69
Visitors: welcome by prior arrange-
ment.

Green Fees: WD £12; WE £15.
Societies: welcome by prior arrangement; packages for golf and catering available; terms on application.
Catering: Fairways Bar and Restaurant.
Hotels: Three Swans, Market Harborough; Rockingham Forest, Corby.

5A 93 Thorney Golf Centre

English Drove, Thorney,
Peterborough, Cambs, PE6 0TJ
☎(01733) 270570, Fax 270842
On A47 E of Peterborough.
Thorney Lakes is parkland members course.
Pro Mark Templeman; Founded 1991/1995
Designed by A. Dow.
18 holes, 6402 yards, S.S.S. 71
Visitors: welcome.
Green Fees: WD £10; WE £16.
Societies: welcome WD; anytime on Fen municipal course: 6104 yards, par 70; packages available; also 9-hole par 3 course; terms on application.
Catering: bar and restaurant.
Practice range, 12 bays floodlit.

5A 94 Thorpe Wood

Nene Parkway, Peterborough, PE3 6SE
☎(01733) 267701, Fax 332774
On A47 to Leicester 2 miles W of Peterborough.
Parkland course.
Pro Roger Fitton; Founded 1975
Designed by Peter Alliss and Dave Thomas
18 holes, 7086 yards, S.S.S. 74
Visitors: welcome.
Green Fees: WD £9.50; WE £12.
Societies: welcome by arrangement up to a year in advance.
Catering: at The Woodman.
Hotels: Moat House.

5A 95 Tilsworth

Dunstable Rd, Tilsworth, Leighton Buzzard, Beds, LU7 9PU
☎(01525) 210721, Fax 210465 ,
Bar/Rest 210722
2 miles N of Dunstable on A5; take Tilsworth/Stanbridge turning.
Parkland course; 13th is 97 yards.
Pro Darren Charlton; Founded 1977
18 holes, 5306 yards, S.S.S. 66
Visitors: welcome except before 10am Sun morning.
Green Fees: WD £10; WE £12.

Societies: welcome WD; terms on application.
Catering: full facilities.
Practice range, open all week.

5A 96 Ullesthorpe

Frolesworth Rd, Ullesthorpe,
Lutterworth, Leics, LE17 5BZ
☎(01455) 209023, Fax 202537, Pro 209150
Close to the M1 and M69, just off the A5.
Parkland course.
Pro David Bowring; Founded 1976
18 holes, 6650 yards, S.S.S. 72
Visitors: welcome except Sun.
Green Fees: WD £20; WE £20.
Societies: golf day packages and overnight accommodation can be organised through the hotel; full clubhouse and hotel facilities for both corporate and society golf days; from £28.
Catering: full hotel and clubhouse facilities.
Hotels: Ullesthorpe Court.

5A 97 Waterbeach Barracks

39th Engineering Regiment,
Waterbeach, Cambs, CB5 9PA
☎(01223) 861048
Fenland course.
Founded 1972
9 holes, 6237 yards, S.S.S. 70
Visitors: HM Forces welcome; civilians must be introduced by and play with a member.
Green Fees: terms on application.
Catering: limited bar available.

5A 98 Wellingborough

Harroween Hall, Great Harroween,
Wellingborough, Northants, NN9 5AD
☎(01933) 673022, Fax 679379, Pro 678752, Sec 677234, Bar/Rest 402612
2 miles N of Wellingborough on A509
Undulating parkland course.
Pro David Clifford; Founded 1893/1975
Designed by Hawtree & Sons
18 holes, 6617 yards, S.S.S. 72
Visitors: welcome WD.
Green Fees: WD £35.
Societies: welcome WD except Tues; full day's golf, bar, restaurant, snooker; from £35.
Catering: full clubhouse facilities available.
Hotels: Foxford; Tudor Gate, Finedon; Kettering Park; Oak House and Hind, both Wellingborough.

5A 99 Western Park

Scudamore Rd, Braunstone Frith,
Leicester, LE3 1UQ
☎(0116) 2872339, Fax 2876158
Off A47 2 miles W of city centre.
Parkland course.
Pro David Butler; Founded 1920
Designed by F.W. Hawtree
18 holes, 6518 yards, S.S.S. 70
Visitors: welcome; must book at WE.
Green Fees: WD £7.50; WE £9.
Societies: welcome by prior arrangement; catering and golf packages available; terms on application.
Catering: full clubhouse facilities.
Hotels: Stakis Hotel.

5A 100 Whaddon Golf Centre

Church St, Whaddon, Nr Royston,
Herts, SG8 5RX
☎(01223) 207325, Fax 207325
4 miles N of Royston off A1198.
Parkland course.
Pro G Huggett; Founded 1990
Designed by Richard Green
9 holes, 905 yards,
Visitors: public pay and play.
Green Fees: WD £2.50; WE £3.
Societies: welcome; terms on application.
Catering: bar snacks.

5A 101 Whetstone

Cambridge Rd, Cosby, Leics, LE9 5SH
☎(0116) 2861424
4 miles from M1 junction 21 SE of Leicester; take A46 to Narborough then signposts for Whetstone.
Wooded parkland course with water features.
Pro David Raitt; Founded 1963
Designed by Nick Leatherland
18 holes, 5795 yards, S.S.S. 68
Visitors: welcome.
Green Fees: WD £14; WE £16.
Societies: welcome by arrangement.
Catering: full bar and catering facilities.
Practice range, 20 bays.
Hotels: Time Out, Blaby.

5A 102 Whittlebury Park Golf & Country Club

Whittlebury, Nr Towcester, Northants,
NN12 8XW
☎(01327) 858092, Fax 858009, Pro 858588
On A413 15 mins from M1 junction 15a.
Parkland/lakeland course.
Founded 1992

Designed by Cameron Sinclair
36 holes 6662 yards, S.S.S. 72
Visitors: welcome.
Green Fees: WD £20; WE £30.
Societies: welcome at all times by prior arrangement; 4 x 9 loops (1905, Royal Whittlewood, Grand Prix, Wedgewood); indoor course; clay pigeon shooting, archery, cricket ground, croquet lawn, corporate hospitality; function suites; terms on application.
Catering: bars, bistros, restaurant.
Hotels: Travelodge, Towcester.

5A 103 **Willesley Park**
Tamworth Rd, Ashby-de-la-Zouch, Leics, LE65 2PF
☎(01530) 411532, Fax 414596, Pro 414820, Sec 414596
2 miles S of Ashby-de-la-Zouch on B5006.
Parkland/heathland course.
Pro C J Hancock; Founded 1921
Designed by C.K. Cotton
18 holes, 6304 yards, S.S.S. 70
Visitors: welcome with h'cap certs.
Green Fees: WD £27.50; WE £32.50.
Societies: welcome Wed, Thurs, Fri; terms on application; from £30.
Catering: clubhouse facilities.
Hotels: Royal; Fallen Knight.

5A 104 **Wyboston Lakes**
Wyboston Lakes, Wyboston, Beds, MK44 3AL
☎(01480) 223004, Fax 407330
Off A1 at St Neots.
Public parkland with lake features.
Pro Paul Ashwell; Founded 1981
Designed by Neil Oackden
18 holes, 5955 yards, S.S.S. 70
Visitors: welcome; bookings taken 7 days in advance for WE.
Green Fees: WD £11; WE £15.
Societies: welcome WD by prior arrangement.
Catering: full catering facilities.
Practice range, 12 bays floodlit.
Hotels: hotel on site offers golf packages.

5B 1 **Abbey Hotel Golf & Country Club**
Dagnell End Rd, Redditch, Worcs, B98 7BD
☎(01527) 63918, Pro 68006
On A441 Redditch to Birmingham road.
Parkland course.
Founded 1985
Designed by Donald Steel
18 holes, 6411 yards, S.S.S. 71

Visitors: welcome subject to course availability.
Green Fees: WD £12.50; WE £15.
Societies: welcome by prior arrangement; special packages with hotel; snooker; gym; swimming pool; sauna.
Catering: bars and restaurant.
Hotels: Abbey Hotel on site.

5B 2 **Ansty Golf Centre**
Brinklow Rd, Ansty, Coventry, Warwicks, CV7 9JH
☎(01203) 621341, Fax 602671
From M6 junction 2 take B4065 to Ansty; turning on to B4029 to Brinklow.
Parkland course.
Pro John Reay; Founded 1990
Designed by D. Morgan
18 holes, 6079 yards, S.S.S. 69
Visitors: pay and play.
Green Fees: WD £9; WE £13.
Societies: welcome with 24 hours notice.
Catering: full facilities.
Practice range, 18 bays.
Hotels: Ansty Hall; Hanover at Hinckley.

5B 3 **Atherstone**
The Outwoods, Atherstone, Warwicks, CV9 2RL
☎(01827) 713110
On A5 in town centre on Coleshill Road.
Parkland course.
Founded 1894
18 holes, 6006 yards, S.S.S. 70
Visitors: welcome.
Green Fees: WD £17; WE £17.
Societies: welcome by arrangement; packages available; full catering facilities; terms on application.
Catering: full catering and bar.
Hotels: Chapel House; Mancetter Manor, both Atherstone.

5B 4 **The Belfry**
Lichfield Rd, Wishaw, N Warwickshire, B76 9PR
☎(01675) 470301, Fax 470301
M42 junction 9 follow A446 towards Lichfield and course is 1 mile on left.
Parkland course courses; Ryder Cup course; 2001 host.
Pro Peter McGovern; Founded 1977
Designed by Peter Alliss & Dave Thomas
Brabazon:18 holes, 6682 yards, S.S.S. 72; Derby: 18 holes, 6009 yards, S.S.S. 72; PGA National: 18 holes, 7072 yards, S.S.S. 72
Visitors: welcome from end of September 98.

Green Fees: WD £75 , WE £75 (Brabazon); WD £35, WE £35 (Derby); WD £60, WE £60 (PGA National).
Societies: welcome; full championship course, clubhouse and hotel facilities; terms on application.
Catering: first-class clubhouse and hotel facilities.
Practice ground.
Hotels: The Belfry.

5B 5 **Belmont Lodge and GC**
Belmont House, Belmont, Hereford, HR2 9SA
☎(01432) 352666, Fax 358090, Pro 352717
1.5 miles from centre of Hereford just off A436 Abergavenny road.
Parkland course with back 9 bordering the river.
Pro Mike Walsh; Founded 1983
Designed by R. Sandow
18 holes, 6511 yards, S.S.S. 71
Visitors: welcome.
Green Fees: WD £10; WE £16.
Societies: welcome; packages can be organised; terms on application.
Catering: full club and hotel facilities.
Practice ground.
Hotels: Belmont Lodge.

5B 6 **Bidford Grange**
Stratford Rd, Bidford on Avon, Warwicks, B50 4LY
☎(01789) 490319, Fax 778184
Off A439 Evesham-Stratford road.
Parkland course with last 4 holes close to River Avon.
Pro Ray Thompson; Founded 1992
Designed by Howard Swan and Paul Tillman
18 holes, 7233 yards, S.S.S. 74
Visitors: welcome.
Green Fees: WD £15; WE £17.50.
Societies: welcome; various packages available, including golf, catering, dinner and accommodation; minimum 12; from £20-£50.
Catering: new clubhouse with spikes bar, restaurant and hotel facilities.
Practice range, 20 bays.
Hotels: Bidford Grange.

5B 7 **Blackwell**
Blackwell, Bromsgrove, Worcs, B60 1PY
☎(0121) 445 1994, Pro 445 3113, Bar/Rest 445 1781
3 miles E of Bromsgrove close to Blackwell village centre.
Parkland course.
Pro Nigel Blake; Founded 1893

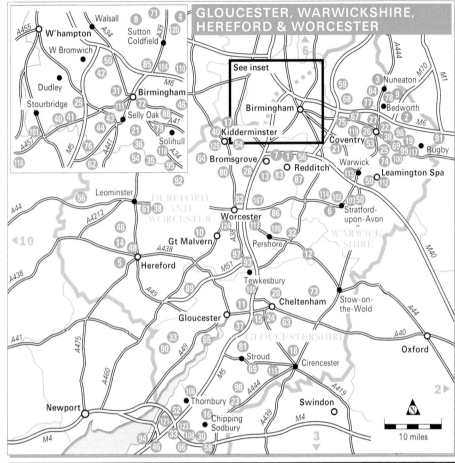

GLOUCESTER, WARWICKSHIRE, HEREFORD & WORCESTER

KEY			
1	Abbey Hotel G &CC	24	Cotswold Hills	49	Herefordshire	75	North Warwickshire	101	Stourbridge
2	Ansty Golf Centre	25	Coventry	50	Hill Top	76	North Worcestershire	102	Stratford Oaks
3	Atherstone	26	Coventry Hearsall	51	Ingon Manor G & CC	77	Nuneaton	103	Stratford-upon-Avon
4	The Belfry	27	Cromwell Course at	52	The Kendleshire	78	Oakridge	104	Sutton Coldfield
5	Belmont Lodge and GC		Nailcote Hall	53	Kenilworth	79	Olton	105	Tewkesbury Park Hotel
6	Bidford Grange	28	Droitwich G & CC	54	Kidderminster	80	Ombersley	106	Thornbury Golf Centre
7	Blackwell	29	Dudley	55	Kings Norton	81	Painswick	107	Tolladine
8	Boldmere	30	Dymock Grange	56	Kington	82	Perdiswell	108	Tracy Park Country Club
9	Bramcote Waters	31	Edgbaston	57	Ladbrook Park	83	Pitcheroak	109	Vale Golf & CC
10	Bransford at Bank House	32	Evesham	58	Lansdown	84	Purley Chase G & CC	110	Walmley
	Hotel	33	Filton	59	Lea Marston Hotel	85	Pype Hayes	111	Warley
11	Brickhampton Court	34	Forest Hills	60	Leamington & County	86	Ravenmeadow	112	Warwick
12	Broadway	35	Fulford Heath	61	Leominster	87	Redditch	113	Warwickshire
13	Bromsgrove Golf Centre	36	Gay Hill	62	Lickey Hills (Rose Hill)	88	Robin Hood	114	Welcombe Hotel
14	Burghill Valley	37	Grange (GPT Golf Club)	63	Lilley Brook	89	Ross-on-Wye	115	Westonbirt
15	Canons Court	38	Grange Golf Centre	64	Little Lakes	90	Royal Forest of Dean	116	Wharton Park
16	Chipping Sodbury	39	Grove Golf Centre	65	Lydney	91	Rugby	117	Whitefields
17	Churchill & Blakedown	40	Habberley	66	Mangotsfield	92	Sapey	118	Widney Manor
18	Cirencester	41	Hagley Country Club	67	Marriott Forest of Arden	93	Sherdons	119	Windmill Village Hotel
19	City of Coventry	42	Halesowen	68	Maxstoke Park	94	Shirehampton Park	120	Wishaw
	(Brandon Wood)	43	Handsworth	69	Memorial Park	95	Shirley	121	Woodlands
20	Cleeve Hill	44	Harborne	70	Minchinhampton	96	Sphinx	122	Woodspring
21	Cocks Moor Woods	45	Harborne Church Farm	71	Moor Hall	97	Stakis Puckrup HI Hotel	123	Worcester G & CC
22	Copt Heath	46	Hatchford Brook	72	Moseley	98	Stinchcombe Hill	124	Worcestershire
23	Cotswold Edge	47	Henbury	73	Naunton Downs	99	Stonebridge	125	Wyre Forest
		48	Hereford Municipal	74	Newbold Comyn	100	Stoneleigh Deer Park		

Designed by H. Fowler and T Simpson 18 holes, 6230 yards, S.S.S. 71
Visitors: welcome WD; with member at WE.
Green Fees: WD £50.
Societies: welcome Wed, Thurs, Fri by prior arrangement with Sec.
Catering: full clubhouse facilities.
Hotels: Perry Hall; Bromsgrove.

5B 8 Boldmere
Monmouth Drive, Sutton Coldfield, W Midlands, B73 6JL
☎(0121) 354 3379
Off A452 Chester Road 6 miles NE of Birmingham.
Parkland course.
Pro Trevor Short; Founded 1936
18 holes, 4493 yards, S.S.S. 62
Visitors: welcome.
Green Fees: WD £8.50; WE £9.
Societies: welcome WD only.
Catering: bar and catering.
Hotels: Parson & Clerk.

5B 9 Bramcote Waters
Bazzard Rd, Bramcote, Nuneaton, Warwickshire, CV11 6QJ
☎(01455) 220807
5 miles SE of Nuneaton off the B4114.
Parkland course.
Pro Nic Gilks; Founded 1995
9 holes, 4992 yards, S.S.S. 62
Visitors: pay and play.
Green Fees: WD £10; WE £11.
Societies: none.
Catering: none.
Hotels: Island Hotel.

5B 10 Bransford at Bank House Hotel
Bank House Hotel, Bransford, Worcester, WR6 5JD
☎(01886) 833551, Fax 832461, Pro 833521, Bar/Rest 833551 x 2017
3 miles W of Worcester on the A4013 Hereford road in Bransford village.
Florida-style course with 14 lakes and 2 island greens.
Pro Craig George/Lysa Jones; Founded 1993
Designed by Bob Sandow
18 holes, 6204 yards, S.S.S. 70
Visitors: welcome.
Green Fees: terms on application.
Societies: welcome; various packages including 2-night golfing break for £150; hotel; clubhouse facilities, outdoor pool, fitness centre; from £25.
Catering: bars, restaurants.
Practice range, 20-bay floodlit range.
Hotels: Bank House Hotel.

5B 11 Brickhampton Court
Brickhampton Court, Cheltenham Road, Churchdown, Glos, GL2 9QF
☎(01452) 859444, Fax 859333
On B4063 between Cheltenham and Gloucester; 3 miles from junction 11 of the M5.
Parkland course.
Pro David Finch; Founded 1995
Designed by S. Gidman
18 holes, 6387 yards, S.S.S. 31
Visitors: welcome.
Green Fees: WD £16; WE £22.50.
Societies: welcome WD; golf and catering packages; also 9-hole Glevum course; on-course refreshments; welcome packs and golf clinics; £21-£37.50.
Catering: clubhouse facilities, bar, restaurant.
Practice range, 26-bay floodlit range; Mizuno teaching academy.
Hotels: Golden Valley; Hatherley Manor; White House.

5B 12 Broadway
Willersey Hill, Broadway, Worcs, WR12 7LG
☎(01386) 858997, Fax 858643, Pro 853275, Sec 853683, Bar/Rest 853561
1.5 miles E of Broadway on A44.
Inland links.
Pro M Freeman; Founded 1896
Designed by James Braid
18 holes, 6216 yards, S.S.S. 70
Visitors: welcome with prior arrangement except before 3pm on Sat in summer.
Green Fees: WD £27; WE £27.
Societies: welcome Wed, Thurs, Fri; terms on application.
Catering: clubhouse facilities.
Hotels: Dormy house on course; Lygon Arms, Broadway.

5B 13 Bromsgrove Golf Centre
Stratford Road, Bromsgrove, Worcestershire, B60 1LD
☎(01527) 575886, Fax 570964
1 mile from Bromsgrove at junction of A38 and A448.
Gently undulating parkland course.
Pro G Long/M Davies; Founded 1992
Designed by Hawtree & Sons
18 holes, 5869 yards, S.S.S. 68
Visitors: pay and play.
Green Fees: WD £12.50; WE £15.50.
Societies: welcome by prior arrangement; group and society packages available; terms on application.
Catering: full facilities with bar and lounge.

Practice range, 41-bay covered floodlit range; large practice bunker.
Hotels: list available on request.

5B 14 Burghill Valley
Tillington Road, Burghill, Hereford, HR4 7RW
☎(01432) 760456, Fax 761654, Pro 760808
4 miles NW of Hereford.
Built around cider orchards, 2 lakes and woods.
Pro Nigel Clarke; Founded 1991
18 holes, 6239 yards, S.S.S. 70
Visitors: welcome.
Green Fees: WD £17; WE £21.
Societies: welcome; golf and catering packages available; from £23.75.
Catering: clubhouse facilities.

5B 15 Canons Court
Canons Court Farm, Bradley, Wotton-under-Edge, Glos, GL12 7PN
☎(01453) 843128, Fax 844151
3 miles from M5 junction 14 on Wotton-under-Edge to N Nibley road.
Parkland course.
Founded 1982
9 holes, 5323 yards, S.S.S. 68
Visitors: public pay and play.
Green Fees: WD £8; WE £10.
Societies: welcome WD; terms on application.
Catering: bar and bar snacks.

5B 16 Chipping Sodbury
Chipping Sodbury, Bristol, Gloucs, BS17 6PU
☎(01454) 319042, Pro 314087, Bar/Rest 315822
Leave M4 junction 18 or M5 junction 14 and from Chipping Sodbury take the Wickwar road; first right turn.
Parkland course; also 9 holes, 1076 yards.
Pro Mike Watts
Designed by Fred Hawtree
18 holes, 6786 yards, S.S.S. 73
Visitors: welcome; after 12 noon at WE.
Green Fees: terms on application.
Societies: welcome WD by prior arrangement.
Catering: full bar and meal service.
Practice ground.
Hotels: Moda; Cross Hands.

5B 17 Churchill & Blakedown
Churchill Lane, Blakedown, Kidderminster, Worcester, DY10 3NB
☎(01562) 700018, Pro 700454

COPT HEATH GOLF

1220 WARWICK ROAD • KNOWLE • SOLIHULL • WEST MIDLANDS • B93

- Enjoy a game at a well known Midlands venue.
- Within half a mile of junction 5 on the M42, the course, basically flat and parkland by nature, is a challenging one.
- Bar and catering facilities are available throughout the day.

Telephone: Professional 01564 776155 • Secretary 01564 772650

Off A456 3 miles NE of Kidderminster; turn under railway viaduct in village of Blakedown.
Undulating parkland course.
Pro Keith Wheeler; Founded 1926
9 holes, 6472 yards, S.S.S. 71
Visitors: welcome WD; WE with a member.
Green Fees: WD £17.50; WE £10.
Societies: welcome by prior arrangement; from £15.
Catering: full facilities except Mon.
Hotels: Cedars.

5B 18 Cirencester

Cheltenham Rd, Bagendon, Cirencester, Glos, GL7 7BH
☎(01285) 652465, Fax 650665, Pro 656145, Bar/Rest 659987
Off A435 Cirencester- Cheltenham road 1.5 miles from Cirencester.
Undulating course.
Pro Peter Garratt; Founded 1893
Designed by James Braid
18 holes, 6020 yards, S.S.S. 69
Visitors: welcome.
Green Fees: WD £20; WE £25.
Societies: welcome by arrangement.
Catering: full facilities.
Hotels: Kings Head.

5B 19 City of Coventry (Brandon Wood)

Brandon Lane, Wolston, Coventry, CV8 3GQ
☎(01203) 543133, Sec 543141
6 miles S of Coventry off A45.
Parkland course.
Pro Chris Gledhill;
Designed by Frank Pennink
18 holes, 6610 yards, S.S.S. 72
Visitors: welcome.
Green Fees: WD £8.45; WE £11.25.
Societies: welcome on application to professional; terms on application.
Catering: clubhouse facilities.
Hotels: Brandon Hall Hotel.

5B 20 Cleeve Hill

Cleeve Hill, Cheltenham, Glos, GL52 3PW
☎(01242) 672025, Fax 672592, Pro 672592
6 miles N of M5; 4 miles from Cheltenham off A46.
Municipal heathland course.
Pro Richard Jenkins; Founded 1891
18 holes, 6411 yards, S.S.S. 71
Visitors: welcome WD; some restrictions WE.
Green Fees: WD £10; WE £12.
Societies: welcome by prior arrangement; catering packages; pool; skittles alley.
Catering: bar snacks.
Hotels: Rising Sun.

5B 21 Cocks Moor Woods

Alcester Rd South, Kings Heath, Birmingham, W Midlands, B14 6ER
☎(0121) 4443584
On A435 near city boundary.
Public parkland course.
Pro Steve Ellis; Founded 1924
18 holes, 5769 yards, S.S.S. 68
Visitors: welcome.
Green Fees: WD £9; WE £9.50.
Societies: welcome by arrangement.
Catering: full clubhouse facilities.

5B 22 Copt Heath

1220 Warwick Rd, Knowle, Solihull, Warwickshire, B93 9LN
☎(01564) 772650, Fax 771022, Pro 776155, Sec 771504
From M42 junction 5 take A4141; course 0.5 miles.
Parkland course.
Pro B J Barton; Founded 1910
Designed by H. Vardon
18 holes, 6508 yards, S.S.S. 71
Visitors: welcome WD.
Green Fees: WD £35; WE £35.
Societies: welcome by prior arrangement with secretary; maximum 36;

---

terms on application; from £35.
Catering: clubhouse facilities.
Hotels: Greswolde Arms; St Johns.

5B 23 Cotswold Edge

Upper Rushmire, Wotton-under-Edge, Gloucestershire, GL12 7PT
☎(01453) 844167, Fax 845120, Pro 844398
On B4058 Wotton-under-Edge/Tetbury road 8 miles from M5 junction 14.
Meadowland course.
Pro David Gosling; Founded 1980
18 holes, 6170 yards, S.S.S. 71
Visitors: welcome WD; WE with member.
Green Fees: WD £15; WE £20.
Societies: welcome WD by prior arrangement; packages available; from £30.
Catering: full clubhouse facilities.
Hotels: Hunters Hall; Calcot Manor.

5B 24 Cotswold Hills

Ullenwood, Cheltenham, Glos, GL53 9QT
☎(01242) 515264, Fax 515264, Pro 515263, Bar/Rest 573210
3 miles S of Cheltenham.
Parkland course on limestone; 1981 English Ladies Amateur.
Pro N Boland; Founded 1902/1976
Designed by M.D. Little
18 holes, 6750 yards, S.S.S. 72
Visitors: welcome by prior arrangement.
Green Fees: WD £24; WE £30.
Societies: welcome Wed and Thurs; packages available; from £24.
Catering: clubhouse facilities.
Hotels: Crest Motel; George Hotel; Lilleybrook; Golden Valley.

5B 25 Coventry

St Martin's Rd, Finham Park, Coventry, Warwicks, CV3 6PJ

☎(01203) 411298, Fax 690131, Pro 411123, Sec 414152, Bar/Rest 414152 Close to A45/A46 junction take A45 towards Birmingham and left at island. Parkland course.
Pro Phil weaver; Founded 1887
Designed by Tom Vardon
18 holes, 6613 yards, S.S.S. 72
Visitors: welcome WD; with member WE.
Green Fees: WD £30; WE £30.
Societies: welcome Mon, Tues, Fri; packages available; from £50-£55.
Catering: clubhouse facilities.
Hotels: Chesford Grange; Old Mill.

5B 26 Coventry Hearsall
Beechwood Ave, Earlsdon, Coventry, CV5 6DF
☎(01203) 672935, Fax 691534, Pro 713156, Sec 713470, Bar/Rest 675809
From A45/A429 towards City Centre turn into Beechwood Avenue.
Parkland course.
Pro Mike Tarn; Founded 1894/1921
18 holes, 6005 yards, S.S.S. 69
Visitors: welcome with member.
Green Fees: terms on application.
Societies: welcome Tues and Thurs; terms on application.
Catering: clubhouse facilities.
Hotels: Hylands Hotel.

5B 27 Cromwell Course at Nailcote Hall
Nailcote Hall Hotel, Nailcote Lane, Berkswell, Warwickshire, CV7 7DE
☎(01203) 466174, Fax 470720
Take A452 Balsall Common junction from B4101 and follow brown signs towards Tile Hall/ Coventry; hotel 1.5 miles on right.
Parkland course; hosts '98 Short Course pro championship.
Pro Sid Mouland; Founded 1994
Designed by Short Course Golf Ltd
9 holes, 1906 yards
Visitors: welcome.
Green Fees: WD £6; WE £6.
Societies: welcome by prior arrangement; terms on application.
Catering: full hotel facilities.
Hotels: Nailcote Hall on site.

5B 28 Droitwich Golf & Country Club
Westford House, Ford Lane, Droitwich, WR9 0BQ
☎(01905) 774344, Fax 797290, Pro 770207
Off A38 1 mile N of town.

Undulating meadowland course.
Pro Chris Thompson; Founded 1897
18 holes, 6058 yards, S.S.S. 69
Visitors: welcome WD with h'cap certs; with member WE.
Green Fees: WD £24.
Societies: welcome Wed and Fri.
Catering: bar, bar meals and restaurant.
Hotels: Raven.

5B 29 Dudley
Turners Hill, Rowley Regis, Warley, W Midlands, B65 9DP
☎(01384) 254020, Sec 233877
1 mile S of town centre.
Undulating parkland course.
Pro Paul Taylor; Founded 1893
18 holes, 5714 yards, S.S.S. 68
Visitors: welcome WD.
Green Fees: WD £18.
Societies: welcome by prior arrangement; packages available for 20 or more; 10% reduction; from £25.
Catering: lunch and evening meals.
Hotels: Travelodge.

5B 30 Dymock Grange
The Old Grange, Dymock, Glos, GL18 2AN
☎(01531) 890840, Fax 890852
On A4172 off the A449 Ledbury-Ross-on-Wye Rd.
Parkland course.
Founded 1995
18 holes, 4600 yards, S.S.S. 65
Visitors: welcome with prior reservation.
Green Fees: WD £10; WE £14.
Societies: welcome by prior arrangement.
Catering: bar, restaurant; fitness centre.

5B 31 Edgbaston
Edgbaston Hall, Church Rd, Edgbaston, Birmingham, B15 3TB
☎(0121) 454 1736, Fax 454 2395, Pro 454 3226, Bar/Rest 454 8014
From city centre take A38 Bristol road; after 1.5 miles turn right into Priory Road (B4217); after mini roundabout, club 100 yards.
Parkland course; with woods and lake.
Pro Andrew Bownes; Founded 1896/1935
Designed by H.S. Colt
18 holes, 6106 yards, S.S.S. 69
Visitors: welcome except Sat comp days before 2pm and Sun before 11.15am.
Green Fees: WD £37.50; WE £50.

Societies: welcome WD except Thurs; packages available including private function room, changing rooms, golf and catering;
minimum 20, maximum 100; £52.50.
Catering: extensive clubhouse facilities; restaurant, bars and private rooms.
Practice range, practice areas and nets.
Hotels: Copperfield House; Portland House; Apollo; Plough & Harrow; Swallow.

5B 32 Evesham
Craycombe Links,Fladbury Cross, Pershore, Worcs, WR10 2QS
☎(01386) 860395, Fax 861356, Pro 861144
3 miles W of Evesham towards Worcester on A4538.
Parkland course by river.
Pro Charles Haynes; Founded 1894
9 holes, 6415 yards, S.S.S. 71
Visitors: welcome with prior arrangement WD; WE with member.
Green Fees: WD £15; WE £15.
Societies: welcome with prior arrangement; terms on application.
Catering: clubhouse facilities.

5B 33 Filton
Golf Course Lane, Filton, Bristol, BS34 7QS
☎(0117) 9692021, Fax 9314359, Pro 9694158, Sec 9694169
M5 junction 16 to A38 at Filton roundabout turn right then 1st right at lights.
Parkland course with views of Brecon Beacons.
Pro Nicky Lums; Founded 1909
Designed by F. Hawtree & Son
18 holes, 6318 yards, S.S.S. 69
Visitors: welcome WD only; member's guest at WE.
Green Fees: WD £20; WE £20.
Societies: welcome by prior arrangement; terms on application.
Catering: full clubhouse facilities.
Hotels: Aztec; Stakis.

5B 34 Forest Hills
Mile End Road, Coleford, Gloucestershire, GL16 7QD
☎(01594) 810620, Fax 810823
On B 4028 to Gloucester 0.5 miles from Coleford town centre.
Meadowland course.
Founded 1992
Designed by Adrian Stiff
18 holes, 5674 yards, S.S.S. 67
Visitors: welcome.

Green Fees: WD £13; WE £15.
Societies: welcome by prior arrangement; terms on application.
Catering: full clubhouse facilities.

5B 35 Fulford Heath
Tanners Green Lane, Wythall,
Birmingham, B47 6BH
☎(01564) 822806, Fax 822629, Pro 822930, Sec 824758
8 miles S of Birmingham.
Parkland course.
Pro D Down; Founded 1933
18 holes, 6216 yards, S.S.S. 70
Visitors: welcome WD; with member at WE.
Green Fees: WD £32.50; WE £11.
Societies: welcome by arrangement on Tues and Thurs; golf and catering packages available; £27.50.
Catering: clubhouse facilities.

5B 36 Gay Hill
Hollywood Lane, Hollywood,
Birmingham, W Midlands, B47 5PP
☎(0121) 430 7077, Fax 436 7796,
Pro 474 6001, Sec 430 8544, Bar/Rest 430 6523
On A435 7 miles from Birmingham city centre and 3 miles from junction 3 of the M42.
Meadowland course.
Pro Andrew Potter; Founded 1913
18 holes, 6532 yards, S.S.S. 71
Visitors: welcome WD; WE with member but not before 12.30pm Sun.
Green Fees: WD £28.50.
Societies: welcome Thurs by prior arrangement.
Catering: full facilities.
Hotels: George.

5B 37 Gloucester
Jarvis Hotel & CC, Robinswood Hill,
Matson Lane, Gloucester,
Gloucestershire, GL4 9EA
☎(01452) 411331, Fax 307212 ,
Bar/Rest 525653
2 miles S of Gloucester on B4073 to Painswick.
Parkland course.
Pro Peter Darnell; Founded 1976
Designed by Donald Steel
18 holes, 6170 yards, S.S.S. 69
Visitors: welcome.
Green Fees: WD £19; WE £25.
Societies: welcome; terms on application.
Catering: full hotel and clubhouse facilities.
Hotels: Jarvis Gloucester Hotel & Country Club.

5B 38 Grange (GPT Golf Club)
Copsewood, Coventry, W Midlands,
CV3 1HS
☎(01203) 563127, Bar/Rest 451465
2.5 from Coventry on A428 Binley rd.
Meadowland course.
Founded 1924
Re-designed by T.J. McAuley
9 holes, 6002 yards, S.S.S. 69
Visitors: welcome WD before 2pm;
except Wed; not Sat; Sun after 11am.
Green Fees: WD £10; WE £10.
Societies: welcome by arrangement with secretary.
Catering: by arrangement only.
Hotels: Hilton.

5B 39 Grove Golf Centre
Fordbridge, Leominster, Herefordshire,
HR6 0LE
☎(01568) 610602
3 miles S of Leominster on A49.
Wooded parkland course.
Designed by J Gaunt/R Sandow
9 holes, 3560 yards, S.S.S. 60
Visitors: public pay and play.
Green Fees: WD £4; WE £5.
Societies: welcome any time; terms on application.
Catering: refreshments.
Practice range, floodlit bays; putting green.

5B 40 Habberley
Low Habberley, Kidderminster, Worcs,
DY11 5RG
☎(01562) 745756
2 miles NW of Kidderminster.
Parkland course.
Founded 1924
9 holes, 5481 yards, S.S.S. 69
Visitors: welcome WD if member of recognised club; WE and Bank Holidays with member only.
Green Fees: WD £10; WE £10.
Societies: welcome by prior arrangement; terms on application.
Catering: clubhouse facilities.
Hotels: Gainsborough; Heath Hotel.

5B 41 Hagley Country Club
Wassell Grove, Hagley, W Midlands,
DY9 9JW
☎(01562) 883701, Pro 883852
4 miles S of Birmingham on A456.
Undulating parkland course.
Pro Ian Clark; Founded 1979
18 holes, 6353 yards, S.S.S. 72
Visitors: welcome WD; WE with a member after 10am.
Green Fees: WD £22.50.

Societies: welcome WD by prior arrangement through the club manager; packages available; also squash.
Catering: bar and restaurant facilities.

5B 42 Halesowen
The Leasowes, Halesowen, west
Midlands, B62 8QF
☎(0121) 550 1041, Pro 503 0593,
Sec 501 3606, Bar/Rest 550 8680
M5 junction 3; A456 Kidderminster 2 miles.
Parkland course.
Pro J Nicholas; Founded 1907
18 holes, 5754 yards, S.S.S. 68
Visitors: welcome; WE with member only; Bank Holidays by arrangement.
Green Fees: WD £18; WE £18.
Societies: welcome by prior arrangement with Sec; packages available for groups of 25 or more; from £18.
Catering: clubhouse facilities except Mon evening.

5B 43 Handsworth
11 Sunningdale Close, Handsworth,
Handsworth, Birmingham, W
Midlands, B20 1NP
☎(0121) 554 0599, Fax 554 3387,
Pro 523 3594, Sec 554 3387
Close to either M5 junction 1 or M6 junction 7 off Hamstead Hill.
Parkland course.
Pro Lee Bashford; Founded 1895
18 holes, 6267 yards, S.S.S. 70
Visitors: welcome WD with h'cap certs.
Green Fees: WD £30.
Societies: welcome WD by arrangement; special packages available; squash.
Catering: full clubhouse facilities except Mon.
Practice range, practice ground.
Hotels: Post House.

5B 44 Harborne
40 Tennal Rd, Birmingham, W
Midlands, B32 2JE
☎(0121) 427 1728, Pro 4273512,
Sec 427 3058, Bar/Rest 428 3373
2 miles SW of city centre adjacent to M5 junction 3.
Parkland course.
Pro Alan Quarterman; Founded 1893
Designed by H.S. Colt
18 holes, 6235 yards, S.S.S. 70
Visitors: welcome WD.
Green Fees: WD £35; WE £35.
Societies: welcome by prior arrangement; terms on application; £30.
Catering: clubhouse facilities.

5B 45 **Harborne Church Farm**
Vicarage Rd, Harborne, Birmingham,
B17 0SN
☎(0121) 427 1204, Fax 428 3126
5 miles SW of Birmingham City centre.
Parkland course.
Pro Paul Johnson; Founded 1926
9 holes, 4882 yards, S.S.S. 64
Visitors: welcome with prior booking.
Green Fees: WD £8; WE £8.50.
Societies: welcome by prior arrangement; terms on application.
Catering: full facilities.

5B 46 **Hatchford Brook**
Coventry Rd, Sheldon, Birmingham,
B26 3PY
☎(0121) 743 9821, Fax 743 3042 ,
Sec 779 3780, Bar/Rest 743 9250
On A45 Birmingham to Coventry road
close to Birmingham airport.
Parkland course.
Pro Mark Hampton; Founded 1969
18 holes, 6155 yards, S.S.S. 69
Visitors: welcome except WE am.
Green Fees: WD £8; WE £8.50.
Societies: welcome by prior arrangement; terms on application.
Catering: full facilities.
Hotels: Metropole; Arden Motel.

5B 47 **Henbury**
Henbury Hill, Westbury-on-Trym,
Bristol, Gloucs, BS10 7QB
☎(0117) 9500044, Pro 9502121,
Bar/Rest 9500660
Leave M5 junction 17, 2nd exit from
roundabout into Crow Lane, course at
top of hill.
Parkland course.
Pro Nick Riley; Founded 1891
18 holes, 6029 yards, S.S.S. 69
Visitors: welcome WD with h'cap
certs.
Green Fees: WD £21; WE £21.
Societies: welcome Tues and Fri by
arrangement.
Catering: full facilities.
Hotels: Ship, Alveston.

5B 48 **Hereford Municipal**
The Racecourse, Holmer Road,
Hereford, HR4 9UD
☎(01432) 278178, Pro 344376
A49 towards Leominster in centre of
race track
Public parkland course.
Pro Phil Brookes; Founded 1983
9 holes, 6120 yards, S.S.S. 69
Visitors: welcome except race days.
Green Fees: WD £5.70; WE £7.60.
Societies: welcome by prior arrange-

ment; packages include 18 holes, coffee and 2-course meal; from £9.95.
Catering: bar and restaurant facilities.
Practice range, practice ground.
Hotels: Starling Gate; Travel Inn.

5B 49 **Herefordshire**
Ravens Causeway, Wormsley,
Hereford, HR4 8LY
☎(01432) 830219, Pro 830465, Sec
830817
Off Roman Road from Hereford in
direction of Weobley.
Parkland course.
Pro D Hemming; Founded 1898
Designed by Major Hutchison
18 holes, 6078 yards, S.S.S. 69
Visitors: welcome WD; WE by
arrangement.
Green Fees: WD £17; WE £20.
Societies: welcome; terms on application.
Catering: clubhouse facilities.

5B 50 **Hill Top**
Park Lane, Handsworth, Birmingham,
W Midlands, B21 8LJ
☎(0121) 554 4463
From M5 junction 1 follow signs for
Handsworth.
Parkland course.
Pro Kevin Highfield; Founded 1980
18 holes, 6208 yards, S.S.S. 69
Visitors: welcome; link card service,
book 8 days in advance.
Green Fees: WD £8.50; WE £9.
Societies: welcome WD by prior
arrangement with the professional;
packages available.
Catering: full clubhouse facilities.
Hotels: Post House, W Bromwich.

5B 51 **Ingon Manor Golf & Country Club**
Ingon Lane, Snitterfield, Nr Stratford
Upon Avon, Warwickshire, CV37 0QE
☎(01789) 731857, Fax 731657, Pro
731938
Signposted from M40 junction 15.
Parkland course.
Pro Craig Phillips; Founded 1993
Designed by David Hemstock
Associates & Colin Geddes
18 holes, 6623 yards, S.S.S. 71
Visitors: welcome.
Green Fees: WD £20; WE £25.
Societies: welcome by prior arrangement; terms on application; packages
available; terms on application.
Catering: full clubhouse and hotel
restaurant and bar facilities.
Hotels: Ingon Manor Hotel.

5B 52 **The Kendleshire**
Henfield Rd, Coalpit Heath, Bristol,
Glos, BS17 2TG
☎(0117) 9567007, Pro 9567000
1 mile from M32.
Parkland course.
Pro Paul Barrington; Founded 1997
Designed by A Stiff
18 holes, 6507 yards, S.S.S. 71
Visitors: welcome WD; WE by
arrangement.
Green Fees: WD £18; WE £24.
Societies: welcome by prior arrangement; packages on request; function
room for 250.
Catering: bar and restaurant facilities.
Practice range, grass.
Hotels: Post House.

5B 53 **Kenilworth**
Crewe Lane, Kenilworth, Warwicks,
CV8 2EA
☎(01926) 854296, Fax 864453, Pro
512732, Sec 858517, Bar/Rest
854038
6 miles from Coventry.
Undulating parkland course.
Pro Steve Yates; Founded 1889/1936
Designed by Hawtree
18 holes, 6413 yards, S.S.S. 71
Visitors: welcome by arrangement.
Green Fees: WD £28; WE £28.
Societies: welcome Wed; packages
available; terms on application.
Catering: clubhouse facilities.
Hotels: Chesford Grange; DeMontfort.

5B 54 **Kidderminster**
Russell Rd, Kidderminster, Worcs,
DY10 3HT
☎(01562) 822303
Course signposted off A449 within 1
mile of town centre.
Parkland course.
Pro Nick Underwood; Founded 1909
18 holes, 6405 yards, S.S.S. 71
Visitors: welcome WD only; WE with
member only.
Green Fees: WD £25.
Societies: welcome Thurs by prior
arrangement.
Catering: full facilities except Mon.
Hotels: Collingdale; Stone Manor.

5B 55 **Kings Norton**
Brockhill Lane, Weatheroak,
Alvechurch, Birmingham, B48 7ED
☎(01564) 826706, Fax 826955, Pro
822635, Sec 826789, Bar/Rest
822821
1 miles N of M42 junc 3 just off A435.
Parkland course; 3 x 9 combinations.

Pro Kevin Hayward; Founded 1892
Designed by F. Hawtree & Son
18 holes, 7057 yards, S.S.S. 74
Visitors: welcome WD.
Green Fees: WD £30.
Societies: welcome by prior arrangement; full catering and golf packages; separate reception room, bar; use of club starter; from £30.
Catering: full clubhouse facilities.
Hotels: Inkford Cottage; Pine Lodge.

5B 56 Kington

Bradnor Hill, Kington, Herefordshire, HR5 3RE
☎(01544) 230340, Fax 340270, Pro 231320, Sec 340270
From A44 take the B4355 Presteigne road for 100 metres and then left to Bradnor Hill.
Mountain links – highest 18-hole course in England.
Pro Dean Oliver; Founded 1925
Designed by C.K. Hutchinson
18 holes, 5228 yards, S.S.S. 68
Visitors: welcome with prior arrangement.
Green Fees: WD £14; WE £18.
Societies: welcome by prior arrangement with Secretary, Mr G Wictome; extensive menu and facilities available; from £14.
Catering: full catering and bar facilities.
Hotels: Royal George.

5B 57 Ladbrook Park

Poolhead Lane, Tamworth-in-Arden, Warwicks, B94 5ED
☎(01564) 742264, Pro 742581, Bar/Rest 742220
Take A435 to Tamworth/Portway; left into Penn Lane; then left into Broad Lane and left into Poolhead Lane.
Parkland course.
Pro Richard Mountford; Founded 1908
Designed by H.S. Colt
18 holes, 6427 yards, S.S.S. 71
Visitors: welcome WD; except Tues am.
Green Fees: WD £25.
Societies: welcome by prior arrangement with the Secretary; full golfing and catering packages; terms on application.
Catering: restaurant and bar facilities.
Hotels: Regency; Plough Inn.

5B 58 Lansdown

Lansdown, Bath, Avon, BA1 9BT
☎(01225) 425007, Fax 339252, Pro 420242, Sec 422138
From M4 junction 18 take A46 towards Bath; at roundabout take A420 towards Bristol; take 1st left and club is 2 miles on right by Bath racecourse.
Elevated parkland course.
Pro Terry Mercer; Founded 1894
Designed by Harry Colt
18 holes, 6316 yards, S.S.S. 70
Visitors: welcome WD; with h'cap certs at WE.
Green Fees: WD £18; WE £30.
Societies: welcome by prior arrangement; from £20.
Catering: clubhouse snacks and meals.
Hotels: Hilton.

5B 59 Lea Marston Hotel & Leisure Complex

Haunch Lane, Lea Marston, Warwickshire, B76 0BY
☎(01675) 470468
1 mile from M42 junction 9 on A4097 Kingsbury road; 1.5 miles from The Belfry.
Parkland course.
Pro Andrew Stokes; Founded 1983
Designed by J.R. Blake
9 holes, 775 yards
Visitors: welcome.
Green Fees: WD £4.25; WE £5.
Societies: welcome by prior arrangement; tennis, crown green bowls; pool; health club; swimming pool.
Catering: bar and restaurant facilities.
Practice range, 26 bays floodlit.
Hotels: Lea Marston on site; golf breaks.

5B 60 Leamington & County

Golf Lane, Whitnash, Leamington Spa, Warwicks, CV31 2QA
☎(01926) 420298, Pro 428014, Sec 425961
6 mins from M40 towards Leamington Spa and then take Whitnash signs.
Parkland course.
Pro Iain Grant; Founded 1908
Designed by H.S. Colt
18 holes, 6437 yards, S.S.S. 71
Visitors: welcome with h'cap certs.
Green Fees: WD £30; WE £40.
Societies: welcome Mon, Wed, Thurs; full golf and catering facilities; from £28.
Catering: clubhouse facilities.
Hotels: Marriott Courtyard.

5B 61 Leominster

Ford Bridge, Leominster, Hereford, HR6 0LE
☎(01568) 612863, Fax 610055, Pro 611402, Sec 610055
3 miles S of Leominster on A49.
Undulating parkland course running alongside River Lugg.
Pro Andrew Farriday; Founded 1903/67/90
Designed by Bob Sandow
18 holes, 6029 yards, S.S.S. 69
Visitors: welcome by arrangement.
Green Fees: WD £17; WE £21.
Societies: welcome WD except Mon; 36 holes of golf; coffee, light lunch and 3-course dinner; fishing on river also available; from £26.
Catering: full bar and bar snacks; restaurant every day except Mon.
Practice range, 18 bays.
Hotels: Castle Pool; Talbot; Royal Oak.

5B 62 Lickey Hills (Rose Hill)

Lickey Hills, Rednal, Birmingham, W Midlands, B45 8RR
☎(0121) 453 3159
M5 junction 4 or M42 junction 1 sign-posted to Lickey Hills Park.
Public parkland course.
Pro Joe Kelly; Founded 1927
Designed by Carl Bretherton
18 holes, 5835 yards, S.S.S. 68
Visitors: welcome.
Green Fees: WD £8.50; WE £8.50.
Societies: welcome by arrangement.
Catering: snacks.
Hotels: Westmead.

5B 63 Lilley Brook

Cirencester Rd, Charlton Kings, Cheltenham, Glos, GL53 8EG
☎(01242) 526785, Fax 256880, Pro 525201, Bar/Rest 580715
2 miles SE of Cheltenham on A435 Cirencester road.
Parkland course.
Pro Forbes Hadden; Founded 1922
Designed by MacKenzie
18 holes, 6212 yards, S.S.S. 70
Visitors: welcome with h'cap certs.
Green Fees: WD £25; WE £30.
Societies: welcome WD by arrangement; packages available; terms on application.
Catering: full clubhouse facilities.
Hotels: Cheltenham Park; Charlton Kings.

5B 64 Little Lakes

Lye Head, Rock, Beweley, Worcs, DY12 2UZ
☎(01299) 266385
A456 2 miles W of Beweley; turn left at Greenhouse and Garden Centre.
Undulating parkland course.

Pro Mark Laing; Founded 1975
Designed by Michael Cooksey
18 holes, 5644 yards, S.S.S. 67
Visitors: welcome.
Green Fees: WD £12; WE £15.
Societies: welcome by prior arrangement; packages available; from £28.
Catering: lunches available.
Hotels: Heath.

5B 65 Lydney
Lakeside Ave, Lydney, Glos, GL15
5QA
☎(01594) 842614
Entering Lydney on A48 from
Gloucester, turn left at bottom of
Highfield Hill and look for Lakeside
Ave on left.
Parkland course.
Founded 1909
9 holes, 5298 yards, S.S.S. 66
Visitors: welcome; WE with member.
Green Fees: WD £10.
Societies: small societies by prior
arrangement; packages available.
Catering: full bar, lunch and dinner
facilities.
Hotels: Speech House.

5B 66 Mangotsfield
Carson's Rd, Mangotsfield, Bristol,
Glos, BS16 9LW
☎(0117) 9565501
From M32 leave at junction for
Filton/Downend; follow sign for
Downend and Mangotsfield.
Hilly meadowland course.
Pro Craig Trewlin; Founded 1975
18 holes, 5290 yards, S.S.S. 66
Visitors: welcome.
Green Fees: WD £10; WE £12.
Societies: welcome by prior arrangement; packages available.
Catering: full clubhouse facilities.
Hotels: Post House.

5B 67 Marriott Forest of Arden
Maxstoke Lane, Meriden, Coventry,
Warwicks, CV7 7HR
☎(01676) 526113, Fax 526125, Pro
0958 632170, Sec 522335, Bar/Rest
522335
Off A45 close to M42 junction 6 or M6
South junction 4.
Championship parkland course; site of
English Open.
Pro Kim Thomas; Founded 1970/91
Designed by Donald Steel
Arden: 18 holes, 7134 yards, S.S.S.
71; Aylesford: 18 holes, 6525 yards,
S.S.S. 71

Visitors: residents and visitors welcome.
Green Fees: terms on application.
Societies: corporate packages can be
booked through golf office; 27 holes,
coffee, buffet lunch, dinner, stroke-
saver and driving range tokens; £125.
Catering: clubhouse and hotel facilities.
Practice range, 6 undercover bays;
teaching facility.
Hotels: Marriott Forest of Arden.

5B 68 Maxstoke Park
Castle Lane, Coleshill, Warwicks, B46
2RD
☎(01675) 466743, Fax 466743, Pro
464915, Bar/Rest 462158
From M6 take Coleshill road and at
high street lights turn towards
Nuneaton; club 2 miles.
Parkland course.
Pro Neil McEwan; Founded 1898/45
Designed by Tom Marks
18 holes, 6442 yards, S.S.S. 71
Visitors: welcome with h'cap certs.
Green Fees: WD £25; WE £25.
Societies: welcome Tues and Thurs;
packages on application; from £25.
Catering: clubhouse facilities.
Practice range, practice area.
Hotels: Lea Marston Hotel.

5B 69 Memorial Park
Memorial Park Golf Office, Kenilworth
Rd, Coventry, W Midlands
☎(01203) 675415
1 mile from the city centre.
Municipal parkland course.
Designed by John Bredemus
18 holes, 2840 yards,
Visitors: welcome.
Green Fees: WD £3.30; WE £3.30.
Societies: welcome; tennis courts;
playground; bowling greens.
Catering: café in park in summer.

5B 70 Minchinhampton
Minchinhampton, Stroud, Glos GL6
9AQ
☎(01453) 832642, Pro 836382 (Old);
834486, Fax 833860, Pro 833860, Sec
833866, Bar/Rest 833858 (Avening/
Cherington)
On Minchinhampton Common 3 miles
SE of Stroud (Old); Between Avening
and Michinhampton off B4014
(Avening/ Cherington)
Commonland course (Old); Parkland
course (Avening/Cherington).
Founded 1889 (Old)
Pro C Steele; Founded 1975 (Avening/
Cherington)

Designed by R Wilson (Old); Designed
by F.W. Hawtree (Avening/Cherington)
Old: 18 holes, 6019 yards, S.S.S. 69;
Avening: 18 holes, 6279 yards, S.S.S.
70; Cherington: 18 holes, 6320 yards,
S.S.S. 70
Visitors: welcome (Old); welcome by
prior arrangement (Avening /
Cherington).
Green Fees: WD £10, WE £13 (Old);
WD £25, WE £30 (Avening /
Cherington).
Societies: welcome by prior arrangement; full range of packages available;
terms on application.
Catering: clubhouse bar and catering
facilities.
Practice ground.
Hotels: Amberley Inn; Bear of
Rodborough; Burleigh House.

5B 71 Moor Hall
Moor Hall Drive, Sutton Coldfield, W
Midlands, B75 6LN
☎(0121) 308 6130, Pro 308 5106
From M42 take A446 to Bassets Pole
roundabout; follow Sutton Coldfield
road and at first lights; course 200
yards on left.
Parkland course.
Pro Alan Partridge; Founded 1932
18 holes, 6249 yards, S.S.S. 70
Visitors: welcome WD; after 12.30pm
Thurs.
Green Fees: WD £30.
Societies: welcome Tues and Wed by
prior arrangement.
Catering: full facilities.
Hotels: Moor Hall.

5B 72 Moseley
Springfield Rd, Kings Heath,
Birmingham, B14 7DX
☎(0121) 444 2115, Fax 441 4662 ,
Sec 444 4957
On Birmingham ring road 0.5 miles E
of Alcester road.
Parkland course.
Pro Gary Edge; Founded 1892
18 holes, 6300 yards, S.S.S. 70
Visitors: welcome WD with letter of
introduction/h'cap certs.
Green Fees: WD £37.
Societies: welcome Wed only by prior
arrangement with secretary.
Catering: full facilities.

5B 73 Naunton Downs
Naunton, Cheltenham, Gloucs, GL54
3AE
☎(01451) 850090, Fax 850091, Pro
850092, Bar/Rest 850093

On B4068 Stow-on-the-Wold to Cheltenham road adjacent to Naunton. Downland course.
Pro Martin Seddon; Founded 1993
Designed by Jacob Pott
18 holes, 6078 yards, S.S.S. 69
Visitors: welcome; WE by arrangement.
Green Fees: WD £19.95; WE £25.
Societies: welcome by prior arrangement; terms on application.
Catering: lounge, spike bars; restaurant facilities; limited Mon.
Hotels: Washbourne Court.

5B 74 **Newbold Comyn**
Newbold Terrace East, Leamington Spa, Warwicks, CV32 4EW
☎(01926) 421157, Sec 422660
Off B4099 Willes road.
Parkland course.
Pro Don Knight; Founded 1972
18 holes, 6259 yards, S.S.S. 70
Visitors: welcome.
Green Fees: WD £8; WE £10.50.
Societies: welcome by prior arrangement; packages on request.
Catering: bar and restaurant.

5B 75 **North Warwickshire**
Hampton Lane, Meriden, W Midlands, CV7 7LL
☎(01676) 522259, Fax 522915, Sec 522915
Off A45 between Coventry and Birmingham.
Parkland course.
Pro David Ingram; Founded 1894
9 holes, 6390 yards, S.S.S. 70
Visitors: WD only by prior arrangement.
Green Fees: WD £18.
Societies: welcome WD by arrangement; maximum 30 players; meals available in restaurant; terms on application.
Catering: restaurant and bar facilities.
Hotels: Manor Hotel; Strawberry Bank.

5B 76 **North Worcestershire**
Frankley Beeches Rd, Northfield, Birmingham, B31 5LP
☎(0121) 475 1026, Fax 476 8681, Pro 475 5721, Sec 475 1047
On A38 from Birmingham.
Parkland course.
Founded 1907
Designed by James Braid
18 holes, 5950 yards, S.S.S. 68
Visitors: welcome WD.
Green Fees: WD £18.50; WE £18.50.

Societies: welcome Tues and Thurs; terms on application.
Catering: full facilities available.
Hotels: Norwood, King's Norton.

5B 77 **Nuneaton**
Golf Drive, Whitestone, Nuneaton, Warwicks, CV11 6QF
☎(01203) 347810, Pro 340201
Leave M6 junction 3 on A444 2 miles S of Nuneaton.
Wooded undulating meadowland course.
Pro Steve Bainbridge; Founded 1906
18 holes, 6480 yards, S.S.S. 71
Visitors: welcome WD; WE only with member.
Green Fees: WD £25.
Societies: welcome by prior arrangement; terms on application.
Catering: full facilities except Mon.
Hotels: Long Shoot; Chase.

5B 78 **Oakridge**
Arley Lane, Ansley Village, Nuneaton, Warwicks, CV10 9PH
☎(01676) 541389, Pro 540542
Off B4112 3 miles W of Nuneaton.
Parkland course.
Pro Ian Sadler; Founded 1993
18 holes, 6242 yards, S.S.S. 70
Visitors: welcome WD; WE only with member.
Green Fees: WD £15; WE £10.
Societies: welcome Mon-Thurs and Fri am.
Catering: full meals and bar except Mon.
Hotels: Marriott Forest of Arden.

5B 79 **Olton**
Mirfield Rd, Solihull, W Midlands, B91 1JH
☎(0121) 705 1083, Fax 711 2010, Bar/Rest 704 1936
2 miles from M42 junction 5 on A41 towards Birmingham.
Parkland course.
Pro Craig Phillips; Founded 1893
18 holes, 6623 yards, S.S.S. 71
Visitors: welcome by arrangement.
Green Fees: WD £30; WE £30.
Societies: welcome WD by prior arrangement; terms on application.
Catering: clubhouse facilities.
Hotels: Ingon Manor.

5B 80 **Ombersley**
Bishops Wood Road, Lineholt, Ombersley, Droitwich, Worcs, WR9 0LE

☎(01905) 620747, Fax 620047, Bar/Rest 620621
Off A449 Kidderminster to Worcester road at A4025.
Rural parkland setting.
Pro Graham Glenister; Founded 1991
Designed by On Course Design (David Morgan)
18 holes, 6139 yards
Visitors: welcome; pay and play.
Green Fees: WD £11.50; WE £15.50.
Societies: welcome; society and corporate packages available; from £16.50.
Catering: restaurant, bar, terrace.
Practice range, 36 bays (20 covered).
Hotels: Hadley Bowling Green Inn.

5B 81 **Painswick**
Painswick Beacon, Painswick, Stroud, Glos, GL6 6TL
☎(01452) 812180
On A46 1 mile N of Painswick.
Commonland course.
Founded 1891
18 holes, 4680 yards, S.S.S. 64
Visitors: welcome WD and Sat; with member at WE.
Green Fees: WD £10; WE £15.
Societies: welcome by prior arrangement with Sec; special packages.
Catering: bar and catering facilities.
Practice range, practice ground.
Hotels: Moat House.

5B 82 **Perdiswell**
Bilford Road, Worcester, Worcs, WR3 8DX
☎(01905) 457189, Fax 756608, Pro 754668
Off main Droitwich road N of Worcester.
Meadowland course; extending to 18 holes in 1999
9 holes, 5870 yards, S.S.S. 68
Visitors: welcome.
Green Fees: WD £7.10; WE £8.20.
Societies: welcome by prior arrangement; catering packages available; discounts.
Catering: bar and snacks.

5B 83 **Pitcheroak**
Plymouth Rd, Redditch, Worcs, B97 4PB
☎(01527) 541043, Sec 541054, Bar/Rest 543868
Signposted from centre of Redditch.
Municipal parkland course.
Pro David Stewart; Founded 1973
9 holes, 4561 yards, S.S.S. 62
Visitors: welcome.

Green Fees: WD £6.50; WE £7.50.
Societies: welcome by prior arrangement.
Catering: bar and restaurant.
Practice range, practice area.
Hotels: Mont Ville.

5B 84 **Purley Chase G & Country Club**

Ridge Lane, Nr Nuneaton,
Warwickshire, CV10 0RB
☎(01203) 393118, Fax 398015, Pro
395348, Bar/Rest 397468
From A5 Mancetter to Atherstone
road; follow signs.
Parkland course.
Pro Gary Carver; Founded 1977
Designed by B. Tomlinson
18 holes, 6772 yards, S.S.S. 72
Visitors: welcome WD; WE afternoons only.
Green Fees: WD £15; WE £25.
Societies: welcome WD; various
packages available; terms on application.
Catering: full clubhouse facilities.
Hotels: Hanover International;
Bosworth Hall.

5B 85 **Pype Hayes**

Eachelhurst Rd, Walmley, Sutton
Coldfield, W Midlands, B76 8EP
☎(0121) 351 1014
Off M6 junction 6 on to Tyburn Rd; 1
mile to Eachelhurst Rd.
Public parkland course.
Pro Jim Bayliss; Founded 1932
18 holes, 5927 yards, S.S.S. 68
Visitors: welcome with prior booking.
Green Fees: WD £8.50; WE £9.
Societies: welcome WD by prior
arrangement.
Catering: cafeteria.
Hotels: Pens Hall.

5B 86 **Ravenmeadow**

Hindlip Lane, Claines, Worcester,
Worcs, WR3 8SA
☎(01905) 757525
4 miles N of Worcester off the A38.
Parkland course.
Pro Graeme Wheelaghan; Founded
1996
9 holes, 5435 yards, S.S.S. 66
Visitors: welcome.
Green Fees: WD £9.75; WE £12.75.
Societies: welcome by prior arrangement; packages available; terms on
application.
Catering: bar and restaurant facilities.
Practice range, 10 bays floodlit.
Hotels: The Founds; Star.

5B 87 **Redditch**

Lower Grinsty Lane, Callow Hill,
Redditch, Worcs, B97 5JP
☎(01527) 543309, Fax 543079, Pro
546372
2 miles W of Redditch.
Parkland course.
Pro Frank Powell; Founded 1913/72
Designed by F. Pennink
18 holes, 6671 yards, S.S.S. 72
Visitors: welcome.
Green Fees: WD £27.50; WE £27.50.
Societies: welcome by prior arrangement; catering packages and reductions available; terms on application.
Catering: full clubhouse facilities.

5B 88 **Robin Hood**

St Bernards Rd, Solihull, W Midlands,
B92 7DJ
☎(0121) 706 0159, Fax 706 0806,
Pro 706 0806, Sec 706 0061
2 miles S of M42 junction 4 & 5.
Parkland course.
Pro A J Harvey; Founded 1893
Designed by H.S. Colt
18 holes, 6635 yards, S.S.S. 72
Visitors: welcome WD.
Green Fees: WD £29; WE £12 with
member.
Societies: welcome Tues, Thurs, Fri
with h'cap certs; packages available;
from £29.
Catering: clubhouse facilities.
Hotels: Arden Hotel.

5B 89 **Ross-on-Wye**

Two Park, Gorsley, Ross-on-Wye,
Hereford, HR9 7UT
☎(01989) 720267, Fax 720212, Pro
720439, Bar/Rest 720457
5 miles N of Ross-on-Wye; close to
M50 junction 3.
Parkland course.
Pro Nick Catchpole; Founded 1903
Designed by C.K. Cotton
18 holes, 6451 yards, S.S.S. 73
Visitors: welcome.
Green Fees: WD £35; WE £35.
Societies: welcome Wed, Thurs, Fri;
packages available for 20+; deposit
required; snooker tables; from £28.
Catering: clubhouse facilities; bar and
restaurant.
Practice range, practice area.
Hotels: Chase Hotel; Royal Hotel.

5B 90 **Royal Forest Of Dean**

Lords Hill, Coleford, Glos, GL16 8BD
☎(01594) 832583, Pro 833689
4 miles from Monmouth; 8 miles from
Ross and Chepstow.

Parkland/meadowland course.
Pro John Hansel; Founded 1973
Designed by John Day of Alphagreen
Ltd
18 holes, 5813 yards, S.S.S. 69
Visitors: welcome.
Green Fees: WD £16.50; WE £18.50.
Societies: welcome by prior arrangement with the hotel; packages available for golf, catering and hotel; swimming pool; tennis; bowls; from £29.
Catering: full bar and restaurant service.
Hotels: Bells, on site.

5B 91 **Rugby**

Clifton Rd, Rugby, Warwicks, CV21
3RD
☎(01788) 544637, Fax 542306, Pro
575134, Sec 542306
On Rugby-Market Harborough road on
right just past railway bridge.
Parkland course.
Pro Andy Peach; Founded 1891
18 holes, 5614 yards, S.S.S. 67
Visitors: welcome WD; WE with a
member.
Green Fees: WD £20; WE £10.
Societies: welcome WD by arrangement; packages available; minimum
12.
Catering: full catering except Sun.
Practice range, practice area.
Hotels: Carlton; Grosvenor.

5B 92 **Sapey Golf**

Upper Sapey, Nr Worcester, Worcs,
WR6 6XT
☎(01886) 853288, Fax 853485, Pro
853567, Sec 853506, Bar/Rest
853567
On A4203 between Bromyard and
Stourport.
Parkland course.
Pro Chris Knowles; Founded 1990
18 holes, 5935 yards, S.S.S. 68
Visitors: welcome.
Green Fees: WD £15; WE £20.
Societies: welcome by prior arrangement; terms on application.
Catering: clubhouse facilities.
Hotels: Hundred House; The Granary.

5B 93 **Sherdons**

Manor Farm, Tredington, Tewkesbury,
Gloucs, GL20 7BP
☎(01684) 274782
2 miles out of Tewkesbury on the A38;
turn off at the Odessa Inn.
Parkland course.
Pro Philip Clark/John Parker; Founded
1995

9 holes, 5308 yards, S.S.S. 66
Visitors: welcome; pay and play.
Green Fees: WD £10; WE £13.
Societies: welcome WD; WE by
arrangement.
Catering: soft drinks, coffee, snacks.
Practice range, 26 floodlit bays.
Hotels: Gubshill Manor.

5B 94 Shirehampton Park
Park Hill, Shirehampton, Bristol, BS11
0UL
☎ (0117) 9823059, Fax 9822083, Pro
9822488, Sec 9822083
2 miles from M5 junction 18 on B4054
through Shirehampton.
Undulating parkland course.
Pro Brent Ellis; Founded 1907
18 holes, 5430 yards, S.S.S. 67
Visitors: welcome.
Green Fees: WD £18; WE £25.
Societies: welcome; snacks, lunch
available; dinner by appt; from £18.
Catering: clubhouse facilities.

5B 95 Shirley
Stratford Rd, Monkspath, Shirley,
Solihull, W Midlands, B90 4EW
☎ (0121) 744 6001, Fax 745 8220
Towards Birmingham off M42 junc 4.
Parkland course.
Pro S Botterill; Founded 1956
18 holes, 6507 yards, S.S.S. 71
Visitors: welcome WD; with member
at WE.
Green Fees: WD £25; WE £25.
Societies: welcome by arrangement;
packages; terms on application.
Catering: restaurant and bar facilities.
Hotels: Regency Hotel.

5B 96 Sphinx
Siddeley Ave, Coventry, Warwicks,
CV3 1FZ
☎ (01203) 458890
4 miles S of Coventry, close to main
Binley Rd.
Parkland course; Founded 1948
9 holes, 4262 yards, S.S.S. 60
Visitors: welcome WD; with member
at WE.
Green Fees: terms on application.
Societies: welcome by arrangement.
Catering: bar and bar meals.

5B 97 Stakis Puckrup Hall Hotel
Puckrup, Tewkesbury, Glos, GL20 6EL
☎ (01684) 296200, Fax 850788
M50 junction 1 towards Tewkesbury
on the A38.

Parkland course.
Pro Kevin Pickett; Founded 1992
Designed by Simon Gidman
18 holes, 6189 yards, S.S.S. 70
Visitors: welcome.
Green Fees: WD £15; WE £20.
Societies: welcome by prior arrange-
ment; full day and half-day packages
can be arranged; £19.50-£45.
Catering: full clubhouse and hotel
facilities.
Hotels: Own Stakis 84-room hotel on
site.

5B 98 Stinchcombe Hill
Stinchcombe Hill, Dursley, Glos, GL11
6AQ
☎ (01453) 542015, Pro 543878
From A38 at Durlsey; right past Post
Office.
Downland course.
Pro Paul Bushell; Founded 1889
Designed by Arthur Hoare
18 holes, 5734 yards, S.S.S. 68
Visitors: welcome.
Green Fees: WD £20; WE £25.
Societies: welcome Mon, Wed and
Fri; catering packages available for 12
or more players; terms on application.
Catering: full facilities and bar.
Practice range, grass.
Hotels: club can provide full list.

5B 99 Stonebridge
Somers Rd, Meriden, Warwicks, CV7
7PL
☎ (01676) 522442
2 miles from M42 junction 6.
Parkland course.
Pro Steve Harrison; Founded 1995
18 holes, 6240 yards, S.S.S. 70
Visitors: welcome; bookings taken 7
days in advance.
Green Fees: WD £13; WE £15.
Societies: welcome Mon to Thurs by
prior arrangement; from £20.
Catering: 2 bars, restaurant and con-
ference facilities.
Practice range, 21 bays floodlit.
Hotels: Strawberry Bank.

5B 100 Stoneleigh Deer Park
The Old Deer Park, Coventry Rd,
Stoneleigh, Warwicks, CV8 3DR
☎ (01203) 639991, Pro 639912,
Bar/Rest 639916
Off A46 or A454 at Stoneleigh village.
Parkland course.
Pro Matt McGuire; Founded 1991
Designed by K. Harrison/Brown
18 holes, 5846 yards, S.S.S. 68
Visitors: welcome.

Green Fees: WD £14.50; WE £22.50.
Societies: welcome with prior
arrangement; packages available;
catering from 8am-9pm; also 9-hole,
1251-yard, par 3 course; from £14.50.
Catering: catering and bar facilities.
Practice area.
Hotels: club can recommend.

5B 101 Stourbridge
Worcester Lane, Pedmore,
Stourbridge, Glos, DY8 2RB
☎ (01384) 393062, Fax 444660, Pro
393126, Sec 395566
1 mile S of Stourbridge on B4147.
Parkland course.
Pro Mark Male; Founded 1892
18 holes, 6231 yards, S.S.S. 70
Visitors: welcome WD; with member
WE.
Green Fees: WD £25; WE £25.
Societies: welcome Tues and Thurs;
packages available; from £25.
Catering: restaurant and bar facilities.
Hotels: Limes, Pedmore; Travelodge,
Hagley.

5B 102 Stratford Oaks
Bearley Road, Snitterfield, Stratford-
upon-Avon, Warwicks, CV37 0EZ
☎ (01789) 731982, Pro 731980
On A34 to Stratford following signs to
Snitterfield.
Parkland course.
Pro Andrew Dunbar; Founded 1989
Designed by Howard Swan
18 holes, 6121 yards, S.S.S. 71
Visitors: welcome with booking.
Green Fees: WD £21; WE £27.50.
Societies: welcome WD by arrange-
ment; catering packages available.
Catering: bar and restaurant facilities.
Practice range, 22 floodlit covered
bays.
Hotels: Arden Valley; Alveston Manor.

5B 103 Stratford-upon-Avon
Tiddington Rd, Stratford-upon-Avon,
Warwicks, CV37 7BA
☎ (01789) 205749, Pro 205677
On B4089 0.5 miles from river bridge.
Parkland course.
Pro David Sutherland; Founded 1894
18 holes, 6303 yards, S.S.S. 71
Visitors: welcome WD; WE by prior
arrangement.
Green Fees: WD £25; WE £35.
Societies: welcome Tues and Thurs
by arrangement; catering packages.
Catering: full bar and catering.
Practice area.
Hotels: many in Stratford.

TEWKESBURY PARK HOTEL
Golf & Country Club

LINCOLN GREEN LANE • TEWKESBURY • GLOUCESTERSHIRE • GL20 7DN

For more information and Golf Society Brochure
Tel: 01684 295405
Fax: 01684 292386

- 6,533 yds, par 73
- 5 par 5s, 4 par 3s
- 6 hole par 3 course
- Practice ground with covered bays
- Putting Green
- Professional Golf Shop
- Leisure Club facilities

Secluded deep within extensive grounds overlooking the Abbey Town of Tewkesbury and set between the Cotswolds and Malvern hills, this picturesque course requires accuracy early on but the later holes offer a welcome relief with their wide fairways. The course has recently been selected to host a qualifying tournament for the Mastercard Tour and holds regular Pro-Am events. Our Golf facilities are complimented by a wide range of hotel facilities including 78 en-suite bedrooms, lounge bar, 120 seater Garden Restaurant, informal Club bar and dining area, and of course the 19th hole.

5B 104 Sutton Coldfield
110 Thornhill Rd, Streetly, Warwicks, B74 3ER
☎(0121) 353 9633, Bar/Rest 353 2014
On B4138 9 miles NE of Birmingham. Heathland course; Sutton Coldfield Ladies (0121) 353 1682.
Pro Jerry Hayes; Founded 1889
18 holes, 6541 yards, S.S.S. 71
Visitors: welcome WD; WE with member only.
Green Fees: WD £25.
Societies: welcome WD by arrangement only.
Catering: full clubhouse facilities. Practice area.
Hotels: Sutton Court; Post House.

5B 105 Tewkesbury Park Hotel
Lincoln Green Lane, Tewkesbury, Glos, GL20 7DN
☎(01684) 295405, Fax 292386, Pro 294892, Sec 299452
0.5 miles S of Tewkesbury on A38; 2 miles from M5 junction 9.
Parkland course.
Pro Robert Taylor; Founded 1976
Designed by Frank Pennink
18 holes, 6533 yards, S.S.S. 72
Visitors: welcome.
Green Fees: WD £15; WE £25.
Societies: welcome WD; packages available; terms on application.
Catering: clubhouse & hotel facilities.
Hotels: 75-bedroom Tewkesbury Park Hotel on site.

5B 106 Thornbury Golf Centre
Bristol Rd, Thornbury, Avon, BS35 3XL
☎(01454) 281144, Fax 281177, Pro 281155, Bar/Rest 281166
Off A38 at Berkeley Vale Motors; 5 miles from M4/M5.
Parkland course.
Pro Simon Hubbard; Founded 1992

Designed by Hawtree
18 holes, 6154 yards, S.S.S. 69
Visitors: welcome by arrangement.
Green Fees: WD £14; WE £16.
Societies: welcome; packages available; terms on application.
Catering: full catering facilities.
Hotels: 11-bedroom lodge on site.

5B 107 Tolladine
The Fairways, Tolladine Rd, Worcester, WR4 9BA
☎(01905) 721074, Pro 726180
M5 junction 6 towards Warndon; club towards Worcester city centre.
Parkland course; steep in parts.
Founded 1898
9 holes, 5432 yards, S.S.S. 67
Visitors: welcome WD except after 4pm Wed; with member at WE.
Green Fees: WD £10; WE £8.
Societies: welcome by prior arrangement; terms on application.
Catering: by prior arrangement.

5B 108 Tracy Park Country Club
Bath Rd, Wick, Bristol, BS15 5RN
☎(0117) 9372251, Fax 9374288, Pro 9373521
Junction 18 on M4, S on A46 towards Bath, right on A420 to Bristol 4 miles.
Parkland course.
Pro Richard Berry; Founded 1975
Designed by Grant Aitken
18 holes, 6430 yards, S.S.S. 71
Visitors: welcome.
Green Fees: WD £20; WE £30.
Societies: welcome; packages available; terms on application.
Catering: clubhouse facilities.

5B 109 Vale Golf & CC
Hill Furze Rd, Bishampton, Pershore, Worcs, WR10 2LZ
☎(01386) 462781, Fax 462597

5 miles from Evesham on A4538; take Bishampton turn.
Parkland course.
Pro Caroline Griffiths; Founded 1991
Designed by M R M Sandow
18 holes, 7114 yards, S.S.S. 74
Visitors: welcome.
Green Fees: WD £18; WE £24.
Societies: welcome WD; terms on application; corporate packages can be arranged; conference and hospitality suites; terms on application.
Catering: clubhouse and country club. Practice range, 20 bays floodlit.
Hotels: club can recommend.

5B 110 Walmley
Brooks Rd, Wylde Green, Sutton Coldfield, Warwickshire, B72 1HR
☎(0121) 373 0029, Fax 377 7272, Pro 373 7103, Sec 377 7272
6 miles N of Birmingham.
Parkland course.
Pro Chris Wicketts; Founded 1902
18 holes, 6559 yards, S.S.S. 72
Visitors: welcome WD; with member at WE.
Green Fees: WD £30; WE £10.
Societies: welcome WD; discounts available for 30+ players; from £30.
Catering: clubhouse facilities.
Hotels: Penns Hall.

5B 111 Warley
Lightwoods Hill, Smethwick, Warley, W Midlands, B67 5ED
☎(0121) 429 2440
Off A465 4.5 miles W of Birmingham behind the Cock & Magpie.
Municipal parkland course; part of Link card system.
Pro David Owen; Founded 1921
9 holes, 5370 yards, S.S.S. 66
Visitors: welcome.
Green Fees: WD £8; WE £8.50.
Societies: none.
Catering: café.

5B 112 Warwick
The Racecourse, Warwick, Warwicks, CV34 6HW
☎(01926) 494316
In centre of Warwick racecourse.
Public meadowland course.
Pro Philip Sharp; Founded 1886
Designed by D.G. Dunkley
9 holes, 5364 yards, S.S.S. 66
Visitors: welcome except on race days.
Green Fees: WD £4; WE £5.
Societies: welcome by arrangement.
Catering: bar.
Practice range, 26 floodlit covered bays.
Hotels: Tudor House.

5B 113 Warwickshire
Leek Woolton, Warwick, Warwickshire, CV35 7QT
☎(01926) 409409, Fax 408409
M49 junction 15 take A46 towards Coventry; turn at signs for Leek Wootton on B4115.
4 x 9 holes; 637 is 4th North.
Pro B Fotheringham; Founded 1993
Designed by K. Litten
18 holes, 7407 yards, S.S.S. 74
Visitors: welcome.
Green Fees: WD £45; WE £45.
Societies: welcome; minimum 12; packages available; private function suites; buggies; coaching clinics; terms on application.
Catering: full clubhouse restaurant and bar facilities.
Practice range, 30 bays – 9 covered.
Hotels: Chesford Grange; Alveston Hall; Charlecote Pheasant; Walton Hall.

5B 114 Welcombe Hotel
Warwick Rd, Stratford-upon-Avon, Warwicks, CV37 0NR
☎(01789) 299012, Fax 414666, Sec 262665, Bar/Rest 295252
5 miles from M40 junction 15; 1.5 miles from Stratford on A439.
Parkland course; being upgraded and remeasured.
Pro Carl Mason/Karen Thatcher; Founded 1956/80
Designed by T.J. McCauley
18 holes, 6274 yards, S.S.S. 70
Visitors: welcome with prior arrangement.
Green Fees: WD £40; WE £40.
Societies: welcome; packages available; discounts available; golf clinics; floodlit tennis courts; corporate days, snooker, fitness room, solarium, conference facilities; terms on application.
Catering: full clubhouse and hotel facilities including Trevelyan Restaurant.
Hotels: Welcombe Hotel; 68 rooms.

5B 115 Westonbirt
Tetbury, Glos, GL8 8QG
☎(01666) 880242
From A433 Tetbury to Bath road turn into Westonbirt village; opposite Arboretum.
Parkland course.
Founded 1934
Designed by Monty Hearn
9 holes, 4504 yards, S.S.S. 61
Visitors: welcome.
Green Fees: WD £7.50; WE £7.50.
Societies: none.
Hotels: Hare and Hounds.

5B 116 Wharton Park
Long Bank, Beweley, Worcs DY12 2QW
☎(01299) 405222, Fax 405121, Pro 405163
On A456 at west end of Beweley by-pass.
Parkland course.
Pro Angus Hoare; Founded 1992
18 holes, 6603 yards, S.S.S. 72
Visitors: welcome.

Green Fees: WD £15; WE £22.
Societies: welcome by prior arrangement; packages available; terms on application.
Catering: clubhouse facilities.
Hotels: Heath Hotel.

5B 117 Whitefields
Coventry Rd, Thurlaston, Nr Rugby, Warwicks, CV23 9JR
☎(01788) 815555, Fax 521695 , Sec 521800
On A45 close to junction with M45.
Parkland course overlooking Draycote Water.
Pro Mark Chamberlain; Founded 1992
Designed by R Mason
18 holes, 6223 yards, S.S.S. 70
Visitors: welcome by prior arrangement.
Green Fees: WD £18; WE £22.
Societies: 3 packages available; terms on application.
Catering: hotel facilities.
Practice range, 16 bays floodlit.
Hotels: Whitefields; 33-room hotel on site.

5B 118 Widney Manor
Saintbury Drive, Widney Manor, Solihull, W Midlands, B91 3SZ
☎(0121) 711 3646, Fax 711 3691
Off M42 junction 4 take Stratford road and then turn right into Monkshall Path Road; signposted for Widney Manor.
Parkland course.
Pro Tim Atkinson; Founded 1993
Designed by Golf Design Group
18 holes, 5001 yards, S.S.S. 65
Visitors: welcome.
Green Fees: WD £9.50; WE £12.50.
Societies: welcome WD but not before 10am at WE; terms on application.
Catering: full facilities.
Practice range, practice area.

WHITEFIELDS
HOTEL, GOLF & COUNTRY
Club

Situated in the heart of the Warwickshire countryside and overlooking the beautiful Draycott Water, Whitefields offers you a warm welcome. Enjoy the luxurious rooms, the fine food and wine in the A La Carte Garden Restaurant, practice on the state of the art new driving range or take up the challenge of the superb 18-hole, 6443 yard, par 71 course.

Accommodation: Societies start at £64.50 P.P. for bed & breakfast & 3 course evening dinner & unlimited golf (based on 2 people sharing).

For more details call **01788 815555,** *or fax* **01788 521695. Whitefields Hotel, Golf & Country Club,** Coventry Road, Thurlaston, Warwickshire CV23 9JR.

5B 119 **Windmill Village Hotel**
Birmingham Road, Allesley, Coventry, Warwicks, CV5 9AL
☎(01203) 404041
On A45 westbound Coventry-Birmingham road.
Part flat, part hilly course.
Pro Robert Hunter; Founded 1990
Designed by Robert Hunter & John Harrhy
18 holes, 5169 yards, S.S.S. 68
Visitors: welcome.
Green Fees: WD £9.95; WE £12.95.
Societies: welcome by arrangement; packages available; swimming pool; snooker; gym; sauna; conference.
Catering: bar and restaurant facilities.
Hotels: Windwill Village on site.

5B 120 **Wishaw**
Bulls Lane, Wishaw, W Midlands, B76 9QW
☎(0121) 351 3221, Pro 3132110
From M42 junction 9 take second left at The Belfry to the Cock at Wishaw; course 0.75 miles.
Parkland course.
Founded 1993
18 holes, 5481 yards, S.S.S. 70
Visitors: welcome.
Green Fees: WD £10; WE £15.
Societies: welcome WD by arrangement; packages available; terms on application.
Catering: restaurant and bar facilities.
Hotels: Belfry; Moor Hall.

5B 121 **Woodlands**
Woodlands Lane, Almondsbury, Bristol, BS32 4JZ
☎(01454) 618121, Fax 619397, Sec 619319
Off A38 at the Aztec roundabout turning left into Woodlands Lane.
Parkland course.
Founded 1989

Designed by C Chapman
18 holes, 6068 yards, S.S.S. 69
Visitors: welcome.
Green Fees: WD £11; WE £13.
Societies: welcome by prior arrangement; terms on application.
Catering: full clubhouse facilities.
Hotels: accommodation on site from late 1998.

5B 122 **Woodspring**
Yanley Lane, Long Ashton, Bristol, Avon, BS18 9LR
☎(01275) 394378, Fax 384473
On A38 near Bristol Airport.
Parkland course; 541/136 on Avon 9.
Pro Nigel Beer; Founded 1994
Designed by P Alliss & C Clark/ D Steel
27 holes, 6587 yards, S.S.S. 70
Visitors: welcome.
Green Fees: WD £25; WE £28.50.
Societies: welcome; catering packages available; contact Kevin Pitts; 3 x 9 courses: Avon, Brunel, Severn; terms on application.
Catering: full clubhouse facilities.
Practice range, 25 bays floodlit.
Hotels: Swallow Royal; Redwood Lodge; Town & Country Lodge; Marriott.

5B 123 **Worcester G & Country Club**
Boughton Park, Bransford Road, Worcester, Worcester, WR2 4EZ
☎(01905) 422555, Fax 749090, Pro 422044, Bar/Rest 421132
From M5 junction 7 follow signs for Worcester West.
Parkland course.
Founded 1898
Designed by Dr. A. MacKenzie (1926)
18 holes, 6251 yards, S.S.S. 70
Visitors: members' guests welcome.
Green Fees: WD £25; WE £25.

Societies: welcome with 12 months prior booking; catering and golf packages can be arranged; jacket and tie required in dining room; from £33.
Catering: full clubhouse restaurant and bar facilities.

5B 124 **Worcestershire**
Wood Farm, Malvern Wells, Worcs, WR14 4PP
☎(01684) 575992, Fax 575992, Pro 564428
2 miles S of Great Malvern; turn off A449 on to B4209.
Parkland course.
Pro Richard Lewis; Founded 1879
Designed by Colt, MacKenzie, Braid; amended by Jiggins and Hawtree
18 holes, 6470 yards, S.S.S. 71
Visitors: welcome if members of clubs; no visitors before 10am WE.
Green Fees: WD £28; WE £30.
Societies: welcome Thurs and Fri; package includes coffee, light lunch and 3-course dinner; £45.
Catering: full catering facilities.
Hotels: Abbey; Foley; Cottage in the Woods.

5B 125 **Wyre Forest**
Zortech Ave, Kidderminster, Worcs, DY11 7EX
☎(01299) 822682, Fax 879433
Take A451 towards Stourport and course is signposted.
Parkland course.
Pro Simon Price; Founded 1994
Designed by Golf Design Group
18 holes, 5790 yards, S.S.S. 68
Visitors: welcome.
Green Fees: WD £8.50; WE £12.
Societies: welcome; terms on application; from £15.
Catering: clubhouse facilities.
Hotels: Heath; Gainsborough; Severn Manor.

6

NORTH MIDLANDS

In the last few years, Staffordshire and Shropshire have made the headlines on account of their golfing sons and daughters. Diane Bailey and Geoffrey Marks became the first to captain victorious Curtis and Walker Cup teams on American soil. David Gilford, a member of Trentham Park, won a place in the Ryder Cup teams in 1991 and 1995 along with Ian Woosnam, whose county golf as an amateur was played for Shropshire in company with Sandy Lyle, who was raised at Hawkstone Park. Hawkstone is part of a hotel complex that provides popular golfing facilities about fourteen miles north of Shrewsbury in an area that is full of largely rural delights. It has recently seen significant change with the addition of a much upgraded second course.

In Shropshire, Bridgnorth is a delight with several holes along the river. But, while Shropshire's courses are relatively few and far between, Staffordshire enjoys quantity as well as quality. It includes Little Aston, Penn, home of the late and great Charlie Stowe, and South Staffordshire at Wolverhampton, as well as the delights of Beau Desert, Drayton Park, Leek, Trentham, Trentham Park, Enville, Uttoxeter (which the locals pronounce Uttcheter), Patshull Park and Newcastle-under-Lyme.

Enville was the home course as a girl of Diane Bailey (née Robb) while Geoffrey Marks has remained loyal all his playing days to Trentham – to the south of Stoke-on-Trent. Enville's two contrasting courses are very good while Trentham is a parkland course with nice changes of level very much like its neighbour, Trentham Park.

Newcastle Municipal is a relatively recent public course that is much used but probably the best courses in this section

are Whittington Barracks, a slightly forbidding name for a moorland retreat that has championship status, and Little Aston, which epitomises the very best of parkland golf, the main hazards taking the form of characteristically large bunkers, a couple of lakes, some majestic trees and a degree of undulation which tests one's judgment of distance.

South of the Mersey, the first ports of call after emerging from the tunnel are the celebrated links of Wallasey and Royal Liverpool. Wallasey is less well known in spite of its association in bygone days with Dr Frank Stableford, mastermind of the excellent scoring system that bears his name – a system less cruel than the rigours of undiluted medal play.

Maybe, he devised the idea from his battles with Wallasey's glorious seaside links and the winds that plague golfers even more. The latest version of the course incorporates rather more of the flat, plain land than it used to, but flatness is also a feature of Royal Liverpool at Hoylake, and few have seen fit to criticise that course in an area that has changed hardly at all in character since the Club was founded in 1869.

As the second oldest seaside course in England, Royal Liverpool wears the local crown but Caldy and Heswall are other Wirral landmarks not far off the road back to Chester where most of the best golfing country lies to the east and south-east.

Sandiway, Delamere Forest, Mere and Eaton at Waverton are all redoubtable courses in beautiful settings, as indeed is Portal at Tarporley, which opened its doors for the first time in 1991. An even more recent creation is Carden Park at Malpas, which has fine teaching facilities.

6A 1 Adlington Golf Centre

Sandy Hey Farm, Adlington, Macclesfield, Cheshire, SK10 4NG
☎ (01625) 850660, Fax 850960, Sec 878468
1 mile S of Poynton on A523 Stockport-Macclesfield road.
Par 3 course.
Pro David Bathgate; Founded 1995
Designed by Hawtree
9 holes, 635 yards
Visitors: public pay and play.
Green Fees: WD £3.50; WE £4.50.
Societies: n/a.
Catering: facilities.
Driving range and golf academy.

6A 2 Alder Root Golf Club

Alder Root Lane, Winwick, Warrington, Cheshire, WA2 8RZ
☎ (01925) 291919, Pro 291932
M62 junction 9 then N on A49, turn left at first set of lights; then 1st right into Alder Root Lane.
Parkland course.
Founded 1993
9 holes, 5834 yards, S.S.S. 68
Visitors: welcome by arrangement.
Green Fees: WD £16; WE £18.
Societies: welcome WD by prior arrangement; full catering and 27 holes of golf; from £24.
Catering: bar and snacks.
Hotels: Winwick Quay.

6A 3 Alderley Edge

Brook Lane, Alderley Edge, Cheshire, SK9 7RU
☎ (01625) 585583
From Alderley Edge turn off A34 to Mobberley/Knutsford on B5085.
Undulating parkland course
Pro: Peter Bowring; Founded 1907
Designed by T. G. Renouf
9 holes, 5823 yards, S.S.S. 68
Visitors: welcome with h'cap certs; restrictions Wed and WE
Green Fees: WD £18; WE £22.
Societies: welcome Thurs by prior arrangement; from £28.
Catering: full catering except Mon.
Hotels: De Trafford Arms.

6A 4 Aldersey Green Golf Club

Aldersey, Chester, Cheshire, CH3 9EH
☎ (01829) 782453; Pro 782157
On A41 Whitchurch road.
Parkland course.
Pro Stephen Bradbury; Founded 1993
18 holes, 6159 yards, S.S.S. 69
Visitors: welcome.
Green Fees: WD £12; WE £15.

Societies: welcome by prior arrangement; 2 packages available WD; 1 at WE; terms on application.
Catering: bar and bar meals.
Hotels: Calverley Arms.

6A 5 Alsager Golf & Country Club

Audley Rd, Alsager, Stoke-on-Trent, Staffs, ST7 2UR
☎ (01270) 875700, Fax 882207, Pro 877432
Leave M6 junction 16 taking A500 towards Stoke for 1 mile; first left turn for Alsager.
Parkland course.
Pro Richard Brown; Founded 1976
18 holes, 6201 yards, S.S.S. 70
Visitors: welcome WD; WE with member.
Green Fees: WD £21.
Societies: welcome Mon, Wed and Thurs; 3 packages available for societies; snooker; bowls; from £27.50.
Catering: clubhouse facilities; banqueting available.
Hotels: Manor Hotel.

6A 6 Altrincham

Stockport Rd, Timperley, Altrincham, Cheshire, WA15 7LP
☎ (0161) 928 0761
On A560 1 mile W of Altrincham.
Undulating parkland course.
Pro Scott Partington; Founded 1935
18 holes, 6162 yards, S.S.S. 69
Visitors: welcome; advance booking at all times.
Green Fees: WD £7.50; WE £10.
Societies: none.
Catering: no catering; facilities at adjacent restaurant.
Hotels: Cresta Court; Woodlands Park.

6A 7 Alvaston Hall Golf Club

Middlewich Road, Nantwich, Cheshire, CW5 6PD
☎ (01270) 624341, Fax 623395, Sec 629444
1 mile from Nantwich on A530 to Middlewich.
Meadowland course.
Founded 1989
Designed by A Lindop
9 holes, 3612 yards, S.S.S. 59
Visitors: welcome.
Green Fees: WD £7; WE £7.
Societies: welcome WD; terms on application.
Catering: full facilities.
Hotels: Alvaston Hall Hotel.

6A 8 Antrobus Golf Club

Foggs Lane, Antrobus, Northwich, Cheshire, CW9 6JQ
☎ (01925) 730890, Fax 730100, Pro 730900, Bar/Rest 730002
From A559 road off M56 junction 10 take second left after Birch and Bottle; left into Foggs Lane.
Parkland course with water features.
Pro Paul Farrance; Founded 1993
Designed by Mike Slater
18 holes, 6220 yards, S.S.S. 71
Visitors: welcome.
Green Fees: WD £18; WE £20.
Societies: welcome every day; packages available; from £26.95.
Catering: full clubhouse facilities.
Hotels: Park Royal, Stretton; Lord Daresbury, Warrington.

6A 9 Aqualate

Stafford Rd, Newport, Shropshire, TF10 9JT
☎ (01952) 811699, Fax 825343
300 yds E of junction of A41 Newport bypass and A518 Newport to Stafford road.
Heathland course.
Pro K Short; Founded 1995
Designed by M D Simmons/T Juhre
18 holes, 5659 yards, S.S.S. 67
Visitors: welcome with a member.
Green Fees: terms on application.
Societies: welcome by arrangement; terms on application.
Catering: clubhouse facilities.
Driving range facilities.
Hotels: Royal Victoria; Adams House, both Newport.

6A 10 Arrowe Park

Arrowe Park, Woodchurch, Birkenhead, Merseyside, L49 5LW
☎ (0151) 677 1527
3 miles from town centre; 1 mile from M53 junction 3 opposite Landicon Cemetery.
Municipal parkland course.
Pro Colin Disbury; Founded 1932
18 holes, 6377 yards, S.S.S. 70
Visitors: welcome.
Green Fees: WD £6.50; WE £6.50.
Societies: welcome by prior arrangement with club Pro.
Catering: restaurant facilities.
Hotels: Arrowe Park Hotel.

6A 11 Arscott

Arscott, Pontesbury, Shropshire, SY5 0XP
☎ (01743) 860114, Fax 860114, Pro 860881

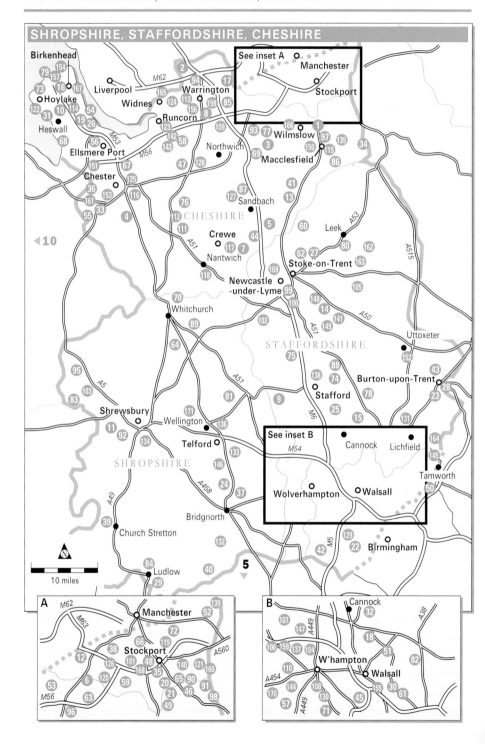

SHROPSHIRE, STAFFORDSHIRE, CHESHIRE

Birkenhead
154
79 157
73 16 167
Hoylake
122 10 14 54
31 19 26
Heswall
68 56
Ellsmere Port
151 67
Chester
36 153 116
161 33
55 4

Liverpool
Widnes
M62
165
Warrington
94 17
113
124 158 85
156 8
Runcorn
123 109
142 58
143
47 128
125
76

Birkenhead
See inset A
Manchester
Stockport

93 77 Wilmslow
69
Macclesfield
41
87 13
127 Sandbach
5
12 CHESHIRE
111
Crewe 44
117 7
Nantwich
118
70
Whitchurch
89
64

2

166 1
3 97 135
150 115 34
86

60
Leek
62 27 80 162
169 Stoke-on-Trent 163
Newcastle
-under-Lyme 99
100 148
102 14 141
149
STAFFORDSHIRE
75
138 88
74 Burton-upon-Trent
81 9 Stafford 78
25 15
A50
Uttoxeter
152
43
28
23
131

95
103
83
Shrewsbury
11
92 134
Wellington
Telford
146
SHROPSHIRE
24
37
39
Church Stretton
132
84 Ludlow
29 40
5

171
136
133

See inset B
M54
Cannock
Lichfield
Wolverhampton Walsall
Tamworth
164
145
50

129
42 22 Birmingham

10 miles

< 10

A

M62
M63
12
53
M56
63
96

Manchester
38
126
101
168
6 120 59

139
52
72
66 119
48 95
140 121 160
20 65 90
21 46 91
49 98
Stockport
A560

B
107
106 159 137
144
170 57

Cannock
32
A38
147 A449
18
104 51
W'hampton 82
110
108 Walsall
130 155 30
71 45 61
A454
A449

1 miles past Hanwood on the A488 road from Shrewsbury to Bishops Castle; signposted at Lea Cross. Parkland course.
Pro Gary Sawyer; Founded 1992
Designed by Martin Hamer
18 holes, 6178 yards, S.S.S. 69
Visitors: welcome by prior arrangement.
Green Fees: WD £14; WE £18.
Societies: welcome WD; packages including golf and catering available; from £20.
Catering: clubhouse facilities.
Hotels: Prince Rupert; Boars Head.

6A 12 Ashton on Mersey

Church Lane, Sale, Cheshire M33 5QQ
☎(0161) 9733220, Pro 973 3727
2 miles from Sale station.
Parkland course.
Pro Michael Williams; Founded 1897
9 holes, 6115 yards, S.S.S. 69
Visitors: welcome except Tues after 3pm (Ladies Day).
Green Fees: WD £18; WE £18.
Societies: welcome by arrangement; terms on application.
Catering: bar snacks and evening meals.
Hotels: Mersey Farm Travelodge.

6A 13 Astbury

Peel Lane, Astbury, Nr Congleton, Cheshire, CW12 4RE
☎(01260) 272772, Pro 298663, Sec 279139, Bar/Rest 299266
1 mile S of Congleton off A34.
Parkland course.
Pro Ashley Salt; Founded 1922
18 holes, 6296 yards, S.S.S. 70
Visitors: welcome with h'cap certs WD; WE with a member.
Green Fees: WD £25; WE £25.
Societies: Thurs only May-October; catering by prior arrangement; from £20.
Catering: facilities available.

6A 14 Barlaston

Meaford Rd, Stone, Staffs, ST15 8UX
☎(01782) 372795, Fax 372867, Sec 372867, Bar/Rest 372867
Between M6 junction 14-15 just off A34 outside Barlaston village.
Picturesque parkland course with water hazards.
Pro Ian Rogers; Founded 1982
Designed by Peter Alliss
18 holes, 5801 yards, S.S.S. 68
Visitors: welcome midweek; some WE restrictions.
Green Fees: WD £18; WE £22.50.

Societies: welcome WD; packages for golf (maximum 27 holes), catering and prizes available; terms on application.
Catering: bar and restaurant facilities.
Hotels: Moat House; Stakis Grand both Stoke; Stone House, Stone.

6A 15 Beau Desert

Rugeley Road, Hazel Slade, Cannock, Staffs, WS12 5PJ
☎(01543) 422773, Fax 451137, Pro 422492, Sec 422626
On A460 between Rugeley and Cannock near Hednesford.
Heathland course.
Pro Barrie Stevens; Founded 1921
Designed by H. Fowler
18 holes, 6310 yards, S.S.S. 71
Visitors: welcome by arrangement.
Green Fees: WD £35; WE £35.
Societies: welcome Mon-Thurs by prior arrangement; packages available; from £49.50.
Catering: facilities available.
Hotels: can be recommended by Sec.

6A 16 Bidston

Bidston Link Road, Wallasey, Merseyside, L46 2HR
☎(0151) 638 3412, Pro 630 6650

Close to M53 junction 1.
Parkland course/links.
Founded 1913
18 holes, 6140 yards, S.S.S. 70
Visitors: welcome WD.
Green Fees: WD £22.
Societies: welcome by prior arrangement; packages available; terms on application.
Catering: full clubhouse facilities.
Hotels: The Bowler Hat.

6A 17 **Birchwood**
Kelvin Close, Birchwood, Warrington, Cheshire, WA3 7PB
☎(01925) 818819, Fax 822403, Pro 816574
Off M62 at junction 11 taking A574 road to Leigh and Science Park North; Club entrance just past Science Park North.
Parkland course with natural water hazards.
Pro Paul McEwan; Founded 1979
Designed by T. J. MacAuley
18 holes, 6727 yards, S.S.S. 73
Visitors: welcome; restrictions on competition days.
Green Fees: WD £26; WE £34.
Societies: welcome Mon, Wed, Thurs; packages can be arranged; from £32.
Catering: full catering facilities.
Hotels: Garden Court, Woolston.

6A 18 **Bloxwich**
136 Stafford Rd, Bloxwich, Walsall, W Midlands, WS3 3PQ
☎(01922) 476593, Fax 476593, Pro 476889, Bar/Rest 405724
1 miles N of Bloxwich on A34 off M6 at junction 10 or 11.
Parkland course.
Pro R J Dance; Founded 1924
Designed by J. Sixsmith
18 holes, 6288 yards, S.S.S. 71
Visitors: welcome midweek; members guests at WE only.
Green Fees: WD £25; WE £25.
Societies: welcome by prior arrangement; reductions for groups; packages available; from £25.
Catering: facilities available.
Hotels: many in local area.

6A 19 **Brackenwood**
Bracken Lane, Bebington, Wirral, Merseyside, L63 2LY
☎(0151) 608 3093, Sec 608 5394
M53 junction 4 to Clatterbridge and Bebington.
Public parkland course.
Pro Ken Lamb; Founded 1933

18 holes, 6045 yards, S.S.S. 70
Visitors: welcome.
Green Fees: WD £6.50; WE £6.50.
Societies: welcome by arrangement.
Hotels: Thornton Hall; Village.

6A 20 **Bramall Park**
20 Manor Rd, Bramhall, Stockport, SK7 3LY
☎(0161) 485 3119, Fax 485 7101, Pro 485 2205, Sec 485 7101
8 miles S of Manchester (club can provide directions from M56 and M63).
Parkland course.
Pro M Proffitt; Founded 1894
Designed by J Braid
18 holes, 6214 yards, S.S.S. 70
Visitors: welcome by arrangement.
Green Fees: WD £25; WE £35.
Societies: welcome Tues and Thurs by prior arrangement; packages available; terms on application.
Catering: clubhouse catering facilities.
Hotels: County, Bramhall; Belfry, Handforth.

6A 21 **Bramhall**
Ladythorn Rd, Bramhall, Stockport, Cheshire, SK7 2EY
☎(0161) 439 4057, Fax 439 0264, Pro 439 1171, Sec 439 6092
Off A5102 S of Stockport.
Parkland course.
Pro R Green; Founded 1905
18 holes, 6340 yards, S.S.S. 70
Visitors: welcome; restrictions Thurs.
Green Fees: WD £24; WE £31.
Societies: welcome on Wed by prior arrangement; golf and catering packages can be arranged; from £24.
Catering: clubhouse facilities.
Hotels: County Hotel, Bramhall.

6A 22 **Brand Hall**
Heron Road, Oldbury, Warley, W Midlands, B68 8AQ
☎(0121) 552 2195, Fax 544 5088
6 miles NW of Birmingham, 1.5 miles from M5 junction 2.
Public parkland course.
Pro Carl Yates
18 holes, 5734 yards, S.S.S. 68
Visitors: welcome; pay and play.
Green Fees: WD £6.60; WE £8.50.
Societies: welcome by arrangement.
Catering: cafe, clubhouse bar.

6A 23 **Branston Golf & Country Club**
Burton Rd, Branston, Burton-on-Trent, Staffs, DE14 3DP

☎(01283) 512211, Fax 566984, Sec 543207
On A5121 off A38 at Burton South.
Parkland course on banks of R Trent; water on 13 holes.
Pro Sean Stiff; Founded 1973
18 holes, 6647 yards, S.S.S. 72
Visitors: welcome WD and afternoons at WE.
Green Fees: WD £25; WE £25.
Societies: welcome by arrangement; terms on application.
Catering: full catering facilities.
Hotels: Riverside; Dog and Partridge.

6A 24 **Bridgnorth**
Stanley Lane, Bridgnorth, Shropshire, WV16 4SF
☎(01746) 763315, Fax 761381, Pro 762045
On road to Broseley, 0.5 miles from Bridgnorth.
Parkland course.
Pro Paul Hinton; Founded 1889
18 holes, 6650 yards, S.S.S. 73
Visitors: welcome.
Green Fees: WD £20; WE £25.
Societies: welcome Tues, Thurs, Fri; reserved tee times and packages available; from £25.
Catering: clubhouse facilities.
Hotels: Parlours Hall; Falcon; Croft.

6A 25 **Brocton Hall**
Sawpit Lane, Brocton, Staffs, ST17 0TH
☎(01785) 662627, Fax 661591, Pro 661485, Sec 661901, Bar/Rest 660357
4 miles S of Stafford off A34.
Parkland course.
Pro R G Johnson; Founded 1894/1923
Designed by Harry Vardon
18 holes, 6064 yards, S.S.S. 69
Visitors: welcome as member's guest.
Green Fees: WD £10; WE £10.
Societies: welcome Tues and Thurs by prior arrangement and with h'cap certss; packages for golf and catering by prior arrangement; from £28.
Catering: full clubhouse bar and restaurant facilities.
Hotels: Tillington Hall; Garth Hotel both Stafford.

6A 26 **Bromborough**
Raby Hall Rd, Bromborough, Wirral, Merseyside, L63 0NW
☎(0151) 334 2155, Fax 334 0303, Pro 334 4499.
Close to M53 junction 5 0.75 miles from A41 Birkenhead to Chester road;

- A complete golf resort, set in 750 acres of beautiful Cheshire countryside
- 18 hole par 72 Cheshire Course
- 18 hole par 72 Nicklaus Course *(opening July '98)*
- 9 hole par 3 Azalea Course
- Europe's first Jack Nicklaus Residential Golf School
- Superb Spa Facilities

*Please call **01829 731000** for a brochure and further information.*

SEE DETAILS OF SPECIAL OFFER ON PAGE 383

0.5 miles from Bromborough station.
Parkland course.
Pro Geoff Berry; Founded 1904
18 holes, 6603 yards, S.S.S. 73
Visitors: welcome WD; by arrangement WE.
Green Fees: WD £28; WE £30.
Societies: welcome Wed; early booking essential.
Catering: extensive catering and bar facilities.
Hotels: Thornton Hall; Village.

6A 27 Burslem
Wood Farm, High Lane, Tunstall,
Stoke-on-Trent, ST6 7JT
☎(01782) 837006
4 miles N of Hanley.
Parkland course.
Founded 1907
11 holes, 5360 yards, S.S.S. 66
Visitors: welcome WD only by prior arrangement.
Green Fees: WD £16.
Societies: WD by prior arrangement; catering to be arranged with the steward; terms on application.
Catering: by arrangement with the steward.

6A 28 Burton-on-Trent
43 Ashby Rd East, Burton-on-Trent,
Derbyshire, DE15 0PS
☎(01283) 568708, Fax 544551, Pro 562240, Sec 544551
On A50 3 miles E of Burton on Trent.
Undulating woodland course.
Pro G Stafford; Founded 1894
Designed by H.S. Colt
18 holes, 6579 yards, S.S.S. 71
Visitors: welcome with h'cap certs.
Green Fees: WD £28; WE £28.
Societies: welcome WD; catering packages available except Mon; snooker; terms on application.
Catering: full facilities except Mon.
Practice range, practice ground.

Hotels: Stanhope Arms; Riverside, both Burton-on-Trent; Newton Park, Newton Solney.

6A 29 Cadmore Lodge
Berrington Green, Tenbury Wells,
Worcester, Worcs, WR15 8TQ
☎(01584) 810044
Off A456 20 miles W of Kidderminster.
Parkland course with lakes.
Founded 1990
Designed by John Weston
9 holes, 5132 yards, S.S.S. 65
Visitors: welcome.
Green Fees: WD £10; WE £14.
Societies: welcome by prior arrangement; packages can be arranged; bowls; tennis; fishing.
Catering: full facilities.
Hotels: Hotel on site.

6A 30 Calderfields
Aldridge Rd, Walsall, W Midlands,
WS4 2JS
☎(01922) 632243, Fax 638787, Pro 613675, Sec 640540, Bar/Rest 646888
On A454 off M6 junctions 7 or 10.
Parkland course with lakes.
Pro Darren Lewis; Founded 1981
Designed by Roy Winter
18 holes, 6509 yards, S.S.S. 71
Visitors: welcome.
Green Fees: WD £15; WE £15.
Societies: welcome every day; packages available; from £15.
Catering: bar and restaurant facilities.
Practice range, 27 bays floodlit; floodlit bunker and putting green.
Hotels: Boundary; Fairview; County.

6A 31 Caldy
Links Hey Rd, Caldy, Wirral, L48 1NB,
Merseyside
☎(0151) 625 5660, Fax 625 7394,
Pro 625 1818

A540 from Chester, turn left at Caldy crossroads.
Seaside/parkland course.
Pro Kevin Jones; Founded 1907
Designed by James Braid, John Salvesen
18 holes, 6668 yards, S.S.S. 73
Visitors: welcome WD; Tues ladies day; WE with a member or after 2pm.
Green Fees: WD £40; WE £35.
Societies: welcome Thurs by arrangement; winter packages available.
Catering: bar snacks all day; dinner by arrangement.
Hotels: Parkgate.

6A 32 Cannock Park
Stafford Rd, Cannock, Staffs WS11 2AL
☎(01543) 578850, Fax 578850, Sec 572800
0.5 miles N of Cannock on A34.
Parkland course.
Pro David Dunk; Founded 1990
Designed by John Mainland
18 holes, 5048 yards, S.S.S. 65
Visitors: welcome; telephone in advance.
Green Fees: WD £7; WE £8.
Societies: welcome by prior arrangement; packages available; terms on application; from £7.
Catering: clubhouse catering facilities.
Hotels: Roman Way; Hollies.

6A 33 Carden Park Hotel, Golf Resort & Spa
Carden Park, Chester, Cheshire, CH3 9DQ
☎(01829) 731600, Fax 731636, Pro 731500, Bar/Rest 731630
On A534 E of Wrexham; 1.5 miles from junction with A41.
Parkland course; Nicklaus course, 7010 yards, opens mid 1998.
Pro David Williams; Founded 1993
Course redesigned several times

18 holes, 6891 yards
Visitors: welcome with h'cap certs.
Green Fees: WD £30; WE £30.
Societies: welcome with h'cap certs and by prior arrangement; packages available for golf and catering; full first-class hotel leisure and catering facilities; terms on application.
Catering: full first-class hotel facilities. Practice range, also 9-hole course available, par 3, £7.50; short game practice area.
Hotels: Carden Park Hotel on site with 192 rooms.

6A 34 Chapel-en-le-Frith
Manchester Rd, Chapel-en-le-Frith, Stockport, Cheshire, SK23 9UH
☎(01298) 812118, Fax 813943
On the road between Whaley Bridge and Chapel.
Parkland course with water hazards.
Pro D Cullen; Founded 1905
18 holes, 6054 yards, S.S.S. 69
Visitors: welcome by prior arrangement.
Green Fees: WD £20; WE £30.
Societies: welcome by prior arrangement; 36 holes of golf; coffee and biscuits on arrival, lunch and 5-course meal; from £35.
Catering: full clubhouse facilities.

6A 35 Cheadle
Cheadle Road, Cheadle, Cheshire, SK8 1HW
☎(0161) 428 2160, Pro 428 9878, Sec + Bar/Rest 491 3873
1.5 miles from M63 junction 11 follow signs for Cheadle; 1 mile S of Cheadle village.
Undulating parkland course.
Founded 1885
Designed by R. Renouf
9 holes, 5006 yards, S.S.S. 65
Visitors: welcome with h'cap certs except Tues and Sat.
Green Fees: terms on application.
Societies: welcome by prior arrangement Mon, Wed, Thurs, Fri; packages can be arranged through the steward; no lunchtime catering Thurs; snooker; terms on application.
Catering: bar and catering facilities, except Thurs.
Hotels: Village, Cheadle.

6A 36 Chester
Curzon Park North, Chester, Cheshire, CH4 8AR
☎(01244) 677760
1 mile from Chester off the A55 behind Chester racecourse.

Parkland course.
Pro George Parton; Founded 1901
18 holes, 6508 yards, S.S.S. 71
Visitors: welcome by arrangement.
Green Fees: WD £23; WE £28.
Societies: welcome by arrangement.
Catering: full facilities.
Hotels: many in Chester.

6A 37 Chesterton Valley Golf Club
Chesterton, Nr. Worfield, Bridgnorth, Shropshire, WV15 5NX
☎(01746) 783682
On B 44176 Dudley-Telford Road.
Heathland course.
Pro Paul Hinton; Founded 1993
Designed by P Hinton
9 holes, 6286 yards, S.S.S. 70
Visitors: pay and play.
Green Fees: WD £6.50; WE £6.50.
Societies: welcome by prior arrangement; terms on application.

6A 38 Chorlton-cum-Hardy
Barlow Hall Rd, Chorlton-cum-hardy, Manchester, M21 7JJ
☎(0161) 881 3139, Fax 881 5830, Pro 881 9911, Sec 881 5830
4 miles S of Manchester close to A5103/A5145 junction.
Parkland course.
Pro David Screeton; Founded 1902
18 holes, 5980 yards, S.S.S. 69
Visitors: welcome by arrangement.
Green Fees: WD £20; WE £25.
Societies: welcome on Thurs by prior arrangement; booking form available from Sec; packages available; terms on application.
Catering: clubhouse facilities.
Hotels: Post House; Britannia both Northenden.

6A 39 Church Stretton
Hunters Moon, Trevor Hill, Church Stretton, Shropshire, SY6 6JH
☎(01694) 722281, Pro 01743 873751, Sec 722633
From A49 into Church Stretton; right at top of town; 1st left into Cardinmill Valley; 100 yards to Trevor Hill.
Hillside course.
Pro Peter Seal; Founded 1898
Designed by James Braid
18 holes, 5020 yards, S.S.S. 65
Visitors: welcome.
Green Fees: WD £12; WE £18.
Societies: welcome by arrangement; some WE available; golf and catering packages by arrangement; from £12.
Catering: clubhouse facilities.

Hotels: Denehurst; Longmynd, both Church Stretton; Stretton Hall, All Stretton.

6A 40 Cleobury Mortimer Golf Club
Wyre Common, Cleobury Mortimer, Shropshire, DY14 8HQ
☎(01299) 271112, Fax 271468, Pro 271628, Bar/Rest 271320
2 miles E of Cleobury Mortimer just off A4117; halfway between Kidderminster and Ludlow.
Parkland course.
Pro Graham Farr; Founded 1993
Designed by EGU
18 holes, 6438 yards, S.S.S. 71
Visitors: welcome by arrangement.
Green Fees: WD £16; WE £19.
Societies: welcome by arrangement; packages involving 18, 27 and 36 holes; catering plus private function room for 90; snooker; from £14.50.
Catering: spike bar, lounge bar and restaurant facilities.
Hotels: Redfern Hotel.

6A 41 Congleton
Biddulph Rd, Congleton, Cheshire, CW12 3LZ
☎(01260) 273540
1 mile SE of Congleton station on A527 Congleton-Biddulph road.
Parkland course.
Pro John Colclough; Founded 1898
9 holes, 5119 yards, S.S.S. 65
Visitors: welcome; Tues Ladies Day.
Green Fees: WD £20; WE £30.
Societies: welcome Mon and Thurs.
Catering: full facilities except Mon.
Hotels: Lion & Swan; Bulls Head.

6A 42 Corngreaves
Corngreaves Road, Cradley Heath, W Midlands, B64 7NL
☎(01384) 567880
2 miles E of Dudley.
Public parkland course.
Pro Carl Yates; Founded 1985
18 holes, 3979 yards, S.S.S. 61
Visitors: welcome.
Green Fees: WD £6.60; WE £7.50.
Societies: welcome by arrangement; packages on request.
Catering: full facilities.

6A 43 The Craythorne
Craythorne Rd, Stretton, Burton-on-Trent, Staffs, DE13 0AZ
☎(01283) 564329, Fax 511908, Pro 533745

300 yards from village after leaving A38 at Stretton signs.
Parkland course.
Pro S Hadfield; Founded 1974
Designed by Cyril Johnson/A A Wright
18 holes, 5306 yards, S.S.S. 67
Visitors: welcome by prior arrangement; h'cap certs required.
Green Fees: WD £18; WE £22
Societies: welcome by prior arrangement; packages available; terms on application.
Catering: full facilities.
Hotels: The Willington.

6A 44 Crewe

Fields Rd, Haslington, Crewe, Cheshire, CW1 5TB
☎(01270) 584227, Fax 584099, Pro 585032, Sec 584099
2 miles NE of Crewe Station off A534.
Parkland course.
Pro Michael Booker; Founded 1911
18 holes, 6424 yards, S.S.S. 71
Visitors: welcome WD; WE with a member.
Green Fees: WD £27.
Societies: welcome Tues; golf and catering packages available; from £25.50.
Catering: clubhouse facilities.
Hotels: Hunter Lodge; Crewe Arms.

6A 45 Dartmouth

Vale St, West Bromwich, W Midlands, B71 4DW
☎(0121) 588 2131
1.5 miles from M5/M6 junction.
Undulating meadowland/parkland course.
Pro Guy Dean; Founded 1910
9 holes, 6036 yards, S.S.S. 72
Visitors: welcome WD h'cap certs; with member only WE
Green Fees: WD £20.
Societies: by arrangement with Pro; packages available; snooker.
Catering: full facilities.
Hotels: Moat House; Albion.

6A 46 Davenport

Worth Hall, Middlewood Rd, Poynton, Stockport, Cheshire, SK12 1TS
☎(01625) 877321, Pro 877319, Sec 876951
From A6 at Hazel Grove take A523 Macclesfield road to Poynton turning left into Park Lane.
Undulating parkland course.
Pro Wyn Harris; Founded 1913
Designed by Fraser Middleton
18 holes, 6067 yards, S.S.S. 69

Visitors: welcome except Sat.
Green Fees: WD £24; WE £30.
Societies: welcome Tues and Thurs by prior arrangement; from £32.50.
Catering: full clubhouse facilities.
Hotels: Belfry; Belgrade.

6A 47 Delamere Forest

Station Rd, Delamere, Northwich, Cheshire, CW8 2JE
☎(01606) 882807, Pro 883307, Sec 883264
From A556 take B5152 to Frodsham; lane to club is 1 mile, next to Delamere station.
Undulating heathland course.
Pro Ellis Jones; Founded 1910
Designed by Herbert Fowler
18 holes, 6305 yards, S.S.S. 70
Visitors: welcome; 2 balls only at WE and Bank Holidays.
Green Fees: WD £30; WE £35.
Societies: welcome Tues and Thurs by arrangement; packages available.
Catering: bar snacks; restaurant.
Hotels: Hartford Hall; Swan; Willington Hall.

6A 48 Didsbury

Ford Lane, Northenden, Manchester, M22 4NQ
☎(0161) 998 9278, Fax 998 9278, Pro 998 2811, Bar/Rest 998 2743
6 miles S of Manchester.
Parkland course.
Pro P Barber; Founded 1891
Designed by G Lowe(1891); G MacKenzie (1921); D Thomas and P Alliss (1973)
18 holes, 6273 yards, S.S.S. 70
Visitors: welcome with h'cap certs.
Green Fees: WD £26; WE £30.
Societies: welcome Thurs and Fri; restricted availability Sun and Mon; catering and golf packages available; minimum 12, maximum 80; from £34.
Catering: full clubhouse facilities.
Hotels: Post House; Britannia, both Northenden.

6A 49 Disley

Stanley Hall Lane, Jackson's Edge, Disley, Cheshire, SK12 2JX
☎(01663) 762071, Pro 762884
Off A6 in Disley village.
Open hillside/parkland course.
Pro Andrew Esplin; Founded 1889
Designed by James Braid
18 holes, 6015 yards, S.S.S. 69
Visitors: welcome WD by prior arrangement.
Green Fees: WD £25; WE £25.

Societies: welcome WD by prior arrangement; catering and golf packages available; from £35.
Catering: clubhouse facilities.
Hotels: Stakis Moorside.

6A 50 Drayton Park

Drayton Park, Tamworth, Staffs, B78 3TN
☎(01827) 251139, Fax 284035, Pro 251478, Bar/Rest 287481
On A4091 at Drayton Park leisure park.
Parkland course.
Pro M W Passmore; Founded 1897
Designed by James Braid
18 holes, 6401 yards, S.S.S. 71
Visitors: welcome WD, except Wed.
Green Fees: WD £29; WE £29.
Societies: welcome Tues and Thurs between May 1 and Sept 30 by prior arrangement with Sec, A O Rammell; minimum of 12 players; catering packages can be arranged; from £26.
Catering: full facilities available.
Hotels: Gungate; Beefeater, both Tamworth.

6A 51 Druids Heath

Stonnall Rd, Aldridge, Walsall, W Midlands, WS9 8JZ
☎(01922) 455595, Pro 459523
Off A452 6 miles NW of Sutton Coldfield.
Undulating course.
Pro Glenn Williams; Founded 1973
18 holes, 6659 yards, S.S.S. 73
Visitors: welcome WD.
Green Fees: WD £25.
Societies: WD by prior arrangement.
Catering: by prior arrangement.
Hotels: Barons Court; Fairlawns.

6A 52 Dukinfield

Yew Tree Lane, Dukinfield, Cheshire, SK10 5DB
☎(0161) 338 2304
From Ashton Road 1 mile then right into Yew Tree Lane; club 1 mile on right on hill behind Senior Service factory.
Hillside course.
Pro Colin Boyle/Jamie Low; Founded 1913
18 holes, 5303 yards, S.S.S. 66
Visitors: welcome WD by prior arrangement.
Green Fees: WD £18.50.
Societies: welcome by prior arrangement with Sec.
Catering: full clubhouse facilities except Mon.
Hotels: Village, Hyde.

6A 53 **Dunham Forest Golf & Country Club**

Oldfield Lane, Altrincham, Cheshire, WA14 4TY

☎(0161) 928 2605, Pro 928 2727

2 miles N of M56 junction 7 towards Manchester and course on left.
Woodland course.
Pro Ian Wrigley; Founded 1961
18 holes, 6636 yards, S.S.S. 72
Visitors: welcome.
Green Fees: WD £40; WE £45.
Societies: welcome WD except Wed; discounts for groups of more than 20; packages available.
Catering: bar and restaurant facilities available.
Hotels: Bowdon; Cresta Court.

6A 54 **Eastham Lodge**

117 Ferry Rd, Eastham, Wirral, L62 0AP

☎(0151) 327 1483, Fax 327 3003, Pro 327 3008, Sec 327 3003

M53 junction 5 to A41 follow signs for Eastham Country Park.
Parkland course; was Port Sunlight GC from 1932-76.
Pro Bob Boobyer; Founded 1976
Designed by Hawtree & Sons
18 holes, 5706 yards, S.S.S. 68
Visitors: welcome WD; with a member only at weekend.
Green Fees: WD £22; WE £10.
Societies: welcome Tues by prior arrangement; some Mon and Fri dates available also; golf and catering packages available; from £18.
Catering: full clubhouse bar and catering facilities.
Hotels: Raby House, Willaston.

6A 55 **Eaton**

Guy Lane, Waverton, Chester, Cheshire, CH3 7PH

☎(01244) 335885, Fax 335782, Pro 335826, Bar/Rest 336862

3 miles SE of Chester off the A41 through the village of Waverton.
Parkland course.
Pro Neil Dunroe; Founded 1965, altered in 1993
Designed by Donald Steel
18 holes, 6562 yards, S.S.S. 71
Visitors: welcome with handicap certificates.
Green Fees: WD £25; WE £30.
Societies: welcome WD except Wed by prior arrangement; full golf and catering packages available; from £25.
Catering: full clubhouse facilities available.
Hotels: Rowton Hall.

6A 56 **Ellesmere Port**

Chester Rd, Childer Thornton, S Wirral, Cheshire, L66 1QH

☎(0151) 339 7689

On M53 W to A41 turn S to Chester for 2 miles; club at rear of St Paul's Church, Hooton.
Municipal parkland/meadowland course.
Pro David Yates; Founded 1971
Designed by Cotton, Pennink, Lawrie & Partners
18 holes, 6432 yards, S.S.S. 71
Visitors: welcome.
Green Fees: WD £6.15; WE £6.85.
Societies: welcome with booking fee of £1.25 per head; winter packages available.
Catering: on request.
Hotels: Brook Meadow; Chimney; Village.

6A 57 **Enville**

Highgate Common, Enville, Stourbridge, W Midlands, DY7 5BN

☎(01384) 872074, Fax 873396, Pro 872585, Bar/Rest 872551

6 miles W of Stourbridge on the A458 to Bridgnorth.
Woodland/heathland course.
Pro Sean Power; Founded 1935
Highgate: 18 holes, 6471 yards, S.S.S. 72; Lodge: 18 holes, 6275 yards, S.S.S. 70
Visitors: welcome WD.
Green Fees: WD £28.
Societies: welcome by prior arrangement and payment of £10 per player deposit; golf and catering packages available; minimum 12 players; 10 per cent reduction for 30 or more; terms on application.
Catering: full clubhouse catering.

6A 58 **Frodsham**

Simons Lane, Frodsham, Cheshire, WA6 6HE

☎(01928) 732159, Pro 739442

Close to M56 junction 12; turn left at lights in Frodsham centre on to B5152.
Parkland course.
Pro Graham Tonge; Founded 1990
Designed by John Day
18 holes, 6298 yards, S.S.S. 70
Visitors: welcome WD except competition days; tee times booked through shop.
Green Fees: WD £30.
Societies: welcome WD by prior arrangement with golf office; packages available.
Catering: full bar and catering.
Hotels: Forest Hills.

6A 59 **Gatley**

Waterfall Farm, off Styal Rd, Heald Green, Cheadle, Cheshire, SK8 3TW

☎(0161) 437 2091, Pro 436 2830

Off Yew Tree Grove and Styal Road, 2 miles from Cheadle and 1 mile from Manchester Airport.
Parkland course.
Pro Simon Reeves; Founded 1912
9 holes, 5909 yards, S.S.S. 68
Visitors: welcome except Tues and Wed.
Green Fees: WD £20; WE £20.
Societies: welcome by prior arrangement with Sec.
Catering: full facilities except Mon.
Hotels: Pymgate Lodge.

6A 60 **Goldenhill**

Mobberley Rd, Goldenhill, Stoke-on-Trent, Staffs, ST6 5SS

☎(01782) 234200, Fax 234303

On A50 between Tunstall and Kidsgrove.
Parkland/meadowland course in old mine basin.
Pro Richard Hulme; Founded 1983
18 holes, 5957 yards, S.S.S. 69
Visitors: welcome; booking system available.
Green Fees: WD £7; WE £7.80.
Societies: welcome by arrangement.
Catering: bar and restaurant.
Practice range, practice ground; putting green.

6A 61 **Great Barr**

Chapel Lane, Great Barr, Birmingham, W Midlands, B43 7BA

☎(0121) 357 1232, Pro 357 5270, Sec 358 4376

Close to M6 junction 7 6 miles NW Birmingham.
Meadowland course.
Pro Richard Spragg; Founded 1961
Designed by J. Hamilton Stutt
18 holes, 6523 yards, S.S.S. 71
Visitors: welcome WD.
Green Fees: WD £25.
Societies: welcome Tues and Thurs by prior arrangement; from £22-£38.
Catering: full clubhouse facilities.
Hotels: Post House.

6A 62 **Greenway Hall**

Stanley Road, Stockton Brook, Stoke-on-Trent, Staffs, ST9 9LJ

☎(01782) 503158, Fax 503158

Off A53 Stoke-Leek road at Stockton Brook.
Parkland course/heathland.
Pro Greg Iron; Founded 1909

18 holes, 5681 yards, S.S.S. 67
Visitors: welcome WD.
Green Fees: WD £14; WE £14.
Societies: welcome by prior arrangement; packages available; terms on application.
Catering: clubhouse facilities.

6A 63 Hale

Rappax Rd, Hale, Altrincham, Cheshire, WA15 0NU
☎(0161) 980 4225, Pro 904 0835
2 miles SE of Altrincham; near Altrincham Priory.
Parkland course.
Pro Mike Grantham; Founded 1903
9 holes, 5780 yards, S.S.S. 68
Visitors: welcome WD except Thurs; with member only at WE.
Green Fees: WD £20; WE £6.
Societies: welcome by prior arrangement; catering available for coffee and lunch; evening meals by prior arrangement with the steward; from £20.
Catering: clubhouse facilities.
Practice ground.
Hotels: Four Seasons, Manchester Airport.

6A 64 Hawkstone Park Hotel

Weston-under-Redcastle, Shrewsbury, Shropshire, SY4 5UY
☎(01939) 200611, Fax 200311
Off A49 12 miles N of Shrewsbury or A442 12 miles N of Telford.
Parkland course.
Pros Paul Wesslingh and Paul Brown; Founded 1935
Hawkstone: 18 holes, 6491 yards, S.S.S. 72; Windmill: 18 holes, 6476 yards, S.S.S. 72
Visitors: welcome with prior booking; h'cap certs required.
Green Fees: WD £28; WE £36.
Societies: welcome by prior arrangement with golf reservation office; terms on application.
Catering: full bar and restaurant facilities.
Practice range, 15 bays; also 6-hole par 3 academy course; putting and pitching green.
Hotels: Hawkstone Park on site; golfing breaks available.

6A 65 Hazel Grove

Buxton Rd, Hazel Grove, Stockport, Cheshire, SK7 6LU
☎(0161) 483 3978, Fax 487 4399, Pro 483 7272, Bar/Rest 483 3217/4399
Off A6 Stockport-Buxton road.

Parkland course.
Pro Mike Hill; Founded 1913
18 holes, 6310 yards, S.S.S. 71
Visitors: welcome by prior arrangement.
Green Fees: WD £25; WE £30.
Societies: welcome Thurs and Fri by prior arrangement; package includes full day of golf and catering; £35.
Catering: full clubhouse bar and restaurant facilities.

6A 66 Heaton Moor

Mauldeth Road, Heaton Mersey, Stockport, Cheshire, SK4 3NX
☎(0161) 432 2134, Pro 432 0846
From M63 junction 12 follow Didsbury signs and Mauldeth Rd is 1.5 miles on right.
Flat, tree-lined parkland course.
Pro Simon Marsh; Founded 1892
18 holes, 5968 yards, S.S.S. 68
Visitors: welcome by prior arrangement.
Green Fees: WD £23; WE £31.
Societies: welcome by prior arrangement; Thurs and Fri preferred; golf and catering packages available; from £33.
Catering: full clubhouse facilities.
Hotels: Rudyard, Heaton Chapel.

6A 67 Helsby

Towers Lane, Helsby, Cheshire, WA6 0JB
☎(01928) 722021, Pro 725457
From M56 junction 14; left to Helsby and then right and right again for Towers Lane.
Parkland course.
Pro M Jones; Founded 1901
Designed by James Braid
18 holes, 6229 yards, S.S.S. 70
Visitors: welcome WD.
Green Fees: WD £22; WE £22.
Societies: welcome Tues and Thurs; packages include full day's golf and catering; from £34.50.
Catering: full clubhouse facilities available.

6A 68 Heswall

Cottage Lane, Gayton, Heswall, Wirral, Cheshire, L60 8PB
☎(0151) 342 1237, Pro 342 7431
M53 junction 4; from roundabout, turn into Well Lane; leads into Cottage Lane.
Parkland course.
Pro Alan Thompson; Founded 1901
18 holes, 6554 yards, S.S.S. 72
Visitors: welcome except Tues.
Green Fees: WD £35; WE £40.

Societies: welcome Wed and Fri only; winter packages available.
Catering: full facilities.
Hotels: Mollington Banastre; Thornton Hall; Parkgate; Travelodge (Gayton); Woodhey; Victoria.

6A 69 Heyrose

Budworth Rd, Tabley, Knutsford, Cheshire, WA16 0HY
☎(01565) 733664, Pro 734267
4 miles W of Knutsford 0.5 miles along Budworth road off Pickmere Lane; M6 junction 19, 1 mile.
Wooded converted farmland course with water features.
Pro Martin Redrup; Founded 1990
Designed by E.L.C.N. Bridge
18 holes, 6515 yards, S.S.S. 71
Visitors: welcome except before 2pm on Sat.
Green Fees: WD £19; WE £24.
Societies: welcome WD by prior arrangement; from £36.
Catering: clubhouse bar and restaurant.
Practice range, practice ground; practice bunkers; putting green; driving net.
Hotels: Cottons, Knutsford; Swan, Bucklow Hill; Old Vicarage, Tabley; Travelodge.

6A 70 Hill Valley Golf & Country Club

Terrick Rd, Whitchurch, Shropshire, SY13 4JZ
☎(01948) 663584, Fax 665927, Pro 663032
Off A49/A41 Whitchurch by-pass.
Undulating parkland course.
Pro Tony Minshall; Founded 1975
Designed by P. Alliss & D. Thomas
18 holes, 6607 yards, S.S.S. 72
Visitors: welcome.
Green Fees: WD £18; WE £12.
Societies: welcome by prior arrangement; packages available; also East course, 5280 yards par 66; health & beauty centre; snooker.
Catering: full clubhouse facilities.
Hotels: motel accommodation at club; Dodington Lodge; Terrick Hall.

6A 71 Himley Hall Golf Centre

Log Cabin, Himley Hall Park, Dudley, W Midlands, DY3 4DF
☎(01902) 895207
From A449 Wolverhampton-Kidderminster road to Dudley on B4176; then into Himley Hall Park.

Public parkland course.
Pro Jeremy Nicholls; Founded 1980
Designed by D.A. Baker
9 holes, 6215 yards, S.S.S. 70
Visitors: welcome.
Green Fees: WD £7.50; WE £8.
Societies: welcome by arrangement.
Catering: cafe and hot meals.
Hotels: Himley House; Park Hall.

6A 72 Houldsworth

Houldsworth Park, Reddish, Stockport,
Cheshire, SK5 6BN
☎(0161) 442 9611, Pro 442 1714,
Sec 442 1712
From M63 junction 13 turn left up to
roundabout then take road to Reddish;
turn left at Houldsworth pub.
Parkland course.
Pro David Naylor; Founded 1911
Designed by T.G. Renouf
18 holes, 6247 yards, S.S.S. 70
Visitors: welcome WD (Ladies days
Tues afternoon).
Green Fees: WD £20; WE £25.
Societies: welcome by prior arrange-
ment.
Catering: full facilities.

6A 73 Hoylake Municipal

Carr Lane, Hoylake, Merseyside, L47
4BG
☎(0151) 632 2956, Bar/Rest 632
4883
Off M53 10 miles SW of Liverpool fol-
lowing signs for Hoylake; 100 yards
beyond Hoylake station.
Municipal parkland course.
Pro Simon Hooton; Founded 1933
Designed by James Braid
18 holes, 6321 yards, S.S.S. 70
Visitors: welcome; book in advance at
WE; Sat from 8.30am.
Green Fees: WD £6.50; WE £6.50.
Societies: welcome by prior arrange-
ment; after 1.30pm at WE.
Catering: hot snacks, meals and bar.
Hotels: Green Lodge.

6A 74 Ingestre Park

Ingestre, Stafford, Staffs, ST18 0RE
☎(01889) 270845, Fax 270845, Pro
270304, Bar/Rest 270061
6 miles E of Stafford off A51 via Great
Haywood and Tixall.
Parkland course in former estate of
Earl of Shrewsbury.
Pro D Scullion; Founded 1977
Designed by Hawtree & Son
18 holes, 6251 yards, S.S.S. 70
Visitors: welcome WD with h'cap
certs; with member at WE.

Green Fees: WD £23; WE £10.
Societies: welcome WD except Wed
with prior arrangement; special pack-
ages available for 15 or more; snooker
room; lounge; from £34.
Catering: bar and restaurant facilities
available.
Practice area.
Hotels: Dower House, Ingestre; Garth,
Tillington Hall, both Stafford.

6A 75 Izaak Walton

Eccleshall Rd, Cold Norton, Stone,
Staffs, ST15 0NS
☎(01785) 760900
On B5026 between Stone and
Eccleshall.
Parkland course.
Pro Julie Brown; Founded 1992
Designed by Mike Lowe
18 holes, 6281 yards, S.S.S. 72
Visitors: welcome.
Green Fees: WD £15; WE £20.
Societies: welcome by prior arrange-
ment; packages for catering and golf
available; full facilities; terms on appli-
cation.
Catering: full clubhouse facilities.
Hotels: Stone House, Stone.

6A 76 Knights Grange Sports Complex

Grange Lane, Winsford, Cheshire,
CW7 2PT
☎(01606) 552780
Course in centre of Winsford.
Public meadowland course.
Pro Graham Moore; Founded 1983
9 holes, 5438 yards, S.S.S. 66
Visitors: welcome.
Green Fees: WD £3.75; WE £5.45.
Societies: welcome by prior arrange-
ment in writing.
Catering: hot drinks and snacks.
Practice area; tennis; bowls.

6A 77 Knutsford

Mereheath Lane, Knutsford, Cheshire,
WA16 6HS
☎(01565) 633355, Pro 755781
2 miles from M6 junction 19; make for
Knutsford entrance to Tatton Park.
Parkland course.
Pro Allan Gillies; Founded 1891
10 holes, 6195 yards, S.S.S. 70
Visitors: welcome WD except Wed.
Green Fees: WD £18; WE £25.
Societies: welcome Thurs by prior
arrangement.
Catering: full facilities.
Hotels: George; Angel; Cottons; Rose
& Crown; Swan.

6A 78 Lakeside (Rugeley)

Rugeley Power Station, Armitage Rd,
Rugeley, Staffs, WS15 1PR
☎(01889) 575667
Between Lichfield and Stafford.
Parkland course.
Founded 1969
18 holes, 5534 yards, S.S.S. 67
Visitors: welcome with a member.
Green Fees: WD on application.
Catering: evening service.

6A 79 Leasowe

Leasowe Rd, Moreton, Wirral L46 3RD
☎(0151) 677 5852, Pro 678 5460
Off M53 1 miles after tunnel; 1 mile W
of Wallasey village.
Links course.
Pro Andrew Ayre; Founded 1891
Designed by John Ball Jnr
18 holes, 6263 yards, S.S.S. 70
Visitors: welcome WD; WE by prior
arrangement.
Green Fees: WD £20.50; WE £25.50.
Societies: welcome by arrangement;
minimum 16 players; not Sat.
Catering: restaurant, bar and snacks.
Large practice area.
Hotels: Leasowe Castle.

6A 80 Leek

Cheddleton Rd, Leek, Staffs ST13 5RE
☎(01538) 385889, Pro 384767, Sec
384779
On A520 0.75 miles S of Leek.
Parkland course.
Pro P A Stubbs; Founded 1892
18 holes, 6240 yards, S.S.S. 70
Visitors: welcome with h'cap certs.
Green Fees: WD £24; WE £24.
Societies: welcome Wed; golf and
catering packages available; from £24.
Catering: full clubhouse facilities.
Hotels: Bank End Farm; Horse
Shoes, Blacksham Moor.

6A 81 Lilleshall Hall

Lilleshall, Newport, Shropshire, TF10
9AS
☎(01952) 604776, Fax 604776, Pro
604104, Bar/Rest 603840
Between A41 and A5 at Sherrifhales.
Parkland course.
Pro Nigel Bramall; Founded 1937
Designed by H.S. Colt
18 holes, 5789 yards, S.S.S. 68
Visitors: welcome WD and WE with a
member.
Green Fees: WD £20; WE £20.
Societies: welcome WD by prior
arrangement; terms on application.
Catering: clubhouse facilities.

6A 82 Little Aston
Roman Road, Streetly, B74 3AN
☎(0121) 353 2066, Fax 353 2942,
Pro 353 0330, Sec 353 2942
4 miles NW of Sutton Coldfield off
A454.
Parkland course.
Pro John Anderson; Founded 1908
Designed by Harry Vardon
18 holes, 6670 yards, S.S.S. 73
Visitors: welcome by arrangement.
Green Fees: WD £50; WE £50.
Societies: welcome Tues, Wed and
Fri by prior arrangement; catering and
golf packages available; from £50.
Catering: full clubhouse facilities.

6A 83 Llanymynech
Pant, Oswestry, Shropshire, SY10 8LB
☎(01691) 830542, Pro 830879, Sec
830983
6 miles S of Oswestry on A483; take
turning at Cross Guns Inn at Pant
Hilltop; 4th hole tee in Wales, green in
England.
Pro Andrew Griffiths; Founded 1933
18 holes, 6114 yards, S.S.S. 69
Visitors: welcome by arrangement.
Green Fees: WD £15; WE £20.
Societies: welcome WD except Thurs;
catering available by prior arrange-
ment; from £15.
Catering: bar and restaurant facilities.
Hotels: many in Oswestry area.

6A 84 Ludlow
Bromfield, Ludlow, Shropshire SY8 2BT
☎(01584) 856285, Pro 856366
1 mile N of Ludlow off A49.
Heathland course.
Pro Russell Price; Founded 1889
18 holes, 6277 yards, S.S.S. 70
Visitors: welcome.
Green Fees: WD £18; WE £24.
Societies: welcome by prior arrange-
ment; terms on application.
Catering: clubhouse facilities.
Hotels: Feathers, Ludlow.

6A 85 Lymm
Whitbarrow Rd, Lymm, Cheshire,
WA13 9AN
☎(01925) 752217, Pro 755054, Sec
755020
5 miles SE of Warrington.
Parkland course.
Pro Steve McCarthy; Founded 1907
18 holes, 6304 yards, S.S.S. 70
Visitors: welcome WD; Thurs ladies
day no visitors before 2.30pm; with
member at WE.
Green Fees: WD £20.

Societies: welcome usually on Wed;
winter packages.
Catering: full meals facilities.
Hotels: Lymm; Statham Lodge.

6A 86 Macclesfield
The Hollins, Macclesfield, Cheshire,
SK11 7EA
☎(01625) 423227, Fax 260061, Pro
616952, Sec 615845
From the southern end of the A523
(Silk Road), turn into Windmill St.
Parkland/heathland course.
Pro Tony Taylor; Founded 1889
Designed by Hawtree & Son
18 holes, 5769 yards, S.S.S. 68
Visitors: welcome.
Green Fees: WD £20; WE £25.
Societies: welcome by arrangement;
packages available; contact Sec;
terms on application.
Catering: full clubhouse facilities.
Hotels: Sutton Hall.

6A 87 Malkins Bank
Betchton Rd, Sandbach, Cheshire,
CW11 4XN
☎(01270) 767878, Pro 765931
1.5 miles from M6 junction 17.
Municipal parkland course course.
Pro David Wheeler; Founded 1980
Designed by Hawtree & Son
18 holes, 5971 yards, S.S.S. 69
Visitors: welcome; booking system in
operation.
Green Fees: WD £6.50; WE £7.50.
Societies: welcome daily.
Catering: bar and catering daily.
Hotels: Old Hall; Saxon Cross Motel.

6A 88 The Manor Golf Club (Kingstone) Ltd
Leese Hill, Kingstone,
Uttoxeter, Staffordshire, ST14 8QT
☎(01889) 563234
On the main Uttoxeter to Stafford road.
Parkland course.
Founded 1992
Designed by David Gough
18 holes, 5360 yards, S.S.S. 69
Visitors: welcome.
Green Fees: WD £10; WE £15
Societies: welcome by arrangement
Catering: bar and catering: facilities
Practice range, 5-bay driving range,
putting green.

6A 89 Market Drayton
Sutton, Market Drayton, Shropshire,
TF9 2HX
☎(01630) 652266

1.5 miles S of Market Drayton.
Undulating meadowland.
Pro Russell Clewes; Founded 1911
18 holes, 6290 yards, S.S.S. 71
Visitors: welcome except Sun.
Green Fees: WD £22; WE £22.
Societies: welcome by arrangement.
Catering: full facilities.
Hotels: bungalow at course (sleeps
six); Bear; Corbet Arms.

6A 90 Marple
Bransfold Rd, Hawk Green, Marple,
Stockport, Cheshire, SK6 7EL
☎(0161) 427 2311, Fax 427 1125,
Pro 427 1195, Sec 427 1125
Signposted from Hawk Green.
Parkland course.
Pro David Myers; Founded 1892
18 holes, 5552 yards, S.S.S. 67
Visitors: welcome except comp days.
Green Fees: WD £20; WE £30.
Societies: welcome by prior arrange-
ment; golf and catering packages
available; from £32.50.
Catering: clubhouse facilities.

6A 91 Mellor & Townscliffe
Tarden, Gibb Lane, Mellor, Stockport,
Cheshire, SK6 5NA
☎(0161) 427 2208, Pro 427 5759,
Sec 442 2208
Off A626 opposite Devonshire Arms
on Longhurst Lane, Mellor.
Parkland/moorland course.
Pro Gary Broadley; Founded 1894
22 holes, 5925 yards, S.S.S. 69
Visitors: welcome except Sat.
Green Fees: WD £20; WE £27.50.
Societies: welcome by prior arrange-
ment; winter packages available.
Catering: full facilities except Tues.
Hotels: Pack Horse Inn.

6A 92 Meole Brace
Meole Brace, Shrewsbury, Shropshire,
SY2 6QQ
☎(01743) 364050
At junction of A5/A49 S of Shrewsbury.
Municipal course with water features.
Pro Stuart McKane; Founded 1976
12 holes, 5830 yards, S.S.S. 68
Visitors: welcome.
Green Fees: WD £5.50; WE £7.
Societies: welcome any time.
Catering: limited.

6A 93 Mere Golf & Country Club
Chester Rd, Mere, Knutsford,
Cheshire, WA16 6LJ

☎(01565) 830155, Fax 830713, Pro 830219
1 mile E of M6 junction 19 on A556; 2 miles W of M56 junction 7.
Parkland course.
Pro Peter Eyre; Founded 1934
Designed by George Duncan and James Braid
18 holes, 6817 yards, S.S.S. 73
Visitors: welcome Mon, Tues and Thurs by prior arrangement.
Green Fees: WD £60; WE £60.
Societies: welcome Mon, Tues and Thurs by arrangement; full range of clubhouse facilities, golf days and golf packages; terms on application.
Catering: bar and restaurant service.
Hotels: Cottons.

6A 94 Mersey Valley
Warrington Rd, Bold Heath, Nr Widnes, Cheshire, WA8 3XL
☎(0151) 424 6060, Fax 424 6060
Leave M62 junction 7; 1.5 miles on A57 towards Warrington.
Parkland course.
Pro Andy Stevenson; Founded 1995
Designed by Mellion Leisure
18 holes, 6374 yards, S.S.S. 70
Visitors: welcome.
Green Fees: WD £15; WE £20.
Societies: welcome by arrangement; deposit required; packages available for 18 and 27 holes of golf with meals; from £26.
Catering: bar and bar snacks; function suite available.
Practice area.
Hotels: Hillcrest, Widnes.

6A 95 Mile End
Mile End, Oswestry, Shropshire, SY11 4JE
☎(01691) 670580, Pro 671246
1 mile SE of Oswestry; signposted from A5.
Parkland course(converted farmland).
Pro Scott Carpenter; Founded 1992
Designed by Michael Price/D Gough
18 holes, 6194 yards, S.S.S. 69
Visitors: welcome.
Green Fees: WD £13; WE £17.
Societies: welcome WD by prior arrangement; terms on application.
Catering: full clubhouse facilities.
Practice range, 12 bays floodlit.
Hotels: Wynnstay; Sweeney Hall.

6A 96 Mobberley
Burleyhurst Lane, Mobberley, Knutsford, Cheshire, WA16 7JZ
☎(01505) 880178, Pro 880188

From M56 junction 6 head towards Wilmslow and after Moat House turn right.
Parkland course.
Pro Robin Welsby; Founded 1995
9 holes, 5542 yards, S.S.S. 67
Visitors: welcome.
Green Fees: WD £12.50; WE £16.
Societies: welcome by prior arrangement.
Catering: bar and restaurant.
Practice range, practice area; indoor teaching facilities.
Hotels: Moat House; Boddington Arms.

6A 97 Mottram Hall Hotel
Wilmslow Road, Mottram St Andrew, Prestbury, Cheshire, SK10 4QT
☎(01625) 820064
From M56 junction 6 follow A538 through Wilmslow; follow signposts.
Parkland/woodland course.
Pro Tim Rastall; Founded 1991
Designed by David Thomas
18 holes, 7006 yards, S.S.S. 74
Visitors: welcome with h'cap certs.
Green Fees: WD £39; WE £44.
Societies: welcome by arrangement; packages available; on-course drink/food buggy; leisure centre.
Catering: full clubhouse and hotel facilities.
Hotels: Mottram Hall on site (133 beds).

6A 98 New Mills
Shaw Marsh, New Mills, High Peak, Cheshire, SK22 3QD
☎(01663) 743485, Pro 746161
0.75 miles from centre of New Mills on St Mary Rd.
Moorland course.
Pro Stephen James; Founded 1907
9 holes, 5633 yards, S.S.S. 67
Visitors: welcome WD and Sat mornings except on competition days.
Green Fees: WD £20.
Societies: welcome WD by prior arrangement; from £26.
Catering: bar and clubhouse catering.
Hotels: Pack Horse; Sportsman; Moorside.

6A 99 Newcastle Municipal
Keele Rd, Newcastle under Lyme, Staffs, ST5 5AB
☎(01782) 627596
Off M6 junction 15, on A525 for 2 miles.
Public parkland course.
Pro Colin Smith; Founded 1975

18 holes, 6396 yards, S.S.S. 70
Visitors: Welcome; book any time.
Green Fees: WD £7.25; WE £8.70.
Societies: welcome on application to local council.
Catering: bar and meals.
Practice range, 26 bays floodlit (01782 717417)
Hotels: Keele Hospitality Inn.

6A 100 Newcastle-under-Lyme
Whitmore Rd, Newcastle-under-Lyme, Staffs, ST5 2QB
☎(01782) 618526
1.5 miles SW of Newcastle-under-Lyme on A53.
Parkland course.
Pro Paul Symonds; Founded 1908
18 holes, 6317 yards, S.S.S. 71
Visitors: welcome WD.
Green Fees: WD £25.
Societies: welcome on Mon all day and Thurs pm; packages on application; snooker.
Catering: bar and restaurant.
Hotels: Post House; Borough Arms.

6A 101 Northenden
Palatine Rd, Northenden, Manchester, M22 4FR
☎(0161) 998 4738, Fax 945 5592, Pro 945 3386, Bar/Rest 998 4079
0.5 miles from M56 junction 9; M63 junction 9.
Parkland course.
Pro Peter Scott; Founded 1913
Designed by T Renouf
18 holes, 6503 yards, S.S.S. 71
Visitors: welcome by arrangement.
Green Fees: WD £25; WE £30.
Societies: welcome Tues and Fri; packages include 27 holes of golf; coffee and bacon sandwich on arrival; light lunch and dinner; £41.
Catering: full clubhouse facilities.
Hotels: Britannia Country House; Post House, Northenden.

6A 102 Onneley
Onneley, Crewe, Cheshire, CW3 5QF
☎(01782) 750577
1 mile from Woore on A51 to Newcastle.
Undulating meadowland course.
Founded 1968
9 holes, 5474 yards, S.S.S. 67
Visitors: welcome WD; WE only with a member.
Green Fees: WD £15.
Societies: welcome by prior arrangement with Sec; from £18.
Catering: clubhouse facilities.
Hotels: Wheatsheaf.

6A 103 Oswestry

Aston Park, Oswestry, Shropshire, SY11 4JJ
☎(01691) 610221, Fax 610535, Pro 610448, Sec 610535
3 miles SE of Oswestry on A5.
Parkland course.
Pro David Skelton; Founded 1930
Designed by James Braid
18 holes, 6024 yards, S.S.S. 69
Visitors: welcome with h'cap certs.
Green Fees: WD £20; WE £28.
Societies: welcome Wed and Fri; packages available; from £31.
Catering: full clubhouse facilities.

6A 104 Oxley Park

Bushbury, Wolverhampton, W Midlands, WV10 6DE
☎(01902) 420506; Pro 425445, Sec 425892
On A449 1 mile N of Wolverhampton.
Parkland course.
Pro Les Burliston; Founded 1913
18 holes, 6222 yards, S.S.S. 70
Visitors: welcome; only with a member at WE in winter.
Green Fees: WD £25; WE £25.
Societies: welcome Wed by arrangement; snooker.
Catering: full clubhouse catering.
Hotels: Mount; Goldthorn; Park Hall.

6A 105 Parkhall

Hulme Road, Weston Coyney, Stoke-on-Trent, Staffs, ST3 5BH
☎(01782) 599584
1 mile outside Longton on A50.
Public moorland course.
Founded 1989
18 holes, 4770 yards, S.S.S. 54
Visitors: welcome.
Green Fees: WD £4.50; WE £5.
Societies: welcome by arrangement.
Catering: none.

6A 106 Patshull Park Hotel Golf and Country Club

Pattingham, Wolverhampton, WV6 7HR
☎(01902) 700100, Fax 700874, Pro 700342
From A41 Wolverhampton-Whitchurch road follow signs to Pattingham.
Parkland course.
Pro R Bissell; Founded 1972
Designed by John Jacobs
18 holes, 6412 yards, S.S.S. 72
Visitors: welcome with h'cap certs.
Green Fees: WD £22.50; WE £27.50.
Societies: welcome by prior arrangement with golf reservations; full day of golf and catering; leisure facilities; banqueting and conference facilities; snooker table; £44.50.
Catering: full clubhouse and hotel facilities.
Practice ground.
Hotels: Patshull Park Hotel on site.

6A 107 Penkridge G & CC

Pottal Pool Rd, Penkridge, Stafford, Staffs, ST19 5RN
☎(01785) 716455
Off A34 at Penkridge/ Rugeley cross roads; turn to Penkridge and course is 0.75 miles on left; from M6 junction 12, take A5 towards Telford, then A449 followed by B5102 towards Cannock, turning left in Pottal Pool Rd after Wolgarston School.
Parkland course.
Pro Andrew Preston; Founded 1995
Designed by John Reynolds
18 holes, 6613 yards, S.S.S. 72
Visitors: welcome.
Green Fees: WD £15; WE £20.
Societies: welcome by arrangement; deposit required; discounts for larger groups; video analysis; from £16.
Catering: clubhouse due for mid 1998.
Practice range, 20 bay.
Hotels: Hatherton Country Hotel.

6A 108 Penn

Penn Common, Penn, Wolverhampton WV4 5JN
☎(01902) 341142, Pro 330472
On A449 2.5 miles W of Wolverhampton at Penn.
Heathland course.
Pro A Briscoe; Founded 1908
18 holes, 6462 yards, S.S.S. 71
Visitors: welcome WD; with member at WE.
Green Fees: WD £20; WE £10.
Societies: welcome Mon, Wed, Fri; reductions for groups of 20+; catering packages available; from £17.
Catering: full clubhouse facilities.

6A 109 Peover

Plumley Moor Road, Lower Peover, Cheshire, WA16 9SE
☎(01565) 723337, Fax 723311
Leave M6 junction 19 to A556; follow signs to Plumley and Lower Peover on Plumley Moor Rd; course 1.5 miles.
Parkland course.
Pro John Watson; Founded 1996
Designed by P Naylor
18 holes, 6702 yards, S.S.S. 72
Visitors: welcome.

Green Fees: WD £16; WE £20.
Societies: welcome WD; packages available on application; from £15.
Catering: full clubhouse facilities.
Hotels: Belle Epoque.

6A 110 Perton Park Golf Club

Wrottesley Park Road, Perton, Wolverhampton, WV6 7HL
☎(01902) 380103, Fax 326219, Pro 380073, Sec 897031, Bar/Rest 380073
Just off the A454 Bridgnorth to Wolverhampton road.
Meadowland course.
Pro Jeremy Harrold; Founded 1990
18 holes, 6620 yards, S.S.S. 70
Visitors: welcome with tee time from starter.
Green Fees: WD £10; WE £15.
Societies: welcome by prior arrangement; golf and catering packages available; from £15.
Catering: full clubhouse facilities available.
Practice range, 18 bay range.

6A 111 Portal Golf & Country Club

Cobblers Cross, Tarporley, Cheshire, CW6 0DJ
☎(01829) 733933, Fax 733928
11 miles SE of Chester off A49 near Tarporley.
Parkland course; 3rd: Haddington's Ground, 602 yards.
Pro Mike Slater; Founded 1989
Designed by Donald Steel
18 holes, 7037 yards, S.S.S. 74
Visitors: welcome by arrangement.
Green Fees: WD £40; WE £40.
Societies: welcome by arrangement; packages available; also Ardene course, par 30; from £35.
Catering: restaurant and bar facilities.
Hotels: The Swan, Tarporley; Wild Boar, Beeston; Nunsmere Hotel.

6A 112 Portal G & Country Club Premier Course

Forest Rd, Tarporley, Cheshire, CW6 0JA
☎(01829) 733884, Fax 733666, Pro 733445, Bar/Rest 733445
1 mile S of Tarporley between Chester and Northwich.
Parkland course.
Pro Judy Statham; Founded 1990
Designed by T Rouse
18 holes, 6508 yards, S.S.S. 72
Visitors: welcome.
Green Fees: WD £22; WE £30.

Societies: welcome by prior arrangement; on application; from £30.
Catering: full clubhouse facilities.
Hotels: Swan, Tarporley; Wild Boar, Beeston.

6A 113 Poulton Park

Dig Lane, Off Crab Lane, Cinnamon Brow, Cheshire, WA2 0SH
☎(01925) 812034, Pro 825220, Sec 822802
3 miles from Warrington off A574.
Parkland course.
Pro Darren Newing; Founded 1978
9 holes, 4978 yards, S.S.S. 66
Visitors: welcome by arrangement.
Green Fees: WD £18; WE £18.
Societies: welcome by prior arrangement; packages for golf and catering available; minimum 8; £20-£26.
Catering: clubhouse facilities.

6A 114 Prenton

Golf Links Rd, Prenton, Birkenhead, Wirral, L42 8LW
☎(0151) 608 1461, Fax 609 1580, Pro 608 1636, Sec 608 1053
From M53 junction 2 take A552 towards Birkenhead.
Parkland course.
Pro Robin Thompson; Founded 1905
Designed by Colt MacKenzie & Co
18 holes, 6429 yards, S.S.S. 71
Visitors: welcome by arrangement.
Green Fees: WD £30; WE £35.
Societies: welcome by prior arrangement; Golf and catering packages available; from £24.
Catering: full clubhouse bar and catering facilities.
Practice range, two practice areas.

6A 115 Prestbury

Macclesfield Rd, Prestbury, Cheshire, SK10 4BJ
☎(01625) 829388, Fax 828241, Pro 828242, Sec 828241, Bar/Rest 829997
2 miles NW of Macclesfield.
Parkland course.
Pro Nick Summerfield; Founded 1920
Designed by Colt & Morrison
18 holes, 6359 yards, S.S.S. 71
Visitors: welcome by prior arrangement on WD; with a member at WE.
Green Fees: WD £38; WE £38.
Societies: welcome Thurs; minimum 20; from £34.
Catering: full clubhouse bar and catering facilities.
Hotels: Bridge; White House, both Prestbury.

6A 116 Pryors Hayes Golf Club

Willington Road, Oscroft, Tarvin, Nr Chester, Cheshire, CH3 8NL
☎(01829) 741250, Fax 741250, Pro 740140, Bar/Rest 741538
5 miles from Chester near Tarvin between A54 and A51.
Parkland course.
Founded 1993
Designed by John Day
18 holes, 6074 yards, S.S.S. 69
Visitors: welcome by prior booking.
Green Fees: WD £15; WE £20.
Societies: welcome every day by prior arrangement; catering and golf packages available; from £17.
Catering: clubhouse facilities.
Hotels: Willington Hall.

6A 117 Queen's Park

Queen's Park Drive, Crewe, Cheshire, CW2 7SB
☎(01270) 662378, Pro 666724, Sec 628352, Bar/Rest 666724
1.5 miles from town centre off Victoria Avenue.
Parkland course.
Pro H Bilton; Founded 1985
9 holes, 4922 yards, S.S.S. 64
Visitors: pay and play; restrictions until 11am Sun.
Green Fees: WD £5; WE £7.
Catering: clubhouse facilities.

6A 118 Reaseheath

Reaseheath College, Nantwich, Cheshire, CW5 6DF
☎(01270) 625131
1 mile from Nantwich on A51 Chester road.
Research course used for greenkeeper training.
Founded 1987
Designed by D. Mortram
9 holes, 3729 yards, S.S.S. 54
Visitors: limited availability.
Green Fees: WD £5; WE £5.
Societies: small groups; minimum 8; by prior arrangement.
Catering: restaurant on site WD.

6A 119 Reddish Vale

Southcliffe Rd, Reddish, Stockport, Cheshire, SK5 7EE
☎(0161) 480 2359, Pro 480 3824, Bar/Rest 480 1521
1.5 miles N of Stockport off B6167 Reddish road.
Undulating course in valley.
Founded 1912
Designed by Dr A. MacKenzie

18 holes, 6086 yards, S.S.S. 69
Visitors: welcome WD (lunchtime restrictions); with member at WE.
Green Fees: WD £22.
Societies: welcome WD by prior arrangement; packages available.
Catering: restaurant and bar service.
Hotels: Belgrade; Old Rectory; Haughton Green.

6A 120 Ringway

Hale Rd, Hale Barns, Altrincham, Cheshire, WA15 8SW
☎(0161) 980 8432, Pro 980 5769, Sec 980 2630, Bar/Rest 904 0940
8 miles S of Manchester 1 mile from M56 junction 6 on the A538 towards Altrincham through Hale Barns.
Parkland course.
Pro Nick Ryan; Founded 1909
Designed by Harry Colt and James Braid
18 holes, 6494 yards, S.S.S. 71
Visitors: welcome except Fri; Tues & Sat are club competition days.
Green Fees: WD £28; WE £34.
Societies: welcome Thurs in summer by prior arrangement; packages available; corporate days organised; snooker.
Catering: full facilities.
Hotels: Cresta Court; Four Seasons; Unicorn.

6A 121 Romiley

Goosehouse Green, Romiley, Stockport, Cheshire, SK6 4LJ
☎(0161) 430 2392
On B6104 off A560 0.75 miles from Romiley station.
Undulating parkland course.
Pro Gary Butler; Founded 1897
18 holes, 6454 yards, S.S.S. 71
Visitors: welcome except Thurs (Ladies day).
Green Fees: WD £30; WE £30.
Societies: welcome Tues and Wed by prior arrangement.
Catering: full clubhouse service.
Hotels: Almonds, Marple.

6A 122 Royal Liverpool

Meols Drive, Hoylake, Wirral, Merseyside, L47 4AL
☎(0151) 632 3101, Fax 632 6737, Pro 632 5868, Bar/Rest 632 3102
On A540 between Hoylake and West Kirby, off junction 2 of M53.
Championship links course.
Pro John Heggarty; Founded 1869
Designed by Robert Chambers & George Morris

18 holes, 7128 yards, S.S.S. 76
Visitors: welcome midweek between 9.30am-1pm and 2pm-4pm except Thurs; limited WE availability.
Green Fees: WD £56; WE £56.
Societies: welcome by prior arrangement only; from £56, including snack lunch except July; full facilities.
Catering: full restaurant and clubhouse facilities.
Practice ground.
Hotels: Thornton Hall, Thornton-le-Hough; Crabwell Manor, Mollington.

6A 123 Runcorn

Clifton Rd, Runcorn, Cheshire, WA7 4SU
☎(01928) 572093, Pro 564791, Sec 574214, Bar/Rest 574214
M56 junction 12; signposted off A557.
Parkland course.
Pro S Dooley; Founded 1909
18 holes, 6035 yards, S.S.S. 69
Visitors: welcome WD except Tues; WE with member.
Green Fees: WD £18; WE £9.
Societies: welcome Mon and Fri; Includes coffee, lunch and dinner for groups of 12 or more; from £25.
Catering: clubhouse facilities.
Hotels: Lord Daresbury, Warrington.

6A 24 St Michael Jubilee

Dundalk Rd, Widnes, Cheshire, WA4 8BS
☎(0151) 424 5636, Pro 424 6230, Sec 424 6461
Close to centre of Widnes off the Runcorn Bridge.
Public parkland course.
Pro Darren Chapman; Founded 1977
18 holes, 5667 yards, S.S.S. 68
Visitors: welcome WD; with bookings at WE.
Green Fees: WD £6; WE £7.
Societies: welcome by arrangement.
Catering: full facilities.
Practice area.
Hotels: Hillcrest.

6A 125 St Thomas's Priory Golf Club

Armitage Lane, Armitage, Nr. Rugeley, Staffordshire, WS15 1ED
☎(01543) 491116, Fax 492244, Pro 492096, Sec 491911, Bar/Rest 491911
1 mile SE of Rugeley on A513; opposite Ash Tree Inn.
Parkland course; 601 is 14th.
Pro Simon Berry; Founded 1995
Designed by Paul Mulholland
18 holes, 5969 yards, S.S.S. 70

Visitors: members' guests only.
Green Fees: terms on application.
Societies: welcome by prior arrangement; terms on application.
Catering: full clubhouse facilities.
Hotels: Riverside Inn; Holiday Inn Express, both Branston.

6A 126 Sale

Sale Lodge, Golf Rd, Sale, Cheshire, M33 2XU
☎(0161) 973 1730, Fax 962 4217, Sec 973 1638, Bar/Rest 973 3404
Close to M63 junction 8.
Parkland course.
Pro Mike Stewart; Founded 1913
18 holes, 6358 yards, S.S.S. 70
Visitors: welcome WD.
Green Fees: WD £28
Societies: welcome by arrangement with the secretary/manager; golf and food packages available on application; terms on application.
Catering: clubhouse facilities.
Hotels: Dane Lodge, Sale.

6A 127 Sandbach

117 Middlewich Rd, Sandbach, Cheshire, CW11 1FH
☎(01270) 762117, Bar/Rest 759227
1 mile N of Sandbach on A533.
Meadowland course.
Founded 1921
9 holes, 5598 yards, S.S.S. 67
Visitors: welcome WD; WE by invitation.
Green Fees: WD £16; WE £16.
Societies: limited; by prior arrangement.
Catering: full facilities except Mon and Tues.
Hotels: Saxon Cross Motel; Old Hall.

6A 128 Sandiway

Chester Rd, Sandiway, Northwich, Cheshire, CW8 2DJ
☎(01606) 883247, Fax 888548, Pro 883180
On A556 14 miles E of Chester, 4 miles from Northwich.
Undulating parkland course.
Pro Bill Laird; Founded 1921
Designed by Ted Ray
18 holes, 6404 yards, S.S.S. 72
Visitors: welcome WD; WE by prior arrangement.
Green Fees: WD £35; WE £40.
Societies: welcome Tues by prior arrangement; packages available; terms on application.
Catering: full clubhouse facilities.
Hotels: Hartford Hall; Oaklands.

6A 129 Sandwell Park

Birmingham Rd, West Bromwich, W Midlands, B71 4JJ
☎(0121) 553 4637, Fax 525 1651, Pro 553 4384, Bar/Rest 525 4151
On A41 Birmingham road, 200 yards from M5 junction 1.
Heathland course.
Pro Nigel Wylie; Founded 1897
Designed by H S Colt
18 holes, 6470 yards, S.S.S. 72
Visitors: welcome WD.
Green Fees: WD £30 .
Societies: welcome WD by prior arrangement; reductions for bigger parties; catering facilities available; from £25.
Catering: full restaurant facilities and two bars.
Hotels: West Bromwich Moat House.

6A 130 Sedgley Golf Centre

Sandyfields Rd, Sedgley, Dudley, W Midlands, DY3 3DL
☎(01902) 880503
Off A463 0.5 miles from Sedgley town centre near Cotwell End Nature reserve.
Parkland course on the side of a valley with mature trees.
Pro Garry Mercer; Founded 1989
Designed by W.G. Cox
9 holes, 6294 yards, S.S.S. 70
Visitors: pay and play course.
Green Fees: WD £5.50; WE £5.50.
Societies: welcome by arrangement; snacks available; terms on application.
Catering: snacks.
Practice range, 16 bays covered and floodlit.

6A 131 Seedy Mill

Elm Hurst, Lichfield, Staffs, WS13 8HE
☎(01543) 417333, Fax 418098
3 miles N of Lichfield off A51.
Parkland course with lakes, ponds and streams.
Pro Richard O'Hanlon; Founded 1991
Designed by Hawtree & Sons
18 holes, 6305 yards, S.S.S. 70
Visitors: welcome; pay and play.
Green Fees: WD £19; WE £24.
Societies: welcome by prior arrangement; limited WE access; packages available for food and golf ranging from £24-£43; corporate days available; also Spires course, par 3; from £24.
Catering: full clubhouse bar and restaurant facilities.
Practice range, 26 bays floodlit.
Hotels: Little Barrow, Lichfield.

6A 132 **Severn Meadows**
Highley, Nr Bridgnorth, Shropshire,
WV16 6HZ
☎(01746) 862212
10 miles N of Bewdley; 8 miles S of
Bridgenorth.
Hilly parkland course in Severn valley.
Pro Martin Payne; Founded 1989
9 holes, 5258 yards, S.S.S. 67
Visitors: welcome WD; pay and play;
must book WE.
Green Fees: WD £12; WE £14.
Societies: welcome by arrangement.
Catering: clubhouse facilities.
Hotels: Bull, Chelmarsh.

6A 133 **Shifnal**
Decker Hill, Shifnal, Shropshire, TF11
8QL
☎(01952) 460467, Fax 460330, Pro
460457, Sec 460330
1 mile N of Shifnal close to M54 junc-
tion 4.
Parkland course.
Pro J Flanagan; Founded 1929/1963
Designed by Frank Pennink
18 holes, 6468 yards, S.S.S. 71
Visitors: welcome by arrangement.
Green Fees: WD £22; WE £22.
Societies: welcome Tues, Wed and
Fri; reductions for groups of 20 or
more; terms on application.
Catering: full clubhouse bar and
catering facilities.
Hotels: Park House.

6A 134 **Shrewsbury**
Condover, Shrewsbury, Shropshire,
SY5 7BL
☎(01743) 872976, Pro 873751, Sec
872977
S of Shrewsbury off A49.
Parkland course.
Pro Peter Seal; Founded 1890/1972
Designed by C.K. Cotton, Pennink,
Lawrie & Partners
18 holes, 6205 yards, S.S.S. 70
Visitors: welcome WD; after 2pm
Wed; WE between 10am-12 noon and
after 2pm.
Green Fees: WD £19; WE £23.
Societies: welcome Mon and Fri; lim-
ited availability Tues, Thurs and Sun
am; packages can be arranged
through the professional; terms on
application.
Catering: full clubhouse facilities.
Hotels: Shrewsbury Hotel.

6A 135 **Shrigley Hall Hotel**
Shrigley Park, Pott Shrigley,
Macclesfield, Cheshire, SK10 5SB
☎(01625) 575757 x 760, Fax
573323, Pro 575626, Sec 575757,
Bar/Rest 575757 x 727
Off A523 Macclesfield road; signpost-
ed Pott Shrigley from Adlington.
Parkland course.
Pro G A Ogden; Founded 1989
Designed by Donald Steel
18 holes, 6281 yards, S.S.S. 71
Visitors: welcome by arrangement.
Green Fees: WD £28/ Fri £35; WE
£35.
Societies: welcome WD by prior
arrangement; packages can be
arranged; terms on application.
Catering: full clubhouse and hotel
facilities.
Practice range, 20-bay floodlit range
opens April 1998.
Hotels: 150-room Shrigley Hall Hotel
on site.

6A 136 **The Shropshire**
Muxton Grange, Muxton, Telford,
Shropshire, TF2 8PQ
☎(01952) 677800, Fax 677622, Pro
677866
From M54/A5 take B5060, turning
right at Granville roundabout; course
opposite equestrian centre.
Parkland course; 3 loops of 9 holes.
Pro Daniel Bateman; Founded 1992
Designed by Martin Hawtree
27 holes, 6637 yards, S.S.S. 72
Visitors: welcome.
Green Fees: WD £15; WE £20.
Societies: welcome everyday; mini-
mum 8; catering and golf packages
available; private room; from £20.
Catering: restaurant and three bars.
Practice range, 30 bays covered flood-
lit.
Hotels: White House, Muxton; Telford
Moat House.

6A 137 **South Staffordshire**
Danescourt Rd, Tettenhall,
Wolverhampton, WV6 9BQ
☎(01902) 751065, Pro 754816
On A41 from Wolverhampton in
Tettenhall; clubhouse and course
behind cricket club.
Parkland course.
Pro Jim Rhodes; Founded 1892
Designed by Harry Vardon (original);
H.S. Colt
18 holes, 6513 yards, S.S.S. 71
Visitors: welcome except Tues am.
Green Fees: WD £34; WE £45.
Societies: welcome except Tues am
and WE.
Catering: clubhouse catering and bar.
Hotels: Mount; Connaught.

6A 138 **Stafford Castle**
Newport Rd, Stafford, Staffs, ST16
1BP
☎(01785) 223821
On A518 1 mile from Stafford Castle.
Parkland course.
Founded 1907
9 holes, 6382 yards, S.S.S. 70
Visitors: welcome by arrangement.
Green Fees: WD £14; WE £14.
Societies: welcome Mon and Fri by
arrangement; terms on application.
Catering: clubhouse restaurant and
bar facilities.
Hotels: Tillington Hall.

6A 139 **Stamford (Stalybridge)**
Oakfield House, Huddersfield Rd,
Stalybridge, Cheshire, SK15 3PY
☎(01457) 836550, Pro 834829,
Bar/Rest 834829
On B6175 NE of Stalybridge.
Parkland/moorland course.
Pro Brian Badger; Founded 1901
18 holes, 5701 yards, S.S.S. 68
Visitors: welcome WD.
Green Fees: WD £20; WE £20.
Societies: welcome by prior arrange-
ment, minimum 12; packages include
27 holes of golf, lunch and dinner;
from £30.
Catering: clubhouse facilities.

6A 140 **Stockport**
Offerton Rd, Offerton, Stockport, SK2
5DB
☎(0161) 427 2001, Fax 449 8293,
Pro 427 2421, Sec 427 8369, Bar/Rest
427 4425
Take A627 Torkington road from A6;
course 1.5 miles on right.
Parkland course.
Pro Mike Peel; Founded 1906
18 holes, 6326 yards, S.S.S. 71
Visitors: welcome by arrangement.
Green Fees: WD £35; WE £45.
Societies: welcome Wed and Thurs;
minimum 20 players; catering and golf
packages available; from £35.
Catering: full clubhouse bar and
restaurant service.
Hotels: Moorside, Disley; Britannia,
Offerton; Alma Lodge, Stockport.

6A 141 **Stone**
The Filleybrooks, Stone, Staffs, ST15
0NB
☎(01785) 813103, Sec 284875
1 miles NW of Stone on A34.
Parkland course.
Founded 1896
9 holes, 6299 yards, S.S.S. 70

THE TYTHERINGTON CLUB

The ideal venue for your golf day or a casual round.
Headquarters of the Women's Professional European Tour.

The Tytherington Club, Dorchester Way, Tytherington, Macclesfield, Cheshire SK10 2JP. Tel: 01625 434562 • Fax: 01625 430882

Visitors: welcome WD; WE only with a member.
Green Fees: WD £20; WE £20.
Societies: welcome by arrangement; catering packages available; terms on application.
Catering: clubhouse catering facilities.
Hotels: Stone House.

6A 142 Styal

Station Road, Styal, Cheshire, SK9 4JN
☎(01625) 530063, Fax 530063
Off M56 junction 5 at Manchester Airport; straight on at roundabout instead of turning to Airport; at end of Ringway road turn right into Styal Road; club 1 mile.
Parkland course.
Pro G Traynor; Founded 1995
Designed by T Holmes
18 holes, 6301 yards, S.S.S. 70
Visitors: welcome.
Green Fees: WD £12; WE £16.
Societies: welcome by prior arrangement; packages available; driving range; from £25.
Catering: clubhouse catering and bar.
Practice range, 24 bays.
Hotels: Stanneylands; Hilton at Manchester Airport.

6A 143 Sutton Hall

Sutton Hall, Aston Lane, Sutton Weaver, Cheshire, WA7 3ED
☎(01928) 790747, Fax 790040, Pro 714872, Sec 790007, Bar/Rest 715530
M56 junction 12, following signs to Frodsham; turn left at swingbridge for course.
Parkland course.
Pro A Roberts; Founded 1995
Designed by S Wundke
18 holes, 6547 yards, S.S.S. 71
Visitors: welcome.
Green Fees: WD £16; WE £20.
Societies: welcome WD; some at WE; packages for catering and golf available for groups of more than 10; groups up to 100 can be catered for; from £20.
Catering: full catering and bar.
Hotels: Forte Crest, Beechwood.

6A 144 Swindon

Bridgnorth Road, Swindon, Dudley, W Midlands, DY3 4PH
☎(01902) 897031, Fax 326219, Pro 896191, Bar/Rest 896765
On B4176 Dudley to Bridgnorth road; 3 miles off A449 at Himley.
Wooded parkland course with exceptional views.
Pro Phil Lester; Founded 1974
18 holes, 6091 yards, S.S.S. 69
Visitors: welcome.
Green Fees: WD £18; WE £27.
Societies: welcome by arrangement with J Smith; terms on application.
Catering: clubhouse facilities.
Practice range, 27 bays; also 9-hole course, par 3.
Hotels: Himley Country Club, Himley.

6A 145 Tamworth Municipal

Eagle Drive, Amington, Tamworth, Staffs, B77 4EG
☎(01827) 53850
From M42 junction 10 proceed towards Tamworth; signposted off B5000 Polesworth road.
Municipal parkland course.
Pro Daryl Scott; Founded 1975
18 holes, 6525 yards, S.S.S. 72
Visitors: welcome.
Green Fees: WD £8.40; WE £8.40.
Societies: welcome WD by appt.
Catering: bar and daily catering.
Hotels: Canada Lodge.

6A 146 Telford Golf & Country Club

Great Hay Drive, Telford, Shropshire, TF7 4DT
☎(01952) 429977, Fax 586602
Off A442 at Sutton Hill S of Telford.
Parkland course.
Pro Ian Duran; Founded 1975
Designed by John Harris
18 holes, 6761 yards, S.S.S. 72
Visitors: welcome.
Green Fees: WD £25; WE £30.
Societies: welcome by prior arrangement; all-day packages; full use of leisure facilities in hotel; from £25.
Catering: full clubhouse and hotel facilities.
Hotels: Telford Country Hotel on site.

6A 147 Three Hammers Golf Complex

Old Stafford Rd, Coven, Staffordshire, WV10 7PP
☎(01902) 790428, Pro 790940
From M54 junction 2 travel N on A449 course 1 mile on right.
Parkland course.
Pro Shaun Bell and Ted Large
Designed by Henry Cotton
18 holes, 1438 yards, S.S.S. 54
Visitors: welcome.
Green Fees: WD £5.50; WE £6.50.
Societies: welcome Mon-Sat.
Catering: bar, bistro, restaurant and private dining facilities.
Practice range, 23-bay floodlit range.

6A 148 Trentham

14 Barlaston Old Rd, Trentham, Stoke-on-Trent, Staffs, ST4 8HB
☎(01782) 642347, Fax 644024, Pro 657309, Sec 658109, Bar/Rest 643623
Off A34 from Stoke to Stone, turn left at Trentham Gardens.
Parkland course.
Pro Sandy Wilson; Founded 1894
18 holes, 6619 yards, S.S.S. 72
Visitors: welcome by prior arrangement.
Green Fees: WD £30; WE £30.
Societies: welcome Mon and Fri by prior arrangement; terms on application.
Catering: clubhouse facilities.
Practice ground.
Hotels: Trentham Hotel; Post House Hotel; Tollgate Leisure.

6A 149 Trentham Park

Trentham Park, Trentham, Stoke-on-Trent, ST4 8AE
☎(01782) 642245, Fax 658800, Pro 642125, Sec 658800, Bar/Rest 644130
On A34 4 miles S of Newcastle; 1 miles from M6 junction 15.
Parkland course.
Founded 1936
18 holes, 6425 yards, S.S.S. 71
Visitors: welcome by prior arrangement.
Green Fees: WD £22.50; WE £30.

The Tytherington

The Tytherington, near Macclesfield in Cheshire, is a modern parkland course and the home of the women's European Tour. Despite being able to boast some of the best golfers in the world, the Tour have had a hard time convincing sponsors to put their money into the women's game and in 1997 lost their main backers, American Express. Their chief executive Terry Coates, who had been given a rough ride throughout the year, also quit.

The Tour Players' Classic, hosted by The Tytherington in May 1997, was one of only three events held in Britain, the others being the Weetabix Women's Open at Sunningdale, and the McDonalds WPGA Championship of Europe at Gleneagles. There is no guarantee that the course will be repeating the experience in 1998, which will sadden the genial Australian Karen Lunn, who came from two strokes adrift on a memorable final day to win the tournament by one shot.

Trailing the Frenchwoman Patricia Meunier-Lebouc by two and the early leader, the German Tina Fischer, by one going into the last round, Lunn fired a one-under-par 71 to clinch the title with a five-under-par 283.

It is apt that the women's tour should base themselves at The Tytherington, for it is a club where male and female golfers pay the same subscriptions and enjoy equal rights. Apart from the men's and ladies' championships, the weekend competitions are played by both sexes in a harmony not evident at many other venues. Built in 1986 by a Cheshire building family, the Seddons, The Tytherington was seen by the local planning authority as a way of preventing further municipal development in an area where Maccles-field, Stockport and Manchester are just a short drive away. The Seddons – by all accounts keen as mustard golfers themselves – jumped at the chance to create a dream course. It may be in the heart of an urban conurbation, but it feels like the country and the Peak District hoves into view from certain vantage points.

The Seddons used the proximity of the course to sell their houses but two owners have come and gone since and the club is now in the hands of The Clubhouse Group, who own courses all over Europe, including The Warwickshire and Castle Royle in Berkshire.

As well as a golf facility, it is also a leisure club and has busy public bars and function rooms which keep the business side of things ticking over nicely. The course, however, is in super shape and is tended lovingly by Mike Goodhind, the UK Greenkeeper of the Year in 1995.

Built on gently undulating parkland, the course looks far more mature than its 12 years. There is gorgeous tree coverage and an imaginative use of water. The club believe they have the best lay-out of any inland course in the north of England, and there is one happy Australian who would certainly agree with that.

Societies: welcome Wed and Fri by prior arrangement; packages for golf and catering available; from £22.50.
Catering: clubhouse facilities.

6A 150 The Tytherington

Dorchester Way, Macclesfield, Cheshire, SK10 2JP
☎(01625) 434562, Fax 430882, Bar/Rest 434327
2 miles from Macclesfield on the A523 Stockport road.
Parkland course; home of WPGA European Tour.
Pro Jonathon Foss; Founded 1986
Designed by Dave Thomas and Patrick Dawson
18 holes, 6765 yards, S.S.S. 74
Visitors: welcome with h'cap certs.
Green Fees: WD £28; WE £34.
Societies: welcome WD by prior arrangement; full facilities for golf and catering packages; private rooms; snooker and pool; health club; tennis; terms on application.
Catering: restaurant, bars and full catering facilities.
Hotels: contact club for details.

6A 151 Upton-by-Chester

Upton Lane, Chester, Cheshire, CH2 1EE
☎(01244) 381183, Pro 381333
Off A41 Chester-Liverpool road near Chester zoo.
Parkland course.
Pro Peter Gardener; Founded 1934
18 holes, 5850 yards, S.S.S. 68
Visitors: welcome except on competition days.
Green Fees: WD £25; WE £25.
Societies: welcome Wed, Thurs and Fri by prior arrangement.
Catering: full clubhouse facilities.
Hotels: Dene; Euromill; Mollington Banastre.

6A 152 Uttoxeter

Wood Lane, Uttoxeter, Staffs, ST14 8JR
☎(01889) 565108, Fax 566552, Pro 564884, Sec 566552
Off B5017 Uttoxeter-Marchington road 0.5 miles along Wood Lane just past the race course.
Parkland course with views over Dove valley.
Pro Adam McCandless; Founded 1972
18 holes, 5475 yards, S.S.S. 68
Visitors: welcome by arrangement.
Green Fees: WD £15; WE £20.
Societies: welcome by prior arrange-

ment; packages available for groups of 10; more than 20 free place for organiser; from £15.
Catering: extended and improved catering and restaurant facilities.
Hotels: White Hart; Bank Hotel, both Uttoxeter.

6A 153 Vicars Cross

Tarvin Rd, Great Barrow, Chester, CH3 7HN
☎(01244) 335174, Pro 335595
On A51 4 miles E of Chester.
Undulating parkland course.
Pro J Forsythe; Founded 1939
Designed by E. Parr
18 holes, 6243 yards, S.S.S. 70
Visitors: welcome except on competition days.
Green Fees: WD £22; WE £22.
Societies: welcome Tues and Thurs April-October except June; full golf and catering packages; from £31.50.
Catering: full clubhouse facilities.

6A 154 Wallasey

Bayswater Rd, Wallasey, Merseyside, L45 8LA
☎(0151) 691 1024, Fax 638 8988, Pro 638 3888
M53 junction 1 to A554 towards New Brighton 0.25 miles on left.
Links course.
Pro Mike Adams; Founded 1891
Designed by Tom Morris Snr
18 holes, 6607 yards, S.S.S. 73
Visitors: welcome by arrangement.
Green Fees: WD £35; WE £35.
Societies: welcome by prior arrangement; packages for groups of 16 or more; catering available; from £30.
Catering: clubhouse facilities.
Hotels: Grove House, Wallasey.

6A 155 Walsall

The Broadway, Walsall, WS1 3EY
☎(01922) 613512, Fax 616460, Pro 626766, Bar/Rest 622710
Off A34 1 mile S of Walsall.
Wooded parkland course.
Pro R Lambert; Founded 1907
Designed by Dr MacKenzie
18 holes, 6257 yards, S.S.S. 70
Visitors: welcome WD; WE as members guest.
Green Fees: WD £33; WE £33.
Societies: welcome WD by prior arrangement; catering and golf packages available for minimum 16; from £30.
Catering: clubhouse facilities.
Hotels: Boundary; County.

6A 156 Walton Hall

Warrington Rd, Higher Walton, Warrington, Cheshire, WA4 5LU
☎(01925) 266775, Pro 263061
1 mile from M56 junction 11.
Scenic parkland course.
Pro John Jackson; Founded 1972
Designed by Dave Thomas
18 holes, 6647 yards, S.S.S. 73
Visitors: welcome.
Green Fees: WD £8; WE £9.80.
Societies: welcome by prior arrangement with the Pro shop; terms on application.
Catering: full catering facilities in season; limited in winter.
Hotels: Lord Daresbury.

6A 157 Warren

The Grange, Grove Rd, Wallasey, Cheshire, L45 0JA
☎(0151) 693 5703
500 yards up Grove Rd by Grove Rd station.
Municipal links.
Pro Stephen Konrad; Founded 1911
9 holes, 5714 yards, S.S.S. 70
Visitors: welcome WD; book at WE.
Green Fees: WD £2.80; WE £2.80.
Societies: welcome by prior arrangement.
Hotels: Grove House.

6A 158 Warrington

London Rd, Appleton, Warrington, Cheshire, WA4 5HR
☎(01925) 261620, Fax 265933, Pro 265431, Sec 261775
On A49 1 mile from M56 junction 10.
Parkland course.
Pro Reay Mackay; Founded 1902
Designed by James Braid
18 holes, 6210 yards, S.S.S. 70
Visitors: welcome by prior arrangement.
Green Fees: WD £25; WE £30.
Societies: welcome on Wed by prior arrangement; summer and winter packages for golf and catering; from £36.
Catering: full clubhouse facilities. Practice ground.
Hotels: Birchdale Hotel, Stockton Heath.

6A 159 Wergs

Keepers Lane, Tettenhall, Wolverhampton, W Midlands, WV6 8UA
☎(01902) 742225, Fax 744748
Off A41 2.5 miles from Wolverhampton.

Open parkland course.
Founded 1990
Designed by C.W. Moseley
18 holes, 6949 yards, S.S.S. 73
Visitors: welcome.
Green Fees: WD £13.50; WE £17.
Societies: welcome WD; after 10am at WE; catering packages available; from £13.50.
Catering: clubhouse catering facilities available.

6A 160 **Werneth Low**

Werneth Low Rd, Hyde, Cheshire, SK14 3AF
☎(0161) 368 2503, Pro 367 9376
2 miles from Hyde town centre via Gee Cross and Joel Lane.
Hilltop course.
Pro Tony Bacchus; Founded 1912
Designed by Peter Campbell
11 holes, 6113 yards, S.S.S. 70
Visitors: welcome except Sun.
Green Fees: WD £18; WE £24.
Societies: WD by prior arrangement.
Catering: full catering facilities available.
Hotels: The Village, Hyde.

6A 161 **Westminster Park**

Hough Green, Chester, Cheshire, CH4 8JQ
☎(01244) 680231, Fax 680231
2 miles W of Chester city centre.
Parkland course.
Pro Jim Law; Founded 1980
9 holes, 1000 yards, S.S.S. 27
Visitors: pay and play.
Green Fees: WD £2.50; WE £2.50.
Societies: none.
Catering: limited soft drinks.

6A 162 **Westwood (Leek)**

Wallbridge, Newcastle Rd, Leek, Staffs, ST13 7AA
☎(01538) 398385, Fax 382485, Pro 398897
On A53 1 mile S of Leek.
Heathland/parkland course.
Pro Neale Hyoe; Founded 1923
18 holes, 6214 yards, S.S.S. 69
Visitors: welcome by prior arrangement.
Green Fees: WD £18; WE £20.
Societies: welcome by prior arrangement; packages available including golf and catering; games/snooker room; from £27.50.
Catering: full clubhouse facilities.
Practice area.
Hotels: The Hatcheries; Bank End Farm; Abbey Inn.

6A 163 **Whiston Hall**

Whiston, Nr Cheadle, Staffs ST10 2HZ
☎(01538) 266260
On A52 midway between Stoke-on-Trent and Ashbourne; 3 miles from Alton Towers.
Parkland/heathland course.
Founded 1971
Designed by Thomas Cooper
18 holes, 5784 yards, S.S.S. 69
Visitors: welcome.
Green Fees: WD £12; WE £16.
Societies: welcome by prior arrangement; packages available both WD and WE; from £33.95.
Catering: full clubhouse facilities.
Hotels: Ashbourne Lodge; Alton Towers.

6A 164 **Whittington Heath**

Tamworth Rd, Lichfield, Staffs, WS14 9PW
☎(01543) 432317, Fax 432317, Pro 432261, Bar/Rest 432212
On A51 Lichfield to Tamworth road.
Heathland course.
Pro A Sadler; Founded 1886
Designed by H S Colt
18 holes, 6490 yards, S.S.S. 71
Visitors: welcome WD with h'cap certs.
Green Fees: WD £24; WE £24.
Societies: welcome Wed and Thurs by arrangement; packages for golf and catering; maximum 50; from £24.
Catering: full clubhouse facilities.
Hotels: Little Barrow, Lichfield.

6A 165 **Widnes**

Highfield Rd, Widnes, Cheshire, WA8 7DT
☎(0151) 4242995
Signposted from the town centre.
Parkland course.
Pro Jason O'Brien; Founded 1924
18 holes, 5729 yards, S.S.S. 68
Visitors: welcome WD except Tues.
Green Fees: WD £22; WE £33.
Societies: welcome Thurs by prior arrangement; from ££30.
Catering: catering and bar facilities.
Hotels: Hillcrest; Everglades.

6A 166 **Wilmslow**

Great Warford, Mobberley, Knutsford, Cheshire, WA16 7AY
☎(01565) 873620, Fax 872172, Sec 872148, Bar/Rest 873973
From A34 Wilmslow-Alderley Edge road take B5085 signposted for Knutsford; Warford Lane 3 miles.
Parkland course.

6A 163 **Whiston Hall**

Pro John Nowicki; Founded 1889
Designed by Alexander Herd
18 holes, 6607 yards, S.S.S. 72
Visitors: welcome by arrangement.
Green Fees: WD £30; WE £40.
Societies: welcome Tues and Thurs by prior arrangement; packages for golf and catering available; minimum 24; from £25.
Catering: full clubhouse facilities.

6A 167 **Wirral Ladies**

93 Bidston Rd, Oxton, Birkenhead, Merseyside, L43 6TS
☎(0151) 6521255, Pro 652 2468
On A41 adjacent to M53 junction 3.
Moorland course.
Pro Angus Law; Founded 1894
Designed by H. Hilton
18 holes, 5182 yards, S.S.S. 66
Visitors: welcome.
Green Fees: WD £20.50; WE £20.50.
Societies: welcome by arrangement.
Catering: full facilities.
Hotels: Bowler Hat.

6A 168 **Withington**

243 Palatine Rd, West Didsbury, Manchester, M20 2UE
☎(0161) 445 9544, Fax 445 5210, Pro 445 4861, Bar/Rest 445 3912
S of Manchester on B5166.
Parkland course.
Pro Bob Ling; Founded 1892
18 holes, 6364 yards, S.S.S. 71
Visitors: welcome by arrangement.
Green Fees: WD £24; WE £30.
Societies: welcome by prior arrangement; 27-hole packages available; from £42.
Catering: full clubhouse facilities.

6A 169 **Wolstanton**

Dimsdale Old Hall, Hassam Parade, Newcastle-under-Lyme, Staffs, ST5 9DR
☎(01782) 622413, Pro 622718, Bar/Rest 616995
0.5 miles off A34, 3 miles from Newcastle.
Parkland course.
Pro Simon Arnold; Founded 1904
18 holes, 5807 yards, S.S.S. 68
Visitors: welcome WD; with member at WE.
Green Fees: WD £20; WE £20.
Societies: welcome WD except Tues; catering packages can be arranged; from £20.
Catering: clubhouse facilities.
Hotels: Friendly Hotel on A34 at Newcastle.

6A 170 Worfield

Roughton, Nr Bridgnorth, Shropshire, WV15 5HE
☎(01746) 716541, Fax 716302, Sec 716372, Bar/Rest 716372
3 miles outside Bridgnorth on A454, Wolverhampton road.
Parkland course.
Pro Stephen Russell; Founded 1991
Designed by T. Williams/D Gough
18 holes, 6801 yards, S.S.S. 73
Visitors: welcome WD; after 12 at WE.
Green Fees: WD £18; WE £22.
Societies: welcome by arrangement; packages arranged through secretary/manager; terms on application.
Catering: full clubhouse facilities.
Practice area.
Hotels: Old Vicarage, Bridgnortrh.

6A 171 Wrekin

Ercall Woods, Wellington, Telford, Shropshire, TF6 5BX
☎(01952) 244032, Pro 223101
Off M54 to B5061 to Golf Links Lane.
Parkland course.
Pro Keith Housden; Founded 1905
18 holes, 5570 yards, S.S.S. 67
Visitors: welcome WD.
Green Fees: WD £20; WE £28.
Societies: welcome WD.
Catering: clubhouse facilities.

6B 1 Alfreton

Highfields, Wingfield Rd, Oakthorpe, Alfreton, Derbys, DE5 7DH
☎(01773) 832070
On Matlock Road 1 mile W of Alfreton.
Parkland course.
Pro Julian Mellor; Founded 1892
11 holes 5393 yards, S.S.S. 66
Visitors: welcome WD; with member at WE.
Green Fees: WD £16; WE £8.
Societies: welcome by prior arrangement; max 36; terms on application.
Catering: clubhouse facilities.
Hotels: Swallow, South Normanton.

6B 2 Allestree Park

Allestree Hall, Allestree Park, Derby, Derbyshire, DE22 2EU
☎(01332) 552971, Fax 541195, Pro 550616
4 miles N of Derby; 1 mile N of A38/A6 junction.
Undulating parkland course.
Pro J Siddons; Founded 1947
18 holes, 5806 yards, S.S.S. 67
Visitors: welcome.
Green Fees: terms on application.
Societies: welcome by prior arrange-
ment; various 18, 27, 36-hole packages available; catering; golf clinics; terms on application.
Catering: clubhouse facilities.
Hotels: International Hotel, Derby.

6B 3 Ashbourne

The Clubhouse, Lichfield Rd, Clifton, Nr Ashbourne, Derbys, DE6 2GJ
☎(01335) 342078, Sec 343457
On A515 2 miles W of Ashbourne.
Parkland course.
Founded 1886/1902
Designed by Frank Pennink
9 holes, 5359 yards, S.S.S. 66
Visitors: welcome WD; with a member at WE.
Green Fees: WD £14; WE £18.
Societies: welcome WD; reductions for groups of more than 20; from £14.
Catering: clubhouse catering and bar.
Hotels: Green Man; Hanover International, both Ashbourne.

6B 4 Ashby Decoy

Burringham Rd, Scunthorpe, Lincs, DN17 2AB
☎(01724) 866561, Fax 271708, Pro 868972, Bar/Rest 842913
From M181, turn right at first three roundabouts; course is 200 yards on rt.
Parkland course.
Pro A Miller; Founded 1936
Designed by Members
18 holes, 6281 yards, S.S.S. 71
Visitors: welcome WD except Tues; with a member WE.
Green Fees: WD £18; WE £18.
Societies: welcome WD except Tues by prior arrangement; various packages on application; £37.
Catering: full clubhouse facilities.
Hotels: Royal; Wortley, both Scunthorpe.

6B 5 Bakewell

Station Rd, Bakewell, Derbys DE451GB
☎(01629) 812307
0.75 miles from Bakewell Square; cross River Wye on A619 Sheffield-Chesterfield Road; up Station Rd, turning right before Industrial estate.
Hilly parkland course.
Founded 1899
Designed by George Low
9 holes, 5240 yards, S.S.S. 66
Visitors: welcome WD; Ladies priority Thurs; WE by prior arrangement.
Green Fees: WD £15; WE £20.
Societies: welcome by arrangement.
Catering: meals and bar except Mon.
Hotels: Rutland Arms.

6B 6 Beeston Fields

Old Drive, Beeston Fields, Nottingham, NG9 3DD
☎(0115) 9257062, Fax 9254280, Pro 9220872
1 mile from Beeston, 5 miles W of Nottingham on south side of A52.
Parkland course.
Pro Alun Wardle; Founded 1923
Designed by Tom Williamson
18 holes, 6404 yards, S.S.S. 71
Visitors: welcome WD (after 3pm Tues) and Sun.
Green Fees: WD £25; WE £25.
Societies: welcome Mon and Wed by prior arrangement; packages available for catering, contact steward; separate dining room; £25-£30.
Catering: clubhouse facilities.
Hotels: Priory Hotel.

6B 7 Belton Park

Belton Lane, Londonthorpe Rd, Grantham, Lincs, NG31 9SH
☎(01476) 567399, Fax 592078, Bar/Rest 563355
From A607 Grantham-Sleaford Road; turn right to Londonthorpe; course 1 mile on left.
Parkland course.
Pro Brian McKee; Founded 1890
Designed by T Williamson/Dave Thomas and Peter Alliss
54 holes 6420 yards, S.S.S. 71.
Visitors: welcome with h'cap certs except Tues.
Green Fees: WD £22; WE £29.
Societies: welcome WD except Tues; by prior arrangement; terms on application.
Catering: full clubhouse facilities.
Practice range, 2 practice areas.
Hotels: Angel & Royal/Kings/Swallow.

6B 8 Belton Woods Hotel & Country Club

Belton, Nr Grantham, Lincolnshire, NG32 2LN
☎(01476) 593200
2 miles E of A1 via Gonerby Moor services; 2 miles N of Grantham on A607 Lincoln Road.
Parkland course with mature trees and ancient woodland.
Pro Tony Roberts; Founded 1991
Lakes: 18 holes, 6781 yards, S.S.S. 73; Woodside: 18 holes, 6605 yards, S.S.S. 73
Visitors: welcome; bookings taken 10 days in advance.
Green Fees: WD £20; WE £20.
Societies: welcome WD by prior arrangement; packages available;

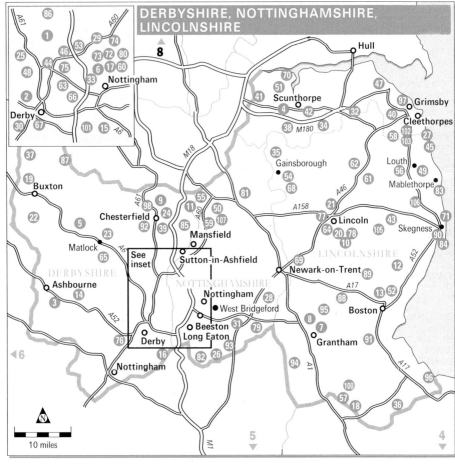

DERBYSHIRE, NOTTINGHAMSHIRE, LINCOLNSHIRE

KEY					
	22 Cavendish	44 Horsley Lodge	65 Matlock	86 Shirland
1 Alfreton	23 Chatsworth	45 Humberston Park	66 Maywood	87 Sickleholme
2 Allestree Park	24 Chesterfield	46 Ilkeston Borough (Pewit)	67 Mickleover	88 Sleaford
3 Ashbourne	25 Chevin	47 Immingham	68 Millfield	89 South Kyme
4 Ashby Decoy	26 Chilwell Manor	48 Kedleston Park	69 Newark	90 Southview
5 Bakewell	27 Cleethorpes	49 Kenwick Park	70 Normanby Hall	91 Spalding
6 Beeston Fields	28 Cotgrave Place Golf &	50 Kilton Forest	71 North Shore	92 Stanedge
7 Belton Park	Country Club	51 Kingsway	72 Nottingham City	93 Stanton-on-the-Wolds
8 Belton Woods Hotel &	29 Coxmoor	52 Kirton Holme	73 Notts	94 Stoke Rochford
CC	30 Derby	53 Leen Valley	74 Oakmere Park	95 Sudbrook Moor
9 Birch Hall	31 Edwalton Municipal	54 Lincoln	75 Ormonde Fields Country	96 Sutton Bridge
10 Blankney	32 Elsham	55 Lindrick	Club	97 Swingtime (Grimsby)
11 Bondhay Golf & CC	33 Erewash Valley	56 Louth Golf Club	76 Pastures	98 Tapton Park Municipal
12 Boston	34 Forest Pines	57 Luffenham Heath	77 Radcliffe-on-Trent	99 Tetney
13 Boston West	35 Gainsborough	58 The Manor Golf Course	78 RAF Waddington	100 Toft Hotel
14 Brailsford	36 Gedney Hill	59 Mansfield Woodhouse	79 Ramsdale Park Golf	101 Trent Lock Golf Centre
15 Bramcote Hills GC	37 Glossop & District	60 Mapperley	Centre	102 Waltham Windmill
16 Breedon Priory	38 Grange Park	61 Market Rasen & District	80 Retford	103 Welton Manor
17 Bulwell Forest	39 Grassmoor Golf Centre	62 Market Rasen Race	81 Ruddington Grange	104 Wollaton Park
18 Burghley Park	40 Grimsby	Course	82 Sandilands	105 Woodhall Spa
19 Buxton & High Peak	41 Hirst Priory	63 Marriott Breadsall Priory	83 Seacroft	106 Woodthorpe Hall
20 Canwick Park	42 Holme Hall	Golf & CC	84 Sherwood Forest	107 Worksop
21 Carholme	43 Horncastle	64 Martin Moor	85	

company days organised; reductions for residents; banqueting facilities for 240; health and sports leisure centres; conference facilities; also Spitfire 9-hole course, 1184 yards, par 3.
Catering: full bar and restaurant facilities.
Practice range, 18 bays floodlit.
Hotels: Belton Woods.

6B 9 Birch Hall
Sheffield Rd, Unstone Green, Sheffield, S18 5DH
☎(01246) 291979, Bar/Rest 291087
Off A61.
Moorland course.
Pro Pete Ball; Founded 1992
Designed by David Tucker
18 holes, 7090 yards, S.S.S. 74
Visitors: welcome.
Green Fees: WD £10; WE £10.
Societies: welcome WD and afternoons at WE; catering on application; from £10.
Catering: clubhouse facilities.
Hotels: Sandpiper.

6B 10 Blankney
Blankney, Lincoln, Lincs, LN4 3AZ
☎(01526) 320263, Fax 322521, Pro 320202
On B1188 10 miles S of Lincoln.
Parkland course.
Pro Graham Bradley; Founded 1903
Designed by Cameron Sinclair (updated Design)
18 holes, 6638 yards, S.S.S. 73
Visitors: welcome by prior arrangement.
Green Fees: WD £20; WE £25.
Societies: welcome by prior arrangement; by arrangement with general manager; from £20.
Catering: clubhouse facilities available.
Hotels: Dover House; Golf Hotel, both Woodhall Spa.

6B 11 Bondhay Golf & Country Club
Bondhay Lane, Whitwell, Worksop, Notts, S80 3EH
☎(01909) 723608, Fax 720226, Sec 724709
Just off A619; 5 minutes from M1 junction 30.
Parkland course.
Pro Martin Bell; Founded 1991
Designed by Donald Steel
18 holes, 6720 yards, S.S.S. 74
Visitors: welcome; advance booking.
Green Fees: WD £20; WE £25.

Societies: welcome by prior arrangement; catering packages by arrangement; also family course £5.
Catering: full bar and restaurant facilities.
Practice range, 15-bay floodlit covered range.
Hotels: Vandykes, Worksop; Beeches, Rotherham.

6B 12 Boston
Cowbridge, Horncastle Rd, Boston, Lincs, PE22 7EL
☎(01205) 350589, Fax 350589, Pro 362306, Bar/Rest 352533
On B1183 2 miles N of Boston.
Parkland course with water on 8 holes.
Pro Terry Squires; Founded 1962
Designed by B.S. Cooper, Extended by Donald Steel
18 holes, 6490 yards, S.S.S. 71
Visitors: welcome by arrangement.
Green Fees: WD £18; WE £18.
Societies: welcome WD except Tues; packages available for 18 holes, lunch and dinner; £36.
Catering: clubhouse facilities.
Hotels: New England; White Hart; Kings Arms, all Boston.

6B 13 Boston West
Hubbert's Bridge, Boston, Lincs, PE20 3QX
☎(01205) 290670
At junction of A1121/B1192 2 miles W of Boston.
Parkland course.
Founded 1995
Designed by Michael Zara
9 holes, 6388 yards, S.S.S. 70
Visitors: welcome.
Green Fees: terms on application.
Societies: welcome at all times; golf and catering packages can be arranged; terms on application.
Catering: full catering facilities.
Hotels: Boston Lodge.

6B 14 Brailsford
Pools Head Lane, Brailsford, Ashbourne, Derbys, DE6 3BU
☎(01335) 360096
Signposted off A52 just before Ashbourne.
Parkland course.
Pro David McCarthy; Founded 1994
9 holes, 6292 yards, S.S.S. 70
Visitors: welcome.
Green Fees: WD £10; WE £15.
Societies: welcome by prior arrangement; reductions for groups of 16 or more of 20%; terms on application.

Catering: no clubhouse; local pub Knights Green.
Practice range, 15 bays floodlit.

6B 15 Bramcote Hills Golf Course
Thoresby Rd, off Derby Rd, Bramcote, Nottingham, Notts, NG9 3EP
☎(0115) 9281880
Leave M1 junction 25 take A52 towards Nottingham past Bramcote Leisure Centre; left after 0.25 miles.
Parkland course.
Founded 1981
18 holes, 1684 yards,
Visitors: welcome; pay and play.
Green Fees: WD £5.50; WE £6.
Societies: welcome.
Catering: none.

6B 16 Breedon Priory
The Clubhouse, Green Lane, Wilson, Nr Derby, DE73 1LG
☎(01332) 863081, Sec 864046
On A453 3.5 miles W of M1 junction 23A.
Parkland course.
Pro Ben Hill; Founded 1991
Designed by D Snell
18 holes, 5530 yards, S.S.S. 67
Visitors: welcome as members' guest.
Green Fees: WD £14; WE £16.
Societies: welcome by prior arrangement; catering and golf packages available; terms on application.
Catering: full clubhouse facilities.

6B 17 Bulwell Forest
Hucknall Rd, Bulwell, Nottingham, NG6 9LQ
☎(0115) 9770576, Pro 9763172
On A611 close to M1 junction 26.
Heathland course.
Pro Lee Rawlings; Founded 1870/1902
18 holes, 5561 yards, S.S.S. 67
Visitors: welcome; restrictions at WE.
Green Fees: WD £10; WE £10.
Societies: welcome WD; after 11am Tues; 2pm Sat and 12 noon Sun; full day packages available; £25.
Catering: clubhouse catering facilities.
Hotels: Moat House; Gateway, both Nottingham.

6B 18 Burghley Park
St Martins Without, Stamford, Lincs, PE9 3JX
☎(01780) 753789, Fax 753789, Pro 762100
On B1081 1 mile S of Stamford.

Parkland course.
Pro Glenn Davies; Founded 1890
Redesigned by Canon J.D. Day in 1936
18 holes, 6236 yards, S.S.S. 70
Visitors: welcome WD with h'cap certs.
Green Fees: WD £20; WE £20.
Societies: welcome WD by prior arrangement; full golf and catering package including insurance; £38.
Catering: clubhouse facilities.
Hotels: The George at Stamford; Garden House; Lady Annes; Crown; Royal Oak, Duddington.

6B 19 Buxton & High Peak

Waterswallows Rd, Fairfield, Buxton, Derbyshire, SK17 7EN
☎(01298) 23453, Fax 26333, Pro 23112, Sec 26263
On A6 Manchester -Derby Road just N of Buxton.
Parkland course.
Pro Gary Brown; Founded 1887
Designed by J Morris
18 holes, 5966 yards, S.S.S. 69
Visitors: welcome by prior arrangement.
Green Fees: WD £25; WE £35.
Societies: welcome by prior arrangement; full golf and catering packages available; £35.
Catering: full clubhouse facilities.
Hotels: Palace Hotel; Hawthorn Farm.

6B 20 Canwick Park

Washingborough Road, Lincoln, Lincoln, LN4 1EF
☎(01522) 522166, Pro 536870, Sec 542912
On B1190 Washingborough Road 2 miles W of Lincoln.
Parkland course.
Pro S J Williamson; Founded 1893/1975
Designed by Hawtree & Partners
18 holes, 6257 yards, S.S.S. 70
Visitors: welcome WD; after 3 at WE.
Green Fees: WD £15; WE £19.
Societies: welcome by prior arrangement; packages available for catering and golf; from £17.
Catering: clubhouse catering facilities.
Hotels: Travel Inn; Branston Hall; Grand, Lincoln.

6B 21 Carholme

Carholme Rd, Lincoln, Lincoln, LN1 1SE
☎(01522) 523725, Fax 533733, Pro 536811

On A57 Worksop Road 1 mile from Lincoln city centre.
Parkland course.
Pro Gary Leslie; Founded 1906
18 holes, 6243 yards, S.S.S. 70
Visitors: welcome by prior arrangement except Sun.
Green Fees: WD £13; WE £16.
Societies: welcome by prior arrangement; catering and golf packages available; terms on application.
Catering: bar and restaurant (except Mon).
Hotels: Delph GH.

6B 22 Cavendish

Gadley Lane, Buxton, Derbys, SK17 6XD
☎(01298) 23494, Fax 79708, Pro 25052, Sec 79708
On outskirts of Buxton off the ring road in direction of A53 Leek.
Moorland/parkland course.
Pro P Hunstone; Founded 1925
Designed by Dr Alister MacKenzie
18 holes, 5721 yards, S.S.S. 68
Visitors: welcome WD.
Green Fees: WD £25.
Societies: welcome by prior arrangement; minimum 16; maximum 27 holes; catering by prior arrangement; from £22.
Catering: full clubhouse facilities available.
Practice area.
Hotels: Leewood; Buckingham; Palace; Portland all Buxton.

6B 23 Chatsworth

Chatsworth Park, Bakewell,
☎(01246) 582204
On Chatsworth Estate.
Parkland course.
9 holes, 5248 yards, S.S.S. 66
Visitors: private; for estate workers only.
Green Fees: terms on application.
Catering: no clubhouse.

6B 24 Chesterfield

Walton, Chesterfield, Derbys, S42 7LA
☎(01246) 279256, Fax 276622, Pro 276297, Bar/Rest 232035
On A632 Matlock Road 1.5 miles S of Chesterfield.
Parkland course.
Pro M McLean; Founded 1897
Designed by H. Colt
18 holes, 6261 yards, S.S.S. 70
Visitors: welcome WD; with member at WE.
Green Fees: WD £25.

Societies: welcome WD by prior application; packages available; from £25.
Catering: full clubhouse facilities.
Hotels: Chesterfield Hotel; Swallow, S Normanton.

6B 25 Chevin

Golf Lane, Duffield, Derbys, DE56 4 EE
☎(01332) 841864, Pro 841112
On A6 5 miles N of Derby outside Duffield.
Hilly parkland course.
Pro Willie Bird; Founded 1894
18 holes, 6057 yards, S.S.S. 69
Visitors: welcome WD except before 9.30am and between 12.30pm and 2pm; WE with member.
Green Fees: WD £27; WE £14.
Societies: welcome WD by prior arrangement with Sec.
Catering: full facilities except Mon. Small practice area.
Hotels: Strutt Arms adjacent.

6B 26 Chilwell Manor

Meadow Lane, Chilwell, Nottingham, Notts, NG9 5AE
☎(0115) 9258958, Fax 9257050, Pro 9258993
4 miles W of Nottingham on A6005 near Beeston.
Parkland course.
Pro Paul Wilson; Founded 1906
18 holes, 6395 yards, S.S.S. 70
Visitors: welcome after 9am WD; after 11am WE.
Green Fees: WD £18; WE £20.
Societies: welcome Mon, Wed, Fri.
Catering: full clubhouse facilities available.
Hotels: Post House; Novotel; Village.

6B 27 Cleethorpes

Kings Rd, Cleethorpes, N E Lincs, DN35 0PN
☎(01472) 812059, Pro 814060
On A1301 1 mile S of Cleethorpes.
Meadowland course.
Pro Paul Davies; Founded 1894
Designed by Harry Vardon (now vastly altered)
18 holes, 6349 yards, S.S.S. 70
Visitors: welcome if member of recognised club; Ladies only Wed.
Green Fees: WD £20; WE £25.
Societies: welcome by prior arrangement.
Catering: full facilities.
Practice area.
Hotels: Kingsway; Wellow.

6B 28 Cotgrave Place Golf & Country Club

Stragglethorpe, Nr Radcliffe on Trent, Nottingham, NG12 3HB
☎(0115) 9333344, Fax 9334567
Off A52 5 miles SE of Nottingham.
Parkland course with lake features; 3 x 9 loops.
Pro G Towse/ R Smith; Founded 1992
Designed by P Alliss/J Small
27 holes 6303 yards, S.S.S. 70
Visitors: welcome.
Green Fees: WD £15; WE £22.
Societies: welcome by prior arrangement; catering and golf packages available by prior arrangement; banqueting facilities available; 27 holes; from £17.50.
Catering: full clubhouse facilities available.
Hotels: Hilton; Moat House; Langar Hall.

6B 29 Coxmoor

Coxmoor Rd, Sutton-in-Ashfield, Notts, NG17 5LF
☎(01623) 557359, Fax 557359, Pro 559906, Bar/Rest 559878
On A611 1.5 miles S of Mansfield.
Heathland course.
Pro D Ridley; Founded 1913
18 holes, 6571 yards, S.S.S. 72
Visitors: welcome WD; with member at WE.
Green Fees: WD £28; WE £28.
Societies: welcome WD except Tues by prior arrangement; golf and catering available; from £18.
Catering: clubhouse catering and bar facilities.
Hotels: Pine Lodge, Mansfield; Cotswold Hotel, Nottingham; Cockcliffe House.

6B 30 Derby

Wilmore Road, Sinfin, Derby, DE24 9HD
☎(01332) 766323, Fax 769004, Pro 766462
2 miles from city centre off Wilmore Road.
Parkland course.
Pro John Siddons; Founded 1923
18 holes, 6163 yards, S.S.S. 69
Visitors: welcome by prior arrangement.
Green Fees: terms on application.
Societies: welcome by prior arrangement; packages available; terms on application.
Catering: full clubhouse facilities available.
Hotels: International, Derby.

6B 31 Edwalton Municipal

Edwalton Village, Nottingham, Notts, NG12 4AS
☎(0115) 9234775
Off A606 from Nottingham at Edwalton Hall.
Parkland course; also par 3 1592 yards.
Pro J Staples; Founded 1981
Designed by Frank Pennink
9 holes, 3336 yards, S.S.S. 36
Visitors: welcome.
Green Fees: terms on application.
Societies: welcome WD.
Catering: lunches and meals available.

6B 32 Elsham

Barton Rd, Elsham, Brigg, Lincs, DN20 0LS
☎(01652) 680291, Pro 680432, Bar/Rest 688382
3 miles N of Brigg on B1206 Road.
Parkland course.
Pro Stewart Brewer; Founded 1901
18 holes, 6406 yards, S.S.S. 71
Visitors: welcome WD except Thurs; with member at WE.
Green Fees: WD £24; WE £18.
Societies: welcome WD except Thurs; full packages of golf and catering available; from £40.
Catering: full clubhouse facilities.
Hotels: Arties Mill, Castlethorpe; Red Lion Hotel, Redbourne; Jolly Miller, Wrawby.

6B 33 Erewash Valley

Golf Club Road, Stanton-by-Dale, Ilkeston, Derbys, DE7 4QR
☎(0115) 9323258, Fax 9322984, Pro 9324667, Sec 9322984
3 miles from M1 junction 25.
Parkland course; 4th hole (Quarry): 92 yards.
Pro Mike Ronan; Founded 1905
Designed by Hawtree
18 holes, 6557 yards, S.S.S. 71
Visitors: welcome WD and pm at WE.
Green Fees: WD £22.50; WE £27.50.
Societies: welcome Mon, Wed, Fri by prior arrangement; catering packages available; snooker; practice grounds; from £22.50.
Catering: restaurant and bar facilities.
Practice ground.
Hotels: Post House; Hilton.

6B 34 Forest Pines

Briggate Lodge Inn, Ermine Street, Nr Brigg, Lincs, DN20 0AQ
☎(01652) 650770, Pro 650756

Take M180 junction 4 and then A15 towards Scunthorpe; club at first roundabout.
Forest course.
Pro David Edwards; Founded 1996
Designed by J Morgan
18 holes, 6882 yards, S.S.S. 73
Visitors: welcome by prior arrangement.
Green Fees: WD £30; WE £35.
Societies: welcome by prior arrangement; 27 holes (Club has Forest course, 3291 yards; Pines course, 3591 yards; Beeches course, 3102 yards), coffee, lunch and evening meal available; accommodation packages; golf schools; from £45.
Catering: restaurant and bar facilities. Practice range, 17 bays floodlit covered.
Hotels: Briggate Lodge Inn, 86-bed hotel on site.

6B 35 Gainsborough

The Belt Road, Thonock, Gainsborough, Lincs, DN21 1PZ
☎(01427) 613088, Fax 810172
Signposted off A631 Gainsborough-Grimsby Road.
US style course with lakes and many bunkers.
Pro Stephen Cooper; Founded 1997 (Karsten Lakes), Founded 1894/1985 (Thonock Park)
Designed by N Coles (Karsten Lakes); Designed by B Waites (Thonock Park, 1985)
Karsten Lakes: 18 holes, 6900 yards, S.S.S. 70; Thonock Park: 18 holes, 6266 yards, S.S.S. 70
Visitors: welcome; with member at WE (Thonock Park).
Green Fees: WD £25; WE £25.
Societies: welcome (welcome WD for Thonock Park); packages for golf and catering can be arranged; snooker tables; menus available for societies in restaurant; from £25.
Catering: full catering and bar service including coffee shop and restaurant. Practice range, 20 bays floodlit.
Hotels: Hickman Hill, Gainsborough.

6B 36 Gedney Hill

West Drove, Gedney Hill, Nr Spalding, Lincs, PE12 0NT
☎(01406) 330922, Fax 330323
On B1166 6 miles from Crowland.
Links style course.
Pro Davud Hutton; Founded 1988
Designed by C. Britton
18 holes, 5285 yards, S.S.S. 66
Visitors: welcome.

Green Fees: WD £6.25; WE £10.50.
Societies: welcome by prior arrangement; catering available; snooker; terms on application.
Catering: clubhouse catering.

6B 37 Glossop & District

Hurst Lane, off Sheffield Rd, Glossop, Derbys, SK13 9PU
☎(01457) 865247, Pro 853117
Off A57 1.5 miles outside Glossop; turn at Royal Oak pub.
Moorland course.
Pro Daniel Marsh; Founded 1894
11 holes 5800 yards, S.S.S. 68
Visitors: welcome; restrictions on Sat.
Green Fees: terms on application.
Societies: welcome by prior arrangement; terms on application.
Catering: clubhouse facilities.
Hotels: Wind in the Willows, Glossop.

6B 38 Grange Park

Butterwick Rd, Messingham, Scunthorpe, N Lincs, DN17 3PP
☎(01724) 762945, Fax 762851
5 miles S of Scunthorpe between Messingham and E Butterwick; 4 miles S of M180 junction 3.
Parkland course.
Pro Leigh Gawley; Founded 1991
Designed by Ray Price
13 holes 4141 yards, S.S.S. 48
Visitors: welcome.
Green Fees: WD £5.50; WE £7.50.
Societies: welcome by prior arrangement; from £5.50.
Catering: by arrangement.
Practice range, floodlit; also par 3 9-hole course (£2.50-£3.50).

6B 39 Grassmoor Golf Centre

North Wingfield Rd, Grassmoor, Chesterfield, Derbys, S42 5EA
☎(01246) 856044, Fax 853933
2 miles S of Chesterfield close to M1 junction 29.
Moorland course.
Pro Peter Goldthorpe; Founded 1992
Designed by Michael Shattock
18 holes, 5723 yards, S.S.S. 69
Visitors: welcome WE; by arrangement.
Green Fees: WD £8.50; WE £8.95.
Societies: welcome.
Catering: full facilities.
Practice range, 25 bays floodlit.
Hotels: Chesterfield.

6B 40 Grimsby

Littlecoates Rd, Grimsby, NE Lincs, N34 4LU

☎(01472) 342823, Fax 342630, Pro 356981, Sec 342630
1 mile W of Grimsby town centre; turn left off A18 at first roundabout; course is 0.75 miles on left.
Undulating parkland course.
Pro Richard Smith; Founded 1922
18 holes, 6098 yards, S.S.S. 69
Visitors: welcome if member of golf club; Ladies Day Tues.
Green Fees: WD £20; WE £25.
Societies: welcome Mon and Fri by prior arrangement.
Catering: full facilities.
Practice ground.
Hotels: Post House.

6B 41 Hirst Priory

Hirst Priory Park, Crowle, N E Lincs, DN17 4BU
☎(01724) 711621, Pro 711619
Off A1161 Crowle to Goole Road from M180 junction 2.
Parkland course.
Pro E D Highfield; Founded 1994
18 holes, 6283 yards, S.S.S. 70
Visitors: welcome.
Green Fees: WD £13.75; WE £17.50.
Societies: welcome WD except Mon and after 11am at WE.
Catering: full facilities except Mon.
Hotels: Red Lion, Epworth.

6B 42 Holme Hall

Holme Lane, Bottesford, Scunthorpe, DN16 3RF
☎(01724) 840909, Fax 862078, Pro 851816, Sec 862078, Bar/Rest 282053
Close to M180 junction 4 for Scunthorpe East.
Heathland course.
Pro R McKiernan; Founded 1908
18 holes, 6404 yards, S.S.S. 71
Visitors: welcome WD; only with member at WE.
Green Fees: WD £20; WE £20.
Societies: welcome WD by arrangement; on application; from £20.
Catering: clubhouse facilities.

6B 43 Horncastle

West Ashby, Horncastle, Lincs, LN9 5PP
☎(01507) 526800
Off A158 W of Horncastle.
Parkland course with water hazards.
Pro E C Wright; Founded 1990
Designed by Ernie Wright
18 holes, 5717 yards, S.S.S. 70
Visitors: welcome.
Green Fees: WD £10; WE £10.

Societies: welcome; packages for golf and catering available; from £10.
Catering: clubhouse facilities.
Practice range, 24 bays floodlit.
Hotels: Admiral Rodney.

6B 44 Horsley Lodge

Horsley Lodge, Smalley Mill Road, Horsley, Derbys, DE21 5BL
☎(01332) 780838, Fax 781118
Off A38 4 miles N of Derby.
Meadowland course.
Pro Paul Kent; Founded 1990
Designed by Peter McEvoy
18 holes, 6400 yards, S.S.S. 71
Visitors: welcome WD, after 2pm WE.
Green Fees: WD £18; WE £18.
Societies: welcome Tues, Thurs or Fri by prior arrangement; packages available; solarium; sauna; conference facilities; from £15.
Catering: clubhouse and à la carte restaurants; bars in 1840 clubhouse.
Hotels: Horsley Lodge on site; residents allowed free round.

6B 45 Humberston Park

Humberston Ave, Humberston, NE Lincs, DN36 4SJ
☎(01472) 210404
Off Humberstone Ave behind the Cherry Garth Scouts Field.
Parkland course.
Founded 1970
9 holes, 3672 yards, S.S.S. 58
Visitors: welcome except Sun am.
Green Fees: WD £8; WE £10.
Societies: welcome by arrangement.
Catering: bar facilities and snacks.

6B 46 Ilkeston Borough (Pewit)

West End Drive, Ilkeston, Derbyshire, DE7 5GH
☎(0115) 9307704
0.5 miles E of Ilkeston.
Municipal meadowland course.
Founded 1920
9 holes, 4116 yards, S.S.S. 60
Visitors: welcome.
Green Fees: WD £6; WE £6.
Societies: welcome WD only by prior arrangement.

6B 47 Immingham

Church Lane, Immingham, Grimsby, Lincs, DN40 2EU
☎(01469) 575298, Fax 577636, Pro 575493
2 miles off M180 behind St Andrew's Church.

Flat parkland course.
Pro Nick Harding; Founded 1975
Designed by Hawtree & Son (front 9),
F. Pennink (back 9)
18 holes, 6215 yards, S.S.S. 70
Visitors: welcome.
Green Fees: WD £15; WE £20.
Societies: welcome; packages available; company days welcome; new clubhouse open mid-1998; terms on application.
Catering: new clubhouse opens 1998.
Practice area.
Hotels: Stallingborough Grange.

6B 48 **Kedleston Park**
Kedleston, Quarndon, Derby, DE22
5JD
☎(01332) 840035, Fax 842329, Pro
841685, Bar/Rest 840634
4 miles N of Derby; from A38 follow
signs to Kedleston Hall.
Parkland course.
Pro David J Russell; Founded 1947
Designed by James Braid and
Morrison & Co
18 holes, 6705 yards, S.S.S. 72
Visitors: welcome by arrangement.
Green Fees: WD £28; WE £28.
Societies: welcome Mon and Fri;
catering packages can be arranged;
from £28.
Catering: full catering facilities.
Hotels: Kedleston House; Midland
Hotel; Mundy Arms.

6B 49 **Kenwick Park**
Kenwick, Nr Louth, Lincs, LN11 8NY
☎(01507) 605134, Fax 606556, Pro
607161, Bar/Rest 608210
1 mile S of Louth.
Rolling parkland course.
Pro Eric Sharp; Founded 1992
Designed by Patrick Tallack
18 holes, 6815 yards, S.S.S. 73
Visitors: welcome.
Green Fees: WD £25; WE £35.
Societies: welcome by prior arrangement; catering and golf packages can be arranged; terms on application.
Catering: clubhouse facilities.
Practice range, driving range.
Hotels: Kenwick Park Hotel.

6B 50 **Kilton Forest**
Blyth Rd, Worksop, Notts, S81 0TL
☎(01909) 472488, Pro 486563, Sec
485994, Bar/Rest 479199
1 mile from Worksop on Blyth Road.
Parkland course.
Pro Peter Foster; Founded 1977
18 holes, 6424 yards, S.S.S. 71

Visitors: welcome; bookings required
at WE.
Green Fees: WD £7.35; WE £10.35.
Societies: welcome by prior arrangement; catering packages available;
terms on application.
Catering: restaurant and bar facilities.
Hotels: Regency; Lion, both Worksop.

6B 51 **Kingsway**
Kingsway, Scunthorpe, N Lincs, DN15
7ER
☎(01724) 840945
Between Berkeley and Queensway
roundabouts S of A18.
Undulating parkland course.
Pro Chris Mann; Founded 1971
Designed by R.D. Highfield
9 holes, 1915 yards, S.S.S. 59
Visitors: welcome.
Green Fees: WD £3.35; WE £3.90.
Societies: none.

6B 52 **Kirton Holme**
Holme Rd, Nr Boston, Lincs, PE20
1SY
☎(01205) 290669
Off A52 4 miles W of Boston.
Parkland course.
Founded 1992
Designed by D.W. Welberry
9 holes, 5778 yards, S.S.S. 68
Visitors: pay and play.
Green Fees: WD £5; WE £5.
Societies: welcome by prior arrangement; maximum 30; meals available;
terms on application.
Catering: full clubhouse facilities.
Hotels: Poacher Inn.

6B 53 **Leen Valley**
Wigwam Lane, Hucknall, Notts, NG15
7TA
☎(0115) 9642037, Fax 9642724, Pro
01623 422764, Bar/Rest 9680968
On B6011 off A611 from Hucknall.
Parkland course; was Hucknall GC.
Pro Shaun Smith; Founded 1994
Designed by Tom Hodgetts
18 holes, 6233 yards, S.S.S. 72
Visitors: welcome.
Green Fees: WD £8.50; WE £9.50.
Societies: welcome; packages can be
arranged; terms on application.
Catering: full clubhouse facilities.
Hotels: Premier Lodge, Hucknall.

6B 54 **Lincoln**
Torksey, Lincoln, Lincs, LN1 2EG
☎(01427) 718210, Pro 718273, Sec
718721, Bar/Rest 718721

On A156 7 miles S of Gainsborough.
Inland links course.
Pro A Carter; Founded 1891/1911
18 holes, 6438 yards, S.S.S. 71
Visitors: welcome by arrangement.
Green Fees: WD £22; WE £22.
Societies: welcome WD by prior
arrangement; catering packages available; from £22.
Catering: full clubhouse dining and
bar facilities.
Practice area.
Hotels: Hume Hall.

6B 55 **Lindrick**
Lindrick Common, Worksop, Notts,
S81 8BH
☎(01909) 485802, Fax 488685, Pro
475820, Sec 475282
On A57 4 miles NW of Worksop.
Heathland course; 1957 Ryder Cup;
1960 Curtis Cup.
Pro Peter Cowen; Founded 1891
Designed by Tom Dunn, Willie Park
and H. Fowler
18 holes, 6606 yards, S.S.S. 72
Visitors: welcome WD except Tues.
Green Fees: WD £45; WE £45.
Societies: welcome by prior arrangement; packages available; from £45.
Catering: full clubhouse facilities.
Practice range, 2 practice areas.
Hotels: Red Lion, Todwick.

6B 56 **Louth Golf Club**
Crowtree Lane, Louth, Lincs, LN11
9LJ
☎(01507) 602554, Fax 603681, Pro
604648, Sec 603681, Bar/Rest 611087
W of Louth close to Hubbards Hills.
Undulating parkland course.
Pro A J Blundell; Founded 1965
Designed by C K Cotton
18 holes, 6424 yards, S.S.S. 71
Visitors: welcome by arrangement.
Green Fees: WD £16; WE £25.
Societies: welcome by prior arrangement; discounts for groups of more
than 25; catering packages available;
from £16.
Catering: all day catering and bar
facilities.
Practice ground.
Hotels: Masons Arms; Beaumont.

6B 57 **Luffenham Heath**
Ketton, Stamford, Lincs, PE9 3UU
☎(01780) 720218, Pro 720298, Sec
720205, Bar/Rest 721095
On A6121 5 miles W of Stamford.
Heathland course.
Pro Ian Burnett; Founded 1911

Designed by James Braid
18 holes, 6273 yards, S.S.S. 70
Visitors: welcome by arrangement.
Green Fees: WD £35; WE £40.
Societies: welcome by prior arrangement with Sec; packages and catering available on application; terms on application.
Catering: full clubhouse facilities.
Hotels: The George at Stamford; Monkton Arms, Glaston.

6B 58 The Manor Golf Course
Laceby Manor, Laceby, Grimsby, Lincolnshire, DN37 7EA
☎(01472) 873468, Fax 276706
On A16 0.5 miles past Oaklands Hotel.
Parkland course.
Founded 1992
Designed by Sir Charles Nicholson and Rushton
18 holes, 6343 yards, S.S.S. 70
Visitors: welcome by arrangement.
Green Fees: WD £14; WE £14.
Societies: welcome by prior arrangement; terms on application.
Catering: full clubhouse facilities.
Hotels: Oaklands.

6B 59 Mansfield Woodhouse
Leeming Lane North, Mansfield Woodhouse, Notts, NG19 9EU
☎(01623) 623521
On A60 Mansfield-Worksop road 2 miles N of Mansfield.
Public parkland course.
Pro L Highfield; Founded 1973
9 holes, 4892 yards, S.S.S. 65
Visitors: welcome except before 11am Sat.
Green Fees: WD £3.20; WE £4.90.
Societies: none.
Catering: clubhouse bar facilities.

6B 60 Mapperley
Central Ave, Plains Rd, Mapperley, Nottingham, NG3 5RH
☎(0115) 9556672, Pro 9556673
Off B684 3 miles NE of Nottingham.
Undulating parkland course.
Pro Malcolm Allen; Founded 1903
18 holes, 6283 yards, S.S.S. 70
Visitors: welcome by prior arrangement.
Green Fees: WD £12; WE £18.
Societies: welcome by arrangement with secretary; packages available; terms on application.
Catering: full clubhouse facilities.
Hotels: many in Nottingham.

6B 61 Market Rasen & District
Legsby Rd, Market Rasen, Lincs, LN8 3DZ
☎(01673) 842319, Pro 842416, Bar/Rest 842416
On A361 1 mile E of Market Rasen.
Heathland course.
Pro A M Chester; Founded 1922
18 holes, 6045 yards, S.S.S. 69
Visitors: welcome with h'cap certs; with member at WE.
Green Fees: WD £18; WE £18.
Societies: welcome Tues and Fri; packages for catering available; from £18.
Catering: full clubhouse facilities.
Hotels: Limes Hotel.

6B 62 Market Rasen Race Course
Market Rasen Race Course, Legsby, Market Rasen, Lincs, LN8 3EA
☎(01673) 843434, Fax 844532
At Market Rasen racecourse; follow signs to golf course from entrance. In centre of racecourse; sandy.
Founded 1989
Designed by Racecourse/Peter Alliss
9 holes, 2377 yards, S.S.S. 45
Visitors: welcome.
Green Fees: terms on application.
Societies: welcome with advance booking.

6B 63 Marriott Breadsall Priory G & CC
Moor Rd, Morley, Derbys, DE7 6DL
☎(01332) 832235, Fax 833509
3 miles NE of Derby off A61 towards Breadsall.
Parkland course.
Founded 1977
Moorland: 18 holes, yards, S.S.S. 68;
Priory: 18 holes, yards, S.S.S. 68
Visitors: welcome by prior arrangement.
Green Fees: terms on application.
Societies: welcome by prior arrangement; packages available; tennis, swimming pool, gym and leisure facilities; terms on application.
Catering: full hotel and clubhouse facilities; 5 bars and 2 restaurants.
Hotels: Marriott Breadsall Priory.

6B 64 Martin Moor
Blankney Rd, Martin Moor, Metheringham, Lincs, LN4 3BE
☎(01526) 378243, Fax 378243
On B1189 2 miles E of Metheringham.
Parkland course.

Pro A Hare; Founded 1992
Designed by S Harrison
9 holes, 6325 yards, S.S.S. 70
Visitors: welcome.
Green Fees: WD £6.50; WE £8.50.
Societies: welcome by prior arrangement; packages available; terms on application.
Catering: clubhouse facilities.
Hotels: Eagle Lodge; golf Hotel; Petwood Hotel, all Woodhall Spa.

6B 65 Matlock
Chesterfield Rd, Matlock, Derbys, DE4 5LZ
☎(01629) 582191, Pro 584934
On Chesterfield Road 1 mile from Matlock.
Moorland course.
Pro Mark Whithorn; Founded 1907
18 holes, 5996 yards, S.S.S. 69
Visitors: welcome WD by prior arrangement.
Green Fees: WD £25; WE £12.50.
Societies: welcome by prior arrangement; parties of more than 12; catering available; £25.
Catering: clubhouse facilities.
Hotels: New Bath, Matlock Bath; Red House, Darley Dale; East Lodge, Rowsley.

6B 66 Maywood
Rushy Lane, Risley, Draycott, Derbys, DE72 3ST
☎(0115) 9392306, Pro 9490043
Off A52 to Risley from M1 junction 25 by the Post House Hotel.
Wooded course with water features.
Pro Colin Henderson; Founded 1990
18 holes, 6424 yards, S.S.S. 72
Visitors: welcome.
Green Fees: WD £15; WE £20.
Societies: welcome by prior arrangement; full day's golf and coffee, light lunch and 4-course evening meal; from £30.
Catering: full bar and catering facilities.
Hotels: Post House; Novotel; Risley Park.

6B 67 Mickleover
Uttoxeter Rd, Mickleover, Derbyshire, DE3 5AD
☎(01332) 513339, Fax 512092, Pro 518662, Sec 512092
On A516/B5020 3 miles W of Derby.
Undulating parkland course.
Pro Tim Coxon; Founded 1923
18 holes, 5708 yards, S.S.S. 68
Visitors: welcome.

Green Fees: WD £22; WE £25.
Societies: welcome Tues and Thurs; packages can be arranged; from £22.
Catering: clubhouse facilities.
Hotels: Mickleover Court; International, Derby.

6B 68 Millfield

Laughterton, Torksey, Nr Lincoln, Lincs, LN1 2LB
☎(01427) 718473
On A113 between A57 and A158 8 miles from Lincoln; 10 miles from Gainsborough.
Inland links course.
Pro Richard Hunter; Founded 1984
18 holes, 6001 yards, S.S.S. 71
Visitors: welcome.
Green Fees: WD £7; WE £7.
Societies: welcome WD by arrangement; tennis, bowls; 2nd 18-hole 4500 yards, par 65 course and 9-hole 1500 yards, par 3 course.
Catering: light refreshments.
Hotels: holiday chalets and log cabins on site.

6B 69 Newark

Kelwick, Coddington, Newark, Notts, NG24 2QX
☎(01636) 626241, Fax 626497, Pro 626492, Sec 626282
On A17 between Newark and Sleaford just past Coddington roundabout.
Parkland course.
Pro Peter Lockley; Founded 1901
18 holes, 6457 yards, S.S.S. 71
Visitors: welcome with h'cap certs; Ladies Day Tues.
Green Fees: WD £22; WE £27.
Societies: welcome WD by prior arrangement; catering packages; snooker; indoor coaching facilities.
Catering: bar and meals.
Practice ground.
Hotels: Robin Hood; George Inn, Leadenham; Travelodge.

6B 70 Normanby Hall

Normanby Park, Normanby, Scunthorpe, N Lincs, DN15 9HU
☎(01724) 720252, Pro 720226
5 miles N of Scunthorpe adjacent to Normanby Hall.
Parkland course.
Pro Chris Mann; Founded 1978
Designed by H.F. Jiggens, Hawtree & Sons
18 holes, 6548 yards, S.S.S. 71
Visitors: welcome; telephone for bookings.
Green Fees: WD £11; WE £13.

Societies: welcome by prior arrangement with the local council.
Catering: full facilities including banqueting at Normanby Hall.
Practice range, practice area.
Hotels: Royal; Wortley House.

6B 71 North Shore

North Shore Rd, Skegness, Lincs, PE25 1DN
☎(01754) 763298, Fax 761902
Just off A16 main Lincoln Road.
Parkland/links course.
Pro John Cornelius; Founded 1910
Designed by James Braid
18 holes, 6257 yards, S.S.S. 71
Visitors: welcome.
Green Fees: WD £18; WE £28.
Societies: welcome by prior arrangement; minimum 12; packages and hotel rates available; from £26.
Catering: full clubhouse catering and bar facilities.
Hotels: North Shore; Crown; Vine.

6B 72 Nottingham City

Lawton Drive, Bulwell, Nottingham, NG6 8BL
☎(0115) 9278021, Fax 9276916, Pro 9272767, Sec 9276916
2 miles from M1 junction 26 follow signs to Bulwell.
Municipal parkland course.
Pro C Jepson; Founded 1910
Designed by H Braid
18 holes, 6218 yards, S.S.S. 70
Visitors: welcome.
Green Fees: WD £10; WE £10.
Societies: welcome by prior arrangement; 18 and 36-hole packages with catering available; terms on application.
Catering: clubhouse facilities.

6B 73 Notts

Hollinwell, Derby Rd, Kirkby-in-Ashfield, Notts, NG17 7QR
☎(01623) 753225, Fax 753655, Pro 753087, Bar/Rest 755640
3 miles from M1 junction 27 off A611.
Heathland course with gorse/heather; lake at Hollinwell.
Pro Brain Waites; Founded 1887/1900
Designed by Willie Park Jnr
18 holes, 7030 yards, S.S.S. 74
Visitors: welcome by prior arrangement.
Green Fees: WD £40; WE £40.
Societies: welcome WD except Fri morning by prior arrangement; packages available for golf and catering; from £40.

Catering: clubhouse facilities.
Hotels: Pine Lodge, Mansfield; Swallow, S Normanton.

6B 74 Oakmere Park

Oaks Lane, Oxton, Notts, NG25 0RH
☎(0115) 9653545, Fax 9655628
Between Blidworth and Oxton.
Parkland course; also Commanders course: 9 holes, 6573 yards, par 72.
Pro Daryl St John Jones; Founded 1977
Designed by Frank Pennink
18 holes, 6612 yards, S.S.S. 72
Visitors: welcome.
Green Fees: WD £16; WE £20.
Societies: welcome; restrictions at WE; packages available; terms on application.
Catering: full clubhouse facilities.
Hotels: Moat House, Nottingham.

6B 75 Ormonde Fields Country Club

Nottingham Rd, Codnor, Ripley, Derbys, DE5 9RG
☎(01773) 742987
On A610 towards Ripley 2 miles from M1 junction 26.
Undulating course.
Pro Peter Buttifant; Founded 1906
18 holes, 6011 yards, S.S.S. 69
Visitors: welcome WD; by prior arrangement WE.
Green Fees: WD £17.50; WE £22.50.
Societies: welcome by arrangement.
Catering: full facilities.

6B 76 Pastures

Pastures, Mickleover, Derby, Derbys, DE3 5DQ
☎(01332) 521074
On A516 4 miles W of Derby.
Undulating meadowland course.
Founded 1969
Designed by Frank Pennink
9 holes, 5095 yards, S.S.S. 64
Visitors: welcome with h'cap certs.
Green Fees: WD £12; WE £12.
Societies: welcome by prior arrangement; packages include lunch and evening meal; from £22.
Catering: limited catering.

6B 77 Pottergate

Moor Lane, Branston, Nr Lincoln, Lincs
☎(01522) 794867
On B1188 in Branston.
Parkland course.
Founded 1992

THE SHERWOOD FOREST GOLF CLUB LTD

EAKRING ROAD, MANSFIELD, NOTTS NG18 3EW

Secretary:	K. Hall	Tel: 01623 626689
Professional:	K. Hall	Tel: 01623 627403
Catering Manageress	D. McCart	Tel: 01623 623327

Full catering service available with dining for up to 100 persons at one sitting. Course is heathland, set in the very heart of Robin Hood country, and was designed by James Braid. Yellow markers distance is 6,294 yds. SSS 71. White markers distance is 6,714 yds. SSS 73.

The Course was the venue for the
**Midland region Qualifying Round for the Open Championship 1990 - 1995
and for the British Open Amateur Seniors Championship 1997.**
Green Fees on application to the secretary.
Within a few miles of places of interest – such as the Major Oak (Robin Hood's Larder).
Newstead Abbey, Thoresby Hall, Clumber Oark, and 14 miles from the centre of Nottingham.

Designed by W Bailey
9 holes, 5096 yards, S.S.S. 66
Visitors: welcome.
Green Fees: WD £8; WE £8.
Societies: welcome.
Catering: bar and snacks available.

6B 78 Radcliffe-on-Trent
Dewberry Lane, Cropwell Rd, Radcliffe on Trent, Notts, NG12 2JH
☎(0115) 9333125, Fax 9116991, Pro 9332336, Sec 9333000, Bar/Rest 9116990
From A52 follow signs to Cropwell Butler.
Wooded parkland course.
Pro Robert Ellis; Founded 1909
Designed by Tom Wilkinson
18 holes, 6381 yards, S.S.S. 71
Visitors: welcome by arrangement.
Green Fees: WD £23; WE £28.
Societies: welcome Wed only; packages available; from £23.
Catering: full clubhouse catering and bar facilities.
Hotels: Westminster Hotel.

6B 79 RAF Waddington
Waddington, Lincoln, Lincs, LN5 9NB
☎(01522) 726854, Fax 726475, Pro

726485, Sec 726488
Off A15 at Bracebridge Heath 3 miles S of Lincoln.
On RAF airfield.
Founded 1972
9 holes, 5558 yards, S.S.S. 69
Visitors: must be accompanied by RAF Waddington member.
Green Fees: WD £4; WE £4.
Societies: by arrangement with captain or secretary; terms on application.
Catering: on application.
Hotels: Moor Lodge; Mill Moor.

6B 80 Ramsdale Park Golf Centre
Oxton Rd, Calverton, Notts, NG14 6NU
☎(0115) 9655600, Fax 9654105
On B6386 10 miles NE of Nottingham.
Parkland course.
Pro Robert Macey; Founded 1992
Designed by Hawtree & Son
18 holes, 6546 yards, S.S.S. 71
Visitors: pay and play.
Green Fees: WD £13.50; WE £15.
Societies: welcome by prior arrangement; packages and catering available; also par 3 course; from £13.50.
Catering: clubhouse facilities.
Hotels: many in local area.

6B 81 Retford
Ordsall, Retford, Notts, DN22 7UA
☎(01777) 703733, Sec 860682
Off A620 midway between Worksop and Gainsborough.
Parkland course.
Pro S Betteridge; Founded 1920
18 holes, 6370 yards, S.S.S. 70
Visitors: welcome by prior arrangement WD; WE with a member.
Green Fees: WD £19; WE £10.
Societies: welcome WD by prior arrangement; discounts for groups of 20 or more; bar and catering packages available; from £19.
Catering: clubhouse facilities.
Practice ground.
Hotels: West Retford; Elms, both Retford; Ye Olde Bell, Barnaby Moor.

6B 82 Ruddington Grange
Wilford Road, Ruddington, Nottingham, Notts, NG11 6NB
☎(0115) 9846141, Pro 9211951, Sec 9214139
Off A52 Grantham Road S of Nottingham.
Parkland course.
Pro Robert Simpson; Founded 1988
Designed by Eddie McCausland, David Johnson

18 holes, 6543 yards, S.S.S. 72
Visitors: welcome with h'cap certs.
Green Fees: WD £15; WE £22.50.
Societies: welcome WD by prior arrangement.
Catering: full facilities and function room.
Practice ground; 24-bay floodlit range at Riverside 2 miles away; also 9-hole pay and play course.
Hotels: Cottage, Ruddington.

6B 83 Sandilands
Roman Bank, Sandilands, Sutton-on-Sea, Mablethorpe, Lincs, LN12 2RJ
☎ (01507) 441432, Sec 441617
On A52 3 miles S of Mablethorpe.
Links course.
Pro S Sherratt; Founded 1901
18 holes, 5995 yards, S.S.S. 69
Visitors: welcome; some WE restrictions.
Green Fees: WD £15; WE £20.
Societies: welcome by prior arrangement.
Catering: clubhouse facilities.
Hotels: Grange and Links.

6B 84 Seacroft
Drummond Rd, Skegness, Lincs, PE25 3AU
☎ (01754) 763020, Fax 763020, Pro 769624
S of Skegness towards Seacroft and Gibraltar Point nature reserve.
Links course.
Pro Robin Lawie; Founded 1895
Designed by Tom Dunn
18 holes, 6479 yards, S.S.S. 71
Visitors: welcome with h'cap certs.
Green Fees: WD £25; WE £30.
Societies: welcome by prior arrangement; deposit required; catering and golf days can be arranged; from £25.
Catering: full clubhouse facilities.
Hotels: Crown; Vine; Links.

6B 85 Sherwood Forest
Eakring Rd, Mansfield, Notts, NG18 3EW
☎ (01623) 23327, Fax 26689, Pro 27403, Sec 26689
Off A617 at Oak Tree Lane to roundabout, second exit, 1 mile to junction, right, club is 500 yards.
Heathland course.
Pro K Hall; Founded 1895
Designed by H.S. Colt, Redesigned by James Braid
18 holes, 6698 yards, S.S.S. 73
Visitors: welcome by prior arrangement with Sec.

Green Fees: WD £35; WE £35.
Societies: terms on application.
Catering: full clubhouse facilities.
Hotels: Pine Lodge; Swallow.

6B 86 Shirland
Lower Delves, Shirland, Nr Alfreton, Derbys, DE55 6AU
☎ (01773) 834935, Sec 832515, Bar/Rest 834969
Off A61 Chesterfield Road turn opposite church in Shirland village.
Parkland course with views over Derbyshire countryside.
Pro Neville Hallam; Founded 1977
18 holes, 6072 yards, S.S.S. 69
Visitors: welcome WD; by prior arrangement at WE.
Green Fees: WD £15; WE £20.
Societies: by prior arrangement with professional; golf and catering packages can be arranged; terms on application.
Catering: full clubhouse facilities.
Hotels: Riber Hall; Swallow Hotel; Higham Farm.

6B 87 Sickleholme
Saltergate Lane, Bamford, Sheffield, S33 0BN
☎ (01433) 651306, Bar/Rest 651252
On A625 14 miles W of Sheffield.
Undulating parkland course.
Pro Patrick Taylor; Founded 1898
18 holes, 6064 yards, S.S.S. 69
Visitors: welcome by prior arrangement; except Wed am.
Green Fees: WD £27; WE £32.
Societies: welcome by prior arrangement; golf and catering packages can be arranged; from £27.
Catering: restaurant and bar facilities available.
Hotels: George; Plough, both Hathersage; Yorkshire Bridge, Bamford.

6B 88 Sleaford
Willoughby Rd, South Rauceby, Sleaford, Lincs, NG34 8PL
☎ (01529) 488273, Fax 488326, Pro 488644
2 miles W of Sleaford at South Rauceby S of the A153 Sleaford to Grantham Road.
Inland links with trees and scrubland.
Pro James Wilson; Founded 1905
Designed by Tom Williamson
18 holes, 6443 yards, S.S.S. 71
Visitors: welcome by prior arrangement.
Green Fees: WD £14; WE £25.

Societies: welcome WD by prior arrangement; packages can be arranged; terms on application.
Catering: restaurant and bar facilities.
Hotels: Carre Hotel; Lincolnshire Oak; Tally Ho Motel.

6B 89 South Kyme
Skinners Lane, South Kyme, Lincoln, LN4 4AE
☎ (01526) 861113
On B1395 4 miles off the A17 midway between Boston and Sleaford.
Fenland course.
Pro Peter Chamberlain; Founded 1990
Designed by Graham Bradley
18 holes, 6597 yards, S.S.S. 71
Visitors: welcome.
Green Fees: WD £10; WE £12.
Societies: terms on application.
Catering: clubhouse facilities.
Practice ground and 6-hole course.

6B 90 Southview
Burgh Rd, Skegness, Lincs, PE25 2LA
☎ (01754) 760589
On the A158 on the outskirts of Skegness signposted to Southview Leisure park.
Parkland course.
Pro Robin Lawie; Founded 1990
9 holes, 4816 yards, S.S.S. 64
Visitors: welcome.
Green Fees: WD £6 per day; WE £6 per round.
Societies: welcome at all times; tuition; swimming pool; sauna; sunbeds; snooker.
Catering: full bar and catering in leisure park.
Hotels: North Shore; Crown; Links.

6B 91 Spalding
Surfleet, Spalding, Lincs, PE11 4EA
☎ (01775) 680386, Pro 680474, Bar/Rest 680234
Off A16 Spalding to Boston Road 4 miles N of Spalding.
Parkland course.
Pro John Spencer; Founded 1908
Designed by Spencer/Price/Ward extension 1993
18 holes, 6478 yards, S.S.S. 71
Visitors: welcome by prior arrangement.
Green Fees: WD £24; WE £30.
Societies: welcome Tues pm and Thurs; catering packages can be arranged; from £18.
Catering: full catering and bar facilities except Tues.
Practice ground.

6B 92 Stanedge

Walton Hay Farm, Stanedge, Chesterfield, Derbys, S45 0LW
☎(01246) 566156, Sec 276568
Off B5057 Darley Dale Road from the A632 Chesterfield-Matlock Road.
Moorland course; being extended 1998.
Founded 1934
9 holes, 4867 yards, S.S.S. 64
Visitors: welcome WD (Fri before 2pm); WE with a member.
Green Fees: WD £15; WE £7.50.
Societies: welcome by arrangement with Sec; catering packages can be arranged; terms on application.
Catering: full clubhouse facilities.
Practice area.
Hotels: Chesterfield Hotel; Olde House, both Chesterfield.

6B 93 Stanton-on-the-Wolds

Stanton-on-the-Wolds, Keyworth, Notts, NG12 5BH
☎(0115) 9372044, Pro 9372390, Bar/Rest 9372264
Off A606 8 miles SE of Nottingham.
Meadowland course.
Pro Nick Hernon; Founded 1906
Designed by Tom Williamson
18 holes, 6437 yards, S.S.S. 71
Visitors: welcome WD; WE with a member.
Green Fees: WD £20.
Societies: welcome by prior arrangement with Sec.
Catering: full bar and catering facilities.
Practice range, practice area; chipping green.
Hotels: Edwalton, Nottingham.

6B 94 Stoke Rochford

Stoke Rochford, Grantham, Lincs, NG33 5EW
☎(01476) 530275, Pro 530218, Sec 567030
6 miles S of Grantham off Northbound A1.
Parkland course.
Pro Angus Dow; Founded 1926/1936
Designed by Major Hotchkin/ C. Turner
18 holes, 6252 yards, S.S.S. 70
Visitors: welcome by prior arrangement.
Green Fees: WD £10; WE £12.
Societies: welcome by prior arrangement; catering packages available; snooker; terms on application.
Catering: full clubhouse bar and restaurant available.
Hotels: many in Grantham.

6B 95 Sudbrook Moor

Charity Street, Carlton Scroop, Nr Grantham, Lincs, NG32 3AT
☎(01400) 250796, Fax 250876
On A607 6 miles NE of Grantham.
Meadowland course in picturesque valley.
Pro Tim Hutton; Founded 1986
Designed by Tim Hutton
9 holes, 4650 yards, S.S.S. 62
Visitors: pay and play.
Green Fees: WD £5; WE £7.
Societies: none.
Catering: coffee shop only.

6B 96 Sutton Bridge

New Rd, Sutton Bridge, Spalding, Lincs, PE 12 9RG
☎(01406) 350323
Off A17 Long Sutton to King's Lynn Road at Sutton Bridge.
Parkland course.
Founded 1914
9 holes, 5770 yards, S.S.S. 68
Visitors: welcome WD by prior arrangement.
Green Fees: WD £17 .
Societies: welcome Tues by prior arrangement; catering can be arranged; from £17.
Catering: bar and restaurant facilities.

6B 97 Swingtime (Grimsby)

Cromwell Rd, Grimsby
☎(01472) 250555, Fax 267447
From A180 follow signs for Auditorium and Leisure centre.
Parkland course.
Pro Stephen Bennett; Founded 1995
9 holes, 4652 yards
Visitors: public pay and play.
Green Fees: WD £9; WE £11.
Societies: none.
Catering: limited.
Practice ground.

6B 98 Tapton Park Municipal

Murray House, Crow Lane, Chesterfield, Derbys, S41 0EQ
☎(01246) 273887, Pro 239500
Signposted in Chesterfield centre.
Municipal parkland course.
Pro Jeremy Tilson; Founded 1934
18 holes, 6025 yards, S.S.S. 69
Visitors: welcome; booking system all week.
Green Fees: WD £5.80; WE £7.50.
Societies: welcome by prior arrangement; packages available; terms on application.
Catering: bar and restaurant facilities available.

6B 99 Tetney

Station Rd, Tetney, Grimsby, Lincs, DN36 5HY
☎(01472) 211644
Off A16 at Tetney; 1.5 miles down Station Rd.
Parkland course.
Pro Jason Abrams; Founded 1994
18 holes, 6100 yards, S.S.S. 69
Visitors: welcome.
Green Fees: WD £10; WE £10.
Societies: welcome with some restrictions at WE; packages available for all-day catering and golf; from £25.
Catering: bar and restaurant facilities available.
Practice ground.

6B 100 Toft Hotel

Toft, Nr Bourne, Lincs, PE10 0XX
☎(01778) 590616, Bar/Rest 590614
6 miles E of Stamford on A6121.
Undulating parkland course with water features.
Pro Mark Jackson; Founded 1988
Designed by Derek and Roger Fitton
18 holes, 6486 yards, S.S.S. 71
Visitors: welcome; tees bookable 14 days ahead.
Green Fees: WD £13.50; WE £18.
Societies: welcome by arrangement.
Catering: full bar and restaurant facilities and function room in hotel.
Hotels: Toft Hotel; golfing packages available.

6B 101 Trent Lock Golf Centre

Lock Lane, Sawley, Long Eaton, Notts, NG10 2FY
☎(0115) 9464398, Fax 9461183, Bar/Rest 9461184
2 miles from M1 junction 25.
Parkland course.
Pro Mark Taylor; Founded 1991
Designed by E.W. McCausland
18 holes, 6211 yards, S.S.S. 71
Visitors: welcome; must book at WE.
Green Fees: WD £10; WE £12.
Societies: welcome by prior arrangement; from £24.95.
Catering: bar snacks, restaurant, private function room.
Practice range, 24 bays floodlit.

6B 102 Waltham Windmill

Cheapside, Waltham, Grimsby, N E Lincs, DN37 0HT
☎(01472) 824109, Pro 823963
In village of Waltham.
Parkland course.
Pro Nigel Burkitt; Founded 1997

Designed by Jim Payne
18 holes, 6333 yards, S.S.S. 70
Visitors: welcome.
Green Fees: WD £18; WE £25.
Societies: welcome WD by prior
arrangement; restrictions at WE; packages available.
Catering: catering, bar and function room.
Practice ground.
Hotels: Brackenborough Arms.

6B 103 **Welton Manor**
Hackthorn Rd, Welton, Lincs, LN2 3PD
☎(01673) 862827
Off A46 Lincoln-Grimsby road.
Undulating parkland course.
Pro Bud Edmondson; Founded 1995
18 holes, 6310 yards, S.S.S. 72
Visitors: welcome; pay and play.
Green Fees: WD £8; WE £10.
Societies: welcome any time by prior arrangement.
Catering: limited; catering available in Welton Manor Sports Club.
Practice range, 8 bays.
Hotels: Four Seasons.

6B 104 **Wollaton Park**
Lime Tree Avenue, Wollaton Park, Nottingham, NG8 1BT
☎(0115) 9784834, Fax 9787574, Sec 9787574, Bar/Rest 9787341

Off slip road from A52 at junction with Nottingham ring road.
Parkland course.
Pro John Lower; Founded 1927
Designed by T. Williamson
18 holes, 6445 yards, S.S.S. 71
Visitors: welcome.
Green Fees: WD £25; WE £25.
Societies: welcome by prior arrangement on Tues and Fri; packages available on application to secretary; from £25.
Catering: clubhouse catering facilities available.
Hotels: Priory Toby, Nottingham.

6B 105 **Woodhall Spa**
The Broadway, Woodhall Spa, Lincs, LN10 6PU
☎(01526) 352511, Fax 352778, Pro 353229
On B1191 19 miles SE of Lincoln.
Heathland course.
Pro Campbell C Elliott; Founded 1905
Designed by Col S.V. Hotchkin
18 holes, 6945 yards, S.S.S. 73
Visitors: welcome by prior arrangement; discount for EGU members.
Green Fees: WD £40; WE £40.
Societies: welcome by prior arrangement; golf and catering by arrangement; from £30.
Catering: full clubhouse facilities.
Hotels: Golf; Petwood House; Eagle Lodge.

6B 106 **Woodthorpe Hall**
Woodthorpe, Alford, Lincs, LN13 0DD
☎(01507), Fax 463664, Sec 463664
Off B1371 3 miles N of Alford.
Parkland course.
Founded 1986
18 holes, 5140 yards, S.S.S. 65
Visitors: welcome WD; by arrangement WE.
Green Fees: WD £10; WE £10.
Societies: welcome WD by prior arrangement; four weeks' notice needed; packages can be arranged for a minimum of 12; from £20.
Catering: Inn on site.

6B 107 **Worksop**
Windmill Lane, Worksop, Notts, S80 2SQ
☎(01909) 472696, Fax 477731, Pro 477732, Sec 477731, Bar/Rest 472513
Off B6034 road to Edwinstowe off the A57.
Heathland course with woods and gorse.
Pro J R King; Founded 1914
18 holes, 6660 yards, S.S.S. 73
Visitors: welcome by prior arrangement.
Green Fees: WD £22.50; WE £30.
Societies: welcome WD by prior arrangement; catering packages can be arranged; terms on application.
Catering: full clubhouse facilities.

THE NORTH WEST

There is a natural desire when heading for Scotland to keep on past those signs for the Lake District, believing that only mountaineers, ramblers, boatmen and water-skiers feel obliged to turn left for the fells and lakes of England's "little Switzerland". The travelling golfer should think about either taking a break or spending some time playing golf in Cumbria, anyway.

It is an area of hidden treasures. There can be few more rewarding moments than standing on the 18th tee at Ulverston Golf Club, in South Lakeland. The hole itself is a downhill par four finishing alongside the clubhouse. To the left and ahead you have the mountains of the Lake District, snow-capped in winter, dappled bright in summer. On the right and lying hundreds of feet below is Morecambe Bay, a tidal estuary alive with bird life and a thriving shrimp industry.

The course itself is invariably in immaculate condition as it sits alongside the quaint old village of Bardsea, with farmland and Birkrigg Common all around. It is parkland with a great diversity of trees and although it may not appear to be particularly long – 6,420 yards – it is cleverly designed without being tricky and there are some memorable holes.

The golfer, leaving Ulverston perhaps to try the unique Windermere course, will also find himself driving close to the car museum and deer park at Holker Hall, Wordsworth's Cottage and Beatrix Potter's cottage. At Windermere he may be forgiven for expecting to find some of her creatures dancing among the rocks, for this undulating 5,006 yards (SSS 65) has a charm of its own. There is no claim from the membership that they belong to a "great" course and its six par threes give an indication of the kind of rock-strewn, mountain-goat country the architect,

George Lowe, had to work with. He did a marvellous job and local hoteliers, advertising their golf packages describe it as "the Gleneagles of the Lake District".

Steven Rooke, the professional, has been there 20 years after a brief flirtation with the European Tour. He says: "It is just a wonderful place to play golf, especially on those summer evenings when the sun is going down and casting its amazing light on the Langdale Pikes."

Alongside the 10th tee, at a high point in the course where the locals sometimes joke that they should be roped together, there is a signpost pointing to the various peaks – Coniston Old Man, Scafell Pike, Great Gable, Helvellyn, High Street and so on. To pause there, to breathe in the rich Lake District air is another of the rewards of Windermere Golf Club.

Another mountain, Blencathra or Saddleback (it is known by both names) dominates Keswick Golf Club, another attractive course well worth a detour. It is part moorland, part parkland with tree-lined fairways and streams to catch the unwary. This is the absolute heart of the Lake District. Derwentwater, regarded as the queen of the lakes, is not far away, green fees are amazingly good value and, although it can be bleak in winter, summer days provide memorable rounds.

Ulverston, Windermere and Keswick are just three of the courses that make the Lake District ideal for a golfing tour but it remains unspoiled and relatively undiscovered. Silloth on Solway, to the North, is a seaside championship course of the highest quality, while Penrith and Kendal have qualities of their own.

The Lake District may not be fashionable for golf. It may be isolated but it would be surprising for anyone to give it a try and then register disappointment.

7 1 **Accrington & District**
New Barn Farm, Devon Ave, West
End, Oswaldtwistle, Accrington, Lancs
BB5 4LS
☎(01254) 232734, Fax 381614, Pro
231091, Sec 381614
On A679 5 miles from Blackburn.
Moorland course.
Pro Bill Harling; Founded 1893
Designed by James Braid
18 holes, 6044 yards, S.S.S. 69
Visitors: welcome.
Green Fees: WD £20; WE £25.
Societies: welcome by arrangement.
Catering: full facilities except Mon and
Thurs.
Practice ground.
Hotels: County; Kendal; Duncan
House.

7 2 **Allerton Municipal**
Allerton Road, Liverpool, Merseyside
L18 3JT
☎(0151) 428 7490, Fax 428 7490, Pro
428 1046, Bar/Rest 428 8510
From end of M62 S on to Queens
Drive, on to the ring road to Yewtree
Road, signposted on Allerton Road.
Parkland course; also 9 holes, 1841
yards, SSS 34.
Pro B Large; Founded 1923
18 holes, 5494 yards, S.S.S. 66
Visitors: welcome.
Green Fees: terms on application.
Societies: welcome WD and WE pm
by arrangement with the professional;
terms on application.
Catering: by arrangement.
Hotels: Redbourne; Grange.

7 3 **Alston Moor**
The Hermitage, Alston, Cumbria, CA9
3DB
☎(01434) 381675
On B6277 1.5 miles S of Alston; sign-
posted from the top of the town.
Parkland and fell course.
Founded 1906/1969
Designed by Members
10 holes, 5518 yards, S.S.S. 67
Visitors: welcome by prior arrange-
ment.
Green Fees: WD £8; WE £10.
Societies: welcome by arrangement;
packages for golf and catering can be
provided; from £8.
Catering: bar and catering facilities.
Hotels: secretary can provide details.

7 4 **Appleby**
Brackenber Moor, Appleby-in-
Westmorland, Cumbria, CA16 6LP

☎(017683) 52922, Pro 51432
On A66 2 miles E of Appleby.
Moorland course.
Pro Paul Jenkinson; Founded 1903
Designed by Willie Fernie of Troon
18 holes, 5901 yards, S.S.S. 68
Visitors: welcome.
Green Fees: WD £14; WE £18.
Societies: welcome by prior arrange-
ment.
Catering: full catering and bar except
Tues.
Practice ground.
Hotels: Tufton Arms; Royal Oak;
Appleby Manor; The Gate.

7 5 **Ashton & Lea**
Tudor Ave, off Blackpool Rd, Lea,
Preston PR4 0XA
☎(01772) 726480, Fax 735762, Pro
720374, Sec 735282
On A5085 3 miles W of Preston.
Parkland course with water features.
Pro M Greenough; Founded 1913
Designed by J. Steer
18 holes, 6346 yards, S.S.S. 70
Visitors: welcome by prior arrange-
ment.
Green Fees: WD £20; WE £23.
Societies: welcome by prior arrange-
ment; packages include golf and cater-
ing; £29.
Catering: full clubhouse facilities
available.
Hotels: Travel Inn, Lea; Marriott,
Broughton.

7 6 **Ashton-in-Makerfield**
Garswood Park, Liverpool Rd, Ashton-
in-Makerfield, Lancs WN4 0YT
☎(01942) 727267, Sec 719330
Off A58 from M6 0.5 miles to course.
Parkland course.
Founded 1902
Designed by F.W. Hawtree
18 holes, 6205 yards, S.S.S. 70
Visitors: welcome WD except Wed;
WE only with a member.
Green Fees: WD £25.
Societies: welcome Tues and Thurs
by prior arrangement.
Catering: full facilities except Mon.
Hotels: Haydock Thistle.

7 7 **Ashton-under-Lyne**
Gorsey Way, Ashton-under-Lyne,
Lancs OL6 9HT
☎(0161) 330 1537, Fax 330 1537,
Pro 308 2095
3 miles from town centre.
Semi-parkland course.
Pro Colin Boyle; Founded 1913

18 holes, 6209 yards, S.S.S. 70
Visitors: welcome by prior arrange-
ment.
Green Fees: WD £25; WE £25.
Societies: welcome Tues, Thurs and
Fri; packages for golf and catering
available; terms on application.
Catering: clubhouse facilities.
Hotels: Broadoak Hotel.

7 8 **Bacup**
Maden Rd, Bacup, Lancs OL13 8HY
☎(01706) 873170
Off A671 7 miles N of Rochdale 0.5
miles from Bacup centre.
Meadowland course.
Founded 1911
9 holes, 6008 yards, S.S.S. 67
Visitors: welcome Wed, Thurs and
Fri, and after competitions at WE.
Green Fees: WD £14; WE £17.
Societies: welcome Wed, Thurs and
Fri by prior arrangement.
Catering: full clubhouse facilities
available.
Hotels: Royal, Waterfoot.

7 9 **Barrow**
Rakesmoor Lane, Hawcoat, Barrow-in-
Furness, Cumbria LA14 4QB
☎(01229) 825444, Pro 832121
From M6 junction 36 take A590 to
Barrow; 3 miles before town follow
Industrial route turning left into Bank
Lane.
Parkland course; being remeasured in
1998.
Pro J McLeod; Founded 1922
18 holes, 6137 yards, S.S.S. 69
Visitors: welcome with h'cap certs
and by prior arrangement.
Green Fees: WD £15; WE £25.
Societies: welcome by prior arrange-
ment with the professional; packages
include a full day's golf and catering;
snooker table; from £26.
Catering: full clubhouse facilities.
Hotels: Lisdowie, Barrow.

7 10 **Baxenden & District**
Top-o'-the Meadow, Wooley Lane, Nr
Accrington, Lancs BB5 2EA
☎(01254) 234555
Take M65 Accrington exit and follow
the signs for Baxenden; course sign-
posted in village.
Moorland course.
Founded 1913
9 holes, 5717 yards, S.S.S. 68
Visitors: welcome WD; with member
only WE.
Green Fees: WD £15.

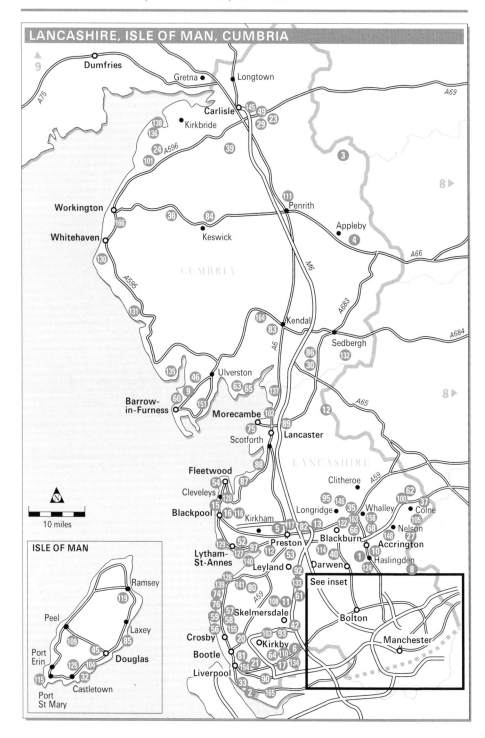

LANCASHIRE, ISLE OF MAN, CUMBRIA

KEY						
1 Accrington & District	35 Clitheroe	69 Greenmount	101 Maryport	134 Sherdley Park
2 Allerton Municipal	36 Cockermouth	70 Haigh Hall	102 Morecambe	135 Silecroft
3 Alston Moor	37 Colne	71 Harwood	103 Mossack Hall	136 Silloth on Solway
4 Appleby	38 Crompton & Royton	72 Haydock Park	104 Mount Murray	137 Silverdale
5 Ashton & Lea	39 Dalston Hall	73 Heaton Park	105 Nelson	138 Solway Village
6 Ashton-in-Makerfield	40 Darwen	74 Hesketh	106 North Manchester	139 Southport & Ainsdale
7 Ashton-under-Lyne	41 Davyhulme Park	75 The Heysham	107 Oldham	140 Southport Municipal
8 Bacup	42 Dean Wood	76 Hillside Golf Club	108 Ormskirk	141 Southport Old Links
9 Barrow	43 Deane	77 Hindley Hall	109 Peel	142 Springfield Park
10 Baxenden & District	44 Denton	78 Horwich	110 Pennington	143 Stand
11 Beacon Park	45 Douglas	79 Houghwood Hall	111 Penrith	144 Standish Court Golf Club
12 Bentham	46 Dunnerholme	80 Hurlston Hall	112 Penwortham	145 Stonyholme Municipal
13 Blackburn	47 Dunscar	81 Huyton & Prescot	113 Pike Fold	146 Stonyhurst Park
14 Blackley	48 Duxbury Park	82 Ingol Golf & Squash	114 Pleasington	147 Swinton Park
15 Blackpool North Shore	49 Eden	Club	115 Port St Mary Golf	148 Towneley
16 Blackpool Park	50 Ellesmere	83 Kendal	Pavilion	149 Tunshill
17 Blundells Hill	51 Fairfield Golf & Sailing	84 Keswick	116 Poulton-le-Fylde	150 Turton
18 Bolton	Club	85 King Edward Bay	117 Preston	151 Ulverston
19 Bolton Old Links	52 Fairhaven	(Howstrake)	118 Prestwich	152 Walmersley
20 Bootle	53 Fishwick Hall	86 Kirkby Lonsdale	119 Ramsey	153 Werneth (Oldham)
21 Bowring	54 Fleetwood	87 Knott End	120 Reach	154 West Derby
22 Brackley	55 Flixton	88 Lancaster	121 Regent Park (Bolton)	155 West Lancashire
23 Brampton	56 Formby	89 Lansil	122 Rishton	156 Westhoughton
24 Brayton Park	57 Formby Golf Centre	90 Lee Park	123 Rochdale	157 Westhoughton Golf
25 Breightmet	58 Formby Hall	91 Leigh	124 Rossendale	Centre
26 Brookdale	59 Formby Ladies	92 Leyland	125 Rowany	158 Whalley
27 Burnley	60 Furness	93 Liverpool Municipal	126 Royal Birkdale	159 Whitefield
28 Bury	61 Gathurst	(Kirkby)	127 Royal Lytham & St	160 Whittaker
29 Carlisle	62 Ghyll	94 Lobden	Annes	161 Wigan
30 Casterton	63 Grange Fell	95 Longridge	128 Saddleworth	162 William Wroe
31 Castle Hawk	64 Grange Park	96 Lowes Park	129 St Annes Old Links	163 Wilpshire
32 Castletown Golf Links	65 Grange-over-Sands	97 Lytham Green Drive	130 St Bees	164 Windermere
33 Childwall	66 Great Harwood	98 Manchester	131 Seascale	165 Woolton
34 Chorley	67 Great Lever & Farnworth	99 Manor (Bolton)	132 Sedbergh	166 Workington
	68 Green Haworth	100 Marsden Park	133 Shaw Hill Hotel G & CC	167 Worsley

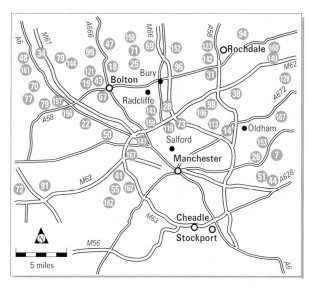

Pro Ray Peters; Founded 1982
Designed by Donald Steel
18 holes, 5931 yards, S.S.S. 69
Visitors: pay and play.
Green Fees: terms on application.
Societies: welcome by prior arrangement; payment required 10 days in advance; terms on application.
Catering: clubhouse facilities.
Practice range, 24 bays floodlit.
Hotels: Lancashire Lodge.

7 12 Bentham

Robin Lane, Bentham, Lancaster,
Lancs LA2 7AG
☎ (015242) 61018, Sec 62455
Between Lancaster and Settle on
B6480 13 miles E of M6 junction 34.
Undulating meadowland course.
Founded 1922
9 holes, 5820 yards, S.S.S. 69
Visitors: welcome.
Green Fees: WD £10; WE £15.
Societies: welcome by arrangement.
Catering: bar and snacks.
Hotels: Bridge, Ingleton; Post House, Lancaster.

7 13 Blackburn

Beardwood Brow, Blackburn, Lancs
BB2 7AX

Societies: welcome WD by arrangement with the secretary; packages include coffee, light lunch, 3-course meal and 27 holes of golf; from £22.
Catering: bar and snacks available; meals to order.
Hotels: Syke Side House, Haslingden.

7 11 Beacon Park

Beacon Lane, Dalton, Up Holland,
Wigan, Lancs WN8 7RU
☎ (01695) 622700, Sec 726298,
Bar/Rest 625551
Off A577 in Up Holland.
Parkland course.

☎(01254) 51122, Fax 665578, Pro 55942
Odd A677 at W end of Blackburn.
Parkland course.
Pro A Rodwell; Founded 1894
18 holes, 6144 yards, S.S.S. 70
Visitors: welcome by prior arrangement.
Green Fees: WD £21; WE £25.
Societies: welcome WD except Tues; catering and golf packages can be arranged; terms on application.
Catering: clubhouse facilities.

7 14 **Blackley**
Victoria Ave East, Blackley, Manchester, M9 7HW
☎(0161) 643 2980, Pro 643 3912, Sec 654 7770, Bar/Rest 653 5707
5 miles N of City centre.
Parkland course.
Pro Andrew Cowan; Founded 1907
18 holes, 6300 yards, S.S.S. 70
Visitors: welcome WD; with member at weekend.
Green Fees: WD £18; WE £12.
Societies: welcome WD except Thurs; golf and catering packages available; from £20.
Catering: full clubhouse catering facilities.
Hotels: Bower Hotel, Chadderton.

7 15 **Blackpool North Shore**
Devonshire Rd, Blackpool, Lancashire, FY2 0RD
☎(01253) 352054, Fax 591240, Pro 354640, Bar/Rest 351017
From M55 junction 4 take Preston New Road to Whitegate Drive and Devonshire Road.
Seaside links course.
Pro Brendan Ward; Founded 1904
18 holes, 6431 yards, S.S.S. 71
Visitors: welcome by prior arrangement; tees reserved for members until 9.30 &12.30-1; not before 2 Thurs and 4 Sat.
Green Fees: WD £25; WE £30.
Societies: welcome WD except Thurs; golf and catering packages available; terms on application.
Catering: catering and bar facilities available daily.
Hotels: many in Blackpool.

7 16 **Blackpool Park**
North Park Drive;Blackpool, Lancs FY3 8LS
☎(01253) 393960, Fax 397916, Pro 391004, Sec 397916, Bar/Rest 396683

2 miles E of Blackpool signposted off M55.
Parkland course.
Pro B Purdie; Founded 1926
Designed by Dr MacKenzie
18 holes, 6192 yards, S.S.S. 69
Visitors: welcome; tee reservations through Blackpool Borough Council.
Green Fees: WD £11; WE £12.
Societies: welcome by prior arrangement with Blackpool Borough Council; terms on application.
Catering: clubhouse facilities.
Hotels: many in Blackpool.

7 17 **Blundells Hill**
Blundells Lane, Rainhill, Liverpool, Merseyside, L35 6NA
☎(0151) 4269040, Fax 01744 28861, Pro 430 0100, Sec 01744 24892, Bar/Rest 426 9040
From M62 junction 7 take A57 towards Prescot; turn left after garage; then left into Blundells Lane.
Parkland course.
Pro R Leach; Founded 1994
Designed by S Marnoch
18 holes, 6256 yards, S.S.S. 70
Visitors: welcome by arrangement.
Green Fees: WD £20. ,WE £30.
Societies: welcome Mon to Thurs; catering and golf packages for a minimum of 12; £28-£35.
Catering: full clubhouse facilities.
Hotels: Ship Inn, Rainhill; Stakis, St Helens; Logwood Mill, Whiston; Hillcrest, Cronton.

7 18 **Bolton**
Lostock Park, Chorley New Rd, Bolton, Lancs BL6 4AJ
☎(01204) 843278, Fax 843067, Pro 843073, Sec 843067
3 miles W of Bolton.
Hilly course.
Pro Robert Longworth; Founded 1891/1912
18 holes, 6237 yards, S.S.S. 70
Visitors: welcome between 10-12 and after 2pm.
Green Fees: WD £29; WE £36.
Societies: welcome Mon, Thurs and some Fris; discounts available for larger groups; packages for golf and catering available; terms on application.
Catering: clubhouse facilities.

7 19 **Bolton Old Links**
Chorley Old Rd, Bolton, Lancs BL1 5SU
☎(01204) 840050, Pro 843089, Sec 842307

On B6226 N of A58 from junction 5 on M61.
Moorland course.
Pro Paul Horridge; Founded 1891
Designed by Dr A. MacKenzie
18 holes, 6406 yards, S.S.S. 71
Visitors: welcome except on competition days; phone in advance.
Green Fees: WD £27.50; WE £35.
Societies: welcome WD by prior arrangement.
Catering: full facilities except Mon.
Practice range, practice ground; indoor practice facilities.
Hotels: Crest; Pack Horse; Last Drop; Moat House.

7 20 **Bootle**
Dunnings Bridge Rd, Bootle, Merseyside L30 2PP
☎(0151) 928 6196, Pro 928 1371
On A565 5 miles from Liverpool.
Municipal seaside links course.
Founded 1934
Designed by F. Stephens
18 holes, 6242 yards, S.S.S. 70
Visitors: welcome.
Green Fees: WD £5.50; WE £6.75.
Societies: welcome by prior arrangement.
Catering: full clubhouse facilities available.
Hotels: Park.

7 21 **Bowring**
Bowring Park Golf Course, Roby Rd, Huyton, Liverpool, Merseyside, L36 4HD
☎(0151) 489 1901
6 miles N of Liverpool.
Municipal parkland course.
Founded 1913
18 holes, 6147 yards, S.S.S. 70
Visitors: welcome.
Green Fees: WD £5.50; WE £6.30.
Societies: welcome by prior arrangement.
Catering: snacks; bar for members only.

7 22 **Brackley**
Bullows Rd, Little Hulton, Worsley, Manchester, M38 9TR
☎(0161) 790 6076
9 miles from Manchester on A6; turn right at White Lion Hotel into Highfield Rd; left into Captain Fold Rd; left into Bullows Rd.
Parkland course.
Pro Mike Higgins; Founded 1976
9 holes, 6006 yards, S.S.S. 69
Visitors: welcome; book at WE.

Green Fees: WD £3.85; WE £6.60.
Societies: welcome by prior arrangement; from £7.
Catering: none.

7 23 Brampton
Brampton, Cumbria, CA8 1HN
☎(016977) 2255, Pro 2000
1.75 miles from Brampton on B6413
Castle Carrock Road.
Moorland course.
Pro Stewart Wilkinson; Founded 1907
Designed by James Braid
18 holes, 6407 yards, S.S.S. 71
Visitors: welcome; tee booked
9.30am-10.30am Mon, Wed, Thurs.
Green Fees: WD £22; WE £28.
Societies: welcome by prior arrangement WD; limited at WE.
Catering: full facilities in refurbished clubhouse.
Practice ground.
Hotels: details of local guest houses and hotels offering reduced fees from club or pro.

7 24 Brayton Park Golf Course
Brayton, Aspatria, Carlisle, Cumbria, CA5 3TD
☎(016973) 20840
Off A596 W of Carlisle.
Parkland course.
Pro Graham Batey; Founded 1978
9 holes, 5042 yards, S.S.S. 64
Visitors: welcome.
Green Fees: WD £7; WE £8.
Societies: welcome by prior arrangement.
Catering: full clubhouse facilities.
Hotels: Kelsey; Wheyrigg; Green Hill.

7 25 Breightmet
Red Lane, Red Bridge, Bolton, Lancs
BL2 5PA
☎(01204) 527381
Off Bury Road in Bolton.
Moorland/parkland course.
Founded 1911
9 holes, 6416 yards, S.S.S. 71
Visitors: welcome by prior arrangement; some restrictions Sat and Wed.
Green Fees: WD £15; WE £18.
Societies: welcome WD; some Suns; packages include full day's golf and catering; snooker; £25-£30.
Catering: full clubhouse facilities.

7 26 Brookdale
Midlock Rd, Woodhouses, Failsworth, Manchester, Manchester, M35 9WQ

☎(0161) 681 4534, Fax 681 4534, Pro 681 2655
From Manchester take A62 turning right at Ashton Rd East; 1 mile turn right into Failsworth Rd; 0.25 miles into Midlock Road.
Parkland course.
Pro Tony Cupello; Founded 1960
Designed by available
18 holes, 5874 yards, S.S.S. 68
Visitors: welcome WD only.
Green Fees: WD £20.
Societies: welcome ,Wed, Thurs, Fri; packages include golf and catering from £33.
Catering: clubhouse facilities.
Hotels: Smokies Park; Bower Hotel.

7 27 Burnley
Glen View, Burnley, Lancs BB11 3RW
☎(01282) 421045, Pro 455266, Sec 451281
Glen View road is off Manchester Road.
Moorland course.
Pro W P Tye; Founded 1905
18 holes, 5911 yards, S.S.S. 69
Visitors: welcome with h'cap certs.
Green Fees: WD £20; WE £25.
Societies: welcome everyday except Sat; h'cap certs required; 36 holes of golf plus meals; £30.
Catering: full facilities.
Hotels: Rosehill House Hotel.

7 28 Bury
Unsworth Hall, Blackford Bridge, Bury, BL9 9TJ
☎(0161) 766 4897, Fax 796 3480, Pro 766 2213
On A57 1.5 miles from M62 junction 17.
Undulating moorland course.
Pro S Crake; Founded 1890
Designed by Dr A Mackenzie
18 holes, 5927 yards, S.S.S. 68
Visitors: welcome except on club comp days.
Green Fees: WD £26; WE £30.
Societies: welcome Wed-Fri; packages include full day's golf and catering £35.
Catering: full clubhouse facilities.
Hotels: Red Hall; Rostrevor.

7 29 Carlisle
Aglionby, Carlisle, Cumbria, CA4 8AG
☎(01228) 513029, Fax 513303, Pro 513241, Sec 513303
On A69 0.25 miles E of M6 junc 43.
Parkland course (Open Championship qualifying course).

Pro John S More; Founded 1909/1940
Designed by T Simpson, MacKenzie Ross/ Frank Pennink
18 holes, 6223 yards, S.S.S. 70
Visitors: welcome except Tues and Sat.
Green Fees: WD £22; WE £30.
Societies: welcome Mon, Wed, Fri by prior arrangement; packages available; club can administer competitions; private dining facilities; terms on application.
Catering: full clubhouse facilities.
Practice area.
Hotels: Cumbrain Hotel, Carlisle; Crown Hotel, Wetherall.

7 30 Casterton
Sedburgh Rd, Casterton, Carnforth, Lancs LA6 2LA
☎(01524) 271592
On A683 Sebergh Road.
Picturesque undulating parkland course.
Pro Roy Williamson; Founded 1946/1993
Designed by W Adamson
9 holes, 5726 yards, S.S.S. 68
Visitors: welcome by prior arrangement; weekend reservations essential.
Green Fees: WD £9; WE £12.
Societies: welcome by arrangement; maximum 20; terms on application.
Catering: light refreshments only.
Hotels: Pheasant, Casterton; Royal, Kirkby Lonsdale.

7 31 Castle Hawk
Chadwick Lane, Heywood Rd, Castleton, OL11 3BY
☎(01706) 640841
Leave Rochdale on Manchester Road towards Castleton; turn right directly before Castleton station.
Undulating parkland/meadowland course.
Pro Michael Vipond; Founded 1965
Designed by T. Wilson
9 holes, 5398 yards, S.S.S. 55
Visitors: welcome.
Green Fees: WD £7; WE £9.
Societies: welcome by prior arrangement.
Catering: restaurant and bar facilities.
Hotels: Royal Toby.

7 32 Castletown Golf Links
Fort Island, Derbyhaven, Castletown, Isle of Man, IM9 1UA
☎(01624) 822201, Fax 824633
1 mile from airport.
Links course.

Pro Murray Crowe; Founded 1892
Designed by MacKenzie Ross
18 holes, 6711 yards, S.S.S. 72
Visitors: welcome; residents have priority at WE.
Green Fees: WD £25; WE £30.
Societies: welcome by prior arrangement; discounts for residents; catering packages available; snooker, sauna, indoor pool; from £25.
Catering: full club and hotel catering restaurant and bar facilities.
Practice ground.
Hotels: Castletown Links.

7 33 Childwall
Naylor's Rd, Liverpool, Merseyside, L27 2YB
☎(0151) 487 0654, Fax 487 0882, Pro 487 9871
5 miles from Liverpool, 2 miles from M62 junction 6.
Parkland course.
Pro Nigel Parr; Founded 1922
Designed by James Braid
18 holes, 6470 yards, S.S.S. 71
Visitors: welcome WD except Tues between 9.45 am and 2pm.
Green Fees: WD £25; WE £35.
Societies: welcome WD except Tues by prior arrangement.
Catering: bar and restaurant facilities.
Practice ground.
Hotels: Logwood Mill; Derby Lodge.

7 34 Chorley
Hall o' th' Hill, Heath Charnock, Lancs PR6 9HX
☎(01257) 480263, Fax 480722, Pro 481245
On A673 100 yds S of A6 junction at Skew Bridge traffic lights.
Heathland course.
Pro Gavin Mutch; Founded 1898
Designed by J.A. Steer
18 holes, 6307 yards, S.S.S. 70
Visitors: welcome WD except Mon by prior arrangement.
Green Fees: WD £27.
Societies: welcome Tues to Fri by prior arrangement.
Catering: full bar and restaurant facilities.
Hotels: Yarrow Bridge; Parkville; Hartwood Hall; Gladmar.

7 35 Clitheroe
Whalley Rd, Pendleton, Clitheroe, Lancs BB7 1PP
☎(01200) 422618, Fax 422282, Pro 424242, Sec 422282
2 miles S of Clitheroe on the

Clitheroe-Whalley Road.
Parkland course.
Pro J E Twissell; Founded 1891/1932
Designed by James Braid
18 holes, 6326 yards, S.S.S. 71
Visitors: welcome by prior arrangement.
Green Fees: WD £28; WE £33.
Societies: welcome by prior arrangement; packages can be arranged for golf and catering from £33.
Catering: full clubhouse facilities.

7 36 Cockermouth
Embleton, Cockermouth, Cumbria, CA13 9SG
☎(017687) 76223, Fax 76941, Sec 76941
3 miles E of Cockermouth.
Fell land course.
Founded 1896
Designed by James Braid
18 holes, 5496 yards, S.S.S. 67
Visitors: welcome by prior arrangement.
Green Fees: WD £15, WE£20.
Societies: welcome; terms on application; from £15.
Catering: clubhouse facilities.
Hotels: Trout; Derwent Lodge, both Cockermouth.

7 37 Colne
Law Farm, Skipton Old Rd, Colne, Lancs BB8 7EB
☎(01282) 863391
From M65 E end travel 1 mile to roundabout, take first exit left.
Moorland course with trees.
Founded 1901
Designed by Club members
9 holes, 5961 yards, S.S.S. 69
Visitors: welcome except comp days; 2 balls only on Thurs.
Green Fees: WD £16; WE £20.
Societies: welcome WD; terms on application; from £16.
Catering: clubhouse facilities.
Practice ground.
Hotels: The Old Stone Trough, Colne.

7 38 Crompton & Royton
High Barn, Royton, Oldham, Lancs OL2 6RW
☎(0161) 624 0986, Fax 624 0986, Pro 624 2154, Bar/Rest 624 9867
Off A627 at Royton centre.
Moorland course.
Pro David Melling; Founded 1908
18 holes, 6224 yards, S.S.S. 70
Visitors: welcome with restrictions at WE and Tues and Wed.

Green Fees: WD £25; WE £30.
Societies: welcome Mon, Thurs and Fri; terms on application.
Catering: clubhouse facilities.

7 39 Dalston Hall
Dalston, Nr Carlisle, Cumbria, CA5 7JX
☎(01228) 710165
From M6 junction 42 to Dalston village; course 0.5 miles on right.
Parkland course.
Founded 1990
Designed by David Pearson
9 holes, 5103 yards, S.S.S. 65
Visitors: welcome; tee booking required at WE and after 4pm WD.
Green Fees: WD £6.50; WE £12.
Societies: welcome by arrangement; packages on application.
Catering: bar and restaurant.
Hotels: Dalston Hall has caravan park.

7 40 Darwen
Winter Hill, Darwen, Lancs BB3 0LB
☎(01254) 701287, Pro 776370, Sec 704367
1.5 miles from Darwen centre.
Moorland/parkland course.
Pro W Lennon; Founded 1893
18 holes, 5863 yards, S.S.S. 68
Visitors: welcome.
Green Fees: WD £20; WE £25.
Societies: welcome by prior arrangement; terms on application.
Catering: clubhouse facilities.
Hotels: Whitehall Hotel & CC.

7 41 Davyhulme Park
Gleneagles Rd, Davyhulme, Urmston, Manchester, M41 8SA
☎(0161) 748 2260, Pro 748 3931
8 miles S of Manchester adjacent to Trafford Hospital in Davyhulme.
Parkland course.
Pro Dean Butler; Founded 1910
18 holes, 6237 yards, S.S.S. 70
Visitors: welcome WD.
Green Fees: WD £24.
Societies: welcome Mon, Tues, Thurs by arrangement.
Catering: full facilities.

7 42 Dean Wood
Lafford Lane, Up Holland, Skelmersdale, Lancs WN8 0QZ
☎(01695) 622219, Fax 622245, Pro 622980
1.5 miles from M6 junction 26 following Up Holland signs.

Castletown

When the weather is fine, the greens holding and there is no wind, seaside links often present fewer problems than other types of course; but the moment the wind stirs it is another matter.

Tales of the 1979 PGA Cup match at Castletown in the Isle of Man centred largely on days of sunshine, the ball running a mile, and agreement that it was an idyllic spot. My baptism was a little more severe, a near gale springing up overnight and rain slanting in from the Irish Sea. The clear outline of mountain peaks disappeared and there was a remoteness, almost a loneliness, on the little peninsula, but not even a princely soaking could dampen my admiration. Castletown's position as one of the great courses of the British Isles is undoubted.

Castletown's hazards are all natural – gorse, bracken, rough, rocks and a beach which gives the course more coastal frontage than perhaps any other in the world. Apart from a clump of forlorn palms behind the eighth green, and some planting to mask the wall behind the fourth there isn't a tree to be seen. Though the golfer has nothing to shield him, there is nothing to obscure the magnificent array of views either; the sea, two great sweeps of bay, the landmark of the castle and, on a good day, the Cumbrian Hills.

In days gone by, it was the residence of the Earl of Derby who, as Lord of Man, started the Derby at Castletown prior to taking it to Epsom. The 10th was the actual site, the hole not surprisingly assuming the name 'Racecourse'.

Castletown deserves undivided attention, although the start is no indication of what lies ahead. The first is a short, uphill par four, one yard, in fact, over the par three limit, and the second a somewhat plain two-shotter. It is when you turn away down the long fifth, a dogleg round the corner of a stone wall, with a second shot between a large mound and an old pill box, that the course really begins. The fifth, not quite such a good par five as the third, sandwiches the fourth where the drive must be left to obtain the correct angle to negotiate the slope of the green and to miss the guardian bunkers on the right. Castletown's short holes make a wonderful set, the sixth, the shortest of them, providing an inviting shot even if the green is encircled by trouble. The same applies to the drive at the seventh and the second shot to a green typical of Mackenzie Ross's imaginative designs.

The eighth is no easier. The fairway may present a nice target at a lower level but it is also alarmingly narrow and the road is only a thin strip separating errant drives from the beach on which balls, pebbles and boulders are indistinguishable. The drive at the ninth must be aimed on the outline of King William's College, a fortress of Manx stone. And at what may have been the home turn in the first Derby down by the 10th green, Castletown Bay hoves in sight. There is no let-up.

At the delightful short 11th and the next two par fours, it is all too simple to let a tee shot drift to the right and, if the 14th is a shade less of a threat in this regard, the tee marker tells the bad news that it is 468 yards. On the 15th, a stone wall denotes out of bounds and the contouring of the greens foil those playing too safe to the left; but the best is yet to come – notably the 17th with its gaping gorge in front of the tee and resplendent rocks to the right. The 18th is a challenging finish, set against the square form of the welcoming Links Hotel.

Those who originally spied out the land knew what they were doing; but a question must be asked of the island's emblem of the Three Legs of Man and its motto "Whichever way you throw me, I shall stand". Did they ever experiment on the championship tee at the 17th with a gale off the sea?

Hilly parkland course.
Pro A B Coup; Founded 1922
Designed by James Braid
18 holes, 6137 yards, S.S.S. 70
Visitors: welcome by prior arrange-
ment.
Green Fees: WD £27; WE £30.
Societies: welcome Mon and Thurs;
terms on application.
Catering: clubhouse facilities.
Practice area; practice nets.
Hotels: Holland Hall; Travel Inn.

7 43 Deane
Broadford Rd, Bolton, Lancs BL3 4NS
☎(01204) 651944, Fax 651808, Sec
651808
1 mile from M61 junction 5.
Undulating parkland course.
Pro David Martindale; Founded 1908
18 holes, 5652 yards, S.S.S. 67
Visitors: welcome by arrangement.
Green Fees: WD £20; WE £25.
Societies: welcome Tues, Thurs, Fri
by prior arrangement; full day package
of golf and catering; £31.
Catering: clubhouse facilities.
Hotels: Beaumont Hotel.

7 44 Denton
Manchester Rd, Denton, Manchester;
Gtr Manchester; M34 2NU
☎(0161) 336 3218, Fax 336 4751,
Pro 336 2070
5 miles SE of Manchester off the A57;
also close to the M66 Denton round-
about.
Parkland course.
Pro Michael Hollingworth; Founded
1909
18 holes, 6541 yards, S.S.S. 71
Visitors: welcome WD; WE only with
a member.
Green Fees: WD £25; WE £30.
Societies: welcome Tues to Fri.
Catering: new clubhouse facilities
opening in May.
Hotels: Stable Gate Travelodge.

7 45 Douglas
Pulrose Rd, Douglas, Isle of Man, IM2
1AE
☎(01624) 675952
1 mile from Douglas town centre, clubhouse near Power Station cooling
tower.
Municipal parkland course.
Pro Kevin Parry; Founded 1927
Designed by Dr A. MacKenzie
18 holes, 5922 yards, S.S.S. 68
Visitors: welcome; advisable to phone
in advance.

Green Fees: WD £7; WE £10.
Societies: welcome by prior arrange-
ment.
Catering: full meals and bar snacks
throughout season.
Hotels: contact local tourist board.

7 46 Dunnerholme
Duddon Rd, Askam-in-Furness,
Cumbria, LA16 7AW
☎(01229) 462675
Take A590 to Askam, turn left over
railway into Duddon Rd, continue down
towards the seashore over the cattle
grid.
Links course.
Founded 1905
10 holes, 6154 yards, S.S.S. 70
Visitors: welcome except before
4.30pm Sun.
Green Fees: WD £12; WE £15.
Societies: welcome by prior arrange-
ment; few restrictions.
Catering: bar and catering facilities.
Hotels: Railway; White Water;
Clarence; Wellington; Abbey House.

7 47 Dunscar
Longworth Lane; Bromley Cross,
Bolton, Lancs BL7 9QY
☎(01204) 598228, Pro 592992, Sec
303321
Off A666 3 miles N of Bolton.
Moorland course.
Pro Gary Treadbold; Founded 1908
Designed by George Lowe
18 holes, 6085 yards, S.S.S. 69
Visitors: welcome by prior arrange-
ment.
Green Fees: WD £20; WE £30.
Societies: welcome by prior arrange-
ment; terms on application.
Catering: clubhouse facilities.
Hotels: Egerton House; Last Drop.

7 48 Duxbury Park
Duxbury Park; Chorley, Lancs PR7
4AS
☎(01257) 265380
1.5 miles S of Chorley on A5106 from
A6.
Municipal parkland course.
Founded 1970
18 holes, 6270 yards, S.S.S. 70
Visitors: welcome; booking system.
Green Fees: WD, terms on applica-
tion.
Societies: welcome WD by prior
arrangement.
Catering: limited at club; facilities
close by.
Hotels: Hartwood Hall; Kilhey Court.

7 49 Eden
Crosby-on-Eden; Carlisle; Cumbria
CA6 4RA
☎(01228) 573003, Fax 818435,
Bar/Rest 573013
From M6 junction 44 take A689 to Low
Crosby and Crosby-on-Eden.
Parkland course.
Pro Steve Harrison; Founded 1991
Designed by E. MacCauslin
18 holes, 6368 yards, S.S.S. 72
Visitors: welcome; booking advisable.
Green Fees: WD £18; WE £23.
Societies: welcome by prior arrange-
ment; discounts available for larger
groups; practice area; driving range;
catering packages; terms on applica-
tion.
Catering: full clubhouse bar and
restaurant facilities.
Hotels: Wall Foot Hotel; Crosby
Lodge; Crown Hotel.

7 50 Ellesmere
Old Clough Lane, Worsley,
Manchester; M28 5HZ
☎(0161) 790 2122, Pro 790 8591,
Sec 790 0554
Off A580 adjacent to M62.
Parkland course.
Pro Terrence Morrey; Founded 1913
18 holes, 6247 yards, S.S.S. 70
Visitors: welcome except on comp
days and Bank Holidays.
Green Fees: WD £20; WE £25.
Societies: welcome Mon, Tues and
Fri; Wed also in winter; 27 holes of
golf plus catering; from £30.
Catering: full clubhouse facilities
available.
Hotels: Novotel, Worsley.

7 51 Fairfield Golf & Sailing Club
"Boothdale", Booth Rd; Audenshaw;
Manchester; M34 5GA
☎(0161) 370 1641, Pro 370 2292,
Sec 336 3950
On A635 5 miles E of Manchester.
Parkland course around reservoir.
Pro S A Pownell; Founded 1892
18 holes, 5664 yards, S.S.S. 68
Visitors: welcome WD; Thurs ladies
day; some weekend restrictions; tele-
phone in advance.
Green Fees: WD £18; WE £24.
Societies: welcome by prior arrange-
ment with the secretary; terms on
application.
Catering: full facilities by prior
arrangement.
Hotels: Village, Hyde; York, Ashton-
under-Lyne.

7 52 Fairhaven

Lytham Hall Park; Ansdell, Lytham-St-
Annes, Lancs FY8 4JU
☎(01253) 736976
On B5261 2 miles from Lytham.
Semi links; Open Championship quali-
fying course.
Pro Brian Plucknett; Founded 1895
Designed by James Braid
18 holes, 6883 yards, S.S.S. 73
Visitors: welcome by arrangement;
restrictions at WE.
Green Fees: WD £35; WE £45.
Societies: welcome by arrangement.
Catering: full facilities except Mon;
banqueting room.
Practice area.
Hotels: Clifton Arms; Grand;
Dalmeney; Fearnlea.

7 53 Fishwick Hall

Glenluce Drive, Farringdon Park;
Preston, Lancs PR1 5TD
☎(01772) 798300 , Pro 795870
From £M6 junction 31 take A59 past
Tickle Trout; Glenluce Drive is 1st left
at top of the hill.
Undulating meadowland/parkland
course.
Pro Mike Hadfield; Founded 1912
18 holes, 6045 yards, S.S.S. 69
Visitors: welcome except between
11.20am-2.00pm.
Green Fees: WD £21; WE £26.
Societies: welcome WD by arrange-
ment.
Catering: full catering facilities.
Hotels: Tickled Trout.

7 54 Fleetwood

Golf House, Princes Way; Fleetwood,
Lancs FY7 8AF
☎(01253) 873114 Fax 773573, Pro
873661, Sec 773573
Off A587 0.5 miles from Fleetwood.
Links course.
Pro S McLaughlin; Founded 1932
Designed by Edwin Steer
18 holes, 6557 yards, S.S.S. 72
Visitors: welcome WD, except Thurs;
some restrictions WE.
Green Fees: WD £24; WE £30.
Societies: welcome by prior arrange-
ment; discounts available for larger
groups; from £24.
Catering: full clubhouse facilities.
Hotels: North Euston; New Boston;
Briardene.

7 55 Flixton

Church Rd, Flixton; Urmston;
Manchester; M41 6EP

☎(0161) 748 2116, Pro 746 7160,
Sec 747 0296
On B5213 5 miles SW of Manchester.
Parkland course.
Pro Danny Proctor; Founded 1893
9 holes, 6410 yards, S.S.S. 71
Visitors: welcome by prior arrange-
ment; WE only with a member.
Green Fees: WD £15; WE £15.
Societies: welcome WD by prior
arrangement; packages available;
terms on application.
Catering: clubhouse facilities.

7 56 Formby

Golf Rd; Formby, Liverpool, Lancs L37
1LQ
☎(01704) 872164
1 mile W of A565 adjacent to
Freshfield station.
Championship links course.
Pro Clive Harrison; Founded 1884
Designed by Willie Park
18 holes, 6993 yards, S.S.S. 74
Visitors: by prior arrangement only.
Green Fees: WD terms on applica-
tion.
Societies: by prior arrangement only;
terms on application.
Catering: full clubhouse facilities.
Practice area.
Hotels: Tree Tops.

7 57 Formby Golf Centre

Moss Side, Formby, Lancs L37 0AF
☎(01704) 875952
On the Formby by-pass.
Parkland course.
Pro Robert Dunbar;
18 holes, 1510 yards
Visitors: welcome; pay and play.
Green Fees: WD £3; WE £3.
Catering: coffee, tea and light refresh-
ments.
Practice range, 24 bays floodlit.

7 58 Formby Hall

Southport Old Road; Formby, Lancs
L37 0AB
☎(01704) 875699
Off Formby by-pass opposite
Woodvale Aerodrome.
Parkland course with 11 lakes.
Pro David Lloyd; Founded 1996
Designed by PSA/Alex Higgins
18 holes, 6892 yards, S.S.S. 73
Visitors: welcome WD; restrictions at
WE.
Green Fees: WD £35.
Societies: welcome by prior arrange-
ment; corporate days available; from
£40.

Catering: 5 bars and 2 restaurants
open from 7.30am-11pm.
Practice range, 31 bays floodlit;
academy.
Hotels: Treetops; many B&Bs can be
recommended.

7 59 Formby Ladies

Golf Rd, Formby, Liverpool,
Merseyside L37 1YH
☎(01704) 873493, Pro 873090,
Bar/Rest 874127
Off A565 5 miles S of Southport.
Seaside links course.
Pro Clive Harrison; Founded 1896
18 holes, 5374 yards, S.S.S. 71
Visitors: welcome by arrangement.
Green Fees: WD £30; WE £35
Societies: welcome by arrangement;
full golf and catering available; terms
on application.
Catering: bar snacks available.
Hotels: Treetops; selection in
Southport.

7 60 Furness

Central Drive, Walney Island, Barrow-
in-Furness, Cumbria LA14 3LN
☎(01229) 471232
Off A590 to Walney Island; 0.5 miles
after end of bridge.
Seaside links course.
Pro Andrew Whitehall; Founded 1872
18 holes, 6363 yards, S.S.S. 71
Visitors: welcome by prior arrangement; some restrictions Wed and WE.
Green Fees: WD £17; WE £17.
Societies: welcome by prior arrangement; must be members of recognised
golf clubs; discounts for groups of
more than 10; from £17.
Catering: clubhouse facilities.
Hotels: White House; Infield GH.

7 61 Gathurst

Miles Lane; Shevington, Wigan, Lancs
WN6 8EW
☎(01257) 252861, Pro 254909, Sec
255235
1 miles S of M6 junction 27.
Parkland course.
Pro David Clarke; Founded 1913
Designed by N Pearson
9 holes, 6089 yards, S.S.S. 7069
Visitors: welcome WD except Wed;
WE with member.
Green Fees: WD £20; WE £10.
Societies: welcome WD except Wed;
27 holes, full day's catering; from £33.
Catering: bar and restaurant facilities.
Hotels: Almond Brook Moathouse
(offers reductions for club visitors).

7 62 Ghyll

Ghyll Brow, Barnoldswick, Colne,
Lancs BB8 6JQ
☎(01282) 842466
A56 to Thornton-in-Craven turn left on
B6252; 1 mile on left opposite Rolls
Royce factory.
Scenic parkland course.
Founded 1907
9 holes, 5770 yards, S.S.S. 67
Visitors: welcome except Tues am;
Fri after 4.30 or Sun.
Green Fees: WD £14; WE £18.
Societies: welcome as with visitors;
reductions for parties of more than 8;
from £14.
Catering: bar catering by arrangement.
Hotels: Stirk House, Gisburn;
Tempest, Elslack.

7 63 Grange Fell

Fell Rd, Grange-over-Sands, Cumbria
LA11 6HB
☎(01539) 532536, Sec 532021
From £M6 junction 36 follow signs to
Barrow until Grange signs; through
town in direction of Cartmel Hillside.
Founded 1952
9 holes, 5312 yards, S.S.S. 66
Visitors: welcome.
Green Fees: WD £12; WE £17.
Societies: none.
Hotels: Netherwood; Grange, both in
Grange-over-Sands; Aynsome,
Cartmel.

7 64 Grange Park

Prescot Rd, St Helens, Merseyside
WA10 3AD
☎(01744) 26318, Fax 26318, Pro
28785, Bar/Rest 22980
M62 junction 7.
Heathland course.
Pro Paul Roberts; Founded 1891
18 holes, 6422 yards, S.S.S. 71
Visitors: welcome WD except Tues;
restrictions at WE.
Green Fees: WD £24; WE £36.
Societies: welcome WD except Tues;
packages including all-day food and
up to 36 holes of golf available; from
£36.
Catering: full clubhouse facilities.
Hotels: Haydock Thistle; Haydock
Moathouse.

7 65 Grange-over-Sands

Meathop Rd, Grange-over-Sands.
Cumbria LA11 6QX
☎(015395) 33180, Fax 33754, Pro
35937, Sec 33754

Off A590 course is located just before
entering town
Parkland course.
Pro S Sumner-Roberts; Founded 1919
18 holes, 5958 yards, S.S.S. 69
Visitors: welcome with h'cap certs.
Green Fees: WD £18; WE £24.
Societies: welcome by appointment;
packages available; from £18.
Catering: full clubhouse facilities.
Hotels: Grange Hotel; Graythwaite
Manor; Clare House.

7 66 Great Harwood

Harwood Bar, Great Harwood, Lancs
BB6 7TE
☎(01254) 884391
Easy access from Clitheroe by-pass.
Parkland course.
Founded 1896
9 holes, 6411 yards, S.S.S. 71
Visitors: welcome WD; restrictions at
WE.
Green Fees: WD £16; WE £22.
Societies: welcome by prior arrangement, catering packages can be
arranged; snooker; from £14.
Catering: clubhouse facilities.
Hotels: Dunkenhalgh, Clayton-le-
Moors.

7 67 Great Lever & Farnworth

Off Plodder Lane, Great Lever, Bolton,
BL4 0LQ
☎(01204) 656137, Fax 652780, Pro
656650, Bar/Rest 656493
From M61 junction 4 take Watergate
Lane to Plodder Lane.
Parkland course.
Pro Tony Howarth; Founded 1917
18 holes, 5986 yards, S.S.S. 69
Visitors: welcome WD with h'cap
certs; restrictions at WE.
Green Fees: WD £16.50; WE £27.
Societies: welcome WD by arrangement; full day packages available for
golf and catering except Mon; £29.50.
Catering: full facilities except Mon.
Practice area.

7 68 Green Haworth

Green Haworth, Accrington, Lancs
BB5 3SL
☎(01254) 237580
From Accrington town centre take
main road to Blackburn; turn left on
Willows Lane; follow road for 2-3
miles; signposted after Red Lion Hotel.
Moorland course.
Founded 1914
9 holes, 5556 yards, S.S.S. 68

Visitors: welcome WD; some restrictions Wed; Sat by prior arrangement.
Green Fees: WD £15; WE £20.
Catering: full facilities; restaurant can
be pre-booked.
Hotels: County, Blackburn.

7 69 Greenmount

Greenhalgh Fold Farm, Greenmount,
Bury, Lancs BL8 4LH
☎(01204) 883712, Pro 888616
Leave M66 at Bury follow signs to
Ramsbottom until Holcombe village.
Undulating parkland course.
Pro Jason Seed; Founded 1920
9 holes, 4980 yards, S.S.S. 64
Visitors: welcome WD; with member
at WE.
Green Fees: WD £15.
Societies: welcome WD except Tues
by prior arrangement.
Catering: full service except Mon;
function suite available.
Hotels: Red Hall; Old Mill; Red Lion.

7 70 Haigh Hall

Haigh Country Park, Aspull, Wigan,
Lancs WN2 1PE
☎(01942) 833337 , Pro 831107
Take M6 junction 27 and B5239 to
Standish; 6 miles NE of Wigan.
Municipal parkland course..
Pro I Lee; Foundcd 1973
18 holes, 6423 yards, S.S.S. 71
Visitors: welcome any time by
arrangement; telephone bookings via
professional.
Green Fees: WD £6.50; WE £9.
Societies: welcome with prior
arrangement with the professional.
Catering: full restaurant and café service.
Hotels: Brocket; Oak; Almond Brook;
Moathouse.

7 71 Harwood

Springfield, Roading Brook Rd;
Harwood, Bolton BL2 4JD
☎(01204) 522878, Sec 524233
4 miles NE of Bolton.
Parkland course extended to 18 holes,
in April 1998.
Pro M Dance; Founded 1926/1998
Designed by Whole New Concept
18 holes, 5851 yards, S.S.S. 69
Visitors: welcome WD; with member
at WE.
Green Fees: WD £15; WE £15.
Societies: welcome by arrangement;
terms on application.
Catering: clubhouse facilities.
Hotels: Last Drop, Bromley Cross.

7 72 Haydock Park

Golborne Park, Newton-le-Willows, Merseyside WA12 0HX
☎(01925) 228525, Bar/Rest 224389
1 mile E of the M6 on A580.
Parkland course.
Pro Peter Kenwright; Founded 1877
18 holes, 6043 yards, S.S.S. 69
Visitors: welcome WD except Tues.
Green Fees: WD £25.
Societies: welcome WD except Tues; from £38.
Catering: full clubhouse facilities.
Hotels: Kirkfield; Post House; Crest.

7 73 Heaton Park

Middleton Rd, Prestwich, Manchester, M25 2SW
☎(0161) 654 9899
On A576 close to M62 junction 19.
Undulating parkland course.
Founded 1912
Designed by J.H. Taylor
18 holes, 5815 yards, S.S.S. 68
Visitors: welcome; advance booking at WE.
Green Fees: WD £9; WE £10.
Societies: welcome by prior arrangement.
Catering: bar and catering in café.
Hotels: Travelodge at Birch Services.

7 74 Hesketh

Cockle Dick's Lane, off Cambridge Rd, Southport, Merseyside PR9 9QQ
☎(01704) 530226, Fax 539250, Pro 530050, Sec 536897, Bar/Rest 531055
On A565 1 mile N of Southport.
Seaside links course with some parkland.
Pro John Donoghue; Founded 1885
Designed by J.O.F. Morris
18 holes, 6522 yards, S.S.S. 72
Visitors: welcome by prior arrangement.
Green Fees: WD £40; WE £50.
Societies: welcome by prior arrangement; inclusive packages for catering and golf available for groups of 12 or more; from £40.
Catering: bar and dining facilities.
Hotels: Prince of Wales; Scarisbrick.

N 75 The Heysham

Trumacar Park, Middleton Rd, Heysham, Lancs LA3 3JH
☎(01524) 851240 Fax 853030, Pro 852000, Sec 851011, Bar/Rest 859154
Off A683 5 miles from M6 junction 34.
Parkland course with some wooded areas.

Pro Ryan Done; Founded 1929
Designed by Alec Herd
18 holes, 6258 yards, S.S.S. 70
Visitors: welcome with h'cap certs.
Green Fees: WD £17; WE £27.
Societies: welcome by arrangement with Sec; discounts for groups of 12 or more; from £22.
Catering: full clubhouse facilities.
Hotels: Strathmore, Morecambe

7 76 Hillside Golf Club

Hastings Road, Hillside, Southport PR8 2LU
☎(01704) 569902, Fax 563192, Pro 568360, Sec 567169 Bar/Rest 568682
On A565 3 miles S of Southport.
Outstanding championship links course.
Pro B Seddon; Founded 1911/1923
Designed by Fred Hawtree
18 holes, 6850 yards, S.S.S. 74
Visitors: restricted; contact Sec.
Green Fees: WD £40; WE £ 50.
Societies: restricted; contact Sec; special approval needed for groups of more than 24; terms on application.
Catering: full bar and restaurant seating 100.
Practice ground.
Hotels: Scarisbrick; Prince of Wales; Metropole.

7 77 Hindley Hall

Hall Lane, Hindley, Wigan, Lancs WN2 2SQ
☎(01942) 255131, Pro 255991
Off A6 from M61 junction 6 then take Dicconson Lane; after 1 mile into Hall Lane; club just after lake.
Moorland course.
Pro Nigel Brazell; Founded 1895
18 holes, 5913 yards, S.S.S. 68
Visitors: welcome if member of a club; check with Sec in advance.
Green Fees: WD £20; WE £27.
Societies: welcome by prior arrangement.
Catering: clubhouse facilities.
Hotels: Georgian House.

7 78 Horwich

Victoria Rd, Horwich, Bolton, Lancs BL6 5PH
☎(01204) 696980
Close to M61 junction 6
Parkland course.
Founded 1895
9 holes, 5404 yards, S.S.S. 67
Visitors: welcome with member or by prior arrangement with Sec.
Green Fees: terms on application.

Societies: welcome WD and occasional Sun by prior arrangement.
Catering: full bar and catering facilities.
Hotels: Swallowfield; Holiday Inn Express.

7 79 Houghwood Hall

Billinge Hill, Crank Rd, Crank, St Helens, Lancs WA11 8RL
☎(01744) 894444
From M6 junction 26 follow signs to Billinge; course 1 mile from Billinge Hospital.
Parkland course with USGA standard greens.
Pro David Clarke; Founded 1996
Designed by N Pearson
18 holes, 6202 yards, S.S.S. 70
Visitors: welcome.
Green Fees: WD £14; WE £17.
Societies: welcome by arrangement; from £17-£30.
Catering: bar and restaurant facilities.
Hotels: Post House, Haydock; Stakis, St Helens.

7 80 Hurlston Hall

Hurlston Lane, Scarisbrick, Lancashire L40 8JD
☎(01704) 840400, Fax 841404, Pro 841149
On A570 8 miles from M58 6 miles from Southport and 2 miles from Ormskirk.
Parkland course with two brooks.
Pro Gerry Bond; Founded 1994
Designed by Donald Steel
18 holes, 6746 yards, S.S.S. 72
Visitors: welcome by prior arrangement; h'cap certs may be required.
Green Fees: WD £25; WE £30.
Societies: registered golf societies welcome by prior arrangement with club office; packages including 36 holes, catering and gourmet dinner can be arranged; satellite TV; golf academy; terms on application.
Catering: full catering facilities with 70-seat restaurant; balcony and patio.
Practice range, 18 bays floodlit, 2 teaching bays.
Hotels: Beaufort Hotel; Scarisbrick; Prince of Wales.

7 81 Huyton & Prescot

Hurst Park, Huyton Lane; Huyton, Liverpool; Merseyside; L36 1UA
☎(0151) 489 3948, Pro 489 2022
10 miles from Liverpool just off M57.
Parkland course.
Pro Malcolm Harrison; Founded 1905

18 holes, 5839 yards, S.S.S. 68
Visitors: welcome WD; WE with member.
Green Fees: WD £22; WE £22.
Societies: by arrangement WD.
Catering: full facilities.
Hotels: Derby Lodge; Hillcrest; Bell Tower.

7 82 Ingol Golf & Squash Club
Tanterton Hall Rd, Ingol, Preston, Lancs PR2 7BY
☎(01772) 734556, Pro 769646
Leave M6 junction32 and turn towards Preston; follow signs for Ingol.
Parkland course.
Pro Robert Eastwood; Founded 1980
Designed by Cotton, Pennink, Lawrie & Partners
18 holes, 6294 yards, S.S.S. 70
Visitors: welcome.
Green Fees: WD £20; WE £25.
Societies: welcome by arrangement but not before 2.30pm at WE; maximum 16; from £18-£35.
Catering: full facilities; bar and function room.
Hotels: Marriott Broughton Park; Barton Grange; Fulwood Park.

7 83 Kendal
The Heights, Kendal, Cumbria LA9 4PQ
☎(01539) 724079, Pro 723499, Sec 733708
To Kendal on A6 signposted in town.
Moorland course; redesigned in late 1998.
Pro David Turner; Founded 1891
18 holes, 5600 yards, S.S.S. 66
Visitors: welcome any time except Sat competition days; by prior arrangement WE.
Green Fees: WD £20; WE £25.
Societies: welcome anytime subject to availability and by prior arrangement; from £27.
Catering: full facilities except Mon.
Hotels: County; Woolpack.

7 84 Keswick
Threlkeld Hall, Threlkeld, Keswick, Cumbria, CA12 4SX
☎(017687) 79013, Pro 79010, Sec 79324
Off A66 4 miles E of Keswick.
Moorland/parkland course.
Pro Craig Hamilton; Founded 1975
Designed by Eric Brown
18 holes, 6225 yards, S.S.S. 72
Visitors: welcome, even most WE.
Green Fees: WD £17; WE £22.

Societies: welcome by prior arrangement with Sec; some WE available; packages for 12 or more.
Catering: bar and dining facilities.
Hotels: Lodore Swiss; Keswick; Borrowdale; Wordsworth; Middle Ruddings.

7 85 King Edward Bay (Howstrake)
Howstrake, Groudle Rd, Onchan, IM3 2JR
☎(01624) 620430, Pro 672709
5 mins from Douglas.
Moorland/seaside course.
Pro Donald Jones; Founded 1893
Designed by T Morris
18 holes, 5485 yards, S.S.S. 65
Visitors: welcome Mon-Sat; after 10am Sun.
Green Fees: WD £12; WE £14.
Societies: welcome; minimum 10; catering packages available; from £10.
Catering: full facilities available, restrictions on Mon.
Hotels: Imperial; Stakis, both Douglas.

7 86 Kirkby Lonsdale
Scalebar Lane, Barbon, Carnforth, Cumbria, LA6 2LE
☎(015242) 76365, Pro 76366
On A683 Sedbergh Road 3 miles from Kirkby Lonsdale.
Parkland course.
Pro Chris Barrett; Founded 1991
Designed by Bill Squires
18 holes, 6472 yards, S.S.S. 71
Visitors: welcome.
Green Fees: WD £18; WE £22.
Societies: welcome by arrangement; terms on application.
Catering: clubhouse facilities.
Hotels: Whoop Hall, Cowan Bridge; Pheasant, Casterton.

7 87 Knott End
Wyreside, Knott End on Sea, Poulton, Lancs, FY6 0AA
☎(01253) 810576, Pro 811365
Take A585 Fleetwood road off M55 and then B2588 to Knott End.
Meadowland course.
Pro Paul Walker; Founded 1911
Designed by James Braid
18 holes, 5832 yards, S.S.S. 68
Visitors: welcome WD not before 9.30 amor between 12.30pm-1.30pm.
Green Fees: WD £20; WE £22.
Societies: welcome by prior arrangement.
Catering: full facilities.
Hotels: Bourne Arms; Seven Stars.

7 88 Lancaster
Ashton Hall, Ashton-with-Stodday, Lancashire, Lancs, LA2 0AJ
☎(01524) 751247, Fax 752742, Pro 751802, Bar/Rest 751105
On A588 2 miles S of Lancaster.
Parkland course.
Pro David Sutcliffe; Founded 1933
Designed by James Braid
18 holes, 6500 yards, S.S.S. 71
Visitors: welcome by prior arrangement with h'cap certs.
Green Fees: WD £32; WE £32.
Societies: welcome by prior arrangement on WD; h'cap certs required; catering and golf packages available; from £32.
Catering: full clubhouse facilities.
Hotels: Dormy House with accommodation for 18.

7 89 Lansil
Caton Rd, Lancaster, Lancs, LA1 3PE
☎(01524) 39269
2 miles E of Lancaster on A683 close to Post House Hotel.
Parkland/meadowland course.
Founded 1947
9 holes, 5608 yards, S.S.S. 67
Visitors: welcome but not before 1pm Sun.
Green Fees: WD £12; WE £12.
Societies: welcome WD by arrangement; catering packages organised with steward.
Catering: meals and bar snacks available.
Hotels: Post House; Farmers Arms.

7 90 Lee Park
Childwall Valley Rd, Gateacre, Liverpool, Merseyside, L27 3YA
☎(0151) 487 3882, Pro 488 0800, Bar/Rest 487 9861
On B5171 off A562 next to Lee Manor High School.
Parkland course.
Founded 1950
Designed by Frank Pennink
18 holes, 6095 yards, S.S.S. 69
Visitors: welcome.
Green Fees: WD £22; WE £27.
Societies: welcome Mon, Thurs and Fri by prior arrangement with Sec.
Catering: bar snacks and meals.
Hotels: Gateacre Hall.

7 91 Leigh
Kenyon Hall, Broseley Lane, Culcheth, Warrington, Cheshire, WA3 4BG
☎(01925) 763130, Fax 765097, Pro 762013, Sec 762943

Off B5217 in Culcheth village.
Parkland course.
Pro Andrew Baguley; Founded 1906
Designed by James Braid
18 holes, 5884 yards, SS.S. 68
Visitors: welcome with h'cap certs or
letter of introduction.
Green Fees: WD £23; WE £33.
Societies: welcome Mon, except BH,
and Tues; catering packages avail-
able; snooker room; 3 practice areas;
2 putting greens; from £23.
Catering: full clubhouse facilities.
Practice range: 3 practice areas; 2
putting greens.
Hotels: Greyhound, Leigh; Thistle,
Haydock.

7 92 Leyland
Wigan Rd, Leyland, Lancs, PR5 2UD
☎(01772) 436457, Pro 423425
On A49 0.25 miles from M6 junction 28.
Meadowland course.
Pro Colin Burgess; Founded 1923
18 holes, 6123 yards, S.S.S. 69
Visitors: welcome WD; WE only with
a member.
Green Fees: WD £25; WE £25.
Societies: welcome by prior arrange-
ment with Sec; packages available on
request.
Catering: full facilities.
Hotels: Jarvis.

7 93 Liverpool Municipal (Kirkby)
Ingoe Lane, Kirkby, Liverpool,
Merseyside, L32 4SS
☎(0151) 546 5435
M57 junction 6, 300 yards on right of
B5192.
Municipal meadowland course.
Pro David Weston; Founded 1966
18 holes, 6706 yards, S.S.S. 72
Visitors: welcome.
Green Fees: WD £6.50; WE £7.50.
Societies: welcome every day; tee
booking required at WE 1 week in
advance.
Catering: bar and cafeteria.
Practice ground.
Hotels: Golden Eagle.

7 94 Lobden
Lobden Moor, Whitworth, Lancashire,
OL12 8XJ
☎(01706) 343228, Fax 643241, Sec
643241
Take A671 from Rochdale to
Whitworth.
Moorland course.
Founded 1888

9 holes, 5697 yards, S.S.S. 68
Visitors: welcome except Sat.
Green Fees: WD £10; WE £15.
Societies: welcome by prior arrange-
ment; terms on application.
Catering: by arrangement with stew-
ard.

7 95 Longridge
Fell Barn, Jeffery Hill, Longridge,
Preston, Lancs, PR3 2TU
☎(01772) 783291
From M6 junction 31a follow signs to
Longridge.
Moorland course with panoramic
views.
Founded 1877
18 holes, 5969 yards, S.S.S. 69
Visitors: welcome.
Green Fees: WD £15; WE £25.
Societies: welcome by written prior
arrangement with Sec; from £30.
Catering: full facilities.
Hotels: Shireburn Arms; Gibbon
Bridge; Black Moss GH.

7 96 Lowes Park
Hill Top, Lowes Rd, Bury, Lancs, BL9
6SU
☎(0161) 764 1231, Fax 763 9503,
Sec 763 9503, Bar/Rest 797 5056
On A56 1 mile N of Bury; turn at Bury
General Hospital into Lowes Road.
Moorland course.
Founded 1930
9 holes, 6014 yards, S.S.S. 69
Visitors: welcome by prior arrange-
ment.
Green Fees: WD £17; WE £23.
Societies: welcome by prior arrange-
ment; package deals available; ladies
only on Wed; terms on application.
Catering: full clubhouse facilities
except Mon.
Practice range, small practice area.
Hotels: Red Hall.

7 97 Lytham Green Drive
Ballam Rd, Lytham, Lancs, FY8 4LE
☎(01253) 734782, Fax 731350, Pro
737379, Sec 737390, Bar/Rest
736087
1 mile from Lytham centre.
Parkland course.
Pro Andrew Lancaster; Founded 1904
Designed by A Herd
18 holes, 6159 yards, S.S.S. 69
Visitors: welcome WD by prior
arrangement.
Green Fees: WD £27.
Societies: welcome WD except Wed;
terms on application.

Catering: full clubhouse facilities.
Hotels: Clifton Arms, Lytham; Fernlea,
St Anne's.

7 98 Manchester
Hopwood Cottage, Rochdale Rd,
Middleton, Manchester, M24 2QP
☎(0161) 643 2718, Fax 643 9174,
Pro 643 2638, Sec 643 3202, Bar/Rest
643 3202
From A627 (M) take A664 for
Middleton.
Parkland/moorland course.
Pro Brian Connor; Founded 1882
Designed by H.S. Colt
18 holes, 6519 yards, S.S.S. 72
Visitors: welcome by arrangement.
Green Fees: WD £30; WE £45.
Societies: welcome by prior arrange-
ment; packages of golf and catering
available on application; £40-£47.
Catering: full clubhouse facilities.
Practice area available to members,
guests and visitors only.
Hotels: Midway; Norton Grange;
Royal Toby.

7 99 Manor (Bolton)
Moors Lane, Kearsley, Bolton, Lancs,
BL4 8SF
☎(01204) 701027
1 mile from M62 junction 17.
Parkland course.
Pro Cornelius O'Neill; Founded 1995
18 holes, 4902 yards, S.S.S. 66
Visitors: welcome; pay and play.
Green Fees: WD £6.50; WE £8.50.
Societies: welcome by arrangement.
Catering: bar and restaurant; function
suites.
Driving range next door.
Hotels: Clifton Park Country House.

7 100 Marsden Park
Downhouse Rd, Nelson, Lancs, BB9
8DG
☎(01282) 614094, Pro 617525
From M65 junction 13 and take B5446
on to Leeds Road and right at second
roundabout.
Parkland course.
Founded 1968/1976
Designed by C.K. Cotton & Partners
18 holes, 5681 yards, S.S.S. 68
Visitors: welcome; pay and play.
Green Fees: WD £7.50; WE £8.65.
Societies: welcome by prior arrange-
ment; golf and catering packages
available on application; from £13.
Catering: catering facilities.
Hotels: The Oaks, Burnley; Great
Marsden, Nelson.

7 101 Maryport

Bank End, Maryport, Cumbria, CA15 6PA
☎(01900) 812605, Sec 815626
N of Maryport turn left off A596 on to the B5300 (Silloth Road).
Seaside links course.
Founded 1905
18 holes, 6088 yards, S.S.S. 69
Visitors: welcome.
Green Fees: WD £15; WE £20.
Societies: welcome by prior arrangement; discounts for groups of 9 or more.
Catering: full clubhouse facilities.
Hotels: Ellenbank; Skimberness Hotel.

7 102 Morecambe

Marine Rd East, Bare, Morecambe, Lancs, LA4 6AJ
☎(01524) 418050, Fax 412841, Pro 415596, Sec 412841, Bar/Rest 412841
On road to Morecambe from A6.
Parkland/links course; no par fives.
Pro Simon Fletcher; Founded 1922
Designed by Dr Clegg
18 holes, 5770 yards, S.S.S. 68
Visitors: welcome by arrangement.
Green Fees: WD £22; WE £27.
Societies: welcome by prior arrangement; terms on application.
Catering: full clubhouse facilities.

7 103 Mossack Hall

Liverpool Rd, Bickerstaffe, Lancs, L39 0EE
☎(01695) 421717, Fax 424961, Pro 424969
From M58 junction 3 take 1st left to Stanley gate Pub; turn left and follow road for 2 miles; club on right.
Meadowland course.
Pro Matthew webb; Founded 1996
Designed by Steve Marnoch
18 holes, 6375 yards, S.S.S. 70
Visitors: welcome by prior arrangement with professional.
Green Fees: WD £20; WE £30.
Societies: welcome by prior arrangement with golf course manager.
Catering: full catering facilities including restaurant; catering for private functions.

7 104 Mount Murray

Santon, IM4 2HT
☎(01624) 661111
On the Castletown road 2 miles from Douglas.
Parkland course.

Pro Andrew Dyson; Founded 1994
18 holes, 6664 yards, S.S.S. 73
Visitors: welcome.
Green Fees: WD £18; WE £24.
Societies: welcome by prior arrangement.
Catering: bistro and restaurant facilities.
Practice range, 20 bays floodlit.
Hotels: Mount Murray (golf packages available).

7 105 Nelson

King's Causeway, Brierfield, Nelson, Lancs, BB9 0EU
☎(01282) 614583, Fax 606226, Pro 617000, Sec 611834
On B6248 off A682 at Brierfield from M65 junction 12.
Moorland course.
Pro Nigel Sumner; Founded 1902
Designed by Dr A MacKenzie
18 holes, 5977 yards, S.S.S. 70
Visitors: welcome.
Green Fees: WD £25; WE £30.
Societies: welcome by prior arrangement; catering and golf packages available; from £25.
Catering: full clubhouse facilities available.
Hotels: Higher Trapp Country House.

7 106 North Manchester

Rhodes House, Manchester Old Rd, Middleton, Manchester, M24 4PE
☎(0161) 643 2941, Pro 643 7094, Sec 643 9033
5 miles N of Manchester off M62 junction 18.
Moorland/parkland course.
Pro Frank Accleton; Founded 1894
18 holes, 6498 yards, S.S.S. 72
Visitors: welcome WD; by arrangement WE.
Green Fees: WD £22; WE £22.
Societies: welcome WD except Tues; terms on application.
Catering: full catering and bar service.
Hotels: Bower, Oldham; Birch, Heywood.

7 107 Oldham

Lees New Rd, Oldham, Lancs, OL4 5PN
☎(0161) 624 4987, Pro 626 8346
Off A669 turning right at Lees.
Moorland/parkland course.
Pro Jason Peel; Founded 1891
18 holes, 5122 yards, S.S.S. 65
Visitors: welcome by prior arrangement.
Green Fees: WD £16; WE £22.

Societies: welcome by arrangement; packages for all day golf and catering; from £22.
Catering: full facilities.
Hotels: Birch Hall.

7 108 Ormskirk

Cranes Lane, Lathom, Ormskirk, Lancs, L40 5UJ
☎(01695) 572112, Pro 572074, Sec 572227
2 miles E of Ormskirk.
Parkland course.
Pro Jack Hammond; Founded 1899
18 holes, 6480 yards, S.S.S. 70
Visitors: welcome.
Green Fees: WD £30; WE & Wed £35.
Societies: welcome by prior arrangement.
Catering: full facilities.
Hotels: Briars Hall.

7 109 Peel

Rheast Lane; Peel; Isle of Man; IM5 1BG
☎(01624) 843456, Bar/Rest 842227
On A1 signposted on outskirts of Peel
Moorland
Pro Murray Crowe; Founded 1895
Designed by A. Herd
18 holes, 5914 yards, S.S.S. 68
Visitors: welcome WD; WE by arrangement.
Green Fees: WD £15; WE £20.
Societies: welcome on application to Sec; packages on request.
Catering: meals and snacks to order; bar.
Hotels: Stakis; Ascot.

7 110 Pennington

Pennington Country Park, St Helen, Leigh, Lancs, WN7 3PA
☎(01942) 682852, Pro 682862
Off A572 to S of Leigh.
Parkland course with ponds and streams.
Pro Tim Kershaw
9 holes, 5790 yards, S.S.S. 68
Visitors: welcome.
Green Fees: WD £3.25; WE £4.50.
Societies: welcome WD by prior arrangement.
Catering: snack bar.
Hotels: Thistle, Haydock.

7 111 Penrith

Salkeld Rd, Penrith, Cumbria, CA11 8SG
☎(01768) 891919, Fax 891919, Bar/Rest 865429

From M6 junction 41 follow signs for Penrith turn left when entering town. Parkland course.
Pro Garry Key; Founded 1890
18 holes, 6047 yards, S.S.S. 69
Visitors: welcome by arrangement.
Green Fees: WD £20; WE £25.
Societies: welcome by prior arrangement with Sec; golf and catering packages available; terms on application.
Catering: clubhouse facilities.
Practice ground.
Hotels: George, Penrith.

7 112 **Penwortham**
Blundell Lane, Penwortham, Preston, Lancs, PR1 0AX
☎(01772) 743207, Fax 744630, Pro 742345, Sec 744630
Off A59 1.5 miles W of Preston.
Parkland course.
Pro N Marshall; Founded 1908
18 holes, 6056 yards, S.S.S. 69
Visitors: welcome WD except Tues.
Green Fees: WD £22.
Societies: welcome WD except Tues by prior arrangement; tee available between 10am-12.30pm and after 2pm; catering packages available; from £22.
Catering: full clubhouse facilities.
Hotels: Carleton; Forte Posthouse both Preston.

7 113 **Pike Fold**
Cooper Lane, Victoria Ave, Blackley, Manchester, M9 2QQ
☎(0161) 740 1136
4 miles N of Manchester off Rochdale road.
Undulating meadowland course.
Founded 1909
9 holes, 5789 yards, S.S.S. 68
Visitors: welcome WD.
Green Fees: WD £15.
Societies: welcome by appointment; catering packages by arrangement with steward.
Catering: full facilities by prior arrangement.
Hotels: Piccadilly; Midland Crown Plaza.

7 114 **Pleasington**
Pleasington, Blackburn, Lancs, BB2 5JF
☎(01254) 202177, Fax 201028, Pro 201630
3 miles SW of Blackburn; from A674 turn north on to road signposted Pleasington Station.
Undulating heathland/parkland course.
Pro G J Furey; Founded 1891

18 holes, 6423 yards, S.S.S. 71
Visitors: welcome by prior arrangement Mon, Wed, Fri.
Green Fees: WD £36.
Societies: welcome Mon, Wed, Fri; some discounts and packages available; from £36.
Catering: full clubhouse facilities.
Hotels: Ellerbeck Hotel, Blackburn.

7 115 **Port St Mary Golf Pavilion**
Port St Mary, Isle of Man, IM9 5EJ
☎(01624) 834932
Just outside Port St Mary; course signposted.
Public seaside links course.
Pro Murray Crowe; Founded 1936
Designed by George Duncan
9 holes, 5418 yards, S.S.S. 66
Visitors: welcome but not before 10.30am at WE.
Green Fees: WD £11; WE £14.
Societies: welcome by arrangement; discounts for 10 or more players.
Catering: bar, café and restaurant.
Hotels: Port Erin; Bay View.

7 116 **Poulton-le-Fylde**
Myrtle Farm, Breck Rd, Poulton-le-Fylde, Lancs, FY6 7HJ
☎(01253) 892444, Sec 893150
0.5 miles N of Poulton town centre.
Municipal meadowland course.
Pro Lewis Ware; Founded 1974
9 holes, 6056 yards, S.S.S. 70
Visitors: welcome.
Green Fees: WD £10; WE £12.
Societies: welcome by prior arrangement; packages available.
Catering: bar and catering facilities.
Practice range, indoor four-bay range.
Hotels: Singleton Lodge.

7 117 **Preston**
Fulwood Hall Lane, Fulwood, Preston, Lancs, PR2 8DD
☎(01772) 700011, Fax 794234, Pro 700022, Bar/Rest 700436
From M6 junction 32 turn towards Preston and after 1.5 miles into Watling St Rd and then into Fulwood Hall Road.
Parkland course.
Pro Andrew Greenbank; Founded 1892
Designed by James Braid
18 holes, 6215 yards, S.S.S. 69
Visitors: welcome WD; some restrictions Tues but with member only at WE.
Green Fees: WD £25.

Societies: welcome WD except Tues; golf and catering packages can be arranged; parties of more than 48 by special arrangement only; from £25.
Catering: bar and restaurant facilities.
Hotels: Broughton Marriott; Barton Grange.

7 118 **Prestwich**
Hilton Lane, Prestwich, Manchester, M25 9XB
☎(0161) 773 2544, Fax 773 1404, Pro 773 1404, Sec 773 2544, Bar/Rest 798 8401
On A6044 1 mile from junction with A56.
Parkland course.
Pro Simon Wakefield; Founded 1908
18 holes, 4806 yards, S.S.S. 63
Visitors: welcome WD with h'cap certs.
Green Fees: WD £16.
Societies: welcome on WD by prior arrangement with professional; 27-hole golf and catering packages available; from £27.50.
Catering: full clubhouse facilities.

7 119 **Ramsey**
Brookfield, Ramsey, Isle of Man, IM8 2AH
☎(01624) 812244, Pro 814736
12 miles N of Douglas; 5 mins from town centre.
Parkland course.
Pro Calum Wilson; Founded 1890
Designed by James Braid
18 holes, 5960 yards, S.S.S. 69
Visitors: welcome; phone in advance.
Green Fees: WD £16; WE £20.
Societies: welcome by arrangement.
Catering: lunches and full facilities.
Hotels: Grand Island.

7 120 **Reach**
De Vere Hotels, East Park Drive, Blackpool, FY3 8LL
☎(01253), Pro 766156
From M55 junction 4, follow signs for Blackpool on A583; at fourth set of lights turn right into South Park Drive; follow signs for zoo.
Parkland course with links characteristics.
Pro Dominik Naughton; Founded 1993
Designed by Peter Alliss and Clive Clark
18 holes, 6232 yards, S.S.S. 72
Visitors: welcome; after 10am Fri.
Green Fees: WD £25; WE £35.
Societies: welcome all year round by prior arrangement; packages avail-

Royal Birkdale

Perhaps it was because I was brought up in the area that I regard the entrance to Royal Birkdale as one of the most spectacular in golf. Even now, all these years on, it is still a thrill to pull off the main Liverpool to Southport Road, to emerge from a blanket of housing to be greeted by the entire course laid out before you, nestling amidst the dunes for which it has rightly become famous.

Birkdale, venue for this year's Open Championship, is recognised among the professionals as one of the fairest courses on the rota. The fairways are free of the pimples of land so often found on links courses, that can lead to a perfectly good drive being dramatically thrown off course and into the rough. There are also few "blind" shots that a golfer has to play, the drive to the tilting fairway at the ninth being the most obvious exception.

Among the famous who sing its praises is Severiano Ballesteros, and I was there in the stands, an excited teenager, when the prodigal Spaniard played his first stroke in Open competition.

The opening hole at Birkdale is one of the toughest. A double dogleg, most of the field had decided that the safest ploy on that burnished summer's day in 1976 was to strike an iron from the tee.

Ballesteros, of course, was having none of it. Among those of us who had sat for hours behind the tee, there was a ripple of anticipation as he pulled out his driver and aimed directly over the dune that protects the left hand side of the fairway.

He cleared it with a masterful shot, and so turned a double dogleg into nothing of the sort. Ballesteros went on to finish second that year, thus beginning his love affair with the Lancashire coastline that would culminate in two Open victories up the road at Lytham in 1979 and 1988.

Birkdale forms part of a chain of wonderful links courses that have made the area a mecca for golfers. Over the boundary fence lies Hillside, itself one of Britain's finest venues; some even prefer it to its more famous neighbour. And within a short drive lie four more courses worthy of any golfer's attention – Southport and Ainsdale, Formby, Hesketh and West Lancs.

My personal favourite, however, remains Birkdale, with its dunes that made it a stadium course long before such terms were invented. It is one of the best spectator courses in the country: the dunes surrounding each green in turn to convert them into amphitheatres.

The best hole? It has to be the 12th, a longish short hole among the finest of its type anywhere. To stand on the medal tee here with the wind blowing and the small green tucked away in the distance is to know intimidation. To then locate the putting surface with your tee shot and walk off with a par is to experience a rare moment of triumph.

METROPOLE HOTEL, SOUTHPORT

Portland Street, Southport PR8 1LL Tel 01704 536836 Fax 01704 549041
RAC/AA 2-star hotel. Centrally situated and close to Royal Birkdale and 5 other championship courses.
Fully licensed with late bar facilities for residents. Full sized snooker table.
Golfing proprieters will assist with tee reservations.

able; leisure club; swimming pool; tennis; squash courts.
Catering: full facilities; spikes bar; 3 restaurants.
Practice range, 18 bays floodlit.
Hotels: De Vere Blackpool on site.

7 121 Regent Park (Bolton)
Links Rd, Lostock, Bolton, Lancs, BL6 4AF
☎(01204) 844170, Pro 842336, Sec 495421
1 mile from M61 junction 6.
Municipal parkland course.
Pro Bob Longworth; Founded 1932
18 holes, 6130 yards, S.S.S. 69
Visitors: welcome; restrictions on Sat.
Green Fees: WD £9; WE £11.
Societies: welcome WD by arrangement.
Catering: bar, restaurant, take away.
Hotels: Forte Crest; Swallowfield.

7 122 Rishton
Eachill Links, Hawthorne Drive, Blackburn, Lancs, BB1 4HG
☎(01254) 884442
3 miles E of Blackburn signposted from church in village.
Meadowland course.
Founded 1928
9 holes, 6097 yards, S.S.S. 69
Visitors: welcome WD; WE with a member.
Green Fees: WD £12.
Societies: welcome with prior arrangement with Sec.
Catering: bar and catering except Mon.
Hotels: Dunkenhalgh.

7 123 Rochdale
Edenfield Rd, Bagslate, Rochdale, Lancs, OL11 5YR
☎(01706) 646024, Fax 643818, Pro 522104, Sec 643818
On A680 3 miles from M62 junction 20.
Parkland course.
Pro Andrew Laverty; Founded 1888
18 holes, 6050 yards, S.S.S. 69
Visitors: welcome by arrangement.
Green Fees: WD £23; WE £27.

Societies: welcome by prior arrangement; terms on application.
Catering: full clubhouse facilities.

7 124 Rossendale
Ewood Lane Head, Haslingden, Rossendale, Lancs, BB4 6LH
☎(01706) 831339, Fax 228669, Pro 213616
16 miles from Manchester off the M66.
Meadowland course.
Pro Stephen Nicholls; Founded 1903
18 holes, 6293 yards, S.S.S. 70
Visitors: welcome except Sat.
Green Fees: WD £22.50; WE £22.50.
Societies: welcome by prior arrangement.
Catering: full facilities except Mon; banqueting facilities.
Hotels: Red Hall; Sykeside.

7 125 Rowany
Rowany Drive, Port Erin, Isle of Man, IM9 6LN
☎(01624) 834072, Bar/Rest 834108
4 miles W of Castletown; located at end of Port Erin promenade.
Parkland/seaside course.
Founded 1895
18 holes, 5881 yards, S.S.S. 69
Visitors: welcome.
Green Fees: WD £7.50; WE £10.
Societies: welcome by arrangement with the Manager (available mornings WD).
Catering: full bar, snacks and restaurant facilities.
Outdoor practice range.
Hotels: Cherry Orchard.

7 126 Royal Birkdale
Waterloo Rd, Birkdale, Southport, Merseyside, PR8 2LX
☎(01704) 567920, Pro 568857
1.5 miles S of Southport on A565.
Open Championship venue 1998; links course.
Pro Richard Bradbeer; Founded 1889
Designed by Hawtree & Taylor
18 holes, 6690 yards, S.S.S. 73
Visitors: h'cap certs required; not Fri or Sat; limited Sun am.
Green Fees: WD £90; WE £110.

Societies: welcome Mon, Wed and Thurs by prior arrangement; from £110.
Catering: full catering facilities.
Hotels: local tourist board can provide detailed list.

7 127 Royal Lytham & St Annes
Links Gate, St Annes on Sea, Lancs FY8 3LQ
☎(01253) 724206
1 mile from centre of Lytham.
Links course; Open Championship venue 2001.
Pro Eddie Birchenough; Founded 1886
18 holes, 6685 yards, S.S.S. 74
Visitors: welcome WD by arrangement; WE dormy house guests only.
Green Fees: WD £80.
Societies: welcome by prior arrangement.
Catering: full catering and bar facilities.
Hotels: Dormy house on site.

7 128 Saddleworth
Mountain Ash, Ladcastle Rd, Uppermill, Oldham, Lancs, OL3 6LT
☎(01457) 873653, Bar/Rest 872059
5 miles from Oldham, signposted off the A670 Ashton-Huddersfield Road at the bend where road crosses railway.
Scenic moorland course.
Pro Tom Shard; Founded 1904
Designed by Dr A. MacKenzie
18 holes, 5976 yards, S.S.S. 69
Visitors: welcome.
Green Fees: WD £23; WE £30.
Societies: welcome WD by prior arrangement; from £34.
Catering: full facilities except Mon.
Hotels: La Pergola.

7 129 St Annes Old Links
Highbury Rd, St Annes, Lytham St Annes, Lancs, FY8 2LD
☎(01253) 723597, Fax 781506, Pro 722432, Bar/Rest 712863
Off A584 coast road at St Anne's.
Championship links course.
Pro G Hardman; Founded 1901

Designed by James Herd
18 holes, 6616 yards, S.S.S. 72
Visitors: welcome except before
9.30am or between 12 noon-1.30pm.
Green Fees: WD £35; WE £35.
Societies: welcome by prior arrangement; packages available; menus on request; separate changing room; snooker; from £35.
Catering: full clubhouse dining and bar facilities.
Practice ground.
Hotels: contact local tourist board.

7 130 St Bees

Station Rd, St Bees, Cumbria, CA27 0EJ
☎(01946) 824300
On B5345 4 miles S of Whitehaven
Seaside course.
Founded 1942
9 holes, 5122 yards, S.S.S. 65
Visitors: welcome except on comp days.
Green Fees: WD £12; WE £12.
Societies: welcome by arrangement with the school.
Catering: no facilities.
Hotels: Queens.

7 131 Seascale

The Banks, Seascale, Cumbria, CA20 1QL
☎(01946) 728202, Fax 728202, Pro 016973 32404
Off A595 at NW edge of Seascale.
Links course.
Pro Jonathen Graham; Founded 1893
Designed by Willie Campbell
18 holes, 6416 yards, S.S.S. 71
Visitors: welcome by prior arrangement.
Green Fees: WD £20; WE £25.
Societies: welcome by prior arrangement; discounts of 10 per cent for 12 or more and 15 per cent for 20 or more; from £20.
Catering: clubhouse facilities.
Practice area for members, guests and visitors only.
Hotels: Lutwidge Arms, Holmnook; Calder House, Seascale; Horse & Groom, Gosforth.

7 132 Sedbergh

Catholes-Abbot Holme, Dent Rd, Sedbergh, Cumbria, LA10 5SS
☎(01539) 621551, Fax 620993, Pro 620993, Sec 620993, Bar/Rest 620993
1 mile from Sedbergh on road to Dent and 5 miles E of M6 junction 37.

New parkland course in Yorkshire Dales National Park.
Pro R Williamson/ J Garner; Founded 1896/1993
Designed by W.G. Squires
9 holes, 5624 yards, S.S.S. 68
Visitors: welcome; by prior arrangement at WE.
Green Fees: WD £14; WE £18.
Societies: welcome by prior arrangement; various packages can be arranged; from £20.
Catering: full catering facilities.
Hotels: George & Dragon, Dent; Bull, Sedbergh; Sec can assist with stay and play breaks.

7 133 Shaw Hill Hotel Golf & Country Club

Preston Rd, Whittle-le-Woods, Nr Chorley, Lancs, PR6 7PP
☎(01257) 269221, Fax 261223, Pro 279222
1 mile N of M61 junction 8 and 2 miles from M6 junction 28.
Parkland course with water hazards.
Pro D Clarke; Founded 1925
Designed by T. McCauley
18 holes, 6239 yards, S.S.S. 73
Visitors: welcome WD only with h'cap certs.
Green Fees: WD £30; WE £30.
Societies: welcome WD with h'cap certs; golf and catering packages can be arranged; terms on application.
Catering: bar, restaurant and à la carte menus available.
Hotels: club has 30 rooms.

7 134 Sherdley Park

Sherdley Park, St Helens, Merseyside, WA9 5DE
☎(01744) 815518, Pro 813149
2 miles S of St Helens on Warrington Road.
Public undulating parkland course.
Pro Peter Parkinson; Founded 1973
Designed by P.R. Parkinson
18 holes, 5974 yards, S.S.S. 69
Visitors: welcome.
Green Fees: WD £7; WE £8.
Societies: welcome by prior arrangement.
Catering: bar and cafeteria.
Practice range, 12 bays floodlit.
Hotels: Stakis, St Helens.

7 135 Silecroft

Silecroft, Cumbria, LA18 4NX
☎(01229) 774250, Sec 774342
On A5093 3 miles N of Millom through Silecroft village towards shore.

Seaside course.
Founded 1903
9 holes, 5877 yards, S.S.S. 68
Visitors: welcome WD; WE and BH not afternoons.
Green Fees: WD £15; WE £15.
Societies: welcome by arrangement.
Catering: limited; Miners Arms provides food.
Hotels: Bankfield; Miners Arms.

7 136 Silloth on Solway

Silloth on Solway, Carlisle, Cumbria, CA5 4BL
☎(016973) 31304, Fax 31782, Pro 32404, Bar/Rest 32442
From Wigton follow B5302 to Silloth.
Championship links course; 1997
British women's strokeplay.
Pro Carl Weatherhead; Founded 1892
Designed by Willie Park Jnr
18 holes, 6614 yards, S.S.S. 72
Visitors: welcome by prior arrangement.
Green Fees: WD £25; WE £30.
Societies: welcome by prior arrangement; full day packages of golf and catering available; Mon catering only by prior arrangement; from £35.
Catering: full bar and catering facilities, except Mon.
Hotels: Wheyrigg Hall, Wigton; Golf Hotel; Queens; Skinburness all Silloth-on-Solway.

7 137 Silverdale

Redbridge Lane, Silverdale, Carnforth, Lancs, LA5 0SP
☎(01524) 701300, Sec 702074, Bar/Rest 702074
3 miles NW of Carnforth by Silverdale station.
Heathland/parkland course.
Founded 1906
12 holes, 5559 yards, S.S.S. 67
Visitors: welcome by prior arrangement; some Sun summer restrictions.
Green Fees: WD £15; WE £18.
Societies: welcome by prior arrangement with Sec, WD and WE packages available; from £22.
Catering: clubhouse facilities.
Hotels: Silverdale Hotel.

7 138 Solway Village Golf Centre

Solway Village, Silloth-on-Solway, Cumbria, CA5 4QQ
☎(016973) 31236
Easy to locate in village of Silloth.
Scenic parkland course.
Founded 1988

9 holes, 4001 yards
Visitors: welcome.
Green Fees: WD £9; WE £9.
Societies: welcome by arrangement.
Catering: bar and restaurant.
Practice range, 4 bays.
Hotels: hotel on site; log cabins; caravans.

7 139 **Southport & Ainsdale**

Bradshaws Lane, Ainsdale, Southport,
Merseyside, PR8 3LG
☎(01704) 578092, Fax 570896, Pro
577316, Sec 578000, Bar/Rest
579422
On A565 3 miles S of Southport, 0.5
miles from Ainsdale station.
Links course.
Pro Mike Houghton; Founded 1907
Designed by James Braid
18 holes, 6583 yards, S.S.S. 73
Visitors: welcome WD between
10am-12 noon and 2.30pm-4.00pm.
Green Fees: WD £35; WE £35.
Societies: welcome WD; terms on
application; from £35.
Catering: full clubhouse facilities.
Hotels: Scarisbrick, Southport.

7 140 **Southport Municipal**

Park Rd West, Southport, Merseyside,
PR9 0JS
☎(01704) 530133, Pro 535286
N end of Promenade.
Public seaside course.
Pro Bill Fletcher; Founded 1914
18 holes, 6139 yards, S.S.S. 69
Visitors: welcome.
Green Fees: WD £6; WE £8.
Societies: welcome by prior booking
at least six days in advance.
Catering: meals and bar facilities.
Hotels: Scarisbrick; Prince of Wales.

7 141 **Southport Old Links**

Moss Lane, Southport, Merseyside,
PR9 7QS
☎(01704) 228207
Off Manchester Rd into Roe Lane and
then into Moss Lane; close to town
centre.
Seaside course.
Founded 1920
9 holes, 6244 yards, S.S.S. 71
Visitors: welcome except Wed and
restrictions at WE.
Green Fees: WD £18; WE £25.
Societies: welcome by arrangement if
party is more than 12; terms on application.
Catering: full facilities except Mon.
Hotels: Richmond House.

7 142 **Springfield Park**

Springfield Park, Bolton Rd, Rochdale,
Lancs, OL11 4RE
☎(01706) 656401, Pro 649801
3 miles from M62.
Parkland course.
Pro David Mills; Founded 1927
18 holes, 5237 yards, S.S.S. 66
Visitors: welcome.
Green Fees: WD £6; WE £10.
Societies: welcome by prior arrangement with the professional; terms on
application.
Catering: none.
Hotels: Midway, Rochdale.

7 143 **Stand**

The Dales, Ashbourne Grove,
Whitefield, Manchester, M45 7NL
☎(0161) 766 2388, Pro 766 2214,
Sec 766 3197
1 mile N of M62 junction 17.
Undulating parkland course.
Pro Mark Dance; Founded 1904
Designed by Alex Herd
18 holes, 6426 yards, S.S.S. 71
Visitors: welcome WD; restricted WE.
Green Fees: WD £25; WE £30.
Societies: welcome Wed and Fri; winter packages.
Catering: full facilities except Mon.
Hotels: Hawthorns.

7 144 **Standish Court Golf Club**

Rectory Lane, Standish, Wigan, WN6
0XD
☎(01257) 425777, Fax 425888
5 mins off M6 junction 27 following
signs for Standish village.
Parkland course.
Pro Tim Kershaw; Founded 1995
Designed by Patrick Dawson
18 holes, 5750 yards, S.S.S. 66
Visitors: welcome by arrangement.
Green Fees: WD £11; WE £16.50.
Societies: welcome by prior arrangement; full day packages available from
£36; from £17.50.
Catering: full clubhouse facilities.
Hotels: Kilbey Court; Wigan Moat
House.

7 145 **Stonyholme Municipal**

St Aidans Rd, Carlisle, Cumbria, CA1
1LF
☎(01228), Pro 625511, Bar/Rest
625512
Off A69 1 mile W of M6 junction 43.
Flat meadowland course.
Pro Stephen Ling; Founded 1974
Designed by Frank Pennink

18 holes, 5787 yards, S.S.S. 68
Visitors: welcome.
Green Fees: WD £7.25; WE £9.
Societies: welcome.
Catering: clubhouse facilities.
Practice range, 16 bays floodlit.
Hotels: Post House.

7 146 **Stonyhurst Park**

c/o The Bayley Arms, Hurst Green,
Blackburn, Lancs, BB7 9QB
☎(01254) 826478
On B6243 Clitheroe-Longridge road.
Parkland course.
Founded 1979
9 holes, 5529 yards, S.S.S. 66
Visitors: welcome except WE; contact
Bayley Arms.
Green Fees: WD £15.
Societies: limited; by prior arrangement only.
Catering: none.
Hotels: Bayley Arms.

7 147 **Swinton Park**

East Lancashire Rd, Swinton,
Manchester, M27 5LX
☎(0161) 794 1785, Fax 281 0698,
Pro 793 8077, Sec 794 0861, Bar/Rest
7941785
On A580 5 miles from Manchester on
Liverpool road.
Parkland course.
Pro Jim Wilson; Founded 1926
Designed by Braid & Taylor
18 holes, 6726 yards, S.S.S. 72
Visitors: welcome WD except Thurs.
Green Fees: WD £25.
Societies: welcome by arrangement
Tues, Wed and Fri.
Catering: bar and restaurant facilities;
function and conference rooms.

7 148 **Towneley**

Towneley Park, Todmorden Rd,
Burnley, Lancs BB11 3ED
☎(01282) 451636, Pro 438473, Sec
414555
From M65 follow signs to Towneley
Hall.
Parkland course.
Founded 1932
Designed by Burnley Council
18 holes, 5811 yards, S.S.S. 69
Visitors: welcome.
Green Fees: WD £8; WE £9.
Societies: welcome by prior arrangement; catering can be arranged with
steward; from £8.
Catering: bar and restaurant facilities.
Practice ground.
Hotels: Alexander.

7 149 **Tunshill**
Kiln Lane, Milnrow; Lancs, OL16 3TS
☎(01706) 342095
From M62 junction 21 take road to
Milnrow and follow Kiln Lane out of the
town to narrow lane for clubhouse.
Moorland course.
Founded 1943
9 holes, 5743 yards, S.S.S. 68
Visitors: welcome WD except Tues
evening; by prior arrangement WE.
Green Fees: WD £15; WE terms on
application.
Societies: welcome WD by arrange-
ment; terms on application.
Catering: restaurant and bar facilities.
Hotels: John Milne, Milnrow.

7 150 **Turton**
Wood End Farm, Chapeltown Rd,
Bromley Cross, Bolton, Lancs BL7 9QH
☎(01204) 852235
4 miles NW of Bolton near Last Drop
Hotel.
Moorland course.
Founded 1908
Designed by James Braid
18 holes, 6159 yards, S.S.S. 68
Visitors: welcome except Wed 11.30-
3 and WE only by arrangement.
Green Fees: WD £16; WE £20.
Societies: welcome by arrangement.
Catering: full catering facilities.
Hotels: Last Drop; Egerton House.

7 151 **Ulverston**
The Clubhouse, Bardsea Park,
Ulverston, Cumbria, LA12 9QJ
☎(01229) 582824, Pro 582806
From M6 junction 36 follow signs for
Barrow on A590 and take A5087 to
Bardsea.
Parkland course.
Pro M R Smith; Founded 1895/1909
Designed by A Herd
18 holes, 6201 yards, S.S.S. 71
Visitors: welcome by prior arrange-
ment.
Green Fees: WD £25; WE £30.
Societies: welcome by prior arrange-
ment; packages for golf and catering
can be arranged; terms on application.
Catering: full clubhouse catering and
bar facilities.

7 152 **Walmersley**
Garretts Close, Walmersley, Bury,
Lancs, BL9 6TE
☎(0161) 764 1429, Fax 01706
826295, Pro 763 9050, Sec 764 7770
Off A56 3 miles N of Bury.
Moorland course.

Pro S Crake; Founded 1906
18 holes, 5341 yards, S.S.S. 67
Visitors: welcome.
Green Fees: WD £20; WE £20.
Societies: welcome Wed-Fri; 27 holes
golf, coffee, light lunch and 4-course
meal; from £26.
Catering: full clubhouse facilities.
Hotels: Red Hall, Bury.

7 153 **Werneth (Oldham)**
Green Lane, Garden Suburb, Oldham,
Lancs, OL8 3AZ
☎(0161) 624 1190, Pro 628 7136
5 miles from Manchester, take A62 to
Hollinwood and then A6104.
Moorland course.
Pro Roy Penney; Founded 1908
18 holes, 5364 yards, S.S.S. 66
Visitors: welcome WD; by arrange-
ment WE.
Green Fees: WD £18.50; WE £18.50.
Societies: welcome Mon, Wed and Fri
by arrangement.
Catering: lunch and meals served
except Mon.
Hotels: Periquito; Smokeys, both
Oldham.

7 154 **West Derby**
Yew Tree Lane, Liverpool, Merseyside,
L12 9HQ
☎(0151) 228 1540, Fax 259 0505,
Pro 220 5478, Sec 254 1034
Follow signs for Knotty Ash to round-
about and then into Blackmoor Drive,
right into Yew Tree Lane.
Flat parkland course with trees.
Pro Andrew Witherup; Founded 1896
18 holes, 6257 yards, S.S.S. 70
Visitors: welcome WD; except Tues.
Green Fees: WD £25; WE £30.
Societies: welcome WD except Tues;
full golf and catering packages avail-
able; from £25.
Catering: bar and restaurant.
Hotels: Derby Lodge, Huyton; Bell
Tower, Knowsley.

7 155 **West Lancashire**
Hall Rd west, Blundellsands,
Liverpool, L23 8SZ
☎(0151) 924 4115, Fax 931 4448,
Pro 924 5662, Sec 924 1076
M57 to Aintree then A5036 to Seaforth
and A565 to Crosby; signposted close
to Hall Rd station.
Links course.
Pro Tim Hastings; Founded 1873
Designed by C.K. Cotton/ D Steel
18 holes, 6768 yards, S.S.S. 73
Visitors: welcome by arrangement.

Green Fees: WD £35; WE £50.
Societies: welcome WD except Tues;
packages available; from £35.
Catering: full clubhouse facilities.
Hotels: Blundellsands Hotel.

7 156 **Westhoughton**
Long Island, Westhoughton, Bolton,
Lancs, BL5 2BR
☎(01942) 811085, Fax 608958, Pro
840545, Sec 608958
Off School Lane, adjacent to Parish
Church in Westhoughton.
Parkland course.
Pro Jason Seed; Founded 1929
9 holes, 5772 yards, S.S.S. 68
Visitors: welcome.
Green Fees: WD £15; WE £15.
Societies: welcome on Thurs; pack-
ages of 9/18 holes, available with
catering; from £25.
Catering: full clubhouse facilities.

7 157 **Westhoughton Golf
Centre**
Wigan Rd, Westhoughton, Nr Bolton,
Lancs, BL8 2BX
☎(01942) 813195
M61 junction 5; travel through
Westhoughton towards Hindley.
Parkland course; home to Hart
Common GC.
Founded 1996
18 holes, 6101 yards, S.S.S. 73
Visitors: welcome.
Green Fees: WD £10.50; WE £13.50.
Societies: welcome by arrangement.
Catering: clubhouse opening April
1998.
Practice range, 26 bays floodlit cov-
ered; also 9-hole par 3 course under
construction.

7 158 **Whalley**
Portfield Lane, Whalley, Blackburn,
Lancs, BB7 9DR
☎(01254) 822236, Pro 824766, Sec
886313
Off A671 one mile SE of Whalley fol-
lowing signs for Sabden.
Parkland course.
Pro H Smith; Founded 1912
9 holes, 6258 yards, S.S.S. 70
Visitors: welcome except Thurs pm
and Sat in summer.
Green Fees: WD £15; WE £20.
Societies: welcome by arrangement
with secretary; catering and packages
on application; from £15.
Catering: clubhouse facilities.
Hotels: Higher Trapp, Simonstone;
Old Stone Manor, Mytton.

7 159 Whitefield
81/83 Higher Lane, Whitefield,
Manchester, M45 7EZ
☎(0161) 766 2728, Fax 767 9502,
Pro 766 3096, Sec 766 2904
On A665 near Whitefield exit from M62.
Parkland course.
Pro Paul Reeves; Founded 1932
18 holes, 6045 yards, S.S.S. 69
Visitors: welcome by arrangement.
Green Fees: WD £25; WE £35.
Societies: welcome WD except Tues;
also some Sat afternoons; groups of
less than 20 players £25; 60 or more
players should contact club for rates;
from £23.
Catering: full clubhouse facilities.

7 160 Whittaker
Whittaker Lane, Littleborough, Lancs,
OL15 0LH
☎(01706) 378310
On Blackstone Edge Old Road, 1.5
miles out of Littleborough; turn right at
High Peak Hamlet.
Moorland course.
Pro P Lunt; Founded 1906
Designed by N P Stott
9 holes, 5606 yards, S.S.S. 67
Visitors: welcome except Tues pm
and Sun.
Green Fees: WD £12; WE £16.
Societies: welcome by prior arrange-
ment with Sec; limited; catering on
application; from £12.
Catering: bar can be arranged.

7 161 Wigan
Arley Hall, Arley lane, Haigh, Wigan,
Lancs, WN1 2UH
☎(01257) 421360
From M6 junction 27 through Standish
on B5239; turn left at Canal Bridge
lights and course is opposite Crawford
Arms.
Parkland course.
Founded 1898
9 holes, 6036 yards, S.S.S. 69
Visitors: welcome any day except
Tues, Wed and Sat.
Green Fees: WD £25; WE £30.
Societies: welcome by prior arrange-
ment; special packages available;
terms on application.

Catering: full catering.
Hotels: Bellingham; Brockett Arms;
Kilhey Court.

7 162 William Wroe
Pennybridge Lane, Flixton,
Manchester, M41 5DX
☎(0161) 748 8680
Leave M63 junction 4 and take B5124
then B5158 to Flixton; 12 miles SW of
Manchester.
Municipal parkland course.
Pro Scott Partington
18 holes, 4264 yards, S.S.S. 61
Visitors: welcome; bookings taken 7
days in advance.
Green Fees: WD £7.50; WE £10.
Societies: welcome with booking a
maximum 7 days in advance.
Catering: local pub.
Hotels: Manor Hey.

7 163 Wilpshire
72 Whalley Rd, Wilpshire, Blackburn,
Lancs, BB1 9LF
☎(01254) 248260, Pro 249558
On A666 4 miles N of Blackburn.
Moorland course.
Pro Walter Slaven; Founded 1890
18 holes, 5802 yards, S.S.S. 69
Visitors: welcome WD; by arrange-
ment at WE.
Green Fees: WD £25.50; WE £30.50.
Societies: welcome WD by appt.
Catering: full facilities.
Hotels: County; Swallow, Salmesbury.

7 164 Windermere
Cleabarrow, Windermere, Cumbria,
LA23 3NB
☎(01539) 443550, Pro 443123, Sec
443123, Bar/Rest 443123
On B5284 1.5 miles from Bowness
towards Kendal.
Undulating parkland course.
Founded 1891
Designed by George Low
18 holes, 5122 yards, S.S.S. 65
Visitors: welcome by arrangement.
Green Fees: WD £23; WE £28.
Societies: welcome by arrangement;
packages can be arranged; from £25.
Catering: bar and snacks.

7 165 Woolton
Doe Park, Speke Rd, Woolton,
Liverpool, L25 7TZ
☎(0151) 486 1601, Fax 486 1664,
Pro 486 1298, Sec 486 2298
6 miles from city centre on road to
Liverpool Airport.
Parkland course.
Pro Alan Gibson; Founded 1901
18 holes, 5724 yards, S.S.S. 68
Visitors: welcome.
Green Fees: WD £20; WE £30.
Societies: welcome; packages can be
arranged; terms on application.
Catering: clubhouse facilities.
Hotels: Redbourne.

7 166 Workington
Branthwaite Rd, Workington, Cumbria,
CA14 4SS
☎(01900) 603460, Pro 67828
Off A595 2 miles SE of Workington.
Undulating meadowland.
Pro Adrian Drabble; Founded 1893
Designed by James Braid
18 holes, 6247 yards, S.S.S. 70
Visitors: welcome with h'cap certs.
Green Fees: WD £17; WE £22.
Societies: welcome by prior arrange-
ment with Pro.
Catering: full facilities except Mon and
Thurs evening.
Practice ground.
Hotels: Washington Central;
Westlands (adjacent).

7 167 Worsley
Stableford Ave, Monton, Eccles,
Manchester, M30 8AP
☎(0161) 789 4202, Fax 789 3200
Follow signs to Monton Green, Eccles
from M62 then to Stableford Ave.
Parkland course.
Pro C Cousins; Founded 1894
Designed by James Braid
18 holes, 6252 yards, S.S.S. 70
Visitors: welcome by prior arrange-
ment.
Green Fees: WD £20; WE £25.
Societies: welcome Wed and Thurs;
tee available 10.15am and 1.35pm;
terms on application.
Catering: clubhouse facilities.
Hotels: Wendover, Monton.

8

THE NORTH EAST

Crossing the Pennines and approaching Yorkshire on the M62 gives a perfect impression of the wild loneliness of the countryside, an impression that can only be reinforced as you travel north. Yet the area around Leeds is blessed with some fine golf courses, few of which are as dominated by a river as Ilkley, particularly the opening holes which have a habit of destroying a score before it has taken shape.

Alwoodley, Moor Allerton, Moortown and Sand Moor formed a distinguished cluster until Moor Allerton sold up and moved out towards Wike. The development of houses on the old course and on part of Sand Moor meant that Moortown became so surrounded that a redesign of their layout was essential. Sand Moor relocated their clubhouse on the other side of Alwoodley Lane and added several new holes but both Moortown and Sand Moor have preserved their reputations.

Neighbouring Bradford boasts West Bowling and the Bradford Club while Halifax is well served and Huddersfield claims Crosland Heath, Woodsome Hall and the Huddersfield GC at Fixby which is probably the pick. Moving south-east, the Sheffield district is full of good things. Hallamshire, Hallowes, Dore & Totley, Abbeydale, Lees Hall and Phoenix constitute the pick; nor must one forget Doncaster Town Moor, Wheatley and the Doncaster Club in the East Riding.

Of the old North Riding courses, Ganton surely wears the crown. Lying in the midst of the lovely Vale of Pickering, it is without doubt one of the finest inland courses in Britain and the only one to have housed the British Amateur championship.

Further north, Catterick Garrison and Richmond stand out along with Bedale and, just to the south, the pleasant nine holes of Ripon City.

Northumberland is a rich tapestry of seascape, woodland, lonely moor and fertile farmland. A welcome addition to the golfing map has been the development at Slaley Hall near Hexham, a comfortable drive west of Newcastle, although the long stretch of Northumberland's coastline, running parallel with the A1, makes it an obvious target for those who like sea air in their nostrils and golf that can be described as off the beaten track.

The best is Berwick-upon-Tweed at Goswick, a course that divides neatly into two, the best and most enchanting being the few holes that nestle between the dunes and open up views of the hallowed, ancient ground of Holy Island. It is the second oldest place in the county where golf is played, the distinction of being the oldest belonging to the little village nine-hole course at Alnmouth.

Crossing the Tyne into Durham marks a distinct change of scenery, although there are two outstanding courses in Seaton Carew, a magnificent links even if its backcloth is industrial, and Brancepeth Castle south-west of Durham, designed by the master, Harry Colt, and of which Leonard Crawley was inordinately fond.

Durham's best news for some time is the opening of The Ramside, a 27-hole course which is attached to the well known Ramside Hall Hotel. Knotty Hill, at nearby Sedgefield, is a most enterprising project comprising 36 holes that is bound to find popularity among local golfers.

From Durham, there is a natural inclination to head towards the sea and sample the coastal chain of courses starting with Hartlepool, the handiwork of James Braid, and then sandwiching Seaton Carew between Hartlepool and the ancient Cleveland Club at Redcar.

8A 1 Abbeydale
Twentywell Lane, Dore, Sheffield, S
Yorks, S17 4QA
☎(0114) 2360763, Pro 2365633.
Off A621 5 miles S of Sheffield.
Parkland course.
Founded 1895
Designed by Nathan Perry
18 holes, 6407 yards, S.S.S. 71
Visitors: welcome by arrangement but
not before 9.30am or between 12 noon
and 1.30pm.
Green Fees: WD £25; WE £35.
Societies: welcome by prior arrange-
ment; terms on application.
Catering: by arrangement; bar and
restaurant facilities.
Hotels: Beauchief; Sheffield Moat
House.

8A 2 Aldwark Manor
Aldwark, Alne, York, YO6 2NF
☎(01347) 838353, Fax 838867,
Bar/Rest 838146.
Off A1 5 miles SE of Boroughbridge;
13 miles NW of York off A19.
Easy walking parkland course built
around the River Ure.
Founded 1978
18 holes 6171 yards, S.S.S. 70
Visitors: welcome WD; some WE
restrictions.
Green Fees: WD £20; WE £25.
Societies: welcome WD; some WE
restrictions; various packages available
involving 18, 29 or 36 holes of golf;
from £22.50.
Catering: full catering in the Victorian
Manor House built in 1856; minimum
12; private dining rooms available; full
restaurant and bar facilities.
Hotels: Aldwark Manor (20 bedrooms).

8A 3 Allerthorpe Park
Allerthorpe Park, Allerthorpe, York,
Yorks, YO4 RL
☎(01759) 306686, Fax 304308.
Off the A1079 York-Hull road 2 miles W
of Pocklington.
Parkland course.
Founded 1994
Designed by J G Hatcliffe & Partners
9 holes, 5514 yards, S.S.S. 67
Visitors: welcome.
Green Fees: WD £14; WE £14.
Societies: welcome by prior arrange-
ment; terms on application.
Catering: clubhouse facilities.

8A 4 Alwoodley
Wigton Lane, Alwoodley, Leeds, W
Yorks, LS17 8SA
☎(0113) 2681680, Fax 2939458, Pro
2689603.
On A61 5 miles N of Leeds.
Heathland/moorland course.
Pro John Green; Founded 1907
Designed by: Dr A. MacKenzie/H. Colt
18 holes, 6686 yards, S.S.S. 73
Visitors: welcome by arrangement.
Green Fees: WD £50; WE £50.
Societies: welcome by prior arrange-
ment; terms on application.
Catering: bar and restaurant facilities;
catering packages by arrangement.
Hotels: Harewood Arms.

8A 5 Ampleforth College
Gilling East, York, York, YO6 5AE
☎(01653) 628555
Entrance opposite church in the centre
of Gilling East.
Parkland course.
Founded 1972
Designed by Ampleforth College
10 holes, 5567 yards, S.S.S. 68
Visitors: welcome by prior arrange-
ment but restrictions between 2pm-
4pm for pupils on WD.
Green Fees: WD £8; WE £12.
Societies: Club will consider applica-
tions.
Catering: none; public house next
door.
Hotels: Worsley Arms, Hovingham.

8A 6 Austerfield Park Country Club
Cross Lane, Austerfield, Doncaster,
Yorkshire, DN10 6RF
☎(01302) 710841, Fax 710841, Sec
710850
Take A614 towards Finningley; Cross
Lane is on right at first roundabout.
Parkland course.
Pro Peter Rothery; Founded 1974
Designed by E.& M. Baker Ltd
18 holes, 6900 yards, S.S.S. 73
Visitors: welcome.
Green Fees: WD £15; WE £19.
Societies: welcome by prior arrange-
ment.
Catering: clubhouse facilities.
Hotels: Crown, Bawtry.

8A 7 Baildon
Moorgate, Baildon, Shipley, Yorkshire,
BD17 5PP
☎(01274) 584266, Fax 530551, Pro
595162, Sec 530551
3 miles N of Bradford off the Bradford-
Ilkley road.
Moorland course laid out as a links
course.

Pro Richard Masters; Founded 1896
Designed by T Morris; modified by J
Braid
18 holes, 6231 yards, S.S.S. 70
Visitors: welcome by prior arrange-
ment.
Green Fees: WD £16; WE £20.
Societies: welcome by prior arrange-
ment; discounts for larger groups;
terms on application.
Catering: clubhouse facilities, catering
packages available.
Hotels: many in local area.

8A 8 Barnsley
Wakefield Rd, Staincross, Nr Barnsley,
S Yorkshire S75 6JZ
☎(01226) 382856, Pro 380358.
On A61 3 miles from Barnsley.
Undulating meadowland course.
Founded 1928
18 holes, 5951 yards, S.S.S. 69
Visitors: welcome.
Green Fees: WD £8; WE £9.
Societies: welcome by prior arrange-
ment; terms on application.
Catering: bar meals.
Practice range, 50 yards from club.
Hotels: Queens; Ardley Moat House.

8A 9 Beauchief
Abbey Lane, Sheffield, S Yorks, S8
0DB
☎(0114) 2620040, Pro 2367274
From M1 junction 33 towards city cen-
tre and follow signs A612 to Bakewell
for 4 miles, turning left into Abbeydale
Road at lights.
Parkland course.
Pro Louis Horsman; Founded 1925
18 holes, 5452 yards, S.S.S. 66
Visitors: municipal pay and play.
Green Fees: WD £8.50; WE £10.
Societies: welcome by prior written
agreement from Sheffield City Council;
Recreation Dept, Town Hall, Sheffield
1; terms on application.
Catering: meals served daily.
Hotels: Beauchief adjacent to course.

8A 10 Bedale
Leyburn Rd, Bedale, N Yorks, DL8
1EZ
☎(01677) 422568, Fax 422451, Pro
422443, Sec 422451
From A1 take A684 through Bedale;
course 400 yards from town centre.
Parkland course.
Pro Tony Johnson; Founded 1894
18 holes, 6565 yards, S.S.S. 71
Visitors: welcome with h'cap certs.
Green Fees: WD £18; WE £28.

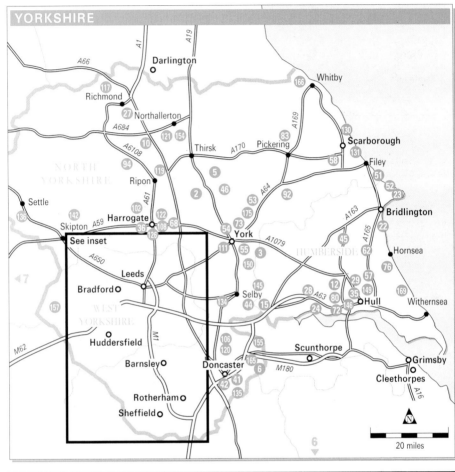

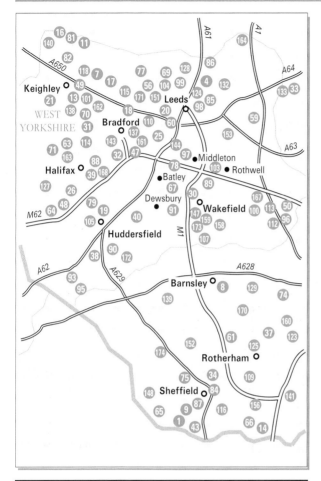

Societies: welcome by prior arrangement; catering and golfing packages available; terms on application.
Catering: clubhouse facilities.
Hotels: Nags Head, Pickhill; White Rose, Leeming Bar.

8A 11 **Ben Rhydding**

High Wood, Ben Rhydding, Ilkley, W Yorkshire, LS29 8SB
☎(01943) 608759
From A65 to Ilkley turn up Wheatley Lane and then into Wheatley Grove, left on to High Wood, club signposted.
Moorland course with mix of light parkland and links.
Founded 1890/1947
Designed by W Dell
9 holes, 4711 yards, S.S.S. 64
Visitors: welcome WD; limited access with member at WE.
Green Fees: WD £10; WE £15.
Societies: very limited access to small parties; terms on application.
Catering: very limited.
Hotels: local tourist office can supply hotels.

8A 12 **Beverley & East Riding**

Anti Mill, Westwood, Beverley, E Yorks, HU17 8PJ
☎(01482) 867190, Fax 868757, Pro 869519, Sec 868757
On B1230 Walkington road 0.5 miles W of town centre
Common pastureland.
Pro Ian Mackie; Founded 1889
Designed by Dr J.J. Fraser
18 holes, 5972 yards, S.S.S. 69
Visitors: welcome.
Green Fees: WD £12; WE £16.
Societies: welcome WD; catering packages can be arranged; from £12.
Catering: clubhouse facilities.
Hotels: Lairgate, Beverley.

8A 13 **Bingley St Ives**

The Golf Clubhouse, Harden, Bingley, BD16 1AT
☎(01274) 562436, Fax 511788, Pro 562506, Sec 511788
Close to A650 Keighley to Bradford road and A629 Bingley to Denholme.
Parkland/moorland/woodland course.
Pro Ray Firth; Founded 1932
Designed by A MacKenzie
18 holes, 6485 yards, S.S.S. 71
Visitors: welcome by arrangement.
Green Fees: WD £24; WE £24.
Societies: welcome by prior arrangement; all day golf and catering packages available; from £36.

Catering: clubhouse facilities.
Hotels: Bankfield; Five Flags; Three Sisters.

8A 14 Birley Wood
Birley Lane, Sheffield, S Yorks, S12 3BP
☎(0114) 2647262
Off A616 4 miles S of Sheffield
Public open course.
Pro Peter Ball; Founded 1974
18 holes, 5008 yards, S.S.S. 65
Visitors: welcome.
Green Fees: WD £8.50; WE £8.90.
Societies: welcome by prior arrangement with the Sheffield Recreation Dept.
Catering: catering at Fairways Inn adjacent to course.

8A 15 Boothferry Park
Spaldington Lane, Howden, Goole, E Yorkshire, DN14 7NG
☎(01430) 430364, Bar/Rest 430371
On B1228 between Howden and Bubwith off M62 junction 37
Meadowland with ponds and ditches.
Pro N Bundy; Founded 1981
Designed by Donald Steel
18 holes, 6651 yards, S.S.S. 72
Visitors: welcome at all times.
Green Fees: WD £8.50; WE £12.50.
Societies: welcome by prior arrangement with the professional; packages can be arranged; terms on application.
Catering: clubhouse facilities.
Hotels: Cave Castle.

8A 16 Bracken Ghyll
Skipton Rd, Addingham, Yorks, LS29 0SL
☎(01943) 831207, Pro 831243
Off A65 Skipton-Leeds road in Addingham.
Undulating parkland course.
Pro Simon Poot; Founded 1993
Designed by OCM Associates
9 holes, 6560 yards, S.S.S. 72
Visitors: welcome by prior arrangement.
Green Fees: WD £10; WE £14.
Societies: welcome; catering and golf packages available; video tuition; indoor practice area; from £10.
Catering: full clubhouse facilities.
Hotels: Craiglands; Devonshire Country House; Randells.

8A 17 Bradford
Hawksworth Lane, Guiseley, Leeds, W Yorks, LS20 8LD
☎(01943) 875570, Fax 875570, Pro 873719, Bar/Rest 873817
Off A6038 3.5 miles NE of Shipley.
Moorland/parkland course.
Pro Sydney Welden; Founded 1862
18 holes, 6303 yards, S.S.S. 71
Visitors: welcome WD by prior arrangement; not Sat; limited Sun.
Green Fees: WD £23; WE £28.
Societies: welcome WD by prior arrangement; catering packages available; terms on application.
Catering: full clubhouse facilities.
Hotels: Marriott Hollins Hall; Chevin Lodge.

8A 18 Bradford Moor
Scarr Hall, Pollard Lane, Bradford, W Yorks, BD2 4RW
☎(01274) 771716, Pro 771718
2 miles from Bradford town centre on Harrogate Rd.
Moorland course.
Pro Ron Hughes; Founded 1907
9 holes, 5900 yards, S.S.S. 68
Visitors: welcome WD; discount before 1.30pm.
Green Fees: WD £12; WE £12.
Societies: welcome WD by prior arrangement; catering and golf packages available; from £16.
Catering: clubhouse facilities.

8A 19 Bradley Park
Bradley Rd, Huddersfield, HD2 2PZ
☎(01484), Fax 451613, Pro 223772
M62 junction 26 in direction of Huddersfield; right at first lights.
Parkland course.
Pro Parnell Reilly; Founded 1973
Designed by Donald Steel
18 holes, 6284 yards, S.S.S. 70
Visitors: welcome by prior arrangement.
Green Fees: WD £10; WE £12.
Societies: welcome WD; catering packages can be arranged; from £10.
Catering: clubhouse facilities.
Practice range, 18 bays floodlit; also 9-hole par 3 course.

8A 20 Brandon
Holywell Lane, Shadwell, Leeds, W Yorks, LS17 8EZ
☎(0113) 2737471
1 mile from N Leeds ring road at Roundhay Park.
Parkland course.
Founded 1967
Designed by George Eric Allamby
18 holes, 4800 yards, S.S.S. 62
Visitors: welcome.

Green Fees: WD £6; WE £7.
Societies: welcome WD by prior arrangement; 10 days notice required; from £6.
Catering: clubhouse snack facilities.
Hotels: White House; Rydal Bank.

8A 21 Branshaw
Branshaw Moor, Oakworth, Keighley, W Yorks, BD22 7ES
☎(01535) 643235, Fax 647441, Pro 647441, Bar/Rest 647441
On B6143 2 miles SW of Keighley.
Moorland course.
Pro Mark Tyler; Founded 1912
Designed by James Braid, A MacKenzie
18 holes, 5870 yards, S.S.S. 69
Visitors: welcome WD; restrictions at WE.
Green Fees: WD £12; WE £15.
Societies: welcome WD by prior arrangement; catering packages available Tues-Fri; from £15.
Catering: clubhouse catering facilities.
Hotels: Three Sisters, Haworth; Newsholme Manor, Oakworth.

8A 22 Bridlington
Belvedere Rd, Bridlington, E Yorks, YO15 3NA
☎(01262) 672092, Fax 606367, Pro 674721, Sec 606367
Off A165 S of town on Bridlington-Hull road.
Open parkland course.
Pro A R A Howarth; Founded 1905
Designed by James Braid
18 holes, 6577 yards, S.S.S. 71
Visitors: welcome by prior arrangement.
Green Fees: WD £14; WE £30.
Societies: welcome by prior arrangement; golf and catering packages available; terms on application.
Catering: full clubhouse facilities available.
Hotels: club can provide list on request.

8A 23 Bridlington Links
Flamborough Road, Marton, Bridlington, E Yorks, YO15 1DW
☎(01262) 401584, Fax 401702
On B1255 just N of Bridlington towards Flamborough Head.
Clifftop links.
Pro Steve Raybould; Founded 1993
Designed by Howard Swan
18 holes, 6719 yards, S.S.S. 72
Visitors: welcome.
Green Fees: WD £12; WE £15.

Alwoodley

Alwoodley is a course of unsuspected beauty. It lies a shortish bus ride from the centre of Leeds, suggesting a setting within sight and sound of urban bustle but those familiar with the glorious Dales country to the north will know how quickly it can be reached and that the Club's attractive name is remarkably descriptive and adapt.

For much of its existence, Alwoodley has been one of the most private clubs in the country where a round for the visitor was very much a privilege. There was no wish or need for the club to seek attention and nobody could blame them for that. But in 1965, they acted as host to the Yorkshire Amateur Championship for what, according to the Golfers Handbook, was the first time and in 1966 the English Women had the pleasure of holding their Championship there.

Alwoodley is a close neighbour of Moortown and Sand Moor, Alwoodley's first secretary being the eminent golf course architect, Dr Alister Mackenzie, who had a hand in the present layout.

Alwoodley, on part of Lord Harewood's Estate, must surely rank as one of the finest inland courses in Britain. The immediate impression surrounds the number of challenging strokes to be met. From the back tees in any sort of wind, a scratch player could well be delighted with a score of 75.

In appearance, the course is a little like Woodhall Spa with an added hint of Walton Heath. Its character is moorland with plenty of heather, gorse, bushes, trees and consuming undergrowth and there is a constant feeling of escape from the city. There is even a fair chance of completing a premature introduction to agricultural surroundings by driving over the hedge on the left of the first tee which is an alarmingly full view of the charming clubhouse but, for all the excellence of the drive and pitch second hole, the course really starts after crossing the road to the third.

This is a five for most people's money and, by the time the first short hole is reached at the seventh, other fives at the fourth, fifth and sixth may also have to be marked down. However, nobody is ever ashamed of a five at the eighth (543 yards), a magnificent hole curving around a wood into which it is so easy to hook. Not that one's troubles end with the drive. The second shot must make a formidable carry or else find a narrow elbow of fairway.

After such a severe beginning, there are mercifully three short ones among three holes around the turn but the 10th is another of Alwoodley's classic doglegs where nobody is quite happy until he has left it behind. This is a sharp left-hander where a long drive is needed to negotiate what can be a full second shot to a green in a hidden dell.

The other is the 15th, with danger this time awaiting the slicer, and a superb approach to an unusually shaped green awaiting everyone; but in between are two grand fours and the longest short hole (211 yards), an exceedingly testing stroke in a crosswind. These holes provide perfect balance to the round which ends with three more par fours, the shortest of which is 435 yards.

Enjoyment will have been increased by the excellence of the lies on springy turf. There will undoubtedly be an urge to return and the completeness of the examination faced is confirmed by the fact that you will probably have used, at some time, every club in the bag.

Not many courses can make claims such as these but an interesting tailpiece is contained in Macken-zie's book on Golf Architecture which informs the reader that at Alwoodley and Moortown "practically every green and every hummock has been artificially made, and yet it is difficult to convince the stranger that this is so".

However, that is a tribute to a good architect and Mackenzie was an undoubted master.

Societies: welcome; summer and winter packages available; driving range; short course; terms on application. **Catering:** full clubhouse facilities. Practice range, 24 bays covered floodlit. **Hotels:** Rags Hotel; Manor Court; Sewerby Grange; North Star, Flamborough.

8A 24 Brough
Cave Rd, Brough, E Yorks, HU15 1HB
☎(01482) 667374, Fax 667291, Pro 667483, Sec 667291
Off A63, 10 miles W of Hull.
Parkland course.
Pro G Townhill; Founded 1893
18 holes, 6134 yards, S.S.S. 69
Visitors: welcome WD except Wed; WE by prior arrangement.
Green Fees: WD £30; WE £30.
Societies: welcome by prior arrangement; full golf and catering packages available; terms on application.
Catering: full clubhouse facilities.
Hotels: Beverley Arms; Walkington Manor.

8A 25 Calverley
Woodhall Lane, Pudsey, Yorks, LS28 5QY
☎(0113) 2564362, Fax 2569244, Pro 2569244, Sec 2569244
Close to M1 & M62 motorways 4 miles for Bradford, 7 miles from Leeds.
Parkland course.
Pro Derek Johnson; Founded 1983
18 holes, 5590 yards, S.S.S. 67
Visitors: welcome; restrictions Sat and Sun am.
Green Fees: terms on application.
Societies: welcome by arrangement; catering packages available for groups up to 30; terms on application.
Catering: full clubhouse facilities.
Large practice ground.
Hotels: Marriott.

8A 26 Castle Fields
Rastrick Common, Rastrick, Brighouse, W Yorks, HD6 3HL
☎(01484) 712108
On A643 1 mile out of Brighouse.
Parkland course.
Founded 1903
6 holes, 4812 yards, S.S.S. 50
Visitors: welcome only with member.
Green Fees: WD £5; WE £7.
Societies: welcome only by prior arrangement with Sec.
Catering: facilities at local Inns within 0.25 miles.

8A 27 Catterick
Leyburn Rd, Catterick Garrison, N Yorks, DL9 3QE
☎(01748) 833401, Fax 833268, Pro 833671, Sec 833268
On B6136 6 miles SW of Scotch Corner.
Parkland/moorland course.
Pro Andy Marshall; Founded 1930
Designed by Arthur day (1938)
18 holes, 6329 yards, S.S.S. 70
Visitors: welcome by prior arrangement.
Green Fees: WD £20; WE £25.
Societies: welcome by prior arrangement; packages can be arranged; 2 practice areas; billiards room; satellite TV; from £20.
Catering: lounge bar, restaurant, bar snacks.
Practice range, 2 practice grounds.

8A 28 Cave Castle Hotel
South Cave, Brough, E Yorks, HU15 2EU
☎(01430) 421286, Bar/Rest 422245
10 miles from Kingston upon Hull.
Parkland course.
Pro Stephen MacKinder; Founded 1989
18 holes, 6524 yards, S.S.S. 71
Visitors: welcome.
Green Fees: WD £12.50; WE £18.
Societies: welcome WD and after 10.30am at WE; special packages available; conference facilities for 250; à la carte restaurant; practice facilities; terms on application.
Catering: full hotel facilities.
Hotels: Cave Castle.

8A 29 Cherry Burton
Leconfield Road, Cherry Burton, Beverley, Yorks, HU17 7RB
☎(01964) 550924
On the B1248 close to Beverley.
Parkland course.
Pro Alex Ashby; Founded 1993
Designed by W Adamson
9 holes, 6480 yards, S.S.S. 71
Visitors: welcome.
Green Fees: WD £7; WE £11.
Societies: welcome by prior arrangement.
Catering: bar and catering facilities.
Practice area.
Hotels: Beverley; Lairgate.

8A 30 City of Wakefield
Lupset Park, Horbury Rd, Wakefield, W Yorkshire, WF2 8QS
☎(01924) 367442, Pro 360282

On A642 2 miles W of Wakefield.
Parkland course.
Pro Roger Holland; Founded 1936
Designed by J S F Morrison
18 holes, 6319 yards, S.S.S. 70
Visitors: welcome.
Green Fees: WD £8; WE £10.
Societies: welcome on WD by prior arrangement; packages can be arranged through the stewardess; terms on application.
Catering: clubhouse facilities.
Hotels: Cedar Court, Wakefield; Forte Post House.

8A 31 Clayton
Thornton View Rd, Clayton, Bradford, W Yorks, BD14 6JX
☎(01274) 880047
On A647 from Bradford following signs for Clayton.
Moorland course.
Founded 1906
9 holes, 5467 yards, S.S.S. 67
Visitors: welcome WD and Sat unless comps.
Green Fees: WD £10; WE £12.
Societies: welcome by arrangement with Sec; catering packages by arrangement; snooker; terms on application.
Catering: bar and bar snacks.
Hotels: Pennine Hilton.

8A 32 Cleckheaton & District
Bradford Rd, Cleckheaton, W Yorks, BD19 6BU
☎(01274) 874118, Pro 851267, Sec 851266
On A638 from M62 junction 26 towards Bradford.
Parkland course.
Pro Mike Ingham; Founded 1900
18 holes, 5860 yards, S.S.S. 68
Visitors: welcome.
Green Fees: WD £24.
Societies: welcome WD by arrangement; catering packages by arrangement; terms on application.
Catering: clubhouse catering and bar.
Hotels: Novotel.

8A 33 Cocksford
Stutton, Tadcaster, N Yorks, LS24 9NG
☎(01937) 834253, Fax 834253, Bar/Rest 530346
In village of Strutton close to A64.
Parkland course with Cock Beck running through it.
Pro Graham Thompson; Founded 1991

Designed by Townend/ Brodigan
18 holes, 5632 yards, S.S.S. 69
Visitors: welcome by arrangement.
Green Fees: WD £17; WE £23.
Societies: welcome by prior arrangement; 27 holes golf; all-day catering; 3rd nine added in 1995 to form Plews and Quarry High courses; £29.
Catering: clubhouse facilities, including bistro and Sparrows restaurant.
Hotels: Club have cottages to rent.

8A 34 Concord Park

Shiregreen Lane, Sheffield, S Yorks, S5 6AE
☎(0114) 2577378, Sec 2349802
Off A6135 3.5 miles N of Sheffield.
Parkland course.
Pro Warren Allcroft; Founded 1952
18 holes, 4872 yards, S.S.S. 64
Visitors: welcome by prior arrangement.
Green Fees: WD £6.95; WE £6.95.
Societies: welcome; from £6.95.
Catering: refreshments in adjacent Sports Centre.

8A 35 Cottingham

Woodhill Way, Cottingham, E Yorks, HU16 5RZ
☎(01482) 842394, Fax 846030, Sec 846030, Bar/Rest 846032
Off A164 4 miles off the M62/A63.
Parkland course.
Pro Chris Gray; Founded 1994
Designed by J Wiles/T Litten
18 holes, 6230 yards, S.S.S. 69
Visitors: welcome by prior arrangement.
Green Fees: WD £12; WE £18.
Societies: welcome by prior arrangement; WD and WE packages available; from £30.
Catering: fully licensed bar and restaurant.
Hotels: Willerby Manor; Jarvis Grange.

8A 36 Crimple Valley

Hookstone Wood Rd, Harrogate, Yorks, HG2 8PN
☎(01423) 883485, Fax 881018
Off A61 1 mile S of town centre.
Parkland course.
Founded 1976
Designed by R Lumb
9 holes, 5000 yards
Visitors: Public pay and play.
Green Fees: WD £7.50; WE £10.
Societies: welcome by arrangement; from £7.50.
Catering: bar and catering facilities.

8A 37 Crookhill Park

Carr Lane, Conisbrough, Nr Doncaster, S Yorks, DN12 2AH
☎(01709) 862979, Sec 01302 780284, Bar/Rest 862974
Off A630 Doncaster to Rotherham road.
Parkland course.
Pro R Swaine; Founded 1976
18 holes, 5849 yards, S.S.S. 68
Visitors: welcome by prior arrangement.
Green Fees: terms on application.
Societies: welcome by prior arrangement with the professional; discounts available depending on group size; terms on application.
Catering: clubhouse facilities.

8A 38 Crosland Heath

Felk Stile Rd, Crosland Heath, Huddersfield, HD4 7AF
☎(01484) 653216, Pro 653877, Sec 653262
Take A62 Huddersfield-Oldham road and follow signs for Countryside Leisure.
Moorland course.
Pro Chris Gaunt; Founded 1913
18 holes, 6004 yards, S.S.S. 70
Visitors: by prior arrangement only; h'cap certs required.
Green Fees: terms on application.
Societies: welcome except Sat by prior arrangement; catering packages by arrangement; terms on application.
Catering: full facilities available except Mon.
Practice ground.
Hotels: Dryclough, Crosland Moor; Durker Roods, Meltham.

8A 39 Crows Nest Park

Coach Road, Hove Edge, Brighouse, W Yorks, HD6 2LN
☎(01422) 201216, Fax 201216, Pro 01484 401121, Bar/Rest 01484 401152
Off M62 at Brighouse follow signs for Bradford; turn left at Ritz.
Parkland course.
Pro Bob Parry; Founded 1985
Designed by W Adamson
9 holes, 6020 yards, S.S.S. 72
Visitors: welcome.
Green Fees: WD £13; WE £16.
Societies: welcome; golf and catering packages available; terms on application.
Catering: clubhouse facilities available.
Practice range, 8 bays floodlit.
Hotels: Lane Head.

8A 40 Dewsbury District

The Pinnacle, Sands Lane, Mirfield, W Yorks, WF14 8HJ
☎(01924) 492399, Fax 492399, Pro 496030, Bar/Rest 491928
2 miles W of Dewsbury off A644; 3 miles from M62 junction 25.
Parkland/moorland course.
Pro N Hirst; Founded 1891
Designed by T Morris / P Alliss
18 holes, 6360 yards, S.S.S. 71
Visitors: welcome WD and after 2.30pm WE.
Green Fees: WD £18; WE £18.
Societies: welcome WD and Sun after 2.30pm; full packages of 27 holes of golf and catering available; from £29.
Catering: full clubhouse facilities.
Practice ground.
Hotels: Five Arches, Mirfield; Woolpack, Whitley.

8A 41 Doncaster

278 Bawtry Rd, Bessacarr, Doncaster, S Yorks, DN4 7PD
☎(01302) 865632, Fax 865994, Pro 868404
On A638 between Doncaster and Bawtry.
Undulating heathland course.
Pro Graham Bailey; Founded 1894
18 holes, 6220 yards, S.S.S. 70
Visitors: welcome.
Green Fees: WD £20; WE £25.
Societies: welcome WD by prior arrangement with Sec; packages by arrangement; terms on application.
Catering: full clubhouse facilities.
Hotels: Punches; Danum.

8A 42 Doncaster Town Moor

Bawtry Rd, Belle Vue, Doncaster, S Yorks
☎(01302) 533778, Pro 535286, Bar/Rest 533167
Next to Doncaster Rovers FC and close to racecourse.
Moorland course.
Pro Steven Poole; Founded 1895
18 holes, 6001 yards, S.S.S. 69
Visitors: welcome; restrictions Sun.
Green Fees: WD £14; WE £16.
Societies: welcome by arrangement; full days golf and catering by arrangement; £25.
Catering: clubhouse facilities.
Hotels: Royal St Leger; Earl of Doncaster.

8A 43 Dore & Totley

Bradway Rd, Sheffield, S Yorks, S17 4QR

☎(0114) 2360492, Fax 2353436, Pro 2366844, Sec 2369872
6 miles S of Sheffield on the B6054 for Bradway.
Parkland course.
Pro G Watkinson; Founded 1913
18 holes, 6256 yards, S.S.S. 70
Visitors: welcome by prior arrangement except Sat; Sun before 10.30am and Wed before 1pm.
Green Fees: WD £20; WE £20.
Societies: welcome except Wed and Sat; summer and winter packages can be arranged through Pro; terms on application.
Catering: full clubhouse facilities.

8A 44 **Drax**
Drax, Nr Selby, N Yorks, YO8 8PQ
☎(01405) 860533
Off A1041 6 miles S of Selby opposite Drax power station.
Tree-lined parkland course.
Founded 1989
9 holes, 5510 yards, S.S.S. 67
Visitors: only with a member.
Green Fees: WD £5; WE £7.
Catering: at Drax Sports and Social Club.

8A 45 **Driffield**
Sunderlandwick, Beverley Rd, Driffield, E Yorks, YO25 7AD
☎(01377) 253116, Fax 240599, Pro 256663
Off A164 Beverley to Driffield road off the first main roundabout.
Mature parkland course.
Pro Gordon Davies; Founded 1934
18 holes, 6215 yards, S.S.S. 70
Visitors: welcome WD 9.30am-12noon & 1.30pm-3pm; WE between 10am-11am.
Green Fees: WD £18; WE £25.
Societies: welcome by prior arrangement with h'cap certs; catering packages available; practice area; from £18.
Catering: clubhouse facilities.
Hotels: Bell, Driffield.

8A 46 **Easingwold**
Stillington Rd, Easingwold, N Yorkshire, YO6 3ET
☎(01347) 821486, Fax 822474, Pro 821964, Sec 822474
On A19 12 miles N of York; 1 miles down Stillington road at S end of Easingwold.
Parkland course.
Pro J Hughes; Founded 1930
Designed by Hawtree

18 holes, 6285 yards, S.S.S. 70
Visitors: welcome by prior arrangement.
Green Fees: WD £25; WE £30.
Societies: welcome by prior arrangement; golf and full catering packages; £38.
Catering: clubhouse facilities.
Hotels: Garth Hotel; The George.

8A 47 **East Bierley**
South View Rd, Bierley, Bradford, W Yorkshire, BD4 6PP
☎(01274) 681023, Sec 683666, Bar/Rest 680450
4 miles S of Bradford.
Parkland course; started as Toftshaw GC in 1904.
Founded 1904/28
9 holes, 4692 yards, S.S.S. 63
Visitors: welcome.
Green Fees: WD £12; WE £15.
Societies: welcome by prior arrangement; terms on application.
Catering: full catering facilities.
Hotels: Tong Village Hotel, Tong; Cedar Court, Bradford.

8A 48 **Elland**
Hammerstones, Leach Lane, Elland, W Yorks, HX5 0TA
☎(01422) 372505, Pro 374886
From M62 junction 24 in direction of Blackley.
Parkland course.
Pro N Kryzwicki; Founded 1910
9 holes, 5630 yards, S.S.S. 66
Visitors: welcome.
Green Fees: WD £14; WE £25.
Societies: welcome Tues, Wed, Fri; catering packages available; from £14.
Catering: clubhouse facilities.
Hotels: Rock Hotel, Holywell Green.

8A 49 **Fardew**
Nursery Farm, Carr Lane, East Morton, Keighley, W Yorks, BD20 5RY
☎(01274) 561229, Fax 561438
1.25 miles from Bingley, then to E Morton.
Parkland course.
Pro Laurie Turner; Founded 1993
Designed by W Adamson
9 holes, 6208 yards, S.S.S. 70
Visitors: pay and play.
Green Fees: WD £14; WE £14.
Societies: welcome by prior arrangement; terms on application
Catering: none; local hotels and inns can supply food.
Open practice ground.
Hotels: Beeches, Keighley.

8A 50 **Ferrybridge 'C'**
Ferrybridge 'C' P.S. Golf Club, Knottingley, WF11 8SQ
☎(01977) 674188
On Castleford-Knottingley road 200 yards from A1.
Founded 1976
Designed by N.E. Pugh
9 holes, 5138 yards, S.S.S. 65
Visitors: only with a member
Green Fees: terms on application.
Societies: welcome by arrangement.

8A 51 **Filey**
West Ave, Filey, N Yorks, YO14 9BQ
☎(01723) 513116, Fax 514952, Pro 513134, Sec 513293, Bar/Rest 513293
1 mile S of Filey.
Links/parkland course.
Pro Gary Hutchinson; Founded 1897
Designed by J Braid
18 holes, 6112 yards, S.S.S. 69
Visitors: welcome by arrangement.
Green Fees: WD £21; WE £30.
Societies: welcome with prior arrangement; catering packages available; from £21.
Catering: clubhouse facilities.
Hotels: White Lodge; Hallam.

8A 52 **Flamborough Head**
Lighthouse Rd, Flamborough, Bridlington, E Yorkshire, YO15 1AR
☎(01262) 850417, Fax 850279, Sec 850333, Bar/Rest 850333
5 miles NE of Bridlington situated on Flamborough headland.
Links course.
Founded 1931
18 holes, 5976 yards, S.S.S. 66
Visitors: welcome.
Green Fees: WD £13; WE £19.
Societies: welcome by arrangement; full day golf and catering available; from £16.
Catering: clubhouse facilities.
Hotels: North Star; Flaneburg.

8A 53 **Forest of Galtres**
Moorlands Rd, Skelton, York, Yorks, YO3 3RF
☎(01904) 766198, Fax 766198, Bar/Rest 750287
Just of A19 Thirsk road through Skelton; 1.5 miles from B1237 York ring road.
Parkland in ancient Forest of Galtres.
Pro Neil Suckling; Founded 1993
Designed by S Gidman
18 holes, 6312 yards, S.S.S. 70
Visitors: welcome.

Green Fees: WD £16; WE £21.
Societies: welcome by prior arrangement only; discounts for groups of 20 or more; from £16.
Catering: full clubhouse facilities.
Hotels: Beechwood Close; Jacobean Lodge; Fairfield Manor.

8A 54 Forest Park

Stockton on Forest, York, YO3 9UW
☎(01904) 400425
2.5 miles from E end of York by-pass
Flat parkland course.
Founded 1991
18 holes, 6660 yards, S.S.S. 72
Visitors: welcome.
Green Fees: WD £16; WE £22.
Societies: welcome; all-day golf and catering packages available; also 9-hole West Course: 6372 yards, par 70; from £33.
Catering: full clubhouse facilities.
Hotels: B&B in Stockton-on-Forest.

8A 55 Fulford

Heslington Lane, Heslington, York, Yorks, YO1 5DY
☎(01904) 413212, Fax 416918, Pro 412882, Sec 413579, Bar/Rest 411503
Off A19 1 mile S of York following sings to University Heathland.
Pro Bryan Hessay; Founded 1909
Designed by Major C. MacKenzie
18 holes, 6775 yards, S.S.S. 72
Visitors: welcome by arrangement.
Green Fees: WD £30; WE £40.
Societies: welcome by prior arrangement; not Tues am; packages can be arranged through Manager; from £30.
Catering: full clubhouse facilities.
Hotels: Stakis; Forte Crest; Almeda GH.

8A 56 Fulneck

The Clubhouse, Fulneck, Pudsey, W Yorks, LS28 8NT
☎(0113) 2565191
Between Leeds and Bradford; at Pudsey cenotaph turn right, then first left into Bankhouse Lane and follow signs.
Undulating wooded parkland course.
Founded 1892
9 holes, 5456 yards, S.S.S. 67
Visitors: welcome WD; with member at WE.
Green Fees: WD £14; WE £7.
Societies: welcome by prior arrangement with Sec; catering packages by arrangement; terms on application.
Catering: by arrangement.

8A 57 Ganstead Park

Longdales Lane, Coniston, Hull, E Yorks, HU11 4LB
☎(01482) 874754, Fax 874754, Pro 811121, Bar/Rest 811280
On A165 Hull-Bridlington road at Ganstead.
Parkland course with water.
Pro Mike Smee; Founded 1976
Designed by Peter Green
18 holes, 6801 yards, S.S.S. 73
Visitors: welcome by prior arrangement.
Green Fees: WD £16; WE £25.
Societies: welcome by prior arrangement; special packages can be arranged; terms on application.
Catering: full clubhouse facilities.
Hotels: Kingstown, Hedon; Tickton Grange, Beverley.

8A 58 Ganton

Ganton, Scarborough, N Yorks, YO12 4PA
☎(01944) 710329, Fax 710922, Pro 710260
On A64 11 miles SW of Scarborough.
Heathland/links course.
Pro Gary Brown; Founded 1891
Designed by Dunn, Vardon, Colt, C.K. Cotton
18 holes, 6734 yards, S.S.S. 74
Visitors: welcome by prior arrangement.
Green Fees: WD £40; WE £45.
Societies: welcome by prior agreement; packages can be organised; terms on application.
Catering: full clubhouse facilities.
Hotels: Crescent, Scarborough; Ganton Greyhound.

8A 59 Garforth

Long Lane, Garforth, Leeds, LS25 2DS
☎(0113) 2862021, Pro 2862063, Sec 2863308
6.5 miles E of Leeds off A642 1 miles from Wass Garage.
Parkland course.
Pro Ken Findlater; Founded 1913
18 holes, 6304 yards, S.S.S. 70
Visitors: welcome WD.
Green Fees: WD £26.
Societies: welcome WD by prior arrangement; terms on application.
Catering: full facilities.
Hotels: Hilton.

8A 60 Gott's Park

Armley Ridge Rd, Leeds, W Yorks, LS12 2QX

☎(0113) 2311896, Bar/Rest 2310492
3 miles W of the city centre.
Parkland course.
Founded 1933
18 holes, 4978 yards, S.S.S. 65
Visitors: welcome.
Green Fees: WD £7; WE £8.50.
Societies: welcome by arrangement.
Catering: Café facilities; bar in evenings and WE.

8A 61 Grange Park

Upper Wortley Rd, Rotherham, S Yorks, S61 2SJ
☎(01709) 558884, Pro 559497
On A629 2 miles W of Rotherham municipal parkland course; private clubhouse.
Pro Eric Clark; Founded 1971
18 holes, 6421 yards, S.S.S. 71
Visitors: welcome.
Green Fees: WD £9.50; WE £10.
Societies: welcome by prior arrangement with Sec; special catering and golf packages available; from £21.
Catering: full bar and catering facilities Tues-Sun; limited Mon.
Practice range, 36 bays, two-tier floodlit covered.
Hotels: Swallow.

8A 62 Hainsworth Park

Brandesburton, Driffield, E Yorks, YO25 8RT
☎(01964) 542362
Just off A165 8 miles N of Beverley.
Parkland course.
Founded 1983
18 holes, 6027 yards, S.S.S. 69
Visitors: welcome by prior arrangement.
Green Fees: WD £14; WE £18.
Societies: welcome by prior arrangement; day tickets available (WD £18, WE £22); from £14.
Catering: full catering and restaurant facilities.
Hotels: Burton Lodge on course.

8A 63 Halifax

Union Lane, Ogden, Halifax, W Yorks, HX2 8XR
☎(01422) 244171, Fax 241459, Pro 240047, Bar/Rest 248108
On A629 4 miles from Halifax.
Moorland course.
Pro Michael Allison; Founded 1895
Designed by W.H. Fowler, James Braid
18 holes, 6037 yards, S.S.S. 70
Visitors: welcome WD; limited at WE.
Green Fees: WD £15; WE £20.

Societies: welcome WD by prior arrangement of Sec; packages available with catering; £24-£32.
Catering: full clubhouse facilities. Driving range 2 miles away.
Hotels: Windmill Court; Holdsworth House; Moorlands.

8A 64 **Halifax Bradley Hall**

Stainland Rd, Holywell Green, Halifax, W Yorks, HX4 9AN
☎(01422) 374108, Pro 370231
On B6112 off A629 Halifax-Huddersfield road.
Moorland/parkland course.
Pro Peter Wood; Founded 1905/24
18 holes, 6213 yards, S.S.S. 70
Visitors: welcome with h'cap certs.
Green Fees: WD £16; WE £24.
Societies: welcome with h'cap certs and by prior arrangement; golf and catering packages; £33.
Catering: full clubhouse facilities.
Hotels: Rock Inn, Holywell Green.

8A 65 **Hallamshire**

The Clubhouse, Sandygate, Sheffield, S Yorks, S10 4LA
☎(0114) 2301007, Fax 2302153, Pro 2305222, Sec 2302153
3 miles W of Sheffield off A57 at Crosspool.
Moorland course.
Pro Geoff Tickell; Founded 1897
Designed by various, including Dr A MacKenzie.
18 holes, 6359 yards, S.S.S. 71
Visitors: welcome; some restrictions at WE.
Green Fees: WD £33; WE £38.
Societies: welcome by arrangement with Sec; packages available; terms on application.
Catering: full clubhouse facilities.
Hotels: Beauchef; Trust House Forte.

8A 66 **Hallowes**

Hallowes Lane, Dronfield, Sheffield, S Yorks, S18 1UA
☎(01246) 413734, Fax 411196, Pro 411196
Take A61 Sheffield -Chesterfield road into Dronfield and turn sharp right under railway bridge.
Undulating moorland course.
Pro Philip Dunn; Founded 1892
18 holes, 6342 yards, S.S.S. 71
Visitors: welcome WD.
Green Fees: WD £24.
Societies: welcome WD by arrangement; day ticket WD £30; catering by arrangement; terms on application.

Catering: full clubhouse facilities.
Practice ground.
Hotels: Chantry.

8A 67 **Hanging Heaton**

White Cross Rd, Bennett Lane, Dewsbury, W Yorks, WF12 7DT
☎(01924) 461606, Fax 430100, Pro 467077, Sec 430100
On A653 Dewbury-Leeds road 0.75 miles from town centre.
Parkland course.
Pro S Hartley; Founded 1922
9 holes, 5902 yards, S.S.S. 69
Visitors: welcome WD; with member at WE.
Green Fees: terms on application.
Societies: welcome by arrangement with Sec; full day packages available; terms on application.
Catering: full clubhouse facilities.

8A 68 **Harrogate**

Forest Lane Head, Harrogate, N Yorks, HG2 7TF
☎(01423) 863158, Fax 860073, Pro 862547, Sec 862999, Bar/Rest 860278
On A59 between Knaresborough and Harrogate.
Parkland course.
Pro Paul Johnson; Founded 1892
Designed by Sandy Herd; revised by Dr A McKenzie
18 holes, 6241 yards, S.S.S. 70
Visitors: welcome by arrangement.
Green Fees: WD £28; WE £40.
Societies: welcome by prior arrangement; packages can be arranged; minimum 12; from £28.
Catering: bar and restaurant.
Practice area.
Hotels: local tourist board can provide brochures.

8A 69 **Headingley**

Back Church Lane, Adel, Leeds, LS16 8DW
☎(0113) 2679573, Fax 2817334, Pro 2675100, Sec 2679573 (Manage
Off A660 Leeds to Otley road.
Undulating parkland course.
Pro Steve Foster; Founded 1892
18 holes, 6298 yards, S.S.S. 70
Visitors: welcome if member of a golf club; by prior arrangement.
Green Fees: WD £30; WE £40.
Societies: welcome by arrangement with the manager; day ticket WD £35; snooker; terms on application.
Catering: full facilities.
Hotels: Village Hotel.

8A 70 **Headley**

Headley Lane, Thornton, Bradford, W Yorks, BD13 3LX
☎(01274) 833481, Fax 833481
4 miles W of Bradford on B6145 in Thornton village.
Moorland course.
Founded 1907
9 holes, 4920 yards, S.S.S. 64
Visitors: welcome WD.
Green Fees: WD £15.
Societies: welcome by arrangement with Sec; special golf and catering packages available; from £15.
Catering: dining room and bar.
Hotels: Guide Post.

8A 71 **Hebden Bridge**

Wadsworth, Hebden Bridge, HX7 8PH
☎(01422) 842896, Sec 842732
In Hebden Bridge, cross Keighley road until Mount Skip Inn.
Upland course on edge of moor.
Founded 1930
9 holes, 5242 yards, S.S.S. 65
Visitors: welcome by prior arrangement.
Green Fees: WD £12; WE £15.
Societies: welcome, preferably on WD; from £12.
Catering: clubhouse facilities.
Hotels: Carlton; White Lion.

8A 72 **Hessle**

Westfield Rd, Cottingham, Hull, E Yorks, HU16 5YL
☎(01482) 650171, Fax 652679, Pro 650190
3 miles SW of Cottingham off A164.
Undulating meadowland; new course opened 1975.
Pro Graeme Fieldsend; Founded 1906
Designed by Peter Alliss & Dave Thomas
18 holes, 6604 yards, S.S.S. 72
Visitors: welcome except Tues 9.15am-1pm or before 11am at WE.
Green Fees: WD £20; WE £28.
Societies: welcome by prior arrangement with Sec; catering packages by arrangement except Mon; terms on application.
Catering: catering except Mon.
Practice ground.
Hotels: Grange Park; Willoughby Manor.

8A 73 **Heworth**

Muncaster House, Muncastergate, York, Yorks, YO3 9JX
☎(01904) 424618, Fax 422389, Pro 422389, Sec 426156

On 1036 Scarborough Malton road 1.5 miles NE of City centre.
Parkland course.
Pro G Roberts; Founded 1911
11 holes 6141 yards, S.S.S. 69
Visitors: welcome by prior arrangement.
Green Fees: WD £12; WE £16.
Societies: welcome by prior arrangement; full catering packages available except Mon; terms on application.
Catering: full clubhouse bar and catering except Mon.

8A 74 Hickleton
Lidget Lane, Hickleton, Nr Doncaster, S Yorks, DN5 7BE
☎(01709) 896081, Fax 896081, Pro 888436
On B6411 Thurnscoe road off the A635 Barnsley road; 4.5 miles from A1 (M) junction 37.
Parkland course.
Pro Paul Shepherd; Founded 1909
Designed by Huggett, Coles & Dyer
18 holes, 6434 yards, S.S.S. 71
Visitors: welcome by prior arrangement.
Green Fees: WD £16; WE £25.
Societies: welcome by prior arrangement; summer packages available; £16-£31.
Catering: bar, with cask beers, and restaurant available.
Hotels: Ardsley House, Barnsley; Doncaster Moat House.

8A 75 Hillsborough
Worrall Rd, Sheffield, S Yorks, S6 4BE
☎(0114) 2343608, Fax 2349151, Pro 2332666, Sec 2349151
Off A6102 Sheffield to Manchester road NW of the city just past Sheffield Wed's football ground, turning right at Horse and Jockey pub.
Undulating wooded parkland and heathland course.
Pro G Walker; Founded 1920
Designed by T Williamson
18 holes, 6216 yards, S.S.S. 70
Visitors: welcome WD and after 2pm at WE.
Green Fees: WD £28; WE £35.
Societies: welcome by prior arrangement with Sec; larger groups can negotiate rates; snooker; catering packages; driving range; terms on application.
Catering: full restaurant and bar service.
Hotels: Queens Ground, Hillsborough; Grosvenor, Sheffield; Tankersley Manor.

8A 76 Hornsea
Rolston Rd, Hornsea, E Yorks, HU11 5DX
☎(01964) 535488, Fax 532020, Pro 534989, Sec 532020
Follow signs to Hornsea Free Port club, 300 yards past port.
Parkland course.
Pro Brian Thompson; Founded 1898
Designed by Harry Vardon/Dr McKenzie/J Braid
18 holes, 6475 yards, S.S.S. 71
Visitors: welcome WD and after 3pm at WE.
Green Fees: WD £19; WE £19.
Societies: welcome by prior arrangement; packages available; from £26.
Catering: full clubhouse facilities.
Hotels: Burton Lodge, Brandesburton; Merlstead, Hornsea.

8A 77 Horsforth
Layton Rise, Horsforth, Leeds, W Yorkshire, LS18 5EX
☎(0113) 2581017, Fax 2586819, Pro 2585200, Sec 2586819, Bar/Rest 2581703
Off A65 towards Ilkley 6 miles from city centre.
Upland/parkland course.
Pro Neil Bell; Founded 1907
18 holes, 6205 yards, S.S.S. 70
Visitors: welcome WD; WE by prior arrangement.
Green Fees: WD £20; WE £30.
Societies: welcome WD by prior arrangement; full packages of golf and catering available; £35.
Catering: full clubhouse facilities.

8A 78 Howley Hall
Scotchman Lane, Morley, Leeds, W Yorks, LS27 0NX
☎(01924) 472432, Fax 478417, Pro 473852, Sec 478417
On B6123 0.75 miles from junction with A650 at Halfway House pub.
Parkland course.
Pro Stephen Spinks; Founded 1900
18 holes, 6346 yards, S.S.S. 71
Visitors: welcome.
Green Fees: WD £21; WE £30.
Societies: welcome by prior arrangement; catering packages available on application; from £25.
Catering: full clubhouse facilities.

8A 79 Huddersfield (Fixby)
Fixby Hall, Lightridge Rd, Huddersfield, W Yorks, HD2 2EP
☎(01484) 420110, Fax 424623, Pro 426463, Sec 426203

From M62 junction 24 follow signs to Brighouse; turn right at traffic lights.
Parkland course.
Pro Paul Carman; Founded 1891
Designed by Herbert Fowler, Amendments by Hawtree
18 holes, 6467 yards, S.S.S. 71
Visitors: welcome; h'cap certs required.
Green Fees: WD £33; WE £40.
Societies: welcome WD except Tues; catering can be organised; from £45.
Catering: full clubhouse bar and restaurant facilities.
Hotels: Pennine Hilton.

8A 80 Hull
The Hall, 27 Packman Lane, Kirkella, Hull, E Yorks, HU10 7TJ
☎(01482) 653026, Fax 658919, Pro 653074, Sec 658919
5 miles W of Hull.
Parkland course.
Pro David Jagger; Founded 1904/21
Designed by James Braid
18 holes, 6246 yards, S.S.S. 70
Visitors: welcome by prior arrangement; with member at WE.
Green Fees: WD £22; WE £22.
Societies: welcome Tues and Thurs by prior arrangement; terms on application.
Catering: full clubhouse facilities.
Hotels: Willerby Manor; Grange Park.

8A 81 Ilkley
Nesfield Rd, Myddleton, Ilkley, W Yorks, LS29 8BL
☎(01943) 607277, Fax 816130, Sec 600214
15 miles N of Bradford.
Parkland course.
Pro John Hammond; Founded 1890
18 holes, 6262 yards, S.S.S. 70
Visitors: welcome by arrangement; h'cap certs required.
Green Fees: WD £35; WE £40.
Societies: welcome WD by arrangement; catering packages can be arranged; £35.
Catering: full clubhouse facilities.

8A 82 Keighley
Howden Park, Utley, Keighley, W Yorks, BD20 6DH
☎(01535) 603179, Pro 665370, Sec 604778
1 mile W of Keighley on the old Keighley-Skipton road.
Parkland course.
Pro Mike Bradley; Founded 1904
18 holes, 6141 yards, S.S.S. 70

River setting at Ilkley

St Andrews, Carnoustie and Prestwick have their famous burns, a fame enhanced by their influence in shaping golfing history. Water hazards take many other forms. In fact, lakes are now the rule rather than the exception on most new courses throughout the world. Sadly, some developers and golf course architects view lake building as essential but a few Clubs such as Ilkley have the grandest and most natural of all water features – a river frequently in full spate.

What makes it even more dramatic is that the Wharfe casts its spell at Ilkley on the opening holes when actions have not yet matched intentions and errors are often beyond redemption. River, Bridge and Island, the names of the first three holes, express the mood although they do not convey the complete picture, a quiet valley set back from a bustling town beneath the vastness and bleakness of the moor.

It is an inspiring setting that occupies the thoughts as the walk back to the first tee is made but it masks the impact of the immediate tasks. The first is 410 yards between trees and the river and the second and third are short holes which test nerve and skill. The tee shot on the second plays over the tributary of the river that creates the island while the third, 206 yards, has the river on both flanks.

The admirable fourth, the first of two par fives in three holes, calls for a short carry on the drive over the tributary of the river as it returns to the main stream which then lingers as far as the seventh, not quite as much of a threat as hitherto although its presence nags. The fifth, 200 yards, and romantically named Kingfisher, maintains the demands of the short holes but direction changes with the seventh, an attractive looking hole with a pleasant raised setting for the green.

As the river pursues its meanderings, its duty done, the eighth turns back, announcing a different tenor to the holes if no lessening of their appeal or challenge. Trees gradually substitute for the river as the principal danger to wayward shots on a succession of par fours. The fours are interrupted by the 13th, a short hole of character, but, after that, a finish begins that strikes another change of scene.

The 14th, 433 yards, is rated the hardest hole of the inward half in spite of a lack of fairway bunkers to plague the drive and the 15th is a quaint short hole with an alarming slope from the back of the green. A putt down the hill on a well shaved surface would have a stimpmeter dancing with joy. Drives from elevated tees are always to be remembered and that from the 16th offers an exciting shot as well as some handsome views.

There is a rural hint to the holes either side of the turn but the 16th and 17th lie in the shadow of a wood, dropping down again to river level. The last three are ideal holes when you need three fours to win the medal or a match, the 18th, back across the road, doglegging gently to the left to a green below a charming clubhouse.

Much of what you see today is the result of the architectural genius of Harry Colt and Alister Mackenzie, the latter based just down the road at Alwoodley. It also served as a base during the formative years of Colin Montgomerie, very much an adopted Yorkshireman, who sharpened his competitive skills on a course that helped make him the best player in Europe.

Ilkley is a shining example of a delightful place to play with a course, testing and enjoyable, that is rightly popular with visitors and well respected in a county of high expectations.

Visitors: welcome except before 9am and between 12.30pm-1.30pm WD; Ladies day Tues; not Sat; by prior arrangement Sun.
Green Fees: WD £22; WE £27.
Societies: welcome by prior arrangement with the manager; day rates available; catering by arrangement; terms on application.
Catering: full bar and catering facilities available 12 noon-2pm & 4.30pm-10.30pm every day except Mon; à la carte menu.
Hotels: Dales Gate.

8A 83 Kirkbymoorside

Manor Vale, Kirkbymoorside, York, YO6 6EG
☎(01751) 431525
On A170 N of Kirkbymoorside Oakland; club moved to present site in 1953.
Founded 1905/53
Designed by T K Cotton
18 holes, 6101 yards, S.S.S. 69
Visitors: welcome after 9.30am and not between 12.30pm-1.30pm.
Green Fees: WD £18; WE £25.
Societies: welcome by prior arrangement; packages available for golf and catering; £26.50.
Catering: full clubhouse facilities available.
Hotels: George & Dragon; Kings Head, both Kirkbymoorside.

8A 84 Knaresborough

Butterhills, Boroughbridge Rd, Knaresborough, N Yorks, HG5 0QQ
☎(01423) 863219, Fax 869345, Pro 864865, Sec 862690, Bar/Rest 860173
On A6055 Boroughbridge Road 2 miles outside Knaresborough.
Parkland course with extensive trees; 17th is 627 yards.
Pro Gary J Vickers; Founded 1920
Designed by Hawtree & Son
18 holes, 6507 yards, S.S.S. 71
Visitors: welcome after 9.30am WD and 10am WE.
Green Fees: WD £22.50; WE £27.50.
Societies: welcome by prior arrangement between April 1 and Oct 31; parties of 12 or more welcome; Mon special rates; full day golf and catering rates available; from £17.
Catering: full restaurant and bar facilities.
Large practice area.
Hotels: Nidd Hall, Harrogate; Dower House, Knaresborough; Crown Hotel, Boroughbridge.

8A 85 Leeds (Cobble Hall)

Elmete Lane, Leeds, W Yorks, LS8 2LJ
☎(0113) 2658775, Fax 2323369, Pro 2658786, Sec 2659203, Bar/Rest 2733933
On A58 Leeds-Wetherby road.
Parkland course with impressive views of Roundhay Park.
Pro Simon Longster; Founded 1896
18 holes, 6078 yards, S.S.S. 69
Visitors: welcome by prior arrangement.
Green Fees: WD £25; WE £25.
Societies: welcome by prior arrangement; packages available; terms on application.
Catering: full restaurant and bar facilities.
Hotels: Weetwood Hall.

8A 86 Leeds Golf Centre

Wike Ridge Lane, Shadwell, Leeds, W Yorks, LS17 9JW
☎(0113) 2886000, Fax 2886185, Bar/Rest 2886160
Just off A61 Harrogate Road, 5 miles N of Leeds.
Open heathland course.
Pro N Harvey, L Scargill, G Day; Founded 1993
Designed by Donald Steel
18 holes, 6482 yards, S.S.S. 72
Visitors: welcome.
Green Fees: WD £12.50; WE £15.
Societies: welcome; restricted numbers at WE; golf and catering packages available; also 12-hole Oaks course; £19.
Catering: full facilities.
Practice range, 20 bays covered floodlit.
Hotels: Harewood Arms; Weetwood Hall, both Leeds.

8A 87 Lees Hall

Hemsworth Rd, Norton, Sheffield, S8 8LL
☎(0114) 2554402, Pro 2507868, Sec 2552900, Bar/Rest 2551526
3 miles S of Sheffield.
Parkland course.
Founded 1907
18 holes, 6171 yards, S.S.S. 69
Visitors: welcome.
Green Fees: terms on application.
Societies: welcome WD by prior arrangement; catering packages by arrangement; snooker; terms on application.
Catering: full facilities except Tues.
Hotels: Grosvenor; Hallam Towers; Sheffield Moat House.

8A 88 Lightcliffe

Knowle Top Rd, Lightcliffe, Halifax, W Yorks, HX3 8RG
☎(01422) 202459
Just off A58 Leeds-Halifax road.
Parkland course.
Pro Robert Kershaw; Founded 1907
9 holes, 5826 yards, S.S.S. 68
Visitors: welcome except on Wed and comp days.
Green Fees: WD £15; WE £15.
Societies: welcome by prior arrangement; terms on application.
Catering: full clubhouse facilities.
Hotels: Trust House, Brighouse.

8A 89 Lofthouse Hill

Leeds Road, Lofthouse, Wakefield, WF3 3LR
☎(01924) 823703, Fax 823703, Pro 820048
Off A61 4 miles from Wakefield.
9-hole extension planned for 1998.
Pro Brian James; Founded 1994
Designed by B J Design
9 holes, 6200 yards, S.S.S. 71
Visitors: welcome WD.
Green Fees: WD £10.
Societies: welcome when extension to course is completed.
Catering: bar and catering facilities.
Practice range, 8 bays floodlit.

8A 90 Longley Park

Maple St, off Somerset Rd, Huddersfield, W Yorks, HD5 9AX
☎(01484) 426932, Pro 422304
0.5 miles from Town centre.
Parkland course.
Pro John Ambler; Founded 1911
9 holes, 5269 yards, S.S.S. 66
Visitors: welcome WD; restricted WE.
Green Fees: WD £13; WE £16.
Societies: welcome by arrangement except Thurs and Sat; catering by arrangement; terms on application.
Catering: full facilities except Mon.
Hotels: George, Huddersfield.

8A 91 Low Laithes

Parkmill Lane, Flushdyke, Ossett, W Yorks, WF5 9AP
☎(01924) 273275, Fax 266067, Pro 274667, Sec 266067, Bar/Rest 267517
Close to M1 junction 40 off A638 towards Dewsbury; turn right at end of slip road.
Parkland course.
Pro Paul Browning; Founded 1925
Designed by MacKenzie
18 holes, 6463 yards, S.S.S. 71

Visitors: welcome WD after 9.30am and not between 12.30pm-1.30pm; WE between 10am-12 noon and after 2pm.
Green Fees: WD £19; WE £32.
Societies: welcome WD by prior arrangement; package includes 27 holes and full catering; £32.
Catering: full clubhouse facilities.
Hotels: Post House; Mews House, both Ossett.

8A 92 Malton & Norton

Welham Park, Malton, N Yorks, YO17 9QE
☎(01653) 692959, Fax 697912, Pro 693882, Sec 697912
From York take the A64 to the centre of Malton, right at traffic lights and right at rail crossing; club is 0.75 miles.
Parkland course.
Pro S I Robinson; Founded 1910
Designed by Hawtree & Son
27 holes (3 loops of 9); Welham: 6456 yards, S.S.S. 71; Park: 6242 yards, S.S.S. 70; Derwent: 6286 yards, S.S.S. 70
Visitors: welcome.
Green Fees: WD £22; WE £28.
Societies: welcome by prior arrangement; full catering packages available; from £22.
Catering: full clubhouse facilities.
Hotels: many in local area.

8A 93 Marsden

Mount Rd, Hemplow, Marsden, W Yorks, HD7 6NN
☎(01484) 844253
Off A62 8 miles from Huddersfield.
Moorland course.
Pro Nick Kryswicki; Founded 1920
Designed by Dr A. MacKenzie
9 holes, 5702 yards, S.S.S. 68
Visitors: welcome WD.
Green Fees: WD £10.
Societies: welcome WD by arrangement; packages available; terms on application.
Catering: clubhouse facilities except Tues.
Hotels: Durker Roods, Meltham.

8A 94 Masham

Burnholme, Swinton Rd, Masham, Ripon, N Yorkshire, HG4 4HT
☎(01765) 689379
Off A6108 10 miles N of Ripon.
Meadowland course.
Founded 1895
9 holes, 6068 yards, S.S.S. 69

Visitors: welcome WD; only with a member at WE.
Green Fees: WD £15.
Societies: welcome by arrangement with Sec; catering packages available; from £15.
Catering: full clubhouse facilities.
Hotels: Kings Head; Bay Horse; White Bear; Bruce Arms all in Marsham.

8A 95 Meltham

Thick Hollins Hall, Meltham, Huddersfield, W Yorks, HD7 3DQ
☎(01484) 850227, Pro 851521
On B6107 6 miles SW of Huddersfield.
Parkland course.
Pro P F Davies; Founded 1908
18 holes, 6305 yards, S.S.S. 70
Visitors: welcome except Wed and Sat.
Green Fees: WD £20; WE £25.
Societies: welcome by prior arrangement; full catering packages available; terms on application.
Catering: full clubhouse facilities.
Hotels: Durker Roods Hall.

8A 96 Mid Yorkshire

Havercroft Lane, Darrington, Nr Pontefract, Yorks, WF8 3BP
☎(01977) 704522, Fax 600823, Pro 600844
400 yards on A1 S from the M62/A1 intersection.
Parkland course.
Pro Alistair Corbett; Founded 1993
Designed by Steve Marnoch
18 holes, 6466 yards, S.S.S. 71
Visitors: welcome WD; restrictions on WE mornings.
Green Fees: WD £18; WE £30.
Societies: welcome WD; WE between 1pm-4.30pm by prior arrangement; conference facilities; catering packages by arrangement; golf clinic; terms on application.
Catering: bar and restaurant facilities.
Practice range, 22 bays floodlit.
Hotels: Darrington.

8A 97 Middleton Park

Ring Rd, Beeston, Leeds, W Yorks, LS10 3TN
☎(0113) 2700449, Pro 2709506
3 miles S of city centre
Public parkland course.
Pro Steve Shaw; Founded 1932
Designed by Leeds City Council
18 holes, 4947 yards, S.S.S. 69
Visitors: welcome WD; book at WE.
Green Fees: WD £7; WE £8.50.
Societies: welcome by arrangement.

8A 98 Moor Allerton

Coal Rd, Wike, Leeds, W Yorks, LS17 9NH
☎(0113) 2661154, Fax 2371124, Pro 2665209, Bar/Rest 2682225
5 miles from Leeds off A61 Harrogate road.
Parkland course.
Pro Richard Lane; Founded 1923
Designed by Robert Trent Jones, Sr.
27 holes (3 x 9 loops forming three different courses): High: 6841 yards, S.S.S. 74; Lakes: 6470 yards, S.S.S. 72; Blackmoor: 6673 yards, S.S.S. 73
Visitors: welcome by prior arrangement.
Green Fees: WD £41; WE £66.
Societies: welcome by prior arrangement; tee times reserved for groups of 12 or more; reductions Nov-March; from £45.
Catering: full clubhouse facilities.
Practice range.
Hotels: Club can provide list of recommended hotels.

8A 99 Moortown

Harrogate Rd, Leeds, W Yorks, LS17 7DB
☎(0113) 2681682, Fax 2680986, Pro 2683636, Sec 2686521, Bar/Rest 2688746
On A61 Harrogate road 1 miles past outer ring road.
Parkland course.
Pro Bryon Hutchinson; Founded 1909
Designed by Dr A. MacKenzie
18 holes, 7020 yards, S.S.S. 73
Visitors: welcome by prior arrangement.
Green Fees: WD £42; WE £45.
Societies: welcome by prior arrangement; day rates also available (50); from £42.
Catering: full clubhouse restaurant and bar facilities.
Hotels: Harewood Arms and others in Leeds area.

8A 100 Normanton

Snydale Rd, Normanton, Wakefield, WF6 1PA
☎(01924) 892943
Off M62 junction 31; 0.5 miles from Normanton centre.
Flat meadowland course.
Founded 1903
9 holes, 5401 yards, S.S.S. 66
Visitors: welcome except Sun.
Green Fees: terms on application.
Societies: welcome WD by prior arrangement.
Catering: full facilities.

8A 101 Northcliffe
High Bank Lane, Shipley, W Yorks,
BD18 4RZ
☎(01274) 584085, Fax 596731, Pro
587193, Sec 596731
On A650 W of Bradford to Saltaire
roundabout.
Undulating parkland course.
Pro M Hillas; Founded 1920
Designed by James Braid/ Harry
Vardon
18 holes, 6104 yards, S.S.S. 69
Visitors: welcome by prior arrangement.
Green Fees: WD £20; WE £25r.
Societies: welcome by prior arrangement; full day's catering and golf package; £35.
Catering: full clubhouse facilities.
Hotels: Bankfield Hotel, Bingley.

8A 102 Oakdale
Oakdale, Harrogate, Yorkshire, HG1
2LN
☎(01423) 567162, Fax 536030, Pro
560510
Turn into Kent Rd from Ripon rd in
Harrogate.
Undulating parkland course with
panoramic views.
Pro Clive Dell; Founded 1914
Designed by Dr A. MacKenzie
18 holes, 6456 yards, S.S.S. 71
Visitors: welcome.
Green Fees: WD £25; WE £30.
Societies: welcome WD by prior
arrangement; catering packages by
arrangement; terms on application.
Catering: full facilities except Mon
lunchtime.
Hotels: Crown; Fern; Majestic;
Studley; Old Swan; Balmoral.

8A 103 The Oaks
Aughton Common, Aughton, York,
Yorks, YO4 4PW
☎(01757) 288577, Fax 289029, Pro
288007, Bar/Rest 288001
On the B1288 1 mile N of Bubwith.
Wooded parkland course with 4 lakes.
Pro Darren Leng; Founded 1996
Designed by J Covey
18 holes, 6743 yards
Visitors: welcome WD.
Green Fees: WD £20.
Societies: welcome by arrangement; packages of golf and catering
available; from £28.
Catering: full bar and catering service;
à la carte restaurant.
Practice area.
Hotels: Loftsome Bridge; Ye Olde Red
Lion.

8A 104 Otley
West Busk Lane, Otley, W Yorks,
LS21 3NG
☎(01943) 461015, Fax 850387, Pro
463403, Sec 465329, Bar/Rest
465453
Off A6038 on the outskirts of the market town of Otley between Leeds and
Bradford.
Parkland course.
Founded 1906
18 holes, 6225 yards, S.S.S. 70
Visitors: welcome except Tues and
Sat.
Green Fees: WD £24; WE £30.
Societies: welcome WD by prior
arrangement with Sec; packages by
arrangement with Sec; terms on application.
Catering: full clubhouse bar and
catering facilities.
Practice ground.
Hotels: Chevin Lodge, Otley; Jarvis
Parkway, Leeds; The Grove, Ilkley.

8A 105 Oulton Park
Pennington Lane, Rothwell, Leeds,
LS26 8EX
☎(0113) 2823152, Fax 2826290
Off M62 junction 30, take A642 to
Rothwell, left at 2nd roundabout.
Parkland course.
Pro Steve Gromett; Founded 1990
Designed by Peter Alliss & Dave
Thomas
18 holes, 6470 yards, S.S.S. 71
Visitors: welcome by prior arrangement.
Green Fees: WD £10; WE £12.
Societies: welcome WD by arrangement; full golf and catering packages
available; also 9-hole course; terms on
application.
Catering: full clubhouse restaurant
and bar facilities.
Practice range, 20 bays.
Hotels: 5-star Oulton Hall on site.

8A 106 Outlane
Slack Lane, Outlane, Huddersfield, W
Yorks, HD3 3YL
☎(01422) 374762, Sec 311789
From M62 take A640 to Rochdale, left
under the motorway through Outlane
village.
Moorland/parkland course.
Pro D M Chapman; Founded 1906
18 holes, 6015 yards, S.S.S. 70
Visitors: welcome by prior arrangement.
Green Fees: WD £18; WE £28.
Societies: welcome by prior arrangement; package details available from

Mrs Caroline Hirst; terms on application.
Catering: full clubhouse facilities.
Hotels: Old Golf House, Outlane.

8A 107 Painthorpe House Golf & Country Club
Painthorpe Lane, Crigglestone,
Wakefield, WF4 5AZ
☎(01924) 255083, Fax 252022
Close to M1 junction 39.
Undulating parkland course.
Founded 1961
9 holes, 4548 yards, S.S.S. 62
Visitors: welcome; restrictions on
Sun.
Green Fees: WD £5; WE £6.
Societies: welcome by arrangement;
terms on application.
Catering: extensive facilities including
four bars, 2 ball rooms and a function
room.

8A 108 Pannal
Follifoot Rd, Pannal, Harrogate,
Yorkshire, HG3 1ES
☎(01423) 871641, Fax 870043, Pro
872620, Sec 872628, Bar/Rest
872629
Off A61 Leeds-Harrogate road 3 miles
S of Harrogate
Moorland/parkland course.
Pro Murray Burgess; Founded 1906
Designed by Sandy Herd
18 holes, 6622 yards, S.S.S. 72
Visitors: welcome by prior arrangement only.
Green Fees: WD £37; WE £45.
Societies: welcome by prior arrangement; catering can be arranged; from
£37.
Catering: full clubhouse bar and
catering facilities.
Hotels: Majestic, Harrogate.

8A 109 Phoenix
Pavilion Lane, Brinsworth, Rotherham,
S Yorks, S60 5PB
☎(01709) 383864, Fax 383788, Pro
382624, Sec 383788
1 mile along Bawtry road turning from
Tinsley roundabout on M1.
Undulating meadowland course.
Pro M Roberts; Founded 1932
18 holes, 6182 yards, S.S.S. 69
Visitors: welcome.
Green Fees: WD £24; WE £32.
Societies: welcome WD by prior
arrangement; packages for golf and
catering available; from £24.
Catering: full catering facilities.
Practice range, 20 bays covered.

8A 110 Phoenix Park

Phoenix Park, Dick Lane, Thornbury, Bradford, W Yorks, BD3 7AT
☎(01274) 615546, Bar/Rest 667573
Off A647 Bradford to Leeds road at Thornbury roundabout.
Undulating parkland course.
9 holes, 4646 yards, S.S.S. 66
Visitors: welcome WD only.
Green Fees: terms on application.
Societies: welcome by prior arrangement.
Catering: catering by prior arrangement.

8A 111 Pike Hills

Tadcaster Rd, Askham Bryan, York, Yorks, YO2 3UW
☎(01904) 706566, Fax 700797, Pro 708756, Sec 700797, Bar/Rest 704416
On A64 4 miles W of York.
Parkland course; formed 1920 as Hob Moor GC, moved 1946.
Pro I Gradwell; Founded 1920/46
18 holes, 6146 yards, S.S.S. 69
Visitors: welcome WD; only with member at WE.
Green Fees: WD £18; WE £18.
Societies: welcome by prior arrangement; packages include full catering and 36 holes of golf; £35.
Catering: full clubhouse facilities.

8A 112 Pontefract & District

Park Lane, Pontefract, W Yorks, WF8 4QS
☎(01977) 798886, Pro 706806, Sec 792241
On B6134 off M62 junction 32.
Parkland course.
Pro Nicholas Newman; Founded 1900
18 holes, 6232 yards, S.S.S. 70
Visitors: welcome WD; by prior arrangement WE.
Green Fees: WD £25; WE £32.
Societies: welcome WD except Wed; packages available; terms on application.
Catering: full facilities.
Hotels: Red Lion; Wentbridge House; Park Side Inn.

8A 113 Pontefract Park

Park Road, Pontefract, W Yorkshire,
☎(01977) 702799
Close to Pontefract racecourse 0.5 miles from M62.
Public parkland course.
9 holes, 4068 yards, S.S.S. 62
Visitors: welcome.
Green Fees: WD £2.80; WE £2.80.

8A 114 Queensbury

Brighouse Rd, Queensbury, Bradford, W Yorks, BD13 1QF
☎(01274) 882155, Pro 816864
From M62 junction 26 take A58 towards Halifax for 3.5 miles then turn to Keighley for 3 miles; also on A647, 4 miles from Bradford.
Undulating parkland course.
Pro Geoff Howard; Founded 1923
9 holes, 5024 yards, S.S.S. 65
Visitors: welcome.
Green Fees: WD £15; WE £30.
Societies: welcome by prior arrangement; packages available; function facilities; terms on application.
Catering: full bar and à la carte restaurant service.
Hotels: Novotel.

8A 115 Rawdon

Buckstone Drive, Rawdon, Leeds, W Yorks, LS19 6BD
☎(0113) 2506040, Pro 2505017, Sec 2506044
On A65 6 miles from Leeds turning left at Rawdon traffic lights.
Undulating parkland course.
Pro Simon Poot; Founded 1896
9 holes, 5982 yards, S.S.S. 69
Visitors: welcome WD.
Green Fees: WD £16.
Societies: welcome WD by prior arrangement; golf and catering packages available; 3 all-weather and 4 grass tennis courts; from £29.
Catering: full facilities except Mon.
Hotels: Peas Hill; Robin Hood.

8A 116 Renishaw Park

Golf House, Mill Lane, Renishaw, Sheffield, S Yorks, S21 3UZ
☎(01246) 432044, Pro 435484
1.5 miles W of the M1 junction 30 on the A6135.
Parkland course.
Pro J Oates; Founded 1911
Designed by Sir G. Sitwell
18 holes, 6262 yards, S.S.S. 70
Visitors: welcome by arrangement.
Green Fees: WD £21; WE £21.
Societies: welcome by arrangement; packages on application; day ticket £29.50; terms on application.
Catering: full clubhouse facilities.
Hotels: Sitwell Arms.

8A 117 Richmond

Bend Hagg, Richmond, N Yorks, DL10 5EX
☎(01748) 825319, Pro 822457, Sec 823231

From A1 Scotch corner follow the Richmond road to lights in town; turn right.
Parkland course; extended to 18 holes in 1970.
Pro Paul Jackson; Founded 1892
Designed by Frank Pennink
18 holes, 5779 yards, S.S.S. 68
Visitors: welcome, except before 3pm on Sun.
Green Fees: WD £20; WE £25.
Societies: welcome by prior arrangement; reduced rates for groups of more than 16; packages available; from £18.
Catering: full bar and restaurant facilities everyday.
Hotels: Turf Hotel; Black Lion; Kings Head.

8A 118 Riddlesden

Howden Rough, Riddlesden, Keighley, W Yorks, BD20 5QN
☎(01535) 602148, Sec 607646
From A650 Bradford road turn into Scott Lane.
Moorland course.
Founded 1927
18 holes, 4295 yards, S.S.S. 61
Visitors: welcome.
Green Fees: WD £10; WE £15.
Societies: welcome on WD by prior arrangement; terms on application.
Catering: clubhouse facilities.
Hotels: Dalesgate Hotel.

8A 119 Ripon City

Palace Rd, Ripon, N Yorks, HG4 3HH
☎(01765) 601987, Pro 600411, Sec 603640, Bar/Rest 603640
On A6108 1 mile N of Ripon.
Undulating parkland course.
Pro Tim Davis; Founded 1908
New 9 holes designed by ADAS
18 holes, 6120 yards, S.S.S. 69
Visitors: welcome with h'cap certs.
Green Fees: WD £18; WE £25.
Societies: welcome by arrangement; packages available for groups of more than 20; £16-50-£23.50.
Catering: full clubhouse facilities.
Hotels: Nags Head; Kirkgate House both Thirsk.

8A 120 Robin Hood

Owston Hall, Owston, Nr Carcroft, Doncaster, S Yorks, DN6 9JF
☎(01302) 722800, Fax 728885
6 miles N of Doncaster on B1220 off the A19.
Parkland course; formerly Owston Park Golf Course.

Founded 1988/1996
Designed by W Adamson
18 holes, 6937 yards, S.S.S. 72
Visitors: welcome.
Green Fees: WD £10; WE £14.
Societies: welcome by prior arrangement; full packages available for 12 or more players; free golf cart available for more than 20; function room with facilities for 60-100; £15-£36.
Catering: full restaurant and bar facilities in 18th century clubhouse.
Hotels: accommodation will be available on site from late 1998.

8A 121 Romanby
Yafforth Road, Northallerton, N Yorks, DL7 0PE
☎(01609) 779988, Fax 779084, Sec 778855, Bar/Rest 777824
On B6271 Northallerton-Richmond road 1 mile NW of Northallerton.
Parkland course.
Pro Tim Jenkins; Founded 1993
Designed by W Adamson
18 holes, 6663 yards, S.S.S. 72
Visitors: welcome.
Green Fees: WD £14; WE £18.
Societies: welcome including WE; Premier Tee and Silver Tee packages available; from £23.50.
Catering: full clubhouse bar and restaurant facilities.
Hotels: Golden Lion.

8A 122 Rother Valley
Mansfield Rd, Wales Bar, Sheffield, Yorks, S31 8PE
☎(0114) 2473000, Fax 2476000
Between Sheffield and Rotherham off M1 junction 31; follow signs for Rother Valley country park.
Parkland with water features.
Pro Jason Ripley; Founded 1996
Designed by M Roe/M Shattock
18 holes, 6602 yards, S.S.S. 72
Visitors: welcome.

Green Fees: WD £10 (£7.50 Mon); WE £16.
Societies: welcome at all times; packages include catering, golf and use of driving range; par 3 course; £10-£30.
Catering: restaurant and bar facilities.
Practice range, 27 bays floodlit.
Hotels: Aston Hall, Sheffield.

8A 123 Rotherham
Thrybergh Park, Doncaster Road, Thrybergh, Rotherham, S Yorks, S65 4NU
☎(01709) 850466, Fax 855288, Pro 850480, Sec 850812
On A630 Doncaster to Rotherham rd.
Parkland course.
Pro Simon Thornhill; Founded 1903
18 holes, 6324 yards, S.S.S. 70
Visitors: welcome by arrangement with Pro or Sec.
Green Fees: WD £28; WE £35.
Societies: welcome except Wed by prior arrangement with Sec; minimum 16; discounts for groups of 40 or more; snooker; terms on application.
Catering: full facilities.
Practice area.
Hotels: Swallow; Moat House; Limes; Brecon.

8A 124 Roundhay
Park Lane, Leeds, Yorks, LS8 2EJ
☎(0113) 2662695, Pro 2661686
4.5 miles from city centre on A58 to Wetherby.
Parkland with mature trees.
Pro Jim Pape; Founded 1922
9 holes, 5322 yards, S.S.S. 65
Visitors: municipal pay and play.
Green Fees: WD £8.50; WE £8.50.
Societies: welcome by arrangement with Pro; packages available on application; from £8.50.
Catering: catering available in restaurant in evenings Tues-Sat; bar.
Hotels: Beechwood.

8A 125 Roundwood
Off Green Lane, Rawmarsh, Rotherham, S Yorks, S62 6LA
☎(01709) 523471
Off A633 2.5 miles N of Rotherham.
Parkland course.
Founded 1977
9 holes, 5713 yards, S.S.S. 67
Visitors: welcome except WE mornings.
Green Fees: WD £12; WE £15.
Societies: welcome WD by prior arrangement; packages available; terms on application.
Catering: bar facilities; catering Wed to Sat.

8A 126 Rudding Park
Follifoot, Harrogate, N Yorks, HG3 1DJ
☎(01423) 872100, Fax 873011, Pro 873400
Off A658 Harrogate by-pass 2 miles S of Harrogate.
Parkland course.
Pro Simon Hotham; Founded 1995
Designed by Hawtree
18 holes, 6871 yards, S.S.S. 73
Visitors: welcome with h'cap certs.
Green Fees: WD £18; WE £24.
Societies: welcome with prior arrangement; packages available; terms on application.
Catering: full clubhouse facilities.
Practice range, 18 covered bays.
Hotels: Rudding Park.

8A 127 Ryburn
The Shaw, Norland, Sowerby Bridge, W Yorks, HX6 3QP
☎(01422) 831355
3 miles S of Halifax.
Hilly moorland course.
Founded 1910
9 holes, 4907 yards, S.S.S. 65
Visitors: welcome WD; WE by arrangement.
Green Fees: WD £14; WE £20.

Societies: welcome by prior arrangement; terms on application.
Catering: catering and bar facilities.
Hotels: The Hobbit Inn.

8A 128 Sand Moor

Alwoodley Lane, Leeds, W Yorks, LS17 7DJ
☎(0113) 2685180, Fax 2685180, Pro 2683925
6 miles from centre of Leeds on A61 N.
Undulating parkland/moorland course.
Pro Peter Tupling; Founded 1926
Designed by A MacKenzie.
18 holes, 6429 yards, S.S.S. 71
Visitors: welcome WD, except 12 noon-1.30pm, Tues 9.30am-10.30am and Thurs 8.30am-12 noon.
Green Fees: WD £30.
Societies: welcome WD by prior arrangement; catering packages by arrangement; terms on application.
Catering: full facilities.
Hotels: Harewood Arms; Parkway; Forte Crest.

8A 129 Sandhill

Middlecliffe Lane, Little Houghton, Barnsley, S72 0HW
☎(01226) 753444, Fax 717420, Bar/Rest 755079
Off A635 Barnsley-Doncaster road near Darfield.
Parkland course.
Founded 1993
Designed by John Royston
18 holes, 6250 yards, S.S.S. 70
Visitors: welcome.
Green Fees: WD £8; WE £11.
Societies: welcome WD; not before 10am Sat or 12 noon Sun; packages available; terms on application.
Catering: full clubhouse facilities available.
Practice range, 18 bays floodlit.
Hotels: Ardsley Moat House.

8A 130 Scarborough North Cliff

North Cliff Ave, Burniston Rd, Scarborough, YO12 6PP
☎(01723) 360786, Fax 362134, Pro 365920
2 miles N of town centre on coast road.
Seaside/parkland course.
Pro Simon Dellor; Founded 1928
Designed by James Braid
18 holes, 6425 yards, S.S.S. 71
Visitors: welcome except before 10am Sun.
Green Fees: WD £18; WE £22.

Societies: welcome by prior arrangement with Sec; packages for groups between 8 and 40; catering packages by arrangement; terms on application.
Catering: full facilities.
Practice area.
Hotels: Park Manor; Headlands.

8A 131 Scarborough South Cliff

Deepdale Ave, Scarborough, YO11 2UE
☎(01723) 360522, Fax 376969, Pro 365150, Sec 374737
1 mile S of Scarborough on the main Filey road.
Parkland/seaside course.
Pro Tony Skingle; Founded 1903
Designed by Dr A. MacKenzie
18 holes, 6039 yards, S.S.S. 69
Visitors: welcome.
Green Fees: WD £20; WE £25.
Societies: welcome WD and WE by prior arrangement; packages available; terms on application.
Catering: full facilities.
Practice ground.
Hotels: Crown; St Nicholas; Southlands; Mount House.

8A 132 Scarcroft

Syke Lane, Scarcroft, Leeds, W Yorks, LS14 3BQ
☎(0113) 2892263, Pro 2892780, Sec 2892311, Bar/Rest 2892883
Off A58 Leeds to Wetherby road turning left at Bracken Fox public house.
Parkland course.
Pro Darren Tear; Founded 1937
Designed by Robert Blackburn
18 holes, 6426 yards, S.S.S. 71
Visitors: welcome; some WE restrictions.
Green Fees: WD £26; WE £40.
Societies: welcome by prior arrangement; packages available for all-day golf and catering for groups of 20 or more; £40.
Catering: full clubhouse facilities.
Hotels: Jarvis, Wetherby; Harewood Arms, Harewood.

8A 133 Scathingwell

Scathingwell Centre, Scathingwell, Tadcaster, Yorks, LS24 9PF
☎(01937) 557878, Fax 557909, Pro 557864
On the A162 3 miles from the A1 between Tadcaster and Ferrybridge.
Parkland course.
Pro Steve Footman; Founded 1993
Designed by I Webster

18 holes, 6771 yards, S.S.S. 72
Visitors: welcome.
Green Fees: WD £16; WE £18.
Societies: welcome by prior arrangement; individual packages can be arranged; summer and winter packages available; terms on application.
Catering: full clubhouse facilities.
Hotels: Hilton, Garforth; Selby Fork Hotel.

8A 134 Selby

Mill Lane, Brayton, Selby, N Yorks, YO8 9LD
☎(01757) 228622, Pro 228785
3 miles SW of Selby; 1 mile E of A19 at Brayton village
Links style course.
Pro Andrew Smith; Founded 1907
Designed by J.H. Taylor & Hawtree Ltd
18 holes, 6249 yards, S.S.S. 70
Visitors: welcome WD with h'cap certs; WE with member.
Green Fees: WD £22.
Societies: welcome Wed, Thurs and Fri by prior arrangement; catering packages by arrangement; snooker; terms on application.
Catering: full facilities.
Practice ground.
Hotels: Londesbro; Selby Fork Motel; The Owl.

8A 135 Serlby Park

Serlby, Doncaster, S Yorks, DN10 6BA
☎(01777) 818268, Sec 01302 536336
3 miles S of Bawtry.
Parkland course.
Founded 1895
Designed by Viscount Galway
9 holes, 5376 yards, S.S.S. 66
Visitors: welcome only with member.
Green Fees: WD £10; WE £15.
Societies: welcome only by prior arrangement with Sec; terms on application.
Catering: clubhouse facilities.
Hotels: Crown, Bawtry; Mount Pleasant; Olde Bell, both Barnaby Moor.

8A 136 Settle

Buckhaw Brow, Settle, Yorks, BD24 0DH
☎(01729) 825288, Fax 823596, Sec 823596
On Kendal Road 1 mile beyond town.
Parkland course.
Founded 1895
Designed by Tom Vardon
9 holes, 5414 yards, S.S.S. 66

Visitors: welcome except Sun.
Green Fees: WD £10; WE £10.
Societies: welcome by prior arrangement; terms on application.
Catering: clubhouse facilities available.
Hotels: Falcon Hotel, Settle; Royal Oak, Settle.

8A 137 The Shay Grange Golf Centre

Long Lane, Off Bingley Road, Bradford, W Yorks, BD9 6RX
☎(01274) 491945, Pro 491547
Off A650 Bradford road at Cottingley.
Parkland course.
Pro John Clapham; Founded 1996
Designed by Tim Colclough
9 holes, 3380 yards, S.S.S. 58
Visitors: pay and play.
Green Fees: WD £10; WE £10.
Societies: welcome by prior arrangement; discounts available including golf and meals at nearby restaurant; from £10.
Catering: limited.
Practice range, 32 bays.
Hotels: Jarvis Bankfield.

8A 138 Shipley

Beckfoot Lane, Cottingley Bridge, Bingley, W Yorks, BD16 1LX
☎(01274) 563212, Fax 568652, Pro 563674, Sec 568652
On A650 6 miles N of Bradford.
Parkland course.
Pro J R Parry; Founded 1896/22
Designed by Colt, Alison and MacKenzie assisted by James Braid
18 holes, 6215 yards, S.S.S. 70
Visitors: welcome except Tues before 3pm and Sat.
Green Fees: WD £27; WE £32.
Societies: welcome Wed, Thurs, Fri; packages available; terms on application.
Catering: full clubhouse facilities available.

8A 139 Silkstone

Field Head, Silkstone, Barnsley, S Yorks, S75 4LD
☎(01226) 790328, Pro 790128
On A628 1 mile from M1.
Undulating meadowland.
Pro Kevin Guy; Founded 1893
18 holes, 6069 yards, S.S.S. 70
Visitors: welcome WD.
Green Fees: WD £27.
Societies: welcome WD by prior arrangement; packages available; terms on application.

Catering: full facilities except Mon.
Practice area.
Hotels: Ardsley Moat House; Brooklands Motel.

8A 140 Silsden

High Brunthwaite, Silsden, Keighley, W Yorks, BD20 0NH
☎(01535) 652998
4 miles from Keighley on A6034 to Silsden, turn E at canal
Moorland/meadowland course.
Founded 1913
14 holes 4870 yards, S.S.S. 64
Visitors: welcome; WE restrictions.
Green Fees: terms on application.
Societies: terms on application.
Catering: clubhouse facilities.
Hotels: Steeton Hall.

8A 141 Sitwell Park

Shrogswood Rd, Rotherham, Yorkshire, S60 4BY
☎(01709) 700799, Fax 703637, Pro 540961, Sec 541046
From M1 junction 33; take 2nd exit at roundabout until signposted; also from M18 junction 1.
Parkland course.
Pro Nick Taylor; Founded 1913
Designed by Dr A. MacKenzie
18 holes, 6209 yards, S.S.S. 70
Visitors: welcome.
Green Fees: WD £24; WE £28.
Societies: welcome by prior arrangement with secretary; discounts for parties of 30+; terms on application.
Catering: clubhouse facilities.
Hotels: Campanile; Beefeater The Brecks.

8A 142 Skipton

North-West By-Pass, Skipton, N Yorks, BD23 1LL
☎(01756) 795657, Fax 796665, Pro 793922
On A65 1 mile N of Skipton.
Undulating parkland course with panoramic views and water.
Pro Peter Robinson; Founded 1896
18 holes, 6049 yards, S.S.S. 69
Visitors: welcome; some restrictions Tues and WE.
Green Fees: WD £23; WE £25.
Societies: welcome WD by prior arrangement with Sec; packages available; snooker and reading rooms; £22.
Catering: dining, banqueting and bar.
Practice range, 0.5 miles away.
Hotels: Hanover, Skipton; Devonshire Arms, Bolton Abbey; Stirk House, Gisburn.

8A 143 South Bradford

Pearson Rd, Odsal, Bradford, BD6 1BJ
☎(01274) 679195, Pro 673346
From Odsal roundabout take Stadium Road and then Pearson Road.
Undulating meadowland course.
Founded 1906
9 holes, 6068 yards, S.S.S. 69
Visitors: welcome WD.
Green Fees: WD £14.
Societies: welcome Tues-Fri by prior arrangement; terms on application.
Catering: full facilities except Mon.
Hotels: Guide Post.

8A 144 South Leeds

Gypsy Lane, off Middleton Ring Rd, Leeds, W Yorks, LS11 5TU
☎(0113) 2700479, Pro 2702598, Sec 2771676
Close to M1 junction 45 and M62 junction 28.
Undulating parkland course.
Pro Mike Lewis; Founded 1914
Designed by Dr A MacKenzie
18 holes, 5769 yards, S.S.S. 68
Visitors: welcome WD; WE only with member.
Green Fees: WD £18; WE £9.
Societies: welcome by prior arrangement; packages can be arranged depending on numbers; terms on application.
Catering: clubhouse facilities.
Practice ground.
Hotels: Oulton Hall; Leeds International Hilton.

8A 145 Spaldington

Spaldington Lane, Howden, E Yorks, DN12 7NP
☎(01757) 288262
Take B1288 out of Howden towards Bubwith and then head for Spaldington.
Parkland course.
Founded 1995
Designed by PMS Golf
9 holes, 3482 yards
Visitors: welcome.
Green Fees: WD £3.50; WE £3.50.
Societies: welcome.
Practice range, 18 bays floodlit.

8A 146 Springhead Park

Willerby Rd, Hull, Yorks, HU5 5JE
☎(01482) 656309, Sec 501126
From A63 follow signs from Humber Bridge to Beverley to major roundabout and then signs to Willerby.
Parkland course.

Pro B Herrington; Founded 1930
18 holes, 6402 yards, S.S.S. 71
Visitors: municipal course; clubhouse access with a member only.
Green Fees: WD £7; WE £8.
Societies: welcome by prior arrangement with Sec; terms on application.
Catering: clubhouse facilities.

8A 147 Springmill
Queens Drive, Osset, W Yorks,
☎(01924) 272515
1 mile from Osset towards Wakefield
Public parkland course.
9 holes, 2330 yards
Visitors: welcome.
Green Fees: terms on application.

8A 148 Stocksbridge & District
30 Royd Lane, Townend, Deepcar, Sheffield, Yorks, S36 2RZ
☎(0114) 2882003, Pro 2882779, Sec 2882408
Close to M1 junction 36.
Moorland course.
Pro Tim Brookes; Founded 1924
Designed by Peter Alliss, Dave Thomas (extension)
18 holes, 5097 yards, S.S.S. 65
Visitors: welcome WD.
Green Fees: WD £26; WE £26.
Societies: welcome WD by prior arrangement; packages include 36 holes of golf and all day catering; £25.
Catering: full clubhouse facilities available.
Hotels: Tankersley Manor; The Wentworth; Ardsley House; Hallam Towers; Grosvenor.

8A 149 Sutton Park
Salthouse Rd, Hull, Yorks, HU8 9HF
☎(01482) 374242, Fax 701428
A165 E to Salthouse Road.
Parkland course.
Pro Paul Rushworth; Founded 1935
18 holes, 6251 yards, S.S.S. 70
Visitors: welcome by prior arrangement.
Green Fees: WD £6.50; WE £8.50.
Societies: welcome by prior arrangement; terms on application.
Catering: bar facilities.

8A 150 Swallow Hall
Swallow Hall, Crockey Hill, York, YO1 4SG
☎(01904) 448889
Off A19 S of York; after 1.5 miles turn left to Wheldrake.

Public parkland course.
Founded 1991
9 holes, 3092 yards
Visitors: welcome.
Green Fees: WD £7; WE £8.
Societies: welcome by arrangement.
Catering: limited.
Practice range.

8A 151 Swingtime (Leeds)
Redcote Lane, Leeds, W Yorks, LS4 2AW
☎(0113) 2633030, Fax 2633044
1.5 miles W of Leeds town centre off Kirkstall Road
Course re-opening in 1998.
Pro Paul Greensmith; Founded 1996
9 holes, yards
Visitors: welcome.
Green Fees: packages available; terms on application.
Catering: full facilities.
Practice range, 30 bays floodlit.

8A 152 Tankersley Park
High Green, Sheffield, S Yorks, S35 4LG
☎(0114) 2468247, Fax 2455586, Pro 2455586
From M1 junction 35A entrance 400 yards.
Parkland course.
Pro Ian Kirk; Founded 1907
Designed by Hawtree
18 holes, 6212 yards, S.S.S. 70
Visitors: welcome WD.
Green Fees: WD £22; WE £22.
Societies: welcome by prior arrangement on WD; catering packages available except Mon; from £22.
Catering: full catering facilities except Mon; bar.
Hotels: Tankersley Manor; Norfolk Arms.

8A 153 Temple Newsam
Temple Newsam Rd, Leeds, W Yorks, LS15 0LN
☎(0113) 2645624, Pro 2647362
On A64 York road 5 miles from Leeds.
Undulating parkland course.
Pro Allan Swaine; Founded 1923
Lady Dorothy: 18 holes, 6094 yards, S.S.S. 69; Lord Erwin: 18 holes, 6153 yards, S.S.S. 69
Visitors: welcome.
Green Fees: terms on application.
Societies: welcome by arrangement; packages available; terms on application.
Catering: full facilities; carvery WE.
Hotels: Windmill; Mercury.

8A 154 Thirsk & Northallerton
Thornton-le-Street, Thirsk, N Yorks, YO7 4AB
☎(01845) 522170, Pro 526216, Sec 525115
Near A19 and A168 2 miles N of Thirsk.
Parkland course.
Pro Robert Garner; Founded 1914/1997
Designed by W Adamson
18 holes, 6495 yards, S.S.S. 70
Visitors: welcome WD; only with member at WE.
Green Fees: WD £20; WE £20.
Societies: welcome WD by prior arrangement; catering packages available; from £20.
Catering: full clubhouse facilities.
Hotels: Golden Fleece; Three Tuns.

8A 155 Thorne
Kirton Lane, Thorne, Doncaster, S Yorks, DN8 5RJ
☎(01405) 815173, Fax 741899, Pro 812084, Sec 812084
From M18 junction 6 to Thorne; signposted.
Parkland course.
Pro Richard Highfield; Founded 1980
Designed by Richard Highfield
18 holes, 5366 yards, S.S.S. 65
Visitors: welcome.
Green Fees: WD £8.75; WE £9.75.
Societies: welcome by prior arrangement; £50 deposit required which is refunded on day; terms on application.
Catering: clubhouse facilities.
Small practice area.
Hotels: Belmont.

8A 156 Tinsley Park
High Hazel Park, Darnall, Sheffield, S Yorks, S9 4PE
☎(0114) 2037435
Take A57 from M1 junction 33.
Parkland course.
Pro R Highfield; Founded 1921
18 holes, 6084 yards, S.S.S. 69
Visitors: welcome.
Green Fees: WD £8.50; WE £8.90.
Societies: welcome by arrangement with the local council.
Catering: full facilities.
Hotels: Royal Victoria.

8A 157 Todmorden
Rive Rocks, Cross Stone Rd, Todmorden, OL14 7RD
☎(01706) 812986
1.5 miles along Halifax road.

Moorland course.
Founded 1895
9 holes, 5878 yards, S.S.S. 68
Visitors: welcome WD except Mon;
WE by arrangement.
Green Fees: WD £15; WE £20.
Societies: welcome WD except Mon
by prior arrangement.
Catering: clubhouse facilities except
Mon.
Hotels: Scaite Cliffe Hall;
Brandschatter Berghoff.

8A 158 **Wakefield**
Woodthorpe Lane, Sandal, Wakefield,
WF2 6JH
☎(01924) 255104, Fax 242752, Pro
255380, Sec 258778
On A61 3 miles S of Wakefield.
Parkland course.
Pro Ian Wright; Founded 1891
Designed by Alex Herd
18 holes, 6613 yards, S.S.S. 72
Visitors: welcome by prior arrange-
ment.
Green Fees: WD £22; WE £30.
Societies: welcome by application to
Sec; catering packages by arrange-
ment; snooker; terms on application.
Catering: full facilities.
Hotels: Cedar Court; Swallow.

8A 159 **Waterton Park**
The Balk, Walton, Wakefield, WF2
6QL
☎(01924) 259525, Fax 256969, Pro
255557, Bar/Rest 255855
Close to M1 junction 39 following
signs for Barnsley and A61; left to
Wakefield and then to Shay Lane.
Parkland on Waterton Hall with trees,
26-acre lake.
Pro Patrick Hall; Founded 1995
Designed by S Gidman
18 holes, 6843 yards, S.S.S. 73
Visitors: welcome as members'
guests only.
Green Fees: WD £15; WE £15.
Societies: none.
Catering: bars and dining room in the
exclusive club house.
Hotels: Waterton Park.

8A 160 **Wath**
Abdy, Blackamoor, Rotherham, S
Yorks, S62 7SJ
☎(01709) 872149, Pro 878677
Off A633 in Wath, 7 miles N of
Rotherham.
Meadowland course.
Pro Chris Bassett; Founded 1904
18 holes, 5801 yards, S.S.S. 68

Visitors: welcome WD; only with a
member WE.
Green Fees: WD £20.
Societies: welcome by prior arrange-
ment; special packages available for
golf and catering; terms on application.
Catering: full facilities.
Hotels: Moat House, Rotherham.

8A 161 **West Bowling**
Newall Hall, Rooley Lane, Bradford, W
Yorks, BD5 8LB
☎(01274) 724449, Pro 728036, Sec
393207
At junction of M606 and Bradford ring
road.
Parkland course.
Pro Ian Marshall; Founded 1898
18 holes, 5769 yards, S.S.S. 68
Visitors: welcome WD; restrictions at
WE.
Green Fees: WD £22; WE £30.
Societies: welcome Wed, Thurs, Fri
by arrangement with the manager;
catering by arrangement; snooker;
terms on application.
Catering: full facilities.
Hotels: Novotel; Norfolk Gardens;
Guide Post; Tong Village; Victoria.

8A 162 **West Bradford**
Chellow Grange, Haworth Rd,
Bradford, W Yorks, BD9 6NP
☎(01274) 542767, Pro 542102
Off B6144 3 miles W of Bradford.
Parkland course.
Pro Nigel Barber; Founded 1900
18 holes, 5723 yards, S.S.S. 68
Visitors: welcome except before
9.30am and between 12 noon-1.30pm.
Green Fees: WD £18; WE £18.
Societies: welcome by arrangement;
packages including catering and golf
with reduced green fees available;
terms on application.
Catering: full clubhouse facilities.

8A 163 **West End (Halifax)**
Paddock Lane, Highroad Well, Halifax,
W Yorks, HX2 0NT
☎(01422) 353608, Fax 341878, Pro
363293, Sec 341878, Bar/Rest
369844
2 miles W of Halifax off Burnley-
Rochdale road.
Parkland course.
Pro David Rishworth; Founded 1906
Designed by Members
18 holes, 5937 yards, S.S.S. 69
Visitors: welcome by prior arrange-
ment.
Green Fees: WD £20; WE £25.

Societies: welcome by prior arrangement with Sec; packages available;
from £20.
Catering: clubhouse facilities.
Hotels: Windmill Court, Halifax.

8A 164 **Wetherby**
Linton Lane, Wetherby, Yorks, LS22
4JF
☎(01937) 583375, Fax 531915, Sec
580089, Bar/Rest 582527
1 mile W of A1 S of Linton village.
Parkland course.
Pro David Padgett; Founded 1910
18 holes, 6235 yards, S.S.S. 70
Visitors: welcome Mon and Tues
afternoons; all day Wed, Thurs, Fri.
Green Fees: WD £25.
Societies: welcome by prior arrange-
ment; packages available; discounts
for groups of 40; terms on application.
Catering: full clubhouse facilities.
Hotels: Linton Springs; Jarvis Resort;
Wood Hall.

8A 165 **Wheatley**
Armthorpe Rd, Doncaster, S Yorks,
DN2 5QB
☎(01302) 831655, Pro 834085
Close to Doncaster racecourse follow-
ing the ring road S; opposite large
water tower.
Undulating parkland; relocated 1933.
Pro Steve Fox; Founded 1913/1933
Designed by George Duncan
18 holes, 6405 yards, S.S.S. 71
Visitors: welcome.
Green Fees: WD £20; WE £30.
Societies: welcome WD by arrange-
ment; day ticket (WD £25); catering by
arrangement; from £20.
Catering: full facilities.
Hotels: Balmoral; Earl of Doncaster;
Punches.

8A 166 **Whitby**
Sandsend Rd, Low Straggleton,
Whitby, N Yorks, YO21 3SR
☎(01947) 602768, Fax 600660, Pro
602719, Sec 600660
On A174 coast road between Whitby
and Sandsend.
Seaside course.
Pro Richard Wood; Founded 1892
18 holes, 6134 yards, S.S.S. 69
Visitors: welcome by prior arrangement.
Green Fees: WD £20; WE £25.
Societies: welcome by prior arrangement; winter and summer packages
available for groups of 8 or more; from
£19.50.

Catering: full facilities.
Practice area.
Hotels: Larpool; Seacliff; White House.

8A 167 **Whitwood**

Altofts Lane, Whitwood, Castleford, W Yorks, WF10 5PZ
☎(01977) 604215, Pro 512835, Bar/Rest 512835
0.5 miles towards Castleford off M62 junction 31.
Parkland course.
Pro Richard Golding; Founded 1986
Designed by Steve Wells (Wakefield Council)
9 holes, 6282 yards, S.S.S. 70
Visitors: welcome; booking system available.
Green Fees: WD £5.90; WE £8.
Societies: welcome by arrangement with the Pro; terms on application.
Catering: available at local inn.
Hotels: Bridge Inn.

8A 168 **Willow Valley Golf & Country Club**

Highmoor Lane, Clifton, Brighouse, W Yorks, HD6 4JB
☎(01274) 878624, Fax 852805
From M62 junction 25 take A644 to Brighouse; turn right at first roundabout.
American parkland style course.
Pro Julian Howarth; Founded 1993
Designed by J Gaunt
18 holes, 7021 yards, S.S.S. 74
Visitors: welcome.
Green Fees: WD £20; WE £24.
Societies: welcome WD; packages available for groups of 12 or more; from £27.50.
Catering: full clubhouse facilities.
Practice range, 24 bays floodlit.
Hotels: Forte Crest; Black Horse Inn; Hartshead Moor.

8A 169 **Withernsea**

Chestnut Ave, Withernsea, E Yorks, HU19 2PG
☎(01964) 612258, Sec 612078
25 miles E of Hull on main road to Withernsea.
Seaside links course.
Pro G Harrison; Founded 1907
9 holes, 6191 yards, S.S.S. 64
Visitors: welcome; after 2pm Sun.
Green Fees: WD £10; WE £10.
Societies: welcome by prior arrangement; catering packages can be arranged; from £10.
Catering: clubhouse facilities.

8A 170 **Wombwell (Hillies)**

Wentworth View, Wombwell, Barnsley, S Yorks, S73 0LA
☎(01226) 754433, Sec 758635
4 miles SE of Barnsley.
Meadowland course.
Founded 1981
9 holes, 4190 yards
Visitors: welcome.
Green Fees: WD £6.30; WE £7.80.
Societies: welcome by prior arrangement; limited catering available; from £6.30.
Catering: bar service only.

8A 171 **Woodhall Hills**

Woodhall Rd, Calverley, Pudsey, W Yorks, LS28 5UN
☎(0113) 2564771, Pro 255462857, Sec 2554594
Take A647 Leeds-Bradford road to Pudsey roundabout; follow signs to Calverley; 0.25 miles past Calverley Golf Club.
Parkland course.
Pro Warren Lockett; Founded 1905
18 holes, 6001 yards, S.S.S. 69
Visitors: welcome.
Green Fees: WD £20.50; WE £25.50.
Societies: welcome by arrangement with secretary/manager; golf and catering packages available for groups of 20 or more; from £27.
Catering: full clubhouse facilities available.
Hotels: Cedar Court, Bradford.

8A 172 **Woodsome Hall**

Fenay Bridge, Huddersfield, W Yorks, HD8 0LG
☎(01484) 602739, Fax 608260, Pro 602034, Bar/Rest 602971
From either M62 junction 23 or 25 towards Huddersfield then A629 towards Sheffield turning right at Farnley Tyas/Honley signs.
Parkland course.
Pro Mike Higginbottom; Founded 1922
Designed by J Braid
18 holes, 6096 yards, S.S.S. 69
Visitors: welcome except Tues.
Green Fees: WD £27.50; WE £35.
Societies: welcome by prior arrangement except Tues and Sat; h'cap certs required; menus for catering packages available from club; TV lounge; halfway bar available; deposit required; terms on application.
Catering: full catering and bar facilities; jacket and tie required.
Practice areas available.
Hotels: Hanover International; Huddersfield Hotel.

8A 173 **Woolley Park**

Woolley Park, New Rd, Woolley, Wakefield, W Yorks, WF4 2JS
☎(01226) 380144, Fax 390295, Sec 382209
From M1 junction 38 follow signs for Woolley Hall; from the A61 Wakefield to Barnsley road take the Woolley signs from the crossroads.
Parkland course.
Pro Jon Baldwin; Founded 1995
Designed by M Shattock
18 holes, 6471 yards, S.S.S. 71
Visitors: welcome.
Green Fees: terms on application.
Societies: welcome by prior arrangement; packages available; terms on application.
Catering: clubhouse facilities.
Practice range, Practice area.

8A 174 **Wortley**

Hermit Hill Lane, Wortley, Sheffield, S35 7DF
☎(0114) 2885294, Pro 2886490, Sec 2888469, Bar/Rest 2882139
Off A629 through Wortley village.
Undulating wooded parkland course.
Pro Ian Kirk; Founded 1894
18 holes, 6035 yards, S.S.S. 69
Visitors: welcome by prior arrangement.
Green Fees: WD £25; WE £30.
Societies: welcome Mon, Wed and Fri by prior arrangement; catering by arrangement except Mon; terms on application.
Catering: clubhouse facilities except Mon.
Hotels: Ardsley Moat House; Brooklands, both Barnsley; Tankersley Manor.

8A 175 **York**

Lords Moor Lane, Strensall, York, Yorks, YO3 5XF
☎(01904) 490304, Fax 491852, Sec 491840
3 miles N of A1237 York ring road from Earswick/Strensall roundabout
Tree-lined heathland course.
Pro T Mason; Founded 1890
Designed by J.H. Taylor (1904)
18 holes, 6302 yards, S.S.S. 70
Visitors: welcome by prior arrangement; with member at WE only.
Green Fees: WD £25.
Societies: welcome except Tues am and Sat; packages can include 27 or 36 holes of golf; some Sun available; catering available; from £32.
Catering: bar and catering facilities.
Practice ground.

THE VICTORIA HOTEL 👑👑👑👑

ETB Commended

BAMBURGH - *"Gem of Northumberland"*

VICTORIA HOTEL
BAMBURGH

Romantic coastal village dominated by its magnificent castle. Scrumptious food in a refreshingly different environment. Golfing Breaks from £35 per person. Tee Times can be arranged. All bedroomsen-suite and tastefully furnished.

Front Street, Bamburgh, Northumberland NE69 7BP. Tel: 01668 214431 Fax 01668 214404

8B 1 Allendale

High Studdon, Allenheads Rd, Allendale, Hexham, Northumberland, N47 9DH
☎ (01434) 683926
On B6295 1.5 miles S of Allendale in the direction of Allenheads.
Hilly parkland course; 7 new tees 1998; new site 1992.
Founded 1907/1992
Designed by Members with advice from English Golf Union and Sports Council
9 holes, 5044 yards, S.S.S. 65
Visitors: welcome except August Bank Holiday Mon.
Green Fees: WD £10; WE £10.
Societies: welcome by arrangement; corporate days welcome; catering by arrangement; from £10.
Catering: clubhouse facilities.
Hotels: Kings Head; Hare & Hounds; Allenheads.

8B 2 Alnmouth

Foxton Hall, Lesbury, Alnmouth, Northumberland, NE66 3BE
☎ (01665) 830231, Fax 830992, Pro 830043
5 miles SE of Alnwick.
Seaside links course with parkland turf.
Founded 1869
Designed by H S Colt
18 holes, 6429 yards, S.S.S. 71
Visitors: welcome Mon, Tues and Thurs; Dormy House guests welcome at all times.
Green Fees: WD £20.
Societies: welcome Mon, Tues, Thurs; day packages available; maximum groups of 30; from £20.
Catering: clubhouse facilities.
Hotels: Foxton Hall has its own Dormy House and self-catering flat.

8B 3 Alnmouth Village

Marine Rd, Alnmouth, Northumberland NE66 2RZ
☎ (01665) 830370
On A1068 from Alnmouth.
Undulating seaside course.
Founded 1869
9 holes, 6078 yards, S.S.S. 70

Visitors: welcome; restrictions on comp days.
Green Fees: WD £15; WE £20.
Societies: welcome with h'cap certs; catering packages by arrangement; from £15.
Catering: catering by prior arrangement.
Hotels: Marine.

8B 4 Alnwick

Swansfield Park, Alnwick, Northumberland NE66 1AT
☎ (01665) 602632, Sec 602499
From A1 S signposted to Willowburn Ave and then into Swansfield Park Road.
7 holes mature parkland; 4 gorse; 7 open parkland course.
Founded 1907/1993
Designed by G Rochester/A Rae
18 holes, 6250 yards, S.S.S. 70
Visitors: welcome by prior arrangement with the starter.
Green Fees: WD £12; WE £16.
Societies: welcome between April 1 and Oct 1 by prior arrangement; packages in season of unlimited golf; full day's catering; minimum 10; £20.
Catering: full clubhouse facilities.
Hotels: White Swans; Royal Oak; Plough; Hotspur.

8B 5 Arcot Hall

Dudley, Cramlington, Northumberland, NE23 7QP
☎ (0191) 2362794, Fax 2170370, Pro 2362147
1.5 miles off A1 near Cramlington.
Parkland course; formerly at Benton; moved to present site in 1948.
Pro Graham Cant; Founded 1909/48
Designed by James Braid
18 holes, 6389 yards, S.S.S. 70
Visitors: welcome WD; restrictions WE.
Green Fees: WD £26; WE £30.
Societies: welcome by prior arrangement on WD; packages available; snooker room; from £26.
Catering: lounge bar and restaurant facilities.
Hotels: Holiday Inn; Swallow Gosforth Park.

8B 6 Backworth

Backworth Welfare, The Hall, Backworth, Shiremoor, NE27 0AH
☎ (0191) 2681048, Sec 2581291
On B1322 1 mile from the A19/A191 junction at Shiremoor crossroads.
Parkland course.
Founded 1937
9 holes, 5930 yards, S.S.S. 69
Visitors: welcome WD except Tues 11am-3pm; restrictions at WE.
Green Fees: WD £12; WE £16.
Societies: welcome by prior arrangement with Sec; packages can be negotiated depending on numbers; terms on application.
Catering: full bar and restaurant facilities.
Hotels: Rex; Park; Stakis Wallsend; Grand.

8B 7 Bamburgh Castle

The Wynding, Bamburgh, Northumberland, NE69 7DE
☎ (01668) 214378, Sec 214321
5 miles E of A1 via B1341 or B1342 into Bamburgh village.
Seaside course.
Founded 1896/04
Designed by George Rochester
18 holes, 5621 yards, S.S.S. 67
Visitors: welcome by prior arrangement except on comp days and BH.
Green Fees: WD £25; WE £30.
Societies: welcome by prior written arrangement with Sec; full catering packages available, except Tues; from £25.
Catering: full catering available except Tues.
Hotels: Victoria; Mizen; Sunningdale; Lord Crewe.

8B 8 Barnard Castle

Harmire Rd, Barnard Castle, DL12 8QN
☎ (01833) 637237, Pro 631980, Sec 638355
On B6278 1 mile N of town signposted Middleton in Teesdale.
Parkland course.
Pro Darren Pearce; Founded 1898/1907
Designed by A S Watson

18 holes, 6406 yards, S.S.S. 71
Visitors: welcome by prior arrangement.
Green Fees: WD £18; WE £25.
Societies: welcome WD by prior arrangement; catering packages available; from £18.
Catering: restaurant and bar facilities. Practice range, practice area.

8B 9 Beamish Park

The Clubhouse, Beamish, Stanley, Co Durham, DH9 0RH
☎(0191) 3701382, Fax 3702937, Pro 3701984
From A1 take A693 towards Stanley and follow the signs for Beamish museum.
Tree lined parkland course.
Pro Chris Cole; Founded 1907/50
Designed by Henry Cotton (part)/W Woodend
18 holes, 6218 yards, S.S.S. 70
Visitors: welcome by arrangement.
Green Fees: WD £16; WE £20.
Societies: welcome by arrangement; on application.
Catering: full clubhouse facilities.
Hotels: Coppy Lodge GH.

8B 10 Bedlingtonshire

Acorn Bank, Bedlington, Northumberland, NE22 5SY
☎(01670) 822457, Pro 822087
Off A189 Ashington road 5 miles N of Newcastle.
Parkland course.
Pro Marcus Webb; Founded 1972
Designed by Frank Pennink
18 holes, 6813 yards, S.S.S. 73
Visitors: welcome by arrangement.
Green Fees: WD £15; WE £20.
Societies: welcome by prior arrangement with professional; packages can be arranged; on application.
Catering: full clubhouse facilities.
Hotels: Swan Inn, Choppington; Half Moon Inn, Stakeford; Holiday Inn, Seaton Born.

8B 11 Belford

South Rd, Belford, Northumberland, NE70 7DP
☎(01668) 213433, Fax 213919
Just off A1 midway between Alnwick and Berwick on Tweed.
Parkland course.
Founded 1993
Designed by Nigel W. Williams
9 holes, 6304 yards, S.S.S. 70
Visitors: welcome.
Green Fees: WD £13; WE £16.

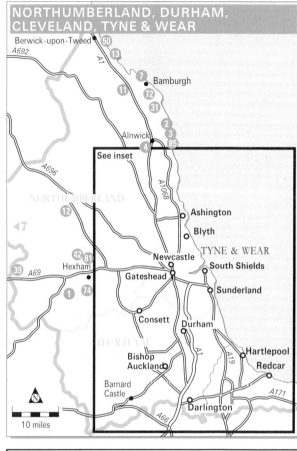

NORTHUMBERLAND, DURHAM, CLEVELAND, TYNE & WEAR

KEY		16	Bishop Auckland	33	Eaglescliffe
1	Allendale	17	Blackwell Grange	34	Elemore
2	Alnmouth	18	Blyth	35	Garesfield
3	Alnmouth Village	19	Boldon	36	George Washington County
4	Alnwick	20	Brancepeth Castle		Hotel & GC
5	Arcot Hall	21	Burgham Park	37	Gosforth
6	Backworth	22	Castle Eden & Peterlee	38	Hall Garth Golf & Country
7	Bamburgh Castle	23	Chester-le-Street		Club
8	Barnard Castle	24	City of Newcastle	39	Haltwhistle
9	Beamish Park	25	Cleveland	40	Hartlepool
10	Bedlingtonshire	26	Close House	41	Heworth
11	Belford	27	Consett & District	42	Hexham
12	Bellingham	28	Crook	43	High Throston
13	Berwick-upon-Tweed	29	Darlington	44	Hobson Municipal
	(Goswick)	30	Dinsdale Spa	45	Houghton-le-Spring
14	Billingham	31	Dunstanburgh Castle	46	Hunley Hall
15	Birtley	32	Durham City	47	Knotty Hill Golf Centre

Societies: welcome by prior arrangement; some WE available; packages include 27 holes plus all-day catering; from £23.
Catering: full clubhouse facilities. 6 indoor 4 outdoor practice bays.
Hotels: Blue Bell; Purdy Travel Lodge.

8B 12 Bellingham

Boggle Hole, Bellingham, Hexham, Northumberland, NE48 2DT
☎(01434) 220152, Sec 220530
Off the B6320 16 miles north-east of Hexham and the A69, on the outskirts of Bellingham.

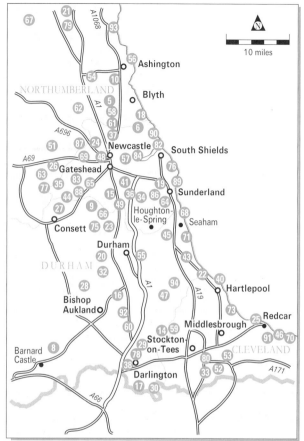

10 miles

48	Linden Hall	64	Ramside	80	Teesside
49	Longhirst Hall	65	Ravensworth	81	Tynedale
50	Magdalene Fields	66	Roseberry Grange	82	Tynemouth
51	Matfen Hall	67	Rothbury	83	Tyneside
52	Middlesbrough	68	Ryhope	84	Wallsend
53	Middlesbrough Municipal	69	Ryton	85	Warkworth
54	Morpeth	70	Saltburn-by-the-Sea	86	Wearside
55	Mount Oswald	71	Seaham	87	Westerhope
56	Newbiggin-by-the-Sea	72	Seahouses	88	Whickham
57	Newcastle United	73	Seaton Carew	89	Whitburn
58	Northumberland	74	Slaley Hall International	90	Whitley Bay
59	Norton Golf Course		Golf Resort	91	Wilton
60	Oak Leaf Golf Complex	75	South Moor	92	Woodham Golf & Country
	(Aycliffe)	76	South Shields		Club
61	Parklands Golf Club	77	Stocksfield	93	Wooler
62	Ponteland	78	Stressholme Golf Centre	94	Wynyard (The Wellington)
63	Prudhoe	79	Swarland Hall		

Rolling parkland course with abundance of natural hazards.
Founded 1893/1996
Designed by E Johnson/I Wilson (96)
18 holes, 6077 yards, S.S.S. 70
Visitors: welcome; booking advisable.
Green Fees: WD £17.50; WE £22.50.

Societies: welcome every day by prior arrangement; catering and golfing packages available; from £17.50.
Catering: full catering and bar facilities.
Practice range, 6 bays floodlit.
Hotels: George; Riverdale; Beaumont.

8B 13 **Berwick-upon-Tweed (Goswick)**
Goswick, Berwick-upon-Tweed, Northumberland, TD15 2RW
☎(01289) 387256, Fax 387256, Pro 387380
1.5 miles from A1; 5 miles S of Berwick-upon-Tweed.
Links course.
Pro Paul Terras; Founded 1890/64
Designed by James Braid/ F Pennick
18 holes, 6462 yards, S.S.S. 71
Visitors: welcome; restrictions between before 10am and between 12noon-2pm at WE.
Green Fees: WD £20; WE £25.
Societies: welcome WD; packages include full day's golf and catering for minimum 10; £25.
Catering: full clubhouse catering and bar facilities.
Practice ground.
Hotels: Blue Bell, Belford; Beadnell Towers, Chathill; Kings Arms; Wallace GH, both Berwick.

8B 14 **Billingham**
Sandy Lane, Billingham, Cleveland, TS22 5NA
☎(01642) 533816, Fax 533816, Pro 557060, Bar/Rest 554494
E of A19 near Billingham Town Centre.
Parkland course.
Pro Mike Ure; Founded 1967
Designed by Frank Pennink
18 holes, 6460 yards, S.S.S. 71
Visitors: welcome.
Green Fees: WD £20; WE £33.
Societies: welcome by prior arrangement with Sec; terms on application.
Catering: full clubhouse facilities.

8B 15 **Birtley**
Birtley Lane, Birtley, Co Durham, DH3 2LR
☎(0191) 4102207
6 miles S of Newcastle off A6127.
Parkland course.
Founded 1921
9 holes, 5660 yards, S.S.S. 67
Visitors: welcome WD; with member at WE.
Green Fees: WD £12.
Societies: welcome WD by prior arrangement; terms on application.
Catering: bar facilities.
Hotels: George Washington County; local B&Bs can be recommended.

8B 16 **Bishop Auckland**
High Plains, Durham Rd, Bishop Auckland, Co Durham, DL14 8DL

☎(01388) 602198, Pro 661618, Sec 663648.
0.5 miles N of town on Durham road.
Parkland course.
Pro David Skiffington; Founded 1894
Designed by James Kay
18 holes, 6399 yards, S.S.S. 71
Visitors: welcome WD except Tues.
Green Fees: WD £20.
Societies: welcome by prior arrangement WD except Tues; special packages for 20+ including 27 holes golf and all-day catering; £27.50.
Catering: full clubhouse facilities.
Practice area.
Hotels: Queens; Park Head, both Bishop Auckland; Old Manor, W Auckland.

8B 17 Blackwell Grange
Briar Close, Blackwell, Darlington, DL3 8QX
☎(01325) 464464, Fax 464458, Pro 462088, Sec 464458
1 mile S of Darlington on A66.
Parkland course.
Pro Ralph Givens; Founded 1930
Designed by Frank Pennink
18 holes, 5621 yards, S.S.S. 67
Visitors: welcome.
Green Fees: WD £16; WE £20.
Societies: welcome WD except Wed; catering packages available; from £16.
Catering: full clubhouse facilities.
Hotels: Blackwell Grange, Darlington.

8B 18 Blyth
New Delaval, Blyth, Northumberland, NE24 4DB
☎(01670) 367728, Pro 356514, Sec 540110
At W end of Plessey Road.
Parkland course.
Pro Andrew Brown; Founded 1905/1976
Designed by Hamilton Stutt & Co
18 holes, 6430 yards, S.S.S. 72
Visitors: welcome WD.
Green Fees: WD £18; WE £18.
Societies: welcome WD by prior arrangement; 3 packages available for society and company days; minimum 10; from £21.
Catering: full clubhouse catering and bar facilities.
Hotels: large number in Whitley Bay.

8B 19 Boldon
Dipe Lane, East Boldon, Tyne & Wear, NE36 0PQ
☎(0191) 5364182, Pro 5365835, Sec 5365360

On A184 1 mile E of A19/A1 junction.
Parkland course.
Pro Richard Phipps
Founded 1912
18 holes, 6338 yards, S.S.S. 70
Visitors: welcome WD with some restrictions; after 3.30 only at WE.
Green Fees: WD £18; WE £22.
Societies: welcome by arrangement; catering packages available; snooker; from £18.
Catering: bar snacks and restaurant facilities.
Practice area.
Hotels: friendly.

8B 20 Brancepeth Castle
Brancepeth Village, Durham, Co Durham, DH7 8EA
☎(0191) 3780075, Fax 3783835, Pro 3780183, Bar/Rest 3783393
On A690 4 miles W of Durham; left at the crossroads before Brancepeth.
Parkland course.
Pro D Howson; Founded 1924
Designed by H.S. Colt
18 holes, 6375 yards, S.S.S. 71
Visitors: welcome by prior arrangement.
Green Fees: WD £29; WE £34.
Societies: welcome WD by prior arrangement; special rates for groups of more than 12 and 30; banqueting facilities available; formal dinners can be arranged; starter available; video service; from £29.
Catering: full clubhouse catering and bar facilities; formal dinner and banquets can be arranged.
Large practice area.
Hotels: Waterside GH.

8B 21 Burgham Park
Near Felton, Morpeth, Northumberland NE65 8QP
☎(01670) 787898, Fax 787164, Bar/Rest 787501
6 miles N of Morpeth off the A1 at Longhorsley road (C137).
Parkland course.
Pro S McNally; Founded 1994
Designed by A Mair
18 holes, 6751 yards, S.S.S. 72
Visitors: welcome.
Green Fees: terms on application.
Societies: welcome except on competition days; catering packages available; terms on application.
Catering: full catering and bar facilities.
Practice area.
Hotels: Sun Inn, Warkworth; Blue Bell, Belford.

8B 22 Castle Eden & Peterlee
Castle Eden, Hartlepool, Cleveland, TS27 4SS
☎(01429) 836220, Fax 836510, Pro 836689, Sec 836510
10 miles S of Sunderland; take slip road off A19 towards Blackhall; 0.25 miles.
Parkland course.
Pro G Laidlaw; Founded 1927
Designed by Henry Cotton (back 9)
18 holes, 6282 yards, S.S.S. 70
Visitors: welcome by prior arrangement.
Green Fees: WD £20; WE £30.
Catering: full clubhouse facilities.
Hotels: Castle Eden Inn.

8B 23 Chester-le-Street
Lumley Park, Chester-le-Street, Co Durham, DH3 4NS
☎(0191) 3883218, Fax 3881220, Pro 3890157
Close to A167 0.5 miles E of Chester-le-Street close to Lumley Castle and Durham CCC ground.
Parkland course.
Pro David Fletcher; Founded 1908
Designed by J.H. Taylor (original 9)/ T Ray
18 holes, 6437 yards, S.S.S. 69
Visitors: welcome by prior arrangement.
Green Fees: WD £20; WE £25.
Societies: welcome by prior arrangement; coffee and catering available depending on numbers; on application.
Catering: full clubhouse facilities.
Hotels: Lumley Castle.

8B 24 City of Newcastle
Three Mile Bridge, Gosforth, NE3 2DR
☎(0191) 2851775, Fax 2840700, Pro 2855481
On B1318 3 miles N of Newcastle.
Parkland course.
Pro A J Matthew; Founded 1892
Designed by Harry Vardon
18 holes, 6528 yards, S.S.S. 71
Visitors: welcome.
Green Fees: WD £24; WE £28.
Societies: welcome by prior arrangement most days; packages on application; from £24.
Catering: full clubhouse facilities.
Hotels: Swallow Gosforth Park.

8B 25 Cleveland
Queen St, Redcar, Cleveland, TS10 1BT
☎(01642) 483693, Fax 471798, Sec 471798

Off A174 following signs for Teesside and Redcar.
Links course.
Pro Stephen Wynn; Founded 1897
18 holes, 6707 yards, S.S.S. 72
Visitors: welcome.
Green Fees: WD £20; WE £30.
Societies: welcome; packages can be arranged depending on numbers; terms on application.
Catering: clubhouse bar and catering facilities.
Hotels: Royal York; Park.

8B 26 Close House

Close House, Heddon-on-the-Wall, Northumberland, NE15 0BH
☎(01661) 852953, Bar/Rest 852255
Off A69 9 miles W of Newcastle.
Parkland/woodland course.
Founded 1965
Designed by Hawtree
18 holes, 5606 yards, S.S.S. 67
Visitors: members' guests only.
Green Fees: WD £6; WE £10.
Societies: welcome WD by prior arrangement; packages available to include all-day catering; corporate days by arrangement; from £18.
Catering: catering and bar facilities in the Mansion House.
Hotels: Copthorne; Novotel, both Newcastle; Holiday Inn, Seaton Burn.

8B 27 Consett & District

Elmfield Rd, Consett, Co Durham, DH8 5NN
☎(01207) 502186, Fax 505060, Pro 580210, Sec 505060
On A691 14 miles N of Durham.
Parkland course.
Pro Craig Dilley; Founded 1911
Designed by Harry Vardon
18 holes, 6023 yards, S.S.S. 69
Visitors: welcome by prior arrangement with Pro.
Green Fees: WD £17; WE £25.
Societies: welcome by prior arrangement with Sec; all-day menu available for £9; from £17.
Catering: full clubhouse facilities.
Hotels: Royal Derwent; Raven.

8B 28 Crook

Low Job's Hill, Crook, Co Durham, DL15 9AA
☎(01388) 762429, Sec 7626177
Bar/Rest 767926
On A690 9 miles W of Durham.
Parkland course, hilly in parts.
Founded 1919
18 holes, 6102 yards, S.S.S. 69

Visitors: welcome by prior arrangement.
Green Fees: WD £14; WE £23.
Societies: welcome WD by prior arrangement; packages on application; from £14.
Catering: clubhouse facilities.
Hotels: Helme Park.

8B 29 Darlington

Haughton Grange, Darlington, Co Durham, DL1 3JD
☎(01325) 288417, Fax 488126, Pro 484198, Sec 355324, Bar/Rest 355324
Between A1 and A66 at N end of Darlington.
Parkland course.
Pro Mark Rogers; Founded 1912
Designed by MacKenzie
18 holes, 6270 yards, S.S.S. 70
Visitors: welcome WD.
Green Fees: WD £20.
Societies: welcome by prior arrangement; packages and special rates for larger groups; from £15.
Catering: full clubhouse facilities.
9-acre practice ground.
Hotels: White Horse; Kings Head, both Darlington; Eden Arms, Rushyford.

8B 30 Dinsdale Spa

Neasham Rd, Middleton-St-George, Darlington, Co Durham, DL2 1DW
☎(01325) 332222, Fax 332297, Pro 332515, Sec 332297
Off the A67 near Teesside Airport midway between Middleton St George and Neasham.
Parkland course.
Pro Craig Imlah; Founded 1910
18 holes, 6090 yards, S.S.S. 69
Visitors: welcome when tee times allow.
Green Fees: WD £20; WE £20.
Societies: welcome by prior arrangement with Sec; catering packages available; from £20.
Catering: full clubhouse bar and catering facilities.
Hotels: Croft Spa; Devenport.

8B 31 Dunstanburgh Castle

Embleton, Alnwick, Northumberland, NE66 3XQ
☎(01665) 576562, Fax 576562
7 miles NE of Alnwick off the A1; follow signs to Embleton.
Seaside links course.
Founded 1900
Designed by James Braid

18 holes, 6298 yards, S.S.S. 70
Visitors: welcome.
Green Fees: WD £15; WE £20.
Societies: welcome by prior arrangement; packages available; separate dining facilities; from £15.
Catering: full clubhouse facilities.
Hotels: Sportsmans Inn; Dunstanburgh Castle, both Embleton.

8B 32 Durham City

Littleburn Farm, Langley Moor, Durham, DH7 8HL
☎(0191) 3780069, Pro 3780029, Sec 3860200
Off A690 2 miles SW of Durham.
Meadowland course.
Pro Steve Carbally; Founded 1887
Designed by C.C. Stanton
18 holes, 6279 yards, S.S.S. 70
Visitors: welcome by prior arrangement.
Green Fees: WD £22; WE £28.
Societies: welcome WD; packages available; terms on application.
Catering: full catering; limited service Mon.
Hotels: Royal County; Three Tuns; Duke of Wellington; Kensington Hall.

8B 33 Eaglescliffe

Yarm Rd, Eaglescliffe, Stockton-on-Tees, Cleveland, TS16 0DQ
☎(01642) 780098, Fax 780238, Pro 790122, Sec 780238
On A135 Stockton to Yarm.
Undulating parkland course.
Pro Paul Bradley; Founded 1914
Designed by James Braid, Modification By H. Cotton
18 holes, 6275 yards, S.S.S. 69
Visitors: welcome.
Green Fees: WD £24; WE £30.
Societies: welcome WD by prior arrangement; packages include 18 holes of golf and 3-course meal; £26.
Catering: full clubhouse facilities.
Hotels: Parkmore.

8B 34 Elemore

Easington Lane, Haughton le Spring, Tyne and Wear,
☎(0191) 5269020
5 miles E of Durham City; W of Easington Lane.
Parkland course.
Founded 1994
18 holes, 5947 yards, S.S.S. 69
Visitors: Pay and play.
Green Fees: WD £8; WE £8.
Societies: welcome by prior arrangement; terms on application.

Catering: bar and function room.
Practice area.
Hotels: Fox and Hounds, Hetton-le-Hole.

8B 35 **Garesfield**
Chopwell, Tyne and Wear, NE17 7AP
☎ (01207) 561309, Fax 561309, Pro 563082, Bar/Rest 561278
On B6315 to High Spen off A694 from A1 at Rowlands Gill.
Undulating wooded parkland course.
Pro David Race; Founded 1922
Designed by William Woodend
18 holes, 6603 yards, S.S.S. 72
Visitors: welcome except before 4.30pm at WE.
Green Fees: terms on application.
Societies: welcome by prior arrangement except Mon and Sat; catering packages can be arranged with the steward; terms on application.
Catering: full clubhouse facilities. except Mon.
Hotels: Towneley Arms, Rowlands Gill.

8B 36 **George Washington County Hotel & GC**
Stonecellar Rd, Washington, Tyne & Wear, NE37 1PH
☎ (0191) 4029988, Fax 4151166, Pro 4178346, Sec 4168341
Signposted from A1(M) and A194.
Parkland course.
Pro Warren Marshall; Founded 1990
18 holes, 6604 yards, S.S.S. 72
Visitors: welcome by prior arrangement; special rates for hotel guests.
Green Fees: WD £20; WE £30.
Societies: welcome by prior arrangement; special rates for groups of more than 15; hotel packages; leisure club; pool; spa; terms on application.
Catering: full clubhouse and hotel facilities.
Practice range, 21 bays floodli; 9-hole pitch and putt.
Hotels: 105-bedroom George Washington County Hotel on site.

8B 37 **Gosforth**
Broadway East, Gosforth, NE3 5ER
☎ (0191) 2853495, Pro 2850553, Bar/Rest 2856710
Off A6125 3 miles N of Newcastle.
Parkland course with stream feature.
Pro Graeme Garland; Founded 1906
18 holes, 6024 yards, S.S.S. 69
Visitors: welcome by prior arrangement.
Green Fees: WD £20; WE £20.

Societies: welcome WD by prior arrangement; catering packages available; discounts for groups of more than 12; from £20.
Catering: full clubhouse facilities.
Hotels: Swallow Gosforth Park; Novotel.

8B 38 **Hall Garth Golf & Country Club**
Coatham Mundeville, Nr Darlington, Co Durham, DL1 3LU
☎ (01325) 320246, Fax 310083, Pro 300400, Sec 300400, Bar/Rest 300400
From A1(M) junction 59 take A167 towards Darlington; top of hill.
Parkland course.
Founded 1995
Designed by B Moore
9 holes, 6621 yards, S.S.S. 72
Visitors: welcome.
Green Fees: WD £10; WE £12.50.
Societies: welcome; packages available; terms on application.
Catering: bar and restaurant facilities on site; hotel on site.
Hotels: Hall Garth, 16th century country house with leisure facilities.

8B 39 **Haltwhistle**
Banktop, Greenhead, Via Carlisle, Cumbria, CA6 7HN
☎ (016977) 47367, Fax 01434 344311, Sec 01434 344000
Off A69 N of Haltwhistle turn right at Greenhead.
Parkland course.
Founded 1967
Designed by members
12 holes, 5522 yards, S.S.S. 69
Visitors: welcome except after 5pm Wed and Fri and before 3pm on Sun.
Green Fees: WD £12; WE £12.
Societies: welcome by prior arrangement; packages include 27 holes of golf and all-day catering; from £20.
Catering: bar and catering facilities.
Hotels: Greenhead Hotel.

8B 40 **Hartlepool**
Hart Warren, Hartlepool, Cleveland, TS24 9QF
☎ (01429) 274398, Fax 274129, Pro 267473
Off A1086 at N edge of Hartlepool.
Seaside links course.
Pro Malcolm Cole; Founded 1906
Designed by James Braid (in Part)
18 holes, 6215 yards, S.S.S. 70
Visitors: welcome; restricted to members guests Sun.

Green Fees: WD £20; WE £30.
Societies: welcome WD by prior arrangement; catering packages available from the steward; snooker; terms on application.
Catering: full clubhouse facilities. except Mon.
Hotels: Staincliffe; Marine; Travelodge.

8B 41 **Heworth**
Gingling Gate, Heworth, Tyne and Wear, NE10 8XY
☎ (0191) 4962137, Sec 4699832
Close to A1 (M) SE of Gateshead.
Parkland course with woods.
Founded 1912
18 holes, 6404 yards, S.S.S. 71
Visitors: welcome but not before 10am at WE.
Green Fees: WD £15; WE £15.
Societies: welcome by prior arrangement; catering packages by arrangement; dining room; from £15.
Catering: bar and restaurant.
Practice range, practice area.
Hotels: George Washington.

8B 42 **Hexham**
Spital Park, Hexham, Northumberland, NE46 3RZ
☎ (01434) 602057, Fax 601865, Pro 604904, Sec 603072
On A69 1 mile W of Hexham.
Undulating parkland course.
Pro Martin Foster; Founded 1907
Designed by Harry Vardon
18 holes, 6301 yards, S.S.S. 68
Visitors: welcome by arrangement.
Green Fees: WD £27; WE £35.
Societies: welcome except WE by arrangement; packages available; from £35.
Catering: clubhouse catering and bar.
Hotels: Beaumont.

8B 43 **High Throston**
Hart Lane, Hartlepool, Co Durham, TS26 0UG
☎ (01429) 275325
From A19N take A179 to Hartlepool.
Parkland course with USGA standard greens.
Founded 1996
Designed by J Gaunt
18 holes, 6247 yards, S.S.S. 71
Visitors: welcome.
Green Fees: WD £15; WE £18.
Societies: welcome by prior arrangement.
Catering: sandwiches, teas, coffee.
Hotels: Raby Arms.

8B 44 Hobson Municipal

Burnopfield, Newcastle-upon-Tyne, NE16 6BZ
☎(01207) 271605, Fax 271609, Sec 570189 Bar/Rest 270941
On main Newcastle-Consett road opposite Hobson Industrial estate.
Parkland course.
Pro J W Ord; Founded 1980
18 holes, 6403 yards, S.S.S. 71
Visitors: pay and play.
Green Fees: WD £11; WE £14.
Societies: welcome by arrangement with the Pro; packages available; terms on application.
Catering: catering and bar facilities.
Hotels: Towneley Arms.

8B 45 Houghton-le-Spring

Copt Hill, Houghton-le-Spring, Tyne and Wear, DH5 8LU
☎(0191) 5841198, Pro 5847421, Sec 5840043
On A1085 Houghton-le-Spring to Seaham Harbour road 0.5 miles from Houghton-le-Spring.
Undulating hillside course.
Pro Kevin Gow; Founded 1908
18 holes, 6443 yards, S.S.S. 71
Visitors: welcome after 9am; WE restrictions.
Green Fees: WD £20; WE £25.
Societies: welcome by prior arrangement; catering packages available; from £27.
Catering: catering and bar facilities available.
Hotels: White Lion; Ramside Hall; Rainton Lodge.

8B 46 Hunley Hall

Brotton, Saltburn-by-the-Sea, N Yorks, TS12 2QQ
☎(01287) 676216, Fax 678250, Pro 677444
Off A174 from Teesside to Brotton into St Margarets Way.
Meadowland course; a further 9 holes planned for 1998.
Pro Andrew Brook; Founded 1993
Designed by J Morgan
18 holes, 6918 yards, S.S.S. 73
Visitors: welcome.
Green Fees: WD £18; WE £25.
Societies: welcome Mon to Sat; packages for 18 and 27 holes of golf and for catering available; terms on application.
Catering: restaurant and bars; members bar; spike bar; all-day catering.
Practice range, 12 bays floodlit.
Hotels: accommodation on site; 3 crowns.

8B 47 Knotty Hill Golf Centre

Sedgefield, Stockton-on-Tees, Cleveland, TS21 2BB
☎(01740) 620320, Fax 622227
On A177 1 mile from Sedgefield 2 miles from A1 (M) junction 60.
Naturally undulating parkland course.
Pro Nick Walton; Founded 1991
Designed by C. Stanton
18 holes, 6577 yards, S.S.S. 71
Visitors: welcome.
Green Fees: WD £12; WE £12.
Societies: welcome WD; terms on application.
Catering: full clubhouse facilities available.
Floodlit practice range; grass tees; chipping and putting areas.
Hotels: Hardwick Hall.

8B 48 Linden Hall

Linden Hall Hotel, Longhorsley, Morpeth, Northumberland, NE65 8XF
☎(01670) 788050
From A1 take A697 to Coldstream until reaching Longhorsley; course 1.5 miles on right.
Parkland course.
Pro David Curry; Founded 1997
Designed by J Gaunt
18 holes, 6809 yards, S.S.S. 73
Visitors: welcome with h'cap certs.
Green Fees: WD £22.50; WE £25.
Societies: welcome by prior arrangement; packages for golf and catering available; corporate days arranged; leisure club, gym in hotel; from £29.50.
Catering: grill room, conservatory and 2 bars.
Practice range, 8 bays.
Hotels: Linden Hall on site.

8B 49 Longhirst Hall

Longhirst Hall, Longhirst, Northumberland, NE61 3LL
☎(01670) 791505
From A1 take signs to Hebron Cockle Park; after 3 miles at T junction follow signs for Longhirst Hall; 7 miles S of Alnwick.
Parkland course.
Founded 1997
18 holes, 6572 yards, S.S.S. 72
Visitors: welcome.
Green Fees: WD £12; WE £16.
Societies: welcome by prior arrangement; packages include golf, catering and some can include accommodation; corporate days can be arranged; from £15.50.
Catering: full facilities in Morpeth Cricket, Hockey and Tennis club.
Hotels: Longhirst Hall on site.

8B 50 Magdalene Fields

Berwick-upon-Tweed, Northumberland TD15 1NE
☎(01289) 306384, Fax 306384, Sec 306130
5 miles from centre of town in direction of coast.
Seaside course with parkland fairways
18 holes, 6407 yards, S.S.S. 71
Visitors: welcome by prior arrangement.
Green Fees: WD £16; WE £18.
Societies: welcome WD; restrictions Sat and Sun; catering packages available; from £16.
Catering: bar and restaurant.
Hotels: Queen's Head, Berwick.

8B 51 Matfen Hall

Matfen Hall, Matfen, Northumberland, NE20 0RQ
☎(01661) 886500, Fax 886146, Pro 886146
Just off B6318 Military road 15 miles W of Newcastle.
Parkland course; 3rd hole is 663 yards.
Founded 1994
Designed by M James/A Mair
18 holes, 6744 yards, S.S.S. 72
Visitors: welcome.
Green Fees: WD £19; WE £25.
Societies: welcome by prior arrangement; golf and catering packages available; par 3 course; practice range; terms on application.
Catering: full bar and restaurant facilities.
Practice range.
Hotels: accommodation available at club from summer 1998; Beaumont, Hexham.

8B 52 Middlesbrough

Brass Castle Lane, Marton, Middlesbrough, TS8 9EE
☎(01642) 311515, Fax 319607, Pro 311766, Sec 316430
1 mile W of A172 5 miles S of Middlesbrough.
Parkland course.
Pro Don Jones; Founded 1908
Designed by James Braid
18 holes, 6215 yards, S.S.S. 69
Visitors: welcome except Tues and Sat.
Green Fees: WD £28; WE £34.
Societies: welcome by prior arrangement; packages of golf and catering available; terms on application.
Catering: full facilities; restaurant service available at 24 hrs notice.
Hotels: Marton Hotel & CC.

8B 53 Middlesbrough Municipal

Ladgate Lane, Middlesbrough, TS5 7YZ
☎(01642) 315533
Access from A19 via A174 to Acklam.
Undulating parkland course.
Founded 1977
Designed by Middlesbrough Borough Council
18 holes, 6333 yards, S.S.S. 70
Visitors: welcome but must arrange starting time.
Green Fees: WD £7.75; WE £9.75.
Societies: welcome by prior arrangement; terms on application.
Catering: catering available; lunches. Driving range.
Hotels: Blue Bell.

8B 54 Morpeth

The Common, Morpeth, NE61 2BT
☎(01670) 519980, Pro 515675, Sec 504942, Bar/Rest 504942
On A197 1 mile S of Morpeth.
Parkland course.
Pro Martin Jackson; Founded 1906
Designed by Harry Vardon (1922)
18 holes, 6104 yards, S.S.S. 70
Visitors: welcome by prior arrangement after 9.30am.
Green Fees: WD £20; WE £25.
Societies: welcome WD by prior arrangement with Sec; packages for golf and catering available; terms on application.
Catering: snacks, bar lunches, dinner available.
Hotels: Waterford Lodge; Queens Head; Linden Hall.

8B 55 Mount Oswald

Mount Oswald Manor, South Rd, Durham, Co Durham, DH1 3TQ
☎(0191) 3867527, Fax 3860975
On A1050 SW of Durham.
Partly wooded parkland course.
Founded 1924
18 holes, 6101 yards, S.S.S. 69
Visitors: welcome; after 10am Sun.
Green Fees: WD £10; WE £12.
Societies: welcome by prior arrangement; special rates for 12 or more; some WE available; function room for 80; other smaller private rooms; packages for golf and catering; from £17.
Catering: full clubhouse catering.
Hotels: Three Tuns.

8B 56 Newbiggin-by-the-Sea

Clubhouse, Newbiggin-by-the-Sea, Northumberland, NE64 6DW
☎(01670) 817344, Fax 520236, Pro 817833
Off A197 following signs for Newbiggin by the Sea from A189 from Newcastle.
Seaside links course.
Pro Richard Guest; Founded 1884
18 holes, 6452 yards, S.S.S. 71
Visitors: welcome after 10am except on comp days.
Green Fees: WD £14; WE £19.
Societies: welcome by prior arrangement with Sec; catering packages available; from £14.
Catering: full clubhouse facilities.
Hotels: Beachcomber.

8B 57 Newcastle United

Ponteland Rd, Cowgate, Newcastle-upon-Tyne, Northumberland, NE5 3JW
☎(0191) 286 4693, Pro 286 9998
1 mile W of the city centre.
Moorland course.
Founded 1892
18 holes, 6612 yards, S.S.S. 71
Visitors: welcome WD; not on WE comp days.
Green Fees: WD £15.50; WE £17.50.
Societies: welcome by arrangement; catering packages by arrangement; snooker; terms on application.
Catering: bar and snacks.
Practice ground.
Hotels: Gosforth Park.

8B 58 Northumberland

High Gosforth Park, Newcastle-upon-Tyne, Tyne and Wear, NE3 5HT
☎(0191) 2362498, Fax 2362498
Off A1 5 miles N of Newcastle.
Parkland course.
Founded 1898
Designed by Members
18 holes, 6629 yards, S.S.S. 72
Visitors: welcome by arrangement.
Green Fees: WD £35; WE £35.
Societies: very limited availability; terms on application.
Catering: full clubhouse catering.
Hotels: Swallow Gosforth Park.

8B 59 Norton Golf Course

Junction Rd, Stockton-on-Tees, Cleveland, TS20 1SU
☎(01642) 676385, Fax 608467, Sec 674636, Bar/Rest 612452
From A177 2miles N of Stockton roundabout.
Parkland course.
Founded 1989
Designed by T Harper
18 holes, 5855 yards, S.S.S. 71
Visitors: public pay and play.
Green Fees: WD £9; WE £10.
Societies: welcome by prior arrangement; packages available both for WD and WE; bookings must be made more than 7 days in advance; from £16.
Catering: full catering facilities.
Hotels: Swallow, Stockton.

8B 60 Oak Leaf Golf Complex (Aycliffe)

School Aycliffe Lane, Newton Aycliffe, Co Durham, DL 5 6QZ
☎(01325) 310820
Take A1 (M) to A68 and then turn into Newton Aycliffe; course on left.
Parkland course.
Pro Clive Burgess
18 holes, 5671 yards, S.S.S. 67
Visitors: welcome; no restrictions.
Green Fees: WD £7; WE £8.
Societies: welcome at off-peak times; minimum of 9 players; deposit required; sports and leisure complex; terms on application.
Catering: bar facilities at leisure complex.
Driving range.
Hotels: Redworth Arms, Redworth; Eden Arms; Gretna Hotel.

8B 61 Parklands Golf Club

High Gosforth Park, Newcastle-upon-Tyne, NE3 5HQ
☎(0191) 2364867, Pro 2364480, Sec 2364480, Bar/Rest 2364480
Off A1 3 miles N of Newcastle.
Parkland course.
Pro Brian Rumney; Founded 1971
18 holes, 6060 yards, S.S.S. 69
Visitors: welcome.
Green Fees: WD £15; WE £18.
Societies: welcome by prior arrangement; catering packages available; terms on application.
Catering: bar and restaurant facilities. Practice range, 45 bays floodlit; also 9-hole pitch and putt.
Hotels: Swallow Gosforth Park.

8B 62 Ponteland

53 Bell Villas, Ponteland, Newcastle-upon-Tyne, Tyne and Wear, NE20 9BD
☎(01661) 822689
On A696 2 miles N of Newcastle Airport.
Parkland course.
Pro Alan Robson-Crosby; Founded 1927
Designed by Harry Ferney
18 holes, 6524 yards, S.S.S. 71

Visitors: welcome Mon-Thurs; Fri, Sat, Sun as members' guest.
Green Fees: WD £22.50; WE £22.50.
Societies: welcome on Tues and Thurs; catering packages can be arranged; from £22.50.
Catering: full clubhouse facilities.

8B 63 **Prudhoe**
Eastwood Park, Prudhoe, Northumberland, NE42 5DX
☎(01661) 832466, Pro 836188
On A695 12 miles W of Newcastle.
Parkland course.
Pro John Crawford; Founded 1930
18 holes, 5862 yards, S.S.S. 68
Visitors: welcome except on competition days.
Green Fees: WD £20; WE £25.
Societies: welcome WD by arrangement; terms on application.
Catering: bar snacks and meals available.
Hotels: Beaumont, Hexham.

8B 64 **Ramside**
Ramside Hall, Carrville, Durham, DH1 1TD
☎(0191) 3865282, Fax 3860399, Sec 3869514
On A690 Sunderland road 400m from A1(M) junction 62.
Parkland course; 3 x 9 loops.
Pro Richard Lister; Founded 1996
Bishops Cathedral: 18 holes, 6183 yards, S.S.S. 69; Cathedral Princess: 18 holes, 6133 yards, S.S.S. 69; Prince Bishops: 18 holes, 6520 yards, S.S.S. 73
Visitors: welcome by prior arrangement.
Green Fees: WD £27; WE £33.
Societies: welcome by prior arrangement; full society and corporate packages available; terms on application.
Catering: full bar and restaurant facilities; hotel restaurant and bar also.
Practice range, 16-bay driving range; golf academy.
Hotels: Ramside Hall.

8B 65 **Ravensworth**
Moss Heaps, Wrekenton, Gateshead, Tyne & Wear, NE9 7UU
☎(0191) 4876014, Pro 4913475, Sec 4887549 Bar/Rest 4820211
Off A1 2 miles S of Gateshead.
Moorland/parkland course.
Pro Shaun Cowell; Founded 1906
18 holes, 5966 yards, S.S.S. 68
Visitors: welcome.
Green Fees: WD £17; WE £25.

Societies: welcome WD by prior arrangement; catering packages available except Mon; terms on application.
Catering: full clubhouse facilities. except Mon.
Hotels: Springfield.

8B 66 **Roseberry Grange**
Grange Villa, Chester-le-Street, Durham, DH2 3NF
☎(0191) 3700670, Pro 3700660, Sec 3702047
3 miles W of Chester-le-Street close to A1 (M) junction.
Parkland course.
Pro Alan Hartley; Founded 1987
18 holes, 6023 yards, S.S.S. 68
Visitors: welcome WD; by prior arrangement WE.
Green Fees: WD £10; WE £10.
Societies: welcome; terms on application.
Catering: full clubhouse facilities.
Hotels: Lumley Castle; Beamish Park.

8B 67 **Rothbury**
Old Race Course, Rothbury, Morpeth, Northumberland, NE65 7TR
☎(01669) 621271, Sec 620718
Off A697 at Weldon Bridge following the signs for Rothbury; 15 miles N of Morpeth.
Flat course alongside river.
Founded 1891
Designed by J B Radcliffe
9 holes, 5681 yards, S.S.S. 68
Visitors: welcome WD; restrictions at WE.
Green Fees: WD £11; WE £16.
Societies: welcome WD by arrangement; catering packages available during the day; by arrangement for evening meals; bar closed between 3pm-7.30pm; reductions for larger groups; from £11.
Catering: clubhouse facilities.
Hotels: Queens Head; Newcastle Hotel, both Rothbury.

8B 68 **Ryhope**
Leechmore Way, Ryhope, Sunderland, Durham, SR2 0DH
☎(0191) 523 7333, Sec 553 6373
Turn off the A19 at Ryhope village towards Hollycarrside.
Course being re-designed.
Founded 1991
Designed by Sunderland Borough Council
9 holes yards, S.S.S. 69
Visitors: welcome.
Green Fees: WD fees on application.

8B 69 **Ryton**
Dr Stanners, Clara Vale, Ryton, Tyne and Wear, NE40 3TD
☎(0191) 4133253, Fax 4131642, Sec 4133737, Bar/Rest 4133737
Off A695 signposted Crawcrook.
Parkland course.
Founded 1891
18 holes, 5950 yards, S.S.S. 69
Visitors: welcome WD; by prior arrangement WE.
Green Fees: WD £15; WE £20.
Societies: welcome; discounts for groups of more than 16; WE available; catering packages; from £12.
Catering: clubhouse facilities.
Hotels: Ryton County Club; Hedgefield; Marriott Gateshead.

8B 70 **Saltburn-by-the-Sea**
Hob Hill, Saltburn-by-Sea, Cleveland, TS12 1NJ
☎(01287) 622812, Pro 624653
On A1268 1 mile from Saltburn.
Parkland course.
Pro Mike Nutter; Founded 1894
18 holes, 5897 yards, S.S.S. 68
Visitors: welcome; restrictions Sun and Thurs; limited Sat.
Green Fees: WD £20; WE £25.
Societies: welcome by prior arrangement; catering available except Mon; terms on application.
Catering: full clubhouse facilities; limited Mon catering.
Hotels: Royal York.

8B 71 **Seaham**
Dawdon, Seaham, Co Durham, SR7 7RD
☎(0191) 5812345, Pro 5130837, Sec 5811268
2 miles NE of the A19.
Heathland course.
Pro Glyn Jones; Founded 1911
Designed by Dr A. MacKenzie
18 holes, 6017 yards, S.S.S. 69
Visitors: welcome.
Green Fees: WD £15; WE £18.
Societies: welcome; terms on application.
Catering: full clubhouse facilities.

8B 72 **Seahouses**
Beadnell Rd, Seahouses, Northumberland, NE68 7XT
☎(01665) 720794
On the B1340 S of Seahouses village.
Links course; upgraded to 18 holes in 1976.
Founded 1913/1976
18 holes, 5462 yards, S.S.S. 67

Visitors: welcome; groups of more than four must book in advance.
Green Fees: WD £16; WE £20.
Societies: welcome by prior arrangement everyday except Sun; packages for catering, golf and local hotels available; from £16.
Catering: full catering service except Tues when limited food is available; full bar in summer.
Hotels: Sunningdale; Beadnell Towers; Sportsman; Blue Bell, Belford.

8B 73 Seaton Carew

Tees Rd, Seaton Carew, Hartlepool, TS25 1DE
☎(01429) 266249, Fax 261040, Pro 890660, Sec 261040
Off A178 3 miles S of Hartlepool.
Championship links course.
Pro Bill Hector; Founded 1874
Designed by Duncan McCuaig
Old: 18 holes, 6613 yards, S.S.S. 72;
Brabazon: 18 holes, 6855 yards, S.S.S. 73
Visitors: welcome WD; WE restricted.
Green Fees: WD £29; WE £40.
Societies: welcome by prior arrangement; catering by arrangement; snooker; from £29.
Catering: full facilities.
Large practice ground.
Hotels: Seaton; Staincliffe Marine.

8B 74 Slaley Hall International Golf Resort

Slaley, Hexham, Northumberland, NE47 0BY
☎(01434) 673350, Fax 673152, Pro 673134
Just off A69; 23 miles from Newcastle.
Wooded, heath and parkland course; European Tour venue.
Pro Mark Stancer; Founded 1989
Designed by Dave Thomas
18 holes, 7021 yards, S.S.S. 74
Visitors: welcome WD by arrangement; hotel residents only at WE.
Green Fees: WD £50; WE £50.
Societies: welcome WD for groups of 9+ by arrangement with the golf office; residential groups may play WE; golf packages available through golf office; residential golf breaks from £110; customised golf days available; video analysis; corporate days; hotel has leisure facilities and spa; from £45.
Catering: full clubhouse and hotel facilities; cocktail bar; Fairways Brasserie; Imperial Restaurant.
Practice range, 8 covered bays opened April 1998.
Hotels: Slaley Hall.

8B 75 South Moor

The Middles, Craghead, Stanley, Co Durham, DH9 6AG
☎(01207) 232848, Fax 284616, Pro 283525, Sec 232848 x 101
Off A693 6 miles W of Chester-le-Street on B6532 1 mile S of Stanley.
Moorland course.
Pro Shaun Cowell; Founded 1923
Designed by Dr A. MacKenzie
18 holes, 6445 yards, S.S.S. 71
Visitors: welcome with h'cap certs or member of a golf club.
Green Fees: WD £15; WE £26.
Societies: welcome WD between 9.30am-11am and 2pm-3.30pm; WE between 10am-11am and 2pm-3.30pm; catering packages available; snooker table; from £15.
Catering: full clubhouse facilities.
Hotels: Lambton Arms; Lumley Castle; South Causey; Harperley Hotel.

8B 76 South Shields

Cleadon Hills, South Shields, Tyne and Wear, NE34 8EG
☎(0191) 4560475, Pro 4560110, Sec 4568942
Close to A19 and A1(M) near Cleadon Chimney.
Heathland links course.
Pro Gary Parsons; Founded 1893
Designed by McKenzie/Baird
18 holes, 6264 yards, S.S.S. 70
Visitors: welcome.
Green Fees: WD £20; WE £25.
Societies: welcome by prior arrangement; terms on application.
Catering: clubhouse catering and bar.
Hotels: Sea Hotel.

8B 77 Stocksfield

New Ridley, Stocksfield, Northumberland, NE43 7RE
☎(01661) 843041, Fax 843046
2 miles from Stocksfield on the New Ridley Road, off the A695 Hexham-Prudhoe Road.
Woodland/parkland course.
Pro S McKenna; Founded 1913/80
Designed by Frank Pennink
18 holes, 6013 yards, S.S.S. 70
Visitors: welcome except Wed and Sat.
Green Fees: WD £18; WE £24.
Societies: welcome by arrangement; special packages with or without catering for 18/27/36 holes available; some reductions for larger groups; from £18.
Catering: full clubhouse facilities.
Hotels: Beaumont, Hexham; Royal Derwent, Allensford.

8B 78 Stressholme Golf Centre

Snipe Lane, Darlington
☎(01325) 461002
2 mile N of Darlington.
Parkland course.
Pro M Watkins; D Paterson; Founded 1976
18 holes, 6229 yards, S.S.S. 69
Visitors: welcome.
Green Fees: WD £9; WE £11.
Societies: welcome by arrangement with professional; terms on application.
Catering: clubhouse facilities.
Practice range, 14 bays floodlit.
Hotels: Blackwell Grange.

8B 79 Swarland Hall

Coast View, Swarland, Morpeth, Northumberland, NE65 9JG
☎(01670) 787010, Bar/Rest 787940
1 mile W of A1 8 miles S of Alnwick.
Parkland course.
Pro David & Linzi Fletcher; Founded 1993
18 holes, 6628 yards, S.S.S. 68
Visitors: welcome.
Green Fees: WD £14; WE £18.
Societies: welcome; packages available for golf/catering; 10% discount for parties of more than 12; from £18.
Catering: full dining and bar facilities.
Practice area.

8B 80 Teesside

Acklam Rd, Thornaby, Stockton, Cleveland, TS17 7JS
☎(01642) 676249, Fax 676252, Pro 673822, Sec 616516
Off A1130 Thornaby-Acklam Road.
Parkland course.
Pro Ken Hall; Founded 1901
18 holes, 6535 yards, S.S.S. 71
Visitors: welcome by arrangement; before 4.30pm WD after 11.30am WE.
Green Fees: WD £26; WE £26.
Societies: welcome WD by prior arrangement; minimum group 10, max 35; from £20.
Catering: full clubhouse facilities.
Hotels: Swallow, Stockton; Golden Eagle, Thornaby.

8B 81 Tynedale

Tyne Green, Hexham, Northumberland, NE46 3HQ
☎(01434) 608154
From A69 Hexham road turn into Countryside Park; course 0.5 miles on S of river Tyne.
Parkland course.
Pro Claire Brown; Founded 1907
9 holes, 5403 yards, S.S.S. 67

Seaton Carew

One of the great joys of golf in the West of Ireland is the feeling of spaciousness and the fact that the views from the links are dominated by natural beauty. For those who never venture further from Donegal than Rosses Point, it might be thought such beauty is an integral part of all courses but one of the game's great strengths is the number of contrasting settings in which it is played. It strikes me therefore that the citizens of Hartlepool are every bit as ardent in counting their blessings over Seaton Carew as the Irish are in their admiration for Tralee or Lahinch.

Modern Seaton Carew is set in surroundings of industrial chimneys and chemical production plants but that has never been, and never will be, a deterrent to golfers. It is something to which you get used in the same way that, by the end of a round at Royal Mid-Surrey, you never notice the aeroplanes or, at West Hill, the trains.

Courses are judged by the challenge and enjoyment they provide and both are high on the list at Seaton Carew whose distinction is heightened by being one of the few outstanding links on the seaboard of eastern England. Its championship qualities have been recognised by the staging of the English Amateur strokeplay and Brit-ish Boys' championships, events that enhanced the courses' admirable and deserved reputation.

Nevertheless, one view from the course is of the swings and roundabouts of the amusement park, a reminder that Seaton Carew's attractions are not all confined to golf. All the same, Seaton Carew, founded in 1874 as the Durham and Yorkshire GC, is the oldest in either county and its seniority undoubtedly adds to its eminence.

The current course is one of 22 holes, a convenient method of giving members playing options rather than an attempt to set new fashions, although the Old Course at St Andrews started as 22 holes. Some prefer the Old course, which plays more or less out and back, although with more variation in direction than on many seaside links but Frank Pennink's design of four new holes gave rise to the championship version of the course which makes it significantly more formidable.

An opening hole named "Rocket" calls to mind that Seaton Carew is very much in railway country but the tempo rises with the long second and the short third which turns back towards the clubhouse. The short sixth also follows the line of the third but the new 10th is the only hole that runs east, a timely signal that the flavour of the golf gains a piquant touch as it nears the sea.

The 10th is a straight par four but the dogleg 11th leads on to another fine par four, aptly named "Beach" on account of its proximity to the fence guarding the shore. By now, the sea buckthorn has begun to dominate and the 13th and 14th, both par fives, are flanked on the right by a hazard that is statistically punishing and physically painful.

There is relief from it at the 208-yard 15th, but there is no escaping the buckthorn on the last three holes which constitute quite a finish. It is particularly easy to become engulfed by it on the right of the 18th, a hole with an unusually contoured fairway but the most renowned hole is the 17th, its title of "Snag" carrying more than a hint of understatement.

It is the second shot, and more especially the distinctive green, which makes demands on our cunning although the drive can become entangled with the same central spine of hillocks encountered on the way out; and the drive can err a little too safely the other way. However, the correct angle for the second shot is essential to hold a green shaped like a scallop shell, bunkered all around and contoured ingeniously on several levels. It wouldn't do if all greens presented such problems but golf would be duller without its teasers and the 17th green at Seaton Carew is as notable an instrument of torture as man can devise.

Visitors: welcome; except before 11am Sun.
Green Fees: WD £10; WE £10.
Societies: welcome by prior arrangement; discounts for groups of more than 10; from £10.
Catering: full clubhouse facilities.
Hotels: Beaumont; County; Royal.

8B 82 Tynemouth

Spital Dene, Tynemouth, North Shields, Tyne & Wear, NE30 2ER
☎(0191) 2574578, Sec 2573381
On A695.
Parkland course.
Pro John McKenna; Founded 1913
Designed by Willie Park
18 holes, 6332 yards, S.S.S. 71
Visitors: welcome WD after 9.30am; after 12.30pm Sun; limited Sat.
Green Fees: WD £15; WE £15.
Societies: welcome WD by prior arrangement; catering packages available; terms on application.
Catering: lunches, teas and snacks available.
Hotels: Park.

8B 83 Tyneside

Westfield Lane, Ryton, Tyne & Wear, NE40 3QE
☎(0191) 4132177, Fax 4132742, Pro 4131600, Sec 4132742, Bar/Rest 4138357
7 miles W of Newcastle off A695 S of river.
Parkland course.
Pro Malcolm Gunn; Founded 1879
Designed by H.S. Colt (1910)
18 holes, 6033 yards, S.S.S. 69
Visitors: welcome.
Green Fees: WD £20; WE £30.
Societies: welcome by prior arrangement; reductions for groups of 18 or more; catering packages available; from £16.
Catering: full clubhouse catering and bar facilities.
Large practice area.
Hotels: Ryton Park; Hedgefield Inn; Copthorne, Newcastle; Marriott, Gateshead; Ravensdene, Gateshead.

8B 84 Wallsend

Bigges Main, Wallsend-on-Tyne, Northumberland, NE28 8SU
☎(0191) 2621973, Pro 2624231
E of Newcastle on coast road to Whitley Bay.
Parkland course.
Pro Ken Phillips; Founded 1905
18 holes, 6606 yards, S.S.S. 72

Visitors: welcome except before 12.30pm WE.
Green Fees: WD £12.50; WE £14.50.
Societies: welcome by prior written arrangement; WD only; terms on application.
Catering: hot and cold snacks available.
Hotels: Stakis.

8B 85 Warkworth

The Links, Warkworth, Morpeth, Northumberland, NE65 0SW
☎(01665) 711596, Sec 711556
Off A1068 at Warkworth; 10 miles N of Morpeth.
Seaside links course.
Founded 1891
Designed by Tom Morris
9 holes, 5870 yards, S.S.S. 68
Visitors: welcome except Tues and Sat.
Green Fees: WD £12; WE £20.
Societies: welcome by prior arrangement with secretary, J A Gray; catering packages available by arrangement with the stewardess; from £12.
Catering: bar and catering facilities in season; by arrangement in winter.
Practice area.
Hotels: Warkworth House; Sun.

8B 86 Wearside

Coxgreen, Sunderland, Tyne & Wear, SR4 9JT
☎(0191) 5342518, Fax 5342518, Pro 5344269
Off A183 towards Chester-le-Street; turn right signposted Coxgreen to T junction; turn left.
Meadowland/parkland course.
Pro Doug Brolls; Founded 1892
18 holes, 6373 yards, S.S.S. 70
Visitors: welcome except on comp days.
Green Fees: WD £25; WE £32.
Societies: welcome on application to Sec; catering packages available; from £25.
Catering: full clubhouse facilities.
Practice range, also 4-hole par 3 practice course.
Hotels: Seaburn.

8B 87 Westerhope

Whorlton Grange, Westerhope, Newcastle-upon-Tyne, NE5 1PP
☎(0191) 2867636, Pro 2860594, Bar/Rest 2869125
On the B6324 5 miles W of Newcastle; close to the Jingling Gate PH.
Wooded parkland course.

Pro N Brown; Founded 1941
Designed by Alexander Sandy Herd
18 holes, 6444 yards, S.S.S. 71
Visitors: welcome.
Green Fees: WD £18; WE £18.
Societies: welcome by prior arrangement; catering packages available; from £18.
Catering: full clubhouse facilities.
Hotels: Airport Moat House; Holiday Inn; Novotel, all Newcastle.

8B 88 Whickham

Hollinside Park, Whickham, Newcastle-upon-Tyne, Tyne & Wear, NE16 5BA
☎(091) 4887309, Fax 4881576, Pro 4888591, Sec 4881576
Off A1 at Whickham; follow signs for Burnopfield, club 1.3 miles.
Parkland course.
Pro Graeme Lisle; Founded 1911
18 holes, 5878 yards, S.S.S. 68
Visitors: welcome.
Green Fees: WD £20; WE £25.
Societies: welcome WD by prior arrangement with Sec; discounts for larger groups; catering packages available; from £14.
Catering: full catering facilities.
Hotels: Gibside Arms, Whickham; Beamish Park; County; Copthorne; Derwent Crossing, all Newcastle.

8B 89 Whitburn

Lizard Lane, South Shields, Tyne & Wear, NE34 7AF
☎(0191) 5292144, Pro 5294210, Sec 5294944
Off coast road mid-way between Sunderland and South Shields.
Parkland course.
Pro David Stephenson; Founded 1932
18 holes, 5900 yards, S.S.S. 69
Visitors: welcome WD; by prior arrangement WE.
Green Fees: WD £18; WE £23.
Societies: welcome WD by prior arrangement; restrictions WE; limited availability WE; discounts for groups of 11 or more; catering packages available by prior arrangement; from £18.
Catering: full clubhouse facilities.
Hotels: Seaburn; Roker.

8B 90 Whitley Bay

Claremont Rd, Whitley Bay, Tyne & Wear, NE26 3UF
☎(0191) 2520180, Fax 2970030, Pro 2525688
N of Town centre.
Simulated links course.

Pro Gary Shipley; Founded 1890
18 holes, 6529 yards, S.S.S. 71
Visitors: welcome WD.
Green Fees: WD £22.
Societies: welcome by prior arrangement; discounts available for larger groups; catering packages available; from £30.
Catering: clubhouse catering facilities.
Hotels: The Grand, Tynemouth; Park; Windsor, both Whitley Bay; Stakis Wallsend.

8B 91 **Wilton**

Wilton, Redcar, Cleveland, TS10 4QY
☎(01642) 465265, Pro 452730
Off A174 Whitby-Redcar road through Lazenby following signs for Wilton Castle.
Parkland course.
Pro Pat Smillie; Founded 1954/66
18 holes, 6145 yards, S.S.S. 69
Visitors: welcome with h'cap certs.
Green Fees: WD £18; WE £24.
Societies: welcome WD except Tues; some Sun by prior arrangement; discounts of £2 for groups of more than 20; Sun £24; catering packages available by arrangement from £7.95-£11.95; from £18.
Catering: full clubhouse facilities.
Hotels: Post House, Thornaby; Marton Way; Blue Bell, both Middlesbrough.

8B 92 **Woodham Golf & Country Club**

Burnhill Way, Newton Aycliffe, Durham, DL5 4PN
☎(01325) 320574, Fax 315254, Pro 315257, Bar/Rest 301551
Off the A167 to Woodham village in Newton Aycliffe.
Parkland course.
Pro Ernie Wilson; Founded 1983
Designed by J. Hamilton Stutt
18 holes, 6771 yards, S.S.S. 72
Visitors: welcome by prior arrangement.
Green Fees: WD £20; WE £24.
Societies: welcome by prior arrangement; some WE available; minimum 12 players; catering packages by arrangement; buggy hire available; practice area; from £15.
Catering: full bar and restaurant facilities.
Practice ground.
Hotels: Eden Arms, Rushyford.

8B 93 **Wooler**

Dod Law, Doddington, Wooler, Northumberland, NE71 6EA
☎(01668) 281791
E of B6525 Wooler-Berwick road; signposted from Doddington village.
Moorland course.
Founded 1976
Designed by Club Members

9 holes, 6372 yards, S.S.S. 70
Visitors: welcome.
Green Fees: WD £10; WE £15.
Societies: welcome by prior arrangement with Sec; catering can be arranged; terms on application.
Catering: bar and catering facilities available.
Hotels: Wheatsheaf; Black Bull; Ryecroft; Tankervill Arms.

8B 94 **Wynyard (The Wellington)**

Wynyard Park, Billingham, TS22 5NQ
☎(01740) 644399, Fax 644592
On A689 at Wynyard Park between A1 and A19.
Parkland course with mature woodlands; extension in 1998.
Founded 1996
Designed by Hawtree & Son
18 holes, 7100 yards, S.S.S. 73
Visitors: members' guests only.
Green Fees: terms on application.
Societies: corporate days only; full corporate golf day organisation and packages available; terms on application.
Catering: full restaurant and bar facilities.
Floodlit driving range; practice ground; short game academy areas.
Hotels: club can supply a list of local hotels.

SCOTLAND

The Borders and south of Scotland are particularly blessed with fine courses. You could stay for a week and play a different East Lothian course of championship standard each day without having to drive for more than twenty minutes. Luffness is enchanting, neither stern nor straightforward, but Gullane Hill is a dominant feature of all three Gullane courses, hiding the road from the holes bordering the Firth of Forth and a series of resplendent views.

On the other side of Gullane Hill lies Muirfield, the third home of the Honourable Company of Edinburgh Golfers and invariably placed top in polls on British courses. It has no enemies, a noble combination of ancient and modern that never disappoints.

Strathclyde casts a comprehensive net over the golfing scene as well as providing more than its share of Britain's great courses. It encompasses the remote outposts of Machrie and Machrihanish, the whole of the area around Glasgow and the veritable treasure trove of Ayrshire.

Prime among its southern defences is Turnberry, one of the world's most spectacular settings for golf. There are few more stirring stretches than that between the short fourth and the short 11th on the Ailsa course, a testing clutch of holes graduating from the relative shelter of the dunes to the rugged, rocky promontory alongside the lighthouse.

Together, the Ailsa and its sister Arran course comprise a wonderful day's golf, a comment pretty commonplace in Ayrshire. Old Prestwick , Royal Troon, Western Gailes, Glasgow Gailes and Prestwick St Nicholas provide a wonderfully rich assortment.

St Andrews, Carnoustie, Gleneagles and Blairgowrie comprise a vivid cross section of the many varied attractions that bring golfers by the thousand to Tayside, Fife and central Scotland every year. Fife itself, quite apart from St Andrews, is as full of good things as a Christmas hamper, the magic carpet ride concentrating on the coastal sweep past Kirkcaldy to the lovely Balcomie links at Crail and then on to the shores of St Andrews Bay.

Downfield is the finest of the courses in the vicinity of Dundee but, by now, sights are set on Carnoustie although not at the cost of by-passing Monifieth or Panmure at Barry which overlap on either side of the Aberdeen railway line. Carnoustie's absence from the Open championship rota since 1975 will happily end in 1999, a decision greeted with acclaim far beyond the Angus coast.

For overseas visitors who tend to prefer inland golf, Gleneagles is still an automatic favourite with its Jack Nicklaus creation, The Monarch. Almost as popular is Blairgowrie at Rosemount in a setting almost as glorious.

In the Highlands and Grampian region by far the fastest and most convenient road to Inverness is the much improved A9 which has no sooner bade farewell to Perth than it has, it seems, found Aviemore beckoning. But the ardent connoisseur will undoubtedly opt for the east coast route starting in Aberdeen and working north round Buchan Ness and then west along the Moray Firth to Inverness. It will, in fact, be hard getting away from Aberdeen after acquaintance with Royal Aberdeen with its valleyed fairways between dunes and an awareness that the Club, founded in 1780, is one of the oldest in the world. A few miles to the north, Cruden Bay represents the model links with mountainous dunes and resplendent views worthy of comparison alongside Turnberry, Tralee and Pebble Beach. Many good things lie ahead, notably Peterhead, Fraserburgh, the Moray Club at Lossiemouth and Nairn, once known freely as the Brighton of the North.

Nairn lies close to Inverness Airport, providing easier access from London for those whose sights are set on Dornoch and Skibo. Nor are those two the end of the northern rainbow. Brora, where the insomniac golfer can play in the famous midnight competition in June, provides the perfect foil for anyone seeking relief from trying to tame Dornoch. Even true lovers of art cannot look at one masterpiece all the time.

9A 1 Baberton
Baberton Ave, Juniper Green,
Edinburgh, EH14 5DU
☎(0131) 4534911, Pro 4533555,
Bar/Rest 4533361
On A70 5 miles W of central
Edinburgh.
Parkland course.
Pro Ken Kelly; Founded 1893
Designed by Willie Park
18 holes, 6123 yards, S.S.S. 70
Visitors: welcome by prior arrange-
ment with the secretary.
Green Fees: WD £18.50; WE £28.50.
Societies: welcome by prior arrange-
ment; catering packages available;
from £18.50.
Catering: full clubhouse facilities.
Hotels: Braid Hills, Edinburgh.

9A 2 Bathgate
Edinburgh Rd, Bathgate, W Lothian
EH48 1BA
☎(01506) 630505, Fax 636775, Pro
630553, Bar/Rest 652232
5 mins E of town centre and station.
Parkland course.
Pro S Strachan; Founded 1892
Designed by Willie Park
18 holes, 6250 yards, S.S.S. 70
Visitors: welcome.
Green Fees: WD £15; WE £30.
Societies: welcome by prior arrange-
ment; full day's catering package
£8.50; priced from £20.
Catering: full clubhouse facilities.
Hotels: Hillcroft; Dreadnought; Kaim
Park; Hilton, Livingston.

9A 3 Braid Hills
Braid Hills Approach Rd, Edinburgh,
EH10 6JY
☎(0131) 4529408, Pro 447 6666, Sec
4452044
On A702 S from City centre.
Hillside course with panoramic views.
Founded 1897
18 holes, 5731 yards, S.S.S. 68
Visitors: welcome.
Green Fees: WD £8; WE £8.
Societies: welcome by prior arrange-
ment; in summer two courses (other
4832 yards, S.S.S. 64); in winter amal-
gamate as one; from £8.
Catering: clubhouse facilities.
Hotels: Braid Hills.

9A 4 Broomieknowe
36 Golf Course Rd, Bonnyrigg,
Midlothian EH19 2HZ
☎(0131) 6639317, Fax 6632152, Pro
6602035, Bar/Rest 6637844

Off A7 at Eskbank Rd roundabout 0.5
miles from Bonnyrigg.
Parkland course.
Pro Mark Patchett; Founded 1906
Designed by James Braid; Alterations
by Hawtree/Ben Sayer
18 holes, 6150 yards, S.S.S. 69
Visitors: welcome.
Green Fees: WD £17; WE £20.
Societies: welcome WD by prior
arrangement; day tickets available for
£25; catering available; from £17.
Catering: clubhouse facilities.
Hotels: Dalhousie Castle.

9A 5 Bruntsfield Links
32 Barnton Ave, Davidsons Mains,
Edinburgh EH4 6JH
☎(0131) 3362006, Fax 3365538, Pro
3364050, Sec 3361479
Off A90 Forth Bridge road 3 miles NW
of Edinburgh city centre; 6 miles from
the airport
Mature parkland with stunning views
Pro Brian Mackenzie; Founded
1761/1898
Designed by Willie Park/ Mackenzie
(22)/ Hawtree (74)
18 holes, 6407 yards, S.S.S. 71
Visitors: welcome by prior arrangement with Secretary or Pro.
Green Fees: WD £36; WE £42.
Societies: welcome by prior written
arrangement; packages available for
lunch, high tea and dinner in the club's
magnificent dining room; jacket and tie
required in clubhouse; from £36.
Catering: full catering and bar.
Hotels: many in the Edinburgh area.

9A 6 Carrickknowe
Glendevon Park, Edinburgh, EH12
5VZ
☎(0131) 3371096
Opposite the Post House Hotel on
Balgreen Road.
Parkland course.
Founded 1933
18 holes, 6166 yards, S.S.S. 70
Visitors: welcome.
Green Fees: WD £7.95; WE £7.95.
Societies: welcome; golf only; £7.95.
Catering: no catering facilities.

9A 7 Castle Douglas
Abercromby Rd, Castle Douglas,
Dumfries & Galloway, DG7 1BA
☎(01556) 502801, Sec 502099
On A713 towards Ayr 400 yards from
the town clock.
Parkland course.
Founded 1905

9 holes, 5408 yards, S.S.S. 66
Visitors: welcome.
Green Fees: WD £12; WE £14.
Societies: welcome; bar meals can be
arranged; from £12.
Catering: bar and bar meals avail-
able.
Hotels: Kings Arms; Imperial; Douglas
Arms.

9A 8 Cogarburn
Hanley Lodge, Newbridge, Midlothian
EH28 8NN
☎(0131) 333 4110, Sec 333 4718,
Bar/Rest 3334110
Close to Edinburgh Airport sliproad off
A8 Glasgow Road.
Parkland course.
Founded 1975
12 holes, 5070 yards, S.S.S. 65
Visitors: welcome but not after 5pm
WD.
Green Fees: WD £10; WE £10.
Societies: welcome by prior arrange-
ment with Sec; catering can be
arranged in new clubhouse; pool table;
from £10.
Catering: full catering and bar facili-
ties.
Hotels: Barnton; Royal Scot.

9A 9 Colvend
Sandyhills, by Dalbeattie, Dumfries &
Galloway DG5 4PY
☎(01556) 630398, Sec 610878
On A710 Solway coast road 6 miles
from Dalbeattie.
Parkland course.
Founded 1905
Designed by Willie Fernie 1905; D
Thomas (1985); J Soutar extension to
18 (1997)
18 holes, 5220 yards, S.S.S. 67
Visitors: welcome.
Green Fees: WD £15; WE £15.
Societies: welcome by prior arrange-
ment; tee reservations require £5 per
head deposit; concession of £2 for
groups of 10 or more; catering pack-
ages available; from £15.
Catering: full catering and bar.
Hotels: Cairngill; Clonyard; Baron's
Craig; Pheasant.

9A 10 Craigentinny
143 Craigentinny Ave, Edinburgh
☎(0131) 556 7501, Sec 657 4815
1 mile from Meadowbank Stadium.
Links course.
Founded 1891
18 holes, 5413 yards, S.S.S. 66
Visitors: public links course.

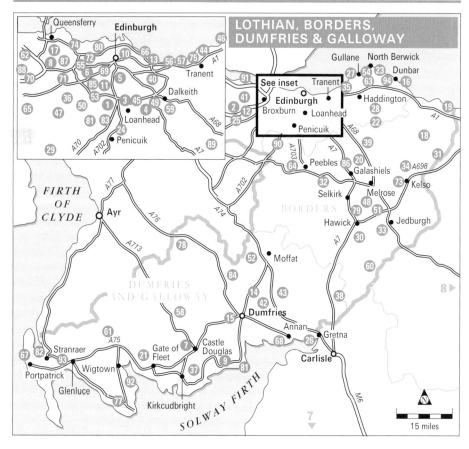

Green Fees: WD £8; WE £8.
Societies: welcome by prior arrangement with Council; on application.
Catering: by prior arrangement.

9A 11 **Craigmillar Park**

1 Observatory Rd, Edinburgh EH9 3HG
☎(0131) 6672499, Pro 6672850, Sec 6670047, Bar/Rest 6672837
From A68 Princes Street turn right at Cameron Toll; course 100yds on right.
Parkland course.
Pro Brian McGhee; Founded 1906
Designed by James Braid
18 holes, 5851 yards, S.S.S. 69
Visitors: welcome WD.
Green Fees: WD £17.50.
Societies: welcome WD by prior arrangement with Sec; separate facilities; catering packages available; from £17.50.
Catering: full catering facilities.
Hotels: Iona Hotel, Edinburgh.

9A 12 **Deer Park Golf & Country Club**

Golf Course Rd, Knightsbridge, Livingston, West Lothian EH54 8PG
☎(01506) 431037, Fax 435608
Leave M8 at junction 3 and follow signs to Knightsbridge; club is signposted.
Parkland course.
Founded 1978
Designed by Charles Lawrie
18 holes, 6677 yards, S.S.S. 72
Visitors: welcome.
Green Fees: WD £17; WE £28.
Societies: welcome by prior arrangement both WD and WE; catering packages available; swimming pool; snooker; squash; sauna; leisure club; from £17.
Catering: full clubhouse and country club facilities.
Hotels: Deer Park; Houston House; Hilton.

9A 13 **Duddingston**

Duddingston Rd West, Edinburgh EH15 3QD
☎(0131) 6611005, Fax 6614301, Pro 6614301, Sec 6617688
2 miles from city centre near A1 turning right at Duddingston crossroads.
Parkland course.
Pro Alastair McLean; Founded 1895
Designed by Willie Park Jnr
18 holes, 6420 yards, S.S.S. 72
Visitors: welcome WD.
Green Fees: WD £27.
Societies: welcome Tues and Thurs by prior arrangement; catering packages can be arranged; from £23.
Catering: full clubhouse facilities.
Hotels: many in Edinburgh.

9A 14 **Dumfries & County**

Edinburgh Rd, Dumfries, Dumfries & Galloway, DG1 1JX
☎(01387) 253585, Pro 268918

KEY		32	Innerleithen	63	North Berwick
1	Baberton	33	Jedburgh	64	Peebles
2	Bathgate	34	Kelso	65	Polkemmet Country Park
3	Braid Hills	35	Kilspindie	66	Portobello
4	Broomieknowe	36	Kingsknowe	67	Portpatrick (Dunskey)
5	Bruntsfield Links	37	Kirkcudbright	68	Powfoot
6	Carrickknowe	38	Langholm	69	Prestonfield
7	Castle Douglas	39	Lauder	70	Pumpherston
8	Cogarburn	40	Liberton	71	Ratho Park
9	Colvend	41	Linlithgow	72	Ravelston
10	Craigentinny	42	Lochmaben	73	The Roxburghe
11	Craigmillar Park	43	Lockerbie	74	Royal Burgess Golfing
12	Deer Park Golf &	44	Longniddry		Society of Edinburgh
	Country Club	45	Lothianburn	75	Royal Musselburgh
13	Duddingston	46	Luffness New	76	St Boswells
14	Dumfries & County	47	Marriott Dalmahoy	77	St Medan
15	Dumfries & Galloway	48	Melrose	78	Sanquhar
16	Dunbar	49	Melville	79	Selkirk
17	Dundas Park	50	Merchants of Edinburgh	80	Silverknowes
18	Duns	51	Minto	81	Southerness
19	Eyemouth	52	Moffat	82	Stranraer
20	Galashiels	53	Mortonhall	83	Swanston
21	Gatehouse-of-Fleet	54	Muirfield – Honourable	84	Thornhill
22	Gifford Golf Club		Company of Edinburgh	85	Torphin Hill
23	Glen		Golfers	86	Torwoodlee
24	Glencorse	55	Murrayfield	87	Turnhouse
25	Greenburn	56	Musselburgh	88	Uphall
26	Gretna	57	Musselburgh Old Course	89	Vogrie
27	Gullane	58	New Galloway	90	West Linton
28	Haddington	59	Newbattle	91	West Lothian
29	Harburn	60	Newcastleton	92	Wigtown & Bladnoch
30	Hawick	61	Newton Stewart	93	Wigtownshire County
31	Hirsel	62	Niddry Castle	94	Winterfield

On A701 Moffat to Edinburgh road 1 mile NE of town centre.
Parkland course; The Wee yin: 90 yards, 14th
Pro Stuart Syme; Founded 1912
Designed by James Braid
18 holes, 5928 yards, S.S.S. 68
Visitors: welcome WD between 9.30am-11am; 2pm-3.30pm; WE not Saturday; Sunday after 10am.
Green Fees: WD £23; WE £26.
Societies: welcome by prior arrangement with Sec; separate facilities; catering packages available; from £23.
Catering: club bar and dining room.
Hotels: Cairndale; Station; Moreig; Balmoral; Edenbank.

9A 15 **Dumfries & Galloway**
Laurieston Ave, Dumfries, Dumfries & Galloway DG2 7NY
☎(01387) 253582, Fax 270297, Pro 256902, Sec 263848
On A75 W of Dumfries.
Parkland course.
Pro Joe Fergusson; Founded 1880
18 holes, 5803 yards, S.S.S. 68
Visitors: welcome except comp days; prior booking essential in summer.
Green Fees: WD £25; WE £30.
Societies: welcome by prior arrangement; catering packages available except Mon; from £25.

Catering: full facilities available; except Mon.
Hotels: Cairndale; Station.

9A 16 **Dunbar**
East Links, Dunbar, E Lothian EH42 1LT
☎(01368) 862317, Fax 865202, Pro 862086
0.5 miles E of Dunbar; 30 miles E of Edinburgh off A1.
Links course.
Pro Derek Small; Founded 1794/1856
Designed by Tom Morris
18 holes, 6426 yards, S.S.S. 71
Visitors: welcome WD by prior arrangement 9.30am-12.30pm & 2pm onwards except Thurs; WE 9.30am-12 noon and after 2pm.
Green Fees: WD £30; WE £40.
Societies: welcome by prior arrangement WD; catering packages available; from £30.
Catering: full clubhouse facilities.
Hotels: Cruachan GH; Royal Mackintosh.

9A 17 **Dundas Park**
Dundas Estate, South Queensferry, W Lothian EH30 9SP
☎(0131) 331 5603
1 mile S of S Queensferry on A8000.

Parkland course.
Founded 1957
9 holes, 6024 yards, S.S.S. 69
Visitors: welcome by arrangement.
Green Fees: WD £8; WE £8.
Societies: welcome by prior arrangement; terms on application.
Catering: snacks in clubhouse.
Practice range.

9A 18 **Duns**
Hardens Rd, Duns, Berwickshire TD11 3HN
☎(01361) 882194, Sec 882717
1 mile W of Duns off A6105 Greenlaw-Duns road, taking junction signposted Longformacus.
Parkland/upland course.
Founded 1894/1921
Designed by A H Scott
18 holes, 6209 yards, S.S.S. 70
Visitors: welcome.
Green Fees: WD £12; WE £12.
Societies: welcome by prior arrangement with Sec; some WE tee-times available; all day golf; limited clubhouse facilities but snack meals can be arranged April-October; from £15.
Catering: snacks and bar in clubhouse during summer.
Hotels: Barniken House.

9A 19 **Eyemouth**
Gunsgreen House, Eyemouth TD14 5DY
☎(01890) 750551, Pro 750004
On A1107 off A1 2.5 miles E of Burmouth.
Seaside course.
Pro Paul Terras; Founded 1884/1996
18 holes, 6472 yards, S.S.S. 66
Visitors: welcome except before 10.30am on Sat; severe restrictions on Sun.
Green Fees: WD £10; WE £10.
Societies: welcome by prior arrangement; catering packages available; pool table; arts; from £10.
Catering: full bar and catering service every day.
Hotels: Home Arms; Contented Sole; Ship; Dolphin.

9A 20 **Galashiels**
Ladhope Recreation Ground, Galashiels, Selkirkshire TD1 2NJ
☎(01896) 753724
On A7 to Edinburgh 0.5 miles N of town centre.
Hilly parkland course.
Founded 1883
Designed by James Braid

East of Scotland

One of the debates in which golfers love to indulge is comparison of the merit of courses which are near neighbours. A sample list might include Hunstanton and Brancaster, Sandwich and Deal, Portush and County Down, Troon and Prestwick, Woking and Worplesdon, Ferndown and Parkstone, Formby and Birkdale, Lahinch and Ballybunion. On a broader canvas, regions also come under the microscope for dissection, not least a comparison between the East and West of Scotland, but one fact to emerge from every debate is that golf in Britain and Ireland is part of a glittering tapestry that no other country can approach. We enjoy a feast of riches.

When people talk about a centre for golfing holidays, Gullane is the first that comes to mind. Within easy reach are Dunbar, North Berwick, Muirfield, Longniddry, Kilspindie and, on the doorstep, Gullane's three beautiful links as well as Luffness. Much is made these days of golf's effect on the environment but Aberlady Bay is a rare bird sanctuary with which golf blends so sympathetically that Gullane and Luffness should be hailed as a model of the harmony that exists with nature.

There is no more natural piece of golfing terrain in the world, a monument to the school of architecture that takes what it finds and leaves well alone. The wind magnifies the defences of a landscape with never a tree to be seen but enjoyment of the surroundings casts an hypnotic spell, diverting the mind from the task in hand. From the firm, sand-based turf, clean striking is essential. Computerised programming, everything measured and predictable, forms no part of golf at the seaside. It is an exercise in improvisation and ingenuity, flighting the ball low to cheat the wind and hold greens with the minimum of give to them.

Rough, bunkers and splendidly rolling ground are the other hazards, although Gullane Hill itself is a prominent feature that gives rise to some spectacularly elevated tees and inviting downhill drives. North Berwick, for the most part, is flat although never dull. It is different, joyously different, a link with history yet enjoying a modern relevance that is enduringly strong. There is a basic simplicity about the look of courses in East Lothian, no mounds or lakes, but looks are deceptive if there is any suggestion that they are straightforward.

North Berwick hugs the coast, similar in shape to the Old course at St Andrews except that the shepherd's crook is reversed, as it were. One rare feature surrounds the stone walls off which many a ball has ricocheted but the best compliment to North Berwick is provided by the countless attempts to reproduce the shaping of some of the greens, notably Redan and Perfection, but the copies are nothing when set against the real thing. Identifying the holes by their names is another pleasant habit that has gone out of fashion but everywhere there are reminders of golf at its best.

If Gullane and North Berwick are the appetising pieces of bread, so to speak, Muirfield is the succulent meat in the geographical sandwich, lying under the lee of Gullane Hill and coming close to rubbing shoulders with North Berwick at the extreme end of the land owned by the Honourable Company of Edinburgh Golfers. Muirfield has many admirers, few, if any, detractors. It is fair and honest but with an ample sprinkling of delightfully challenging shots and no recourse to water or artificially constructed hazards. They belong to a world from which East Lothian is mercifully far distant.

18 holes, 5185 yards, S.S.S. 67
Visitors: welcome.
Green Fees: WD £10; WE £14.
Societies: welcome by prior arrangement with Sec; package deals available; terms on application.
Catering: full clubhouse facilities.
Hotels: Abbotsford Arms; Kingsknowes; Kings.

9A 21 **Gatehouse-of-Fleet**

Laurieston Rd, Gatehouse-of-Fleet
☎(01557) 814766, Sec 450260, Bar/Rest 814459
From A75 into Gatehouse-of-Fleet follow signs for Laurieston; course 0.5 miles.
Parkland course with stunning views.
Founded 1921
9 holes, 5042 yards, S.S.S. 64
Visitors: welcome.
Green Fees: WD £10; WE £10.
Societies: welcome by prior arrangement; local hotels can provide catering arrangements; terms on application.
Catering: none at course.
Hotels: Masonic Arms; Murray Arms.

9A 22 **Gifford Golf Club**

Edinburgh Road, Gifford, E Lothian
EH41 4QN
☎(01620) 810267, Fax 810267
On A1 4 miles from the market town of Haddington.
Undulating parkland course in Lammermuir foothills.
Founded 1904
Designed by Willie Watt
9 holes, 6255 yards, S.S.S. 70
Visitors: welcome.
Green Fees: WD £10; WE £10.
Societies: welcome; discounts for larger groups; from £10.
Catering: full facilities at village hotels; clubhouse.
Hotels: Goblin Ha'; Tweeddale Arms.

9A 23 **Glen**

East Links, Tantallon Terrace, North Berwick, E Lothian EH39 4LE
☎(01620) 892726, Fax 895288, Pro 894596, Sec 895288, Bar/Rest 892221
Signposted from A198 1 miles E of town centre.
Seaside links course.
Founded 1906
Designed by MacKenzie Ross
18 holes, 6043 yards, S.S.S. 69
Green Fees: WD £17; WE £20.
Societies: welcome by prior arrange-

ment; catering packages available; from £17.
Catering: full clubhouse facilities.
Hotels: Marine; Belhaven; Golf.

9A 24 **Glencorse**

Milton Bridge, Pencuik, Midlothian
EH26 0RD
☎(01968) 677189, Fax 674399, Pro 676481, Bar/Rest 677177
On A701 Peebles road 9 miles S of Edinburgh.
Parkland course with stream on 10 holes.
Pro C Jones; Founded 1890
Designed by Willie Park Jnr
18 holes, 5217 yards, S.S.S. 66
Visitors: welcome; restrictions on comp days.
Green Fees: WD £18; WE £24.
Societies: welcome Mon-Thurs and Sun afternoon by prior arrangement; packages for golf and catering also available for parties of 10 or more; from £18.
Catering: full clubhouse catering and bar packages.
Practice range: Glencorse range 0.5 miles from course; 30 floodlit bays.
Hotels: Royal Hotel, Pencuik.

9A 25 **Greenburn**

6 Greenburn Rd, Fauldhouse EH47 9AY
☎(01501) 770292, Pro 771187
4 miles S of M8 junction 4 and 5.
Parkland/moorland course.
Pro M Leighton; Founded 1953
18 holes, 6046 yards, S.S.S. 70
Visitors: welcome by prior arrangements; WE 9am-10am and 2pm-3pm.
Green Fees: WD £17; WE £25.
Societies: welcome WD by prior arrangement; catering packages available; terms on application.
Catering: full clubhouse facilities.
Practice area.
Hotels: Hillcroft.

9A 26 **Gretna**

"Kirtle View", Gretna, Dumfriesshire
DG16 5HD
☎(01461) 338464
0.5 miles W of Gretna on S side of A75; 1 mile from M74/A75 junction.
Parkland course.
Founded 1991
Designed by Nigel Williams/ Bothwell
9 holes, 6430 yards, S.S.S. 71
Visitors: welcome except on comp days.
Green Fees: WD £8; WE £10.

Societies: welcome by prior arrangement; catering packages by arrangement; terms on application.
Catering: catering by arrangement.
Practice range.
Hotels: many hotels in local area.

9A 27 **Gullane**

West Links Rd, Gullane, E Lothian
EH31 2BB
☎(01620) 842255, Fax 842327, Pro 843111
Leave the A1 S to the A198.
300-year-old seaside links course;
Open qualifying course.
Pro Jimmy Hume; Founded 1882
(Course 1), Founded 1898 (Course 2),
Founded 1910 (Course 3)
Course 1: 18 holes, 6466 yards, S.S.S. 71
Course 2: 18 holes, 6244 yards, S.S.S. 71
Course 3: 18 holes, 5252 yards, S.S.S. 68
Visitors: welcome with h'cap certs by prior arrangement.
Green Fees: WD £54, WE £67 (Course 1); WD £23, WE £29 (Course 2); WD £14, WE £18 (Course 3).
Societies: welcome by prior arrangement; corporate days can be arranged; also conference day packages with exclusive use of the first-class accommodation in the Members' clubhouse for seminars/conferences for 12-24; Heritage of Golf Museum; coaching clinics; terms on application.
Catering: full clubhouse catering facilities in the Members' clubhouse.
Hotels: Club can provide a list in Gullane, North Berwick and Aberlady.

9A 28 **Haddington**

Amisfield Park, Whittinghame Dr, Haddington EH41 4PT
☎(01620) 826058, Fax 826580, Pro 822727, Sec 823627
0.75 miles E of Haddington just off the A1; 17 miles E of Edinburgh.
Parkland course.
Pro John Sandilands; Founded 1865
18 holes, 6317 yards, S.S.S. 70
Visitors: welcome WE pre-booking essential.
Green Fees: WD £17; WE £21.
Societies: welcome; full days golf; catering packages available in the season by arrangement Oct-March; from £25.
Catering: full catering and bar facilities April-Sept.
Hotels: Plough; Maitlandfield.

9A 29 **Harburn**
West Calder, W Lothian, EH55 8RS
☎(01506) 871582, Fax 871131, Sec
871131, Bar/Rest 871256
On B7008 off A705 from M8 junction
4.
Parkland course.
Pro Stephen Mills; Founded 1933
18 holes, 5921 yards, S.S.S. 68
Visitors: welcome except on comp
days.
Green Fees: WD £16; WE £21.
Societies: welcome except on comp
days; packages for Mon-Thurs; Fri,
Sat and Sun available including day's
golf, lunch and high tea; separate
changing facilities; from £30.
Catering: full clubhouse facilities.
Hotels: Bankton House; Livingston
Hilton.

9A 30 **Hawick**
Vertish Hill, Hawick, Roxburgh TD9
0NY
☎(01450) 372293, Sec 374947
Just S of Hawick on A7.
Parkland course.
Founded 1877
18 holes, 5933 yards, S.S.S. 69
Visitors: welcome; restrictions until
after 3.30pm on some Sats; not before
10.30am Sun.
Green Fees: WD £18; WE £24.
Societies: welcome by arrangement;
catering packages in season; separate
facilities; terms on application.
Catering: full clubhouse facilities in
summer.
Hotels: Kirkland; Mansfield House;
Elmsfield.

9A 31 **Hirsel**
Kelso Rd, Coldstream, Berwickshire,
TS12 4NJ
☎(01890) 882678, Fax 882233, Sec
882233
On A697 through Coldstream; golf
club is signposted.
Parkland course.
Founded 1948
18 holes, 6092 yards, S.S.S. 69
Visitors: welcome.
Green Fees: WD £18; WE £25.
Societies: welcome by arrangement
two months in advance; catering and
golf packages available; more than 10
players must book tee times 2 months
in advance; 2-10 must book 10 days in
advance; no starts before 10am; terms
on application.
Catering: full clubhouse facilities.
Hotels: Tillmouth park; Collingwood
Arms; Cross Keys.

9A 32 **Innerleithen**
Leithen Water, Leithen Road,
Innerleithen, Peebleshire EH44
6NL
☎(01896) 830951, Sec 830071
0.75 miles from town centre down
Leithen Road.
Heathland/parkland course.
Founded 1886
Designed by Willie Park
9 holes, 6056 yards, S.S.S. 69
Visitors: welcome.
Green Fees: WD £11; WE £14.
Societies: welcome but groups of
more than six should book; maximum
42; from £11.
Catering: by arrangement.
Hotels: Corner House; Traquar Arms.

9A 33 **Jedburgh**
Dunion Rd, Jedburgh, Roxburghshire,
TD8 6LA
☎(01835) 863587
0.75 mile W of Jedburgh on Hawick
road.
Undulating parkland course.
Founded 1892
9 holes, 5555 yards, S.S.S. 67
Visitors: welcome except on comp
days; WE booking advisable.
Green Fees: WD £12; WE £12.
Societies: welcome with at least 2
weeks' notice; catering and bar facili-
ties available between May and
September; from £12.
Catering: available in season.
Hotels: Royal; Jedforest.

9A 34 **Kelso**
Racecourse Rd, Kelso, Roxburgh,
TD5 7SL
☎(01573) 223009, Sec 223259
1 mile N of Kelso inside National Hunt
racecourse.
Flat parkland course.
Founded 1887
Designed by James Braid
18 holes, 6046 yards, S.S.S. 69
Visitors: welcome.
Green Fees: WD £14; WE £18.
Societies: welcome by prior arrange-
ment; includes all day golf; catering
packages available; notice needed for
Mon or Tues; from £20.
Catering: clubhouse facilities except
Mon and Tues.
Hotels: Cross Keys; Queen's Head.

9A 35 **Kilspindie**
The Clubhouse, Aberlady, EH32 0QD
☎(01875) 870216, Pro 870695, Sec
870358

Off A198 North Berwick Road immedi-
ately E of Aberlady; private road leads
to the club.
Seaside course.
Pro Graham Sked; Founded 1867
Designed by Ross & Sayers;
Extended by Willie Park
8 holes, 5471 yards, S.S.S. 66
Visitors: welcome by prior arrange-
ment.
Green Fees: WD £20; WE £25.
Societies: welcome by prior arrange-
ment; catering packages available;
terms on application.
Catering: full catering facilities with
bar and dining room.
Practice range.
Hotels: Kilspindie House.

9A 36 **Kingsknowe**
326 Lanark Rd, Edinburgh EH14 2JD
☎(0131) 441 1144, Fax 441 2079,
Pro 441 4030, Sec 441 1145
On A70 on the SW outskirts of
Edinburgh.
Undulating parkland
Pro Andrew Marshall; Founded 1908
Designed by Alex Herd, James Braid,
J.C. Stutt
18 holes, 5979 yards, S.S.S. 69
Visitors: welcome by prior arrange-
ment with Pro.
Green Fees: WD £18; WE £25.
Societies: welcome by prior applica-
tion to Sec; full day's golf and catering
available; separate changing; from £18.
Catering: full clubhouse catering and
bar facilities.
Hotels: Orwell Lodge; Edinburgh Post
House.

9A 37 **Kirkcudbright**
Stirling Crescent, Kirkcudbright, DG6
4EZ
☎(01557) 330314
Off A711 road from the A75 Dumfries-
Stranraer Road.
Parkland course.
Founded 1893
18 holes, 5739 yards, S.S.S. 69
Visitors: welcome; some restrictions
Tues/Wed.
Green Fees: WD £18; WE £18.
Societies: welcome by prior arrange-
ment; full day £23; from £18.
Catering: clubhouse facilities.
Hotels: Royal; Selkirk; Commercial.

9A 38 **Langholm**
Whitaside, Langholm, Dumfriesshire
DG13 0JR
☎(013873) 81247; Sec 80673

Off the A7 Edinburgh-Carlisle road in centre of Langholm; follow signs Hillside course.
Founded 1892
9 holes, 5744 yards, S.S.S. 68
Visitors: welcome.
Green Fees: WD £10; WE £10.
Societies: welcome by prior arrangement; catering by arrangement; £10.
Catering: clubhouse facilities.
Hotels: Eskdale; Buck; Crown.

9A 39 Lauder

Galashiels Rd, Lauder, TD2 6QD
☎(01578) 722526, Fax 722526
On A68 30 miles S of Edinburgh; 0.5 miles outside Lauder.
Parkland course.
Founded 1896
Designed by W. Park of Musselburgh
9 holes, 6002 yards, S.S.S. 70
Visitors: welcome except before noon Sun and 5.30pm-7.30pm Wed.
Green Fees: WD £10; WE £10.
Societies: welcome by prior arrangement; golf only available; from £10.
Catering: arranged with local hotels.
Hotels: Lauderdale; Eagle; Black Bull.

9A 40 Liberton

297 Gilmerton Rd, Edinburgh EH16 5UJ
☎(0131) 664 3009, Fax 666 0853, Pro 664 1056, Bar/Rest 664 8580
Exit Edinburgh city by-pass at Gilmerton A7 junction; course 3 miles towards city.
Parkland course.
Pro Iain Seith; Founded 1920
18 holes, 5306 yards, S.S.S. 66
Visitors: welcome.
Green Fees: WD £17; WE £25.
Societies: welcome WD by prior written arrangement; 36 holes of golf, coffee, lunch, high tea; max 40; £33.
Catering: full clubhouse facilities.

9A 41 Linlithgow

Braehead, Golf Course Rd, Linlithgow, W Lothian, EH49 6QF
☎(01506) 671044, Fax 842764, Pro 844356, Sec 842585
Approx 10 miles from Edinburgh on M9.
Undulating parkland course.
Pro Steve Rosie; Founded 1913
Designed by Robert Simpson of Carnoustie
18 holes, 5729 yards, S.S.S. 68
Visitors: welcome except Sat and comp days.
Green Fees: WD £17; WE £25.

Societies: welcome by arrangement with Sec; catering packages available except Tues; from £17.
Catering: full clubhouse facilities.
Hotels: Star & Garter; West Port.

9A 42 Lochmaben

Castlehill Gate, Lochmaben, Lockerbie, Dumfries & Galloway DG11 1NT
☎(01387) 810552
4 miles from the A74 at Lockerbie on the A709 road to Dumfries.
Parkland course; extended in 1993.
Founded 1926
Designed by James Braid
18 holes, 5387 yards, S.S.S. 66
Visitors: welcome except competition days.
Green Fees: WD £16; WE £20.
Societies: welcome by prior arrangement; catering packages available; caddie car hire; from £16.
Catering: full clubhouse facilities.
Practice area.
Hotels: Balcastle; Queens; Somerton House.

9A 43 Lockerbie

Corrie Rd, Lockerbie, Dumfriesshire DG11 2ND
☎(01576) 203363, Fax 203363
Leave M74 at Lockerbie and course is signposted.
Tree-lined parkland course with pond in play on 3 holes.
Founded 1889
Designed by James Braid (original 9)
18 holes, 5463 yards, S.S.S. 66
Visitors: welcome; booking advisable.
Green Fees: WD £18.
Societies: welcome by prior arrangement; 36 holes of golf; morning coffee, light lunch; evening meal (£30 Sat); from £25.
Catering: full clubhouse facilities.
Hotels: Queens; Kings; Ravenshill; Dryfesdale.

9A 44 Longniddry

Links Rd, Longniddry, E Lothian EH32 0NL
☎(01875) 852141, Fax 853371, Pro 852228, Bar/Rest 852623
On B6363 in Longniddry village from the A1.
Parkland and links course.
Pro John Gray; Founded 1921
Designed by Harry Colt
18 holes, 6219 yards, S.S.S. 70
Visitors: welcome WD; h'cap certs required; WE by arrangement.

Green Fees: WD £27; WE £35.
Societies: welcome by prior arrangement and with h'cap certs; catering packages can be arranged with the clubmaster; tee times between 9.30am and 4pm; deposit of £10 per person required; credit cards accepted; max 40; from £38.
Catering: full clubhouse facilities.
Hotels: Kilspindie House; Maitlandfield; Greencraigs.

9A 45 Lothianburn

106 Biggar Rd, Edinburgh, EH10 7DU
☎(0131) 445 5067, Pro 445 2288, Bar/Rest 445 2206
On A702 Biggar to Carlisle road, 200 yards from City by-pass at Lothianburn exit.
Hilly course.
Pro Kurt Mungall; Founded 1893/1928
Designed by James Braid (1928)
18 holes, 5568 yards, S.S.S. 69
Visitors: welcome WD up to 4.30pm; WE with member.
Green Fees: WD £15.
Societies: welcome WD by prior arrangement with Sec; discounts for more than 16 in a party; catering packages by arrangement; from £13.
Catering: clubhouse facilities.
Hotels: Braid Hills.

9A 46 Luffness New

Aberlady, E Lothian, E32 0QA
☎(01620) 843114, Fax 842933, Sec 843336, Bar/Rest 843376
1 mile outside Aberlady on the A198 Gullane road.
Links course.
Founded 1894
Designed by Tom Morris (1894)
18 holes, 6123 yards, S.S.S. 69
Visitors: welcome WD only; gentlemen only.
Green Fees: WD £35.
Societies: welcome WD by prior arrangement; full day's golf £50; catering by arrangement; from £35.
Catering: smoke room; dining room; lunch daily; high tea/dinner by arrangement (min 10).
Practice range: 5-hole course.
Hotels: Marine, N Berwick; Golf, Greywalls (Gullane).

9A 47 Marriott Dalmahoy

Kirknewton, Midlothian, EH27 8EB
☎(0131) 3358010, Fax 3353203, Sec 3334105
On A71 7 miles W of Edinburgh
Rolling parkland course.

Pro Stuart Callan; Founded 1927
Designed by James Braid
East: 18 holes, 6677 yards, S.S.S. 72;
West: 18 holes, 5185 yards, S.S.S. 66
Visitors: welcome WD by prior
arrangement and with h'cap cert;
members and residents only at WE.
Green Fees: WD £48 (East); £32
(West).
Societies: welcome WD by arrange-
ment; corporate days can be organ-
ised; catering and residential pack-
ages; lleisure facilities, including
indoor heated pool, spa, sauna, ten-
nis, gym, health & beauty salon; terms
on application.
Catering: facilities in the Long
Weekend Restaurant.
Practice range, 12 bays all-weather
floodlit.
Hotels: Marriott Dalmahoy.

9A 48 **Melrose**
Dingleton, Melrose, Roxburghshire
☎(01896) 822855, Sec 822758
2 miles N of St Boswell off the A68
Newcastle-Edinburgh Road; 0.5 miles
S of Melrose.
Undulating wooded parkland course.
Founded 1880
9 holes, 5579 yards, S.S.S. 68
Visitors: welcome WD; Sat very limit-
ed; some Sun available.
Green Fees: WD £15; WE £15.
Societies: welcome by arrangement;
catering can be arranged; from £15.
Catering: by arrangement.

9A 49 **Melville**
South Melville, Lasswade, EH18 1AN
☎(0131) 654 8038, Fax 654 0814,
Sec 654 0224
Off the Edinburgh city by-pass on the
Galashiels A7 road.
Parkland course.
Founded 1995
Designed by P Campbell/G Webster
9 holes, 4310 yards, S.S.S. 62
Visitors: welcome.
Green Fees: WD £12; WE £16.
Societies: welcome by prior arrange-
ment Mon-Thurs; minimum 10, maxi-
mum 20; from £12.
Catering: snacks available.
Practice range: 34 bays; 22 covered,
12 outdoor.
Hotels: Eskbank; Dalhousie Castle.

9A 50 **Merchants of Edinburgh**
10 Craighill Gardens, Edinburgh,
EH10 5PY

☎(0131) 447 1219, Pro 447 8709
Off A701 S of Edinburgh.
Hilly parkland course
Pro N E M Colquhoun; Founded 1907
18 holes, 4889 yards, S.S.S. 64
Visitors: welcome WD before 4pm.
Green Fees: WD £15.
Societies: welcome WD before 4pm
by prior arrangement; catering pack-
ages can be arranged; from £15.
Catering: available except Thurs; full
bar facilities.
Hotels: Braid Hills.

9A 51 **Minto**
Minto Village, by Denholm, Hawick,
Roxburghshire TD9 8SH
☎(01450) 870220, Sec 862611
5 miles NE of Hawick leaving A698 at
Denholm.
Parkland course.
Founded 1928
18 holes, 5453 yards, S.S.S. 68
Visitors: welcome by arrangement.
Green Fees: WD £15; WE £20.
Societies: welcome by prior arrange-
ment; packages available; from £15.
Catering: full clubhouse facilities.
Practice range.
Hotels: contact the Scottish Tourist
Board.

9A 52 **Moffat**
Coatshill, Moffat, Dumfriesshire DG10
9SB
☎(01683) 220020
Leave A74 (M74) at Beattock; take
A701 to Moffat for 1 mile; club is sign-
posted.
Moorland course with tree plantations,
spectacular views.
Founded 1884
Designed by Ben Sayers
18 holes, 5263 yards, S.S.S. 67
Visitors: welcome except Wed pm.
Green Fees: WD £17.50; WE £25.50.
Societies: welcome by prior arrange-
ment except Wed; includes 2 rounds
of golf, morning coffee; snack lunch;
evening dinner; from £30.
Catering: full clubhouse facilities.
Hotels: Beechwood Country; Moffat
House; Annandale Arms; Balmoral;
Buchanan; Star.

9A 53 **Mortonhall**
231 Braid Rd, Edinburgh, EH10 6PB
☎(0131) 447 6974, Fax 447 8712,
Pro 4475185
On A702 2 miles S of the city.
Moorland course.
Pro Douglas Horn; Founded 1892

Designed by James Braid & Fred
Hawtree
18 holes, 6557 yards, S.S.S. 71
Visitors: welcome by prior arrange-
ment.
Green Fees: WD £25; WE £30.
Societies: welcome WD by arrange-
ment; terms on application.
Catering: bar and catering facilities.
Hotels: Braid Hills.

9A 54 **Muirfield – Honourable Company of Edinburgh Golfers**
Muirfield, Gullane, E Lothian EH31
2EG
☎(01620) 842123
On the A198 to the NE of Gullane
Links; staged 14 Open Championships
since 1892.
Founded 1744
Designed by Tom Morris
18 holes, 6970 yards, S.S.S. 73
Visitors: welcome only Tues and
Thurs.
Green Fees: WD £60.
Societies: welcome on Tues and
Thurs only by prior arrangement; no
more than 12 golfers allowed; must
have h'cap certs; 18 max for men;
terms on application.
Catering: full catering and bar service
(ladies may not lunch in clubhouse).
Practice range.
Hotels: Greywalls; Kilspindie House.

9A 55 **Murrayfield**
Murrayfield Rd, Edinburgh EH12 6EU
☎(0131) 337 3478
2 miles W of city centre.
Parkland course.
Founded 1896
18 holes, 5725 yards, S.S.S. 68
Visitors: welcome only with member.
Green Fees: terms on application.
Societies: limited.
Catering: bar snacks; dining room;
meals served daily except Mon.
Hotels: Ellersly House; Murrayfield.

9A 56 **Musselburgh**
Monktonhall, Musselburgh, E Lothian
EH21 6SA
☎(0131) 665 2005, Pro 665 7055
On B6415 to Musselburgh from the
end of the A1 Edinburgh by-pass.
Parkland course.
Pro Fraser Mann; Founded 1938
Designed by James Braid
18 holes, 6614 yards, S.S.S. 73
Visitors: welcome by prior arrange-
ment.

~Tweed Valley Hotel~

If you are looking for superb courses, set amongst beautiful scenery, in one of the country's most unexplored areas - you've just hit a hole-in-one in the Scottish Borders.

We will arange golf for individuals or parties on over 17 courses!

And for parties of four or more, staying for at least 3 nights DB&B, we can even arrange your own mini-tournament; to include a celebration drink for all at our welcoming nineteenth hole, a special Tweed Valley Hotel engraved glass goblet for the winner.

See our voucher at the back of this Guide for special golf packages, or contact:-
TWEED VALLEY HOTEL, Walkerburn, Peebleshire EH43 6AA. Tel: 01896 870636.

Green Fees: WD £18; WE £22.
Societies: welcome by prior arrangement; catering packages available; terms on application.
Catering: bar and restaurant facilities.
Hotels: Kings; Manor; Woodside.

9A 57 **Musselburgh Old Course**
10 Balcarres Rd, Musselburgh, E Lothian EH21 7RG
☎(0131) 665 6981
7 miles E of Edinburgh on A199 at Musselburgh racecourse.
Seaside links course.
9 holes, 5380 yards, S.S.S. 67
Visitors: welcome WD; not before 1pm at WE.
Green Fees: WD £5; WE £5.
Societies: welcome by prior arrangement; terms on application.
Catering: catering facilities.

9A 58 **New Galloway**
New Galloway, Castle Douglas, Kirkcudbrightshire DG7 3RN
☎(01644) 420737, Fax 420244, Sec 430455
On A713 to New Galloway.
Moorland course.
Founded 1902
Designed by G Baillie
9 holes, 5006 yards, S.S.S. 67
Visitors: welcome.
Green Fees: WD £10; WE £10.
Societies: welcome by prior arrangement with Sec; catering packages can be organised; from £10.
Catering: bar and snack facilities available.
Hotels: Kenmure Arms; Cross Keys; Kalmar.

9A 59 **Newbattle**
Abbey Rd, Dalkeith, Midlothian EH22 3AD

☎(0131) 663 2123, Pro 660 1631, Sec 663 1819, Bar/Rest 6632123
On A7 7 miles SW of Edinburgh; taking Newbattle exit at Eskbank roundabout.
Undulating parkland course.
Pro David Torrance; Founded 1935
18 holes, 6025 yards, S.S.S. 70
Visitors: welcome WD up to 4pm.
Green Fees: WD £16; WE £16.
Societies: welcome Mon-Fri by prior arrangement between 9am-10am and 2pm-4pm; catering packages available; terms on application.
Catering: full clubhouse facilities.
Hotels: Lugton; Eskbank.

9A 60 **Newcastleton**
Holm Hill, Newcastleton, Roxburghshire TD9 0QD
☎(013873) 75257
On A7 25 miles N of Carlisle; 10 miles from Canonbie/Newcastleton junction.
Hilly course.
Founded 1894
Designed by J. Shade (74)
9 holes, 5748 yards, S.S.S. 68
Visitors: welcome.
Green Fees: WD £7; WE £8.
Societies: welcome by prior arrangement; packages can be arranged with local hotel; from £7.
Catering: facilities at Liddlesdale Hotel.
Hotels: Liddlesdale; Grapes.

9A 61 **Newton Stewart**
Kirroughtree Ave, Minnigaff, Newton Stewart DG8 6PF
☎(01671) 402172
Close to A75 Carlisle-Stranraer road; 1 mile from town centre.
Parkland/hill course.
Founded 1896/1992
18 holes, 5887 yards, S.S.S. 69
Visitors: welcome.
Green Fees: WD £14; WE £17.

Societies: welcome by prior arrangement; catering by prior arrangement with the steward; terms on application.
Catering: full clubhouse facilities available.
Hotels: Glencalm; Crown.

9A 62 **Niddry Castle**
Castle Rd, Winchburgh, W Lothian EH52 6RQ
☎(01506) 891097
On B9080 in centre of village; 5 miles from Newbridge interchange.
Parkland course.
Founded 1982
Designed by Derek Smith
9 holes, 5518 yards, S.S.S. 67
Visitors: welcome WD; by arrangement at WE.
Green Fees: WD £12; WE £12.
Societies: welcome WD by prior arrangement; full catering packages by arrangement; £12.
Catering: full clubhouse facilities.
Hotels: Tally-ho, Winchburgh.

9A 63 **North Berwick**
New Club House, Beach Rd, North Berwick, E Lothian, EH39 4BB
☎(01620) 894766, Fax 893274, Pro 893233, Sec 892135/895050
In North Berwick take the last left turn before the town centre.
Links course.
Pro D Huish; Founded 1832
Designed by MacKenzie Ross
18 holes, 6420 yards, S.S.S. 70
Visitors: welcome by prior arrangement.
Green Fees: WD £30; WE £30.
Societies: welcome by prior arrangement; catering packages can be arranged; from £30.
Catering: full clubhouse facilities available.
Hotels: Marine Hotel; many B&Bs in the area.

9A 64 Peebles
Kirkland St, Peebles, EH45 8EU
☎(01721) 72(0197, Sec 720099
Located on NW side of Peebles off
A72; signposted; 23 miles S of
Edinburgh.
Undulating parkland course.
Founded 1892
Designed by James Braid; Alterations
by H.S. Colt
18 holes, 6160 yards, S.S.S. 69
Visitors: welcome by prior arrange-
ment.
Green Fees: WD £17; WE £23.
Societies: welcome by prior arrange-
ment except on Sat; new clubhouse
opened in 1997; catering packages
available by arrangement; terms on
application.
Catering: full clubhouse facilities
available.
Hotels: Peebles Hotel Hydro; Park;
Kingsmuir; Greentree.

9A 65 Polkemmet Country Park
Park Centre, Polkemmet Country
Park, Bathgate, W Lothian, EH47 0AD
☎(01501) 743905, Bar/Rest 744441
Park is on the N side of the B7066
midway between Harthill and
Whitburn.
Parkland course.
Founded 1981
Designed by W Lothian District
Council
9 holes, 6531 yards
Visitors: welcome; no restrictions.
Green Fees: WD £3.40; WE £4.20.
Societies: welcome except at WE;
limited; from £3.40.
Catering: bar and restaurant facilities
available.
Hotels: Eillcroft, Whitburn; Holiday
Inn; Dreadnought both Bathgate.

9A 66 Portobello
Stanley St, Portobello, Edinburgh,
EH15 1JJ
☎(0131) 669 4361
On A1 E of Edinburgh, off Milton
Road.
Parkland course.
Founded 1826
9 holes, 4504 yards, S.S.S. 64
Visitors: welcome.
Green Fees: WD £4; WE £4.
Societies: welcome by prior arrange-
ment; restrictions Sat in summer;
catering packages available by prior
application; from £4.
Catering: by prior arrangement.
Hotels: Kings Manor.

9A 67 Portpatrick (Dunskey)
Golf Course Rd, Portpatrick, Stranraer,
Wigtownshire DG9 8TB
☎(01776) 810273, Fax 810811
Follow A77 or A75 to Stranraer and
then follow signs for Portpatrick; on
entering village turn right at the War
Memorial.
Links style cliff-top course.
Founded 1903
Designed by Dunskey Estate/W M
Hunter of Prestwick
18 holes, 5910 yards, S.S.S. 68
Visitors: welcome with h'cap certs.
Green Fees: WD £18; WE £21.
Societies: welcome by prior arrange-
ment; h'cap certs required; catering
packages available; weekly tickets;
day rates; also Dinvin course: 1504
yards, par 3; from £18.
Catering: full clubhouse facilities;
meals until 9pm daily.
**Practice range.
Hotels: Fernhill; Portpatrick;
Downshire; Harbour House; Mount
Stewart.

9A 68 Powfoot
Cummertrees, Annan, Dumfriesshire,
DG12 5QE
☎(01461) 700227, Fax 700276, Pro
700327, Sec 700276
Off A75 road to Annan/Dumfries taking
the 2nd turning for Annan until signs
for Cummertrees and Powfoot on the
B724; 3 miles later sharp left after rail-
way bridge.
Links course.
Pro Gareth Dick; Founded 1903
Designed by James Braid
18holes, 6266 Yards, S.S.S. 71
Visitors: welcome except Sat and
before 2pm on Sun.
Green Fees: WD £23; WE £23.
Societies: welcome by prior arrange-
ment; terms on application.
Catering: full clubhouse facilities.
Hotels: Cairndale, Dumfries;
Carrutherstown.

9A 69 Prestonfield
6 Priestfield Rd N, Edinburgh EH16
5HS
☎(0131) 667 1273, Pro 667 8597,
Sec 667 9665
Close to Commonwealth Games pool.
Parkland course.
Pro Graeme MacDonald; Founded
1920
Designed by James Braid
18 holes, 6212 yards, S.S.S. 70
Visitors: welcome by arrangement.
Green Fees: WD £20; WE £30.

Societies: welcome WD starting from
9.30am and 2pm; catering packages
available; terms on application.
Catering: full catering except Mon.
Hotels: Prestonfield House; March
Hall; Rosehall.

9A 70 Pumpherston
Drumshoreland Rd, Pumpherston, W
Lothian, EH53 0LH
☎(01506) 432869
400 yards, E of the Village cross.
Undulating parkland course.
Founded 1895
9 holes, 5434 yards, S.S.S. 66
Visitors: welcome with a member.
Green Fees: terms on application.
Societies: welcome WD by arrange-
ment; max party 24; bar snacks and
meals to order; terms on application.
Catering: clubhouse facilities.

9A 71 Ratho Park
Ratho, Newbridge, Midlothian EH28
8NX
☎(0131) 333 2566, Fax 333 1752,
Pro 333 1406, Sec 333 1752, Bar/Rest
333 1752
Adjacent to Edinburgh Airport 8 miles
W of Edinburgh.
Parkland course.
Pro Alan Tate; Founded 1928
Designed by James Braid
18 holes, 5900 yards, S.S.S. 68
Visitors: welcome by prior arrange-
ment with the Prol.
Green Fees: WD £35;WE £35.
Societies: welcome Tues, Wed, Thurs
by prior arrangement; packages for
golf and catering available for groups
of 12 or more; terms on application.
Catering: full clubhouse bar and
restaurant facilities.

9A 72 Ravelston
24 Ravelston Dykes Rd, Blackhall,
Edinburgh, EH4 5NZ
☎(0131) 3152486
From city centre turn left at Blackhall
junction then across the crossroad and
turn right 100 yards further on.
Parkland course.
Founded 1912
Designed by James Braid
9 holes, 5200 yards, S.S.S. 65
Visitors: welcome WD by prior
arrangement.
Green Fees: WD £15.
Societies: small groups welcome by
prior arrangement; from £15.
Catering: snacks and bar available.
Hotels: Garden Court Holiday Inn.

Southerness

Nothing like enough golfers are acquainted with the delights of Southerness which lies on the silent, sandy stretches of the Solway Firth about 15 miles south of Dumfries. This is largely because the south-west corner of Scotland is not the best known golfing area of a country that has so much to offer, although those aware of its charm find it rich in quality and enjoyment and hard to believe that its reputation has not spread further.

As with so many courses around our shores, much of its appeal lies in its out of the way position but it still makes a convenient beginning or end to any golfing tour. The drive from Carlisle is by no means arduous but, by the time that one turns off the main road down a long, narrow lane towards the sea, there is a growing impatience to see what lies beyond.

Before the days of a new clubhouse, built in 1974 close to the position of the old sixth hole, journey's end was less pretentious. The small community dominated by the Paul Jones Hotel consisted of a field of caravans, a few shops and a clubhouse which had more the look of some rustic cricket pavilion. A notice invited visitors to settle green fees with the caretaker in the village shop across the road and the path to the first tee was through some quaint little paddock.

However, one round on the course, laid out by Mackenzie Ross shortly after the last war, is sufficient to appreciate its merits and indicate, rather like Dornoch at the opposite end of the country, that it is well worthy of having won its championship spurs. By a happy coincidence, Dornoch was awarded the British Amateur Championship in 1985, the same year in which the Scottish Golf Union took the Scottish Amateur to Southerness constructed for about £2,000 around 1947. The staging of the championship bestowed a posthumous tribute to Mackenzie Ross, who resurrected Turnberry at more or less the same time as he paid his regular visits to Southerness.

By the current rating, there is only one par five but the weight of the challenge is marked by having eight holes between 405 and 470 yards, many with fine natural greens angled to ensure the best chance of finishing near the hole comes from drives correctly positioned. There is no great feeling that the fairways are narrow but gorse and heather can swallow up wayward shots and there is a tough start including the longest hole, the fifth, with its elevated and quaintly shaped green.

The eighth, taking aim on the lighthouse, begins the stretch along the shore but the pick of the holes are the dogleg 12th and the 13th and the old 18th, a formidable 467 yards. The 17th green, perched above the beach, also gives the best view of the splendour of the setting. Leagues of golden sand slip westwards along the coast of Kirkcudbright. The peaks of Cumberland stand strong against the peaceful waters of the Firth and, inland, the simple green landscape completes a feeling of escape that causes as much surprise as finding a golf course to match its majestic surroundings.

9A 73 **The Roxburghe**
Sunlaws House, Kelso, Roxburghshire
TD5 8JZ
☎(01573) 450333, Fax 450611
On A698 between Jedburgh and Kelso.
Woodland/parkland course.
Pro Gordon Niven; Founded 1997
Designed by Dave Thomas
18 holes, 6873 yards, S.S.S. 73
Visitors: welcome by arrangement.
Green Fees: WD £30; WE £40.
Societies: welcome by arrangement;
packages available; tennis court;
terms on application.
Catering: full facilities; cocktail bar;
spikes bar; restaurant.
Practice range.
Hotels: Sunlaws House (on site).

9A 74 **Royal Burgess Golfing Society Of Edinburgh**
181 Whitehouse Rd, Edinburgh EH4
6BY
☎(0131) 339 2075, Pro 339 6474,
Bar/Rest 339 2012
W side of Edinburgh on the
Queensferry road, 100 yds from
Barnton roundabout.
Parkland course.
Pro George Yuille; Founded 1735
Designed by Tom Morris
18 holes, 6494 yards, S.S.S. 71
Visitors: welcome by prior arrange-
ment; no lady members.
Green Fees: WD £37; WE £55.
Societies: welcome WD by prior
arrangement; catering by arrange-
ment; terms on application.
Catering: clubhouse lunches and bar
snacks.
Hotels: Barnton; Royal Scot.

9A 75 **Royal Musselburgh**
Prestongrange House, Prestonpans, E
Lothian EH32 9RP
☎(01875) 810276, Fax 810276, Pro
810139, Bar/Rest 813671
On B1361 North Berwick Road.
Parkland course.
Pro John Henderson; Founded
1774/1926
Designed by James Braid
18 holes, 6237 yards, S.S.S. 70
Visitors: welcome by prior arrange-
ment.
Green Fees: WD £20; WE £35.
Societies: welcome WD except Fri
afternoons by prior arrangement;
catering can be arranged; £35 per day
for golf; from £20.
Catering: full catering facilities avail-
able.
Hotels: Marine Hotel; Golf Inn.

9A 76 **St Boswells**
Braeheads, St Boswells, Melrose,
Roxburghshire TD6 0DE
☎(01835) 823527
Off the A68 in St Boswells.
Parkland course.
Founded 1899
Designed by William Park, Altered by
John Shade (1956)
9 holes, 5250 yards, S.S.S. 66
Visitors: welcome by prior arrange-
ment.
Green Fees: WD £15; WE £15.
Societies: welcome by prior arrange-
ment if more than six in party; catering
can be arranged in advance; from £15.
Catering: bar and light snacks avail-
able at WE; other times by arrange-
ment.
Hotels: Buccleuch Arms.

9A 77 **St Medan**
Monreith, Port William, Newton
Stewart, Wigtownshire, DG8 8NJ
☎(01988) 700358
Off the A747 3 miles S of Port William
following the A714 from Newton
Stewart.
Links course.
Founded 1905
9 holes, 4454 yards, S.S.S. 63
Visitors: welcome.
Green Fees: WD £12; WE £12.
Societies: welcome by prior arrange-
ment; terms on application.
Catering: clubhouse facilities.

9A 78 **Sanquhar**
Old Barr Rd, Sanquhar, Dumfries,
DG4 6JZ
Club ((01659) 50577, Sec 58181
Off A76, 0.5 miles from Sanquhar.
Parkland course.
Founded 1894
9 holes, 5594 yards, S.S.S. 68
Visitors: welcome.
Green Fees: WD £10; WE £12.
Societies: welcome by arrangement;
catering by arrangement; snooker;
bowls; darts; from £10.
Catering: clubhouse facilities.
Hotels: Blackaddie; Glendyne;
Nithsdale.

9A 79 **Selkirk**
The Hill, Selkirk, TD7 4NW
☎0750) 20621
0.5 miles S of Selkirk on A7
Heathland.
Founded 1883
Designed by Willie Park
9 holes, 5620 yards, S.S.S. 67

Visitors: welcome WD by arrangement except Mon pm; WE by arrangement.
Green Fees: WD £15; WE £15.
Societies: welcome WD; some WE;
catering packages by arrangement;
from £15.
Catering: bar open evenings and WE;
at other times by arrangement.
Hotels: Heatherlie; Woodburn; Glen
all Selkirk.

9A 80 **Silverknowes**
Silverknowes, Parkway, Edinburgh,
EH4 5ET
☎(0131) 336 5359, Pro 336 3843
W end of Edinburgh off Cramond
Foreshore
Municipal links course.
Founded 1958
18 holes, 6202 yards, S.S.S. 70
Visitors: welcome by prior arrange-
ment.
Green Fees: WD £8; WE £8.
Societies: welcome by prior arrange-
ment; terms on application.
Catering: clubhouse facilities.
Hotels: Commodore, adjacent.

9A 81 **Southerness**
Southerness, Kirkbean, Dumfries,
Dumfries, DG2 8AZ
☎(01387) 880677, Fax 880644
On A710 15 miles S of Dumfries
Links on Solway Firth.
Founded 1947
Designed by MacKenzie Ross
18 holes, 6566 yards, S.S.S. 72
Visitors: welcome by prior arrange-
ment; h'cap certs required.
Green Fees: WD £28; WE £40.
Societies: welcome by prior arrange-
ment; packages available; from £28.
Catering: full catering facilities.
Hotels: Cairndale; Clonyard; Cavens
House; Paul Jones Hotel.

9A 82 **Stranraer**
Creachmore, Leswalt, Stranraer DG9
0LF
☎(01776) 870245, Fax 870445, Sec
870445
On A718 to Kirkcolm 3 miles from
Stranraer.
Parkland/seaside course; on present
site since 1951.
Founded 1905/1951
Designed by James Braid
18 holes, 6308 yards, S.S.S. 72
Visitors: welcome except at members'
times; not before 9.15am or between
12.30pm-1.30pm and 5pm-6pm.
Green Fees: WD £18; WE £23.

Societies: welcome by arrangement; same restrictions apply as to visitors; catering can be arranged; separate locker rooms; terms on application.
Catering: full catering and bar service.
Hotels: North West Castle; Kelvin House; Fernhill.

9A 83 Swanston
111 Swanston Rd, Edinburgh EH10 7DS
☎(0131) 445 2239: Pro 445 4002
S side of the city on the lower slopes of Pentland Hills.
Hillside course
Pro Ian Taylor; Founded 1927
Designed by Herbert More
18 holes, 5004 yards, S.S.S. 65
Visitors: welcome WD; some WE restrictions.
Green Fees: WD £15; WE £20.
Societies: welcome by prior arrangement; catering and golf packages available; from £15.
Catering: full facilities.
Hotels: Braid Hills; Newland Inn.

9A 84 Thornhill
Blacknest, Thornhill, Dumfriesshire, DG3 5DW
☎(01848) 330546
Off A76 at Thornhill 14 miles N of Dumfries
Moorland/parkland course.
Founded 1893
18 holes, 6085 yards, S.S.S. 69
Visitors: welcome by prior arrangement.
Green Fees: WD £18; WE £20.
Societies: welcome by prior arrangement; catering packages can be arranged through the steward; terms on application.
Catering: full clubhouse facilities.
Hotels: George; Gillbank.

9A 85 Torphin Hill
Torphin Rd, Colinton, Edinburgh EH13 0PG
☎(0131) 441 1100, Pro 441 4061, Sec 441 4061
SW of Colinton village.
Hilly course.
Pro Jamie Browne; Founded 1895
18 holes, 4580 yards, S.S.S. 66
Visitors: welcome except before 2pm at WE.
Green Fees: WD £12; WE £20.
Societies: welcome WD by prior arrangement; terms on application.
Catering: clubhouse facilities.
Hotels: Braid Hills.

9A 86 Torwoodlee
Edinburgh Road, Galashiels, TD1 2NE
☎(01896) 752660
2 miles outside Galashiels on the main Edinburgh road.
Parkland course.
Pro R Elliot; Founded 1895
Designed by Willie Park (new layout, John Gurner)
18 holes, 6087 yards, S.S.S. 68
Visitors: welcome by prior arrangement.
Green Fees: WD £16; WE £20.
Societies: welcome by prior arrangement; packages for golf and catering available; from £20.
Catering: full clubhouse facilities.
Hotels: Kingsknowe, Galashiels; Burts, Melrose.

9A 87 Turnhouse
154 Turnhouse Rd, Edinburgh EH12 0AD
☎(0131) 339 1014, Pro 3391 7701
On A9080 W of city near the airport.
Parkland/heathland course.
Pro John Murray; Founded 1909
18 holes, 6153 yards, S.S.S. 70
Visitors: welcome by arrangement.
Green Fees: WD £18;WE £18.
Societies: welcome by prior arrangement; catering packages available everyday; terms on application.
Catering: full facilities everyday.
Hotels: Royal Scot; Posthouse; Stakis.

9A 88 Uphall
Houston Mains, Uphall, W Lothian, EH52 6JT
☎(01506) 856404, Fax 855358, Pro 855553
On A899 200 yards W of Uphall; 0.5 miles from M8 junction 3; 15 miles W of Edinburgh.
Tree-lined parkland course.
Pro Gordon Law; Founded 1895
18 holes, 5592 yards, S.S.S. 67
Visitors: welcome by prior arrangement except on comp days.
Green Fees: WD £14; WE £18.
Societies: welcome by prior arrangement; catering packages available; snooker; disabled facilities; from £14.
Catering: full bar and catering facilities.
Hotels: Houston House.

9A 89 Vogrie
Vogrie Estate Country Park, Gorebridge, Lothian, EH23 4NN
☎(01875) 821716, Sec 8217986

Off A68 Jedburgh Road.
Parkland course.
Founded 1989
9 holes, 5060 yards, S.S.S. 66
Visitors: public pay and play.
Green Fees: terms on application.
Societies: welcome; some restrictions; terms on application.
Catering: tea room in park.

9A 90 West Linton
Medwyn Road, West Linton, Peeblshire EH46 7HN
☎(01968) 660463, Pro 660256, Sec 660970, Bar/Rest 660589
Off A702 at West Linton.
Moorland course.
Pro I Wright; Founded 1890
Designed by Braid/Millar/Fraser
18 holes, 6132 yards, S.S.S. 69
Visitors: welcome WD and after 1pm on non-comp WE.
Green Fees: WD £18; WE £28.
Societies: welcome WD by prior arrangement with Sec; catering packages available; from £18.
Catering: full clubhouse facilities.
Hotels: Gordon Arms.

9A 91 West Lothian
Airngath Hill, Linlithgow, W Lothian EH49 7RH
☎(01506) 826030, Fax 826030, Pro 825060
Take A706 from Linlithgow to Bo'ness for 2.5 miles, and then turn right to the Golf Club.
Parkland course.
Pro Neil Robertson; Founded 1892
Designed by W Park (1892)/ J Adams (1923)/F Middleton (1975)
18 holes, 6046 yards, S.S.S. 71
Visitors: welcome by prior arrangement.
Green Fees: WD £15; WE £20.
Societies: welcome WD and non-competition WE by prior arrangement; catering packages by prior arrangement; from £15.
Catering: clubhouse facilities.
Hotels: Richmond Park; Earl o'Moray.

9A 92 Wigtown & Bladnoch
Lightlands Terrace, Wigtown, Dumfries & Galloway DG8 9EF
☎(01988) 403354
On A746 0.25 miles from town centre.
Parkland course.
Founded 1960
9 holes, 5462 yards, S.S.S. 67
Visitors: welcome.
Green Fees: WD £10; WE £10.

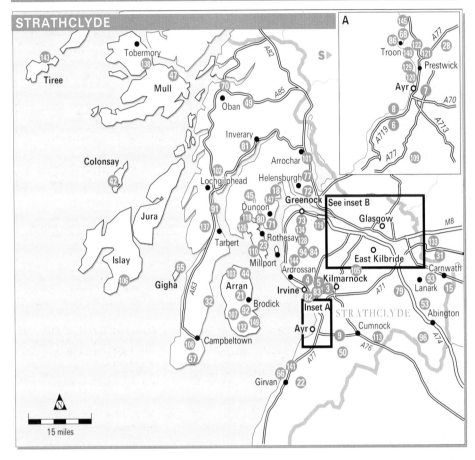

STRATHCLYDE

A

Tobermory
Tiree
Mull
Oban
Inverary
Colonsay
Arrochar
Lochgilphead
Helensburgh
Greenock
Dunoon
Rothesay
Tarbert
Millport
Ardrossan
Islay
Gigha
Arran
Irvine
Brodick
Campbeltown
Girvan

Troon
Prestwick
Ayr
See inset B
Glasgow
East Kilbride
Carnwath
Kilmarnock
Lanark
Abington
STRATHCLYDE
Cumnock
Inset A
Ayr

15 miles

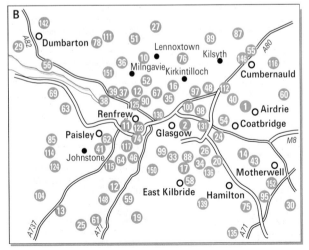

B

Dumbarton
Lennoxtown
Kilsyth
Milngavie
Kirkintilloch
Cumbernauld
Renfrew
Airdrie
Paisley
Coatbridge
Glasgow
Johnstone
Motherwell
East Kilbride
Hamilton

Societies: welcome by prior arrangement; packages with local hotels; terms on application.
Catering: clubhouse facilities.
Hotels: Conifers Leisure Park.

9A 93 **Wigtownshire County**
Mains of Park, Glenluce, Newton Stewart, Wigtownshire, DG8 0NN
☎ (01581) 300420
On the A75 8 miles E of Stranraer.
Links course.
Founded 1894
Designed by G Cunningham/C Hunter
18 holes, 5847 yards, S.S.S. 68
Visitors: welcome.
Green Fees: WD £17.50; WE £19.50.
Societies: welcome by prior arrangement; discounts for groups of 10 or more; catering packages available; from £17.50.
Catering: clubhouse facilities.

KEY							
1	Airdrie	30	Carluke	61	Eastwood	92	Lamlash	123	Ralston
2	Alexandra Park	31	Carnwath	62	Elderslie	93	Lanark	124	Ranfurly Castle
3	Annanhill	32	Carradale	63	Erskine	94	Largs	125	Renfrew
4	Ardeer	33	Cathcart Castle	64	Fereneze	95	Larkhall	126	Rothesay
5	Auchenharvie Golf	34	Cathkin Braes	65	Gigha	96	Leadhills	127	Rouken Glen
	Complex	35	Cawder	66	Girvan	97	Lenzie	128	Routenburn
6	Ayr Belleisle	36	Clober	67	Glasgow	98	Lethamhill	129	Royal Troon
7	Ayr Dalmilling	37	Clydebank & District	68	Glasgow (Gailes)	99	Linn Park	130	Ruchill
8	Ayr Seafield	38	Clydebank Municipal	69	Gleddoch Country Club	100	Littlehill	131	Sandyhills
9	Ballochmyle	39	Clydebank Overtoun	70	Glencruitten	101	Loch Lomond	132	Shiskine
10	Balmore	40	Coatbridge	71	Gourock	102	Lochgilphead	133	Shotts
11	Barshaw	41	Cochrane Castle	72	Greenock	103	Lochranza	134	Skelmorlie
12	Bearsden	42	Colonsay	73	Greenock Whinhill	104	Lochwinnoch	135	Strathaven
13	Beith	43	Colville Park	74	Haggs Castle	105	Loudoun Golf Club	136	Strathclyde Park
14	Bellshill	44	Corrie	75	Hamilton	106	Machrie Bay	137	Tarbert
15	Biggar	45	Cowal	76	Hayston	107	Machrie Hotel & G Links	138	Tobermory
16	Bishopbriggs	46	Cowglen	77	Helensburgh	108	Machrihanish	139	Torrance House
17	Blairbeth	47	Craignure	78	Hilton Park	109	Maybole	140	Troon Municipal
18	Blairmore & Strone	48	Crow Wood	79	Hollandbush	110	Millport	141	Turnberry Hotel
19	Bonnyton	49	Dalmally	80	Innellan	111	Milngavie	142	Vale of Leven
20	Bothwell Castle	50	Doon Valley	81	Inverary	112	Mount Ellen	143	Vaul
21	Brodick	51	Dougalston	82	Irvine	113	New Cumnock	144	West Kilbride
22	Brunston Castle	52	Douglas Park	83	Irvine Ravenspark	114	Old Course Ranfurly	145	Western Gailes
23	Bute	53	Douglas Water	84	Kilbirnie Place	115	Paisley	146	Westerwood Hotel Golf
24	Calderbraes	54	Drumpellier	85	Kilmacolm	116	Palacerigg		& Country Club
25	Caldwell	55	Dullatur	86	Kilmarnock (Barassie)	117	Pollok	147	Whinhill
26	Cambuslang	56	Dumbarton	87	Kilsyth Lennox	118	Port Bannatyne	148	Whitecraigs
27	Campsie	57	Dunaverty	88	Kirkhill	119	Port Glasgow	149	Whiting Bay
28	Caprington	58	East Kilbride	89	Kirkintilloch	120	Prestwick	150	Williamwood
29	Cardross	59	East Renfrewshire	90	Knightswood	121	Prestwick St Cuthbert	151	Windyhill
		60	Easter Moffat	91	Kyles of Bute	122	Prestwick St Nicholas	152	Wishaw

Hotels: Glenbay; Kelvin, both Glenluce; North West Castle, Stranraer.

9A 94 Winterfield

North Rd, Dunbar, E Lothian EH42 1AU
☎ (01368) 862280, Pro 863562, Sec 865119
Off A1 to Dunbar; club 0.5 miles from High Street.
Links course.
Pro Kevin Phillips; Founded 1935
18 holes, 5155 yards, S.S.S. 64
Visitors: welcome; WE restrictions.
Green Fees: WD £11.50; WE £13.75.
Societies: welcome by prior arrangement with Pro; packages available for 18 or 36 holes of golf plus catering; from £11.50.
Catering: full clubhouse facilities.
Hotels: Bayswell; Hillside; Goldenstones; Craigengelt; Royal Mackintosh.

9B 1 Airdrie

Rochsoles, Airdrie, ML6 0PQ
☎ (01236) 762195, Pro 754360
N of Airdrie on Glenmavis road.
Parkland course.
Pro Gregor Monks; Founded 1877
Designed by James Braid
18 holes, 6004 yards, S.S.S. 69
Visitors: welcome by letter of introduction.

Green Fees: WD £15; WE £15.
Societies: welcome WD by arrangement with Sec; catering packages can be arranged; snooker; from £15.
Catering: full clubhouse facilities.
Hotels: Tudor; Kenilworth.

9B 2 Alexandra Park

Alexandra Park, Sannox Gdns, Glasgow, G31 8SE
☎ (0141) 556 1294, Pro 770 0519
Off M8 before Blochairn.
Wooded parkland course.
Pro Alistair Baker; Founded 1818
Designed by Graham McArthur
9 holes, 4016 yards
Visitors: welcome.
Green Fees: terms on application.
Societies: none.
Hotels: Copthorne; Kelvin Park; Stakis Ingram Hotel; Central; Courtyard.

9B 3 Annanhill

Irvine Rd, Kilmarnock, Ayrshire, KA1 4RT
☎ (01563) 521644, Sec 525557
1 mile N of Kilmarnock on the A71 Irvine road.
Parkland course.
Founded 1957
Designed by J. McLean
18 holes, 6269 yards, S.S.S. 70
Visitors: welcome by prior arrangement.

Green Fees: WD £10; WE £15
Societies: welcome by prior arrangement; catering can be arranged; terms on application.
Catering: full clubhouse facilities.
Hotels: Howard Park; Portman.

9B 4 Ardeer

Greenhead, Stevenston, Ayrshire, KA20 4JX
☎ (01294) 464542, Pro 601327, Sec 465316
Follow A78 signs for Largs and Greenock on High road by-passing Stevenston; turn right in Kerelaw Rd.
Parkland course; Founded 1880
18 holes, 6630 yards, S.S.S. 72
Visitors: welcome except Sat.
Green Fees: WD £12; WE £20.
Societies: Welcome Sun-Fri; full day's golf (£30 on Sun); packages available for groups of 12 or more; from £25.
Catering: full catering facilities.

9B 5 Auchenharvie Golf Complex

Moor Park Rd West, Brewery Park, Stevenston, Ayrshire, KA20 3HU
☎ (01294) 603103
Links/parkland course.
Founded 1981
Designed by Michael Struthers
9 holes, 5130 yards, S.S.S. 66
Visitors: welcome.

Green Fees: WD £4.30; WE £6.40.
Societies: welcome by prior arrangement; from £4.30.
Catering: clubhouse bar.
Driving range.

9B 6 Ayr Belleisle

Belleisle Park, Doonfoot Rd, Doonfoot, Ayr, Ayrshire, KA7 4DU
☎(01292) 441314, Fax 442632, Sec 441258, Bar/Rest 442331
Follow signs for Burns Cottage Drive on A719 1.5 miles S of Ayr.
Parkland course/on same site as Ayr Seafield.
Pro David Gemmel; Founded 1927
Designed by James Braid & Stutt
18 holes, 6431 yards, S.S.S. 71
Visitors: public pay and play.
Green Fees: WD £17; WE £17.
Societies: welcome; 7 day advance booking system; catering by arrangement in local hotels; separate locker room; from £17.
Catering: limited facilities.
Practice range at Prestwick Golf Centre.
Hotels: Belleisle.

9B 7 Ayr Dalmilling

Westwood Ave, Ayr, Strathclyde, KA8 0QY
☎(01292) 263893, Fax 610543
On A77 1 mile N of Ayr near race-course.
Parkland course/meadowland
Pro Philip Cheyney; Founded 1960
18 holes, 5724 yards, S.S.S. 68
Visitors: welcome by prior arrangement.
Green Fees: WD £10; WE £10
Societies: welcome by at least seven days prior arrangement; catering packages involving snacks/lunches/high tea available; terms on application.
Catering: full clubhouse facilities.

9B 8 Ayr Seafield

Belleisle Park, Doonfoot Rd, Ayrshire, KA7 4DU
☎(01292) 441258, Fax 442632
1.5 miles S of Ayr on A719 following signs for Burns Cottage Drive.
Parkland/seaside course; on same site as Ayr Belleisle.
Pro David Gemmel; Founded 1927
Designed by J Braid
18 holes, 5481 yards, S.S.S. 68
Visitors: welcome.
Green Fees: WD £11; WE £11
Societies: welcome by prior arrangement; seven-day booking system in

operation; catering can be arranged in the local hotels; from £11.
Catering: limited.
Practice range at Prestwick Golf Centre.
Hotels: Belleisle.

9B 9 Ballochmyle

Ballochmyle, Mauchline, Ayrshire, KA5 6LE
☎(01290) 550469, Fax 553150
On B705 off A76 1 mile S of Mauchline; following signs for Ballochmyle Hospital.
Inland/parkland course.
Founded 1937
18 holes, 5972 yards, S.S.S. 69
Visitors: welcome except Sat.
Green Fees: terms on application.
Societies: welcome Mon, Tues, Thurs, Fri and Sun; tee times available between 9am-10am and 2pm-3pm WD; Sun 10am-10.45am and 2.30pm-3.15pm; catering packages available; terms on application.
Catering: full clubhouse facilities.
Hotels: Royal; Dumfries Arms.

9B 10 Balmore

Balmore, Torrance, Stirlingshire, G64 4AW
☎(01360) 620240
2 miles N of Glasgow on A807 off A803.
Parkland course.
Founded 1906
Designed by James Braid
18 holes, 5542 yards, S.S.S. 67
Visitors: welcome by introduction of a member.
Green Fees: terms on application.
Societies: none.
Catering: full clubhouse facilities.

9B 11 Barshaw

Barshaw Park, Glasgow Rd, Paisley, Renfrewshire
☎(0141) 889 2908, Sec 884 2533
1 mile before Paisley Cross off the A737.
Meadowland course.
Founded 1920
18 holes, 5703 yards, S.S.S. 67
Visitors: welcome.
Green Fees: WD £7; WE £7
Societies: limited.
Catering: limited.
Hotels: Water Mill; Brablock.

9B 12 Bearsden

Thorn Rd, Bearsden, Glasgow, G61 4BP

☎(0141) 942 2351, Sec 942 2381
1 mile N of Bearsden Cross on Thorn Rd.
Parkland course; 9 holes, 16 tees;
Founded 1891
9 holes, 6014 yards, S.S.S. 69
Visitors: welcome only as members' guest.
Green Fees: terms on application.
Societies: welcome only by prior arrangement; terms on application.
Catering: light meals and snacks available.
Hotels: Black Bull; Burnbrae.

9B 13 Beith

Threepwood Rd, Beith, Ayrshire, KA15 2JR
☎(01505) 503166
2 miles S of Linwood about 1 mile E of Beith.
Hilly parkland course.
Founded 1896
18 holes, 5616 yards, S.S.S. 68
Visitors: welcome.
Green Fees: WD £15; WE £20.
Societies: welcome by written prior arrangement; catering packages by arrangement; from £15.
Catering: full catering facilities.

9B 14 Bellshill

Community Rd, Orbiston, Bellshill, Lanarkshire, ML4 2RZ
☎(01698) 745124
Between Bellshill and Strathclyde Country Park lose to M74 junction 5 for the A725 or the A725 junction on the A8.
Parkland course.
Founded 1905
18 holes, 6315 yards, S.S.S. 70
Visitors: welcome by prior arrangement; restricted Sat.
Green Fees: WD £18; WE £25.
Societies: welcome by prior written arrangement; tee off after 1.30pm Sun; all inclusive packages available for 18 and 36 holes of golf; from £18.
Catering: full catering facilities.
Hotels: Bothwell Bridge; Moorings House; Silvertrees.

9B 15 Biggar

The Park, Broughton Rd, Biggar, Lanarkshire, ML12 6QX
☎(01899) 220618, Pro 220319, Sec 220566
Off the A702 0.5 miles from the town centre.
Parkland course.
Founded 1895

Designed by Willie Park
18 holes, 5537 yards, S.S.S. 68
Visitors: welcome by prior arrangement.
Green Fees: WD £8; WE £9.
Societies: welcome by prior arrangement; packages for golf and catering may be available in 1998; terms on application.
Catering: full clubhouse facilities available.
Hotels: Elphinstone; Clydesdale; Tinto.

9B 16 Bishopbriggs
Brackenbrae Rd, Bishopbriggs, Glasgow, G64 2DX
☎(0141) 772 1810 Fax 762 2532;Sec 772 8938, Bar/Rest 7721810
On A803 4 miles north of Glasgow turning 200 yards short of the Bishopbriggs cross.
Parkland course.
Founded 1906
Designed by James Braid
18 holes, 6041 yards, S.S.S. 69
Visitors: welcome only by prior arrangement.
Green Fees: terms on application.
Societies: welcome Tues, Wed, Thurs only; apply to Sec at least 1 month in advance; terms on application.
Catering: catering facilities.

9B 17 Blairbeth
Fernbrae Ave, Rutherglen, G73 4SF
☎(0141) 634 3355, Sec 569 7266
1 mile S of Rutherglen off Stonelaw Rd.
Parkland course.
Founded 1910/57
18 holes, 5518 yards, S.S.S. 68
Visitors: welcome either as member's guest or by prior arrangement.
Green Fees: terms on application.
Societies: terms on application.
Catering: clubhouse facilities.
Hotels: Kings Park.

9B 18 Blairmore & Strone
Strone, By Dunoon, Argyll, PA23 8TJ
☎(01369) 840676
On A880 0.75 miles N of Strone and 5 miles N of Dunoon.
Undulating moorland/parkland course with views of Clyde.
Founded 1896
Designed by J Braid
9 holes, 4224 yards, S.S.S. 62
Visitors: welcome; some restrictions Sat and Mon evening.
Green Fees: WD £8; WE £10.

Societies: welcome by prior arrangement with Sec; from £8.
Catering: bar facilities in summer.

9B 19 Bonnyton
Kirtonmoor Road, Eaglesham, Glasgow, G76 0QA
☎(01355) 302781, Fax 303151, Pro 302256
1 mile S of Eaglesham; 10 miles S of Glasgow.
Moorland course.
Pro Kendal McWade; Founded 1957
18 holes, 6255 yards, S.S.S. 71
Visitors: welcome by arrangement.
Green Fees: terms on application.
Societies: welcome Mon and Thurs by prior arrangement; catering packages can be arranged; terms on application.
Catering: full clubhouse facilities.
Hotels: Stakis West Point, E Kilbride.

9B 20 Bothwell Castle
Blantyre Rd, Bothwell, Glasgow, G71 8PJ
☎(01698) 853177, Fax 854052, Pro 852052, Sec 854052
3 miles N of Hamilton on the A9071 from the M74 junction 5.
Parkland course.
Pro Adam McCloskey; Founded 1922
18 holes, 6243 yards, S.S.S. 70
Visitors: welcome WD 9.30am-3.30pm.
Green Fees: WD £20.
Societies: welcome WD by written prior arrangement; catering packages by arrangement; from £20.
Catering: full clubhouse facilities.
Hotels: Silvertrees; Bothwell Bridge.

9B 21 Brodick
Brodick, Isle of Arran, KA27 8DL
☎(01770) 302349, Pro 302513
1 mile N of Pier.
Parkland/links course.
Founded 1897
18 holes, 4736 yards, S.S.S. 64
Visitors: welcome by prior arrangement.
Green Fees: WD £14; WE £17.
Societies: welcome by prior written arrangement; catering packages available; from £14.
Catering: full clubhouse facilities.

9B 22 Brunston Castle
Bargany, Dailly, By Girvan, Ayrshire, KA26 9RH
☎(01465) 811471, Fax 811545

Off the A77 at Girvan then on to B741 to Dailly.
Parkland course.
Pro Derek McKenzie; Founded 1992
Designed by Donald Steel
18 holes, 6681 yards, S.S.S. 73
Visitors: welcome.
Green Fees: WD £26; WE £30.
Societies: welcome by prior arrangement with Pro; includes a full day's golf; company days; pro-ams also catered for; golf clinics; catering packages; 10% discount for larger groups; £5 pp deposit required; from £40.
Catering: full clubhouse facilities with restaurant.
Hotels: Brunston Castle Holiday Resort; Kings Arms, Girvan; Malin Court, Turnberry.

9B 23 Bute
Kingarth, Isle of Bute, Strathclyde
☎(01700), Sec 504369
In Stravanan Bay off A845 Rothesay-Kilchattan Bay road.
Links course.
Founded 1888
9 holes, 4994 yards, S.S.S. 64
Visitors: welcome, but not before 12.30pm on Sat.
Green Fees: WD £6; WE £6.
Hotels: Kingarth; St Blanes.

9B 24 Calderbraes
57 Roundknowe Rd, Uddingston, G71 7TS
☎(01698) 813425
Close to start of M74; 4 miles from Glasgow.
Hilly parkland course.
Founded 1891
9 holes, 5186 yards, S.S.S. 67
Visitors: public.
Green Fees: WD £12; WE £12.
Societies: welcome WD by prior arrangement; maximum 20; catering packages available; from £12.
Catering: full bar and catering facilities.
Hotels: Redstones.

9B 25 Caldwell
Uplawmoor, Renfrewshire, G78 4AU
☎(01505) 850329, Fax 850604, Pro 850616, Sec 850366
Off A736 5 miles SW of Barrhead; 12 miles NE of Irvine.
Moorland course.
Pro Stephen Forbes; Founded 1903
18 holes, 6228 yards, S.S.S. 70
Visitors: welcome WD but advisable to check in advance.

Green Fees: terms on application.
Societies: welcome WD except Thurs by prior arrangement; catering by arrangement; terms on application.
Catering: clubhouse facilities.
Hotels: Uplawmoor; Dalmeny Park.

9B 26 Cambuslang
30 Westburn Drive, Cambuslang, Glasgow, G72 7NA
☎(0141) 641 3130, Sec 6413130, Bar/Rest 6413130
Off main Glasgow to Hamilton road at Cambuslang.
Parkland course.
Founded 1891
9 holes, 6072 yards, S.S.S. 69
Visitors: welcome by written application to secretary.
Green Fees: terms on application.
Societies: apply in writing to secretary; catering by arrangement; terms on application.
Catering: full clubhouse facilities.
Hotels: Cambus Court.

9B 27 Campsie
Crow Rd, Lennoxtown, Glasgow, G65 7HX
☎(01360) 310244, Pro 310920
On B822 to N of Lennoxtown.
Hillside/parkland course.
Pro Mark Brennan; Founded 1897
Designed by W Auchterlonie
18 holes, 5509 yards, S.S.S. 67
Visitors: welcome WD; WE by prior arrangement after 4pm.
Green Fees: WD £12; WE £15.
Societies: welcome by prior arrangement with Sec; full day's golf; catering: by arrangement; from £20.
Catering: clubhouse facilities.
Hotels: Glazert Country House Hotel, Lennoxtown.

9B 28 Caprington
Ayr Rd, Kilmarnock, Ayrshire, KA1 4UW
☎(01563) 523702
On Ayr road S of Kilmarnock.
Parkland course.
18 holes, 5781 yards, S.S.S. 68
Visitors: welcome.
Green Fees: terms on application.
Societies: apply to Sec; terms on application.
Catering: clubhouse facilities.

9B 29 Cardross
Main Rd, Cardross, Dumbarton, G82 5LB

☎(01389) 841213, Fax 841754, Pro 841350, Sec 841754
On A814 to Helensburgh 18 miles from Glasgow.
Parkland course.
Pro Robert Farrell; Founded 1895
Designed by James Braid
18 holes, 6469 yards, S.S.S. 71
Visitors: welcome WD.
Green Fees: WD £25.
Societies: none.
Catering: full clubhouse facilities.
Hotels: Cameron House; Kirkton House.

9B 30 Carluke
Mauldslie Rd, Hallcraig, Carluke, ML8 5HG
☎(01555) 770574, Pro 751053, Sec 773086, Bar/Rest 771070
Easy access from both M74 and M8; from M74 leave at junction 7 and take the Lanark turn until lights at Garron Bridge; left on to A71 and then on to B7011; club 2.5 miles.
Parkland course.
Pro Ricky Forrest; Founded 1894
18 holes, 5853 yards, S.S.S. 68
Visitors: welcome WD 9am-4pm.
Green Fees: WD £18.
Societies: welcome by prior arrangement; maximum 24; from £18-£25.
Catering: full clubhouse facilities.
Hotels: Popinjay; Cartland Bridge.

9B 31 Carnwath
1 Main St, Carnwath, Strathclyde, ML11 8JX
☎(01555) 840251
5 miles NE of Lanark.
Undulating parkland course.
Founded 1907
18 holes, 5953 yards, S.S.S. 69
Visitors: welcome except Sat or after 4pm WD.
Green Fees: WD £20; WE £30.
Societies: welcome WD except Tues and Thurs by prior arrangement; catering by arrangement; from £20.
Catering: catering except Tues and Thurs.
Hotels: Tinto, Symington.

9B 32 Carradale
Carradale, Campbeltown, Argyll, PA28 6SA
☎(01583) 431643
Off B842 from Campbeltown in Kintyre.
Difficult scenic course with sea views;
Founded 1906
9 holes, 4784 yards, S.S.S. 63

Visitors: welcome.
Green Fees: WD £8; WE £8.
Societies: welcome by prior arrangement; catering in local hotels; from £8.
Catering: catering in local hotels.
Hotels: Carradale; Ashbank.

9B 33 Cathcart Castle
Mearns Rd, Clarkston, Glasgow, G76 7YL
☎(0141) 638 9449, Pro 638 3436
On B767 1 mile from Clarkston.
Undulating parkland course.
Founded 1895
18 holes, 5832 yards, S.S.S. 68
Visitors: welcome if introduced by a member.
Green Fees: WD £25; WE £25.
Societies: welcome Tues and Thurs by arrangement with Sec; day ticket £35; catering by prior arrangement; from £25.
Catering: clubhouse facilities.
Hotels: Redhurst; Macdonald; Busby.

9B 34 Cathkin Braes
Cathkin Rd, Rutherglen, Glasgow, G73 4SE
☎(0141) 634 4007, Pro 634 0650, Sec 634 6605
On B759 SE of Glasgow between A749 and B766.
Moorland course.
Pro Stephen Bree; Founded 1888
Designed by James Braid
18 holes, 6208 yards, S.S.S. 71
Visitors: welcome WD.
Green Fees: WD £25.
Societies: welcome WD by prior arrangement; packages available; from £25.
Catering: full catering facilities.
Hotels: Stuart; Bruce; Burnside; Busby.

9B 35 Cawder
Cadder Rd, Bishopbriggs, Glasgow, G64 3QD
☎(0141) 772 7101, Pro 772 7102, Sec 772 5167
Off A803 Glasgow-Kirkintilloch road 0.5 miles E of Bishopbriggs.
Parkland course.
Pro Ken Stevley; Founded 1933
Designed by Donald Steel (Cawder)
Designed by James Braid (Keir)
Cawder: 18 holes, 6295 yards, S.S.S. 71; Keir: 18 holes, 5870 yards, S.S.S. 68
Visitors: welcome WD by arrangement with Sec.
Green Fees: WD £26.

Societies: welcome WD by prior arrangement with Sec; day ticket £31; catering packages by arrangement; from £26.
Catering: full catering facilities.
Hotels: Black Bull; Glazert Country House; Crow Wood House.

9B 36 Clober
Craigton Rd, Milngavie, G62 7HP
☎(0141) 956 1685, Pro 956 6963, Bar/Rest 9561685
7 miles NW of Glasgow.
Parkland course.
Pro Alan Tait; Founded 1952
Designed by Lyle Family
18 holes, 4963 yards, S.S.S. 65
Visitors: welcome WD until 4pm.
Green Fees: terms on application.
Societies: welcome WD by prior arrangement; catering packages available; terms on application.
Catering: full clubhouse facilities.
Hotels: Black Bull; Crosskeys; Burnbrae.

9B 37 Clydebank & District
Glasgow Rd, Hardgate, Clydebank, Dumbartonshire, G81 5QY
☎(01389) 873289, Fax 800098, Pro 878686, Sec 873407
Off A82 turning right at Hardgate; 10 miles W of Glasgow.
Parkland course.
Pro D Pirie; Founded 1905
Designed by Committee members
18 holes, 5825 yards, S.S.S. 68
Visitors: welcome WD.
Green Fees: WD £15.
Societies: welcome WD by prior arrangement; terms on application.
Catering: full clubhouse facilities.
Small practice area.
Hotels: West Hills; Boulevard; Radnor; Duntugher; West Highways.

9B 38 Clydebank Municipal
Overtoun Rd, Dalmuir, Clydebank, G81 3RE
☎(0141) 952 8698, Sec 941 1331, Bar/Rest 9528698
8 miles W of Glasgow.
Municipal parkland course.
18 holes, 5349 yards, S.S.S. 67
Visitors: welcome except between 11am-2pm at WE.
Green Fees: terms on application.
Societies: contact local district council; terms on application.
Catering: snack and café facilities available.
Hotels: Radnor.

9B 39 Clydebank Overtoun
Overtoun Rd, Clydebank, Dumbartonshire, G81 3RE
☎(0141) 952 6372
5 minutes from Dalmuir station.
Municipal parkland course.
Pro Ian Toy; Founded 1928
18 holes, 5349 yards, S.S.S. 66
Visitors: welcome.
Green Fees: WD £6.55; WE £7.
Societies: welcome by arrangement; limited facilities.
Catering: café only.

9B 40 Coatbridge
Townhead Rd, Coatbridge, Lanark, ML5 2HX
☎(01236) 421492
In Coatbridge town.
Public parkland course.
Pro George Weir; Founded 1971
18 holes, 6026 yards, S.S.S. 69
Visitors: welcome.
Green Fees: terms on application.
Societies: welcome by prior arrangement.
Catering: full facilities.
Practice range, 18 bays floodlit.

9B 41 Cochrane Castle
Scott Ave, Craigston, Johnstone, PA5 0HF
☎(01505) 320146, Fax 325338, Pro 328465
0.5 miles off Beith Road in Johnstone.
Parkland course.
Pro Jason Boyd; Founded 1895
Designed by Charles Hunter of Prestwick; Altered by James Braid
18 holes, 6226 yards, S.S.S. 71
Visitors: welcome WD; with member at WE.
Green Fees: WD £17.
Societies: none.
Catering: full clubhouse facilities.
Hotels: Bird in Hand; Lynnhurst, both Johnstone.

9B 42 Colonsay
Isle of Colonsay, Argyll, PA61 7YP
☎(01951) 200316 Fax 200353
2 miles W of Scalascraig pier; car ferry two-and-a-half-hour journey from mainland.
Natural machair course.
Founded 1880
18 holes, 4775 yards, S.S.S. 72
Visitors: welcome.
Green Fees: WD £5; WE £5.
Catering: all facilities at Colonsay Hotel; courtesy car provided to course.
Hotels: The Colonsay Hotel.

9B 43 Colville Park
New Jerviston House, Merry St, Motherwell, Lanarkshire, ML1 4UG
☎(01698) 263017, Fax 230418, Pro 265779, Sec 265378
1 mile NE of Motherwell railway station.
Parkland course.
Pro Alan Forrest; Founded 1923
Designed by James Braid
18 holes, 6265 yards, S.S.S. 70
Visitors: welcome as member's guest only.
Green Fees: WD £2; WE £3.
Societies: welcome by written prior arrangement; catering packages can be arranged; maximum 36; £20.
Catering: full clubhouse facilities available.
Hotels: Old Mill; Moorings; Silvertrees.

9B 44 Corrie
Sannox, Isle of Arran, KA27 8JD
☎(01770) 810223
7 miles N of Brodick on A84 coast road.
Picturesque undulating course.
Founded 1892
9 holes, 3896 yards, S.S.S. 61
Visitors: welcome except for some Thurs and Sat afternoons.
Green Fees: WD £7; WE £7.
Societies: welcome by prior arrangement; catering by arrangement; maximum normally 12.
Catering: catering available in season April-Oct.

9B 45 Cowal
Ardenslate Rd, Dunoon, Argyll, PA23 8NN
☎(01369) 702216, Fax 705673, Pro 702395, Sec 705673, Bar/Rest 702426
From the Shore road turn up Kirn Brae.
Heath/parkland course.
Pro Russell Weir; Founded 1891
Designed by James Braid
18 holes, 6063 yards, S.S.S. 70
Visitors: welcome.
Green Fees: WD £16; WE £24.
Societies: welcome; packages include transport, catering, and 18 holes of golf; from £27.
Catering: full clubhouse catering.
Hotels: local tourist office can provide details.

9B 46 Cowglen
301 Barrhead Rd, Glasgow, G43 1EU
☎(0141) 632 0556, Pro 649 9401

S side of Glasgow following signs for Burrell Collection.
Undulating parkland course.
Pro John McTear; Founded 1906
18 holes, 5976 yards, S.S.S. 69
Visitors: welcome if introduced by a member.
Green Fees: WD £22.
Societies: welcome by prior arrangement with Sec; catering packages available; from £22.
Catering: clubhouse facilities.
Hotels: Tinto.

9B 47 **Craignure**

Scallastle, Craignure, Isle of Mull, PA65 6AY
☎(01680) 812487;
1 mile from Oban/Mill ferry terminal.
Links course built on estuary of Scallastle River; Founded 1895/1979
9 holes, 5072 yards, S.S.S. 65
Visitors: welcome except on comp days.
Green Fees: WD £12; WE £12.
Societies: welcome by arrangement; weekly ticket (£45) available; £12.
Catering: limited clubhouse facilities.
Hotels: Isle of Mull; Craignure Inn.

9B 48 **Crow Wood**

Garnkirk House, Cumbernauld Rd, Muirhead, Glasgow, G69 9JF
☎(0141) 779 2011, Fax 779 9148, Pro 779 1943, Sec 779 4954
Off A80 Stirling road midway between Stepps and Muirhead 5 miles N of Glasgow.
Parkland course.
Pro Brian Moffat; Founded 1925
Designed by James Braid
18 holes, 6261 yards, S.S.S. 70
Visitors: welcome WD.
Green Fees: WD £20.
Societies: welcome WD only by prior arrangement; catering can be arranged; from £20.
Catering: full clubhouse facilities.
Practice range available.
Hotels: Garfield House, Stepps; Crow Wood House, Muirhead.

9B 49 **Dalmally**

'Orchy Bank', Dalmally, Argyll, PA33 1AS
☎(01838) 200370
2 miles W of Dalmally Village on A85.
Parkland course.
Founded 1987
Designed by C MacFarlane Barrow
9 holes, 4514 yards, S.S.S. 63
Visitors: welcome.

Green Fees: WD £10; WE £10.
Societies: welcome by prior arrangement; bar snacks and meals can be arranged; £8.
Catering: by arrangement; bar facilities.
Hotels: Glen Orchy Lodge.

9B 50 **Doon Valley**

Hillside Park, Patna, Ayrshire, KA6 7JT
☎(01292) 531607, Sec 550411
On A713 Ayr to Castle Douglas road 10 miles S of Ayr.
Undulating parkland course.
Founded 1927
Course redesigned by E Ayrshire Council
9 holes, 5856 yards, S.S.S. 69
Visitors: welcome WD; WE by arrangement.
Green Fees: WD £9; WE £9.
Societies: welcome WD; some WE by prior arrangement; day ticket for golf; catering available by arrangement; £15.
Catering: bar open evenings WD; all day WE.
Practice range opening 1999.
Hotels: Smithson Farm B&B; Bellsbank House; Parsons Lodge.

9B 51 **Dougalston**

Strathblane Rd, Milngavie, Glasgow, G62 8HJ
☎(0141) 956 5750, Fax 956 6480
On A81 NW of Glasgow out of Milngavie going to Aberfoyle.
400-acre parkland course.
Founded 1978
Designed by John Harris
18 holes, 6354 yards, S.S.S. 72
Visitors: welcome WD.
Green Fees: WD £14.
Societies: welcome WD by prior arrangement; packages available for 18 or 36 holes; full day or part-day catering; 10 per cent deposit required; from £15.
Catering: full clubhouse catering.
Hotels: Black Bull; Burnbrae, both Milngavie.

9B 52 **Douglas Park**

Hillfoot, Bearsden, Glasgow, G61 2TJ
☎(0141) 942 2220, Pro 942 1482
6 miles N of Glasgow adjacent to Hillfoot station off Milngavie road.
Undulating parkland course.
Pro D B Scott; Founded 1897
18 holes, 5962 yards, S.S.S. 69
Visitors: members guests only; occa-

sional overseas visitors if course is quiet.
Green Fees: terms on application.
Societies: welcome Wed and Thurs only; full day's golf £28; catering can be arranged; from £21.
Catering: full catering and licensed facilities.
Hotels: Burnbrae; Black Bull.

9B 53 **Douglas Water**

Ayr Rd, Rigside, Lanark, ML11 9NY
☎(01555) 88036, Sec 01698 792249
On A70 7 miles SW of Lanark.
Undulating parkland course.
Founded 1922
Designed by Striking Coal Miners 1921
9 holes, 5890 yards, S.S.S. 69
Visitors: welcome except on competition days.
Green Fees: terms on application.
Societies: welcome by prior arrangement with Sec; terms on application.
Catering: limited.

9B 54 **Drumpellier**

Drumpellier Ave, Coatbridge, ML5 1RX
☎(01236) 424139; Pro 432971, Sec 428723
On A89 8 miles E of Glasgow.
Parkland course.
Pro David Ross; Founded 1894
Designed by W. Fernie
18 holes, 6227 yards, S.S.S. 70
Visitors: welcome WD.
Green Fees: WD £22.
Societies: welcome WD by prior arrangement; catering packages available; pool table; from £22.
Catering: full clubhouse catering facilities.
Hotels: Georgian.

9B 55 **Dullatur**

Glen Douglas Drive, Dullatur, Glasgow, G68 0AR
☎(012367) 23230, Fax 27271
1.5 miles from Cumbernauld village.
Parkland course.
Pro Duncan Sinclair; Founded 1896
Designed by J Braid
Antonine: 18 holes, 5940 yards, S.S.S. 69; Carrickstone: 18 holes, 6204 yards, S.S.S. 70
Visitors: welcome except on competition days.
Green Fees: WD £15; WE £20.
Societies: welcome except on comp days; catering packages available from £12.50; from £15.

Catering: full clubhouse facilities.
Hotels: Castlecary House.

9B 56 Dumbarton
Broadmeadows, Dumbarton,
Dumbartonshire, G82 2BQ
☎(01389) 732830, Sec 765995
Off A82 15 miles NW of Glasgow.
Meadowland course.
Founded 1888
18 holes, 6017 yards, S.S.S. 69
Visitors: welcome WD.
Green Fees: WD £18.
Societies: welcome by arrangement;
catering by arrangement; from £18.
Catering: full clubhouse facilities.

9B 57 Dunaverty
Southend by Campbeltown, Argyll,
PA28 6RW
☎(01586) 830677
On B842 10 miles S of Campbeltown.
Undulating seaside course.
Founded 1889
18 holes, 4799 yards, S.S.S. 63
Visitors: welcome.
Green Fees: WD £13; WE £13.
Societies: limited availability; strictly
by prior arrangement; day ticket
£19.50; weekly £50; from £13.
Catering: snacks available.
Hotels: Argyll.

9B 58 East Kilbride
Chapelside Rd, Nerston, G74 4PF
☎(013552) 20913, Pro 22192, Sec
47728
In Nerston 10 miles SE of Glasgow.
Parkland course.
Pro Willie Walker; Founded 1900/67
Designed by Fred Hawtree
18 holes, 6419 yards, S.S.S. 71
Visitors: welcome WD by prior
arrangement with Sec.
Green Fees: WD £20.
Societies: welcome WD by prior writ-
ten arrangement; catering packages
available; pool room; from £20.
Catering: lounges and dining room
facilities in clubhouse.
Hotels: Stakis Westpoint; Bruce;
Stuart; Crutherland House.

9B 59 East Renfrewshire
Loganswell, Pilmuir, Newton Mearns,
Glasgow, G77 6RT
☎(01355) 500256; Pro 500206, Sec
0141 333 9989, Bar/Rest 500258
On A77 Glasgow to Kilmarnock road 2
miles S of Newton Mearns.
Moorland course.

Pro Gordon D Clarke; Founded 1922
Designed by James Braid
18 holes, 6097 yards, S.S.S. 70
Visitors: welcome by prior arrange-
ment with Pro.
Green Fees: WD £30; WE £30.
Societies: welcome Tues and Thurs
by arrangement with Sec; catering and
bar facilities by prior arrangement with
the clubhouse manager; from £30.
Catering: full clubhouse facilities.
Free practice area.

9B 60 Easter Moffat
Mansion House, Plains, by Airdrie,
Lanarkshire, ML6 8NP
☎(01236) 842289, Pro 843015, Sec
842878
2 miles E of Airdrie on the old
Edinburgh-Glasgow road.
Moorland/parkland course.
Pro Brian Dunbar; Founded 1922
18 holes, 6240 yards, S.S.S. 70
Visitors: welcome.
Green Fees: WD £15; WE £15.
Societies: welcome WD by prior
arrangement; day tickets £20; catering
by arrangement; from £15.
Catering: clubhouse facilities.
Hotels: Tudor Hotel, Airdrie.

9B 61 Eastwood
Loganswell, Newton Mearns, Glasgow,
G77 6RX
☎(01355) 500261, Pro 500285, Sec
500280
On A77 from Glasgow; 3 miles S of
Newton Mearns.
Moorland/parkland course.
Pro Alan McGinness; Founded 1893
Designed by J. Moon
18 holes, 5864 yards, S.S.S. 69
Visitors: welcome WD.
Green Fees: WD £24.
Societies: welcome WD by prior
arrangement; catering packages by
arrangement; from £24.
Catering: clubhouse facilities.
Hotels: Redhurst; Macdonald.

9B 62 Elderslie
63 Main Rd, Elderslie, Renfrewshire,
PA5 9AZ
☎(01505) 323956, Bar/Rest 322835
On A737 between Paisley and
Johnstone.
Undulating parkland course.
Founded 1909
18 holes, 6175 yards, S.S.S. 70
Visitors: welcome WD.
Green Fees: WD £20.
Societies: welcome Mon, Wed and Fri

by prior arrangement; day ticket £30;
catering by arrangement; snooker;
from £20.
Catering: full clubhouse facilities.
Hotels: Glasgow Airport hotels.

9B 63 Erskine
Bishopton, Renfrewshire, PA7 5PH
☎(01505) 862302, Pro 862108
Off Erskine Toll Bridge and turn left
along B815 for 1.5 miles.
Parkland course.
Pro Peter Thomson; Founded 1904
18 holes, 6241 yards, S.S.S. 70
Visitors: welcome if introduced by or
playing with a member.
Green Fees: terms on application.
Societies: welcome by prior arrange-
ment; catering by prior arrangement
only; terms on application.
Catering: meals served to members
or their guests only.
Hotels: Erskine; Crest.

9B 64 Fereneze
Fereneze Ave, Barrhead, Glasgow,
G78 1HJ
☎(0141) 881 1519, Pro 881 7058,
Sec 887 4141
9 miles SW of Glasgow near Barrhead
station.
Moorland course.
Pro Darren Robinson; Founded 1904
18 holes, 5962 yards, S.S.S. 71
Visitors: welcome by prior arrange-
ment or with member.
Green Fees: terms on application.
Societies: welcome WD only by prior
arrangement; catering by arrange-
ment; terms on application.
Catering: full clubhouse facilities
available; WD evening meals by
arrangement.
Hotels: Dalmeny Park.

9B 65 Gigha
Isle of Gigha, Kintyre, Argyll PA41 7AA
☎(01583) 505287
Ferry from Tayinloan takes 20 mins;
0.5 miles N from Gigha Post Office.
Parkland course
Founded 1988
Designed by Members
9 holes, 5042 yards, S.S.S. 65
Visitors: welcome.
Green Fees: WD £10; WE £10.
Societies: welcome; day ticket £15;
meals and bar at Gigha Hotel; from
£10.
Catering: meals and bar at the Gigha
Hotel.
Hotels: Gigha; Tayinloan.

9B 66 Girvan

Girvan, Ayrshire, KA26 9HW
☎(01465) 714346, Bar/Rest 714272.
Off A77 Stranraer to Ayr road.
Seaside links/parkland course.
Founded pre-1877.
Designed by James Braid
18 holes, 5064 yards, S.S.S. 64
Visitors: welcome by prior arrangement.
Green Fees: WD £12; WE £12.
Societies: welcome by prior arrangement; catering by arrangement; from £12.
Catering: catering by arrangement.
Hotels: Turnberry Hotel; Kings Arms.

9B 67 Glasgow

Killermont, Bearsden, Glasgow, G61 2TW
☎(0141) 942 1713, Fax 942 0770, Pro 942 8507, Sec 942 2011.
6 miles NW of Glasgow near Killermont Bridge taking the A81 or A806.
Parkland course.
Pro Jack Steven; Founded 1787/1905
Designed by Tom Morris Snr
18 holes, 5968 yards, S.S.S. 69
Visitors: welcome by prior arrangement.
Green Fees: WD £42; WE £42.
Societies: none.
Catering: lunches and high teas by application.
Hotels: Grosvenor; Burnbrae; Black Bull; Pond.

9B 68 Glasgow (Gailes)

Gailes, by Irvine, Ayrshire, KA11 5AE
☎(01294) 311258, Fax 0141 942;
Pro 311561 0770, Sec 0141 942 011, Bar/Rest 311347
2 miles S of Irvine on A78.
Championship seaside links
Pro Jack Steven; Founded 1787/1892
Designed by Willie Park, Jr.
18 holes, 6513 yards, S.S.S. 72
Visitors: welcome by prior arrangement with Sec or introduced by a member.
Green Fees: WD £42; WE £47.
Societies: welcome by arrangement with Sec only; WD day tickets £52; catering by arrangement; from £42.
Catering: full clubhouse facilities.
Hotels: Hospitality Inn, Irvine; Marine, Troon.

9B 69 Gleddoch Country Club

Langbank, Renfrewshire, PA14 6YE
☎(01475) 540304 Fax 540459 Pro 540704

M8 to Greenock; first turning to Langbank Houston on B789.
Parkland/moorland course.
Pro Keith Campbell; Founded 1975
Designed by Hamilton Stutt
18 holes, 6357 yards, S.S.S. 71
Visitors: welcome by prior arrangement with Pro.
Green Fees: terms on application.
Societies: welcome; catering packages by arrangement; terms on application.
Catering: clubhouse facilities.
Hotels: Glenddoch House.

9B 70 Glencruitten

Glencruitten Rd, Oban, Argyll, PA34 4PU
☎(01631) 562868, Pro 564115, Sec 564604
1 mile from the Town Centre.
Parkland course.
Pro Graham Clark; Founded 1900
Designed by James Braid
18 holes, 4250 yards, S.S.S. 63
Visitors: welcome except comp days.
Green Fees: WD £15; WE £15.
Societies: welcome by prior arrangement; discounts available; full catering packages by arrangement; from £13.50.
Catering: full clubhouse facilities.
Hotels: Kilchrenan House; Barriemore, both Oban.

9B 71 Gourock

Cowal View, Gourock, Renfrewshire, PA19 1HD
☎(01475) 631001, Pro 636834
2 miles uphill from Gourock station.
Moorland course.
Pro Gavin Coyle; Founded 1896
Designed by Henry Cotton
18 holes, 6512 yards, S.S.S. 73
Visitors: welcome by arrangement with Pro shop.
Green Fees: WD £18; WE £22.
Societies: welcome by prior arrangement; day tickets available WD £27; WE £29; catering by prior arrangement; from £18.
Catering: bar lunches and high teas; dinners by arrangement.
Hotels: Gantock.

9B 72 Greenock

Forsyth St, Greenock, Renfrewshire, PA16 8RE
☎(01475) 720793
1 mile SW of the town on the main road to Gourock.
Moorland course.

Pro Stewart Russell; Founded 1890
Designed by James Braid
18 holes, 5838 yards, S.S.S. 69
Visitors: welcome by prior arrangement with Sec.
Green Fees: terms on application.
Catering: full clubhouse facilities.
Hotels: Tontine.

9B 73 Greenock Whinhill

Beith Rd, Greenock, Renfrewshire, PA16 9LN
☎(01475) 724694, Pro 721064, Sec 633258
Off Largs Road.
Parkland course.
Founded 1911
Designed by W Fernie
18 holes, 5504 yards, S.S.S. 68
Visitors: welcome.
Green Fees: WD £6 WE £6.
Societies: none.
Catering: by arrangement.
Hotels: Stakis Gantock.

9B 74 Haggs Castle

70 Dumbreck Rd, Glasgow, G41 4SN
☎(0141) 427 0480, Fax 427 1157;
Pro 427 3355, Sec 427 1157
Close to M77 junction 1.
Parkland course.
Pro J McAlister; Founded 1910
Designed by Peter Alliss & Dave Thomas
18 holes, 6464 yards, S.S.S. 72
Visitors: welcome by arrangement.
Green Fees: WD £27; WE £27.
Societies: welcome WD only by arrangement with Sec; catering by arrangement; terms on application.
Catering: full clubhouse facilities.
Hotels: Shenbrooke Castle, Pollockshields.

9B 75 Hamilton

Riccarton, Ferniegair, Hamilton, Lanarkshire, ML3 7UE
☎(01698) 282872, Pro 282324, Sec 459557
Off A74 between Larkhill and Hamilton.
Parkland course.
Pro Maurice Moir; Founded 1892
Designed by James Braid
18 holes, 6264 yards, S.S.S. 71
Visitors: welcome by prior arrangement.
Green Fees: terms on application.
Societies: by arrangement with Sec; catering packages by arrangement; terms on application.
Catering: clubhouse facilities.

9B 76 Hayston
Campsie Rd, Kirkintilloch, Glasgow,
G66 1RN
☎(0141) 776 1244, Fax 775 0723,
Pro 775 0882, Sec 775 0723
7 miles N of Glasgow.
Parkland course.
Pro Steve Barnett; Founded 1926
Designed by James Braid
18 holes, 6042 yards, S.S.S. 70
Visitors: welcome by prior arrange-
ment on WD only.
Green Fees: WD £20.
Societies: welcome Tues and Thurs
by prior arrangement; day ticket £30;
maximum 24; catering by arrange-
ment; from £20.
Catering: full clubhouse facilities.
Hotels: Kincaid House.

9B 77 Helensburgh
25 East Abercromby St, Helensburgh,
Argyll, G84 9JD
☎(01436) 674173, Fax 671170, Pro
675505
Follow A82 to Helensburgh; signpost-
ed in town.
Moorland course.
Pro David Fotheringham; Founded
1893
Designed by James Braid
18 holes, 6104 yards, S.S.S. 70
Visitors: welcome WD.
Green Fees: WD £15; WE £15.
Societies: welcome by prior arrange-
ment; includes food and golf; from
£35.
Catering: full clubhouse dining facili-
ties.
Hotels: Commodore, Helensburgh;
Camerous House, Balloch.

9B 78 Hilton Park
Stockiemuir Rd, Milngavie, Glasgow,
G62 7HB
☎(0141) 956 5124, Pro 956 5125,
Sec 956 4657
On A809 8 miles N of Glasgow.
Meadowland course; also Allander
course: 5374 yards, S.S.S. 66
Pro Billy McCondichie; Founded 1927
Designed by James Braid
18 holes, 6054 yards, S.S.S. 6670
Visitors: welcome WD by prior
arrangement.
Green Fees: WD £20.
Societies: welcome WD; day rate of
approx £26; catering by arrangement;
from £20.
Catering: full catering facilities avail-
able.
Hotels: Kirkhouse; Black Bull; County
Club.

9B 79 Hollandbush
Acretophead, Lesmahagow, S
Lanarkshire, ML11 0JS
☎(01555) 893484, Pro 893646, Sec
820222, Bar/Rest 893546
Off M74 at Lesmahagow; course
between Lesmahagow and Coalburn.
Parkland courses on edge of moorland
Pro Ian Rae; Founded 1954
Designed by K Pate/ J Lawson
18 holes, 6218 yards, S.S.S. 70
Visitors: public municipal course.
Green Fees: terms on application.
Societies: none.
Catering: full clubhouse facilities.
Practice range available.
Hotels: Shawlands; Popinjay.

9B 80 Innellan
Knockamillie Rd, Innellan, Argyll
☎(01369) 830242
4 miles S of Dunoon.
Parkland course.
Founded 1891
9 holes, 4878 yards, S.S.S. 63
Visitors: welcome anytime except
Mon evening.
Green Fees: terms on application.
Societies: welcome by prior arrange-
ment; catering by arrangement; terms
on application.
Catering: by prior arrangement.
Hotels: Esplanade; Slatefield;
Rosscalm.

9B 81 Inverary
Inverary, Argyll, Argyll
☎(01499) 302508
SW corner of town on Lochgilphead
Road.
Parkland course.
Founded 1993
Designed by Watt Landscaping
9 holes, 5700 yards, S.S.S. 68
Visitors: welcome except comp days.
Green Fees: WD £10; WE £10.
Societies: welcome by prior arrange-
ment; golf only; catering available by
special arrangement with local hotels;
from £10.
Catering: none.
Hotels: Loch Fynn; George; Great
Inn.

9B 82 Irvine
Bogside, Irvine, N Ayrshire, KA12 8SN
☎(01294) 275979, Pro 275626
On the road from Irvine to Kilwinning,
turn left after Ravespark academy and
carry straight on for 0.5 miles over the
railway bridge.
Links course.

Pro Keith Erskine; Founded 1887
Designed by James Braid
18 holes, 6408 yards, S.S.S. 73
Visitors: welcome; but not before 3pm
WE.
Green Fees: WD £30; WE £45.
Societies: welcome by arrangement
with Sec; catering packages by
arrangement; from £30.
Catering: full clubhouse facilities.
Hotels: Hospitality Inn; Golf Hotel.

9B 83 Irvine Ravenspark
13 Kidsneuk Lane, Irvine, Ayrshire,
KA12 8SR
☎(01294) 271293, Pro 276467
On A78 midway between Irvine and
Kilwinning.
Municipal parkland course.
Pro M Bond; Founded 1907
18 holes, 6429 yards, S.S.S. 71
Visitors: welcome; not before 2.30
Sat.
Green Fees: WD £9; WE £13.
Societies: welcome by prior
arrangement with Sec for Sun; cater-
ing packages by arrangement; from
£15.50.
Catering: full clubhouse facilities.
Hotels: Hospitality Inn; Annfield;
Redburn; Golf Inn.

9B 84 Kilbirnie Place
Largs Rd, Kilbirnie, Ayrshire, KA25
7AJ
☎(01505) 683398, Sec 683283
On the main Largs road on the out-
skirts of Kilbirnie.
Parkland course.
Founded 1922
18 holes, 5517 yards, S.S.S. 69
Visitors: welcome WD.
Green Fees: WD £10.
Societies: welcome by prior arrange-
ment; on application; from £18.
Catering: full facilities.
Hotels: Ryan.

9B 85 Kilmacolm
Porterfield Rd, Kilmacolm,
Renfrewshire, PA13 4PD
☎(01505) 872139, Fax 874007; Pro
872695
From M8 Glasgow Airport follow the
main signs to Irvine; turn off 2nd junc-
tion and follow A761 to Kilmacolm.
Moorland course.
Pro David Stewart; Founded 1890
Designed by James Braid
18 holes, 5961 yards, S.S.S. 69
Visitors: welcome some WD by prior
arrangement.

Green Fees: WD £20.
Societies: welcome Tues, Wed, Thurs by prior arrangement; packages and prices depend on numbers; terms on application.
Catering: full clubhouse facilities.
Hotels: many in Glasgow, Renfrew and Paisley.

9B 86 Kilmarnock (Barassie)
Hillhouse Rd, Barassie, Troon, Ayrshire, KA10 6SY
☎(01292) 313920, Fax 313920, Pro 311322, Bar/Rest 311077
2 miles N of Troon directly opposite Barassie railway station.
Championship links course.
Pro Gregor Howie; Founded 1887
Designed by Matthew M. Monie
18 holes, 6817 yards, S.S.S. 72
Visitors: welcome WD except Wed; ladies reduced fees; not before 8.30am or between 12.30pm-1.30pm.
Green Fees: WD £32.50.
Societies: welcome WD except Wed by arrangement; catering can be arranged with club caterer; dining room; television lounge; 9-hole course, 2888 yards, par 34; from £32.50.
Catering: full clubhouse dining and bar; jacket and tie in dining room.
Hotels: South Beach; Prestland House, both Troon.

9B 87 Kilsyth Lennox
Tak-Ma-Doon Rd, Kilsyth, Glasgow, G65 0HX
☎(01236) 824115, Sec 823213.
On A80 12 miles from Glasgow.
Moorland/parkland course.
Founded 1907
18 holes, 5912 yards, S.S.S. 70
Visitors: welcome by prior arrangement with Sec or starter.
Green Fees: WD £16; WE £18.
Societies: welcome by arrangement with Sec; from £16.
Catering: clubhouse facilities.

9B 88 Kirkhill
Greenlees Rd, Cambuslang, Glasgow, G72 8YN
☎(0141) 641 3083, Pro 641 7972, Sec 641 8499, Bar/Rest 641 3083
Follow East Kilbride road from Burnside, take first turning on left past Cathkin by-pass roundabout.
Meadowland course.
Pro Duncan Williamson; Founded 1910
Designed by James Braid
18 holes, 5900 yards, S.S.S. 69

Visitors: welcome by arrangement.
Green Fees: WD £20; WE £20.
Societies: welcome by prior arrangement; catering by prior arrangement with caterer; from £15.
Catering: full facilities by prior arrangement; snacks and bar meals available.
Hotels: Kings Park; Burnside; Stuart; Bruce.

9B 89 Kirkintilloch
Todhill, Campsie Rd, Kirkintilloch, Glasgow, G66 1RN
☎(0141) 776 1256, Sec 775 2387
1 miles from Kirkintilloch on road to Lennoxtown.
Parkland course.
Founded 1895
Designed by James Braid
18 holes, 5269 yards, S.S.S. 66
Visitors: welcome with letter of introduction.
Green Fees: WD £18; WE £18.
Societies: welcome by prior arrangement; day ticket from £28; catering by arrangement; from £18.
Catering: clubhouse facilities; restrictions Mon and Tues.
Hotels: Garfield, Stepps.

9B 90 Knightswood
Lincoln Ave, Knightswood, G13
☎(0141) 959 6358, Sec 959 6495
From City Centre go W along Great Western Road through Knightswood past the cross and then left into Lincoln Avenue.
Flat parkland course.
Founded 1920
9 holes, 5584 yards, S.S.S. 64
Visitors: welcome, except Wed and Fri from 7.45am-8.45am and 10am-11am.
Green Fees: WD £6.50; WE £6.50.
Societies: welcome with same restrictions as visitors; from £6.50.
Catering: limited.
Hotels: Charing Cross Tower Hotel.

9B 91 Kyles of Bute
The Moss, Kames, Tighnabruaich, Argyll, PA21 2EE
☎(01700) Sec 811603
On B3836 on the road from Dunoon to Tighnabruaich, B8000 to Millhouse.
Undulating moorland course.
Founded 1907
9 holes, 4748 yards, S.S.S. 64
Visitors: welcome all times except Wed evenings and Sun 9.30am-1pm.
Green Fees: WD £8; WE £10.

Societies: welcome by arrangement with Sec; from £8.
Catering: snacks when available.
Hotels: Royal; Kames; Kilfenan.

9B 92 Lamlash
Lamlash, Brodick, Isle of Arran, KA27 8JU
☎(01770) 600296, Fax 600296, Sec 600272
3 miles S of pier terminal at Brodick.
Undulating heathland course.
Founded 1889
Designed by W Auchterlonie/W Fernie
18 holes, 4640 yards, S.S.S. 64
Visitors: welcome.
Green Fees: WD £10; WE £12.
Societies: welcome; day tickets WD £14, WE £18; catering by arrangement; from £10.
Catering: full clubhouse facilities.
Hotels: Glenisle; Lilybank; Marine.

9B 93 Lanark
The Moor, Whitelees Rd, Lanark, S Lanarkshire, ML11 7RX
☎(01555) 663219, Fax 663219, Pro 661456, Bar/Rest 665261
Take A73 or A72 to Lanark; turn left in town for Whitelees road.
Moorland course.
Pro Alan White; Founded 1851
Designed by T Morris
18 holes, 6423 yards, S.S.S. 71
Visitors: welcome WD; with member at WE.
Green Fees: WD £24; WE £4.
Societies: welcome by prior arrangement on WD; larger groups welcome Mon-Wed; max 12 Thurs & Fri; catering by arrangement; from £24.
Catering: full clubhouse facilities.
Hotels: Cartland Bridge; Popinjay; Tinto.

9B 94 Largs
Irvine Rd, Largs, Ayrshire, KA30 8EU
☎(01475) 674681, Fax 673594, Pro 686192, Sec 673594, Bar/Rest 687390
On A78 1 mile S of Largs.
Parkland/woodland course.
Pro Bob Collinson; Founded 1891
18 holes, 6115 yards, S.S.S. 71
Visitors: welcome by arrangement.
Green Fees: WD £25; WE £35.
Societies: welcome Tues and Thurs by prior arrangement; packages for 18 and 36 holes of golf plus catering; from £30.
Catering: full clubhouse facilities.
Hotels: Priory House; Haylie; Queens.

Loch Lomond

Golf courses are no different from paintings in giving rise to likes and dislikes. There are those who rave about the extravagance of multi-million-pound ventures although they may be far beyond their financial reach; and there are others who believe that the soundly designed and sensibly built creations highlighting the natural look, represent far better value for money.

The last few years in Britain and Ireland have seen examples of both but it has also been a period in which new courses have made the news for all the wrong reasons. Dreams all too quickly turned to nightmares, hopes to disillusionment.

Even making allowance for the recession, much of the damage was self-inflicted through a lack of proper understanding of the market, insufficient research, application of the wrong principles and scant knowledge of what British golfers need and can afford.

Developers, armed with a copy of the Royal & Ancient's pamphlet "Demand for Golf", and a vision of what they had seen and heard about the game in America and Japan, leapt to the conclusion that what works there would work here. Nothing could be further from the truth. However, rescue packages have come to the aid of several afflicted courses which undoubtedly deserved a reprieve – none more so than Loch Lomond on whose bonny, bonny banks Tom Weiskopf, one of the best professional golfers turned architect, has produced an eye catching 18-holes to test and dazzle the best.

Admittedly, his canvas is flanked by a frame of gold although wise heads warn of midges in summer. A stunning setting anywhere in the world is a great asset for a new course, a fact that raises the thought as to what opinion would have made of the actual courses at Pebble Beach, Gleneagles or Killarney if they had been created in Hackney Marshes instead.

Be that as it may, Loch Lomond will stand comparison in any contest, the first golfing requirement being definite control from the tee to hit largely well-guarded fairways. Since the hardest part of the game is to aim straight and hit straight, those finding the fairways should always have a decided advantage over those who do not. Weiskopf, in his time, was as handsome a player as there was and, not surprisingly, his design at Loch Lomond owes nothing to gimmickry.

It would be hard to find a challenge to Loch Lomond in terms of beauty but the Carnegia Links (or Skibo) on the Dornoch Firth in Sutherland manages it easily. Featured later in the book, it is the first links course to be built in Scotland or England for half a century and, considering the demands of ecologists and environmentalists, could well be one of the last.

9B 95 Larkhall

Burnhead Rd, Larkhall, Lanarkshire
☎(01698) 881113
Take M8 to Larkhall exit then head SW
on B7019.
Municipal parkland course.
9 holes, 6423 yards, S.S.S. 71
Visitors: pay and play.
Green Fees: WD £3.75; WE £3.75.
Societies: welcome by arrangement;
limited catering; from £3.75.
Catering: bar.

9B 96 Leadhills

Leadhills, Biggar, Lanarkshire, ML12
6XR
☎(01659) 74324
On B797 in Leadhills village 6 miles
from A74 at Abington.
Moorland course; highest course in
Scotland.
Founded 1935
9 holes, 4100 yards, S.S.S. 62
Visitors: welcome.
Green Fees: WD £5; WE £5.
Societies: welcome; catering organ-
ised in local hotel; from £5.
Catering: local hotel.
Hotels: Hopetoun Arms.

9B 97 Lenzie

19 Crosshill Rd, Lenzie, Glasgow, G66
5DA
☎(0141) 776 1535, Pro 777 7748,
Sec 776 6020
10 miles NE of Glasgow; leave M8 at
Stirling junction then head for
Kirkintilloch.
Parkland course.
Pro J McCallum; Founded 1889
18 holes, 5984 yards, S.S.S. 69
Visitors: welcome by prior arrange-
ment.
Green Fees: WD £18; WE £18.
Societies: welcome by prior arrange-
ment with club Sec; catering packages
by prior arrangement; professional can
assist on society days with golf clinic,
etc; from £18.
Catering: full clubhouse facilities
available.
Hotels: Moodiesburn, Moddiesburn;
Garfield, Stepps.

9B 98 Lethamhill

Cumbernauld Rd, Glasgow, G33 1AH
☎(0141) 770 6220
On A80 adjacent to Hogganfield Loch.
Municipal parkland course.
18 holes, 5836 yards, S.S.S. 70
Visitors: welcome.
Green Fees: WD £6.50; WE £6.50.

9B 99 Linn Park

Simshill Rd, Glasgow, G44 5EP
☎(0141) 637 5871
Off M74 S of Glasgow
Public parkland course.
Founded 1925
Designed by Glasgow Parks
18 holes, 5005 yards, S.S.S. 65
Visitors: welcome.
Green Fees: WD £5.50; WE £5.50.
Societies: welcome by prior applica-
tion; from £5.50.
Catering: clubhouse.

9B 100 Littlehill

Auchinairn Rd, Bishopbriggs,
Glasgow, G74 1UT
☎(0141) 772 1916
3 miles N of city centre.
Public parkland course.
Founded 1924
Designed by James Braid
18 holes, 6228 yards, S.S.S. 70
Visitors: welcome.
Green Fees: terms on application.
Societies: apply to Council for full
details.
Catering: clubhouse facilities; except
Mon; WE only in the winter.

9B 101 Loch Lomond

Rossdhu House, Luss by Alexandria,
Dunbartonshire, G83 8NT
☎(01436) 655555, Pro 655540
On the A82 on the W bank of Loch
Lomond.
Championship parkland course; host
of Loch Lomond Classic.
Pro Colin Campbell; Founded 1995
Designed by Tom Weiskopf and Jay
Morrish
18 holes, 7060 yards, S.S.S. 72
Visitors: private; with member only.
Green Fees: WD £100; WE £100.
Societies: none.
Catering: first-class clubhouse facili-
ties.
Hotels: Cameron House.

9B 102 Lochgilphead

Blarbuie Road, Lochgilphead, Argyll,
PA31 8LE
☎(01546) 602340, Sec 603840
Follow signs for Argyll & Bute Hospital
from the centre of Lochgilphead.
Hilly parkland course.
Founded 1891/1963
Designed by Dr Ian MacCammond
9 holes, 4484 yards, S.S.S. 63
Visitors: welcome.
Green Fees: WD £10; WE £10.
Societies: welcome; weekly ticket of

£30; reductions for groups registered
with the club; from £10.
Catering: bar facilities; catering by
arrangement.
Hotels: Stag; Argyll'Lochgair.

9B 103 Lochranza

Lochranza, Isle of Arran, KA27 8HL
☎(01770) 830273, Fax 830600
In Lochranza opposite the distillery.
Grassland course with rivers/trees: 3
holes on seashore.
Founded 1991
Designed by Iain M. Robertson
9 holes, 5484 yards, S.S.S. 70
Visitors: welcome between April and
late October.
Green Fees: WD £10; WE £10.
Societies: welcome by arrangement;
day ticket £15; packages can include
accommodation, meals, ferry, distillery
visit and golf; from £10.
Catering: snacks available.
Hotels: Hotel/GH packages available.

9B 104 Lochwinnoch

Burnfoot Rd, Lochwinnoch,
Renfrewshire, PA12 4AN
☎(01505) 842153, Fax 843668, Pro
843029
On A760 10 miles S of Paisley.
Parkland course.
Pro Gerry Reilly; Founded 1897
18 holes, 6243 yards, S.S.S. 71
Visitors: welcome WD before 4pm.
Green Fees: WD £15.
Societies: welcome by prior arrange-
ment WD; catering packages; from
£15.
Catering: clubhouse facilities.
Hotels: Lindhurst.

9B 105 Loudoun Golf Club

Galston, Ayrshire, KA4 8PA
☎(01563) 820551, Sec 821993
On A71 5 miles E of Kilmarnock.
Parkland course; Founded 1909
18 holes, 6016 yards, S.S.S. 68
Visitors: welcome WD by prior
arrangement.
Green Fees: WD £17.
Societies: welcome WD by prior
arrangement; catering packages can
be arranged; from £17.
Catering: full catering facilities.
Hotels: Loudoun Mains, Newmilns;
Fox Bar, Kilmarnock.

9B 106 Machrie Bay

Sheeans, Pirnmill, Brodick, Isle of
Arran, KA27 8HM

Machrie

Machrie's charm lies in its out of the way setting. Lapped on one side by the Atlantic and separated from the mainland by a sea voyage (or a short aeroplane hop from Glasgow), its delights are little known.

They are certainly not as well known as they deserve to be, because the course is in the very best tradition of seaside links. However, by developing its assets a little more than in the past, the Island of Islay is putting itself far more on the map; and without wishing to spoil a way of life by causing a golfing invasion to its shores, the recommendation for its golf is based on happy personal experience that it would be churlish not to pass on.

After years of acting as co-tenants to grazing sheep and cattle, golfers owe something of a transformation to the former owners of Bowmore Distillery who bought the course and hotel, and added a cluster of cottages alongside which are an ideal base for whatever form of holiday you seek on Islay.

It is a wide choice but, as golfers have supported the distillers' product ever since man first took three putts, there is a delicious aptness about the change. However, Machrie's new look was not confined to new management. It has six new holes which add enormously to its rating as a test of golf. Some of the eccentricities that grew up before there was much in the way of machinery or golf course architects have been reduced; gone are one or two, though not all, of the blind shots into crater-like greens – a type of hole not so favourably looked upon as it once was; in their place have arisen a new second, 10th, 11th, 12th, 13th and 14th that offer, in distillers' language, a smoother blend.

The first, a gentle opener, has an inviting drive from a raised tee, but the second quickly gets down to the real golfing business. The first of the alterations, it is a winding dogleg to the left, the dogleg taking the form of a fast-flowing brook with plans for extending the hole to par five.

Anyone with thoughts of getting home in two will need a strong nerve as well as two good shots, although the third and fourth are less stern. The fifth is a fine short hole and the sixth typical of Machrie's natural blessings with a drive to the left providing the correct approach and view of a green in a dell.

In its early days in the last century, the drive at the seventh over a vast sandhill was rather more formidable than it is now; all the same, it can still strike fear at the beginning of a stretch of three holes, all par fours, which follow the line of a glorious sandy beach.

The 10th tee is a notable example even if it is not time to be distracted. A marvellous natural short hole at the furthest limit of the course marks the introduction to the new golfing country; this is nicely demanding but, at the same time, there is a pleasant scenic change to the hills and lonely peat moors.

The 11th requires a strong second to a long green with a heathery drop to the left and the not so short par-three 12th, is even tougher. The main feature of the 13th, a par five bending left, is the amphitheatre in which the green is situated, while the 14th is perhaps the hardest of all the par fours. A long drive is necessary to get a view of the flag outlined against the skyline.

After a spell where stout hitting is essential, the last four holes are not quite as severe; nevertheless, the need for good judgment is paramount and, against any sort of wind, the 16th and 18th, in particular, can pose much greater problems. However, if your score doesn't turn out quite the way you planned, there are ample consolations.

There is no shortage of spirituous assistance to help forget the bad round – and celebrate the good – and the atmosphere of the Club and hotel is wonderfully friendly and informal.

☎(01770) 850232, Sec 850247,
Bar/Rest 840213
9 miles W of Brodick.
Links course.
Founded 1900
Designed by William Fernie
9 holes, 4400 yards, S.S.S. 62
Visitors: welcome
Green Fees: WD £5; WE £5.
Societies: welcome by prior arrangement; only limited catering available; from £5.
Catering: tea room.
Hotels: Lochranza; Kinloch; Catacoc Bay.

9B 107 **Machrie Hotel & Golf Links**
The Machrie Hotel & Golf Course, Port Ellen, Isle of Islay, Argyll, PA42 7AN
☎(01496) 302310 Fax 302404, Sec 302409
Ferry from Kennacraig (2hrs) or plane from Glasgow (30 mins).
Traditional links course.
Founded 1891
Designed by Willie Campbell/ Donald Steel
18 holes, 6226 yards, S.S.S. 70
Visitors: welcome; residents receive discounts.
Green Fees: WD £20; WE £20.
Societies: welcome by prior arrangement; day rates available; also accommodation and golf packages can be arranged; hotel can also advise on air packages from Glasgow; conference facilities; own beach; salmon & trout fishing; snooker; from £20.
Catering: full clubhouse and hotel catering and bar facilities with à la carte restaurant.
Hotels: Machrie Bay Hotel.

9B 108 **Machrihanish**
Machrihanish, Campbeltown, Argyll, PA28 6PT
☎(01586) 810213, Fax 810221, Pro 810277
5 miles W of Campbeltown on B843.
Seaside links course.
Pro Ken Campbell; Founded 1876
18 holes, 6228 yards, S.S.S. 71
Visitors: welcome by prior arrangement.
Green Fees: WD £23; WE £23.
Societies: welcome by prior arrangement with club Pro; some WE available; catering by prior arrangement; some air packages available; accommodation packages also on offer; from £23.
Catering: full clubhouse facilities.

9B 109 **Maybole**
Memorial Park, Maybole, Ayrshire, KA19
☎(01292) 612000
9 miles S of Ayr on main Stranraer road.
Hillside course with splendid views.
Founded 1905
9 holes, 5304 yards, S.S.S. 65
Visitors: welcome.
Green Fees: WD £7; WE £7.
Societies: welcome; book through S Ayrshire District Council; day ticket from £11; from £7.
Hotels: many in local area; Abbotsford.

9B 110 **Millport**
Golf Rd, Millport, Isle of Cumbrae, KA28 0HB
☎(01475) 530311, Fax 530306, Pro 530305, Sec 530306
10 mins ferry crossing from Largs in Ayrshire; 4 miles from the Ferry Terminal.
Heathland course.
Pro Ken Docherty; Founded 1888
Designed by James Braid
18 holes, 5828 yards, S.S.S. 69
Visitors: welcome.
Green Fees: WD £14.50; WE £24.50.
Societies: welcome by prior arrangement; catering packages by arrangement; from £14.50.
Catering: full facilities.
Large practice area.

9B 111 **Milngavie**
Laighpark, Milngavie, Glasgow, G62 8EP
☎(0141) 956 1619; Fax 956 4252
Off A809 NW of Glasgow; club can provide detailed directions.
Moorland course.
Founded 1895
Designed by J Braid
18 holes, 5818 yards, S.S.S. 68
Visitors: welcome by prior arrangement.
Green Fees: WD £20; WE £20.
Societies: welcome by prior arrangement; packages ranging from £9 can be arranged including 4-course dinner; from £20.
Catering: full clubhouse facilities available.
Hotels: Black Bull; Burnbrae, both Milngavie.

9B 112 **Mount Ellen**
Johnstone Rd, Johnstone House, Gartcosh, Glasgow, G69 8EY

☎(01236) 872277, Fax 872249, Pro 872632
From M8 N and A89 take B752 N to Gastosh on to B804 in direction of Glenboig.
Parkland course.
Pro Iain Bilsborough; Founded 1905
18 holes, 5525 yards, S.S.S. 67
Visitors: welcome WD only.
Green Fees: WD £12.
Societies: welcome by prior arrangement; on application; terms on application.
Catering: full clubhouse facilities.
Hotels: Garsfield House, Stepps; Moodiesburn House, Moodiesburn.

9B 113 **New Cumnock**
Lochill, Cumnock Rd, New Cumnock, Ayrshire, KA18 4BQ
☎(01290) 338848, Sec 423659
On the A76 1 mile to the NW of New Cumnock.
Parkland course.
Founded 1901
Designed by W Fernie
9 holes, 5176 yards, S.S.S. 66
Visitors: welcome; tickets available from the Lochside Hotel next to course.
Green Fees: WD £6; WE £6.
Societies: none.
Catering: limited; Lochside Hotel next door.
Hotels: Lochside Hotel.

9B 114 **Old Course Ranfurly**
Ranfurly Place, Bridge of Weir, Renfrewshire, PA11 3DE
☎(01505) 613612, Fax 613214, Sec 613214
5 miles W of Glasgow Airport.
Heathland course.
Founded 1905
Designed by W Park Jnr
18 holes, 6061 yards, S.S.S. 69
Visitors: welcome by arrangement WD; with member WE.
Green Fees: WD £20.
Societies: welcome by written prior arrangement WD; day ticket of £30 available; from £20.
Catering: full clubhouse facilities.
Hotels: Normandy, Renfrew; Glyn Hill, Paisley.

9B 115 **Paisley**
Braehead, Paisley, PA2 8TZ
☎(0141) 884 2292, Fax 884 3903, Pro 884 4114; Sec 884 3903
Leave M8 junction 27 follow B778 to Braehead.

Moorland course.
Pro Gordon Stewart; Founded 1895/1951
18 holes, 6466 yards, S.S.S. 72
Visitors: welcome WD before 4pm.
Green Fees: WD £20.
Societies: welcome by prior arrangement WD; day ticket £28; catering can be provided by arrangement; snooker; from £20.
Catering: full clubhouse facilities. Two practice grounds.
Hotels: Watermill.

9B 116 Palacerigg

Palacerigg Country Park, Cumbernauld, G67 3HU
☎(01236) 734969, Fax 721461, Pro 721461
Take A80 to Cumbernauld and follow signs for Country Park.
Wooded parkland course.
Pro/Starter John Murphy; Founded 1974
Designed by Henry Cotton
18 holes, 6444 yards, S.S.S. 71
Visitors: welcome.
Green Fees: terms available on application.
Societies: welcome WD by prior arrangement; range of packages available; full day's golf and catering; £28.
Catering: full clubhouse facilities; restrictions Mon/Tues.
Hotels: Castlecarry; Moodiesburn; Cumbernauld Travel Inn.

9B 117 Pollok

90 Barrhead Rd, Glasgow, G43 1BG
☎(0141) 632 1080, Fax 649 1398, Sec 632 4351
Course lies four miles south of the city of Glasgow off M77 junction 2 on B736.
Wooded parkland course.
Founded 1892
18 holes, 6257 yards, S.S.S. 70
Visitors: welcome WD; gentlemen only.
Green Fees: WD £30.
Societies: welcome by prior arrangement with Sec; day rate £40; from £30.
Catering: full clubhouse catering facilities.
Hotels: Albany; Macdonald; Marriott.

9B 118 Port Bannatyne

Bannatyne Mains Rd, Port Bannatyne, Isle of Bute, PA20 0PH
☎(01700) 504544, Sec 502009

2 miles N of Rothesay on Isle of Bute above the village of Port Bannatyne.
Hilly seaside course.
Founded 1912
Designed by James Braid
13 holes, 5085 yards, S.S.S. 65
Visitors: welcome.
Green Fees: WD £14; WE £14.
Societies: welcome by prior arrangement; reductions for groups of 30-39 to £10; for more than 40, £8; from £10.
Catering: new clubhouse opens March 1998.
Hotels: Ardmory House; Royal; Ardbeg.

9B 119 Port Glasgow

Devol Farm Industrial Estate, Port Glasgow, Renfrewshire, PA14 5XE
☎(01475) 704181
On M8 towards Greenock SW of Glasgow in the town of Port Glasgow.
Undulating course.
Founded 1895
18 holes, 5712 yards, S.S.S. 68
Visitors: WD until 3.55pm; WE by introduction.
Green Fees: terms on application.
Societies: welcome by prior arrangement on non-comp days; catering by arrangement; terms on application.
Catering: clubhouse facilities.
Hotels: Clune Brae; Star.

9B 120 Prestwick

2 Links Rd, Prestwick, Ayrshire, KA9 1QG
☎(01292) 477404, Fax 477255, Pro 479483
1 mile from Prestwick Airport adjacent to Prestwick station.
Links course; hosted first Open Championship in 1860.
Founded 1851
Designed by Tom Morris
18 holes, 6544 yards, S.S.S. 73
Visitors: welcome by arrangement.
Green Fees: terms on application.
Societies: welcome by prior arrangement; terms on application.
Catering: full clubhouse facilities; dining room men only; Cardinal room.
Hotels: Parkstone; Fairways; Golf View; North Beach.

9B 121 Prestwick St Cuthbert

East Rd, Prestwick, Ayrshire, KA9 2SX
☎(01292) 477101, Fax 671730
Take A77 to Whitletts roundabout and then follow signs for Heathfield Estate.
Parkland course.

Founded 1899
Designed by Stutt & Co
18 holes, 6470 yards, S.S.S. 71
Visitors: welcome WD; only with member at WE.
Green Fees: WD £22.
Societies: welcome by prior arrangement; day ticket £30; meal packages from £10.50; from £22.
Catering: full clubhouse facilities.
Hotels: St Nicholas; Golf.

9B 122 Prestwick St Nicholas

Grangemuir Rd, Prestwick, Ayrshire, KA9 1SN
☎(01292) 477608, Fax 678570
From Prestwick town centre take the road to Ayr; turn right at Grangemuir road junction; proceed under railway bridge to course.
Links course.
Founded 1851/1892
Designed by C. Hunter & J Allan
18 holes, 5952 yards, S.S.S. 69
Visitors: welcome WD and Sun afternoon; prior booking essential.
Green Fees: WD £30; WE £35.
Societies: welcome WD and some Sun afternoons by prior arrangement; catering by arrangement; from £30.
Catering: full clubhouse refurbishment completed spring 1998.
Hotels: Parkstone.

9B 123 Ralston

Strathmore Ave, Ralston, Paisley, Renfrewshire, PA1 3DT
☎(0141) 882 1349, Sec 882 1503
Off the main Paisley to Glasgow road.
Parkland course.
Founded 1904
18 holes, 6029 yards, S.S.S. 69
Visitors: organised parties only.
Green Fees: terms on application.
Societies: welcome by prior arrangement; catering by arrangement; terms on application.
Catering: full clubhouse facilities.
Hotels: Abbey.

9B 124 Ranfurly Castle

Golf Rd, Bridge of Weir, Renfrewshire, PA11 3HN
☎(01505) 612609, Pro 614797
From the M8 take the Irvine road to Bridge of Weir; turn left at Prieston road and at top of the rise the clubhouse is on right.
Spacious heathland course.
Pro Tom Eckford; Founded 1889/1904
Designed by Andrew Kirkaldy & Willie Auchterlonie

18 holes, 6284 yards, S.S.S. 71
Visitors: welcome WD.
Green Fees: WD £25.
Societies: welcome Tues by prior
arrangement; clubhouse catering by
arrangement; from £25.
Catering: full clubhouse bar and
restaurant service.
Hotels: Glynhill, Renfrew; Stakis,
Glasgow Airport.

9B 125 Renfrew

Blythswood Estate, Inchinnan Rd,
Renfrew, RA4 9EG
☎(0141) 886 6692, Fax 886 1808,
Pro 885 1754
Leave M8 motorway at junction 26
then A8 to Renfrew, turning to club at
Stakis Glasgow Airport Hotel.
Parkland course.
Pro Stuart Kerr; Founded 1894
Designed by John Harris
18 holes, 6818 yards, S.S.S. 73
Visitors: welcome if introduced by a
member
Green Fees: terms on application.
Societies: welcome Mon, Tues and
Thurs by arrangement; catering by
arrangement; day ticket £35; from £25.
Catering: full clubhouse bar and
catering facilities.
Hotels: Dean Park; Glynhill; Stakis
Glasgow Airport.

9B 126 Rothesay

Canada Hill, Rothesay, Isle of Bute,
PA20 9HN
☎(01700) 502244, Fax 503554, Pro
503554, Sec 503554
30 minutes by steamer from Wemyss
Bay.
Undulating parkland course.
Pro Jim Dougal; Founded 1892
Designed by James Braid
18 holes, 5395 yards, S.S.S. 66
Visitors: public.
Green Fees: WD £15; WE £24.
Societies: welcome by prior arrange-
ment; catering by arrangement; from
£15.
Catering: full clubhouse facilities in
the season April-October.
Hotels: club will supply comprehen-
sive list of local hotels.

9B 127 Rouken Glen

Stewarton Rd, Thornliebank, Glasgow,
G46 7UZ
☎(0141) 638 7044
5 miles S of Glasgow.
Parkland course.
Pro Kendal McReid; Founded 1922

18 holes, 4800 yards, S.S.S. 64
Visitors: welcome.
Green Fees: terms on application.
Societies: welcome by prior arrange-
ment; terms on application.
Catering: full facilities.
Practice range, 18 bays floodlit.
Hotels: The MacDonalds.

9B 128 Routenburn

Largs, Ayrshire, KA30 8SQ
☎(01475) 673230, Pro 687240
1 mile north of Largs turning left at first
major turning on the Greenock road.
Seaside hill course.
Pro Greig McQueen; Founded 1914
Designed by James Braid
18 holes, 5680 yards, S.S.S. 68
Visitors: welcome WD by prior
arrangement.
Green Fees: terms on application.
Societies: welcome WD by prior
arrangement; catering packages by
prior arrangement; terms on application.
Catering: full facilities except Thurs.

9B 129 Royal Troon

Craigend Rd, Troon, Ayrshire, KA10
6EP
☎(01292) 311555, Fax 318204, Pro
313281, Bar/Rest 317578
3 miles from A77 and Prestwick
Airport.
Championship links course; host of
1997 Open.
Pro Brian Anderson; Founded 1878
Designed by local members
18 holes, 7079 yards, S.S.S. 73
Visitors: Mon, Tues and Thurs only;
maximum handicap 18.
Green Fees: WD £100.
Societies: welcome by prior arrangement; includes lunch and coffee; also
Portland course: 18 holes, 6274 yards,
par 71; £100.
Catering: full bar and restaurant service.
Hotels: Marine; Piersland House.

9B 130 Ruchill

Brassey Street, Maryhill, Glasgow,
G20
☎(0141) 770 0519
2.5 miles NW of Glasgow off Bearsden
road.
Municipal parkland course.
Founded 1928
9 holes, 4480 yards, S.S.S. 61
Visitors: public.
Green Fees: terms on application.
Societies: contact city council.

9B 131 Sandyhills

223 Sandyhills Rd, Glasgow, G32 9NA
☎(0141) 778 1099, Sec 778 0787,
Bar/Rest 778 1179
E side of Glasgow from Tollcross road,
turn left at Killin St and right into
Sandyhills Road.
Parkland course.
Founded 1905
18 holes, 6237 yards, S.S.S. 70
Visitors: welcome by prior arrange-
ment.
Green Fees: terms on application.
Societies: welcome by prior arrange-
ment; catering packages available;
terms on application.
Catering: full clubhouse catering facili-
ties.
Hotels: Hilton; Moat House; Marriott,
all in Glasgow.

9B 132 Shiskine

Blackwaterfoot, Isle of Arran, KA27
8HA
☎(01770) 860226, Fax 860205, Pro
860392, Sec 860293
300 yards off B880 in Blackwaterfoot.
Seaside course with magnificent
views.
Founded 1896
Designed by Original 9: W Fernie;
upgraded to 12: W Park
12 holes, 2990 yards, S.S.S. 42
Visitors: welcome; h'cap certs
required in July and August period.
Green Fees: WD £12; WE £15.
Societies: welcome by prior arrangement with match secretary; packages
available with Kinloch Hotel for
travel, accommodation and golf;
day tickets available (WD £18, WE
£20); also weekly and fortnightly tickets; tennis and bowls; maximum parties of 24 unless by prior agreement;
from £12.
Catering: tea room, lunches, high
teas and restaurant facilities; bar at
Kinloch Hotel 500 yards.
Hotels: Kinloch Hotel.

9B 133 Shotts

Blairhead, Shotts, N Lanarkshire, ML7
5BJ
☎(01501) 820431, Pro 822658
Take M8 to junction 5; then A7057 to
Shotts; 1.5 miles to course.
Heathland/parkland course.
Pro John Strachan; Founded 1895
Designed by James Braid
18 holes, 6125 yards, S.S.S. 70
Visitors: welcome WD; Sat after
4.30pm and Sun by prior arrangement.
Green Fees: WD £20; WE £20.

Royal Troon

Until 1989, post-war Open championships at Royal Troon (Royal since 1978), had been notable for comfortable winning margins rather than hairsbreadth finishes, although Tom Watson's fourth success in 1982 was one slight exception. It was the least glorious of the five he won, a number of players letting slip better chances than Watson.

Of Troon's three previous Opens, Bobby Locke won by two strokes in 1950, Arnold Palmer in by six in 1962 and Tom Weiskopf by three in 1973. However, it was all change in 1989. Not only did that Open see the first three-way tie in the championship's history, it witnessed the first foreshortened play-off over four holes.

The 18th was certainly the place to be for the last hour and a half, first as the play-off took shape and then as it reached its climax. Until the final few minutes, Mark Calcavecchia had not exactly looked the likely winner. Having pitched his ball full toss into the cup for an eagle two at the 12th and added birdies on the 16th and 18th, he was one behind Greg Norman with two holes of the play-off remaining. Then, Norman took three from the back of the 17th green, drove into a far distant bunker from the 18th tee and Calcavecchia, keeping out of trouble, was home.

Troon is a fair and honest course which begins along the beach and reaches its peak, to my mind, with the stretch from the seventh to the 13th. The start and finish are good but I like the variety which these middle holes provide. It is a curious fact that when Palmer spreadeagled the field in 1962, he failed to get a birdie on any of the first three holes in the four rounds but the 11th was where the drama unfurled.

The hole, hugging the railway line, had only recently been increased from a shortish par four to a par five. It quickly proved a hole to be feared, as Palmer recalled on the eve of the championship twenty-seven years later. "My motive was to get it behind me as quickly as I could," but, unlike Jack Nicklaus who ran up a 10 there on the final day, Palmer undoubtedly got the 11th before it got him.

Having had to qualify with everyone else, Palmer had an eagle and three birdies in five rounds, his only par coming when he hit perhaps his best second shot and just overran the green.

Societies: welcome WD; full day's golf and catering included in packages; visitors' locker room; £30.
Catering: full clubhouse facilities.
Practice range available.
Hotels: Golden Circle, Bathgate; Travelodge, Newhouse; Hillcroft, Whitburn.

9B 134 Skelmorlie
Skelmorlie, Ayrshire, PA17 5ES
☎(01475) 520152
1 mile from Wemyss station.
Parkland/moorland course; five additional holes planned 1998.
Founded 1891
Designed by James Braid
13 holes, 5104 yards, S.S.S. 65
Visitors: welcome except Sat during season.
Green Fees: terms on application.
Societies: welcome by prior arrangement except Sat; catering by arrangement; terms on application.
Catering: full clubhouse facilities.
Hotels: Haywood.

9B 135 Strathaven
Overton Ave, Glasgow Rd, Strathaven, ML10 6NL
☎(01357) 520539, Fax 520421, Pro 521812, Sec 520421, Bar/Rest 520422
On A723 East Kilbride road on outskirts of the town.
Tree-lined undulating parkland course.
Pro Matt McCrorie; Founded 1908
Designed by William Fernie of Troon, Extended to 18 holes by JR Stutt
18 holes, 6224 yards, S.S.S. 70
Visitors: welcome WD until 4pm.
Green Fees: WD £20.
Societies: welcome Tues by prior arrangement with Sec; catering by prior arrangement; club can organise morning coffee, hot and cold snacks, lunches, high teas and dinners; from £20.
Catering: full clubhouse facilities available.
Hotels: Strathhaven; Springvale.

9B 136 Strathclyde Park
Mote Hill, Hamilton, Lanarkshire, ML3 6BY
☎(01698) 429350
1.5 miles from M74 close to Hamilton Ice rink.
Public parkland course.
9 holes, 6350 yards, S.S.S. 70
Visitors: welcome.
Green Fees: WD £3; WE £3.50.

Societies: welcome; catering by prior arrangement; from £3.
Catering: catering by prior arrangement.
Practice range available.
Hotels: Travelodge.

9B 137 Tarbert
Kilberry Rd, Tarbert, Argyll, PA29 6XX
☎(01880) 820565
1 mile from A83 to Campbeltown from Tarbert, on B8024.
Hilly seaside course.
9 holes, 4460 yards, S.S.S. 63
Visitors: welcome by prior arrangement.
Green Fees: WD £8; WE £8.
Societies: welcome WD; day ticket for £15; from £10.
Catering: full clubhouse facilities available.
Hotels: Stonefield Castle; West Loch.

9B 138 Tobermory
Erray Rd, Tobermory, Isle of Mull, PA75 6PR
☎(01688) 302338, Fax 302140
Signposted in Tobermory.
Clifftop heathland course with views over Sound of Mull.
Founded 1896
Designed by David Adams (1935)
9 holes, 4890 yards, S.S.S. 64
Visitors: welcome.
Green Fees: WD £12; WE £12.
Societies: welcome; catering on application to Sec; from £12.
Catering: clubhouse facilities.
Practice range.
Hotels: Western Isles; Fairways (on course).

9B 139 Torrance House
Strathaven Rd, East Kilbride, Glasgow, G75 0QZ
☎(01355) 249720, Sec 248638
On the A726 on the outskirts of East Kilbride travelling S to Strathaven.
Municipal parkland course.
Founded 1969
Designed by Hawtree & Sons
18 holes, 6476 yards, S.S.S. 71
Visitors: welcome; advance booking system.
Green Fees: WD £16; WE £16.
Societies: welcome by prior arrangement by calling (01355) 806271; catering packages by prior arrangement; from £16.
Catering: full clubhouse facilities available.
Practice range 1 mile from club.

9B 140 Troon Municipal
Harling Drive, Troon, Ayrshire, KA10 6NE
☎(01292) 312464
100 yards from the railway station.
Links course.
Founded 1905
Darley: 18 holes, 6360 yards, S.S.S. 71; Lochgreen: 18 holes, 6822 yards, S.S.S. 72; Fullerton: 18 holes, 4869 yards, S.S.S. 63
Visitors: welcome.
Green Fees: terms on application.
Societies: welcome by prior arrangement; catering by arrangement; terms on application.
Catering: full clubhouse facilities.

9B 141 Turnberry Hotel
Turnberry Hotel, Turnberry, Ayrshire, KA26 9LT
☎(01655) 331000, Fax 331706
On A77 15 miles SW of Ayr.
Championship seaside links; Open venue.
Pro Brian Gunson; Founded 1897
Designed by MacKenzie Ross (Ailsa)
Ailsa: 18 holes, 6976 yards, S.S.S. 74; Arran: 18 holes, 6014 yards, S.S.S. 69
Visitors: hotel residents only.
Green Fees: WD £80; WE £80.
Societies: only if society is resident in hotel.
Catering: full clubhouse restaurant and bar; first-class hotel facilities.
Hotels: Turnberry Hotel Golf Courses & Spa.

9B 142 Vale of Leven
Northfield Rd, Bonhill, Alexandria, Dumbartonshire, G83 9ET
☎(01389) 752351, Pro 755012
Off A82 Glasgow to Dumbarton road at signs marked Bonhill & Alexandria.
Moorland course with views of Loch and Ben Lomond.
Pro Gordon Brown; Founded 1907
18 holes, 5162 yards, S.S.S. 66
Visitors: welcome except Sat.
Green Fees: WD £15; WE £18.
Societies: welcome by prior arrangement; catering packages by prior arrangement with club caterers; £15.
Catering: full clubhouse and bar facilities.
Hotels: Balloch; Duck Bay Marina; Lomond Park; Tullichewan.

9B 143 Vaul
Scarinish, Isle of Tiree, Argyll, PA77 6XH
☎(01879) 220334

On the E end of the Island 3 miles from the pier and 5 miles from the airport; 40-minute flight from Glasgow; 50 miles W of Oban by ferry.
Links course.
Founded 1920
9 holes, 5674 yards, S.S.S. 68
Visitors: welcome.
Green Fees: WD £5; WE £5.
Societies: welcome by prior arrangement; weekly and fortnightly tickets available; from £5.
Catering: catering at Lodge Hotel.
Hotels: Lodge; Glassary GH; Kirkapol GH.

9B 144 **West Kilbride**
33-35 Fullerton Drive, Seamill, W Kilbride, Ayrshire, KA23 9HT
☎(0294) 823911, Fax 823911, Pro 823042, Bar/Rest 823128.
On A78 Androssan to Largs road at Seamill.
Flat seaside links course alongside Firth of Clyde.
Pro Graham Ross; Founded 1893
Designed by Tom Morris
18 holes, 6452 yards, S.S.S. 70
Visitors: welcome WD after 9.30am.
Green Fees: WD £35.
Societies: welcome Tues and Thurs only by arrangement; catering to be arranged with the caterer; from £35.
Catering: full clubhouse facilities.
Hotels: Seamill Hydro.

9B 145 **Western Gailes**
Gailes, Irvine, Ayrshire, KA11 5AE
☎(01294) 311357, Sec 311649
On A78 5 miles N of Troon.
Championship links; Open qualifying course.
Founded 1897
18 holes, 6714 yards, S.S.S. 72
Visitors: welcome WD except Thurs; no lady visitors on Tues.
Green Fees: WD £52.
Societies: welcome by prior arrangement WD except Thurs; day tickets from £84; catering by arrangement; from £52.
Catering: clubhouse catering and bar.

9B 146 **Westerwood Hotel Golf & Country Club**
St Andrews Drive, Cumbernauld, G68 0EW
☎(01236) 457171, Fax 738478, Pro 725281
Signposted off the A80 13 miles from Glasgow.
Parkland course.

Pro Steve Killin; Founded 1989
Designed by Seve Ballesteros and Dave Thomas
18 holes, 6616 yards, S.S.S. 73
Visitors: welcome.
Green Fees: WD £22.50; WE £27.50.
Societies: welcome by prior arrangement; packages available; hotel leisure facilities; residents discounts; from £22.50.
Catering: full clubhouse catering.
Practice range available.
Hotels: Westerwood Hotel on site.

9B 147 **Whinhill**
Beith Road, Greenock, Renfrewshire
☎(01475) 721064
Just outside Greenock on old Largs road.
Parkland course.
18 holes, 5434 yards, S.S.S. 68
Visitors: welcome.
Green Fees: terms on application.
Societies: none.
Catering: small clubhouse for members only.

9B 148 **Whitecraigs**
72 Ayr Rd, Giffnock, G46 6SW
☎(0141) 639 4530, Pro 639 2140, Bar/Rest 693 4530
On A77 7 miles S of Glasgow.
Parkland course.
Pro Alistair Forrow; Founded 1905
18 holes, 6013 yards, S.S.S. 70
Visitors: welcome by member's introduction only.
Green Fees: WD £35; WE £35.
Societies: welcome Wed only; catering by arrangement; day tickets from £45; from £35.
Catering: full clubhouse facilities available.
Hotels: Macdonald.

9B 149 **Whiting Bay**
Golf Course Rd, Whiting Bay, Isle of Arran, KA27 8QT
☎(01770) 700487, Sec 700307
8 miles S of Brodick.
Undulating heathland course.
Founded 1895
18 holes, 4405 yards, S.S.S. 63
Visitors: welcome.
Green Fees: WD £11; WE £22.
Societies: welcome by prior arrangement with Sec; discounts available for groups of 10 or more; from £11.
Catering: clubhouse catering and bar facilities.
Hotels: Cameronia; Grange House; Kiscadale; Royal.

9B 150 **Williamwood**
Clarkston Rd, Netherlee, Glasgow, G44 3YR
☎(0141) 637 1783, Fax 637 6688, Pro 637 2715
5 miles S of Glasgow.
Wooded parkland course.
Founded 1906
Designed by James Braid
18 holes, 5878 yards, S.S.S. 69
Visitors: welcome by introduction only.
Green Fees: WD on application.
Societies: welcome WD by arrangement; catering by arrangement; terms on application.
Catering: full clubhouse facilities available.
Hotels: Macdonald, Giffnock; Redhurst, Clarkston.

9B 151 **Windyhill**
Baljaffray Rd, Bearsden, Glasgow, G61 4QQ
☎(0141) 942 2349, Fax 942 5874, Pro 942 7157, Sec 942 5874
1 mile N of Bearsden.
Parkland course.
Pro Gary Collinson; Founded 1908
Designed by James Braid
18 holes, 6254 yards, S.S.S. 70
Visitors: welcome WD.
Green Fees: WD £20.
Societies: welcome by prior arrangement; discounts available for larger groups; catering available by arrangement; £20.
Catering: full bar and restaurant facilities.
Practice range available.
Hotels: Black Bull, Milngavie; Jury's Pond Hotel, Glasgow.

9B 152 **Wishaw**
Lower Main Street, Wishaw, Lanarkshire, ML2 7PL
☎(01698) 372869, Pro 358247
15 miles SW of Glasgow; 5 miles from M74 Motherwell junction.
Parkland course.
Pro John Campbell; Founded 1897
Designed by James Braid
18 holes, 6100 yards, S.S.S. 69
Visitors: welcome WD until 4pm; not Sat and by prior arrangement Sun.
Green Fees: WD £13; WE £26.
Societies: welcome WD; Sun only by special arrangement; day's golf; catering packages by arrangement; from £21.
Catering: full clubhouse facilities available.
Hotels: Wishaw Town Hotel.

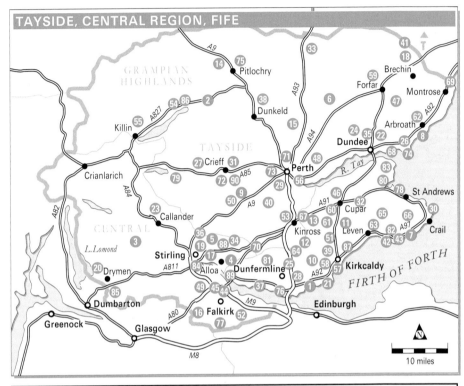

TAYSIDE, CENTRAL REGION, FIFE

GRAMPIAN HIGHLANDS

TAYSIDE

CENTRAL

L.Lomond

FIRTH OF FORTH

R. Tay

10 miles

KEY		19	Bridge of Allan	37	Dunfermline	56	King James VI	75	Pitlochry
1	Aberdour	20	Buchanan Castle	38	Dunkeld & Birnam	57	Kinghorn	76	Pitreavie (Dunfermline)
2	Aberfeldy	21	Burntisland	39	Dunnikier Park	58	Kirkcaldy	77	Polmont
3	Aberfoyle	22	Caird Park	40	Dunning	59	Kirriemuir	78	St Andrews
4	Alloa	23	Callander	41	Edzell	60	Ladybank	79	St Fillans
5	Alva	24	Camperdown	42	Elie	61	Leslie	80	St Michaels
6	Alyth		(Municipal)	43	Elie Sports Club	62	Letham Grange	81	Saline
7	Anstruther	25	Canmore	44	Falkirk	63	Leven	82	Scoonie
8	Arbroath	26	Carnoustie Golf Links	45	Falkirk Tryst	64	Lochgelly	83	Scotscraig
9	Auchterarder	27	Comrie	46	Falkland	65	Lundin	84	Stirling
10	Auchterderran	28	Cowdenbeath	47	Forfar	66	Lundin Ladies	85	Strathendrick
11	Balbirnie Park	29	Craigie Hill	48	Glenalmond	67	Milnathort	86	Taymouth Castle
12	Ballingry	30	Crail Golfing Society	49	Glenbervie	68	Monifieth	87	Thornton
13	Bishopshire	31	Crieff	50	Gleneagles Hotel	69	Montrose Links Trust	88	Tillicoultry
14	Blair Atholl	32	Cupar	51	Glenrothes	70	Muckhart	89	Tulliallan
15	Blairgowrie	33	Dalmunzie	52	Grangemouth	71	Murrayshall	90	Whitemoss
16	Bonnybridge	34	Dollar	53	Green Hotel	72	Muthill		
17	Braehead	35	Downfield	54	Kenmore Golf Course	73	North Inch		
18	Brechin	36	Dunblane New	55	Killin	74	Panmure		

9C 1 Aberdour

Seaside Place, Aberdour, Fife, KY3 0TX
☎(01383) 860688, Fax 860050, Pro 860256, Sec 860080, Bar /Rest 860256
In Aberdour village on coast route to Burntisland.
Parkland/seaside course with views of River Forth.

Pro Gordon McCallum; Founded 1896
Designed by Peter Robertson & Joe Anderson
18 holes, 5460 yards, S.S.S. 66
Visitors: welcome WD and by prior arrangement.
Green Fees: WD £17; WE £28.
Societies: welcome except Sat by prior arrangement; catering by arrangement with the clubmaster;

maximum parties of 24 on Sun; from £17.
Catering: full clubhouse catering.
Hotels: Woodside.

9C 2 Aberfeldy

Taybridge Rd, Aberfeldy, Perthshire, PH15 2BH
☎(01887) 820535, Sec 829509

Follow signs from A9 at Ballinluig through the centre of Aberfeldy for Weem and first right at Wades Bridge. Parkland course.
Founded 1895
Designed by Souters
18 holes, 5283 yards, S.S.S. 66
Visitors: welcome.
Green Fees: WD £14; WE £14.
Societies: welcome by prior arrangement; catering by arrangement; terms on application.
Catering: full facilities.
Hotels: Palace; Crown, both Aberfeldy.

9C 3 **Aberfoyle**
Braeval, Aberfoyle, Stirlingshire, FK8 3UY
☎(01877) 382493, Sec 382638, Bar/Rest 382809
1.5 miles from Aberfoyle on the main Stirling road.
Parkland course.
Founded 1890
Designed by James Braid
18 holes, 5218 yards, S.S.S. 66
Visitors: welcome; some restrictions at WE.
Green Fees: WD £12; WE £16.
Societies: welcome by prior arrangement; full day £16; WE full day £24; restrictions on numbers; from £12.
Catering: full clubhouse facilities.
Hotels: Rob Roy Motor Inn; Forth Inn.

9C 4 **Alloa**
Schawpark, Sauchie, Clackmannanshire FK10 3AX
☎(01259) 722745, Pro 724476
On the A908 1 mile N of Alloa; 8 miles E of Stirling.
Undulating parkland course.
Pro Bill Bennett; Founded 1891
Designed by James Braid
18 holes, 6229 yards, S.S.S. 71
Visitors: welcome.
Green Fees: WD £25; WE £30.
Societies: welcome WD by arrangement; catering available by prior arrangement; snooker room; from £25.
Catering: full clubhouse facilities.
Hotels: Harviestoun; Royal Oak; Dunmar House; Claremont Lodge.

9C 5 **Alva**
Beauclerc St, Alva, Clackmannanshire FK12 5LH
☎(01259) 760431
On A91 Stirling to St Andrews road; follow signs for Alva Glen as club car park is at entrance to Glen Hillside.

Sloping fairways/plateau greens.
Founded 1901
9 holes, 4846 yards, S.S.S. 64
Visitors: welcome.
Green Fees: terms on application.
Societies: welcome by prior arrangement; facilities limited; no pro shop, no equipment for hire; terms on application.
Catering: bar snacks only; clubhouse open for 7pm each night and from noon at WE.
Hotels: Alva Glen.

9C 6 **Alyth**
Pitcrocknie, Alyth, Perthshire, PH11 8HF
☎(01828) 632668, Fax 633491, Pro 632411, Sec 632268, Bar/Rest 633490
1 mile SE of Alyth on the B954.
Parkland course with views over Angus & Perthshire.
Pro Tom Melville; Founded 1894
Part designed by James Braid
18 holes, 6205 yards, S.S.S. 71
Visitors: welcome by prior arrangement.
Green Fees: WD £18; WE £23.
Societies: welcome by prior arrangement; catering available by prior arrangement; Pro can assist with golf clinics; day and weekly tickets; from £18.
Catering: full clubhouse facilities.
Hotels: Lands of Loyal; Alyth; Lossett.

9C 7 **Anstruther**
Marsfield, Shore Rd, Anstruther, Fife, KY10 3DZ
☎(01333) 310956, Fax 312283, Sec 312283
Turn off main road at Craw's Nest Hotel.
Seaside course.
Founded 1890
9 holes, 4588 yards, S.S.S. 63
Visitors: welcome.
Green Fees: WD £12; WE £15.
Societies: none.
Catering: snacks and lunches.
Hotels: Craw's Nest.

9C 8 **Arbroath**
Elliot, Arbroath, Angus, DD11 2PE
☎(01241) 872069, Pro 875837
Take A92 from Dundee N and turn right 2 miles before Arbroath.
Seaside links course.
Pro Lindsay Ewart; Founded 1903
Designed by James Braid
18 holes, 6185 yards, S.S.S. 69

Visitors: welcome; not before 9.30am WE.
Green Fees: WD £13; WE £18.
Societies: welcome by prior arrangement; catering by arrangement; terms on application.
Catering: full clubhouse facilities.
Hotels: Seaforth; Cliffburn; Viewfield.

9C 9 **Auchterarder**
Orchil Rd, Auchterarder, Perthshire, PH3 1LS
☎(01764) 662804, Fax 662804, Pro 663711
Off the A9 next to Gleneagles Hotel.
Wooded heathland course.
Pro Gavin Baxter; Founded 1892
Designed by Bernard Sayers
18 holes, 5775 yards, S.S.S. 68
Visitors: welcome by prior arrangement or with a member.
Green Fees: WD £15; WE £22
Societies: welcome by prior arrangement with Sec; catering and golf packages by arrangement.
Catering: full catering and bar.
Hotels: Cairn Lodge; Colliearn House; Duchally.

9C 10 **Auchterderran**
Woodend Rd, Cardenden, Fife, KY5 0NH
☎(01592) 721579
On main Lochgelly to Glenrothes road at N end of Cardenden.
Parkland course.
Founded 1904
9 holes, 5250 yards, S.S.S. 66
Visitors: welcome.
Green Fees: WD £9; WE £12.50
Societies: welcome by arrangement; catering by arrangement; from £9.
Catering: bar and snacks facilities available; meals cooked to order.
Hotels: Bowhill; Central.

9C 11 **Balbirnie Park**
Balbirnie Park, Markinch, Glenrothes, Fife, KY7 6NR
☎(01592) 612095, Pro 752006, Sec 752006, Bar /Rest 752006
2 miles E of Glenrothes.
Scenic parkland course.
Pro Craig Donnelly; Founded 1983
18 holes, 6197 yards, S.S.S. 70
Visitors: welcome by arrangement.
Green Fees: WD £24; WE £30.
Societies: welcome by prior arrangement; catering packages by arrangement; terms on application.
Catering: full clubhouse facilities; all-day catering.

Buchanan Castle

Scotland's celebrated reputation for the variety and quality of its golf courses is centred very largely around its coastline. Apart from Gleneagles, Blairgowrie and, more recently, Loch Lomond, there are few hidden jewels in its central heartland but the joy of exploring fresh territory lies in the pleasant surprises it brings forth.

The name of Buchanan Castle had been familiar to me for years. In the heyday of Eric Brown, the Club and his association with it was mentioned every time he played. Going back further, the connection of John M Bannerman was even better known as the factor for the Estate of the Dukes of Montrose who allowed the course, designed by James Braid, to be opened in 1936.

Bannerman who, for a long time, held the record for the most number of Scottish rugby caps, was later Lord Bannerman after standing for Parliament as a Liberal. However, it was his influence which helped Buchanan Castle to flourish amid the scenic glories of the Trossachs which receive thousands of visitors each year. For most, there is little thought of golf but it is a convenient port of call to those heading north and one that would grace the most distinguished itinerary.

Its charms are gentler than the championship links, its overall length, in fact, being modest by modern standards. Its character is that of a peaceful parkland with an air of antiquity lent by some handsome trees and the Castle that is reminiscent of Brancepeth in Durham.

For those with a lively imagination, there is the belief that the course might be in the grounds of your country home. This complies with the feeling of intimacy, but it would be wrong to suggest that it is devoid of demand or challenge. It requires thought, decision and the shotmaking ability and control to avoid the myriad snares that line its path.

The first is a case in point, the opening drive having to negotiate the giant tree that forms the right angled dogleg. Confidence is not always an abundant commodity on the first tee and it is easy to play too safe, leaving the green out of reach although there is no respite on the second and third which are similarly testing par fours, the third with a stream crossing the fairway.

It is a course of fast-flowing brooks, attractive bridges and strategic trees or copses, the stream on the third reappearing to tease on the drive and pitch fifth. A drive that tempts you to cut the corner is the best feature of the par-five sixth which is a little dull near the green. However, the scene is quickly transformed on the seventh which is a classic dogleg round a majestic wood, only the most solid drive bringing the green into view or range. Fours are greatly to be prized.

Good judgment and a sound nerve are requirements of the short eighth where the tee shot is over water and then follows two more attractive fours, the ninth curving right. The 12th returns close to the clubhouse, leaving a finishing loop of six holes that offer variety, and opportunity as well as a capacity to come to grief. Length is supplied by the 13th and 14th but there is considerably less freedom on the 15th, where the gap between trees on either side of the tee can seem alarmingly narrow.

There is a rural tinge to the setting of the green but the 16th, which turns about, is an excellent short hole, while the 17th and 18th maintain the need for strong hitting. Nevertheless, there is nothing too daunting on a course so eminently suitable for the vast legions of golfers whose enjoyment is so often eroded elsewhere by an impression of mission impossible.

9C 12 Ballingry

Lochore Meadows Country Park,
Crosshill, By Lochgelly, Ballingry, Fife,
KY5 8BA
☎(01592) 414300, Fax 414345
W of M90 between Lochgelly and
Ballingry.
Parkland course.
Founded 1981
9 holes, 6484 yards, S.S.S. 71
Visitors: welcome; book tees at WE.
Green Fees: WD on application.
Societies: welcome by prior arrangement; angling, wind-surfing; terms on application.
Catering: catering and bar facilities in café in park centre.
Hotels: Navitie House.

9C 13 Bishopshire

Kinnesswood by Kinross, Tayside,
Tayside
☎(01592) 780203
3 miles E of Kinross off M90.
Upland course.
Founded 1903
Designed by W. Park
10 holes, 4784 yards, S.S.S. 64
Visitors: welcome; restrictions after 5pm Fri.
Green Fees: WD £6; WE £7.
Societies: limited by arrangement; catering by arrangement or at local hotels; from £6.
Catering: available at the Lomond Hotel 400 yards away.
Hotels: Lomonda; Scotlandwell Inn.

9C 14 Blair Atholl

Blair Atholl, Perthshire, PH18 5TG
☎(01796) 481407
On A9 5 miles N of Pitlochry.
Parkland course.
Founded 1896
9 holes, 5710 yards, S.S.S. 68
Visitors: welcome except comp days.
Green Fees: WD £13; WE £16
Societies: welcome by prior arrangement only; catering by arrangement; from £13.
Catering: clubhouse facilities.
Hotels: Atholl Arms; Tilt.

9C 15 Blairgowrie

Rosemount, Blairgowrie, Perthshire,
PH10 6LG
☎(01250) 872383, Fax 875451, Pro
873116, Sec 872622, Bar/Rest 875527
1 mile S of Blairgowrie off the A93; 15
miles N of Perth.
Heathland course with pine, heather,
silver birch, broom.

Pro Charles Dernie; Founded 1974
(Lansdowne), 1889 (Rosemount)
Designed by Thomas/Alliss
Lansdowne: 18 holes, 6913 yards,
S.S.S. 72; Rosemount: 18 holes, 6590
yards, S.S.S. 72
Visitors: welcome by arrangement;
some restrictions Wed, Fri and WE.
Green Fees: WD on application.
Societies: welcome with same restrictions as visitors; catering packages by arrangement; also 9-hole Wee course, 2327 yards, par 32, designed by Old Tom Morris in 1889; terms on application.
Catering: full clubhouse facilities.
Hotels: Kinloch House; Moorfield House; Altamount House; Angus; Royal.

9C 16 Bonnybridge

Larbert Rd, Bonnybridge, Stirlingshire,
FK4 1NY
☎(01324) 812822
On B816 3 miles W of Falkirk.
Undulating moorland course.
Founded 1925
9 holes, 6128 yards, S.S.S. 69
Visitors: welcome with a member or by letter of introduction.
Green Fees: WD £10; WE £10.
Societies: none.
Catering: meals at WE; bar facilities; limited in winter.
Hotels: Royal.

9C 17 Braehead

Cambus, by Alloa
☎(01259) 725766, Pro 722078
On A907 Stirling-Alloa Road about 1.5
miles W of Alloa.
Parkland course.
Pro Paul Brookes; Founded 1891
18 holes, 6086 yards, S.S.S. 69
Visitors: welcome.
Green Fees: WD £18; WE £24.
Societies: welcome seven days by prior arrangement; catering packages by arrangement; from £24 per day.
Catering: full catering facilities.
Practice range.
Hotels: Royal Oak; Dunmar House.

9C 18 Brechin

Trinity, by Brechin, Angus, DD9 7PD
☎(01356) 622383, Pro 625270, Sec
622326
1 mile outside Brechin on the A90
road to Aberdeen.
Rolling parkland course.
Pro Stephen Rennie; Founded 1893
Part designed by James Braid

18 holes, 6096 yards, S.S.S. 70
Visitors: welcome; restrictions Sat
and Sun 10am-12 noon & 2.30pm-4.30pm.
Green Fees: WD £14; WE £18.
Societies: welcome WD by prior arrangement; packages for eight or more include all catering and 2 rounds of golf; £25.
Catering: full clubhouse facilities.
Practice range.
Hotels: Northern Hotel.

9C 19 Bridge of Allan

Sunnlaw, Bridge of Allan, Stirlingshire
☎(01786) 832332
3 miles N of Stirling.
Undulating course; one of toughest
par 3s in Scotland.
Founded 1895
Designed by Old Tom Morris
9 holes, 5120 yards, S.S.S. 65
Visitors: welcome WD and Sun.
Green Fees: WD on application.
Societies: by prior arrangement;
terms on application.
Catering: bar facilities.
Hotels: Royal.

9C 20 Buchanan Castle

Drymen, Glasgow, G63 0HY
☎(01360) 660307, Fax 870382, Pro
660360, Bar/Rest 660369
On A811 Glasgow to Aberfoyle road;
entrance just before Drymen.
Secluded parkland course with stunning views.
Pro Keith Baxter; Founded 1936
Designed by James Braid
18 holes, 6059 yards, S.S.S. 69
Visitors: welcome by arrangement.
Green Fees: WD £30; WE £30.
Societies: welcome Thurs by prior arrangement; full day's golf £40; catering by arrangement with Clubmaster; from £30.
Catering: full clubhouse facilities.
Hotels: Buchanan Arms; Winnock Hotel.

9C 21 Burntisland

Dodhead, Burntisland, Fife, KY3 9EY
☎(01592) 874093, Pro 872116
On B923 0.5 miles E of Burntisland.
Parkland course.
Pro J Montgomery ; Founded 1897
Designed and re-worked by J Braid
18 holes, 5965 yards, S.S.S. 70
Visitors: welcome except comp days.
Green Fees: WD on application.
Societies: welcome except on comp days; contact manager for starting

times; £5 per head deposit; catering packages by arrangement; terms on application.
Catering: full clubhouse bar and catering: facilities 8am-8pm.
Hotels: Inchview; Kingswood.

9C 22 Caird Park
Mains Loan, Dundee, Tayside, DD4 9BX
☎(01382) 453606
Via Kingsway to the NE of the town.
Parkland course.
Pro J Black; Founded 1926
18 holes, 6352 yards, S.S.S. 70
Visitors: public.
Green Fees: WD £13; WE £22.
Societies: book through Dundee City Council Leisure and Parks dept; terms on application.
Catering: by prior arrangement; bar and lounge facilities.
Hotels: Swallow; Kingsway.

9C 23 Callander
Aveland Rd, Callander, Perthshire, FK17 8EN
☎(01877) 330090, Fax 330062, Pro 330975, Bar/Rest 331718
Off A84 at the E end of Callender.
Parkland course.
Pro William Kelly; Founded 1890
Designed by Tom Morris (1890); Redesigned by W Fernie
18 holes, 5151 yards, S.S.S. 66
Visitors: welcome by prior arrangement.
Green Fees: WD £26; WE £31.
Societies: welcome by prior arrangement; catering packages by arrangement; from £26.
Catering: full catering facilities.
Hotels: Abbotsford Lodge; Myrtle Inn; Dreadnought.

9C 24 Camperdown (Municipal)
Camperdown Park, Dundee, Tayside, DD2 4TF
☎(01382) 623398
At Kingsway junction of the Coupar-Angus Road.
Parkland/ wooded course.
Pro Roddy Brown; Founded 1959
Designed by Eric Brown
18 holes, 6561 yards, S.S.S. 72
Visitors: welcome; pay and play.
Green Fees: WD £15; WE £15.
Societies: welcome by prior arrangement; on application; from £15.
Catering: clubhouse facilities.
Hotels: Swallow.

9C 25 Canmore
Venturefair Ave, Dunfermline, Fife, KY12 0PE
☎(01383) 724969
On A823 1 mile N of Dunfermline.
Undulating parkland course.
Founded 1897
18 holes, 5432 yards, S.S.S. 66
Visitors: welcome WD; Sat after 4pm; not on comp days.
Green Fees: WD £12; WE £18.
Societies: welcome by prior arrangement; catering and day rates by arrangement; from £12.
Catering: full clubhouse facilities.
Hotels: several in Dunfermline.

9C 26 Carnoustie Golf Links
Links Parade, Carnoustie, Angus, DD7 7PH
(01241) 853789, Fax 852720, Sec 853249
On A930 12 miles E of Dundee.
Open Championship links.
Pro Lee Vannet; Founded 1842
Designed by A Robertson; Tom Morris; James Braid
18 holes, 6941 yards, S.S.S. 75
Visitors: welcome by prior arrangement; WE restrictions.
Green Fees: WD £52; WE £52.
Societies: welcome by prior arrangement; catering by arrangement; also Burnside course: 18 holes, 6020 yards; Buddon Links: 18 holes, 5420 yards; from £52.
Catering: full clubhouse facilities.

9C 27 Comrie
Laggan Braes, Comrie, Perthshire, PH6 2LR
☎(01764) 670055, Sec 670941
On A85 7 miles W of Crieff; course signposted from village.
Slightly undulating parkland course.
Founded 1891
9 holes, 6040 yards, S.S.S. 70
Visitors: welcome; restrictions after 4.30pm Mon and Tues.
Green Fees: WD £10; WE £12.
Societies: welcome by arrangement; catering by arrangement; from £10.
Catering: light refreshments, coffee, teas available.
Hotels: Royal; Comrie; Mossgiel GH; Langower GH.

9C 28 Cowdenbeath
Seco Place, Cowdenbeath, Nr Dunfermline, Fife, KY4 8PD
☎(01383) 511918
6 miles E of Dunfermline.

Parkland course; re-opening in summer 1998 as 18 holes.
Founded 1990/1998
18 holes, yards, S.S.S. 71
Visitors: welcome.
Green Fees: WD £7; WE £12.
Societies: welcome by arrangement; catering by arrangement; from £7.
Catering: bar and snacks available.
Practice range.
Hotels: Halfway House; Kingseat.

9C 29 Craigie Hill
Cherrybank, Perth, Perthshire, PH2 0NE
☎(01738) 624377, Pro 622644, Sec 620829
1 mile W of Perth with easy access from A9 and M90.
Hilly course.
Founded 1909
Designed by W. Ferne and J. Anderson
18 holes, 5386 yards, S.S.S. 67
Visitors: welcome; bookings required Sun.
Green Fees: WD £15; WE £20.
Societies: welcome WD and some Sun by prior arrangement; catering by arrangement; from £15.
Catering: full facilities.
Hotels: Lovat.

9C 30 Crail Golfing Society
Balcomie Clubhouse, Fifeness, Crail, KY10 3XN
☎(01333) 450686, Fax 450416, Pro 450960, Bar/Rest 450278
11 miles SE of St Andrews on A917.
Seventh oldest club in world; moved from Sauchope in 1895.
Pro Graeme Lennie; Founded 1786/1895
Designed by Tom Morris
18 holes, 5922 yards, S.S.S. 69
Visitors: welcome.
Green Fees: WD £20; WE £25.
Societies: welcome; catering by arrangement; new 18-hole course called Craighead available for limited play in 1998; terms on application.
Catering: full service with views over course and N Sea.
Hotels: club can supply detailed list.

9C 31 Crieff
Perth Rd, Crieff, Perthshire, PH7 3LR
☎(01764) 652397, Fax 655096, Sec 652909
On A85 on the E edge of Crieff.
Parkland ferntower course.
Pro David Murchie; Founded 1891

Carnoustie

It is going to be a special and emotional moment at next year's Open Championship when Carnoustie is returned to active service. For 24 years it will have been missing from the rota, an absence that has been keenly felt by those who consider the event to be the most important title in world golf.

For great events demand great golf courses to host them and Carnoustie is surely that. Indeed, a straw poll of those who will participate next year would perhaps declare it the finest of all.

Approaching the course for the first time, one would never believe it to be the case. The buildings are grey and drab, the old clubhouse which thankfully has been demolished was quite simply a disgrace.

Soon after it lost the Open in 1975, Carnoustie fell into a state of wilful neglect that matched its surroundings. Thankfully, that has not been the case for some time now. The fairways are protected in the winter and the rewards are obvious during the growing months. It has long been a pleasure to play again.

Carnoustie depends less than most links courses for the wind to blow for protection but when the elements do play a part it can be completely unforgiveable.

Two years ago at the Scottish Open it made a fool of Colin Montgomerie and wrecked his confidence a week before the Open. Yet it can so easily make a player who successfully completes its challenge.

Tom Watson was regarded as something of a choker until he won the 1975 Open at Carnoustie. He left the Tay estuary with the feeling that if he could conquer Carnoustie he could hold his own anywhere. And over the next seven years he would prove it, taking such a hold over the game that he won seven more majors, including four Opens.

Watson's victory was not, however, the most memorable of the five Carnoustie Opens. That surely came in 1953 when Ben Hogan made his only visit to the championship.

He came early to accustom himself to the smaller 1.62in British ball and left with both public and press in thrall. Perhaps only Arnold Palmer's first visit in 1960 compares in terms of impact.

Whether Hogan liked Carnoustie or not is a matter of some dispute. But the sixth became known thereafter as Hogan's alley, in tribute to the way he played this long par five. Two bunkers dissect the fairway and a player has two options: to play away from the boundary fence to the right of the hazards or play straight for a narrow sliver of land, taking on both the sand and the out of bounds. Guess which route Hogan chose – all four days at that – and never once missed his target?

It is the finish, though, which so often wrecks cards. The 15th and 16th are brutishly long and then the Barry Burn winds and twists its way over the final two holes to add further devilry.

Suffice to say, if the wind is blowing, any player who stands on the 15th tee needing four pars to win the Open will have fully deserved the trophy for completing the task.

Designed by Old Tom Morris / R Simpson (1914) / J Braid (1924) / J Stark & J Freeman (1980)
18 holes, 6450 yards, S.S.S. 71
Visitors: welcome.
Green Fees: WD £20; WE £28.
Societies: welcome; catering by arrangement; also 9-hole Dornock course £9 (9 holes); £14 (18 holes); from £20.
Catering: full clubhouse facilities.
Hotels: Crieff Hydro; Murray Park; Foulford Inn.

9C 32 **Cupar**
Hilltarvit, Cupar, KY15 5JT
☎(01334) 653549, Fax 653549, Sec 654101
25 miles on Ceres Rd; SE outskirts of Cupar; 9 miles from St Andrews.
National Trust parkland course; oldest 9-hole course in country.
Founded 1855
Designed by Alan Robertson
9 holes, 5074 yards, S.S.S. 65
Visitors: welcome except Sat.
Green Fees: WD £12; WE £15.
Societies: welcome; discounts available; private room; catering by arrangement; from £12.
Catering: snacks and meals.
Hotels: Eden House.

9C 33 **Dalmunzie**
Spittal of Glenshee, Blairgowrie, Perthshire, PH10 7QG
☎(01250) 885226
On A93 Blairgowrie to Braemar Rd; 18 miles N of Blairgowrie.
Hilly upland course.
Founded 1922
Designed by Alister MacKenzie
9 holes, 4070 yards, S.S.S. 60
Visitors: welcome.
Green Fees: WD on application.
Societies: welcome by arrangement; discounts of 10% for more than 10 and 20% on WD; terms on application.
Catering: facilities in hotel.
Hotels: Dalmunzie House.

9C 34 **Dollar**
Brewlands House, Dollar, Stirlingshire, FK14 7EA
☎(01259) 742400, Sec 743581
In Dollar signposted 0.5 miles off A91.
Hillside course; 2nd, Brae, is 97 yards.
Founded 1890
Designed by Ben Sayers
18 holes, 5242 yards, S.S.S. 66
Visitors: welcome except comp days.
Green Fees: WD £12; WE £20.

Societies: welcome by prior arrangement; packages (WD £30, WE £35) include 36 holes of golf and full day's catering; maximum 36.
Catering: full clubhouse facilities.
Hotels: Castle Campbell Hotel.

9C 35 **Downfield**
Turnberry Ave, Dundee, Tayside, DD2 3QP
☎(01382) 825595, Fax 813111, Pro 889246, Bar/Rest 811055
Follow Kingsway to A923; right into Faraday St then first left to Harrison Road; left at Dalmahoy Drive and sharp left to club.
Championship parkland course; Qualifying course for 1999 Open.
Pro Kenny Hutton; Founded 1932
Designed by C.K. Cotton
18 holes, 6822 yards, S.S.S. 73
Visitors: welcome WD; restrictions at WE.
Green Fees: WD £25; WE £30
Societies: welcome by arrangement; special packages available for golf and catering; terms on application.
Catering: full clubhouse facilities.
Hotels: Gourdie; Swallow, both Dundee; Invercarse at Inchture.

9C 36 **Dunblane New**
Perth Rd, Dunblane, Stirlingshire, FK15 0LJ
☎(01786) 823711, Fax 825946
6 miles N of Stirling on the old A9 at Fourways roundabout.
Parkland course.
Pro Bob Jamieson; Founded 1923
18 holes, 5957 yards, S.S.S. 69
Visitors: welcome WD; restrictions at WE.
Green Fees: WD £18; WE £27.
Societies: welcome Mon, Thurs and Fri by prior arrangement; catering packages by arrangement; tennis and squash adjacent; terms on application.
Catering: full clubhouse facilities.
Hotels: Dunblane Hydro; Stirling Arms.

9C 37 **Dunfermline**
Pitfirrane, Crossford, Dunfermline, Fife, KY12 8QW
☎(01383) 723534, Pro 729061
On S of A994 2 miles W of Dunfermline on the road to the Kincardine Bridge.
Parkland course.
Pro Steven Craig; Founded 1887
Designed by J.R. Stutt & Sons
18 holes, 6126 yards, S.S.S. 70

Visitors: welcome WD between 10am-12noon and 2pm-4pm; Sun at WE.
Green Fees: WD £20; WE £25.
Societies: welcome by arrangement; day ticket WD £30; Sun £35; catering by arrangement; snooker; from £20.
Catering: bar and restaurant facilities.
Hotels: Keavil; Pitfirran Arms; The Maltings.

9C 38 **Dunkeld & Birnam**
Fungarth, Dunkeld, Perthshire, PH8 0HU
☎(01350) 727524, Fax 728660, Sec 727564
On the A923 1 mile N of Dunkeld.
Heathland course with panoramic views.
Founded 1892
9 holes, 5322 yards, S.S.S. 67
Visitors: welcome.
Green Fees: WD £11; WE £16.
Societies: welcome by prior arrangement; catering packages by prior arrangement; from £11.
Catering: full bar and catering facilities.
Hotels: Royal Dunkeld; Stakis Dunkeld House Resort.

9C 39 **Dunnikier Park**
Dunnikier Way, Kirkcaldy, Fife, KY1 3LP
(01592) 261599, Pro 642121, Sec 642541
Leave A92 at Kirkcaldy West roundabout and join B981 for 1 mile.
Parkland course.
Pro Gregor Whyte; Founded 1963
Designed by R Stutt
18 holes, 6601 yards, S.S.S. 72
Visitors: welcome; invitation needed for clubhouse.
Green Fees: WD on application.
Societies: welcome by prior arrangement with Sec; catering packages by arrangement; changing facilities limited (council owned); minimum12, maximum 30; terms on application.
Catering: full catering facilities.
Hotels: Dunnikier House; Dean Park.

9C 40 **Dunning**
Rollo Park, Dunning, Perth, PH2 0RG
☎(01764) 684747, Sec 684237
Off A9 9 miles SW of Perth.
Parkland course.
9 holes, 4836 yards, S.S.S. 63
Visitors: welcome except on comp days.

Green Fees: WD £10; WE £12.
Societies: welcome WD and most Sun; WD price £14; from £10.
Catering: soft and hot drinks in clubhouse; meals by prior application; also in village hotels.
Small practice area.

9C 41 **Edzell**
High St, Edzell, by Brechin, Angus, DD9 7HT
☎(01356) 648235, Fax 648094, Pro 648462, Sec 647283, Bar/Rest 647241
Take B996 off the A90 at the North end of the Brechin by-pass.
Parkland course.
Pro Alastair Webster; Founded 1895
Designed by Bob Simpson
18 holes, 6348 yards, S.S.S. 71
Visitors: welcome.
Green Fees: WD on application.
Societies: welcome; some restrictions; by prior arrangement with Sec; catering by prior arrangement; driving range; terms on application.
Catering: full clubhouse bar and restaurant facilities.
Practice range, opened 1997.
Hotels: Glenesk; Central, both Edzell.

9C 42 **Elie**
Golf House Club, Elie, Leven, Fife, KY9 1AS
☎(01333) 330327, Fax 330895, Pro 330955, Sec 330301
On A915 12 miles S of St Andrews.
Links course; Ladies club: Elie & Earlsferry GC.
Pro Robin Wilson; Founded 1875
18 holes, 6241 yards, S.S.S. 70
Visitors: welcome after 10am; ballot in July & August; no Sun visitors June-Sept.
Green Fees: WD £36 WE £40.
Societies: welcome except in June, July and August; day rates (WD £45, WE £55); catering by arrangement with Steward; from £36.
Catering: full catering and bar.
Hotels: Golf, Elie; Craw's Nest, Anstruther.

9C 43 **Elie Sports Club**
Elie, Fife, KY9 1AS
☎(01333) 330955
On A917 10 miles S of St Andrews.
Seaside course.
Pro Robin Wilson
9 holes, 4354 yards, S.S.S. 64
Visitors: welcome.
Green Fees: WD £7; WE £7.

Societies: welcome by prior arrangement; packages available; terms on application.
Catering: clubhouse facilities.
Hotels: Golf; Old Manor; Lundin Links.

9C 44 **Falkirk**
136 Stirling Rd, Camelon, FK2 7YP
☎(01324) 611061, Fax 639573, Sec 634118
On A9 1.5 miles N of Falkirk.
Parkland course.
Founded 1922
Designed by James Braid
18 holes, 6230 yards, S.S.S. 70
Visitors: welcome WD; not Sat.
Green Fees: WD £15.
Societies: welcome WD and Sun by prior arrangement; catering by arrangement; £30.
Catering: full clubhouse facilities.
Hotels: Stakis Park Hotel.

9C 45 **Falkirk Tryst**
86 Burnhead Rd, Larbert,, FK5 4BD
☎(01324) 562415, Fax 562091, Pro 562091, Sec 562054, Bar /Rest 570436
On A88 5 miles N of Falkirk close to the A9 Falkirk-Stirling road.
Links course.
Founded 1885
18 holes, 6053 yards, S.S.S. 69
Visitors: welcome WD by prior arrangement.
Green Fees: WD £16.
Societies: welcome WD by prior arrangement; catering packages by arrangement; from £16.
Catering: full facilities.
Hotels: Stakis Park; Airth Castle, Airth; Plough, Stenhousemuir; Commercial, Larbert.

9C 46 **Falkland**
The Myre, Falkland, Cupar, Fife, KY15 7AA
☎(01337) 857404
In the Howe of Fife near to Freuchie and Auchtermuchty.
Parkland course.
Founded 1976
9 holes, 5140 yards, S.S.S. 65
Visitors: welcome except on comp days.
Green Fees: WD £8; WE £12.
Societies: welcome by prior arrangement; packages available; terms on application.
Catering: full facilities during summer; restricted in winter.
Hotels: Hunting Lodge.

9C 47 **Forfar**
Cunninghill, Arbroath Rd, Forfar, Angus, DD8 2RL
☎(01307) 462120, Fax 468495, Pro 465683, Sec 463773
From A90 to Forfar centre; 1 mile E of town on A932 Arbroath road.
Heathland course with tree-lined fairways.
Pro Peter McNiven; Founded 1871
Designed by James Braid
18 holes, 6052 yards, S.S.S. 69
Visitors: welcome by prior appointment.
Green Fees: WD £16; WE £20.
Societies: welcome between 10am-11.30am and 2.30pm-4pm except Sat morning; day tickets available; catering by arrangement; from £16.
Catering: full clubhouse facilities.
Hotels: Chakelbank, Forfar; James House, Letham.

9C 48 **Glenalmond**
Glenalmond, Perthshire, Tayside
☎(01738) 880270, Sec 880424
Moorland course; part of Glenalmond Trinity College.
Founded 1923
9 holes, 4801 yards, S.S.S. 68
Visitors: members only.
Green Fees: terms on application.

9C 49 **Glenbervie**
Stirling Rd, Larbert, Stirlingshire, FK5 4SJ
☎(01324) 562983, Fax 551504, Pro 562725, Sec 562605
M876 junction 2 left on to A9; club 300 yards.
Parkland course.
Pro John Phillas; Founded 1932
Designed by James Braid
18 holes, 6423 yards, S.S.S. 71
Visitors: welcome WD.
Green Fees: WD £30
Societies: welcome Tues and Thurs by prior arrangement; packages for 18/36 holes of golf and catering; from £44.
Catering: full clubhouse facilities.

9C 50 **Gleneagles Hotel**
Gleneagles Hotel, Auchterarder, Perthshire, PH3 1NF
☎(01764) 662231, Fax 662134
Halfway between Perth and Stirling on the A9.
Inland links/moorland course.
Pro Greg Schofield; Founded 1919 (Kings), 1917 (Queens), 1993 (Monarchs)

Designed by James Braid (Kings, Queens); Designed by Jack Nicklaus (Monarchs)
Kings: 18 holes, 6471 yards, S.S.S. 69; Monarchs: 18 holes, 7080 yards, S.S.S. 74; Queens: 18 holes, 5965 yards, S.S.S. 69
Visitors: members and hotel guests only.
Green Fees: WD £80; WE £80.
Societies: welcome if resident; catering packages by arrangement; also 9-hole, par 3 course; country club; health spa; clay target, shooting school; equestrian centre; terms on application.
Catering: full clubhouse bar and grill facilities; full hotel restaurant, conference centre and bars.
Practice range, for members and residents only.
Hotels: Gleneagles Hotel.

9C 51 **Glenrothes**

Golf Course Rd, Glenrothes, Fife, KY6 2LA
☎(01592) 758686, Sec 754561
Leave M90 at junction 3; A92 for Glenrothes; follow signs for Whitehill Industrial Estate.
Parkland course.
Founded 1958
Designed by J.R. Stutt
18 holes, 6444 yards, S.S.S. 71
Visitors: welcome.
Green Fees: WD £12; WE £16.
Societies: welcome by prior arrangement; catering available by arrangement with steward; groups of 12-40 only; day tickets available; terms on application.
Catering: full bar and catering facilities.
Hotels: Holiday Inn; Rescobie Hotel.

9C 52 **Grangemouth**

Polmonthill, by Falkirk, Stirlingshire, FK2 0YE
☎(01324) 711500, Pro 503840
M9 junction 4; follow signs to Polmonthill.
Parkland course.
Pro Stuart Campbell; Founded 1973
Designed by Sportwork
18 holes, 6314 yards, S.S.S. 71
Visitors: welcome.
Green Fees: WD £11.50; WE £14.50.
Societies: welcome by prior arrangement; catering by prior arrangement; from £11.50.
Catering: clubhouse facilities available.
Hotels: Inchrya; Grange; Lea Park.

9C 53 **Green Hotel**

2 The Muirs, Kinross, KY13 7AS
☎(01577) 862237, Fax 863180, Pro 865125, Sec 863407, Bar/Rest 862234
Opposite Green Hotel.
Parkland course.
Pro Stuart Gerraghy; Founded 1991
Designed by Sir David Montgomery
Blue: 18 holes, 6438 yards, S.S.S. 71; Red: 18 holes, 6256 yards, S.S.S. 71
Visitors: welcome.
Green Fees: WD £15; WE £25.
Societies: welcome; catering in hotel or clubhouse by arrangement; swimming pool; squash; tennis; from £15.
Catering: full facilities at hotel and clubhouse.
Hotels: Green Hotel.

9C 54 **Kenmore Golf Course**

Kenmore, Aberfeldy, Perthshire, PH15 2HN
☎(01887) 830226, Fax 830211, Bar/Rest 830775
On A827 through Kenmore village.
Slightly undulating parkland course.
Pro Alex Marshall; Founded 1992
Designed by R. Menzies and Partners
9 holes, 6052 yards, S.S.S. 69
Visitors: welcome.
Green Fees: WD £11; WE £12.
Societies: welcome by arrangement; catering packages available; £18.
Catering: full service.
Hotels: Kenmore.

9C 55 **Killin**

Killin, Perthshire, FK21 8TX
☎(01567) 820312, Sec 820705
W end of Loch Tay on A827 Killin to Aberfeldy road.
Parkland course; 5th/14th is The Dyke, 96 yards.
Founded 1913
Designed by John Duncan of Stirling
9 holes, 5016 yards, S.S.S. 65
Visitors: welcome.
Green Fees: WD £12; WE £12.
Societies: welcome by prior arrangement; full packages available; minimum 8; from £12.
Catering: full catering and bar facilities.
Hotels: Bridge of Lochay; Killin; Clachaig.

9C 56 **King James VI**

Moncreiffe Island, Perth, Perthshire, PH2 8NR
☎(01738) 625170, Fax 445132, Pro 632460, Sec 445132

In the centre of the River Tay; access by footpath from Tay Street or Shore Road.
Parkland course; one of only two courses on river island in the world.
Pro A Coles; Founded 1858/1897
18 holes, 6038 yards, S.S.S. 68
Visitors: welcome by prior arrangement.
Green Fees: WD £18; WE £20.
Societies: welcome by prior arrangement with the Pro; catering by arrangement; from £18.
Catering: full facilities.
Hotels: Salutation; Royal George; Isle of Skye.

9C 57 **Kinghorn**

Macduff Crescent, Kinghorn, Fife, KY3 9RE
☎(01592) 890345, Pro 890978
Off A92 3 miles W of Kirkcaldy.
Undulating links course.
Founded 1887
Designed by layout recommended by Tom Morris
18 holes, 5166 yards, S.S.S. 66
Visitors: welcome.
Green Fees: WD £9; WE £12.
Societies: welcome by prior written arrangement; groups of 12-30; catering packages by arrangement; from £9.
Catering: full catering facilities.
Hotels: Kingswood; Longboat.

9C 58 **Kirkcaldy**

Balwearie Rd, Kirkcaldy, Fife, KY2 5LT
☎(01592) 260370, Fax 203258, Pro 203258, Sec 205240
On A92 at W end of town.
Parkland course.
Pro Scott McKay; Founded 1904
Designed by Tom Morris
18 holes, 6038 yards, S.S.S. 69
Visitors: welcome; some restrictions Sat.
Green Fees: WD £16; WE £22.
Societies: welcome by prior arrangement; restrictions Sat; day rates and catering packages available; from £16.
Catering: full clubhouse facilities.
Hotels: Parkway Hotel; Dunnikier House.

9C 59 **Kirriemuir**

Northmuir, Kirriemuir, Angus, DD8 4LN
☎(01575) 573317, Fax 574608, Sec 575905, Bar/Rest 572144
N of Kirriemuir and accessible from A90 Dundee-Aberdeen road.
Parkland course.

Pro Anthony Caira; Founded 1908
Designed by James Braid
18 holes, 5510 yards, S.S.S. 67
Visitors: welcome.
Green Fees: WD £16; WE £16.
Societies: welcome by prior arrangement; day tickets available; catering and hospitality packages available; £5 pp deposit required; from £16.
Catering: full catering packages.
Hotels: Airlie Arms; Thrums: Castleton Park; Chapelbank.

9C 60 Ladybank

Annsmuir, Ladybank, Fife, KY15 7RA
☎ (01337) 830320, Fax 831505, Pro 830725, Sec 830814, Bar/Rest 830814
In Ladybank off A914 between Glenrothes and Dundee.
Heathland course.
Pro Martin Gray; Founded 1879
Designed by Tom Morris
18 holes, 6641 yards, S.S.S. 72
Visitors: welcome WD and some Sun by arrangement; h'cap certs required.
Green Fees: WD £28; WE £35.
Societies: welcome WD by prior arrangement with the club Pro; catering packages available; names and handicaps of all players required 7 days before arrival; dining room for 80; from £28.
Catering: full clubhouse bar and catering facilities.
Hotels: club can provide a list of local hotels, GH and self-catering accommodation.

9C 61 Leslie

Balsillie, Leslie, Fife, KY6 3EZ
☎ (01592) 620040
Leave M90 at junctions 5 or 7; Leslie 11 miles.
Undulating course.
Founded 1898
9 holes, 4940 yards, S.S.S. 64
Visitors: welcome.
Green Fees: WD £8; WE £10.
Societies: welcome by arrangement; catering by arrangement; from £8.
Catering: clubhouse facilities.
Hotels: Greenside; Rescobie.

9C 62 Letham Grange

Letham Grange, Colliston, by Arbroath, Angus, DD11 4RL
☎ (01241) 890373, Fax 890414, Pro 890377, Sec 872914
Follow Lenham Grange signs in Arbroath from Dundee-Arbroath road.
Parkland course.

Pro Steven Moir; Founded 1985 (Old); 1988 (New)
Designed by Donald Steel & G.K. Smith (Old); Designed by T MacAuley (New)
Old: 18 holes, 6968 yards, S.S.S. 73; New: 18 holes, 5528 yards, S.S.S. 68
Visitors: welcome; some restrictions at WE.
Green Fees: WD £24, WE £35 (Old); WD £15.50, WE £15.50 (New); combination rates available £31).
Societies: welcome by prior arrangement; catering packages available; contact Catherine Grainger at club; from £24.
Catering: full clubhouse facilities. Large practice area.
Hotels: 4-star Lenham Grange.

9C 63 Leven

PO Box 14609, Links Rd, Leven, Fife, KY8 4HS
☎ (01333) 426096, Fax 424229, Sec 424229
Enter Leven on A915 from Kirkcaldy and follow signs to the Beach.
Seaside links course.
Founded 1820
18 holes, 6436 yards, S.S.S. 70
Visitors: welcome; not before 9.30am WD; 10.30am WE.
Green Fees: WD £24; WE £28.
Societies: welcome by prior arrangement; catering packages by arrangement; snooker table; from £24.
Catering: full catering facilities.
Hotels: Lundin Links Hotel; Old Manor.

9C 64 Lochgelly

Cartmore Rd, Lochgelly, Fife, KY5 9PB
☎ (01592) 780174, Sec (01383) 512238
On A910 2 miles NE of Cowdenbeath.
Parkland course.
Founded 1896/1911
18 holes, 5454 yards, S.S.S. 67
Visitors: welcome.
Green Fees: WD on application.
Societies: welcome by prior arrangement; terms on application.
Catering: by arrangement.

9C 65 Lundin

Golf Rd, Lundin Links, Fife, KY8 6BA
☎ (01333) 320202, Fax 329743, Pro 320051
On seaward side of the village on East Neuk Coast Road from Kirkcaldy.
Seaside links course.

Pro David Webster; Founded 1868
Designed by James Braid
18 holes, 6394 yards, S.S.S. 71
Visitors: welcome between 9am-3.30pm Mon-Thurs; 9am-3pm Fri; after 2.30pm Sat; not Sun.
Green Fees: WD £27; WE £37.
Societies: welcome by prior arrangement with Sec; WD ticket of £36; catering packages by arrangement; from £27.
Catering: full facilities.
Hotels: Lundin Links; Old Manor.

9C 66 Lundin Ladies

Woodielea Road, Lundin Links, Fife, KY8 6AR
☎ (01333) 320832
Off Leven Road A915 in middle of Loudin Links.
Parkland course.
Founded 1891
Designed by James Braid
9 holes, 4730 yards, S.S.S. 67
Visitors: welcome.
Green Fees: WD £8; WE £9.50.
Societies: welcome except Wed April-August; from £8.
Catering: not available.
Hotels: Loudin Links; Old Manor.

9C 67 Milnathort

South St, Milnathort, Kinross, KY13 2AW
☎ (01577) 864069, Fax 0131 345 4907, Sec 0131 4430070
1 mile N of Kinross leaving M90 at junction 6/7.
Undulating course with trees; new tees/greens planned.
Founded 1890
9 holes, 5993 yards, S.S.S. 68
Visitors: welcome.
Green Fees: WD £15; WE £18.
Societies: welcome by prior arrangement; catering by arrangement with clubmaster; from £15.
Catering: clubhouse facilities. Practice range.
Hotels: Jolly Beggars; Thistle; Royal.

9C 68 Monifieth

Medal Starters Box, Princes St, Monifieth, Angus, DD5 4AW
☎ (01382) 532678, Fax 535553, Pro 532945, Sec 535553
5 miles E of Dundee on coast.
Links course.
Pro Ian McLeod; Founded 1850
Medal: 18 holes, 6655 yards, S.S.S. 72
Visitors: welcome.

Green Fees: WD £26; WE £30.
Societies: welcome; composite tickets available with Ashludie Course (18 holes, 5123 yards, par 68) WD £33, WE £36; from £26.
Catering: clubhouse facilities.
Practice range.
Hotels: Panmure packages available; Woodlands.

9C 69 Montrose Links Trust
Traill Drive, Montrose, Angus, DD10 8SW
☎(01674) 672634, Fax 671800, Sec 672932
Turn off Dundee-Aberdeen A90 at Brechin and take A935 to Montrose.
Links course.
Founded 1562
18 holes, 6470 yards, S.S.S. 71
Visitors: welcome; but nor before 2.30pm Sat or 10am on Sun.
Green Fees: WD £18; WE £25.
Societies: welcome by prior arrangement; same restrictions as for visitors; facilities available at the 3 clubs adjacent to courses (Montrose Caledonia GC (01674) 672313; Montrose Mercantile GC 672408; Royal Montrose 672376); also Broomfield course: 4788 yards, par 66/67; from £18.
Catering: catering at member clubs.
Hotels: Park Hotel; Links.

9C 70 Muckhart
Drumburn Rd, Muckhart, by Dollar, Clackmannanshire, FK14 7JH
☎(01259) 781423, Pro 781493
Off A91 3 miles E of Crieff; S of Muckhart; signposted.
Heathland course on rising ground.
Pro Keith Salmon; Founded 1908/1971
18 holes, 6034 yards, S.S.S. 70
Visitors: welcome.
Green Fees: WD £15; WE £22.
Societies: welcome; catering by arrangement; £10 addition for playing 9-hole course; day rates WD £22; WE £30; from £15.
Catering: full catering and bar facilities.

9C 71 Murrayshall
Murrayshall Country House Hotel, Scone, Perthshire, PH2 7PH
☎(01738) 551171, Fax 552595, Pro 552784
On A94 Cupar-Angus road 4 miles from Perth by Scone.
Parkland course.

Pro Alan Reid; Founded 1981
Designed by J. Hamilton Stutt
18 holes, 6441 yards, S.S.S. 72
Visitors: welcome.
Green Fees: WD £22; WE £27.
Societies: welcome; packages by arrangement; from £22.
Catering: full facilities and hotel bar and restaurants.
Hotels: Murrayshall on site.

9C 72 Muthill
Peat Rd, Muthill, by Crieff, Perthshire, PH5 2DA
☎(01764) 681523
From Crieff course is on right before Muthill at Bowling Green.
Parkland course.
Founded 1935
9 holes, 4700 yards, S.S.S. 63
Visitors: welcome.
Green Fees: WD £12; WE £12.
Societies: none.
Catering: full clubhouse facilities available.
Hotels: Drummond Arms.

9C 73 North Inch
Perth & Kinross Council, 3 High Street, Perth, Perthshire, PH1 5JU
☎(01738) 475000, Pro 636481
N of Perth adjacent to Gannochy Trust Sports Complex.
Tree-lined course running alongside river.
18 holes, 5178 yards, S.S.S. 65
Visitors: welcome.
Green Fees: WD £6; WE £8.
Societies: welcome by prior arrangement; some summer restrictions apply; from £6.
Catering: catering at Bell's Sports Complex.

9C 74 Panmure
Burnside Road, Barry, Angus, DD7 7RT
☎(01241) 853120, Fax 859737, Pro 852460, Sec 855120
Off A930 2 miles W of Carnoustie.
Seaside course.
Pro Neil MacKintoch; Founded 1845
18 holes, 6317 yards, S.S.S. 71
Visitors: welcome except for Sat.
Green Fees: WD £30; WE £30.
Societies: welcome by arrangement; catering packages by arrangement; day ticket £45; from £30.
Catering: full facilities.
Practice range.
Hotels: Carlogie; Panmure; Station; Woodlands.

9C 75 Pitlochry
Golf Course Rd, Pitlochry, Perthshire, PH16 5QY
☎(01796) 472792
A9 to Pitlochry then via Atholl Rd, Larchwood Rd to Golf Course road.
Hill course.
Pro George Hampton; Founded 1908
Designed by Willie Fernie of Troon; Modernised by Major C. Hut
18 holes, 5811 yards, S.S.S. 69
Visitors: welcome by arrangement with the Pro.
Green Fees: WD £20; WE £25.
Societies: welcome by arrangement; catering by arrangement with Steward; terms on application.
Catering: full clubhouse facilities.

9C 76 Pitreavie (Dunfermline)
Queensferry Rd, Dunfermline, Fife, KY11 5PR
☎(01383) 722591, Fax 722591, Pro 723151
M90 N of Forth Road Bridge; 3rd exit signposted Dunfermline; club 3 miles.
Parkland course.
Pro Colin Mitchell; Founded 1922
Designed by Dr A. MacKenzie
18 holes, 6032 yards, S.S.S. 69
Visitors: welcome.
Green Fees: WD £16; WE £30.
Societies: welcome; catering by arrangement; terms on application.
Catering: full clubhouse facilities.
Hotels: Pitbauchlie House; King Malcolm.

9C 77 Polmont
Manuelrigg Maddiston, by Falkirk, Stirlingshire, FK2 0LS
☎(01324) 711277
4 miles S of Falkirk, 1st right after Fire Brigade HQ.
Undulating parkland course.
Founded 1904
9 holes, 6062 yards, S.S.S. 69
Visitors: welcome except on Sat.
Green Fees: WD £14; WE £16.
Societies: welcome by prior arrangement; catering by arrangement with Sec; from £14.
Catering: clubhouse facilities.
Hotels: Inchrya Grange; Polmont.

9C 79 St Fillans
South Loch Earn Rd, St Fillans, Perthshire, PH6 2NJ
☎(01764) 685312
On A85 at E end of the village.
Parkland course; Founded 1903
Designed by W Auchterlonie

St Andrews

Golfers go to St Andrews as Moslems flock to Mecca, Mormons descend on Salt Lake City and Roman Catholics gather in St Peter's Square. It is as much a shrine as any religious centre, indeed, its symbolic importance grows more not less.

Every golf course in the world owes something to the Old Course. Whether by accident or design, it embraces nearly all the elements on which sound, traditional golf-course architecture is based. In discussing the qualifications for an architect long ago, Tom Simpson said: "Above everything else, he must understand the message of the Old Course."

Some architects have even gone to the lengths of building replicas of some of the holes. Charles Blair Macdonald, a figure of enormous influence in shaping golf in America, repaid his love of St Andrews by building a course on the lines of the old, classic links at The National Golf Links of America on Long Island. Among the holes he built were copies of St Andrews' 11th and 17th. Augusta's fourth hole also bears more than a little resemblance to St Andrews' 11th. They are fine holes but, however much of a compliment they may be, the best holes are always those which owe nothing to imitation and everything to Nature.

Modern machinery has simplified golf course architecture in the sense that nothing is now impossible. However, it has allowed some architects to drift away from the age-old tenets which St Andrews holds dear. This syndrome is typified by greens in the middle of lakes, huge carries to greens, enormous bunkers shaped like eccentric jig-saw pieces and railway sleepers by the train load. Television and resort developers are largely to blame for this 'stadium golf'.

Horror-provoking stretches of water, roller-coaster fairways and penal hollows make only the publicity men happy. Golf,

even professional golf, is played for pleasure and there is no pleasure in losing ball after ball or feeling that the impossible is being attempted.

However, there are signs that sanity is being restored. The 1986 US Open at Shinnecock Hills brought forth *cris de coeur* from such players as Lee Trevino, Hale Irwin, David Graham and Jack Renner. Shinnecock is one the oldest courses in the America, the Club in fact, being the first to be 'formalised' in the United States. Everyone liked the course for different reasons. Trevino saw Shinnecock's greatness in the fact that it favoured no particular group of players. Graham liked the idea that it allowed you to hit the ball low with the chance to run the ball on to the green, if you wanted to. It gave the player desirable options, and made a break from all-or-nothing shots typical of many new courses.

Curtis Strange endorsed this view a year later, following his record-breaking 62 over the Old Course in the 1987 Dunhill Cup, when he declared: "They should come to St Andrews and be reminded what traditional design is all about."

Maybe the developments in course architecture in the last few years are part of a passing phase. Fashion exists in golf course architecture just as it does in clothes, motor cars or buildings but golf courses are more permanent. It needs visits to St Andrews to understand that simplicity is the best basic art and that the game is better when the player has to formulate his strategy on the tee, choosing how to play a hole from as many as four or five options.

St Andrews is planning for the future, not just living in the past, but it needs a shrewd mind to understand that what one might term traditional architecture is still the best and St Andrews is still its most faithful standard-bearer.

9C 78 St Andrews

St Andrews Links Management Committee, Pilmour Cottage, St Andrews, Fife, KY16 9JA
☎ (01334) 466666, Fax 477036, Pro 475757, Sec 475757, Bar/Rest 473107
60 miles north of Edinburgh via A91 to St Andrews; turning to course is on the left before the town; by rail to Leuchars on Edinburgh-Dundee main line.
Green Fees: apply for details.
Societies: welcome; terms on application.
Catering: clubhouse facilities and in local hotels.
Hotels: full range in St Andrews from B&B to international standard.

Old Course
18 holes, 6566 yards, S.S.S. 72
Most famous Championship links in the world.
Founded 1400
Designed by Nature and Tom Morris, A. Robertson, A. MacKenzie
Visitors: welcome with h'cap certs; no play on Sun.

Balgove Course
9 holes, 1530 yards
Founded 1974
Visitors: welcome; children under 16 reduced prices.
Green Fees: WD £7; WE £7.

Eden Course
18 holes, 6112 yards, S.S.S. 70
Founded 1914
Designed by HS Colt
Visitors: public.

Jubilee Course
18 holes, 6805 yards, S.S.S. 72
Founded 1897/1989
Designed by J Angus/ Donald Steel (1989)
Visitors: welcome.

New Course
18 holes, 6604 yards, S.S.S. 72
Founded 1895
Designed by Old Tom Morris
Visitors: welcome.

Strathyrum Course
18 holes, 5094 yards, S.S.S. 65
Founded 1993
Designed by Donald Steel
Visitors: welcome.

9 holes, 5796 yards, S.S.S. 67
Visitors: welcome.
Green Fees: WD £12; WE £16.
Societies: welcome by arrangement; maximum 16; catering by arrangement; from £12.
Catering: catering facilities; no bar; unlicensed.
Hotels: Achray; Four Seasons; Drummond Arms.

9C 80 St Michaels

Leuchars, Fife, KY16 0DX
☎ (01334) 839365, Fax 838666, Sec 838666
5 miles from St Andrews on main road to Dundee.
Undulating parkland course.
Founded 1903
18 holes, 5802 yards, S.S.S. 68
Visitors: welcome except before 12 noon on Sun.
Green Fees: WD £15; WE £15.
Societies: welcome by written prior arrangement; restrictions on Sun; 36 holes of golf and full catering; £25.
Catering: full facilities.
Hotels: St Michaels Inn; many in St Andrews.

9C 81 Saline

Kinneddar Hill, Saline, Fife, KY12 9LT
☎ (01383) 852591; Sec: 852344
5 miles NW of Dunfermline.
Hillside course.
Founded 1912
9 holes, 5304 yards, S.S.S. 66
Visitors: welcome except Sat.
Green Fees: WD £9; WE £11.
Societies: welcome WD and Sun only; maximum 24; catering packages by arrangement; terms on application.
Catering: full catering.
Hotels: Saline Castle; Campbell; Pitbauchly.

9C 82 Scoonie

North Links, Leven, Fife, KY8 4SP
☎ (01333) 307007, Fax 307008, Pro 427437
10 miles SW of St Andrews.
Parkland course.
Founded 1951
18 holes, 4979 yards, S.S.S. 65
Visitors: welcome by arrangement with Sec except Thurs and Sat.
Green Fees: WD on application.
Societies: welcome by appointment with Sec; groups of 12-30; catering by arrangement; terms on application.
Catering: full clubhouse facilities.
Hotels: Caledonian.

9C 83 Scotscraig

Golf Rd, Tayport, Fife, DD6 9DZ
☎ (01382) 552515, Pro 552855
On B946 3 miles from S end of Tay Road Bridge.
Links/seaside course.
Pro Stuart Campbell; Founded 1817
18 holes, 6550 yards, S.S.S. 72
Visitors: welcome WD and by prior arrangement at WE.
Green Fees: WD £27; WE £32.
Societies: welcome by prior arrangement; packages by arrangement; day tickets WD £36; WE £44; from £27.
Catering: full catering facilities.
Hotels: Seymour; Scores; Rusacks; Russell.

9C 84 Stirling

Queens Rd, Stirling, Stirlingshire, FK8 3AA
☎ (01786) 464098, Pro 471490
On A811 1 mile W of town.
Parkland course.
Pro Ian Collins; Founded 1869
Designed by J Braid/H Cotton
18 holes, 6438 yards, S.S.S. 71
Visitors: welcome WD; some WE restrictions.
Green Fees: WD £20.
Societies: welcome WD by prior arrangement; day ticket £30; catering by arrangement; pool table; from £20.
Catering: full clubhouse facilities.
Hotels: Golden Lion.

9C 85 Strathendrick

Glasgow Rd, Drymen, Stirlingshire, G63 0AA
☎ (01360) 660675
Off A811 1 mile S of Drymen; 17 miles N W of Glasgow.
Hilly moorland course.
Founded 1901
9 holes, 5116 yards, S.S.S. 64
Visitors: welcome WD 8.30am-2.30pm May-Sept.
Green Fees: WD on application.
Societies: limited access by prior arrangement; terms on application.
Catering: none.
Hotels: Buchanan Arms; Winnock.

9C 86 Taymouth Castle

Kenmore, by Aberfeldy, Tayside, PH15 2NT
☎ (01887) 830228, Fax 830228, Bar/Rest 830397
5 miles W of Aberfeldy on the A827.
Parkland course.
Pro Alex Marshall; Founded 1923
Designed by James Braid

18 holes, 6066 yards, S.S.S. 69
Visitors: welcome.
Green Fees: WD £17; WE £21.
Societies: welcome by prior arrangement; packages available; from £17.
Catering: full clubhouse facilities.
Hotels: Kenmore.

9C 87 **Thornton**

Station Rd, Thornton, Fife, KY1 4DW
☎(01592) 771111, Fax 774955, Pro
771173, Bar/Rest 771161
1 mile off the A92 road at the
Redhouse roundabout midway
between Kirkcaldy and Glenrothes.
Parkland course.
Founded 1921
Designed by Members
18 holes, 6177 yards, S.S.S. 69
Visitors: welcome.
Green Fees: WD £14; WE £20.
Societies: welcome; catering packages by arrangement; from £14.
Catering: full clubhouse facilities; new clubhouse opened in Dec 1997.
Hotels: Crown, Thornton; Rescobie; Albany, both Glenrothes; Royal, Dean Park, both Kirkcaldy.

9C 88 **Tillicoultry**

Alva Rd, Tillicoultry, FK13 6BL
☎(01259) 750124
9 miles E of Stirling on the A91.
Undulating parkland course.
Founded 1899
Designed by Peter Robertson, Braids
Hill G.C. Edinburgh
9 holes, 5358 yards, S.S.S. 66
Visitors: welcome by arrangement.
Green Fees: WD £10; WE £16.
Societies: welcome by arrangement
with Sec; catering by prior arrangement; terms on application.
Catering: restaurant and bar facilities.

9C 89 **Tulliallan**

Alloa Rd, Kincardine on Forth, FK10
4BB
☎(01259) 730396, Pro 730798
0.5 miles N of the Kincardine Bridge
on the Alloa road.
Parkland course.
Pro Stephen Kelly; Founded 1902
18 holes, 5965 yards, S.S.S. 69
Visitors: welcome by arrangement.
Green Fees: WD £15; WE £20.
Societies: welcome by prior arrangement except Sat; day tickets WD:
£27.50; WE: £35; WD maximum 40;
Sun max 24; from £15.
Catering: full clubhouse facilities.
Hotels: Powfoulis Manor.

9C 90 **Whitemoss**

Whitemoss Road, Dunning,
Perthshire, PH2 0QX
☎(01738) 730300, Fax 730300
1 mile off the A9; 2 miles past the
Gleneagles Hotel.
Parkland course.
Founded 1994
18 holes, 5955 yards, S.S.S. 68
Visitors: welcome by arrangement.
Green Fees: WD £15; WE £15.
Societies: welcome by prior arrangement; catering packages available by
prior arrangement; day tickets £20;
from £15.
Catering: full facilities.
Hotels: Gleneagles.

9D 1 **Abernethy**

Nethybridge, Inverness-shire, PH25
3DE
☎(01479) 821305
On B970 Grantown-on-Spey to Boat of
Garten road.
Undulating course with views of Spey
valley.
Founded 1893
9 holes, 4986 yards, S.S.S. 66
Visitors: welcome with Sun restrictions.
Green Fees: WD £10; WE £14.
Societies: welcome by arrangement
with Sec; packages available; terms
on application.
Catering: full clubhouse facilities in
season.
Hotels: Nethybridge; Mountview;
Heatherbrae.

9D 2 **Aboyne**

Formaston Park, Aboyne,
Aberdeenshire, AB34 5HP
☎(013398) 86328, Pro 87078
Off A93 from Aberdeen; take first turning on right after entering village.
Undulating parkland course.
Pro Dennis Wright; Founded 1883
18 holes, 5975 yards, S.S.S. 69
Visitors: welcome.
Green Fees: WD £18; WE £22.
Societies: welcome by prior arrangement except Sun; day tickets available
(WD £23, WE £27); catering packages
by arrangement between April and
October; from £18.
Catering: full summer facilities.
Hotels: Charleston; Birse Lodge;
Huntly Arms.

9D 3 **Alford**

Montgarrie Rd, Alford, AB33 8AE
☎(019755) 62178, Fax 62178

On A944 in the village of Alford 25
miles W of Aberdeen.
Parkland course.
Founded 1982
Designed by David Hurd
18 holes, 5402 yards, S.S.S. 65
Visitors: welcome; some restrictions
on club comp days.
Green Fees: WD £12; WE £19.
Societies: welcome by prior arrangement; day tickets available (WD £17,
WE £24); shotgun starts can be organised for a minimum of 50 players;
catering packages by arrangement;
from £12.
Catering: full clubhouse facilities
available.
Hotels: Kildrummy Castle; Forbes
Arms.

9D 4 **Alness**

Ardross Rd, Alness, Ross-shire
☎(01349) 883877
On A9 10 miles N of Dingwall.
Extending to 18 holes in 1998.
Founded 1904
Designed by John Sutherland
9 holes, 4946 yards, S.S.S. 64
Visitors: welcome except 4.30pm-
7.30pm Mon.
Green Fees: WD £8; WE £10.
Societies: welcome by prior arrangement; catering by prior arrangement;
terms on application.
Catering: by prior arrangement.
Hotels: Commercial Hotel.

9D 5 **Askernish**

Lochboisdale, Askernish, South Uist,
Western Isles, HS81 5SY
☎(01878) 700301, Fax 700309
Take the ferry from Oban to
Lochboisdale; course is 5 miles N of
Lochboisdale.
Links course; most Western course in
Scotland; 18 tees.
Pro M McPhee; Founded 1891
Designed by Tom Morris
9 holes, 5042 yards, S.S.S. 67
Visitors: welcome.
Green Fees: WD £10; WE £10.
Societies: welcome; terms on application.
Catering: by prior arrangement.
Hotels: Lochboisdale Hotel.

9D 6 **Auchenblae**

Myreside, Auchenblae, Laurencekirk,
Kincardineshire, AB30 1BU
☎(01561) 320002
2 miles W of Fordoun off A94.
Parkland course.

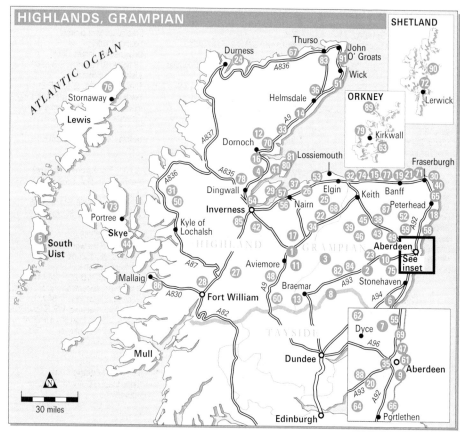

HIGHLANDS, GRAMPIAN

1	Abernethy	20	Deeside	39	Insch	58	Newburgh-on-Ythan	77	Strathlene
2	Aboyne	21	Duff House Royal	40	Inverallochy	59	Newmachar	78	Strathpeffer Spa
3	Alford	22	Dufftown	41	Invergordon	60	Newtonmore	79	Stromness
4	Alness	23	Dunecht House	42	Inverness	61	Northern	80	Tain
5	Askernish	24	Durness	43	Inverurie	62	Oldmeldrum	81	Tarbat
6	Auchenblae	25	Elgin	44	Isle of Skye	63	Orkney	82	Tarland
7	Auchmill	26	Forres	45	Keith	64	Peterculter	83	Thurso
8	Ballater	27	Fort Augustus	46	Kemnay	65	Peterhead	84	Torphins
9	Balnagask	28	Fort William	47	King's Links	66	Portlethen	85	Torvean
10	Banchory	29	Fortrose & Rosemarkie	48	Kingussie	67	Reay	86	Traigh Golf Course
11	Boat of Garten	30	Fraserburgh	49	Kintore	68	Rothes	87	Turriff
12	Bonar Bridge & Ardgay	31	Gairloch	50	Kirkcaldy	69	Royal Aberdeen	88	Westhill
13	Braemar	32	Garmouth & Kingston	51	Lybster	70	Royal Dornoch	89	Westray
14	Brora	33	Golspie	52	McDonald	71	Royal Tarlair	90	Whalsay
15	Buckpool (Buckie)	34	Grantown-on-Spey	53	Moray	72	Shetland	91	Wick
16	Carnegie Club	35	Hazlehead	54	Muir of Ord	73	Skeabost		
17	Carrbridge	36	Helmsdale	55	Murcar	74	Spey Bay		
18	Cruden Bay	37	Hopeman	56	Nairn	75	Stonehaven		
19	Cullen	38	Huntly	57	Nairn Dunbar	76	Stornoway		

9 holes, 4496 yards, S.S.S. 63
Visitors: welcome except Wed and Fri evenings between 5.30pm-9pm.
Green Fees: WD £8; WE £10.
Societies: welcome WD by prior

arrangement; limited catering; terms on application.
Catering: village hotels provide catering
Hotels: Drumtochty; Thistle.

9D 7 Auchmill
Bonny View, Auchmill, AB16 7FQ
☎(01224) 715214, Pro 714577
5 miles N of Aberdeen
Municipal parkland course.

18 holes, 5560 yards, S.S.S. 69
Visitors: welcome.
Green Fees: WD £4.45; WE £4.45.
Societies: only with prior arrangement through council.
Catering: limited.

9D 8 **Ballater**

Victoria Rd, Ballater, Aberdeenshire, AB35 5QX
☎(013397) 55567, Fax 55057, Pro 55658, Bar/Rest 56241
42 miles W of Aberdeen on the A93.
Heath/parkland course.
Pro Billy Yule; Founded 1891
Designed by James Braid/H Vardon
18 holes, 6112 yards, S.S.S. 69
Visitors: welcome by arrangement.
Green Fees: WD £18; WE £22.
Societies: welcome by arrangement; catering and day rates; from £18.
Catering: bar and catering facilities.
Hotels: club can provide comprehensive list.

9D 9 **Balnagask**

St Fitticks Rd, Balnagask, Aberdeen, AB24
☎(01224) 876407
2 miles SE of the city.
Municipal seaside course.
Founded 1955
Designed by Hawtree & Son
18 holes, 5986 yards, S.S.S. 69
Visitors: welcome.
Green Fees: WD £4.45; WE £4.45
Societies: welcome by prior arrangement with the council.
Catering: by arrangement with the council.
Hotels: Caledonian.

9D 10 **Banchory**

Kinneskie Rd, Banchory, Kincardineshire, AB31 3TA
☎(01330) 822365, Fax 822491, Pro 822447, Bar/Rest 822274
100 yards off the A93, the main Aberdeen to Braemar road.
Parkland course course; 16th hole, Doo'cot is 88 yards.
Pro David Naylor; Founded 1905
18 holes, 5775 yards, S.S.S. 68
Visitors: welcome; booking advisable on Thurs and at WE.
Green Fees: WD £19; WE £21.
Societies: welcome; catering packages by prior arrangement; terms on application.
Catering: full catering, lounge and dining room facilities
Hotels: Burnett Arms; Tor-na-coille; Banchory Lodge.

9D 11 **Boat of Garten**

Boat of Garten, Inverness-shire, PH24 3BQ
☎(01479) 831282, Fax 831523, Bar/Rest 831731
2 miles E of A9 30 miles S of Inverness.
Heathland course.
Pro James Ingram; Founded 1898
Designed by James Braid
18 holes, 5866 yards, S.S.S. 69
Visitors: welcome WD 9.30am-6pm; WE 10am-4pm.
Green Fees: WD £21; WE £26.
Societies: welcome by prior arrangement; day tickets available (WD £26, WE £31); catering by arrangement; separate changing rooms; from £21.
Catering: full clubhouse facilities.
Hotels: The Boat; Craigand.

9D 12 **Bonar Bridge & Ardgay**

Market Stance, Migdale Rd, Bonar Bridge, Sutherland, IV24 3EJ
☎(01863) 766199, Fax 766738, Sec 766375
Off A836 at Bonar Bridge 0.5 miles up Migdale Rd; 12 miles W of Dornoch.
Parkland course.
Founded 1904
9 holes, 5284 yards, S.S.S. 63
Visitors: welcome.
Green Fees: WD £10; WE £10.
Societies: welcome WD by prior arrangement; terms on application.
Catering: clubhouse facilities in season.

9D 13 **Braemar**

Cluniebank Rd, Braemar, Aberdeenshire, AB35 5XX
☎(013397) 41618, Sec (01224) 704471
Signposted from the village centre; turn left opposite Fife Arms Hotel.
Parkland course.
Founded 1902
Designed by Joe Anderson
18 holes, 4935 yards, S.S.S. 64
Visitors: welcome.
Green Fees: WD £13; WE £16.
Societies: welcome; packages include 36 holes of golf and catering; from £20; WE £32.
Catering: full clubhouse facilities.
Hotels: Invercauld Arms; Fife Arms; Moorfield House.

9D 14 **Brora**

43 Golf Rd, Brora, Sutherland, KW9 6QS
☎(01408) 621417, Fax 622157, Pro 621423

On A9 N of Inverness; turn right over bridge in centre of Brora.
Traditional links course.
Founded 1891
Designed by James Braid
18 holes, 6110 yards, S.S.S. 69
Visitors: welcome.
Green Fees: WD £18; WE £18.
Societies: welcome by prior arrangement; on application; from £18.
Catering: clubhouse facilities.
Practice range.
Hotels: Royal Marine; Links.

9D 15 **Buckpool (Buckie)**

Barhill Rd, Buckie, Banffshire, AB56 1DU
☎(01542) 832236, Fax 832236
Turn off the A98 at Buckpool.
Links course.
Founded 1933/65
Designed by Hawtree & Taylor
18 holes, 6257 yards, S.S.S. 70
Visitors: welcome.
Green Fees: WD £10; WE £12.
Societies: welcome by prior arrangement; packages include 36 holes of golf with full catering; WE discounts for groups of more than 20; from £22.
Catering: full clubhouse facilities.
Hotels: Marine, Buckie.

9D 16 **Carnegie Club**

Skibo Castle, Dornoch, Sutherland, IV25 3RQ
☎(01862) 894600, Fax 894601, Pro 881260
Take A9 towards Wick from Inverness; 1st left after Dornoch Bridge signposted Meikle Ferry North; continue for 1 mile and turn right at Green Sheds.
Links course; new 9-hole parkland course (members course) opens 1998.
Pro Willie Milne; Founded 1994
Designed by Donald Steel
18 holes, 6671 yards, S.S.S. 72
Visitors: WD only teeing off between 11am-12 noon; by arrangement only.
Green Fees: WD £130.
Societies: WD only teeing off between 11am-12 noon; includes soup, sandwiches and a special gift pack; £130.
Catering: full facilities in the club.
Hotels: Morangie House; Mansfield House, both Tain; Royal Golf; Burghfield, both Dornoch.

9D 17 **Carrbridge**

Inverness Rd, Carrbridge, Inverness-shire, PH23 3AU
☎(01479) 841623, Sec 841506

Carnegie Golf Links

Long ago, the American golf course architect, Perry Maxwell, wrote: "Nature must precede the architect in laying out the course. The site of a golf course must be there, not brought there. In this way, it will have its own character, distinct from any other in the world."

It is a message too often overlooked by modern architects who are slaves to the bulldozer. It never occurs to some to work any other way but the Carnegie Golf Links at Skibo, the first links to be built in Britain for over half a century, relies entirely upon nature, a perfect blend with the landscape – and what a landscape. Few places where golf is played can rival the majesty of a Highland setting, magnified by the clear, northern light.

It was a magic first discovered by Andrew Carnegie, whose golfing interests only took shape once he had amassed his considerable fortune in America. To prove his intent, he engaged John Sutherland, the famous Secretary at Royal Dornoch, to lay out nine holes so that he could learn the game and thus accept Royal Dornoch's invitation to membership, an honour he later repaid with the presentation of the Carnegie Shield which remains the Club's foremost annual competition.

Virtually nothing of the old layout was evident when the new Carnegie links was born in 1992 as the centrepiece of the Carnegie Club, membership of which enjoys use of the incomparable castle and the many blessings of a vast and varied estate. In order to accommodate 18 holes, the utmost had to be made of the slender finger of land running from the Inverness road and surrounded on three sides by water including Loch Evelix, a salmon loch and haven for aquatic birds.

Everything about Skibo was sympathetically thought out, even the character of the clubhouse, designed along the lines of the farm steading which it replaced. From here, the first hole makes its way parallel with a line of low sandhills which gives the dogleg second its feature and the green on the short third an elevated Rye-like perch. Then, it is over the old ferry road to exploit the stretch of water, crossed by the Dornoch Firth bridge, with contrasting short par fours.

The short sixth lies in the heart of the rare and protected lichen heath with its 120 species but, for golfers, it is the presence of gorse, heather and a strain of strong rough which makes steering a straight course both wise and welcome. After the drive on the seventh takes you back onto the higher ground, the eighth hugs the curve of Loch Evelix, a hole extolling more the inland beauty. However, the ninth, 12th, 13th and 14th are set against a mountain backdrop and, as the short 15th beckons, the scene changes yet again.

Water flanks this attractive hole beside the clubhouse, as it does the left of the short par-four 17th, the 17th tee offering perhaps the best opportunity of assimilating the full glory of the setting.

In its short life, the course has been called "Heaven on Earth", "a dream come true", and "maybe the last consummate private golf sanctuary in all the British Isles". Jim Achenbach felt that the course blends so unobtrusively into the landscape, "it looks as if it could have been built by shepherds two centuries ago" but, where the finish is concerned, Bob McCoy, who has seen more of the finest courses than anyone, believes, "the final three holes could develop into one of the best finishing stretches in golf".

The 18th, a par five, swings left-handed across a salt marsh and alongside an estuary to the Firth to a green on a lonely point, watched over by a clubhouse with perhaps the best outlook in the world.

Off A9 25 miles S of Inverness.
Parkland course/heathland course.
Founded 1980
9 holes, 5402 yards, S.S.S. 68
Visitors: welcome.
Green Fees: WD £10; WE £12.
Societies: limited to small groups.
Catering: tea, coffee and snacks.
Hotels: Contact Carrbridge Tourist
Association.

9D 18 **Cruden Bay**

Aulton Rd, Cruden Bay, Peterhead,
Aberdeenshire, AB42 7NN
☎(01779) 812285, Fax 812945, Pro
812414
Off A90 10 miles from Peterhead; or
from Aberdeen off A90 then A975.
Championship links course.
Pro Robbie Stewart; Founded 1899
Designed by Tom Morris & Archie
Simpson
Main course: 18 holes, 6395 yards,
S.S.S. 72; St Olaf: 9 holes, 5106
yards, S.S.S. 65
Visitors: welcome; restrictions until
after 9.30am Mon; after 10.30am Tues
and at WE (Main); welcome (St Olaf).
Green Fees: WD £35, WE £45 (Main);
WD £10, WE £20 (St Olaf).
Societies: welcome WD except Wed
by prior arrangement; h'cap certs
needed; minimum 16 players; catering
by prior arrangement; from £25 (Main);
welcome (St Olaf).
Catering: full clubhouse facilities.
Practice range, covered bays.
Hotels: club can provide list.

9D 19 **Cullen**

The Links, Cullen, Buckie, Banffshire,
AB56 2UU
☎(01542) 840685, Sec 840174
Off the A98 at the western end of the
town on the Moray Firth coastline.
Traditional links course with natural
rock landscaping.
Founded 1879.
Designed by Tom Morris (original 9
holes); Charles Neaves
18 holes, 4610 yards, S.S.S. 62
Visitors: welcome WD; some WE
restrictions July/August.
Green Fees: WD £10; WE £13.
Societies: welcome by prior arrange-
ment; restrictions on Wed and Sat;
day tickets available (WD £15, WE
£18); catering packages by arrange-
ment; from £10.
Catering: clubhouse catering and bar.
Hotels: Cullen Bay; Royal Oak;
Bayview; Three Kings; Grant Arms;
Seafield Arms; Waverley.

9D 20 **Deeside**

Golf Rd, Bieldside, Aberdeen,
Aberdeenshire, AB15 9DL
☎(01224) 869457, Pro 861041
On A93 3 miles W of Aberdeen.
Parkland course.
Pro F J Coutts; Founded 1903
18 holes, 5971 yards, S.S.S. 69
Visitors: welcome after 9am WD and
4pm Sat; letter of introduction needed.
Green Fees: WD £25; WE £30.
Societies: welcome Thurs only by
arrangement; catering packages by
arrangement; also 9-hole course, 3316
yards, SSS 36; terms on application.
Catering: full facilities.
Hotels: Cults; Bieldside Inn.

9D 21 **Duff House Royal**

The Banyards, Banff, Banffshire, AB45
3SX
☎(01261) 812062, Pro 812075
On A98.
Parkland course.
Pro R Strachan; Founded 1909
Designed by Dr A. & Major C.A.
MacKenzie
18 holes, 6161 yards, S.S.S. 70
Visitors: welcome except before
11am and between 12.30pm-3.30pm
WE and in July/August.
Green Fees: WD £14; WE £20.
Societies: welcome by prior arrange-
ment; catering and day packages by
application; terms on application.
Catering: full facilities.
Hotels: Banff Springs; County; Fife
Lodge.

9D 22 **Dufftown**

Tomintoul Road, Dufftown, Keith,
Banffshire, AB55 4BX
☎(01340) 820325, Fax 820325, Sec
820227
On A9009 1 mile S of Dufftown.
Moor/parkland course; Founded 1896
Designed by A Simpson
18 holes, 5308 yards, S.S.S. 67
Visitors: welcome.
Green Fees: WD £10; WE £10.
Societies: welcome by prior arrange-
ment; discounts for groups of more
than 12; catering by prior arrange-
ment; from £10.
Catering: clubhouse bar and catering.
Hotels: Fife Arms; Craigellachie.

9D 23 **Dunecht House**

Dunecht, Skene, Aberdeenshire, AB3
7AX
☎(01224)
Course on B994 to Dunecht.

Inland wooded course; Founded 1925
9 holes, 6270 yards, S.S.S. 70
Visitors: no visitors; private.
Green Fees: terms on application.

9D 24 **Durness**

Balnakeil, Durness, Sutherland, IV27
4PN
☎(01971) 511364
57 miles NW of Lairg on A838; turn
left in village square.
Links/parkland course.
Founded 1988
Designed by F Keith, L Ross,
I Morrison
9 holes, 5555 yards, S.S.S. 69
Visitors: welcome.
Green Fees: WD £12; WE £12.
Societies: welcome; terms on applica-
tion.
Catering: clubhouse facilities.
Hotels: Cape Wrath; Parkhill;
Rhiconich.

9D 25 **Elgin**

Hardhillock, Birnie Rd, Elgin, Moray,
IV30 3SX
☎(01343) 542338, Fax 542341, Pro
542884
On A941 Birnie road.
Parkland course.
Pro Ian Rodger; Founded 1906
Designed by John MacPherson
18 holes, 6411 yards, S.S.S. 71
Visitors: welcome.
Green Fees: WD £21; WE £27.
Societies: welcome by prior arrange-
ment with Sec David Black; discounts
of 10% for larger groups; catering by
arrangement; from £21.
Catering: clubhouse bar and catering.
Hotels: Sunnighill; Laichmoray; Eight
Acres; Mansion House; Rothes Glen.

9D 26 **Forres**

Muiryshade, Forres, IV36 0RD
☎(01309) 672949, Fax 672250, Pro
672250
On A96 26 miles E of Inverness; 1
mile S of Forres.
Parkland course.
Pro Sandy Aird; Founded 1889
Designed by James Braid
18 holes, 6141 yards, S.S.S. 69
Visitors: welcome by prior arrange-
ment with the professional.
Green Fees: WD £14; WE £14.
Societies: welcome by prior arrange-
ment; maximum number 60; terms on
application.
Catering: full clubhouse facilities.
Hotels: Ramnee.

Cruden Bay

Cruden Bay is no place for those who like their golf to be an exercise of dull predictability in a sheltered setting. However, if you are a romantic imbued with a sense of adventure and a belief that the game should be primarily a test of ingenuity and adaptability in which the wind plays a leading role, it is heaven on earth.

Nowhere is the spirit of seaside links better embodied or more faithfully preserved than on a stretch of the Aberdeenshire coastline where the dunes contain a turbulent air and the holes portray an excitement that matches the mood. There are those who will say that some are unfair and old-fashioned but the sign of a great course is one that has stood the test of time. Cruden Bay has certainly done that.

It has neither seen nor needed much adjustment to combat the relentless march of the steel shaft and the modern ball although there are some elements of the course that have evoked cries for change. Over the eighth, they have had their way but holes such as the 14th and 15th are those on which Cruden Bay's fame is based.

Change them and you inject a note of anonymity but one landmark which has sadly disappeared is the hotel, an edifice of pink Peterhead granite known as the "Palace in the Sandhills". In terms of position, it rivalled Turnberry, looking down on the links and capturing the coastal splendour at a glance. In the pre-war days of seaside holidays at home, it was fashionable and popular but at least its disappearance meant that the clubhouse could fill the gap it left, the old clubhouse down below remaining as a reminder of an era when its needs were less.

There is an inviting start to the round from an elevated tee that immediately indicates the special nature of the golf and its surroundings, the second and third continuing parallel with the main street – a scene familiar in so many towns or villages in Scotland which are known to the world for

their golf. The third is typical of a number of imaginatively shaped greens that may lie hidden from the striker but which lose nothing in terms of challenge or devilment.

They overlook the fun which is paramount and which Cruden Bay offers in abundance but they may wish that the stern demands of the short fourth were not so visible. Beside a picturesque creek and the cottages of Port Ellen, they involve a mighty carry from the back tee and a high premium on being straight.

The course now turns to follow the line of the shore, the fifth tempting with a drive between the dunes, the sixth a par five to a heavily defended green and the seventh, a par four swinging left to a green in the hills. Some of the original menace of the eighth has been lost by the removal of a hill to fill a hollow and by the realignment of the green of which Tom Simpson, its designer, was justly proud. It is as well that artists do not suffer a desire by people to tamper with their work but the ninth marks a change in the character of the terrain which, having scaled the hill, plunges down for five holes that are interesting if not remarkable.

The most remarkable and unique part comes with the narrow neck between a mountain and the shore occupied by the 14th and 15th, the artery that reconnects with the main heartland which is impossible to by-pass. A shallow valley, highlighting the drive at the 14th, is vital to hit if the second is to be broached successfully, a towering shot over a marker-post on the top of the ridge which must drop on to, or run down to, a beautiful green nestling in a hollow.

Here, there is no alternative to a blind shot that can be thrilling; nor is there much alternative at the 15th, another blind shot round a stony escarpment of the mountain. It is a little like threading a ball through the eye of a needle, a tall order for the weaker brethren but that helps Cruden Bay stand apart.

9D 27 **Fort Augustus**

Markethill, Fort Augustus, Inverness-shire, PH32 4DT
☎(01320) 366600, Sec 366309
0.75 miles S of Fort Augustus on A82
Moorland course.
Founded 1905
Designed by Dr Lean
9 holes, 5452 yards, S.S.S. 67
Visitors: welcome.
Green Fees: WD £10; WE £10.
Societies: welcome by prior arrangement; on application; from £8.
Catering: limited.
Hotels: Lovat Arms; Richmond House.

9D 28 **Fort William**

North Rd, Torlundy, Inverness-shire, PH33 6SN
☎(01397) 704464, Fax 705893, Sec 702404
On A82 2 miles N of Fort William.
Parkland course.
Founded 1975
Designed by J.R. Stutt
18 holes, 6217 yards, S.S.S. 71
Visitors: welcome.
Green Fees: WD £15; WE £15.
Societies: welcome by arrangement; golf packages only; no catering; £15.
Catering: no catering.
Hotels: Milton; Moorings.

9D 29 **Fortrose & Rosemarkie**

Ness Rd East, Fortrose, Ross-shire, IV10 8SE
☎(01381) 620529, Fax 620529, Pro 620529 (Shop)
Off A832 to Fortrose off the A9 at Tope roundabout.
Links course on headland; stunning views.
Founded 1888
Redesigned by James Braid
18 holes, 5858 yards, S.S.S. 69
Visitors: welcome.
Green Fees: WD £16; WE £22.
Societies: welcome by prior arrangement with Sec; day tickets available (WD £22, WE £30); from £22.
Catering: clubhouse facilities.
Hotels: Royal; Kinkell House.

9D 30 **Fraserburgh**

Philnorth, Fraserburgh, Aberdeenshire, AB43 8TL
☎(01346) 516616, Pro 517898, Bar/Rest 518287
S of first roundabout when entering Fraserburgh and then first right.
Links course.
Founded 1881

Designed by James Braid
18 holes, 6278 yards, S.S.S. 70
Visitors: welcome.
Green Fees: WD £15; WE £23.
Societies: welcome by prior arrangement; catering packages by arrangement; also 9-hole course, 6800 yards; from £15.
Catering: bar and dining room facilities.
Hotels: Royal; Tufted Duck, both Fraserburgh.

9D 31 **Gairloch**

Gairloch, Ross-shire, IV21 2BE
☎(01445) 712407, Sec 781346
On A832 60 miles W of Inverness.
Seaside course with stunning views; 7th hole, An Dun, is 91 yards.
Founded 1898
Designed by Captain A W Burgess
9 holes, 4514 yards, S.S.S. 64
Visitors: welcome.
Green Fees: WD £13.50; WE £13.50.
Societies: welcome by prior arrangement 2 months before date; weekly ticket: £49; catering by prior arrangement; from £13.50.
Catering: clubhouse facilities.
Hotels: Gairloch; Myrtle Bank Millcroft; Old Inn; Gairloch Sands.

9D 32 **Garmouth & Kingston**

Spey St, Garmouth, Morayshire, IV32 7NJ
☎(01343) 870388, Fax 870388, Sec 870231
3 miles N of A96 at Mosstodloch cross roads.
Links/parkland course; new layout in spring 1998.
Founded 1932
Designed by George Smith
18 holes, 5874 yards, S.S.S. 67
Visitors: welcome by prior arrangement.
Green Fees: WD £12; WE £18.
Societies: welcome by prior arrangement; catering by arrangement; games room; terms on application.
Catering: bar and dining room facilities.
Hotels: Garmouth; Gordon Arms, Fochabers.

9D 33 **Golspie**

Ferry Rd, Golspie, Sutherland, KW10 6ST
☎(01408) 633266, Fax 633393
On A9 to Golspie.
Links course.
Founded 1889

Designed by James Braid
18 holes, 5890 yards, S.S.S. 68
Visitors: welcome.
Green Fees: WD £18; WE £18.
Societies: welcome by prior arrangement; day tickets: WD £20; WE £25; discounts for groups of 10 or more; catering by arrangement; from £18.
Catering: bar and catering facilities.
Hotels: Stags Head; Golf Links; Ben Bhraggie; Sutherland Arms.

9D 34 **Grantown-on-Spey**

Golf Course Rd, Grantown-on-Spey, Morayshire, PH26 3HY
☎(01479) 872079, Fax 873725, Pro 8723986
On NE of town, signposted off the Grantown-Nairn/Forres road.
Parkland/woodland course.
Pro Bill Mitchell; Founded 1890
Designed by Willie Park /James Braid/AC Brown
18 holes, 5710 yards, S.S.S. 67
Visitors: welcome except before 10am at WE.
Green Fees: WD £18; WE £23.
Societies: welcome by prior arrangement except before 10am at WE; catering by arrangement; from £18.
Catering: full bar and catering facilities.
Practice range.
Hotels: Culdearn House; Garth; Muckrach Lodge.

9D 35 **Hazlehead**

Hazlehead Park, Aberdeen, AB15 8BD
☎(01224) 310711, Sec 315747
4 miles NW of the city centre.
Municipal moorland courses.
Pro Ian Smith
18 holes, 6304 yards, S.S.S. 68
Visitors: welcome.
Green Fees: WD £7.65; WE £7.65.
Societies: apply to council; two other courses: 18 holes, 6045 yards, S.S.S. 68; 9 holes, 2770 yards, S.S.S. 34; terms on application.
Catering: available nearby.
Hotels: Treetops; Belvedere; Queens.

9D 36 **Helmsdale**

Golf Rd, Helmsdale, Sutherland, KW8 6JA
☎(01431) 821650
Off A9 in village of Helmsdale.
Moorland course.
Founded 1895
9 holes, 3720 yards, S.S.S. 60
Visitors: welcome.

Green Fees: WD £6; WE £6.
Societies: welcome by application; day ticket £12; weekly £30; from £6.
Catering: none.
Hotels: Navidale; Bridge; Belgrave.

9D 37 Hopeman
Hopeman, Morayshire, IV30 2YA
☎(01343) 830578, Fax 830152
On B9012 7 miles N of Elgin.
Seaside links-type course.
Founded 1923
Designed by J. MacKenzie
18 holes, 5531 yards, S.S.S. 67
Visitors: welcome except some Sat comp days.
Green Fees: WD on application.
Societies: welcome by prior arrangement with Sec; catering packages by arrangement; pool table; terms on application.
Catering: full catering facilities.
Hotels: Station.

9D 38 Huntly
Cooper Park, Huntly, Aberdeenshire, AB54 4SH
☎(01466) 792643, Pro 794181
On A96 0.5 miles from the town centre through school arch.
Parkland course.
Founded 1892
18 holes, 5399 yards, S.S.S. 66
Visitors: welcome except comp days.
Green Fees: WD £13; WE £20.
Societies: welcome by prior arrangement with Sec; catering packages by arrangement in the summer; from £13.
Catering: practice area.
Hotels: full facilities; some winter restrictions.

9D 39 Insch
Golf Terrace, Insch, Aberdeenshire
☎(01464) 820363
Off A96 28 miles NW of Aberdeen.
Parkland course with water hazards; extended 1997.
18 holes, 5395 yards, S.S.S. 67
Visitors: welcome.
Green Fees: WD on application.
Societies: by arrangement with Sec; catering by arrangement; snooker; darts; terms on application.
Catering: clubhouse facilities.
Hotels: Commercial; Station.

9D 40 Inverallochy
Inverallochy, Nr Fraserburgh, AB43 8XY
☎(01346) 582000

4 miles SE of Fraserburgh.
Seaside links course.
Founded 1888
18 holes, 5244 yards, S.S.S. 65
Visitors: welcome by prior arrangement except before 10am at WE.
Green Fees: WD £10; WE £15.
Societies: welcome by prior arrangement; catering by arrangement; terms on application.
Catering: catering and licensed bar.
Hotels: Tufted Duck.

9D 41 Invergordon
King George St, Invergordon, Ross-shire, N17 0BD
☎(01349) 852715
Off B817 from A9 to Invergordon.
Parkland course; extended to 18 holes, 1996.
Founded 1893
Designed by J Urquhart; Extended by A Rae 1996
18 holes, 6030 yards, S.S.S. 69
Visitors: welcome.
Green Fees: WD £12; WE £12.
Societies: welcome by prior arrangement with Sec; day ticket £15; catering by arrangement; from £12.
Catering: bar and bar meals service.
Hotels: Kincraig; Marine.

9D 42 Inverness
Culcabock Rd, Inverness, IV2 3XQ
☎(01463) 233422, Pro 231989, Sec 239882
1 mile W of A9 near Raigmore Hospital.
Parkland course.
Pro Alistair Thomson; Founded 1883
18 holes, 6226 yards, S.S.S. 70
Visitors: welcome; restrictions on Sat comp days.
Green Fees: WD £21; WE £25.
Societies: welcome by prior arrangement; limited; clubhouse being redeveloped until 1999; terms on application.
Catering: restrictions because of clubhouse work.
Hotels: Kingsmills; Craigmonie; Inverness Thistle.

9D 43 Inverurie
Blackhall Rd, Inverurie, AB51 9WB
☎(01467) 624080, Pro 620193, Sec 623053, Bar/Rest 620207
17 miles W of Aberdeen off the A96.
Slightly wooded parkland course.
Founded 1923
Designed by G. Smith and J.M. Stutt
18 holes, 5711 yards, S.S.S. 65

Visitors: welcome.
Green Fees: WD £18; WE £24.
Societies: welcome by prior arrangement; some discounts for larger groups; catering packages by arrangement; from £14.
Catering: full bar and catering.
Hotels: Strathburn; Kintore Arms.

9D 44 Isle of Skye
Sconser, Isle of Skye, IV48 8TD
☎(01478) 650351, Fax 650351, Sec 650235
On A87 between Skye Bridge and Portree.
Parkland course.
Founded 1964
Designed by Dr F. Deighton
9 holes, 4677 yards, S.S.S. 64
Visitors: welcome.
Green Fees: WD £10; WE £10.
Societies: welcome by arrangement with Sec; discounts for groups of 15 or more; from £10.
Catering: by arrangement.
Hotels: Sligachan Hotel; Sconser Lodge.

9D 45 Keith
Fife Park, Keith, Banffshire, AB55 3DF
☎(01542) 882469
A96 to Keith; course 0.5 miles.
Parkland course.
Founded 1965
18 holes, 5802 yards, S.S.S. 68
Visitors: welcome.
Green Fees: WD £10; WE £12.
Societies: welcome by prior arrangement; day tickets WD £12; WE £15; catering packages by arrangement; pool table; from £10.
Catering: clubhouse facilities.
Hotels: Fife Arms; Grampian; Royal; Ugie House, all in Keith.

9D 46 Kemnay
Monymusk Road, Kemnay, Aberdeenshire, AB51 5RA
☎(01467) 642225, Sec 643746
On A96 15 miles N of Aberdeen; turn on to B994.
Parkland course.
Pro Ronnie McDonald; Founded 1908
Designed by Greens of Scotland Ltd (new Course)
18 holes, 5903 yards, S.S.S. 68
Visitors: welcome except on comp days.
Green Fees: WD £12; WE £14.
Societies: welcome by prior arrangement; day tickets available; catering by arrangement; from £12.

Catering: full clubhouse facilities.
Hotels: Park Hill Lodge; Grant Arms; Burnett Arms.

9D 47 King's Links

Golf Rd, King's Links, Aberdeen, AB24 5QB
☎(01224) 632269
Close to Pittodrie Stadium in the E of the city.
Municipal seaside course.
18 holes, 6384 yards, S.S.S. 71
Visitors: welcome.
Green Fees: WD on application.
Societies: welcome by prior arrangement; terms on application.

9D 48 Kingussie

Gynack Rd, Kingussie, Inverness-shire, PH21 1LR
☎(01540) 661600, Fax 662066, Bar/Rest 661374
Off A9 and turn in to club at Duke of Gordon Hotel.
Scenic hilly course.
Founded 1891
Designed by Vardon & Herd
18 holes, 5555 yards, S.S.S. 67
Visitors: welcome.
Green Fees: WD £13.50; WE £15.50.
Societies: welcome by prior arrangement; day tickets (WD £16.50, WE £20.50); reductions for 20 or more golfers; from £15.50.
Catering: clubhouse facilities.
Hotels: Silverfjord; Scot House.

9D 49 Kintore

Balbithan Rd, Kintore, Inverurie, Aberdeenshire, AB51 0UR
☎(01467) 632631
Off A96 12 miles N of Aberdeen.
Undulating moorland course.
Founded 1911
18 holes, 6019 yards, S.S.S. 69
Visitors: welcome except Mon & Wed 4.30pm-6pm and after 4.30pm Fri.
Green Fees: WD £15; WE £20.
Societies: welcome by prior arrangement; catering by arrangement; day tickets available; terms on application.
Catering: full clubhouse facilities.
Practice nets.
Hotels: Toryburn; Thainstone; Crown.

9D 50 Lochcarron

East End, Lochcarron, IV 54
☎(01520) 722257
0.5 miles E of Lochcarron.
Parkland/links course.
Founded 1908

9 holes, 3578 yards, S.S.S. 60
Visitors: welcome except Sat 2-5pm.
Green Fees: WD £7.50; WE £7.50.
Societies: welcome by prior arrangement; catering by arrangement at village hotel; weekly ticket £20; from £7.50.
Catering: no clubhouse facilities; catering at local hotels.
Hotels: Rockvilla Hotel.

9D 51 Lybster

Main St, Lybster, Caithness, KW1 6BL
On A9 13 miles S of Wick.
Moorland course; smallest in Scotland.
Founded 1926
9 holes, 3796 yards, S.S.S. 62
Visitors: welcome; honesty box.
Green Fees: WD £5; WE £5.
Societies: welcome except Sat evening (club comp).

9D 52 McDonald

Hospital Rd, Ellon, Aberdeenshire, AB41 9AW
☎(01358) 720576, Fax 720001, Pro 722891, Bar/Rest 723741
Off A90 16 miles N of Aberdeen.
Parkland course.
Pro Ronnie Urquhart; Founded 1927
18 holes, 5991 yards, S.S.S. 69
Visitors: welcome by prior arrangement.
Green Fees: WD £14; WE £16.
Societies: welcome by prior arrangement; day tickets available (WD £20, Sat £24, Sun £30); from £14.
Catering: full clubhouse facilities.
Hotels: Buchan Hotel; New Inn; Station Hotel.

9D 53 Moray

Stotfield Rd, Lossiemouth, Moray, IV31 6QS
☎(01343) 812018, Fax 815102, Pro 813330, Bar/Rest 812338
At Lossiemouth turn off from A96.
Links course.
Pro Alistair Thomson; Founded 1972
New: 18 holes, 6005 yards, S.S.S. 69;
Old: 18 holes, 6667 yards, S.S.S. 72
Visitors: welcome after 10am; not between 1pm-2pm and not after 4pm.
Green Fees: WD £17, WE £25 (New); WD £30, WE £40 (Old).
Societies: welcome by prior arrangement; some discounts available for larger groups; day tickets WD £22, WE £30 (New); WD £40, WE £50 (Old); from £30.
Catering: full clubhouse facilities.
Hotels: Stotfield; Skerry Brae.

9D 54 Muir of Ord

Great North Rd, Muir of Ord, Ross-shire, IV6 7SX
☎(01463) 870825, Pro 871311
15 miles N of Inverness.
Moorland/parkland course with links-type fairways.
Pro Graham Vivers; Founded 1875
Part designed by James Braid
18 holes, 5557 yards, S.S.S. 68
Visitors: welcome but not before 11am at WE and on comp days.
Green Fees: WD £12.50; WE £16.50.
Societies: welcome by prior arrangement; discounts available for groups of more than 15; daily and weekly tickets available; snooker and pool tables; from £12.50.
Catering: bar and catering facilities.
Hotels: Ord Arms; Priory.

9D 55 Murcar

Bridge of Don, Aberdeen, Aberdeenshire, AB23 8BD
☎(01224) 704354, Fax 704370, Pro 704370
On A92 3 miles from Aberdeen on road to Fraserburgh.
Seaside course.
Pro Gary Forbes; Founded 1909
Designed by Archie Simpson
18 holes, 6241 yards, S.S.S. 71
Visitors: welcome; restrictions Sat until 4pm; Sun & Tues am; Wed pm.
Green Fees: WD £28; WE £43.
Societies: welcome WD with prior arrangement with Sec; daily tickets WD £38; catering packages by arrangement; from £28.
Catering: full clubhouse facilities.
Hotels: Mill of Mundurno.

9D 56 Nairn

Seabank Rd, Nairn, IV12 4HB
☎(01667) 453208, Fax 456328, Pro 452787, Bar/Rest 452103
Off A96 at Nairn Old Parish Church.
Championship links; 1990 Walker Cup venue.
Pro Robin Fyfe; Founded 1887
Designed by Tom Morris, James Braid, A Simpson
18 holes, 6745 yards, S.S.S. 72
Visitors: welcome by prior arrangement.
Green Fees: WD £50; WE £50.
Societies: welcome by prior arrangement; h'cap certs required; catering packages by arrangement; £50.
Catering: full clubhouse facilities.
Practice range.
Hotels: Golf View; Newton; Altonburn; Ramleh.

9D 57 Nairn Dunbar
Lochloy Rd, Nairn, IV12 5AE
☎(01667) 452741, Fax 456897, Pro
453964
0.5 miles E of Nairn on A96.
Links course.
Pro Brian Mason; Founded 1899
18 holes, 6712 yards, S.S.S. 71
Visitors: welcome.
Green Fees: WD £23; WE £28.
Societies: none.
Catering: full clubhouse facilities
available.
Hotels: Golf View; Links; Claymore.

9D 58 Newburgh-on-Ythan
The Links, Newburgh, Aberdeenshire,
AB41 6FD
☎(01358) 789058, Fax 789956, Sec
789956
From A90 12 miles N of Aberdeen to
A975 to Newburgh.
Links course; new 9 holes, added
1996.
Founded 1888/1996
Designed by Greens of Scotland
(Aberdeen)
18 holes, 6162 yards, S.S.S. 70
Visitors: welcome.
Green Fees: WD £15; WE £20.
Societies: welcome by prior arrange-
ment; full day's golf and catering pack-
ages available; from £22.
Catering: full clubhouse facilities
available.
Hotels: Udny Arms; Ythan Hotel.

9D 59 Newmachar
Swailend, Newmachar, Aberdeen,
AB21 7UU
☎(01651) 863002, Fax 863055, Pro
863222, Bar/Rest 863302
12 miles N of Aberdeen off A947
Aberdeen-Banff road.
Parkland course.
Pro P Smith; Founded 1990
Designed by Dave Thomas
Hawkshill: 18 holes, 6623 yards,
S.S.S. 73; Swailend: 18 holes, 6388
yards, S.S.S. 70
Visitors: welcome but h'cap certs are
required.
Green Fees: WD £25, WE £30
(Hawkshill); WD £15, WE £20
(Swailend).
Societies: welcome by prior arrange-
ment; from £25 (Hawkshill); from £15
(Swailend).
Catering: full clubhouse facilities
available.
Practice range, 12 bays.
Hotels: Dunavon House; Kirkhill;
Marriott, Dyce.

9D 60 Newtonmore
Golf Course Rd, Newtonmore,
Highland, PH20 1AT
☎(01540) 673328, Pro 673611, Sec
673878
2 miles S of Newtonmore off the A9.
Moorland/parkland course.
Pro Bob Henderson; Founded 1893
Designed by James Braid
18 holes, 6029 yards, S.S.S. 68
Visitors: welcome.
Green Fees: WD £13; WE £15.
Societies: welcome by prior arrange-
ment with Sec; day tickets available;
catering packages by arrangement;
pool table; from £13.
Catering: full clubhouse facilities;
some restrictions Tues.
Hotels: Glen; Balavil Sports; Lodge;
Mains.

9D 61 Northern
Golf Rd, Kings Links, Aberdeen, AB24
5QB
☎(01224) 636440, Sec 622679
East of City.
Municipal seaside course.
18 holes, 6270 yards, S.S.S. 69
Visitors: welcome.
Green Fees: WD £7.80; WE £7.80.
Societies: welcome by arrangement;
terms on application.
Catering: full facilities at WE; by
arrangement WD.

9D 62 Oldmeldrum
Kirk Brae, Oldmeldrum,
Aberdeenshire, AB51 0DJ
☎(01651) 872648, Pro 873555
On A947 from Aberdeen
Parkland course; extended to 18 holes
in 1994.
Founded 1885/1994
18 holes, 5988 yards, S.S.S. 69
Visitors: welcome by prior arrange-
ment.
Green Fees: WD £12; WE £18.
Societies: welcome by prior arrange-
ment with Sec Mrs M Smith; catering
packages by arrangement; from £12.
Catering: full facilities.
Hotels: Meldrum House; Meldrum
Arms; Redgarth; Cromlet Hill B&B.

9D 63 Orkney
Grainbank, Kirkwall, Orkney, KW15
1RD
☎(01856) 872457, Fax 874165, Sec
874165
W boundary of Kirkwall.
Parkland course.
Founded 1889

18 holes, 5411 yards, S.S.S. 67
Visitors: welcome.
Green Fees: WD £10; WE £10.
Societies: welcome; day's golf;
snacks and meals can be arranged at
lunchtime during the summer; games
room; from £10.
Catering: full clubhouse facilities.

9D 64 Peterculter
Oldtown, Burnside Rd, Peterculter,
Aberdeen, AB14 0LN
☎(01224) 735245, Fax 735580, Pro
734994, Bar/Rest 735744
A93 to Royal Deeside into Peterculter
turning left before Rob Roy Bridge.
Undulating scenic parkland course on
banks of River Dee.
Pro Dean Vannet; Founded 1989
Designed by E. Lappin/Greens of
Scotland
18 holes, 5947 yards, S.S.S. 69
Visitors: welcome
Green Fees: WD £12; WE £16.
Societies: welcome WD by prior
arrangement; day tickets (WD £18,
WE £21); catering by prior arrange-
ment; from £12.
Catering: full clubhouse facilities.
Hotels: Golden Arms.

9D 65 Peterhead
Craigewan Links, Peterhead,
Aberdeenshire, AB42 1LT
☎(01779) 472149, Fax 480725, Sec
480725
On A92 and A975, 30 miles N of
Aberdeen.
Seaside links course.
Founded 1841
Designed by Willie Park and James
Braid
18 holes, 6173 yards, S.S.S. 71
Visitors: welcome; some Sat restric-
tions.
Green Fees: WD £22; WE £27.
Societies: welcome by arrangement
with Sec; restrictions Sat; catering
packages by arrangement; also 9-hole
course, 2400 yards, S.S.S. 60; from
£22.
Catering: new clubhouse with full
facilities.
Hotels: Palace; Waterside Inn.

9D 66 Portlethen
Badentoy Rd, Portlethen,
Aberdeenshire, AB12 4YA
☎(01224) 781090, Fax 781090, Pro
782571, Bar/Rest 782575
On A90 6 miles S of Aberdeen.
Parkland course.

Pro Muriel Thomson; Founded 1986
Designed by Donald Steel
18 holes, 6707 yards, S.S.S. 72
Visitors: welcome WD 9.30am-3pm;
not Sat; Sun after 1pm.
Green Fees: WD £14; WE £21.
Societies: welcome by prior arrangement with Sec; catering packages available; WD ticket £21; pool table; from £14.
Catering: full clubhouse facilities.

9D 67 Reay

The Clubhouse, Reay, by Thurso, Caithness, KW14 7RE
☎(01847) 811288, Sec 811537
11 miles W of Thurso.
Seaside links course.
Founded 1893
18 holes, 5884 yards, S.S.S. 68
Visitors: welcome except comp days.
Green Fees: WD £15; WE £15.
Societies: welcome by prior arrangement with Sec; catering by prior arrangement; from £15.
Catering: full clubhouse facilities.
Hotels: Forss House, Forss; Park Hotel, Thurso; Melvich Hotel, Melvich.

9D 68 Rothes

Blackhall, Rothes, Aberlour, Banffshire, AB38 7AN
☎(01340) 831443, Sec 831277
10 miles S of Elgin on A941 at S end of the town.
Parkland course.
Founded 1990
Designed by John Souter
9 holes, 4972 yards, S.S.S. 65
Visitors: welcome.
Green Fees: WD £8; WE £10.
Societies: welcome by prior arrangement; packages for golf and catering can be arranged; terms available on application.
Catering: full bar facilities evenings and WE.
Hotels: Ben Aigen; Eastbank; Rothes Glen, all Rothes; Craigellachie Hotel, Craigellachie.

9D 69 Royal Aberdeen

Balgownie, Bridge of Don, Aberdeen, AB23 8AT
☎(01224) 702571
2 miles N on the main road from Aberdeen on the A92 to Fraserburgh.
Seaside links course.
Pro R MacAskill; Founded 1780
Designed by Robert Simpson and James Braid
18 holes, 6372 yards, S.S.S. 71

Visitors: welcome WD; WE restrictions.
Green Fees: WD £40; WE £60.
Societies: welcome by prior arrangement WD; day ticket £60; also Silverburn shorter course for high handicappers, 4066 yards; from £40.
Catering: dining room; lounge and bar.
Hotels: Atholl; Marcliffe; Udny Arms.

9D 70 Royal Dornoch

Golf Rd, Dornoch, Sutherland IV25 3LW
☎(01862) 810219, Fax 810792, Pro 810902, Sec 811220, Bar/Rest 810371
45 miles N of Inverness off A9.
Championship links course.
Pro W E Skinner; Founded 1877
Designed by Tom Morris, John Sutherland, George Duncan
18 holes, 6514 yards, S.S.S. 72
Visitors: welcome with h'cap certs.
Green Fees: WD £45; WE £55.
Societies: welcome by prior arrangement; h'cap certs required; catering by prior arrangement; three-day tickets and combination tickets with Struie course also available; from £45.
Catering: full clubhouse facilities.
Hotels: club can provide a list of local hotels, GH and B&Bs.

9D 71 Royal Tarlair

Buchan St, Macduff, Aberdeenshire, AB44 1TA
☎(01261) 832897
On A98 48 miles from Aberdeen.
Parkland course.
Founded 1923
Designed by George Smith
18 holes, 5866 yards, S.S.S. 68
Visitors: welcome.
Green Fees: WD £10; WE £13.
Societies: none.
Catering: full catering and bar.
Hotels: Highland Haven; Banff Springs.

9D 72 Shetland

Dale, Gott by Lerwick, Shetland Is
☎(01595) 840369
3 miles N of Lerwick.
Undulating moorland course.
Founded 1891
Designed by Fraser Middleton
18 holes, 5776 yards, S.S.S. 69
Visitors: welcome.
Green Fees: WD £12; WE £12.
Societies: welcome by arrangement; weekly ticket £35; from £12.
Catering: bar and snacks.
Hotels: Lerwick; Grand; Queens

9D 73 Skeabost

Skeabost Bridge, Isle of Skye, IV51 9NP
☎(01470) 532322, Bar/Rest 532202
40 miles from Kyle of Lochlaish.
Parkland course.
Founded 1984
9 holes, 3224 yards, S.S.S. 59
Visitors: welcome.
Green Fees: WD on application.
Catering: bar and restaurant in the hotel April-Oct.
Hotels: Skeabost (26 beds).

9D 74 Spey Bay

Spey Bay, Fochabers, Moray, IV32 7PJ
☎(01343) 820424
Turn off A96 near Fochabers Bridge, follow B9104 Spey Bay road to coast.
Links course.
Founded 1907
Designed by Ben Sayers
18 holes, 6092 yards, S.S.S. 69
Visitors: welcome; restrictions on Sun; Tues pm and Thurs pm.
Green Fees: WD on application.
Societies: welcome by application; day packages available; tennis; petanque; putting; terms available on application.
Catering: full facilities; meals and bar all day; bar lunches in winter.
Practice range.
Hotels: Spey Bay.

9D 75 Stonehaven

Cowie, Stonehaven, Kincardineshire, AB39 3RH
☎(01569) 762124, Fax 765973
N of Stonehaven on A92; signposted at the mini roundabout near the Leisure Centre.
Parkland course on cliffs overlooking Stonehaven Bay.
Founded 1888
Designed by A. Simpson
18 holes, 5103 yards, S.S.S. 65
Visitors: welcome except before 4pm Sat and on comp days.
Green Fees: WD £15; WE £20.
Societies: welcome WD and Sun; catering on application to Sec; terms on application.
Catering: full facilities.
Hotels: Heugh; County; Station; Crown.

9D 76 Stornoway

Castle Grounds, Stornoway, Isle of Lewis, HS2 0XP
☎(01851) 702240

0.5 miles outside Stornoway in the grounds of Lews Castle.
Parkland course.
Founded 1890
Designed by J.R. Stutt
18 holes, 5252 yards, S.S.S. 66
Visitors: welcome except on Sun.
Green Fees: WD £12; WE £12.
Societies: welcome by prior written arrangement with Sec; special rates by application; from £12.
Catering: bar and bar snacks.
Hotels: Caberfeidh; Royal; Seaforth.

9D 77 **Strathlene**
Portessie, Buckie, Banffshire, AB56 2DJ
☎(01542) 831798, Sec 834170
Off the Elgin-Banff coast route 2 miles E of Buckie Harbour.
Undulating moorland/seaside course.
Founded 1877
Designed by Alex Smith
18 holes, 5936 yards, S.S.S. 69
Visitors: welcome except before 9.30am and between 12 noon-2pm at WE.
Green Fees: WD £12; WE £16.
Societies: welcome by prior arrangement; catering by arrangement; day and weekly tickets available; terms on application.
Catering: full facilities; two bars and meals.
Practice range.
Hotels: St Andrews.

9D 78 **Strathpeffer Spa**
Strathpeffer, Ross-shire, IV14 9AS
☎(01997) 421219;   Pro 421011
5 miles N of Dingwall.
Upland course.
Founded 1888
Designed by W. Park
18 holes, 4813 yards, S.S.S. 64
Visitors: welcome except before 10am Sun.
Green Fees: WD £14; WE £14;
Societies: welcome by prior arrangement; packages available for golf and catering; £29.
Catering: full facilities.
Hotels: Ben Wyvis; Highland; Holly Lodge.

9D 79 **Stromness**
Ness, Stromness, Orkney, K16 3DU
☎(01856) 850772, Sec 850622
Situated at the S end of town bordering Hoy Sound.
Parkland course.
Founded 1890

18 holes, 4762 yards, S.S.S. 63
Visitors: welcome.
Green Fees: WD £12; WE £12.
Societies: welcome; catering packages by arrangement; tennis; pool table; darts and bowls; terms on application.
Catering: Stromness; Royal.

9D 80 **Tain**
Chapel Road, Tain, Ross-shire, IV19 1PA
☎(01862) 892314
35 miles N of Inverness on A9; 0.25 miles from Tain.
Parkland/links course.
Founded 1890
Designed by Tom Morris
18 holes, 6271 yards, S.S.S. 70
Visitors: welcome.
Green Fees: WD on application.
Societies: welcome by prior arrangement; discount of 25% for groups of 10 or more; catering by arrangement; terms on application.
Catering: full facilities.
Hotels: Morangie; Mansfield House, both Tain; Royal; Carnegie Lodge, both Tain.

9D 81 **Tarbat**
1 East Tarrel Cottages, Portmahomack, Ross-shire, IV20 1SL
☎(01862) 871349
9 miles east of Tain on the B9165 off the A9.
Seaside links course.
Founded 1909
Designed by J. Sutherland
9 holes, 5082 yards, S.S.S. 65
Visitors: welcome; some restrictions on Sat comp days.
Green Fees: WD £10; WE £10.
Societies: welcome by prior arrangement with Sec; catering by arrangement; local hotels provide full meal and bar service; from £10.
Catering: limited facilities; see local hotels.
Practice ground.
Hotels: Castle; Caledonian; Oyster Catcher.

9D 82 **Tarland**
Aberdeen Rd, Tarland, Aboyne, Aberdeenshire, AB34 4YN
☎(01339) 881413, Sec 881571
5 miles NW of Aboyne; 30 miles W of Aberdeen.
Parkland course.
Founded 1908
Designed by Tom Morris

9 holes, 5875 yards, S.S.S. 68
Visitors: welcome.
Green Fees: WD £12; WE £15.
Societies: welcome by prior arrangement; terms on application.
Catering: full facilities June-Sept; otherwise by arrangement.
Hotels: Aberdeen Arms; Commercial.

9D 83 **Thurso**
Newlands of Geise, Thurso, Caithness, KW14 7XF
☎(01847) 893807
2 miles SW from centre of Thurso on B870.
Parkland course.
Founded 1893
Designed by W. Stuart
18 holes, 5828 yards, S.S.S. 69
Visitors: welcome.
Green Fees: WD on application.
Societies: welcome by prior arrangement; terms on application.
Catering: full facilities.
Hotels: Park Hotel.

9D 84 **Torphins**
Bog Rd, Torphins, Aberdeenshire, AB31 4JU
☎(01339) 882115, Sec 882402
☎signposted in village; 6 miles W of Banchory on A980.
Parkland course with Highland views.
Founded 1896
9 holes, 4738 yards, S.S.S. 63
Visitors: welcome.
Green Fees: WD £10; WE £12.
Societies: welcome by prior arrangement; catering packages at WE; from £10.
Catering: full facilities at WE.
Hotels: Learney Arms.

9D 85 **Torvean**
Glenurquhart Rd, Inverness, Inverness-shire, IV3 6JN
☎(01463) 225651, Fax 225651, Pro 711434, Bar/Rest 236648
On A82 Fort William road approx 1 mile from Inverness Town Centre.
Municipal parkland course.
Founded 1962
Designed by T Hamilton
18 holes, 5784 yards, S.S.S. 68
Visitors: welcome; tee bookings advisable.
Green Fees: WD £12; WE £14.
Societies: welcome by arrangement with Highland Council, Town Hal, Inverness; terms on application.
Catering: meals by arrangement.
Hotels: Loch Ness.

9D 86 **Traigh Golf Course**

Traigh, Arisaig, by Mallaig, Arisaig,
Inverness-shire, PH39 4NT
☎(01687) 450337, Sec 450645
On the A830 Fort William to Mallaig
road.
Links course.
Founded 1995
Designed by John Salvesen
9 holes, 4912 yards, S.S.S. 65
Visitors: welcome.
Green Fees: WD £10; WE £12.
Societies: welcome by arrangement.
Catering: clubhouse snacks.
Hotels: Arisaig Hotel; Arisaig House;
Marine; Glas na Cardoch; West
Highland.

9D 87 **Turriff**

Rosehall, Turriff, Aberdeenshire, AB53
4HD
☎(01888), Pro 563025, Sec 562982
On B9024 1 mile up Huntly road.
Meadowland/parkland course.
Pro Robin Smith; Founded 1896
18 holes, 6107 yards, S.S.S. 69
Visitors: welcome except before
10am WE; h'cap certs required.
Green Fees: WD £16; WE £21.
Societies: welcome by arrangement
with Sec; day tickets available (WD
£20, WE £27); from £16.
Catering: by prior arrangement.
Hotels: Union; White Heather.

9D 88 **Westhill**

Westhill Heights, Skene,
Aberdeenshire, AB32 6RY
☎(01224), Pro 740159, Sec 742567
Course is on A944, 6 miles from
Aberdeen.
Undulating parkland/moorland course.
Pro M McDonald; Founded 1977
Designed by Charles Lawrie
18 holes, 5849 yards, S.S.S. 69
Visitors: welcome except Sat.
Green Fees: WD £12; WE £15.
Societies: welcome WD and Sun by
prior arrangement; catering packages
by special arrangement; terms on
application.
Catering: bar facilities
Hotels: Broadstreik Inn; Westhill Inn.

9D 89 **Westray**

Tulloch's Shop, Westray, Orkney,
KW17 2DH
☎(01857) 677373, Sec 677211
0.5 miles from Pierowall village.
Links course.
Founded 1890
9 holes, 4810 yards
Visitors: welcome.
Green Fees: WD £3; WE £3.
Societies: welcome by prior arrange-
ment; only limited catering available;
from £3.
Catering: by prior arrangement.
Hotels: Cleaton House.

9D 90 **Whalsay**

Skaw Taing, Island of Whalsay,
Shetland, ZE2 9AL
☎(01806), Sec 566450
At N end of Island.
Moorland course.
Founded 1975
18 holes, 6009 yards, S.S.S. 68
Visitors: welcome; restrictions on
comp days.
Green Fees: WD £10; WE £10.
Societies: welcome by prior arrange-
ment; packages available; terms on
application.
Catering: bar and catering facilities
available.
Hotels: Hotels on Shetland.

9D 91 **Wick**

Reiss, Wick, Caithness, KW1 4RW
☎(01955) 602726, Sec 602935
On A9 3 miles N of Wick.
Links course.
Founded 1870
Designed by McCulloch
18 holes, 5976 yards, S.S.S. 70
Visitors: welcome.
Green Fees: WD £15; WE £15.
Societies: welcome by prior arrange-
ment; catering by prior arrangement;
pool table; terms on application.
Catering: bar and catering facilities
available.
Hotels: Mackays.

WALES

The journalist Peter Corrigan once wrote that exploring Wales in search of golfing experiences, even for a Welshman like himself, was like stumbling upon a row of Rembrandts in the attic. It is a lovely simile and one that is easily justified when one considers the praise lavished upon virtually every other part of the United Kingdom while Wales stands largely ignored.

Why this should be so is baffling. Is not Royal Porthcawl fit to rank alongside the very best links courses in the British Isles? Does Aberdovey not have greens in January so good that you have to wait until August to find putting surfaces in comparable condition at most other courses? Is not Royal St David's fit to compare with the course it sought to emulate, Royal St George's? To all these questions one can give positive answers and yet the stampede among touring golfers to anywhere but Wales seemingly goes on. Perhaps the absence of any high-profile event explains it. The European Tour has an English Open, Scottish Open, Irish Open, but no – yes, you've guessed it – Welsh Open. The Open Championship itself has been to all corners of the Kingdom, including Northern Ireland, but never Wales, and it never will now either.

To be fair to the Royal and Ancient, nothing would please them more than to visit Porthcawl every seven years but the course could not cope with the space demands that a modern championship makes. The first also crosses over the 18th fairway, which would be a nightmare for spectators.

But to deny it merit on such grounds is ludicrous, for there are few better places to lengthen the stride than Porthcawl. This is one of those rare links courses where the sea is visible on every hole. Over the first three holes, which are all adjoined to the rugged edge of Rest Bay, it can be painfully too close. Porthcawl is laid out in the classic triangular links shape, thereby giving as fair a test as possible in windy conditions. Some of the holes away from the sea have an almost moorland feel to them, beset as they are by bracken, heather and gorse.

The finish is magnificent. The 18th goes back towards the sea, the wind, and the setting sun. On a gorgeous, languid summer's day, nowhere is more appealing.

Royal St David's, or Harlech, to call it by its less formal name, lies in the shadow of the imposing castle that was built by Edward I in the 13th century to keep an eye on the Welsh. Now the castle keeps watch over all golfers, as they try to master a course that has been described as the world's toughest par 69. It has its share of fine dune holes and the spectacular backdrop of the Snowdonia mountains completes a majestic picture.

Aberdovey was close to the heart of the doyen of golf writers, Bernard Darwin, and many others since, including Ian Woosnam who, when he still lived in Oswestry, used to travel over each week during the winter.

If these are the big three of Welsh golf then Southerndown in the South, Ashburnham in the West, Conway to the North and Llanymynech to the east all emphasise that fine courses lie all over the Principality.

The latter is a lovely place to spend a sunny day. Part of its boundary is Offa's Dyke and sumptuous views surround every hole. It is also unique in that it lies literally on the Welsh border: on the fourth hole you tee off in Wales and putt out in England.

10 1 Aberdare

Abernant, Aberdare, Mid-Glam, CF44 0RY
☎(01685) 871188, Fax 872 797, Pro 878735, Sec 872797
0.5 miles E of Aberdare, 12 miles NW of Pontypridd.
Mountain course with parkland features.
Pro A W Palmer; Founded 1921
18 holes, 5875 yards, S.S.S. 69
Visitors: welcome with a member.
Green Fees: WD £8; WE £10.
Societies: welcome by prior arrangement with Sec; from £12.
Catering: bar and dining room, snooker available.
Practice area.
Hotels: Baverstock.

10 2 Aberdovey

Aberdovey, Gwynedd, LL35 0RT
☎(01654) 767210, Fax 767027, Pro 767602, Sec 767493
On A493 W of Aberdovey, adjacent to station.
Pro John Davies; Founded 1892
18 holes, 6445 yards, S.S.S. 71
Visitors: welcome with h'cap certs.
Green Fees: WD £25; WE £25.
Societies: welcome by prior arrangement; h'cap certs needed; terms on application.
Catering: clubhouse facilities.
Practice area.
Hotels: Trefeddian; Bodfor; Plas Penhelig; Brodawell.

10 3 Abergele & Pensarn

Tan-y-Gopa Rd, Abergele, Denbighshire, LL28 8DS
☎(01745) 824034, Pro 823813, Bar/Rest 826716
A55 at Abergele/Rhuddlan exit; through town; first left past the police station
Parkland course.
Pro I R Runcie; Founded 1910
Designed by Hawtree & Sons
18 holes, 6520 yards, S.S.S. 71
Visitors: welcome by arrangement.
Green Fees: WD £23; WE £29.
Societies: welcome by arrangement; members have priority until 10.15am and until 2pm in afternoon; 27 holes of golf; light lunch, 3-course meal; £32.
Catering: full clubhouse facilites.
Hotels: Kinmel Manor; Colwyn Bay; Dol Hyfryd.

10 4 Abersoch

Golf Rd, Abersoch, Gwynedd, LL53 7EY
☎(01758) 712622
6 miles from Pwhelli; 1st left through the village.
Seaside links course.
Founded 1910
Designed by Harry Vardon
18 holes, 5671 yards, S.S.S. 68
Visitors: welcome with h'cap certs.
Green Fees: WD £18; WE £20.
Societies: welcome by prior arrangement; from £25.
Catering: full facilities.
Hotels: Deucoch; Linksway.

10 5 Aberystwyth

Bryn y-Mor, Aberystwyth, Dyfed, SY23 3QD
☎(01970) 615104, Fax 615104, Pro 625301
N end of the promenade behind the seafront hotels; access road adjacent to cliff railway; 1 mile from the town centre.
Undulating meadowland course.
Pro Kevin Bayliss; Founded 1911
Designed by Harry Vardon
18 holes, 6150 yards, S.S.S. 71
Visitors: welcome; some WE restrictions.
Green Fees: WD £15; WE £20.
Societies: welcome by prior arrangement; packages available.
Catering: bar and restaurant facilities.
Practice ground.
Hotels: apply to Sec for details.

10 6 Alice Springs

Court Wyndermere, Bettws Newydd, Usk, Monmouthshire, NP5 1JY
☎(01873) 880708, Fax 880838, Pro 880914, Sec 880244
3 miles N of Usk and 8 miles N of Abergavenny on B4598.
Parkland course.
Pro Paul Williams; Founded 1986
Designed by Keith R. Morgan
18 holes, 5596 yards, S.S.S. 67
Visitors: welcome; book at WE and Bank Holidays.
Green Fees: WD £15; WE £18.
Societies: welcome by prior arrangement; packages available from Karen Lloyd; driving range.
Catering: full catering and bar facilities; £5 deposit needed per player to reserve tee-time; terms on application.
Hotels: Curt Bleddybn; The Court.

10 7 Allt-y-Graban

Allt-y-Graban Rd, Pontlliw, Swansea, SA4 1 DT
☎(01792) 885757
M4 junction 47 take A48 to Pontlliw.
Parkland course.
Founded 1993
Designed by F.G. Thomas
9 holes, 4453 yards, S.S.S. 63
Visitors: welcome.
Green Fees: WD £7; WE £8.
Societies: welcome; minimum 10; catering by arrangement; from £6.
Catering: clubhouse facilites.
Hotels: Forest Motel.

10 8 Anglesey

Station Rd, Rhosneigr, LL64 5QX
☎(01407) 810219, Fax 811202, Pro 811202, Sec 811202
8 miles SE of Holyhead; on A4080 off A5 between Gwalchmai and Bryngwran.
Links course with dunes and heather.
Pro P Lovell; Founded 1914
18 holes, 6300 yards, S.S.S. 68
Visitors: welcome.
Green Fees: WD £15; WE £20.
Societies: welcome by prior arrangement; packages and reductions available for more than 10 players; terms on application.
Catering: clubhouse bar and catering facilities.
Hotels: Trecastell; Maelog Lake; Gadleys Country House; Eryl Mor.

10 9 Ashburnham

Cliffe Terrace, Burry Port, Camarthenshire, SA16 0HN
☎(01554) 832466, Sec 832269
4 miles from Llanelli; 9 miles from M4.
Championship links.
Founded 1894
18 holes, 6936 yards, S.S.S. 74
Visitors: welcome by prior arrangement.
Green Fees: WD £27.50.
Societies: welcome WD by prior arrangement
Catering: full facilities.
Hotels: Ashburnham.

10 10 Bala

Penlan, Bala, Gwynedd, LL23 7YD
☎(01678) 520359, Fax 521361
Off the main Bala-Dolgellau road.
Upland course with Snowdonia views.
Pro Tony Davies; Founded 1973
10 holes, 4790 yards, S.S.S. 64
Visitors: welcome; some WE restrictions.
Green Fees: WD £12; WE £15.
Societies: welcome by prior arrangement; terms on application.
Catering: bar with snacks available.

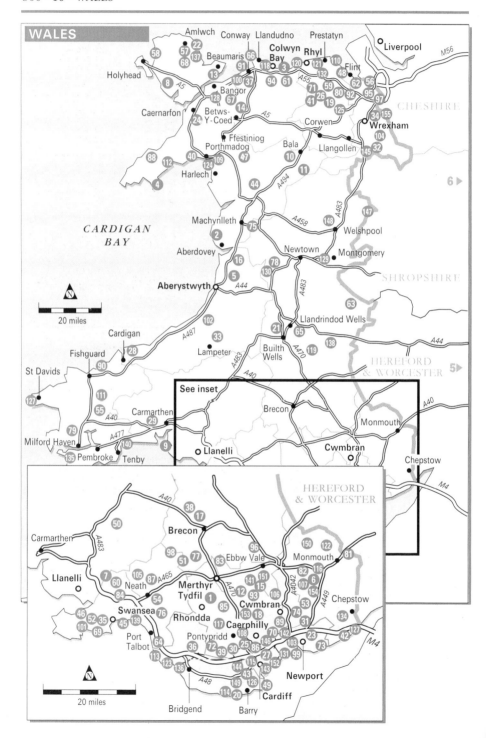

KEY								
1	Aberdare	33	Cilgwyn	64	Lakeside	97	Padeswood & Buckley	128	St Deiniol
2	Aberdovey	34	Clay's Farm Golf Centre	65	Llandrindod Wells	98	Palleg	129	St Giles
3	Abergele & Pensarn	35	Clyne	66	Llandudno (Maesdu)	99	Parc Golf	130	St Idloes
4	Abersoch	36	Coed-y-Mwstwr GC	67	Llanfairfechan	100	Penmaenmawr	131	St Mellons
5	Aberystwyth	37	Conwy	68	Llangefni (Public)	101	Pennard	132	St Melyd
6	Alice Springs		(Caernarvonshire)	69	Llangland Bay	102	Penrhos Golf & Country	133	St Pierre Hotel G & CC
7	Allt-y-Graban	38	Cradoc	70	Llanishen		Club	134	Shirenewton Golf Club
8	Anglesey	39	Creigiau	71	Llannerch Park	103	Peterstone G & Country	135	South Pembrokeshire
9	Ashburnham	40	Criccieth	72	Llantrisant & Pontyclun		Club	136	Southerndown
10	Bala	41	Denbigh	73	Llanwern	104	Plassey	137	Storws Wen
11	Bala Lake Hotel	42	Dewstow	74	Llanyrafon	105	Pontardawe	138	Summerhill Golf Club
12	Bargoed	43	Dinas Powis	75	Machynlleth	106	Pontnewydd	139	Swansea Bay
13	Baron Hill	44	Dolgellau	76	Maesteg	107	Pontypool	140	Tenby
14	Betws-y-Coed	45	Earlswood	77	Merthyr Tydfil (Cilsanws)	108	Pontypridd	141	Tredegar & Rhymney
15	Blackwood	46	Fairwood Park	78	Mid-Wales Golf Centre	109	Porthmadog	142	Tredegar Park
16	Borth & Ynyslas	47	Ffestiniog	79	Milford Haven	110	Prestatyn	143	Trefloyne
17	Brecon	48	Flint	80	Mold	111	Priskilly Forest Golf Club	144	Vale of Glamorgan Golf
18	Bryn Meadows G & CC	49	Glamorganshire	81	Monmouth	112	Pwllheli		and Country Club
19	Bryn Morfydd Hotel	50	Glynhir	82	Monmouthshire	113	Pyle & Kenfig	145	Vale of Llangollen
20	Brynhill	51	Glynneath	83	Morlais Castle	114	Radyr	146	Virginia Park
21	Builth Wells	52	Gower	84	Morriston	115	RAF St Athan	147	Welsh Border Golf
22	Bull Bay	53	Greenmeadow	85	Mountain Ash	116	Raglan Parc Golf Club		Complex
23	Caerleon	54	Grove	86	Mountain Lakes	117	Rhondda	148	Welshpool
24	Caernarfon	55	Haverfordwest	87	Neath	118	Rhosgoch	149	Wenvoe Castle
25	Caerphilly	56	Hawarden	88	Nefyn & District	119	Rhos-on-Sea	150	Wernddu Golf Centre
26	Caerwys Nine Of Clubs	57	Henllys Hall	89	Newport	120	Rhuddlan	151	West Monmouthshire
27	Cardiff	58	Holyhead	90	Newport (Pembs)	121	Rhyl	152	Whitchurch (Cardiff)
28	Cardigan	59	Holywell	91	North Wales	122	The Rolls of Monmouth	153	Whitehall
29	Carmarthen	60	Inco	92	Northop Country Park	123	Royal Porthcawl	154	Woodlake Park Golf Club
30	Castell Heights	61	Kinmel Park Golf	93	Oakdale	124	Royal St David's	155	Wrexham
31	Celtic Manor		Complex	94	Old Colwyn	125	Ruthin Pwllglas		
32	Chirk	62	Kinsale	95	Old Padeswood	126	St Andrews Major		
		63	Knighton	96	Old Rectory Hotel	127	St Davids City		

10 11 Bala Lake Hotel

Bala, Gwynned, LL23 7YF
☎(01678) 520344
Off the B4403 1.5 miles from Bala.
Parkland course.
Founded 1960
9 holes, 3818 yards, S.S.S. 61
Visitors: welcome.
Green Fees: terms on application.
Societies: welcome by arrangement.
Catering: full facilities.
Hotels: Bala Lake Hotel.

10 12 Bargoed

Heolddu, Bargoed, CF8 9GF
☎(01443) 830143 , Pro 836411
10 miles from Caerphilly.
Part moorland/mountain course.
Pro Clive Coombes; Founded 1912
18 holes, 6049 yards, S.S.S. 70
Visitors: welcome WD; with member only at WE.
Green Fees: WD £17; WE £17.
Societies: welcome by prior arrangement.
Catering: bar facilities and evening meals.
Hotels: Maes Manor; Park.

10 13 Baron Hill

Beaumaris, Anglesey, N Wales, LL58 8YW
☎(01248) 810231

A545 from Menai Bridge to Beaumaris; course just before Beaumaris.
Heathland course.
Founded 1895
9 holes, 5596 yards, S.S.S. 67
Visitors: welcome by arrangement with Sec; h'cap certs required; restrictions Tues and Sun.
Green Fees: WD £13; WE £13.
Societies: welcome by prior arrangement; bar and catering packages available; terms on application.
Catering: clubhouse facilites.
Hotels: Bull's Head; Bishop's Gate; Bulkeley.

10 14 Betws-y-Coed

The Clubhouse, Betws-y-Coed, Gwynedd, LL24 0AL
☎(01690) 710556
Off A470 or A5 opposite Midland Bank in village centre.
Parkland course.
Founded 1971
9 holes, 4998 yards, S.S.S. 63
Visitors: welcome.
Green Fees: WD £15; WE £20.
Societies: welcome by prior arrangement; catering and bar packages available; terms on application.
Catering: clubhouse facilites.
Hotels: Glen Aber; Four Oaks; Gwydir; Waterloo.

10 15 Blackwood

Cwmgelli, Blackwood, Gwent, NP2 1EL
☎(01495) 223152, Sec 222121
0.25 miles N of Blackwood on the A4048 Blackwood-Tredegar road.
Parkland course.
Founded 1914
9 holes, 5304 yards, S.S.S. 66
Visitors: welcome WD; with a member at WE.
Green Fees: WD £13; WE £13.
Societies: welcome by prior arrangement; terms on application.
Catering: clubhouse facilites.
Hotels: Maes Manor.

10 16 Borth & Ynyslas

Borth, Ceredigion, SY24 5JS
☎(01970) 871202, Fax 871202, Pro 871557
8 miles S of Macynlleth; 4 miles N of Aberyswyth on A487.
Links course.
Pro J G Lewis; Founded 1885
18 holes, 6116 yards, S.S.S. 70
Visitors: welcome by arrangement.
Green Fees: WD £18; WE £22.
Societies: welcome; minimum 8 in summer, 6 in winter; catering packages available; from £10.
Catering: bar and catering facilities.
Hotels: Black Lion, Talybont; Belle View, Aberyswyth; Ynyshir Hall.

10 17 **Brecon**
Newton Park, Llanfaes, Brecon,
Powys, LD3 8PA
☎(01874) 622004
50 yards, from A40 on W of town.
Parkland course by R Usk and Tarrell.
Founded 1902
Designed by J Braid
9 holes, 5256 yards, S.S.S. 66
Visitors: welcome.
Green Fees: WD £10; WE £10.
Societies: welcome by arrangement;
catering packages available; terms on
application.
Catering: catering facilities available.
Hotels: Peterstone Court.

10 18 **Bryn Meadows G & CC**
The Bryn, Hengoed, Mid-Glam, CF8
7SM
☎(01495) 225590, Pro 221905, Sec
227276
Off A469 15 miles from Cardiff.
Parkland course.
Pro Bruce Hunter; Founded 1973
Designed by E. Jefferies & B. Mayo
18 holes, 6156 yards, S.S.S. 70
Visitors: welcome WD.
Green Fees: WD £17.50.
Societies: welcome WD by arrange-
ment; special golf packages; new gym;
indoor pool; jacuzzi; pool table.
Catering: full facilities.
Practice area.
Hotels: Bryn Meadows.

10 19 **Bryn Morfydd Hotel**
Llanrhaeadr, Denbighshire, LL16 4NP
☎(01745) 890280, Fax 890488
Off A525 between Denbigh and Ruthin
Parkland course; also Duchess
course: 1049 yards, par 3; £5.
Founded 1982/92
Designed by Alliss/Thomas (Duchess
course); Muirhead/Henderson
18 holes, 5760 yards, S.S.S. 67
Visitors: welcome.
Green Fees: WD £12; WE £16.
Societies: welcome by arrangement;
packages available; from £20.
Catering: full clubhouse and hotel
facilities.
Hotels: 3-star hotel on site.

10 20 **Brynhill**
Port Rd, Barry, CF62 8PN
☎(01446) 735061, Pro 733660, Sec
720277
M4 junction 33 take signs for Barry
and Cardiff Airport on to the A4050.
Undulating meadowland course;
redesigning in 1998.

Pro Peter Fountain; Founded 1921
Designed by G.K. Cotton
18 holes, 5947 yards, S.S.S. 68
Visitors: welcome except Sun; h'cap
certs may be required.
Green Fees: WD £20; WE £25.
Societies: welcome WD by prior
arrangement; from £17.
Catering: lunches, afternoon teas and
dinners.
Driving range 500 yards.
Hotels: Mount Sorrel; International;
Copthorne.

10 21 **Builth Wells**
Golf Club Rd, Builth Wells, Powys,
LD2 3NF
☎(01982) 553296, Fax 551064
On A483 Builth-Landovery road just
after River Irfon bridge on outskirts of
Builth.
Parkland course; no par 5s.
Pro Roy Truman; Founded 1923
18 holes, 5376 yards, S.S.S. 67
Visitors: welcome with h'cap certs.
Green Fees: WD £13; WE £23.
Societies: welcome; packages and
reductions available; terms on applica-
tion.
Catering: clubhouse bar and catering.
Hotels: Pencerrig House; Caerberis
Manor; Greyhound Hotel; Cedars GH.

10 22 **Bull Bay**
Bull Bay Rd, Amlwch, Anglesey, LL68
9RY
☎(01407) 830960, Fax 832612, Pro
831188; Bar/Rest 830213
On A5025 via Benllech and course is
1 mile beyond Amlwch.
Clifftop heathland course, northern-
most course in Wales
Pro John Burns; Founded 1913
Designed by Herbert Fowler and
Walton Heath
18 holes, 6217 yards, S.S.S. 70
Visitors: welcome by prior arrange-
ment.
Green Fees: WD £15; WE £15.
Societies: welcome; meals can be
provided; from £13.
Catering: clubhouse facilities.
Hotels: Trecastell; Bull Bay

10 23 **Caerleon**
Broadway, Caerleon, Newport, Gwent,
NP6 1AY
☎(01633) 420342
3 miles from M4 junction 25 for
Caerleon.
Parkland course.
Pro Fraser Scott; Founded 1974

Designed by D. Steel
9 holes, 5800 yards, S.S.S. 68
Visitors: welcome.
Green Fees: WD £5.40; WE £6.80.
Societies: welcome by arrangement.
Catering: snacks and bar.
Practice range, 12 bays floodlit.
Hotels: Priory.

10 24 **Caernarfon**
Aberforeshore, Llanfaglan, Gwynedd,
LL54 5RP
☎(01286) 678359, Fax 672535, Pro
673783
A470 from A55 at Caernarfon towards
Porthmadog; at new road bridge turn
right, club 1.5 miles.
Parkland course.
Pro Aled Owen; Founded 1907/1981
18 holes, 5891 yards, S.S.S. 68
Visitors: welcome.
Green Fees: WD £17; WE £22.
Societies: welcome; special rates for
10 or more players; full facilities avail-
able; terms on application.
Catering: full catering and bar facili-
ties.
Hotels: Celtic Royal; Seiont Manor;
Bryn Eisteddfod; Erw Fair, all
Caernarfon; Eryl Mor, Bangor.

10 25 **Caerphilly**
Pencapel, Mountain Rd, Caerphilly,
Mid-Glam, CF83 1HJ
☎(01222) 883481, Pro 869104, Sec
863441
On A469 7 miles from Cardiff; 250
yards from rail and bus stations.
Steep wooded mountainside course; 5
new holes by mid-1999.
Pro Richard Barter; Founded 1905
Designed by Fernie (original 9)
13 holes, 6039 yards, S.S.S. 71
Visitors: welcome WD; WE only with
a member.
Green Fees: WD £20.
Societies: limited numbers by
arrangement only.
Catering: bar and dining room.
Hotels: Mount; Greenhill; Moat House;
Cedar Tree.

10 26 **Caerwys Nine Of Clubs**
Caerwys, Mold, Flintshire, CH7 5AQ
☎(01352) 720692
1.5 miles S of the A55 midway
between St Asaph and Holywell.
Undulating parkland course.
Founded 1988
Designed by Eleanor Barlow
9 holes, 3080 yards, S.S.S. 60
Visitors: welcome.

Aberforeshire, Caernarfon, Gwynedd LL54 5RP
Tel: 01286 678359

Less than a mile from the historic royal town of Caernarfon we can offer a delightful, 18-hole, 5746yd parkland course. Designed to provide panoramic views of Snowdonia, the Menai Straits & Anglesey, come & relax & enjoy our beautifully sculptured & well manicured course. Full tuition & equipment is always available from our resident PGA professional, & a warm Welsh welcome & hot meal awaits you in the clubhouse.

Green Fees: WD £6; WE £7.
Societies: welcome by prior arrangement.
Catering: light refreshments.

---

10 27 Cardiff
Sherborne Ave, Cyncoed, Cardiff, CF2 6SJ
☎(01222) 753067, Fax 752134, Pro 754772, Sec 753320 Bar/Rest 689375
3 miles N of Cardiff, 2 miles W of Pentwyn of A48(M), M4 junction 29.
Undulating parkland course.
Pro Terry Hanson; Founded 1922
18 holes, 6013 yards, S.S.S. 70
Visitors: welcome.
Green Fees:
Societies: welcome by prior arrangement; terms on application.
Catering: clubhouse facilites.
Hotels: Post House, Pentwyn

---

10 28 Cardigan
Gwbert-on-Sea, Cardigan, Ceredigion, SA43 1PR
☎(01293) 612035, Fax 621775, Pro 615359, Sec 621775
3 miles N of Cardigan.
Links/parkland course with view of River Teifi.
Pro C Parsons; Founded 1895
Designed by Hawtree
18 holes, 6687 yards, S.S.S. 72
Visitors: welcome.
Green Fees: WD £16; WE £21.
Societies: welcome by prior arrangement; packages and catering available; satellite TV; pool table; squash courts; terms on application.
Catering: clubhouse facilites.
Hotels: Cliff Hotel; Gwbert Hotel.

---

10 29 Carmarthen
Blaenycoed Rd, Carmarthen, Carmarthenshire, SA33 6EH
☎(01267) 281214, Pro 281493, Sec 281588
4.5 miles N of town.
Upland course.
Pro Pat Gillis; Founded 1929
Designed by J H Taylor
18 holes, 6210 yards, S.S.S. 71

Visitors: welcome; ladies day Tues.
Green Fees: WD £18; WE £25.
Societies: welcome WD; packages and discounts available; terms on application.
Catering: full clubhouse facilites.
Hotels: Falcon; Ivy Bush; Forge Motel.

---

10 30 Castell Heights
Blaengwynlais, Caerphilly, Mid-Glamorgan, CF8 1NG
☎(01222) 886666, Fax 863243, Sec 861128, Bar/Rest 886686
4 miles from M4 junction 32 on the Tongwynlais-Caerphilly road.
Mountainside course.
Pro Sion Bebb; Founded 1982
9 holes, 5376 yards, S.S.S. 66
Visitors: welcome.
Green Fees: WD £5.50; WE £6.50.
Societies: welcome by arrangement; WD only in summer.
Catering: bar and bar snacks.
Practice range, 6 bays.

---

10 31 Celtic Manor
Catsash Road, Coldra Woods, Newport, Gwent, NP6 2YQ
☎(01633) 413000
M4 junction 24 to A48 towards Newport for 0.25 miles; turn right at Royal Oak following AA signs.
Parkland course; also Coldra Woods course, 4000 yards; new course 1999.
Pro Ian Woosnam (Touring pro); Founded 1995
Designed by Robert Trent-Jones Snr & Jnr
18 holes, 6950 yards, S.S.S. 74
Visitors: welcome by prior arrangement.
Green Fees: terms on application.
Societies: welcome by prior arrangement; company days and society packages available; computerised tuition, driving range; two leisure clubs with swimming pools; largest clubhouse in Britain; terms on application.
Catering: full clubhouse and hotel facilities.
Practice range, two-tier range.
Hotels: Celtic Manor Hotel &CC with 73 bedrooms.

---

10 32 Chirk
Chirk, Nr Wrexham, Flintshire, LL14 5AD
☎(01691) 774407, Fax 773878, Bar/Rest 774243
5 miles S of Wrexham just off A5.
Parkland course; 2 holes greater than 600 yards.
Pro Mark Maddison; Founded 1991
18 holes, 7045 yards, S.S.S. 73
Visitors: welcome.
Green Fees: terms on application.
Societies: welcome; full clubhouse facilities; terrace; buggies; driving range; also 9-hole Mine Rock course, par 3; from £20.
Catering: clubhouse facilities; spike bar, restaurant; snacks and meals Practice range, 15 undercover floodlit bays; practice bunker.
Hotels: Golden Pheasant, Glyn Cieriog.

---

10 33 Cilgwyn
Llangybi, Lampeter, Ceredigion, SA48 8NN
☎(01570) 493286
4 miles N of Lampeter on A485.
Parkland course.
Founded 1905/1977
9 holes, 5309 yards, S.S.S. 67
Visitors: welcome.
Green Fees: WD £10; WE £15.
Societies: welcome; minimum of 10 players; bar and restaurant packages available; from £8.
Catering: clubhouse facilities.
Hotels: Falcondale; Black Lion both Lampeter.

---

10 34 Clay's Farm Golf Centre
Bryn Estyn Road, Wrexham, Wrexham, LL13 9UB
☎(01978) 661406, Fax 661417, Bar/Rest 661416
From A483 Wrexham-Chester road, take A534 for Nantwich and Wrexham Industrial Estate; 2 miles, turn to golf centre.
Parkland course.
Pro D Larvin; Founded 1991
Designed by R D Jones
18 holes, 5794 yards, S.S.S. 67
Visitors: welcome all times.

CRADOC GOLF CLUB invites you to the beautiful Brecon Beacons National Park. Our 18 hole, Parklands Course will delight individual golfers and golf societies alike.

Cradoc offers spectacular views of the Brecons, a superb, scrupulously tended course, a separate practice ground, and a friendly welcome & home cooked food in the clubhouse.

Just 2 miles from Brecon, Cradoc Golf Club is within easy reach of South Wales, the South West, &The Midlands. **For bookings or more details call 01874-623658.**

Green Fees: WD £13; WE £18. **Societies:** welcome by prior arrangement; minimum 12; deposit required; practice balls, 18-27 holes of golf; light lunch; 3-course dinner; from £24. **Catering:** catering facilities. **Hotels:** Cross Lane, Marchweil; Holt Lodge, Wrexham.

10 35 Clyne
118/120 Owls Lodge Lane, Mayals, Swansea, SA3 5DP
☎(01792) 401989, Fax 401078, Pro 402094, Bar/Rest 403534
M4 to Swansea; exit for Mumbles at Blackpill head for Gower and then first right into Owls Lodge Lane.
Moorland course.
Pro Mark Bevan; Founded 1920
Designed by H.S. Colt/Harris
18 holes, 6334 yards, S.S.S. 71
Visitors: welcome with h'cap certs.
Green Fees: WD £25; WE £30.
Societies: welcome WD except Tues; catering packages and reductions for more than 20 players; from £21.
Catering: clubhouse facilities
Practice area.
Hotels: Marriott, Swansea; St Anne's, Mumbles.

10 36 Coed-Y-Mwstwr Golf Club
The Club House, Coychurch, Nr Bridgend, CF35 6AF
☎(01656) 862121
From M4 junction 35 turn towards Bridgend and then into Coychurch.
Parkland course.
Founded 1994
9 holes, 5834 yards, S.S.S. 68
Visitors: welcome with h'cap certs.
Green Fees: WD £15; WE £15.
Societies: welcome by prior arrangement; packages available; terms on application.
Catering: clubhouse facilities.
Hotels: Coed-y-Mwstwr.

10 37 Conwy
(Caernarvonshire)
Beacons Way, Morfa,Conwy, Gwynedd, LL32 8ER
☎(01492) 593400, Fax 593363, Pro 593225, Sec 592423
Just off A55 at Conwy.
Links course.
Pro P Lees; Founded 1890
18 holes, 6647 yards, S.S.S. 72
Visitors: welcome with h'cap certs.
Green Fees: WD £25; WE £30.
Societies: welcome with prior arrangement through Sec; catering available; from £25.
Catering: clubhouse facilities.
Practice ground.
Hotels: Royal; Esplanade, both Llandudno.

10 38 Cradoc
Penoyre Park, Cradoc, Brecon, Powys, LD3 9LP
☎(01874) 623658, Pro 625524, Bar/Rest 624396
Take B 4520 road to Upper Chapel past Brecon Cathedral and turn left to Cradoc village.
Parkland course.
Pro Richard W Davies; Founded 1967
Designed by C.K. Cotton
18 holes, 6301 yards, S.S.S. 72
Visitors: welcome by prior arrangement.
Green Fees: WD £20; WE £25.
Societies: welcome with prior arrangement through Sec; packages available; terms on application.
Catering: clubhouse facilities.
Hotels: Peterstone Court; Llangoed Hall; Castle of Brecon; Lansdown.

10 39 Creigiau
Creigiau, Cardiff, CF4 8NN
☎(01222) 890263, Fax 890263, Pro 891909, Bar/Rest 891243
4 miles NW of Cardiff towards Llantrisant.
Parkland course.
Pro Ian Luntz; Founded 1926
18 holes, 6063 yards, S.S.S. 70
Visitors: welcome WD except Tues; WE with member.
Green Fees: WD £26; WE £26.
Societies: welcome by prior arrangement; maximum 40.
Catering: bar and full catering facilities.

Practice range, 22 indoor and 8 outdoor bays.
Hotels: Friendly Hotel; Miskin Manor; Park; Royal; Angel.

10 40 Criccieth
Ednyfed Hill, Criccieth, Gwynedd, LL52
☎(01766) 522154
On A497 4 miles from Portmadoc; turn right past Memorial Hall; course 0.5 miles.
Undulating hilltop course.
Founded 1904
18 holes, 5787 yards, S.S.S. 68
Visitors: welcome.
Green Fees: WD £14; WE £18.
Societies: welcome by prior arrangement.
Catering: full bar and catering facilities.
Hotels: George IV; Bron Eifion; Marine; Lion.

10 41 Denbigh
Henllan Rd, Denbigh, LL16 5AA
☎(01745) 814159, Fax 814888, Sec 816669, Bar/Rest 816664
0.5 miles from Denbigh on B5382.
Parkland course.
Pro Mike Jones; Founded 1922
Designed by John Stockton
18 holes, 5712 yards, S.S.S. 68
Visitors: welcome with prior arrangement.
Green Fees: WD £22; WE £27.
Societies: welcome; packages and catering available; from £22.
Catering: clubhouse facilities available.
Hotels: Talardy Park; Oriel House, both St Asaph.

10 42 Dewstow
Caerwent, Newport, Monmouthshire, NP6 4AH
☎(01291) 430444, Fax 425816
Off A48 between Newport and Chepstow.
Parkland course.
Pro Gareth Bebb/Kim Dobson; Founded 1988
Park: 18 holes, 6176 yards, S.S.S. 69;

Old: 18 holes, 6091 yards, S.S.S. 70
Visitors: welcome.
Green Fees: WD £12; WE £16.
Societies: welcome WD; some restrictions at WE; packages available; from £20.
Catering: full bar and restaurant facilities.
Practice range, 26 bays floodlit covered.
Hotels: Beaufort; Old Course

10 43 **Dinas Powis**

Golf House, Old Highwalls, Dinas Powis, CF64 4AJ
☎(01222) 512727, Fax 512727, Pro 513682, Bar/Rest 514128
Centre of Dinas Powys 5 miles from Cardiff.
Parkland course; 90 yards 7th.
Pro Gareth Bennett; Founded 1914
18 holes, 5486 yards, S.S.S. 67
Visitors: welcome with h'cap certs.
Green Fees: WD £20; WE £27.
Societies: welcome by prior arrangement and with h'cap certs; terms on application.
Catering: clubhouse facilities.
Hotels: many in Cardiff.

10 44 **Dolgellau**

Pencefn, Golf Rd, Dolgellau, Gwynedd, LL40 2ES
☎(01341) 422603
0.5 miles N of Dolgellau.
Parkland course.
Founded 1911
9 holes, 4671 yards, S.S.S. 63
Visitors: welcome by prior arrangement.
Green Fees: WD £13; WE £16.
Societies: welcome by prior arrangement; catering packages available; from £13.
Catering: clubhouse facilities.
Hotels: Royal Ship Hotel, Dolgellau

10 45 **Earlswood**

Jersey Marine, Neath, W Glamorgan, SA10 6JP
☎(01792) 321578 , Sec 812198
Signposted off B 4290 road off the A483 Neath-Swansea road.
Parkland course.
Pro Mike Day; Founded 1993
18 holes, 5174 yards, S.S.S. 68
Visitors: welcome.
Green Fees: WD £8; WE £8.
Societies: welcome by prior arrangement; packages available; terms on application.
Catering: by arrangement with Sec.

10 46 **Fairwood Park**

Blackhills Lane, Upper Killay, Swansea, SA2 7JN
☎(01792) 297849, Fax 297849, Pro 203648, Sec 203648, Bar/Rest 203648
Turn into Blackhills Lane opposite Swansea Airport.
Parkland championship course.
Pro James Hughes; Founded 1969
Designed by Hawtree & Co
18 holes, 6741 yards, S.S.S. 72
Visitors: welcome by prior arrangement.
Green Fees: WD £25; WE £30.
Societies: welcome by prior arrangement; terms on application.
Catering: clubhouse facilities.
Hotels: Winston Hotel, Bishopston; Langrove Hotel, Parkmill; Hillcrest, Mumbles.

10 47 **Ffestiniog**

Clwb Golff Ffestiniog, Y Cefn, Ffestiniog, Gwynned,
☎(01766) 762637
On the B4391 1 mile from Ffestiniog.
Scenic mountain course.
Founded 1893
9 holes, 5032 yards, S.S.S. 65
Visitors: welcome; some WE restrictions.
Green Fees: WD £10; WE £10.
Societies: welcome by prior arrangement.
Catering: clubhouse facilities by arrangement; bar.
Hotels: Abbey Arms; The Pengwren.

10 48 **Flint**

Cornist Park, Flint, Flintshire, CH6 5HJ
☎(01352) 732327, Fax 811885, Sec 812974
1 mile from centre of Flint.
Parkland course.
Founded 1965
Designed by H Griffith
9 holes, 5980 yards, S.S.S. 69
Visitors: welcome.
Green Fees: WD £10; WE £10.
Societies: welcome WD by arrangement; terms on application; £25.
Catering: clubhouse facilities.
Hotels: Springfield, Halkyn.

10 49 **Glamorganshire**

Lavernock Rd, Penarth, CF64 5UP
☎(01222) 707048, Fax 701185, Pro 707401, Sec 701185, Bar/Rest 701033
5 miles SW of Cardiff just off M4 junction 33.

Parkland course.
Pro Andrew Kerr-Smith; Founded 1890
Designed by W East & T Simpson
18 holes, 6056 yards, S.S.S. 70
Visitors: welcome by arrangement.
Green Fees: WD £28; WE £30.
Societies: welcome Thurs and Fri only; packages available; reductions for more than 60; from £22.
Catering: clubhouse facilities.
Hotels: Walton House Hotel; Raisdale, both Penarth.

10 50 **Glynhir**

Glynhir Rd, Llandybie, Ammanford, Carmarthenshire, SA18 2TF
☎(01269) 850472, Fax 851365, Pro 851010, Sec 851365
3.5 miles from Ammanford; off A483 towards Llandello.
Parkland course.
Pro Duncan Prior; Founded 1967
Designed by F.W. Hawtree
18 holes, 5996 yards, S.S.S. 69
Visitors: welcome except Sun with h'cap certs.
Green Fees: WD £16; WE £22.
Societies: welcome by arrangement; Tues and Fri; terms on application.
Catering: clubhouse facilities.
Hotels: The Mill at Glynhir (next to course); Cawdor Arms; White Hart Inn; Plough Inn, all Llandello.

10 51 **Glynneath**

Pen-y-craig, Pontneathvaughan, Nr Glynneath, W Glamorgan, SA11 5HH
☎(01639) 720452, Sec 720679
From A465 road at Glynneath take B4242 for 1.5 miles to Pontneathvaughan.
Parkland and wooded hilltop course.
Founded 1931
Designed by Cotton, Pennink, Lawrie & Partners
18 holes, 5707 yards, S.S.S. 68
Visitors: welcome; no restrictions.
Green Fees: WD £12; WE £20.
Societies: welcome; catering available; from £12.
Catering: clubhouse facilities.
Hotels: Baverstock.

10 52 **Gower**

Cefn Goleu, Three Crosses, Gowerton, Swansea, SA4 3HS
☎(01792) 872480, Fax 872480, Pro 879905
Take A484 towards Gowerton and then take B4295 to Penclawdd; 1 mile turn to Three Crosses.

Parkland course with lakes.
Pro Mark Whittingham; Founded 1995
Designed by Donald Steel
18 holes, 6441 yards, S.S.S. 73
Visitors: welcome.
Green Fees: WD £14; WE £16.
Societies: welcome by prior arrangement; maximum 60; from £16.50.
Catering: bar and catering facilities.
Hotels: The Mill at Glynhir; Winston, Bishopston.

10 53 Greenmeadow

Treherbert Road, Croesyceiliog, Cwmbran, Gwent, NP44 2BZ
☎(01633) 869321, Fax 868430
Off A4042 5 miles N of M4 junction 26.
Parkland course.
Founded 1978
18 holes, 6078 yards, S.S.S. 70
Visitors: welcome.
Green Fees: WD terms on application.
Societies: welcome by prior arrangement; packages available; professional clinics; tennis courts; private function rooms.
Catering: full clubhouse facilities.
Practice range, 26 bays covered and floodlit.
Hotels: Parkway; Commodore.

10 54 Grove

South Cornelly, Nr Bridgend, Mid Glamorgan, CF33 4RP
☎(01656) 788771, Fax 788414, Sec 788300
Off M4 junction 37 near the Glamorgan Heritage Coast at Porthcawl.
Parkland course with water features.
Founded 1997
18 holes, 6128 yards, S.S.S. 69
Visitors: welcome; bookings essential.
Green Fees: WD £10; WE £10.
Societies: welcome by prior arrangement.
Catering: bar and restaurant; function rooms.

10 55 Haverfordwest

Arnolds Down, Haverfordwest, Pembrokeshire, SA61 2XQ
☎(01437) 763565, Fax 764143, Pro 768409, Sec 764523
1 miles E of Haverfordwest on A40.
Parkland course.
Pro Alex Pile; Founded 1904
18 holes, 6005 yards, S.S.S. 69
Visitors: welcome by prior arrangement.

Green Fees: WD £18; WE £22.
Societies: welcome by arrangement; catering packages available; terms on application.
Catering: bars, bar snacks and dining room.
Hotels: Mariners.

10 56 Hawarden

Groomsdale Lane, Hawarden,Deeside, Flintshire, CH5 3EH
☎(01244) 531447, Pro 520809
Off A55 at Ewloe towards Hawarden; Groomsdale Lane opposite police station after playing fields.
Undulating parkland course.
Pro Alec Rowlands; Founded 1911/1950
18 holes, 5894 yards, S.S.S. 68
Visitors: welcome.
Green Fees: WD £16; WE £20.
Societies: welcome by prior arrangement with Sec.
Catering: bar and limited catering facilities; meals by arrangement.
Hotels: St David's Park, Ewloe.

10 57 Henllys Hall

Beaumaris, Anglesey, Gwynedd, LL58 8HU
☎(01248) 810412, Fax 811511
4 miles from A55.
Parkland course with Snowdonia views and water features.
Pro Peter Maton; Founded 1997
Designed by Roger Jones
18 holes, 6098 yards, S.S.S. 71
Visitors: welcome by prior arrangement.
Green Fees: terms on application.
Societies: welcome by prior arrangement; catering and hotel packages terms on application; sun room; fitness centre; tennis court; swimming pool; leisure centre (under construction).
Catering: full hotel facilities.
Hotels: Henllys Hall on site.

10 58 Holyhead

Trearddur Bay, Holyhead, Anglesey, LL65 2YG
☎(01407) 763279, Fax 763279, Pro 762022, Bar/Rest 762119
4 miles off the A5 after turning left at the Valley traffic lights.
Undulating heathland
Pro Steve Elliott; Founded 1912
Designed by James Braid
18 holes, 6060 yards, S.S.S. 70
Visitors: welcome.
Green Fees: terms on application.
Societies: welcome by arrangement.

Catering: full bar and catering facilities
Practice range, 0.5 miles away – 10 bays.
Hotels: Treardurr Bay; Anchorage; Beach; also dormy house on site.

10 59 Holywell

Brynford, Nr Holywell, Flintshire, CH8 8LQ
☎(01352) 713937, Fax 713937, Pro 710040
From A55 at Holywell exit take A5026, then take Brynford signs.
Natural moorland/links type course around quarries.
Pro Jim Law/Sean O'Connor; Founded 1906
18 holes, 6164 yards, S.S.S. 70
Visitors: welcome.
Green Fees: WD £15; WE £20.
Societies: welcome by arrangement with Sec; catering packages available; snooker; reduced rates for groups of 20; from £15.
Catering: full catering facilities and bar.
Hotels: club can recommend hotels.

10 60 Inco

Clydach, Swansea, W Glamorgan, SA6 5EU
☎(01792) 844216 , Sec 843336
2 miles N of M4 junction 45.
Parkland course with river and trees featured.
Founded 1965
Extended from 12-18 holes in 1997
18 holes, 6064 yards, S.S.S. 69
Visitors: welcome.
Green Fees: terms on application.
Societies: welcome by prior arrangement.
Catering: catering by arrangement.

10 61 Kinmel Park Golf Complex

Bodelwyddan, Denbighshire, LL18 5SR
☎(01745) 833548
Just off A55 between St Asaph and Abergele.
Parkland course.
Pro Peter Stebbings; Founded 1988
Designed by Peter Stebbings
9 holes, 3100 yards,
Visitors: pay and play
Green Fees: WD £3.50; WE £3.50.
Societies: welcome; Peter Stebbings Golf Academy; Roberto's Italian restaurant; terms on application.
Catering: restaurant, bar.

10 62 Kinsale

Llanerchymor, Holywell, Flintshire, CH8 9DX
☎(01745) 561080, Fax 561079
Off A548 coast road at turning for Maes Pennant.
Parkland course.
Pro Alec Backhurst; Founded 1994
Designed by Ken Smith
9 holes, 6005 yards, S.S.S. 70
Visitors: welcome; pay and play.
Green Fees: WD £5.75; WE £8.50.
Societies: welcome by arrangement.
Catering: café facilities; Kinsale Hall next door for bar and restaurant.
Practice range, 12 bays floodlit.
Hotels: Kinsale Hall.

10 63 Knighton

The Ffrydd, Knighton, Powys, LD7 1DL
☎(01547) 528646, Sec 520297
SW of Knighton off the A488 Shrewsbury-Llandrindod Wells road at junction with A4113.
Upland course.
Founded 1913
Designed by Harry Vardon
9 holes, 5338 yards, S.S.S. 66
Visitors: welcome.
Green Fees: WD £8; WE £10.
Societies: welcome by prior arrangement; terms on application.
Catering: clubhouse facilities.
Hotels: Red Lion; Knighton Hotel.

10 64 Lakeside

Water St, Margam, Port Talbot, SA13 2PA
☎(01639) 899959, Sec 883486
0.5 miles from M4 junction 38 off A48 to Margam Park.
Parkland course.
Pro M Wootton; Founded 1992
Designed by M Wootton/D.T. Thomas
9 holes, 4390 yards, S.S.S. 61
Visitors: welcome.
Green Fees: WD £9; WE £9.
Societies: welcome except Sun; golf and meal; £14.
Catering: catering available.
Hotels: Twelve Knights; Seabank; Esplanade.

10 65 Llandrindod Wells

☎ House, Llandrindod Wells, Powys, LD1 5NY
☎(01597) 822010, Fax 823873, Pro 822247, Sec 823873, Bar/Rest 824487
Signposted in the town.
Parkland course.

Pro Shop: Phil Davies; Founded 1905
Designed by Harry Vardon
18 holes, 5759 yards, S.S.S. 69
Visitors: welcome.
Green Fees: WD £12; WE £20.
Societies: welcome by prior arrangement with Sec; terms on application.
Catering: clubhouse facilities
Hotels: Metropole; Montpellier; Griffin House; Penybont.

10 66 Llandudno (Maesdu)

Hospital Rd, Llandudno, Gwynedd, LL30 1HU
☎(01492) 876016, Fax 871570, Pro 875195, Sec 876450
A55 to Conwy-Deganwy exit, then A546 to clubhouse.
Parkland course.
Pro Simon Boulden; Founded 1915
Designed by Tom Jones
18 holes, 6545 yards, S.S.S. 72
Visitors: welcome by arrangement.
Green Fees: WD £25; WE £30.
Societies: welcome everyday; maximum 36 at WE; 50 in week; no concessions; from £25.
Catering: catering and bar facilities.
Hotels: Royal; Esplanade; Risboro.

10 67 Llanfairfechan

Llannerch Road, Llanfairfechan, Conwy, LL33 0EB
☎(01248) 680144 , Sec 680524
S of A55 in Llanfairfechan.
Parkland course.
Founded 1972
9 holes, 3119 yards, S.S.S. 57
Visitors: welcome.
Green Fees: WD £5; WE £10.
Societies: welcome by prior arrangement; catering by arrangement; terms on application.
Catering: some catering and bar facilities.
Hotels: Split Willow.

10 68 Llangefni (Public)

Llangefni, Anglesey, LL77 8YQ
☎(01248) 722193
On the outskirts of Llangefni towards Amlwch.
Parkland course.
Pro Paul Lovell
Founded 1983
Designed by Hawtree & Sons
9 holes, 2934 yards, S.S.S. 56
Visitors: welcome.
Green Fees: WD £3; WE £3.
Societies: welcome by prior arrangement.
Catering: in local café.

10 69 Llangland Bay

Llangland Bay, Swansea, SA3 4QR
☎(01792) 366023, Sec 361721
6 miles W of Swansea
Seaside parkland course.
Pro Mark Evans; Founded 1904
18 holes, 5857 yards, S.S.S. 69
Visitors: welcome.
Green Fees: WD terms on application.
Societies: welcome by prior arrangement; maximum 36; catering packages available by prior arrangement; terms on application.
Catering: clubhouse facilities.
Hotels: Llangland Bay; Osborne.

10 70 Llanishen

Cwm, Lisvane, Cardiff, CF4 5UD
☎(01222) 752205, Fax 755078, Pro 755076, Sec 755078
5 miles N of Cardiff, 1 mile N of Llanishen.
Parkland course.
Pro R A Jones; Founded 1905
18 holes, 5296 yards, S.S.S. 66
Visitors: welcome WD; WE only with a member.
Green Fees: WD £28; WE £14.
Societies: welcome Wed and Thurs afternoons; packages available with catering; from £18.
Catering: clubhouse facilities.
Hotels: Cardiff Bay; Angel; Manor House; New House.

10 71 Llannerch Park

North Wales Golf Range and Course, St Asaph, Denbighshire, LL17 0BD
☎(01745) 730805
On A525 between St Asaph and Trefnant.
Parkland course.
Pro Michael Jones; Founded 1988
9 holes, 1587 yards
Visitors: public pay and play.
Green Fees: WD £2.50; WE £2.50.
Catering: refreshments.

10 72 Llantrisant & Pontyclun

Lanlay Rd, Talbot Green, Mid-Glam, CF72 8HZ
☎(01443) 222148, Pro 228169, Sec 224601
M4 junction 34 then A4119 to Talbot Green.
Parkland course.
Founded 1927
12 holes, 5712 yards, S.S.S. 68
Visitors: welcome WD; with member at WE.
Green Fees: WD £20; WE £15.

Societies: welcome; menus available at all times; from £15.
Catering: bar and restaurant facilities.
Hotels: Miskin Manor.

10 73 Llanwern

Tennyson Ave, Llanwern, Newport, NP6 2DY
☎(01633) 412380, Fax 412029, Pro 413233, Sec 412029, Bar/Rest 413278
1 mile from M4 junction 24.
Parkland course.
Pro Stephen Price; Founded 1928
18 holes, 6177 yards, S.S.S. 69
Visitors: welcome WD; only with member at WE.
Green Fees: WD £20; WE £10.
Societies: welcome Wed, Thurs, Fri with prior arrangement; reduced rates for golf and catering for more than 20; terms on application.
Catering: catering available.
Hotels: Stakis Country Court; Hilton National.

10 74 Llanyrafon

Llanfrechfa Way, Cwmbran, NP44 8HT
☎(01633) 874636
N to Pontypool off the M4 junction 26.
Parkland course.
Pro Dave Woodman; Founded 1981
9 holes, 2566 yards, S.S.S. 54
Visitors: welcome.
Green Fees: WD £2.70; WE £3.30.
Societies: welcome by arrangement.
Catering: terms on application.

10 75 Machynlleth

Newtown Road, Machynlleth, Powys, SY20 8DU
☎(01654) 702000
0.5 miles out of town on the A480 Newtown road.
Parkland course.
Founded 1905
Designed by James Braid
9 holes, 5726 yards, S.S.S. 67
Visitors: welcome.
Green Fees: WD £12; WE £15
Societies: welcome; 10% reduction for groups of 8 or more; terms on application.
Catering: clubhouse facilities.
Hotels: Wynnstay, Plas Dolguog.

10 76 Maesteg

Mount Pleasant, Neath Rd, Maesteg, Mid-Glam, CF34 9PR
☎(01656) 732037, Pro 735742, Sec 734106

Adjacent to B4282 main Maesteg to Port Talbot road 0.5 miles from Maesteg.
Hilltop course with forest views down the valley.
Pro John Black; Founded 1912
Designed by James Braid (1945)
18 holes, 5939 yards, S.S.S. 69
Visitors: welcome.
Green Fees: WD £17; WE £20.
Societies: welcome by prior arrangement.
Catering: bar meals available except Mon.
Practice ground.
Hotels: Heronstone, Bridgend; Aberavon, Port Talbot; Greenacres GH, Maesteg.

10 77 Merthyr Tydfil (Cilsanws)

Cloth Hall Lane, Cefn Coed, Merthyr Tydfil, Mid-Glam, CF48 2NU
☎(01685) 723308
2 miles N of Merthyr on Cilsanws Mountain in Cefn Coed.
Mountain top heathland course.
Founded 1908
18 holes, 5622 yards, S.S.S. 69
Visitors: welcome except on Sun competition days.
Green Fees: WD £10; WE £15.
Societies: welcome by prior arrangement; meals available; terms on application.
Catering: clubhouse facilities.
Hotels: Mount Dolu Lodge.

10 78 Mid-Wales Golf Centre

Maesmawr, Caersws, Nr Newtown, Powys,
☎(01686) 688303
6 miles W of Newtown
Farmland course.
Pro Philip Parkin; Founded 1992
Designed by Jim Walters
9 holes, 2554 yards, S.S.S. 54
Visitors: welcome.
Green Fees: WD £6; WE £8.
Societies: welcome by prior arrangement.
Catering: light snacks and bar.
Practice range, 12 bays floodlit.
Hotels: Maesmawr Hall.

10 79 Milford Haven

Woodbine House, Hubberston, Milford Haven, SA73 3RX
☎(01646) 692368, Pro 697762
0.75 miles W of town on road to Dale.
Meadowland course.
Founded 1913

Designed by David Snell
18 holes, 6035 yards, S.S.S. 70
Visitors: welcome.
Green Fees: WD £15; WE £20.
Societies: welcome at all times; terms on application.
Catering: restaurant facilities.
Driving and practice area.
Hotels: Lord Nelson; Sir Benfro; Little Haven.

10 80 Mold

Cilcain Rd, Pantymwyn, Mold, Flintshire, CH7 5CH
☎(01352) 741513, Pro 740318
3 miles from Mold; leave on Denbigh road; turn left after 100 yards, and follow road for 2.5 miles.
Undulating parkland course.
Pro Neil Coulson; Founded 1909
Designed by Hawtree
18 holes, 5528 yards, S.S.S. 67
Visitors: welcome
Green Fees: WD £16; WE £18
Societies: welcome by prior arrangement; catering packages by arrangement.
Catering: full facilities.
Practice ground.
Hotels: Bryn Awel.

10 81 Monmouth

Leasebrook Lane, Monmouth, Monmouthshire, NP5 3SN
☎(01600) 712212
Signposted from the Monmouth-Ross on Wye (A40) road.
Undulating parkland course.
Founded 1896
18 holes, 5698 yards, S.S.S. 69
Visitors: welcome; Bank Holiday with a member only.
Green Fees: WD £15; WE £15.
Societies: welcome with prior arrangement with the secretary Mrs E Edwards; packages available; from £18.
Catering: clubhouse facilities.

10 82 Monmouthshire

Llanfoist, Abergavenny, Monmouthshire, NP7 9HE
☎(01873) 852606, Fax 852606, Pro 852532, Bar/Rest 853171
2 miles SW of Abergavenny.
Parkland course; three successive par 5s: 6, 7 ,8
Founded 1892
Designed by James Braid
18 holes, 5978 yards, S.S.S. 70
Visitors: welcome byarrangement.
Green Fees: WD £25; WE £30.

Societies: welcome Mon and Fri by prior arrangement; 10% reduction if more than 25 in party; terms on application.
Catering: full clubhouse facilities.

10 83 Morlais Castle

Pant, Dowlais, Merthyr Tydfil, Mid-Glam, CF48 2UY
☎(01685) 722822
Follow signs for Brecon Mountain Railway.
Moorland course.
Pro P Worthing; Founded 1900
18 holes, 6320 yards, S.S.S. 71
Visitors: welcome except Sat pm and Sun am.
Green Fees: WD £14; WE £16.
Societies: welcome WD by prior arrangement with Sec.
Catering: full catering and bar facilities in new clubhouse.
Practice ground.
Hotels: Treganna.

10 84 Morriston

160 Clasemont Rd, Morriston, Swansea, W Glamorgan, SA6 6AJ
☎(01792) 771079, Fax 795628, Pro 772335, Sec 795628
3 miles N of Swansea city centre on A4067.
Parkland course.
Pro Darryl Rees; Founded 1919
18 holes, 5755 yards, S.S.S. 68
Visitors: welcome.
Green Fees: WD £21; WE £30.
Societies: welcome by prior arrangement only.
Catering: lunches and bar facilities available.
Hotels: Dragon; Dolphin; Forest Motel; Hilton; Holiday Inn.

10 85 Mountain Ash

The Clubhouse, Cefn Pennar, Mountain Ash, Mid-Glam, CF45 4DT
☎(01443) 472265, Fax 479459, Pro 478770, Sec 479459
Off A470 Cardiff to Abercynon road at Mountain Ash – follow signs to Cefn Pennar.
Mountain heathland course.
Founded 1908
18 holes, 5553 yards, S.S.S. 67
Visitors: welcome.
Green Fees: WD £15; WE £18.
Societies: welcome; special packages available from secretary; terms on application.
Catering: clubhouse facilities
Hotels: Baverstocks, Aberdare.

10 86 Mountain Lakes

Blaengwynlais, Nr Caerphilly, Mid-Glam, CF83 1NG
☎(01222) 861128, Fax 869030, Pro 886666, Bar/Rest 886686
4 miles from M4 junction 32 on Tongwynlais-Caerphilly road.
Parkland course.
Pro S Bebb; Founded 1989
Designed by R Sandow/ J Page
18 holes, 6343 yards, S.S.S. 73
Visitors: welcome.
Green Fees: WD £15; WE £15.
Societies: welcome by prior arrangement; terms on application; function, conference facilities; from £19.95.
Catering: restaurant and bar facilities.
Practice range, 15 bays.
Hotels: New Country House.

10 87 Neath

Cadoxton, Neath, SA10 8AH
☎(01639) 643615, Pro 633693, Sec 632759
2 miles from Neath in Cadoxton Mountain.
Pro E M Bennett; Founded 1934
Designed by James Braid
18 holes, 6490 yards, S.S.S. 72
Visitors: welcome WD; with member at WE.
Green Fees: WD £20; WE £20.
Societies: welcome by arrangement with Sec; terms on application.
Catering: full clubhouse facilities
Hotels: Castle, Neath.

10 88 Nefyn & District

Morfa Nefyn, Pwllheli, Gwynedd, LL53 6DA
☎(01758) 720966, Pro 720102, Bar/Rest 720218
1 mile W of Nefyn; 18 miles W of Caernarfon.
Seaside clifftop course on Llyn peninsula.
Pro John Froom; Founded 1907
New: 18 holes, 6548 yards, S.S.S. 71;
Old: 18 holes, 6201 yards, S.S.S. 71
Visitors: welcome by prior arrangement.
Green Fees: WD £30; WE £35.
Societies: welcome by prior arrangement except for 2 weeks in August; 10 per cent reduction for larger groups; snooker table; terms on application.
Catering: full clubhouse facilities.
Hotels: Nanhoron, Nefyn.

10 89 Newport

Great Oak, Rogerstone, Newport, Gwent, NP1 9FX

☎(01633) 892683, Fax 896676, Pro 893271, Sec 892643, Bar/Rest 894496
3 miles from Newport M4 junction 27 on B4591.
Parkland course.
Pro Paul Mayo; Founded 1903
18 holes, 6431 yards, S.S.S. 71
Visitors: welcome by prior arrangement.
Green Fees: WD £30; WE £30.
Societies: welcome Wed, Thurs, Fri and some Sun; h'cap certs required; discounts available at off-peak times; from £30.
Catering: full clubhouse facilities.
Hotels: Harris Hotel, Newport.

10 90 Newport (Pembs)

Newport, Pembrokeshire, SA42 0NR
☎(01239) 820244, Fax 820244
Follow signs for Newport Sands from Newport.
Seaside course.
Pro Colin Parsons; Founded 1925
Designed by James Braid
9 holes, 5815 yards, S.S.S. 68
Visitors: welcome.
Green Fees: WD £15; WE £15.
Societies: welcome by prior arrangement.
Catering: full bar and restaurant facilities.
Hotels: self-catering flats on site.

10 91 North Wales

72 Bryniau Rd, West Shore, Llandudno, Gwynedd, LL30 2DZ
☎(01492) 875325, Fax 875325, Pro 876878, Bar/Rest 875342
2 miles from A55 on A546 Llandudno/Deganwy road.
Links course.
Pro Richard Bradbury; Founded 1894
Designed by Tancred Cummins
18 holes, 6247 yards, S.S.S. 71
Visitors: welcome.
Green Fees: WD £23; WE £30.
Societies: welcome with h'cap certs; menu, practice area and snooker; from £23.
Catering: full bar and restaurant facilities.
Hotels: many in Llandudno.

10 92 Northop Country Park

Northop, Nr Chester, Flintshire, CH7 6WA
☎(01352) 840440, Fax 840445
Off A55 at Northop/Connahs Quay exit; entrance is on slip road.
Parkland course.

Pro Matthew Pritchard; Founded 1994
Designed by John Jacobs
18 holes, 6735 yards, S.S.S. 73
Visitors: welcome by prior arrangement.
Green Fees: WD £28; WE £35.
Societies: welcome by prior arrangement WD; catering packages available; corporate days arranged; tennis; gym; sauna.
Catering: full restaurant facilities; bar; terrace.
Practice range, 8 bays.
Hotels: St Davids Park, Ewloe.

10 93 **Oakdale**
Llwynon Lane, Oakdale, Gwent, NP2 0NF
☎(01495) 220044, Pro 220440
M4 junction 28 then A467 to Crumlin and B4251 to Oakdale.
Parkland course.
Founded 1990
Designed by Ian Goodenough
9 holes, 2688 yards, S.S.S. 56
Visitors: welcome.
Green Fees: WD £4; WE £4.
Societies: welcome by prior arrangement.
Catering: snacks in clubhouse.
Practice range, 18 bays floodlit.
Hotels: The Old Forge.

10 94 **Old Colwyn**
Woodland Ave, Old Colwyn, Clwyd, LL29 9NL
☎(01492) 515581
Off A55 at Old Colwyn exit towards Old Colwyn.
Undulating meadowland course.
Founded 1907
Designed by J Braid
9 holes, 5263 yards, S.S.S. 66
Visitors: welcome; by arrangement at WE.
Green Fees: WD £10; WE £15.
Societies: welcome by arrangement; reductions for 10 or more players; menus by arrangement; terms on application.
Catering: full clubhouse facilities.
Hotels: Bodelwyddan Castle has reduced rates for golfers; Lyndale.

10 95 **Old Padeswood**
Station Rd, Padeswood, Mold, Clwyd, CH7 4JL
☎(01244) 547701, Pro 547401, Sec 550414
On A5118 between Penyfford and Mold close to A55.
Meadowland course in valley.

Pro Tony Davies; Founded 1933/1978
Designed by Arthur Joseph
18 holes, 6685 yards, S.S.S. 72
Visitors: welcome.
Green Fees: WD £18; WE £20.
Societies: welcome WD; restaurant, bar, also par 3 course; from £18.
Catering: full clubhouse facilities
Practice range, par 3 course.
Hotels: any in Chester/ Wrexham/ Mold.

10 96 **Old Rectory Hotel**
Llangattock, Crickhowell, Powys, NP8 1PH
☎(01873) 810373, Fax 810373
A40 to Crickhowell.
Parkland course.
Founded 1968
9 holes, 2600 yards, S.S.S. 54
Visitors: welcome.
Green Fees: WD £5; WE £5.
Societies: terms on application; bars, meals and restaurant available.
Catering: bar and restaurant.
Hotels: Old Rectory Hotel; 15 en suite rooms.

10 97 **Padeswood & Buckley**
The Caia, Station Lane, Padeswood, Mold, Flintshire, CH7 4JD
☎(01244) 550537, Fax 541600, Pro 543636, Bar/Rest 556072
Off Penyfford-Mold road A5118 at Old Padeswood turning; club 50 yards, further on.
Parkland course alongside River Alyn.
Pro D V Ashton; Founded 1933
Designed by Williams Partnership
18 holes, 5982 yards, S.S.S. 70
Visitors: welcome.
Green Fees: WD £20; WE £20.
Societies: welcome WD; packages include 28 holes of golf; coffee on arrival, light lunch and dinner; from £33.
Catering: full clubhouse facilities and restaurant.
Hotels: St David's Park, Ewloe; Beaufort Palace, New Brighton.

10 98 **Palleg**
Palleg Rd, Lower Cwmtwrch, Swansea, SA9
☎(01639) 842193
Off Swansea- Brecon road.
Meadowland course.
Pro Sharon Roberts; Founded 1930
Designed by C.K. Cotton
9 holes, 6418 yards, S.S.S. 72
Visitors: welcome with h'cap certs WD; with member at WE.

Green Fees: WD £13; WE £18.
Societies: welcome by prior arrangement; terms on application.
Catering: clubhouse facilities.
Hotels: Y Stycle, Upper Cwmtwrch; Dab-Yr-Ogof Cafes, Abercrane.

10 99 **Parc Golf**
Church Lane, Coedkernew, Newport, Gwent, NP1 9TU
☎(01633) 680933, Fax 681011, Pro 680955, Sec 681011
M4 junction 28; on to A48 towards Cardiff for 1.5 miles.
Parkland course.
Pro John Skose; Founded 1989
Designed by B. Thomas & T. Hicks
18 holes, 5619 yards, S.S.S. 68
Visitors: welcome WD; WEs by arrangement.
Green Fees: WD £11; WE £13
Societies: welcome by arrangement.
Catering: full facilities.
Practice range, 38 bays floodlit.
Hotels: Coach & Horses, Castleton.

10 100 **Penmaenmawr**
Conway Rd, Penmaenmawr, Conwy, LL34 6RD
☎(01492) 623330
3 miles W of Conwy on A55 to Dwygyfylchi.
Undulating parkland course.
Founded 1910
9 holes, 5350 yards, S.S.S. 66
Visitors: welcome except Sat.
Green Fees: WD £12; WE £18.
Societies: welcome by prior arrangement; inclusive package of 27 holes, lunch and dinner; from £25.
Catering: bar and restaurant.
Hotels: Caerlyr Hall.

10 101 **Pennard**
2 Southgate Rd, Southgate, Swansea, W Glamorgan, SA3 2BT
☎(01792) 233131, Pro 233451
8 miles W of Swansea via A4067 and B4436.
Undulating seaside.
Pro Mike Bennett; Founded 1896
18 holes, 6265 yards, S.S.S. 72
Visitors: welcome.
Green Fees: WD £24; WE £30.
Societies: welcome by prior arrangement; minimum group 12; snooker; squash; from £16.
Catering: bar snacks; lunches and evening meals.
Practice area.
Hotels: Osborne; Winston; Nicholaston; Cefn Goleua; Fairy Hill.

St. David's Park Hotel and Northop Country Park Golf Club offer luxury accommodation and superb facilities second to none, including our:

- 18 Hole Championship Golf Course
- Pavilion Style Clubhouse and Excellent Pro-Shop
- Luxurious Health Club Facilities and Tennis Courts
- Renowned Restaurants and the Club Cafe

*Please call **01244 520800** for a brochure and further information.*

SEE DETAILS OF SPECIAL OFFER ON PAGE 383

10 102 Penrhos Golf & Country Club
Llanrhystud, Nr Aberystwyth, Cardiganshire, SY23 5AY
☎ (01974) 202999, Fax 202100
9 miles S of Aberystwyth on A487; take Llanrhystud turning on to B4337.
Parkland course.
Pro Paul Diamond; Founded 1991
Designed by Jim Walters
18 holes, 6641 yards, S.S.S. 72
Visitors: welcome except Sun am.
Green Fees: WD £17; WE £22.
Societies: welcome by arrangement; catering packages available; £17–£38.
Catering: full clubhouse facilities.
Hotels: Marine; Conrah Country both Aberystwyth; Plas Morfa, Llanon

10 103 Peterstone G & Country Club
Peterstone Wentloog, Cardiff CF3 8TN
☎ (01633) 680009, Fax 680563, Pro 680072
Take A48 towards Cardiff from M4 junction 28 turning left to Marshfield; course 2.5 miles.
Parkland/links course.
Pro Richard Harries; Founded 1990
Designed by Bob Sandow
18 holes, 6555 yards, S.S.S. 72
Visitors: welcome.
Green Fees: WD £16.50; WE £22.50.
Societies: welcome Mon-Fri; full packages; corporate days; photographs; starter; half-way house; on-course competition; presentation evenings; terms on application.
Catering: full bar and restaurant facilities; Fairways restaurant.
Hotels: Wentloog; Travelodge; Moat House.

10 104 Plassey
The Plassey Golf Course, Eyton, Wrexham, Flintshire, LL13 0SP
☎ (01978) 780020

2 miles SW of Wrexham signposted from A483.
Parkland course.
Founded 1992
Designed by K Williams
9 holes, 4616 yards,
Visitors: pay and play; telephone first.
Green Fees: WD £8; WE £8.
Societies: unlimited access; terms on application.
Driving range.
Hotels: caravan site with swimming pool; visitors can play in comps.

10 105 Pontardawe
Cefn Llan, Pontardawe, Swansea, SA8 4SH
☎ (01792) 863118, Fax 830041, Pro 830977
From M4 junction 45 take A4067 to Pontardawe.
Moorland course.
Pro Gary Hopkins; Founded 1924
18 holes, 6038 yards, S.S.S. 70
Visitors: welcome WD with h'cap certs.
Green Fees: WD £20; WE £20.
Societies: welcome by arrangement; prices vary depending on numbers; catering by arrangement; from £18.
Catering: full clubhouse facilities.
Hotels: Pen-yr-Alt.

10 106 Pontnewydd
West Pontnewydd, Cwmbran, Gwent, NP44 1AB
☎ (01633) 482170
Follow signs for West Pontnewydd or Upper Cwmbran; W slopes of Cwmbran.
Meadowland course.
Founded 1875
10 holes, 5353 yards, S.S.S. 67
Visitors: welcome WD; WE with member.
Green Fees: WD terms on application.

Societies: welcome by prior arrangement.
Catering: limited.
Hotels: Parkway; Commodore.

10 107 Pontypool
Lasgarn Lane, Trevethin, Pontypool, Gwent, NP4 8TR
☎ (01495) 763655
Off A4042 at St Cadoc's Church in Pontypool.
Mountain course.
Pro James Howard; Founded 1919
18 holes, 5963 yards, S.S.S. 69
Visitors: welcome by arrangement.
Green Fees: WD £20; WE £20.
Societies: welcome by prior arrangement; packages available; terms on application.
Catering: full catering facilities.
Hotels: Three Salmons; Glyn-yr-Avon, both Usk; Parkway, Cwmbran.

10 108 Pontypridd
Ty-Gwyn, The Common, Pontypridd, Mid-Glam, CF37 4DJ
☎ (01443) 402359, Fax 491622, Pro 491210, Sec 409904
12 miles NW of Cardiff E of Pontypridd off A470.
Mountain course.
Pro Wade Walters; Founded 1905
Designed by Bradbeer
18 holes, 5881 yards, S.S.S. 66
Visitors: welcome with h'cap certs
Green Fees: terms on application.
Societies: welcome by arrangement with the Secretary, Vikki Hooley; packages available; terms on application.
Catering: clubhouse facilities.

10 109 Porthmadog
Morfa Bychan, Porthmadog, Gwynedd, LL49 9UU
☎ (01766) 512037, Fax 514638, Pro 513828, Sec 514124

RAGLAN PARC GOLF CLUB
Offering a 6604 yd, par 73 parkland course in truly historic surroundings.
Full catering & bar facilities. Visitor & society bookings most welcome.

Parc Lodge, Raglan, Monmouthshire, NP5 2ER. Tel: (01291) 690077

1 mile W of Porthmadog High Street after turning towards Black Rock Sands.
Parkland/links course.
Pro Pete Bright; Founded 1902
Designed by James Braid
18 holes, 6363 yards, S.S.S. 71
Visitors: welcome by arrangement.
Green Fees: WD £20; WE £26.
Societies: welcome by prior arrangement; discounts for groups of more than 16; catering available; terms on application.
Catering: clubhouse facilities.
Hotels: Tydden Llwyn; Sportsmans.

10 110 Prestatyn
Marine Rd East, Prestatyn, Denbighshire, LL19 7HS
☎(01745) 854320, Fax 888353, Pro 852083, Sec 888353, Bar/Rest 886172
Off A548 coast road to Prestatyn.
Championship links.
Pro M L Staton; Founded 1905
Designed by S. Collins
18 holes, 6808 yards, S.S.S. 73
Visitors: welcome except Sat and Tues morning.
Green Fees: WD £20; WE £25.
Societies: welcome except Sat and Tues am by prior arrangement; 27 holes; lunch and dinner; from £30.
Catering: clubhouse facilities.
Hotels: Talardy; Traeth Ganol; Sands, all Prestatyn; Craig Park, Dyserth.

10 111 Priskilly Forest Golf Club
Castlemorris, Haverfordwest, Pembrokeshire, SA62 5EH
☎(01348) 840276
On B4331 towards Mathry off A40 at Letterstone
Picturesque mature parkland course.
Founded 1992
Designed by J. Walters
9 holes, 5738 yards, S.S.S. 68
Visitors: welcome.
Green Fees: WD £10; WE £10.
Societies: welcome by arrangement; limited catering facilities; from £10.
Catering: licensed bar and tea rooms.
Hotels: Priskilly Forest GH on site.

10 112 Pwllheli
Golf Rd, Pwllheli, Gwynedd, LL53 5PS
☎(01758) 612520, Fax 701644, Sec 701644, Bar/Rest 701633
Turn into Cardiff Road in town centre; bear right at the first fork; course signposted
Parkland/links.
Pro Doug Verity; Founded 1900
Designed by Tom Morris Extended By James Braid
18 holes, 6200 yards, S.S.S. 69
Visitors: welcome.
Green Fees: WD £20; WE £25.
Societies: welcome most days by prior arrangement.
Catering: full facilities.
Hotels: Caeau Capel, Nefyn; Bryn Eisteddfod, Clynnogfawr; Nanhoron, Morfa.

10 113 Pyle & Kenfig
Waun-y-Mer, Kenfig, S Wales, CF33 4PU
☎(01656) 783093, Fax 772822, Pro 772446, Bar/Rest 771788
M4 junction 37 through Porthcawl and follow signs
Links/downland.
Pro Robert Evans; Founded 1922
Designed by H. Colt
18 holes, 6688 yards, S.S.S. 73
Visitors: welcome.
Green Fees: WD £30; WE £30.
Societies: welcome by arrangement; prices vary according to numbers; terms on application.
Catering: full bar and catering facilities.
Hotels: Fairways; Atlantic; Seabank.

10 114 Radyr
Drysgol Rd, Radyr, Cardiff, CF4 8BS
☎(01222) 842408, Fax 843914, Pro 842476, Bar/Rest 842735
4 miles from M4 junction 32; 8 miles from Cardiff.
Parkland course.
Pro R Butterworth; Founded 1902
18 holes, 6078 yards, S.S.S. 70
Visitors: welcome by prior arrangement.
Green Fees: WD £34; WE £34.
Societies: welcome with prior

arrangement; catering packages available; separate facilities for parties of 35-40; dining room for 100; terms on application.
Catering: full dining and bar facilities available.
Extensive practice ground.
Hotels: Quality Inn.

10 115 RAF St Athan
St Athan, Barry, Vale of Glamorgan, CF62 4WA
☎(01446) 751043, Sec 797186
1st right after St Athan village on Cowbridge road.
Parkland course.
Pro Neil Gillette; Founded 1982
9 holes, 6542 yards, S.S.S. 72
Visitors: welcome except Sun am.
Green Fees: WD £10; WE £15.
Societies: welcome by arrangement with Sec.
Catering: full facilities available, except Mon.

10 116 Raglan Parc Golf Club
Parc Lodge, Raglan, Monmouthshire, NP5 2ER
☎(01291) 690077
0.5 miles from Raglan at junction of A40 and A449.
Undulating parkland course.
Founded 1994
18 holes, 6604 yards, S.S.S. 72
Visitors: welcome; booking advisable.
Green Fees: WD £20; WE £20.
Societies: welcome by prior arrangement; packages of coffee, light lunch and 3 course meal; from £30.
Catering: bar, snacks and light meals.

10 117 Rhondda
Golf House, Penrhys, Mid-Glamorgan, CF43 3PW
☎(01443) 433204, Fax 441384, Pro 441385, Sec 441384
On Penrhys road between Rhondda Fach and Rhondda Fawr.
Mountain course.
Pro Rhys Davies; Founded 1910
18 holes, 6205 yards, S.S.S. 70
Visitors: welcome WD; restrictions WE.

Green Fees: WD £20; WE £25.
Societies: welcome by prior arrangement; terms on application.
Catering: full clubhouse bar and catering facilities.
Hotels: Heritage Park.

10 118 Rhos-on-Sea

Penrhyn Bay, Llandudno, Conwy, LL30 3PU
☎(01492) 549100, Pro 548115, Bar/Rest
From A55 take Old Colwyn exit and follow coast road to Penrhyn Bay; course between Rhos-on-Sea and Llandudno.
Links course.
Pro Richard Hughes; Founded 1899
Designed by J J Simpson
18 holes, 6064 yards, S.S.S. 69
Visitors: welcome.
Green Fees: WD £10; WE £20.
Societies: welcome everyday but only with prior arrangement; catering terms on application; from £10.
Catering: full clubhouse facilities.
Hotels: own dormy house hotel.

10 119 Rhosgoch

Rhosgoch, Builth Wells, Powys LD23JY
☎(01497) 851251
Off B4594 at turning to Clyro between Erwood and Kington.
Parkland course.
Founded 1984
Designed by Herbie Poore
9 holes, 5078 yards, S.S.S. 67
Visitors: welcome.
Green Fees: WD £7; WE £10.
Societies: welcome by prior arrangement; terms on application.
Catering: bar and snacks.

10 120 Rhuddlan

Meliden Rd, Rhuddlan, Denbighshire, LL18 6LB
☎(01745) 590217, Fax 590472, Pro 590898
Off A55 3 miles N of St Asaph.
Parkland course.
Pro Andrew Carr; Founded 1930
Designed by Hawtree & Co
18 holes, 6482 yards, S.S.S. 71
Visitors: welcome; only with a member Sun.
Green Fees: WD £24; WE £30.
Societies: welcome WD by arrangement.
Catering: lunch and dinner daily; bar facilities.
Hotels: Plas Elwy (packages available).

10 121 Rhyl

Coast Rd, Rhyl, Denbighshire, LL18 3RE
☎(01745) 353171, Pro 360007, Sec 334136
1 mile from station on A548 Prestatyn road.
Seaside links course.
Pro Tim Leah; Founded 1890
Redesigned by James Braid
9 holes, 6165 yards, S.S.S. 70
Visitors: welcome.
Green Fees: WD £12; WE £15.
Societies: welcome by prior arrangement; discount of 20 per cent for parties of more than 20 players; full catering packages available; snooker; from £12.
Catering: full catering facilities.
Hotels: Grange; Marina.

10 122 The Rolls of Monmouth

The Hendre, Monmouth, Monmouthshire, NP5 4HG
☎(01600) 715353, Fax 713115
4 miles NW of Monmouth on the B4233.
Parkland course.
Founded 1982
Designed by Urbis Planning
18 holes, 6733 yards, S.S.S. 73
Visitors: welcome by arrangement.
Green Fees: WD £32; WE £37.
Societies: welcome by prior arrangement; special offers on Mon; coffee on arrival, lunch, 18 holes, for £26; terms on application.
Catering: full catering facilities available.
Hotels: Talacher Farm House; Riverside.

10 123 Royal Porthcawl

Rest Bay, Porthcawl, Mid-Glam, CF36 3UW
☎(01656) 782251, Fax 771687, Pro 773702
M4 junction 37 and follow signs for Porthcawl/Rest Bay.
Championship links course.
Pro Peter Evans; Founded 1891
Designed by Charles Gibson
18 holes, 6685 yards, S.S.S. 74
Visitors: welcome Mon afternoon, Tues, Thurs, Fri; h'cap certs required.
Green Fees: WD £50; WE £50.
Societies: welcome by arrangement; restaurant and bar facilities; from £50.
Catering: full restaurant and bar service.
Hotels: club has own Dormy House from £25 pp; Atlantic; Fairways.

10 124 Royal St David's

Harlech, Gwynedd, LL46 2UB
☎(01766) 780203, Fax 781110, Pro 780857, Sec 780361, Bar/Rest 780182
On the A496 Lower Harlech road under the Castle.
Championship links course.
Pro John Barnett; Founded 1894
18 holes, 6427 yards, S.S.S. 72
Visitors: welcome; booking essential.
Green Fees: WD £30; WE £35.
Societies: welcome; booking essential; 10% reduction for more than 40 players; £5 deposit per player 2 months before visit; from £30.
Catering: full catering facilities.
Hotels: Rum Hole; St David's, both Harlech.

10 125 Ruthin Pwllglas

Ruthin Pwllglas, Ruthin, Denbighshire, LL15 7AR
☎(01824) 702296
On A494 2.5 miles S of Ruthin; right fork before Pwllglas village.
Parkland/meadowland course.
Pro Michael Jones; Founded 1906
Designed by David Lloyd Rees
10 holes, 5418 yards, S.S.S. 66
Visitors: welcome.
Green Fees: WD £12.50; WE £18.
Societies: welcome by prior arrangement.
Catering: bar and catering facilities.
Hotels: Ruthin Castle.

10 126 St Andrews Major

Coldbrook Rd East, Nr Cadoxton, Barry, S Glamorgan, CF6 3BB
☎(01446) 722227
From M4 junction 33 follow signs to Barry and Cardiff Airport; turn left to Sully.
Parkland course.
Founded 1993
Designed by MRM Leisure
9 holes, 5862 yards, S.S.S. 68
Visitors: pay and play
Green Fees: WD £10; WE £13.
Societies: welcome.
Catering: bar and restaurant facilities.
Hotels: Copthorne.

10 127 St Davids City

Whitesands, St Davids, Pembrokeshire, SA62 6PT
☎(01437) 721751, Sec 720312
2 miles W of St Davids following signs for Whitesands Bay.
Links course; most westerly Welsh course.

St Pierre

In the summer of 1987, St Pierre celebrated its 25th anniversary. In a game which goes back centuries, that might not seem much of a landmark, but St Pierre earned itself pride of place by being the first postwar championship course to be built in Britain – the herald of a new era.

In the winter of 1961-62, Ken Cotton was invited to design two courses in the border country of England and Wales, one in the old deer park alongside the main road from Chepstow to Newport and the other in unpromising woodland at Ross-on-Wye. He thought a visit to see how it was done would be a good experience for a young writer – and how right he was.

The two courses could not possibly have been more of a contrast. St Pierre was largely ready-made in terms of fairways whereas Ross-on-Wye, a miracle of enterprise by a devoted band, had to be stripped root by root before the holes took shape.

That Cotton succeeded in both instances showed that he was a master of his craft. You can only judge the results if you knew the original terrain, the difficulties encountered and the budgets available. Both St Pierre and Ross-on-Wye were built on the thinnest of shoestrings. Bill Graham, who had dreamed of a course in the lovely park at St Pierre, drove past one day, and discovering that it was on the market, proved himself a man of action by buying it.

The land, the ancient manor house where the Crown Jewels were stored during the Battle of Agincourt, and the cost of construction of the course came to something under £30,000. However absurdly modest that seems nowadays, one or two sacrifices had to be made but Graham's reasons for purchasing had to be commercially based and there he showed how valid his instincts were. Floodlit golf proved to be one of his few ideas to misfire. When St Pierre was built the motorway systems were already well launched, and the opening of the Severn Bridge only a few years away. St Pierre was, and is, wonderfully accessible from London, Birmingham and Bristol, as well as South Wales.

It wasn't given long to settle down before it was much in demand. Dunlop made it a frequent home for their much lamented Masters and in 1980 the Ladies Golf Union paid it the ultimate compliment by holding the Curtis Cup there. Regular calls have been made upon it by organisers of small tournaments and company days, all of whom flock to take advantage of its residential amenities and a host of other sporting facilities. The latest compliment was paid to it by the announcement of the staging of the 1996 Solheim Cup, the ladies' equivalent of the Ryder Cup which the Europeans won at Dalmahoy in 1992.

The addition of the second course brought alteration to Cotton's original design, and more land was purchased on higher ground. However, nothing destroyed Cotton's first impression that, for Club golfers at large, it is a delightful place to play.

Stately ancient trees feature strongly. After a mild introduction to them at the first, the second is dominated by them, although there follows a break on the loftier reaches of the third to the sixth. At the sixth, the eye is caught by the distant sights but, with the seventh, the trees return and, from then on, there is no let-up.

Several recent changes and a few new back tees have made the professionals flex their muscles a little more. However, one hole where no change is contemplated, and certainly none required, is the 18th across the lake. One of golf's oldest cliches is that nothing is certain until the last putt is holed; nowhere is it more apt than at St Pierre.

Founded 1902
9 holes, 6117 yards, S.S.S. 70
Visitors: welcome; some restrictions
Fri pm.
Green Fees: WD £12; WE £12.
Societies: welcome by arrangement.
Catering: at the Whitesands Bay
Hotel adjacent to course.
Hotels: Whitesands Bay; Old Cross;
St Nons; Warpool Court.

10 128 **St Deiniol**
Pen y Bryn, Bangor, Gwynedd, LL57
1PX
☎(01248) 353098
From A5/A55 intersection follow
A5122 for 1 mile to E of Bangor.
Undulating parkland course; views of
Menai and Snowdonia.
Founded 1906
Designed by James Braid
18 holes, 5654 yards, S.S.S. 67
Visitors: welcome; WE restrictions.
Green Fees: WD £12; WE £16.
Societies: welcome by appointment;
packages vary; terms on application.
Catering: full clubhouse facilities; no
catering Mon.
Hotels: Eryl Mon.

10 129 **St Giles**
Pool Rd, Newtown, Powys, SY16 3AJ
☎(01686) 625844
1 mile E of Newtown on A483.
Riverside/parkland course.
Pro D P Owen; Founded 1895
9 holes, 6006 yards, S.S.S. 69
Visitors: welcome.
Green Fees: terms on application.
Societies: welcome by arrangement;
packages include refreshments; from
£14.
Catering: clubhouse facilities with bar
and restaurant.
Hotels: Elephant and Castle.

10 130 **St Idloes**
Penrallt, Llanidloes, Powys, SY18 6LG
(Club(01686) 412559, Sec 413219
Off A470 at Llanidloes; 1 mile down
B4569.
Undulating course; superb views from
hill plateau.
Founded 1906
Designed by Members
9 holes, 5510 yards, S.S.S. 66
Visitors: welcome.
Green Fees: WD £10.50; WE £12.50.
Societies: welcome; packages avail-
able; terms on application.
Catering: clubhouse facilities
Hotels: Mount Inn; Unicorn; Lloyds.

10 131 **St Mellons**
St Mellons, Cardiff, CF3 8XS
☎(01633) 680401, Fax 681219, Pro
680101, Sec 680408
Close to M4 junctions 28 (W); 30 (E).
Parkland course.
Pro Barry Thomas; Founded 1964
18 holes, 6275 yards, S.S.S. 70
Visitors: welcome WD.
Green Fees: WD £26; WE £26.
Societies: welcome Tues and Thurs;
packages vary according to numbers;
terms on application.
Catering: clubhouse facilities.

10 132 **St Melyd**
The Paddock, Prestatyn,
Denbighshire, LL19 9NB
☎(01745) 854405
On A547 on the main Prestatyn to
Meliden road.
Undulating parkland course.
Pro Andrew Carr; Founded 1922
9 holes, 5839 yards, S.S.S. 68
Visitors: welcome except Thurs
(Ladies day) and Sat.
Green Fees: WD £12; WE £16.
Societies: welcome except Thurs and
Sat.
Catering: full facilities except Tues.
Hotels: Nant Hall; Graig Park.

10 133 **St Pierre Hotel Golf & CC**
St Pierre Park, Chepstow,
Monmouthshire, NP6 6YA
☎(01291) 625261, Fax 629975
2 miles from Chepstow on A49.
Parkland course.
Founded 1962
Designed by Bill Cox
New: 18 holes, 5762 yards, S.S.S. 73;
Old: 18 holes, 6700 yards, S.S.S. 73
Visitors: welcome with h'cap certs.
Green Fees: terms on application.
Societies: welcome WD; WE resi-
dents only; packages available; terms
on application.
Catering: full facilities.
Hotels: St Pierre.

10 134 **Shirenewton Golf Club**
Shirenewton, Nr Chepstow, Gwent,
NP6 6RL
☎(01291) 641642
Off M4 take A48 towards Newport on
reaching Chirk take road to
Shirenewton (2.5 miles).
Parkland course.
Pro Mark Kedward; Founded 1995
Designed by M. Weeks/Tony Davies
18 holes, 6658 yards, S.S.S. 72

Visitors: welcome.
Green Fees: WD £10; WE £10.
Societies: welcome by prior arrange-
ment.
Catering: full facilities.
Practice range, opening summer 1998.
Hotels: self-catering accommodation
on site.

10 135 **South Pembrokeshire**
Defensible Barracks, Military Rd,
Pembroke Dock, Pembrokeshire,
SA72 6SE
☎(01646) 621453
Main A477 road from Carmarthen to
Pembroke dock; 100 yards, after town
boundary sign turn right to Pembroke.
Parkland course.
Founded 1970
18 holes, 6100 yards, S.S.S. 70
Visitors: welcome.
Green Fees: WD £16; WE £20.
Societies: welcome by prior arrange-
ment; catering packages available;
some discounts for larger groups; from
£16.
Catering: clubhouse facilities.
Hotels: Coach House; Cleddau
Bridge; Kings Arms.

10 136 **Southerndown**
Ewenny, Bridgend, Mid-Glam, CF32
0QP
☎(01656) 880476, Fax 880317, Pro
880326
4 miles from Bridgend on the coast
road to Ogmore-by-Sea.
Links/downland course.
Pro Denis McMonagle; Founded 1906
Designed by W. Herbert Fowler, Willie
Park, H.S. Colt
18 holes, 6417 yards, S.S.S. 72
Visitors: welcome; WE only with a
member.
Green Fees: WD £25; WE £35.
Societies: welcome WD by prior
arrangement; h'cap certs required.
Catering: full facilities.
Hotels: Sea Lawns; Sea Bank;
Heronston; Great House.

10 137 **Storws Wen**
Brynteg, Yns Mon, Anglesey, LL78
8JY
☎(01248) 852673, Bar/Rest 853892
Follow the A5025 to Amlwch and then
the B5108 to Llangefni; course 1.5
miles on right before California Hotel.
Parkland course.
Founded 1996
Designed by K Jones
9 holes, 5002 yards, S.S.S. 65

Visitors: welcome.
Green Fees: WD £15; WE £18.
Societies: welcome by arrangement.
Catering: clubhouse facilities.
Hotels: Bryntiyon; Glanrafon; Bay Court; California.

10 138 Summerhill Golf Club
Hereford Road, Clifford, Hay-on-Wye, HR3 5EW
☎(01497) 820451, Fax 820451
On B4352 from Hay towards toll bridge.
Parkland course.
Pro Graham Priday; Founded 1994
9 holes, 5858 yards, S.S.S. 68
Visitors: welcome.
Green Fees: terms on application.
Societies: welcome by prior arrangement; private function room; catering packages.
Catering: full facilities.
Hotels: Kilvert; Swan.

10 139 Swansea Bay
Jersey Marine, Neath, W Glamorgan, SA10 6JP
☎(01792) 812198, Pro 816159, Sec 814793
From A483 take B4290 to Jersey Marine.
Links course.
Pro Mike Day; Founded 1892
18 holes, 6605 yards, S.S.S. 72
Visitors: welcome with h'cap certs.
Green Fees: WD £16; WE £22.
Societies: welcome by arrangement; packages by arrangement; terms on application.
Catering: full clubhouse facilities.
Hotels: many in Swansea area.

10 140 Tenby
The Burrows, Tenby, Pembrokeshire, SA70 7NP
☎(01834) 842978, Fax 842978, Pro 844447
On A477 to Tenby W of town.
Championship links; oldest in Wales.
Pro Mark Hawkey; Founded 1888
18 holes, 6224 yards, S.S.S. 71
Visitors: welcome with h'cap certs.
Green Fees: WD £22; WE £26.
Societies: welcome by arrangement; catering packages by arrangement.
Catering: full facilities.
Hotels: club can provide a list.

10 141 Tredegar & Rhymney
Cwmtysswg, Rhymney, NP2 3BQ
☎(01685) 840743, Fax 843440

On B4256 1.5 miles from Rhymney.
Undulating mountain course.
Founded 1921
12 holes, 6120 yards, S.S.S. 67
Visitors: welcome.
Green Fees: WD £12; WE £15
Societies: welcome except Sun am.
Catering: bar and snacks; meals by prior arrangement.
Hotels: Red Lion, Tredegar.

10 142 Tredegar Park
Bassaleg Rd, Newport, Gwent, NP9 3PX
☎(01633) 895219, Fax 897152, Pro 894517, Sec 894433
Leave M4 junction 27 to Newport; 1st rt at Western Ave and right at end of Western Ave.
Parkland alongside River Ebbw.
Pro M Morgan; Founded 1923
Designed by James Braid
18 holes, 6095 yards, S.S.S. 70
Visitors: welcome with h'cap certs and member of golf club.
Green Fees: WD £25; WE £30.
Societies: welcome by prior arrangement; minimum group 16; from £35.
Catering: restaurant and bar facilities.
Practice ground.
Hotels: Celtic Manor.

10 143 Trefloyne
Trefloyne Park, Penally, Tenby, Pembrokeshire
☎(01834) 842165
Off A4139 Tenby to Pembroke road at Penally.
Parkland course.
Pro S Laidler; Founded 1997
18 holes, 6635 yards, S.S.S. 73
Visitors: welcome.
Green Fees: WD £17.50; WE £22.
Societies: welcome by prior arrangement; minimum 8.
Catering: catering by arrangement; light refreshments.
Practice ground.

10 144 Vale of Glamorgan Golf and Country Club
Hensol Park, Hensol, S Glamorgan, CF7 8JY
☎(01443) 222221, Fax 222220
From M4 junction 34 follow signs to Pendoylan.
Parkland course.
Pro Peter Johnson; Founded 1993
Designed by P. Johnson
18 holes, 6401 yards, S.S.S. 71
Visitors: welcome WD; with member at WE.

Green Fees: WD £30; WE £30.
Societies: welcome by arrangement with Adrian Davies; full society packages; function room; computer analysis; £25-£39.
Catering: full clubhouse facilities and bars.
Practice range, 20 bays.
Hotels: Miskin Manor.

10 145 Vale of Llangollen
The Club House, Holyhead Rd, Llangollen, Denbighshire, LL20 7PR
☎(01978) 860613, Fax 860906, Pro 860040, Sec 860906
1.5 miles E of Llangollen on the A5.
Parkland course set in floor of a valley.
Pro David Vaughan; Founded 1908
18 holes, 6656 yards, S.S.S. 73
Visitors: welcome with h'cap certs.
Green Fees: WD £20; WE £25.
Societies: welcome WD; 30 holes of golf with catering organised by steward; from £25.
Catering: clubhouse facilities.
Hotels: Bryn Howel; Tyn-y-Wew; Wild Pheasant, all Llangollen.

10 146 Virginia Park
Virginia Park, Caerphilly, Mid-Glam, CF8 3SW
☎(01222) 863919
In centre of town next to Caerphilly recreation centre.
Parkland course.
Founded 1992
9 holes, 4661 yards, S.S.S. 66
Visitors: welcome.
Green Fees: WD £11; WE £11.
Societies: welcome by arrangement.
Catering: full bar and refreshments.
Practice range, 22 bays floodlit.

10 147 Welsh Border Golf Complex
Bulthy Farm, Bulthy, Middletown, Nr Welshpool, Powys, SY21 8ER
☎(01743) 884247
Via A458 Shrewsbury/Welshpool road following sign from Middletown.
Parkland course.
Pro Andy Griffiths; Founded 1991
Designed by Andrew Griffiths
9 holes, 6012 yards, S.S.S. 69
Visitors: welcome.
Green Fees: WD £10; WE £10.
Societies: welcome by prior arrangement; also academy course, 1614 yards, par 30.
Catering: bar and restaurant facilities.
Practice range, 10 bays floodlit.
Hotels: Rowton Castle; Bulthy Farm.

10 148 Welshpool

Golfa Hill, Welshpool, Powys SY21 9AQ
☎(01938) 850249
On the A458 out of Welshpool towards
Dolgellau.
Hilly course.
Founded 1931
Designed by James Braid
18 holes, 5708 yards, S.S.S. 69
Visitors: welcome.
Green Fees: terms on application.
Societies: welcome by prior arrange-
ment; terms on application; from £18.
Catering: clubhouse facilities.
Hotels: Gorfa; Royal Oak, both
Welshpool.

10 149 Wenvoe Castle

Wenvoe, Cardiff, CF5 6BE
☎(01222) 591094, Fax 594371, Pro
593649, Sec 594371, Bar/Rest
594371
Follow signs for Cardiff Airport from
M4 junction 33.
Parkland course.
Pro R P Day; Founded 1936
Designed by J Braid
18 holes, 6422 yards, S.S.S. 71
Visitors: welcome WD only.
Green Fees: WD £24.
Societies: welcome WD; minimum 16;
catering packages available; from £18.
Catering: clubhouse facilities.

10 150 Wernddu Golf Centre

Old Ross Rd, Abergavenny,
Monmouthshire, NP7 8NG
☎(01873) 856223, Fax 852177
1.5 miles NE of Abergavenny on
B4521 off A405.
Parkland course; 18th is 615 yards.
Pro Alan Ashmead; Founded 1992
Designed by G. Watkins/A Ashmead
18 holes, 5403 yards, S.S.S. 67
Visitors: welcome.
Green Fees: WD £15; WE £15.
Societies: welcome; maximum 24;
terms on application; from £15.
Catering: bar snacks.
Practice range, 26 bays floodlit.
Hotels: Great George.

10 151 West Monmouthshire

Golf Road, Nantyglo, Gwent, NP3 4QT
☎(01495) 310233, Fax 311361, Pro
313052, Sec 310126
A465 Heads of Valley road, western
valley A467 to Semtex roundabout;
follow Winchestown signs.
Mountain heathland course; highest in
England and Wales.
Founded 1906
18 holes, 6118 yards, S.S.S. 69
Visitors: welcome; with member Sun.
Green Fees: WD £15; WE £15.
Societies: welcome WD by prior
arrangement; package includes meals;
minimum 20; from £20.
Catering: full clubhouse facilities
available.

10 152 Whitchurch (Cardiff)

Pantmawr Rd, Whitchurch, Cardiff,
CF4 6XD
☎(01222) 620125, Fax 529860, Pro
614660, Sec 620985, Bar/Rest
618287
400 yards, along A470 towards Cardiff
from M4 junction 32.
Parkland course.
Pro Eddie Clark; Founded 1915
Redesigned by James Braid/F Johns
18 holes, 6321 yards, S.S.S. 71
Visitors: welcome.
Green Fees: WD £30; WE £35.
Societies: welcome Thurs; reductions
for groups over 60 and between 24-
40; minimum 24; from £16.
Catering: full clubhouse facilities
available.
Hotels: Quality Inn; Friendly Hotel;
Masons Arms.

10 153 Whitehall

The Pavilion, Nelson, Treharris, Mid-
Glam, CF46 6ST
☎(01443) 740245
Off A470 at Treharris and Nelson exit.
Mountain course.
Founded 1922
9 holes, 5666 yards, S.S.S. 68
Visitors: welcome WD; with captain's
permission at WE.

Green Fees: WD £15; WE £20.
Societies: welcome by arrangement
with Sec; catering packages by
arrangement.
Catering: clubhouse facilities.
Hotels: Llechwen Hall, Pontypridd.

10 154 Woodlake Park Golf Club

Glascoed, Pontypool, Monmouthshire,
NP4 0TE
☎(01291) 673933, Fax 672764
3 miles W of Usk overlooking
Llandegfedd reservoir.
Undulating parkland course.
Pro Adrian Pritchard; Founded 1993
Designed by M.J. Wood and H.N.
Wood
18 holes, 6284 yards, S.S.S. 72
Visitors: welcome WD; with booking
at WE.
Green Fees: WD £20; WE £20.
Societies: welcome by prior arrange-
ment; catering and golf packages
available; snooker; pool table; from
£20.
Catering: full clubhouse bar and
restaurant facilities.
Practice range, nets available.
Hotels: Three Salmon; Rat Trap; New
Court and Greyhound Inn, all Usk.

10 155 Wrexham

Holt Rd, Wrexham, Flintshire, LL13
9SB
☎(01978) 261033, Fax 364268, Pro
351476, Sec 364268, Bar/Rest
358705
2 miles NE of Wrexham on A534.
Sandy parkland course.
Pro Roy Young; Founded 1906/1924
Designed by James Braid
18 holes, 6233 yards, S.S.S. 70
Visitors: welcome with handicap certificates.
Green Fees: WD £25; WE £30.
Societies: welcome WD except Tues;
27 holes of golf; coffee on arrival; light
lunch, evening meal; £32.
Catering: full clubhouse catering facilities.

NORTHERN IRELAND

Discussion on comparative merits of golf courses is always fierce although rarely conclusive. Golfers are influenced by a multitude of factors, from how they played to the condition of the greens and the beauty of the setting. Where the debate surrounds courses that are near neighbours, passions are liable to be even more frenzied but, while Royal Portrush and Royal County Down cannot quite be classed as neighbours, they lie roughly equidistant on either side of Belfast and as a result tend to split opinion nicely.

This is not the place to fuel the argument about their merits but there is not the slightest doubt that both are in the classic mould and nobody should visit Ulster and play one without the other. Few big cities can boast two championship links within such easy reach of its centre.

Royal County Down is at Newcastle, an attractive holiday town nestling in the romantic shadow of the Mountains of Mourne. Mountains make an imposing backcloth to golf anywhere and one is always aware of their brooding presence at Newcastle, with sun and cloud casting ever-changing patterns and colours. They make the ninth particularly imposing but an equally dominant impression of the course is forged by the massive sand dunes that line so many of the fairways together with the heather and gorse that magnify and punish errant shots.

They place huge demands on bold, forceful driving, although the varied nature of the shots to the greens gives an important added dimension that increases the regret that circumstances beyond its control have denied Royal County Down more major championships. The British Amateur of 1970 and the Curtis Cup match two years earlier were events enhanced by the quality of its challenge but the same applies to Royal Portrush – the only Irish Club to have housed the Open Championship in 1951. It saw Max Faulkner emerge as champion, although his win marked the beginning of a drought where British victories were concerned, which lasted until Tony Jacklin won in 1969.

Portrush also saw the crowning of Catherine Lacoste as British Women's champion, many of the noble holes bringing out the best in a supreme striker, and in 1993 the British Men's Amateur Open returned after a gap of 33 years. The spectacular part is down by the shore not far from the Giant's Causeway. Holes entitled Purgatory and Calamity convey the true picture.

However, it must not be thought that golf in the Province is confined to Newcastle and Portrush – superb as they are. Lovers of links golf have a splendid example in Portstewart and another in Castlerock – both close to Portrush. Belfast itself is well served, Royal Belfast, with excellent views of the city, and Malone being the pick.

There is also Balmoral, the home club of the late Fred Daly, Holywood and Shandon Park, which used to stage the Gallaher's Ulster Open at a time when a young Tony Jacklin was taking his first steps on to the world golfing stage.

Clandeboye and Bangor are towns on the fringe of the Belfast district with splendid courses and the best of the new courses are Blackwood, with 36 holes and a driving range, and Rockmount on rolling agricultural land. Lastly, I well remember journeys to Lurgan when Frank Pennink was redesigning the course; and a sentimental mention for Warrenpoint near the border with the Republic, the course that raised Ronan Rafferty.

11 1 Aberdelghy
Bell's Lane, Lambeg, Co Antrim, N
Ireland
☎(01846) 662738
Between Dunmurry and Lambeg off the
Belfast-Lisburn road.
Municipal parkland course.
Founded 1986
9 holes, 4384 yards, S.S.S. 65
Visitors: welcome.
Green Fees: WD £6.50; WE £7.50.
Societies: welcome; discounts for
groups of 15 or more.

11 2 Ardglass
Castle Place, Ardglass, Co Down,
BT30 7TP
☎(01396) 841219, Fax 841841, Pro
841022
On B1 7 miles from Downpatrick; 30
miles S of Belfast.
Seaside course.
Pro Philip Farrell; Founded 1896
18 holes, 6065 yards, S.S.S. 69
Visitors: welcome WD; Sun afternoon.
Green Fees: WD £14; WE £20.
Societies: welcome by prior arrange-
ment WD and Sun am; packages on
application; £12-18.
Catering: full facilities.
Hotels: Burrendale; Slieve Danard;
Burford Lodge GH.

11 3 Ashfield
Freeduff, Cullyhanna, Co Armagh
☎(01693) 868180, Fax 868111
Parkland course.
Founded 1990
18 holes, 5620 yards, S.S.S. 67
Visitors: welcome.
Green Fees: WD £10; WE £12.
Societies: terms on application.
Catering: clubhouse facilities.

11 4 Ballycastle
Cushendall Rd, Ballycastle, Co Antrim,
BT54 6QP.
☎(012657) 62536, Fax 69909, Pro
62506
On A2 between Portrush and
Cushendall.
Mixture of parkland, links and heath
course.
Pro Ian McLaughlin; Founded 1890
18 holes, 5629 yards, S.S.S. 68
Visitors: welcome by prior arrange-
ment; some WE restrictions.
Green Fees: WD on application.
Societies: welcome by arrangement;
WE restrictions; terms on application.
Catering: full clubhouse facilities.
Hotels: Marine.

11 5 Ballyclare
25 Springvale Rd, Ballycare, BT39
9JW
☎(01960) 324542, Fax 322696, Sec
322696
1.5 miles N of Ballyclare at Five
Corners.
Parkland course.
Founded 1923
Designed by Tom McCauley
18 holes, 5745 yards, S.S.S.71
Visitors: welcome.
Green Fees: WD £15; WE £20.
Societies: welcome by prior arrange-
ment; minimum 20 players; catering by
arrangement; snooker; from £13.
Catering: bar and restaurant service.
Practice range.
Hotels: Country House; Dunadry Inn;
Chimney Corner; Five Corners B&B;
Fairways B&B.

11 6 Ballyearl Golf and Leisure Centre
585 Doagh Rd, Newtownabbey,
Belfast, BT36 8RZ
☎(01232) 848287
1 mile N of Mossley off B59.
Public parkland course.
9 holes, 4724 yards
Visitors: welcome.
Green Fees: WD £3; WE £4.
Catering: full facilities.
Practice range.

11 7 Ballymena
128 Raceview Rd, Ballymena
☎(01266) 861487, Pro 861652,
Bar/Rest 862087
2.5 miles E of the town on the A42 to
Brough Shane and Carnlough.
Heathland/parkland course.
Founded 1902
18 holes, 5299 yards, S.S.S. 67
Visitors: welcome Tues, Sat.
Green Fees: WD £15; WE £20.
Societies: welcome by prior arrange-
ment with the Hon Secretary.
Catering: full clubhouse bar and
restaurant facilities.
Hotels: Adair Arms; Tullyglass House;
Leighinmohr; The Country House.

11 8 Balmoral
518 Lisburn Rd, Belfast, BT9 6GX
☎(01232) 381514, Pro 667747,
Bar/Rest 668540
2 miles S of Belfast city centre; immediately beside the King's Hall on the
Lisburn road opposite Balmoral Halt
station.
Parkland course.

Pro Geoff Blakeley; Founded 1914
18 holes, 6276 yards, S.S.S. 70
Visitors: welcome except Sat and
after 3pm Sun.
Green Fees: WD £20; WE £30.
Societies: welcome by prior arrange-
ment Mon and Thurs; special pack-
ages are available.
Catering: full clubhouse bar and
restaurant facilities.
Hotels: Forte Crest; Europa; Plaza;
York; Balmoral; Beechlawn.

11 9 Banbridge
116 Huntly Rd, Banbridge, Co Down,
BT32 3UR
☎(018206) 62342, Fax 69400, Sec
62211, Bar/Rest 62211
1 mile N of Banbridge.
Parkland course.
Founded 1913
Extension by F Ainsworth
18 holes, 5047 yards, S.S.S. 67
Visitors: welcome; dress code.
Green Fees: WD £15; WE £20.
Societies: welcome by prior arrangement; must be GUI recognised societies; catering by arrangement; from
£12.
Catering: lounge and bar facilities
available.
Hotels: Belmont; Downshire.

11 10 Bangor
Broadway, Bangor, Co Down, BT20
4RH
☎(01247) 270922, Fax 453394, Pro
462164, Bar/Rest 270483
0.75 miles S of town centre.
Parkland course.
Pro Blake Campbell
Founded 1903
Designed by James Braid
18 holes, 6410 yards, S.S.S. 71
Visitors: welcome except Sat; ladies
have priority Tues.
Green Fees: WD £17.50; WE £25.
Societies: welcome by prior arrange-
ment except Tues and Sat; catering by
arrangement; from £15.
Catering: full bar and catering facili-
ties.
Hotels: Marine Court; Royal.

11 11 Belvoir Park
73 Church Rd, Newtownbreda,
Belfast, BT8 4AN
☎(01232) 491693, Fax 646113, Pro
646714, Bar/Rest 641159
4 miles from Belfast off the Ormeau
road.
Parkland course.

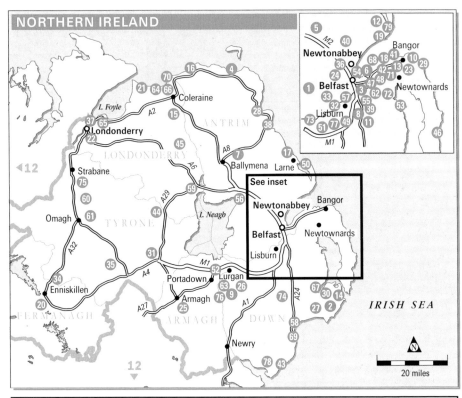

NORTHERN IRELAND

KEY		16	Bushfoot	33	Edenmore Golf Course	50	Larne	67	Ringdufferin
1	Aberdelghy	17	Cairndhu	34	Enniskillen	51	Lisburn	68	Royal Belfast
2	Ardglass	18	Carnalea	35	Fintona	52	Lurgan	69	Royal County Down
3	Ashfield	19	Carrickfergus	36	Fortwilliam	53	Mahee Island	70	Royal Portrush
4	Ballycastle	20	Castle Hume	37	Foyle	54	Mallusk	71	Scrabo
5	Ballyclare	21	Castlerock	38	Garron Tower	55	Malone Golf Club	72	Shandon Park
6	Ballyearl Golf and	22	City of Derry	39	Gilnahirk	56	Massereene	73	Silverwood
	Leisure Centre	23	Clandeboye	40	Greenisland	57	Mount Ober	74	Spa
7	Ballymena	24	Cliftonville	41	Helen's Bay	58	Mourne	75	Strabane
8	Balmoral	25	County Armagh	42	Holywood	59	Moyola Park	76	Tandragee
9	Banbridge	26	Craigavon	43	Kilkeel	60	Newtownstewart	77	Temple
10	Bangor	27	Crossgar	44	Killymoon	61	Omagh	78	Warrenpoint
11	Belvoir Park	28	Cushendall	45	Kilrea	62	Ormeau	79	Whitehead
12	Bentra	29	Donaghadee	46	Kirkistown Castle	63	Portadown		
13	Blackwood	30	Downpatrick	47	The Knock	64	Portstewart		
14	Bright Castle	31	Dungannon	48	Knockbracken Golf & CC	65	Radisson Roe Park Hotel		
15	Brown Trout	32	Dunmurry	49	Lambeg	66	Rathmore		

Pro Maurice Kelly; Founded 1927
Designed by H.S. Colt
18 holes, 6516 yards, S.S.S. 71
Visitors: welcome.
Green Fees: WD £33; WE £38.
Societies: only 6 per month permitted
by prior arrangement with the club
Secretary.
Catering: full facilities supplied by
Countryside Cuisine.
Practice range.
Hotels: La Mon House; Stormont.

11 12 **Bentra**
1 Slaughterford Rd, Whitehead, Co
Antrim, BT38 9TG
☎(019603) 78996
5 miles N of Carrickfergus on Larne
road.
Municipal parkland course.
9 holes, 6084 yards, S.S.S. 68
Visitors: pay and play.
Green Fees: WD £7; WE £10.50.
Societies: welcome but tee times cannot be reserved.

Catering: bar and snacks at Bentra
roadhouse.
Practice range, 200 yards, 10 bays.
Hotels: Magheramorne House; Coast
Road; Dobbins, Carrickfergus.

11 13 **Blackwood**
150 Crawfordsburn Rd, Clandeboye,
Bangor, BT19 1GB
☎(01247) 852706, Fax 853785
On A2 towards Bangor from Belfast

turn to Newtonards; course 1.5 miles. Heathland/parkland course.
Pro Tony White; Founded 1994
Designed by Simon Gidman
18 holes, 6337 yards, S.S.S. 70
Visitors: welcome; pay and play.
Green Fees: WD £14; WE £18.
Societies: welcome by prior arrangement.
Catering: bar, snacks and restaurant facilities.
Practice range, 25 bays floodlit.
Hotels: Clandeboye Lodge.

11 14 Bright Castle
14 Coniamstown Rd, Bright, Co Down, Co Down
☎(01396) 841319
5 miles S of Downpatrick.
Parkland course; 16th hole, par 6, is 735 yards.
Founded 1970
Designed by Arnold Ennis
18 holes, 7143 yards, S.S.S. 74
Visitors: welcome.
Green Fees: terms on application.
Societies: welcome by prior arrangement; catering by arrangement; terms on application.
Catering: bar and catering facilities.
Hotels: Abbey Lodge, Downpatrick.

11 15 Brown Trout
209 Agivy Road, Aghadowey, Nr Coleraine, Co Londonderry, BT51 4AP
☎(01265) 868209, Fax 868878
7 miles S of Coleraine on the intersection of A54 & B66.
Parkland course.
Pro Ken Revie; Founded 1973
Designed by Bill O'Hara Snr
9 holes, 5510 yards, S.S.S. 68
Visitors: welcome.
Green Fees: WD £10; WE £15.
Societies: welcome by prior arrangement; catering packages by arrangement; private room for meals and presentations; accommodation for small groups; from £7.
Catering: full catering and bar facilities.
Hotels: Brown Trout Country Inn on site.

11 16 Bushfoot
50 Bushfoot Rd, Portballintrae, Co Antrim, BT57 8RR
☎(012657) 31317, Fax 31852, Bar/Rest 32588
4 miles E of Portrush on the coast.
Seaside links course.
Founded 1890

9 holes, 5914 yards, S.S.S. 67
Visitors: welcome except on competition days.
Green Fees: WD £13; WE £16.
Societies: welcome by prior arrangement.
Catering: bar, restaurant, function room; snooker room.
Hotels: Bayview; Beech; Bushmills Inn; Causeway.

11 17 Cairndhu
192 Coast Rd, Ballygally, Larne, Co Antrim, BT40 2QG
☎(01574) 583324, Fax 583324
4 miles N of Larne on the Glens of Antrim coast road.
Parkland course.
Pro Bob Walker; Founded 1928/1958
Designed by John S.F. Morrison
18 holes, 5611 yards, S.S.S. 69
Visitors: welcome.
Green Fees: WD £15; WE £20.
Societies: welcome by prior arrangement; discounts for groups of 20 or more; from £15.
Catering: clubhouse facilities.
Hotels: Highways; Londonderry Arms; Ballygally Holiday Aparts.

11 18 Carnalea
Station Rd, Bangor, Co Down, BT19 1EZ
☎(01247) 465004, Fax 273989, Pro 270122, Sec 270368, Bar/Rest 461901
1.5 miles from Bangor adjacent to Carnalea station.
Parkland course on shore of Belfast Lough.
Pro Thomas Loughran; Founded 1927
18 holes, 5574 yards, S.S.S. 67
Visitors: welcome; Sat after 2.30pm.
Green Fees: WD £13; WE £17.
Societies: welcome except Sat; catering by arrangement; from £13.
Catering: bar and restaurant facilities.
Hotels: Royal; Marine Court; Crawfordsburn Inn.

11 19 Carrickfergus
35 North Rd, Carrickfergus, Co Antrim, BT38 8LP
☎(019603) 63713, Pro 51803, Bar/Rest 51868
Odd A2 9 miles NE of Belfast on the North Rd; 1 mile from Shore Road.
Parkland/meadowland course.
Pro Ray Stephenson; Founded 1926
18 holes, 5623 yards, S.S.S. 68
Visitors: welcome except Sat.
Green Fees: WD £14; WE £20.

Societies: welcome WD by arrangement.
Catering: full facilities.
Hotels: Coast Road; Dobbins; Glenavna; Quality Inn.

11 20 Castle Hume
Castle Hume, Enniskillen, Co Fermanagh, BT93 7ED
☎(01365) 327077, Fax 327076
5 miles from Enniskillen on the Donegal road.
Parkland course.
Pro Gareth McShea; Founded 1991
18 holes, 6492 yards, S.S.S. 72
Visitors: welcome
Green Fees: WD £12; WE £18.
Societies: welcome; minimum group of 12; from £10.
Catering: bar and restaurant.
Hotels: Fort Lodge; Killyhevlin.

11 21 Castlerock
65 Circular Rd, Castlerock, Co Londonderry, BT51 4TJ
☎(01265) 848215, Fax 848314, Pro 848314, Sec 848314, Bar/Rest 848004
Off A2 6 miles W of Coleraine.
Links course.
Pro Robert Kelly; Founded 1901
Designed by Ben Sayers
18 holes, 6687 yards, S.S.S. 72
Visitors: welcome by arrangement with Pro.
Green Fees: WD £25; WE £35.
Societies: welcome by prior arrangement; catering by prior arrangement; from £25.
Catering: full catering facilities.
Hotels: GolfLodge.

11 22 City of Derry
49 Victoria Rd, Londonderry, BT47 2PU
☎(01504) 346369, Pro 311496, Bar/Rest 311610
On main Londonderry-Strabane road three miles from Craigavon Bridge.
Parkland course; also 9-hole pay and play Dunhugh course.
Pro Michael Docherty; Founded 1912
18 holes, 6429 yards, S.S.S. 71
Visitors: welcome WD before 4.30pm; WE by prior arrangement.
Green Fees: WD £20; WE £25.
Societies: welcome WD; limited WE availability.
Catering: full facilities.
Practice range.
Hotels: Everglades; Broomhill House; White Horse Inn; Waterfoot.

11 23 Clandeboy Ava

Tower Rd, Conlig, Newtownards, Co Antrim, BT23 3PN
☎(01247) 271767, Fax 473711, Pro 271750, Bar/Rest 270992
In village of Conlig off the Belfast-Bangor road at Newtonards.
Parkland course.
Pro Peter Gregory; Founded 1933
Designed by Baron von Limburger
Ava: 18 holes, yards, S.S.S. 73;
Dufferin: 18 holes, yards, S.S.S. 73
Visitors: welcome; Sat restrictions.
Green Fees: WD £20, WE £20 (Ava); WD £25, WE £25 (Dufferin).
Societies: welcome WD except Thurs; packages include golf and food; from £20 (Ava); from £25 (Dufferin).
Catering: full clubhouse dining and bar facilities.
Hotels: Clandeboye Lodge; Marine Court; Crawfordsburn Inn.

11 24 Cliftonville

44 Westland Rd, Belfast, BT14 6NH
☎(01232) 744158, Sec 746595
From Belfast take Antrim road for two miles then turn into Cavehill Rd and left again at Fire Station.
Parkland course.
Pro Peter Hanna; Founded 1911
9 holes, 5706 yards, S.S.S. 70
Visitors: welcome except Tues afternoon and Sat.
Green Fees: WD £12; WE £15.
Societies: welcome by arrangement with secretary J M Henderson.
Catering: bar facilities.
Practice range.
Hotels: Lansdowne Court.

11 25 County Armagh

The Demesne, Newry Rd, Armagh, Co Armagh, BT10 1EN
☎(01861) 522501, Pro 525861
Off Newry Rd 0.25 miles from the city.
Parkland course.
Pro Alan Rankin; Founded 1893
18 holes, 6212 yards, S.S.S. 69
Visitors: welcome except 12 noon-2pm Sat; 12 noon-3pm Sun.
Green Fees: WD £15; WE £25.
Societies: welcome by arrangement except Sat.
Catering: full facilities except Mon.
Practice range.
Hotels: Charlemont Arms; Drumshill House.

11 26 Craigavon

Turmoyra Lane, Silverwood, Lurgan, Craigavon, Co Armagh, BT66 6NG
☎(01762) 326606
Off M1 from Belfast at A76 junction 10; continue for 500 yards on the sliproad; first right into Kiln road and then right again.
Public parkland course.
Pro Des Paul
18 holes, 6118 yards, S.S.S. 72
Visitors: welcome; phone at WE.
Green Fees: WD £10.50; WE £ 13.50.
Societies: welcome mainly Sun by arrangement; 12 hole pitch and putt; 9-hole putting green; ski centre.
Catering: full facilities at Silverwood Golf and Ski Centre.
Practice range, 5 bays floodlit.
Hotels: Silverwood.

11 27 Crossgar

231 Derryboye Rd, Crossgar, Co. Down, BT30 9DL
☎(01396) 831523, Pro 831629
From Belfast 5 miles S of Saintfield close to town of Crossgar.
Parkland course.
Founded 1993
Designed by John Cuffey
9 holes, 4580 yards, S.S.S. 63
Visitors: welcome.
Green Fees: WD £9; WE £11.
Societies: welcome by prior arrangement; from £8.
Catering: small restaurant and bar.
Hotels: Millbrook Lodge, Ballynahinch.

11 28 Cushendall

Shore Rd, Cushendall, Ballymena, Co Antrim, BT44 0QG
☎(012667) 71318, Sec 58366
On main Antrim coast road 25 miles N of Larne.
Parkland course.
Founded 1937
Designed by Daniel Delargy
9 holes, 4384 yards, S.S.S. 63
Visitors: welcome; start sheet on Thurs, Sat, Sun.
Green Fees: WD £10; WE £15.
Societies: welcome on application to secretary Mr S McLaughlin; catering packages available in summer; from £10.
Catering: full catering in summer; bar facilities.
Hotels: Thornlea.

11 29 Donaghadee

84 Warren Rd, Donaghadee, Co Down, BT21 0PQ
☎(01247) 888697, Fax 888891, Pro 882392, Sec 883624, Bar/Rest 882519
6 miles S of Bangor on the coast road.
Part links and inland course.
Pro Gordon Drew; Founded 1899
18 holes, 5570 yards, S.S.S. 69
Visitors: welcome by prior arrangement.
Green Fees: WD £14; WE £18.
Societies: welcome Mon, Wed, Fri by prior arrangement; discounts for groups of 24 or more; catering packages available by arrangement; from £14.
Catering: clubhouse facilities.
Hotels: Copeland.

11 30 Downpatrick

43 Saul Rd, Downpatrick, Co Down, BT30 6PA
☎(01396) 615947, Pro 615167, Bar/Rest 615244
23 miles SE of Belfast off A24 and A7.
Parkland course.
Founded 1930
Designed by Hawtree & Sons
18 holes, 6299 yards, S.S.S. 69
Visitors: welcome; some WE restrictions.
Green Fees: WD £15; WE £20.
Societies: welcome by prior arrangement.
Catering: full facilities.
Hotels: Denvir; Abbey Lodge.

11 31 Dungannon

34 Springfield Lane, Mullaghmore, Dungannon, Co Tyronne, BT70 1QX
☎(01868) 727338, Bar/Rest 722098
0.5 miles from Dungannon on Donaghmore road.
Parkland course.
Founded 1890
18 holes, 6046 yards, S.S.S. 69
Visitors: welcome; restrictions Tues (Ladies Day).
Green Fees: WD £15; WE £18.
Societies: welcome by prior arrangement except Tues and Sat.
Catering: full facilities.
Hotels: Cohananon Autolodge; Inn on the Park; Glengarron.

11 32 Dunmurry

91 Dunmurry Lane, Dunmurry, BT17 9JS
☎(01232) 610834, Fax 602540, Pro 621314, Sec 621402, Bar/Rest 301124
Follow signs for Dunmurry from the M1; turn left at first traffic lights.
Parkland course.
Pro J Dolan; Founded 1905
Designed by T.J. McAuley
18 holes, 5832 yards, S.S.S. 68

Visitors: welcome by prior arrangement.
Green Fees: WD £17; WE £26.50.
Societies: welcome WD by prior written arrangement; packages on application; from £16.
Catering: full clubhouse facilities.
Hotels: Forte Crest; Beech Lawn.

11 33 Edenmore Golf Course
Edenmore House, 70 Drumnabreeze Rd, Maralin, Co. Armagh, BT67 0RH
☎(01846) 611310
M1 from Belfast to junction 5 for Moira to Maralin.
Parkland course.
Founded 1992
Designed by Frank Ainsworth
9 holes, 6244 yards, S.S.S. 70
Visitors: welcome except Sun; members have priority before 1pm on Sat.
Green Fees: WD £10; WE £15.
Societies: welcome by prior arrangement; packages on request; private dinners for groups of 25-80.
Catering: full restaurant facilities available.
Hotels: Seagoe, Portadown; White Gables, Hillsborough; Silverwood, Lurgan.

11 34 Enniskillen
Castlecoole, Enniskillen, Co Fermanagh, BT74 6HZ
☎(01365) 325250
1 miles from Enniskillen off Tempo Road.
Parkland course.
Founded 1896
Designed by Dr Dixon & George Mawhinney/ T.J. McAuley
18 holes, 6189 yards, S.S.S. 69
Visitors: welcome.
Green Fees: WD £12; WE £15.
Societies: welcome by arrangement; catering by arrangement with the steward; snooker.
Catering: full catering and bar facilities.
Hotels: Fort Lodge; Ashbury; Killyhevlin; Railway; Belmore Court.

11 35 Fintona
Ecclesville Demesne, Fintona, Co Tyrone, BT78 2BJ
☎(01662) 841480, Pro 840777
9 miles SW of Omagh
Parkland course.
Founded 1904
9 holes, 5866 yards, S.S.S. 70
Visitors: welcome WD.
Green Fees: WD £15.

Societies: welcome by prior arrangement; packages for groups of more than 20; £10.
Catering: full facilities.
Hotels: Royal Arms; Silver Birches.

11 36 Fortwilliam
8A Downview Ave, Belfast, B15 4EZ
☎(01232) 370770, Fax 781891, Pro 770980, Bar/Rest 370072
3 miles from Belfast centre off the Antrim road.
Parkland course.
Pro Peter Hanna; Founded 1891
Designed by Butchart
18 holes, 5973 yards, S.S.S. 69
Visitors: welcome
Green Fees: WD £21; WE £28.
Societies: welcome by prior arrangement; discounts for groups of more than 15; catering packages available by arrangement; from £18.
Catering: clubhouse facilities.
Hotels: Lansdowne Court; Chimney Corner.

11 37 Foyle
12 Alder Road, Londonderry, Co Londonderry, BT48 8DB
☎(01504) 352222, Fax 353967
2 miles N of Londonderry off Culmore road.
Parkland course.
Pro Kieran McLoughlin; Founded 1994
Designed by F Ainsworth
18 holes, 6678 yards, S.S.S. 71
Visitors: welcome.
Green Fees: WD £12; WE £15.
Societies: welcome; bookings taken 12 months in advance; discount for groups of 14 or more; packages with hotels and catering available; also 9-hole par 3 course; from £12.
Catering: restaurant and bar facilities. Practice range, 19 bays covered and floodlit.
Hotels: Waterfoot Hotel & CC; Whitehorse Inn.

11 38 Garron Tower
St Macnissi's College, Carnlough, Co Antrim, BT44 0JS
☎(01232) 85202
Playing facilities at Cushendall and Ballycastle Golf Clubs.
Founded 1968

11 39 Gilnahirk
Manns Corner, Upper Braniel Rd, Gilnahirk, Castlereagh, Belfast, BT5 7TX

☎(01232) 448477
3 miles from Belfast off Ballygowan road.
Public moorland course.
Pro Kenneth Gray; Founded 1983
9 holes, 5924 yards, S.S.S. 68
Visitors: welcome.
Green Fees: WD £8.15; WE £9.70
Societies: welcome by prior arrangement.
Catering: full catering facilities.
Hotels: Stormont.

11 40 Greenisland
156 Upper Rd, Greenisland, Carrickfergus, Co Antrim, BT38 8RW
☎(01232) 862236
8 miles N of Belfast; 2 miles from Carrickfergus.
Parkland course.
Founded 1894
Designed by C Day
9 holes, 5624 yards, S.S.S. 69
Visitors: welcome.
Green Fees: WD £12; WE £18.
Societies: welcome by prior arrangement; on application; from £12.
Catering: full clubhouse facilities.
Hotels: Coast Road Hotel; Glenavna.

11 41 Helen's Bay
Golf Rd, Helen's Bay, Bangor, Co Down, BT19 1TL
☎(01247) 852601, Fax 852815, Sec 852815, Bar/Rest 852816
4 miles W of Bangor off the B20; adjacent to Crawfordsburn Country Park.
Parkland course on shores of Belfast Lough.
Founded 1896
9 holes, 5181 yards, S.S.S. 67
Visitors: welcome except Tues and Sat; restrictions Thurs pm and Fri summer am.
Green Fees: WD £12; WE £15.
Societies: welcome by prior arrangement Sun, Mon, Wed, Thurs morning and Fri; minimum 10 maximum 40; private room for dining or presentations; catering packages available; from £12.
Catering: full bar and restaurant facilities.
Hotels: Crawfordsburn Old Inn; Clandeboye Lodge; Marine Court; Culloden.

11 42 Holywood
Nuns Walk, Demesne Rd, Holywood, Co Down, BT18 9LE
☎(01232) 423135, Fax 425040, Pro 425503, Bar/Rest 426832
On A2 6 miles E of Belfast.

Undulating course.
Pro Michael Bannon; Founded 1904
18 holes, 6028 yards, S.S.S. 68
Visitors: welcome except Sat.
Green Fees: WD £15; WE £20.
Societies: welcome except Thurs, Sat and BH
Catering: bar and catering facilities.
Hotels: Culloden.

11 43 Kilkeel

Mourne Park, Kilkeel, Co Down, BT34 4LB
☎(016937) 62296, Fax 65095, Sec 63787
3 miles W of Kilkeel; 45 miles S of Belfast.
Parkland course.
Founded 1948/1993
Designed by Lord Justice Babbington, Eddie Hackett
18 holes, 6615 yards, S.S.S. 72
Visitors: welcome by prior arrangement.
Green Fees: WD £16; WE £18.
Societies: welcome by prior arrangement; catering available on application; from £14.
Catering: full clubhouse facilities.
Practice range, close to course.
Hotels: Kilmurey Arms; Cronfield Arms; Slieve Donard; Burrendale.

11 44 Killymoon

200 Killymoon Rd, Cookstown, Co Tyrone, BT80 8TW
☎(016487) 63762, Pro 63460, Bar/Rest 62254
Off A29 0.5 miles S of Cookstown.
Parkland course.
Pro Gary Chambers; Founded 1889
Designed by Hugh Adair
18 holes, 5486 yards, S.S.S. 69
Visitors: welcome except Sat.
Green Fees: WD £21; WE £25.
Societies: welcome except Thurs and Sat by prior arrangement; from £25.
Catering: full facilities.
Hotels: Glenavon; Greenvale; Royal.

11 45 Kilrea

38 Drumagarner Rd, Kilrea, Co Londonderry, Co Londonderry
☎(01265) 821048
0.5 miles from Kilrea Village on Maghera road.
Parkland course.
Founded 1919
9 holes, 4514 yards, S.S.S. 62
Visitors: welcome except after 4.30pm Tues and Wed and Sat pm.
Green Fees: WD £10; WE £12.50.

Societies: welcome by prior arrangement; limited catering; from £10.
Catering: limited.
Hotels: Port Neal Lodge.

11 46 Kirkistown Castle

142 Main Rd, Cloughey, Co Down, BT22 1JA
☎(01247) 771233, Fax 771699, Pro 771004, Sec 771136
A20 from Belfast to Kircubbin; follow signs to Newtonards and Portaferry; then B173 to Cloughey.
Links course.
Pro John Peden; Founded 1902
Designed by B. Polley
18 holes, 6125 yards, S.S.S. 70
Visitors: welcome.
Green Fees: WD £13; WE £25.
Societies: welcome WD by prior arrangement; packages for groups of 16 or more.
Catering: full facilities.
Hotels: Portaferry.

11 47 The Knock

Summerfield, Upper Newtownards Rd, Dundonald, BT16 0QX
☎(01232) 482249, Fax 483251, Pro 483825, Sec 483251, Bar/Rest 480915
4 miles E of Belfast off the Upper Newtonards road.
Parkland course.
Pro Gordon Fairweather; Founded 1895
Designed by Colt, MacKenzie & Allison
18 holes, 6435 yards, S.S.S. 71
Visitors: welcome every day except Sat.
Green Fees: WD £20; WE £25.
Societies: welcome Mon and Thurs; discounts available for groups of more than 40; catering packages available; from £18.
Catering: full bar and restaurant facilities.
Hotels: Stormont; Clandeboye; Strangford.

11 48 Knockbracken Golf & Country Club

Ballymaconaghy Rd, Knockbracken, Belfast, BT8 4SB
☎(01232) 792108, Pro 795666
Near Four Winds restaurant on SE outskirts of the city.
Pro Geoff Loughrey
18 holes, 5391 yards, S.S.S. 68
Visitors: welcome
Green Fees: WD £9; WE £13.

Societies: welcome by prior arrangement; packages on request; putting green; ski slopes.
Catering: full bar and restaurant facilities.
Practice range, 25 bays floodlit.

11 49 Lambeg

Aberdelly, Bells Lane, Lambeg, Lisburn, Co. Antrim, BT27 4QH
☎(01846) 662738, Fax 603432
Off the main Lisburn road at Bells Lane in Lambeg.
Parkland course.
Pro Ian Murdoch; Founded 1986
9 holes, 4139 yards, S.S.S. 62
Visitors: welcome except Sat am.
Green Fees: WD £7; WE £9.
Societies: welcome except Sat am.
Catering: snacks available.
Hotels: Forte Post House.

11 50 Larne

54 Ferris Bay Rd, Islandmagee, Larne, BT40 3RT
☎(01396) 724234
From Belfast N to Carrickfergus and 6 miles from Whithead; from Larne S along the coast road to Islandmagee.
Seaside course at N tip of Islandmagee peninsula.
Founded 1894
Designed by Babington
9 holes, 6288 yards, S.S.S. 69
Visitors: welcome except Sat.
Green Fees: WD £8; WE £15.
Societies: welcome except Sat.
Catering: full clubhouse facilities available.
Hotels: Magheramorne House.

11 51 Lisburn

68 Eglantine Rd, Lisburn, Co Antrim, BT27 5RQ
☎(01846) 677216, Fax 603608, Pro 677217, Bar/Rest 677218
Take Springfield roundabout exit from M1 in direction of Hillsborough.
Parkland course.
Pro Blake Campbell; Founded 1905/1973
Designed by Hawtree & Sons
18 holes, 6647 yards, S.S.S. 72
Visitors: welcome WD before 3pm; WE with member.
Green Fees: WD £25; WE £12.
Societies: welcome Mon and Thurs before 3pm; discounts for groups of 20 or more; from £25.
Catering: clubhouse facilities available.
Hotels: White Gables Hotel.

11 52 Lurgan

The Demesne, Lurgan, Co Armagh, BT67 9BN
☎(01762) 325306, Fax 325306, Pro 321068, Sec 322087, Bar/Rest 322087
Centre of Lurgan off Windsor Avenue past park gates and down road between Park Lake and Brownlow House.
Parkland course.
Pro Des Paul; Founded 1893
Designed by Frank Pennink
18 holes, 6257 yards, S.S.S. 70
Visitors: welcome except Tues, Wed and Sat; restrictions Fri pm.
Green Fees: WD £15; WE £20.
Societies: welcome by prior arrangement as guest policy; discounts for groups of 50 or more; catering packages available; from £15.
Catering: restaurant and lounge bar available.
Hotels: Ashburn; Silverwood; Carngrove; Seagoe.

11 53 Mahee Island

Comber, Newtownards, Co Down, BT23 6ET
☎(01238) 541234
Turn left 0.5 miles from Comber off Comber to Killyleagh road.
Parkland/seaside course.
Pro Archie McCracken; Founded 1929
9 holes, 5590 yards, S.S.S. 67
Visitors: welcome; restrictions Wed and Sat.
Green Fees: WD £10; WE £15.
Societies: welcome WD except Mon; alternate Sun by prior arrangement; catering by prior arrangement; from £10.
Catering: by prior arrangement; no bar.
Hotels: Old Schoolhouse; Lisbarnet House.

11 54 Mallusk

City of Belfast Golf Course, Mal, Newtownabbey, Co. Antrim, BT36 2RF
☎(01232) 843799
From Belfast on A8 to Antrim; course just before Chimney Corner Hotel.
Parkland course.
Founded 1992.
9 holes, 4444 yards, S.S.S. 62
Visitors: welcome except Sat before 11.30am.
Green Fees: WD £6.29; WE £8.75.
Societies: welcome by prior arrangement.
Catering: none.
Hotels: Chimney Corner.

11 55 Malone Golf Club

240 Upper Malone Rd, Dunmurry, Belfast, BT17 9LB
☎(01232) 612695, Fax 431394, Pro 614917, Sec 612758, Bar/Rest 614916
5 miles from Belfast city centre
Parkland course.
Pro Michael McGee; Founded 1895/1962
Designed by Fred Hawtree/ Comdr. J Harris
18 holes, 6599 yards, S.S.S. 71
Visitors: welcome; start sheet operates Wed pm, Sat, Sun am.
Green Fees: WD £32; WE £32.
Societies: welcome Mon and Thurs by prior arrangement; catering packages by prior arrangement; also Edenderry course: 9 holes, 3160 yards, par 72; from £32.
Catering: full clubhouse catering and bar facilities.
Two practice grounds.
Hotels: Wellington Park; Beechlawn.

11 56 Massereene

51 Lough Rd, Antrim, Co Antrim, BT41 4DQ
☎(01849) 428096, Pro 464074
1 mile S of town; 3.5 miles from Aldergrove Airport.
Parkland course.
Pro Jim Smyth; Founded 1895
Designed by F.W. Hawtree
18 holes, 6559 yards, S.S.S. 71
Visitors: welcome WD and WE; Sat restrictions.
Green Fees: WD £20; WE £25.
Societies: welcome by prior arrangement; from £15.
Catering: full facilities.
Hotels: Dunadry; Deerpark.

11 57 Mount Ober

24 Ballymaconaghy, Knockbracken, Belfast BT8 4SB
☎(01232) 795666, Fax 705862, Pro 701648, Sec 401811, Bar/Rest 792100
Off Four Winds roundabout.
Parkland course.
Pro G Loughrey/S Rourke; Founded 1985
18 holes, 5391 yards, S.S.S. 68
Visitors: welcome except Sat.
Green Fees: WD £11.
Societies: welcome except Sat; catering packages; function rooms; 10% discount in pro shop; from £11.
Catering: full clubhouse facilities.
Practice range, floodlit bays.
Hotels: La Mon House; Stormont Hotel.

11 58 Mourne

36 Golf Links Rd, Newcastle, Co Down, BT33 0AN
☎(01396) 723889
Playing facilities at Royal Co Down.

11 59 Moyola Park

Shanemullagh, Castledawson, Magherafelt, Co Londonderry, BT45 8DG
☎(01648) 468468, Fax 468468, Pro 468830
Off the M2 Belfast-Coleraine road at Magherafelt roundabout.
Mature parkland course.
Pro Vivian Teague; Founded 1976
Designed by Don Patterson
18 holes, 6491 yards, S.S.S. 71
Visitors: welcome byarrangement.
Green Fees: WD £16; WE £25.
Societies: welcome by prior arrangement only; discounts available; packages by arrangement; from £16.
Catering: clubhouse facilities.

11 60 Newtownstewart

38 Golf Course Rd, Newtownstewart, Omagh, Co Tyrone, BT78 4HU
☎(016626) 61466, Sec 71487
2 miles SW of Newtonstewart on B84.
Parkland course.
Founded 1914
Designed by Frank Pennink
18 holes, 5341 yards, S.S.S. 69
Visitors: welcome.
Green Fees: WD £10; WE £15.
Societies: welcome if affiliated to the GUI; 25% discount on groups of 20 or more; catering packages by arrangement; from £10.
Catering: bar and restaurant facilities.
Practice range.
Hotels: Hunting Lodge Hotel; Chalets close to clubhouse.

11 61 Omagh

83a Dublin Rd, Omagh, Co Tyrone, BT78 1 HQ
☎(01662) 241442, Fax 241442, Bar/Rest 243160
On A5 on outskirts of Omagh.
Parkland course.
Founded 1910
18 holes, 5674 yards, S.S.S. 68
Visitors: welcome WD except Tues; WE with member.
Green Fees: WD £10; WE £10 with member.
Societies: welcome WD by prior arrangement.
Catering: clubhouse facilities.
Hotels: Royal Arms.

11 62 Ormeau

50 Park Rd, Belfast, BT7 2FX
☎(01232) 641069, Fax 640250, Pro
640999, Sec 640700, Bar/Rest
641999
Adjacent to Ormeau road alongside
Ravenhill Rd and Park Rd.
Parkland course.
Pro Bertie Wilson; Founded 1892
9 holes, 4862 yards, S.S.S. 65
Visitors: welcome.
Green Fees: WD £9; WE £11.
Societies: welcome mainly Thurs and
Sun; packages available; terms on
application.
Catering: full bar and catering facilities.
Hotels: Stormont Hotel.

11 63 Portadown

192 Gilford Rd, Portadown, Craigavon,
Co Armagh, BT63 5LF
☎(01762) 355356, Pro 334655,
Bar/Rest 352214
3 miles from Portadown on Gilford
road.
Parkland course.
Pro Paul Stevenson; Founded 1908
18 holes, 5649 yards, S.S.S. 70
Visitors: welcome by arrangement.
Green Fees: WD £17; WE £ 21.
Societies: welcome by prior written
arrangement; catering packages by
prior arrangement; snooker; squash;
from £16.
Catering: bar and restaurant facilities.
Hotels: Seagoe; Bonnview.

11 64 Portstewart

117 Strand Rd, Portstewart, Co
Londonderry, BT55 7PG
☎(01265) 832015, Pro 832601
4 miles W of Portrush.
Links course.
Pro Alan Hunter; Founded 1894
18 holes, 6779 yards, S.S.S. 73
Visitors: welcome WD on application.
Green Fees: WD £40; WE £35.60.
Societies: welcome WD by prior
booking; also 9-hole course: 5124
yards, par 64, S.S.S. 64 .
Catering: full facilities in season.
Hotels: Edgewater.

11 65 Radisson Roe Park Hotel

Roe Park, Limavady, Co Derry, BT49
9LB
☎(015047) 22222
On the A2 Londonderry-Limavady
road 16 miles from Londonderry.
Parkland course.

Pro Seamus Duffy; Founded 1993
18 holes, 6309 yards, S.S.S. 71
Visitors: welcome.
Green Fees: WD £20; WE £20.
Societies: welcome by prior arrangement; catering packages available;
from £15.
Catering: restaurant and bar facilities.
Practice range, 10 covered floodlit
bays.
Hotels: Radisson Roe Park Hotel on
site.

11 66 Rathmore

Bushmills Rd, Portrush
☎(01265) 822996
Playing facilities at Royal Portrush;
Founded 1947

11 67 Ringdufferin

Ringdufferin Rd, Toye, Killyleagh, CO
Down, BT30 9PH
☎(01396) 828812, Fax 828812
2 miles N of Killyleagh on the Comber
road.
Parkland course.
Founded 1992
Designed by F Ainsworth
9 holes, 5136 yards, S.S.S. 66
Visitors: welcome.
Green Fees: WD £10; WE £10.
Societies: welcome; catering by
arrangement; from £9.
Catering: clubhouse facilities.
Hotels: Dufferin Arms.

11 68 Royal Belfast

11 Station Rd, Craigavad, Holywood,
Co Down, BT18 0BP
☎(01232) 428165, Fax 421404, Pro
428586, Bar/Rest 428307
2 miles E of Holywood on A2.
Parkland course.
Pro Chris Spence; Founded 1881
Designed by H.C. Colt/ Donald Steel
(1988)
18 holes, 6306 yards, S.S.S. 71
Visitors: welcome except Wed or Sat
before 4.30pm; h'cap certs required.
Green Fees: WD £30; WE £40.
Societies: welcome by arrangement.
Catering: full facilities.
Hotels: Culloden.

11 69 Royal County Down

Newcastle, BT33 0AN, Co Down
☎(013967) 23314, Fax 26281, Pro
22419
On A24 30 miles S of Belfast.
Links course.
Pro Kevan Whitson; Founded 1889

Designed by Tom Morris Senior
18 holes, 7037 yards, S.S.S. 73
Visitors: welcome WD except Wed;
other days by prior arrangement.
Green Fees: WD £60; WE £70.
Societies: welcome by prior arrangement with Sec; day tickets (WD £90,
WE £100); also 18-hole Annesley
Links course; from £60.
Catering: full clubhouse facilities.
Hotels: Slieve Donard; Burrendale;
Brook Cottage; Glassdrumman Lodge.

11 70 Royal Portrush

Bushmills Rd, Portrush, Co Antrim,
BT56 8JR
☎(01265) 822311, Fax 823139, Pro
823335
1 mile from Portrush off A1.
Championship links; 1951 Open
course.
Pro Dai Stevenson; Founded 1888
Designed by H.S. Colt
18 holes, 6818 yards, S.S.S. 73
Visitors: welcome WD between
9.10am-11.50am and except Wed and
Fri after 2pm; restrictions at WE.
Green Fees: WD £55; WE £65.
Societies: none.
Catering: clubhouse redevelopment in
1998 restricts availability; local hotels
can provide meals.
Two practice grounds.
Hotels: club can provide list.

11 71 Scrabo

233 Scrabo Rd, Newtownards, Co
Down, BT23 4SL
☎(01247) 812355, Pro 817848, Sec
816516
Off A20 10 miles E of Belfast; near
Scrabo Tower.
Hilly parkland course.
Pro Paul McCrystal; Founded 1907
18 holes, 5699 yards, S.S.S. 71
Visitors: welcome WD except Wed.
Green Fees: WD £15; WE £20.
Societies: welcome anyday except
Sat; not in June; from £13.
Catering: full bar and restaurant.
Hotels: Strangford Arms; George; La
Mon House.

11 72 Shandon Park

73 Shandon Park, Belfast,, BT5 6NY
☎(01232) 793730, Fax 402773, Pro
797859, Sec 401856
3 miles from city centre via Knock dual
carriageway.
Parkland course.
Pro Barry Wilson; Founded 1926
Designed by Brian Carson

18 holes, 6282 yards, S.S.S. 70
Visitors: welcome WD and Sun.
Green Fees: WD £22; WE £27.
Societies: welcome Mon and Fri only by prior arrangement; reductions for groups of more than 24 and 40.
Catering: meals and bar snacks.
Hotels: Stormont.

11 73 **Silverwood**
Tormoyra Lane, Silverwood, Lurgan, Co Armagh, BT66 6NG
☎(01762) 326606
Playing facilities at Craigavon.
Founded 1984

11 74 **Spa**
20 Grove Rd, Ballynahinch, Co Down, BT24 8PN
☎(01238) 562365, Fax 564158
0.5 miles from Ballynahinch; 11 miles S of Belfast.
Wooded parkland course.
Founded 1907/1987
Designed by F Ainsworth
18 holes, 6003 yards, S.S.S. 72
Visitors: welcome except Sat.
Green Fees: WD £15; WE £20.
Societies: welcome except Sat; discounts for parties of more than 16; 10% reduction for groups of more than 30; catering packages by arrangement; from £15.
Catering: full clubhouse facilities.
Hotels: White Horse; Millbrook.

11 75 **Strabane**
Ballycolman, Strabane, Co Tyrone, BT82 9PH
☎(01504) 382007, Fax 382007, Bar/Rest 382271
1 mile from Strabane on Dublin road beside church and schools.

Parkland course.
Founded 1908
Designed by Eddie Hackett
18 holes, 5854 yards, S.S.S. 69
Visitors: welcome WD; WE by prior arrangement.
Green Fees: WD £12; WE £14.
Societies: wecome by arrangement with Sec.
Catering: fll facilities.
Hotels: Fir Trees Lodge.

11 76 **Tandragee**
Market Hill Rd, Tandragee, Co Armagh, BT62 2ER
☎(01762) 840727, Fax 840664, Pro 841761, Sec 841272, Bar/Rest 841763
On B3 in Tandragee.
Parkland course.
Founded 1922
Designed by F. Hawtree
18 holes, 5747 yards, S.S.S. 69
Visitors: welcome WD 10.30am-2pm and WE after 3pm.
Green Fees: WD £15; WE £20.
Societies: welcome by prior arrangement; catering by prior arrangement; from £15.
Catering: full bar and restaurant facilities.
Hotels: Carngrove; Seagoe; Bannview.

11 77 **Temple**
60 Church Rd, Boardmills, Lisburn, Co Down, BT27 6UP
☎(01846) 639213, Fax 638637
On main Ballynahinch road out of Belfast.
Parkland course.
Pro Joe McBride; Founded 1994
9 holes, 5451 yards, S.S.S. 66
Visitors: welcome except Sat am in summer.

Green Fees: WD £10; WE £14.
Societies: welcome by arrangement; from £16.
Catering: full facilities.
Hotels: Ivanhoe; Millbrook.

11 78 **Warrenpoint**
Lower Dromore Rd, Warrenpoint, Co Down, BT34 3LN
☎(016937) 53695, Fax 52918, Pro 52371
5 miles from Newry on Warrenpoint road.
Parkland course.
Pro Nigel Shaw; Founded 1893
18 holes, 6161 yards, S.S.S. 70
Visitors: welcome by prior arrangement.
Green Fees: WD £20; WE £27.
Societies: welcome by prior arrangement.
Catering: full facilities.
Hotels: Canal Court, Newry.

11 79 McCrae's Brae, Whitehead, Co Antrim, BT38 9NZ
☎(01960) 353792, Fax 353631, Pro 353118, Sec 353631
On the Co Antrim coast between Larne and Carrickfergus.
Parkland course.
Pro Colin Farr; Founded 1904/1975
Designed by A B Armstrong
18 holes, 6080 yards, S.S.S. 69
Visitors: welcome WD; WE with a member.
Green Fees: WD £12; WE £18.
Societies: welcome WD and Sun 10.30am-12 noon by prior arrangement; catering by prior arrangement; from £12
Catering: full clubhouse facilities.
Hotels: Coast Road; Magheramorne.

12

REPUBLIC OF IRELAND

The golf on the west coast of Ireland has now become so popular that the names of the great courses trip off the tongue as readily as those in Scotland. Ballybunion, Waterville, Killarney, and Tralee has become an established foursome for the golfing tourist, and one that every player should experience at least once. As Peter Dobereiner once wrote, no player is qualified to talk about golf courses until he has been to Kerry because he has not experienced the upper range of quality.

But what about the lesser known east coast? True, Portmarnock is established and Druid's Glen has achieved deserved fame through its recent staging of the Irish Open. Outside these two, however, there are other gems that any golfer should be happy to welcome on to an itinerary.

The east coast starts, of course, with the benefit of being much more accessible. Flights are now cheap and plentiful to Dublin and the courses mentioned here are all within an hour's drive of the airport, or the car ferry port Dun Laoghaire.

The European is situated to the south of Dublin in Brittas Bay, Wicklow, and is a modern links with a lovely story to boot. It was conceived, designed, nurtured and continues to be owned by a grand man called Pat Ruddy. At a time when Mount Juliet and the K Club were being built at a cost in the region of £30 million apiece, Ruddy was constructing his course at a fraction of the price.

True, there is no lavish clubhouse, or five-star hotel. But if you like your golfing welcome to be unpretentious and friendly, this is about as good as it gets. And whisper it quietly. The course, as well, is better than either of the aforementioned. Four holes on the back nine run hard against the sea and on a clear sunny day are as spectacular as the sea holes at Turnberry, or indeed anywhere else.

Now, I can hear you remark: what do you mean a clear, sunny day? Do they have such things in Ireland? Yes they do, sir, and here is another reason for visiting the east coast – it is far drier than the west. Two years ago, the European saw rain on just one day out of 120.

The Links at Portmarnock is not to be confused with the course that has long been considered, and rightly so, among Ireland's finest. This is another new links, albeit one that was built on a much more lavish budget than Ruddy's. Its start is plain and ordinary, rather like that at Ballybunion, and after five holes you're wondering what the fuss is about. Then it opens out, the fairways are dune-lined, the sea is audible, and suddenly you're fully in agreement with bores like me who think the only true golf is links golf.

North of Dublin is County Louth, or Baltray as it is often called, and it is geographically the middle member of the formidable trinity of traditional links courses on this coast with Royal County Down to the north and Portmarnock to the south.

It is not as famous as either, which is odd. Its views are magnificent and its holes challenging, calling for every shot a golfer can possess. The greens are considered among the best in Ireland and the four short holes are not far behind, with each played from a different direction.

There are five par fives which can provide sanctuary, not to mention the note of delightful non-conformity that is often to be found on old links courses. And a splendid idea too: Lord save us from architects who think courses somehow incomplete if they don't feature four par fives, four par threes and 10 par fours!

12 1 Abbeyleix
Stradbally Rd, Abbeyleix, Co Laois
☎(0502) 31450, Sec 31051
0.5 miles off Main Street.
Parkland course; Founded 1895
9 holes, 5626 yards, S.S.S. 68
Visitors: welcome.
Green Fees: WD £8; WE £10.
Societies: welcome.
Hotels: Hibernian; Killeshin;
Montague; Globe House.

12 2 Achill Island
Keel, Achill, Co Mayo
☎(098) 43456
Via Castlebar or Westport.
Seaside course.
Founded 1952
Designed by P. Skerrit
9 holes, 5378 yards, S.S.S. 66
Visitors: welcome.
Green Fees: WD £5; WE £5.
Catering: full clubhouse facilities
available.
Hotels: Atlantic; McDowalls;
Slievemore; Strand; Gray's GH.

12 3 Adare Golf Club
Adare Manor, Adare, Co Limerick
☎(061) 395044, Fax 396987, Sec
396204
10 miles from Limerick on the Killarney
Road.
Parkland course built round castle/fri-
ary ruins.
Founded 1995
Designed by Robert Trent Jones, Sr.
18 holes, 7138 yards, S.S.S. 69
Visitors: welcome WE with member
or prior arrangement.
Green Fees: WD £30.
Societies: welcome by prior arrange-
ment; catering packages can be
arranged; terms on application.
Catering: clubhouse facilities avail-
able.
Hotels: Dunranen Arms; Woodlands.

12 4 Ardee
Town Parks, Ardee, Co Louth,
☎(041) 53227, Fax 56137, Bar/Rest
56283
0.25 miles N of town on Mullinstown
Road.
Parkland course.
Founded 1911
Designed by Eddie Hackett
18 holes, 5500 yards, S.S.S. 69
Visitors: welcome WD.
Green Fees: WD £15.
Societies: welcome Mon-Sat by prior
arrangement.
Catering: full facilities available.

12 5 Arklow
Abbeylands, Arklow, Co Wicklow
☎(0402) 32492, Fax 32492, Sec
32971
Signposted from town centre after
turning at bridge.
Links course.
Founded 1927
Designed by Hawtree & Taylor
18 holes, 5604 yards, S.S.S. 69
Visitors: welcome by arrangement
Green Fees: WD £ 18; WE £ 18
Societies: welcome by prior arrange-
ment; welcome WD and Sat morning;
deposit of £75 required; catering pack-
ages; from £18.
Catering: bar and restaurant facilities.
Practice range; practice bunkers and
nets.
Hotels: Arklow Bay.

12 6 Ashbourne
Archerstown, Ashbourne, Co Meath
☎(01) 8352005, Fax 8352005,
Bar/Rest 8352562
On N2 12 miles from Dublin.
Parkland course with water features.
Pro John Dwyer; Founded 1994
Designed by Des Smyth
18 holes, 5872 yards, S.S.S. 70
Visitors: welcome.
Green Fees: WD £17; WE £20.
Societies: welcome WD; golf and
catering packages available; terms on
application.
Catering: full bar and restaurant ser-
vice.
Practice area.
Hotels: Ashbourne House.

12 7 Ashford Castle
Cong, Co Mayo
☎(092) 46003
27 miles N of Galway on shores of
Lough Corrib.
Parkland course.
Founded 1972
Designed by Eddie Hackett
9 holes, 4506 yards, S.S.S. 70
Visitors: welcome.
Green Fees: WD £15; WE £15.
Societies: welcome by prior arrange-
ment.
Catering: bar facilities.
Hotels: Ashford Castle; packages
available.

12 8 Athenry
Palmerstown, Oranmore, Co Galway
☎(091) 94466, Sec 751405
5 miles from Athenry on N6 Galway-
Dublin road.
Parkland course.
Founded 1902
Designed by Eddie Hackett
18 holes, 5552 yards, S.S.S. 69
Visitors: welcome except Sun.
Green Fees: WD £12; WE £12.
Societies: welcome by prior arrange-
ment.
Catering: full bar and catering facili-
ties.

12 9 Athlone
Hodson Bay, Athlone, Co Roscommon
☎(0902) 92073, Fax 94080, Pro
92868, Bar/Rest 92235
3 miles N of Athlone on the
Roscommon Road.
Parkland course; all Ireland finals
course 1998.
Pro Martin Quinn; Founded 1892
Designed by J McAllister
18 holes, 5935 yards, S.S.S. 71
Visitors: welcome; some restrictions
Tues and Sun.
Green Fees: WD £15; WE £18.
Societies: welcome by prior arrange-
ment; discount for groups of more than
40; catering packages available; terms
on application.
Catering: full clubhouse facilities.
Hotels: Hodson Bay; Prince of Wales;
Shamrock; Royal Hoey.

12 10 Athy
Geraldine, Athy, Co Kildare
☎(0507) 31729, Bar/Rest 31464
On T6 2 miles N of Athy.
Undulating parkland course.
Founded 1906
18 holes, 5500 yards, S.S.S. 69
Visitors: welcome WD.
Green Fees: terms on application.
Societies: welcome Sat mornings.
Catering: by arrangement with the
steward.

12 11 Balbriggan
Blackhall, Balbriggan, Co Dublin
☎(01) 8412173, Fax 8413927, Sec
8412229
0.75 miles S of Balbriggan on the N1
Dublin-Belfast Road.
Parkland course.
Founded 1945
Designed by R. Stilwell, J. Paramour
18 holes, 5922 yards, S.S.S. 71
Visitors: welcome WD except Tues.
Green Fees: WD £15.
Societies: welcome by prior arrange-
ment with Sec; discounts for more
than 30 players; from £16.
Catering: full clubhouse facilities.

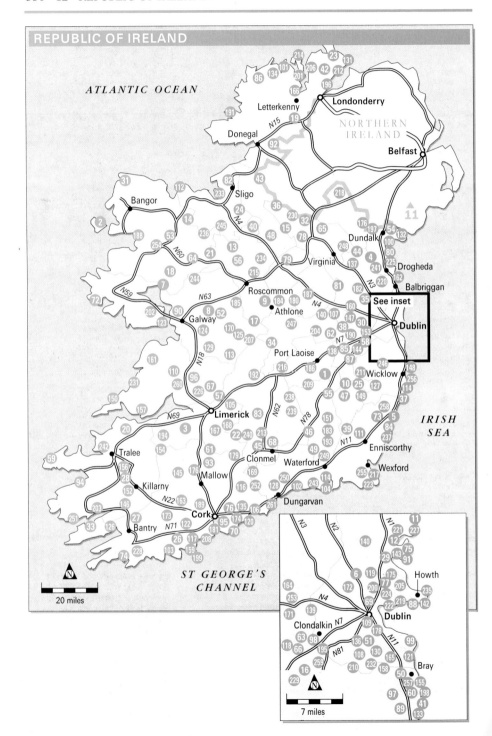

REPUBLIC OF IRELAND

ATLANTIC OCEAN

Londonderry

Letterkenny

NORTHERN IRELAND

Donegal

Belfast

Sligo

Bangor

Dundalk

Drogheda

Balbriggan

Virginia

Roscommon

Athlone

See inset

Dublin

Galway

Port Laoise

Wicklow

Limerick

Tralee

Clonmel

Waterford

Enniscorthy

Mallow

Killarny

Dungarvan

Wexford

IRISH SEA

Cork

Bantry

ST GEORGE'S CHANNEL

20 miles

Clondalkin

Howth

Dublin

Bray

7 miles

KEY

1. Abbeyleix
2. Achill Island
3. Adare Golf Club
4. Ardee
5. Arklow
6. Ashbourne
7. Ashford Castle
8. Athenry
9. Athlone
10. Athy
11. Balbriggan
12. Balcarrick
13. Ballaghaderreen
14. Ballina
15. Ballinamore
16. Ballinascorney
17. Ballinasloe
18. Ballinrobe
19. Ballybofey & Stranorlar
20. Ballybunion
21. Ballyhaunis
22. Ballykisteen Golf & Country Club
23. Ballyliffin
24. Ballymote
25. Baltinglass
26. Bandon
27. Bantry Bay
28. Beaufort
29. Beaverstown
30. Beech Park
31. Belmullet
32. Belturbet
33. Berehaven
34. Birr
35. The Black Bush
36. Blacklion
37. Blainroe
38. Bodenstown
39. Borris
40. Boyle
41. Bray
42. Buncrana
43. Bundoran
44. Cabra Castle
45. Cahir Park
46. Callan
47. Carlow
48. Carrickmines
49. Carrick-on-Shannon
50. Carrick-on-Suir
51. Castle
52. Castle Barna
53. Castlebar
54. Castleblayney
55. Castlecomer
56. Castlerea
57. Castletroy
58. Castlewarden Golf & Country Club
59. Ceann Sibeal (Dingle)
60. Charlesland
61. Charleville
62. Cill Dara
63. Clane
64. Claremorris
65. Clones
66. Clongowes
67. Clonlara
68. Clonmel
69. Clontarf
70. Cobh
71. Coldwinters
72. Connemara
73. Coollattin
74. Coosheen
75. Corballis
76. Cork
77. Corrstown
78. County Cavan
79. County Longford
80. County Louth
81. County Meath (Trim)
82. County Sligo
83. County Tipperary Golf & Country Club
84. Courtown
85. Craddockstown
86. Cruit Island
87. Curragh
88. Deer Park Hotel
89. Delgany
90. Delvin Castle
91. Donabate
92. Donegal
93. Doneraile
94. Dooks
95. Douglas
96. Dromoland Castle
97. Druids Glen
98. Dublin Mountain
99. Dun Laoghaire
100. Dundalk
101. Dunfanaghy
102. Dungarvan
103. Dunmore
104. Dunmore East Golf & Country Club
105. East Clare
106. East Cork
107. Edenderry
108. Edmondstown
109. Elm Park
110. Ennis
111. Enniscorthy
112. Enniscrone
113. Esker Hills Golf & Country Club
114. The European Club
115. Faithlegg
116. Fermoy
117. Fernhill
118. Finnstown Fairways
119. Forrest Little
120. Fota Island
121. Foxrock
122. Frankfield
123. Galway
124. Galway Bay Golf & Country Club
125. Glasson G & CC
126. Glengarriff
127. Glenmalure
128. Gold Coast Golf and Leisure
129. Gort
130. Grange
131. Greencastle
132. Greenore
133. Greystones
134. Gweedore
135. Harbour Point
136. Hazel Grove
137. Headfort
138. Heath
139. Hermitage
140. Highfield
141. Hollywood Lakes
142. Howth
143. The Island Golf Club
144. The K Club
145. Kanturk
146. Kenmare
147. Kilcock
148. Kilcoole
149. Kilkea Castle
150. Kilkee
151. Kilkenny
152. Killarney Golf Club
153. Killeen
154. Killeline
155. Killiney
156. Kilorglin
157. Kilrush
158. Kilternan Golf & Country Club
159. Kinsale
160. Knockanally Golf & Country Club
161. Lahinch Golf Club
162. Laytown & Bettystown
163. Lee Valley
164. Leixlip
165. Leopardstown Golf Centre
166. Letterkenny
167. Limerick
168. Limerick County Golf & Country Club
169. Lismore
170. Loughrea
171. Lucan
172. Luttrellstown Castle
173. Macroom
174. Mahon
175. Malahide
176. Mallow
177. Mannan Castle
178. Milltown
179. Mitchelstown
180. Moate
181. Monkstown
182. Moor Park
183. Mount Juliet
184. Mount Temple
185. Mountbellew
186. Mountrath
187. Mullingar
188. Mulranny
189. Muskerry
190. Naas
191. Narin & Portnoo
192. Nenagh
193. New Ross
194. Newcastle West
195. Newlands
196. North West
197. Nuremore
198. Old Conna
199. Old Head Links
200. The Open Golf Centre
201. Otway
202. Oughterard
203. Parknasilla
204. Portarlington
205. Portmarnock Golf Club
206. Portsalon
207. Portumna
208. Raffeen Creek
209. Rathdowney
210. Rathfarnham
211. Rathsallagh House
212. Redcastle
213. Rockwell
214. Rosapenna
215. Roscommon
216. Roscrea
217. Rosslare
218. Rossmore
219. Royal Dublin Golf Club
220. Royal Tara Golf Club
221. Rush
222. St Annes
223. St Helen's Bay
224. St Margaret's Golf & Country Club
225. Seapoint
226. Shannon
227. Skerries
228. Skibbereen & West Cabbery
229. Slade Valley
230. Slieve Russell Golf & Country Club
231. Spanish Point
232. Stackstown
233. Strandhill
234. Strokestown
235. Sutton
236. Swinford
237. Tara Glen
238. Templemore
239. Thurles
240. Tipperary
241. Townley Hall
242. Tralee
243. Tramore
244. Tuam
245. Tubbercurry
246. Tulfarris Hotel & Country Club
247. Tullamore
248. Virginia
249. Waterford
250. Waterford Castle Golf & Country Club
251. Waterville Golf Links
252. West Waterford
253. Westmanstown
254. Westport
255. Wexford
256. Wicklow
257. Woodbrook
258. Woodenbridge
259. Woodlands
260. Woodstock
261. Youghal

12 12 Balcarrick

Corballis, Donabate, Co Dublin
☎(01) 8436957, Sec 8408260
Founded 1972
9 holes, 6362 yards, S.S.S. 73
Visitors: welcome.
Green Fees: WD £10; WE £15.

12 13 Ballaghaderreen

Aughalista, Ballaghaderreen, Co Roscommon
☎(0907) 60295, Sec 60717
3 miles from Ballaghaderreen.
Parkland course.
Founded 1937

9 holes, 5363 yards, S.S.S. 66
Visitors: welcome.
Green Fees: WD £6; WE £6.
Societies: welcome by prior arrangement.
Catering: bar and snack facilities.

12 14 Ballina

Mossgrove, Shanaghy, Ballina, Co Mayo
☎(096) 21050, Fax 21050
On the outskirts of Ballina on the Bonniconlon Road.
Parkland course.
Founded 1910

Designed by Eddie Hackett
9 holes, 6103 yards, S.S.S. 69
Visitors: welcome.
Green Fees: WD £12; WE £12.
Societies: welcome; reductions for groups of 12 or more; from £12.
Catering: full clubhouse facilities.
Hotels: Downhill; Bartra House.

12 15 Ballinamore

Creevy, Ballinamore, Co Leitrim
☎(078) 44346
1.5 miles NW of Ballinamore.
Parkland course.
Founded 1939

Designed by Arthur Spring
9 holes, 4782 yards, S.S.S. 66
Visitors: welcome.
Green Fees: WD £10; WE £10.
Societies: welcome; special deals depending on numbers; catering packages also available; terms on application.
Catering: bar and catering facilities.
Hotels: Commercial; McAllisters; Slieve-an-Iaraim.

12 16 **Ballinascorney**
Bohernabreena, Tallaght, Co Dublin
☎(01) 4512082
10 miles SW of Dublin.
Parkland course.
Founded 1971
18 holes, 5648 yards, S.S.S. 67
Visitors: welcome WD.
Green Fees: terms on application.
Catering: bar facilities.

12 17 **Ballinasloe**
Rossgloss, Ballinasloe, Co Galway
☎(0905) 42126, Fax 42538
2 miles off the N6 on the Portumna Road.
Parkland course.
Founded 1894
Designed by Eddie Connaughton
18 holes, 5865 yards, S.S.S. 70
Visitors: welcome Mon-Sat.
Green Fees: WD £14; WE £12.
Societies: welcome Mon-Sat; catering packages available; terms on application.
Catering: bar and restaurant facilities available.
Practice area.
Hotels: Haydens; East County; Gullanes.

12 18 **Ballinrobe**
Castlebar Road, Ballinrobe, Co Mayo
☎(092) 41448
30 miles from Galway.
Parkland course set in beautiful scenery.
Founded 1895
9 holes, 5540 yards, S.S.S. 68
Visitors: welcome; some restrictions Tues and Sun.
Green Fees: terms on application.
Societies: welcome WD by arrangement; catering packages by arrangement; fishing can be organised; terms on application.
Catering: bar and restaurant facilities available.
Hotels: Lakeland.

12 19 **Ballybofey & Stranorlar**
Stranorlar, Ballybofey, Co Donegal
☎(074) 31093
Signposted off Strabane-Balleybofey Road; 14 miles from Strabane.
Parkland course.
Founded 1957
Designed by P.C. Carr
18 holes, 5437 yards, S.S.S. 69
Visitors: welcome.
Green Fees: terms on application.
Societies: welcome by prior arrangement.
Catering: bar facilities; meals by arrangement.

12 20 **Ballybunion**
Sandhill Rd, Ballybunion, Co Kerry
☎(068) 27146, Fax 27387, Bar/Rest 27611
20 miles N of Tralee.
Traditional links course.
Pro Brian O'Callaghan; Founded 1893
Designed by Simpson McKenna
Old: 18 holes, 6593 yards, S.S.S. 72;
Cashen: 18 holes, 6216 yards, S.S.S. 72
Visitors: welcome WD; limited at WE.
Green Fees: WD £55, WE £55 (Old); WD £30; WE £30 (Cashen).
Societies: WD by arrangement; from £55; both courses £72.
Catering: full catering facilities.
Hotels: club can provide detailed list; some golf packages available.

12 21 **Ballyhaunis**
Coolnaha, Ballyhaunis, Co Mayo
☎(0907) 30014, Fax 81829
2 miles from Ballyhaunis on N83.
Parkland course.
Pro David Carney; Founded 1929
9 holes, 5413 yards, S.S.S. 68
Visitors: welcome Mon-Sat; with member Sun.
Green Fees: WD £10; WE £10.
Societies: welcome Mon-Sat by prior arrangement; reductions for groups of more than 20; from £10.
Catering: full catering facilities available.
Hotels: Cill Aodain; Belmont.

12 22 **Ballykisteen G & Country Club**
Ballykisteen, Co Tipperary
☎(062) 51439, Sec 52877
3 miles from Tipperary on the Limerick Road.
Parkland course.
Founded 1994
Designed by Des Smyth

18 holes, 6765 yards, S.S.S. 73
Visitors: welcome.
Green Fees: WD £15; WE £20.
Societies: welcome.
Catering: bar and restaurant.

12 23 **Ballyliffin**
Ballyliffin, Carndonagh P.O, Co Donegal
☎(077) 76119, Fax 76672, Sec 74417
8 miles from Buncrana.
Seaside links course.
Founded 1947
21 holes, 6384 yards, S.S.S. 72
Visitors: welcome.
Green Fees: WD £10; WE £15.
Societies: welcome by prior arrangement.
Catering: bar snacks and meals.

12 24 **Ballymote**
Carrigans, Ballymote, Co Sligo
☎(071) 83158, Bar/Rest 83089
Off N4 15 miles S of Sligo Town.
Parkland course.
Founded 1993
9 holes, 5302 yards, S.S.S. 65
Visitors: welcome.
Green Fees: WD £7; WE £7.
Societies: welcome; discount for groups of more than 20.
Catering: at local restaurant.
Hotels: Sligo Park; Tower Hotel, Sligo; Noreen Mullen GH; Eileen Cahill GH.

12 25 **Baltinglass**
Baltinglass, Co Wicklow
☎(0508) 81350, Sec 81514
40 miles S of Dublin.
Parkland course.
Founded 1928
Designed by Dr. W.G. Lyons, Hugh Dark and Col. Mitchell
9 holes, 5554 yards, S.S.S. 69
Visitors: welcome.
Green Fees: WD £10; WE £12.
Societies: three welcome per month; terms on application.
Catering: by arrangement.

12 26 **Bandon**
Castlebernard, Bandon, Co Cork
☎(023) 41111, Fax 44690, Pro 42224
2 miles W of Bandon.
Parkland course.
Pro Paddy O'Boyle; Founded 1909
18 holes, 5663 yards, S.S.S. 69
Visitors: welcome by prior arrangement.
Green Fees: WD £12; WE £15.

Societies: welcome between March and October on WD, except Wed, and Sat; catering packages available; from £10.
Catering: full bar and catering facilities.

12 27 Bantry Bay
Donemark, Bantry, Co Cork
☎(027) 50579, Fax 50579
2 km NW of Bantry on the Killarney Road.
Clifftop parkland course with views of Bantry Bay/Beara.
Pro Finbar Condon; Founded 1975
Designed by E Hackett & C O'Connor Jnr
18 holes, 5910 yards, S.S.S. 72
Visitors: welcome WD 8.30am-4.30pm; by arrangement WE and Bank Holidays.
Green Fees: WD £18; WE £20.
Societies: welcome by prior arrangement; catering packages available; from £12.
Catering: full catering facilities.
Hotels: West Lodge; Bantry Bay; Reendesert; Ballylickey Manor; Seaview.

12 28 Beaufort
Churchtown, Beaufort, Killarney, Co Kerry
☎(064) 44440, Fax 44752
7 miles W of Killarney off the N72.
Parkland course.
Pro Hugh Duggan; Founded 1995
Designed by Arthur Spring
18 holes, 6605 yards, S.S.S. 72
Visitors: welcome.
Green Fees: WD £25; WE £30.
Societies: welcome; discounts available for groups of more than 20 and more than 50; from £25.
Catering: full bar and catering.
Hotels: Europe; Great Southern; Dunloe Castle.

12 29 Beaverstown
Beaverstown, Donabate, Co Dublin
☎(01) 8436439
15 miles N of Dublin; 3 miles from Dublin Airport.
Parkland course.
Founded 1984
Designed by Eddie Hackett
18 holes, 5874 yards, S.S.S. 71
Visitors: welcome WD
Green Fees: WD £12; WE £20
Societies: welcome by prior arrangement; terms on application.
Catering: full facilities.

12 30 Beech Park
Johnstown, Rathcoole, Co Dublin
☎(01) 4580522, Fax 4588365, Bar/Rest 4580100
3km from Rathcoole village off the Naas dual carriageway.
Parkland course.
Founded 1974
Designed by Eddie Hackett
18 holes, 5762 yards, S.S.S. 70
Visitors: welcome Mon, Thurs and Fri.
Green Fees: WD £22.
Societies: welcome Mon, Thurs, Fri; catering packages available; from £19.
Catering: full bar and catering.
Hotels: Green Isle; City West; Bewleys; Ambassador.

12 31 Belmullet
Carne, Belmullet, Co Mayo
☎(097) 82292, Sec 81136
1.5 miles W of Belmullet.
Seaside links course.
Founded 1925
Designed by Eddie Hackett
18 holes, 6058 yards, S.S.S. 72
Visitors: welcome.
Green Fees: WD £15; WE £15.

12 32 Belturbet
Erne Hill, Belturbet, Co Cavan
☎(049) 22287, Sec 22498
0.5 miles on the Cavan Road from Belturbet.
Parkland course.
Founded 1950
9 holes, 5347 yards, S.S.S. 65
Visitors: welcome.
Green Fees: terms on application.
Societies: welcome by prior arrangement.
Catering: full facilities.

12 33 Berehaven
Millcove, Castletownbere, Co Cork
☎(027) 70700
On the main Castletownbere Road 20 miles W of Glengarriff.
Links course.
Founded 1993
9 holes, 4759 yards, S.S.S. 64
Visitors: welcome.
Green Fees: WD £10; WE £10.
Societies: on application; tennis fishing, swimming, sailing available.
Catering: clubhouse facilities.

12 34 Birr
The Glenns, Birr, Co Offaly
☎(0509) 20082, Pro 21606, Sec 20092

2.5 miles W of Birr on the Banagher Road.
Parkland course.
Founded 1893
18 holes, 5748 yards, S.S.S. 70
Visitors: welcome; booking essential at WE.
Green Fees: WD £12; WE £15.
Societies: welcome by prior arrangement; discounts available depending on numbers; catering packages available; terms on application.
Catering: full catering facilities.
Hotels: Dooleys; County.

12 35 The Black Bush
Thomastown, Dunshaughlin, Co Meath
☎(01) 8250021, Fax 8250400
0.5 miles E of Dunshaughlin on Ratoath Road.
Parkland course.
Founded 1987
Designed by Robert Brown
18 holes, 6360 yards
Visitors: welcome.
Green Fees: WD on application
Societies: welcome WD; catering packages available; also 9-hole course; terms on application.
Catering: full catering facilities.
Practice range.

12 36 Blacklion
Toam, Blacklion, Co Cavan
☎(072) 53024
Off the Sligo-Enniskillen Road at Blacklion.
Parkland course.
Founded 1962
Designed by Eddie Hackett
9 holes, 5605 yards, S.S.S. 69
Visitors: welcome.
Green Fees: WD £8; WE £10.
Societies: welcome by arrangement.
Catering: full facilities.

12 37 Blainroe
Blainroe, Co Wicklow
☎(0404) 68168, Fax 69369, Sec 67022
3 miles S of Wicklow on coast Road.
Seaside course.
Founded 1978
Designed by Hawtree & Sons
18 holes, 6171 yards, S.S.S. 72
Visitors: welcome by prior arrangement.
Green Fees: WD £18; WE £25.
Societies: welcome by prior arrangement; catering packages available.
Catering: full clubhouse facilities.

12 38 Bodenstown
Bodenstown, Sallins, Co Kildare
☎(045) 97096
5 miles N of Naas.
Parkland course.
Founded 1973
36 holes, 6321 yards, S.S.S. 73
Visitors: welcome; members only on
Old course at WE.
Green Fees: WD £10; WE £10.
Societies: welcome by prior arrangement.
Catering: full catering facilities.

12 39 Borris
Deer Park, Borris, Co Carlow
☎(0503) 73143
16 miles from Carlow off the Dublin
Road.
Parkland course.
Founded 1902
9 holes, 5596 yards, S.S.S. 69
Visitors: welcome.
Green Fees: WD £12; WE £12.
Societies: welcome; terms on application.
Catering: bar and catering facilities
available.
Hotels: Lord Bagenal; Seven Oaks;
Newpark.

12 40 Boyle
Knockadoo Brusna, Boyle, Co
Roscommon
☎(079) 62594, Sec 62192
2 miles S of Boyle on the N61
Roscommon Road.
Parkland course.
Founded 1911/1972
Designed by Eddie Hackett
9 holes, 4914 yards, S.S.S. 66
Visitors: welcome.
Green Fees: WD £8; WE £8.
Societies: welcome by prior arrangement; discounts and catering packages available; from £8.
Catering: full bar and catering facilities.
Hotels: Forest Park; Royal.

12 41 Bray
Ravenswell Rd, Bray, Co Wicklow
☎(01) 2862484, Sec 2888435
Off the L29 from Dublin.
Parkland course.
Founded 1897
9 holes, 5782 yards, S.S.S. 70
Visitors: welcome WD except Mon.
Green Fees: WD £17.
Societies: welcome by prior arrangement; must be affiliated to GUI.
Catering: limited facilities.

12 42 Buncrana
Buncrana, Co Donegal,
☎(077) 62279
Parkland course.
9 holes, 4250 yards, S.S.S. 62
Visitors: welcome.
Green Fees: WD £6; WE £6.

12 43 Bundoran
Great Northern Hotel, Bundoran, Co
Donegal
☎(072) 41302, Fax 42014
22 miles N of Sligo.
Links/parkland course.
Pro David Robinson; Founded 1894
Designed by Harry Vardon
18 holes, 5599 yards, S.S.S. 70
Visitors: welcome by arrangement.
Green Fees: WD £16; WE £18.
Societies: welcome by prior arrangement.
Catering: limited on course to snacks;
hotel on site for meals.
Hotels: Great Northern on course;
Holyrood; Addingham; Fox's Lair;
Marlborough; Atlantic.

12 44 Cabra Castle
Kingscourt, Co Cavan
☎(042) 67030
6 miles S of Carrickmoss.
Parkland course.
Founded 1977
9 holes, 5308 yards, S.S.S. 68
Visitors: welcome; only with a member on Sun.
Green Fees: terms on application.
Societies: welcome by prior arrangement except Sun.
Catering: full facilities.

12 45 Cahir Park
Kilcommon, Cahir, Co Tipperary
☎(052) 41474, Sec 41601
1 mile S of Cahir on Clogheen Road.
Parkland course.
Founded 1965
Designed by Eddie Hackett
9 holes, 5446 yards, S.S.S. 69
Visitors: welcome; by prior arrangement at WE.
Green Fees: WD £10; WE £10.
Societies: welcome on Sat by prior
arrangement; catering packages can
be arranged with 72 hours notice;
terms on application.
Catering: bar facilities.

12 46 Callan
Geraldine, Callan, Co Kilkenny
☎(056) 25136, Bar/Rest 54362
10 miles S of Kilkenny; 0.5 miles from
Callan.
Parkland course.
Founded 1929
Designed by Des Smyth
9 holes, 5722 yards, S.S.S. 68
Visitors: welcome.
Green Fees: terms on application.
Societies: welcome WD and Sat am.
Catering: bar facilities.

12 47 Carlow
Deerpark, Dublin Rd, Carlow, Co
Carlow
☎(0503) 31695, Fax 40065, Pro
41745, Sec 31353
1 mile from Carlow station off Naas to
Dublin Road.
Undulating parkland.
Founded 1899
Designed by Tom Simpson
18 holes, 5844 yards, S.S.S. 71
Visitors: welcome.
Green Fees: WD £20; WE £25.
Societies: welcome WD by prior
arrangement.
Catering: full catering facilities.

12 48 Carrick-on-Shannon
Woodbrook, Carrick-on-Shannon, Co
Roscommon
☎(079) 67015
3 miles W of Carrick on N4.
Parkland course.
Founded 1910
Designed by Eddie Hackett
9 holes, 5545 yards, S.S.S. 68
Visitors: welcome.
Green Fees: WD £10; WE £10.
Societies: welcome by prior arrangement with Sec.
Catering: full bar and catering facilities.

12 49 Carrick-on-Suir
Garravoone, Carrick-on-Suir, Co
Tipperary
☎(051) 640047, Fax 640558, Sec
640558
15 miles from Waterford.
Parkland course.
Founded 1939
Designed by Edward Hackett
18 holes, 6061 yards, S.S.S. 71
Visitors: welcome except before 1pm
Sun.
Green Fees: WD £12; WE £14.
Societies: welcome; catering packages; private rooms; group discounts;
from £12.
Catering: full catering facilities.
Hotels: Carraig.

12 50 Carrickmines

Golf Lane, Carrickmines, Dublin 18
☎(01) 2955972
8 miles S of Dublin.
Heath/parkland course.
Founded 1900
9 holes, 6103 yards, S.S.S. 69
Visitors: welcome except Wed and Sat.
Green Fees: WD £20; WE £20.
Societies: none.
Catering: limited.

12 51 Castle

Woodside Drive, Rathfarnham, Dublin
☎(01) 4904207, Fax 4920264
Turn left after Terenure and take 2nd right.
Parkland course.
Founded 1913
Designed by H.S. Colt
18 holes, 5653 yards, S.S.S. 69
Visitors: welcome WD.
Green Fees: WD £25.
Societies: welcome by prior arrangement only.
Catering: full facilities.

12 52 Castle Barna

Daingean, Co Offaly
☎(0506) 53384, Fax 53077
7 miles S of N6 at Tyrellspass.
Parkland course.
Founded 1996
Designed by A Duggan
18 holes, 6200 yards, S.S.S. 72
Visitors: welcome; restrictions Sun am.
Green Fees: WD £7; WE £9.
Societies: welcome by arrangement.
Catering: coffee shop.

12 53 Castlebar

Rocklands, Castlebar, Co Mayo
☎(094) 21649
1.25 miles from town centre.
Parkland course.
Founded 1910
18 holes, 5698 yards, S.S.S. 70
Visitors: welcome WD.
Green Fees: WD £12; WE £15.
Societies: welcome by prior arrangement.
Catering: by arrangement.

12 54 Castleblayney

Onomy, Castleblayney, Co Monaghan
☎(042)
Almost in Castleblayney town centre.
Parkland course.
Founded 1984

Designed by Bobby Browne
9 holes, 4923 yards, S.S.S. 66
Visitors: welcome.
Green Fees: WD £5; WE £8.
Societies: welcome by prior arrangement.
Catering: full facilities.
Hotels: Glencarn; Central.

12 55 Castlecomer

Drumgoole, Castlecomer, Co Kilkenny
☎(056) 41139
On N7 10 miles N of Kilkenny.
Parkland course.
Founded 1935
Designed by Pat Ruddy
9 holes, 5923 yards, S.S.S. 71
Visitors: welcome Mon-Sat by prior arrangement.
Green Fees: WD £8; WE £10.
Societies: welcome except Sun.
Catering: by arrangement.

12 56 Castlerea

Clonalis, Castlerea, Co Roscommon
☎(0907) 20068
On main Dublin-Castlebar Road.
Parkland course.
Founded 1905
9 holes, 4974 yards, S.S.S. 66
Visitors: welcome.
Green Fees: terms on application.
Societies: welcome by prior arrangement; catering packages by arrangement.

12 57 Castletroy

Castletroy, Co Limerick
☎(061) 335753, Fax 335753, Pro 330450, Bar/Rest 335261
3 miles from Limerick on N7.
Parkland course.
Pro Kevin Bennis; Founded 1937
18 holes, 5793 yards, S.S.S. 71
Visitors: welcome by prior arrangement.
Green Fees: WD £22; WE £22.
Societies: welcome by prior arrangement; £15.
Catering: full catering facilities.
Hotels: Castletroy Park; Kilmurry Lodge.

12 58 Castlewarden Golf & Country Club

Castlewarden, Straffan, Co Kildare
☎(01) 4589254, Fax 458924, Pro 4588219
Between Rathcoole and Kill.
Moorland course.
Founded 1989

Designed by Tommy Halpin;
Redesigned By R.J. Browne (1992)
18 holes, 6008 yards, S.S.S. 71
Visitors: welcome Mon, Thurs, Fri WE with member.
Green Fees: WD £12.
Societies: welcome Mon, Thurs, Fri and some Sat mornings.
Catering: full facilities.
Practice area.

12 59 Ceann Sibeal (Dingle)

Ballyougheragh, Tralee, Co Kerry
☎(066) 56225, Fax 56409, Sec 56408
1.5 miles from Ballyferriter.
Traditional links course.
Pro Dermot O'Connor; Founded 1924
Designed by Eddie Hackett (72)/Christy O'Connor (88)
18 holes, 6690 yards, S.S.S. 71
Visitors: welcome.
Green Fees: WD £21; WE £21.
Societies: welcome; catering packages by arrangement; day ticket £27; from £21.
Catering: full bar and restaurant service.
Hotels: Skellig; Benners.

12 60 Charlesland

Charlesland, Greystones, Co Wicklow
☎(01) 2874350, Fax 2874360, Bar/Rest 2876764
Off the N11 Dublin-Wexford Road at Delgarny turning.
Parkland course.
Pro Paul Heeney; Founded 1992
Designed by E Hackett
18 holes, 6739 yards, S.S.S. 72
Visitors: welcome.
Green Fees: WD £23; WE £28.
Societies: welcome by prior arrangement; discounts for groups of 20 or more; terms on application.
Catering: full facilities.
Hotels: La Touche; Charlesland.

12 61 Charleville

Smiths Rd, Ardmore, Charleville, Co Cork
☎(063) 81257
On main road from Cork to Limerick.
Parkland course.
Founded 1909
18 holes, 6430 yards, S.S.S. 70
Visitors: welcome by prior arrangement.
Green Fees: terms on application.
Societies: welcome except Sun by prior arrangement.
Catering: bar and restaurant service.

12 62 Cill Dara

Kildare, Co Kildare
☎(045) 21433
1 mile E of Kildaire.
Moorland course.
Founded 1920
9 holes, 5738 yards, S.S.S. 70
Visitors: welcome.
Green Fees: terms on application.
Societies: welcome by prior arrangement; catering packages available.
Catering: clubhouse facilities.

12 63 Clane

Clane, Co Kildare
☎(01) 6286608
Playing facilities at Clongowes.
Founded 1976

12 64 Claremorris

Rushbrook, Castlemagarett,
Claremorris, Co Mayo
☎(094) 71527, Sec 71868
1.5 miles from Claremorris on Galway Road.
Parkland course.
Founded 1917
9 holes, 5600 yards, S.S.S. 69
Visitors: welcome except Sun.
Green Fees: WD £8; WE £8.
Societies: welcome WD by prior arrangement; catering packages by arrangement.
Catering: by arrangement.

12 65 Clones

Hilton Park, Clones, Co Monaghan
☎(047) 56017, Fax (042) 42333, Sec (042) 42333
3 miles from Clones.
Parkland course.
Founded 1913
9 holes, 5206 yards, S.S.S. 67
Visitors: welcome.
Green Fees: WD £10; WE £10.
Societies: welcome by prior arrangement with the secretary; catering by arrangement; also 9-hole course: 2608 metres, par 34; from £5.
Catering: clubhouse facilities.
Hotels: Lennard Arms; Creighton; Hibernian; Riverdale.

12 66 Clongowes

Naas, Co Kildare
☎(045) 68202
Parkland course.
Founded 1966
9 holes, 5400 yards, S.S.S. 65
Visitors: welcome by prior arrangement.

Green Fees: terms on application.
Societies: terms on application.
Catering: full facilities.

12 67 Clonlara

Clonlara Golf and Leisure, Clonlara, Co Clare
☎(061) 354141, Fax 354143, Bar/Rest 354191
7 miles NE of Limerick on the Corbally-Killaloe Road.
Woodland/parkland course.
Pro Noel Cassidy; Founded 1993
12 holes, 5187 yards, S.S.S. 69
Visitors: welcome; pay and play.
Green Fees: WD £5; WE £5.
Societies: welcome by prior arrangement; discounts for groups of 20 or more; tennis; sauna; games room; fishing; terms on application.
Catering: bar facilities; catering by order.
Hotels: self-catering accommodation on site.

12 68 Clonmel

Lyreanearla, Mountain Rd, Clonmel, Co Tipperary
☎(052) 21138, Fax 24050, Pro 24050, Sec 24050
3 miles from Clonmel.
Parkland course.
Pro Robert Hayes; Founded 1911
Designed by Eddie Hackett
18 holes, 5845 yards, S.S.S. 70
Visitors: welcome; restrictions on Mon.
Green Fees: WD £18; WE £20.
Societies: welcome except Sun; terms on application.
Catering: full clubhouse facilities available.
Hotels: Clonmel Arms; Minella; Hearns; Hanora's Cottage.

12 69 Clontarf

Donnycarney House, Malahide Rd, Co Dublin
☎(01) 8331892, Fax 8831933, Pro 8331877, Bar/Rest 8330622
2.5 miles NE of city centre off Malahide Road.
Parkland course.
Pro Joe Craddock; Founded 1912
18 holes, 5433 yards, S.S.S. 68
Visitors: welcome.
Green Fees: WD £26; WE £35.
Societies: welcome Tues or Fri; packages include catering; from £30.
Catering: full clubhouse facilities available.
Hotels: Skylon.

12 70 Cobh

Ballywilliam, Cobh, Co Cork
☎(021) 812399
1 mile E of Cobh.
Public parkland course.
Founded 1987
Designed by Eddie Hackett
9 holes, 4366 yards, S.S.S. 63
Visitors: welcome WD; by prior arrangement WE.
Green Fees: terms on application.
Societies: welcome Mon-Sat; terms on application.
Catering: bar facilities.

12 71 Coldwinters

Newtown House, St Margaret's, Co Dublin
☎(01) 8640324, Fax 8341400
Parkland course; also 9-hole course, 2163 metres, par 31.
Pro Roger Yates
18 holes, 5973 yards, S.S.S. 69
Visitors: welcome; pay and play.
Green Fees: WD £8.50; WE £12.50.
Societies: welcome by prior arrangement.
Catering: clubhouse facilities.
Hotels: many in Dublin.

12 72 Connemara

Ballyconneely, Clifden, Co Galway
☎(095) 23602, Fax 23662, Pro 23502, Bar/Rest 23502
Signposted from Clifden.
Links course.
Pro Hugh O'Neill; Founded 1973
Designed by Eddie Hackett
18 holes, 6611 yards, S.S.S. 75
Visitors: welcome.
Green Fees: WD £25; WE £25.
Societies: welcome; minimum parties of 20; catering packages available; from £13.
Catering: full bar and restaurant facilities.
Hotels: Rock Glen; Abbey Glen; Foyles; Alcock & Brown; Ballinahynch.

12 73 Coollattin

Coollattin, Shillelheh, Co Wicklow
☎(055) 26302, Bar/Rest 29125
12 miles SW of Aughrim.
Parkland course.
Founded 1922
9 holes, 5688 yards, S.S.S. 70
Visitors: welcome WD.
Green Fees: WD £10; WE £10.
Societies: welcome WD by prior arrangement.
Catering: bar and snacks; meals by arrangement.

12 74 **Coosheen**
Coosheen, Schull, Co Cork
☎ (028) 28182, Fax 28573
1 mile E of Schull.
Seaside parkland course.
Founded 1989
Designed by Daniel Morgan
9 holes, 3982 yards, S.S.S. 61
Visitors: welcome.
Green Fees: WD £10; WE £10.
Societies: welcome; from £10.
Catering: full bar and restaurant.
Hotels: East End; West Cork;
Westlodge.

12 75 **Corballis**
Dunabate, Co Dublin
☎ (01) 8436583
N of Dublin on Belfast Road.
Links course.
Founded 1971
Designed by City Council
18 holes, 4971 yards, S.S.S. 64
Visitors: public pay and play.
Green Fees: WD £8; WE £10.
Societies: none.
Catering: snack facilities.
Hotels: Dunes.

12 76 **Cork**
Little Island, Cork, Co Cork
☎ (021) 353451, Fax 353410, Pro
353421
5 miles E of Cork City off N25.
Parkland/heathland course.
Pro Peter Hickey; Founded 1888
Designed by Alister MacKenzie
18 holes, 6119 yards, S.S.S. 72
Visitors: welcome.
Green Fees: WD £35; WE £40.
Societies: welcome by prior arrange-
ment; minimum 20; catering packages
by arrangement; from £24.
Catering: bar and catering facilities.
Hotels: Ashborune House; Silver
Springs; Jurys.

12 77 **Corrstown**
Corrstown, Kilsallaghan, Co Dublin
☎ (01) 8640533, Bar/Rest 8640534
Parkland course.
Founded 1993
27 holes, 5584 yards, S.S.S. 69
Visitors: with a member only.
Green Fees: WD £8; WE £8.

12 78 **County Cavan**
Arnmore House, Drumelis, Cavan, Co
Cavan
☎ (049) 31541, Fax 31541, Pro
31388, Bar/Rest 31283
1 mile from Cavan on the Killeshandra
Road.
Parkland course.
Pro Ciaran Carroll; Founded 1894
Designed by E Hackett
18 holes, 5634 yards, S.S.S. 69
Visitors: welcome.
Green Fees: terms on application.
Societies: welcome; restrictions Wed
and Sun.
Catering: full catering facilities.
Hotels: Farnham Arms; Kilmore.

12 79 **County Longford**
Glack, Longford
☎ (043) 46310, Sec 45556
E of Glack off the Dublin-Sligo N4 rd.
Undulating parkland course.
Founded 1894
Designed by E. Hackett
18 holes, 5494 yards, S.S.S. 69
Visitors: welcome.
Green Fees: terms on application.
Societies: welcome by prior arrange-
ment.
Catering: clubhouse catering facilities.

12 80 **County Louth**
Baltray, Drogheda, Co Louth
☎ (041) 22329, Fax 22969, Pro
22444, Bar/Rest 22442
5 miles NE of Drogheda.
Links course.
Pro Paddy McGuirk; Founded 1892
Designed by Tom Simpson
18 holes, 6783 yards, S.S.S. 72
Visitors: welcome by prior arrange-
ment.
Green Fees: WD £40; WE £50.
Societies: welcome by prior arrange-
ment; catering packages by arrange-
ment; from £40.
Catering: full bar and catering facili-
ties.
Hotels: Boyn Valley.

12 81 **County Meath (Trim)**
Newtownmoynagh, Trim, Co Meath
☎ (046) 31463, Bar/Rest 36842
3 miles from Trim on the Longwood
Road.
Parkland course.
Founded 1898
Designed by Eddie Hackett
18 holes, 6720 yards, S.S.S. 72
Visitors: welcome; restrictions Thurs,
Sat, Sun.
Green Fees: terms on application.
Societies: welcome Mon-Sat by prior
arrangement.
Catering: full bar and catering facili-
ties.

12 82 **County Sligo**
Rosses Point, Co Sligo
☎ (071) 77134, Fax 77460, Pro
77171, Sec 77186, Bar/Rest 77186
5 miles N of Sligo.
Links course.
Pro Leslie Robinson; Founded 1894
Designed by Colt & Alison
18 holes, 6043 yards, S.S.S. 72
Visitors: welcome; no fourballs Tues;
not before 10.30 Sun.
Green Fees: WD £27; WE £35.
Societies: welcome by prior arrange-
ment; special rates and packages for
12 or more players; from £23.
Catering: full clubhouse facilities.
Practice area.
Hotels: Tower Hotel; Sligo Park; Yeats
Country Hotel; Ballincar House.

12 83 **County Tipperary Golf & Country Club**
Dundrum, Cashel, Co. Tipperary
☎ (062) 71116, Fax 71366
6 miles W of Cashel.
Parkland course.
Founded 1993
Designed by Philip Walton
18 holes, 6709 yards, S.S.S. 72
Visitors: welcome.
Green Fees: WD £20; WE £24.
Societies: welcome; discounts for
groups of more than 12; from £17.
Catering: full catering and bar facili-
ties.
Hotels: Dundrum House on site.

12 84 **Courtown**
Kiltennel, Gorey, Co Wexford
☎ (055) 25166, Fax 25553
Leave N11 at Gorey following the
Road to Courtown Harbour.
Parkland course.
Pro John Coone; Founded 1936
Designed by Harris &
Associates/Henry Cotton
18 holes, 5898 yards, S.S.S. 71
Visitors: welcome; some restrictions
Tues and WE.
Green Fees: WD £18; WE £23.
Societies: welcome by prior arrange-
ment with secretary/manager; reduc-
tions for groups of more than 20.
Catering: full catering and bar facili-
ties.
Hotels: Marlfield; Courtown; Bayview.

12 85 **Craddockstown**
Craddockstown, Naas, Co Kildare
☎ (045) 97610
Parkland course.
Founded 1983

County Louth

There are certain courses throughout Britain and Ireland where a sense of expectancy reaches a peak at a specific point near journey's end; when turning off the main road at Wadebridge for St Enodoc, for instance, or when a long drive nears its end along the only road to Southerness, a superb links on the Solway Firth, which in 1985 hosted the Scottish Amateur for the first time.

A similar sense of anticipation accompanies the last lap to Brancaster which takes you past the church and down through the marsh lined by tall rushes; and there is a less glamorous approach beyond the level crossing to the Royal Cinque Ports Golf Club at Deal. The twisty conclusion to the journey to Rye is another example. But there are few sights as thrilling as the links of County Louth at Baltray at last coming into view.

It is a fine, challenging course in the traditional mould of dunes, undoubtedly one of my favourites and one whose rating within Ireland is not as high as it should be. It is worthy of the best, full of variety and contrast with always the magnificence of its distant views.

Although there have been modifications, one or two made necessary by moving the clubhouse some years ago, there is still an authentic touch of Tom Simpson about it that bears the unmistakable mark of quality. If I had to exemplify it, I would point to the long third which, after a reasonably straight forward drive, reveals hidden talents once the brow of dunes has been scaled. Beautifully natural humps and hollows make careful placing of the second shot essential and, for those attempting to get home in two, there is only a narrow path between salvation and ruin. An attractive small green is not easy to hit.

The curving first and testing second make a nice introduction but the fourth, a short par four, offers some relief before the first of four first class short holes. The fifth and seventh, sandwiched around another fine par five, demand well-controlled, truly hit iron shots which the eighth and ninth are no easy fours.

A sense of space becomes more apparent on the second half which, having begun with a hole alongside the clubhouse, works its way towards the sea by means of the dogleg par-five 11th. It is then that a special character is lent by the 12th, 13th and 14th which, from a combination of factors, comprise a notable trio. They emphasise the merit of great par fours, not perhaps daunting in terms of yardage but rewarding in the satisfaction they give by being played properly, as they must be if they are to yield a par or a birdie.

Changes to the course have resulted in two short holes in the last four but the 16th is appealing and the 18th the last of five par fives. Baltray, as the course is more conveniently called after the local fishing village, has a championship cloak without a doubt and it also has its less forbidding side which makes it popular for a day out.

Harry Bradshaw's winning aggregate of 291 in the 1947 Irish Professional championship tells a tale or two about its full blown potential. It is also rare among Irish clubs in having two legendary Irish women golfers as members. Val Reddan, as Clarrie Tiernan, won the Irish title twice and was also the first Irish woman to play in the Curtis Cup. After the war, she was confronted by her new local rival Philomena Garvey in the final of the Irish, not, as would have been most appropriate, at Baltray, but at Lahinch. After the longest final, Garvey won at the 39th, the first of her 15 victories.

Continuing the feminine influence, Mrs Josephine Connolly founded the East of Ireland Men's championship played annually at Baltray, an event by which Irish golfers set great store. It can claim father and son winners in Joe and Roddy Carr, but when you speak of the course you speak of distinction. Its list of champions is no more than it deserves.

DEER PARK HOTEL & GOLF COURSES

IRELAND'S LARGEST GOLF COMPLEX. Not just any Golf Hotel, but the largest golf complex in Ireland. Situated on the grounds of Howth Castle, the Hotel offers 78 superb en-suite bedrooms. Awarded 3 stars by the RAC, the hotel has no less than 4 separate parkland courses all within its grounds. Only 9 miles from Dublin City/Airport the hotels additional features include an indoor swimming pool complex, sauna, steam room and Rhododendron gardens.

Exceptional value golf breaks available.
For details call: **The Deer Park Hotel & Golf Courses**
Howth, Co. Dublin, Ireland.
Tel: (01) 8322624 • Fax: (01) 8392405 • E-mail: sales@deerpark.iol.ie

---

18 holes, 6134 yards, S.S.S. 72
Visitors: welcome.
Green Fees: WD £12; WE £15.

12 86 Cruit Island

Kincasslagh, Letterkenny, Co Donegal
☎(075) 43296, Sec 48151
6 miles from Dungloe opposite the Viking House Hotel.
Links course.
Founded 1986
9 holes, 4860 yards, S.S.S. 64
Visitors: welcome.
Green Fees: WD £7; WE £10.
Societies: welcome by prior arrangement; catering packages available by arrangement; from £8.
Catering: bar and catering facilities. Practice area.
Hotels: Viking House; Ostan na Rosann.

12 87 Curragh

Curragh, Co Kildare
☎(045) 441714, Fax 441714, Sec 441238
2 miles SE of Newbridge.
Parkland course.
Pro Gerry Burke; Founded 1883
Designed by David Ritchie
18 holes, 6035 yards, S.S.S. 71
Visitors: welcome by prior arrangement.
Green Fees: WD £18; WE £22.
Societies: welcome by prior arrangement Mon-Fri & Sat morning; from £16.
Catering: full clubhouse facilities available.
Hotels: Standhouse; Keadeen.

12 88 Deer Park Hotel

Deer Park Hotel, Howth, Co Dublin
☎(01) 8322624, Fax 8326039, Sec 8326039
9 miles E of the City centre.

Parkland course; 2 x 9-hole courses; 12-hole pitch and putt.
Founded 1973
Designed by Fred Hawtree
18 holes, 6770 yards, S.S.S. 71
Visitors: welcome; restrictions Sun am.
Green Fees: WD £9; WE £12.
Societies: welcome WD by prior arrangement; catering packages available by prior arrangement; function rooms.
Catering: full restaurant and bar facilities.
Hotels: Deer Park on site.

12 89 Delgany

Delgany, Co Wicklow
☎(01) 2874536, Fax 2873977
Off N11 1 mile past Glenview Hotel.
Parkland course.
Pro Gavin Kavanagh; Founded 1908
Designed by H Vardon
18 holes, 5474 yards, S.S.S. 68
Visitors: welcome.
Green Fees: WD £23; WE £23.
Societies: welcome by prior arrangement; from £23.
Catering: full bar and catering facilities.
Hotels: Glenview; Delgany Inn.

12 90 Delvin Castle

Delvin Castle, Delvin, Westmeath
☎(044) 64315
On N52 in the village of Delvin.
Mature parkland with lakes.
Founded 1995
Designed by J Day
18 holes
Visitors: welcome; restrictions Wed and Sun.
Green Fees: WD £10; WE £12.
Societies: welcome by prior arrangement.
Catering: full bar and catering service available.

12 91 Donabate

Donabate, Balcarrick, Co Dublin
☎(01) 8436346, Sec 8431264
1 mile N of Swords on the Dublin-Belfast Road.
Parkland course.
Founded 1925
18 holes, 5704 yards, S.S.S. 69
Visitors: welcome WE with a member.
Green Fees: WD £18; WE £12.
Societies: welcome by prior arrangement.
Catering: clubhouse catering facilities.

12 92 Donegal

Murvagh, Laghey, Co Donegal
☎(073) 34054, Fax 34377
8 miles from Donegal on the Ballyshannon Road.
Links course.
Founded 1960/73
Designed by Eddie Hackett
18 holes, 6547 yards, S.S.S. 75
Visitors: welcome.
Green Fees: WD £18; WE £25.
Societies: welcome by prior arrangement; discounts for more than 16 golfers; snooker; from £18.
Catering: full bar and restaurant facilities.
Practice range, large practice ground.
Hotels: Sandhouse.

12 93 Doneraile

Doneraile, Co Cork
☎(022) 24137
Off T11 28 miles from Cork; 9 miles from Marlow.
Parkland course.
Founded 1927
9 holes, 5055 yards, S.S.S. 67
Visitors: welcome.
Green Fees: terms on application.
Societies: welcome by prior arrangement
Catering: full clubhouse facilities available.

12 94 Dooks
Glenbeigh, Co Kerry
☎(066) 68205, Fax 68476
On the N70 between Killonglin and
Glenbeigh.
Links course.
Founded 1889
Designed by Eddie Hackett/Donald
Steel
18 holes, 6010 yards, S.S.S. 68
Visitors: welcome.
Green Fees: WD £20; WE £20.
Societies: welcome by prior arrangement; from £20.
Catering: full clubhouse facilities.
Hotels: Towers; And na si; Bianconi.

12 95 Douglas
Douglas, Co Cork
☎(021) 895297
3 miles from Cork; 0.5 miles past
Douglas village.
Parkland course.
Founded 1909
18 holes, 5664 yards, S.S.S. 69
Visitors: welcome; reservations needed at WE.
Green Fees: terms on application.
Societies: welcome by prior arrangement before start of the season.
Catering: catering facilities.

12 96 Dromoland Castle
Newmarket-on-Fergus, Co Clare
☎(061) 368444, Fax 368498
14 miles from Limerick on N18 and 6
miles from Shannon on N19.
Parkland course.
Pro Philip Murphy; Founded 1963
Designed by Wigginton
18 holes, 5719 yards, S.S.S. 71
Visitors: welcome.
Green Fees: WD £22; WE £24.
Societies: welcome by prior arrangement; catering packages available;
leisure, spa and health studios; from
£22.
Catering: full clubhouse facilities.
Practice area.
Hotels: Clare Inn; Oakwood Arms;
Limerick Inn.

12 97 Druids Glen
Newtonmountkennedy, Co Wicklow
☎(01) 2873600, Fax 287399
Signposted from N11 from Dublin taking
Newtonmountkenndey/Glengalaugh
junction.
Parkland course; European Tour
venue.
Pro Eamonn Darcy; Founded 1993

Designed by T Craddock & P Ruddy
18 holes, 7026 yards, S.S.S. 73
Visitors: welcome.
Green Fees: WD £75; WE £75.
Societies: welcome everyday by prior
arrangement; minimum 20 players;
catering packages by arrangement;
from £65.
Catering: full clubhouse bar and
restaurant facilities.
Practice range, practice facilities and
3-hole academy.
Hotels: Glenview; Tinakilly.

12 98 Dublin Mountain
Gortlum, Brittas, Co Dublin
☎(01) 4582622
Undulating parkland course.
Founded 1993
18 holes, 5433 yards, S.S.S. 69
Visitors: welcome.
Green Fees: terms on application.
Societies: on application.
Catering: clubhouse facilities.

12 99 Dun Laoghaire
Eglinton Park, Tivoli Rd, Dun
Laoghaire, Co Dublin
☎(01) 2805116, Fax 2804868, Pro
2801694, Sec 2803916, Bar/Rest
2801055
7 miles S of Dublin; 0.5 miles from
Ferry port.
Parkland course.
Pro Owen Mulhall; Founded 1910
Designed by H S Colt
18 holes, 5298 yards, S.S.S. 68
Visitors: welcome except Thurs and
Sat.
Green Fees: WD £26; WE £26.
Societies: welcome by prior arrangement with the manager; discounts for
groups of 30 or more; from £26.
Catering: full clubhouse facilities.
Hotels: Royal Marine; Rochestown;
Killiney Castle.

12 100 Dundalk
Blackrock, Dundalk, Co Louth
☎(042) 21731, Fax 22022, Pro 22102
2 miles S of Dundalk taking the coast
Road to Blackrock.
Parkland course.
Pro James Cassidy; Founded 1904
Designed by Dave Thomas & Peter
Alliss
18 holes, 6160 yards, S.S.S. 72
Visitors: welcome.
Green Fees: WD £18; WE £20.
Societies: welcome by prior arrangement; catering packages by arrangement; from £18.

Catering: bar and restaurant facilities.
Large practice area.
Hotels: Fairway.

12 101 Dunfanaghy
Dunfanaghy, Letterkenny, Co Donegal
☎(074) 36335, Pro 36488
On N56 from Letterkenny 0.5 miles E
of Dunfanaghy.
Seaside links course.
Founded 1904
Designed by H Vardon
18 holes, 5006 yards, S.S.S. 66
Visitors: welcome except on captain
and president's day.
Green Fees: WD £11.50; WE £14.50.
Societies: welcome by prior arrangement; discounts for groups of more
than 12 and 20; from £8.
Catering: full clubhouse facilities
available.
Hotels: Arnolds; Carrig Rua; Port-n-
Blagh; Shandon.

12 102 Dungarvan
Knocknagranagh, Dungarvan, Co
Waterford
☎(058) 43310, Fax 44113, Pro
44707, Bar/Rest 41605
2.5 miles E of Dungarvan on the N25
Waterford to Rosslare Road.
Parkland course.
Pro David Hayes; Founded 1924/1993
Designed by Maurice Fives
18 holes, 6708 yards, S.S.S. 73
Visitors: welcome; booking needed at
WE.
Green Fees: WD £15; WE £20.
Societies: welcome by prior arrangement; catering packages available;
from £13.
Catering: full clubhouse facilities
available.
Practice range, 1 mile.
Hotels: Clonea Strand; Gold Coast;
Lawlors: Park.

12 103 Dunmore
Dunmore House, Muckross, Clonakilty,
Co Cork
☎(023) 33352
Signposted 3 miles from Clonakilty.
Hilly Open course.
Founded 1967
Designed by E. Hackett
9 holes, 4464 yards, S.S.S. 61
Visitors: welcome.
Green Fees: WD £10; WE £10.
Societies: welcome by prior arrangement.
Catering: bar and restaurant facilities
in Dunmore House.

12 104 Dunmore East Golf & Country Club

Dunmore East, Co Waterford
☎(051) 383151, Fax 383151
In the village of Dunmore East.
Seaside parkland course.
Founded 1993
Designed by Eamon Condon & Assoc
18 holes, 6059 yards, S.S.S. 71
Visitors: welcome.
Green Fees: WD £10; WE £12.
Societies: welcome by prior arrangement; terms on application.
Catering: full clubhouse facilities.
Hotels: Ivory Lodge; Dunmore Holiday Villas; Haven.

12 105 East Clare

Coolreigh, Bodyke, Co Clare
☎(061) 921322, Fax 921717, Sec 921388
15 miles E of Ennis.
Parkland course.
Founded 1997
Designed by A Spring
9 holes, 5922 yards, S.S.S. 71
Visitors: welcome.
Green Fees: WD £12; WE £15.
Societies: welcome; discounts for groups of 25 or more; from £12.
Catering: limited.
Hotels: Smyths Village.

12 106 East Cork

Gortacrue, Midleton, Co Cork
☎(021) 631687, Fax 613695, Pro 633667, Bar/Rest 631273
Leave Cork to Waterford at Midleton; course 2 miles on the Fermou Road.
Parkland course.
Pro Don MacFarlane; Founded 1970
Designed by Edward Hackett
18 holes, 5774 yards, S.S.S. 67
Visitors: welcome with prior booking.
Green Fees: WD £15; WE £15.
Societies: welcome by prior arrangement; minimum 10 players; £12.
Catering: full clubhouse facilities.
Hotels: Commodore; Midleton Park; Garryvoe.

12 107 Edenderry

Kishawanny, Edenderry, Co Offaly
☎(0405) 31072
Off the R402 to Edenderry from the N4.
Parkland course.
Founded 1947
Designed by E Hackett
18 holes, 6029 yards, S.S.S. 72
Visitors: welcome.
Green Fees: WD £12; WE £14.

Societies: welcome except Thurs and Sun; from £10.
Catering: clubhouse facilities.
Hotels: Wells; Tullamore Court.

12 108 Edmondstown

Edmondstown Rd, Rathfarnham, Co Dublin
☎(01) 4932461, Fax 4933152, Pro 4941049, Sec 4931082, Bar/Rest 4933205
8 miles SW of City centre.
Parkland course.
Pro Andrew Crofton; Founded 1944
Designed by McAlister
18 holes, 5663 yards, S.S.S. 70
Visitors: welcome.
Green Fees: WD £25; WE £30.
Societies: welcome; terms on application.
Catering: full facilities.
Practice ground.
Hotels: many in Dublin.

12 109 Elm Park

Nutley Lane, Donnybrook
☎(01) 2693438, Pro 2692650
2 miles from City centre.
Parkland course.
Founded 1925
Designed by Fred Davies
18 holes, 5422 yards, S.S.S. 68
Visitors: welcome by prior arrangement.
Green Fees: terms on application.
Societies: welcome Tues.
Catering: full facilities.

12 110 Ennis

Drumbiggle, Ennis, Co Clare
☎(065) 29211, Fax 41848, Pro 20690, Sec 24074, Bar/Rest 24074
1 mile from town centre.
Parkland course.
Pro Martin Ward; Founded 1912
18 holes, 5275 yards, S.S.S. 68
Visitors: welcome.
Green Fees: WD £18; WE £18.
Societies: welcome by prior arrangement; minimum group 10; £16.
Catering: full clubhouse facilities.
Hotels: Auburn Lodge; Old Ground; West County.

12 111 Enniscorthy

Knockmarshal, Enniscorthy, Co Wexford
☎(054) 33191, Fax 33191
1 mile from town on the Newross-Waterford Road.
Parkland course.

Pro Martin Sludds; Founded 1926
Designed by E. Hackett
18 holes, 6115 yards, S.S.S. 72
Visitors: welcome by prior arrangement.
Green Fees: WD £14; WE £16.
Societies: welcome by prior arrangement; from £14.
Catering: full facilities.
Hotels: Murphy Floods.

12 112 Enniscrone

Enniscrone, Co Sligo
☎(096) 36297, Fax 36657
7 miles from Ballina.
Championship links course.
Pro Charlie McGoldrick; Founded 1918/31
Designed by E. Hackett
18 holes, 6720 yards, S.S.S. 72
Visitors: welcome by prior arrangement.
Green Fees: WD £18; WE £24.
Societies: welcome by prior arrangement; minimum 12; catering packages by arrangement; from £13.
Catering: full bar and catering.
Practice area.
Hotels: Downhill, Ballina; Atlantic; Benbulbow; Castle, all Enniscrone.

12 113 Esker Hills G & CC

Tullamore, Co Offaly
☎(0506) 55999, Fax 55989
2.5 miles W of Tullamore.
Undulating parkland course.
Founded 1996
Designed by C O'Connor jnr
18 holes, 6612 yards, S.S.S. 70
Visitors: welcome.
Green Fees: WD £15; WE £15.
Societies: welcome by arrangement.
Catering: coffee shop facilities.

12 114 The European Club

Brittas Bay, Co Wicklow
☎(0404) 47415, Fax 47449
Midway between Wicklow and Arklow S of Dublin.
Links course.
Founded 1993
Designed by Pat Ruddy
18 holes, 6850 yards, S.S.S. 73
Visitors: welcome by prior arrangement.
Green Fees: WD £35; WE £35.
Societies: welcome by prior arrangement; minimum group 24; from £18.
Catering: full clubhouse facilities.
Practice range, practice ground.
Hotels: Tinakilly House; Grand, Wicklow; Hunters, Ashford.

Fota Island Golf Club

HOME OF THE IRISH AMATEUR OPEN

Located 12 km east of Cork City. Tel: +353 21 883710 • E-mail: fotagolf@iol.ie

12 115 Faithlegg
Faithlegg House, Co. Waterford
☎(051) 382241, Fax 382664
6 miles from Waterford city centre on
the banks of the Suir.
Parkland course.
Founded 1993
Designed by Patrick Merrigan
18 holes, 6057 yards, S.S.S. 72
Visitors: welcome.
Green Fees: WD £20; WE £20.
Societies: welcome by prior arrangement; packages available; terms on
application.
Catering: full bar and restaurant facilities.
Practice area.

12 116 Fermoy
Corrin, Fermoy, Co Cork
☎(025) 31472
2 miles from Fermoy off Cork-Dublin
Road.
Undulating parkland course.
Founded 1893
Designed by Commander Harris
18 holes, 5795 yards, S.S.S. 70
Visitors: welcome WD.
Green Fees: terms on application.
Societies: welcome WD and Sat am.
Catering: by arrangement.

12 117 Fernhill
Carrigaline, Co Cork
☎(021) 373103, Fax 371011
Parkland course.
Founded 1994
18 holes
Visitors: welcome.
Green Fees: terms on application.
Societies: on application.

12 118 Finnstown Fairways
Finnstown Fairways Country House,
Lucan, Co Dublin
☎(01) 6280644

N4 to Lucan and then left for
Newcastle Road.
Mature trees on a parkland course.
Founded 1991
Designed by Bobby Brown
9 holes, 5172 yards, S.S.S. 64.
Visitors: welcome.
Green Fees: WD £16; WE £16.
Societies: welcome by prior arrangement; maximum 30 players; from £26.
Catering: full hotel facilities.
Hotels: Finnstown Country House.

12 119 Forrest Little
Forest Little, Cloghran, Co Dublin
☎(01) 8401763, Fax 8401000, Pro
8407670
0.5 miles beyond Dublin Airport on the
Dublin-Belfast Road, take 1st turn left.
Parkland course.
Founded 1940
Designed by Fred Hawtree
18 holes, 5865 yards, S.S.S. 70
Visitors: welcome WD.
Green Fees: terms on application.
Societies: welcome normally Mon and
Thurs afternoon.
Catering: snacks and restaurant.

12 120 Fota Island
Fota Island, Carrigtwohill, Co Cork
☎(021) 883700, Fax 883713, Pro
883710
Take N25 E from Cork City towards
Waterford and Rosslare; after 9 miles
take the exit for Cobh/Fota, course 0.5
miles.
Parkland course.
Pro Kevin Morris; Founded 1993
Designed by Peter McEvoy and
Christy O'Connor Jnr
18 holes, 6901 yards, S.S.S. 74
Visitors: welcome.
Green Fees: WD £32; Fri £37.
Societies: welcome by prior arrangement; packages available on application; from £26.

Catering: full facilities.
Hotels: Midleton Park; Ashbourne
House; Jury's Cork.

12 121 Foxrock
Torquay Rd, Dublin, Co Dublin
☎(01) 2893992, Fax 2894943, Pro
2893414, Bar/Rest 2897523
About 6 miles from Dublin; turn right
off T7 just past Stillergan on the
Leopardstown Road then left into
Torquay Road.
Parkland course.
Founded 1893
9 holes, 5667 yards, S.S.S. 69
Visitors: welcome Mon, Wed am,
Thurs, Fri and Sun with a member.
Green Fees: WD £20; WE £10.
Societies: welcome Mon and Thurs.
Catering: snacks.

12 122 Frankfield
Frankfield, Douglas, Co Cork
☎(021) 363124
10 miles S of Cork.
Parkland course.
Founded 1984
9 holes, 4621 yards, S.S.S. 65
Visitors: welcome.
Green Fees: terms on application.
Catering: lunches.

12 123 Galway
Blackrock, Salthill, Co Galway
☎(091) 522033, Fax 529783, Pro
523038, Bar/Rest 521827
3 miles W of Galway.
Tight tree-lined parkland course.
Pro Don Wallace; Founded 1895
Designed by A MacKenzie
18 holes, 5832 yards, S.S.S. 71
Visitors: welcome.
Green Fees: WD £17; WE £17.
Societies: welcome WD by prior
arrangement; catering packages by
arrangement; from £15.

Catering: full catering facilities.
Hotels: Salthill; Galway Bay; Jameson's; Spinnaker.

12 124 Galway Bay Golf & Country Club

Renville, Oranmore, Co Galway
☎(091) 521159
From Galway take coast road through Oranmore signposted from there.
Seaside parkland course.
Founded 1993
Designed by Christy O'Connor Jnr
18 holes, 6533 yards, S.S.S. 72
Visitors: welcome with h'ap certs.
Green Fees: WD £20; WE £25.
Societies: welcome by arrangement.
Catering: restaurant; spikes bar; bar.
Practice range, practice bays.

12 125 Glasson G & CC

Glasson, Athlone, Co Westmeath
☎(0902) 85120, Fax 85444
6 miles N of Athlone on the N55.
Parkland course.
Founded 1994
Designed by C O'Connor
18 holes, 7120 yards, S.S.S. 72
Visitors: welcome.
Green Fees: WD £25; WE £28.
Societies: welcome by prior arrangement; catering packages by arrangement; from £23.
Catering: full clubhouse facilities.

12 126 Glengarriff

Glengarriff, Co Cork
☎(027) 63150
On T65 55 miles W of Cork.
Seaside course.
Founded 1936
9 holes, 4094 yards, S.S.S. 66
Visitors: welcome.
Green Fees: terms on application.
Societies: welcome by prior arrangement; special packages available.

12 127 Glenmalure

Greenane, Rathdrum, Co. Wicklow
☎(0404) 46679, Fax 46783, Sec 46783
2 miles W of Rathdrum.
Parkland course.
Founded 1993
Designed by Pat Suttle
18 holes, 5850 yards, S.S.S. 66
Visitors: welcome.
Green Fees: WD £12; WE £18.
Societies: welcome by prior arrangement; discounts depending on group numbers; from £12.

Catering: full facilities.
Hotels: self-catering lodge accommodation on site.

12 128 Gold Coast Golf and Leisure

Ballinacourty, Dungarvan, Co. Waterford
☎(058) 44055, Fax 43378, Bar/Rest 42249
Located 3 miles from Dungarvan.
Parkland course by the sea.
Founded 1937/97
Designed by Capt. R. Hewson/Maurice Fives
18 holes, 6171 yards, S.S.S. 70
Visitors: welcome by prior arrangement.
Green Fees: WD £15; WE £18.
Societies: welcome by prior arrangement; discounts depending on size of group and date of visit.
Catering: full facilities.
Practice range, driving range near golf course.
Hotels: Goldcoast Hotel; Goldcoast Holiday homes; Clonea Strand.

12 129 Gort

Castlequarter, Gort, Co Galway
☎(091) 632244
Off Kilmacduagh Road.
Parkland course.
Founded 1924/1996
Designed by C O'Connor Jnr
18 holes, 5979 yards, S.S.S. 67
Visitors: welcome; some restrictions Sun morning.
Green Fees: WD £12; WE £12.
Societies: welcome by prior arrangement; deposit of £Ire100 in advance; catering packages available; from £10.
Catering: lunches and snacks available.
Hotels: Sullivans, Gort.

12 130 Grange

Rathfarnham, Dublin
☎(01) 4932889, Fax 4939490, Pro 4932299, Sec 4979266, Bar/Rest 4931404
7 miles S from city.
Parkland course.
Founded 1910
Designed by James Braid
18 holes, 5517 yards, S.S.S. 69
Visitors: welcome WD except Tues and Wed afternoon.
Green Fees: WD £28; WE £12.
Societies: welcome Mon and Thurs by prior arrangement.
Catering: full facilities.

12 131 Greencastle

Greencastle, Moville, Co Donegal
☎(077) 81013, Sec 82280
On L85 23 miles NE of Londonderry through Moville.
Public seaside course.
Founded 1892
Designed by Eddie Hackett (new 9 Holes)
18 holes, 5211 yards, S.S.S. 67
Visitors: welcome.
Green Fees: WD £10; WE £15.
Societies: welcome by prior arrangement.
Catering: bar and catering facilities.

12 132 Greenore

Greenore, Co Louth
☎(042) 73678
15 miles out of Dundalk on the Newry Road.
Wooded seaside course.
Founded 1896
Designed by Eddie Hackett
18 holes, 6506 yards, S.S.S. 71
Visitors: welcome WD; by prior arrangement at WE.
Green Fees: terms on application.
Societies: welcome by arrangement.
Catering: full facilities.

12 133 Greystones

Greystones, Co Wicklow
☎(01) 2874136, Fax 2873749, Pro 2875308, Sec 2828684
N11 out of Dublin towards Wexford.
Parkland course.
Founded 1895
18 holes, 5401 yards, S.S.S. 68
Visitors: welcome Mon, Tues and Fri.
Green Fees: WD £20; WE £24.
Societies: welcome by arrangement.
Catering: full facilities.

12 134 Gweedore

Derrybeg, Letterkenny, Co Donegal
☎(075) 31140, Fax 31666
L82 from Letterkenny or T72 from Donegal.
Seaside course; Founded 1926
Designed by Eddie Hackett
9 holes, 6150 yards, S.S.S. 69
Visitors: welcome.
Green Fees: WD £7; WE £8.
Societies: welcome at WE.
Catering: lunches at WE.

12 135 Harbour Point

Little Island, Cork, Co Cork
☎(021) 353094, Fax 354408, Pro 353719

The K Club

Tom Lehman was unequivocal. "I have stayed in many fine hotels but this unquestionably is the finest," he said. And to whom was he conferring this lavish honour? The K Club, a splendid five-star establishment in the heart of Kildare, about an hour's drive from Dublin. When he heard the compliment Dr Michael Smurfit, chairman of Ireland's largest and most successful company, must have purred. This was his dream, his master plan when he set out some 10 years ago to find a site that would provide unrivalled sporting facilities.

At the time the hotel was a dilapidated country house, surrounded by mature woodland and gently rolling terrain. Four years later, complete with its 18 holes, it opened to general acclaim. The golf course? Now, it would take something otherworldly to be considered Ireland's finest, let alone the world's, but what we can say is that it is a worthy contributor to parkland play in the Emerald isle.

It is for its links courses that Ireland has become rightly so revered; the K Club, alongside Mount Juliet and Druid's Glen, form a splendid trinity that state defiantly that the inland golf is not bad either. The course was designed by Arnold Palmer and makes good use of the River Liffey that meanders gently through its acres. One of the best holes is the eighth, with the Liffey hugging its entire left-hand side. The hole is known as the 'Half Moon', taking its name from the crescent shape of the fairway.

The K Club only opened in 1991 but it was always Dr Smurfit's intention to host major tournaments and for the last three years the course has successfully staged one of Europe's biggest events, the European Open.

The glittering prize, however, hangs within reach. At the time of writing it had not been decided which Irish course would host the 2005 Ryder Cup but the K Club was a short odds favourite.

Certainly the players could ask for no better place to stay than the on-site hotel. And the course is capable of holding large gatherings of spectators. I dare say the craic would be quite mighty too.

As for the finish, that is certainly worthy of holding such an event, the punishing last four holes coming to a wonderful crescendo with an 18th that would undoubtedly be the scene of memorable drama. A par five of 518 yards, a drive down the middle to the left-hand side of the fairway brings the green tantalisingly into view. But here's the rub: the left-hand side of the fairway by the green and the left of the putting surface itself are both protected by water.

Under normal circumstances, therefore, it is a very demanding second shot; under the unique pressure of the Ryder Cup, it would call for all the skills that a player has to offer, and anyone who found the green would rightly be acclaimed.

Now, is that not how it should be when it comes to golf's most charismatic competition?

6 miles E of Cork.
Parkland course.
Pro Brendan McDaid; Founded 1991
Designed by Paddy Merrigan
18 holes, 6063 yards, S.S.S. 72
Visitors: welcome.
Green Fees: WD £20; WE £22.
Societies: welcome; minimum nine;
reductions for groups of more than 20
and 40; from £17.
Catering: full facilities.
Hotels: John Barley Corn; Ashbourne
House; Midleton Park; Fitzpatricks
Silver Springs.

12 136 Hazel Grove
Mt Seskin Rd, Jobstown, Tallaght,
Dublin
☎(01) 4520911, Sec 4522931
On the Blessington Road 2.5 miles
from Tallaght.
Parkland course.
Founded 1988
Designed by Jim Byrne
11 holes, 5030 yards, S.S.S. 67
Visitors: welcome Mon, Wed, Fri; not
after 12 Tues, not after 11 Sat.
Green Fees: WD £10; WE £10.
Societies: welcome by prior arrange-
ment; maximum 50 players; Sat morn-
ing maximum 40; catering packages
available.
Catering: bar, function room.
Large practice ground.

12 137 Headfort
Kells, Co Meath
☎(046) 40146, Fax 49282, Pro 40639
N3 from Dublin on Cavan route.
Parkland course.
Pro Brendan McGovern; Founded
1928
18 holes, 5973 yards, S.S.S. 71
Visitors: welcome.
Green Fees: WD £15; WE £18.
Societies: welcome by prior arrange-
ment; catering package by arrange-
ment.
Catering: full facilities.
Hotels: Headfort Arms.

12 138 Heath
The Heath, Portlaoise, Co Laois
☎(0502) 46533, Pro 46622
4 miles NE of Portlaoise off the main
Dublin to Cork/Limerick Road.
Heathland course.
Founded 1930
18 holes, 5721 yards, S.S.S. 70
Visitors: welcome WD WE by prior
arrangement.
Green Fees: terms on application.

Societies: welcome by prior arrange-
ment.
Catering: full facilities.
Practice range, available.

12 139 Hermitage
Lucan, Co Dublin
☎(01) 6268491, Pro 6268072,
Bar/Rest 6268396
8 miles from Dublin; 1 mile from
Lucan.
Parkland course.
Pro Simon Byrne; Founded 1905
Designed by Eddie Hackett
18 holes, 6051 yards, S.S.S. 71
Visitors: welcome WD.
Green Fees: WD £32.
Societies: welcome WD by arrange-
ment; five golf and meal packages; lat-
est tee time 1.45pm; from £32.
Catering: full clubhouse catering facili-
ties.
Hotels: Finnstown; Bewley; Spa;
Morans Red Cow; Green Isle.

12 140 Highfield
Carbury, Co Kildare
☎(0405) 31021
In Carbury.
Parkland course.
Founded 1992
18 holes, 5707 yards, S.S.S. 70
Visitors: welcome.
Green Fees: WD £7; WE £10.

12 141 Hollywood Lakes
Hollywood, Ballyboughal, Co Dublin
☎(01) 8433406, Fax 8433002,
Bar/Rest 8433407
15 minutes N of Dublin Airport via N1
and R129 to Ballyboughal.
Parkland course.
Founded 1991
Designed by Mel Flanagan
18 holes, 6246 yards, S.S.S. 72
Visitors: welcome except Sat and
Sun before 12.30.
Green Fees: WD £17; WE £22.
Societies: welcome by prior arrange-
ment; reductions for larger groups;
catering packages by arrangement;
early bird rates between 8am and
10am Mon-Fri; from £17.
Catering: full facilities.
Practice range, practice bar.
Hotels: Grove; Grand; Airport.

12 142 Howth
Carrickbrack Rd, Sutton, Dublin
☎(01) 8323055, Fax 8321793, Pro
8392617

Situated on Howth Head on the NE of
Dublin.
Heathland course.
Pro John McGuirk; Founded 1912
Designed by James Braid
18 holes, 5672 yards, S.S.S. 69
Visitors: welcome WD except Wed.
Green Fees: WD £20/22 Fri.
Societies: welcome WD except Wed;
reductions on numbers over 25 and
35; catering packages by arrange-
ment; from £20.
Catering: bar and restaurant.
Practice ground.
Hotels: Marine; Sutton Castle; Howth
Lodge; Bailey Court.

12 143 The Island Golf Club
Corballis, Donabate, Co Dublin
☎(01) 8436462, Fax 8436860, Sec
8453418, Bar/Rest 8436104
Leave N1 1 mile beyond Swords at
Donabate signpost then L91 for 3
miles and turn right at sign.
Seaside course.
Founded 1890
Designed by F. Hawtree & Eddie
Hackett
18 holes, 6053 yards, S.S.S. 72
Visitors: welcome by prior arrange-
ment.
Green Fees: WD £27; WE £30.
Societies: welcome Mon, Tues and
Fri by prior arrangement.
Catering: full facilities.

12 144 The K Club
Kildaire Hotel & County Club, Straffan,
Co Kildare
☎(01) 6017300, Fax 6017399
22 miles from Dublin via N7 Naas
Road.
Parkland course.; 606 is 7th.
Pro Ernie Jones; Founded 1991
Designed by Arnold Palmer
18 holes, 7159 yards, S.S.S. 74
Visitors: welcome by prior arrange-
ment.
Green Fees: WD £120; WE £120.
Societies: welcome groups of 16 or
more; catering packages by arrange-
ment; from £80.
Catering: full clubhouse catering facili-
ties, bar, coffee shop.
Practice range, available.
Hotels: Kildaire Hotel & Country Club
5 star on site.

12 145 Kanturk
Fairyhill, Kanturk, Co Cork
☎(029) 50534, Sec 50588
1 mile from Kanturk via Fairyhill Road.

Parkland course.
Founded 1973
Designed by Richard Barry
18 holes, 6262 yards, S.S.S. 69
Visitors: welcome except on competition dates.
Green Fees: WD £10; WE £10.
Societies: welcome by prior arrangement with the secretary; catering packages by arrangement through the secretary; from £8.
Catering: full facilities.
Hotels: Duhallow Park; Assolas.

---

12 146 **Kenmare**
Killowen Rd, Kenmare, Co Kerry
☎(064) 41291, Fax 42061
Off the N22 Cork to Killarney Road and then on to the R569.
Parkland course on the mouth of a river.
Pro Charlie McCarthy; Founded 1903
Designed by Eddie Hackett
18 holes, 6003 yards, S.S.S. 69
Visitors: welcome.
Green Fees: WD £16; WE £16.
Societies: welcome by prior arrangement; minimum 18 players; catering by arrangement; from £13.
Catering: full catering facilities available.
Hotels: Park; Kenmare Bay; Sheen Falls.

---

12 147 **Kilcock**
Gallow, Kilcock, Co Meath
☎(01) 6284074
2 miles N of Kilcock.
Parkland course.
Founded 1985
Designed by Eddie Hackett
18 holes, 5775 yards, S.S.S. 70
Visitors: welcome WD; WE by prior arrangement.
Green Fees: terms on application.
Societies: welcome by prior arrangement.
Catering: bar snacks.

---

12 148 **Kilcoole**
Kilcoole, Co Wicklow
☎(01) 2872066
21 miles S of Dublin on coast.
Parkland course.
Founded 1992
9 holes, 5506 yards, S.S.S. 69
Visitors: welcome except Sat and Sun am.
Green Fees: WD £12; WE £14.
Societies: welcome by prior arrangement.
Catering: clubhouse facilities.

12 149 **Kilkea Castle**
Castle Dermot, Co Kildare
☎(0503) 45156
40 miles from Dublin.
Parkland course.
Founded 1994
Designed by McDadd & Cassidy
18 holes, 6200 yards
Visitors: welcome; booking always advisable.
Green Fees: WD £25; WE £30.
Societies: welcome by prior arrangement.
Catering: full facilities.

---

12 150 **Kilkee**
East End, Kilkee, Co Clare
☎(065) 56048, Fax 56041
400 yards from town centre.
Meadowland course.
Founded 1896
Designed by McAlister
18 holes, 5537 yards, S.S.S. 69
Visitors: welcome.
Green Fees:
Societies: welcome by prior arrangement; restrictions in July and early August; catering packages by arrangement.
Catering: full facilities.

---

12 151 **Kilkenny**
Glendine, Kilkenny, Co Kilkenny
☎(056) 65400, Pro 61730
1 miles NW of Kilkenny off the Castlecorner Road.
Parkland course.
Founded 1896
18 holes, 5857 yards, S.S.S. 70
Visitors: welcome.
Green Fees: WD £16; WE £18.
Societies: welcome by prior arrangement; mainly on Sat am.
Catering: clubhouse facilities.

---

12 152 **Killarney Golf Club**
Mahoney's Point, Killarney, Co Kerry
☎(064) 31034, Fax 33065, Pro 31615, Bar/Rest 36602
2 miles W of Killarney on the N70.
Parkland and lakeside course.
Pro Tony Covemy; Founded 1939
Designed by Sir Guy Campbell & Henry Longhurst
Killeen: 18 holes, 6474 yards, S.S.S. 73; Mahony Point: 18 holes, 6164 yards, S.S.S. 72
Visitors: welcome by prior arrangement.
Green Fees: WD £38; WE £38.
Societies: welcome by prior arrangement with handicap certificates; dis-

counts for groups of 20 or more; from £38.
Catering: full clubhouse facilities.
Hotels: club can provide a list.

---

12 153 **Killeen**
Kill, Co Kildare
☎(045) 66003
N7 to Kill village then head to Straffan.
Parkland course.
Founded 1991
18 holes, 4989 yards, S.S.S. 66
Visitors: welcome.
Green Fees: WD £11; WE £13.
Societies: welcome.
Catering: full bar and catering.

---

12 154 **Killeline**
Newcastle West, Co. Limerick
☎(069) 61600
On the edge of Newcastle West.
Parkland course.
Founded 1993
Designed by E Hackett
18 holes, 6720 yards, S.S.S. 72
Visitors: welcome.
Green Fees: WD £12; WE £12.
Societies: welcome at all times by arrangement; catering packages by arrangement; from £10.
Catering: full facilities.
Hotels: Courtney Lodge; Rathkeale House; Devon Inn.

---

12 155 **Killiney**
Ballinclea Rd, Killiney, Co Dublin
☎(01) 2852823, Bar/Rest 2851983
3 miles from Dun Laoghaire.
Parkland course.
Founded 1903
9 holes, 5655 yards, S.S.S. 70
Visitors: welcome.
Green Fees: WD £20; WE £20.
Societies: none.
Catering: full clubhouse facilities.
Hotels: Killiney Castle; Killiney Court.

---

12 156 **Killorglin**
Steelroe, Killorglin, Co. Kerry
☎(066) 61979, Fax 61437
On the N70 Tralee Road 3km from the bridge at Killorglin.
Parkland course.
Pro John Gleeson; Founded 1992
Designed by Eddie Hackett
18 holes, 6467 yards, S.S.S. 71
Visitors: welcome.
Green Fees: WD £14; WE £16.
Societies: welcome; terms on application.
Catering: full clubhouse facilities.

Hotels: Bianncoi Inn; Riverside House; Grove Lodge; Fairways B&B; Laune Bridge; Fern Rock.

12 157 **Kilrush**
Parknamoney, Kilrush, Co Clare
☎(065) 51138, Fax 52633, Sec 59005
0.5 miles from Kilrush on N68 from Ennis.
Parkland course.
Pro Sean O'Connor; Founded 1934
Designed by Dr A Spring (Extended in 1994)
18 holes, 5986 yards, S.S.S. 70
Visitors: welcome.
Green Fees: WD £16; WE £18.
Societies: welcome by prior arrangement; from £10.
Catering: full clubhouse facilities available.
Hotels: Halpins; Stella Maris; Bellbridge.

12 158 **Kilternan Golf & Country Club**
Kilternan Hotel, Enniskerry Road, Co Dublin
☎(01) 2955559, Fax 2955670, Pro 2952986
On N11 S of Dublin.
Hilly parkland course.
Pro Gary Headley; Founded 1988
Designed by E Hackett
18 holes, 4952 yards, S.S.S. 67
Visitors: welcome.
Green Fees: WD £16; WE £20.
Societies: welcome by prior arrangement; leisure club; tennis courts; workout studios; from £13.50.
Catering: full facilities in hotel.
Hotels: Kilternan Hotel on site; golf packages available.

12 159 **Kinsale**
Farrangalway, Kinsale, Co Cork
☎(021) 774722m, Pro 773258
3 miles N of Kinsale on Cork Road.
Parkland course.; club founded 1912.
Pro Ger Broderick; Founded 1994
Designed by J Kenneally
18 holes, 6609 yards, S.S.S. 72
Visitors: welcome.
Green Fees: WD £20; WE £25.
Societies: welcome by prior arrangement; restricted to 11.30am-1.30pm only at WE; catering by arrangement; also 9-hole course available, 3 miles E of Kinsale at Ringenane £12; from £18.
Catering: full clubhouse facilities.
Hotels: Actons; Trident; Blue Haven.

12 160 **Knockanally Golf & Country Club**
Donadea, North Kildare
☎(045) 69322
3 miles off the main Dublin-Galway Road between Kilcock and Enfield.
Parkland course.
Founded 1985
Designed by Noel Lyons
18 holes, 6424 yards, S.S.S. 72
Visitors: welcome.
Green Fees: WD £15; WE £20.
Societies: welcome by prior arrangement everyday.
Catering: full clubhouse facilities.

12 161 **Lahinch Golf Club**
Lahinch, Co Clare
☎(065) 81003, Fax 81592
34 miles from Shannon Airport.
Seaside course.
Founded 1892
Designed by JD Harris/Donald Steel (Castle); Designed by Tom Morris (1892), redesigned by Dr. A. MacKenzie (Old)
Castle: 18 holes, 5138 yards, S.S.S. 70; Old: 18 holes, 6633 yards, S.S.S. 73
Visitors: welcome.
Green Fees: WD £40; WE £40.
Societies: welcome except Sun.
Catering: full facilities.

12 162 **Laytown & Bettystown**
Bettystown, Co Meath
☎(041) 27563, Fax 28506, Pro 28793, Sec 27170, Bar/Rest 27534
45 miles N of Dublin Airport.
Links course.
Pro Robert Browne; Founded 1909
18 holes, 5668 yards, S.S.S. 69
Visitors: welcome by prior arrangement.
Green Fees: terms on application.
Societies: welcome WD and some Sat; terms on application.
Catering: full bar and catering facilities.

12 163 **Lee Valley**
Clashanure, Ovens, Co Cork
☎(021) 331721, Fax 331695, Pro 331758
On main Cork-Killarney Road.
Parkland course.
Pro John Savage; Founded 1993
Designed by Christy O'Connor Jnr
18 holes, 6715 yards, S.S.S. 72
Visitors: welcome by prior arrangement.
Green Fees: WD £20; WE £25.

Societies: welcome by arrangement.
Catering: full clubhouse facilities.
Hotels: Blarney Park; Farran House.

12 164 **Leixlip**
Leixlip, Co Kildare
☎(01) 6244978, Sec 6246185, Bar/Rest 6247040
Off N4 past Lucan.
Parkland course.
Founded 1994
Designed by E Hackett
18 holes, 6068 yards, S.S.S. 70
Visitors: welcome.
Green Fees: WD £13; WE £16.
Societies: welcome by prior arrangement; discounts for groups of more than 20; from £13.
Catering: clubhouse facilities.
Hotels: Becketts; Springfield; Spa.

12 165 **Leopardstown Golf Centre**
Foxrock, Dublin
☎(01) 2895341
5 miles S of Dublin.
Parkland course.
18 holes, 5384 yards, S.S.S. 66
Visitors: welcome.
Green Fees: terms on application.
Societies: welcome Sun morning.
Catering: café and restaurant facilities.

12 166 **Letterkenny**
Barnhill, Letterkenny, Co Donegal
☎(074) 21150
On T72 2 miles N of Letterkenny.
Parkland course.
Founded 1913
Designed by E. Hackett
18 holes, 6239 yards, S.S.S. 71
Visitors: welcome.
Green Fees: terms on application.
Societies: welcome by arrangement.
Catering: bar and snacks available; meals by arrangement.

12 167 **Limerick**
Ballyclough, Co Limerick
☎(061) 415146, Pro 412492
S of the city on Fedamore Road.
Parkland course.
Founded 1891
18 holes, 5938 yards, S.S.S. 71
Visitors: welcome before 4pm WD except Tues.
Green Fees: WD £20; WE £12.
Societies: welcome Mon, Wed, Fri mornings.
Catering: full facilities.

Macroom Golf Club
Lackaduve, Macroom, Co. Cork.

Macroom Golf Club is a magnificent parkland course situated within the castle grounds on the winding banks of the Sullane. The Kerry mountains to the West & the great old trees provide a stunning backdrop for our 18 hole par 72 course. With green-fees of just £13.00 during the week and £16.00 at weekends, and full catering facilities available your guaranteed a warm welcome.

Phone for more details on 026-41072 or fax 0126-41391.
Special society rates & group catering available upon request.

---

12 168 Limerick County Golf & Country Club
Bellyneety, Co Limerick
☎(061) 351881, Fax 351384
5 miles S of Limerick towards Bruff/Kilmallock.
Parkland course.
Founded 1994
Designed by Des Smyth
18 holes, 6191 yards, S.S.S. 74
Visitors: welcome.
Green Fees: WD £20; WE £25.
Societies: welcome; deposit required; from £18.
Catering: full facilities.
Practice range, golf school.
Hotels: Castleray Park; Woodlands; Jurys.

12 169 Lismore
Lismore, Co Waterford
☎(058) 54026, Sec 54222
0.5 miles from Lismore on Killarney Road.
Parkland course.
Founded 1965
Designed by Eddie Hackett
9 holes, 5291 yards, S.S.S. 67
Visitors: welcome; some Sun reserved.
Green Fees: WD £8; WE £10.
Societies: welcome by arrangement.
Catering: clubhouse facilities.

12 170 Loughrea
Loughrea, Co Galway
☎(091) 41049
On L11 1 mile N of Loughrea.
Meadowland course.
Founded 1924
Designed by Eddie Hackett
18 holes, 5176 yards, S.S.S. 68
Visitors: welcome.
Green Fees: terms on application.
Societies: welcome by prior arrangement.
Catering: clubhouse facilities.

12 171 Lucan
Celbridge Rd, Lucan, Co Dublin
☎(01) 6280246, Fax 6282929, Sec 6282106
Take the N4 from Dublin and turn of at Celbridge.
Parkland course.
Founded 1897
18 holes, 5994 yards, S.S.S. 71
Visitors: welcome.
Green Fees: WD £20; WE £1620.
Societies: welcome by arrangement.
Catering: full bar and restaurant service.

12 172 Luttrellstown Castle
Castleknock, Dublin 15
☎(01) 8089988
Leave N1 at M50 intersection following southbound signs, exit M50 at Castleknock.
Parkland course.
Pro Graham Campbell; Founded 1993
Designed by Dr Nick Bielenberg/Edward Connaughton
18 holes, 6367 yards, S.S.S. 73
Visitors: welcome.
Green Fees: WD £40; WE £45.
Societies: welcome; terms on application.
Catering: full clubhouse facilities.
Hotels: Liffey Valley; Kildaire Hotel & CC; Conrad International; on site accommodation in 2 courtyard apartments.

12 173 Macroom
Lackaduv, Macroom, Co Cork
☎(026) 41072, Fax 41391
On main Cork/Killarney road on the outskirts of the town.
Parkland course.
Founded 1924
Designed by J Kennealy (new 9 holes)
18 holes, 5574 yards, S.S.S. 70
Visitors: welcome; some WE restrictions.

Green Fees: WD £13; WE £16.
Societies: welcome by prior arrangement between March-October; from £11.
Catering: full facilities.
Hotels: Castle.

12 174 Mahon
Clover Hill, Blackrock, Co Cork
☎(021) 362480, Sec 362727
2 miles SE of Cork
Municipal parkland course.
Founded 1980
18 holes, yards, S.S.S. 62
Visitors: welcome WD WE by prior arrangement.
Green Fees: WD £8.50; WE £9.50.
Catering: bar, snacks, lunch and dinner by arrangement.

12 175 Malahide
Beechwood, The Grange, Malahide, Co Dublin
☎(01) 8461611, Fax 8461270, Pro 8460002, Bar/Rest 8461067
8 miles N of Dublin; 1 mile S of Malahide.
Parkland course.
Pro David Barton; Founded 1892/1990
Designed by Eddie Hackett
18 holes, 6066 yards, S.S.S. 72
Visitors: welcome Mon, Thurs, Fri and Sat up to 9.30.
Green Fees: WD £30; WE £40.
Societies: welcome Mon, Thurs, Fri and Sat morning; discounts available; catering by arrangement; from £30.
Catering: full bar and restaurant facilities.
Hotels: Grand Hotel; Portmarnock Links.

12 176 Mallow
Ballyellis, Mallow, Co Cork
☎(022) 21145, Fax 42501, Pro 43424, Sec 42501

Mallow Golf Club
BALLYELLIS, MALLOW, Co. CORK. Tel: 00 353 22 21145, Fax:00 353 22 42501.

This majestic parkland course with exceptional views of both the Mushera and the distant Galtee mountains boasts an idyllic rural setting, set in the heart of the Blackwater Valley.

Course Length: 6518 yds, Par 72. **Clubhouse Dress:** Smart Casual, no denim jeans.
Visitors: Welcome at all times but pre-booking is essential. **Green Fees:** £20 w/days; £25 w/ends.

1.5 km from Mallow on the Killanvullen Road.
Parkland course.
Pro Sean Conway; Founded 1892/1947
Designed by Commander J.D. Harris
18 holes, 5960 yards, S.S.S. 72
Visitors: welcome WD; WE restrictions.
Green Fees: WD £20; WE £25.
Societies: welcome WD by prior arrangement; packages available; from £20.
Catering: full clubhouse facilities.
Hotels: Longueville House; Hibernian.

12 177 Mannan Castle
Donaghmoyne, Carrickmacross, Co Monaghan
☎(042) 63308, Fax 63195, Sec 62531
4 miles NE of Carrickmacross on the Crossmaglen Road.
Parkland course.
Founded 1994
Designed by F Ainsworth
9 holes, 6008 yards, S.S.S. 71
Visitors: welcome.
Green Fees: WD £10; WE £10.
Societies: welcome WD and Sat mornings; from £8.
Catering: clubhouse facilities.

12 178 Milltown
Lower Churchtown Rd, Milltown, Co Dublin
☎(01) 4976090, Fax 4976008, Pro 4977072
3 miles S of the city centre via Ranelagh village.
Parkland course.
Founded 1907
Designed by F E Davies
18 holes, 5638 yards, S.S.S. 69
Visitors: welcome except Tues and Sat; with a member on Sun.
Green Fees: WD £28; WE £28.
Societies: welcome by prior arrangement; catering packages by prior arrangement; private function room; from £28.
Catering: bar and restaurant facilities.
Hotels: Berkeley Court; Jury's; Herbert Park; Montrose.

12 179 Mitchelstown
Mitchelstown, Co Cork
☎(025) 24072
1 mile from Mitchelstown off the N1 Dublin to Cork Road.
Parkland course.
Founded 1908
Designed by David Jones
18 holes, 5148 yards, S.S.S. 67
Visitors: welcome.
Green Fees: WD £10; WE £10.
Societies: welcome except Sun; catering packages available.
Catering: full facilities.

12 180 Moate
Aghanargit, Moate, Co Westmeath
☎(0902) 81271, Sec 81270
On Dublin-Galway Road.
Parkland course.
Founded 1900
Designed by B Browne (1993 extension)
18 holes, 5752 yards, S.S.S. 70
Visitors: welcome.
Green Fees: WD £10; WE £13.
Societies: welcome except after 12.30pm at WE; catering packages available; caddy hire; visitors locker room; from £10.
Catering: full bar and catering facilities.
Hotels: Grand.

12 181 Monkstown
Parkgariffe, Monkstown, Co Cork
☎(021) 841376, Fax 841376, Pro 841686, Sec 841225, Bar/Rest 841098
11 miles E of Cork; turn right off the Rochestown Road at the Rochestown Inn.
Parkland course.
Pro Matt Murphy; Founded 1908/71
Designed by Peter O'Hare/Tom Carey
18 holes, 5669 yards, S.S.S. 70
Visitors: welcome.
Green Fees: WD £23; WE £26.
Societies: welcome by prior arrangement; from £18.
Catering: restaurant and bar facilities available.
Practice ground.
Hotels: Rochestown Park.

12 182 Moor Park
Mooretown, Navan, Co Meath
☎(046) 27661
Parkland course.
Founded 1993
18 holes, 5600 yards, S.S.S. 69
Visitors: welcome.
Green Fees: terms on application.

12 183 Mount Juliet
Thomastown, Co Kilkenny
☎(056) 24455, Fax 24522
Signposted in Thomastown off the main Dublin-Waterford Road.
Parkland course; assoc with David Leadbetter Academy.
Founded 1992
Designed by Jack Nicklaus
18 holes, 7112 yards, S.S.S. 74
Visitors: welcome by prior arrangement.
Green Fees: WD £70; WE £75.
Societies: welcome by prior arrangement; WE price of £50; minimum 20 players; from £45.
Catering: full facilities.
Practice ground with driving bays and 18 hole putting green.
Hotels: Mount Juliet.

12 184 Mount Temple
Mount Temple Village, Moate, Co Westmeath
☎(0902) 81545, Fax 81957, Sec 81841
4 miles off the main N6 Dublin-Galway route in Mount Temple Village.
Combination of links and parkland course.
Founded 1991
Designed by Robert J. Brown and Michael Dolan
18 holes, 5872 yards, S.S.S. 71
Visitors: welcome; by arrangement at WE.
Green Fees: WD £14; WE £16.
Societies: welcome by prior arrangement; from £14.
Catering: catering and wine licence; pub 100 yards.
Practice range, 3 hole practice area.
Hotels: Hudson Bay; Prince of Wales; Royal Hoey; Shamrock Lodge; Bloomfield House.

12 185 Mountbellew

Shankhill, Mountbellew, Co Galway
☎(0905) 79259, Sec 79622
On T4 28 miles E of Galway.
Undulating meadowland course.
Founded 1929
18 holes, 5143 yards, S.S.S. 66
Visitors: welcome.
Green Fees: WD £8; WE £8.
Societies: welcome by prior arrangement.
Catering: catering by arrangement; snacks.

12 186 Mountrath

Knockinina, Mountrath, Co Laois
☎(0502) 32558, Sec 32421
0.5 miles off the main Dublin-Limerick Road.
Undulating parkland course.
Founded 1929
18 holes, 5493 yards, S.S.S. 69
Visitors: welcome; some WE restrictions.
Green Fees: WD £10; WE £10.
Societies: welcome WD by prior arrangement; discounts for larger groups; from £10.
Catering: full clubhouse facilities available.
Hotels: Killeshin; Montague; Leix Co; Grants; Racket Hall.

12 187 Mullingar

Belvedere, Mullingar, Co Westmeath
☎(044) 48366, Fax 41499
3.5 miles from Mullingar on the N52.
Parkland course.
Founded 1894
Designed by James Braid
18 holes, 6468 yards, S.S.S. 70
Visitors: welcome.
Green Fees: WD £20; WE £25.
Societies: welcome by prior arrangement; packages available; terms on application.
Catering: full clubhouse facilities.

12 188 Mulranny

Mulranny, Westport, Co Mayo
☎(098) 36262, Sec 41568
15 miles from Westport.
9 hole links course.
Founded 1968
9 holes, 6255 yards, S.S.S. 69
Visitors: welcome.
Green Fees: WD £8; WE £8.
Societies: welcome by prior arrangement; from £7.
Catering: full clubhouse facilities available.
Hotels: many in Westport.

12 189 Muskerry

Carrigrohane, Co Cork
☎(021) 385297, Pro 381445
7 miles W of Cork near Blarney.
Parkland course.
Founded 1897
18 holes, 5786 yards, S.S.S. 71
Visitors: welcome WD except Wed afternoons; Thurs mornings and after 3.30pm Fri.
Green Fees: WD £17; WE £20.
Societies: welcome by prior arrangement.
Catering: full facilities.

12 190 Naas

Kerdiffstown, Naas, Co Kildare
☎(045) 74644, Sec 76737
Between Johnstown and Sallins.
Parkland course.
Founded 1886
Designed by Arthur Spring
18 holes, 5660 yards, S.S.S. 69
Visitors: welcome Mon, Wed, Fri and Sat.
Green Fees: WD £12; WE £15.
Societies: welcome Mon, Wed, Fri and Sat morning.
Catering: bar; meals by prior arrangement.

12 191 Narin & Portnoo

Portnoo, Co Donegal
☎(075) 45107, Bar/Rest 45332
From Donegal via Ardara.
Seaside course.
Founded 1930
18 holes, 5322 yards, S.S.S. 68
Visitors: welcome; some summer restrictions.
Green Fees: terms available on application.
Societies: welcome by prior arrangement.
Catering: full bar facilities.

12 192 Nenagh

Beechwood, Nenagh, Co Tipperary
☎(067) 31476, Sec 32547
4 miles E of Nenagh.
Parkland course.
Founded 1892
Designed by Alister MacKenzie (original 9), E. Hackett (addition)l
18 holes, 5491 yards, S.S.S. 68
Visitors: welcome but by prior arrangement at WE.
Green Fees: WD £12; WE £15.
Societies: welcome by prior arrangement.
Catering: full facilities.
Practice range, large practice ground.

12 193 New Ross

Tinneranny, New Ross, Co Wexford
☎(051) 21433
1 mile from town centre off Waterford Road.
Parkland course.
Founded 1905
9 holes, 5172 yards, S.S.S. 69
Visitors: welcome; some Sun restrictions.
Green Fees: WD £8; WE £12.
Societies: welcome by arrangement.
Catering: clubhouse facilities.

12 194 Newcastle West

Ardagh, Co Limerick
☎(069) 76500
Off N21 2 miles beyond Rathkeale.
Parkland course.
Founded 1939/94
Designed by Arthur Spring
18 holes, 6317 yards, S.S.S. 72
Visitors: welcome.
Green Fees: WD £18; WE £18.
Societies: welcome by prior arrangement; catering packages by arrangement; from £12.
Catering: bar and restaurant.
Hotels: Courtenay Lodge; Rathkeale House; Devon Inn.

12 195 Newlands

Clondalkin, Dublin
☎(01) 4593157, Pro 4593538, Sec 4513436
6 miles from city centre.
Parkland course.
Founded 1926
Designed by James Braid
18 holes, 5696 yards, S.S.S. 70
Visitors: welcome.
Green Fees: WD £25; WE £25.
Societies: welcome WD.
Catering: full facilities.

12 196 North West

Lisfannon, Fahan, Co Donegal
☎(077) 61715, Bar/Rest 61841
2 miles S of Buncrana.
Seaside links course.
Founded 1892
18 holes, 5968 yards, S.S.S. 69
Visitors: welcome.
Green Fees: WD £10; WE £15.
Societies: welcome by prior arrangement WD WE in the summer.
Catering: bar and restaurant.

12 197 Nuremore

Carrickmacross, Co Monaghan
☎(042) 61438, Sec 62125

1 mile S of Carrickmacross.
Parkland course.
Founded 1964
Designed by Eddie Hackett
18 holes, 6246 yards, S.S.S. 74
Visitors: welcome.
Green Fees: WD £15; WE £18.
Societies: welcome by prior arrangement.
Catering: clubhouse and hotel facilities.

12 198 Old Conna
Ferndale Road, Bray, Co Dublin
☎(01) 2826055, Fax 2825611, Pro 2820822, Bar/Rest 2820038
12 miles from Dublin.
Parkland course.
Founded 1977
18 holes, 5590 yards, S.S.S. 71
Visitors: welcome Mon, Thurs and Fri.
Green Fees: WD £20; WE £20.
Catering: bar and full meal service.

12 199 Old Head Links
Old Head Golf Links
Kinsale, Co Cork
☎(021) 778444, Fax 778022
20 miles S of Cork.
Clifftop setting on Atlantic promontory.
Founded 1996
Designed by J Carr/R Kirby
18 holes, 6756 yards, S.S.S. 72
Visitors: welcome.
Green Fees: WD £50; WE £60.
Societies: welcome by prior arrangement; from £50.
Catering: bar and light meals; full restaurant service.

12 200 The Open Golf Centre
Newtown House, St Margaret's, Co Dublin
☎(01) 8640324, Fax 8341400
4 miles from Dublin adjacent to Dublin Airport.
Parkland course.
Pro Robin Machin; Founded 1993
Designed by Martin Hawtree
27 holes, 6570 yards
Visitors: welcome.
Green Fees: WD £8.50; WE £12.50.
Societies: welcome by prior arrangement; from £8.50.
Catering: full facilities.
Practice range, 15 bays.
Hotels: Forte Crest.

12 201 Otway
Saltpans, Rathmullan, Co Donegal
☎(074) 58319, Sec 58235

15 miles NE of Letterkenny by Lough Swilly.
Links course.
Founded 1893
9 holes, 4234 yards, S.S.S. 60
Visitors: welcome.
Green Fees: terms on application.
Societies: welcome.
Hotels: Fort Royal; Rathmullan House; Pier Hotel.

12 202 Oughterard
Gortreevagh, Oughterard, Co Galway
☎(091) 82131
1 mile from Oughterard on N59.
Mature parkland course with elevated greens.
Founded 1973
Designed by Hawtree/Hackett
18 holes, 6089 yards, S.S.S. 69
Visitors: welcome.
Green Fees: terms on application.
Societies: welcome WD.
Catering: bar snacks; full a la carte menu.

12 203 Parknasilla
Parknasilla, Sneem, Co Kerry
☎(064) 45122
2 miles E of Sneem on the Ring of Kerry Road.
Undulating seaside course.
Founded 1974
9 holes, 4652 yards, S.S.S. 65
Visitors: welcome.
Green Fees: terms on application.

12 204 Portarlington
Garryhinch, Portarlington, Co Offaly
☎(0502) 23115, Sec 23044
On L116 between Portarlington and Mountmellick.
Parkland course.
Founded 1909
18 holes, 6004 yards, S.S.S. 71
Visitors: welcome.
Green Fees: WD £14; WE £17.
Societies: welcome; from £14.
Catering: bar and restaurant facilities.
Hotels: East End Hotel.

12 205 Portmarnock Golf Club
Portmarnock, Co Dublin
☎(01) 8462968, Fax 8462601, Pro 8462634, Bar/Rest 8462783
From Dublin along the coast road to Baldoyle and on to Portmarnock.
Seaside links course.
Founded 1894
Designed by W.G. Pickeman and George Ross

27 holes, 6497 yards, S.S.S. 75
Visitors: welcome.
Green Fees: WD £40; WE £50.
Societies: welcome Mon, Tues and Fri by prior arrangement.
Catering: full facilities.

12 206 Portsalon
Portsalon, Fanad, Co Donegal
☎(074) 59459, Fax 59459
20 miles N of Letterkenny.
Seaside links course.
Founded 1891
Designed by Mr Thompson of Portrush
18 holes, 5880 yards, S.S.S. 68
Visitors: welcome by prior arrangement.
Green Fees: WD £12; WE £15.
Societies: welcome by prior arrangement; from £10.
Catering: full facilities.
Hotels: Fort Royal; Rathmullan House; Pier Hotel.

12 207 Portumna
Ennis Rd, Portumna, Co Galway
☎(0509) 41059
1.5 miles from Portumna on Ennis Road.
Parkland course.
Founded 1913
18 holes, 5474 yards, S.S.S. 67
Visitors: welcome Mon-Sat.
Green Fees: WD £10; WE £10.
Societies: welcome by prior arrangement with Sec; special packages available; terms on application.
Catering: restaurant and bar.
Practice area.
Hotels: Shannon Oaks.

12 208 Raffeen Creek
Ringaskiddy, Co Cork
☎(021) 378430
1 mile from Ringaskiddy ferry.
Seaside/parkland course with water.
Founded 1988
Designed by Eddie Hackett
9 holes, 5098 yards, S.S.S. 68
Visitors: welcome WD; WE afternoon only.
Green Fees: WD £10; WE £10.
Societies: welcome by arrangement.
Catering: bar food.

12 209 Rathdowney
Rathdowney, Portlaoise, Co. Laois
☎(0505) 46170, Sec 46233
Off the N7 in Rathdowney.
Parkland course.
Founded 1930

Designed by Eddie Hackett
18 holes, 5894 yards, S.S.S. 71
Visitors: welcome; some Sun restrictions.
Green Fees: WD £10; WE £10.
Societies: welcome by prior arrangement with the secretary; bar and catering packages by prior arrangement; from £8.
Catering: clubhouse facilities.
Hotels: Leix Co; Woodview GH.

12 210 **Rathfarnham**
Newtown, Rathfarnham
☎(01) 4931201
2 miles from Rathfarnham.
Parkland course.
Founded 1899
Designed by John Jacobs
9 holes, 5833 yards, S.S.S. 70
Visitors: welcome WD except Tues.
Green Fees: WD £20.
Societies: welcome by prior arrangement only.
Catering: lunch and dinners.

12 211 **Rathsallagh House**
Dunlavin, Co Wicklow
☎(045) 403316, Fax 4033295
32 miles SW of Dublin.
Parkland course.
Founded 1994
Designed by Peter McEvoy
18 holes, 6916 yards, S.S.S. 74
Visitors: welcome.
Green Fees: WD £20; WE £35.
Societies: welcome by arrangement.

12 212 **Redcastle**
Redcastle, Moville, Co Donegal
☎(077) 82073
Parkland course.
Founded 1983
9 holes, yards, S.S.S. 70
Visitors: public.

12 213 **Rockwell**
Cashel, Co Tipperary
☎(062) 61444
Parkland course.
Founded 1964
9 holes, 3782 yards, S.S.S. 60
Visitors: welcome by arrangement.
Green Fees: terms on application.
Societies: on application.

12 214 **Rosapenna**
Rosapenna Hotel, Downings, Co Donegal
☎(074) 55301, Fax 55128

25 miles from Letterkenny.
Links course.
Pro Don Patterson; Founded 1893
Designed by Tom Morris (1893), Re-Designed by Braid & Vardon (
18 holes, 6271 yards, S.S.S. 71
Visitors: welcome.
Green Fees: WD £18; WE £20.
Societies: welcome but must have handicap certificate.
Catering: full hotel bar and restaurant facilities.
Hotels: Rosapenna Hotel (4 star) on site.

12 215 **Roscommon**
Mote Park, Roscommon, Co Roscommon
☎(0903) 26382, Sec 26927
0.25 miles from Roscommon Town.
Parkland course.
Founded 1904/1996
Designed by Eddie Connaughton
18 holes, 6040 yards, S.S.S. 69
Visitors: welcome except Tues and Sun.
Green Fees: WD £15; WE £15.
Societies: welcome by prior arrangement; catering by arrangement; from £10.
Catering: full bar and catering facilities.
Hotels: Abbey; Royal; Regans; Gleesons.

12 216 **Roscrea**
Derryvale, Roscrea, Co Tipperary
☎(0505) 21130
2 miles E of Roscrea on N7.
Parkland course.
Founded 1892
Designed by A. Spring
18 holes, 5708 yards, S.S.S. 70
Visitors: welcome.
Green Fees: terms on application.
Societies: welcome by prior arrangement.
Catering: bar and restaurant facilities.

12 217 **Rosslare**
Rosslare Strand, Co Wexford
☎(053) 32113, Fax 32203, Pro 32238, Sec 32203, Bar/Rest 32460
6 miles from the Rosslare ferry terminal; 10 miles S of Wexford.
Seaside links course.
Pro Austin Skerritt; Founded 1905/1992
Designed by Hawtree & Taylor (old), Christy O'Connor Jnr (new)
18 holes, 6577 yards, S.S.S. 72
Visitors: welcome.

Green Fees: WD £22; WE £30.
Societies: welcome by prior arrangement; catering packages by arrangement.
Catering: full clubhouse facilities.
Hotels: Kellys Resort.

12 218 **Rossmore**
Rossmore Park, Cootehill Road, Monaghan, Co Monaghan
☎(047) 81316, Sec 81473
1.5 miles on the Cootehill Road out of Monaghan town.
Parkland course.
Founded 1916
Designed by Des Smyth
18 holes, 5507 yards, S.S.S. 68
Visitors: welcome.
Green Fees: WD £15; WE £15.
Societies: welcome; from £10.
Catering: full bar and restaurant facilities.
Hotels: Four Seasons.

12 219 **Royal Dublin Golf Club**
North Bull Island, Dollymount, Dublin 3
☎(01) 8337153, Fax 8336504, Pro 8336477, Sec 8336346, Bar/Rest 8333370
NE from Dublin along the coast Road to Bull Wall.
Links course.
Pro Leonard Owens; Founded 1885
Designed by H.S. Colt
18 holes, 6330 yards, S.S.S. 73
Visitors: welcome WD except Wed, Sun 10am-12 noon and after 4pm on Sat.
Green Fees: WD £50; WE £60.
Societies: welcome but must book a year in advance; catering by prior arrangement; from £33.
Catering: full clubhouse facilities, bar and restaurant.
Hotels: Marine; Hollybrook; Howth Lodge.

12 220 **Royal Tara Golf Club**
Bellinter, Navan, Co Meath
☎(046) 25244, Sec 25508, Bar/Rest 25508
Off N3 30 miles N of Dublin.
Parkland course.
Founded 1923
Designed by Des Smyth Golf Design
27 holes, 5917 yards, S.S.S. 71
Visitors: welcome by arrangement.
Green Fees: WD £14; WE £18.
Societies: welcome Mon, Thurs, Fri and Sat by arrangement.
Catering: full bar and catering facilities.

ST. HELEN'S BAY GOLF & COUNTRY CLUB.
St. Helen's, Kilrane, Rosslare Harbour, Co. Wexford, Ireland. Tel: 053-33669/33234. Fax: 053-33803.

Located beside beautiful St. Helen's Bay, 14 holes actually overlook the coast. The course is designed to be at one with nature, taking advantage of onshore winds & gently sloping land. St. Helen's incorporates 9 water features, 5000 trees and even offers on site accommodation in the course cottages.

12 221 Rush
Rush, Co Dublin
☎(01) 8437548, Fax 8438711, Sec 8438711
Off the Dublin-Belfast Road at Blakes Cross.
Links course.
Founded 1943
9 holes, 5598 yards, S.S.S. 69
Visitors: welcome.
Green Fees: WD £15; WE £15.
Societies: welcome by prior arrangement.
Catering: full facilities.

12 222 St Annes
North Bull Island, Dollymount, Dublin 3
☎(01) 8332797, Fax 8334618, Pro 8336471, Sec 8336471, Bar/Rest 8530671
5 miles N of Dublin City.
Links course.
Pro Paddy Skerritt; Founded 1921
Designed by Eddie Hackett
18 holes, 5713 yards, S.S.S. 69
Visitors: welcome.
Green Fees: WD £24; WE £30.
Societies: welcome; Sat rate of IR£650 available; from £24.
Catering: full facilities.
Practice area.
Hotels: Marine; St Lawrence; Forte Posthouse; Grand; Sutton Castle.

12 223 St Helen's Bay
St Helen's, Kilrane, Rosslare Harbour, Co. Wexford
☎(053) 33234, Fax 33803 Pro 33669
5 minutes from the Rosslare ferryport in the village of Kilrane.
Links/parkland course mixture.
Pro Paul Roche; Founded 1993
Designed by Philip Walton
18 holes, 6091 yards, S.S.S. 72
Visitors: welcome.
Green Fees: terms on application.
Societies: welcome by prior arrangement; packages available; tennis; accommodation on site; terms on application.
Catering: full clubhouse dining and bar facilities.
Hotels: Great Southern; Rosslare; Devereux; Ferrycarrig.

12 224 St Margaret's Golf & Country Club
St Margaret's, Co Dublin
☎(01) 864-0400, Fax 864-0289
4 miles W of Dublin Airport.
Parkland course.
Founded 1992
Designed by Ruddy & Craddock
18 holes, 6917 yards, S.S.S. 73
Visitors: public.
Green Fees: WD £40; WE £40.
Societies: welcome by prior arrangement; corporate days available; £35 for parties of more than 30; from £35.
Catering: 2 bars and 2 restaurants.
Hotels: Forte Crest; Grand, Malahide.

12 225 Seapoint
Termonfeckin, Co. Louth
☎(041) 22333, Fax 22331
In Termonfeckin off the N1 Dublin to Drogheda Road.
Championship links course.
Founded 1993
Designed by Des Smyth, Declan Branigan
18 holes, 6339 yards, S.S.S. 74
Visitors: welcome.
Green Fees: WD £20; WE £25.
Societies: welcome WD by arrangement; discounts for larger groups.
Catering: bar and restaurant facilities.
Driving range.

12 226 Shannon
Shannon Airport, Co Clare
☎(061) 471849, Fax 471507, Pro 471551
0.5 miles from Shannon Airport.
Woodland/parkland course.
Founded 1966
18 holes, 6186 yards, S.S.S. 74
Visitors: welcome WD.
Green Fees: WD £20; WE £25.
Societies: welcome by prior arrangement.
Catering: bar snacks and meals.

12 227 Skerries
Hacketstown, Skerries, Co Dublin
☎(01) 8491204, Fax 8491567, Pro 8490925, Sec 8491567, Bar/Rest 8493135

N of Dublin Airport off the Belfast Road.
Parkland course.
Pro Jimmy Kinsella; Founded 1906
18 holes, 6081 yards, S.S.S. 72
Visitors: welcome.
Green Fees: terms on application.
Societies: welcome on Mon and Thurs by prior arrangement; terms on application.
Catering: full facilities.
Hotels: Trusthouse Forte, Dublin Airport.

12 228 Skibbereen & West Cabbery
Licknavar, Skibbereen, Co Cork
☎(028) 21227, Fax 22994
2 miles from Skibbereen on the Baltimore Road.
Parkland course.
Founded 1905
Designed by Eddie Hackett
18 holes, 6069 yards, S.S.S. 68
Visitors: welcome with handicap certificate.
Green Fees: WD £12; WE £16.
Societies: welcome by prior arrangement; from £12.
Catering: full clubhouse facilities.
Hotels: West Cork; Eldon; Casey's; Baltimore Harbour; Celtic Ross.

12 229 Slade Valley
Lynch Park, Brittas, Co Dublin
☎(01) 4582207, Fax 4582183
8 miles W of Dublin off N4.
Undulating parkland course.
Founded 1970
Designed by W.D. Sullivan and D. O'Brien
18 holes, 5337 yards, S.S.S. 68
Visitors: welcome WD; WE with a member.
Green Fees: WD £20.
Societies: welcome by prior arrangement with Sec.
Catering: full WE facilities.
Hotels: Green Isle; Downshire House.

12 230 Slieve Russell Golf & Country Club
Ballyconnell, Co Cavan

A golfing trip around Ireland

The first lesson that has to be learned about golf in Ireland is that, in order to derive the greatest benefit, it is better not to be in too much of a hurry. Settle in to the pace of life. Don't plan an impossible itinerary. Travel can be slow and golfing destinations remote but that is part of their attraction and you will soon adapt.

This certainly applies to the coastal sweep that begins in Dublin and ends in Galway, a journey that incorporates many wonderful courses particularly out west where giant dunes, lonely beaches and wild winds lend an accompaniment to the play that is quite uplifting. Ballybunion, Lahinch, Tralee and Waterville are fit for giants, places that pose the ultimate in challenge although beguiling enough to soften failure.

For those arriving at Shannon Airport, the decision is whether to head north or south of the great Estuary which runs into Limerick. Greater by far are the number of courses to the south-west but Lahinch, the St Andrews of Ireland, because of its discovery by officers of the Black Watch, is as fine an example of links golf as could be imagined.

Ballybunion's Old course is an undoubted monument that has brought deserved fame to the little seaside town. It involves a little more climbing than on other links although some of the high spots enhance the spectacular views. Nearby Tralee, the work of Arnold Palmer, is a course of two parts, a front nine of more open land and a back nine dominated by majestic dune country involving many demanding strokes.

Some of the greens on the outward half enjoy settings on the edge of the sea which are captivating if the wind is not severe but beauty of the setting is a recurring theme all over the south-west of Ireland, and it certainly applies to Waterville, the inspira-

tion of a local man, J.A. Mulcahy.

Killarney, scene of the 1996 Curtis Cup, continues to be highly popular with its scenic glories. It is an ideal port of call for those enjoying the delights of Kerry but there are other inland delights such as Little Island (Cork) and Carlow, set in a lovely old deer park, and three new creations, St Helen's Bay at Rosslare, Faithlegg in County Waterford and The European Club in County Wicklow.

The Irish course which has seen more great events than any other is Portmarnock, many Irish Opens, the Canada Cup, British Amateur and the Walker Cup head the impressive list, a tribute to the formidable test of golf.

Royal Dublin, older than Portmarnock, is another noble links and a word for Sutton, the nine hole course famous for its association with Joe Carr. It stands on Cush Point looking across the narrow estuary to Portmarnock where Carr was born. It is such a short, compact little course that it used to be said that if Carr shouted "Fore", everybody ducked; but if it is enchantment that you want, the Island at Malahide offers the perfect retreat among its lonely dunes. Further up the coast, Baltray, or County Louth, represents as fine a tract of land as any in a country renowned for great courses.

Many of Dublin's other courses are more parkland in character but out on the west coast the feature of the courses is again one of grandeur and beauty. Connemara, Donegal, Rosapenna and Westport are the main attraction and there are few lovelier spots where the game is played than County Sligo at Rosses Point, home of the late Cecil Ewing, another giant of Irish golf. In 1991, the Club housed the Home Internationals, a wonderfully friendly environment for a unique gathering.

☎(049) 26444, Fax 26474, Pro 26458
90 miles SW of Belfast.
Parkland course.
Founded 1992
Designed by Paddy Merrigan
18 holes, 6413 yards, S.S.S. 74
Visitors: welcome; book in advance.
Green Fees: terms on application.
Societies: welcome by prior arrangement.
Catering: full facilities.

12 231 Spanish Point
Spanish Point, Miltown Malbay, Co Clare
☎(065) 84198
2 miles from Milton Malbay; 8 miles from Lahinch.
Seaside course.
Founded 1896
9 holes, 3574 yards, S.S.S. 58
Visitors: welcome.
Green Fees: terms on application.
Societies: welcome.
Catering: light snacks only.

12 232 Stackstown
Kellystown Road, Rathfarnham
☎(01) 4941993, Pro 4944561, Bar/Rest 4942338
8 miles S of Dublin off the N81 and R115
Hilly course with panoramic views.
Founded 1976
18 holes, 5789 yards, S.S.S. 71
Visitors: welcome WD; by prior arrangement WE.
Green Fees: WD £14; WE £18.
Societies: welcome by prior arrangement.
Catering: bar snacks and full meals.

12 233 Strandhill
Strandhill, Co Sligo
☎(071) 68188, Fax 68811, Pro 68725
5 miles W of Sligo.
Links course.
Founded 1932
18 holes, 5516 yards, S.S.S. 68
Visitors: welcome.
Green Fees: WD £15; WE £15.
Societies: welcome by prior arrangement; from £15.
Catering: full facilities.
Hotels: Ocean View; Tower.

12 234 Strokestown
Strokestown, Co Roscommon
☎(078) 33100
Parkland course.
Founded 1992

9 holes, 5226 yards, S.S.S. 67
Visitors: welcome by arrangement.
Green Fees: terms on application.

12 235 Sutton
Cush Point, Sutton, Dublin 13
☎(01) 8322965, Fax 8321603, Pro 8321703
7 miles NE of city centre.
Seaside links course.
Founded 1890
9 holes, 5226 yards, S.S.S. 67
Visitors: welcome; restrictions Tues and Sat.
Green Fees: WD £15; WE £20.
Societies: welcome by prior arrangement.
Catering: clubhouse facilities.

12 236 Swinford
Brabazon Park, Swinford, Co Mayo
☎(094) 51378, Sec 51502
1 km S of Swinford on the Kiltimagh Road.
Parkland course.
Founded 1922
9 holes, 5542 yards, S.S.S. 68
Visitors: welcome.
Green Fees: WD £10; WE £10.
Societies: welcome except Sun; special packages available; from £10.
Catering: full catering; lounge bar.
Hotels: Cill Aodain; Breaffy; Welcome Inn.

12 237 Tara Glen
Ballymoney, Courtown, Co Wexford
☎(055) 25413
Parkland course.
Founded 1993
9 holes
Visitors: welcome by prior arrangement.
Green Fees: terms on application.

12 238 Templemore
Manna South, Templemore, Co Tipperary
☎(0504) 31400, Fax 31913, Sec 31720
0.5 miles S of town centre off the N62.
Parkland course.
Founded 1972
9 holes, yards, S.S.S. 67
Visitors: welcome.
Green Fees: WD £5; WE £10.
Societies: welcome by prior arrangement.
Catering: limited.
Hotels: Templemore Arms; Grants; Anner: Hayes; Munster.

12 239 Thurles
Turtulla, Thurles, Co Tipperary
☎(0504) 21983, Fax 24647, Sec 24599
1 mile from Thurles towards the main Cork-Dublin road.
Parkland course.
Pro Sean Hunt; Founded 1909/44
Designed by J McAllister
18 holes, 6465 yards, S.S.S. 71
Visitors: welcome except Sun.
Green Fees: WD £20; WE £20.
Societies: welcome except Sun; from £18.
Catering: full facilities.
Practice range, 200 yards from club.
Hotels: Anner; Hayes.

12 240 Tipperary
Rathanny
☎(062) 51119
1 mile from the town on the Glen of Aherlow Road.
Parkland course.
Founded 1896
18 holes, 5807 yards, S.S.S. 71
Visitors: welcome; some Sun restrictions.
Green Fees: WD £10; WE £10.
Societies: welcome by prior arrangement.
Catering: bar and snacks available.

12 241 Townley Hall
Townley Hall, Tullyallen, Drogheda, Co Louth
☎(041) 42229
Parkland course.
Founded 1994
18 holes, 4978 Yards
Visitors: welcome.
Green Fees: WD £5; WE £5.

12 242 Tralee
West Barrow, Ardfert, Co Kerry
☎(066) 36379, Fax 36008, Bar/Rest 36074
8 miles from Tralee on the Churchill Road.
Links course.
Founded 1896/1984
Designed by Arnold Palmer Design
18 holes, 6192 yards, S.S.S. 73
Visitors: welcome.
Green Fees: WD £45; WE £45.
Societies: welcome by prior arrangement; discounts available for larger groups; from £45.
Catering: full clubhouse facilities.
Two practice grounds.
Hotels: Mount Brandon; Grand; Abbeygate.

12 243 **Tramore**

Newtown Hill, Tramore, Co Waterford
☎(051) 386170, Fax 390961, Pro
381706, Bar/Rest 381247
7 miles S of Waterford on coast road.
Parkland course.
Pro Danny Kiely; Founded 1894
Designed by Tibbett (1936/7)
18 holes, 6055 yards, S.S.S. 73
Visitors: welcome; pre booking advisable.
Green Fees: WD £25; WE £30.
Societies: welcome by prior arrangement; full catering packages available; from £22.
Catering: catering and bar facilities.
Hotels: Grand; Majestic; O'Sheas.

12 244 **Tuam**

Barnacurragh, Tuam, Co Galway
☎(093) 28993, Fax 26003, Pro 24091
1 miles outside Tuan on the Athenwy
Road.
Parkland course.
Pro Larry Smyth; Founded 1907
Designed by E Hackett
18 holes, 6045 yards, S.S.S. 71
Visitors: welcome.
Green Fees: WD £12; WE £14.
Societies: welcome by prior arrangement except on Sat afternoon and Sun; discounts for groups of more than 20; deposit of £50 required; catering by arrangement; from £10.
Catering: full clubhouse bar and restaurant facilities.
Practice range, practice ground.
Hotels: Imperial.

12 245 **Tubbercurry**

Ougham, Tubbercurry, Co Sligo
☎(071) 85849, Sec 86124
0.5 miles from town on the Ballymote Road.
Parkland course.
Founded 1991
Designed by Eddie Hackett
9 holes, 5490 yards, S.S.S. 69
Visitors: welcome; Sun by arrangement.
Green Fees: WD £10; WE £10.
Societies: welcome except Sun; discounts available; catering by arrangement; from £10.
Catering: full bar and restaurant facilities.
Hotels: Conleys.

12 246 **Tulfarris Hotel & Country Club**

Blessington, Co Wicklow
☎(045) 64612

6 miles from Blessington off N81.
Parkland course.
Founded 1989
Designed by Eddie Hackett
9 holes, 5612 yards, S.S.S. 69
Visitors: welcome; some Sun restrictions.
Green Fees: terms on application.
Societies: welcome by prior arrangement.
Catering: restaurant and bar facilities.

12 247 **Tullamore**

Brookfield, Tullamore, Co Offaly
☎(0506) 21439, Pro 51757
3.5 miles S of Tullamore off the R451
to Kinnity from the N52.
Parkland course.
Founded 1886
Designed by James Braid/ P
Merrigan(redesign)
18 holes, 6434 yards, S.S.S. 70
Visitors: welcome; some Tues, Sat
and Sun restrictions.
Green Fees: WD £16; WE £25.
Societies: welcome by prior arrangement; terms on application.
Catering: full bar and restaurant facilities.

12 248 **Virginia**

Virginia, Co Cavan
☎(049) 47235
50 miles N of Dublin on the main
Dublin-Cavan Road.
Meadowland course.
Founded 1946
9 holes, 4900 yards, S.S.S. 62
Visitors: welcome.
Green Fees: terms on application.
Catering: in Park Hotel.

12 249 **Waterford**

Newrath, Waterford, Co Waterford
☎(051) 876748, Fax 853405, Pro
854256, Bar/Rest 874182
On N9 from Dublin 1 mile from
Waterford or N25 from Rosslare.
Parkland course.
Pro Eammon Condon; Founded 1912
Designed by Cecil Barcroft And Willie
Park/ James Braid
18 holes, 5722 yards, S.S.S. 70
Visitors: welcome.
Green Fees: WD £22; WE £27.
Societies: welcome by arrangement
with secretary/manager; terms on
application.
Catering: full clubhouse facilities
available.
Hotels: Jurys; Tower; Granville;
Bridge.

12 250 **Waterford Castle Golf & Country Club**

The Island, Ballinakill, Co. Waterford
☎(051) 871633, Fax 879316
2 miles from Waterford on the
Dunmore East Road.
Parkland course on island in River
Suir.
Founded 1993
Designed by Des Smyth and Declan
Brannigan
18 holes, 6303 yards, S.S.S. 73
Visitors: welcome by arrangement.
Green Fees: WD £18; WE £20.
Societies: welcome by arrangement.
Catering: clubhouse facilities.

12 251 **Waterville Golf Links**

Rink of Kerry, Waterville, Co Kerry
☎(066) 74102, Fax 74482
1 mile W of Waterville half way
through the Ring of Kerry.
Links course.
Pro Liam Higgins; Founded 1901/1972
Designed by E. Hackett
18 holes, 7184 yards, S.S.S. 74
Visitors: welcome.
Green Fees: WD £50; WE £50.
Societies: welcome by prior arrangement; discount 10% for 20 or more
players; from £50.
Catering: full clubhouse facilities.
Practice range, open to green fee paying players and members.
Hotels: Waterville House; Butler
Arms; Bay View.

12 252 **West Waterford**

Coolcormack, Dungarvan, Co
Waterford
☎(058) 43216, Fax 44343, Sec
41475
3 miles W of Dungarvan off the N25
on the Aglish Road.
Parkland course.
Founded 1993
Designed by Eddie Hackett
18 holes, 6802 yards, S.S.S. 74
Visitors: welcome.
Green Fees: WD £18; WE £22.
Societies: welcome everyday by prior
arrangement; from £15.
Catering: full clubhouse facilities
everyday.
Hotels: Lawlors; Park; Clonea Strand.

12 253 **Westmanstown**

Clonsilla, Dublin
☎(01) 8205817, Fax 8207891, Sec
8210562, Bar/Rest 8207888
Off Dublin Road in Lucan village following the signs for Clonsilla.

Parkland course.
Founded 1988
Designed by Eddie Hackett
18 holes, 5819 yards, S.S.S. 70
Visitors: welcome WD.
Green Fees: WD £20.
Societies: welcome by prior arrangement.
Catering: full clubhouse facilities available.

12 254 **Westport**

Carrowholly, Westport, Co Mayo
☎(098) 25113, Fax 27217, Pro 27481, Sec 26134
2 miles from Westport.
Parkland course.
Founded 1908
Designed by Hawtree & Son
18 holes, 6959 yards, S.S.S. 73
Visitors: welcome.
Green Fees: terms on application.
Societies: welcome by prior arrangement; special packages available.
Catering: lounge bar and dining facilities.

12 255 **Wexford**

Mulgannon, Wexford
☎(053) 42238, Pro 46300, Sec 44611
In Wexford town.
Parkland course.
Founded 1960
Designed by J. Hamilton Stutt & Co (original), Des Smyth (new
18 holes, 5578 yards, S.S.S. 70
Visitors: welcome; restrictions Wed evening and Thurs.
Green Fees: WD £14; WE £15.
Societies: welcome by prior arrangement; discounts for larger groups.
Catering: bar and snacks.

12 256 **Wicklow**

Dunbur Rd, Wicklow, Co Wicklow
☎(0404) 67379, Pro 66122, Sec 69386
On L29 32 miles from Dublin.
Seaside course.
Founded 1904
18 holes, 5695 yards, S.S.S. 70
Visitors: welcome WD.
Green Fees: WD £15.
Societies: welcome by prior arrangement.
Catering: full clubhouse facilities.

12 257 **Woodbrook**

Dublin Rd, Bray, Co Wicklow
☎(01) 2824799
11 miles S of Dublin on N11.
Parkland course.
Founded 1921
18 holes, 5996 yards, S.S.S. 71
Visitors: welcome by arrangement.
Green Fees: WD £25; WE £35.
Societies: welcome Mon, Thurs and Fri by prior arrangement.
Catering: full clubhouse facilities.

12 258 **Woodenbridge**

Woodenbridge, Arklow, Co Wicklow
☎(0402) 35202, Fax 31402, Sec 31571
45 miles S of Dublin on N11 to Arklow.
Parkland course.
Founded 1884
18 holes, 6316 yards, S.S.S. 70
Visitors: welcome except Thurs and Sat.
Green Fees: WD £20; WE £20.
Societies: welcome WD by prior arrangement.
Catering: full clubhouse facilities.
Practice ground.

12 259 **Woodlands**

Coill Dubh, Naas, Co Kildare
☎(045) 60777
On outskirts of Naas.
Parkland course.
Founded 1985
9 holes, 5202 yards, S.S.S. 68
Visitors: welcome.
Green Fees: WD £6; WE £7.
Societies: welcome with prior arrangement.

12 260 **Woodstock**

Woodstock House, Shanaway Road, Ennis, Co Clare
☎(065) 29463, Fax 20304, Sec 22148
In Ennis.
Parkland course.
Founded 1993
18 holes, 5879 yards, S.S.S. 71
Visitors: welcome.
Green Fees: WD £18; WE £18.
Societies: welcome with prior arrangement; terms on application.

12 261 **Youghal**

Knockaverry, Youghal, Co Cork
☎(024) 92787, Fax 92641, Pro 92590
On N25 between Rosslare and Cork.
Parkland course.
Pro Liam Burns; Founded 1898
Designed by Commander Harris
18 holes, 5646 yards, S.S.S. 70
Visitors: welcome.
Green Fees: WD £14; WE £14.
Societies: welcome by prior arrangement.
Catering: full clubhouse facilities available.
Hotels: Walter Raleigh; Hilltop; Devonshire Arms.

INDEX

C

D

I

J

K

Q

R

T

Y